The Rorschach: A Comprehensive System, in two volumes
  by John E. Exner, Jr.
Theory and Practice in Behavior Therapy
  by Aubrey J. Yates
Principles of Psychotherapy
  by Irving B. Weiner
Psychoactive Drugs and Social Judgment: Theory and Research
  edited by Kenneth Hammond and C. R. B. Joyce
Clinical Methods in Psychology
  edited by Irving B. Weiner
Human Resources for Troubled Children
  by Werner I. Halpern and Stanley Kissel
Hyperactivity
  by Dorothea M. Ross and Sheila A. Ross
Heroin Addiction: Theory, Research and Treatment
  by Jerome J. Platt and Christina Labate
Children's Rights and the Mental Health Profession
  edited by Gerald P. Koocher
The Role of the Father in Child Development
  edited by Michael E. Lamb
Handbook of Behavioral Assessment
  edited by Anthony R. Ciminero, Karen S. Calhoun, and Henry E. Adams
Counseling and Psychotherapy: A Behavioral Approach
  by E. Lakin Phillips
Dimensions of Personality
  edited by Harvey London and John E. Exner, Jr.
The Mental Health Industry: A Cultural Phenomenon
  by Peter A. Magaro, Robert Gripp, David McDowell, and Ivan W. Miller III
Nonverbal Communication: The State of the Art
  by Robert G. Harper, Arthur N. Wiens, and Joseph D. Matarazzo
Alcoholism and Treatment
  by David J. Armor, J. Michael Polich, and Harriet B. Stambul
A Biodevelopmental Approach to Clinical Child Psychology: Cognitive Controls and Cognitive Control Theory
  by Sebastiano Santostefano
Handbook of Infant Development
  edited by Joy D. Osofsky
Understanding the Rape Victim: A Synthesis of Research Findings
  by Sedelle Katz and Mary Ann Mazur
Childhood Pathology and Later Adjustment: The Question of Prediction
  by Loretta K. Cass and Carolyn B. Thomas
Intelligent Testing with the WISC-R
  by Alan S. Kaufman
Adaptation in Schizophrenia: The Theory of Segmental Set
  by David Shakow
Psychotherapy: An Eclectic Approach
  by Sol L. Garfield
Handbook of Minimal Brain Dysfunctions
  edited by Herbert E. Rie and Ellen D. Rie
Handbook of Behavioral Interventions: A Clinical Guide
  edited by Alan Goldstein and Edna B. Foa
Art Psychotherapy
  by Harriet Wadeson
Handbook of Adolescent Psychology
  edited by Joseph Adelson
Psychotherapy Supervision: Theory, Research and Practice
  edited by Allen K. Hess

D1637142

Continued on back

HANDBOOK OF CLINICAL
BEHAVIOR THERAPY

HANDBOOK OF CLINICAL BEHAVIOR THERAPY

Edited by

SAMUEL M. TURNER

KAREN S. CALHOUN

HENRY E. ADAMS

A WILEY-INTERSCIENCE PUBLICATION

JOHN WILEY & SONS   New York • Chichester • Brisbane • Toronto

Library of Congress Cataloging in Publication Data:

Main entry under title:
Handbook of clinical behavior therapy.

   (Wiley series on personality process)
   "A Wiley-Interscience publication."
   Includes indexes.
   1. Behavior therapy. 2. Psychology, Pathological.
I. Turner, Samuel M., 1944- II. Calhoun, Karen S.
III. Adams, Henry E., 1931- [DNLM: 1. Behavior
therapy—Handbooks. WM425 T952h]

RC489.B4H37   616.89'142   80-16841
ISBN 0-471-04178-5

Printed in the United States of America

10 9 8 7 6 5 4 3 2 1

Contributors

GENE G. ABEL, M.D., Professor of Psychiatry, Columbia University College of Physicians and Surgeons

HENRY E. ADAMS, PH.D., Professor of Psychology, University of Georgia

W. STEWART AGRAS, M.D., Professor of Psychiatry, Stanford University School of Medicine

ROBERT P. ARCHER, PH.D., Director, Early Intervention Project, Florida Mental Health Institute

ALFRED A. BAUMEISTER, PH.D., Professor of Psychology and Human Development, George Peabody College for Teachers of Vanderbilt University

JUDITH V. BECKER, PH.D., Assistant Professor of Psychiatry, Columbia University College of Physicians and Surgeons

BRUCE L. BIRD, PH.D., Assistant Professor of Neurology, The Johns Hopkins University School of Medicine

KAREN S. CALHOUN, PH.D., Associate Professor of Psychology, University of Georgia

TRACEY POTTS CARSON, PH.D., Department of Psychology, University of Georgia

MICHAEL F. CATALDO, PH.D., Assistant Professor of Psychiatry, The Johns Hopkins University School of Medicine

THOMAS J. COATES, PH.D., Assistant Professor of Psychiatry and Behavioral Sciences, The Johns Hopkins University School of Medicine

ALAN M. DELAMATER, M.S., Department of Psychology, University of Georgia

LEONARD H. EPSTEIN, PH.D., Associate Professor of Psychiatry, Psychology, and Epidemiology, University of Pittsburgh School of Medicine

REX FOREHAND, PH.D., Professor of Psychology, University of Georgia

DAVID FOY, PH.D., Associate Professor, University of Mississippi Medical Center and Jackson VA Medical Center

GEROME GILMORE, M.S., Department of Psychology, Virginia Commonwealth University

NATHAN HARE, PH.D., Adjunct Assistant Professor of Clinical Psychology, Binghamton Psychiatry Center and State University of New York at Binghamton

MICHEL HERSEN, PH.D., Professor of Psychiatry and Psychology, Western Psychiatric Institute & Clinic, University of Pittsburgh School of Medicine

RUSSELL T. JONES, PH.D., Assistant Professor of Psychology, University of Pittsburgh

WILLIAM M. KALLMAN, PH.D., Assistant Professor of Psychology, Virginia Commonwealth University

ALAN E. KAZDIN, PH.D., Professor of Psychology, Pennsylvania State University

DEAN G. KILPATRICK, PH.D., Professor of Psychiatry and Behavioral Sciences, Medical University of South Carolina

ROBERT L. KOEGEL, PH.D., Associate Professor of Autism, Social Process Research Institute, University of California at Santa Barbara

DAVID L. KUPFER, M.S., Department of Psychology, University of Georgia

BENJAMIN B. LAHEY, PH.D., Associate Professor of Psychology, University of Georgia

CRAIG LEFEBVRE, M.S., Department of Psychology, North Texas State University

DONALD J. LEVIS, PH.D., Professor of Psychology, State University of New York at Binghamton

BRUCE J. MASEK, PH.D., Assistant Professor of Medical Psychology, The Johns Hopkins University School of Medicine

VICTOR MEYER, PH.D., Reader in Psychology, Middlesex Hospital Medical School

PETER M. MILLER, PH.D., Director, Sea Pines Behavioral Institute

DAVID MOSTOFSKY, PH.D., Professor of Psychology, Boston University

LYNN H. PARKER, PH.D., Instructor in Psychiatry, The Johns Hopkins University School of Medicine

DAVID C. RIMM, PH.D., Professor of Psychology, North Texas State University

DENNIS C. RUSSO, PH.D., Assistant Professor of Psychology, Harvard Medical School

KURT SALZINGER, PH.D., Professor of Psychology, Polytechnic Institute of New York

LAURA SCHREIBMAN, PH.D., Associate Professor of Psychology, Claremont Men's College

RICHARD B. STUART, D.S.W., Professor of Family and Community Medicine, University of Utah School of Medicine

ELLIE T. STURGIS, PH.D., Assistant Professor of Psychology, University of North Carolina at Chapel Hill

PATRICIA B. SUTKER, PH.D., Associate Dean, College of Medicine, Professor of Psychiatry and Behavioral Sciences, Medical University of South Carolina

CARL E. THORESON, PH.D., Professor of Education and Psychology, Stanford University

DAVID TOLLINSON, PH.D., Assistant Professor of Psychiatry, Medical College of Georgia

SAMUEL M. TURNER, PH.D., Associate Professor of Psychiatry and Psychology, Western Psychiatric Institute & Clinic, University of Pittsburgh School of Medicine

KAREN C. WELLS, PH.D., Assistant Professor of Psychiatry, Children's Hospital, National Medical Center, George Washington School of Medicine

JOELLEN WERNE, M.D., Clinical Assistant Professor of Psychiatry, Stanford University School of Medicine

BRUCE WETHERBY, PH.D., Assistant Professor of Psychology and Human Development, George Peabody College for Teachers of Vanderbilt University

JOHN P. WINCZE, PH.D., Associate Professor of Psychiatry, Brown University Medical School and Providence VA Medical Center

Series Preface

This series of books is addressed to behavioral scientists interested in the nature of human personality. Its scope should prove pertinent to personality theorists and researchers as well as to clinicians concerned with applying an understanding of personality processes to the amelioration of emotional difficulties in living. To this end, the series provides a scholarly integration of theoretical formulations, empirical data, and practical recommendations.

Six major aspects of studying and learning about human personality can be designated: personality theory, personality structure and dynamics, personality development, personality assessment, personality change, and personality adjustment. In exploring these aspects of personality, the books in the series discuss a number of distinct but related subject areas: the nature and implications of various theories of personality; personality characteristics that account for consistencies and variations in human behavior; the emergence of personality processes in children and adolescents; the use of interviewing and testing procedures to evaluate individual differences in personality; efforts to modify personality styles through psychotherapy, counseling, behavior therapy and other methods of influence; and patterns of abnormal personality functioning that impair individual competence.

IRVING B. WEINER

University of Denver
Denver, Colorado

Preface

The field of behavior therapy has witnessed a dramatic increase in its literature, as have virtually all academic areas, within recent years. In fact, the information explosion has been so extensive in this field that the proliferation of journals, books, and other written works has made it next to impossible to keep abreast of our rapidly changing discipline. In part, the explosion of information in behavior therapy can be explained by the increasing areas for its applicability, and by the expansion of its theoretical bases, contributing to new empirical findings.

Over the past few years behavior therapy has matured considerably and has become a legitimate therapeutic modality increasingly used by clinicians who are not necessarily trained in applied behavior analysis. There is no single model of behavior therapy; rather, it represents the application of principles grounded in basic experimental psychology. As a testament to the maturity of the field, numerous models are being included under the behavioral umbrella. The field of health care, or behavioral medicine, for example, is currently receiving phenomenal growth and acceptance.

This anthology presents an overview of various treatment approaches being used in the field for specific disorders. The treatment of clinically significant problems is rarely accomplished with the utilization of a single therapeutic technique. Our intention was to design a book to present the clinician, educator, and student with an accurate picture of how various clinical syndromes are handled with behavioral intervention strategies, empirical evidence of their efficacy, and knowledge of the theoretical foundation for the various techniques. Therefore, the chapters are appropriately arranged to deal with specific clinical syndromes. Each chapter includes a discussion of behavioral strategies that are appropriate for each disorder or class of behavior. It is hoped that this book will serve as a valuable reference for behavioral clinicians and others interested in behavioral treatments, and as a training tool for teaching graduate students and other trainees in the application of behavioral treatment principles.

We wish to express our thanks to the numerous contributors who endeavored to make their manuscripts fit our restricted criteria. We also gratefully acknowledge

John Wiley and Sons, the publisher, for the support and understanding they demonstrated over the course of this long project. Finally, we express our appreciation to Michele Cassidy who spent many hours typing the manuscript and to Deborah C. Beidel, Barbara Duffy Stewart, Karen Ketchum, Harry Sherick, and Janet Twomey for their technical assistance.

SAMUEL M. TURNER
KAREN S. CALHOUN
HENRY E. ADAMS

Pittsburgh, Pennsylvania
Athens, Georgia
October 1980

Contents

HANDBOOK OF CLINICAL
BEHAVIOR THERAPY

CHAPTER 1

Historical Perspectives and Current Issues in Behavior Therapy

Karen S. Calhoun and Samuel M. Turner

The field of behavior therapy has become the most rapidly growing system of therapy in psychology and related professions. A wide variety of mental health professionals are engaged in the practice of behavior therapy. Trends in the training of mental health professionals, including the development of didactic and practicum experiences in behavioral intervention, reflect this increased acceptance of the principles and methods of behavior therapy and are a tribute to their acknowledged effectiveness in clinical use. The growth and increased sophistication of behavioral approaches has been stimulated by a vastly increased literature in the area of the application and analysis of behavior. The chapters that follow summarize new developments and ongoing work in the major areas in which behavior therapy is currently applied. These chapters are designed to give students of various disciplines, as well as professionals engaged in the practice of behavior therapy, a central source of current information on clinical techniques, research results, and theoretical developments.

TERMINOLOGICAL ISSUES

The history of the behavioral movement has been marked by vigorous and healthy dialogues ranging from arguments concerning the theoretical foundations to disagreements about terminology. The issues in terminology center in the various terms used to refer to intervention approaches, including behavior modification, behavior therapy, and applied behavior analysis. In a recent discussion, Wilson (1978) noted that many behaviorists do not use the term therapy because it smacks of the medical model that many behaviorists roundly reject. However, the term "medical model" has been used in numerous ways and has different implications to different people. In our opinion, behaviorists reject what Kazdin (1978a) refers to as the "intrapsychic disease model." The concept of an underlying pathogen in this model is embodied in the concept of intrapsychic conflict. It is this conceptualization that behaviorists uniformly reject, not the possibility that certain behavior patterns are associated with biological factors.

In attempting to distinguish among terms, Franzini and Tilker (1972) suggested that the term behavior modification be used to describe efforts to alter social institutions or groups of people. The change agent in such an endeavor would more appropriately be called a behavioral consultant as opposed to a therapist. Behavior therapy, on the other hand, should be used to label direct attempts to alter the behavior of an individual. While such a differentiation is logical, in the short history of the behavioral movement both terms have been used in both of these contexts. Furthermore, a therapist is a consultant, and the prescription for institutional or large group change can also be viewed as therapeutic. Franzini and Tilker (1972) also suggested that the application of techniques of operant psychology where such mediational constructs as anxiety are disavowed, be labeled as applied behavior analysis. Yet, the application of most behavioral strategies includes some operant aspects.

The term "behavior therapy" has often been used in a more general, inclusive way. Wolpe (1969) defined it as "the use of experimentally established principles of learning for the purpose of changing unadaptive behavior." The term seems to have been first used by Lindsley, Skinner, and Solomon (1953) in their application of operant conditioning procedures with psychotic patients. Somewhat later, Lazarus (1958) and Eysenck (1959) also independently used the term.

From the very beginning of the behavioral movement differentiations among the various terms have never been widely accepted. Ullmann and Krasner (1965), in one of the most influential early works in the field, *Case Studies in Behavior Modification,* failed to distinguish among the various terminologies, preferring instead to use them interchangeably. While a case can be made for differentiating the use of the terms *behavior modification, behavior therapy,* and *applied behavior analysis,* we believe that such a differentiation is of no practical value. The fact that these terms exist is a reflection of the diverse foundations of the behavioral approaches, which can be considered one of its strengths. In the clinical arena, the most effective interventions usually represent a combination of strategies embodying the diverse theoretical notions that have led to the terminological confusion. We have elected to use the term t .erapy in the title of this book to reflect the clinical nature of the work presented. However, from a philosophical perspective, we use the terms interchangeably as is the case with most of our contributors.

MODELS OF BEHAVIOR THERAPY

Some current developments in behavior therapy were surprisingly anticipated by early thinkers (Franks, 1969). A good example is Pliny the Elder's suggestion for the use of aversion in treating alcoholics (i.e., putting spiders in their cups). Although many such interesting examples can be found, they lack the continuity necessary to be regarded as part of a stream of development leading directly to modern behavior therapy. For these roots, we must look to developments in the nineteenth and early twentieth centuries, beginning with scientific and philosophical interest in the concept of the conditional reflex.

Classical Conditioning

Kazdin (1978a) has critically examined the historical factors influencing the growth of behaviorism in general and behavior modification in particular. According to Kazdin, one of the seminal factors contributing to the emergence of the behavioral movement was the conditioning or reflexology movement in Russia. From this work the classical conditioning model was developed. Russian scientists began programs of careful experimentation to study behavior and subjective processes. Sechenov, the "father of Russian physiology," was interested in psychological phenomena. He developed the theory that all behavior is reflexive and that humans learn through association the complex reflexes making up their behavior. His emphasis on scientific experimentation and the role of the environment in determining behavior greatly influenced later scientists (Kazdin, 1978a). Pavlov and Bechterev were especially influenced by Sechenov's work. They both studied learned reflexes, but with differing emphases. Bechterev was interested in applying his "reflexology" to psychiatric disorders. However, it is Pavlov's work in the development of conditioned reflexes that is more generally recognized as antecedent to behavior therapy techniques. Of course, every psychologist is familiar with his famous experiments on conditioned reflexes (Pavlov, 1927). This work, which was soon called "classical conditioning," along with his emphasis on a systematic approach to research, made an important impact on psychology in the early twentieth century. Later in life, Pavlov became interested in the relationship between learning and psychopathology in humans. He suggested that there were relationships between behavioral disorders and inhibitory and excitory processes in the central nervous system.

Another major source of influence in the early twentieth century was the "behaviorism" of J. B. Watson, whose dissatisfaction with the focus of psychology at the time and its basic method of introspection, led him to advocate the study of observable behavior using objective methods. He used procedures developed in the study of animal behavior to examine the learning process and stressed learning as the determinant of abnormal behavior, incorporating the Russians' conditioning work into his ideas. His classic study with Rayner (Watson & Rayner, 1920) illustrated how fear or phobic reactions as well as simple motor habits could be developed in a child. Briefly, Little Albert, a five-year-old boy with no prior fear of rabbits served as the subject in this experiment. Little Albert was placed in a room where a loud noise was paired with the presentation of a white furry rabbit. Soon, Little Albert developed a conditioned fear of the rabbit. Furthermore, through the process of stimulus generalization, other white furry objects also produced this fear reaction. This study was a powerful demonstration of the acquisition of fear in the classical conditioning paradigm.

The classical conditioning model is an associationist approach to learning in which particular responses are explained on the basis of the arrangement of prior stimulation, the biological state of the organism, and the individual's response repertoire (Kanfer & Phillips, 1970). We will not repeat the classical conditioning paradigm here, as it appears in most general psychology text and in numerous other sources (e.g., Bellack, & Hersen, 1977; Kanfer & Phillips, 1970). The classical conditioning model has had enormous influence in clinical psychology and psychiatry.

This model is used by behavior therapists to explain many types of neurotic and phobic behavior, as well as more benign types of fears seen in clinical populations. A major reason for its widespread acceptance in explaining fear and avoidance behavior is that, for a long period of time, it was considered the only type of learning model for modifying autonomic or involuntary responses. With respect to treatment strategies, aversive conditioning procedures embodying escape, avoidance, and punishment paradigms have their roots in classical conditioning. Further, counterconditioning treatments (e.g., desensitization), and other treatments of stimulus control have strong elements of classical conditioning. Of course, these techniques as well as other behavioral strategies also have various components of operant conditioning, whether acknowledged or not (Kanfer & Phillips, 1970).

Operant Conditioning

Perhaps the best-known and most influential model in behavior therapy is operant or instrumental conditioning. This particular model is often seen as being synonymous with behavior modification or analysis. In fact, the lay public as well as some nonbehavioral professionals of various disciplines frequently have failed to recognize the existence of other models in behavior therapy. The operant approach to human behavior is ultraenvironmental, and it fit well into the general movement of behaviorism in the early twentieth century. The seminal work in operant psychology was conducted by E. L. Thorndike. But the popularization and extension of operant principles was carried out by a man whose name is now often cited synonymously with operant principles, B. F. Skinner. The basic operant approach is presented in Skinner's classic work, *Behavior of Organisms,* published in 1938.

Operant principles and methodology have had a profound effect not only on behavioral psychology, but on psychology in general. In fact, the writings of Thorndike and Skinner were important in moving psychology away from introspectionism and toward a more objective and empirical stance. Operant theory, like its old foe, psychoanalytic theory, is a comprehensive set of principles designed to account for all human behavior.

In the classical conditioning model the emphasis is on the stimulus, whereas in operant conditioning the emphasis is on the response. The basic principle of the operant approach is that behavior is a function of its consequences. Specifically, this involves the manipulation of reinforcement and punishment. Although there are many early demonstrations of operant principles with humans, Lindsley (1956) is usually given the credit for the first systematic demonstration in a clinical population. Today, operant principles are widely used in clinical settings, and as mentioned earlier, are actually part of most behavioral intervention programs. Such treatment procedures as extinction, programmed positive reinforcement, shaping, and chaining are examples. The most comprehensive application of operant principles in the clinical arena is the token economy (Ayllon & Azrin, 1968). Token economies have been used widely in various residential settings and in the classroom. Operant conditioning has had a profound impact in education, most strikingly demonstrated in the teaching machine technology or programmed learning. Today, operant principles are being employed in the treatment and prevention of general health problems, in industry, and in a wide variety of other settings.

Social Learning Theory

Social learning theory (Bandura, 1969, 1977) is in many respects a synthesis of operant and classical conditioning. Nevertheless, social learning theory also represents a major shift away from a peripheral concept of behavior by acknowledging the role of central mechanisms. Specifically, the theory provides a theoretical framework to account for such phenomena as no-trial learning and the acquisition of language. Moreover, social learning theory introduced the concepts of cognitive control and reciprocal determinism to behavioral theory. According to Bandura (1969), social learning theory emphasizes the prominent roles played by vicarious, symbolic, and self-regulatory processes. This is in contrast to both operant and classical conditioning where the individual is viewed as a passive actor in the environment. In the social learning framework, the individual is accorded a much more active role in creating his own environment. The acknowledgement that learning can occur purely as a function of cognitive activities was, indeed, a radical departure from strict behavioral doctrine. Perhaps even more radical is the notion of symbolic control of behavior, and the premise that a direct linkage between external stimuli and overt behavior is mediated by cognitive processes. It is important to note that social learning theory is a much more "common sense" approach to understanding behavior and is much more consonant with the Western view of man.

In the early development of social learning theory, there was heavy emphasis on the direct experience of antecedents and consequences in the acquisition and maintenance of behavior. Yet, the role of vicarious processes was also stressed. In fact, Bandura (1969) argues that virtually all behavior learned through direct experience can be learned through observation. The vicarious learning processes are referred to in various literature by such names as modeling, imitation, identification, and observational learning.

The impact of social learning principles in the clinical setting is enormous, not the least reason for which is its rational, believable explanation of behavior that appeals to the public. A recent review of the clinical uses of modeling is provided by Rosenthal (1976).

Cognitive Behavior Modification and Self-Control

The acceptance of the role of cognitive variables in behavioral theory and therapy has been very slow and grudgingly given. From the very beginning of the behavioral movement, cognitive behaviors and other private events were viewed as outside the realm of behavioral research because they were not subject to direct observation, measurement, and manipulation. Yet, the use of such variables has been widespread in many behavioral treatment strategies. Examples of the use of cognitive variables in behavioral techniques include imagery in desensitization and sexual change therapies, and self-verbalization in thought-stopping and other covert strategies (Kazdin, 1978a).

The introduction of the concept of self-control and self-control strategies for modifying behavior in the early sixties signaled a movement toward a more cognitive emphasis in behavior therapy. Although Skinner, as early as 1953, discussed the concept of self-control, formal acceptance occurred much later (e.g., Ferster, Nurnberger, & Levitt, 1962; Goldiamond, 1965; Kanfer & Karoly, 1972). The notion embodied in self-control is that the individual is capable of controlling or changing his own behavior by the manipulation of rewards and punishments. A major concept in the notion of self-control is self-reinforcement, a phenomenon that has raised much controversy in behavior therapy. The controversy centers around whether or not self-reinforcement occurs in the absence of external factors (cf. Bandura, 1978; Jones, Nelson & Kazdin, 1977; Rachlin, 1974). Despite this controversy, there are many treatment strategies based on the model. Such procedures are frequently employed in obesity programs, sexual change programs, and programs to improve academic and study behavior.

Although the acceptance of self-control programs represents a major shift in behavioral theory, there are at least some ties to traditional operant theory, which is not the case with purely cognitive strategies. Cognitive behavioral theories (e.g., Beck, 1970, 1976; Ellis, 1971; Mahoney & Thorenson, 1974; Meichenbaum, 1977) have essentially taken behavior therapy back to what has always been the domain of psychology—a focus on internal processes and their influence on behavior. The cognitive therapies are aimed at modifying thinking processes, but more importantly for behaviorism, they emphasize the cognitive mediation of the learning process. Kanfer (1977) argues that despite this fact, behavior therapy has maintained most of its characteristic features. To be sure, the infusion of cognitive and self-control concepts in behavior therapy has helped to moderate the perception of behavior therapy as mechanistic. However, it remains to be seen whether behavior therapy can maintain its rigid objectivism while accommodating such ideas.

Recently, Bandura (1977) proposed a self-efficacy theory of behavior change. Essentially, Bandura argues that all behavior change procedures achieve their effects by modifying "self-efficacy" and that perceived self-efficacy is the determinant of all behavioral responses. Although peripheral influences are acknowledged, the core of the theory is the existence of a mediational construct, self-efficacy. Presently, Bandura's theory is only partially supported by empirical evidence, and there is no doubt that in the years to come this particular theory will receive much attention within behavior therapy.

The emergence of the cognitive movement has not gone unchallenged (cf. Ledwidge, 1978, 1979; Wolpe, 1976a,b). These approaches are seen by some as representing a return to traditional psychotherapy and an abandonment of proven behavioral techniques. And, in fact, many of the proponents of the cognitive approach are indeed individuals whose training and earlier identification have been in traditional areas. For some, the appeal of the cognitive approaches may be the things they have in common with other approaches. For example, treatment methods such as transactional analysis tend to change attitudes and self-report whereas behavioral techniques emphasize changing behavior (Kazdin, 1978b). Perhaps cognitive methods have appeal because they seem to bridge the gap left by behaviorists who have underestimated the lag between behavior change and attitude change. Regardless of its appeal, the cognitive approach is in a very early stage of development, having failed as yet even to clearly define what cognition is. Conceptual and methodological problems also make empirical validation difficult.

CURRENT ISSUES

The history of the behavioral movement has been marked by numerous controversies, many of them pseudoissues. One example of this is the outcome issue. Whether behavior therapy is more effective than psychotherapy is a meaningless question, particularly in view of the way such evaluations have been conducted. Many different behavioral strategies (and psychotherapy strategies as well) are used with ill-defined patient populations and by therapists with different levels of expertise. Needless to say, the results of such studies provide little useful information, and certainly do not answer the question of which modality is superior, behavior therapy or psychotherapy. For a discussion of comparative evaluations of behavior therapy with other modalities, see Kazdin and Wilson (1978).

Another current example of the types of pseudoissues leading to controversy among behavior therapists is the question concerning the importance of the therapist-client relationship. Traditionally, relationship variables have received little attention by behaviorists, leading to charges that behavior therapy is technique-oriented and mechanistic. However, the relationship has received occasional mention (Goldfried & Davison, 1976) and those of us involved in training and supervision have long recognized that a good working relationship is basic to any effective treatment. This fact is currently being discussed more openly by behaviorists (Hersen & Kazdin, in press), but we should not allow it to become a devisive issue. Few adequately trained behavior therapists would argue that a good relationship is not a necessary condition in working with clients. However, behavior therapists operate on the premise that the client-therapist relationship is not the active ingredient in therapy. It is a necessary but not a sufficient condition for behavior change. Nevertheless, the therapist-client relationship is an appropriate subject for empirical study. It is probably accurate to say that this controversy has altered only the description of what behavior therapists say they do in therapy rather than what they actually do. A good relationship has always been important in effective intervention.

CURRENT STATUS OF BEHAVIOR THERAPY

The term behavior therapy has become increasingly less meaningful because it has been expanded to include a broad range of conceptual approaches and procedures. No longer can the term be used to designate an approach with a well-delineated conceptual base. No longer is it possible to designate practitioners who can be clearly identified on the basis of any given set of criteria as behavior therapists. Without clear definitions of terms, any intervention method can be labeled as "behavior therapy" without fear of challenge, a condition that could cause the public image of behavior therapy to suffer considerably.

In attempting to clearly identify a set of general characteristics unique to behavior therapy, Kazdin and Hersen (in press) were able to suggest only the following:

1. A strong commitment to empirical evaluation of treatment and intervention techniques.
2. A general belief that therapeutic experiences must provide opportunities to learn adaptive or prosocial behavior.
3. Specification of treatment in operational and, hence, replicable terms.
4. Evaluation of treatment effects through multiple-response modalities, with particular emphasis on overt behavior.

Even these criteria, however, may not be unique to behavior therapy. For example, commitment to empirical evaluation of treatment is not exclusive to behaviorists, although it certainly receives strong support from them. Noticeably absent from this list is any reference to behavior therapy's traditional ties to learning and experimental psychology. This apparently represents a recent shift in the thinking of at least one of the authors. Kazdin (1978b), in a similar list of characteristics, includes "Reliance upon basic research in psychology as a source of hypotheses about treatment and specific therapy techniques" (p. 375). We wonder if it is desirable to discard basic assumptions that have proven useful without a sufficient empirically validated replacement.

Early behaviorists were most adamant in their view of the new therapy's basis in experimental psychology, and more specifically, in learning theory. In a manner typical of the era, Eysenck (1959) asserted that behavior modification procedures could be distinguished from others in that they are based on modern learning theory. This assertion was vigorously challenged in numerous sources (e.g., Breger & McGaugh, 1965, 1966; Wiert, 1967). Essentially, the gist of the antagonists' arguments is that a learning theory formulation of mental disorders is not possible because of inadequacies in the theories, and that behavioral therapeutic strategies do not represent direct application of specific theory. Today, most behaviorists would not argue this point inasmuch as it is generally recognized that many behavioral strategies are not direct applications of a specific theory of learning. However, the principles of learning (e.g., operant conditioning, classical conditioning) served a crucial function in guiding the development and utilization of behavioral intervention strategies. The fact that the strategies and the manner in which they were implemented frequently did not strictly adhere to the model is relatively insignificant in this context. The use of such principles do provide an experimental base for the field.

Another reason for the strong allegiance to a learning model by early behaviorists is that learning theory served as a "flag" for behaviorists to rally around in the face of widespread opposition to behavioral approaches by their more traditionally oriented colleagues (London, 1972). This fact no doubt helped behavior therapy to survive its infancy. However, Bellack and Hersen (1977) argue that the battle has essentially been won and the "flag" is no longer needed. Most behavior therapists now accept the fact that the many treatment procedures grouped under the behavioral rubric are not based on any one specific learning principle. Indeed, there is no one unified theory of learning but rather a group of theories that account for various aspects of the learning process. These theories have certainly had an important impact on the behavioral revolution, and their influence is evident in the various behavioral treatment techniques. In the chapters that follow, it can be seen that commitment to both empiricism and basic principles of learning and experimental psychology are still strong among those who identify with behavior therapy.

The fact that behavior therapy is no longer truly recognizable as a specific entity has a number of implications for the field. The inclusion of a wide diversity of methods and conceptual ideas both reflect and enhance the general acceptance of behavior therapy by professionals and the public at large. This diversity, an inevitable function of the field's maturation, reveals both negative and positive aspects. We no longer need to fight the kinds of pitched battles in defense of behavior therapy that were common in the early development of the field. However, to the extent that wide acceptance means acceptance of watered-down versions of bits and pieces of methods and jargon, behavior therapy may have lost more than it has gained. Without acceptance of the basic scientific approach to the development and evaluation of intervention methods, acceptance of a few techniques will not further the development of the field.

The current state of behavior therapy reflects in part a breakdown of the notion of orientations, alignments characterized by allegiance to a particular set of intervention methods and conceptions. This sort of loyalty to different existing treatment approaches has plagued the mental health professions from the beginning and has been one of the major factors preventing progress in the development and refinement of new techniques as well as a factor in slowing progress in the understanding of psychopathology. Ideally, orientations should not be centered around intervention methods but around scientific approaches to the study and understanding of the etiology of behavior. Intervention methods should develop out of this understanding. Without this base, behavior therapy is left in the position for which we have criticized other approaches—that of attempting to treat all problems with the same methods. One of the great strengths of behavior therapy is the ability to tailor treatment methods to the specific problems of the individual. Since this requires a thorough assessment of behavior, we have seen rapid growth in the development of innovative assessment methods that have in turn increased our understanding of etiology.

The development of behavior therapy has to a large extent followed the general trend of other clinical sciences, such as medicine, since methods of treatment have commonly been developed and implemented in advance of the basic etiological knowledge, upon which those methods should be based. Thus, gaining the basic scientific knowledge of behavioral disorders as well as empirically evaluating treatment methods is essential if we are to have a true science of human behavior.

REFERENCES

Ayllon, A., & Azrin, N. *The token economy: A motivational system for therapy and rehabilitation.* Englewood Cliffs, N.J.: Prentice-Hall, 1968.

Bandura, A. *Principles of behavior modification.* New York: Holt, Rinehart & Winston, 1969.

Bandura, A. *Social learning theory.* Englewood Cliffs, N.J.: Prentice-Hall, 1977.

Bandura, A. Self-efficacy: Toward a unifying theory of behavioral change. *Psychological Review,* 1977, **84**, 191–215.

Beck, A. T. Cognitive therapy: Nature and relation to behavior therapy. *Behavior Therapy,* 1970, **1**, 184–200.

Beck, A. T. *Cognitive therapy and the emotional disorders.* New York: International Universities Press, 1976.

Bellack, A. S., & Hersen, M. *Behavior modification: An introductory textbook.* Baltimore: Williams & Wilkins, 1977.

Breger, L., & McGaugh, J. Critique and reformulation of "learning theory" approaches to psychotherapy and neuroses. *Psychological Bulletin,* 1965, **63**, 338–358.

Breger, L., & McGaugh, J. Learning theory and behavior therapy: A reply to Rachman and Eysenck. *Psychological Bulletin,* 1966, **65**, 170–173.

Ellis, A. *Growth through reason. Verbatim cases in rational emotive therapy.* Palo Alto, CA: Science and Behavior Books, 1971.

Eysenck, H. J. Learning theory and behavior therapy. *Journal of Mental Sciences,* 1959, **105**, 61–75.

Eysenck, H. J. Behavior therapy as a scientific discipline. *Journal of Consulting and Clinical Psychology,* 1971, **36**, 314–319.

Ferster, C. B., Nurnberger, J. I., & Levitt, E. G. The control of eating. *Journal of Mathematics,* 1962, **1**, 87–107.

Ferster, C. B., & Skinner, B. F. *Schedules of reinforcement.* New York: Appleton, 1957.

Franks, C. M. *Behavior therapy: Appraisal and status.* New York: McGraw-Hill, 1969.

Franzini, L. R., & Tilker, H. A. On the terminological confusion between behavior therapy and behavior modification. *Behavior Therapy,* 1972, **3**, 279–282.

Goldfried, M. R., & Davison, G. C. *Clinical behavior therapy.* New York: Holt, Rinehart & Winston, 1976.

Goldiamond, I. Self-control procedures in personal behavior problems. *Psychological Reports,* 1965, **17**, 851–868.

Hersen, M. Limitations and problems in the clinical application of behavioral techniques in psychiatric settings. *Behavior Therapy,* 1979, **10**, 65–80.

Jones, R. T., Nelson, R. E., & Kazdin, A. E. The role of external variables in self-reinforcement: A review. *Behavior Modification,* 1977, **1**, 147–178.

Kanfer, F. H. The many faces of self-control, or behavior modification changes its focus. In R. B. Stuart (Ed.), *Behavioral self-management.* New York: Brunner/Mazel, 1977.

Kanfer, F. H., & Karoly, P. Self-control: A behavioristic excursion into the lion's den. *Behavior Therapy,* 1972, **3**, 398–416.

Kanfer, F. H., & Phillips, J. S. *Learning foundations of behavior therapy.* New York: Wiley, 1970.

Kazdin, A. E. *History of behavior modification.* Baltimore: University Park Press, 1978. (a)

Kazdin, A. E. The application of operant techniques in treatment rehabilitation and education. In S. L. Garfield & A. E. Bergin (Eds.), *Handbook of psychotherapy and behavior change.* New York: Wiley, 1978. (b)

Kazdin, A. E., & Hersen, M. The current status of behavior therapy. *Behavior Modification,* in press.

Kazdin, A. E., & Wilson, G. T. *Evaluation of behavior therapy: Issues, evidence, and research strategies.* Cambridge, Mass.: Ballinger, 1978. (b)

Krasner, L. On the death of behavior modification: Some comments from a mourner. *American Psychologist,* 1976, **31**, 387–388.

Lazarus, A. A. New methods in psychotherapy: A case study. *South Africa Medical Journal,* 1958, **33**, 660–664.

Ledwidge, B. Cognitive behavior modification: A step in the wrong direction? *Psychological Bulletin,* 1978, **85**, 353–375.

Ledwidge, B. Cognitive behavior modification or new ways to change minds: Reply to Mahoney and Kazdin. *Psychological Bulletin,* 1979, **86,** 1050–1053.

Lindsley, O. R. Operant conditioning methods applied to research in chronic schizophrenia. *Psychiatric Research Reports,* 1956, **5,** 118–139.

Lindsley, O. R., Skinner, B. F., & Solomon, H. C. *Studies in behavior therapy. Status report* **1**. Waltham, MA: Metropolitan State Hospital, 1953.

London, P. The end of ideology in behavior modification. *American Psychologist,* 1972, **27,** 913–920.

Mahoney, M. J., & Thorensen, C. E. (Eds.), *Self-control: Power to the person.* Monterey, CA: Brooks/Cole, 1974.

Meichenbaum, D. H. *Cognitive behavior modification.* New York: Plenum, 1977.

Pavlov, I. *Conditioned reflexes.* New York: Oxford University Press, 1927.

Rosenthal, T. L. Modeling therapies. In M. Hersen, R. M. Eisler, & P. M. Miller (Eds.), *Progress in behavior modification,* Vol. 12. New York: Academic Press, 1976.

Skinner, B. F. *The behavior of organisms.* New York: Appleton, 1938.

Ullmann, L. P., & Krasner, L. (Eds.), *Case studies in behavior modification.* New York: Holt, Rinehart & Winston, 1965.

Watson, J. B., & Rayner, R. Conditioned emotional reactions. *Journal of Experimental Psychology,* 1920, **3,** 1–14.

Wiert, W. M. Some recent criticism of behaviorism and learning theory with special reference to Breger and McGaugh and to Chomsky. *Psychological Bulletin,* 1967, **67,** 214–225.

Wilson, G. T. On the much discussed nature of the term "behavior therapy." *Behavior Therapy,* 1978, **9,** 89–98.

Wolpe, J. *The practice of behavior therapy.* New York: Pergamon, 1969.

Wolpe, J. Behavior therapy and its malcontents—I. Denial of its bases and psychodynamic fusionism. *Journal of Behavior Therapy and Experimental Psychiatry,* 1976, **7,** 1–5. (a)

Wolpe, J. Behavior therapy and its malcontents—II. Multimodal electicism, cognitive exclusivism and "exposure" empiricism. *Journal of Behavior Therapy and Experimental Psychiatry,* 1976, **7,** 109–116. (b)

CHAPTER 2

Phobic Disorders

David C. Rimm and R. Craig Lefebvre

When an individual shows an intense fear response to a stimulus or situation that by social consensus isn't particularly dangerous or frightening, that individual may be said to be suffering from a phobia or phobic disorder. In defining or describing phobias, it is common for writers to add that phobics themselves view their fears as irrational or in some sense disproportionate to the likelihood that the situation really is threatening or dangerous (Beck, 1976; DSM-III, 1980).

It is not uncommon for writers of a Freudian persuasion to incorporate the notion of displacement into their descriptions of phobic reactions (e.g., DSM-II, 1968; Fenichel, 1945; Wolberg, 1967). In their view, what the phobic really fears are unconscious thoughts or impulses, typically of a sexual or aggressive nature, that originate during early childhood. Inasmuch as these thoughts or impulses are totally unacceptable to the individual, he displaces the fear to previously neutral situations or objects. This view of phobias is a good illustration of an all-too-common practice in the traditional psychiatric approaches to diagnoses: the intertwining of *description* (i.e., phobias as irrational or exaggerated fears) with *theorizing* (i.e., phobias as *displaced* fear reactions). It is noteworthy that DSM-III (1980), the most recently American Psychiatric Association Diagnostic Manual, omits the notion of displacement when phobic reactions are described. Instead, it describes phobic disorders as

Persistent and irrational fear of a specific object, activity, or situation that results in a compelling desire to avoid the dreaded object, activity, or situation (the phobic stimulus) . . . when the avoidance behavior or fear is a significant source of distress to the individual or interferes with social or role functioning, a diagnosis of a Phobic Disorder is warranted (DSM-III, p. 225).

As we just noted, the Freudian view of phobias assumes they are symptomatic of unconscious conflicts. Later we make the case that the psychoanalytic conceptualization of phobias is of limited value, at best. This notwithstanding, conflict most certainly does play a critical role in fear reactions that can be labeled as phobias (Costello, 1970; Hayes, 1976). To illustrate, consider a woman who lives in the heart of Manhattan. She is very much a "city girl" and has absolutely no interest in exploring the countryside, hiking, camping, and furthermore, she finds zoos a monumental bore. When questioned, she does indicate that she is very much afraid of harmless snakes, and when asked to approach a caged garden snake, she refuses even to touch the cage, let alone handle or touch the snake. Can this person be described as "snake phobic"? The answer must be, not necessarily. After all, there is nothing in the situation that would make approaching and handling the snake particularly rewarding (in Hayes' words, there is no "approach contingency"). Ergo, how can we be sure her fear really is that intense? But now, let us suppose that we set up a powerful approach contingency. If she touches the snake, for 10 seconds, barehanded, we convince her that we will reward her with $5000. Assuming that she isn't independently wealthy, if she *still* refuses, she may be legitimately labeled snake phobic. If this same Manhattanite verbalized an intense fear of going above the third floor of any building, this would, in all likelihood, qualify as a phobia, given the obvious approach contingencies associated with living and/or working in high-rise buildings in the Big Apple. The reader should note that the conflict we are presently discussing is very much in the behaviorist tradition and that no reference is made to unconscious motivation.

DESCRIPTION OF PHOBIC DISORDERS

What are the manifestations of a phobic reaction? *Behaviorally,* the most common response is avoidance of a specific situation, or escape if the individual unexpectedly encounters that situation. *Physiological responses* when one is exposed to the phobic stimuli (real or imagined) are varied but typically include increases in heart rate, increased muscle tension, constriction of peripheral blood vessels (which accounts for why our hands are sometimes cold when we are frightened), and changes in respiration (Rachman, 1974). *Cognitive* responses might include verbalizations such as "something terrible will happen," "I've got to get out of here," "I'm terrified," or images of catastrophic consequences (person "sees" self falling off the building and hears a thud on the sidewalk below) (Beck, 1976; Ellis, 1973; Rimm, Janda, Lancaster, Nahl, & Dittmar, 1977). The verbalizations might be overt, as with a client telling the therapist about his experiences, or they might be covert (i.e., what the client thinks in the phobic situation). As Lick and Katkin (1976) note, clients typically show phobic manifestations in all three spheres or systems—behavioral, physiological, cognitive. It should be noted, however, that *changes* in any one of these response systems do not necessarily correlate with changes in the other response systems (Hodgson & Rachman, 1974). We return to this point when we discuss the two-factor theory of fear acquisition and maintenance later in this chapter.

The above discussion suggests several ways in which clinicians and researchers may assess the degree to which an individual is fearful in a given situation. Behaviorally, how willing is the subject to approach a harmless snake or the edge of a building, or how much agitation does the person show while making a speech or taking an examination? (Sometimes the approach contingencies are so strong, phobics feel compelled to remain in the target situation, in which case the assessor must look for behavioral symptoms of fear other than escape or avoidance.) A good example of one such measure is Paul's Timed Behavioral Checklist (Paul, 1966) used to assess speech anxiety. Physiologically, does the subject's heart rate (or frontalis muscle tension) show a marked increase when confronted with the phobic situation? Electrophysiological recording devices are commonly used for making such measurements. Cognitively, does the individual verbalize fear vis-à-vis the phobic stimulus? A client may indicate fear via a rough screening device such as the Fear Survey Schedule (Wolpe & Lang, 1964). The FSS lists a large number of common fear-producing situations or stimuli and the client indicates on a five-point scale how fearful he is in each. Similarly, clients may rate their fear level (say on a 10-point scale) while in an actual phobic situation.[1] We should mention that whereas researchers typically do rely on behavioral and physiological as well as self-report measures in assessing phobic responding, clinicians typically limit themselves to self-report. As a rule, practicing clinicians don't have the equipment or facilities to allow for the sophisticated assessment procedures afforded to researchers. Hopefully, this will not always be the case.

INCIDENCE

How common are phobic disorders? This question raises a seeming paradox: experience would seem to suggest they are very common and some research findings corroborate this. For example, Brandon (1960) reported that 38% of the females and 20% of the males in an urban community in England reported phobic symptoms. On the other hand, diagnoses of phobias (or phobic neurosis, phobic disorder) are rather rare among clinical populations, with most studies citing between a 3 to 12% incidence rate in outpatient psychiatric populations (DSM-III, 1980; Eiduson, 1968; Frazier & Carr, 1967; Marks, 1970). One obvious reason for this apparent contradiction is that whereas many individuals will readily acknowledge having fears that society considers irrational, in most cases those fears don't especially interfere with the individual's daily functioning (Rimm et al., 1977). Even when the phobia does interfere with one's daily functioning, hospitalization would rarely be required. Further, were an individual with phobic symptoms to end up in a mental hospital, there is certainly no guarantee that he would receive the phobic diagnosis. The distinction between certain types of phobias (especially agoraphobia and pervasive social phobias) and so-called anxiety neuroses can be quite nebulous. In fact, whether a particular patient is seen as suffering from a phobia or anxiety neurosis will depend in part on the orientation of the psychologist or psychiatrist making the diagnosis. Traditionally, the anxiety experienced by the anxiety neurotic is thought to be "free floating" (Buss, 1966), that is, not triggered by specific sets of environmental stimuli or events. But recall that behaviorally oriented clinicians are inclined to view *all* behavior as directly or indirectly triggered by environmental events. In other words, whereas a psychodynamically oriented clinician might diagnose a particularly anxious patient as suffering from anxiety neurosis, a behaviorist might well label the same patient as phobic.

---

[1] The technology of behavioral assessment is becoming increasingly sophisticated and complex, and a thorough discussion of the assessment of phobic behavior is well beyond the scope of this chapter. The interested reader, however, is referred to the *Handbook of behavioral assessment* (edited by Ciminero, Calhoun, & Adams, 1977) and *Behavioral assessment: A practical handbook* (edited by Hersen & Bellack, 1976).

Consider the following case history (taken from Rimm's files, published in Rimm & Somervill, 1977, pp. 63–64):

J.R., age 40, had spent most of his adult life in a mental institution in the Southwest. The diagnosis, unchanged throughout his many hospitalizations, was anxiety neurosis. At age 18 he entered college, intending to become a minister. Although above average in intelligence he found college distasteful and after one year he dropped out. He soon married and is the father of two children. Interestingly, his wife, who had been diagnosed as schizophrenic, was not hospitalized, while J.R., a neurotic, remained in an institution.

His chief complaint was what he described as ever-present anxiety. Often he seemed unable or unwilling to see any connection between external events and his level of anxiety. Yet from all observable indications, his distress was markedly influenced by external events, and in a strikingly predictable manner. He showed much more anxiety after spending time with his wife, who most observers described as a shrew. He became visibly shaken whenever the subject of his children was broached; he believed himself to be inadequate as a father. He evidenced a reaction best described as panic whenever his therapist raised the possibility that he might get better and leave the hospital. He had no history of employment, his family relationships were highly unsatisfactory, and his only friends were in the hospital. When interacting with his friends, or engaging in nondemanding, routine hospital activities, he appeared to be relatively calm.

The case of J.R. was not presented to convince the reader that the diagnostic category "anxiety neurosis" is therefore invalid, but rather to point up the fact that many persons with this label could as readily be diagnosed as phobic. We might point out that the ambiguity in differential diagnoses has led to the dropping of "anxiety neurosis" in the DSM-III nomenclature, and the term "generalized anxiety reaction" (referring to anxiety that does not have situational or object constraints) substituted in its place.

TYPES OF PHOBIAS

In principle there are as many different phobias as there are discrete stimuli or situations. Table 1 lists some of the more common phobias (and some exotic ones as well).

However, factor analytic studies suggest that fears tend to cluster; that is, they are interrelated within individuals (Hallam & Hafner, 1978; Landy & Gaupp, 1971; Rubin, Lawlis, Tasto, & Namenek, 1969). The results of Landy and Gaupp (1971), who used college students as subjects, are typical: the fear clusters include animate nonhuman organisms, interpersonal events, the unknown, noise, and medical-surgical procedures. Miller, Barrett, Hampe, and Noble (1972) found three main clusters of fears in children: physical injury, natural events, and psychological stress. Note that Miller et al. did not obtain an "interpersonal" or "social" factor in their sample. This is consistent with Rachman's (1974) observation that there are developmental changes in relation to the objects that individuals fear. Typically as the child matures, fears of natural events (e.g., storms, the dark) diminish, while interpersonal fears (e.g., social evaluation) increase.

Table 1.   Phobic Diagnoses and Their Translation

Acrophobia	Fear of heights
Agoraphobia	Fear of open places
Ailurophobia	Fear of cats
Aquaphobia	Fear of water
Claustrophobia	Fear of closed spaces
Cynophobia	Fear of dogs
Decidophobia	Fear of making decisions
Mysophobia	Fear of dirt and germs
Ophidophobia	Fear of snakes
Pyrophobia	Fear of fire
Xenophobia	Fear of strangers

Often a distinction is made between simple and complex phobias. Simple phobias (e.g., fear of heights, fear of snakes) are relatively more circumscribed, and therefore probably somewhat easier for afflicted individuals to cope with than complex phobias which include pervasive social phobias and agoraphobia. Complex phobias are in general less responsive to systematic desensitization than simple phobias (Goldstein & Chambless, 1978). Agoraphobics and social phobics are also more likely than simple phobics to show prolonged physiological arousal (as measured by GSR responses) in the absence of the eliciting stimuli (Lader & Matthews, 1968). Perhaps relatedly, agoraphobics frequently find it difficult to relate their anxiety to external events in a systematic or predictable manner (Goldstein & Chambless, 1978). This lack of predictability leads to the development of the "fear of fears" so characteristic of agoraphobics, and the pervasive anxiety that so often results in the misdiagnosis of these patients.

Agoraphobia is commonly defined as the "fear of open spaces," but this can be very misleading.[2] It implies, after all, that a typical agoraphobic would be terrified if left alone on a deserted prairie in the Texas panhandle, but would be very comfortable on a crowded New York subway. In fact, if anything, the opposite is true, especially if our agoraphobic happens to be familiar with the panhandle of Texas. What exactly is the clinical picture of agoraphobia? In severe cases, the individual may literally be housebound to the point of being fearful even of going outside to the mailbox or to pick up the morning paper. For the agoraphobic housewife, keeping the kitchen stocked with basic foodstuffs such as bread or milk may be virtually overwhelming, and she may spend much of her day planning strategies wherein others go to the market for her. In contrast to other phobics, agoraphobics are far more likely to report physical symptoms associated with intense anxiety, for example, difficulty breathing, feelings of dizziness (Hallam & Hafner, 1978). What situations do agoraphobics find especially frightening? Obviously it varies considerably from case to case, but as Hallam and Hafner note, travel in public conveyances is high on the list, as are open spaces, and *confined*

---

[2] Literally translated agoraphobia is "the fear of the market place," a definition that as it turns out is more descriptive.

spaces; ergo, the crowded subway that is an irritant to most people is literally a terrifying experience to the typical agoraphobic. Relative to most other phobics, agoraphobics are more likely to verbalize fears of illness and death. As we noted earlier, agoraphobics show a fear of fear, manifested frequently in statements like "My God . . . if I go outside, I might panic . . . what if I fainted?" One has the impression that some agoraphobics believe they will literally die of fear and it is useful, therapeutically, to point out that while panic is a most aversive experience, it isn't fatal. (We realize that chronic intense anxiety can in the long run be fatal. However, the intense anxiety associated with agoraphobia is of an acute, intermittent nature.) Another theme common in agoraphobia is concern with loss of control. By loss of control the client might be referring to fainting, but he could also mean screaming, crying, or even impulsive violence (self-directed, e.g., jumping in front of a subway train; or directed toward others, e.g., impulsively attacking another with a sharp object). It is not unlikely that agoraphobics' fears of crowds, public conveyences, and so forth, at least in some measure are mediated by their literally obsessive concern with panic and/or losing control. In addition, agoraphobic behavior may be maintained by social reinforcers provided by important people in the client's environment. For example, the client's spouse may assume responsibility for performing activities the client might find distasteful (i.e., shopping for food, clothes, etc.). Agoraphobia is one of the most incapacitating phobias and, not surprisingly, it is commonly associated with relatively high levels of depression (Hallam & Hafner, 1978).

From the above the reader may get the impression that among phobics, only agoraphobics show truly intense and debilitating anxiety. Clearly, this is not the case. Consider, for example, the fear of harmless snakes. As the reader may know, many behavior therapy studies dealing with the evaluation of treatment interventions have used snake-phobic (or at least snake-avoidant) subjects because they are fairly common in the general population and because the fear is relatively easy to assess in a laboratory situation. Frequently, it has been argued that such studies are lacking in inherent validity because the subjects aren't true phobics (e.g., Cooper, Furst, & Bridger, 1969), that is, it is a "normal fear" or that somehow the fear of harmless snakes doesn't constitute a real problem. For some subjects this may be true to some extent, but be advised that for many individuals, fear of harmless snakes is most debilitating. Consider Mahoney's comments (personal communication, cited in Rimm, 1976) regarding a case history (Mahoney, 1971).

When her husband's boss and wife came over for dinner, they sat quietly at the table, watching the last few minutes of the news on television. The announcer made some reference to a snake (Mahoney does not recall whether one was actually shown) at which point she panicked, screamed, and turned the table upside down, literally spilling its contents all over the guests and floor.

Incidentally, the female in question, who was a voluntary participant in a research project, did eventually overcome her fear via sequential treatment involving desensitization, symbolic modeling, live modeling, and participant modeling (we'll describe each of these later in the chapter). Bandura (1978) in responding to Cooper, Furst, and Bridger (1969) makes a very cogent point: In the case of individuals having intense fears of harmless snakes, the problem . . . is not that they will have much commerce with reptiles should they expand their range of activities. Rather, because of their phobic dread of snakes they cannot perform their vocational activities or force themselves to do so under heavy stress costs; they cannot venture into, and enjoy, the outdoors; and they are frequently tormented by intrusive, frightening thoughts and recurrent nightmares [p. 67].

Bandura's comments are apropos in other types of phobias as well, whether simple or complex. So often what is truly debilitating about intense phobias isn't the individual's reaction while in the phobic situation, even if such a reaction is typically one of pure panic. Rather it is the dread phobics experience in anticipating possible confrontations with the phobic situation, and further, the complex and often exhausting rituals they go through to avoid such confrontations. To illustrate, recently Rimm treated a middle-aged male who was fearful when driving across high bridges. He'd go miles out of his way to avoid such bridges, but when this wasn't possible he would experience dread from the moment he got into his car until he had crossed the bridge (and if the return trip involved the same bridge, this would be sufficient to ruin an otherwise pleasant trip or vacation). When phobic individuals are embarrassed about their fears, and therefore attempt to hide them (not at all uncommon), the problem is further compounded. Several years ago Rimm treated a woman intensely fearful of flying (the case is described in Rimm and Somervill, 1977). She had acquired the fear during a particularly turbulent flight the previous year, and because she viewed her problem as silly and as a sign of weakness, she avoided telling her husband about it. Her husband, who had been working some months as a consultant in a remote part of South America was at a loss as to why his wife kept putting off flying down there to join him and began questioning whether she still loved him. Finally, in a letter, she told him of her flying phobia, but that in spite of this she would join him. His response, to her surprise, was understanding and supportive; but now, having made the plane reservation she experienced almost continuous dread. By the time Rimm saw her she wasn't sleeping or eating well and had lost considerable weight. She noted that her close friends, who normally saw her as a person of considerable composure, were lately telling her she was a nervous wreck and should seek help.

A second dichotomy for the broad classification of phobias has been put forth by Martin Seligman (de Silva, Rachman, & Seligman, 1977; Seligman, 1971). According to his hypothesis, phobias are *prepared* or *unprepared*. Preparedness refers to an innate predisposition toward learning to fear certain types of stimuli or stimulus configurations. Presumably, during the course of our evolution, avoiding certain stimuli or situations (e.g., high places, snakes, spiders) had survival value and by natural selection, the predisposition to avoid those stimuli was programmed into our nervous systems. If Seligman's hypothesis is correct, one would expect that a high proportion of clinical phobias would be prepared and that is precisely what de Silva et al. (1977) found. (In their sample of 69 phobics, 66 were prepared.) Another obvious prediction was that prepared phobias would be more difficult to eliminate than unprepared phobias. This was not confirmed, however. If anything, the unprepared phobias were more resistant to elimination using behavior therapy techniques. Elsewhere, Rachman and Seligman (1976) have noted that behavior therapy techniques might be more appropriate for prepared than unprepared phobias. On the basis of limited case history data, they raise the possibility that broader rehabilitation programs might be required in the case of unprepared phobias. Laboratory research of the preparedness model for phobias has not provided unequivocal evidence for its usefulness. Olman, Erixon, and Lofberg (1975) have demonstrated in an adult population that a fear response can be elicited equally well to human faces, houses, and snakes after repeated pairings of these stimuli to electric shocks. An additional finding was that the fear reactions to houses and faces were extinguished more quickly than fear reactions to snakes. Needless to say, at this stage no definitive statement can be made regarding the role that preparedness has in the etiology and treatment of phobias. Nevertheless, Seligman and his colleagues have raised a very intriguing question.

THE ETIOLOGY OF PHOBIAS

The Psychodynamic View

The psychodynamic view of the etiology of phobias is well-illustrated by a case described by Nemiah (1978). A female client participates in a forbidden sexual encounter that happens to occur on a boat. The memory of the encounter generates painful anxiety. In order to cope with this anxiety, the client displaces it (unconsciously) to the *memory* of the boat, inasmuch as the boat is an emotionally neutral stimulus. This attempt at coping with the anxiety is not terribly successful, however, because she finds it difficult *not* to recall the image of the boat. She then employs the defense mechanism of projection, wherein the anxiety is projected or transferred to actual boats. Thus she has provided herself with a class of stimuli (real boats) that can be avoided. Our boat phobic pays an obvious price, however; she must avoid places where she might encounter boats, and she is fearful that she might see boats depicted on TV or in the newspapers.

Why was the client in such conflict about the sexual encounter in the first place? According to early psychoanalytic formulations (see Nemiah, 1978), phobias reflected poorly resolved oedipal conflicts. More contemporary psychodynamic writers note that the early childhood conflict considered to be critical in the development of subsequent phobias might not be limited to sexuality, that is, conflicts about aggression or dependency might also have an important etiological significance.

While a thorough critique of the above is beyond the scope of this chapter, we would like to point to one observation frequently noted in the behavior therapy literature (e.g., Bandura, 1969; Lazarus, 1971; Wolpe, 1973). If the psychodynamic formulation was generally accurate, direct so-called symptomatic treatment (e.g., using systematic desensitization) should either be ineffective, or if it is effective in alleviating the phobic symptom, a new substitute symptom should surface. After all, the underlying problem has not been treated. However, there is presently a wealth of clinical and experimental data (e.g., Bandura, 1969; Lazarus, 1971; Rimm & Masters, 1979; Wolpe, 1973) suggesting that behavioral techniques are often quite effective in removing or reducing phobic behaviors and that symptom substitution (as it is commonly called) almost never occurs. Largely because of such evidence, the doctrine of symptom substitution is no longer given widespread credence. Interestingly, however, the psychodynamic interpretation of the etiology of phobias is still considered credible by much of the psychiatric establishment. (Nemiah's account of the boat phobic is presented in the chapter on Psychoneurotic Disorders in the 1978 *Harvard guide to modern psychiatry,* edited by Nicholi.)

Behavioral Views—The Classical Behavioral Interpretation

You may recall from your introductory psychology course a famous experiment (demonstration might be a better word, since it wasn't well controlled) conducted by John Watson and Rosalie Rayner (1920). A 5-year-old child, Albert, was simultaneously exposed to a white rat, paired with a loud sound. After several such pairings, the rat came to elicit a fear response from Albert, who prior to the experience had shown no fear at all of the animal. This illustrates classical or Pavlovian conditioning (Pavlov, 1927), and for many years behaviorists viewed the little Albert experience as prototypic of the way in which people acquire fears (whether irrational or not). O. H. Mowrer (1947, 1960) put forth a major modification, or addition, in his famous *two-factor theory.* The question that Mowrer addressed is a very reasonable one: it is well known that fears conditioned in the laboratory may undergo *extinction.* That is, if you present the so-called conditioned stimulus (e.g., the white rat in Albert's case) repeatedly, without the unconditioned stimulus (the loud sound), the emotional response would gradually die away. Why then are fear responses in the real world seemingly so resistant to extinction? After all, we have all known phobics who are repeatedly exposed to the feared stimulus but remain phobics. The reason for this, according to Mowrer, is that when the individual confronts the phobic situation and begins to experience anxiety or fear, the habitual response of escape or avoidance follows. Associated with such escape or avoidance is fear reduction, and it is this reduction in fear or anxiety that reinforces the tendency to avoid the phobic situation. This then makes it impossible for the fear to undergo extinction. The term "two-factor theory" is used to indicate that two types of learning are involved in the acquisition and maintenance of phobic behavior: classical conditioning, which is responsible for the acquisition of the fear response, and operant conditioning, wherein the escape or avoidance behavior is reinforced and maintained.

In recent years, the two-factor theory has undergone considerable criticism (e.g., Herrnstein, 1969; Rachman, 1976). If avoidance behavior is driven by a fear response, then the correspondence between fear level and the probability or strength of an avoidance response ought to be very high. Often, however, this is not the case (see Rachman, 1976). Consider the number of times you have approached a situation, or taken on a task, in spite of intense feelings of fear.

The Vicarious Acquisition of Phobias

While it may be that some phobic reactions are acquired by a more or less *direct* process of classical conditioning, there is laboratory and clinical evidence that fears may also be learned through a process of *vicarious* conditioning (Bandura & Rosenthal, 1966; Berger, 1962). Thus, observing another person supposedly receiving electric shock paired with a certain stimulus can cause an observer to develop an autonomic response (suggesting anxiety) in the presence of the same stimulus. The observed aversive experience can be psychological as well as physical (e.g., observing another person experience repeated failures, Craig & Weinstein, 1965). In the typical laboratory investigation, emotional reactions acquired by vicarious conditioning are mild and probably readily extinguishable. In clinical settings, however, one may come upon individuals showing intense and enduring phobic reactions acquired by vicarious conditioning. For example, Rimm (1973) treated a woman intensely fearful of seeing any manifestation of mutilation (e.g., a dead animal beside the road, a movie depicting blood or mutilization). The phobia interfered with her life in that she dreaded riding in a car (especially in rural settings) lest she see a dead animal, and she avoided movies and TV shows that most would consider totally innocuous (and which she might otherwise have enjoyed). She readily traced her phobia to an event she had witnessed two years prior to treatment: her husband accidentally running over a small child.

How important is vicarious conditioning relative to direct conditioning in the acquisition of phobas? In one investigation (Rimm et al., 1977), among 45 phobic subjects only 3 (6.7%) were able to relate vicarious experiences to the development of their fear, whereas 16 (35.6%) were able to account for their fears in terms of direct experiences (e.g., an acrophobic reporting falling out of a tree). It should be pointed out, however, that the subjects used by Rimm et al. were not intensely phobic; that is, most would not have sought help in overcoming their fears. The relative contribution of vicarious experiences in the etiology of phobias found in a clinical setting may be greater. We have known many clients who have developed debilitating phobias as a consequence of seeing movies of a particularly frightening nature (Alfred Hitchcock's *Psycho* or *The Birds* or more recently, *Jaws*).

Cognitive Factors in the Acquisition of Phobias

In recent years many behavior therapists have come to view cognitions (i.e., thoughts, images) as playing a major role in the development and maintenance of maladaptive behaviors (Bandura, 1969, 1977a; Beck, 1976; Mahoney, 1974; Meichenbaum, 1977). Thus far we've suggested two ways in which fear responses may be acquired—via direct experience (i.e., first order classical conditioning), and via vicarious experience (i.e., vicarious conditioning). In recent years many behavior therapists have come to view *cognitions,* that is, thoughts and images, as playing an important role in the development and maintenance of maladaptive behaviors (e.g., Bandura, 1969, 1977; Beck, 1976; Ellis, 1962; Ellis & Grieger, 1977; Mahoney, 1974; Meichenbaum, 1977; Rimm & Masters, 1974, 1979). The so-called cognitive-learning perspective would emphasize the role of either overt or covert verbal instruction in the acquisition of phobic responses. That is, a person might develop an intense fear of an object or situation merely as a consequence of being *told* that the object or situation was dangerous. It is assumed that after receiving such instruction, the individual engages in a process of active rehearsal whenever he is confronted with the phobic situation; for example, people afraid of flying might say to themselves "flying is dangerous . . . the plane might crash."

In addition, cognitively oriented clinicians view the phobic thoughts as a result of specific, discrete, and relatively automatic internal dialogues in which information about the phobic stimulus is processed. Further, this internal dialogue is under the control of an idiosyncratic psychological system that is usually found to contain one or more of the following distortions (Beck, 1976; Sokolov, 1972). *Personalization,* the most common cognitive style in phobics (Beck, 1976), is characterized by the client interpreting events in terms of some personal meaning. Personalization manifests itself most often as an "inner drama" in which the client identifies with the "victim" of the feared stimulus (e.g., people who die in an airplane crash). *Polarized* or dichotomous thinking occurs whenever the client construes events in opposites. *Arbitrary inference* involves jumping to a conclusion when there is no supporting evidence, or even contradictory evidence exists. *Overgeneralization* occurs when the client makes an unjustified (based on empirical evidence) generalization on the basis of a single incident.

At this time, cognitive theories dealing with the development of phobias have received very little notice in the experimental literature. Wade, Malloy, and Proctor (1977) found that negative imagery associated with a phobic stimulus (snake) was significantly correlated with both self-reported fear of the snake and subsequent avoidance behavior in a test situation. May (1977) has found that phobic thoughts produce as much anxiety as the actual phobic stimuli. May's conclusions are that there may be a significant role played by cognitive processes in the development of phobias, but we caution the reader against drawing an "arbitrary inference" from these data.

In the cognitive-learning view, self-verbalizations play a critical role in mediating the fear response. If the individual were somehow induced into *not* engaging in such self-verbalization, the fear response would be greatly attenuated. We have more to say about the methods of cognitive-learning therapy in the treatment section of this chapter.

The reader should be aware that the role of cognitions in mediating maladaptive behavior, including phobic responses, is presently a subject of heated debate. Some writers take the position that conscious thoughts play a key role in virtually everything a human being does (Lazarus, 1977). On the other side of the coin, certain so-called radical behaviorists (Rachlin, 1977) voice serious reservations about the scientific or practical value of attempting to deal with unseen entities such as thoughts and images. Something of an intermediate position is taken by others such as Wolpe (1978) who, while stressing the role of direct (and possibly vicarious) experience in the acquisition and maintenance of maladaptive patterns of human behavior, nevertheless notes that some problem behavior may reflect irrational or distorted thinking. Our own clinical and research experiences suggest that frequently fear and avoidance behavior associated with phobias does, at least in part, reflect conscious thinking. When such seems to be the case, this does not necessarily mean that the fear was *acquired* via cognitive learning. Thus as a consequence of falling out of a tree (direct experience), a person may now experience a moderate degree of anxiety, not in and of itself incapacitating, whenever he observes stimuli associated with high places. However, there is research evidence (Horowtiz & Becker, 1971; Horowitz, Becker, & Moskowitz, 1971) that anxiety may itself act as the cue and/or driving force for ruminative thinking (e.g., "my God, I might fall and be killed") that leads to levels of anxiety that truly are incapacitating.

APPROACHES TO TREATMENT

A detailed exposition of psychodynamic approaches to the treatment of phobias is clearly beyond the scope of the present chapter and text. The orthodox psychoanalytic approach to phobias, as well as most other psychological disorders, stresses the gaining of insight as client and therapist laboriously attempt to "undercover" and "work through" the unconscious conflicts of which the phobia is symptomatic (see Freud, 1968; Fenichel, 1945). More contemporary psychodynamic approaches (e.g., Alexander, French, et al., 1945; Wachtel, 1977), while operating under similar theoretical assumptions, tend in practice to provide a more "here and now" problem-solving orientation that is so characteristic of the behavioral approaches.

The principle behavioral approaches to the treatment of phobias include *systematic desensitization, assertive training, implosive therapy, flooding* (which is closely related to implosive therapy), and *modeling*. The cognitive-learning approaches include a variety of techniques often subsumed under the label of cognitive restructuring, as well as thought-stopping. What follows is a description and evaluation of each of these treatments.

Systematic Desensitization

Systematic desensitization was the first widely used behavior therapy technique aimed at alleviating phobias. It was developed by Joseph Wolpe (Wolpe, 1958, 1973), a psychiatrist. Typically the technique involves having the client imagine scenes related to his phobia while in a state of deep relaxation. Relaxation may be induced in a variety of ways, but most commonly some adaption of Jacobson's procedure is used (Jacobson, 1938, 1964). Clients are asked to tense and relax voluntary muscles following some prescribed order (see Goldfried & Davison, 1976; Rimm & Masters, 1979; Wolpe, 1973).[3] Having achieved a state of deep relaxation, clients are then asked to imagine the aforementioned scenes in hierarchal order, beginning with the scene judged by the client to be the least fear inducing. When the client can imagine that scene without experiencing anxiety, the next scene is presented. If anxiety is experienced (usually indicated by the client's raising a finger), the scene may be presented again in its original form, or perhaps modified so as to be less threatening to the client, or a prior scene may be presented—procedures vary somewhat from therapist to therapist. In any event, the immediate goal is to complete the entire hierarchy so that any of the hierarchy scenes may be imagined without experiencing noticeable anxiety. The number of scenes (items) per hierarchy varies considerably depending on the pervasiveness of the phobia, but 15 to 20 scenes would be typical. Ordinarily one can expect to complete one to three hierarchy items per 50-minute session.

[3] Borkovec and Sides (1979) reviewed a number of studies that have investigated the effects of procedural variables on the client's ability to relax. They conclude that the more successful treatments include more sessions of relaxation training (mean = 4.5), with the therapist actually administering the relaxation protocol (versus playing a tape), and with the client controlling the progress of training.

There is evidence that the nature of the treatment rationale given the client may play an important role in treatment outcome (Rosen, 1976). For example, a credible therapy rationale is more likely to be associated with improvement than, for example, a rationale that characterizes desensitization as an "experimental" procedure. The therapeutic rationale most often given by therapists derives from Wolpe's theoretical interpretation of desensitization. For Wolpe (1958, 1973), systematic desensitization reflects an underlying process of *reciprocal inhibition*. According to Wolpe, deep-muscle relaxation induces excitation in the parasympathetic branch of the autonomic nervous system, and this parasympathetic excitation has the psychophysiological effect of inhibiting activity in the sympathetic branch of the autonomic nervous system. According to Wolpe, it is sympathetic nervous activity that is the substrate or basis for anxiety, thus deep-muscle relaxation has the more or less automatic effect of reducing or inhibiting anxiety. In desensitization, Wolpe assumes that this state of anxiety inhibition is conditioned to each of the hierarchy scenes, so that the client experiences relaxation instead of anxiety when confronted with the phobic stimuli in the real world. Naturally, the specifics of the therapeutic rationale are geared to the level of sophistication of the particular client; that is, one need not load a client down with neurophysiological jargon. Under the Wolpe rationale, the main ideas to be presented to the client are that the client will visualize heretofore frightening scenes in *graduated* fashion, while the client is relaxed, so that the client learns to experience relaxation instead of anxiety in the presence of phobic stimuli. This is often referred to as the *counterconditioning* rationale. (Counterconditioning means learning to experience one set of emotional responses for another in the presence of a given set of stimuli; reciprocal inhibition is a special case or instance of counterconditioning with relaxation utilized to counteract the anxiety.)

There are, as it turns out, other theoretical interpretations of what precisely is happening to the client undergoing systematic desensitization, and the therapeutic rationales deriving from these competing theories would obviously differ from that of Wolpe. One influential alternative theory has been put forth by Goldfried and Trier (1974) who stress the acquisition of active coping skills rather than the passive, automatic learning of a response that inhibits anxiety. The Goldfried and Trier treatment rationale provides clients the expectation that desensitization will teach them how to cope with or "relax away" anxiety. The treatment procedure itself differs somewhat from Wolpe's version of desensitization. Where with the Wolpean approach every effort is made to keep anxiety at the lowest possible level, under the coping approach it is necessary that clients experience some degree of anxiety while imagining hierarchy scenes (as we noted, the client's task is to reduce the anxiety). The Goldfried and Trier approach to desensitization bears a similarity to Suinn and Richardson's Anxiety Management Training (Suinn & Richardson, 1971) and Meichenbaum's Stress Innoculation Training (Meichenbaum, 1977), although the latter is more explicitly cognitive in nature.

There are other theoretical conceptualizations of systematic desensitization. For example, Ellis and his followers (Ellis, 1962) would argue that desensitization in effect discourages the client from engaging in self-verbalizations that lead to anxiety. Bandura has also provided an essentially cognitive interpretation of desensitization (Bandura, 1977b). Desensitization, by lowering physiological arousal vis-à-vis the phobic stimuli, enhances the client's belief that he/she can in fact cope with the phobic situation, which in turn leads to more effective functioning in the phobic situation. Both Ellis and Bandura are partial to therapeutic techniques other than desensitization for reducing phobic behavior, hence they have not provided specific therapeutic rationales to be used with desensitization. Another interpretation, also cognitive in nature, is that systematic desensitization functions as a placebo. Thus Kazdin and Wilcoxon (1976) point out that when desensitization has been compared with a placebo judged by subjects as equally credible as desensitization, typically desensitization is *not* found to be superior. Note that Kazdin and Wilcoxon are not saying that desensitization therefore is nothing more than a placebo—such a contention would be virtually impossible to prove. What they are saying is that presently such an interpretation can't be ruled out.

Implosive Therapy and Flooding

Both implosive therapy and flooding, like desensitization, involve exposing the client, through mental images, to phobic-relevant stimuli.[4] An important difference is that whereas desensitization (à la Wolpe at least) requires that the client experience minimal anxiety, in implosive therapy and flooding the therapist deliberately attempts to generate very high levels of anxiety. Recall from our discussion of the two-factor theory that escape from or avoidance of the phobic stimulus tends to reinforce phobic behavior by preventing extinction of the fear response. The rationale behind implosive therapy and flooding is that if the client can be induced to remain in the phobic situation (through mental images) in spite of very high levels of anxiety, extinction of the anxiety will result.

Sometimes in the behavior therapy literature the terms "implosive therapy" and "flooding" are used interchangeably, but in our view there are some important theoretical and procedural differences. Flooding involves having the client imagine what is tantamount to the most frightening items on a desensitization hierarchy without first having worked one's way up the hierarchy. Implosive therapy may involve this as well, but in addition, clients are asked to imagine scenes or situations derived from psychoanalytic theory. According to Thomas Stampfl (see Stampfl, 1961, 1967; Stampfl & Levis, 1967a, 1967b, 1968), most phobic behavior in adults arises as a result of traumatic learning experiences occurring in childhood. Consistent with psychoanalytic theory, such experiences are often associated with conflicts centering around themes of rejection, dependency, aggression, orality, anality, sexuality, loss of impulsive control, and guilt (Hogan, 1968; Stampfl, 1967). As we suggested, the therapist may present imaginal scenes not unlike those high on a desensitization hierarchy, but in short order the client is asked to imagine scenes that the therapist *assumes* reflect the client's unconscious fears and conflicts that are presumed to form the basic core of the client's phobia. To illustrate, consider the following scene, illustrating a theme of rejection.

Shut your eyes and imagine that you are a baby in your crib. You are in a dark, shabby, dirty room. You are alone and afraid. You are hungry and wet. You call for

---

[4] Occasionally, flooding procedures with human subjects involve exposure to actual phobic stimuli, as opposed to imaginal exposure. For obvious reasons, animal investigations of flooding always involve exposure to the actual anxiety-eliciting stimuli.

your mother, but no one comes. If only someone would change you; if only they would feed you and wrap you in a warm blanket. You look out the window of your room into the house next door, where a mother and father are giving another baby love, warmth and affection. Look how they love the baby. You are crying for your mother now. "Please mother, please come and love me." But no one comes. Finally, you hear some steps. They come closer, and closer, and closer. You hear someone outside your door. The door slowly opens. Your heart beats with excitement. There is your mother coming to love you. She is unbuttoning her blouse. She takes out her breast to feed you. Then she squirts your warm milk on the floor and steps on it. Look, see her dirty heel mark in your milk. She shouts, "I would rather waste my milk than give it to you. I wish you were never born; I never wanted you" [Hogan, 1969, p. 181].

Typically, scenes such as the above are presented very dramatically so as to elicit maximum anxiety. Whereas in desensitization, hierarchy items are presented for no more than 20 or 30 seconds, in implosive therapy (as well as flooding) the duration of scene exposure is far longer, often lasting for many minutes. The basic idea is to present the scene for whatever duration is required to allow for extinction to occur. The judgment that extinction has in fact occurred is based upon the therapist's observation that overt signs of anxiety (e.g., difficulty in breathing, tightening of one's mouth, clenching of fists) have greatly diminished. Such a judgment may be difficult to make, especially for beginning therapists.[5] What are the consequences of terminating a scene prior to extinction? For flooding (and we assume this also applies to implosive therapy) evidence suggests that a process of *sensitization* may be the result (Rachman, 1969; Baum, 1970), wherein the client's negative emotionality may actually be enhanced. In one investigation (McCutcheon & Adams, 1975), a 20-minute implosion session was associated with an increase in anxiety as measured by the GSR, with a behavioral test of fear failing to indicate improvement. When the duration of treatment was increased to 60 minutes, physiological arousal initially increased but then decreased. Following the 60-minute session, subjects did show reductions in fear as measured by the behavioral test. This increase and subsequent decrease in emotionality during the course of a single session of implosive therapy is well illustrated in a study by Orenstein and Carr (1975). Referring to Figure 1, note that heart rate increased during the first 10 minutes or so, remaining at a high level for the subsequent 10 minutes; this was followed by a relatively rapid return to a rate nearly as low as the pretreatment baseline.

The reader is cautioned *not* to interpret the above findings to mean that some fixed duration of implosive therapy, for example, 30 minutes will always be ideal. Keep in mind that these results are averaged across many subjects. Depending on the individual case, 25 to 30 minutes may be more than adequate, or it may be insufficient. As we noted earlier, the therapist must carefully monitor the individual client's anxiety level.

How effective is implosive therapy? As it turns out, the results tend to be mixed (see Rimm & Masters, 1979). Positive findings have been reported by Hogan and Kirchner (1967), Levis and Carrera (1967), McCutcheon and Adams (1975),

---

[5] Gauthier and Marshall (1977) report that terminating the scene based on an observer's noting anxiety reduction is superior to termination of the scene based on either electrophysiological measurement of heart rate or subjective report.

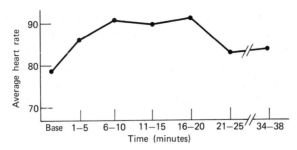

FIGURE 1.   Average heart rate during implosive therapy (adapted from Orenstein & Carr, 1975).

and Orenstein and Carr (1975), whereas essentially negative results were obtained by Fazio (1970) and Hodgson and Rachman (1970). Because procedures tend not to be standardized across investigations, conclusions regarding the general efficacy of implosive therapy are difficult to draw; durations of treatment vary from study to study. Additionally, the investigations vary considerably with respect to the degree to which psychoanalytic themes are or are not incorporated; that is, what one writer may call implosive therapy others might refer to as flooding. Several investigations have compared implosive therapy with systematic desensitization (e.g., Borkovec, 1970, 1972; Hekmat, 1973; McGlynn, 1968) and again the results are conflicting—sometimes desensitization is found to be superior and sometimes no significant treatment differences are reported. Interestingly no study has yet reported implosive therapy to be superior to desensitization (Rimm & Masters, 1979).

As we have noted, flooding (also referred to as response prevention inasmuch as treatment prevents avoidance or escape responses) differs from implosive therapy in that the former does not employ themes derived from psychoanalytic theory. Basically, then, flooding involves the relatively straightforward presentation (usually through mental images) of stimuli likely to elicit high levels of anxiety. The scenes are not embellished in any particular way nor are they presented in an especially dramatic fashion.[6] A variety of investigations and case histories suggest that flooding, like implosive therapy, may be of value in treating phobic reactions (e.g., Meyer, Robertson, & Tatlow, 1975; Wijesinghe, 1974; Yule, Sacks, & Hersov, 1974). When logistics allow, flooding may be conducted *in vivo,* where the situations or scenes are real rather than imagined. In three studies comparing imaginal and *in vivo* flooding (Boulougouris & Bassiakos, 1973; Emmelkamp & Wessels, 1975; Watson, Mullet, & Pillay, 1973), both modes of presentation were effective in reducing anxiety in agoraphobic subjects, but greater therapeutic progress was associated with "live practice," that is, having the subjects go outside. Whether *in vivo* flooding is in general superior to imaginal flooding is an interesting practical question awaiting an answer (Rimm & Masters, 1979).

We noted earlier that implosive therapy presented over short durations may be ineffective (and even harmful). There is evidence from animal studies (Baum,

[6] Two recent studies have concluded that the use of so-called horrifying scenes in flooding adds little to therapeutic effectiveness, and in some cases may actually impair successful treatment (Foa, Blau, Prout, & Latimer, 1977; Marshall, Gauthier, Christie, Currie, & Gordon, 1977).

1969) that brief periods of flooding may be similarly ineffective. Baum found that avoidance responding in rats was not extinguished following flooding sessions of 1-minute duration, but that extinction did occur as a result of exposure to the feared stimulus of 3–5 minutes. Findings with animals also suggest that engaging in activities not fear-related during flooding enhances the positive effects of flooding. As always, care must be exercised in generalizing to humans, but it may be that flooding in humans would be more effective were clients instructed to engage in activities such as exploration or assertion or even eating while exposed to the objects of their fear.

Imagery in Therapy

Systematic desensitization, implosive therapy, and flooding techniques have in common their reliance on the generation of vivid images by the client. While the use of imagery has been challenged as being nonbehavioristic (Locke, 1971), many practicing behavioral clinicians employ imagery-based techniques. Lang (1977) has conceptualized the image as being controlled by identifiable external stimuli (such as instructions) and measurable by the emotional responses of the client. In practice, this analysis indicates that effective imagery therapy is dependent on the skill of the therapist in *composing* and *delivering* imagery instructions, and on the ability of the client to *respond emotionally* to the image (Lang, 1977). In systematic desensitization then, the therapist's primary task is to develop stimuli (instructions) that are specific to the phobia and its context. For example, an instruction "Imagine that you are standing on a stage and about to begin your speech to a class of 20 students" is preferable to "Imagine that you are going to give a speech." Flooding and implosive therapy differ from systematic desensitization in that in these latter techniques the instructions emphasize the emotional responses of the subject with the environmental stimuli receiving somewhat less attention. Thus instructions take the form of "As you begin your speech, you notice your hands sweating and trembling, your heart is racing, your mouth has suddenly become dry, and you cannot swallow, and so on." Again, specific instructions are preferable to general ones such as "You become quite anxious." In practice, the clinician should attempt to specify both the stimulus and the response; while research into Lang's analysis of fear imagery has not yet appeared, we believe that the specification he encourages is advisable in clinical practice.

Modeling Procedures

During the past decade, modeling procedures have been increasingly used by behavior therapists in tackling a variety of clinical problems. The two most commonly used in dealing with phobic behavior are *graduated modeling* and *participant modeling.*

In *graduated modeling,* the client or subject observes a model (live or on film or TV) going through a series of behaviors or interactions vis-à-vis the phobic situation, graduated with respect to the degree of fear likely to be elicited. For example, Bandura, Grusec, and Menlove (1967) had children who were dog phobic observe live peer models interact with a dog. During the first treatment session, the model merely patted and fed the dog, which was confined to a pen. By the fifth session, treatment had progressed to the stage where the model-dog interactions occurred outside the pen, and during the final two sessions, the model actually climbed into the pen with the dog. As Bandura (1971) notes, had the children been asked to view these latter interactions at the outset of treatment, they would probably have refused even to look. By presenting ever-more threatening situations in a graduated manner (similar to what is done in desensitization), most of the children were willing to view a given interaction when it occurred. Results of the modeling procedure were most impressive. In a test situation, the children's approach behaviors vis-à-vis the dog virtually doubled, with improvement generalizing to a dog very different in appearance. In a related study, Bandura and Menlove (1968) compared the above treatment procedure with one wherein the child observed several different models (with both age and sex varying) interacting with a variety of different dogs (small, large, and also varying with respect to fearsomeness). In terms of the child's subsequent willingness to remain alone in a room while confined in the pen with a dog, the multiple-model/multiple-dog condition was far more effective. For example, at a follow-up, whereas about half the subjects in the multiple condition were willing to engage in the above interaction, less than 20% of the single-model/single-dog children were willing to be left alone in the pen with the dog.

Among the several procedures presented in this chapter as ways of reducing phobic reactions, participant modeling is probably the most potent. To illustrate participant modeling, assume the client is fearful of harmless snakes. The therapist selects a harmless snake (preferably one that is docile—small boas are excellent for this purpose, although it is advisable *not* to indicate to the client that the snake is a boa lest this evoke cinematographical images of heros being attacked by mammoth constrictors) which is placed in a cage in the corner of the room. The client observes the therapist calmly and confidently go through a graduated series of interactions with the snake, such as approaching and touching the cage, touching and holding the snake while wearing gloves, touching and holding the snake without gloves (see Rimm & Masters, 1979 for more detail). The client observes the graduated modeling from whatever distance he finds comfortable, preferably with the door open so the client knows escape is possible. When the client reports being able to observe the most fearsome therapist-snake interaction with reasonable comfort, the therapist then "talks" the client through a similar series of interactions, with the *client* determining the pace. The therapist, who initially at least is in close physical proximity with the client (so that the client knows the therapist is there to take the snake in hand if necessary), provides ongoing praise and social support. The therapist might also provide physical contact with the client (e.g., putting an arm around the shoulder of the client, a powerful gesture of reassurance).[7]

Participant modeling, which has also been employed with individuals having

---

[7] Participant modeling is sometimes called "contact desensitization," in part because of the physical contact between therapist and client. The process of generalization of treatment gains (a very important goal for the client) has been found to be enhanced by the use of client-controlled interactions with the phobic stimulus while the therapist is out of the room. Even one additional hour of independent exposure has been shown to produce better generalization than no extra contact (Bandura, Jeffery, & Gajdos, 1975; Smith & Coleman, 1977).

fears of other small animals, as well as water (Hunziker, 1972) and high places (Ritter, 1969a, 1969b), can be highly effective even with very brief treatments. For example, Bandura, Blanchard, and Ritter (1969), working with severely incapacitated snake phobics, reported that each of their subjects freely interacted with snakes following no more than 5 hours of treatment (mean treatment time was approximately 2 hours). Very rapid improvement in snake-avoidant subjects via participant modeling has been reported by others as well (Rimm & Madieros, 1970; Rimm & Mahoney, 1969).

In the aforementioned discussion of modeling, the models showed no fear, while evidencing considerable skill in interacting with the phobic object,—handling a snake with confidence and authority. That is, the models displayed *mastery.* Another strategy involves the use of a *coping model,* someone who is initially a bit awkward in the situation and who does evidence some fear, but who during the course of the modeling sequence overcomes the fear, showing a commensurate increase in skills. There is some evidence that the coping strategy may be the more effective of the two (Kazdin, 1973; Meichenbaum, 1971). Why this should be the case is not presently clear, although it may be, as Kazdin (1974) suggests, that subjects see coping models as more similar to themselves, for if an initially frightened model can readily overcome fear, the subject can likely overcome his/her fear as well. If one chooses to employ a coping strategy, it is essential that the model really *does* overcome the fear and/or skills deficiency. As an example, in one study using participant modeling (Howard, 1975), one of the two therapists, who served as a coping model, had a fear of the phobic stimulus (laboratory rat) which he did not overcome: his subjects showed little improvement.

Cognitive Approaches

As we noted earlier, cognitive learning approaches assume that to a large extent phobias are mediated by conscious thoughts. If this is correct, a reasonable therapeutic strategy would be to modify or eliminate such thoughts, and this is the goal of cognitive learning therapies. Among the most influential of these approaches is Albert Ellis' Rational-Emotive Therapy (Ellis, 1962, 1971, 1977). The essence of RET can be seen in the A-B-C-D-E paradigm illustrated in the following example of a client with a fear of public speaking.

A. *Activating experience.* An actual external event, the audience stares at the client with indifferent expressions.

B. *Belief.* The chain of self-verbalizations in which the person engages in response to A; for example, "They look bored . . . they think I'm a terrible speaker . . . I'll fail this course and flunk out of college . . . I'll be a failure."

C. *Consequences.* The emotions and behaviors resulting from B; for example, the person feels fear and finally panic . . . he/she blocks and becomes dysfluent or even incoherent.

D. *Disputation* of B by therapist and/or client—the therapist assists the client in challenging B; the client comes to believe, instead, that the indifferent expressions do not necessarily indicate boredom or hostility . . . that they probably don't think he/she is a terrible speaker, and even if they did, it doesn't follow that the client will therefore flunk out of college and, further, that not succeeding at a specific task does not make one a total failure.

E. *Effect* of D.   The client no longer feels dread at the prospect of making a speech. He/she enjoys life more fully and, indeed, is now a more effective public speaker.

Homework is an important part of RET. Frequently, clients are assigned books or chapters Ellis and his associates have written (Ellis, 1975; Ellis & Harper, 1975; Ellis, Wolpe, & Mosely, 1972). Homework may also include a kind of *in vivo* desensitization; for instance, the speech phobic might be encouraged to make speeches to real or imagined audiences. While doing this, the client is expected to observe and dispute any irrational or self-defeating thoughts he experiences.

The RET approach to phobias emphasizes restructuring the client's thinking so that the phobic situation is now perceived as less threatening. Thus individuals fearful of public speaking might be taught to say to themselves just prior to making a speech, "I'll probably do okay, but even if I don't, it isn't the end of the world." Meichenbaum's *stress innoculation* training (Meichenbaum, 1974, 1977), while it includes important elements of RET, has a somewhat different emphasis. In addition to helping clients realize that dire consequences aren't likely to occur when they are in the phobic situation, clients are also taught active coping skills. While the coping skills might include something as simple as taking a deep breath when the client experiences anxiety in the target situation, the major emphasis is on conscious thought as a means of controlling one's feelings and behavior. For example, in the case of the speech-anxious client, the therapist might model the following verbalizations that the client is to employ prior to or during a speech:

"You might as well relax . . . worrying won't do any good."
"Focus on what you have to do."
"Tension is normal when a person makes a speech."

Once the client is proficient in the use of such coping tactics, the therapist might provide what Meichenbaum calls *application training*. In application training the client is exposed to a stressful situation such as unpredictable electric shock (Klepac, 1975; Meichenbaum & Cameron, 1972a), immersing one's hand in ice water (Turk, 1976), or an imagined stressful event (Suinn, 1975). The client's task is to use his newly acquired coping skills to reduce the anxiety. The presumption is that application training will further enhance the client's ability to use coping skills, and that this ability will generalize to the phobic situation.

As we have noted earlier, many of the phobic clients' complaints involve excessive rumination about possible or anticipated exposure to the phobic stimulus. This sort of worrying is not oriented toward problem solving and is clearly self-defeating. The technique of thought-stopping can often be successfully applied to such behavior (see Rimm & Masters, 1974, 1979, for a review of this literature). Thought-stopping consists of asking the client to engage in the anxiety-inducing thoughts and, after a short period of time, the therapist suddenly shouts, "STOP" (any loud noise may be substituted in its place). This will usually result in the client's reporting an interruption or cessation of the thoughts, and the procedure is repeated several more times. As success experiences accumulate, the focus of control shifts from the therapist to the client so that the client comes to control the interruptions. The goal of thought-stopping is for the client to stop phobic ruminations by emitting a subvocal "stop," and appropriate fading procedures to accomplish this should be implemented by the therapist.

Thought-stopping, while eliminating much of the conditioned anxiety, usually does not eliminate some residual anxiety that may be triggering the ruminations (recall the studies of Horowitz and his associates). Covert assertion has been suggested as a technique to be used adjunctively with thought-stopping (Rimm & Masters, 1974, 1979). After successful completion of the thought-stopping procedure, the client is asked to imagine a situation in which the ruminative behavior occurs. Instructions are then given to stop any obsessive thoughts that might occur, and to immediately make an assertive statement appropriate to the situation (see Rimm, 1973, for case examples). Again, the goal is for the client to execute these behaviors covertly.

How effective are the cognitive learning approaches in dealing with phobic individuals? Available evidence tends to be supportive (e.g., DiLoreto, 1971; Fremouw & Zitter, 1978; Meichenbaum & Cameron, 1972a, 1972b; Moleski & Tosi, 1976; Trexler & Karst, 1972), although negative findings have been reported in the literature (e.g., Straatmeyer & Watkins, 1974). Most writers agree that a good deal of additional research is needed before definitive statements regarding the efficacy of any of the cognitive learning approaches can be made (Mahoney, 1974; Meichenbaum, 1977; Rimm & Masters, 1979; Trexler, 1977).

Which Approach to Use?

In this section we presented several major treatment interventions potentially useful in dealing with phobic clients: systematic desensitization, implosive therapy (and flooding), modeling, cognitive-learning approaches. Given the present state of the art/science, there is no real basis for making any categorical statements regarding which approach is best. It is possible that as empirical evidence mounts, one strategy will emerge as clearly superior. It is just as likely, however, that future research findings will establish a basis for matching a given client with a given treatment approach; for example, client A's phobia would be best treated with desensitization, whereas client B's phobia is most likely to be alleviated using a cognitive approach. The increasing emphasis on behavioral assessment within the domain of behavior therapy may make such a matching possible.

An initial attempt at such a matching procedure is described by Tucker, Shearer, and Murray (1977). In this study, they found that subjects who exhibited anxiety primarily through imagery ("Saw" themselves dying on the street, falling off the building) responded better to treatments that were primarily verbal in nature (such as stress inoculation training, cognitive restructuring, and thought-stopping). Other subjects whose anxiety was ruminative in nature (worrying incessantly about coming into contact with the phobic stimulus and the dire consequences of such a meeting) profited more from imagery therapies, systematic desensitization, anxiety management training, flooding, implosive therapy. Obviously, results such as this are in need of replication.

Case Histories

The following are some abbreviated case histories of phobic clients we have worked with.

A 38-year-old female had been fearful of snakes since she was a child. She could not recall any single traumatic event that might have precipitated her fear, but did note that as a child she was told that girls were supposed to be afraid of snakes. She wished to overcome her fear so that her 11-year-old son would not acquire it from her vicariously. Following 1½ hours of participant modeling, she was able to handle a harmless snake comfortably. She was delighted with her improvement.

A 45-year-old air force veteran was fearful of loud noises and high places. He had flown some fifty combat missions (as a bombardier) without apparent incident, but within two to three months after his discharge, he began to experience his fears. Now, three years later, he sought help indicating his fears were seriously interfering with his life. He traced his phobias directly to his combat experiences, that is, seeing height-related cues and hearing antiaircraft fire while performing his bombardier functions. Treatment, which extended over a two-month period, included systematic desensitization with separate hierarchies developed for the acrophobia and fear of loud noises. At the termination of treatment and at a six-month follow-up, he reported that loud noises (e.g., a jackhammer) no longer bothered him and at the follow-up he noted that he had volunteered to help paint his community water tower and that he was able to engage in such activity with little discomfort.

A 21-year-old female college student (Rimm, 1973) had been intensely fearful of the dark for the past six months. She stated that her problem began when an intruder had attempted to rape her. Since then she would lie awake at night obsessed with the possibility that someone would try and break in, or that someone might be hiding in the closet. Each night she would repeatedly check her windows and her closet, and this activity, coupled with her emotional arousal, was seriously interfering with her sleep. Treatment involved the use of thought-stopping and covert-assertion, a cognitive approach designed to assist her in controlling her frightening thoughts (see Rimm & Masters, 1979). Within two sessions she reported she was able to sleep. Six months after the termination of treatment she reported that the fear continued to present no problem, and that she was sleeping well.

The aforementioned case histories illustrate the use of three different approaches with three different clients. In the case below, several different strategies were employed with the same client.

The client, a 47-year-old female, reported several phobias, but the one that concerned her the most was fear of not being able to swallow. She reported having this fear for the past two years, and was not able to relate its onset to any specific environmental event. Like many phobics, she viewed her fears as an indication of a generalized trait of personal incompetence, and during the first few sessions she ruminated on this perceived incompetence, suggesting that because she was so incompetent perhaps she didn't deserve to overcome her phobias. RET was employed to deal with this self-defeating attitude, and within three sessions she was able to accept her fears, while allowing that they were "darn inconvenient" (but not a sign that she was worthless or an incompetent human being). Treatment for her fear of not being able to swallow included thought-stopping (i.e., whenever she began to ruminate about not being about to swallow) and desensitization, employed as a coping strategy. The latter required that she imagine hierarchy scenes (e.g., eating in a restaurant) and that she relax away any anxiety she might experience. Within a month she reported being able to eat a meal in a restaurant and enjoy it. A similar approach was also successfully employed for her fears of driving on an interstate highway and flying in an airplane.

REFERENCES

Alexander, F., French, T., et al. *Psychoanalytic therapy*. New York: Ronald Press, 1946.

American Psychiatric Association. *Diagnostic and statistical manual of mental disorders* (2nd edition). Washington, D.C., 1968.

American Psychiatric Association. *Diagnostic and statistical manual of mental disorders* (3rd edition). Washington, D.C., 1980.

Bandura, A. *Principles of behavior modification*. New York: Holt, Rinehart & Winston, 1969.

Bandura, A. Psychotherapy based on modeling principles. In A. E. Bergin & S. L. Garfield (Eds.), *Handbook of psychotherapy and behavior change*. New York: Wiley, 1971.

Bandura, A. Self-efficacy: Toward a unifying theory of behavioral change. *Psychological Review*, 1977, **84**, 191–215. (a)

Bandura, A. *Social learning theory*. Englewood Cliffs, N.J.: Prentice-Hall, 1977. (b)

Bandura, A. Reflections on self-efficacy. Unpublished manuscript, Stanford University, 1978.

Bandura, A., Blanchard, E. B., & Ritter, R. The relative efficacy of desensitization and modeling approaches for inducing behavioral, affective, and attitudinal changes. *Journal of Personality and Social Psychology*, 1969, **13**, 173–199.

Bandura, A., Grusec, J. E., & Menlove, F. L. Vicarious extinction of avoidance behavior. *Journal of Personality and Social Psychology*, 1967, **5**, 16–23.

Bandura, A., Jeffery, R. W., & Gajdos, E. Generalizing change through participant modeling with self-directed mastery. *Behaviour Research and Therapy*, 1975, **13**, 141–152.

Bandura, A., & Menlove, F. L. Factors determining vicarious extinction of avoidance behavior through symbolic modeling. *Journal of Personality and Social Psychology*, 1968, **8**, 99–108.

Bandura, A., & Rosenthal, T. L. Vicarious classical conditioning as a function of arousal level. *Journal of Personality and Social Psychology*, 1966, **3**, 54–62.

Baum, M. Extinction of an avoidance response following response prevention: Some parametric investigations. *Canadian Journal of Psychology*, 1969, **23**, 1–10.

Baum, M. Extinction of avoidance responding through response prevention (flooding). *Psychological Bulletin*, 1970, **74**, 276–284.

Beck, A. T. *Cognitive therapy and the emotional disorders*. New York: International Universities Press, 1976.

Berger, S. M. Conditioning through vicarious instigation. *Psychological Review,* 1962, **69**, 450–466.

Borkovec, T. D. The comparative effectiveness of systematic desensitization and implosive therapy and the effect of expectancy manipulation on the elimination of fear. Unpublished doctoral dissertation, University of Illinois, Urbana, 1970.

Borkovec, T. D. Effects of expectancy on the outcome of systematic desensitization and implosive treatments for analogue anxiety. *Behaviour Research and Therapy,* 1979, **17**, 119–125.

Borkovec, T. D., & Sides, J. K. Critical procedural variables related to the physiological effects of progressive relaxation: A review: *Behavior Therapy,* in press.

Boulougouris, J. C. & Bassiakos, L. Case histories and shorter communications: Prolonged flooding in cases with obsessive-compulsive neurosis. *Behavior Research and Therapy,* 1973, **11**, 227–231.

Brandon, S. An epidemiological study of maladjustment in childhood. Unpublished M.D. thesis, University of Durham, England, 1960.

Buss, A. H. *Psychopathology.* New York: Wiley, 1966.

Ciminero, A. R., Calhoun, K. S., & Adams, H. E., (Eds.), *Handbook of behavioral assessment.* New York: Wiley, 1977.

Cooper, A., Furst, J. B., & Bridger, W. H. A brief commentary on the usefulness of studying fears of snakes. *Journal of Abnormal Psychology,* 1969, **74**, 413–414.

Costello, C. G. Classification and psychopathology. In C. G. Costello (Ed.), *Symptoms of psychopathology: A handbook.* New York: Wiley, 1970.

Craig, K. D., & Weinstein, M. S. Conditioning vicarious affective arousal. *Psychological Reports,* 1965, **17**, 955–963.

de Silva, P., Rachman, S., & Seligman, M. E. P. Prepared phobias and obsessions: Therapeutic outcome. *Behaviour Research and Therapy,* 1977, **15**, 65–77.

DiLoreto, A. O. *Comparative Psychotherapy: An experimental analysis.* Chicago: Aldine-Atherton, 1971.

Eiduson, B. The two classes of information in psychiatry. *Archives of General Psychiatry,* 1968, **18**, 405–419.

Ellis, A. *Reason and emotion in psychotherapy.* New York: Lyle Stuart, 1962.

Ellis, A. (Ed.), *Growth through reason: Verbatim cases in rational-emotive therapy.* Palo Alto, Calif.: Science & Behavior Books, 1971.

Ellis, A. *Humanistic psychotherapy: The rational-emotive approach.* New York: Julian Press, 1973.

Ellis, A. *How to live with a "neurotic": At home and at work.* New York: Crown, 1975.

Ellis, A. The basic clinical theory of rational-emotive therapy. In A. Ellis & R. Grieger (Eds.), *Handbook of rational-emotive therapy.* New York: Springer, 1977.

Ellis, A. & Grieger, R. (Eds.), *Handbook of rational-emotive therapy.* New York: Springer, 1977.

Ellis, A., & Harper, R. A. *A new guide to rational living.* Englewood Cliffs, N.J.: Prentice-Hall, 1975.

Ellis, A., Wolfe, J. L., & Moseley, S. *How to raise an emotionally healthy, happy child.* North Hollywood: Wilshire, 1972.

Emmelkamp, P. M. G., & Wessels, H. Flooding in imagination vs. flooding *in vivo:* A comparison with agoraphobics. *Behaviour Research and Therapy,* 1975, **13**, 7–15.

Fazio, A. F. Treatment components in implosive therapy. *Journal of Abnormal Psychology,* 1970, **76**, 211–219.

Fenichel, O. *The psychoanalytic theory of neurosis.* New York: Norton, 1945.

Foa, E. B., Blau, J. S., Prout, M., & Latimer, P. Is horror a necessary component of flooding (implosion)? *Behaviour Research and Therapy,* 1977, **15**, 397–402.

Frazier, S. H., & Carr, A. C. Phobic reaction. In A. M. Freedman & H. I. Kaplan (Eds.), *Comprehensive textbook of psychiatry.* Baltimore: Williams & Wilkins, 1967.

Fremouw, W. J., & Zitter, R. E. A comparison of skills training and cognitive restructuring-relaxation for the treatment of speech anxiety. *Behavior Therapy,* 1978, **9**, 248–259.

Freud, S. *A general introduction to psychoanalysis.* New York: Washington Square Press, 1968.

Gauthier, J., & Marshall, W. L. The determination of optimal exposure to phobic stimuli in flooding therapy. *Behaviour Research and Therapy,* 1977, **15**, 403–410.

Goldfried, M. R., & Davison, G. C. *Clinical behavior therapy.* New York: Holt, Rinehart & Winston, 1976.

Goldfried, M. R., & Trier, C. S. Effectiveness of relaxation as an active coping skill. *Journal of Abnormal Psychology,* 1974, **83**, 348–355.

Goldstein, A. J., & Chambless, D. L. A reanalysis of agoraphobia. *Behavior Therapy,* 1978, **9**, 47–59.

Hallam, R. S., & Hafner, R. J. Fears of phobic patients: Factor analyses of self-report data. *Behaviour Research and Therapy,* 1978, **16**, 1–6.

Hayes, S. C. The role of approach contingencies in phobic behavior. *Behavior Therapy,* 1976, **7**, 28–36.

Hekmat, H. Systematic versus semantic desensitization and implosive therapy: A comparative study. *Journal of Consulting and Clinical Psychology,* 1973, **40**, 202–203.

Herrnstein, R. Method and theory in the study of avoidance. *Psychological Review,* 1969, **76**, 49–69.

Hersen, M., & Bellack, A. S. (Eds.), *Behavioral assessment: A practical handbook.* New York: Pergamon Press, 1976.

Hodgson, R. J., & Rachman, S. An experimental investigation of the implosion technique. *Behaviour Research and Therapy,* 1970, **8**, 21–27.

Hodgson, R., & Rachman, S. Desynchrony in measures of fear. *Behaviour Research and Therapy,* 1974, **2**, 319–326.

Hogan, R. A. The implosive technique. *Behaviour Research and Therapy,* 1968, **6**, 423–432.

Hogan, R. A. Implosively oriented behavior modification: Therapy considerations. *Behaviour Research and Therapy,* 1969, **7**, 177–184.

Hogan, R. A., & Kirchner, J. H. A preliminary report of the extinction of learned fears via short term implosive therapy. *Journal of Abnormal Psychology,* 1967, **72**, 106–111.

Horowitz, M. J., & Becker, S. S. Cognitive response to stress and experimental demand. *Journal of Abnormal Psychology,* 1971, **78**, 86–92.

Horowitz, M. J., Becker, S. S., & Moskovitz, M. L. Intrusive and repetitive thought after stress: A replication study. *Psychological Reports,* 1971, **29**, 763–767.

Howard, G. Participant modeling in the treatment of rat phobias. Unpublished doctoral dissertation, Southern Illinois University, 1975.

Hunziker, J. C. The use of participant modeling in the treatment of water phobias. Unpublished master's thesis, Arizona State University, 1972.

Jacobson, E. *Progressive relaxation.* Chicago: University of Chicago Press, 1938.

Jacobson, E. *Anxiety and tension control.* Philadelphia: Lippincott, 1964.

Kazdin, A. E. Covert modeling and the reduction of avoidance behavior. *Journal of Abnormal Psychology,* 1973, **81**, 87–95.

Kazdin, A. E. Comparative effects of some variations of covert modeling. *Journal of Behavior Therapy and Experimental Psychiatry.* 1974, **5**, 225–231.

Kazdin, A. E., & Wilcoxon, L. A. Systematic desensitization and nonspecific treatment effects: A methodological evaluation. *Psychological Bulletin,* 1976, **83**, 729–758.

Klepac, R. Successful treatment of avoidance of dentistry by desensitization or by increasing pain tolerance. *Journal of Behavior Therapy and Experimental Psychiatry,* 1975, **6**, 307–310.

Lader, M. H., & Matthews, A. M. A physiological model of phobic anxiety and desensitization. *Behaviour Research and Therapy,* 1968, **6**, 411–421.

Landy, F. J., & Gaupp, L. A. A factor analysis of the fear survey schedule–III. *Behaviour Research and Therapy,* 1971, **9**, 89–93.

Lang, P. J. Imagery in therapy: An information processing analysis of fear. *Behavior Therapy,* 1977, **8**, 862–886.

Lazarus, A. A. *Behavior therapy and beyond.* New York: McGraw-Hill, 1971.

Lazarus, A. A. Has behavior therapy outlived its usefulness? *American Psychologist,* 1977, **32**, 550–554.

Levis, D. J., & Carrera, R. N. Effects of 10 hours of implosive therapy in the treatment of outpatients: A preliminary report. *Journal of Abnormal Psychology,* 1967, **72**, 504–508.

Lick, J. R., & Katkin, E. S. Assessment of anxiety and fear. In M. Hersen & A. S. Bellack (Eds.), *Behavioral assessment: A practical handbook.* New York: Pergamon Press, 1976.

Locke, E. Is "behavior therapy" behavioristic? (An analysis of Wolpe's psychotherapeutic methods). *Psychological Bulletin,* 1971, **76**, 318–327.

McCutcheon, B. A., & Adams, H. E. The physiological basis of implosive therapy. *Behaviour Research and Therapy,* 1975, **13**, 93–100.

McGlynn, F. D. Systematic desensitization, implosive therapy and the aversiveness of imaginal hierarchy items. Unpublished doctoral dissertation, University of Missouri, Columbia, 1968.

Mahoney, M. J. Sequential treatments for severe phobia. *Journal of Behavior Therapy and Experimental Psychiatry,* 1971, **2**, 195–197.

Mahoney, M. J. *Cognition and behavior modification.* Cambridge, Mass.: Ballinger, 1974.

Marks, I. M. Agoraphobic syndrome (phobic anxiety state). *Archives of General Psychiatry,* 1970, **23**, 539–553.

Marshall, W. L., Gauthier, J., Christie, M. M., Currie, D. W., & Gordon, A. Flooding therapy: Effectiveness, stimulus characteristics and the value of brief *in vivo* exposure. *Behaviour Research and Therapy,* 1977, **15**, 79–87.

May, J. R. Psychophysiology of self-regulated phobic thoughts. *Behavior Therapy,* 1977, **8**, 150–159.

May, J. R. A psychophysiological study of self and externally regulated phobic thoughts. *Behavior Therapy,* 1977, **5**, 849–861.

Meichenbaum, D. Examination of model characteristics in reducing avoidance behavior. *Journal of Personality and Social Psychology,* 1971, **17**, 298–307.

Meichenbaum, D. *Cognitive behavior modification.* Morristown, N.J.: General Learning Press, 1974.

Meichenbaum, D. *Cognitive behavior modification: An integrative approach.* New York: Plenum Press, 1977.

Meichenbaum, D., & Cameron, R. An examination of cognitive and contingency variables in anxiety relief procedures. Unpublished manuscript, University of Waterloo, 1972. (a)

Meichenbaum, D., & Cameron, R. Reducing fears by modifying what clients say to themselves: A means of developing stress inoculation. Unpublished manuscript, University of Waterloo, 1972. (b)

Meyer, V., Robertson, J., & Tatlow, A. Home treatment of an obsessive-compulsive disorder by response prevention. *Journal of Behavior Therapy and Experimental Psychiatry,* 1975, **6**, 37–38.

Miller, L. C., Barrett, C. L., Hampe, E., & Noble, H. Factor structure of childhood fears. *Journal of Consulting and Clinical Psychology,* 1972, **39**, 264–268.

Moleski, R., & Tosi, D. J. Comparative psychotherapy: Rational-emotive therapy versus systematic desensitization in the treatment of stuttering. *Journal of Consulting and Clinical Psychology,* 1976, **44**, 309–311.

Mowrer, O. H. On the dual nature of learning. A reinterpretation of "conditioning" and "problem-solving." *Harvard Educational Review,* 1947, **17**, 102–148.

Mowrer, O. H. *Learning theory and the symbolic processes.* New York: Wiley, 1960.

Nemiah, J. C. Psychoneurotic disorders. In A. M. Nicholi (Ed.), *The Harvard guide to modern psychiatry.* Cambridge, Mass.: Belknap Press, 1978.

Nicholi, A. M. (Ed.), *The Harvard guide to modern psychiatry.* Cambridge, Mass.: Belknap Press, 1978.

Olman, A., Erixon, G., & Lofberg, I. Phobias and preparedness: Phobic versus neutral pictures as conditioned stimuli for human autonomic responses. *Journal of Abnormal Psychology,* 1975, **84**, 41–45.

Orenstein, H., & Carr, J. Implosion therapy by tape-recording. *Behaviour Research and Therapy,* 1975, **13**, 177–182.

Paul, G. L. *Insight vs. desensitization in psychotherapy: An experiment in anxiety reduction.* Stanford, Calif.: Stanford University Press, 1966.

Pavlov, I. P. *Conditioned reflexes: An investigation of the physiological activity of the cerebral cortex* (translated by G. V. Anrep). London and New York: Oxford University Press, 1927.

Rachlin, H. Reinforcing and punishing thoughts. *Behavior Therapy,* 1977, **8**, 659–665.

Rachman, S. Treatment by prolonged exposure to high intensity stimulation. *Behaviour Research and Therapy,* 1969, **7**, 295–302.

Rachman, S. *The meanings of fear.* Baltimore: Penguin, 1974.

Rachman, S. The passing of the two-stage theory of fear and avoidance. *Behaviour Research and Therapy,* 1976, **14**, 125–131.

Rachman, S., & Seligman, M. E. P. Unprepared phobias: "Be prepared." *Behaviour Research and Therapy,* 1976, **14**, 333–338.

Rimm, D. C. Thought-stopping and covert assertion in the treatment of phobias. *Journal of Consulting and Clinical Psychology,* 1973, **41**, 466–467.

Rimm, D. C. Discussion: Behavior therapy. Some general comments and a review of selected papers. In R. L. Spitzer & D. F. Klein (Eds.), *Evaluation of Psychological therapies*. Baltimore: The Johns Hopkins University Press, 1976.

Rimm, D. C., Janda, L. H., Lancaster, D. W., Nahl, M., & Dittmar, K. An exploratory investigation of the origin and maintenance of phobias. *Behaviour Research and Therapy*, 1977, **15**, 231–238.

Rimm, D. C., & Madieros, D. C. The role of muscle relaxation in participant modeling. *Behaviour Research and Therapy*, 1970, **8**, 127–132.

Rimm, D. C., & Mahoney, M. J. The application of reinforcement and participant modeling procedures in the treatment of snake-phobic behavior. *Behaviour Research and Therapy*, 1969, **7**, 369–376.

Rimm, D. C., & Masters, J. C. *Behavior therapy: Techniques and empirical findings*. New York: Academic Press, 1974.

Rimm, D. C., & Masters, J. C. *Behavior therapy: Techniques and empirical findings* (2nd edition) New York: Academic Press, 1979.

Rimm, D. C., & Somervill, J. W. *Abnormal psychology*. New York: Academic Press, 1977.

Ritter, B. Eliminating excessive fears of the environment through contact desensitization. In J. D. Krumboltz & C. E. Thoreson (Eds.), *Behavioral counseling: Cases and techniques*. New York: Holt, Rinehart & Winston, 1969. (a)

Ritter, B. Treatment of acrophobia with contact desensitization. *Behaviour Research and Therapy*, 1969, **7**, 41–45. (b)

Rosen, G. M. Subjects' initial therapeutic expectancies and subjects' awareness of therapeutic goals in systematic desensitization: A review. *Behavior Therapy*, 1976, **7**, 14–27.

Rubin, S. E., Lawlis, G. F., Tasto, D. L., & Namenek, T. Factor analysis of the 122 item fear survey schedule. *Behaviour Research and Therapy*, 1969, **7**, 381–386.

Seligman, M. E. P. Phobias and preparedness. *Behavior Therapy*, 1971, **2**, 307–320.

Smith, G. P., & Coleman, R. E. Processes underlying generalization through participant modeling with self-directed practice. *Behaviour Research and Therapy*, 1977, **15**, 204–206.

Sokolov, A. N. *Inner speech and thought*. New York: Plenum Press, 1972.

Stampfl, T. G. Implosive therapy: A learning theory derived psychodynamic therapeutic technique. In Lebarba & Dent (Eds.), *Critical issues in clinical psychology*. New York: Academic Press, 1961.

Stampfl, T. G. Implosive therapy, Part I: The theory. In S. G. Armitage (Ed.), *Behavioral modification techniques in the treatment of emotional disorders*. Battle Creek, Mich.: V. A. Publication, 1967.

Stampfl, T. G., & Levis, D. J. Essentials of implosive therapy: A learning theory-based psychodynamic behavioral therapy. *Journal of Abnormal Psychology*, 1967, **72**, 496–503. (a)

Stampfl, T. G., & Levis, D. J. Phobic patients: Treatment with the learning theory approach of implosive therapy. *Voices: The Art and Science of Psychotherapy*, 1967, **3**, 23–27. (b)

Stampfl, T. G., & Levis, D. J. Implosive therapy. A behavioral therapy? *Behaviour Research and Therapy*, 1968, **6**, 31–36.

Straatmeyer, A. J., & Watkins, J. T. Rational-emotive therapy and the reduction of speech anxiety. *Rational Living*, 1974, **9**, 33–37.

Suinn, R. M. Anxiety management training for general anxiety. In R. M. Suinn & R. G. Weigel (Eds.), *The innovative psychological therapies: Critical and creative contributions*. New York: Harper & Row, 1975.

Suinn, R. M., & Richardson, F. Anxiety management training: A nonspecific behavior therapy program for anxiety control. *Behavior Therapy*, 1971, **2**, 498–510.

Trexler, L. D. A review of rational-emotive psychotherapy outcome studies. In J. L. Wolfe & E. Brand (Eds.), *Twenty years of rational therapy*. New York: Institute for Rational Living, 1977.

Trexler, L. D., & Karst, T. O. Rational-emotive therapy, placebo, and no-treatment effects on public-speaking anxiety. *Journal of Abnormal Psychology*, 1972, **79**, 60–67.

Tucker, D. M., Shearer, S. L., and Murray, J. D. Hemispheric specialization and cognitive behavior therapy. *Cognitive Therapy and Research*, 1977, **1**, 263–273.

Turk, D. An expanded skills training approach for the treatment of experimentally induced pain. Unpublished doctoral dissertation, University of Waterloo, 1976.

Wachtel, P. L. *Psychoanalysis and behavior therapy*. New York: Basic Books, 1977.

Wade, T. C., Malloy, T. E., & Proctor, S. Imaginal correlates of self-reported fear and avoidance behavior. *Behaviour Research and Therapy*, 1977, **15**, 17–22.

Watson, J. P., Mullett, G. E., & Pillay, H. The effects of prolonged exposure to phobic situations upon agoraphobic patients treated in groups. *Behaviour Research and Therapy*, 1973, **11**, 531–545.

Watson, J. B., & Rayner, R. Conditioned emotional reactions. *Journal of Experimental Psychology*, 1920, **3**, 1–14.

Wijesinghe, B. A vomiting phobia overcome by one session of flooding with hypnosis. *Journal of Behavior Therapy and Experimental Psychiatry*, 1974, **5**, 169–170.

Wolberg, L. R. *The technique of psychotherapy* (2nd edition). New York: Grune & Stratton, 1967.

Wolpe, J. *Psychotherapy by reciprocal inhibition*. Stanford, Calif.: Stanford University Press, 1958.

Wolpe, J. *The practice of behavior therapy* (2nd edition). New York: Pergamon, 1973.

Wolpe, J. Cognition and causation in human behavior and its therapy. *American Psychologist*, 1978, **33**, 437–446.

Wolpe, J., & Lang, P. J. A fear survey schedule for use in behavior therapy. *Behaviour Research and Therapy*, 1964, **2**, 27–30.

Yule, W., Sacks, B., & Hersov, L. Successful flooding treatment of a noise phobia in an eleven-year-old. *Journal of Behavior Therapy and Experimental Psychiatry*, 1974, **5**, 209–211.

CHAPTER 3

Pervasive ("Free-Floating") Anxiety: A Search for a Cause and Treatment Approach

Nathan Hare and Donald J. Levis

One of the most common problems seen by mental health practitioners is that of pervasive or chronic anxiety. The classification system of DSM-II referred to this condition as anxiety neurosis and defined it as follows:

> This neurosis is characterized by anxious over-concern extending to panic and frequently associated with somatic symptoms. Unlike Phobic neurosis (q.v.), anxiety may occur under any circumstances and is not restricted to specific situations or objects. This disorder must be distinguished from normal apprehension of fear, which occurs in realistically dangerous situations.

The first systematic accounts of anxiety neurosis appeared in an unpublished paper by Stille in 1863 who described the condition of "palpitation of the heart" in Civil War soldiers. A few years later, Da Costa (1871) provided a published account of Stille's work along with some of his own conclusions about the disorder. As a result, this clinical condition was referred to as Da Costa's syndrome until the term anxiety neurosis was coined by Freud in 1895 (see Pitts, 1971).

Since its isolation as a syndrome, recognition of anxiety neurosis has increased markedly. Available evidence suggests that as many as 10 million Americans suffer from this disorder. Furthermore, anxiety neurotics outnumber practicing physicians by 40 to 1 and represent as much as 30% of the patients seeking help from primary care physicians (Pitts, 1971). In light of the above, it is surprising that a thorough review of the current psychological and psychiatric literature revealed that relatively little systematic research has been conducted on this topic. This observation is especially true for students investigating the efficacy of various treatment modalities. Cautela (1966), for example, concluded that "no general method for treating pervasive anxiety has been proposed." Relatively little has been accomplished since his statement.

Perhaps part of the problem in stimulating interest in generating conceptual and treatment models of anxiety neurosis resides in the inherent difficulty of isolating specific stimulus patterns eliciting the anxiety state. In fact, it is just this etiological difficulty that gives anxiety neurosis its definitional properties and makes it distinct from other nosologies that also are associated with persistent anxiety reactions.

The main purpose of this chapter, then, is to provide an overview of the existing literature in the hope of generating a greater interest in isolating effective treatment methods for anxiety neurosis. A review of the existing biological and psychological theories of the problem is provided, followed by an analysis of the various treatment methods designed to alleviate the problem. Finally, an attempt is made to reconceptualize the problem from a new-learning based perspective with suggestive treatment implications and clinical examples.

CONCEPTUAL MODELS

Biological Theories

Our review yielded two systematically presented biological theories of anxiety neurosis. The first theory conceptualizes anxiety symptoms as being related to abnormal rises in blood lactate. Pitts, who suggested this possibility (Pitts, 1969; Pitts, 1971; Pitts & McClure, 1967), argued from data (Jones & Mellersh, 1946) which showed that following a standard exercise procedure, anxiety neurotics displayed an abnormal rise in blood lactate (a normal by-product of glucose metabolism). He concluded that the high levels of blood lactate may be responsible for producing the anxiety symptoms. At a clinical level this excess of lactate is assumed to bind calcium ions in the intercellular fluid preventing the calcium ions from being utilized in the normal fashion during nerve transmission. This emphasis on calcium ions resulted from an observation that anxiety symptoms are similar to symptoms produced by hypocalcemia.

Support for Pitts' theory comes from an experiment by Pitts and McClure (1967). Fourteen anxiety neurotics and 10 normal controls were given 20-minute infusions of one of three solutions while being observed by an experimenter blind to experimental and subject conditions. The three solutions were 500 mM sodium lactate; 500 mM sodium lactate with 20 mM calcium chloride added; or 555 mM glucose with 167 mM sodium chloride. The subjects reported the symptoms they experienced under each of these conditions. It was shown that the lactate produced reliably more anxiety symptoms than either the lactate and calcium chloride or the glucose solutions. This was true for both anxiety neurotic and normal subjects. In some neurotic subjects, the lactate solution resulted in actual anxiety attacks. More symptoms were produced by the lactate in anxiety neurotics than in normals. The lactate solution containing calcium chloride generated fewer symptoms which in turn provides evidence for the theory of calcium binding.

The above data, unfortunately, do not provide an explanation as to how anxiety neurotics produce more lactate than normals. It has been tentatively postulated that this phenomenon may be due to an over production of adrenalin since this substance accelerates glucose metabolism. With this mechanism in mind, Pitts proposes the use of B-adrenergic blockers (such as propranol) for the treatment of anxiety neurosis.

The second major physiological theory of pervasive anxiety is presented by Lader and Mathews (1968). This theory was based on earlier experimental work involving psychophysiological investigations of anxiety neurotics (Lader & Wing,

1966). In a classic monograph, Lader and Wing demonstrated that patients suffering from anxiety states had higher rates of spontaneous skin conductance fluctuations (a measure believed to correlate with arousal) than normals. The patients and the normals were matched for age and sex. In a later portion of the study all subjects were given 20 presentations of a tone stimuli in order to investigate how rapidly skin conductance responses to the tones habituated. It was shown that the patients with anxiety states habituated significantly more slowly than the normals. From these data Lader and Wing hypothesized that anxiety neurotics are chronically overaroused and suffer from deficits in the mechanism of habituation.

Lader and Mathews' theory suggests that the repeating of a stimulus for a certain level of arousal (such as the anxiety neurotic) actually serves to maintain or even increase the already high arousal level. According to these theorists almost any environmental or ideational stimulus could serve to maintain or increase arousal in the anxiety neurotic. They point out that arousal above a critical level would be experienced as a "panic attack."

Treatment of anxiety states according to Lader and Mathews should involve a procedure designed to lower the state of hyperarousal. They suggested the use of Jacobson's (1938) muscle relaxation technique. It is pointed out that the effects produced by this treatment are not due to removal of muscle tension, but rather, due to the procedure's ability to lower the level of spontaneous skin conductance fluctuations. It will be recalled that Lader and Mathews equate skin conductance fluctuations with arousal.

The two biological theories presented are not necessarily incompatable, as the theories may simply be considering different aspects of the same problem. Pitts maintained that abnormally high lactate production caused binding of calcium in a physiologically inactive form which, in turn, may effect nerve transmission. Lader and Mathews postulated that persistent anxiety states result from chronic hyperarousal of the autonomic nervous system. It may be that the hyperarousal observed by Lader and Mathews resulted from the process outlined by Pitts and his fellow investigators. More experiment work should be undertaken to clarify these issues.

The data upon which both theories are based suffers from the same problems. That is, the population samples used already were manifesting the anxiety reaction. Therefore, it is impossible to discern whether the investigators were observing basic physiological differences between different groups or the end result of a disease process or conditioning phenomenon in a population that began as normals. Both Pitts (1971) and Lader and Wing (1966) addressed this problem by suggesting anxiety neurosis is an inherited disorder. In support of this claim, Lader and Wing investigated the psychophysiological characteristics of several sets of monozygotic and dizygotic twins. They found high correlations in the number of spontaneous fluctuations, skin conductance fluctuation rate, and pulse rate in the monozygotic twins. These correlations were higher for the monozygotic twins than the dizygotic twins suggesting heredity played a part. Pitts (1971) cites data presented by Cohen, Bahal, Kilpatrick, Reed, and White (1951) that also pointed toward a genetic factor. Cohen and his group found that the incidence of anxiety neurosis in the general population was 4.7%. However, 48 and 61% of the children of a family in which one or both parents respectively have the problem also suffer from the disease. Collectively these data are used in support of a genetic factor, although the data represent too few subjects to be conclusive. In addition, control conditions for ruling out environmental factors were lacking, such as locating monozygotic pairs raised apart.

PSYCHOLOGICAL THEORIES

Psychoanalytic Theory

As with the biological theories, there have been few psychological theories of anxiety neurosis. Freud first separated the syndrome of anxiety neurosis from the general concept of neurasthenia in 1894 (Freud, 1924). In general, the major difference is that in neurasthenia the neurotic state presents itself as emergency discharges other than anxiety alone, with general inhibition of ego functions. Later writers (see Fenichel, 1945) point out that the concept of neurasthenia, and thus possibly its differentiation from anxiety neurosis, is ill defined.

Analytic theory suggests that the problem of anxiety neurosis develops, as does all neurotic conditions, as a result of a conflict between the instinctual drives of the id and the ego (Freud, 1927). According to this formulation, as the ego begins to develop, the infant learns that its instinctual urges may be dangerous and thus must be controlled (Freud, 1936). Because of inability of the infant to satisfy instinctual needs, its first experience is one of trauma. These instinctual strivings are learned to be dangerous because of the pairing of trauma with the strivings. As the ego develops, the child learns to not only use portions of the traumatic anxiety as a signal to activate defensive action in order to avoid further anxiety, but it also learns to gratify instinctual needs through other means (Freud, 1936). Fenichel (1945) noted that once the ego has developed to this point, instinctual impulses should no longer be frightening. He further stated that because of strong fears over loss of love or castration, the ego does not allow discharge of normal excitements. When this happens a state of being "damned up" is created. Freud (1924) originally attributed this state to the practice *coitus interruptus* and other sexual acts that prevented completed sexual discharge. Later theorizing included other unexpressed instinctual needs than sexual ones (Fenichel, 1945).

Because of the state of being "damned up," ego control becomes difficult. Fenichel (1945) noted the behavioral similarities between patients suffering from this state and those with a traumatic neurosis. He described the anxiety neurotic engaged in a struggle for control of unacceptable impulses as follows:

The neurotic, being engaged in an inner defense struggle, becomes restless, agitated, upset, and feels that he needs some change but does not know what it should be [p. 187].

These symptoms are then followed by the development of anxiety attacks that Fenichel saw as the way great amounts of excitement are manifested. To repeat, anxiety neurosis results from the inability of the individual to discharge anxiety resulting from conflicts between the instinctual demands of the id and the sanctions placed on gratification of these impulses by the ego. This condition is unlike other neurotic conditions in that no specific psychological defenses are present to aid in the control of this conflict (Kolb, 1968). Likewise, the anxiety is not displaced from the internal conflict to external events and objects representative of the conflict which occurs in anxiety hysteria (Jones, 1913). Research evidence in support of this analytic model has not been forthcoming, nor have data been provided which support the effectiveness of treating anxiety neurosis with psychoanalysis.

Behavioral Theories

Behaviorally oriented clinicians have not presented elaborate theories regarding the etiology of anxiety neurosis. Only two briefly presented theories have appeared, one by Wolpe (1958) and the other by Costello (1971).

Wolpe (1958) prseented a theory based upon conditioning principles to account for the development of pervasive anxiety, a term he preferred instead of "free-floating" anxiety. He argued that conditioning of anxiety responses not only occurs to well-defined stimulus configurations, as in the case of a phobic reaction, but also occurs in response to less salient environmental cues. Extreme examples of such cues would be light, light and shade contrasts, amorphous noise, spatiality, and the passage of time.

For Wolpe there is no sharp dividing line between specific anxiety-evoking stimuli and stimuli conditioned to pervasive anxiety. From his clinical work he observed that for one patient anxiety increased in the presence of any very large object; another experienced an uncomfortable intrusiveness of all sharp contrasts in the visual field like printed words on a page; and a third was overwhelmed by physical space. Anxiety frequently increases in such cases when the outside world makes its impact, when noises are heard, or when the subject wakes up and when the day goes on. Wolpe also observed that patients felt less anxious when they lie down and close their eyes. He suggested the latter may be explained to some extent on the basis of perseveration due to prolonged reverberation of the effects of the stimulus in the nervous system.

Wolpe's clinical experience led him to postulate two factors that are responsible for determining whether pervasive anxiety will be part of the patient's neurosis. The first factor involves the intensity of the anxiety reaction at the time of conditioning—the greater the magnitude or intensity of the effect, the more stimulus aspects are likely to be included in the conditioned stimulus complex. The second factor is the postulated lack of clearly defined environmental stimuli at the time of acquisition.

Costello (1971) provided an alternative theory of pervasive anxiety which argues against a conditioning explanation of etiology. That is to say, according to this position the development of pervasive anxiety is not due to the effects of CS-UCS pairings and to the generalization of these effects as suggested by Wolpe but rather develops because of constitutional reasons that in all probability are primarily genetic. Costello based this premise partially on the Lader and Wing (1966) data presented earlier in this chapter which suggested that anxious patients do not habituate autonomic responding readily to simple tone stimuli. In a sense Costello's model is mislabeled by us and perhaps should have been included under the section of biological theories. However, we chose to include it under behavioral models because he attempted to illustrate how the constitutional factor integrates with behavioral development.

To account for the interaction of behavioral and physiological stress reactions, Costello's theory relies upon the information-processing model developed by Teichner (1968). According to Teichner, sensory processes are involved with signals from the external world and the internal biological world. Such stimuli are stored in short-term memory (STM) and from there to an attentional mechanism where they are compared with stimuli stored in long-term memory (LTM). When some level of matching between STM and LTM stimuli has occurred, the organism will be engaged in some action. When the matching has not been reached at a desired level, the organism experiences discomfort and the search for additional information in the environment or in LTM memory. This process continues until sufficient matching occurs to permit behavioral action.

According to Costello, the anxiety neurotic has a constitutional overreactive autonomic nervous system (ANS). As such the stimuli for this individual's external and internal world are not readily associated with some appropriate action so they do not result in representations in LTM. Therefore the individual is likely to become engaged in perseverative information-processing activity that cannot be resolved because of a lack of LTM encoding. Discomfort should result because of the inability to match STM and LTM stimuli. Costello characterized such individuals as being constantly in a "novel" situation and as being exposed to stimuli that are neutral for the majority of people but act as aversive unconditioned stimuli for the anxiety neurotic.

Both of the above theories suffer from a lack of supporting data. However, both suggest that traditional behavioral therapeutic approaches emphasizing the stimulus-response analysis of anxiety conditions (i.e., systematic desensitization) will be ineffective in dealing with pervasive anxiety problems. The available data (Lazarus, 1963), as well as statements by well-known advocates of behavioral treatment of anxiety states (Gelder, 1969) suggest this to be the case. For example, Gelder (1969) commented, in relation to treatment of generalized anxiety, that:

Unless these situational elements can be identified, behavior therapy as such cannot be used [p. 693].

Perhaps it is because of behavioral clinicians' inability to identify clear stimulus antecedents to pervasive anxiety problems that only a few behaviorally based treatment strategies have appeared in the literature. Difficulties with treatment of these problems are not limited to the newer behavioral approaches since reports of patients treated with more traditional treatment techniques (Miles, Barrabee, & Finesinger, 1951) found 42% of 62 patients essentially unimproved after treatment. Considering this information, the popular treatment techniques for these disorders will now be discussed.

TREATMENT APPROACHES

Psychopharmacological

By far the most popular treatment of pervasive anxiety involves the use of anti-anxiety medication. Although barbiturates had been used for some time for the treatment of anxiety, the introduction of meprobamate in 1955 was felt by some

(Berger, 1954) to be the beginning of an era in which common anxiety symptoms could be efficiently treated. Reports suggested that this drug removed anxiety symptoms without unwanted side effects such as drowsiness (Greenblatt & Shader, 1974). Later, the first of the benzodiazepines (chlordiazepoxide) was introduced and it is these drugs that have taken the forefront in the treatment of anxiety although the authors of one classic text (Goodman & Gilman, 1970) state the reason for this popularity is unknown. This popularity has reached astounding proportions as studies of prescription drug use have shown. Greenblatt and Shader (1974) summarize these statistics. Their summary indicates that prescriptions of antianxiety agents account for almost 30% of new psychotropic drug prescriptions (prescriptions for psychotropic drugs represent 17% of all prescriptions written in 1967 according to several sources; see Greenblatt & Shader, 1974). The summary further cites statistics showing that in an average year 5–15% of American adults take antianxiety agents (Gottschalk, Bates, Fox, & James, 1971; Mellinger, Balter, & Manheimer, 1971).

Review of psychopharmacology textbooks (Goodman & Gilman, 1970; Greenblatt & Shader, 1974; Hollister, 1973; Tinklenberg, 1977) suggested many possible reasons for the popularity of the benzodiazepines in the treatment of anxiety. Foremost is the conclusion from available reports that these compounds are very safe, carrying almost no risk of death due to overdose of these drugs alone. This is not true of other antianxiety agents (meprobamate and barbiturates) that carry substantial risk of lethality when taken in quantity. However, deaths have been noted when benzodiazepines have been combined with other drugs. Hollister (1973) noted in his review that when these drugs are overdosed in combination with other drugs the effects of the second drug is usually predominant. Other reasons noted by experts for the popularity of benzodiazepines includes the long half-life of the drugs (except for oxazepam and flurazepam) which provides for long duration of effects with a single dose; low risk of physical tolerance; and the fact that the drugs themselves do not stimulate the production of enzymes that speed their own metabolism. Although one of the reported advantages of benzodiazepines is low potential of physical tolerance, some literature suggested this can occur. In addition, psychological addiction has become a problem with these drugs (Barchas, Berger, Ciaranello, & Elliott, 1977). It is generally believed that actual physical addiction to the benzodiazepines only occurs with very high doses taken over long periods of time (Greenblatt & Shader, 1974; Tinklenberg, 1977). Smith and Wesson (1970) concluded that it requires doses of 300 to 600 mg/day of chloridazepoxide and 80 to 120 mg/day of diazepam to produce addiction. These authors further stated that these dosages must be taken for at least 40 days before the problem develops. The incidence of this problem is unclear. However, figures available suggest that benzodiazepines addiction is implicated in approximately 20.5% of a group of patients admitted to hospitals because of drug abuse (Swanson, Weddige, & Morse, 1973). A study conducted in Sweden (Allgulander, 1978) found benzodiazepines in the blood and urine of 24 of 43 patients admitted to the hospital because of dependence on sedative and hypnotic drugs. Thus it would seem abuse of these drugs may be a problem. The medical sequelae of withdrawal from these substances when actual physical tolerance is present may be quite severe. Hollister, Motzenbecker, and Degan (1961) reported that symptoms including depression, insomnia, agitation, seizures, and loss of appetite were experienced by patients shifted from chlordiazepoxide to a placebo after one to seven months of the drug. Dosage levels ranged from 100 to 600 mg/day. A review of case studies by Greenblatt and Shader (1974) noted symptoms of delirium tremens, agitation, depression, hallucinations, and in one case death following withdrawal. Considering these data, nonmedical practitioners might be wise to consult a physician in cases where possible physical addiction is suspected. Noted psychopharmacologists (see Hollister, 1977) recommend care in prescribing drugs to the patients with so-called abuse prone personality.

There are five major benzodiazepines used in the treatment of anxiety symptoms. These are chlordiazepoxide (Librium); diazepam (Valium); oxazepam (Serax); clorazepate (Tranxene); and flurazepam (Dalmane). Of the five, the first four are used in the treatment of daytime anxiety symptoms while the fifth, flurazepam, is extremely short acting and used as a hypnotic. All of the benzodiazepines have similar properties although there are some variations between them. For example, both chlordiazepoxide and diazepam are stored in the tissues of the body and produce pharmacologically active metabolites, thereby producing long-lasting effects after the initial dose (Hollister, 1973). Oxazepam, on the other hand, produces no active metabolites (itself being a metabolite of diazepam) and therefore having a relatively short duration of action. The complete chemistry of these drugs is beyond the scope of this chapter and the reader interested in this aspect is referred to Greenblatt and Shader (1974) for discussion of this topic.

The mechanism of action of the benzodiazepines is believed to be due to effects on the limbic system (Greenblatt & Shader, 1974). Animal studies (Jwahara, Oishi, Yamazaki, & Sakai, 1972; Schallek & Thomas, 1971; Steiner & Hummel, 1968) have shown a reduction in spontaneous hippocampal electrical activity and changes in response to external stimulation. Other studies have shown that benzodiazepines produce changes in the amygdalahippocampus circuit. Drug doses reduce hippocampal discharge when the amygdala is stimulated (Morillo, Revzin, & Knauss, 1962). Greenblatt and Shader (1974) speculates that this finding suggests that the drug's antianxiety effects are due to a "pharmacologic amyglalectomy."

Research has suggested that these drugs produce two major behavioral effects (Greenblatt & Shader, 1974). First, the compounds reduce hostile behavior, and second they increase the frequency of behaviors that have been suppressed by punishment, fear, or frustration. However, it should be noted that under some circumstances aggressive behavior has been enhanced (Fox & Snyder, 1969). Although the parameters of this effect are not completely understood, it is important to note that increases in human aggressive behavior have been observed with administration of the benzodiazepines (DiMascio, Shader, & Giller, 1970). It is generally believed that this occurs when hostility has been suppressed by anxiety (Greenblatt & Shader, 1974). Thus, when the anxiety is reduced by the drug, the hostility comes forward.

Clinical studies using these drugs have produced mixed results regarding their effectiveness. Many of these inconclusive results may be due to the problems in the study of anxiety and its treatment (Hollister, 1973; Greenblatt & Shader, 1974). For example, the episodic nature of anxiety symptoms poses a problem as drug-placebo differences can be hidden simply because the anxiety reaction of the control patients has waned because of their natural time course. Similarly, the objective, reliable measurement of anxiety symptoms is also problematic. Additionally, nonspecific environmental factors (physician attributes, capsule vs. tablet, sex, etc.) have produced differences (Rickels, 1968). In spite of these problems, in a review of almost 100 studies comparing various benzodiazepines with placebos, Greenblatt and Shader concluded that the drugs are more effective than placebos. Their conclusions were based on the studies global rating of improvement. These reviewers found that a number of studies demonstrated a "drug washout" effect (loss of drug-placebo differences over time) which they attribute to the cyclic nature of anxiety symptoms. Based on these findings the authors suggested that antianxiety drugs are probably most helpful when taken during acute anxiety episodes instead of continuously.

The literature reviewed also suggested that the benzodiazepines were more effective than barbiturates (according to patient reported, when both drugs were given in a "cross-over design"). One problem with these studies is the possible pharmacological nonequivalence of benzodiazepine and barbiturate dose levels. One study (Lader & Wing, 1966) attempted to establish dose equivalence through the use of preliminary "staircase bioassay" of the two drugs, amylobarbitone sodium and chlordiazepoxide. Subjects of the study were anxiety neurotics. When physiological measures of anxiety (skin conductance fluctuations) were considered, there were no differences between the two drugs of pharmacological equivalent dose levels. When patient preference was considered, there were no differences between the two drugs. No consistent drug differences were shown when psychiatrist ratings were considered. Thus, when appropriate dose levels are given, there may be no differences between benzodiazepines and barbiturate compounds. This latter conclusion differs from that reached by Greenblatt and Shader (1974). However, as Greenblatt and Shader pointed out, the benzodiazepine drugs are much safer than the barbiturates, resulting in little danger with overdose. Thus, they may be the drugs of choice in the treatment of anxiety.

Reviews of studies comparing the effectiveness of the various benzodiazepine derivatives revealed little difference between them (Greenblatt & Shader, 1974). Studies in which differences were found generally failed to provide pharmacologically equivalent dosages of the drugs or failed to consider differences in plasma half-life and production of active metabolites.

The appropriate administration of antianxiety agents are not covered in this chapter. Those readers with interests in this area are referred to the several excellent texts on the topic (Hollister, 1973; Shader & Greenblatt, 1975; Slaby, Lieb, & Tancredi, 1975; Tinklenberg, 1977).

One area of importance with these and other psychotropic drugs is side effects. Epidemiological studies of patients using chlordiazepoxide and diazepam have shown that drowsiness is by far the most common side effect of the drug (Miller, 1973; Svenson & Hamilton, 1966). This side effect is apparently dose related with 80 gm/day or more of chlordiazepoxide and 20 mg/day or more of diazepam producing the effect in over 10% of the patients sampled (Boston Collaborative Drug Surveillance Program, 1973). Other side effects reported by Svenson and Hamilton (1966) include (in descending order of frequency) ataxia (1.70%); paradoxical excitement (0.70%); dizziness (0.64%); constipation (0.40%); appetite stimulation (0.36%); nausea or vomiting (0.34%); and muscular weakness (0.30%). Other side effects such as weight gain occurred with a frequency of less than 0.30%. Greenblatt and Shader (1974) found in their review of the literature that events such as hepatoxicity, hematologic effects, allergic reactions, and cytogenetic effects have been reported at the case study level. Summarizing, it would appear that other than drowsiness, side effects are rather uncommon with these drugs.

Behavioral

Although a variety of psychotherapy techniques including psychoanalytic and other insight-oriented approaches have been applied to the treatment of anxiety neurosis, little or no serious attempt has been made to evaluate treatment effectiveness for this disorder or to suggest change in technique to accommodate this unique problem. As noted earlier, even the behavioral-oriented techniques have been remiss in providing outcome studies. This sad state of affairs makes it impossible to provide a literature review in which a solid, data-based conclusion can be reached.

Therefore, a decision has been made to limit the following review of psychological treatment techniques of pervasive anxiety to the behavioral-therapy literature. Even though the vast majority of papers in this area dealt with case reports, some attempt was made to suggest specialized treatment techniques for this problem. It is our hope such a review will enhance more interest and stimulate systematic work in this area.

Organization of this literature review proved difficult given the apparent unrelatedness of the various approaches and the finding that many of the suggestions offered involved a combination of different treatment techniques frequently presented in a single case report. In an attempt to provide some structure for our review the reports are initially organized in terms of the relatedness of the available evidence to theory. The reader should not necessarily assume that the author of a given report was stimulated by the theory in question or would agree to our suggested relevance.

It will be recalled that Wolpe's theory of pervasive anxiety hypothesized that less salient environmental cues such as light, amorphous noise, spatiality, or passage of time have been conditioned to the anxiety response. Except for the presence of clearly defined environmental stimuli at the time of acquisition, the conditioned anxiety response involved in anxiety neurosis is assumed to be controlled by the same learning principles governing specific-defined fear responses.

Wolpe's (1958) strategy to deconditioned anxiety essentially involves a counterconditioning approach which attempts to pair the anxiety response with a response that is directly inhibitory or antagonistic to it. Since fear or anxiety is believed to affect the sympathetic section of the autonomic nervous system, effective counterconditioners are viewed by Wolpe as involving the parasympathetic section, which essentially operates in opposition to the sympathetic system. The relaxation response that comes under the control of the parasympathetic system is seen by Wolpe as an excellent inhibitor of conditioned anxiety. From this formulation, one cannot both be afraid and relax at the same time.

The above reasoning led Wolpe (1958) to develop his well-known technique of systematic desensitization that incorporates a relaxation counterconditioner and encompasses three procedural steps. First, the therapist trains the patient in deep-muscle relaxation involving the progressive contrasting and relaxing of the different muscle groups originally as suggested by Jacobson (1938). Next, the therapist's task is to construct a list of anxiety-producing situations in order of their increasing level of anxiety elicitation to the patient. Lastly, the first and second steps are combined into a third step in which the patient is asked to imagine for a short time period (3–5 seconds) experiencing an item on the hierarchy that, in turn, is followed by the instructional set to relax. Each hierarchy item is experienced one by one and separately counterconditioned by relaxation training, starting with the lowest item and moving upward on the anxiety scale. The procedure continues until evidence exists that the relaxation response becomes dominant.

It should be noted that Wolpe (1958) has suggested other counterconditioning procedures as well as other counterconditioning agents like sexual pleasure, eating, and anxiety relief. But the most widely used technique emanating from his approach is systematic desensitization.

Costello's (1971) theory of pervasive anxiety, although radically different from that proposed by Wolpe, leads to a similar counterconditioning treatment strategy. It will be recalled that Costello based his position on the premise that ordinary environmental stimulation functions as an unconditioned stimulus (UCS) for the anxiety neurotic because of constitutional differences in autonomic activity. In theory, these UCSs can repeatedly condition other stimuli with the end result being the elicitation of high levels of autonomic activity produced by stimuli uncorrelated with the patient's behavior. The therapy approach adopted by Costello is to provide the patient with a repertoire of "coping" behavior to counteract (or countercondition) the anxiety reaction. Despite marked differences in suggested etiology between theories, Wolpe could readily interpret Costello's "coping" behavior, training strategy from his counterconditioning viewpoint.

A literature review of the relevant studies bearing on the above and related issues will now follow. For organization purposes, studies were grouped under the following five headings: (a) modified systematic desensitization procedures; (b) chemical counterconditioner facilitators; (c) relaxation training as a counterconditioning approach; (d) "packaged" coping strategies; and (e) miscellaneous approaches.

Modified Systematic Desensitization Procedures

Treatment of pervasive anxiety via the standard, systematic desensitization procedure becomes problematic since the stimuli eliciting the anxiety response remains undetected and from Wolpe's viewpoint is amorphous. To deal with this problem, Goldfried (1971) modified Wolpe's procedure to broaden generalization of the counterconditioning agent to encompass all anxiety arousing situations. In this respect, he viewed his approach as training the patient in anxiety-inhibiting coping skills. To achieve this objective, Goldfried recommended four procedural modifications to the traditional systematic desensitization technique. First, a different rationale is given to the patient. Basically, the patient is told that he has to learn to respond to various situations with tension or anxiety. Therefore, treatment is geared to teaching the patient to successfully cope with these situations so that he will no longer respond with anxiety. Second, the patient is told during relaxation training that the tension phase of the relaxation procedure is designed to teach him to recognize tension so that the tension can serve as a cue to relax. Third, the stimuli in the desensitization hierarchy are deemphasized so that the patient learns to respond with relaxation to the proprioceptive cues of anxiety rather than with relaxation to other stimulus cues. Goldfried points out that the hierarchy items only need reflect increasing amounts of anxiety rather than make sense thematically. Finally, a modification is made in the presentation of hierarchy items in that patients are encouraged to keep imagining a scene even if it produces anxiety. During this, the patient is instructed to use his relaxation skills to cope with the tension. Goldfried believes that this procedure is a more accurate real-life analog since patients cannot always avoid anxiety-arousing situations in reality. Thus the patient is taught an active coping skill to deal with anxiety. The patient, once trained, is instructed to use these tactics in life situations.

Two experimental studies have tested Goldfried's notions. Goldfried and Trier (1974) used college students with public-speaking anxiety. These investigators found that the self-control relaxation procedure was more effective in reducing speech anxiety when compared to a standard systematic desensitization or a discussion-group control procedure. The authors noted that upon follow-up the subjects who received the self-control procedure reported more improvement than the other groups. Other than subject self-report, no other measures were taken. Zemore (1975) used college students fearful of both examinations and public speaking. A Goldfried style self-control group, a standard systematic desensitization group, and a no-treatment control group were used. Only one of the subject's fears was treated. The results indicated that with both active treatments, both treated and untreated fears improved relative to the control group. Thus, in this study the self-control procedure was not shown to be superior with multiphobic subjects. It should also be pointed out, however, that the self-control coping procedure has yet to be attempted with anxiety neurotic patients and final judgment should await such an analysis.

Suinn and Richardson (1971) present a treatment approach for nonspecific anxiety called *Anxiety Management Training* (AMT) which is somewhat similar to that presented by Goldfried. The originators of this technique view their approach as similar to systematic desensitization but without the use of hierarchies specific to problem areas. They feel that the use of anxiety hierarchies prevents generalization of treatment effects to new problem areas of the patient's life. Basically, AMT involved teaching the patient to recognize the initial cues of anxiety and use these to serve as discriminative stimuli for competing responses such as relaxation. Suinn and Richardson believe that many patients become overwhelmed with anxiety simply because they fail to recognize its initial symptoms. Anxiety Management Training sensitizes them to these cues. Procedurally, patients are first asked to visualize past events that arouse anxiety. The patients are then taught to use competing responses when these feelings occur. The authors suggest two such responses—relaxation or success feelings. Following their presentation of the technique, Suinn and Richardson present data from a study comparing this technique with standard systematic desensitization. Subjects of the study were college students with anxiety over learning mathematics. The data supported the notion that AMT was an effective anxiety reduction procedure but no more effective than standard desensitization. The procedure has not been used with patients classified as anxiety neurotics, although at a theoretical level the procedure would appear to have merit.

Chemical Counterconditioner Facilitators

Wolpe (1958, 1969, 1973), aware of the stimulus specificity issue in treating pervasive anxiety, realized the limited usefulness of systematic desensitization. Instead, he recommended the use of carbon dioxide therapy which requires the patient to inhale a mixture of 70% carbon dioxide and 30% oxygen. Wolpe suggested that from one to four inhalations be given during each treatment. He reported that following each inhalation, the patient breathed very heavily for 5 to 15 seconds and reported feeling flushed, having tingling sensations, and experiencing visual sensations such as colored lights. Following each session, Wolpe reported that his patients generally experienced a considerable lessening of the anxiety symptoms. Unfortunately, these effects appeared in some patients to last only until the patient is reexposed to a specific anxiety arousing stimulus which reestablished the anxiety reaction. Wolpe's solution to this problem is to provide additional carbon dioxide treatments, but he agreed that if this situation materializes again the treatment is hardly worthwhile under such circumstances.

Wolpe's (1958) rationale for the use of treatment is based upon his assumption that carbon dioxide therapy results in a reciprocal inhibition of the anxiety response. He argued that processes antagonistic to anxiety can be found both in the excitation that goes with intense respiratory stimulation and in association with the complete muscle relaxation that high concentrations of carbon dioxide produce. He concluded that at present it is not possible to say which of these processes is the effective one and both might play a part. Nevertheless, Wolpe did lean toward the viewpoint that respiratory excitation is the critical change agent. As far as other strategies go, Wolpe noted that the most profound relaxation, obtained by Jacobson's method or by the use of tranquilizing drugs, has not been shown to be effective for the treatment of pervasive anxiety.

Carbon dioxide therapy was also used by Slater and Leavy (1966) who reported data from 12 neurotic patients treated. For control purposes, the subjects spent some sessions breathing only air and other sessions deep breathing such that hyperventilation was produced. The latter procedure was used to investigate the possibility that hyperventilation was the effective component of anxiety reduction. Subjects' anxiety ratings before and after treatment indicated that the carbon dioxide-oxygen mixture produced significantly more anxiety reduction than either air alone, or the hyperventilation procedure. An independent observer's rating of the patient's anxiety level failed to differentiate the three procedures. Comparison of anxiety ratings following the CO_2 treatment with the anxiety rating 24 hours later failed to show lasting treatment effects over time. The authors felt that the treatment effects observed resulted from an increase in CO_2 concentration in the brain tissue. This increased concentration was believed to produce cortical inhibition.

Costello (1964) suggested therapeutic administration of another chemical agent, LSD-25. He believed it may be helpful in cases where the stimulus complex cannot be adequately broken down for systematic desensitization. During these sessions, the patient is given the drug while the therapist presents complex stimulus material hypothesized to be related to the patient's anxiety symptoms. In addition, the therapist provides support and suggestion to "face whatever ideas, thoughts, or pictures presented themselves." Costello reported that patients experienced considerable anxiety reduction following this treatment, although during treatment itself they may become quite agitated. Costello justified the use of the drug in that it allows the patient to contact all of the stimulus complex to which the anxiety responses are linked. In a sense this approach can be viewed as an extinction procedure as opposed to a counterconditioning strategy. Conceptually, Costello proposed a model based on Osgood's theory of representational mediation (Osgood, 1956)ˈ in order to explain the development of stimulus complexes. Although Costello's treatment approach is interesting, the use of LSD-25 may prove difficult for therapists because of current legal restrictions.

Relaxation Training as a Counterconditioner Approach

If chronic tension or pervasive anxiety is viewed as an anxiety response to a wide variety of diffused stimuli, training patients to relax in the presence of the anxiety stimuli makes theoretical sense. The extent to which deep-muscle relaxation reduces at least the autonomic portion of the anxiety response has been well documented in the literature. The procedure was originally developed and researched by Jacobson (1938). Jacobson's relaxation procedure stemmed from his observation that in almost every emotion there is an increase in striate muscle tension. He reasoned that a reduction in the striate muscle response should produce the opposite of tension, that is, relaxation. Several studies (Connor, 1974; Mathews & Gelder, 1969; Paul, 1969) have shown that relaxation training produces several changes in the autonomic nervous system's response. Perhaps the most consistent changes that have been shown following this procedure are a reduction in spontaneous skin conductance fluctuations and a reduction in skin conductance response to anxiety-evoking stimuli. Considering Lader and Wing's (1966) conceptualization of chronic anxiety as lack of modulation in the autonomic nervous system, these studies provide support for the apparent effectiveness of relaxation procedures with anxiety problems.

The question of whether or not relaxation training is effective in nonspecific, anxiety stimulus situations characteristic of pervasive anxiety, however, is still unanswered. Two studies (Johnson & Spielberger, 1968; Stoudenmire, 1972) related to this question have measured the effects of relaxation procedures on state and trait anxiety reactions. In both studies, it was suggested that relaxation training effected only state or situationally bound anxiety. Conceptually, pervasive anxiety reactions are probably more reflective of trait anxiety, and if so relaxation training may not prove effective. On the other hand, one could take the position that pervasive anxiety actually reflects the responding to a wide variety of specific stimulus situations that only spuriously give the impression of trait or continuous, nonspecific anxiety responding. If the latter is the case, then training patients to relax to each specific stimulus situation or perhaps to the antecedent cues of anxiety response itself may prove beneficial.

The use of relaxation training to counteract pervasive anxiety has been one of the most frequently applied behavioral strategies. Cautela (1965) reported a case study of a 33-year-old janitor who suffered from chronic anxiety for over five years. Prior to Cautela's treatment, the patient had undergone two years of dynamically oriented therapy that resulted in only minimal relief. Cautela utilized two tactics to overcome the chronic tension. The first was relaxation therapy and autosuggestion (visualizing the work situation while relaxation training was given). The second strategy involved instructing the patient to engage in an anxiety competitive response (eating a candy bar) when he began to feel fearful. The patient reported considerable improvement following six weeks of treatment.

Although it is difficult to isolate the importance of the relaxation ingredient in Cautela's treatment package, some support for relaxation training at the case study level was noted by Dawley (1973). He successfully treated a chronic anxiety case through the use of self-administered relaxation therapy by instructing the patient in this procedure and providing audio tapes for practicing.

The more systematic work done in evaluating relaxation training has focused on enhancing its effectiveness through the use of biofeedback procedures. Three studies using this strategy and concerned with the treatment of chronic tension have appeared (Acosta, Yamamoto, & Wilcox, 1978; Raskin, Johnson, & Rondestvedt, 1973; Townsend, House, & Addario, 1975). Two of the studies (Acosta et al. 1978; Raskin et al. 1973) involved a multiple case study design while the Townsend et al. (1975) investigation utilized a group therapy control group. The two case study reports utilized a frontalis muscle feedback procedure on patients reporting a variety of tension-related symptoms (headaches, insomnia, free-floating anxiety, etc.). The Acosta et al. study used both diagnosed schizophrenic and neurotic patients, while the Raskin et al. study used only pervasive-anxiety patients. Many of Raskin's patients were receiving concurrent chlordiapoxide (40 to 80 mg/day) treatment. Acosta et al. reported that their patients were able to significantly lower frontalis muscle tension over 10 weekly sessions. The patients' diagnosis did not affect the outcome. Data were not reported on the effects of the training sessions outside the laboratory. However, Raskin et al. did address this issue. They found that patients receiving such treatment reported that they were able to control excessive situational anxiety using the procedures they had learned. Some of the patients indicated that they were able also to control sleep disturbance symptoms. However, these effects were transient in the sense that only one patient reported a lessening of the chronic anxiety symptoms.

In the Townsend et al. controlled study, patients received nine 20-minute EMG feedback sessions. Taped self-relaxation instructions were also provided during this period. Two weeks of self-practice (without taped instructions) then followed. During this same period, the control group patients received 16 sessions of traditional group psychotherapy. Assessment of these procedures indicated that patients in the feedback group showed significantly reduced EMG levels and less mood disturbance than the control group. Transient reductions from baseline were also shown in both state and trait anxiety by the feedback group but not the comparison group.

Overall, these studies suggest that biofeedback-assisted relaxation training may be of benefit to patients suffering from chronic anxiety. (Please note that the above three studies reviewed did not use patients specifically diagnosed as suffering from anxiety neurosis, although all had problems with chronic tension or pervasive anxiety.) However, the results of these studies suggest that benefits are far from dramatic since none of the patients showed long-lasting effects over time. Blanchard and Epstein (1977), following a review of the literature, suggested several reasons why this may be the case. Foremost of these is the specificity of the training to the muscle on which feedback is given and the lack of correlation between the construct anxiety and muscle tension alone (Epstein, 1976).

Studies investigating the effectiveness of the EMG biofeedback relaxation procedure have not shown consistent findings. A study by Reinking and Kohl (1975) found that there were no differences in reported levels of relaxation between several feedback and nonfeedback relaxation conditions. There were differences in favor of feedback procedures when EMG levels were concerned. Specifically, the biofeedback procedures produced faster training and lower EMG readings. One should note that these lower readings were only for the muscle on which training was given (frontalis) and thus these readings were not representative of other muscle groups.

Beiman, Israel, and Johnson (1978) compared the effects of self-relaxation and EMG biofeedback with both live and taped instructions. Using measures of general autonomic arousal (skin conductance fluctuations and respiration), it was shown that there were no differences between the self-relaxation and biofeedback procedures. Live presentation was found to be superior, however. Thus, the literature is unclear concerning the effectiveness of biofeedback-assisted relaxation training or, for that matter, relaxation training per se.

"Packaged" Coping Strategies

Cautela (1966) was one of the first to present a "package" treatment approach for pervasive anxiety problems. His approach included the following components. The first component involved reassurance therapy in which the patient is instructed to call the therapist at any time when in need. The second component consisted of a modified desensitization procedure, in which the patient is asked to imagine anxiety-eliciting scenes until he can imagine the scene without experiencing anxiety. When this occurs the next, more anxiety-provoking scene is presented. The third component encompassed relaxation therapy in which the patient is taught to use covert verbal responses (previously paired with relaxation) to quell anxiety experienced in real life situations. The final component used was assertive training. Cautela included this latter component because he believed the procedure was indicated in all the cases of pervasive anxiety he has treated. Following presentation of the various procedures, Cautela reviewed two cases in which these procedures were used successfully. At the case study level, effectiveness was reported but no empirical studies have been undertaken using the procedures in this "package" form. Cautela's use of assertive training as part of his package has some indirect empirical support. A study using psychiatric patients demonstrated that an assertive training group reduced patient's trait anxiety levels (Percell, Berwick, & Beigel, 1974).

Using a different package strategy Meichenbaum and Turk (1976) present a self-management procedure called *Stress Inoculation Training* for anxiety-ridden patients. These authors reported that they have successfully used this program with patients suffering from free-floating anxiety. Treatment consists of three phases. First, the patient is given a didactic session on the nature of the stress response. Included in this are discussions of possible coping responses such as planning escape routes, relaxation techniques, cognitive self-reinforcement statements, and so forth. Second, these ideas are rehearsed. Emphasis is placed on the patient's self-dialogue during the confrontations with a stressor. An attempt is made to have the patient refrain from negative or anxiety-increasing self-statements. Finally, the patient's abilities are tested using laboratory anxiety-arousing stimuli (films, threats of electric shock, etc.). As of yet no published research has appeared on this technique. Like the Goldfried or Suinn and Richardson procedure, it could be effective with anxiety-neurotic patients.

Miscellaneous Approaches

Other clinicians have published suggestions for treatment of anxiety neurosis that do not readily reflect our previous subheadings. Girodo (1974), for example, suggested that yoga meditation be used with these patients. Nine anxiety-neurotic patients were trained in this procedure for four months. Five of the patients showed improvement with this treatment on an Anxiety Symptom Questionnaire (ASQ). Following this, the four patients who failed to improve were given flooding or implosive therapy (generally around situations involving the expression of anger). With this latter extinction approach these patients also improved. Analysis of the patient pretreatment data revealed that the subgroup of patients who responded to yoga meditation had been experiencing symptoms for a shorter period of time (14.2 vs 44.2 months) and experienced more cognitive symptoms (apprehension, worry, etc.). The patients who required flooding therapy were symptomatic for a longer period of time and had fewer cognitive symptoms. Although no control groups were used these therapeutic tactics appear beneficial and should be subject to more controlled research.

Another technique suggested by Serber, Goldstein, Piaget, and Kort (1969) consisted of teaching the patient normal expression of emotion. These authors recommended first teaching the patient the nonverbal components of affective behavior and then having the patient add verbalization while imagining scenes relevant to the problems. Three case reports presented suggest that this tactic produces considerable anxiety reduction in selected cases.

On the other hand, Kass, Rogers, and Feldman (1973) argued for the use of antianxiety responses already available to the patient. For example, in one case presented by these authors the patient imagined engaging in sitting-up exercises. In all cases reported, relief of monosituational anxiety was reported using this tactic in place of deep-muscle relaxation. Kass et al. reported that the technique is faster since the training period necessary for deep-muscle techniques is eliminated.

Rubin (1972) developed a strategy for using verbally suggested anxiety inhibitors. Rubin recommended that the patient be hypnotized and then given suggestions to attend to responses incompatible with the anxiety response in a given situation. For example, a patient fearful of showers may receive a suggestion to liken the feeling of the shower to raindrops (which the patient enjoyed). Rubin reported good results at the case study level using this procedure. His case reports also indicated that he has been successful with patients suffering from more complex neurotic conditions than monosituational phobias. It should be emphasized, as pointed out by Rubin, that embedded in the procedure, is an implosion or flooding procedure (Stampfl & Levis, 1967). The extent to which extinction contributes to the technique's apparent success is as of yet unresolved. Finally, Gershman and Stedman (1971) presented two case studies in which oriental defense exercises (Kung Fu or Karate) were used as inhibitors of the anxiety response. Both were found to be effective for this purpose. In both cases the exercises were used *in vivo*.

In summary, although some of the approaches described emanated directly from theory and others represented clever and plausible treatment suggestions, the lack of systematically controlled outcome research with anxiety neurotic patients prevents us from making any concise empirical statements. Unless such work is forthcoming, treatment recommendations for dealing with pervasive anxiety will be as elusive as is the current problem of identifying the stimulus situations eliciting this reaction.

PERVASIVE ANXIETY: A REFORMULATION OF THEORY AND TREATMENT

As noted in the previous review of the literature, the major barrier in developing viable conceptual and treatment models of anxiety neurosis resides in the apparent difficulty in isolating specific stimulus patterns responsible for eliciting the anxiety state. It is precisely this lack of stimulus specificity that separates this reaction from other nosologies.

Wolpe (1958) argued that pervasive anxiety is a result of conditioning sequences similar to that postulated for other nosologies where a well-defined stimulus configuration functions as the elicitor of the anxiety response. On this point, we are in full agreement. Wolpe further postulated that the learning of pervasive anxiety differs from other neurotic conditioning sequences in that the original conditioning pairing was more intense, and conditioning failed to occur to a clearly defined stimulus complex at the time of acquisition. Although such reasoning seems plausible, we do not feel the conditioning literature of the laboratory supports such a contention. Intense UCS presentation should result in better long-term storage of the conditioning sequence and better discriminability. If as Wolpe suggested the CSs do involve less salient environmental cues such as light, amorphous noise, and the passage of time, then should not exposure to such cues result in fast extinction of the emotional response once the UCS is eliminated? Humans are constantly exposed throughout life to such cues in the absence of any danger. Because of extended CS exposure to such stimuli a learning approach would expect a rapid extinction effect of any previously conditioned emotional response. As has been argued elsewhere (Levis & Hare, 1977; Stampfl & Levis, 1967), psychopathology tends to maintain itself over time precisely because the patient is able to prevent exposure and subsequent extinction to a large part of the original CS complex.

Costello's (1971) theory of pervasive anxiety appears even less tenable to us. His basic premise that ordinary environmental stimuli function as UCSs for the anxiety neurotics because of constitutional differences in autonomic activity not only seems premature on data grounds but also relegates the model to one that is difficult to test. Although constitutional differences may well enhance ease of conditionability, we know of no infrahuman or human laboratory data which suggest that genetics can transform ordinary environmental stimuli into pain-producing UCSs.

An attempt will now be made to provide yet a different theoretical perspective. The theory of pervasive anxiety to be proposed is derived from a more general model of psychopathology and treatment approach developed by Stampfl (Levis, 1980, a; Levis & Hare, 1977; Stampfl & Levis, 1967, 1969, 1973). The model involves an extension to human psychopathology of Mowrer's two-factor theory of avoidance learning (Mowrer, 1947, 1960) and Solomon and Wynne's (1954) conservation of anxiety hypothesis.

In most cases maladaptive behavior is viewed as a learned response which reflects an end product of antecedent, aversive conditioning events. Symptoms are viewed as avoidance behavior, designed to escape conditioned stimuli capable of eliciting a secondary aversive source of drive, such as fear. Such avoidance behavior not only prevents escape from aversive CSs but also permits the avoidance of other emotionally conditioned stimuli which are also part of the original CS chain. It should be noted that symptomatic behavior may involve other drive states in addition to fear (e.g., sex, anger, pleasure) and more complex learning paradigms then simple avoidance learning (e.g., approach-avoidance conflict paradigms, see Levis & Hare, 1977).

A critical ingredient of the theory is that conditioning of the emotional state occurs to a complex set of stimuli involving both external and internal stimulation. Furthermore, many of these conditioned multiple-stimulus patterns are believed to be stored in long-term memory and arranged in a serial sequence in terms of their emotional loading and accessibility (recovery). Many of these internal stored cues (thoughts, images, memories) are believed to be representations of early conditioning sequences. Therefore, the model clearly suggests it is misleading to assume that a given discrete stimulus is the only cue responsible for eliciting symptomatic behavior.

The task of therapy is viewed conceptually as blocking or circumventing the avoidance behavior to permit more full exposure to the CS complex in order to allow extinction of the emotional responses to these cues. Since acquisition occurred historically, the UCS is no longer present. Repetition of the total CS complex will therefore result in the unlearning of the conditioned reaction. Once the drive value of the CS is extinguished, the symptom (the avoidance behavior) will also extinguish (Mowrer, 1947).

Returning to the issue of pervasive anxiety, the assumption is made that specific CS patterns are indeed responsible for eliciting the anxiety reaction, and that they remain undetected because of the patient's avoidance behavior. The anxiety neurotic's inability to pinpoint a concrete fear-stimulus situation is designed to protect the individual from being fully exposed to these aversive cues. Clinically, such patients are not only unable to verbalize a pattern to their anxiety reaction but also frequently report the absence of any early childhood memories. In a sense they have built a psychological protective wall around themselves to prevent decoding of the avoided CS patterns. Thus by focusing on their chronic anxiety state, the critical cues are effectively masked. In other words, the anxiety reaction itself or more precisely the *consistent focusing on the anxiety state can be conceptualized as the symptom or defensive reaction protecting the individual from the impact of the remaining CS elements.*

Much in the same way the obsessive individual relies upon repetitive counting to block "dangerous" thoughts about sex or aggression, the anxiety neurotic is believed to ward off fear cues by being concerned with the anxiety reaction itself. Conceptualizing an emotional response as a defense may appear at first to be an unusual strategy, but when analyzing the cases of individuals who routinely engaged in angry, hostile behaviors this concept has some clinical support. Clinical inference suggests that such behaviors frequently are repeated in order to prevent exposure to cues associated with feelings of closeness, pleasure, and love (see Levis, 1980, b). Therefore, the argument is advanced that the anxiety-neurotic anxiety reaction is elicited by partial exposure to previously conditioned external or internal CS patterns. Once the emotional reaction is elicited the anxiety neurotic attempts to avoid or escape exposure to the aversive CS patterns by focusing on the consequences of the anxiety reaction itself. Once elicited, the individual has a convenient excuse for behaviorally removing himself/herself from the eliciting situational cues. Furthermore, the sensory consequences of autonomic and central nervous system reactivity may function itself as a cue for repeated anxiety arousal (Stampfl & Levis, 1967). For example, an anxiety neurotic client treated by the second author was able to generate a full-blown anxiety attack through heightening autonomic and central nervous system reactivity by engaging in physical exertion (e.g., running up a flight of stairs).

A learning analysis would also suggest that the continual focusing on the anxiety reaction itself should produce an extinction reaction resulting in further exposure to the avoided CS patterns. This latter CS exposure, in turn, should reestablish the anxiety reaction and if continually experienced, it would again lead to greater extinction of the CS pattern. Such a cycle should repeat itself until complete extinction is finally achieved. From such an analysis one would expect more spontaneous remission with this nosology when compared to more intact avoidance behavior reflected in phobic and obsessive-compulsive nosologies.

If the above theoretical model is deemed to have merit then the task of deriving treatment implications may prove worthwhile. *The first implication of the model is for the therapist to assume that specific external and internal cue patterns are eliciting the anxiety reaction.* This assumption has proven useful clinically for the authors. In each pervasive anxiety case we have treated, a well-defined set of anxiety-eliciting CSs have been detected. First of all, observation suggests that despite the patient's verbal report, no evidence exists that the individual is under a continued chronic state of anxiety. Many periods throughout a given day are relatively free of anxiety responding. Second, a careful observational analysis tends to reveal a pattern of responding that appears to be triggered by certain situational cues. For example, a female patient treated by the first author complained of almost constant anxiety, tension, and fears of death from heart failure. Further analysis revealed that the anxiety reaction was used as a convenient excuse to avoid driving a car and leaving home. Furthermore, considerable secondary gain was achieved through her symptom in that it kept her younger son at home most of the time. Additional analysis revealed that the patient manifested considerable ambivalent feelings (love-hate reactions) toward her children and toward her role as a mother and housewife. The anxiety attacks appeared to help her avoid confronting these specific fears.

A case treated by the second author provided another example. Analysis revealed that anxiety reactions reported focused around situations where the patient was exposed to people such as in a classroom setting, restaurant, and store. With each anxiety attack the individual frequently would avoid the stimulus situation in question and return home. The patient initially reported being unaware that the anxiety reactions were stimulus-bound. Later in treatment it appeared that the cues being avoided elicited feelings of rejection, loss of control, expression of anger, and fear of sexual contact with individuals other than her husband.

A second treatment implication from the model is that once the situational cues are isolated, exposure to them should produce an initial increase in anxiety level and a subsequent extinction effect via the principle of nonreinforced CS exposure. At a clinical level of analysis the authors have found considerable success in treating pervasive anxiety by using the technique of implosive therapy (Stampfl & Levis, 1967).

Implosive therapy is an extinction technique designed to confront the patient via imagery or *in vivo* presentation with those cues hypothesized to be responsible for eliciting anxiety and subsequent avoidance behavior. Unlike other nosologies, a basic underlying cue area is not readily identifiable for the anxiety neurotic. The most common themes uncovered in our clinical work are how this area relates to fears of failure and rejection, loss of control, expression of anger, and fear of sexual involvement. In many ways, pervasive anxiety produces avoidance of situational cue areas frequently noted with agoraphobia. That is to say, anxiety neurotics frequently avoid exposing themselves to new situations involving contact with people.

Conformation for determining the merit of the hypothesized cues can be obtained by exposing the patient to scenes depicting the suspected avoided cues. If anxiety markedly increases or if increased defense patterns are noted, support for repeated exposure to these cue areas is obtained. Frequently, such exposure will elicit a recovery of memory relating to additional feared events. This new material then can be included in other scenes until eventual extinction is achieved.

In order to generate reasonable hypotheses about what cues are being avoided, we recommend that a careful history be taken before treatment begins. Furthermore, it has proven clinically useful to solicit the aid of the patient to rate on a 10-point scale their anxiety reaction to various stimulus situations which they daily confront. By training them to keep a careful diary of when they experience substantial anxiety, decoding of the eliciting cues becomes much easier.

It would follow from the above that the more clearly a subject perceives the anxiety-eliciting stimuli when followed by nonreinforcement, the more rapid the extinction of the emotional response will be (see Lowenfeld, Rubenfeld, & Guthrie, 1956; Wall & Guthrie, 1959). However, it has been the authors clinical experience that when dealing with problems of pervasive anxiety, patients frequently display difficulties in autonomic perception (see Borkovec, 1976). Simply stated, these individuals are unable to appropriately label internal states. Thus their referent to the anxiety reaction appears to have little to do with experiencing the actual sensory consequences of their physiological arousal. If such is the case, additional protection against quick extinction of the anxiety reaction is maintained.

Thus the final implications of the model to be discussed center on the possibility that the individual's perception of the anxiety response may be a form of avoidance behavior and the anxiety reaction itself may also function as a CS. If such is the case, then focusing upon the sensory consequences of the patient's anxiety response should enhance the extinction of this response. Imaginal scenes can be introduced in which the patient is asked to visualize his heart pounding, feel an increase in muscular tension, and/or see perspiration flowing out of his body. It also appears clinically useful to instruct the patient to try to increase his anxiety reaction when actually experiencing an attack. Those subjects who have tried this approach frequently reported that it produced a paradoxical effect in that it stopped the anxiety reaction rather than enhanced it. If relaxation training proves successful in reducing pervasive anxiety, it may well be effective because the training phase of this procedure requires considerable focusing on tensing various muscle groups that frequently are affected by the anxiety response.

It should be noted that the merits of the above theory have yet to be demonstrated through controlled research. However, the proposed model does generate a number of differential predictions that can be contrasted with those produced from Wolpe and Costello's positions. Those readers interested in a detailed description of the clinical administration of implosive therapy are referred to Levis (1980, b), and those interested in a recent summary of the available clinical treatment studies (see Levis and Hare, 1977).

OVERVIEW

Prior to undertaking the task of preparing this chapter, it was the author's hope that a careful review of the literature would uncover sufficient data for us to make specific treatment recommendations. It is clear from the review provided that insufficient evidence exists to even draw tentative conclusions. The various theoretical models offered to account for the development of pervasive anxiety are also in need of more substantial empirical validation. The current state of affairs permits only suggestive and speculative inferences.

It is our contention that an identifiable stimulus situation can be isolated to account for the elicitation of the anxiety response. Clearly, more empirical work is needed on this topic. Isolation of such cues would then permit the use of a number of techniques like systematic desensitization and implosive therapy. It is also possible that individuals suffering from this disorder show anomalies of autonomic functioning (Lader & Wing, 1966). If this latter point is substantiated, the etiology may be biochemical, genetic, or learned avoidance. Whatever the cause, the anxiety response itself may function as a cue for both conditioning new stimuli and for eliciting and increasing the level of arousal. Relaxation training or direct focusing on the concomitance of the anxiety response may prove beneficial.

The behavior approaches to treatment of this disorder have involved the use of a single procedure or packaged treatment approaches. Detailed clinical usage of each strategy can be obtained by referring to the appropriately provided references.

Hopefully, this chapter will result in providing a renewed interest in this important clinical problem both at a theoretical and treatment level of analysis.

REFERENCES

Acosta, F. X., Yamamoto, J., & Wilcox, S. A. Application of electromyographic biofeedback to the relaxation training of schizophrenic neurotic, and tension headache patients. *Journal of Consulting and Clinical Psychology*, 1978, **46**, 383–384.

Allgulander, C. Dependence on sedative and hypnotic drugs. *ACTA Psychiatrica Scandinavica Supplementum*, 1978, 270.

Barchas, J. D., Berger, P. A., Ciaranello, R. D., & Elliott, G. R. (Eds.), *Psychopharmacology from theory to practice*. New York: Oxford University Press, 1977.

Beiman, I., Israel, E., & Johnson, S. A. Error during training and posttraining effects of live and taped extended progressive relaxation, self-relaxation, and electromyogram biofeedback. *Journal of Consulting and Clinical Psychology*, 1978, **46**, 314–321.

Berger, F. M. The pharmacological properties of 2-methyl-2-*n*-propyl-1, 3-propanediol dicarbomate (Miltown), a new interneuronal blocking agent. *Journal of Pharmacology and Experimental Therapeutics*, 1954, **112**, 413–423.

Blanchard, E. B. & Epstein, L. H. The clinical usefulness of biofeedback. In M. Hersen, R. M. Eisler, & P. M. Miller (Eds.), *Progress in behavior modification volume 4*. New York: Academic Press, 1977.

Borkovec, T. D. Physiological and cognitive processes in the regulation of anxiety. In G. E. Schwartz & D. Shapiro (Eds.), *Consciousness and self-regulation*. New York: Plenum, 1976.

Boston Collaborative Drug Surveillance Program: Clinical depression of the central nervous system due to diazepamand chlordiazepoxide in relation to cigarette smoking and age. *New England Journal of Medicine*, 1973, **288**, 277–280.

Cautela, J. R. The application of learning theory "as a last resort" in the treatment of a case of anxiety neurosis. *Journal of Clinical Psychology*, 1965, **21**, 448–452.

Cautela, J. R. A behavior therapy approach to pervasive anxiety. *Behaviour Research and Therapy*, 1966, **4**, 99–109.

Cohen, M. E., Bahal, D. W., Kilpatrick, A., Reed, E. W., & White, P. D. The high familial prevalence of neurocirculatory asthenia (anxiety neurosis, effort syndrome). *American Journal of Human Genetics*, 1951, **3**, 126–158.

Connor, W. H. Effects of brief relaxation training on autonomic response to anxiety-evoking stimuli. *Psychophysiology*, 1974, **11**, 591–599.

Costello, C. G. Lysergic acid diethylamide (LSD-25) and behavior therapy. *Behaviour Research and Therapy*, 1964, **2**, 117–130.

Costello, C. G. Anxiety and the persisting novelty of input from the autonomic nervous system. *Behavior Therapy*, 1971, **2**, 321–333.

Da Costa, J. M. On irritable heart; a clinical form of functional cardiac disorder and its consequences. *American Journal of Medical Science*, 1871, **61**, 17–52.

Dawley, H. H. Self-administered relaxation in the reduction of anxiety. *Newsletter for Research in Mental Health and Behavioral Sciences*, 1973, **15**, 17–19.

DiMascio, A., Shader, R. I., & Giller, D. R. Emotional states. In R. I. Shader, A. DiMascio & associates. Baltimore: Williams & Wilkins, 1970.

Epstein, L. H. Psychophysiological measurement in assessment. In M. Hersen & A. S. Bellack (Eds.), *Behavioral assessment: A practical handbook*. New York: Pergamon, 1976.

Fenichel, O. *The psychoanalytic theory of neurosis*. New York: Norton, 1945.

Fox, K. A., & Snyder, R. L. Effects of sustained low doses of diazepam on aggression and mortality in grouped male mice. *Journal of Comparative and Physiological Psychology*, 1969, **69**, 663–666.

Freud, S. The justification for detaching from neurasthenia a particular syndrome: The anxiety-neurosis. In J. Riviere (Ed.), *Collected papers, volume 1*. New York: The International Psycho-Analytical Press, 1924.

Freud, S. *The ego and the id*. London: Hogarth Press, 1927.

Freud, S. *The problem of anxiety*. New York: Norton, 1936.

Gelder, M. Behavior therapy for anxiety states. *British Medical Journal*, 1969, **1**, 691–694.

Gershman, L., & Stedman, J. M. Oriental defense exercises as reciprocal inhibitors of anxiety. *Journal of Behavior Therapy and Experimental Psychiatry*, 1971, **2**, 117–119.

Girodo, M. Yoga meditation and flooding in the treatment of anxiety neurosis. *Journal of Behavior Therapy and Experimental Psychiatry*, 1974, **5**, 157–160.

Goldfried, M. R. Systematic desensitization as training in self-control. *Journal of Consulting and Clinical Psychology*, 1971, **37**, 228–234.

Goldfried, M. R., & Trier, C. S. Effectiveness of relaxation as an active coping skill. *Journal of Abnormal Psychology*, 1974, **83**, 348–355.

Goodman, L. S., & Gilman, A. *The Pharmacological Basis of Therapeutics* (4th edition). New York: Macmillan, 1970.

Gottschalk, L. A., Bates, D. E., Fox, R. A., & James, J. M. Psychoactive drug use. Patterns found in samples from a mental health clinic and a general medical clinic. *Archives of General Psychiatry*, 1971, **25**, 395–397.

Greenblatt, D. J., & Shader, R. I. *Benzodiazepines in clinical practice*. New York: Raven Press, 1974.

Hollister, L. E. *Clinical use of psychotherapeutic drugs*. Springfield, Ill.: Charles C. Thomas, 1973.

Hollister, L. E. Valium: A discussion of current issues. *Psychosomatics*, 1977, **18**, 1–15.

Hollister, L. E., Motzenbecker, F. P., & Degan, R. O. Withdrawal reactions from chlordiazepoxide (Librium). *Psychopharmacologia*, 1961, **2**, 63–68.

Jacobson, E. *Progressive relaxation*. Chicago: The University of Chicago Press, 1938.

Johnson, D. T., & Spielberger, C. D. The effects of relaxation training and passage of time on measures of state- and trait-anxiety. *Journal of Clinical Psychology*, 1968, **24**, 20–23.

Jones, E. The relation between anxiety neurosis and anxiety hysteria. *Papers on psychoanalysis*. New York: Wood and Co., 1913.

Jones, M., & Mellersh, V. Comparison of exercise response in anxiety states and normal controls. *Psychosomatic Medicine*, 1946, **8**, 180–187.

Jwahara, S., Oishi, H., Yamazaki, S., & Sakai, K. Effects of chlordiazepoxide upon spontaneous alternation and the hippocampal electrical activity in white rats. *Psychopharmacologia*, 1972, **24**, 496–507.

Kass, D. J., Rogers, H. E., & Feldman, S. E. Deconditioning anxiety by individualized inhibitors. *Journal of Behavior Therapy and Experimental Psychiatry,* 1973, **4**, 361–363.

Kolb, L. C. *Noyes' modern clinical psychiatry* (7th edition). Philadelphia: W. B. Saunders Company, 1968.

Lader, M. H., & Mathews, A. M. A physiological model of phobic anxiety and desensitization. *Behaviour Research and Therapy,* 1968, **6**, 411–421.

Lader, M. H., & Wing, L. Physiological measures, sedative drugs, and morbid anxiety. *Maudsley Monographs,* London: Oxford, 1966.

Lazarus, A. A. The results of behavior therapy in 126 cases of severe neurosis. *Behaviour Research and Therapy,* 1963, **1**, 69–79.

Levis, D. J. The infrahuman avoidance model of symptom maintenance and implosive therapy. In J. D. Keehn (Ed.), *Psychopathology in animals.* New York: Academic Press, 1980. (a)

Levis, D. J. Implementing the technique of implosive therapy. In E. B. Foa & A. Goldstein (Eds.), *Handbook of behavioral interventions.* New York: Wiley, 1980. (b)

Levis, D. J., & Hare, N. A review of the theoretical rational and empirical support for the extinction approach of implosive (flooding) therapy. In M. Hersen, R. M. Eisler, & P. M. Miller (Eds.), *Progress in behavior modification, volume 4.* New York: Academic Press, 1977.

Lowenfeld, J., Rubenfeld, S., & Guthrie, G. M. Verbal inhibition in subception. *Journal of General Psychology,* 1956, **54**, 171–176.

Mathews, A. M., & Gelder, M. G. Psycho-physiological investigations of brief relaxation training. *Journal of Psychosomatic Research,* 1969, **13**, 1–12.

Meichenbaum, D., & Turk, D. The cognitive-behavioral management of anxiety, anger, and pain. In P. O. Davidson (Ed.), *The behavioral management of anxiety, depression and pain.* New York: Brunner/Mazel, 1976.

Mellinger, G. D., Balter, M. B., & Manheimer, D. I. Patterns of psychotherapeutic drug use among adults in San Francisco. *Archives of General Psychiatry,* 1971, **25**, 385–394.

Miles, H. H. W., Barrabee, E. L., & Finesinger, J. E. Evaluation of psychotherapy with follow-up study of 62 cases of anxiety neurosis. *Psychosomatic Medicine,* 1951, **13**, 83–105.

Miller, R. R. Drug surveillance utilizing epidemiologic methods: A report from the Boston Collaborative Drug Surveillance Program. *American Journal of Hospital Pharmacy,* 1973, **30**, 584–592.

Morillo, A., Revzin, A. M., & Knauss, T. Physiological mechanisms of action of chlordiazepoxide in cats. *Psychopharmacologia,* 1962, **3**, 386–394.

Mowrer, O. H. On the dual nature of learning—A reinterpretation of "conditioning" and "problem-solving." *Harvard Educational Review,* 1947, **17**, 102–148.

Mowrer, O. H. *Learning theory and behavior.* New York: Wiley, 1960.

Osgood, C. E. Behaviour theory and the social sciences. *Behavioural Science,* 1956, **1**, 167–185.

Paul, G. L. Physiological effects of relaxation training and hypnotic suggestion. *Journal of Abnormal Psychology,* 1969, **74**, 425–427.

Percell, L. P., Berwick, P. T., & Beigel, A. The effects of assertive training on self-concept and anxiety. *Archives of General Psychiatry,* 1974, **31**, 502–504.

Pitts, F. N. The biochemistry of anxiety. *Scientific American,* 1969, **220**, 69–75.

Pitts, F. N. Biochemical factors in anxiety neurosis. *Behavior Science,* 1971, **16**, 82–91.

Pitts, F. N., & McClure, J. Lactate metabolism in anxiety neurosis. *New England Journal of Medicine,* 1967, **277**, 1329–1336.

Raskin, M., Johnson, G., & Rondestvedt, J. W. Chronic anxiety treated by feedback-induced muscle relaxation. *Archives of General Psychiatry,* 1973, **28**, 263–267.

Reinking, R. H., & Kohl, M. L. Effects of various forms of relaxation training on physiological and self-report measures of relaxation. *Journal of Consulting and Clinical Psychology,* 1975, **43**, 595–600.

Rickels, K. *Non-specific factors in drug therapy.* Springfield, Ill.: Charles C. Thomas, 1968.

Rubin, M. Verbally suggested responses for reciprocal inhibition of anxiety. *Journal of Behavior Therapy and Experimental Psychiatry,* 1972, **3**, 273–277.

Schallek, W., & Thomas, J. Effects of benzodiazepines on spontaneous electrical activity of subcortical areas in brain of cat. *Archives of International Pharmacodynamics,* 1971, **192**, 321–337.

Serber, M., Goldstein, P. G., Piaget, G., & Kort, F. The use of implosive-expressive therapy in anxiety reactions. In R. D. Rubin & C. M. Franks (Eds.), *Advances in behavior therapy.* New York: Academic Press, 1969.

Shader, R. I., & Greenblatt, D. J. The psychopharmacologic treatment of anxiety states. In R. I. Shader, (Ed.), *Manual of psychiatric therapeutics.* Boston: Little, Brown, 1975.

Slaby, A. E., Lieb, J., & Tancredi, L. R. *Handbook of psychiatric emergencies.* Flushing, N.Y.: Medical Examination Publishing Company, 1975.

Slater, S. L., & Leavy, A. The effects of inhaling a 35 per cent CO_2-65 per cent O_2 mixture upon anxiety level in neurotic patients. *Behaviour Research and Therapy,* 1966, **4**, 309–316.

Smith, D. E., & Wesson, D. R. A new method for treatment of barbiturate dependence. *Journal of the American Medical Association,* 1970, **213**, 294–295.

Solomon, R. L., & Wynne, L. C. Traumatic avoidance learning: The principle of anxiety conservation and partial irreversibility. *Psychological Review,* 1954, **61**, 353–385.

Stampfl, T. G., & Levis, D. J. Essentials of implosive therapy: A learning-theory-based psychodynamic behavioral therapy. *Journal of Abnormal Psychology,* 1967, **72**, 496–503.

Stampfl, T. G., & Levis, D. J. Learning theory: An aid to dynamic therapeutic practice. In L. D. Eron & R. Callahan (Eds.), *Relationship of theory to practice in psychotherapy.* Chicago: Aldine, 1969.

Stampfl, T. G., & Levis, D. J. *Implosive therapy: Theory and technique.* Morristown, N.J.: General Learning Press, 1973.

Steiner, F. A., & Hummel, P. Effects of nitrazepam and phenobarbital on hippocampal and lateral geniculate neurons in the cat. *International Journal of Neuropharmacology,* 1968, **7**, 61–69.

Stille. Unpublished paper, 1863. Cited in Da Costa, J. M. On irritable heart, a clinical form of functional cardiac disorder and its consequences. *American Journal of Medical Science,* 1871, **61**, 17–52.

Stoudenmire, J. Effects of muscle relaxation training on state- and trait anxiety in introverts and extroverts. *Journal of Personality and Social Psychology,* 1972, **24**, 273–275.

Suinn, R. M., & Richardson, F. Anxiety management training: A nonspecific behavior therapy program for anxiety control. *Behavior Therapy,* 1971, **2,** 498–510.

Svenson, S. E., & Hamilton, R. G. A critique of overemphasis on side effects with the psychotropic drugs: An analysis of 18,000 chlordiazepoxide-treated cases. *Current Therapy Research,* 1966, **8,** 455–464.

Swanson, D. W., Weddige, R. L., & Morse, R. M. Abuse of prescription drugs. *Mayo Clinic Proceedings,* 1973, **48,** 359–367.

Teichner, W. H. Interaction of behavioral and physiological stress reactions. *Psychological Review,* 1968, **75,** 271–291.

Tinklenberg, J. R. Antianxiety medications and the treatment of anxiety. In J. D. Barchas, P. A. Berger, R. D. Ciaranello, & G. R. Elliott (Eds.), *Psychopharmacology from theory to practice.* New York: Oxford University Press, 1977.

Townsend, R. E., House, J. F., & Addario, D. A comparison of biofeedback-mediated relaxation and group therapy in the treatment of chronic anxiety. *The American Journal of Psychiatry,* 1975, **132,** 598–601.

Wall, H. N., & Guthrie, G. M. Extinction of responses to subceived stimuli. *Journal of General Psychology,* 1959, **60,** 205–210.

Wolpe, J. *Psychotherapy by reciprocal inhibition.* Stanford: Stanford University Press, 1958.

Wolpe, J. *The practice of behavior therapy.* New York: Pergamon, 1969.

Wolpe, J. *The practice of behavior therapy.* New York: Pergamon Press, 1973.

Zemore, R. Systematic desensitization as a method of teaching a general anxiety-reducing skill. *Journal of Consulting and Clinical Psychology,* 1975, **43,** 157–161.

CHAPTER 4

Obsessive-Compulsive Disorders

Ellie T. Sturgis and Victor Meyer

The term obsessive-compulsive has been applied to a variety of cognitive and motor behavior problems encountered in psychiatric practice. Although many definitions of the disorder have been proposed in the literature, certain features appear to be constant across descriptions. The Diagnostic and Statistical Manual of mental disorders (DSM-III, 1980) description of the disorder is:

> The essential features are recurrent obsessions or compulsions. Obsessions are recurrent, persistent ideas, thoughts, images, or impulses that are egodystonic, that is, they are not experienced as voluntarily produced, but rather as thoughts that invade consciousness and are experienced as senseless or repugnant. Attempts are made to ignore or suppress them. Compulsions are repetitive and seemingly purposeful behaviors that are performed according to certain rules or in a stereotyped fashion. The behavior is not an end in itself, but is designed to produce or to prevent some future event or situation. However, the activity is not connected in a realistic way with what it is designed to produce or prevent, or may be clearly excessive. The act is performed with a sense of subjective compulsion coupled with a desire to resist the compulsion (at least initially). The individual generally recognizes the senselessness of the behavior (this may not be true for young children) and does not derive pleasure from carrying out the activity, although it provides a release of tension (DSM-III, 1980, p. 234).

This definition of obsessive-compulsive behavior brings up several important points for discussion. First, either obsessions or compulsions alone or combined may be regarded as pathological entities; thus the problem behaviors may be cognitive, motor, or combined responses. Second, both obsessions and compulsions typically are recognized by the individual as being nonsensical or not fitting with his/her views of reality. Third, the difficulties are not under voluntary control but have an intrusive quality to them, often becoming evident on some occasions and absent on others. Fourth, efforts are made by the individual to resist engaging in the maladaptive responses.

The discrimination of obsessive-compulsive from schizophrenic, retardation, and organic disorders can become muddled when the patterns are severe, but generally several factors are useful in making a differential diagnosis. The obsessive-compulsive patient is usually in contact with reality except in the area of the obsession or compulsion, labels the aberrant cognitive and/or motor pattern as nonsensical and unwanted, tries to resist engaging in the maladaptive response, and experiences marked anxiety when prevented from obsessing or ritualizing.

Schizophrenia, while also a disorder of cognitive, motor, and emotional response systems, is characterized by more pervasive dissociation from reality and an apparent belief in and comfort with the emitted maladaptive response. In addition, the role of anxiety is more ambiguous. Overall intelligence levels of obsessionals are usually average or above, a useful factor in differentiating the disorder from retardation. Retardates and organics lack the feelings of resistance to the stereotypic behaviors that are commonly experienced by obsessionals and compulsives (DSM-III, 1980).

The psychological literature has grouped diverse behaviors into the category of obsessive-compulsive disorder. For the purpose of this discussion, the phenomena are divided into two response modes, cognitive and motor behaviors. Under the rubric cognitive behaviors, we discuss obsessional thoughts, ruminations, and cognitive rituals. The section on motor behaviors includes compulsive rituals and behavioral avoidances.

Cognitive Behavior Patterns

Obsessions have already been defined as recurrent, persistent ideas, thoughts, images, or impulses that come to the person's awareness. The most common examples of obsessional thoughts include senseless, repetitive thoughts of contamination, dread, guilt, or urges to kill, attack, injure, confess, or steal (Metzner, 1963). Ruminations are defined as intrusive, forced preoccupations with thoughts about a particular topic or problem (Nemiah, 1975). Ruminations are characterized by prolonged spells of brooding, doubting, and speculation without ever reaching definite conclusions. Often the individual is unable to terminate his preoccupation, even when he realizes the problem is insoluble. We define a cognitive ritual as an elaborate series of mental actions that the individual feels compelled to complete. The distinguishing feature of the cognitive ritual is that it can be described and consists of a number of discrete steps that must be completed in a specified manner if they are to be effective. An example of this behavior is the silent recitation of a particular prayer, series of statements, or series of numbers. Cognitive rituals differ from obsessions and ruminations for they have a pattern and a point of termination if performed appropriately.

Motor Behavior Patterns

The behavioral manifestations of the disorder include compulsive rituals and avoidances. Rituals are elaborate, often very time-consuming behavior chains. Ritualistic activities frequently are associated with everyday tasks such as eating, toileting, grooming, dressing, and performing sexual activities. The most common forms of compulsions are handwashing, counting, checking, and touching (DSM-III, 1980). Behavioral avoidance responses are substitute actions that an individual performs rather than performing a more appropriate response. Performance of the maladaptive avoidance response is seen as less anxiety provoking or more comfortable than performance of the more adaptive response. The difficulty with the use of avoidance is that the resultant actions are less effective for the individual than the avoided responses would be.

EPIDEMIOLOGY

It is a rare individual who has not at some period of his/her life experienced some form of obsessional thinking or exhibited some compulsive form of behavior. However, the individual who exhibits pathological obsessional or ritualistic difficulties may be handicapped to the extent he/she can no longer function in everyday life. The frequency of the disorder is unknown, but it is thought to occur in about 0.05% of the total population or 5% of the total neurotic population (Black, 1974). The onset of the disorder usually occurs in preadolescence but can occur at any age.

Early descriptions based upon clinical observations indicate there are more female obsessionals than males (Nemiah, 1975). This conclusion, however, may be an artifact of sampling procedures. More recent examinations indicate that the larger the group sampled, the more closely the sex ratio approaches unity. Black (1974) reports a tabulation of 11 studies involving 1336 individuals. Results indicated 49% of the patients treated were male and 51% female. Such findings tend to confirm the view that based on the available evidence, there is no reason to suppose females are more predisposed to obsessional disorders than are males (DSM-III, 1980).

It has also been commonly assumed that obsessional states occur more frequently in middle- to upper-class patients (Nemiah, 1975). The results are again equivocal. Black (1974) summarized six studies and showed that two studies did not support the socioeconomic hypothesis while four did. At present, because of the lack of data describing sampling and control procedures, the interpretation of these findings should be made with caution.

Intelligence is another area of interest for individuals who study obsessional states. A number of individuals have considered obsessionals to be more intelligent than other patient populations (Nemiah, 1975). Black (1974) again summarized two psychometric studies which found that obsessional neurotics performed better on various tests of intelligence than did anxiety neurotics and hysterics. The latter two groups did not differ from one another. Aside from these two studies, most conclusions regarding intelligence come from clinical impression. Thus, one should accept with caution the tentative suggestion that obsessionals differ from normal and neurotic controls in intellectual functioning.

ETIOLOGY

Explanations of obsessive-compulsive disorders fall into three major categories. These categories include biological models, psychodynamic models, and learning experimental models of behavior. In the following section, each of these models is discussed.

Biological Models

Efforts to discover a biological basis for obsessive-compulsive disorders have been disappointing. The research has shown some similarities with behaviors associated with encephalitis, basal ganglia disease, and temporal lobe lesions; however, the vast majority of obsessive-compulsive individuals have demonstrated no evidence of neural pathology (Nemiah, 1975). The results of genetic studies have also been meager. Despite extensive and painstaking work involving the collection of twin data, only three cases of twins have been reported in which monozygosity and the diagnosis of obsessive-compulsive disorder have both been reliably determined (Black, 1974).

The relationship of depression to obsessive-compulsive disorders has been investigated since the 1940s. Black (1974) reports three familial studies which suggest a moderate link between the two disorders. Rosenberg (1968) compared the frequency of depression in obsessional and anxiety neuroses. He found 34% of the obsessionals and 25.7% of the anxiety neurotics required treatment for moderately severe depressive illness. Although more obsessionals became depressed, the difference between the two groups of neurotics was not significant. Gittleson (1966) reported 31.2% of the subjects studied showed obsessional symptoms during periods of depression. In 51% of these patients with obsessional symptomatology, the content of the obsessional thoughts was suicidal, homicidal, or both. Among the patients with obsessions, the incidence of a premorbid obsessional personality was twice as great as in individuals without obsessions. Our clinical impression is that obsessions, rituals, and depression may be related, but such a relationship varies among individuals. Depression is a negatively valenced affective state. For individuals who are more likely to obsess or ritualize in times of stress, depressive periods are likely to exacerbate obsessive-compulsive symptoms. Another subset of patients appear to experience depression as a result of increased obsessive or compulsive symptoms. Increased obsessing, ruminating, or ritualizing is effective in reducing life's normally experienced reinforcements; thus depression is a result of or is secondary to the obsessional-compulsive problem. For the first subgroup who experience obsessive-compulsive symptoms secondary to a fundamental depression, therapy designed to alleviate the depression is recommended (i.e., antidepressants, depression management training, personal effectiveness training). In the group experiencing depression secondary to obsessions and/or rituals, treatment designed to change the primary symptoms is recommended. A final group which we have observed does not appear to experience depression, regardless of the obsessive-compulsive problem. Thus depression and obsessive-compulsive symptoms are related for some individuals, although the nature of the relationship is unclear at present. It may be that there is some biological mechanism which predisposes the individual to depressive and/or obsessive-compulsive symptomatology. However, at present, our knowledge is insufficient to propose the nature of the mechanism. Currently, it is believed that psychological formulations of the abnormality are more valuable than are biological theories.

Psychoanalytic Models

Both obsessions and compulsions are similar to the other neurotic symptoms for they are viewed as reflecting the operation of intrapsychic mechanisms. Each neurotic disorder ostensibly protects the individual from recognizing the true source of his/her anxieties, yet it allows the anxiety some measure of release without damaging the self-image or provoking social rebuke. In the case of obsessions and compulsions, tension is controlled, symbolized, and periodically discharged through a series of repetitive actions or cognitions.

Freud viewed obsessions and compulsions as previously repressed thoughts, hostility feelings, and guilt that became reactivated. In order to counteract the feelings, yet to give partial ventilation to the ideas and emotions experienced, the client employs four defense mechanisms—isolation, displacement, reaction formation, and undoing.

Through "undoing" the individual disconnects the association that previously existed between a forbidden thought and its accompanying affect. For example, an individual might have obsessional thoughts of violence without experiencing the parallel emotion. By isolating an affect from its associated thought, the individual avoids confronting the real connection between them. However, isolation may not be completely successful and some residuals of the feelings and thoughts may continue to be experienced as stressful. Displacement may then be necessary.

"Displacement" enables an individual to use a substitute activity or thought as a means of attacking tensions. The substitute activity or cognition camouflages the real discomfort and allows an alternate focus of attention. The individual may become obsessed with some trivial thought and thereby manages to divert himself/herself from true but uncomfortable reflection.

"Reaction formation" furthers the process of self-deception. The individual thinks and behaves in ways that are diametrically opposite to the true, but forbidden, impulses and ideas. When this mechanism is employed, not only are feelings and thoughts disconnected, but the contents of these emotions and cognitions are twisted into exact opposites. Thus, instead of expressing an urge to soil and be messy, a person might become compulsively neat and clean.

"Undoing" parallels reaction formation. Having failed to reverse attitudes and emotions beforehand, the patient finds he/she must gain forgiveness for the transgressions. Through an undoing gesture, the individual attempts to pay penance for forbidden thoughts and often seeks a "magical" way of restoring himself/herself to a state of purity. For example, by compulsive handwashing, the patient endures the discomfort and embarrassment of the ritual and at the same time symbolically cleanses himself/herself for past misdeeds and evil intentions. However, since the true source of tension was not dealt with through the maneuver, the relief is only temporary, and the act must be repeated time and time again.

Although the emphases of the varied psychoanalytic theorists vary, most of them view obsessions and compulsions as means of isolating and controlling conflicts and anxiety concerning painful interpersonal experiences. Many clinicians perceive a symbolic relationship between symptoms and the emotional forces being expressed through them. Some analysts hypothesize the toilet-training period and the accompanying struggles between the mother and child to be critical in the development of obsessional and compulsive symptoms. (See Fenichel, 1945; Millon, 1969; and Sullivan, 1954 for more thorough explanations.)

Behavioral Models

Cognitive Responses

The existence of obsessions, ruminations, and cognitive rituals, being subvocal and private in nature, provides the behavioral clinician with a reminder of the limits to which animal analogues can be applied to human behavior. Rachman (1971) considers obsessions and ruminations to be noxious conditioned stimuli acquired via classical conditioning procedures. Ruminations are aversive endogenous or self-produced stimuli to which the patient does not habituate. Theoretically, the processes of habituation and sensitization interact to produce a response to repeated stimulation (Groves and Thompson, 1970). The magnitude of a response to repetitive stimuli is a function of the frequency and intensity of a stimulus and the excitability of the organism at the time of stimulation. Rachman maintains that ruminations are likely to produce sensitization because of their special significance to the individual. The ruminations have acquired special significance via classical conditioning paradigms. Sensitization is also facilitated by disturbed mood states (anxiety, agitated depression). The sensitizing effects of repeated ruminations and mood disturbances interact, increasing the arousal of the individual and potentiating the tendency to ruminate further. The discomfort produced by the aversive thoughts may increase until the person asks someone else to reassure him or until he makes a physical response to reduce the discomfort. The temporary relief achieved by the motor act or reassurance terminates an aversive state and makes this resolution pattern likely to be repeated the next time a disturbing thought occurs (Rachman, 1976). Cognitive rituals are considered to be similar to motoric rituals except they are performed cognitively rather than motorically. Such rituals are presently thought to develop in ways similar to motor rituals (see following section).

Motor Responses

Compulsive or ritualistic behavior has been produced experimentally in humans and animals for several decades. Currently, there appear to be four models to account for motor responses becoming fixated and compulsive in nature: (*a*) responses with double reinforcement properties; (*b*) punished instrumental avoidance responses; (*c*) previously learned avoidance responses which reemerge during times of stress; and (*d*) schedule-induced or adjunctive behaviors.

DOUBLE REINFORCEMENT THEORY. Responses with double reinforcement properties include responses that are associated with both positive reinforcement training and negative reinforcement training. A positive approach response can become fixated when it also becomes an avoidance or escape response, so that the response that satisfies the approach response (positive reinforcement) also reduces a learned drive or anxiety (negative reinforcement). Farber (1948) showed that a group of rats who were shocked after the choice point in a T-maze while running to a food reward took longer to extinguish the running response than did a control group that ran to the food without the presence of the shock. Herrnstein and Sidman (1958) trained a group of rats to avoid a shock by bar-pressing in response to a clicker cue. When the cue and shock contingencies (negative reinforcement schedule) were later superimposed on a bar-press procedure to obtain food (positive reinforcement schedule), there was an increased response rate to the clicker cue. Control groups not previously trained in avoidance conditioning decreased the response rate under such conditions. A human analogue to behavior stereotypy having positive and negative reinforcement properties has been provided by Metzner (1963) in his discussion of compulsive masturbation. Punished sexual behavior may lead to the development of anxiety attributed to the sexual drive. "Compulsive" masturbation reduces sexual drive, conditions anxiety, and also provides positive feelings. It becomes an escape response that also satisfies sexual urges and is pleasurable.

PUNISHED AVOIDANCE THEORY. An instrumental avoidance response may become fixated by being punished or becoming an unsuccessful avoidance response. Solomon, Kamin, & Wynne (1953) discovered that if shock is delivered after an avoidance response is made, the result consisted of faster, more stereotypic, unsuccessful avoidances. Maier (1949) employed a discrimination situation to assess the punishment paradigm. The animals first learned to respond to soluble discrimination problems. The same animals were then exposed to insoluble problems in which the solutions were presented in a random sequence. If the animal was forced to make a response in the insoluble situation, the majority of the animals developed stereotyped, rigid responses and were unable to switch to new responses even when the problem was later made soluble. A human analogue to this type of situation occurs whenever a person faces a situation over which he/she has no control or in which the reinforcement contingencies are altered. An example of the evolution of such a problem is illustrated in the case of an office worker whose initial job involved the checking of figures entered upon a data sheet. Accuracy was the target behavior that was stressed and which avoided the displeasure of the supervisor and ensured the maintenance of a job. Her position was then changed to a supervisory position in which she was responsible for a number of clerks and she was given more general duties. Because of the increased responsibilities and her determination to do well in the new job, she became increasingly stressed. The previous avoidance to stress involved the checking and rechecking of figures, so the individual continued to attend carefully to detail, becoming increasingly bogged down, losing track of the general office responsibilities, and becoming the subject of a number of reprimands, thus further increasing the checking behavior. Her general adaptation to life began to suffer and the checking-rechecking behavior pattern generalized even further, causing further stress and eventual hospitalization.

REEMERGENCE OF AVOIDANCE THEORY. A third type of fixated behavior includes the reappearance of previously successful avoidance responses during periods of stress. Fonberg (1956) demonstrated that a learned response previously successful in avoiding painful stimuli may later reappear when the animal is placed in a different anxiety-provoking situation. If the animal is placed in an insoluble problem situation and is unable to develop an appropriate avoidance response, he often readopts a response from his habit hierarchy that has in the past proved successful. This response may be totally inappropriate in the current conflict situation. One patient recently treated at the Middlesex Hospital had been trained as an audiology technician, a job requiring the checking and rechecking of signal levels in a signal detection experiment. However, she overgeneralized the response and during any stress situation at work, home, or traveling, she was compelled to recheck any action she performed until she was sure the response was correct. This rechecking often took hours at a time. The increased checking caused increased stress in her life and thus, paradoxically, the urge to check increased even more.

SCHEDULE-INDUCED THEORY. A final type of fixated behavior that has been shown in the analogue setting is the emergence of schedule-induced or adjunctive behaviors. Superstitious behaviors fall under the rubric of schedule-induced behaviors. When reinforcement is partial and delivered on an intermittent schedule, not only do targeted terminal responses occur, but other behaviors not correlated with the reinforcement also occur regularly. These behaviors are often unique to the individual and occur at times when the reinforcement is unlikely to be delivered (Staddon, 1977). In pigeons, intermittent schedules induce nonreinforced behaviors such as facing the wall, pecking the floor, preening, flapping wings, and locomotion (Staddon & Simmelhag, 1971). In rats, intermittent reinforcement schedules can induce such behaviors as polydipsia, grooming, and running (Staddon, 1977). Humans who were placed on a variety of schedules while playing slot machines and poker developed an assortment of interim activities such as varied movements, playing, and bizarre behaviors (Clarke, Gannon, Hughes, Keogh, Singer, & Wallace, 1977; Wallace, Singer, Wayner, & Cook, 1975). The role of adjunctive behaviors in the development of ritualistic behaviors has not yet been demonstrated in clinical cases, but seems to be a fruitful avenue for investigation. Rituals acquired as schedule-induced behaviors would not be reinforced directly, but they would develop during the acquisition and maintenance of other independent behaviors.

Regardless of the way in which fixated cognitive or motor patterns of behavior are acquired, maintenance of the response pattern may occur for several reasons. The role of anxiety and its relation to abnormal behavior has been debated since the late 1950s. The most common type of obsessional-compulsive disorder occurs in the context of anxiety, for execution of the ritual or request for reassurance diminishes the emotional arousal of the individual and is negatively reinforcing. Typical examples of anxiety-reducing rituals are washing and straightening. Anxiety-reducing rituals may develop as a consequence of chance associations between the ritual behavior and the reduction of anxiety. Wolpe (1958) provided an example of an anxiety-reducing ritual. The client described was an 18-year-old male who complained of a severe hand-washing compulsion that was stimulated by a fear of contamination by urine. After urinating, he would spend up to 45 minutes cleansing the genitals and 2 hours washing his hands. After completing the ritual, he experienced a cessation of anxiety until the next exposure.

In addition to anxiety-reducing rituals, some rituals and obsessions appear to be anxiety elevating. In the case of anxiety-elevating obsessions, it is the consequence of the thought or action that is disturbing and causes discomfort (Wolpe, 1958). Taylor (1963) has provided a clear case of anxiety-elevating obsessions in which the discomfort experienced came as a consequence of rituals. A 40-year-old woman had compulsively plucked her eyebrows for 31 years. The result of this action was strong social disapproval. While disapproval generally decreases the frequency of a behavior, Taylor proposed that the delay between the execution of the act and the delivery of the criticism reduced the potency of the criticism, thus it was not strong enough to alter the behavior. A second interpretation for the results is that the immediate and momentary consequence of the ritual was anxiety reduction. Moreover, once the client realized he/she had ritualized, anxiety increased as a function of the social/environmental consequences of compulsive behavior. However, the most immediate result, anxiety reduction, served to maintain the maladaptive response. Roper, Rachman, and Hodgson (1973) conducted an experiment to determine whether the execution of a potentially harmful act produced discomfort and whether the act of checking produced relief. They found a difference between "checkers" and "washers." A checking ritual was found to reduce discomfort in most clients, but in a minority of the subjects, discomfort was actually increased by execution of the ritual. Anxiety was reduced by washing for all subjects whose main ritual was washing. When the study was replicated in the homes of the clients, no differences were found between washers and checkers. It seems that some checkers do not feel compelled to ritualize when away from home because they are not responsible for the well being of others. Further research is being conducted in an attempt to elucidate the relationship between obsessions, ruminations, rituals, avoidances, and anxiety. Robertson (1978) is currently investigating the effects of ritual performance and prevention upon heart rate and subjective ratings of anxiety in compulsive patients.

Maintenance of maladaptive cognitive and motor behaviors can also result from the avoidance of other stressful situations. A side effect of being a severe obsessional or ritualizer is that the individual has little time to engage in other activities including working, relating with others, raising a family, managing a household, and so forth. If the individual is deficient in skills required for daily living, performance of the maladaptive responses allows the individual to escape or avoid other more stressful situations that might well be anxiety producing, and thus the maladaptive response is negatively reinforced by its escape or avoidance characteristic.

Finally, positive reinforcement may be involved in the maintenance of the disorder. Being labeled the "sick" individual may result in significant attention and concern by family members and others important to the person. Other people's responses to the disability, including the responses of the government in monetary terms, are critical in assessing variables which are maintaining the disorder.

To summarize, obsessions and ruminations are noxious conditioned stimuli acquired via association with aversive unconditioned stimuli. Because of the interaction of mood state and the sensitization to ruminations, the arousal experienced fails to habituate. Physical rituals and requests for reassurance may reduce the aversive state, thus reinforcing their occurrence and continuing the perceived effectiveness of the ritualistic behavior. Motor responses may become fixated (a) because one response acquires both positive and negative reinforcing properties; (b) because a previously successful avoidance response becomes unsuccessful and is punished, thus increasing the aversive state and increasing the likelihood of the emission of an avoidance response; (c) when a previously successful avoidance response reemerges in times of stress; and (d) as an adjunctive or schedule-induced behavior. Anxiety has been proposed to play a critical role in the development and maintenance of fixated behaviors. Secondary or social reinforcement as well as the escape or avoidance of aversive consequences are all important factors influencing the maintenance of the aberrant cognitive and motor responses. The validity of all of these models has not yet been demonstrated. Further research is sorely needed in the investigation of these areas. Although an understanding of the disorder is not a necessary precursor for effective treatment, it does make the treatment process a more sensible, goal-oriented endeavor.

TREATMENT

Physical Treatments

Physical treatments of obsessive-compulsive patients have involved drugs, electrical lesions, and surgical lesions. Although double-blind control studies are needed to evaluate physical treatment effectiveness, we do have some indications of promising avenues. The use of tricyclic antidepressants in the treatment of the disorder has largely been disappointing. However, recent studies have indicated treatment with clomipramine and imipramine, both inhibitors of serotonin and catecholamine reuptake, is promising. Clomipramine, although widely used in Europe, has not been approved for use in the United States because of associated deaths. The use of imipramine has replaced clomipramine in the States. Although clomipramine is a more potent serotonin uptake inhibitor, both seem equally effective as antidepressants, and are not different in the speed of onset or the incidence or types of side effects (Rack, 1973). It is possible that the effectiveness of the tricyclics stems from the associated sedative effect that eliminates spontaneous panic attacks rather than through the antidepressant action (Cobb, 1977; Zitrin and Klein, 1975). Turner, Hersen, Bellack, and Wells (1979) suggest that antidepressant medications have no direct effect on obsessive-compulsive behavior but may be of utility in treating symptoms of depression secondary to the obsessional disorder. Use of MAO inhibitors that help to lift the depressive component of the illness do not help pure obsessional states (Cobb, 1974). The use of minor tranquilizers such as diazepam are useful in reducing anxiety and behavioral avoidances, but they do not effect a change in ritualistic behaviors. Use of CO_2 abreaction and ECT are contraindicated unless there is clear evidence of a serious depressive element.

Treatment by leucotomy has long been a method used to treat the disorder. Freeman and Watts (1950) hypothesized leucotomies were successful because, although the ideas and compulsive rituals continued, their aversiveness was reduced. Sykes and Tredgold (1964) indicated improvement following leucotomies was correlated with decreased tension, scrupulousness, and a decline in standards to a point that fell in line with those of society. They found that all patients improved for a time but only 50% maintained the improvement over a 10-year period. Contraindications for leucotomies include a 1.5–4% death rate during surgery, an increase in susceptibility to epileptic seizures, dangers from wound complications, the presence of permanent brain damage, and the fact that prognosis is largely dependent upon the social environment of the patient. Patients with a stable home environment, work available or waiting to be resumed, and supportive systems outside the home have a better postleucotomy prognosis than do unmarried people, or people with unstable home environments, with no work available, and with less supportive social systems. Furthermore, the effects of the leucotomy may result from the patient being adjusted to live with the obsessions, since he is less anxious and less reactive to stimuli, rather than to a change being made in the obsessional disorder itself (Cobb, 1977; Sternberg, 1974).

Psychotherapy

Treatment of obsessional and compulsive disorders with traditional psychotherapy has been unrewarding. Comparisons of different treatment are of little value because the severity of the illness prior to treatment has not been controlled and because patients were often treated according to the ideas prevailing at the time of treatment and according to the different biases of the therapists. However, taking all of these variables into account the follow-up studies which have been completed suggest that in general, five years after treatment about 25% of the patients will have recovered or markedly improved, 50% will have shown minimal improvement, and 25% will be no better or worse. Studies have shown better results the longer the term of follow-up. Psychotherapy also seems to be more effective in altering obsessions than it is with rituals (Cawley, 1974).

Behavior Therapy

The behavioral methods used in treating obsessive and compulsive problems have included a variety of procedures. The plethora of treatment modes employed suggests that on the whole, treatment efforts have had limited success and therapists have continually searched for new and better treatment approaches. In this section, the rationale and salient features of the most popular approaches will be discussed, and conclusions will be drawn concerning the overall effectiveness of behavioral procedures used in treatment.

Treatment of cognitive disorders has included procedures involving reciprocal inhibition or systematic desensitization, exposure, modeling, response prevention, aversion relief, thought-stoppage, shaping, distraction, and instructions. Treatment of motoric problems has included reciprocal inhibition or systematic desensitization, exposure, modeling, response prevention, aversion relief, thought-stoppage, shaping, instructions, punishment, and time-out. In short, the modes of treatment of cognitive and motor disorders overlap considerably. Little systematic work has been done to differentiate the particular methods of treatment that are most effective for the different facets of the obsessive-compulsive complex.

The treatment methods can be categorized according to purpose. These categories include the treatment of anxiety related to the obsessive-compulsive difficulties, decreasing the rate of abnormal behavior while establishing more appropriate responses, and teaching control of maladaptive responses.

Anxiety Related Treatment

As was discussed in an earlier section, anxiety is hypothesized to play a major role in the development and/or maintenance of obsessions, ruminations, rituals, and avoidances. Methods used to modify anxiety include systematic desensitization, exposure, modeling, response prevention, and aversion relief.

DESENSITIZATION. Use of desensitization procedures is based on the assumption that anxiety is prominent in learned neurotic reactions. The reaction is viewed as continuing because of the principle of anxiety reduction. According to this principle, there are two components of a compulsive neurosis, the conditioned emotional response (anxiety) and another response instrumental in reducing the anxiety, a conditioned-avoidance response. This second response may be a motor act or a thought (Wolpe, 1958). Wolpe made the original attempt to treat the disorder by reducing the anxiety using the evocation of responses inhibitory to the anxiety. Inhibiting responses include relaxation, drug-induced relaxation, coping assertive statements, humor, and so on. Once inhibitory responses are learned, the individual is gradually exposed to more and more threatening stimuli in imagination or in vivo until he/she no longer experiences anxiety when faced with the threatening stimuli. Thus, the client has no need to engage in the anxiety-reducing, ritualistic, or ruminative behavior. The effectiveness of treating the anxiety versus the maladaptive behavior appears to be a function of the duration of the illness. Walton and Mather (1964) suggest anxiety inhibition to be effective in alleviating compulsive habits if the persons involved were in the early, acute stage of the disorder but to be insufficient in treating chronic cases of more than a few months duration. They have hypothesized that over time, the motor response may become partly autonomous of the original anxiety.

Gentry (1971) provides an example of an obsessional case treated with desensitization procedures. The patient was a 26-year-old married female who referred herself for treatment. Early symptoms included a phobic avoidance of being touched on the breasts, a fear of growths that she felt in the breasts whenever she touched herself or was touched by someone or something, and a compulsive ritual for checking her breasts to alleviate fears of cancer. The ritual involved physical manipulation of the breast area to ascertain whether a lump actually did exist. The symptoms caused the patient considerable anxiety, depression, and interferred with daily chores, child care, the maintenance of interpersonal relationships, and sexual activity. Treatment was designed to relieve the anxiety associated with tactile stimulation of the breasts, to alleviate obsessional fears concerning breast cancer, and to terminate "checking behavior." Treatment occurred during 11 sessions. The imaginal hierarchy progressed from reading an article on breast cancer to pulling a blanket over her chest and sleeping on her stomach. The in vivo hierarchy ranged from laying her arms across the breast without pressure to moving the hands from the neck to the waist while pressing the body quite tightly. Between presentations of the anxiety-evoking images or in vivo exercises the patient was instructed to relax, imagine calming, pleasant scenes, and to think of things other than the obsession. By the eleventh session all treatment goals were attained. At one-year follow-up the patient reported she was free of the fears, had resumed sexual relations with her husband, and was coping well with life.

EXPOSURE. Exposure procedures may involve rapid and prolonged contact with threatening stimuli or may be slowed and of a short duration. The stimuli may or may not be hierarchically arranged. During exposure conditions, the individual actually comes into contact with the discomfort-evoking stimuli. If the individual is unable to make contact with the feared stimulus, the therapist may break down the procedure into smaller steps or may model the appropriate response, but actual contact remains the treatment goal. The characteristics of exposure vary across studies, but the key element in the procedure is actual contact. The methods are hypothesized to work because the conditioned avoidance responses become ineffective and eventually are extinguished; the conditioned emotional responses are ineffective in terminating contact and thus gradually extinguish, and/or the feared consequences do not occur, resulting in a change in cognitive perception of the stimuli that lead to behavioral changes in the individual. Rachman, Hodgson, & Marks (1971) compared exposure or flooding and modeling with relaxation in 10 patients. Both exposure and flooding were found to be superior to relaxation but did not differ from each other in general effectiveness with compulsive patients.

MODELING. Modeling procedures are also designed to reduce anxiety responses. During modeling the client witnesses another individual in contact with feared stimuli, learns ways to manipulate the stimuli, and perceives that disastrous consequences do not result from contact with the stimuli. Modeling is hypothesized to be effective because of vicarious extinction of fear responses, the acquisition of new behavior, and the transmission of useful information (Roper, Rachman, & Marks, 1975). Rachman, Hodgson, and Marks (1971) found modeling and exposure to be equally effective but both were superior to relaxation in reducing compulsive behavior. Roper, Rachman, and Marks (1975) found participant modeling involving exposure to be more effective than passive modeling without exposure.

RESPONSE PREVENTION. Most of the experiments involving exposure and/or modeling have encouraged, but not enforced, response prevention. The theoretical basis for response prevention has its origin in a technique for altering fixated behavior developed by Maier and Klee (1945). Previous work had shown that rats who had developed stereotypic motor responses under insoluble conditions would not abandon these responses when faced with a soluble problem. In the soluble discrimination problem Maier and Klee manually guided the rats to jump to the correct window each time they were frustrated. A rat attempting to carry out a stereotypic response would be stopped by the experimenter and prevented from completing the fixated response. Then, the rat had to avoid jumping or to jump toward the correct window. Guidance led to an abandonment of fixated responses but did not facilitate the acquisition of new responses. Reinforcing trial and error learning was needed to build in the responses. The human analogue for guidance was first introduced by Meyer (1966). With this procedure the client is exposed to stimuli which typically elicit compulsive ritualistic responses. The individual is not allowed to ritualize but has the opportunity to learn alternate, adaptive responses. It is important that the rituals be prevented on each occasion either by the patient alone or with the help of a significant other if treatment is to be effective. This procedure involves exposure, modeling, guidance, support, and a method of altering faulty cognitions by demonstrating the nonoccurrence of feared consequences.

The effectiveness of response prevention and prolonged exposure (flooding) were examined by Turner, Hersen, Bellack, and Wells (1979) in a series of three controlled single case studies. One of the cases will be described below. The patient described was a 66-year-old married female who had difficulties with excessive washing and checking behaviors for 40 years. Over the years the problem generalized to the extent she was unable to perform household duties. Symptoms upon admission included checking and extensive cleaning and washing rituals. The patient was taking thioridazine. 50 mg, bid, imipramine 50 mg, bid, tripexyphenidyl HCl 2m. q am. and 4 mg hs. All medications were discontinued upon admission. Data collected included observer recordings of checking and washing behavior performed by observers, self-reported daily urges to check and wash, anxiety ratings, and Beck Depression Inventory scores. Baseline measures were taken for 7 days, 24 hour response prevention and exposure was instituted for 14 days, baseline measures were taken for 6 days, response prevention was instituted for 20 days, baseline measures were taken for 7 days, flooding procedures were instituted for 7 days, and baseline recordings were made for another 2 days. During response prevention a staff member was assigned to the patient on a 24 hour-a-day basis. Instructions included preventing the patient from ritualizing via distraction, redirection, and cajoling methods. Actual physical prevention was not required. Exposure to feared objects encountered in the course of daily activity was performed. Flooding procedures were conducted in one hour daily sessions and consisted of in vivo exposure to feared objects. The patient was seen in outpatient follow-up treatment on a weekly basis. Self-report data were obtained during these sessions. Results of treatment and follow-up are presented in Figure 1. The patient responded well to the response prevention treatment. The addition of flooding did not appear to contribute significantly to outcome. However, the elements of flooding are part of the response prevention program since the patient is consistently exposed to stimuli eliciting compulsive behavior without the oportunity to ritualize. In an earlier study, Mills, Agras, Barlow, and Mills (1973) demonstrated that exposure implemented before response prevention increases rather than decreases ritualistic behavior.

AVERSION RELIEF. Modeling, exposure, and response prevention are all based on the assumption that anxiety is altered by becoming ineffective in causing conditioned avoidance responses or by becoming unnecessary since more adaptive coping mechanisms have developed. Aversion relief procedures attempt to alter and reverse the negative valence of anxiety-producing stimuli. The patient is placed in an uncomfortable situation such as receiving mild, electrical shock. Termination of the aversive state is paired with exposure to the obsessional thoughts or feared stimuli. The occurrence of the previously negative event is reinforcing, for it is paired with the termination of an aversive state (Solyom, 1969). In all of the anxiety-related treatments, the goal is to make the obsessional- or ritualistic-eliciting stimuli less aversive so the occurrence of the maladaptive response is unnecessary in escaping or avoiding the discomfort. Solyom (1969) provides one of the few examples of an obsessive-compulsive neurosis treated by aversive relief. A 49-year-old married woman was hospitalized because she experienced obsessional thoughts and frequently ritualized. Feelings of depression and inadequacy were also problematic. She reported a 30-year history of obsessional thoughts and compulsive

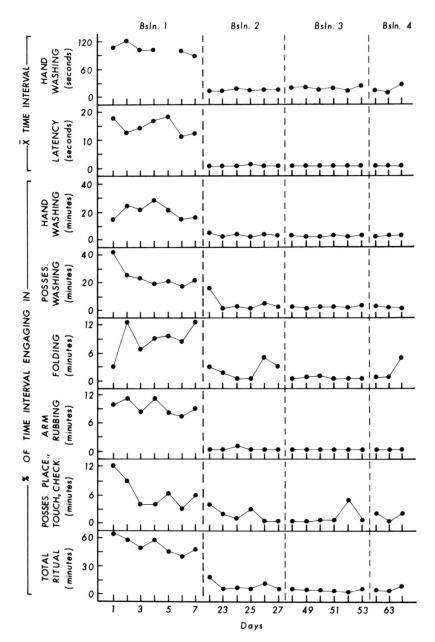

FIGURE 1.   Mean time engaged in handwashing, mean latency for checking, and percentage of observation intervals engaged in handwashing, possession marking, folding, arm rubbing, possession touching, placing checking, and total rituals (Turner, Hersen, Bellack, & Wells, 1979).

rituals and had been treated with psychotherapy, insulin shock, ECT, and major and minor tranquilizers. An analysis of obsessional thoughts indicated they centered around sexual objects or the use of "refined" words for common objects. Ritualistic activities included a mean of 399 hand-washes per day. (Additional descriptions are provided in the article.) During treatment the patient was required to write several narratives of her obsessional experiences, describing in detail the anxiety-producing event, the rumination, the increase of anxiety, and the resulting ritual. These were tape-recorded by the patient. The stories were then played back to her through earphones. Aversion relief (the cessation of digitally administered electroshock) was paired with the description of the anxiety-producing event, rumination, increases of experienced anxiety, or ritual. The purpose of the procedure was to provide reciprocal inhibition of anxiety stimuli and responses. The hand-washing ceased after 20 sessions, and gradually other rituals followed suit. The patient was discharged after 10 weeks of inpatient treatment. Following a stressful period one year later the obsessions returned, but within five treatment sessions the obsessions were eliminated. At two-year follow-up the patient continued to be markedly improved.

Reduction of Maladaptive Responses

Methods used to decrease the rate of obsessions or compulsions have included punishment and time-out procedures. Punishment paradigms are designed to decrease the maladaptive response by making the aversive consequences contingent upon the occurrence of the inappropriate response. The only way the client can avoid experiencing aversive consequences is by eliminating the obessions and/or compulsive rituals. The use of time-out procedures is employed to remove possible sources of positive reinforcement following the maladaptive response. Attention, reassurance, or other desirable consequences are altered so they are only available when the person does not obsess, ruminate, or ritualize. Thus, time-out procedures are designed to eliminate sources of secondary reinforcement. Animal analogue, involving the use of positive reinforcement and punishment to change fixated responses have had contradictory results. Maier and Ellen (1955) studied the effects of different amounts of reward and punishment on fixations in rats and concluded that all the conditions were largely ineffective in modifying behavior. Knopfelmacher (1953) suggested that punishment weakens fixated responses in rats whereas Maier and Klee (1943) showed that punishment increased the strength of a fixation. The results of these studies are insufficient to support or contraindicate the use of therapy based on reinforcement conditions. Three uncontrolled single case studies (Melamed & Seigel, 1975; O'Brien & Raynes, 1973; & Saper, 1971) have shown shaping procedures and contingent punishment to be effective in reducing maladaptive responses.

Increase of Self-Control

The final category of treatment used in the therapy of obsessive-compulsive problems includes use of procedures designed to increase self-control over the problem. Most of us worry, dwell on unnecessary topics, and occasionally show repetitive patterns that are not always most adaptive. The difference between the "normal" individual and the person with obsessive or compulsive problems is that the normal person has a degree of control over the response and is able to regulate its occurrence. Treatment procedures designed to teach control over the relevant responses include distraction, thought-stopping, thought-switching, and shaping the desired response. Distraction procedures are usually used in conjunction with other procedures but their purpose is to help the person switch his attention from the troubling response and to attend to other stimuli. Thought-stopping techniques have been used with cognitive disorders and are designed to help the person "turn off" the troubling responses. The therapist initially interrupts the thought pattern by using loud noises, distractions, and occasionally electric shock. The patient first models the response and eventually imitates it subvocally.

The use of thought-stopping in the treatment of ruminations has been investigated by Lombardo and Turner (1979) in a controlled single case study. The client was a 25-year-old male, day hospital patient with a nine-year history of rumination and a history of several psychiatric hospital admissions. He ruminated over fantasized heterosexual relations a great deal of the time, and the ruminations resulted in feelings of depression. People the client had met during his hospitalization two years earlier comprised the subject for the rumination. Active attempts to control the thoughts by shifting attention to other activities were unsuccessful. The patient remained on 100 mg Tofranil per day throughout the study. Treatment consisted of: (a) having the patient monitor and record the frequency and duration of the ruminations for 6 days; (b) training in the procedure of thought stopping for 11 days; (c) instructions to refrain from thought stopping for 10 days; and (d) resumption of the procedure for 13 days. Results of the study and follow-up are illustrated in Figure 2. From this study one can see that thought-stopping treatment produced dramatic decreases in ruminative activity for this

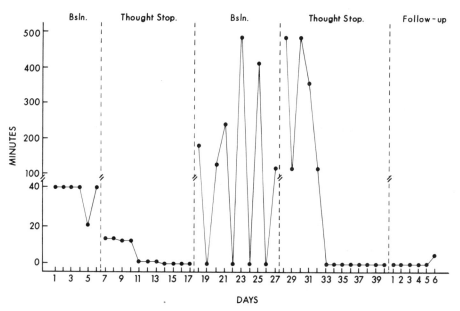

FIGURE 2. Duration of obsessive rumination during baseline, treatment, and six week follow-up (Lombardo & Turner, 1979).

patient. Decreases appeared to be related to continual use of the procedure since the ruminations resumed during the reversal period. The treatment employed in this study involved a variety of components including training on emitting neutral thoughts, the covert stopping of the aversive thought-shifting to a pleasant scene to reinforce the stopping behavior.

Thought-switching procedures include distraction and thought-stoppage paradigms; they also have the person voluntarily induce the troublesome cognition, stop the cognition, distract himself, reward himself when applicable, and reinduce the troublesome cognition. The purpose of this training is to enable the person to obsess or ruminate when it is appropriate to do so and to be able to concentrate on other activities when it is not appropriate to ruminate. Shaping procedures are used to gradually change the topography of the emitted behavior until it approximates a more normal response. Delay and positive reinforcement procedures are useful in the shaping procedures. Once a target behavior is established, the individual's maladaptive responses are gradually changed until they approximate the desired response.

EVALUATION CRITERIA

In order to assess the efficacy of any treatment technique, the dependent variables, which are relevant to the procedures, should be examined. This assessment should include the degree of experimental control exercised, the number and ages of the subjects used, the maladaptive response patterns targeted for treatment, the duration of the disorder, the prevalence of previous treatment, the methods and goals of treatment, the experimental results, and the follow-up results, when available.

Since the advent of the use of behavior therapy with obsessive-compulsive disorders in 1960, a total of 49 treatment studies have been carried out. A brief description of each treatment study is presented with its results in Tables 1-4. Studies are assigned to the tables representing the degree of experimental control present. A summary of the findings is presented in this section.

Twenty-five (51%) of the studies are classified as uncontrolled single case studies, ten (20%) are controlled single case studies, four (8%) are uncontrolled group studies, and ten (20%) are controlled group studies. A total of 172 clients have been treated—37% male and 63% female. The mean age when seeking treatment is 34 with a history of symptoms duration averaging 11 years. Thirty percent of the clients had obsessive thoughts, 20% experienced chronic rumination, 1% showed cognitive rituals, 73% exhibited motor rituals, and 10% demonstrate behavioral avoidances. From these figures it can be seen that the categories of classification are not mutually exclusive. The treatment complex including modeling, exposure, and response prevention (total, partial, or encouraged) is most popular, having been used with 30, 53, and 41% of the patients, respectively. These procedures are often used together as a package. Only a few case studies have isolated the contribution of each component. Reciprocal inhibition, systematic desensitization, and in vivo desensitization (10, 12, 5% respectively) follow in popularity, with thought-stoppage having been used with 11% of the patients. The remainder of the studies have used other techniques, but those have primarily been tested in

Table 1. Uncontrolled Single Case Studies

Author	Subject Characteristics			Target Behavior	Treatment	Result	Follow-Up
	Sex	Age	Duration (years)				
Bevan, 1960	F	29	1.3	Ruminations	Reciprocal inhibition with chlorpromazine	Marked improvement	1 year; maintenance
Walton, 1960	M	33	[a]	Obsessions Compulsions	Reciprocal inhibition c Largactil; exposure	Asymptomatic	7 months; relapse
					Reciprocal inhibition c Largactil; change of cognitions	Asymptomatic	4 months; maintenance
Walton & Mather, 1963	M	30s	1.6	Ruminations Rituals	Reciprocal inhibition c assertion	Asymptomatic	[a]
	M	30	5	Obsessions Rituals	Reciprocal inhibition c assertion	Asymptomatic	1 year; maintenance
	F	24	6	Obsessions Rituals	Systematic desensitization	Partial reduction anxiety; no change rituals	[a]
	F	48	26	Ruminations Rituals	In vivo desensitization	No change	[a]
	F	[a]	10	Obsessions Rituals	In vivo desensitization, reinforcement normal behavior	Improved	[a]
	M	[a]	3	Obsessions Rituals	Systematic desensitization	Asymptomatic	[a]
Haslam, 1965	F	25	6	Obsessions Rituals	Reciprocal inhibition c Largactil, exposure	Asymptomatic	1 year; asymptomatic
Meyer, 1966	F	33	3	Obsessions Rituals	In vivo exposure, response prevention	Marked improvement	1.2 years; maintenance
	F	47	36	Obsessions Rituals Avoidances	In imaginal and in vivo exposure, response prevention	Marked improvement	1.9 years; maintenance

86

Reference	Sex	Age	Sessions	Symptoms	Treatment	Outcome	Follow-up
Solyom, 1969	F	49	30	Obsessions Rituals	Reciprocal inhibition, aversion relief	Asymptomatic	1 year; relapse 5 additional sessions 3 years; asymptomatic [a]
Furst & Cooper, 1970	F	52	18	Obsessions Rituals	Systematic and in vivo desensitization	No change	[a]
	M	28	10	Obsessions Rituals	Systematic and in vivo desensitization	No change	[a]
Gentry, 1970	F	26	3	Obsessions Rituals Avoidances	Systematic and in vivo desensitization	Asymptomatic	1 year; asymptomatic
Lautch, 1970	M	40	35	Obsessions Rituals Avoidances	Reciprocal inhibition c Thiopentane	Marked improvement	1 year; maintenance
Stern, 1970	M	27	8	Ruminations	Reciprocal inhibition c Brevital, thought-stopping	Improved	[a]
Wisocki, 1970	M	27	3	Obsessions Rituals	Relaxation, thought-stopping, covert sensitization and reinforcement	Improved	1 year; maintenance
Saper, 1971	F	26	15	Hair pulling	Reinforcement to reduce pulls	Marked improvement	[a]
	F	15	4	Hair pulling	Reinforcement to reduce pulls	No change	[a]
	M	40	25	Obsessions Rituals	Systematic desensitization	Terminated	[a]
	F	28	3	Obsessions	Systematic desensitization reinforcement	Improved	[a]
Yamagami, 1971	M	24	8	Cognitive rituals	Thought-stopping	Marked improvement	7 months; maintenance
Rackensperger & Feinberg, 1972	F	26	2	Rituals	Systematic and in vivo desensitization	Improved	6 months; maintenance
Rainey, 1972	M	25	12	Obsessions Rituals	Self-monitoring, exposure, response prevention	Asymptomatic	1.5 years; asymptomatic
Meyer, 1973	F	38	[a]	Obsessions	Delay therapy	Asymptomatic	2 years; asymptomatic
O'Brien & Raynes, 1973	F	38	[a]	Rituals	Baseline, relaxation, aversion, time-out	Asymptomatic	[a]

Table 1. (Continued)

Author	Subject Characteristics			Target Behavior	Treatment	Result	Follow-Up
	Sex	Age	Duration (years)				
Orwin, 1973	F	24	0.75	Rituals	Random punishment, time-out	Asymptomatic	3 months; asymptomatic
	F	26	10	Obsessions Rituals	Reciprocal inhibition CO_2 inhalation, exposure, modeling	Improved	[a]
Solyom & Kingstone, 1973	M	23	2	Obsessions Rituals	Aversion relief	Asymptomatic	4 years; asymptomatic
Hallam, 1974	F	15	3	Ruminations Rituals	Extinction, social skills training, response cost	Marked improvement	14 months; improved
Anthony & Edelstein, 1975	F	24	3	Ruminations	Thought-stopping	Asymptomatic	6 months; asymptomatic
Melamed & Seigel, 1975	M	63	0.75	Rituals	Shaping, response prevention	Asymptomatic	8 months; asymptomatic
Meyer, Robertson, & Tatlow, 1975	F	45	30	Ruminations Rituals	Exposure, modeling, response prevention	Asymptomatic	8 months; asymptomatic
MacNeil & Thomas, 1976	F	21	4	Hair pulling	Self-monitoring, response cost	Asymptomatic	7 months; asymptomatic
Horton & Johnson, 1977	M	38	0.6	Ruminations	Thought-stopping, intrusion control, assertive training	Marked improvement	7 months; asymptomatic

[a] Unable to determine from data provided.

Table 2. Controlled Single Case Studies

	Subject Characteristics						
Author	Sex	Age	Duration (years)	Target Behavior	Treatment	Result	Follow-Up
Bailey & Atchinson, 1969	M	33	5	Rituals	Baseline	52% AM 71% PM	[a]
					Extinction and shaping PM, no change AM	52% AM 21% PM	
					Extinction and shaping AM and PM	52% AM 20% PM; improved	
Rachman, Hodgson, & Marzillier, 1970	M	20	5	Obsessions Rituals	Implosion-contamination and horror	Adverse effect	6 months; maintenance
					Modeling and exposure	Marked improvement	
					Response prevention	Maintenance	
					Modeling and response prevention	Maintenance	
Mahoney, 1971	M	22	[a]	Ruminations	Baseline	8–9 ruminations/week	2 months; maintenance
					Attentional distraction	14–10 ruminations/week	
					Self-punishment	4–0 ruminations/week	
					Self-monitoring ruminations and reinforcement positive statements	0–1 rumination/week; 0 PSStatements	
					Self-monitoring ruminations and primed reinforcement positive self-statements	0–0 ruminations/week; 14–30 PSStatements	
Tanner, 1971	F	24	4	Rituals	Baseline, self-monitoring	Some reduction rituals	[a]
					Relaxation, self-monitoring	Decrease rituals	
					Desensitization to performance of rituals, self-monitoring	Marked decrease rituals	
Gullick & Blanchard, 1973	M	33	0.05	Ruminations	Baseline	$X = 31$	9 months; asymptomatic
					Psychotherapy and thought-stopping	Slight decrease	

Table 2. (Continued)

Author	Subject Characteristics			Target Behavior	Treatment	Result	Follow-Up
	Sex	Age	Duration (years)				
					Reversal	X = 41	
					Psychotherapy	X = 20	
					Reversal	X = 13	
					Psychotherapy	X = 0	
Mills, Agras, Barlow, Mills, 1973	F	31	2	Rituals	Exposure	7.7 rituals; 8 urges	[a]
					Exposure and response prevention	0 6.5	
					Baseline	1 3.6	
	F	32	5	Obsessions Ruminations Rituals	Baseline and exposure	38.4 rituals; similar urges	[a]
					Instructions	25.1 similar	
					Response prevention	0 increased	
					Probe	12.6 decreased	
					Response prevention	0 increased	
					Probe	11.2 4.3	
					Instructions	4.4 3.1	
	F	25	3	Ruminations Rituals	Baseline and exposure	38.2 rituals; decline urges	[a]
					Placebo	47.8 rituals; no change	
					Response prevention	0	
					Placebo	41–25 urges	
						2.8	
						about same baseline	
					Baseline	0–1	
						about same baseline	
	M	20	1.5	Obsessions Rituals	Baseline and exposure	25.5 rituals; 9.4 urges	[a]
					Placebo	20.2 no change	

Study	Sex	Age	Duration	Behavior	Treatment	Results	Follow-up
					Placebo, exposure, and response prevention	0	no change
					Placebo and exposure	3 0	
					Baseline and exposure	1.5 0	
	M	15	[a]	Rituals	Baseline	6–8 night 3–7 day	[a]
					Response prevention	0 0–4	
					Baseline	0 0	
Stern & Marks, 1973	F	31	19	Ruminations	Baseline	8 preoccupation; 1 hour day	3 months; 1 preoccupation
				Rituals	Contract	8–3	10 minutes/day
						60–11 minutes	
Samaan, 1975	F	42	[a]	Ruminations	Baseline	15/week	20 months; 0–1 week
					Thought-stopping	4.5	
					Baseline	6	
					Exposure	2	
Hay, Hay, & Nelson, 1977	F	27	6	Obsessions	Self-monitoring	20–40	6 months; no change
				Rituals	Covert modeling	20–0	
					Coping statements	20–40	
Lombardo & Turner, 1979	M	25	9	Ruminations	Self-monitoring	37 minutes	6 weeks; 0–5 day
					Thought-stopping	17–0	
					Withdrawal	0–500	
					Thought-stopping	500–0	
Turner, Hersen, Bellack, & Wells, 1979	M	44	10	Rituals	Withdrawal medication	Considerable decrease in target behaviors	3 months; maintenance
					Baseline		
					Exposure		
					Response prevention		
					Baseline		
	M	51	lifelong	Rituals	Baseline	30% intervals ritualizing	[a]
				Avoidances			

Table 2. (Continued)

	Subject Characteristics			Target				
Author	Sex	Age	Duration (years)	Behavior	Treatment	Result	Follow-Up
	F	66	40	Rituals	Response prevention	9%	
					Baseline	15%	
					Response prevention	6%	
					Flooding and response prevention	8%	
					Baseline	11%	
					Antidepressant therapy	12%	
					Discontinued medication	High ritual level	11 weeks; slight increase
					Baseline		
					Response prevention		
					Baseline		
					Response prevention		
					Baseline		
					Flooding		
					Baseline		

[a] Unable to determine from data provided.

Table 3. Uncontrolled Group Studies

Author	Subject Characteristics			Target Behavior	Treatment	Result	Follow-Up
	Sex	Age	Duration				
Levy & Meyer, 1971	1M 7F	$X = 35.8$	$X = 17$	Rituals	Modeling, exposure, response prevention	2 asymptomatic 3 much improved 3 improved	1–6 years; $X = 2.5$ years 1 asymptomatic 5 much improved 2 improved
Boulougouris & Bassiokos, 1973	2M 1F	$X = 38.3$	$X = 15.7$	2 Obsessions 3 Rituals 2 Avoidances	Systematic and *in vivo* exposure, encouraged response prevention	3 much improved	9 months; maintenance
Meyer, Levy, & Schnurer, 1974	4M 11F	$X = 34.3$	$X = 15.6$	Rituals	Exposure, modeling, and response prevention	3 asymptomatic 7 much improved 5 improved	0–6 years; $X = 1.6$ years 2 asymptomatic 6 much improved 2 improved 2 no change 3 no follow-up

Table 4. Controlled Group Studies

Author	Subject Characteristics			Target Behavior	Treatment	Result	Follow-Up
	Sex	Age	Duration (years)				
Cooper, Gelder, & Marks, 1965	1M 9F	38	10	10 rituals	Reciprocal inhibition and imaginal exposure	10% much improved 20% improved	1 year 33% much improved 22% improved 33% improved
	9 control				Supportive treatment	44% improved	
Rachman, Hodgson, & Marks, 1971	0M 5F	36	10.4	9 obsessions 9 rituals 2 avoidances	Baseline Relaxation 5 flooding	No change No change 1 asymptomatic 1 much improved 1 slightly improved 2 no change	See Marks, Hodgson, & Rachman, 1975
	1M 4F	35	11.4		5 modeling	1 asymptomatic 2 much improved 1 improved 1 no change No significant difference between flooding and modeling	
Hodgson, Rachman, & Marks, 1972	1M 4F	32	8	2 obsessions 2 ruminations 4 rituals 3 avoidances	As above plus 5 modeling and flooding (with relaxation)	4 much improved 1 no change Combined treatment superior to either alone	See Marks, Hodgson, & Rachman, 1975
Rachman, Marks, & Hodgson, 1973	1M 4F	29	13	4 obsessions 5 rituals 1 avoidance	As above plus 5 modeling and flooding (without relaxation)	1 much improved 2 improved 2 no change	See Marks, Hodgson, & Rachman, 1975
Stern, Lipsedge, & Marks, 1973	6M 5F	33	12	11 ruminations	Thought-stopping, thought control	4 much improved 3 improved 4 no change No significant difference between treatments	[a]

Study	Sample			Symptoms	Treatment	Results	Follow-up
Hackman & McLean, 1975	2M 8F	30.2	3.7	10 ruminations	Crossover design; Flooding; Thought-stopping	No significant difference between treatments	
Marks, Hodgson, & Rachman, 1974	Follow-up of 1971, 1972, and 1973 studies					Two year — After 3 weeks: MI No. 2, Im. 4, M.I. 8; Im No. 0, Im. 1, M.I. 0; No No. 3, Im. 2, M.I. 0. Two year: MI No. 1, Im. 1, M.I. 12 (28); No. 5, Im. 1 (3); M.I. 0 (12) [a]	6 Months: No. 1, Im. 1, M.I. 12; No. 1, Im. 1, M.I. 0; No. 5, Im. 0, M.I. 0
Roper, Rachman, & Marks, 1975	A: 2M 3F; B: 1M 4F	32.6; 66.4	5.2; 13.8	A B: 5 3 obsessions, 1 2 ruminations, 2 2 avoidances, 3 4 rituals	A: Passive observation and response prevention; B: Participant modeling and response prevention	Two Year — A: 1 much improved, 3 improved, 1 no change; B: 4 much improved, 0 improved, 1 no change	6 months: 1 much improved, 3 improved, 1 no change; 3 much improved, 1 improved, 1 no change
Rabavilas, Boulougouris, & Stephanis, 1978	8M 4F	30.3	8.1	Ruminations	Latin square; Long and short fantasy; Long and short practice	6 improved, 4 moderate improvement, 2 no change; Long practice superior to other forms treatment	Maintenance
Foa & Goldstein, 1978	11M 10F	35	12	Rituals	Exposure to therapist baseline; Exposure and response prevention baseline	No change, 18 markedly symptomatic, 3 moderately symptomatic; 18 asymptomatic, 2 improved, 1 no change	3 months to 3 years; X = 1.25 years; Maintenance

[a] Unable to determine from data provided.

95

uncontrolled single case studies. The prognosis for the disorder has improved in recent years with 25% of the patients being asymptomatic, 37% markedly improved (at least 75% reduction in symptomatology and life-style interference), 23% improved, and 15% showing no change or rated as worse at the end of treatment. The range of follow-up data extends from 0 to 6 years with the mean follow-up time per person being 11 months. Such findings may be regarded as positive when compared with earlier studies using a variety of physical and traditional treatment procedures. Lewis (1936) found a cure or much improved rate of 46% at 5-year follow-up; Pollitt (1957) a rate of 60% in leucotomized patients and 45% in nonleucotomized patients at 3 to 15-year follow-up; Kringlen (1965) a rate of 19% at 13 to 20-year follow-up; and Grimsham (1965) a rate of 40% at 0 to 10-year follow-up. It appears on the whole that behavior therapy techniques have a success rate at least equivalent to the leucotomy procedures and are more effective than other techniques. However, it is dangerous to make these assumptions comparing technique effectiveness without comparing them in a controlled study under standardized conditions and criteria.

CLINICAL IMPRESSIONS

Although a total of 46 studies have investigated the effectiveness of behavioral treatments on obsessional and compulsive disorders, Paul's (1969) ultimate question for research has not yet been answered. We cannot yet answer "what treatment, by whom, is most effective for a particular individual with a specific problem, under what set of circumstances, and how does it come about" (p. 44). The current trend is for the studies to become more carefully controlled and some of these questions should be answered as time passes.

At the Middlesex Hospital, treatment of the cognitive and motor abnormalities continues to incorporate exposure, modeling, and response prevention. Since the initial uncontrolled group studies, a number of controlled studies have begun including a comparison of exposure, modeling, and 24-hour response prevention with exposure, modeling, and 1-hour response prevention. During 24-hour prevention a therapist or nurse therapist remains with the patient during all waking hours to prevent the occurrence of rituals. The patient is left alone when sleeping, but frequent, unannounced checks are performed by the therapist to make sure the patient is not ritualizing. Preliminary results of this study indicate that 24-hour response prevention is slightly more effective in controlling obsessions and rituals after the termination of treatment, but this difference is not impressive at six month follow-up (Robertson, 1978). Clinical impression, however, still favors use of 24-hour response prevention in very difficult cases. One-hour supervision seems appropriate if the urge to ritualize subsides during the interval, if the person can leave the task and not return to it later to undo whatever he/she did during exposure, and if the individual understands the importance of reducing rituals to zero from the beginning of treatment and feels he/she can refrain from the rituals. In cases in which the above criteria cannot be met, we prefer the use of continuous supervision. However, further evaluation of this preference is planned.

One change that has occurred is that the treatment is now more comprehensive than it was initially. In the earlier days of response prevention, elimination of ritualistic behavior was the treatment goal and little effort was made to rehabilitate clients. Results of such an approach were disappointing, for patients frequently relapsed. Current thinking indicates that those who do well in treatment also make drastic changes in their lives. Assessment now includes a thorough evaluation of family, social, vocational, educational, and financial assets and deficits. Treatment is provided in these areas, if necessary, in addition to the treatment of the ritualistic and obsessional behaviors. The goal of treatment is to facilitate the return to the home and community in a ritual or obsession-free state. Whenever possible, treatment is also conducted in the home environment and involves the efforts of significant others when applicable and possible. The role of anxiety, secondary reinforcement, and the organization of life around the disorder are assessed, and treatment is designed to intervene in any areas deemed appropriate.

Another change in therapeutic approach is seen in the treatment of ruminations. Treatment of ruminations using thought-switching has been evaluated in pilot work with four individuals and is encouraging. Controlled evaluation of the procedure is in progress, but final results are not yet available. The hypothesis behind treatment is that the ruminator has no control over his thought processes and this lack of control is unpleasant and may be anxiety provoking. The procedure incorporates thought-stopping, coping statements, thought-switching, self-reinforcement, and when the client becomes relaxed, reelicitation or reinitiation of the rumination. Treatment continues along these lines until the person is able to voluntarily invoke a rumination, think about it, terminate it upon demand, and control the ruminations as others do.

Cases that continue to present the most significant treatment problems include those for whom the deviant behavior is the predominant or only activity in life, and individuals whose obsessions can be classified as overvalued ideas. The first category has been addressed in the section discussing the need for comprehensive assessment and treatment. For these cases elimination of the obsessional ritualistic behavior alone is only the first step in treatment. If other problems (social, interpersonal, vocational, familial, etc.) are not attended to, the probability of relapse is quite high. Overvalued ideas were first documented by Foa (1979) and are defined as actual beliefs that the fears experienced are realistic. Overvalued ideas seem to border on being delusional at times. The individuals maintain that their fears are realistic and that ritualistic behavior actually prevents the occurrence of disastrous consequences. Most obsessionals state their fears are senseless or assign a low probability of occurrence to them. Individuals with overvalued ideas believe there is a high probability of their occurrence. Foa found that individuals with overvalued ideas do not show habituation of anxiety responses between sessions whereas individuals who respond well in treatment do show a gradual habituation response. It is possible that a combination of cognitive restructuring plus exposure, modeling, and/or response prevention will be more effective in the treatment of overvalued ideas.

Treatment of cognitive and motor abnormalities has made major strides since its beginning in 1961. Studies have become more controlled, begun to evaluate the effectiveness of treatment components, and more effective treatments are under development. Better definitions of targeted behaviors, the use of multiple baselines in the introduction of multicomponent procedures, further investigation of the interrelationship between the response exhibited (cognitive, motoric, and autonomic), and continued validation of current thought will improve knowledge concerning the condition. However, now the time has come to put down the pen, cease being obsessional about the words written here, and to begin to exhibit controlled but nonstereotypic motor responses designed to investigate some of the questions still remaining.

REFERENCES

Anthony, J., & Edelstein, B. A. Thought-stopping treatment of anxiety attacks due to seizure-related obsessive ruminations. *Journal of Behavior Therapy and Experimental Psychiatry,* 1975, **6**, 343–344.

Bailey, J., & Atchinson, T. The treatment of compulsive hand-washing using reinforcement principles. *Behaviour Research and Therapy,* 1969, **7**, 327–329.

Bevan, J. R. Learning theory applied to the treatment of a patient with obsessional ruminations. In H. J. Eysenck (Ed.), *Behaviour therapy and the neuroses.* Oxford: Pergamon Press, 1960.

Black, A. The natural history of obsessional neurosis. In H. R. Beech, (Ed.), *Obsessional states.* London: Methuen, 1974.

Boulougouris, J. C., & Bassiokos, L. Prolonged flooding in cases with obsessive-compulsive neuroses. *Behaviour Research and Therapy,* 1973, **11**, 227–231.

Cawley, R. Psychotherapy and obsessional disorders. In H. R. Beech (Ed.), *Obsessional states.* London: Methuen, 1974.

Clarke, J., Gannon, M., Hughes, I., Keogh, C., Singer, G., & Wallace, M. Adjunctive behavior in humans in a group gambling situation. *Physiology and Behavior,* 1977, **18**, 159–161.

Cobb, J. Drugs in treatment of obsessional and phobic disorders with behavioural therapy—possible synergies. In J. C. Boulougouris & A. D. Rabavilas (Eds.), *The treatment of phobic and obsessive-compulsive disorders.* Oxford: Pergamon Press, 1977.

Cooper, J. E., Gelder, M. G., & Marks, I. M. Results of behaviour therapy in 77 psychiatric patients. *British Medical Journal,* 1965, **1**, 1222–1225.

Farber, I. F. Response fixation under anxiety and nonanxiety conditions. *Journal of Experimental Psychology,* 1948, **38**, 111–131.

Fenichel, O. *The psychoanalytic theory of neuroses.* New York: Norton, 1945.

Foa, F. B. Failure in treating obsessive-compulsives. *Behaviour Research and Therapy,* 1979, **17**, 169–175.

Foa, F. B., & Goldstein, A. Continuous exposure and complete response prevention in the treatment of obsessive-compulsive neuroses. *Behavior Therapy,* 1978, **9**, 821–829.

Fonberg, F. On the manifestation of conditioned defensive reactions to stress. In J. Wolpe, *Psychotherapy by reciprocal inhibition.* Stanford, Calif.: Stanford University Press, 1958.

Freeman, W., & Watts, J. W. *Psychosurgery* (2nd edition). Oxford: Oxford University Press, 1950.

Furst, J. B., & Cooper, A. Failure of systematic desensitization in two cases of obsessional-compulsive neurosis marked by fear of insecticides. *Behaviour Research and Therapy,* 1970, **8,** 203–206.

Gentry, W. D. In vivo desensitization of an obsessive cancer fear. *Journal of Behavior Therapy and Experimental Psychiatry,* 1970, **1,** 315–318.

Gittleson, N. L. The effects of obsessions in depressive psychosis. *British Journal of Psychiatry,* 1966, **112,** 253–259.

Grimshaw, L. The outcome of obsessional disorder: A follow-up study in 100 cases. *British Journal of Psychiatry,* 1965, **111,** 1051–1056.

Groves, P., & Thompson, R. F. Habituation: A dual process theory. *Psychological Review,* 1970, **77,** 419–450.

Gullick, E. I., & Blanchard, E. B. The use of psychotherapy and behavior therapy in the treatment of an obsessional disorder: An experimental case study. *Journal of Nervous and Mental Diseases,* 1973, **156,** 427–431.

Hackman, A., & McLean, C. A comparison of flooding and thought-stopping. *Behaviour Research and Therapy,* 1975, **13,** 263–270.

Hallam, R. S. Extinction of ruminations: A case study. *Behavior Therapy,* 1974, **5,** 565–568.

Haslam, M. T. The treatment of an obsessional patient by reciprocal inhibition. *Behaviour Research and Therapy,* 1965, **2,** 213–216.

Hay, W. M., Hay, L. R., & Nelson, R. O. The adaptation of covert modeling procedures to the treatment of chronic alcoholism and obsessive compulsive behavior: Two case reports. *Behavior Therapy,* 1977, **8,** 70–76.

Herrnstein, R. J., & Sidman, M. Avoidance conditioning as a factor in the effects of unavoidable shocks on food-reinforced behavior. *Journal of Comparative and Physiological Psychology,* 1958, **51,** 380–385.

Hodgson, R., Rachman, S., & Marks, I. M. The treatment of chronic obsessive-compulsive neurosis: Follow-up and the further findings. *Behaviour Research and Therapy,* 1972, **10,** 181–189.

Horton, A. M., & Johnson, C. H. The treatment of homicidal obsessional ruminations by thought-stopping and covert assertion. *Journal of Behavior Therapy and Experimental Psychiatry,* 1977, **8,** 339–340.

Knopfelmacher, F. Fixations, position stereotypes and their relation to the degree and pattern of stress. *Quarterly Journal of Experimental Psychology,* 1953, **5,** 108–127.

Kringlen, E. Obsessional neurotics: A long term follow-up. *British Journal of Psychiatry,* 1965, **111,** 709–722.

Lautch, H. Videotape recording as an aid to behaviour therapy. *British Journal of Psychiatry,* 1970, **117,** 207–208.

Levy, R., & Meyer, V. Ritual prevention in obsessional patients. *Proceedings of the Royal Society of Medicine,* 1971, **64,** 115–120.

Lewis, A. J. Problems of obsessional illness. *Proceedings of the Royal Society of Medicine,* 1936, **29,** 325–326.

Lombardo, T. W., & Turner, S. M. Use of thought-stopping to control obsessive ruminations in a chronic schizophrenic patient, *Behavior Modification,* 1979, **3,** 267–272.

MacNeil, J., & Thomas, M. R. Treatment of obsessive-compulsive hair pulling (trichotillomania) by behavioral and cognitive contingency manipulation. *Journal of Behavior Therapy and Experimental Psychiatry,* 1976, **7,** 391–392.

Mahoney, M. J. The self-management of covert behavior: A case study. *Behavior Therapy,* 1971, **2**, 575–578.

Maier, N. R. F. *Frustration: The study of behavior without a goal.* New York: McGraw-Hill, 1949.

Maier, N. R. F., & Ellen, P. Studies of abnormal behavior in the rat. XXIII. The prophylactic effects of "guidance" in reducing rigid behavior. *Journal of Abnormal and Social Behavior,* 1952, **47**, 109–116.

Maier, N. R. F., & Klee, J. B. Studies of abnormal behavior in the rat. XVII. Guidance versus trial and error in the alteration of habits and fixations. *Journal of Psychology,* 1945, **19**, 133–163.

Marks, I. M., Hodgson, R., & Rachman, S. Treatment of chronic-obsessive compulsive neuroses by in vivo exposure. A two-year follow-up and issues in treatment. *British Journal of Psychiatry,* 1975, **127**, 349–364.

Melamed, B. G., & Siegel, L. J. Self-directed in vivo treatment of an obsessive-compulsive checking ritual. *Journal of Behavior Therapy and Experimental Psychiatry,* 1975, **6**, 31–35.

Metzner, R. Some experimental analogues of obsession. *Behaviour Research and Therapy,* 1963, **1**, 231, 236.

Meyer, R. G. Delay therapy: Two case reports. *Behavior Therapy,* 1973, **4**, 709–711.

Meyer, V. Modification of expectancies in cases with obsessional rituals. *Behaviour Research and Therapy,* 1966, **4**, 273–280.

Meyer, V., & Levy, R. Modification of behavior in obsessive-compulsive disorders. In H. E. Adams & I. P. Unikel (Eds.), *Issues and trends in behavior therapy.* Springfield, Ill.: C. C. Thomas, 1973.

Meyer, V., Levy, R., & Schnurer, A. The behavioral treatment of obsessive-compulsive disorders. In H. R. Beech (Ed.), *Obsessional states.* London: Methuen, 1974.

Meyer, V., Robertson, J., & Tatlow, A. Home treatment of an obsessive-compulsive disorder by response prevention. *Journal of Behavior Therapy and Experimental Psychiatry,* 1975, **6**, 37–38.

Millon, T. *Modern psychopathology: A biosocial approach to maladaptive learning and functioning.* Philadelphia: W. B. Saunders Company, 1969.

Mills, H. L., Agras, W. S., Barlow, D. H. & Mills, J. R. Compulsive rituals treated by response prevention: An experimental analysis. *Archives of General Psychiatry,* 1973, **38**, 524–529.

Nemiah, J. C. Obsessive-compulsive neurosis. In A. M. Freedman, H. I. Kaplan, & B. J. Saddock, (Eds.), *Comprehensive textbook of psychiatry/II,* Vol. 1. Baltimore: Williams & Wilkins, 1975.

O'Brien, J. S., & Raynes, A. F. Treatment of compulsive verbal behavior with response contingent punishment and relaxation. *Journal of Behavior Therapy and Experimental Psychiatry,* 1973, **4**, 347–352.

Orwin, A. Augmented respiratory relief. A new use for CO_2 therapy in the treatment of phobic conditions: A preliminary report on two cases. *British Journal of Psychiatry,* 1973, **122**, 171–173.

Paul, G. L. Behavior modification research design and tactics. In C. M. Franks, (Ed.), *Behavior therapy: Appraisal and status.* New York: McGraw-Hill, 1969.

Pollitt, J. Natural history of obsessional states. *British Medical Journal,* 1957, **1**, 195–198.

Rabavilas, A. D., Boulougouris, J. C., & Stephanis, C. Compulsive checking diminished when overchecking instructions were disobeyed. *Journal of Behavior Therapy and Experimental Psychiatry*, 1977, **8**, 111–112.

Rachman, S. Obsessional ruminations. *Behaviour Research and Therapy*, 1971, **9**, 229–235.

Rachman, S. The modification of obsessions: A new formulation. *Behaviour Research and Therapy*, 1976, **14**, 437–443.

Rachman, S., Hodgson, R., & Marks, I. M. The treatment of chronic obsessional-compulsive neurosis. *Behaviour Research and Therapy*, 1971, **9**, 237–247.

Rachman, S., Hodgson, R., & Marzillier, J. Treatment of an obsessional-compulsive disorder by modeling. *Behaviour Research and Therapy*, 1970, **8**, 385–392.

Rachman, S., Marks, I. M., Hodgson, R. The treatment of obsessive-compulsive neurotics by modeling and flooding in vivo. *Behaviour Research and Therapy*, 1973, **11**, 463–471.

Rack, P. H. Clomipramine in the treatment of obsessional states with special reference to the Leyton Obsessional Inventory. *Journal of International Medical Research*, 1973, **1**, 332, 397–402.

Rackensperger, W., & Feinberg, A. M. Treatment of a severe hand-washing compulsion by systematic desensitization: A case report. *Journal of Behavior Therapy and Experimental Psychiatry*, 1972, **3**, 123–127.

Rainey, C. A. An obsessional neurosis treated by flooding in vivo. *Journal of Behavior Therapy and Experimental Psychiatry*, 1972, **3**, 117–121.

Robertson, J. Personal communication, 1978.

Roper, G., Rachman, S., & Hodgson, R. An experiment of obsessional checking. *Behaviour Research and Therapy*, 1973, **11**, 271–277.

Roper, G., Rachman, S., & Marks, I. M. Passive and participant modeling in exposure treatment of obsessive-compulsive neurotics. *Behaviour Research and Therapy*, 1975, **13**, 271–277.

Rosenberg, C. M. Complications of obsessional neurosis. *British Journal of Psychiatry*, 1968, **114**, 477–478.

Samaan, M. Thought-stopping and flooding in a case of hallucinations, obsessions, and homicidal-suicidal behaviors. *Journal of Behavior Therapy and Experimental Psychiatry*, 1975, **6**, 65–67.

Saper, B. A report on behavior therapy with outpatient clinic patients. *Psychiatric Quarterly*, 1971, **45**, 209–215.

Solomon, R. S., Kamin, L. J., & Wynne, L. C. Traumatic avoidance learning: The outcome of several extinction procedures with dogs. *Journal of Abnormal and Social Psychology*, 1953, **48**, 291–301.

Solyom, L. A case of obsessive neurosis treated by aversion relief. *Canadian Psychiatric Association Journal*, 1969, **14**, 623–626.

Solyom, L., & Kingstone, F. An obsessive neurosis following morning glory seed ingestion treated by aversion relief. *Journal of Behavior Therapy and Experimental Psychiatry*, 1973, **4**, 293–295.

Staddon, J. F. R. Schedule induced behavior. In W. K. Honig & J. F. R. Staddon, (Eds.), *Handbook of operant conditioning*. New York: Appleton-Century-Crofts, 1977.

Staddon, J. F. R., & Simmelhag, V. L. The "superstition" experiment: A reexamination of its implications for the principles of adaptive behavior. *Psychological Review*, 1971, **78**, 1–43.

Stern, R. Treatment of a case of obsessional neurosis using thought-stopping techniques. *British Journal of Psychiatry*, 1970, **117**, 441–442.

Stern, R. S., Lipsedge, M. S., & Marks, I. M. Obsessive ruminations: A controlled trial of thought-stopping technique. *Behaviour Research and Therapy*, 1973, **11**, 659–662.

Stern, R. S., & Marks, I. M. Contract therapy in obsessive-compulsive neurosis with marital discord. *British Journal of Psychiatry*, 1973, **123**, 681–684.

Sternberg, M. Physical treatments in obsessional disorders. In H. R. Beech, (Ed.), *Obsessional states*. London: Methuen, 1974.

Sullivan, H. S. *Clinical studies in psychiatry*. New York: Wiley, 1956.

Sykes, M. K., & Tredgold, R. F. Restricted orbital undercutting. A study of its effects on 350 patients over the ten years 1951–1960. *British Journal of Psychiatry*, 1964, **110**, 609–640.

Tanner, B. A. A case report on the use of relaxation and systematic desensitization to control multiple compulsive behaviors. *Journal of Behavior Therapy and Experimental Psychiatry*, 1971, **2**, 262–272.

Taylor, J. G. A behavioural interpretation of obsessive-compulsive neurosis. *Behaviour Research and Therapy*, 1963, **1**, 237–244.

Turner, S. M., Hersen, M., Bellack, A. S., & Wells, K. C. Behavioral treatment of obsessive-compulsive neurosis. *Behaviour Research and Therapy*, 1979, **17**, 95–106.

Wallace, M. & Singer, G., Wayner, M. J., & Cook, P. Adjunctive behavior in humans during game playing. *Physiology and Behavior*, 1975, **14**, 651–654.

Walton, D. The relevance of learning theory to the treatment of an obsessive-compulsive state. In H. J. Eysenck (Ed.), *Behaviour therapy and the neuroses*. Oxford: Pergamon Press, 1960.

Walton, D., & Mather, M. D. The application of learning principles to the treatment of obsessive-compulsive states in the acute and chronic phases of illness. *Behaviour Research and Therapy*, 1963, **1**, 163–174.

Wisocki, P. A. Treatment of obsessive-compulsive behaviour by covert sensitization and covert reinforcement: A case report. *Journal of Behavior Therapy and Experimental Psychiatry*, 1970, **1**, 233–239.

Wolpe, J. *Psychotherapy by reciprocal inhibition*. Stanford, California: Stanford University Press, 1958.

Yamagami, T. The treatment of an obsession by thought-stopping. *Journal of Behavior Therapy and Experimental Psychiatry*, 1971, **2**, 133–135.

Zitrin, C. M. & Klein, D. F. Imipramine, behavior therapy, and phobias. *Psychopharmacology Bulletin*, 1975, **11**, 41–42.

CHAPTER 5

Disorders of Social Behavior: A Behavioral Approach to Personality Disorders

Samuel M. Turner and Michel Hersen

The class of psychological disturbance generally referred to as personality or character disorders is one of the least understood and researched of all the psychiatric disorders. Yet, this group of disorders represents the single largest group of patients seen by psychologists and psychiatrists (Salzman, 1974). In this chapter we review some of the major personality disorder syndromes, briefly describe some of the major diagnostic categories, outline what we feel are unifying characteristics of the different syndromes, present a behavioral formulation of these disorders, and review the current behavioral literature in this area. The antisocial personality (i.e., sociopathy) is not covered here inasmuch as Chapter 23 is devoted entirely to this disorder. Similarly, we do not include episodic disturbances or syndromes that are not well-defined or where there is considerable evidence linking the syndrome to more severe mental disorders (i.e., Cyclothymic Personality). Juvenile delinquency and other adolescent problems are only given cursory attention as they are dealt with in Chapters 20 and 23.

The concept of personality has a long and controversial history within psychology. As Adams (in press) points out, the major reason for the heated controversy around the term personality is because psychologists do not agree as to what it really means. Indeed, Allport (1937) describes 50 different definitions of personality. Despite the multitude of definitions, there are aspects of the term personality with which most psychologists agree. Most psychological theorists would argue that the behaviors comprising what we consider to be the personality of an individual are those that specifically are stable across time and situation. As an example, an individual possessing the trait or characteristic of assertiveness is considered to be assertive regardless of situation and to remain so over time. Likewise, the individual possessing the trait of dependency is expected to exhibit dependent behavior regardless of situational factors, albeit perhaps in different patterns.

The American Psychiatric Association's Diagnostic and Statistical Manual (DSM-III, APA, 1980), describes personality disorders as "enduring patterns of perceiving, relating to, and thinking about the environment and oneself, and are exhibited in a wide range of important social and personal contexts" (p. 305).

Moreover, these characteristics are considered to be fixed traits that collectively form the individual's personality. The ramifications of such a view are discussed in a later section. At this point, we discuss some of the major specific syndromes that are classified as personality disorder.

PERSONALITY DISORDER

Hysterical Personality

Perhaps the best-known, and certainly the oldest of the identified personality disorders is the hysterical personality. Actually, the term hysteria has been used in many contexts throughout recorded history, and it is derived from the Greek word *hystera* which means uterus. The hysterical disorders were initially believed to be due to the misplacement or wandering of the womb, hence the disorder was believed to occur solely in women. More recently, hysterical symptoms have been identified in children as well as adult males (Abse, 1974).

The terminological confusion surrounding this label has been particularly problematic with respect to diagnosis, and the lack of homogeneity in most groups of patients so labeled has been the subject of concern. Chodoff (1974) lists the following five semantic meanings of the term: (*a*) to relate to conversion disorders; (*b*) Briquet's Syndrome; (*c*) a personality disorder; (*d*) a specific pathological psychodynamic pattern manifesting itself as a personality trait; and (*e*) a colloquialism used to describe undesirable behavior. For a most enlightening and readable historical account of the term hysteria, the interested reader is referred to Veith (1965).

For our purposes here, the term hysterical is used to refer to a group of behaviors that seem to be relatively stable characteristics of certain individuals. The hysterical personality is to be distinguished from hysterical neurosis, which is characterized by conversion symptoms and hysteria (Briquet's Syndrome) as well as multiple vague physical complaints. (For a discussion of Briquet's Syndrome see Rounsville, Harding, & Weissman, 1979; Woodruff, Goodwin & Guze, 1974). The hysterical personality is consistently described as excitable, vain, attention seeking, egocentric, emotionally labile, dependent, and self-dramatizing. Such individuals are also noted by many clinicians to be sexually seductive, but ineffectual in sexual relations. There has been at least one experimental study of this notion. O'Neil and Kempler (1969) compared hysterical and normal females under neutral and sexually provocative stimuli in a paired-associative learning task. Hysterical females avoided or failed to attend to sexual stimuli under the provocative condition, but not under the neutral condition. This effect was not shown for the normal group. The experimenters concluded that the hysteric is accepting of sexual self-reference only when conditions are irrelevant or neutral. When they are sexually provocative, the hysteric denies or avoids.

Many behavioral characteristics have been ascribed to the hysteric from time to time. Alarcon (1973) surveyed the available literature and concluded that there are seven main behavioral characteristics of the hysterical personality disorder. They are as follows: histrionic behavior, emotional lability, dependency, excitability, egocentricity, suggestibility, and seductiveness.

Obsessive-Compulsive Personality

The obsessive-compulsive personality is also known as the anankastic personality. The word anankastic is derived from the Greek word meaning rigid or coercive. The obsessive-compulsive personality is characterized by rigid adherence to a given set of standards. The obsessive-compulsive personality is generally perfectionistic, orderly, overly conscientious, concerned with detail, inhibited, and unable to relax. When forced to work under conditions that they cannot control, the obsessive-compulsive may become anxious and disorganized (Freedman, Kaplan, & Sadock, 1972). To further complicate matters, the obsessive-compulsive may demand the same unrealistically high-moral standards and concern for detail from others (Adams, in press). Needless to say, attempts to demand from others such rigid behavior are likely to lead to interpersonal difficulty.

Much attention has been given to the notion that the obsessive-compulsive personality is a precursor or sets the stage for the development of an obsessive-compulsive neurosis. However, to date the empirical evidence for such a relationship remains equivocal. A review of research concerning this issue is provided by Black (1974).

Passive-Aggressive Personality

The passive-aggressive personality is described as being both passive and aggressive. These individuals attempt to control their environments through passive manipulation of others. Aggression is frequently expressed in a passive fashion through pouting, procrastination, obstructionalism, intentional inefficiency, and stubbornness. They are further characterized as resenting authority figures, lacking in assertiveness, lacking self-confidence, and generally dependent (DSM-III, APA, 1980).

Freedman, Kaplan, and Sadock (1972) describe two subtypes of passive-aggressive personality: passive-dependent and passive-aggressive. The passive-dependent type is indecisive, dependent, and in need of constant support. The passive-aggressive type expresses hostility and aggression covertly. This kind of individual is generally compliant but when threatened will evince pouting, stubbornness, procrastination, obstructionism, and intentional inefficiency. As can be seen, these behaviors have been used to describe the entire syndrome, and at this point there is little empirical evidence to support subtyping. The passive-aggressive individual most likely displays the particular behavior pattern (dependent or aggressive) that produces the best results in a particular situation.

The individual who displays this behavior pattern is particularly annoying, and not surprisingly, frequently unpopular. In fact, Pasternack (1974) considers maladaptive social relationships to be the most salient characteristic of this syndrome.

Paranoid Personality

The paranoid personality is characteristically suspicious, argumentative, hypersensitive, aggressive, rigid, and possesses an exaggerated sense of importance. Such persons are also noted to be envious of others, sometimes litigious, and extremely sensitive to criticism. This individual's whole being is characterized by defensiveness. According to Salzman (1974), these individuals make extensive use of the defense mechanism of projection, and while paranoid personalities do not show frank delusions, they do engage in referential thinking and view the environment in a suspicious fashion.

Individuals diagnosed as having paranoid personalities are noted to have fragmented and inflammable interpersonal relationships. They rarely show humor and are restrained and rigid. The relationship of homosexual feelings to the paranoid disorders has long been the subject of controversy and speculation. While the exact relationship is still not clear, these particular feelings are now considered to be part of a broad-based pattern of self-doubt (Salzman, 1974). The relationship of the paranoid personality to the various forms of paranoid psychoses remains equivocal at this time.

Schizoid Personality

Individuals evincing this behavior pattern are described as shy, oversensitive, and seclusive. They are noted to avoid competitive or close relationships and to present an image of detachment. Behavioral abnormalities are noted to appear in early childhood as the schizoid is shy, considered an outsider, underachieves, and pursues solitary interests. There is also a marked absence of the ability to display emotionality. The relationship of this particular pattern of behavior to schizophrenia has long been a topic of speculation.

In the DSM-III (APA, 1980), the term schizoid has been deleted in favor of two new terms: *introverted personality disorder* and *schizotypal disorder*. The introverted personality disorder fits the description given above. The term schizotypal is reserved for individuals who exhibit the above symptomatology in addition to various other unusual forms of communication and behavior. This group includes the previous diagnostic categories of latent and borderline schizophrenia. This distinction is made because it is felt that there is sufficient evidence to suggest a relationship to schizophrenia in this group of individuals. This stance is obviously a controversial one and, in our opinion, still requires empirical verification.

In any event, the schizoid personalities are grossly deficient in interpersonal skill and their typical response to stress is withdrawal. Heterosexual relationships are particularly problematic among this group because of their lack of emotionality and their inability to form intimate relationships. Consequently, they are typically slow to engage in courtship, and in many instances refrain totally.

TRADITIONAL APPROACHES TO TREATMENT

Psychodynamic Treatment

The personality disorders have long been one of the primary types of disorders found in patients treated by psychodynamic modes of therapy, particularly psychoanalysis. In fact, much of psychoanalytic theory of treatment is based on the treatment of hysterical disorders (Adams, in press). Given that these disorders have been recognized for a long period of time, it is surprising that there is little in the way of systematic evaluation of psychodynamic approaches. However, it is clear that the goal of psychodynamic treatment is to elucidate the particular character structure of the individual such that he gains insight into the meaning of his behavior. These types of therapies are particularly concerned with the therapist-patient relationship, and attempt to use the relationship to resolve the patient's interpersonal difficulties (e.g., aggressiveness, dependency, manipulation). For a general discussion of psychodynamic approaches see Lion (1974), and Salzman (1974).

Therapeutic Community

Therapeutic communities and milieu therapy have been used to treat personality disorders in residential as well as outpatient (day hospital) programs. Such programs attempt to use the structure of the therapeutic community or milieu to help the patient become aware of and understand the effects of his deviant behavior. Since the community encourages interaction, it is assumed that the activities of the milieu will foster the learning of more adaptive ways of interacting (Liebman & Hedlund, 1974). Therapeutic communities would appear to be ideal settings to deal with personality disorders, since patients are available for long periods of time and a pool of people are available for interacting with the patient. However, although therapeutic communities are structured with specific methods (Kraft, 1966; Stainbrook, 1967), they do not appear to make direct efforts to eliminate specific inappropriate behaviors or to specifically teach new skills. Rather, the milieu is assumed to spontaneously produce those effects.

Pharmacological Treatment

The dominant position within psychology and psychiatry has been that personality disorders result from abnormalities in the socialization process. Yet, speculation concerning an organic etiology has existed in the psychiatric literature for some time, particularly in relation to the episodic disorders. Although pharmacological intervention is used in many personality disorders (e.g., Freedman, Kaplan, & Sadock, 1972), it is considered adjunctive rather than primary. Pharmacological intervention is typically aimed at controlling such symptoms as anxiety and depression. (For a review of pharmacological intervention in personality disorders see Covi & Alessi, 1974.)

RECONCEPTUALIZATION OF PERSONALITY DISORDER

Basic to the notion that the individual possesses a stable and enduring personality is that the personality is comprised of traits that together define its nature. Traits are enduring characteristics that an individual will exhibit in most, if not all, situations. Until recently, this conceptualization of the individual as consisting of a variety of enduring traits was most prevalent in psychology. Moreover, these traits and attributes were thought to be a function of various needs and of intrapsychic conflict. For the psychodynamic theorist, learning occurred only through the process of being integrated into the personality characteristics of the individual. Little attention was given to the surrounding environment.

In his now classic work entitled, *Personality and Assessment,* Mischel (1968) concluded from a large survey of the available literature that behavior was largely a function of situation, and that little of the variance in behavior can be accounted for by traits or personality characteristics. While this conclusion has been subjected to severe criticism, it has basically been upheld within some limits. New evidence has emerged to suggest that some behavior can be explained by predisposition or traits, while others can only be explained by situation (Bowers, 1973; Endler, 1973; Mischel, 1973). Moreover, the evidence suggests that it is the psychopathological behaviors that tend to be displayed consistently across time and situation (Bowers, 1973).

The diagnostic classifications described in this chapter would appear to represent those individuals who seem to display various deviant behaviors in a consistent fashion. The question that arises at this juncture is: do individuals with personality disorders possess a set of traits that predispose them to behave in a certain fashion regardless of situational context? Before we attempt to answer this question, we would like to examine the context in which an individual is identified as having a personality disorder. The personality disorder, unlike the neurotic disorder, does not cause subjective distress, and individuals with such problems do not consider themselves to be deviant in any way. Individuals with a personality disorder experience subjective distress as a function of the manner in which others respond to them (Adams, in press).

From the above description of how the personality-disordered individual experiences stress, it can be discerned that it is in the interpersonal context. That is to say, it is the inability to maintain satisfactory interpersonal relations and to extract gratification from the environment that leads these individuals to experience subjective distress. Therefore, behaviors in which the personality disorder are apparently deficient would appear to be social in nature.

The statements made above concerning the existence of behavioral consistency will undoubtedly cause some behaviorists to raise their eyebrows. However, behavioral consistency is certainly not antithetical to all behavioral theory or theorists (Eysenck, 1970; Eysenck & Eysenck, 1969). Perhaps our colleagues who are more operantly inclined look upon this notion with more reluctance than others; yet, data would seem to dictate that our theories are in need of revision to accommodate these findings. Moreover, operant theory itself already provides the mechanism to allow for behavioral consistency through the development and influence of prior reinforcement history. Behaviors that have been reinforced in the past have a higher likelihood of being displayed when stimulus conditions are appropriate. For instance, if a class of behaviors that we label dominant is reinforced by significant others (e.g., family) in various situations, then those dominant behaviors are now more likely to be displayed in similar situations than other submissive behaviors.

Bandura and Walters (1963), in their book *Social Learning and Personality Development,* present a comprehensive system to account for personality development using principles of social learning theory. For reasons unknown to us, this work has received little attention from behavioral theorists. We will briefly present very selected parts of their theory of the socialization process. For a complete account the interested reader is referred to Bandura and Walters (1963). Essentially, Bandura and Walters employ the principles of operant conditioning and observational learning to account for personality development. An individual's repertoire of behaviors is acquired through the process of reward and punishment (direct and vicarious), with maintenance determined by schedules of reinforcement to which they have been subjected. An important element in this account of social development is the notion that most social behavior is controlled by what they refer to as combined schedules of reinforcement. Combined schedules are made up of a mixture of variable interval and variable ratio schedules, which are capable of sustaining low rates of responding as well as high rates of responding over long periods of time (p. 6). Bandura and Walters further argue that children are trained or socialized under these combined schedules that permit behaviors to be sustained at any rate. They give the example of a mother who ignores mild attention-seeking behavior and responds only to intense, frequent occurrences of attention seeking. This mother will produce children who will display persistent attention-seeking behavior at the rate and intensity that has brought reward. They state:

One may suspect the most troublesome behavior has been rewarded on a combined schedule by which undesirable responses of high magnitude and frequency are unwittingly reinforced. The behavior is thus persistent, difficult to extinguish, and baffling for the parents. Perhaps the genesis of much aggressive behavior is to be found in the use of schedules which reward only responses of high magnitude. These could be attention seeking, food seeking, and other so-called dependency responses, as well as responses of the kind more usually regarded as "aggressive" [Bandura & Walters, 1963, p. 7].

The social milieu is replete with various combined schedules of reinforcement due to the complexity of social demands. It seems likely to us that the behavior patterns we have described as personality disorders are acquired under these circumstances and generalize to other situations through the process of stimulus generalization and discrimination. Furthermore, habit hierarchies of behaviors are likely produced with a particular behavior being dominant in more than one hierarchy. Consequently, this dominant behavior (or group of behaviors) may be elicited in many diverse social situations. If this is so, then we have the mechanism to account for behavioral consistency.

At this point, we have acknowledged that there are behavioral characteristics that do appear to remain more or less stable across time and situation. When these characteristics are repeatedly displayed in social intercourse, the individual is said to have a personality characterized by some dominant pattern (e.g., dependency, aggression). These behaviors are a function of an intricate reinforcement history characterized by complex combined schedules of reinforcement. When using this formulation to account for persistent behavior patterns of a problematic nature, we believe the outlook toward treatment is somewhat more optimistic than traditional conceptualizations have allowed. Inasmuch as the disorder is identified and defined as a disorder of social behavior, perhaps the obvious treatment strategy to come to mind is social skills training. Various operant strategies would also seem appropriate. Before discussing behavioral treatments that seem to us to be most appropriate, at this point we would like to review the available literature on behavioral treatment of the personality disorders.

THE BEHAVIORAL APPROACH

Two primary approaches have been used by behaviorists in treating personality disorders: contingency management and social skills training. Of course, in the more comprehensive programs, elements of both have been combined in order to achieve maximum efficacy (e.g., Kass, Silvers, & Abrams, 1972). In some instances (e.g., Boren & Colman, 1970), only the operant approach has been carried out to evaluate and demonstrate its controlling effects over targeted behaviors. In general, the operant approach has proven quite effective in reducing and eliminating excesses in behavior (e.g., verbal and physical aggression) evidenced by juvenile delinquents, delinquent and acting-out soldiers, and individuals with hysterical personality disorders. Such excesses in behavior have been controlled via instructions, feedback (negative and positive), time-out, token economy, response cost, and contingency contracting. Application of operant techniques has had its most consistent effect in residential (e.g., Cohen & Filipczak, 1971) and inpatient-type settings (cf. Marks, Cameron, & Silberfeld, 1971; Pieczenik & Birk, 1974). In dealing with excesses in behavior, the framework and inherent control of the institutional setting are facilitative.

Often, the social skills approach has been employed in complementary fashion with contingency management techniques. It is absolutely clear that by decreasing the aversive aspects of the personality disorder's behavior, only one-half of the job has been accomplished. To achieve some semblance of permanence and to ensure generalization outside of the institutional setting, new patterns of behavior are required. A careful behavioral analysis of the personality disorder invariably reveals very severe deficits (e.g., Freedman, Rosenthal, Donahoe, Schlundt, & McFall, 1978). It is not so much that the current behavior of the individual is aversive to "polite society," but that he or she simply does not possess a different (and more acceptable) repertoire of responses (cf. Blanchard & Hersen, 1976). The repetitive and inadequate pattern displayed represents a case of faulty learning and overlearning that has been reinforced, albeit only periodically (i.e., by a partial reinforcement schedule).

Most recently, social skill training techniques have been used with increasing regularity to teach new behaviors in a variety of individuals bearing diagnoses of a personality disorder (e.g., Argyle, Trower, & Bryant, 1974; Foy, Eisler, & Pinkston, 1975; Hersen, 1979; Marzillier, Lambert, & Kellett; 1976; Ollendick & Hersen, 1979). Among the disorders treated are: explosive personalities, chronically angry individuals, juvenile delinquents, and those labeled passive or socially inadequate. Generally, the skills approach (formerly referred to as assertiveness training) has consisted of instructions, behavior rehearsal, practice, modeling, and social reinforcement contingent on evidence of small improvements. Not only have clients and patients been taught to express angry feelings in socially acceptable ways, but they have been taught to express positive feelings as well when indicated (see Bellack & Hersen, 1979).

In considering the behavioral approach to the personality disorder, we examined case reports, within-subject analyses (single and group), short-term group outcome studies, and longer-term group outcome studies. Our review is not exhaustive but focuses on the most relevant strategies used to date. Most of the review of these case reports is devoted to evaluation of the work done with adults. Indeed, there is a vast literature on behavioral strategies implemented with junvenile delinquents, which has received periodic and very satisfactory review (see Braukmann & Fixsen, 1975; Burchard & Harig, 1976). To replicate these excellent reviews would serve no useful purpose. Rather, when looking at juvenile delinquency as an example of personality disorders, we selected prototypical programs (CASE II MODEL: Cohen & Filipczak, 1971; Achievement Place: Phillips, 1968) and evaluated their therapeutic contribution.

Operant Strategies

In an integrated series of reports, Colman and his colleagues (Boren & Colman, 1970; Colman, 1971; Colman & Baker, 1969; Colman & Boren, 1969) have described the development and implementation of an operantly-run psychiatric ward for delinquent soldiers hospitalized at Walter Reed General Hospital. Throughout the course of the study, 48 soldiers, diagnosed as cases of character and behavior disorders, participated. These soldiers, as a consequence of their acting-out behavior in the military (e.g., suicidal threats, homicidal threats, interpersonal difficulties with peers and authority figures) had been hospitalized. As indicated by Colman (1971), the subjects in his study typify those individuals who frequently receive administrative discharges from the service. They also constitute 40% of the psychiatric admissions to general hospitals serving the army. Generally, these soldiers have had lengthy histories of failure in school, difficulties with the law, job problems, and overall interpersonal maladjustment.

The behavioral unit was a 24-hour point economy, with points awarded for educational, occupational, and "group skills." In light of the soldiers' deficient histories in school, considerable emphasis was given to educational activities. Points were exchangeable for a large menu of reinforcers such as television time, passes, and additional educational opportunities. The system also involved fines for inappropriate behavior but apparently were infrequently applied. In addition, the ward was organized on a levels basis, with level II patients essentially given "carte blanche" privileges after evidencing 10 weeks of appropriate behavior. However, to maintain level II status, patients had to evince leadership qualities (e.g., teaching courses, running the unit in the evenings). The ward staff consisted of two sergeants, one occupational therapist, a psychiatric resident, a psychiatrist, and nine enlisted men who served as psychiatric technicians. The follow-up team involved two social workers (one full-time; one half-time) and a psychologist.

Although most of the empirical data reported by Colman and colleagues resulted from within-subject analyses, data for a comparable group of soldiers treated on a traditional psychiatric ward at Walter Reed were available. However, data from the two groups are not directly comparable inasmuch as the traditional group only spent an average of four weeks in the hospital. By contrast, soldiers on the behavioral unit spent an average of 16 weeks and were followed up periodically at 3-month intervals. At the conclusion of their hospital stay, one-half of the soldiers on the traditional unit had received administrative discharges from the service. None received such a discharge from the behavioral unit. At the three-month posthospital follow-up, the success rate (i.e., functioning in the army or having successfully completed a tour of duty) for the behavioral unit was 69.5%; 30.5% had failed (i.e., been administratively discharged, AWOL, or in the stockade). By contrast, the respective success and failure rates for the traditionally treated group were much poorer: 28.3% and 71.7%. It is clear that those treated behaviorally did better; but, of course, the extra time and attention afforded patients on the behavioral unit are a confound and do not allow for a definitive comparative statement of superiority.

In a number of within-subject analyses, Boren and Colman (1970) first documented that by increasing the number of points awarded from 4 to 20 to 30, an increased percentage of men participated in one of the ward activities (e.g., a one-half mile run). The addition of a model who participated in the run did not yield a further increment. This may have been due to the fact that the model was an officer and a physician, thus a definite authority figure. Considering the soldiers' past relationship with authority figures, the negative effects of modeling are understandable.

In the second experiment (an A-B-A-B design), the imposition of a 10-point fine for remaining in bed not only failed to improve attendance at the ward unit meeting, but actually led to a substantial decrease in attendance. As noted by Boren and Colman (1970), "These patients reportedly had past histories of destructive behavior in response to aversive control. Thus, working with physically mature and aggressive individuals in the open setting decreased the possible utility of punishment" (p. 32). In a third experiment, a chaining procedure was implemented to increase attendance at the unit meeting. In order to earn points for any other activity during the day, attendance at the meeting was required. As might be expected, this contingency resulted in an increase in attendance from 38 to 87%. In the fourth experiment, an individual versus a group contingency was contrasted with regard to increasing verbal participation at the unit meeting. Results indicated the superiority of the individual contingency. And finally, in the fifth study, point reinforcement was shown to be much more effective in eliciting soldiers' comments about their personal problems in group meetings than a social reinforcement contingency consisting of approving comments from the staff.

From these five experiments, it is clear that contingency management techniques (e.g., token economy) are efficacious with this type of subject population. However, social reinforcement, modeling, and punishment strategies (i.e., fines) do not appear to modify behavior. The soldiers' prior reinforcement histories undoubtedly, in part, account for these findings. Certainly, the greater the structure imposed (in the form of a very specific positive contingency), the better the results appear to be.

A substantial number of inmates in correctional facilities also bear the diagnostic labels of personality and character disorders. In attempts to remediate some of the behavioral problems evidenced by such inmates, token economies have been established in these settings (cf. Bassett & Blanchard, 1977; Bassett, Blanchard, & Koshland, 1975; Lawson, Greene, Richardson, McClure, & Padina, 1971). The establishment of contingency management programs in institutional settings has come under considerable criticism in the last few years (see Hersen, 1976; Kazdin, 1977 for discussion of the issues). Not only have criticisms been leveled at the artificial state of deprivation brought about by the token economy, but concern has been expressed over those very behaviors that have been selected for change. In some instances, the token economy in penal settings has been directed toward maintaining "institutional tranquility" rather than toward teaching inmates behaviors that will enhance their success in regular society. Indeed, in a socially significant within-subject analysis, Bassett and Blanchard (1977) demonstrated that in the absence of close supervision by the investigators, staff at the penal farm (program run under token economic lines) substantially increased their use of response cost (i.e., fines). By contrast, when the investigators were present, response cost levies dropped considerably. Thus, it is undeniable that the possibility for abusing contingency management systems in penal systems is very much present.

Very cognizant of these viable criticisms of the application of token economy in prisons, Bassett et al. (1975) developed a 16-hour-per-day supervised contingency management environment (in a county penal farm) that was devoted to targeting behaviors that might be of value in the "free world" (e.g., viewing and understanding television news programs; increasing attendance at evening remedial education courses). In the first within-subject analysis, the effects of instructions, noncontingent quizzes, and contingent quizzes (points awarded for correct answers) were evaluated with respect to the percentage time for watching television news programs and understanding the content of that news. The results of the study indicated that the contingency condition led to the best results. In the second within-subject analysis, awarding of bonus points for attending remedial education classes proved effective in increasing the number of participants.

In discussing the value of their work, Bassett et al. (1975) argue:

. . . what these two studies show, and the relatively novel contribution they make, is that it is possible to target and increase the rates of behavior which have potential benefits to prisoners once they return to the "free world" *while they are still incarcerated.* This last point is a large part of what rehabilitation should be about, in our opinion. This study has shown that it is possible, and we believe is highly desirable, to maintain adaptive "free world" behaviors at a high rate while a man is in prison through the use of contingent reinforcement [p. 647].

However, to ensure generalization into the community postprison, such behaviors, of course, would have to be prompted, modeled, and reinforced. Given that many prisoners return to their former peer groups, this is a rather unlikely consequence.

Let us now turn to the use of operant techniques with juvenile delinquents. Probably the most exciting of these programs developed was the CASE II MODEL (Contingencies Applicable to Special Education-Motivationally Oriented Designs for an Ecology of Learning) by Cohen and Filipczak (1971) at the National Training School for Boys in Washington, D.C. During the project year, 41 convicted male juvenile offenders participated. Offenses included assault, homicide, robbery, housebreaking, petty larceny, auto theft, and so forth. The mean age of these boys was 16.9. Despite the wide differences of their legal offenses, they all shared a common feature—failure in school.

Thus, Cohen and Filipczak (1971) developed a 24-hour-a-day living and learning environment using a point economy system. As in most such economies, points were exchangeable for material goods and privileges. However, to motivate these boys, deprivation tactics were not employed. Rather, points had purchase power for luxuries not readily available (e.g., special meals, private rooms, special leisure time activities). The most unusual feature of CASE II was that most points were earned for displaying academic achievements. As Cohen and Filipczak (1971) argued:

> . . . educational behavior is functionally related to its consequences and that—by setting up a situation in which appropriate consequences are made contingent upon changing behavioral requirements—these behaviors can be established, altered, maintained, and transferred [pp. 5–6].

Indeed, the investigators were able to confirm the aforementioned with their data.

Using teaching machines (i.e., programmed self-instruction), a sequentially arranged course of instruction was established. However, individual attention to students was available when needed. Topics covered were as follows: reading, language usage, science, social studies, and mathematics. To move up the sequence of programmed instruction, a 90% level or better was required for a passing mark. Of course, as the student moved up in the sequence, the educational material was made progressively more difficult (i.e., shaping).

Pre-post data for 19 boys who spent more than 90 days in the program showed a 16.2 increment in IQ scores (i.e., an increase of more than one standard deviation). Ninety percent of 36 students in a six-month period evidenced a *four year* grade level increase in at least one subject. Without going into further laborious detail, these are typical of the kinds of results obtained by the investigators.

Unfortunately, no formal comparison group was planned on a prospective basis. Nevertheless, the results for CASE II were far superior to those obtained in the regular National Training School (NTS) Program for boys who had committed similar offenses. Also, despite the fact that education in CASE II was specifically targeted, comparative recidivism data for CASE II and NTS students definitely indicated superiority for those attending CASE II (i.e., two-thirds less recidivism for the first year postprogram). However, by the third year the rates were equal. Nonetheless, these figures are most impressive given that no specific effort was directed to maintain gains in the natural environment. Moreover, even at the third year postprogram follow-up, there was considerable evidence of retention at the educational-academic level for CASE II students. We certainly consider CASE II as a landmark program of behavioral application.

Another landmark program, involving the use of operant principles in treating juvenile delinquents, was developed by psychologists at the University of Kansas (Phillips, 1968; Phillips, Phillips, Fixsen, & Wolf, 1971; Phillips, Phillips, Wolf, & Fixsen, 1973). This program is based "in a home-style" residence and is referred to as *Achievement Place*. The concept of a home-style residence with "house parents" was intended to overcome the deleterious effects of placing juvenile offenders into larger institutions, where further instances of criminal behavior invariably are learned by modeling older peers.

Boys attending Achievement Place were between 12 to 14 years of age and had committed the following offenses: theft, truancy, fighting, and general disruptive behavior. The two house parents administered points to the boys for engaging in positive behaviors (e.g., reading books—5 to 10 points per page; performing homework—500 per day; doing dishes—500 to 1000 per meal; maintaining personal neatness—500 per day). Infractions of the rules led to fines (e.g., speaking aggressively—20 to 50 points; stealing, lying, or cheating—10,000 points; being late—10 points per minute).

In one set of nicely designed within-subject analyses, Phillips (1968) documented the controlling effects of the point economy for reducing hostile statements, improving punctuality, decreasing the use of the word "ain't," and improving bathroom cleanliness. In a second series of studies, Phillips et al. (1971) showed that the point economy increased promptness at meals, increased the boy's personal savings, and improved attendance at televised news programs. In still a third investigation, use of a "manager" selected from the group of boys to administer the point economy (i.e., to supervise tasks, award points, levy fines) was evaluated (Phillips, et al., 1973). The manager elected by peers proved to be more effective than one who had been selected via auction by bidding the most points for that position.

As previously summarized elsewhere,

Taken together, the studies conducted by Phillips and his colleagues illustrate the comprehensive use of operant techniques with regard to most aspects of predelinquents' lives in a home-style residential setting. These studies are particularly important inasmuch as they show the efficacy of operant techniques in reversing the usual negative reinforcement contingencies operating in institutional settings for the delinquent. The data clearly indicate that comprehensive behavioral programs for delinquents can be directed toward shaping and reinforcing behaviors that are considered to be appropriate for extra-institutional living in the community [Bellack & Hersen, 1977, pp. 357–358].

Social Skills Training

Since the earlier study carried out by Eisler, Hersen, and Miller (1974), several experimental, single case analyses (Hersen & Barlow, 1976) have appeared in the literature documenting the effectiveness of social skills training for reducing aggressiveness and teaching alternative modes of responses to individuals labeled passive-aggressive (Elder, Edelstein, & Narick, 1979; Foy, Eisler, & Pinkston, 1975; Frederiksen, Jenkins, Foy, & Eisler, 1976; King, Liberman, Roberts, & Bryan, 1977). Not only do these single case analyses show the value of teaching such individuals more socially appropriate ways of expressing angry feelings, but they underscore the importance of delineating aggressiveness and assertiveness (cf. De Giovanni & Epstein, 1978). Both types of responses, of course, are effective in bringing about behavioral change in one's interpersonal partner. However, as previously noted by Hersen (1979), "only assertiveness is both effective and appropriate."

Foy et al. (1975) describe a study in which modeled assertion was effective in reducing explosive rages in a 56-year-old, twice-married carpenter. Dealing with perceived "unreasonable demands from others," this patient typically responded with verbal abuse and assaultiveness. He had beaten his wife on a number of occasions and was separated from her at the time of the study.

A baseline assessment of role-played situations depicting conflictual relationships evidenced the following behaviors that needed modification: hostile comments, com-

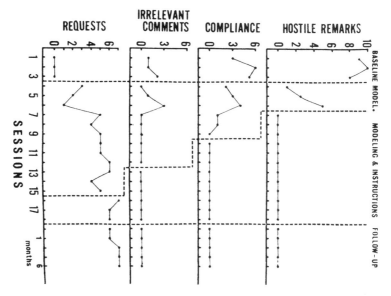

FIGURE 1. Target assertive behaviors during the four phases. From Foy et al., 1975.

pliance with unreasonable requests, irrelevant comments, and absence of requests for the interpersonal partner to change his/her behavior. Thus, each of the four behaviors was targeted for change in a multiple baseline design across behaviors. As is apparent from the data presented in Figure 1, modeling led to changes in the four targeted behaviors, with consolidation of gains achieved with the addition of instructions. Five follow-ups conducted over a six-month period showed that gains were maintained. Also, on the basis of the patient's verbal report, general interpersonal functioning in work and home-related situations seemed to have undergone improvement.

In an extension of this work, Frederiksen et al. (1976) applied social skills training, consisting of instructions, feedback, behavior rehearsal, and modeling, to decrease verbal abusiveness in two hospitalized psychiatric patients. Using a multiple baseline design across subjects, the following behaviors were targeted for change: eye contact, irrelevant and hostile comments, inappropriate and appropriate requests. As a consequence of treatment, all targeted behaviors improved both in training and in generalization scenes that were role played. Also, not only was there generalization of improvements from an original to a new role model (during the course of role-played interactions), but there was good evidence of generalization to stage *in vivo* situations on the ward that previously might have elicited inappropriate outbursts.

King et al. (1977) employed a variant of social skills training (i.e., personal effectiveness training) in a case of a 25-year-old married male, who periodically displayed rage reactions in spite of the fact that generally he was described as "docile and passive." Hierarchies of items in three different settings in which he experienced difficulties were constructed. Thus the dependent measure in each setting was the number of items successfully completed in the hierarchy. The effects of training were evaluated in a multiple baseline design across settings, with resulting data attesting to the controlling effects of the skills strategy on a time-lagged basis.

In a more recent study, Elder et al. (1979) reported on the use of a multiple baseline design across behaviors to evaluate the effects of social skill training in four aggressive adolescent psychiatric inpatients. Resulting data indicated the efficacy of the approach both in terms of trained and untrained situations. Moreover, generalization to the ward setting was observed, as indicated by a decreased need to find and seclude these patients in the token economy program. At the three-month posttreatment follow-up, three of the four patients had been discharged from the hospital and subsequently remained in the community for nine months.

Let us now turn to the evaluation of the skills training approach in controlled group outcome studies in which a number of behavioral and nonbehavioral treatments for personality disordered individuals have been contrasted. Argyle, Bryant, and Trower (1974) compared social skills training with psychoanalytically oriented psychotherapy in a crossover design that controlled for drug effects and spontaneous improvements. Patients treated experienced interpersonal difficulties and ranged in age from 17 to 50. After a three week period of assessment, four patients received 6 sessions of social-skills treatment over a period of six weeks or 18 sessions of psychotherapy over a period of six weeks. Subsequently, some six weeks later, another set of four patients was assigned to the two therapies.

The primary dependent measure used to evaluate results of this study was a 17-item social skill rating scale. Results of the study showed that both social skills and psychotherapy were equally effective in bringing about behavioral change. However, considering that psychotherapy patients had three times as much therapy, the skills approach appears to be more cost effective. But, given the small numbers of patients treated in this investigation, results must be interpreted with some caution.

In a relatively recent study, Trower, Yardley, Bryant, and Shaw (1978) evaluated the effects of systematic desensitization and social skills training with 20 phobic patients and 20 socially unskilled patients (some of whom had personality disorders). Ten patients in each of the two diagnostic categories received 10 sessions of skills training or systematic desensitization. Results revealed that systematic desensitization and skills training were equally effective for phobic patients. However, for socially unskilled patients, the skills approach proved to be superior. Thus, when skill deficits are present, a remedial procedure that teaches individuals new behaviors is indicated (see Hersen, 1979).

Somewhat less positive findings were obtained by Marzillier et al. (1976) in a study contrasting desensitization, social skills training, and a waiting list control condition conducted with 21 patients diagnosed as socially inadequate. Both systematic desensitization and social skills treatment resulted in improvements in the social lives of patients that were maintained for the social skill training group at the six-month follow-up. However, neither of the two treatments resulted in greater anxiety reduction, clinical adjustment, or improved social skills than the waiting list controls.

On the other hand, Ollendick and Hersen (1979) recently showed that social skills training (consisting of instructions, feedback, modeling, behavior rehearsal, social reinforcement, and graduated homework assignments) was superior to a discussion or control condition for juvenile delinquents who were residents of a training center. Delinquents in the skills condition evidenced the following improvements: a learning of new interpersonal skills, a reduced state of anxiety, an increase in their locus of internal control, and better adjustment to the institutional program.

Finally, in an earlier study contrasting assertion training (conducted in a group context) with a placebo group condition for male volunteers reporting problems expressing anger in inappropriate fashion, a significant improvement of the assertion training group over the placebo condition was evidenced (Rimm, Hill, Brown, & Stuart, 1974). That is, assertion training conducted over a total of eight hours led to improvements in *subjective* measures of discomfort and anger. However, there are some methodological problems with this study in that the three therapists were the same for both treatment conditions.

Combined Approaches

During the course of clinical practice, behavioral techniques rarely are applied in singular fashion. Rather, they tend to be used concurrently or in sequence. At times, they even may be applied in conjunction with drugs (cf. Liberman & Davis, 1975) or within the context of other ongoing programs (e.g., as supplements to an inpatient ward milieu). This is the case for the behavioral group treatment of hysterical personality disorder described by Kass et al. (1972). That is, a pilot study, using several behavioral strategies concurrently in the context of inpatient milieu therapy, was conducted with five young women, each of whom had made suicidal gestures and presented with histrionic features. Admittedly, this particular type of personality disorder is exceedingly difficult to treat successfully with traditional psychotherapeutic strategies.

Very much aware of this problem, Kass et al. (1972) arranged a program that included the following features: (*a*) the five patients lived together in a large room; (*b*) were expected to identify those behaviors (i.e., hysterical) considered maladaptive; (*c*) were asked to make up daily schedules that were most likely to elicit each other's adaptive responses; (*d*) were asked to provide positive and negative feedback, fines, and other environmental contingencies to extinguish unadaptive behavior (e.g., suicidal threats, hostility, aggressiveness, pouting, seductiveness, manipulativeness, etc.); and (*e*) were asked to learn new and more adaptive behaviors. Behavioral techniques included: assertiveness training, feedback, negative practice, response cost, role playing, and desensitization.

Apparently, four of the five patients showed considerable symptomatic improvement, learned new and more adaptive behavioral repertoires, and did well 18 months posthospital discharge. Kass et al. (1972) contend:

. . . we have operationally defined hysteria as the type of behaviors which emerge when the patient is required to adhere to a schedule that demands responsible self-assertion. We have thus concerned ourselves with deficits, excesses, or misdirected (indirect, displaced) forms of assertion or aggression, such as the expression of suicidal impulses, physical complaints, sarcasm, withdrawal of interest, and so on. By arranging a corrective feedback system, we have assisted patients in recognizing these behaviors as unwanted—a big step towards gaining control over them. Instead of the symptomatic control of others, the patient moves towards self-control, which in this context means simply the recognition and direct expression of her needs and wishes [pp. 49–50].

However, despite the clinical successes attained, there are few hard data presented to confirm these clinical impressions.

In an empirical study, in which several behavioral techniques were combined, Sloane, Staples, Cristol, Yorkston, and Whipple (1975) contrasted short-term psychoanalytically oriented psychotherapy with behavior therapy and a waiting list control condition. Of the 94 patients in this study, one-third had diagnoses of personality disorder, while two-thirds were labeled neurotic. From the results obtained, very specific statements as to the effects of treatment on personality disorder alone are not available. Also, given that desensitization, assertivenesss training, and aversion therapy were combined in many instances, the specific effects of each strategy on personality disordered individuals are not known.

In any event, patients in behavior therapy had an average of 13.2 one hour treatment sessions; patients in psychotherapy had an average of 14.2 one hour treatment sessions. In general, the results showed that both behavior therapy and psychotherapy patients were significantly more improved than waiting list controls on a four month pre-post basis. Behavior therapy patients showed improvement on target symptoms, work adjustment, and social adjustment. Psychotherapy patients showed little improvement on work adjustment and none on social functioning. However, at the one-year follow-up there were fewer differences between behavior therapy and psychotherapy patients. Sloane et al. (1975) concluded that, "There was very little difference between the two active treatment groups in amount of improvement, although it is tempting to argue that behavior therapy was somewhat more effective than psychotherapy" (p. 376). Our analysis of these results is similar, but we would argue that the behavioral approach is both more direct and effective in bringing about social adjustment in personality disordered and neurotic individuals.

Summary of Behavioral Treatment

Behavioral intervention strategies, primarily contingency management procedures and social skills training, have been employed in inpatient and outpatient settings with favorable results. The comprehensive residential programs described by Colman (1971), Cohen and Filipczak (1971), Phillips and his colleagues (Phillips, 1968; Phillips et al., 1971; Phillips et al., 1973) are particularly impressive. The fact that the studies reported here cover a wide variety of patients (juveniles, military, adult psychiatric inpatients and outpatients) as well as diverse diagnostic categories (e.g., hysterical, passive-aggressive) lend support to the use of behavioral techniques with the personality disorders.

As alluded to previously, simply decreasing or controlling deviant behaviors in these individuals represents only part of the job. Therefore, programs or strategies combining contingency management procedures and social skills training are more likely to produce favorable results. However, it should be pointed out that the studies reported here are plagued by many of the same problems seen in other areas of the clinical literature. In some instances, the diagnostic categories employed in the studies are mixed, and in some instances, it is not clear just what specific behavior is modified. Thus, we cannot answer the all-important question of what particular procedure is most effective in treating what particular disorder. As a further cautionary note, it seems that aversive procedures are particularly inappropriate in treating the personality disorder (e.g., Colman, 1971). Similarly, the importance of interpersonal relationship variables in the therapeutic process on outcome is evident (e.g., Colman, 1971; Pieczenik & Birk, 1974). In this regard, it is interesting to note that Elery Phillips in a recent address at the 1978 AABT (Association for Advancement of Behavior Therapy) convention commented that in the Achievement Place Model, he found that one of the most crucial variables in relation to positive outcome was the relationship between peer counselor and resident. In fact, according to Phillips, this is the single most important variable. Thus it behooves the behavioral clinician to be cognizant of this issue.

The socially deviant or antisocial behavior exhibited by the personality disorder varies in intensity from mild to severe. They may show simple obnoxious, verbal behavior toward others, or exhibit dangerous physical aggression. They may also exhibit superficial wrist cutting behavior or more serious attempts to take their own life by ingesting toxic substances. With the more severely disordered individual, particularly the hysteric, care must be exercised in attempting to bring high-rate deviant behaviors under control. An example of the suicidal gesture in the hysterical patient will serve to illustrate our point. It seems clear that in many cases these gestures are attempts to exert control over the environment (Bostock & Williams, 1974). But the more severe cases of this nature present problems that may make the use of operant strategies detrimental. Attempts to get this operant behavior under control could further frustrate such patients, driving them to make more serious suicidal attempts or to resort to other more deviant behavior. For the most severe cases of personality disorder, we are of the opinion that structured environments such as the ones described above are more likely to produce favorable results. For those individuals, sufficient control of the environment is necessary in order to allow for the learning of new responses to replace the more deviant ones.

SUMMARY

Despite the difficulty in diagnosing the syndromes typically referred to as personality disorders in the psychiatric nomenclature, it would appear that such disorders *do in fact exist*. There has been considerable controversy over whether or not behavior is a function of certain characteristics or traits that are consistent across time and situation, or whether behavior is solely a function of situational stimuli. It appears that at least some behaviors in some individuals remain fairly consistent across time and situation whereas some behavior appears situationally specific.

Moreover, those studies supporting consistency demonstrate that it is more likely to occur when pathological behavior is evident.

The concept of personality or behavioral consistency is not antithetical to behavioral theory. To the contrary, behavioral theory provides a much more parsimonious explanation for personality disorders in that they are defined in terms of social behavior. Social behavior is a function of the individual's complex social learning history and the schedules of reinforcement to which he has been subjected.

Behavioral strategies, primarily contingency management and social skills training, have shown some promise in remediating personality difficulties. This is true when treatment is carried out on an outpatient basis or in a residential setting with a variety of populations. Treatment of the severe personality disorder, when such problems as suicide or aggression are exhibited, is best conducted in a residential setting where environmental contingencies may be controlled by the therapist.

ACKNOWLEDGMENT

The authors thank Karen Ketchum for her assistance in preparing this chapter.

REFERENCES

Abse, D. W. Hysterical Conversion and dissociative syndromes and the hysterical character. In S. Arieti and E. Brody (Eds.), *American Handbook of Psychiatry,* 1974, **111**, 155–194.

Adams, H. E. *Psychology of abnormal behavior.* Dubuque, Iowa: Wm. C. Brown, in press.

Allport, G. W. *Personality: A psychological interpretation.* New York: Holt, Rinehart, & Winston, 1937.

Alarcon, R. D. Hysteria and hysterical personality. *Psychiatric Quarterly,* 1973, **47**, 258–275.

American Psychiatric Association. Diagnostic and statistical manual of mental disorders (DSM-III). Washington, D.C.: American Psychiatric Association, 1980.

Argyle, M., Bryant, B., & Trower, P. Social skills training and psychotherapy. *Psychological Medicine,* 1974, **4**, 435–443.

Argyle, M., Trower, P., & Bryant, B. Exploration in the treatment of personality disorders and neuroses by social skills training. *British Journal of Medical Psychology,* 1974, **47**, 63–72.

Bandura, A., & Walters, R. H. *Social learning and personality development.* New York: Holt, Rinehart, & Winston, 1963.

Bassett, J. E., & Blanchard, E. B. The effect of the absence of close supervision on the use of response cost in a prison token economy. *Journal of Applied Behavior Analysis,* 1977, **10**, 375–379.

Bassett, J. E., Blanchard, E. B., & Koshland, E. Applied behavior analysis in a penal setting: Targeting "free world" behaviors. *Behavior Therapy,* 1975, **6**, 639–648.

Bellack, A. S., & Hersen, M. (Eds.). *Research and practice in social skills training.* New York: Plenum Press, 1979.

Bellack, A. S., & Hersen, M. *Behavior modification: An introductory textbook.* Baltimore, Md.: Williams & Wilkins, 1977.

Black, A. The natural history of obsessional neurosis. In H. R. Beech (Ed.), *Obsessional States.* London: Methuen, 1974.

Blanchard, E. B., & Hersen, M. Behavioral treatment of hysterical neurosis: Symptom substitution and symptom return reconsidered. *Psychiatry,* 1976, **39**, 118–129.

Boren, J. J., & Colman, A. D. Some experiments on reinforcement principles within a psychiatric ward for delinquent soldiers. *Journal of Applied Behavioral Analysis,* 1970, **3**, 29–37.

Bostock, T., & Williams, C. L. Attempted Suicide as an operant behavior. *Archives of General Psychiatry,* 1974, **31**, 482–486.

Bowers, K. *Situationism in psychology:* An analysis and a critique. *Psychological Review,* 1973, **80**, 307–336.

Braukmann, C. J., & Fixsen, D. L. Behavior modification with delinquents. In M. Hersen, R. M. Eisler, & P. M. Miller (Eds.), *Progress in behavior modification: Volume 1.* New York: Academic Press, 1975.

Burchard, J. D., & Harig, P. T. Behavior modification and juvenile delinquency. In H. Leitenberg (Ed.), *Handbook of behavior modification and behavior therapy.* Englewood Cliffs, N.J.: Prentice-Hall, 1976.

Chodoff, P. The diagnosis of hysteria: An overview. *American Journal of Psychiatry,* 1974, **131**, 1073–1078.

Cohen, H. L., & Filipczak, J. *A new learning environment.* San Francisco: Jossey–Bass, 1971.

Colman, A. D. *The planned environment in psychiatric treatment: A manual for ward design.* Springfield, Ill.: Charles C. Thomas, 1971.

Colman, A. D., & Baker, S. L. Utilization of an operant conditioning model for the treatment of character and behavior disorders in a military setting. *American Journal of Psychiatry,* 1969, **125**, 1395–1403.

Colman, A. D., & Boren, J. J. An information system for measuring patient behavior and its use by staff. *Journal of Applied Behavior Analysis,* 1969, **2**, 207–214.

Covi, L., & Alessi, L. Pharmacological treatment of personality disorders. In J. R. Lion (Ed.), *Personality disorder: Diagnosis and management.* Baltimore, Md.: Williams & Wilkins, 1974.

De Giovanni, I. S., & Epstein, N. Unbinding assertion and aggression in research and clinical practice. *Behavior Modification,* 1978, **2**, 173–192.

Eisler, R. M., Hersen, M., & Miller, P. M. Shaping components of assertiveness with instructions and feedback. *American Journal of Psychiatry,* 1974, **131**, 1344–1347.

Elder, J. P., Edelstein, B. A., & Narick, M. M. Social skills training in the modification of aggressive behavior of adolescent psychiatric patients. *Behavior Modification,* 1979, **3**, 161–178.

Endler, N. S. The person versus the situation—a pseudo issue? A response to Alka. *Journal of Personality,* 1973, **41**, 287–303.

Eysenck, H. J. *The structure of human personality.* London: Methuen, 1970.

Eysenck, H. J., & Eysenck, S. B. G. *Personality structure and measurement.* London: Kegan Paul, 1969.

Foy, D. W., Eisler, R. M., & Pinkston, S. Modeled assertion in a case of explosive rages. *Journal of Behavior Therapy and Experimental Psychiatry,* 1975, **6**, 135–137.

Frederiksen, L. W., Jenkins, J. O., Foy, D. W., & Eisler, R. M. Social-skills training to modify abusive verbal outbursts in adults. *Journal of Applied Behavior Analysis,* 1976, **9**, 117–125.

Freedman, A., Kaplan, M., & Sadock, B. *Modern synopsis of comprehensive textbook of psychiatry.* Baltimore, Md.: Williams & Wilkins, 1972.

Freedman, B. J., Rosenthal, L., Donahoe, C. P., Schlundt, D. G., & McFall, R. M. A social-behavioral analysis of skill deficits in delinquent and nondelinquent adolescent boys. *Journal of Consulting and Clinical Psychology,* 1978, **46**, 1448–1462.

Hersen, M. Token economies in institutional settings. *Journal of Nervous and Mental Disease,* 1976, **162**, 206–211.

Hersen, M. Modification of skill deficits in psychiatric patients. In A. S. Bellack & M. Hersen (Eds.), *Research and practice in social skills training.* New York: Plenum Press, 1979.

Hersen, M., & Barlow, D. H. *Single case experimental designs: Strategies for studying behavior change.* New York: Pergamon Press, 1976.

Kass, D. J., Silvers, F. M., & Abrams, G. M. Behavioral group treatment of hysteria. *Archives of General Psychiatry,* 1972, **26**, 42–50.

Kazdin, A. E. *The token economy: A review and evaluation.* New York: Plenum Press, 1977.

King, L. W., Liberman, R. P., Roberts, J., & Bryan, E. Personal effectiveness: A structured therapy for improving social and emotional skills. *European Journal of Behavioural Analysis and Modification,* 1977, **2**, 82–91.

Kraft, A. M. The therapeutic community. In S. Arieti (Ed.), *American handbook of psychiatry.* New York: Basic Books, 1966.

Lawson, R. B., Greene, R. T., Richardson, J. S., McClure, G., & Padina, R. J. Token economy program in a maximum security correctional hospital. *Journal of Nervous and Mental Disease,* 1971, **152**, 199–205.

Liberman, R. P., & Davis, J. Drugs and behavior analysis. In M. Hersen, R. M. Eisler, and P. M. Miller (Eds.), *Progress in behavior modification: Volume I.* New York: Academic Press, 1975.

Liebman, M. C., & Hedlund, D. A. Therapeutic community and milieu therapy of personality disorders. In J. R. Lion (Ed.), *Personality disorder: Diagnosis and management.* Baltimore, Md.: Williams & Wilkins, 1974.

Lion, J. R. Diagnosis and treatment of personality disorders. In J. R. Lion (Ed.), *Personality disorder: Diagnosis and management.* Baltimore, Md.: Williams & Wilkins, 1974.

Marks, I. M., Cameron, P. M., & Silberfeld, M. Operant therapy for an abnormal personality. *British Medical Journal,* 1971, **1**, 647, 648.

Marzillier, J. S., Lambert, C., & Kellett, J. A controlled evaluation of systematic desensitization and social skills training for socially inadequate psychiatric patients. *Behaviour Research and Therapy,* 1976, **14**, 225–238.

Mischel, W. *Personality and assessment.* New York: John Wiley, 1968.

Mischel, W. Toward a cognitive social learning reconceptualization of personality. *Psychological Review,* 1973, **80**, 252–283.

Ollendick, T. H., & Hersen, M. Social skills training for juvenile delinquents. *Behaviour Research and Therapy,* 1979, **17**, 547–555.

O'Neil, M., & Kempler, B. Approach and avoidance responses of the hysterical personality to sexual stimuli. *Journal of Abnormal Personality,* 1969, **74**, 300–305.

Pasternack, S. A. The explosive, antisocial, and passive-aggressive personalities. In J. R. Lion (Ed.), *Personality disorder: Diagnosis and management.* Baltimore, Md.: Williams & Wilkins, 1974.

Phillips, E. L. Achievement place: Token reinforcement procedures in a home-style rehabilitation setting for "predelinquent" boys. *Journal of Applied Behavior Analysis,* 1968, **1**, 213–223.

Phillips, E. L., Phillips, E. A., Fixsen, D. L., & Wolf, M. M. Achievement place: Modification of the behaviors of predelinquent boys within a token economy. *Journal of Applied Behavior Analysis,* 1971, **4**, 45–59.

Phillips, E. L., Phillips, E. A., Wolf, M. M., & Fixsen, D. L. Achievement place: Development of the elected manager system. *Journal of Applied Behavior Analysis,* 1973, **6**, 541–561.

Pieczenik, S., & Birk, L. Behavior therapy of personality disorders. In J. R. Lion (Ed.), *Personality disorders: Diagnosis and management.* Baltimore, Md.: Williams & Wilkins, 1974.

Rimm, D. C., Hill, G. A., Brown, N. N., & Stuart, J. E. Group-assertive training in treatment of expression of inappropriate anger. *Psychological Reports,* 1974, **34**, 791–798.

Rounsville, B., Harding, P., & Weissman, M. Single case study: Briquet's syndrome in a man. *Journal of Nervous and Mental Disease,* 1979, **167**, 364–367.

Salzman, L. Other character-personality syndromes: Schizoid, inadequate, passive aggressive, paranoid, dependent. In S. Arieti and E. Brody (Eds.), *American Handbook of Psychiatry,* 1974, **111**, 224–234.

Sloane, R., Staples, F. R., Cristol, A. H., Yorkston, N. J., & Whipple, K. Short-term analytically oriented psychotherapy versus behavior therapy. *American Journal of Psychiatry,* 1975, **132**, 373–377.

Stainbrook, E. Milieu therapy—the hospital as a therapeutic community. In A. Freedman & H. Kaplan (Eds.), *Comprehensive Textbook of Psychiatry.* Baltimore, Md.: Williams & Wilkins, 1967.

Trower, P., Yardley, K., Bryant, B. M., & Shaw, P. The treatment of social failure. A comparison of anxiety-reduction and skills-acquisition procedures on two social problems. *Behavior Modification,* 1978, **2**, 41–60.

Veith, I. *Hysteria: The history of a disease.* Chicago: The University of Chicago Press, 1965.

Woodruff, R. A., Goodwin, D. W., & Guze, S. B. *Psychiatric diagnosis.* New York: Oxford University Press, 1974.

CHAPTER 6

Affective Disorders Behavioral Perspectives

Tracey Potts Carson and Henry E. Adams

Affective disorders, while historically viewed as perplexing and relatively impregnable to direct intervention, have been recognized in recent years as solvable human dilemmas. As a subset of emotional disorders involving specifically the emotions of depression and elation, affective disturbances have been a subject of rigorous investigation. Primarily, this investigation has focused on depressive phenomena. In reference to the pathological extreme of elation—known as mania or manic behavior—the available literature is sparse. Mania has not been considered a separate nosological entity, but instead has been traditionally linked with psychotic levels of depression under the rubric of manic-depressive psychoses, and more recently, bipolar affective disorders. In fact, not until the draft version of the DSM-III has psychiatric nomenclature officially recognized mania as an individual grouping of disordered behavior independent of an alternation with depressive episodes.

Research pertaining to depression seems to have burgeoned during the past decade—on sociopsychological, genetic, biochemical, pharmacological, neurophysiological, and crosscultural fronts. During this period, we have witnessed a significant increase in the attention behaviorists have devoted to the problem of depression, with a concomitant flooding of empirical investigation. As a consequence, we now have preliminary data to supplement theoretical debate and thus make initial attempts to evaluate various hypothetical constructions.

Any discourse on depression must consider the current major applications of this term. The word *depression* has been variously utilized to refer to (*a*) a set of specific behavioral events that tend to occur in a cluster and are at least moderately correlated; and (*b*) a discrete disease entity involving consistent internal events and behavioral manifestations. We adhere to the first interpretation, for reasons that will become clear in the course of our discussion. Psychiatric nomenclature ascribes to the latter usage, proposing that there exists within some individuals a distinct psychiatric illness (depression), which may be conceptualized like any other medical disease. Although this disease model of depression is somewhat in vogue, there are serious limitations to its singular application. For example, a treatment approach that emphasizes biological abnormalities could have the adverse consequence of excusing the depressed patient from attending to psychosocial variables relevant to his/her psychological distress. Depressed individuals who adopt a medical explanation for their distress and consider themselves to be victims of a physical illness may assume a very passive stance in ameliorating their life situations. Antidepressant medication may in turn acquire magical, curative attributes, at the expense of self-help efforts. Finally, relevant situational problems and behavioral deficiencies are likely to remain unchanged with an exclusively medical treatment plan.

Unfortunately, psychiatric education and diagnostic practice does not reflect much of what we now know about depression (Akiskal & McKinney, 1975). It is commonly acknowledged that individuals diagnosed as depressed do not share a homogeneous set of symptoms but instead manifest varying combinations of the symptoms suggestive of depression. In fact, any two individuals diagnosed as depressed by psychiatric criteria may present very dissimilar clinical pictures. Further, the correlation among behaviors symptomatic of depression, while usually statistically significant, is not sufficient to predict the occurrence of one depressed behavior based on the observation of another (Lewinsohn, 1975a). The concept of a discrete disease entity is not logically consistent with such variance in symptomatology across individuals. Most importantly, the disease model does not take into account the substantial body of data that implicates psychosocial factors in the causation and maintenance of depression.

The proposition that clinical depression reflects an underlying medical condition also implies a clear-cut distinction between normal and abnormal depression. The fact is we have no precise criteria for distinguishing normal from pathological depression. All people are subject to occasional bouts of sadness, variation in the intensity of sadness they experience, as well as oscillations in mood (Hinsie & Campbell, 1960; Wessman & Ricks, 1966). Certainly, moods of profound sadness with concomitant decreases in activity level and physiological change are not limited to individuals who are judged to require professional attention. In fact, a clinical picture of severe depression is considered normal in the context of certain stressors, such as the loss of a significant loved one. An acute grief reaction following a poignant loss may even be regarded as adaptive, and there seems to be little qualitative variation in symptomatology between grief and pathological depression. In the case of bereavement following a significant loss, the *duration* of the characteristic symptoms primarily determines the need for professional intervention. For example, a full depressive syndrome that is evidenced one month following the death of a loved one is considered to be a normal grief response; whereas, the same symptomatology several months subsequent to the loss warrants professional concern.

In practice, an individual's emotional behavior is evaluated with reference to several dimensions including intensity, duration, variability, and appropriateness. Thus, when emotional responses are judged to be of extreme intensity, variability, and/or duration relative to the environmental context, the individual is considered to be manifesting a disorder of affect.

Our criticism of the disease model of depression should not imply that biological and psychological perspectives are mutually incompatible. We mostly contest a heavy emphasis on medical intervention that obviates a rigorous investigation of interpersonal and experiential stressors operating in the depressed individual's life.

There is evidence suggesting that biological factors become operative at extreme levels of depression, and that their correction may be prerequisite for effective psychotherapeutic engagement. For such extreme cases, appropriate medication may be a necessary but not sufficient ingredient of successful intervention.

The purpose of this chapter is to address the problem of affective disorders from a social-learning perspective. This discourse is focused primarily on depression because of the relative paucity of literature pertaining to mania. Various issues relevant to the subject of affective disorders are delineated and discussed, with special attention given to major behavioral formulations of depression. Finally, we present a strategy for clinical intervention with depressed persons, which takes into account the heterogeneity of this group. Our discussion begins with a careful definition of the affective disorders.

DEFINITION OF AFFECTIVE DISORDERS

A pervasive *disturbance of mood* is commonly considered to be an essential, if not the primary, feature of affective disorders. Nevertheless, many patients otherwise meeting the criteria of being clinically depressed do not acknowledge a mood abnormality (Beck, 1967). This is especially the case in non-Western cultures (Marsella, 1979). Many depressed individuals instead emphasize various bodily ailments such as headaches, insomnia, fatigue, poor appetite, and constipation. Therefore, the common tendency to equate depression or affective disorder with subjective reports of mood alteration would appear to be in error. Because current nosological criteria for the affective disorders place an emphasis on mood *as described by the patient,* the diagnostic system does not adequately account for numerous depressed and elated persons who fail to acknowledge the pertinent emotional experience. In a behavioral approach, the traditional criteria for affective disorders must be revised such that there is less reliance on the patient's self-description of mood and increased attention to bodily functioning and behavioral events.

The discrepancy between acknowledged and inferred mood for some depressed or elated patients can best be explained by examining the components of an emotional response. As affective disorders by definition involve salient emotional behavior, it follows that our knowledge of *emotion* should be useful in clarifying the parameters of affective regulation. Depression and elation, emotions associated with the affective disorders, should be identifiable according to criteria established for all emotional responses.

Emotion may be operationally defined as the activity and reactivity of tissues and organs innervated by the autonomic nervous system that are associated with specific behavior patterns and/or subjective experiences of the individual (Adams, in press; Spielberger, 1966). Thus activity or reactivity of the autonomic nervous system is a necessary condition for an emotional response, but not sufficient in itself. Additionally, physiological change must be accompanied by a subjective report of emotional experience and/or observable emotional behavior—preferably, but not necessarily, both. This definition specifies three channels for assessment of the emotional response system: subjective report, behavioral, and physiological.

Specific patterns of autonomic nervous system activity or reactivity, behavioral events, and subjective reports differentiate between the various subsystems of emotion—such as anxiety, depression, anger, and elation. In general though, the differentiation of emotions is determined by behavior and/or subjective report, since specific patterns of autonomic nervous system response, with few exceptions, have not yet been clearly associated with specific types of emotions. Nevertheless, physiological change is essential to any emotional response.

If one applies the criteria for an emotional response to the measurement of affective behavior, it is possible to identify an affective disturbance without a subjective report of emotional discomfort by focusing on observable emotional behavior as well as somatic manifestations of physiological activity. As a consequence, it is possible to measure affect in individuals who do not have the use of language to communicate their mood as well as in individuals who do not verbally acknowledge their mood. According to our definition, emotion/affect always involves autonomic nervous system functioning, and, with some variation across individuals, it is expressed behaviorally and/or by verbal report. This definition, while arbitrary in some respects, conceptualizes affective responses as psychophysiological phenomena. The definition, by design, does not specify a temporal sequence or causal relationship for bodily events, behavior, and subjective experience—which remains a thorny theoretical problem.

We next address the clinical signs of depression and mania consistent with the above definition.

CLINICAL SIGNS OF AFFECTIVE DISORDERS

Throughout the psychiatric and psychological literature, it is difficult to find a single symptom or symptom combination that is universally ascribed to depression (Rehm, 1976). This also seems to be the case for mania. Nevertheless, there are a number of clinical signs that *generally* contribute to a diagnosis of depression or mania. Table 1 lists those behaviors that, in varying combinations, commonly con-Zeiss (1976) and would only add to their listing the observation that many destitute a depressive syndrome. We borrow this table from Lewinsohn, Biglan, & pressed individuals exhibit psychomotor agitation (e.g., hand wringing, pacing, restlessness). Table 2 presents in similar outline the common constituents of a manic syndrome. Individuals diagnosed as manic manifest combinations of these relevant clinical signs.

As we indicated in the previous section, physiological activity or reactivity is an essential component of any emotion. Somatic symptoms of the affective disorders may provide an indirect index of physiological change. We have also indicated that specific patterns of autonomic nervous system response, with few exceptions, have not yet been identified for specific types of emotion. A review of these exceptions will direct us to peripheral physiological measures that may discriminate depressed from nondepressed individuals.

A number of studies have investigated the relationship between depression and physiological responsivity. While a high level of autonomic arousal has been associated with agitated and retarded depression (e.g., Gatchel, McKinney, & Koe-

Table 1. Symptoms of Depression[a]

Dysphoria	Behavioral Deficits	Behavioral Excesses	Somatic Symptoms	"Cognitive" Manifestations
Feelings dominated by sadness and blueness	Minimal social participation—"I do not like being with people"	Complaints about:	Headaches	Low self-evaluation: feelings of failure, inadequacy, helplessness and powerlessness
Loss of gratification—"I no longer enjoy the things I used to"	Sits alone quietly, stays in bed much of time, does not communicate with others, does not enter into activities with others	Material problems—money, job, housing	Sleep disturbances: restless sleep, waking during night, complete wakefulness, early morning awakening	Negative expectation—"Things will always be bad for me"
Professes to have little or no feeling	Inability to do ordinary work	Material loss—money, property	Fatigue—"I get tired for no reason"	Self-blame and self criticism —"People would despise me if they knew me"
Feels constantly fatigued—"Everything is an effort"	Decreased sexual activity	The demands of others	Gastrointestinal—indigestion, constipation, weight loss	
Loss of interest in food, drink, sex, etc.	Psychomotor retardation. Speech slow, volume of speech decreased, monotone speech, whispering	Noise	Dizzy spells	
Feeling of apathy and boredom	Gait and general behavior retarded[b]	Memory, inability to concentrate, confusion	Loss of libido	
	Does not attend to grooming; neglect of personal appearance	Lack of affection from others —"No one cares about me"	Tachycardia	
	Lack of mirth response	Being lonely	Chest sensations	
		Expresses feelings of guilt and concern about:	Generalized pain	
		Making up wrongs to others	Urinary disturbances	
		Suffering caused to others		
		Not assuming responsibilities		
		Welfare of family and friends		
		Indecisiveness—"I can't make up my mind anymore"		
		Crying, weepy, screaming. Suicidal behavior—"I wish I were dead." "I want to kill myself"		

[a] From Lewinsohn, Biglan, & Zeiss (1976). Reproduced by permission.

[b] Gait and general behavior may alternatively be agitated.

Table 2. Symptoms of Mania[a]

Euphoria	Behavioral Deficits	Behavioral Excesses	Somatic Symptoms	Cognitive Manifestations
Excessively elated, expansive, or irritable mood	Exercises minimal judgment	Hyperactivity	Decreased need for sleep—may reduce average sleep time substantially and still feel energetic	High self-evaluation ranging from uncritical self-confidence to grandiosity
Full of energy	Limited concentration span—easily distracted by irrelevant stimuli	Excessive involvement in activities without regard to possible consequences: buying sprees, reckless driving, foolish investments, nightly partying	Weight loss	Feelings of power, special knowledge or ability
Unselective, persistent enthusiasm for relating to others	Neglect of personal appearance and grooming	Flamboyant, disorganized, or bizarre activities: wearing strange garments, wearing excessive, poorly applied makeup, distributing gifts and advice to passing strangers		
		Speech loud, rapid. May be difficult to interpret because of fast pace		
		Impulsive decisions		

[a] Adapted from American Psychiatric Association (1978).

bernick, 1977; Goldstein, 1965; Lader & Wing, 1969; Lewinsohn, Lobitz, & Wilson, 1973; Martin & Davies, 1965; Rimón, Stenbäck, & Huhmar, 1967; Suarez, Crowe, & Adams, 1978), this does not differentiate depression from other behavioral disorders. However, two recent studies (Schwartz, Salt, Mandel, & Klerman, 1976; Teasdale & Bancroft, 1977) have presented evidence suggesting that physiological indices can be used to specifically detect depressed affect.

Schwartz et al. (1976) found that patterns of facial electromyographic (EMG) activity differentiated depressed from nondepressed subjects. Comparisons were made across three affective imagery conditions (happy, sad, angry) and four muscle sites (frontalis, corrugator, masseter, and depressor). While both subject groups showed similar patterns of activity during sad and angry imagery conditions, nondepressed subjects more reliably generated the pattern associated with happy affect than did depressed subjects. Depressed subjects, in turn, more reliably generated a sad pattern of activity. Furthermore, when asked to imagine a typical day, depressed subjects approximated a sad pattern of activity, while nondepressed subjects evidenced "a miniature happy pattern" (Schwartz et al., 1976, p. 491). Depressed subjects evidenced an attenuated ability to generate facial activity associated with happy affect. This study suggests that facial EMG may be used to index affective states. Interestingly, changes in facial musculature were not readily detectable by direct observation.

Teasdale and Bancroft (1977) examined the covariation between corrugator EMG and subjective ratings of mood. Subjects were five female psychiatric patients evidencing mild to moderate symptoms of depression. Like Schwartz et al. (1976), the investigators found that corrugator EMG activity was higher when subjects engaged in unhappy thought than it was during engagement in happy thought. Furthermore, they demonstrated that higher corrugator EMG was temporally associated with self-report of depressed mood. Results from both of these investigations suggest that facial EMG may be useful as an index of normal and clinical affective states.

CLASSIFICATION OF AFFECTIVE DISORDERS

Psychiatric nomenclature is now regulated by the American Psychiatric Association's Diagnostic and Statistical Manual II (DSM-III, APA, 1980). The DSM-III corresponds with the international medical diagnoses established by the World Health Organization. This section will address the classification of affective disorders both for the DSM-II and the version DSM-III. As will be obvious, the two manuals produce comparable difficulties for reliably placing affective events into categories.

Let us first consider two basic principles of classification. First of all, reliable implementation of any classification system requires, at least, that the component categories of the system represent mutually exclusive, operationally defined subsets of the relevant phenomena (Adams, Doster, & Calhoun, 1977). Second, an effective taxonomic system does not employ theoretical inferences as classifying principles until and unless such inferences have withstood the test of empirical validation (Kety, 1965). At the very least, it is essential that category criteria be sufficiently objective and homogeneous to facilitate reliable assignment of persons or behavior to appropriate categories. Stated otherwise, any two clinicians adhering to the same classification system should be able to arrive at the same diagnosis for a particular person or group of responses. It has been demonstrated that the APA classification system falls considerably short of rendering such reliability (Zigler & Phillips, 1961; Zubin, 1967).

It is not our task here to provide a comprehensive review of the principles of classification (the reader is referred to Adams et al., 1977; Bruner, Goodnow, & Austin, 1965; Kety, 1965; Mayr, 1952; Plutnik, 1968; Robbins, 1966; and Stengel, 1959, for further discussion of taxonomic principles). Nor can we, within the limits of this chapter, thoroughly review the various dilemmas generated by traditional psychiatric nomenclature (see Adams et al., 1977). We have briefly addressed the topic of classificatory principles to establish a framework from which to evaluate traditional diagnostic groupings of the affective disorders, for the DSM-II and DSM-III respectively.

DSM-II

The proposed divisions of affective phenomena within the DSM-II do not represent homogeneous sets of observable behavior that are exclusive from one another; rather, these divisions are mutually distinct only in terms of questionable theoretical postulates. Consequently, the assignment of a patient to a particular division is determined by considerations that cannot be observably verified, such as assumed etiology, the vague neurotic/psychotic distinction, and premorbid personality. An etiological index—presence or absence of precipitating stress—is employed as a major criterion variable in differentiating these categories of affective disorders, despite the fact that the etiology of affective anomalies remains undetermined to date. While avoiding such terms as "reactive" and "endogenous," the APA diagnostic manual still adheres to the endogenous-reactive dichotomy (Akiskal & McKinney, 1975). For example, a defining attribute of manic-depressive illnesses (manic type, depressed type, circular type) and involutional melancholia is that they do "not seem to be related directly to a precipitating life experience" (APA, 1968, pp. 35–36). In contrast, the psychotic depressive reaction and depressive neurosis are defined as "attributable to some experience . . . to an identifiable event" (APA, 1968, pp. 38, 40). In fact, the only distinction made between manic-depression, depressed type, and the psychotic depressive reaction is that the latter is said to be "more easily attributable to precipitating stress" (APA, 1968, p. 37). Thus, the degree of ease with which clinicians can personally establish a relationship between a patient's emotional state and environmental events largely determines their resultant diagnosis.

Leff, Roatch, and Bunney (1970) have established that the likelihood of discovering significant stressful events preceding instances of affective disorders is directly determined by the comprehensiveness of the search. Additionally, it has been demonstrated that the frequency and kinds of psychosocial stress preceding "reactive" and "endogenous" depressions are not significantly different (Kendell & Gourlay, 1970; Paykel, Myers, Dienelt, Klerman, Lindenthal & Pepper, 1969; Thomson & Hendrie, 1972). Thus, reliance on assumed etiological distinctions to define the affective disorders is essentially anachronistic at this point.

The affective disorders are further categorized with reference to the arbitrary neurotic/psychotic dichotomy. Beck (1967) has found that patients with diagnoses of neurotic- and psychotic-depressive reactions evidence the same clinical symptoms; the only difference between these two classifications being that the symptoms are judged to be present with greater severity for the psychotically depressed patients. Thus, in application, the sole criterion for differentiating neurotic and psychotic depression is a subjective judgment of severity. It is not surprising that various investigators (e.g., Akiskal & McKinney, 1975; Mendelson, 1967) have commented on the lack of consensus about the clinical boundaries of "neurotic" and "psychotic" depressions, given that the DSM-II does not base the neurotic/psychotic distinction on differential symptomatology. Furthermore, considering the varied connotations associated with the terms neurosis and psychosis, the practical utility of superimposing such labels on affective phenomena is highly questionable.

DSM-III

The DSM-III may facilitate more reliable diagnosis for the affective disorders because greater attention has been given to operationalizing definitions of the designated categories. However, these categories are still confounded by theoretical distinctions and thus likely to create some confusion in application. The two major divisions for the affective disorders, episodic and chronic, seem to be distinguishable only in terms of severity of symptomatology; the overlap in objective criteria for these divisions being substantial.

According to the draft manual, the Episodic Affective Disorders are more severe than the Chronic Affective Disorders. Thus, while the behavioral indicants of episodic and chronic disturbances are practically indistinguishable, chronic syndromes are by definition less severe manifestations of mood abnormality. Further, the "chronic" classification requires that affective symptomatology has been evidenced continually for at least two years. In fact, the diagnosis of a chronic disorder is not applicable if there is an intervening period of "normal" mood lasting two months or longer. There is no specified duration of symptomatology for the episodic disorder, though it is described as "a sustained disturbance" (APA, 1978, p. E:1).

To add to the confusion, episodic disorders have been placed on a severity continuum, ranging from moderate to psychotic. In practice, it may be extremely difficult to differentiate a recurrent episodic disorder of moderate severity from a chronic affective disorder.

Like the DSM-II, the DSM-III employs etiological assumptions to index affective anomalies. For example, the depressive syndrome that can be attributed to "an identifiable psychosocial stressor" is categorized as an Adjustment Disorder with Depression (APA, 1978, p. N:8). By implication, the episodic and chronic disorders are not linked to identifiable stressors. Neither is the Atypical Depressive Disorder, "a residual category for classifying individuals with depressive features that cannot be classified as an Episodic or Chronic Affective Disorder or as an Adjustment Disorder" (APA, 1978, p. E:27).

The DSM-III further divides Episodic and Chronic Affective Disorders into manic, depressive, and bipolar subtypes. A bipolar affective disorder is reserved for individuals who evidence both manic and depressive behavior, concurrently or in alternation. The distinction between bipolar and nonbipolar (i.e., unipolar) depression, while common practice, is not reliably based on differential behavioral indicants, duration, or rate of recurrence. And unfortunately, a diagnosis of unipolar depression apparently requires a prediction that manic behavior will not be manifested in the future. Nevertheless, bipolar and unipolar depression seem to be differentially responsive to pharmacological agents. The data relevant to this bipolar/unipolar dichotomy, while not yet conclusive, suggest that it may be a valid classification distinction (Depue & Monroe, 1978).

Theoretical assumptions regarding a functional relationship between schizophrenic and affective symptomatology are incorporated into the DSM-III. For example, if intense and sustained depression is evidenced by a schizophrenic, residual subtype, episodic and chronic diagnoses are precluded. A diagnosis of Adjustment Disorder with Depressed Mood is to be made if the depressive syndrome is reactive to psychosocial stress. If not judged to be reactive, the depression is diagnosed as an Atypical Depressive Disorder. These classificatory specifications imply that the affective disorder preceded by a period of schizophrenic behavior is objectively, qualitatively different from the typical affective disorder. Additionally, presumed etiology (reactive, not reactive) is a major determinant for diagnosis.

Consider next the Schizoaffective classification, which essentially represents a catch-bag for symptomatology not neatly fitting into either affective or schizophrenic categories. If an affective syndrome precedes or develops concurrently with one or more schizophrenic symptoms, a diagnosis of Schizoaffective Disorder is to be made (APA, 1978, p. DD:1). In our opinion, this is analogous to generating a diagnosis of multiple sclerosis-influenza for the individual who has multiple sclerosis and develops influenza. The point is, schizophrenic and affective syndromes may be manifested concurrently yet still be independent of one another. The schizoaffective classification assumes, a priori, that concurrent affective and schizophrenic behaviors covary and are functionally related. Until it has been demonstrated empirically that this is a valid assumption, both affective disorder and schizophrenia should be diagnosed when their separate criteria have been met.

In summary, the draft version of the DSM-III improves upon its predecessor by providing operational criteria for the affective disorders. However, theoretical assumptions still confound the validity and reliability of the proposed classification system.

THEORETICAL CONSIDERATIONS

Several explanations of depressive behavior—its cause and its maintenance—have recently been formulated within a social-learning paradigm. The fundamental premise underlying various behavioral formulations is that depression, as a set of behaviors, is a natural consequence of anomalous reinforcement conditions. Accordingly, the primary task of clinical and research efforts is to identify and account for those anomalies of reinforcement in the depressed individual's life that elicit and maintain his affective disturbance.

Eastman (1976) has recently presented a commendable review of six behavioral formulations of depression, concluding that current literature displays "a curious narrowness of outlook regarding reinforcement parameters" (p. 280). Unfortunately, as he has accurately commented, several formulations are sufficiently complex in their expression to obscure accurate interpretation; this is partially consequent to the tendency of many theorists to incorporate many distinct formulations under the guise of any one theoretical position. Nevertheless, despite its current imperfections behavioral theory on depression has inspired considerable conceptual, experimental, and clinical productivity (McLean, 1976). The various behavioral models of depression, along with the empirical literature they have generated, do direct us to a preliminary set of reinforcement conditions most likely to be involved in the predisposition to and precipitation of depressive episodes. We regard this as a promising springboard for further understanding of depressive phenomena. In the section that follows, we address those reinforcement variables that seem to be implicated thus far in the major behavioral models.

Low Rate of Response-Contingent Positive Reinforcement

Lewinsohn and his associates (e.g., Lewinsohn, 1974; Lewinsohn, Biglan, & Zeiss, 1976; Lewinsohn, Weinstein, & Shaw, 1969) profess that a low rate of response-contingent positive reinforcement (RCPR) is a causal and maintaining factor in depression. Dysphoria and depressive behaviors are thought to result consequent to a reduction in the frequency and/or quality of response-elicited reinforcement. It is not the absolute rate of reinforcement per se that is implicated in the development and maintenance of depression, but rather the rate of positive reinforcement acquired contingent upon one's behavior. In other words, the behavior of depressed persons may be attributed to the contingency and rate of reinforcement allotted to them by a nonreinforcing environment.

A low rate of RCPR may result consequent to a slow, insidious reduction of available reinforcers (and thus be difficult to initially detect) or may alternatively be caused by the highly visible withdrawal of a pivotal reinforcer (e.g., death of a loved one, financial disaster, public humiliation, loss of employment). "Success depression" may be attributed to the inadequacy of postsuccess rewards relative to the level of reinforcement expected from an achievement (Lewinsohn, 1974).

According to this formulation, when the net gains for responding adaptively to one's environment are considerably less than the rewards for noninitiation of goal-seeking behavior, depression will result. Cognitive changes—pessimism, guilt, helplessness, hopelessness—are thought to be secondary elaborations of the dysphoria instigated by a low rate of RCPR. A corollary tenet of the RCPR formulation stipulates that the severity of depressive symptomatology covaries directly with the rate of contingent positive reinforcement. Further, the emission of depressive behavior is maintained not only by a sustained low rate of response-produced reinforcement, but also by the social attention and sympathy depression initially elicits from the environment (Burgess, 1969; Lewinsohn et al., 1969; Liberman & Raskin, 1971).

Lewinsohn and his colleagues contend that an index of pleasant events can be used to approximate measurement of contingent positive reinforcement. This approach assumes that when an individual engages in an activity he/she positively evaluates, he/she receives positive reinforcement on a contingent basis. MacPhillamy and Lewinsohn (1971) have constructed an index of 320 empirically derived pleasant activities, supposedly representing the universe of pleasant events. Their method of investigation rests on the assumption that the rate of RCPR is positively correlated with scores on this Pleasant Events Schedule. As has been acknowledged by MacPhillamy and Lewinsohn (1974), the enjoyability ratings obtained from subjects on the Pleasant Events Schedule are partially a function of activity level *prior* to experimental participation. That is, low activity rates may preclude the opportunity to adequately differentiate among environmental events.

In one series of studies (Lewinsohn & Graf, 1973; Lewinsohn & Libet, 1972), Lewinsohn and his associates found that positive mood and frequency of participation in pleasant activities were positively correlated for depressed, psychiatric control, and normal control groups, with no significant differences between groups. Crosslagged correlations failed to confirm the prediction that a decrease in activity level usually precedes a drop in mood. Results from a later series of correlational studies (Lewinsohn & MacPhillamy, 1974; MacPhillamy & Lewinsohn, 1974) indicated that the average amount of participation is pleasurable activities and the subjective enjoyability of potentially reinforcing events are both lower in depressed subjects relative to psychiatric and normal controls.

It should be noted that most empirical investigations of Lewinsohn's formulations (e.g., Brenner, 1975; Lewinsohn & Graf, 1973; Lewinsohn & Libet, 1972; Lewinsohn & MacPhillamy, 1974; MacPhillamy & Lewinsohn, 1974; Sheslow & Erickson, 1975) rely on correlational analysis. While it is possible that depression is causally related to a loss or low rate of RCPR, the correlational data offered in support of this assumption does not lend direct support to Lewinsohn's position, is not inconsistent with the predictions of other models, and simply confirms what one would expect given the stereotypic disengagement from the environment characteristic of depression. Blaney (1977), in a critique of this empirical work, comments, ". . . perhaps the theory should be treated as a characterization of the depressed person's interaction with his environment rather than as a hypothesis concerning the causal antecedents of the depressive episode" (p. 210). As Blaney also indicates, Lewinsohn would do well to devote more attention to the circumstances that effect a drop in the rate of response-contingent positive reinforcement.

Inadequate Social Reinforcement

The above formulation ascribed depression to prevailing environmental contingencies, which by virtue of inappropriate timing, rate, or quality decrease the instrumental value of a competent behavioral repertoire. Alternatively, another view of depression focuses on the individual's inability to elicit reinforcement from the environment consequent to a skill deficit. Any omission in the behavioral repertoire that curtails efficacious interaction with the environment may be considered a skill deficit. Primary attention has been devoted to the hypothesized link between social skill deficits and depression.

According to a majority of behavioral theorists (e.g., Hersen, Eisler, Alford, & Agras, 1973; Lewinsohn & Graf, 1973; Lewinsohn, Weinstein, & Alper, 1970; Lewinsohn et al., 1969; Liberman & Raskin, 1971; McLean, Ogston, & Grauer, 1973;

Patterson & Hops, 1972; Shipley & Fazio, 1973), an inadequacy in the frequency or quality of social reinforcement is causally related to the instigation and maintenance of depression. Depression is thought to result when an individual has lost some ability to elicit positive reactions from others, such that he/she experiences an inability to effectively control the consequences of interpersonal encounters. Along this line, the depressed person may not have the instrumental skills to avoid or remedy negative interpersonal exchanges.

McLean (1976), a major proponent of the Interpersonal Disturbance Model of depression, emphasizes the depressogenic function of "coercive communication patterns" (p. 64). He reports that approximately 70% of the clients referred to his program have become depressed consequent to prolonged marital discord. It is the weaker participant in coercive exchanges who typically develops depressive behavior (McLean, 1976); possibly as respondents to the aversive stimuli generated by marital friction, possibly as a desperate strategy to establish some control over the dominating spouse (e.g., through guilt induction). A functional analysis of the depressed client's interactions with significant others is thus considered requisite to adequate assessment procedures. Similarly, modification of the client's maladaptive interpersonal encounters is best achieved by involving in the therapeutic plan those people whose interactions with the patient are problematic.

Lewinsohn and his associates have shown considerable interest in the social skills of depressed individuals, speculating that a social skill deficit could be a major antecedent to a low rate of RCPR. Social skills is operationally defined by this group as the ability to emit behaviors that elicit positive (and avoid negative) reactions from the social environment (Lewinsohn, 1974). While the RCPR hypothesis addresses reinforcement in general, social reinforcement is thought to be particularly relevant to mood fluctuation.

According to the Lewinsohn research team (Lewinsohn & Shaffer, 1971; Lewinsohn et al., 1970; Libet & Lewinsohn, 1973; Libet, Lewinsohn, & Javorek, 1973; Shaffer & Lewinsohn, 1971) the social behavior of a significant number of depressives elicits a lower rate of social reinforcement relative to nondepressives. Empirically, they have found that in small group interactions: (a) depressed individuals emit verbal behaviors toward other people at approximately half the rate of nondepressed controls (Libet & Lewinsohn, 1973; Shaffer & Lewinsohn, 1971); (b) in response to behavior directed toward them, depressed individuals reciprocate fewer positive reactions relative to control subjects (Libet & Lewinsohn, 1973); (c) depressed subjects are three times slower than nondepressed subjects to respond to verbalizations directed toward them (Libet & Lewinsohn, 1973); and (d) depressed males—but not females—distribute their responses to a fewer number of group members relative to nondepressed controls. On the basis of these findings, the Lewinsohn group suggests that depressed individuals are less active interpersonally, provide less reinforcement for others, miss chances to emit and elicit behavior, and have a restricted interpersonal range (only demonstrated for male depressives). Thus, depressed individuals are less likely than nondepressed individuals to maintain the behavior of others toward them; consequently, a lower frequency of social reinforcement would be expected for them.

Lewinsohn (1974) further hypothesizes that the relationships of depressed persons lacks reciprocity and stability relative to nondepressed individuals. In a relationship that lacks reciprocity, the amount of effort (number of behaviors) an individual invests in an interaction to gain rewards is characteristically greater or less than the effort extended by his/her partner. That is, one member of the dyad is doing much more for the other person than the other person is doing for him. Libet and Lewinsohn (1973) and Shaffer and Lewinsohn (1971) have collected data suggesting that the relationships of depressives may be less reciprocal.

Ekman and Friesen (1974) have also examined the interpersonal skills of individuals who are depressed, focusing specifically on two categories of hand movement that accompany conversation. Relative to nondepressed persons, depressed individuals seldom utilize illustrators (gestures facilitating communication) but display numerous adaptors (hand motions that essentially distract from the conversation). Interestingly, this trend is reversed with clinical improvement. Hinchliffe, Lanceshire, and Roberts (1971) compared the speech rate of depressed and nondepressed subjects. Depressed subjects spoke more slowly than the comparison group of normals. In contrast to the results reported by Libet and Lewinsohn (1973), Shaffer and Lewinsohn (1971), and Hinchliff et al. (1971); Coyne (1976a) did not find depressed persons to be lower in verbal activity level or rate of positive response.

It is not surprising that individuals *when depressed* manifest varying social skill problems, as depression by definition involves behavioral inefficiency. In order to establish any directional relationship between a lack of social skill and depression, it must be demonstrated that social ineffectiveness was characteristic of the depressed individual prior to the onset of dysphoria. Independent support for the role of social skill deficits in precipitating depression also requires that the identified skill deficiency or deficiencies be exclusively relevant to depression. As Becker (1977) has commented, other psychopathological groups are even less interpersonally skilled than depressives. What then, if any, are the skill deficits that may be specifically implicated in the development of depression?

Coyne (1976a, 1976b) suggests that those individuals who become depressed lack the specific skills requisite to eliciting support from others when life becomes stressful. His proposal is inherently very viable. Paykel et al. (1969) found that depressed patients reported having experienced a number of stressful life events during the six months prior to depression onset which was three times that reported by matched nondepressed controls. Given that only a minority of persons who experience significant stress become depressed (Brown, Harris, & Peto, 1973; Klerman, 1974; Paykel, 1973), how do those people who experience stress and become clinically depressed differ from those who experience stress and do not? Coyne (1976a) provides one reasonable answer. Stressful events evoke stronger needs for social support and nurturance. Those individuals who become depressed in response to life stress events do not have the ability to elicit the support they need without also inducing negative affect in others.

Depressive symptoms are seen by Coyne as instrumental, albeit usually unsuccessful, behaviors that are designed to extract support and reassurance from others. The actual, rather than intended, reaction of others to depressed behavior has been examined in recent studies (e.g., Coyne, 1976a, Hammen & Peters, 1978). It has been demonstrated that depressed patients evoke significantly more depression, anxiety, hostility, and rejection from normal subjects than do nondepressed patients and normal controls (Coyne, 1976a). Further, depressive behavior may be more likely to elicit negative feelings and rejection in mixed-sex dyads (Hammen & Peters, 1978). These studies do not identify what aspect(s) of the behavior of depressed individuals provokes mood changes in others. Coyne (1976a) speculates that, "the solution may lie in the nonreciprocal, high disclosure of intimate problems . . . [and] that some of the inappropriate topics of conversation introduced by depressed persons [may] have inherently depressing qualities" (p. 193).

Coyne seems to be suggesting that a social skill deficit (inability to effectively request support) is implicated in the development of depression; while a behavioral excess (some unspecified aspect of depressive behavior, perhaps excessive, intimate self-disclosure) contributes to the maintenance of depression. Depressive behavior, by virtue of its aversive impact on others, alienates those members of the social environment from whom support is desired, thereby rendering the depressed person even more deprived of social reinforcement and leading him to amplify his depressive requests for support. Finally, Coyne (1976a) suggests that depressed individuals lack the "special social skills" necessary to circumvent or "overcome the effects of their mood-induction on others" (p. 192).

Aberrant Cognitive Mediation of Reinforcement

Beck (1967, 1976) conceptualizes most depression as primary thought disorders, involving not a conceptual distortion but a distortion of content. While environmental events may precipitate depression, it is the depressed individual's idiosyncratic perception and appraisal of such events that render them depression-inducing. Precipitating stress, according to Beck, merely stimulates heretofore dormant, negative cognitive patterns. In turn, depressive affect and behavior are secondary to the activation of these negative cognitions. Essentially an individual is prone to depression by virtue of aberrant cognitive mediation of reinforcement. Environmental experience is distorted by a "constellation of enduring negative attitudes" and negative self-statements. The cognitive approach to depression is not exclusively Beck's (e.g., Ellis, 1962; Valins & Nisbett, 1971); however, Beck has made the most active effort to elucidate the cognitive biases specific to depression.

According to Beck, stressful life events precipitate severe affective reactions only in the person who has a predepressive cognitive organization. For the individual predisposed to depressive episodes, cognition is dominated by a "cognitive triad" involving negative views of the self, the world, and the future. A crucial characteristic of the depressed patient's cognitions (cognitions typically involving themes of low self-regard, ideas of deprivation, self-blame and self-criticism, overwhelming problems or responsibilities, self-injunctions, and escapist desires) is that they show a "systematic error" or reality distortion in terms of a bias against oneself (Beck, 1967). The depression-prone individual selectively attends to the negative aspects of an event. Along this line, Lishman (1972) and Lloyd and Lishman (1975) have demonstrated that depressed subjects manifest a special proclivity to attend to and recall the negative features of information provided to them. Additionally, the depressed individual tends to assume excessive causal responsibility for events which are negatively evaluated, without adequate consideration of alternative sources of causality.

The logical distortions inherent in depression cognitions "may be classified as paralogical (arbitrary inference, selective abstraction, and overgeneralization), stylistic (exaggeration), or semantic (inexact labelling)" (Beck, 1967, p. 234). The depressed individual magnifies the meaning of any situation that represents loss and actually seems to be preoccupied with a sense of loss, such that hypothetical and pseudo losses are construed and experienced as if they were actual events (Beck, 1974). It is not psychosocial stress that provokes depressive reactions, but the illogical cognitive processing of such events in line with dominating negative self-statements.

Beck and Rush (1976) provide a review of naturalistic, experimental, and psychotherapeutic outcome studies that lend indirect support to their position. Experimental procedures effecting a change in mood by cognitive means are especially supportive of Beck's formulation. A cognitive procedure developed by Velten (1968) has been demonstrated to produce depression and elation of mood in normally functioning individuals, independent of any change in activity level, across several studies (Aderman, 1972; Hale & Strickland, 1976; Potts, 1977; Strickland, Hale, & Anderson, 1975; Velten, 1968; Tucker, 1975). Furthermore, this mood manipulation procedure has been shown to successfully induce opposite mood states in characteristically depressed and elated subjects (Coleman, 1975).

Utilizing Velten's (1968) technique, Potts (1977) found that experimentally induced negative affect effected a decrease in the subjective enjoyability of previously pleasant events, and experimentally induced positive affect increased the subjective enjoyability of activities. Similarly, Strickland et al. (1975) have shown that the induction of depressive affect with Velten's (1968) statements decreases the interest subjects report to have in various social and physically involving activities. An individual can thus experience a change in mood as well as desire for activity by focusing his/her attention on mood relevant statements. Furthermore, one study (Aderman, 1972) suggests that behavioral changes might accompany the cognitive induction of mood. Aderman (1972), using Velten's procedure, found that college males who read the elation statements were significantly more likely to volunteer for a postexperimental task (another experiment) than those who had read depression statements.

The results of these investigations, along with other studies that have successfully employed cognitive strategies to induce mood (e.g., Batsel, 1976; Moore, Underwood, & Rosenhan, 1975), challenge strongly anticognitive formulations of depression. These studies suggest a direction of influence in the relationship between cognitions, affect, and behavior that is not addressed by most behavioral theorists. They do not, however, preclude the reverse temporal sequence. Results from future studies employing cognitive mood manipulation procedures would be strengthened by the inclusion of behavioral dependent measures.

Expectation of Noncontrol Over Reinforcement

According to the original learned helplessness model of depression, the motivational, cognitive, and emotional deficits of the depressed individual may be attributed to his/her having learned that outcomes are independent of his/her responses and are thus uncontrollable. The hypothesis partially resembles Lewinsohn's RCPR formulation, in that it focuses on the effects of response-reinforcement contingencies. However, there are some basic differences (see Becker, 1977, and Blaney, 1977 for further comparison of these two models). Lewinsohn's model focuses on the depressogenic consequences of positive reinforcement deprivation, with relative inattention to the direct effects of aversive events. In contrast, Seligman's (1975) model of human helplessness has been extrapolated from animal studies involving inescapable, unavoidable aversion and has been only weakly generalized to the situation of uncontrollable positive reinforcement. Further, as stated earlier, Lewinsohn would predict depression if the consequences for not responding to one's environment are greater than the consequences for responding. In contrast, Seligman would not predict the onset of depression if the individual expects that—by either responding or not responding—he/she can still demonstrate control over reinforcers.

Seligman's formulation is essentially cognitive "in that it postulates that mere exposure to uncontrollability is not sufficient to render an individual helpless; rather, the organism must come to expect that outcomes are uncontrollable in order to exhibit helplessness" (Abramson, Seligman, & Teasdale, 1978, p. 50). An individual must perceive and come to *expect* noncontingency between responses and outcomes. Abramson et al. (1978) cite Bandura's (1977) recent article, which proposes that the outcome expectations characteristic of learned helplessness may result consequent to the individual's lack of capabilities ("efficacy-based futility") or an unresponsive, possibly punishing, environment.

Generalization of the animal helplessness paradigm to human depression has not fared well in empirical examinations. Even those studies conducted in Seligman's laboratory provide only minimal support, if any, for the learned helplessness model of depression (Costello, 1978). Abramson et al. (1978) acknowledge the inadequacies of Seligman's (1975) original helplessness model for clinical depression. First of all, even when people learn that events occur independent of their actions, they do not reliably demonstrate depressive affect. Secondly, the model does not explain the lowered self-esteem (e.g., self-blame, guilt) characteristic of the depressed person. Consider the contradiction between feeling guilty and responsible for some predicament, and at the same time believing that one's actions have no impact on one's environment. As Abramson et al. (1978) admit, the model does not account for the tendency of many depressed individuals to attribute failure to themselves and to in fact assume excessive responsibility for failure.

The Seligman group now proposes a reformulation of their original theory that supposedly remedies previous inadequacies. According to the reformulated model, the *attribution* an individual makes for the lack of contingency between his/her responses and outcomes is crucial in determining whether the perception of noncontingency becomes an expectation of noncontingency. The expectation of noncontingency, as stated above, is considered essential to the symptoms of helplessness.

In a complicated discourse, Abramson et al. (1978) explain how they have incorporated a complex, cognitive process into the previous model. They specify that depression results only "when highly desired outcomes are believed improbable or highly aversive outcomes are believed probable, and the individual expects that no responses in his/her repertoire will change their likelihood" (Abramson et al., 1978, p. 68). Further, they speculate that depressed people are more likely to attribute failure to internal, global, and stable factors (e.g., lack of intelligence or charm) and success to external, specific, and unstable factors (e.g., being lucky on one task).

In summary, this reformulated theory of learned helplessness requires that an individual be exposed to a series of noncontingent outcomes, perceive the noncontingency, and have the relevant "attributional style" in order to be susceptible to depression. One's attributions ultimately determine vulnerability to depression.

The revised learned helplessness model has already engendered considerable criticism (e.g., Buchwald, Coyne, & Cole, 1978; Wortman & Dintzer, 1978) on many grounds. Abramson et al. (1978) correctly acknowledge that they are providing post hoc explanations for existing data. The population of depressives to which this formulation supposedly applies is curiously limited. Seligman (1978) suggests that learned helplessness is a model relevant to that *subclass* of depressions caused by helplessness cognitions. While he argues that it is not circular to state that learned helplessness is specifically applicable to helplessness depressions, we are not convinced.

Aversive Control

Aversive stimuli, especially conditioned aversive stimuli, may exert a depressogenic effect on behavior (Ferster, 1973). There is some evidence that depressed individuals, in comparison to nondepressed individuals, are particularly sensitive to aversive stimulation. For example, depressed subjects show a greater increase in electrodermal responding during administration of electric shock relative to psychiatric and normal controls (Lewinsohn et al., 1973). Depressed subjects in the Lewinsohn et al. (1973) study were selected on the basis of Byrne Scale (Byrne, 1961) scores and postinterview ratings on the Feelings and Concerns Checklist (Grinker, Miller, Sabshin, Nunn, & Nunnally, 1961). Contrary to experimental predictions depressed subjects did not show a greater anticipatory response to shock, nor a less complete return to baseline following the aversive stimulus.

Zuckerman, Persky, and Curtis (1968) subdivided male psychiatric patient and normal male control groups on the basis of anxiety, hostility, and depression. Irrespective of original diagnoses, subjects were assigned to affect subgroups based on nonvalidated self-report scales as well as ratings of "overt, observed, or admitted behavior" and "covert, inferred, or potential behaviors." The authors found that rated overt depression (in patients only) was positively correlated with spontaneous GSR fluctuations prior to ($p \leq .05$) and after ($p \leq .05$) exposure to coldpressor stress. The results of this study, however, are tempered by seemingly unreliable subject selection criteria.

Gatchel, McKinney, and Koebernick (1977), similar to Lewinsohn et al. (1973), demonstrated greater electrodermal responding by depressed subjects to uncontrollable aversive stimuli (a loud noise) in comparison to nondepressed subjects. The final sample in this study consisted of eighteen depressed and eighteen nondepressed college students, selected on the basis of Beck Depression Inventory (Beck, Ward, Mendelson, Mock, & Erbaugh, 1961) scores. Interestingly, in the experimental condition allowing control over (i.e., escape from) the aversive stimulus, depressed subjects did not show greater electrodermal responding relative to nondepressed subjects.

Suarez, Crowe, and Adams (1978) have investigated the physiological responses of depressed and nondepressed subjects during presentation of mildly aversive stimuli. Four subject groups were included in the study: student-depressed, nonstudent-depressed, student-nondepressed, and nonstudent-nondepressed. The Beck Depression Inventory (Beck et al., 1961), the MMPI, and the Depression Thermometer (self-rating scale for depression intensity) were used to differentiate depressed students and nonstudents from nondepressed students and nonstudents. Both skin resistance level (SRL) and skin resistance responses (SRR) were measured throughout baseline periods and during an audiotaped presentation of neutral and depressive statements. Only the nonstudent depressed group showed a differential physiological response to the neutral and negative statements, displaying a significant larger number of SRR during negative, as opposed to neutral, statements.

Given the autonomic overresponsivity of depressed persons demonstrated in these studies, one would predict that depressed individuals have developed strategies to avoid aversive situations. Along this line, Suarez et al. (1978) propose a passive avoidance model for depression and question the passive, nonresponsive state attributed to depressive behavior by the learned helplessness model. In a second experiment, they assessed avoidance behavior in both active and passive paradigms, where subjects could avoid a noxious buzzer by emitting the correct response (active avoidance) or by not responding (passive avoidance). Depressed groups demonstrated inferior active and superior passive avoidance learning in comparison to nondepressed control groups. According to the authors, the depressed individual has learned that he/she can control aversive stimuli by not responding. On the other hand, if this passive avoidance strategy is unsuccessful, the individual will engage in active responding to manipulate the situation. In this experiment, depressed subjects were able to learn the active avoidance response, but did so with a higher number of errors compared to nondepressed subjects, due to a higher rate of responding.

Having demonstrated that depressed subjects are more sensitive to aversive stimuli, Suarez et al. (1978) postulate that behavioral suppression may be a strategy that has been acquired by the depressed person to avoid noxious events. The depressed groups' higher rate of responding during active avoidance challenges a nonresponsive characterization of depressed individuals, and may also be a function of this greater sensitivity to aversive stimuli. The Suarez et al. (1978) study suggests that depressed persons can and will engage actively with their environment if passive strategies become ineffective.

Forrest and Hokanson (1975) suggest that depressive responses may have acquired "arousal-reducing properties" by virtue of being instrumental in terminating or avoiding aversive interpersonal encounters. They theorize that "one component of depression may be related to the instrumental value that depressive, self-demeaning displays have in controlling aversiveness and threat from others" (p. 347). In a relevant study, the authors confirmed their prediction that depressed individuals utilize self-harming behaviors more frequently than normals when subject to interpersonal aggression. Following electric shock from an aggressive partner, depressed and nondepressed subjects had the choice of counter-responding with shock, self-shock, or a friendly gesture. Depressed subjects showed significantly more rapid reduction of autonomic arousal following self-shock, relative to their arousal reduction following aggressive and friendly counterresponses. In contrast, the nondepressed group showed rapid reduction of autonomic arousal only after engaging in aggressive retaliation.

Depressive behaviors (e.g., passive avoidance, self-punishment) may represent strategies that have acquired reinforcing properties by facilitating avoidance or escape from more noxious stimuli. It is predictable that avoidance of social situations would in turn result in isolation and eventually less skill acquisition for the depressed person (Lewinsohn, 1974).

Loss of Reinforcer Effectiveness

Costello (1972a, 1972b) proposes that a pervasive loss of reinforcer *effectiveness*, rather than an actual decrease in the *rate* of reinforcement, causes depression. Previously effective reinforcers may lose their potency by way of endogenous biological changes and/or the disruption of a behavioral chain (Costello, 1972a). The term "behavioral chain" does not have a precise referent in Costello's (1972a) discourse; however, Eastman (1976) suggests that Costello is referring to a "network" of closely interconnected behaviors, stimuli, and reinforcers. According to Costello's elaborate but untestable hypothesis, the loss of any one component of a behavioral chain (e.g., a reinforcer or discriminative stimulus) disrupts the effectiveness of all remaining reinforcers. Costello implies that the stimuli, responses, and reinforcers in an individual's life are mutually interdependent, such that all connections between them must remain intact lest reinforcers lose their potency. Further, Costello (1972b) speculates that for depressed individuals the mutual interdependence among components of a behavioral chain is particularly strong.

Becker (1977) aptly questions why the response chains of depressed people are assumed to be unusually rigid and constricted relative to nondepressed persons. Lazarus (1972), in his critique of Costello's (1972a) speculative paper, questions the treatment relevance of Costello's formulation. How does one repair a broken behavioral chain?

It goes without saying that a salient feature of depressive behavior is an apparent loss of interest in reinforcers. As Lazarus (1972) points out, "it is usually difficult to determine whether . . . [this] is an effect or a cause of depression" (p. 249). Two studies (Potts, 1977; Strickland, et al., 1975) have shown that the cognitive induction of depressed affect reduces the hedonic relevance of previously enjoyable events, thus suggesting that cognitive set may mediate the effectiveness of reinforcers.

COMMENTARY

While we have attempted to reduce the overlap inherent in existing formulations, some redundancy has been inevitable, given the complexity of each position. Only one of the above-mentioned theorists has attempted to account for manic behavior.

Beck (1967) attributes the subacute manic reaction to maladaptive cognitive patterns characterized by "exaggerated ideas of personal abilities, minimization of external obstacles, and overly optimistic expectations" (p. 270). According to Beck, such patterns lead to the observable manifestations of mania.

To our knowledge, behaviorists have not yet investigated the problem of mania, nor arrived at any firm formulations for this disorder. Interestingly, in his well-known abnormal psychology text, Coleman (1976) has proposed one possible behavioristic formulation for the manic reaction. He speculates that manic behavior might be conceptualized as an attempt to obtain desired reinforcers via an indiscriminate rise in activity level. Similar to depressed individuals, manic persons might be responding to an inadequate rate, quality, or contingency of positive reinforcement. Both manic and depressive behavior might represent desperate (albeit topographically different) strategies to elicit reinforcement from the environment. Of course, this behavioral formulation of mania would still have to account for the euphoria characteristic of most manic individuals (Coleman, 1976).

To date, Coleman's speculation stands as the sole attempt to account for manic phenomena within a behavioral paradigm. We would contend that this relative inattention to manic disorders is most likely hindering our search for the parameters of affective regulation.

MODIFICATION OF AFFECTIVE DISORDERS

To date, there is only a smattering of controlled outcome research examining the application of behavioral treatment strategies to depression. A valid demonstration of the efficacy or any antidepressive behavioral approach will require more rigorous investigative efforts. Though the results of many narrative reports, single case designs, and small group studies appear promising, a majority of these are handicapped by a lack of sufficient experimental control. Regrettably, the published literature does not address the possible application of behavioral treatment to mania.

Garfield (1978) has recently discussed a number of methodological inadequacies apparent in research involving clinical diagnosis. His comments are all too appropos to the accumulating body of depression research—both behavioral and nonbehavioral. Indeed, methodological flaws across several depression studies limit the opportunity to gain an organized compilation of data from past research. To begin with, the selection of depressed subjects is too often based on a single screening measure, frequently a self-report index of mood. Furthermore, subject selection criteria vary from one investigation to the next, reflecting the lack of consensus about requirements for a representative depressed sample. Significant variation in sampling procedures across studies may result in very diverse subject groups. Along this line, basic subject data is often too meager to confirm or disconfirm the possibility of substantial dissimilarity between the depressed subject groups of different studies.

All too many outcome studies rely totally on self-report measures and clinical judgment for improvement criteria. As a result, there is a scarcity of objective behavioral measurement. We would concur with Lewinsohn (1974) that observable behavior must be included as an outcome measure of depression treatment studies.

Without a systematic demonstration of behavioral change, the success of any intervention remains questionable. Finally, the frequent practice of administering multicomponent therapeutic programs in outcome research makes it extremely difficult to isolate the critical ingredient(s) of any treatment package. We would suggest that future outcome research on depression utilize multiple criterion measures for subject selection, provide basic descriptive data about subjects, include behavioral baseline and outcome measures, more clearly define target behaviors and therapeutic strategies, and attend more carefully to the provision of adequate control conditions.

We turn now to our strategy for intervention with depressed individuals. Our approach is geared toward rectification of those problems that *cause* and *maintain* depressive behavior. From the behavioral formulations of depression, we extrapolate four distinct factors most often implicated as causal and maintaining factors: a nonreinforcing environment, a skill deficit, aberrant cognitions, and autonomic overresponsivity. Given the heterogeneity of the depressed population, it is doubtful that any one of these depressogenic factors will be common to all depressed individuals. Similarly, it is unlikely that any one treatment procedure will be universally applicable to this group. The clinician must determine *for each individual client* which of these factor(s) are operating to precipitate and maintain a depressive orientation to the environment. Treatment planning should correspond directly with such formulation. For example, if poor social skills are pivotal in the onset and maintenance of a person's depression, he/she will require social skills training. Each depressogenic factor requires alternative modification procedures, thus the accuracy of the clinician's formulation for a particular client determines the efficacy of the corresponding treatment program.

In the section that follows, we discuss the appropriate treatment methods for each depressogenic factor.

Nonreinforcing Environment

An individual will experience his/her environment as nonreinforcing if competent, goal-directed behavior does not elicit a sufficient level of positive reinforcement. Similarly, the individual will conclude that it is essentially futile to act on the environment when his/her efforts routinely meet with little success. It may be that desirable behavior is not recognized by significant members of his/her social environment (e.g., family members, close friends, employer). Alternatively, the client's sources of reinforcement may be limited such that the total range, quantity, or quality of contingent positive reinforcement is insufficient.

Bandura (1977) aptly summarizes what must be done to rectify an individual's disengagement from the environment: ". . . to change outcome-based futility necessitates changes in prevailing environmental contingencies that restore the instrumental value of the competencies that people already possess" (pp. 204–205). Most importantly, if the rectification of a nonreinforcing environment becomes the focus of treatment, it must first be determined that the client has the skills necessary to draw reinforcement from social interactions and various activities. Procedures to modify the nonreinforcing environment include contingency management and activity schedules.

Contingency Management

Contingency management procedures may be useful in altering a lack of contingent positive external reinforcement for desirable behavior. "Contingency management" involves the contingent administration of rewards for targeted adaptive behavior in combination with the withdrawal of reinforcement following maladaptive (e.g., depressed) behavior (Rimm & Masters, 1974). Although this treatment may be utilized by the therapist himself within sessions, it is advisable to involve family members or significant others in the program in order to effect natural contingencies in the environment. Therapy may involve reinstatement of former reinforcers or the development of new rewards. When employing contingency management procedures, it is necessary to concretely define the target desirable behaviors and to identify effective reinforcers for the individual. Reinforcers may be material (e.g., money, trips, gifts), social (e.g., praise, attention, smiles, physical contact), or preferred activities (Rimm & Masters, 1974).

Individual case studies (Burgess, 1969; Hersen et al., 1973; Liberman & Raskin, 1971; Reisinger, 1972) have demonstrated the effectiveness of a contingency management approach with clients who evidence high-frequency depressive behavior and comparable low-frequency task-oriented behavior. Burgess (1969) describes six cases where therapist or mate reinforcement for action-oriented behaviors, combined with inattention to depressive behaviors, effected positive behavior change and a client-reported decrease in depression level. As she points out, if goal-directed behavior has been extinguished through a loss of positive reinforcement, the appropriate strategy may be to gradually reinstate such behavior via contingent reward for approximations to the desired outcome (Burgess, 1969).

Liberman and Raskin (1971) summarize several cases that responded favorably to therapist contingency management. Additionally, they report successful modification of a depressed individual's behavior through training members of the patient's family in principles and methods of reinforcement control. The family was instructed to provide immediate attention for constructive behavior (e.g., household responsibilities, child care) and to gradually ignore all depressive behavior. Utilizing an A-B-A design, Hersen et al. (1973) demonstrated the effectiveness of a token economy program for increasing work behaviors of three depressed hospitalized patients. Most important, the increase in target work behaviors was accompanied by a decrease in depressed behavior. Reisinger (1972) modified the depressed behavior of a hospitalized 21-year-old female patient by dispensing token and/or social reinforcement for appropriate smiling as well as response cost for excessive crying. Using a modified reversal design, he demonstrated the control that therapeutic procedures established over target responses. The author did not comment on other behavioral changes but concluded that the treatment was successful in alleviating this woman's depression. No follow-up data were obtained.

Lewinsohn (1974) reports that application of the Premack principle in the treatment of depression has yielded promising results with several cases. The Premack principle states that a low-frequency activity or behavior may be reinforced by a high-frequency behavior if the occurrence of the latter is made contingent on the emission of the former. According to Lewinsohn (1974), this variation of contingency management is useful with depressed persons who are poorly motivated to follow through with treatment recommendations and homework assignments. A high-frequency behavior of many depressed people is depressed talk (e.g., complaints, worry statements, self-derogatory comments). The Lewinsohn group has found it useful to make therapy time for such talk contingent upon an increase of adaptive low-frequency behaviors (e.g., engagement in pleasant activities, assertive verbalizations). For example, with one client (Flippo & Lewinsohn, 1969) the therapy time allowed for high-rate depressive talk was directly proportional to the number of activities she engaged in between sessions. Theoretically, homework activities acquired reinforcing value by earning the client time for an established high-frequency behavior.

Contingency management techniques are employed to reinforce and thereby reinstate a constructive behavioral repertoire. The instrumental value of nondepressed, adaptive behavior is restored through systematic manipulation of environmental contingencies.

Activity Schedules

A nonreinforcing environment may be directly modified by involving the depressed client in potentially rewarding activities. Potentially rewarding events are likely to function as positive reinforcers for the behavior they require. Logically, a person should feel less depressed when engaged in an enjoyable activity. Empirically, involvement in pleasant activities is correlated with a nondepressed mood state (Lewinsohn & Graf, 1973; Lewinsohn & Libet, 1972).

In working with depressed patients, Lewinsohn and his colleagues identify potential reinforcers for each patient and then increase his/her daily activity level relative to these reinforcing events. They have developed a quantitative approach to identify those activities that are relevant to the patient's mood. During the diagnostic phase, the patient completes a Pleasant Events Schedule (PES) (MacPhillamy & Lewinsohn, 1971). This PES is an empirically derived instrument listing a variety of pleasurable social and solitary activities. Each item of the inventory receives an enjoyability and frequency rating from the patient, and those 160 activities obtaining the highest combined scores comprise his/her personalized Activity Schedule. Then, on a daily basis, the depressed person completes a depression inventory and monitors target behaviors from his/her Activity Schedule. From this daily monitoring of mood and activities, those events most highly correlated with a nondepressed mood state can be identified.

Usually, the number of mood-related activities for a given patient ranges from 10 to 20 (Lewinsohn, 1975b). During treatment, the patient is instructed to increase the frequency of these mood-relevant activities. It may be equally therapeutic, however, to increase the frequency of all activities from the patient's Activity Schedule that have high enjoyability ratings (Lewinsohn et al., 1976).

How does the therapist motivate the depressed client to follow this activity-oriented treatment regimen? Lewinsohn et al. (1976) outline various techniques to encourage patient engagement in pinpointed activities. For the patient who is not easily persuaded to break a pattern of inertia, Lazarus (1974) recommends that the therapist personally take him/her into potentially rewarding activities until he/she is mobilized to act independently.

The therapeutic utility of systematically increasing the depressive's rate of engagement in pleasant activities has not yet been empirically demonstrated. Experimentally, depressed subjects have become more depressed after following instructions to increase participation in such activities (Hammen & Glass, 1975). For the depressed individual who does not have the social skills or other competencies to consistently derive benefits from targeted activities, more frequent engagement in such activities may actually become aversive. Skill deficits should be remedied before activity level becomes a focus of treatment, as the depressed person must have the ability to cope effectively with his/her environment before placing more demands on him/her to cope. Similarly, physiological and cognitive anomolies should be modified prior to increasing the depressed person's activity level. A higher activity level may increase exposure to anxiety-arousing stimuli for the autonomically overresponsive depressive. Illogical processing of events will, in turn, limit beneficial effects of increased activity and will first require cognitive therapy.

Skill Deficit

Skill training for the depressed client will be warranted whenever he/she lacks some instrumental behavior or ability necessary to satisfactorily engage the environment. A skill deficit may involve study skills, writing skills, conflict-resolution skills, problem-solving skills, decision-making skills, and so on. Assertiveness training has been recommended as a useful treatment for many depressives who manifest some inability to control interpersonal situations (Wolpe, 1958, 1969; Wolpe & Lazarus, 1966). For the depressed mother who cannot manage the behavior of her youngsters, parent training will be warranted. The depressed individual who has lost important skills consequent to physical illness or injury may require occupational and academic training (Lewinsohn, 1975a), concomitant with an introduction to new, alternative sources of reinforcement in the community.

A number of depressed individuals evidence longstanding decision-making and problem-solving difficulties. Shipley and Fazio (1973) conducted two controlled experiments designed to evaluate the efficacy of a "functional problem-solving approach" to treating depression in comparison to a waiting list control condition. Twenty-four depressed college students were randomly assigned to either the treatment or the control group. For subjects in the treatment group, the therapist (a) recommended functional problem-solving alternatives for individual problems to promote more skillful manipulation of the environment; (b) discussed subsequent outcomes of these recommendations and generated new alternatives; and (c) instructed the client to have "isolation depression"—to confine depressed behavior to therapy sessions and thereby gain control of this behavior while avoiding environmental reinforcement for depressive symptoms. The authors extrapolated this treatment plan from an outline prepared by Kanfer and Phillips (1970). Control subjects did not meet with the therapist but completed pre- and postmeasures. After three weeks of treatment, posttreatment depression scores indicated no improvement for the waiting list control group but significant improvement for the treatment group. Subsequently, the control group was offered the same treatment, after which their depression scores dropped significantly as well. As this study used nonclinical depressives, the investigators were cautious in generalizing conclusions to the treatment of clinical depression. They used additional groups in their second study, to control for nonspecific effects from therapist support and treatment expectancies, and found that support and expectancy variables were not confounding treatment effects.

As noted earlier, many investigators have addressed themselves to the interpersonal deficiencies manifested by depressed individuals. A variety of social skill deficits have been discussed, though there has been no demonstration that any of these are specific to depression. Of course, not all depressed persons lack social skills, and the specific nature of the deficits varies substantially across those individuals who do (Lewinsohn et al., 1976). "It is therefore essential to specifically describe and delineate the particular social skill problems manifested by a given depressed individual and to focus interventions on the modification of the behavior relevant to these areas" (Lewinsohn et al., 1976, pp. 121–122).

The Lewinsohn group has developed an objective, replicable approach to target interpersonal problems for the depressed patient (Lewinsohn, 1974; Lewinsohn et al., 1976). With a majority of depressed patients they have treated, they have found it necessary to focus on problematic social interactions. Their approach to the social behavior of depressed persons is summarized (Lewinsohn, 1974, 1975a; Lewinsohn et al., 1976) and exemplified (Lewinsohn & Atwood, 1969; Lewinsohn & Shaw, 1969; Lewinsohn et al., 1969; Martin, Weinstein, & Lewinsohn, 1968) elsewhere. Like McLean (1976) they (e.g., Lewinsohn et al., 1976) have noted that many depressed individuals have serious marital problems that are related to their depression. Home observations during diagnostic, treatment, and follow-up phases of therapeutic contact have been extremely useful for identifying problematic family interchanges, defining treatment goals, and assessing behavior change (Lewinsohn, 1974; Lewinsohn & Shaffer, 1971). Home observations also communicate to the patient that his/her problem is related to patterns of interaction with others. All findings consequent to observer coding are shared with the patient and family through graphs and other visual aids.

To date, it has not been empirically demonstrated that modification of the depressive's social behavior is associated with an improvement in mood (Lewinsohn et al., 1976). Nevertheless, if the depressed person evidences impaired social skills, his/her interpersonal behavior must be altered to facilitate effective adjustment to the social environment. There is no model of social skills training specifically designed for depressed clients. Obviously, the type of intervention will vary according to the particular need of the client.

Lewinsohn and his colleagues typically focus antidepression treatment on the depressed individual's social skills, communication patterns with significant others, and activity level. Operating on the assumption that depressed individuals are less socially skillful than their nondepressed peers, Lewinsohn et al. (1970) investigated a behavioral approach to the group treatment of depressed individuals that was designed to increase interpersonal efficiency. Subjects were nine depressed individuals; no control groups were used. Two observers rated each group member according to the frequency, range, and quality of his/her interactions. Subsequently, each member was given individual feedback accompanied by graphs and data that were used to define specific behavioral problems and goals to be attained in his/her group interactions. Other group members were used to effect desired behavior change through differential reinforcement of appropriate and inappropriate social behaviors. Posttreatment measures on the MMPI D Scale, Grinker's Feelings & Concerns Checklist, and an Interpersonal Behavior Scale indicated improvement for the majority of group members in the direction of less depression and improved social skills.

McLean et al. (1973) conducted an experimental study to evaluate the relative effectiveness of a structured form of communication training with depressed patients complaining of problematic marital communication. Twenty married depressives and their spouses were randomly assigned to either a behavioral treatment group (training in social-learning principles, modeling of conflict resolution via negative cueing, and reciprocal behavioral contracts) or a conventional comparison group. Several objective measures of depression and interaction obtained prior to and immediately after treatment indicated improvement of treatment group subjects over controls. Furthermore, this improvement was maintained at a three-month follow-up. The authors speculated that negative cueing made couples more aware of the effects their interactions had on one another; however, the relative impact of each component of the behavioral treatment can not be determined from this study.

Aberrant Cognitions

If treatment focuses on the depressed client's cognition, attitudes, and beliefs, it must first be demonstrated that he/she has a smoothly functioning behavioral repertoire (McLean, 1976). His/her negative cognitions are not necessarily inaccurate and changeworthy. For example, the socially awkward depressive who berates him/herself after most social contacts may be accurately perceiving his/her own interactional ineptness. The appropriate treatment in this case would be social skills training rather than cognitive modification.

Beck (1967, 1976) employs a myriad of techniques to alter negative cognitive sets. The ultimate goal of all treatment procedures is to systematically induce "fundamental attitude change" (Beck, 1976, p. 74). Beck's therapy package focuses on modifying both overt and covert behavior, though overt behavioral assignments (e.g., graded task assignments, activity schedules) are included merely to generate data contradictory to the client's negative self-perception. Cognitive modification procedures teach the patient that his/her depression is related to maladaptive thought patterns and train him/her to identity and logically challenge the erroneous assumptions underlying these cognitions. Basic assumptions are conceptualized as hypotheses that must be tested. The patient learns to challenge the validity of his/her negative attitudes by examining disconfirmatory data. For example, the patient's belief that he/she cannot do anything well can be challenged by confronting him/her with prior and ongoing success experiences. Similarly, the attitude that nothing is pleasant may be contradicted by engaging the patient in some enjoyable activity or through guided imagery of pleasant events (Beck, 1976). Beck's (1976) "Mastery and Pleasure Therapy" is designed to heighten awareness of successful and/or enjoyable experiences. The patient records all daily activities and is trained to recognize those events that represent mastery or pleasure. Lazarus (1968, 1974) employs a technique called "time projection" to facilitate the experience of pleasure. This is an imagery exercise requiring the patient to project himself/herself forward in time and to view himself/herself engaged in a successful, rewarding activity.

While cognitive therapy for depression stems primarily from Beck's work, alternative cognitive restructuring approaches (c.f. Mahoney, 1974; Meichenbaum, 1974) may be used to modify a depressogenic misperception of environmental events. The self-regulation literature (e.g., Bandura, 1969; Kanfer, 1970a, 1970b, 1971; Kanfer & Karoly, 1972a, 1972b) is also directly relevant to cognitive treatment for depression. Training effective patterns of self-regulation alters covert activity by effecting greater accuracy in self-monitoring, self-evaluation, and self-reinforcement.

Jackson (1972) successfully treated a depressed female for whom compliments served as a discriminative stimulus for self-criticism, making social reinforcement largely ineffective. The ultimate objective was to increase the frequency and accuracy of contingent self-reinforcement. The subject was assisted in setting up realistic, less stringent standards for self-award. Behavioral goals of graded difficulty were determined for the self-dispensation of tangible self-reinforcements and positive self-statements. Components of this procedure included training in self-monitoring, objective self-evaluation of behavior, and self-administration of reinforcement for appropriate behavior.

Like other cognitive approaches, self-regulation training serves to make the depressed person more aware of the positive aspects of life events and his/her own behavior. Mathews (1977), who conceptualizes depression in terms of a self-regulatory dysfunction, defines self-regulation as "the processes by which an individual alters and maintains his behavior in the absence of immediate environmental support" (p. 82). Inaccurate self-monitoring, unrealistically high standards, an excess of self-punishment, and/or a deficit of self-reward are all internal events that may predispose a person to depression (Mathews, 1977). All will lower the total amount of contingent positive reinforcement experienced by the individual. Self-regulation training is applied to rectify faulty patterns of self-monitoring, self-evaluation, and self-reinforcement and thereby restore appropriate self-control over one's own behavior. It may also be useful as an adjunct to contingency management procedures, as it teaches skills that can compensate for deficits in environmental reinforcement.

Automatic negative thoughts and depressive ruminations are common to the depressed population. They may be indirectly eliminated by altering erroneous underlying attitudes and faulty self-regulation patterns. Alternatively, the depressed person can be taught to directly control the occurrence of depressed thoughts through thought-stoppage (Wolpe, 1958, 1969; Wolpe & Lazarus, 1966) and a programmed increase of positive cognitions.

Wanderer (1972) reports on the successful application of a thought-stoppage procedure in treating ruminating depressed persons. With this approach, the client is instructed to relax and then to concentrate on the unpleasant ideation. Without warning, the therapist disrupts ongoing depressive rumination by producing a loud noise and shouting, "Stop!" at the client. The client then learns to interrupt his/her own negative thoughts by overtly and then covertly yelling, "Stop!" while actively engaged in depressive ideation.

Todd (1972) and Seitz (1971) utilized Homme's (1965) extension of the

Premack Principle to increase positive self-evaluative statements. In both cases, a list of positive self-statements was elicited with considerable effort from chronically depressed patients. The occurrence of cigarette smoking (a high-frequency behavior) was then made contingent upon the reading of these personalized statements. Both authors report favorable outcomes utilizing this coverant control technique.

Mahoney (1971) treated a 22-year-old man suffering from numerous self-defeating obsessions with a combination of thought-stoppage and Homme's (1965) extension of the Premack Principle. The client was instructed to snap a rubber band placed around his wrist whenever an obsessional thought occurred, and additionally, to make cigarette smoking contingent upon engaging in positive thought. A total cessation of obsessional thought occurred by the sixth week of treatment; and the cigarette contingency, which was gradually faded out, produced an increased rate of positive self-thought. This client remained free of his obsessions at a four-month follow-up.

Unfortunately, the application of these techniques to disrupt or replace depressive rumination has received only preliminary study with case reports. Thus, such treatment should be implemented secondary to those cognitive approaches that have been subjected to more extensive investigation with depressed persons.

Autonomic Overresponsivity

Antianxiety procedures should be employed in cases of autonomic overresponsivity or neurophysiological hyperactivity. The interactive effects of depression and anxiety are as yet undetermined; however, a depressive's extreme anxiety responses are likely to interfere with his/her social functioning and therefore warrant early attention during therapeutic contact. Wolpe and Lazarus (1966) contend that severe and prolonged anxiety is a major cause of depression. The anxiety must be deconditioned, usually by systematic desensitization to anxiety-arousing stimuli or assertiveness training. Assertiveness training is recommended for the depressed person who evidences a conditioned anxiety response to interpersonal situations requiring assertive behavior (Wolpe, 1972). The learned assertive response is theoretically incompatible with habitual anxiety responses and thus accomplishes conditioned inhibition of the anxiety response habit (Wolpe, 1972).

Phobias, which involve excessive fear and avoidance of innocuous stimuli, may be causally related to depression by virtue of restricting the client from potentially rewarding activities. This is especially true for the depressive social phobic or agoraphobic. Systematic and/or in vivo desensitization is warranted whenever the depressed person's avoidance of anxiety-arousing stimuli is limiting his/her range of reinforcement. Wanderer (1972) reports the successful application of systematic desensitization in treating a depressed patient who feared various modes of travel, particularly airplane transportation. Deconditioning of the anxiety response exposed the patient to a wide range of pleasurable activities previously inaccessible by association with the feared stimuli.

We recently treated a young woman whose long-standing depression was both caused and maintained by phobic responses. Initially, she was phobic to the burn scars she had sustained from an accident. The woman had eventually become phobic of all social contacts, as she feared that her scars would be detected even when covered completely by clothing. When the client first contacted us, she was unemployed and her activity level was extremely low. Social skills observed in various interactions with psychology graduate students were very good, except when comments were made to the client about her appearance. Additionally, the client frequently engaged in rumination about her scar tissue.

Systematic and in vivo desensitization with this woman resulted in a total cessation of phobic behavior. Hierarchies were based on self and others being exposed to her scars as well as feared social exchanges. Assertiveness training provided her with appropriate responses when others would inadvertently stare at her scars or comment about them. Three months after the treatment program was initiated, the client no longer evidenced depressed behavior, had secured a job she enjoyed, and was engaged in a high rate of social activity.

Flooding, response prevention, and implosive therapy can also be used to extinguish anxiety and phobic behavior. Hannie and Adams (1974) investigated the effectiveness of flooding therapy (FT) relative to supportive therapy (ST) and no treatment (NT) in alleviating agitated depression (i.e., depression secondary to prolonged anxiety). Twenty-one anxious, depressed females were randomly assigned to one of the three conditions. Pre- and posttreatment measures included the Multiple Affect Adjective Checklist (MAACL), the Mental Status Schedule (MSS), the Fear Survey Schedule III (FSS), and the WAIS Digit Symbol Subtest (DS). On scales of the MSS and the MAACL, the FT group showed more positive change than the control groups. The authors concluded that FT was more effective than either control condition for reducing anxiety and depressive symptomatology.

As we have noted earlier, depressed individuals show more sensitivity to noxious stimulation than do nondepressed persons. The procedures mentioned above can also be employed to reduce an excessive arousal response to situations that are objectively aversive. For example, the depressed person who evidences debilitating anxiety in reaction to aversive social interactions can be taught assertive counterresponses and/or desensitization to counteract disruptive arousal and consequent avoidance. As we have also previously stated, social skills training may be necessary once avoidance behavior has been eliminated, if isolation from interpersonal contacts has prevented the acquisition of important interactional skills.

Being relaxed is negatively correlated with being depressed (Lewinsohn, 1975a; Lewinsohn & Graf, 1973). For many depressed persons, the state of relaxation is difficult to achieve. Relaxation skills should be taught to all those depressed clients who manifest physiological hyperactivity. High autonomic arousal may be experienced as chronic tension and anxiety or, alternatively, as fatigue and lethargy. This condition should preferrably be documented through physiological assessment.

CASE MANAGEMENT

We are advocating a treatment strategy that relies heavily on an accurate formulation for each clinical case. Formulation entails a conceptual process whereby etiological and maintaining factors are proposed, hopefully based on empirical data. The formulation of a case specifies causal and maintaining factors as well as functional relationships among various problems. Diagnosis, on the other hand, should involve a judgment as to whether a client's assessed behavior corresponds with the objective signs of a particular classification.

We are suggesting that when a client evidences a variety of symptoms the clinician should be sensitive to the interdependence of the target behaviors. For example, an individual may present depressive mood, sleep disorder, and impotence. It would be foolish to attempt to modify the impotence or sleep disturbance if they are a direct function of the depression. In a similar fashion, to treat depression when it is elicited as a function of another disorder is equally shortsighted. This does not mean that various difficulties could not be treated simultaneously in those few circumstances where it is warranted.

We are also suggesting that the varied behavioral manifestations of clinical depression are related for each client to common precipitating and maintaining events. If modification procedures focus on the common denominators of depressive symptomatology, rather than on individual depressive behaviors, successful outcome can be more parsimoniously achieved. Given that most depression is time-limited (Beck, 1967), mere alleviation of depressive symptoms does not constitute effective treatment. The client must learn from therapy those skills necessary to cope more effectively with stress that might arise in the future, so that he/she will be less susceptible to events that previously precipitated depression.

REFERENCES

Abramson, L. Y., Seligman, M. E. P., & Teasdale, J. D. Learned helplessness in humans: Critique and reformulation. *Journal of Abnormal Psychology,* 1978, **87**, 49–74.

Adams, H. E. *Psychology of abnormal behavior.* Dubuque, Iowa: Wm. C. Brown, in press.

Adams, H. E., Doster, J. A., & Calhoun, K. S. A psychologically based system of response classification. In A. R. Ciminero, K. S. Calhoun, & H. E. Adams (Eds.), *Handbook of behavioral assessment.* New York: Wiley, 1977.

Aderman, D. Elation, depression, and helping behaviors. *Journal of Personality and Social Psychology,* 1972, **24**, 91–101.

Akiskal, H. S., & McKinney, W. T. Overview of recent research in depression. *Archives of General Psychiatry,* 1975, **32**, 285–305.

Akiskal, H. S., & McKinney, W. T. Depressive disorders: Toward a unified hypothesis. *Science,* 1973, **182**, 20–29.

American Psychiatric Association. *Diagnostic and statistical manual of mental disorders* (DSM-II). Washington, D.C.: American Psychiatric Association, 1968.

American Psychiatric Association. *Diagnostic and statistical manual of mental disorders* (DSM-III). Washington, D.C.: American Psychiatric Association, 1980.

Bandura, A. *Principles of behavior modification.* New York: Holt, Rinehart & Winston, 1969.

Bandura, A. Self-efficacy: Toward a unifying theory of behavioral change. *Psychological Review,* 1977, **84**, 191–215.

Batsel, W. M. Cognitive alteration of depressive affect: A false-feedback experiment. Unpublished doctoral dissertation, University of Texas at Austin, 1976.

Beck, A. T. *Depression: Causes and treatment.* Philadelphia: University of Pennsylvania Press, 1967.

Beck, A. T. The development of depression: A cognitive model. In R. J. Friedman & M. M. Katz (Eds.), *The psychology of depression: Contemporary theory and research.* New York: Winston-Wiley, 1974.

Beck, A. T. *Cognitive therapy and the emotional disorders.* New York: International University Press, 1976.

Beck, A. T., & Rush, A. J. Research on suicide, depression, and anxiety. Paper presented at the meeting of the American Association of Behavior Therapy, New York, December, 1976.

Beck, A. T., Ward, C. H., Mendelson, M., Mock, J., & Erbaugh, J. An inventory for measuring depression. *Archives of General Psychiatry,* 1961, **4**, 561–571.

Becker, J. *Affective disorders.* Morristown, N.J.: General Learning Press, 1977.

Blaney, P. H. Contemporary theories of depression: Critique and comparison. *Journal of Abnormal Psychology,* 1977, **86**, 203–223.

Brenner, B. Enjoyment as a preventative of depression affect. *Journal of Community Psychology,* 1975, **3**, 346–357.

Brown, G. W., Harris, T. O., & Peto, J. Life events and psychiatric disorders, part 2: Nature and causal link. *Psychological Medicine,* 1973, **3**, 159–176.

Bruner, J. W., Goodnow, J. J., & Austin G. A. *A study of thinking.* New York: Science Editions, 1965.

Buchwald, A. M., Coyne, J. C., & Cole, C. S. A critical evaluation of the learned helplessness model of depression. *Journal of Abnormal Psychology,* **87**, 180–193.

Burgess, E. P. The modification of depressive behaviors. In R. D. Rubin & C. M. Franks (Eds.), *Advances in behavior therapy.* New York: Academic Press, 1969.

Byrne, D. Repression-sensitization as a dimension of personality. In B. A. Maher (Ed.), *Progress in experimental personality research.* New York: Academic Press, 1964.

Coleman, J. C. *Abnormal psychology in modern life* (5th edition). Glenview, Ill.: Scott, Foresman, 1976.

Coleman, R. E. Manipulation of self-esteem as a determinant of mood of elated and depressed women. *Journal of Abnormal Psychology,* 1975, **84**, 693–700.

Costello, C. G. Depression: Loss of reinforcers or loss of reinforcer effectiveness? *Behavior Therapy,* 1972, **3**, 240–247.

Costello, C. G. Reply to Lazarus. *Behavior Therapy,* 1972, **3**, 251–253.

Costello, C. G. A critical review of Seligman's laboratory experiments on learned helplessness and depression in humans. *Journal of Abnormal Psychology,* 1978, **87**, 21–31.

Coyne, J. C. Depression and the response of others. *Journal of Abnormal Psychology,* 1976, **85**, 186–193. (a)

Coyne, J. C. Toward an interactional description of depression. *Psychiatry,* 1976, **39**, 28–40. (b)

Depue, R. A., & Monroe, S. M. The unipolar-bipolar distinction in the depressive disorders. *Psychological Bulletin,* 1978, **85**, 1001–1029.

Eastman, C. Behavioral formulations of depression. *Psychological Review,* 1976, **83**, 277–291.

Ekman, P., & Friesen, W. V. Non-verbal behavior in psychopathology. In R. J. Friedman & M. M. Katz (Eds.), *The psychology of depression: Contemporary theory and research.* New York: Winston-Wiley, 1974.

Ellis, A. *Reason and emotion in psychotherapy.* New York: Lyle Stuart, 1962.

Ferster, C. B. A functional analysis of depression. *American Psychologist,* 1973, **28,** 857–870.

Flippo, J., & Lewinsohn, P. M. Unpublished manuscript, University of Oregon, 1969.

Forrest, M. S., & Hokanson, J. E. Depression and autonomic arousal reduction accompanying self-punitive behavior. *Journal of Abnormal Psychology,* 1975, **84,** 346–357.

Garfield, S. L. Research problems in clinical diagnosis. *Journal of Consulting and Clinical Psychology,* 1978, **46,** 596–607.

Gatchel, R. J., McKinney, M. E., & Koebernick, L. F. Learned helplessness, depression and physiological responding. *Psychophysiology,* 1977, **14,** 25–31.

Goldstein, I. B. The relationship of muscle tension and autonomic activity to psychiatric disorders. *Psychosomatic Medicine,* 1965, **27,** 39–52.

Grinker, R. R., Miller, I., Sabshin, M., Nunn, R., & Nunnally, J. C. *The phenomena of depression.* New York: Harper & Row, 1961.

Hale, W. D., & Strickland, B. R. The induction of mood states and their effect on cognitive and social behaviors. *Journal of Consulting and Clinical Psychology,* 1976, **55,** 144.

Hammen, C. L., & Glass, D. R. Depression, activity, and evaluation of reinforcement. *Journal of Abnormal Psychology,* 1975, **84,** 718–721.

Hammen, C. L., & Peters, S. D. Differential responses to male and female depressive reactions. *Journal of Consulting and Clinical Psychology,* 1977, **45,** 994–1001.

Hannie, T. J., & Adams, H. E. Modification of agitated depression by flooding: A preliminary study. *Journal of Behavior Therapy and Experimental Psychiatry,* 1974, **5,** 161–166.

Hersen, M., Eisler, D., Alford, G. S., & Agras, W. S. Effect of token economy on neurotic depression: An experimental analysis. *Behavior Therapy,* 1973, **4,** 382–397.

Hinchliffe, M. K., Lancashire, M., & Roberts, F. J. Depression: Defense mechanisms in speech. *British Journal of Psychiatry,* 1971, **118,** 471–472.

Hinsie, L., & Campbell, R. *Psychiatric dictionary.* London: Oxford University Press, 1960.

Homme, L. E. Perspectives in psychology: XXIV: Control of coverants, the operants of the mind. *Psychological Record,* 1965, **15,** 501–511.

Jackson, B. Treatment of depression by self-reinforcement. *Behavior Therapy,* 1972, **3,** 298–307.

Kanfer, F. H. Self-regulation: Research, issues and speculations. In C. Neuringer & J. L. Michael (Eds.), *Behavior modification in clinical psychology.* New York: Appleton-Century-Crofts, 1970. (a)

Kanfer, F. H. Self-monitoring: Methodological limitations and clinical applications. *Journal of Consulting and Clinical Psychology,* 1970, **35,** 148–152. (b)

Kanfer, F. H. The maintenance of behavior by self-generated stimuli and reinforcement. In A. Jacobs & L. B. Sachs (Eds.), *The psychology of private events: Perspectives on covert response systems.* New York: Academic Press, 1971.

Kanfer, F. H., & Karoly, P. Self-control: A behavioristic excursion into the lion's den. *Behavior Therapy,* 1972, **3,** 398–416. (a)

Kanfer, F. H., & Karoly, P. Self-regulation and its clinical applications. In R. C. Johnson, P. O. Mokecki, & O. P. Mower (Eds.), *Conscience, contract and social reality: Theory and research in behavioral science.* New York: Holt, Rinehart & Winston, 1972. (b)

Kanfer, F. H., & Phillips, J. S. *Learning foundations of behavior therapy.* New York, Wiley, 1970.

Kendell, R., & Gourlay, J. The clinical distinction between psychotic and neurotic depressions. *British Journal of Psychiatry,* 1970, **117,** 257–266.

Kety, S. S. Problems in psychiatric nosology from the viewpoint of the biological sciences. In M. M. Katz, J. O. Cole, & W. E. Barton (Eds.), *The role and methodology of classification in psychiatry and psychopathology.* Chevy Chase, MD: National Institute of Mental Health, 1965.

Klerman, G. L. Depression in adaptation. In R. J. Friedman & M. M. Katz (Eds.), *The psychology of depression: Contemporary theory and research.* New York: Wiley, 1974.

Lader, M. H., & Wing, L. Physiological measures in agitated and retarded depressed patients. *Journal of Psychiatric Research,* 1969, **7,** 89–100.

Lazarus, A. A. Learning theory and the treatment of depression. *Behaviour Research & Therapy,* 1968, **6,** 83–89.

Lazarus, A. A. Some reactions to Costello's paper on depression. *Behavior Therapy,* 1972, **3,** 248–250.

Lazarus, A. A. Multimodel behavioral treatment of depression. *Behavior Therapy,* 1974, **5,** 549–554.

Leff, M., Roatch, J., & Bunney, W. E., Jr. Environmental factors preceding the onset of severe depressions. *Psychiatry,* 1970, **33,** 293–311.

Lewinsohn, P. M. Clinical and theoretical aspects of depression. In K. S. Calhoun, H. E. Adams, & K. M. Mitchell (Eds.), *Innovative treatment methods in psychopathology.* New York: Wiley, 1974.

Lewinsohn, P. M. The behavioral study and treatment of depression. In M. Hersen, R. Eisler, & P. Miller (Eds.), *Progress in behavior modification,* Vol. 1. New York: Academic Press, 1975. (a)

Lewinsohn, P. M. Engagement in pleasant activities and depression level. *Journal of Abnormal Psychology,* 1975, **84,** 729–731. (b)

Lewinsohn, P. M., & Atwood, G. E. Depression: A clinical-research approach. *Psychotherapy: Theory, research, and practice,* 1969, **6,** 166–171.

Lewinsohn, P. M., Biglan, A., & Zeiss, A. M. Behavioral treatment of depression. In P. O. Davidson (Ed.), *The behavioral management of anxiety, depression, and pain.* New York: Brunner/Mazel, 1976.

Lewinsohn, P. M., & Graf, M. Pleasant activities and depression. *Journal of Consulting and Clinical Psychology,* 1973, **41,** 261–268.

Lewinsohn, P. M., & Libet, J. Pleasant events, activity schedules, and depression. *Journal of Abnormal Psychology,* 1972, **79,** 291–295.

Lewinsohn, P. M., Lobitz, C., & Wilson, S. "Sensitivity" of depressed individuals to aversive stimuli. *Journal of Abnormal Psychology,* 1973, **81,** 259–263.

Lewinsohn, P. M., & MacPhillamy, D. J. The relationship between age and engagement in pleasant activities. *Journal of Gerontology,* 1974, **29,** 290–294.

Lewinsohn, P. M., & Shaffer, M. The use of home observations as an integral part of the treatment of depression: Preliminary report and case studies. *Journal of Consulting and Clinical Psychology,* 1971, **37,** 87–94.

Lewinsohn, P. M., & Shaw, D. A. Feedback about interpersonal behavior as an agent of behavior change: A case study in the treatment of depression. *Psychotherapy and Psychosomatics,* 1969, **17,** 82–88.

Lewinsohn, P. M., Weinstein, M. S., & Alper, T. A behaviorally oriented approach to the group treatment of depressed persons: A methodological contribution. *Journal of Clinical Psychology,* 1970, **26**, 525–532.

Lewinsohn, P. M., Weinstein, M. S., & Shaw, D. A. Depression: A clinical-research approach. In R. D. Rubin & C. M. Franks (Eds.), *Advances in behavior therapy,* 1968. New York: Academic Press, 1969.

Liberman, R. P., & Raskin, D. E. Depression: A behavioral formulation. *Archives of General Psychiatry,* 1971, **24**, 515–523.

Libet, J., & Lewinsohn, P. M. The concept of social skills with special reference to the behavior of depressed persons. *Journal of Consulting and Clinical Psychology,* 1973, **40**, 304–312.

Libet, J., Lewinsohn, P. M., & Javorek, F. The construct of social skill: An empirical study of several measures on temporal stability, internal structure, validity, and situational generalizability. Unpublished manuscript, University of Oregon, 1973.

Lishman, W. A. Selective factors in memory: II, Affective disorder. *Psychological Medicine,* 1972, **2**, 248–253.

Lloyd, G. G., & Lishman, W. A. Effect of depression on the speed of recall of pleasant and unpleasant experiences. *Psychological Medicine,* 1975, **5**, 173–180.

MacPhillamy, D. J., & Lewinshon, P. M. Depression as a function of levels of desired and obtained pleasure. *Journal of Abnormal Psychology,* 1974, **83**, 651–657.

MacPhillamy, D. J., & Lewinsohn, P. M. The pleasant events schedule. Unpublished manuscript, University of Oregon, 1971.

Mahoney, M. J. The self-management of covert behavior: A case study. *Behavior Therapy,* 1971, **2**, 575–578.

Mahoney, M. J. *Cognitive and behavior modification.* Cambridge, Mass.: Bellinger Publishing, 1974.

Marsella, A. J. Depressive experience and disorder across cultures. In H. Triandis & J. Draguns (Eds.), *Handbook of cross-cultural psychology,* Boston: Allyn & Bacon, 1979.

Martin, I., & Davies, B. M. The effect of Na amytal in autonomic and muscle activity of patients with depressive illness. *British Journal of Psychiatry,* 1965, **111**, 168–175.

Martin, M. L., Weinstein, M., & Lewinsohn, P. M. The use of home observation as an integral part of the treatment of depression: The case of Mrs. B. Unpublished manuscript, University of Oregon, 1968.

Mathews, C. O. A review of behavioral theories of depression and a self-regulation model for depression. *Psychotherapy, Theory, Research & Practice,* 1977, **14**, 79–85.

Mayr, E. Concepts of classification and nomenclature in higher organisms and microorganisms. *Annals of the New York Academy of Science,* 1952, **56**, 391–397.

McLean, P. Therapeutic decision-making in the behavioral treatment of depression. In P. O. Davidson (Ed.), *The behavioral management of anxiety, depression, and pain.* New York: Brunner/Mazel, 1976.

McLean, P., Ogston, K., & Grauer, L. A behavioral approach to the treatment of depression. *Journal of Behavior Therapy and Experimental Psychiatry,* 1973, **4**, 323–330.

Meichenbaum, D. *Cognitive behavior modification.* Morristown, N.J.: General Learning Press, 1974.

Mendelson, M. Neurotic depressive reaction. In A. Freedman & H. I. Kaplan (Eds.), *Comprehensive textbook of psychiatry*. Baltimore, Md.: Williams & Wilkins, 1967.

Moore, B. S., Underwood, B., & Rosenhan, D. L. Affect and altruism. *Developmental Psychology*, 1973, **8**, 99–104.

Patterson, G. R., & Hops, H. Coercion, a game for two: Intervention technique for marital conflict. In R. E. Ulrich & P. Mountjoy (Eds.), *The experimental analysis of social behavior*. New York: Appleton-Century-Crofts, 1972.

Paykel, E. S. Life events and acute depression. In J. P. Scott & E. C. Sonay (Eds.), *Separation and depression: Clinical and research aspects*. Washington: American Association for the Advancement of Science, 1973.

Paykel, E. S., Myers, J. K., Dienelt, M. W., Klerman, G. L., Lindenthal, J. J., & Pepper, M. P. Life events and depression: A controlled study. *Archives of General Psychiatry*, 1969, **21**, 753–760.

Pehm, L. P. Assessment of depression. In M. Hersen & A. S. Bellack (Eds.), *Behavioral assessment: A practical handbook*. New York: Pergamon Press, 1976.

Plutchik, R. *Foundations of experimental research*. New York: Harper & Row, 1968.

Potts, T. L. Activity valence as a function of mood change. Unpublished master's thesis, University of Georgia, 1977.

Reisinger, J. The treatment of "Anxiety-Depression" via positive reinforcement and response cost. *Journal of Applied Behavior Analysis*, 1972, **5**, 125–130.

Rimm, D. C., & Masters, J. C. *Behavior therapy: Techniques and empirical findings*. New York: Academic Press, 1974.

Rimón, R., Stenbäck, A., & Huhmar, E. Electromyographic findings in depressive patients. *Journal of Psychosomatic Research*, 1967, **10**, 159–170.

Robbins, L. L. A historical review of classification of behavior disorders and one current perspective. In L. D. Eron (Ed.), *The classification of behavior disorders*. Chicago: Ardine, 1966.

Schwartz, G. E., Fair, P. L., Salt, P., Mandel, M. R., & Klerman, G. L. Facial muscle patterning to affective imagery in depressed and nondepressed subjects. *Science*, 1976, **192**, 489–491.

Seitz, F. C. A behavior modification approach to depression: A case study. *Psychology*, 1971, **8**, 58–63.

Seligman, M. E. P. *Helplessness: On depression, development, and death*. San Francisco: Freeman, 1975.

Seligman, M. E. P. Comment and integration. *Journal of Abnormal Psychology*, 1978, **87**, 165–179.

Shaffer, M., & Lewinsohn, P. M. Interpersonal behaviors in the home of depressed versus nondepressed psychiatric and normal controls: A test of several hypotheses. Paper presented the meeting of the Western Psychological Association, San Francisco, April, 1971.

Sheslow, D. V., & Erickson, M. T. An analysis of activity preference in depressed and nondepressed college students. *Journal of Counseling Psychology*, 1975, **22**, 329–332.

Shipley, C. R., & Fazio, A. F. Pilot study of a treatment for psychological depression. *Journal of Abnormal Psychology*, 1973, **82**, pp. 372–376.

Spielberger, C. D. (Ed.). *Anxiety & behavior*. New York: Academic, 1966.

Stengel, E. Classification of mental disorders. *Bulletin of the World Health Organization*, 1959, **21**, 601–663.

Strickland, B. R., Hale, W. D., & Anderson, L. K. Effect of induced mood states on activity and self-recorded affect. *Journal of Consulting and Clinical Psychology,* 1975, **43**, 587.

Suarez, Y., Crowe, M. J., & Adams, H. E. Depression: Avoidance learning and physiological correlates in clinical and analog populations. *Behaviour Research and Therapy,* 1978, **16**, 21–31.

Teasdale, J. D., & Bancroft, J. Manipulation of thought content as a determinant of mood and corrugator electromyographic activity in depressed patients. *Journal of Abnormal Psychology,* **86**, 235–241.

Thomson, K., & Hendrie, H. Environmental stress in primary depressive illness. *Archives of General Psychiatry,* 1972, **26**, 130–132.

Todd, F. J. Coverant control of self-evaluative responses in the treatment of depression: A new use of an old principle. *Behavior Therapy,* 1972, **3**, 91–94.

Tucker, J. A. The effects of sexual arousal and depression on the eating behavior of obese and normal individuals. Unpublished honor's thesis, Duke University, 1975.

Valins, S., & Nisbett, R. E. *Attribution process in the development and treatment of emotional disorders.* New York: General Learning Press, 1971.

Velten, E. A laboratory task for induction of mood states. *Behaviour Research and Therapy,* 1968, **6**, 473–482.

Wanderer, Z. W. Existential depression treated by desensitization of phobias: Strategy and transcript. *Journal of Behavior Therapy and Experimental Psychiatry,* 1972, **3**, 111–116.

Wessman, A. E., & Ricks, D. F. *Mood and personality.* New York: Holt, Rinehart & Winston, 1966.

Wolpe, J. *Psychotherapy by reciprocal inhibition.* Stanford, Calif.: Stanford University Press, 1958.

Wolpe, J. *The practice of behavior therapy.* Oxford: Pergamon, 1969.

Wolpe, J. Neurotic depression: Experimental analog, clinical syndromes, and treatment. *American Journal of Psychotherapy,* 1972, **25**, 362–368.

Wolpe, J., & Lazarus, A. A. *Behavior therapy techniques: A guide to the treatment of neuroses.* Oxford: Pergamon, 1966.

Wortman, C. B., & Dintzer, L. Is an attributional analysis of the learned helplessness phenomenon viable: A critique of the Abramson-Seligman-Teasdale reformulation. *Journal of Abnormal Psychology,* 1978, **87**, 75–90.

Zigler, E., & Phillips, L. Psychiatric diagnosis and symptomatology. *Journal of Abnormal and Social Psychology,* 1961, **63**, 69–75.

Zubin, L. Classification of the behavior disorders. *Annual Review of Psychology,* 1967, **18**, 373–406.

Zuckerman, M., Persky, H., & Curtis, G. C. Relationships among anxiety, depression, hostility, and autonomic variables. *The Journal of Nervous & Mental Disease,* 1968, **146**, 481–487.

CHAPTER 7

Remedying Schizophrenic Behavior

Kurt Salzinger

"I see nobody on the road," said Alice.

"I only wish I had such eyes," the King remarked in a fretful tone. "To be able to see Nobody! And at that distance too! Why, it's as much as I can do to see real people, by this light!"

LEWIS CARROLL, *Through the Looking-glass*

Nothing summarizes the controversy raging around the diagnostic category of schizophrenia as well as does the quotation above. Many is the investigator who has concluded that seeing schizophrenia is like seeing nobody "and at that distance too!" The feeling is quite definite, the proof hard to come by.

The controversy about this diagnostic category, as about others, is not abating. DSM III (The Diagnostic and Statistical Manual, 1980)—the latest American Psychiatric Association official document describing all the permissible diagnostic categories—is now being prepared. It is an attempt to arrive at a new consensus, based on majority rule of the committee to be sure and under the constant influence of various pressures from members of the psychiatric profession; but it will be, for the first time, buttressed by some empirical data concerning the reliability and validity of the various categories. The controversy, however, is continuing. This is so, to take but one example, because the greater use of *recent* research results in the constitution of diagnostic categories has laid them open to the uncertainty of passing the test of replication, and as such the research results are bound to be inconsistent across studies with regard to at least some categories. Of course, the alternative of continuing to accept the traditional lack of reliability and validity in this area is equally unacceptable. In addition, there are the more severe critics of the psychiatric system of classification who believe that DSM III, based as it is on the medical model, will harbor the same difficulties (e.g., no consideration is given to social or behavioral variables), as the older systems. Detailed criticisms of this kind are to be found in Salzinger (1977, 1978a), Schacht and Nathan (1977) and Zubin (1977–1978).

Given these difficulties, we will, although presenting the criteria for the diagnosis of schizophrenia based on DSM III, urge that the reader view that description only as furnishing general guidelines for identifying people who emit certain kinds of aberrant behaviors and, in the absence of data of a physiological nature, insist that the emphasis be on behavior; the transformation of the adjective "schizophrenic" to the noun "schizophrenic," although saving time and space, too often results in the false attribution of behaviors to people who do not in fact emit them. This springs from the fact that the category of schizophrenia even in DSM III is defined by the presence of a minimal *number* of symptoms and other characteristics in various subcategories rather than by the presence of particular markers. In other words, different patients who bear the name "schizophrenic" do not need to show the same symptoms or other characteristics. The assumption of the intersubstitutability of these various characteristics still needs to be tested; if it is unwarranted, then the classification is wrong. All in all, in suggesting that there might be a common core to what we call schizophrenia, this chapter is alerting the reader to the need to look for common behaviors rather than simply assume the presence of these categories of behavior.

How then do we use the diagnostic category that does, after all, in some vague way, define the boundaries of this chapter? We use it in several ways:

1. As a convenient way of finding certain aberrant *behavior*.
2. As a convenient starting point to find *people* belonging to a group characterized by a single disorder.
3. As a source of ideas for the treatment of people characterized by the diagnostic category. Such ideas are embodied in various theories of schizophrenia even though they are not often transformed into therapeutic practice. If a given theory states that schizophrenia is caused by an underlying deficit in stimulus reception, stimulus processing, or stimulus integration, then one should be able to focus treatment on that deficit. Such an approach allows one to test the validity of a theory as well as to evaluate the effectiveness of particular forms of treatment. Behavior modification, because of its explicitness, is particularly valuable in this regard as is shown below.

A TENTATIVE DESCRIPTION OF SCHIZOPHRENIA

Let us now, having cautioned the reader, present the diagnostic descriptions according to DSM III. These disorders are characterized first by a general disorganization of the previous level of functioning that cannot be explained in the same way as can the conditions listed in the Organic Mental Disorders Section of DSM III. Schizophrenic disorders involve at least one of the following: delusions (a belief unwarranted by the facts that someone else is controlling one, that insignificant events are in some way personally related to one, that other people can hear one's thoughts, and other bizarre beliefs of that kind), hallucinations (typically auditory and consisting of voices talking about one in the absence of the appropriate stimulation—usually in an insulting fashion; hallucinations other than auditory are rare and suggest that the disorder is probably organic in origin, rather than schizophrenic), or formal thought disorder (typically detected when the interviewer fails to understand what the patient is saying; examples of such difficulties are the use of incidental, noncontextually determined associations, vague statements, and obscure or stereotyped phrases). Noted for its absence in this array of critical aspects of schizophrenia is the affect category—either its shallowness or inappropriateness. The drafters of DSM III state that they had to omit affective disturbance from consideration because of the general difficulty in judging it reliably and because of the production of the same shallowness of affect by "antipsychotic" drugs as is supposedly produced by schizophrenia.

A refinement of the diagnostic system is the establishment of what has come to be called the Research Diagnostic Criteria (RDC). The RDC states in an explicit fashion the minimal symptoms and other characteristics that must be found in order to place a patient in a particular diagnostic category. According to this system, people are classified as schizophrenic if they manifest at least one of the three classes of symptoms listed above, that is, delusions, hallucinations, or formal thought disorder. In addition, they must show signs of the disorder for at least two weeks, and the symptoms must not be traceable to any of the Organic Mental Disorders listed in DSM III. The general category of schizophrenia is broken down into subcategories by the phenomenology of the disorder. The DSM III categories are sometimes given new names but their definition is very much the same as used in the older DSM booklets. A case in point is the category of the disorganized schizophrenic which was called "hebephrenic." Such patients are characterized by so-called silly affect and incoherence. Other categories of schizophrenia are catatonia (dominated by a marked decrease in reactivity to the environment, muteness, or bizarre postures), paranoia (dominated by false beliefs of persecution or of improbable power and ability), undifferentiated (substituted for the category formerly labelled "mixed" and used if all of the above categories seem to be present in a particular case, or for cases that meet the general criteria of schizophrenia but meet none of the specific criteria listed above). A final category is that of "residual," to be used when no "prominent psychotic symptoms" are noticeable but a previous episode containing some of the above-listed symptoms occurred, with some lesser signs of the disorder still present.

Finally, two other related categories now separated from the schizophrenic disorders are mentioned; they are schizoaffective disorder—manic or depressed. These two disorders are being kept separate from the main category of schizophrenia as well as from the main category of affective disorders (manic-depressive disorders). Essentially, the manic subtype of schizoaffective disorder is characterized by more than usual verbal and nonverbal activity, inflated self-esteem, and a smaller need for sleep, in addition to the general schizophrenic features mentioned above; patients suffering from the depressed subtype of schizoaffective disorder are characterized as being sad, blue, and "depressed," in addition to having the general schizophrenic characteristics. Whether the decision to separate the schizoaffective behaviors from the rest of schizophrenia is wise or not, only time will tell. Clearly, however, what future research tells us about "schizophrenics" according to DSM III may well be different from what we learned from research according to DSM II or DSM I.

So much then for the phenomenology of schizophrenia. We must take note here that what is missing from this description is almost as important as what is there; for example, the frequency of occurrence expected for each of the listed behaviors, the methods by which one is to ascertain the information, and the conditions under which one would expect the same behavior to be nonpathognomonic. Nevertheless, the explicitness, if not the arbitrariness, of the criteria is an improvement in the diagnostic system.

DSM III characterizes patients in terms of another dimension, namely the course of illness. Here, note is taken of the speed of onset and duration; that is, whether the disorder had been going on for two years or more or whether it took less than three months between the first signs of the disorder and the full-blown psychotic symptoms; the first kind of patient would be called chronic, the second acute. Between the two extremes are subacute (duration of five months) and subchronic (closer to chronic in duration). Another part of this dimension is the category "in remission." It is not entirely clear how this category (defined vaguely in terms of time since the last episode and the number of episodes before) is to be differentiated from the diagnosis of "no mental disorder." One gets the general impression that the drafters of DSM III wish to make up for the imprecision of definition of each category by having a large number of them.

THE SIGNIFICANCE OF PSYCHIATRIC DIAGNOSIS

We have given several reasons for the usefulness of psychiatric diagnosis above. Here, we will review some recent developments—not all scientific—that have lent added impetus to the renewed interest in psychiatric diagnosis and psychiatric treatment. The medical model is returning to power, in part, because of the advances in genetics and the biochemistry of the functioning organism. The work in the biochemistry of psychopathology was stimulated to a large degree by the discovery of a number of drugs that seemed to make psychotic patients more amenable to hospitalization. More restrictive measures (straightjackets) were hardly used after the introduction of the "antipsychotic" drugs. Moreover, this introduction of drugs was eventually followed by a great exodus of the patient population from the state hospital to the community. This migration is often attributed solely to the advent of drug therapy. However, it is to be noted that at the very same time, other means of intervention also came to the fore, particularly in such forms as milieu therapy, starting in England but quickly spreading to this country, group therapy, and behavior modification. Inspired by Skinner (1954) and Lindsley (1956), who put psychotic patients into cubicles and observed their behavior much the same way as they had the behavior of other organisms, behavior theorists used behavior theory not only as a way of changing the verbal behavior (Krasner, 1958; Salzinger, 1959) of patients, and not only in the course of diagnostic interviews (Salzinger & Pisoni, 1958, 1960, 1961), but also as a means of directly attacking the patients' inactivity and other bizarre behaviors (Ayllon and Azrin, 1968).

In addition to these changes in treatment, other events and issues occupied our society. While therapies for abnormal behaviors changed, our concepts of civil rights and our attitudes toward various groups such as Blacks, other ethnic groups, and women underwent a revolutionary change that eventually affected our attitudes toward the civil rights of mental patients. As a result, we now have lawyers representing the rights of patients in the hospitals, with special laws and regulations spelling out the rights of patients, including their right to know what treatment they are getting. As a result of suing for the right to treatment, patients could no longer be held in hospitals against their will without therapy. "Custodial" treatment was no longer held to be sufficient. One might have expected that development to result in refinement of various methods of therapy, but that did not happen because of a general tightening of governmental belts—correctly or not, people have been increasingly objecting to the ever-increasing tax burden. Instead of improvement of treatment methods, government officials found the solution of releasing patients into the community very agreeable since not only did it get them out of having to cope with the burden of running large state hospitals with all their upkeep costs, but it allowed them, by cutting down the number of attendants, occupational therapists, psychiatrists, psychologists, ground keepers, and so forth, to reduce the operating cost of such facilities.

One other variable influencing the reduction of hospital populations that is not often mentioned is the general reduction in birthrate during the depression; the net effect of that was a general decrease in the number of people reaching the age of high-incidence of schizophrenia at just about the time of the large-scale use of antipsychotic drugs.

In sum, although inspired not altogether for the right reasons, the modification and attempted improvement of the diagnostic system is clearly needed as the variety of treatments has become greater than in earlier times when custodial treatment only was given to all patients. Of course, the scientific reason for diagnostic classification is always the same: the construction of homogeneous groups so that each patient can serve as a replication for every other one in that group. From the practical point of view of improved treatment, this means appropriate matching of treatment to type of disorder. But there is also a political reason for the emphasis on psychiatric diagnosis and on drug treatment, namely the struggle for government insurance, which is sure to come in the next few years. Who will be able to decide on patient care and who will be compensated for it? The rise of a large number of new therapies, ranging from scream therapy through "group grope," acupuncture, nude marathons, and various and sundry other social therapies, in addition to the further development of the more classical social therapies, have made it clear that these many different ways of treating the psychologically infirm can be effectively carried out by people other than physicians. The interest in drug therapy and in improving psychiatric diagnosis is part of the psychiatrists' attempt to retain their powerful position vis-à-vis the treatment of the mentally ill.

DRUG TREATMENT FOR ACUTE PSYCHOTIC BEHAVIOR

The patients who left the hospitals in droves are now in the communities, often in the big cities, living in neglected ways and generally making enough of a nuisance of themselves so that the community in general is asking that the patients be removed from their neighborhoods. Perhaps even more important in all of this is the fact that the patients who continue to go to clinics to get their drugs do not seem to be faring any better than those who were not given the drugs. Moreover, the side effects, many of which were seen in the hospitals, not only continue requiring that the patients be watched very carefully, but in addition there is a new kind of side effect that has made its appearance of late and that is *tardive dyskinesia,* a form of involuntary muscle movement involving the face and arms and sometimes other parts of the body. That reflexive kind of motion involved is so debilitating that people under treatment sometimes are unable to keep their jobs, when the effect of the antipsychotic drug is supposed to make it possible for them to work.

Although noting these deleterious effects of drugs, articles continue to speak of the revolution in pharmacotherapy. Berger (1978) states (p. 974): "The drug treatments are not a panacea. The medications sometimes cause irreversible side effects, and they are not helpful for all patients. . . . Despite their limitations, psychotherapeutic drugs relieve a great deal of human suffering." The article presents the change in patient population in public mental hospitals and shows the drop beginning in 1956 when the drugs were introduced in large numbers and incorrectly attributes that drop in population to the drugs alone when in fact many other changes (enumerated above) had taken place at the same time.

There is another development which suggests that the drugs are not all that they have been built up to be; after the rise of the civil liberty proponents who objected to the incarceration of patients because they had been given custodial care only, that is, had not been given any active treatment, a second wave of lawyers are now objecting to the fact that patients have somehow lost the right to refuse treatment. A review of such a case (Zander, 1977; U.S. Court of Appeals, 1977), *Okin v. Rogers,* is presented in the July–August 1977 *Mental Disability Law Reporter* along with a brief description of the research on fluphenazine, a commonly used antipsychotic drug. Although no conclusion has been reached in the case as of this writing, the judge of the United States District Court for the District of Massachusetts, did order the Boston Hospital in question to refrain "from forcibly . . . medicating the [patients] . . . except where there is a serious threat of, or a result of, extreme violence, personal injury or attempted suicide."

There are rumblings coming from the citadel itself; psychiatrists such as Engel (1977) from the University of Rochester are making clear their dissatisfaction with the medical model as it now exists. Engel complained that psychiatrists are trying to reenter the halls of classical medicine by strict adherence to the medical model. He says (p. 130): "The historical fact we have to face is that in modern Western society biomedicine not only has provided a basis for the scientific study of disease, it has also become our culturally specific perspective about disease, that is, our folk model." Engel goes on to point out that the medical model "has acquired the status of *dogma*" (the italics are the author's). Engel challenges Kety's (1974) argument that schizophrenia, like diabetes, will ultimately be reduced to its biochemical source of difficulty. He contends that in both cases the biochemical fault constitutes but one cause of the disorder. The medical-model approach makes no attempt to obtain the relevant behavioral data in as scientific a way as it does the biochemical data. In failing here, it ignores a problem equally critical in the diagnosis of diabetes. Engel points out (p. 132): "Thus, virtually each of the symptoms classically associated with diabetes may also be expressions of or reactions to psychological distress, just as ketoacidosis and hypoglycemia may induce psychiatric manifestations."

In a recent paper, Salzinger (in press) made a similar point about the precision of the biochemical studies and the ambiguity of the behavioral data to which those biochemical results were being correlated. Salzinger argued that it is critical to uncover the *behavioral* mechanisms that converted the biochemical or neurophysiological deficit into the behavioral fault on the basis of which the mental patient has been identified. No theory of schizophrenia is complete that fails to state by what behavioral mechanism the hypothesized defect or deficit is converted into abnormal behavior. Specification of such a mechanism allows one to try behavioral interventions. For example, if we assume that the schizophrenic's behavior of hallucinating is due to a greater sensitivity to minimal-magnitude stimuli, then we might, by means of behavior therapy, train a group of such patients to attend primarily to stimuli of greater magnitude. The dependent variables would be not only the responses to the stimuli we trained the schizophrenic patients to ignore, and those to stimuli we trained them to attend to, but also the frequency of hallucinations before and after the training. We talk more about such theoretically based behavior therapy; here we point it out only to indicate the importance of having appropriate behavioral information for behavioral intervention. It also follows, as Engel says in his article, that the medical (actually he uses the term "biomedical" in the way we use the term "medical") model is inadequate to deal with psychopathology because of its limitation to what he calls the reductionistic approach, in which only the biological is considered in studying the disorder. No matter what the primary and what the secondary causes, it is the patient's behavior that calls our attention to them and it is the patient's behavior that we must evaluate to determine the effectiveness of our interventions. Engel argues in much the same way.

But let us return to consideration of the efficacy of drugs. An important article by Gunderson (1977) reviews a number of studies examining the question of what psychosocial treatment contributes toward the improvement of the schizophrenic patient treated by drugs. Note how defensively this hypothesis is stated. It reflects the thinking in this area of clinical functioning as well as research, at least in the medical community. The results of this review, nestled as it is, in the psychiatric literature among repeated testimonials to the effectiveness of the drugs and their contributions to this new millennium of drug treatment will come as a surprise. First of all, Gunderson found, and apparently without too much trouble, studies that showed that drugs actually interfered with the psychosocial treatment that was effective when used alone; he also found that the effectiveness of drugs varied with the social context in which they were administered.

Like Engel, Gunderson (1977) laments the failure of the medical model to require specification of social intervention in precise scientific terms. With this inadequate specification of what was involved, psychosocial treatment was found to be inadequate to cause any effect beyond that produced by the drugs. Too often such studies were conducted in state hospitals in which psychosocial treatment meant merely more staff without any specification of more program; the places in which psychosocial treatment was administered were typically viewed as control wards both in the eyes of the staff and the patients. Gunderson raises an additional point. All schizophrenic patients are not the same before drug treatment. Some are more likely to benefit from it than others; there is evidence, for example, that paranoid patients are more likely to benefit from psychosocial treatment and less likely to improve because of drug treatment.

A factor not always taken into account in evaluation studies is the length of time of follow-up. Those treated by drugs alone appear to be less well off after a longer follow-up period than they were on a short-term basis. The reason for this is fairly obvious; since short-term follow-up does not include the necessary adjustment that an improved patient must make in order to survive in the community, such problems do not appear until later. Since drugs can only, at best, alleviate some troublesome emotions or change a person's response to stimulation, rather than teach anyone a new way to behave or adjust to an environment, it is not surprising that a psychosocial technique that specifically takes up such problems of living should in the long run be superior to drug therapy. Why must new behavior be involved in the treatment of schizophrenic patients? Because it is inconceivable that most of the psychotic patients who come to be given drugs in these studies, with all their bizarre behaviors—hallucinations, delusions, and confusing communication patterns—should ever have had the opportunity to learn how to get along in our very complex society.

Let us look at a recent study on the treatment of acute schizophrenia without drugs. Note first that if you ask any psychiatrist, and many a psychologist, what to do for an acute schizophrenic episode the answer will be clear and forceful: drug the afflicted person to produce the quickest and best help you can! Carpenter, McGlashan, and Strauss (1977) compared 2 groups of patients—one group of 49 acute schizophrenic patients in a program that emphasizes psychosocial treatment and another of 73 similar patients given the usual drug program with nurse support. A general outcome measure (based on an assessment of work function, social function, and time in hospital) used to compare the two groups showed a small but significant superiority in the psychosocial over the drug group. Length of treatment stay in the hospital was approximately the same in the 2 groups; drugged patients had a greater likelihood of being depressed after their psychosis had subsided than the other group. Finally, this study also found that patients whose drug regimen was discontinued because of the research design did not relapse. Interpreting this study most generously from the drug point of view, we must conclude that acute schizophrenic patients given drugs fared no better than those who were treated by means of a psychosocial program.

Let us now look at a case study of the interaction of the administration of phenothiazines and a social skills training program. Hersen, Turner, Edelstein, and Pinkston (1975) report the case of a 27-year-old, single, Black male who was admitted to the psychiatry service of a veterans administration center with a diagnosis of schizophrenia, catatonic type, withdrawn. When admitted, he was partially mute, unresponsive, and hallucinating. At the time of his admission he had been in outpatient treatment that consisted of large doses of thorazine and stelazine. He had been treated in the hospital for a period of 88 days some 3 years before when he had had a schizophrenic episode. During his earlier hospitalization, he was treated with drugs and after discharge, he was continued in drug treatment for the 3 years preceding the current hospitalization. He was also seen in "supportive" psychotherapy as an outpatient. During that period he was never able to lead a normal life, being reclusive throughout and having no job. The ultimate deterioration that ensued resulted in his current hospitalization.

Although his drug treatment was not discontinued entirely, it was reduced sufficiently so that he was not so drowsy as to be completely unresponsive. He was then placed in a general token economy program; in it, he was able to earn points that were exchangeable for more concrete rewards. Although he was earning points, the quality of his work in the token economy was not very good. It was at this point that the investigators decided to conduct a behavioral analysis of the patient's specific problems. Note that the early treatment with this patient was through a token economy, a form of treatment that changes the patient's environment to be generally responsive to his actions; that constitutes a profound change in the life of the patient whose major difficulty often is lack of interaction with the environment. It is also one of the difficulties of back wards of state hospitals in which patients' actions have virtually no effect, so that eventually the patients cease to interact with their environment even if they did so when they first entered the hospital. In addition to the general reinforcement contingencies of the token economy, one can form-fit a behavior modification program to the particular problems of a given patient. This requires a behavioral analysis examining the variables currently controlling the patient's problematic behavior.

The behavioral analysis in this case arrived at the general conclusion that the patient required social skills training. The patient was trained through instructions, behavioral rehearsal, feedback, and modeling on four of eight scenes. The other four scenes served as generalization situations, in order to test whether the training given in the first four scenes carried over to other situations. The therapists demonstrated that the patient improved such assertive behaviors as increased eye contact, reduction of voice fadings, and increase in making requests; furthermore, generalization was demonstrated in the group psychotherapy sessions in which the patient initiated conversations more frequently.

Toward the end of the social skills training program, the patient was given job retraining by being allowed to work in a Goodwill Industries two-week training program. The patient subsequently found a job in the community that he eventually changed for one that paid better, was closer to home, and had a number of his friends working there. The patient's adjustment to his natural environment continued for at least 22 weeks following his discharge from the hospital. The study showed that the simple administration of drugs even when accompanied by so-called supportive psychotherapy is not enough to help a psychotic patient remain in the community. What is needed is specific help based on a behavioral analysis of the difficulties of that patient. That analysis must then be followed by modification of the patient's behavior; in this case, by slowly fading in new stimulus, controls. In this instance, this was accomplished by going from scenes that were almost completely artificial, to a protected job, to a job on the outside, and finally to a job that made still further demands on the patient. As for the drugs used here, by closely observing the patient's behavior and seeing the effect of the variations of the dosage and its interaction with the behavioral program, it was possible to make most effective use of the drugs as well as of the behavioral program.

What can we conclude so far? Drugs are not all that some have claimed they are. The advent of drugs was not the only factor that changed concomitant with the reduction in psychiatric hospital populations; drugs do not always help, nor do they help every type of schizophrenic patient. Sometimes they seem to interfere with the help that patients might have gotten from other kinds of therapy, and finally, as is shown in greater detail below, the kinds of psychosocial therapies to which they were often compared were grossly inadequate. Thus, we must conclude it is not obvious that drugs are necessary for patients in the acute stage. But what about the use of drugs to keep patients from becoming worse?

MAINTENANCE OF BEHAVIOR THROUGH THE USE OF DRUGS

We have shown above that the effect of drugs is not an unmixed blessing. Nevertheless, treatment of psychosis in general, and of schizophrenia in particular, is not much affected by research results. The immediate consequences of the treatment under one's own supervision (and which change in behavior might well be due to other factors than the drug treatment) are much more important than the more remote research findings. As a result, the use of drugs for acute psychotic episodes continues unabated. In this section, we will examine the use of drugs in maintenance therapy. We have already pointed out that drugs have very potent side effects. Some deleterious effects are more prone to occur when the drugs are used for longer periods of time. It is axiomatic that these effects take longer to discover.

Tobias and MacDonald (1974) wrote a critical review of the area and found, even though a majority of the studies they examined concluded that drug withdrawal results in clinical relapse, or at least in behavioral deterioration, that these conclusions were not warranted because of errors in design, procedure, analysis, or interpretation of the data collected. Even a mere listing of all the errors in these studies would take up too much space in this chapter, but it is instructive to look at some of them. To begin with, many of the publications are mere case studies and do not make use of the double-blind design (i.e., where neither the patient nor the therapist knows who is getting an active drug and who is getting a placebo—although side effects, and sometimes even main effects make it possible for clinicians to uncover who is getting the active drug and who the placebo); definitions of what constitutes a chronic and an acute patient vary from three months to two years of sickness, thus making studies incomparable; dosages vary from study to study and even within studies—checks on actual intake of drugs are sometimes effective although it is difficult to generalize from these studies to actual clinical treatment where the absence of such checks means that various patients are getting different dosages; differences in attitude or bias of therapists measured in some studies have been shown to be significant factors in what the therapists do, and perhaps even more important, in their evaluation of clinical outcome; the milieu was found to be more important in changing the behavior of patients than the usual drug studies allowed for, and wards that use milieu-therapy principles show smaller differences between drug and placebo groups than those that do not; there are problems of differential drop-out rates between drug and placebo groups: although some placebo patients are given drugs when they appear to have a relapse and are therefore dropped from the placebo group, change of a drug patient who appears to have a relapse to a placebo simply does not occur, with the consequence that no conclusions can be drawn about these patients' states at a later time. The judgment of what constitutes a relapse is a changeable thing as shown by a study (Serafetinides, Collins, & Clark, 1972) that took patients on drug treatment and abruptly withdrew medication in 57 patients, substituting no placebo, for a period of 12 weeks for "drying out." They found only one clinical relapse. This last result should be instructive for those people who are told that patients cannot be taken off drugs for purposes of trying out other treatments because of the high relapse rate that is "known" to result. Sometimes the experiments that investigate the effectiveness of maintenance of drug treatment use measures that have poor reliability, or report none. The measures very often have not been validated in any way; sometimes, when several hospitals are used in comparisons, the rates of placebo relapses vary all the way from 12 to 68%, suggesting that there are differences in patients, and in relapse criteria, but even more important, suggesting that the different environments of the different hospitals may account for a very large difference in relapse—certainly as large as any drug-placebo difference reported.

Davis, Gosenfeld, and Tsai (1976) responded to the Tobias and MacDonald (1974) review by admitting that many of the studies cited did indeed contain errors but insisted that these errors increase the variance and thereby probably acted to decrease the chances of finding a significant difference between the drug and placebo groups. They also presented what they called "controlled" studies according to which, adding up all the results, only 20% of the patients on drugs relapsed as opposed to 52% who were on placebo. Even if we accept these results (and they are questionable), we should note that as many as half the patients now getting drugs clearly do not need them and that 20% who do get active drugs relapse and therefore needlessly leave themselves open to the side effects of the drugs.

MacDonald and Tobias (1976) responded to Davis et al. (1976). First, they pointed out that unreliability does not always increase general variance thereby making the finding of significant differences between groups less likely. They showed that *systematic* unreliability actually gives rise to a spurious finding of difference when in fact there is none. They also point out that the use by Davis et al. of the relapse criterion as their measure of the efficacy of drug maintenance uses the weakest link in any argument for drugs. This is so because relapse is defined differently by various investigators, never mind clinicians; it has poor reliability, and it is based on a patently false assumption that level of functioning can be reduced to one sick-well dimension.

An important study of the effect of maintenance of psychotropic drugs in the presence of active environmental treatment programs was undertaken by Paul, Tobias, and Holly (1972). They used what they called a "triple-blind" design, in which patients, clinical staff administering the drugs (or placebos), and the observers collecting data on the patients were not only unaware as to who received an active drug and who a placebo, but did not even know that a drug study was being conducted. Four different assessment instruments were employed to arrive at some global estimate of functioning in chronic patients, some of which measured bizarre behaviors, others low-level, and still others higher-level social functioning; these measures were obtained by watching the patients on the ward, or through a structured interview; the fourth assessment device sampled behavior periodically. Reliability estimates were obtained on all of the measures for the people using the measurement instruments and were found to be very high (.87 and higher).

Patients were given two different behavioral treatments (one consisting of milieu therapy and one of social learning or behavior therapy); and they were equated in terms of a number of background variables such as age, sex, socioeconomic status, marital status, race, presence of precipitating factors, prior somatotherapy, medical problems, length of hospitalization, score on a process-reactive continuum, and nature of symptom onset; they also checked the baseline functioning of the four groups. Finally, the two types of social treatment groups were randomly divided into those that had their drug treatment continued and those who were abruptly switched to a placebo. The results were quite clear: over a period of 4½ months there was an increase in adaptive behavior and a decrease in bizarre behavior as a function of the treatment programs. (It is of incidental interest to note that these patients had been hospitalized for an average of 17 years without showing a change in their behavior.) No significant interaction was found between the two treatment programs and the maintenance of the drug treatment. Bizarre behavior declined from an average of 51% of the time engaged in it during the baseline period to an average of 22% of the time 18 weeks later. The only effect of continuation of the drug treatment was to retard the patients' progress in response to the social treatment programs.

Drug treatment both for controlling acute episodes and for maintenance of improvement in the case of chronic patients must be questioned, whether we use the criterion of cost (i.e., the side effects, more of which we hear about as length of treatment continues) or the criterion of effectiveness.

THE PLACE OF A BEHAVIORAL CONCEPTION OF SCHIZOPHRENIA

It will be useful at the outset to make clear that behavior theory must be considered with reference to schizophrenia whether we call it a disease, a disorder, evil behavior, criminal behavior, stupid behavior, poor manners, or whatnot. At a time when it has become clear that even physiological aspects of our behavior can be modified in a lawful way by the principles of behavior theory, it is long past the time for argument. In other words, at least at one level, it does not matter whether the "urcause" is physiological, biochemical, or electrical, whether some neural damage was done to the fetus or the adult, whether a genetic effect is manifested, or whether a transient environmental change is visible. In all of these cases, we must contend, as suggested above, with a behavioral mechanism (Salzinger, in press). It is never enough to say that something is caused by a physical deficit or fault. We must always ask, "How does it affect behavior?" It will be the contention of this chapter that the proper way of answering that question is by stating how the usual controls of behavior are modified by the defect that is hypothesized.

To clarify this point, let us talk about a defect that we all know about—nearsightedness. It demonstrates the rather important interaction of the physical defect and the requirements of the environment that make up the reinforcement contingencies critical to behavior theory. Nearsighted people often fail to be stimulated by the same stimuli as people whose vision is normal. If the individuals in question do not realize they are nearsighted then their responses will appear to be peculiar to other members of our society. For example, people who continue to drive while nearsighted (and not wearing glasses) might get into a fatal accident, injure themselves while working on machines, appear to be nonresponsive to greetings from friends, and so on. The extent to which their behavior is "different" will depend on the extent to which visual stimuli control our behavior. Thus, one could conceive of living in a society of blind people where being nearsighted would, rather than constituting a problem, be an asset. However, if the society were set up so that all the important discriminative stimuli (which is what we are talking about here) were other than visual, then being sighted would not help very much at all. One reason being nearsighted or blind is a problem is that in our society a large number of discriminative stimuli are visual.

Let us now consider nearsighted people from the point of view of the consequences of their behavior. What if most of the consequences of our behavior, or merely the important ones, were visual; it must be remembered that much of our behavior is governed by conditioned reinforcers and that many of those are visual. That means that we might continue to emit responses even though the reinforcer by which those responses would ordinarily be controlled were already available. People who cannot see far enough would also act as if they were under extinction much of the time even though visually reinforced, with the result that they would emit other responses than those appropriate, and the reinforcement control of their behavior would be less precise. The weakened discriminative and reinforcing control of the nearsighted people's behavior, whose vision was not corrected by eyeglasses, would then be aversive to those who would deal with them. The result would be a host of untoward consequences of a second order such as: people might avoid them, would prefer not to spend time with them, would not choose them for certain tasks with the further consequence that the nearsighted would then be exposed to more aversive stimuli than the normally sighted; they would be under the control of punishing stimuli much of the time, with consequent emotional behavior that might further alienate them from people and from other sources of positive reinforcement, and so forth. It is not very difficult to imagine a situation in which one could predict how a physical deficit would affect someone's behavior through the mechanism of the reinforcement contingency.

Note that sometimes one can make up directly for a deficit—as in this case, with eyeglasses. In other cases, it might take the form of assessing the stimuli to which one cannot react, as in blindness, and then seek out substitutes for those. It is also important to note that all physical deficits are not equal; for example, in our society physical prowess is not critical; in fact, we do not ordinarily look upon lack of physical prowess as a deficit. In a hunting and gathering society, however, that might indeed be a significant deficit because of the reinforcers in the society that are contingent on it.

To return to schizophrenia, when we know what the deficit is that we need to remedy, then we can go about the task of building the requisite prosthetic device. By proper behavioral testing we have one very important route to discovery of that deficit. It means that our behavior research should focus on particular basic functions to find that deficit. When we find such a deficit, it will have some very important implications for the use of behavior therapy. We are suggesting that we use behavior therapy along theoretical lines. By this time there are a number of theories that specify a particular basic deficit. The implication of such a deficit is to modify the behavior of schizophrenic patients by attacking that deficit rather than by changing each class of behavior separately. More about that later.

A behavioral conception for the amelioration of schizophrenia is most appropriate when the theory about its inception is environmental, without benefit of any special kind of *Anlage,* that is, any special genetic makeup that makes some people susceptible to schizophrenia and some not. It is, however, also useful for theories that give a place both to genetics and the environment. Zubin (1976) has recently come up with a theory of schizophrenia of that kind. It uses a vulnerability concept in conjunction with the idea of time-limited episodes. According to Zubin it takes less of a precipitating incident to make some people become schizophrenic than others. Obviously this theory takes the genetic makeup into account, but it also gives a place to environment in the form of precipitating incidents. One of the few attempts at objectifying such precipitating incidents is the method of critical life events (Dohrenwend & Dohrenwend, 1974). That method asks what environmental events precede psychological (and physical) ailments. Although at the moment the method is a listing of events that on a statistical basis are likely to precede problems of various kinds, it nevertheless will eventually lend itself to individual use as well. For our purposes here we can say that this approach is a first approximation to gaining an understanding of the effect of the environment in causing psychological problems. Completely environmentally caused schizophrenia theories are very rare but they do exist. Ullmann and Krasner (1975), for example, maintain that schizophrenia is essentially the product of the extinction of attending responses, particularly those attending responses that are normally controlled by social stimuli. This theory makes it quite clear how one should apply behavior therapy to help a schizophrenic patient.

Finally, there is another way of conceptualizing the role of behavior therapy in remedying schizophrenic behavior, and that is to ignore the putative causes of schizophrenia altogether, applying behavior therapy that is an all-purpose technique of altering behavior—to increase, decrease, or change behavior and/or its stimulus control and to eliminate problems on a completely empirical basis. That point of view suggests that diagnosis, with all of its theoretical baggage, serves only to call attention to possible behaviors and distracts the therapist from the behaviors that actually occur. It is of some interest to note that this is exactly how behavior therapy has been most frequently employed with schizophrenic patients. Certainly that is the way behavior modification began. This is not to say that one should modify each response class separately and apart from every other one. The normal methods of behavior analysis are still called for in this approach. Some response classes constitute "opportunity responses" in that they open up other situations to individuals making possible the reinforcement of many other desirable responses. Thus a man who has no difficulty getting along with strangers once he is with them in a social situation but who is terribly afraid to go out of his house would no doubt benefit greatly from having that fear extinguished (by whatever method the behavior therapist finally decides upon). For this man it would certainly be more important to work on that response, rather than, for example, his habit of chain smoking—a response that might be taken care of at a later time; if he does learn to conquer his fear of leaving his house first, he might also be more likely to follow a program made up by his therapist for giving up smoking afterward. The rules of response and stimulus generalization would also have to be taken into consideration, as would questions of incompatibility of different responses that together might play an important role in the particular responses that the man emits or fails to emit.

BEHAVIORAL TREATMENT

With the above as an orientation as to how behavior modification could possibly be used, we shall describe some of the common methods of treatment in use and show how they relate to the empirical or the theory-based approach to schizophrenia.

We have already pointed out the significant role that variables outside of the science play with respect to the concepts in diagnosis. We need to do the same with respect to the utilization of behavior modification in patients in the state mental hospitals. The first patients on whom such new techniques were tried out were the chronic back ward patients. These patients were made available to psychologists for this new form of treatment because the psychiatrists found themselves unable to cope with them and also because most of the psychiatrists wanted to deal with patients that could at least be talked to so that they might try out their psychoanalysis-based therapies, if the insulin and electroshock treatments caused no changes. These patients also presented some of the largest problems of taking care of themselves, since they were usually unkempt and poorly clothed, refusing to eat or throwing food around, and in some cases presenting serious problems of safety both for the staff and the other patients in becoming violent.

In addition to these nonscientific factors, Skinner (1954) and Lindsley (1956), as stated above, turned their attention to the study of the psychiatric patient by observing regressed, noncommunicative patients in cubicles that strongly resembled the Skinner box, used to study the behavior of pigeons and rats, in order to find out how the behavior of psychotic patients varied with reinforcement contingencies. These studies showed that even the most regressed, mute and unkempt patients who had been kept away from the outside world could respond to reinforcement contingencies carefully constructed according to the principles of behavior theory. At the same time the principles of behavior theory were also applied to the verbal behavior of schizophrenics; here, even short periods of application of the reinforcement procedure caused changes in various classes of verbal response (Krasner, 1958; Salzinger, 1959, 1969) such as affect responses which had been deemed diagnostic and prognostic for schizophrenia (Salzinger & Pisoni, 1958, 1960, 1961; Salzinger, Portnoy, & Feldman, 1964). It was not merely simple knob-pulling behavior as used by Skinner and Lindsley that could be changed. Relatively complicated verbal behavior also could be modified.

Publishing in the second volume of the new *Journal of the Experimental Analysis of Behavior,* Ayllon and Michael (1959) showed the possibility of interfering with such long standing behaviors in chronic and acute schizophrenic patients as hoarding, avoidance of self-feeding, and the associated delusion about feeling that one is being poisoned. In 1960, Isaacs, Thomas, and Goldiamond showed that it is possible to take acute psychotic patients and reinstate their speech. The two patients in question had been mute for 14 and 19 years respectively. The procedures employed were the classical ones for operant conditioning: the experimenters shaped the responses by reinforcing ever-closer approximations to the desired response, first by reinforcing the patient's looking at the reinforcer (the gum), then moving the lips and looking at the gum, then looking at the gum and making a vocalization, and finally repeating the experimenter's saying gum. The last part also made use of approximation conditioning; the experimenter accepted relatively remote approximations to the word "gum" at first, gradually making the matching accuracy requirement more precise by reinforcing ever closer approximations to the word "gum."

The promotion of generalization from the experimental situation to others, which continues to be a problem today as it did earlier, was not left to chance but was brought about in an explicit planned for manner. When the patients did not yet speak on the ward even though they did in the experimental sessions, a generalization promotion program was instituted. A ward nurse was introduced into the experimental situation and the patient's speaking in response to the nurse's questions was reinforced in the presence of the experimenter. Other staff members on the ward were instructed to withhold objects requested by the patient until the patient spoke.

Sherman (1965) used a similar set of principles to instate speech in mute schizophrenics; in addition to using imitation procedures, he employed fading principles. Thus, in getting the patients to say particular words, he first said the entire word and gradually less and less of that word until he simply asked the patient to name the object. Sherman also demonstrated the effectiveness of the reinforcement contingency by reversing it for a time by reinforcing the patient for every period of 30 seconds when he did *not* speak in response to the stimulus that had earlier evoked speech.

Token Economies

Many demonstrations of the effectiveness of behavior therapy techniques in individual case studies followed the studies described. A number of journals exist today that specialize in behavior modification, and many articles continue to be published in the more general journals also; we have many books on behavior therapy today; courses in the area are taught at almost all universities, and many graduate programs have sprung up. A specific development is particularly related to schizophrenic patients, not in a theoretical but in a practical way. A great need exists to do something with schizophrenic patients best characterized as being unresponsive to their environment. A specialized form of behavior modification designed to deal with such patients is the token economy. It became so successful that today it is used in schools, camps, and even in families as a way of coping.

In 1965, Ayllon and Azrin described the first token economy. This was followed by a book by the same authors (Ayllon & Azrin, 1968) and in the same year Atthowe and Krasner (1968) published their report on the token economy. Since then other books have been published on the nature of token economies. Schaeffer and Martin (1969) were the first in being both specific and generally prescriptive as to what to do. The latest (Paul & Lentz, 1977) is a most comprehensive study of a token economy. Its characteristics are studied by contrasting it to milieu therapy. Paul and Lentz use generally accepted measures of patient functioning in addition to the usual behavior theory measures that concentrate on measuring specific behaviors as they respond to changes in reinforcement contingencies. The study presents detailed aspects of the evaluation schemes used, the program for the token economy, and, because it is compared to milieu therapy, some valuable ways of differentiating between them. A six-year study, it presents a detailed comparison of the results for years of follow-up, including follow-up into the community. It took a large number of precautions to assure that the different treatment groups being compared were comparable to begin with, regarding patient characteristics and staff members' characteristics. The behavior of the latter was strictly governed and observed to make sure that they followed exactly the kind of program called for by the particular approach being tested. The results of this study were thus quite clear: the token economy was clearly superior to the milieu therapy technique and the traditional hospital program. The superiority showed itself in the functioning within the hospital and in the production of a higher-release rate from the hospital. Comparison of those who were released by the different programs showed no difference in rates of rehospitalization or functioning in the community. The superior results of the token economy were produced in a more efficient and cost-effective manner than the milieu therapy effects because the staffing was the same across the treatment conditions being compared. The results were independent of demographic characteristics of the patients, and even the severity of their initial condition. Perhaps most important, the results produced by the token economy occurred in the relative absence of psychotropic drugs. One is led to the conclusion that at least with respect to the chronically hospitalized patient, the treatment of choice is the token economy. It is not possible to present a complete description of the results or even the procedures; the interested reader is urged to consult the book *Psychosocial Treatment of Chronic Mental Patients: Milieu Versus Social-Learning Program* by Paul and Lentz (1977).

In the interest of presenting some of the procedures that constitute an effective token economy, we will present important parts of the *Manual* describing the rules and procedures employed. The *Social-Learning Program Manual,* as the token economy is referred to, begins by explaining the principles of reinforcement and is the book used by the ward staff. It first defines positive and negative reinforcers. It defines them in the usual operant way in terms of an increase in frequency of response. It also discusses three principles of reducing frequency of response: punishment (which the *Manual* labels "negative reinforcement" but explains must be contingent on the occurrence of the response in order to reduce response rate), response cost (in which positive reinforcers are not given out or are taken away as a consequence of the emission of a response), and extinction.

The *Manual* discusses the necessity of reinforcing the target behavior immediately, the association of the discriminative stimulus with primary reinforcers to produce conditioned reinforcers, and the association of a conditioned reinforcer with a number of situations and other primary and conditioned reinforcers to become a generalized reinforcer such as attention or money. The *Manual* also discusses shaping (the approximation conditioning we mentioned above with respect to the acquisition of speech in mute patients), prompting of responses by way of instructions, and modeling (demonstrating the responses to be emitted). Specific examples are provided and it is suggested that the instructions and prompts be faded out gradually. The reasons for using tokens are explained. The reasons being that one can give them out immediately after the response occurs and that they have a consistent value irrespective of the patient's current condition of satiation or deprivation. The Manual stresses, as it should, that tokens are to be accompanied by social reinforcement.

Shaping of responses takes the form of first giving patients tokens for merely attending an activity; during the course of the activity special color chips are given as "shaping" chips; these are exchanged later into the tokens administered at the end of the activity period. Thus, the shaping chips serve merely to bridge the gap between the behavior of a given activity and the end of the activity when the tokens, which act essentially as money, are given out to the patients. As mentioned above, all tokens are accompanied by social reinforcement. The latter process is obviously very important since schizophrenic patients who make up the larger part of chronic mental patient groups seem not to respond to social reinforcers to begin with; they obviously need to learn to respond to social stimuli in general and to social reinforcers in particular. The tokens are gradually thinned out as the patients improve so that the reinforcers are given out after increasingly longer periods of delay following the behavior. Patients are not forced to do anything. After they sample the activities during which they can earn tokens, they are encouraged to choose whatever they wish to do; the reinforcers are allowed to take over control. Inappropriate behavior, with the exception of violent behavior that has to be handled on an immediate basis to prevent harm to people or objects, is typically handled by the method of extinction; that is, nobody pays any attention to those behaviors nor are any tokens given out at such times. Destructive behaviors are followed by "time-out"; during such times the patient cannot receive any positive reinforcers or avoid any negative reinforcers; this is accomplished by having the patient removed to a place where those conditions prevail (e.g., a room in isolation). Furthermore, response cost is also used in some of these cases; patients emitting asocial behaviors have to pay token charges. Finally, these contingencies are accompanied with prompts and instructions consisting of advice in terms of reinforcement contingencies. What distinguished this particular study, and other token economies, is the recording of the token exchanges, behaviors, and relevant criteria for the delivery of the tokens. This is the best way in which one can keep track of what is happening to the patient, and even more important, whether one is being effective in treating that patient. Paul and Lentz stress that recording must be made as the actions occur thus maintaining accuracy.

The Manual presents the program content in great detail. Different living quarters are available; the six-bed dorms are fairly barren but require no payment of tokens. On the other hand, as the rooms become more private—going from a six-bed room dorm to four- to two- and to one-bed rooms—the number of tokens that the patient must pay increases. People in the rented rooms also have the privilege of sleeping longer in the morning. Five minutes after waking the patient, the staff members (Paul and Lentz call them "change agents") return to deliver a token if the patient is out of bed, or explain why the token is not being given if the patient is still in bed. The staff member also prompts the patient to get up "now" to be able to receive the tokens that are scheduled for later activities such as dressing, grooming, and making of beds. For some patients these activities require shaping; for others, the tokens can simply be given for the completed activities.

This precise specification of activity goes on to cover meals and class periods of which there are three, containing instruction in communication skills—reading, writing, and speaking—elementary mathematics, practical home economics, and grooming; participation in these various classes is on the basis of the patient's need; patients receive one token for attending and one for cooperating. During the class period, the staff member presents the shaping chips, referred to above, to shape appropriate behavior; at the end of the period the shaping chips are exchanged for a token. Informal interactions are programmed for four to five periods during the day at which time all recreational facilities within the unit are available. A community meeting is scheduled once a week during which the patients can earn tokens. General announcements are made at that time, covering job openings, residents moving up in step level (those who have earned more tokens and are therefore ready to advance to a new level of performance) or about to be released. Their names are announced and they are given social approval; new residents are formally introduced, and program changes are discussed at that time.

Small group meetings are scheduled for individual and interpersonal problem behaviors. There are different level groups, depending on the level reached by each patient, meeting several times a week. Residents participate in dealing not only with their own problems but also with those of others. The prerelease groups include the relatives of the patients about to be released, whenever possible. The description of the program includes activity periods (crafts, gym, shopping trips), canteen time (cigarettes, candies, cosmetics, grooming aids, soaps, inexpensive clothing, and the use of a safety deposit box and token bank is allowed at this time), housekeeping and odd jobs (dusting, sweeping, etc.), free periods during which no tokens can be earned but social reinforcement continues, weekend activity periods, bedtime routine and bathing, and individual assignments. Beginning with the second performance level, all sorts of jobs at the unit or outside with other units of the psychiatric center are available, and finally passes are given—a center pass, a downtown pass, or an overnight pass—at different levels in exchange for tokens earned. There is simply not enough space here to describe this token economy in the rich detail in which it is outlined in Paul and Lentz's book. Anyone interested in starting a token economy should read that book. The idea of calling it a Social-Learning Program is also an excellent idea. It stresses the behavior that is to be acquired rather than the types of reinforcers that are dispensed.

The Paul–Lentz book is of course a good example of the empirical approach to the problem of helping the schizophrenic patient. The only questions that are asked about the patients concern the inadequacies of their behaviors, given the rules of our society. Thus, we expect people in general to keep clean, to be able to socialize with others, to get and hold a job, not to be violent, and so on. The approach taken does not concern itself with the possible original causes of the problems because knowing them would not help in deciding how to get a particular patient to rise earlier in the morning or to talk to other patients. The important questions here are: what are useful reinforcers; how can one best shape the desired behavior; and finally how can one best maintain it on the outside? The same general approach has been taken by many other psychologists. In a book edited by DiScipio (1974), we find a number of articles each attacking one or more of the empirical problems that one needs to confront in dealing with this therapeutic approach. That includes not only particular patient responses, but also the problem of how to maintain the behavior of the attendants who must mete out the reinforcers in a specific and reliable way. In a review of the token economies, Gripp and Magaro (1974) took practitioners of behavior therapy to task for not isolating the variables that caused the changes in the patients. They present different experimental paradigms that would specify which aspects of the token economy do what, and they asked for evaluation. Paul and Lentz more than any others have responded to those questions and have shown at least some of the ways in which the token economy can be made to work.

Liberman (1974, 1976) has written a series of reviews of behavior therapy and schizophrenia. It is instructive to quote from one of them (Liberman, 1976, p. 75): "Behavior therapy should be viewed as a clinical strategy for understanding and responding to the problems that individuals present in mental health settings rather than as a collection of techniques for certain problems." Liberman points out that behavior analysis presents guidelines for changing "deviant behavior," and it develops "cause and effect links between environmental events and behavior" (Liberman, 1976, p. 75). Finally, he states quite boldly that the social environment is most important in determining behavior. He talks of "behaviors of interest" and he includes in his listing of behaviors the "subjectively reported states and complex social interactions" (p. 75), underscoring the importance of the reliable measurement of each response class. These descriptions of the behaviors that interest behavior modifiers are quite accurate. No bar is laid between any behavior that can be specified and the behavior analyst's willingness to try to modify it. This is quite different from the stereotype many antibehaviorists hold about behavior modification. Although it is true that the first responses that were modified were such responses as cleaning up, grooming, and making one's bed, the lierature shows that many other responses are being conditioned as well. I say "as well" because the responses, looked down upon by many people unsympathetic to the behavioral approach, are in fact very important for those chronic patients who are incapable of emitting them. First they have to be trained to emit these before they can begin to engage in more socially significant behavior.

What are the behaviors that have been conditioned? Grooming behavior, making of beds, reduction of delusions (as measured by the amount of rational as opposed to delusional talk engaged in by the patient; e.g., Liberman, Teigen, Patterson, & Baker, 1973), reduction of disturbances in thinking (which some still consider to be central in the schizophrenic's difficulties; Meichenbaum, 1969), self instruction (Meichenbaum and Cameron, 1973, 1974), reduction in destructive behavior (Liberman, 1974), social skills training (Hersen & Bellack, 1977) or as it is also called assertiveness training or personal effectiveness (King, Liberman, Roberts, & Bryan, 1977), skill training for community living (Goldstein, Sprafkin, & Gershaw, 1976), reduction in hallucinations (Baker, 1975), and increase in affect responses (Salzinger & Pisoni, 1958, 1960, 1961; Salzinger, Portnoy, & Feldman, 1964). It is to be noted that the major force behind the latter experiments was to illustrate the effect of the interviewer on the reliability and validity of information.

Although some of the responses conditioned are recognizable symptoms of schizophrenia, it is interesting to note that the responses chosen, whether specific or general, were typically those that impinge on the social environment either by annoying people around them and/or otherwise further isolating the patients from society. The disturbance in thinking might be thought to be an exception, but since it is manifested in verbal behavior, much of which is vocal (therefore being a major social response), and because it affects the way in which such an individual solves problems of everyday living, it would also impinge on the social environment.

Another way to classify the responses listed above is in terms of their being merely symptomatic, or central in getting along. People who have hallucinations often get along in the outside world; one often hears the patients who have finally come to a hospital reporting that they "had their voices" for years or at least months before entering the hospital. In contrast, personal effectiveness is bound to be noticed by people around the patient and therefore have a direct effect on their environment. From that point of view it might be argued that social skills training ought to be the response to be modified, particularly, since the modification of those behaviors often result in the attenuation of such symptoms as hallucinations and delusions. The point is that all responses are not equal. Some are more socially significant and some are so-called opportunity responses—responses that make available to the person a large number of additional reinforcers when the person emits other behavior that is well practiced. Thus, a man terrified to leave his house but perfectly at ease in interacting with people outside if someone else takes him would profit greatly by being trained to leave his house by himself.

Verbal Control of Behavior

Meichenbaum's (1974) approach to what he calls "cognitive" behavior modification might be considered to concentrate on such an opportunity response. He maintains that behavior theory is unable to explain some of the changes that take place when behavior modification techniques are employed. His point is that this is due to the fact that people "talk to themselves" and that this talk must be taken into account. I disagree with Meichenbaum that behavior theory is not capable of dealing with that problem. I believe that verbal behavior to oneself is a very powerful kind of discriminative stimulus and that therapy ought to take advantage of that. In my writings on verbal behavior I stressed such effects (viz. Salzinger, 1969, 1978b) and so did Staats (1972) in an article he entitled "Language Behavior Therapy."

It is of some interest to describe the procedure that Meichenbaum and Cameron (1973) used to show the effect of training schizophrenic self-talk. They employed a digit symbol substitution test and an auditory distraction digit recall test. Without describing these tasks in detail, it is sufficient to indicate that both require the successful subject to pay attention and to withstand distractions—tasks on which schizophrenic patients usually do not do well. The self-talk training took place by having the experimenter model what to do, followed by the patient doing the task of talking out loud, followed by doing the same task but this time whispering, and finally repeating the task while talking to self. The modeled statements were:

What is it I have to do? I'm supposed to fill in these numbered boxes with symbols. Now look up at the code of symbols and numbers. Good. The first symbol I have to look for goes with number 94. It's three lines. That's it. Now quickly to the next one, number 24 has a circle with a dot in it. Just continue this way until I finish the line. I'm getting it. Let me see how many I can get. Remember, I must go quickly, but also carefully.

Such instructions that the schizophrenic patients learned to repeat significantly improved their performance by comparison to two control groups. One was the practice control group (given the same amount of practice on the task as the self-instruction group but without any special instructions), the other was merely a pretest-posttest control. Similar kinds of self-instructions were taught to another group of schizophrenic patients, and they were shown to improve with respect to "sick talk," a response class reliably defined and apparently consisting of incoherent and irrelevant answers to interview questions. The results were again positive.

We need to add here that the important aspect of self-talk taught to these patients was not confined to using such response-produced stimulation in guiding their behavior included learning to respond to appropriate external discriminative stimuli as well. Thus they learned to monitor the external signs of success of their behavior and to become sensitive to the interpersonal discriminative stimuli supplied by others. Teaching self-talk is also not that far removed from the idea of teaching the patient behavioral analysis in order to better handle a new situation. Patients who learn, not only to talk to themselves but also how to manipulate the conditions surrounding them, will clearly be far ahead in dealing with the community in which increasingly the schizophrenics find themselves. Meichenbaum has taught us that one must not assume that schizophrenic patients are so different from other people as to make impossible their using verbal behavior to regulate their behavior. In fact, all the reports that we get from schizophrenic patients who tell us that their "voices" told them to do such and such demonstrate vividly how schizophrenic patients already talk to themselves. We must add to this that the naïve escape from verbal behavior of some of the early behaviorists of this generation was based on the erroneous assumption that language behavior is somehow basically different from other behavior and as such, even attempts to investigate it would sully one's reputation as a behaviorist. Of course, Skinner (1957) made clear over two decades ago that the same principles can be applied to speech as to other behavior and that private events, many of which are verbal, can be analyzed behaviorally. In addition, there are quite a few experiments (Salzinger, 1969, 1978b) not all of which have been performed by behaviorists that are nevertheless relevant in understanding how language behavior may be used to guide one's behavior.

Social Skills Training

All of this brings us to the final topic of behavior modification in regard to schizophrenic patients: social skills training, also called assertiveness training, personal effectiveness, and structured learning therapy. Talking to self is often a part of this kind of procedure. Even those psychologists who have been persuaded by the data about drug-effectiveness (and I have tried to show a lot of reasons for questioning the data in an earlier part of the chapter) are aware of the fact that drugs alone cannot bridge that gaping chasm that separates the psychiatric state hospital from the community which the patients are returned to and are expected to live in without difficulty or preparation (e.g., Bellack, Hersen, & Turner, 1976; Hersen & Bellack, 1976; Liberman, Lillie, Falloon, Vaughn, Harpin, Leff, Hutchison, Ryan, & Stoute, in preparation).

Bellack, Hersen and Turner (1976) present three case studies of social skills training, one male and two female schizophrenic patients. The training consisted of instructions, feedback, and modeling. The target behaviors were selected on the basis of role-playing interactions in which the patient had to emit some assertive responses; in one interaction the patient is expected to commend someone for a favor done and in another one, to respond to a slight done to him or her. Assertiveness by the patients was measured by counting the following: frequency of eye contact, speech duration, appropriate intonation, appropriate smiles (during commendation scene), and appropriate physical gestures during the hostile scene. Training was done independently of the generalization testing by using new scenes for the latter. The training results were positive for all three subjects, although only partial for the male patient. Generalization was successful, showing that such training does not merely train the subject to parrot verbal responses. An 8- to 10-week follow-up showed that the effects lasted for the two female subjects. Although only a case study, it had the advantage of following patients in a multiple baseline setup demonstrating that the responses being worked on changed whereas others did not.

A final point needs to be made concerning the empirical use of behavior therapy. As noted above, there has been a change from isolated, not terribly meaningful response classes, to socially significant response classes in recent years, with the social skills training approach being a very obvious recent example. These opportunity responses have a certain efficiency that other responses lack; when they are modified, so are a whole additional set of responses thus generally speeding up the recovery of the patient.

Theoretically Motivated Behavior Modification

Having shown that behavior modification can be usefully applied to the behavior of even chronic schizophrenic patients, we can return to a consideration of theories of schizophrenia. Here I find myself in partial disagreement with Meichenbaum and Cameron (1973) who said, after listing a number of theories then extant, that it would not be possible to interpret their results in terms of any of the theories they had named. They are right that one cannot go from the typical behavior modification study to a theory of schizophrenia. It does not follow, however, that one cannot so design the behavior modification program as to test the theories, and what is probably even more important, to find a response class whose modification, because of its theoretical import, would also change a whole set of other responses. Let us look at some examples.

Suppose we took seriously the many arousal theories of schizophrenia, namely that at least some schizophrenics are suffering from overarousal. We could choose such people, subject them to desensitization therapy, and then measure to see whether they are not merely more relaxed but also show a reduction in hallucinations or delusions, and so on. If we took seriously the Immediacy Hypothesis (Salzinger, 1973; Salzinger, Portnoy, & Feldman, 1978), we might try to condition subjects to respond to less immediate stimuli, gradually training them to respond to more and more remote ones. We could then test the validity of this theory by determining whether the other difficulties associated with schizophrenia are more efficiently eliminated by this procedure than by the more empirical approach we now use.

Some Case Studies

It is useful to cite some additional case studies to show in somewhat more concrete terms what the various techniques are like when applied to specific patients. Liberman, Wallace, Teigen, and Davis (1974) present a number of interesting cases stemming from their own clinical research unit at Camarillo State Hospital. Essentially that unit has an individualized token economy, meaning that in addition to general rules, which if followed will result in positive reinforcement, there are special programs for individual patients depending on each one's special problem.

Let us begin by looking at the delusional speech problem of a 64-year-old white male patient who had been hospitalized for a period of some 16 years. That patient was receiving no medication and some 15 years earlier had received a prefrontal lobotomy—clearly not successful. His diagnosis was schizophrenia, paranoid type. The specific behaviors worked on were: high frequency of delusional speech, habitual carrying around of a large briefcase filled with garden tools, newspaper clippings, and personal articles. The newspaper clippings apparently supported the delusions. It should be noted that carrying around one's possessions is probably not very uncommon in mental hospitals, the basic problem frequently being that there is no place in which one can keep one's private and cherished possessions. In other words, it is not at all obvious that carrying around one's possessions is a personal problem at all; more than likely, it simply reflects the fact that if one leaves something personal and valuable around in such a hospital, it is very likely to be stolen. The final problem was a deficit in social and task-oriented skills.

Since this patient liked to stay up late and have midnight snacks, permission to do so was used as a reinforcer. It was made contingent on avoiding talk about delusions in the course of interviews. The procedure was successfully generalized to a party that contained all sorts of people the patient was meeting for the first time. Beginning with a baseline collected over a period of 13 days with almost seven delusional statements per day, the number dropped to almost three per day when only one category of delusional statements was included in the contingency over a period of 12 days. Most interesting in this case study, a procedure was employed that is usual when the operant conditioning procedure is used, namely the reversal or removal of the reinforcement contingency. By the end of the experiment, the reinforcement contingency had been applied to all categories of delusion, with the result that for a period of 44 days approximately one delusional statement per day was emitted by the patient. When the reinforcement contingency was removed, the number of delusional statements climbed back up to almost five delusional statements per day in a period of 12 days. This procedure showed, as no control group of different patients could, that it is the specific contingency that improved the behavior of the patient. After that the contingency was reinstituted and then slowly faded out. Reinstitution of the contingency reduced the frequency of delusional statements to less than 1 per day and the gradual fading of the contingency over 16 days produced a frequency of less than 2 per day.

The patient was given a place to store his tools so that they would not be stolen, was given the opportunity to engage in his old hobby and was reinforced for that by tokens, and was given a programmed course in social relations. The carrying of the briefcase that contained not only his valuable tools but also the newspaper clippings supporting his delusions decreased remarkably even though not specifically worked on, apparently as his rate of discussing delusions decreased. After the course of treatments was completed, he was discharged to a board-and-care home. Seventeen months follow-up shows that his rate of delusional talk is "acceptably low," meaning that he was able to exist in the community without any complaints; he was also described as pursuing gardening "with a flourish," maintaining his interest in photography, and keeping up his social interactions with people.

A second case dealt with a 39-year-old white female patient hospitalized for a period of some 18 years; she was divorced, mother of a child, and had graduated from a junior college; her diagnosis was schizophrenia, catatonic (withdrawn). The problem behaviors were self-inflicted cigarette burns in which she burned both herself and her clothing. In addition, she apparently engaged men in sexual advances altogether too frequently. A reinforcement contingency acting directly on her problems was instituted. She obviously found smoking positively reinforcing and so a reinforcement schedule was instituted in which delivery of cigarettes was contingent on not burning herself or her clothing. Each day, the patient was given a set of clothing without burn holes (thus eliminating old burn holes as discriminative stimuli for further burning activity); each hour the patient's clothes were inspected for burns during a conversation with a staff member; each time she had remained burn-free for the past hour, she was given a half cigarette and praised for her appearance; if she had burned herself, she was given no further cigarettes for the remainder of the day. Finally, if by 9:00 P.M. she had not burned herself, she was given a bonus of five cigarettes.

As for her inappropriate sexual advances, appropriate male-female social behaviors were modeled for her, and when she behaved appropriately, she was given cookies, candy, and puffs of a cigarette while a male whom she preferred sat with her. The results were quite impressive. Self-inflicted burns changed from one a day during an eight day baseline determination to 0.24 burns/day for the 46-day treatment regimen; during the last 14 days of her stay in the unit, she remained completely burn-free. Her inappropriate sexual advances were reduced from 3.47 observed incidents per day to an average of 0.86 per day for the last seven days of treatment. She was discharged to a nursing home and one month later follow-up indicated no incidents of self-inflicted burns. Apparently, her self-inflicted burns constituted the major reason for her continued hospitalization for the past 18 years.

A third case was a 41-year-old single white male with an eighth-grade education who had been in the hospital for all but 3 of the previous 29 years. His diagnosis was schizophrenia, residual type. His problems were listed as being nonassertiveness—leaving himself open to exploitation as in giving away his money, cigarettes, and even clothing, poor grooming, being unshaved, uncombed, with dirty clothing, and generally looking disheveled, and finally, noncompliance with his work assignments. Assertive responses were conditioned under natural circumstances with praise by staff and natural consequences from having asserted himself serving as reinforcers. Initially, staff prompted the appropriate response under conditions set up to produce the discriminative stimuli under which assertive responses are appropriate; for example, in the hospital canteen, the waitress would ignore the patient's order or give the patient cold coffee when hot coffee was requested. The prompts to assert oneself were slowly faded out and here too baseline data were collected; at first, the patient never asserted himself under the conditions described; then he began to do so when prompted, and finally he learned to assert himself most of the time without any prompts. Other situations included having fellow patients request cigarettes and having a student volunteer obviously cheat at cards. The latter two situations were used to test for generalization and showed that although no special training took place for these cases, the patient definitely learned to assert himself in those situations, too.

The patient's other problem behaviors were dealt with by means of the token reinforcers available in the token economy. These behaviors changed so that during the last two weeks before discharge, the patient completed some 80% of his grooming tasks and became a reliable messenger for the unit thus carrying out at least one major assigned chore. At nine-months follow-up, he worked as a messenger, used public transportation to visit his mother on weekends, and was not exploited by residents in the board-and-care home in which he was living after discharge.

SUMMARY AND CONCLUSIONS

Beginning with a discussion of the treatments now used most frequently with schizophrenic patients, this chapter went on to describe how behavior modification techniques are being used to remedy the behavior of patients described as being schizophrenic. Here we raised the problem of the very definition of what schizophrenia means. We also described the empirical nature of the typical behavior modification process when applied to such patients. Finally, we raised the question of whether the time had not come for behaviorists to begin to look for more efficient ways of changing the behavior of schizophrenic patients by beginning to test the theories of schizophrenia that have shown on the basis of behavioral data that certain classes of response control may be at the center of the problem faced by such individuals. I believe that the next phase of behavior modification in schizophrenia will surely take such an approach.

REFERENCES

American Psychiatric Association. *Diagnostic and Statistical Manual,* third edition (DSM-III). Washington, D.C.: American Psychiatric Association, 1980.

Atthowe, J. M., Jr. & Krasner, L. Preliminary report on the application of contingent reinforcement procedures (token economy) on a "chronic" psychiatric ward. *Journal of Abnormal Psychology,* 1968, **73,** 37–43.

Ayllon, T., & Azrin, N. *The token economy.* New York: Appleton-Century-Crofts, 1968.

Ayllon, T., & Michael, J. The psychiatric nurse as a behavioral engineer. *Journal of the Experimental Analysis of Behavior,* 1959, **2,** 323–334.

Baker, R. Behavioural techniques in the treatment of schizophrenia. In A. Forrest & J. Affleck (Eds.), *New perspectives in schizophrenia.* Edinburgh: Churchill Livingstone, 1975.

Bellack, A. S., Hersen, M., & Turner, S. M. Generalization effects of social skills training in chronic schizophrenics: An experimental analysis. *Behaviour Research and Therapy,* 1976, **14,** 391–398.

Berger, P. A. Medical treatment of mental illness. *Science,* 1978, **200,** 974–981.

Davis, J. M., Gosenfeld, L., & Tsai, C. C. Maintenance antipsychotic drugs do prevent relapse: A reply to Tobias and MacDonald. *Psychological Bulletin,* 1976, **83,** 431–447.

DiScipio, W. J. *The behavioral treatment of psychotic illness.* New York: Behavioral Publications, 1974.

Dohrenwend, B. S., & Dohrenwend, B. P. (Eds.), *Stressful life events.* New York: Wiley, 1974.

Engel, G. L. The need for a new medical model: A challenge for biomedicine. *Science,* 1977, **196,** 129–136.

Goldstein, A. P., Sprafkin, R. P., & Gershaw, N. J. *Skill training for community living: Applying structured learning therapy.* New York: Pergamon Press, 1976.

Gripp, R. F., & Magaro, P. A. The token economy program in the psychiatric hospital: A review and analysis. *Behaviour Research and Therapy,* 1974, **12,** 205–228.

Gunderson, J. G. Drugs and psychosocial treatment of schizophrenia revisited. *Psychiatry Digest: Journal of Continuing Education in Psychiatry,* December 1977, **37,** 25–40.

Hersen, M., & Bellack, A. S. Social skills training for chronic psychiatric patients: Rationale, research findings, and future directions. *Comprehensive Psychiatry,* 1976, **17,** 559–580.

Hersen, M., & Bellack, A. S. Assessment of social skills. In A. R. Ciminero, K. S. Calhoun, & H. E. Adams (Eds.), *Handbook for behavioral assessment.* New York: Wiley, 1977.

Hersen, M., Turner, S. M., Edelstein, B. A., & Pinkston, S. G. Effects of phenothiazines and social skills training in a withdrawn schizophrenic. *Journal of Clinical Psychology,* 1975, **31,** 588–594.

Isaacs, W., Thomas, J., & Goldiamond, I. Application of operant conditioning to reinstate verbal behavior in psychotics. *Journal of Speech and Hearing Disorders,* 1960, **25,** 8–12.

Kety, S. From rationalization to reason. *American Journal of Psychiatry,* 1974, **131,** 957–963.

King, L. W., Liberman, R. P., Roberts, J., & Bryan, E. Personal effectiveness: A structured therapy for improving social and emotional skills. *European Journal of Behavioral Analysis and Modification,* 1977, **2**, 82–91.

Krasner, L. Studies of the conditioning of verbal behavior. *Psychological Bulletin,* 1958, **55**, 148–170.

Liberman, R. P. Behavior modification of schizophrenia. In W. J. DiScipio (Ed.), *Behavioral treatment of psychotic illness.* New York: Behavioral Publications, 1974.

Liberman, R. P. Behavior therapy for schizophrenia. In L. J. West & D. E. Flinn (Eds.), *Treatment of schizophrenia: Progress and prospects.* New York: Grune & Stratton, 1976.

Liberman, R. P., Lillie, F., Falloon, I., Vaughn, C., Harpin, E., Leff, J., Hutchison, W., Ryan, P., & Stoute, M. Social skills training for schizophrenic patients and their families. In preparation.

Liberman, R. P., Teigen, J., Patterson, R., & Baker, V. Reducing delusional speech in chronic paranoid schizophrenics. *Journal of Applied Behavior Analysis,* 1973, **6**, 57–64.

Liberman, R. P., Wallace, C., Teigen, J., & Davis, J. Interventions with psychotic behaviors. In K. Calhoun, H. Adams, & K. Mitchell (Eds.), *Innovative treatment methods in psychopathology.* New York: Wiley, 1974.

Lindsley, O. R. Operant conditioning methods applied to research in chronic schizophrenia. *Psychiatric Research Reports, 5.* American Psychiatric Association, 1956.

MacDonald, M. L., & Tobias, L. L. Withdrawal causes relapse? Our response. *Psychological Bulletin,* 1976, **83**, 448–457.

Meichenbaum, D. H. The effects of instructions and reinforcement on thinking and language behavior of schizophrenics. *Behaviour Research and Therapy,* 1969, **7**, 101–114.

Meichenbaum, D. H., *Cognitive behavior modification.* Morristown, N.J.: General Learning Press, 1974.

Meichenbaum, D. H., & Cameron, R. Training schizophrenics to talk to themselves: A means of developing attentional controls. *Behavior Therapy,* 1973, **4**, 515–534.

Meichenbaum, D. H., & Cameron, R. The clinical potential of modifying what clients say to themselves. *Psychotherapy: Theory, Research & Practice,* 1974, **11**, 103–117.

Paul, G. L. & Lentz, R. J. *Psychosocial treatment of chronic mental patients.* Cambridge, Mass.: Harvard University Press, 1977.

Paul, G. L., Tobias, L. L., & Holly, B. L. Maintenance psychotropic drugs in the presence of active treatment programs. *Archives of General Psychiatry,* 1972, **27**, 106–115.

Salzinger, K. Experimental manipulation of verbal behavior: A review. *Journal of General Psychology,* 1959, **61**, 65–94.

Salzinger, K. The place of operant conditioning of verbal behavior in psychotherapy. In C. M. Franks (Ed.), *Behavior therapy: Appraisal and status.* New York: McGraw-Hill, 1969.

Salzinger, K. *Schizophrenia: behavioral aspects.* New York: Wiley, 1973.

Salzinger, K. But is it good for the patients? Paper presented at the American Psychological Association meetings, San Francisco, California, August, 1977.

Salzinger, K. A behavioral analysis of diagnosis. In R. L. Spitzer & D. F. Klein (Eds.), *Critical issues in psychiatric diagnosis.* New York: Raven Press, 1978. (a)

Salzinger, K. Language behavior. In A. C. Catania & T. A. Brigham (Eds.), *Handbook of applied behavior analysis*. New York: Irvington/Naiburg, 1978. (b)

Salzinger, K. The behavioral mechanism to explain abnormal behavior. *Annals of the New York Academy of Sciences,* in press.

Salzinger, K., & Pisoni, S. Reinforcement of affect responses of schizophrenics during the clinical interview. *Journal of Abnormal and Social Psychology,* 1958, **57**, 84–90.

Salzinger, K., & Pisoni, S. Reinforcement of verbal affect responses of normal subjects during the interview. *Journal of Abnormal and Social Psychology,* 1960, **60**, 127–130.

Salzinger, K., & Pisoni, S. Some parameters of the conditioning of verbal affect responses in schizophrenic subjects. *Journal of Abnormal and Social Psychology,* 1961, **63**, 511–516.

Salzinger, K., Portnoy, S., & Feldman, R. S. Experimental manipulation of continuous speech in schizophrenic patients. *Journal of Abnormal and Social Psychology,* 1964, **68**, 508–516.

Salzinger, K., Portnoy, S., & Feldman, R. S. Communicability deficit in schizophrenics resulting from a more general deficit. In S. Schwartz (Ed.), *Language and cognition in schizophrenia*. Hillsdale, N.J.: Lawrence Erlbaum Associates, 1978.

Schacht, T., & Nathan, P. E. But is it good for the psychologists? Appraisal and status of DSM III. *American Psychologist,* 1977, **32**, 1017–1025.

Schaeffer, H. H., & Martin, P. L. *Behavioral therapy*. New York: McGraw-Hill, 1969.

Serafetinides, E. A., Collins, S., & Clark, M. L. Haloperidol, clopenthixol, and chlorpromazine in chronic schizophrenia. *Journal of Nervous and Mental Disease,* 1972, **154**, 31–42.

Sherman, J. A. Use of reinforcement and imitation to reinstate verbal behavior in mute psychotics. *Journal of Abnormal Psychology,* 1965, **70**, 155–164.

Skinner, B. F. A new method for the experimental analysis of the behavior of psychotic patients. *Journal of Nervous and Mental Diseases,* 1954, **120**, 403–406.

Skinner, B. F. *Verbal behavior*. New York: Appleton-Century-Crofts, 1957.

Staats, A. Language behavior therapy: A derivative of social behaviorism. *Behavior Therapy,* 1972, **3**, 165–192.

Tobias, L. L., & MacDonald, M. L. Withdrawal of maintenance drugs with long-term hospitalized mental patients: A critical review. *Psychological Bulletin,* 1974, **81**, 107–125.

Ullmann, L. P., & Krasner, L. *A psychological approach to abnormal behavior*. Englewood Cliffs, N.J.: Prentice-Hall, 1975.

U.S. Court of Appeals: First Circuit. *Robert Okin et al.* v. *Ruby Rogers et al. Mental Disability Law Reporter,* 1977, July–August, 43–52.

Zander, T. K. Prolixin decanoate: A review of the research. *Mental Disability Law Reporter,* 1977, July–August, 37–42.

Zubin, J. The role of vulnerability in the etiology of schizophrenic episodes. In L. J. West & D. E. Flinn (Eds.), *Treatment of schizophrenia*. New York: Grune & Stratton, 1976.

Zubin, J. But is it good for science? *The Clinical Psychologist,* 1977–78, **31**, 1–7.

CHAPTER 8

Substance Abuse

Peter M. Miller and David W. Foy

The use and abuse of substances that are harmful to physical and psychological health is a serious and pervasive clinical and social problem. Recently, public and professional concern has been focusing away from individual addictions (e.g., alcoholism) and toward overall substance use and total health care. Cigarette smoking, overeating, drug use and abuse, and excessive alcohol consumption are all targets of intervention. This focus is, in part, a function of the multiple substance abuses in our society today and the relationship among these abuses within individuals. Thus, treatment of one abuse without at least monitoring others is no longer acceptable. By modifying one abuse professionals often unwittingly cause other abuses to increase in severity. Clinically, for example, treated drug abusers increase their alcohol consumption and treated smokers gain weight.

Fortunately, from a social learning viewpoint, the understanding and treatment of various substance abuses is similar (Miller, 1978). For that reason this chapter focuses primarily on the abuse of alcohol with the assumption that the techniques described are equally applicable to drug, cigarette, and food abuse.

DEFINITION OF ALCOHOL ABUSE

A standardized definition of alcoholism is necessary for three reasons. First, clinicians must be able to identify (i.e., screen individuals with alcohol problems from among clinical populations). Second, clinicians must provide a baseline from which change can be evaluated. Third, standard definitions enable comparison of the efficacy of treatment strategies across different populations.

Several diagnostic classifications have been proposed. The Diagnostic and Statistical Manual of the American Psychiatric Association (1968) defines alcoholism as drinking that chronically interferes with physical, personal, or social functioning. Alcoholism is further divided into three classifications. *Episodic Excessive Drinking* refers to intoxication as frequently as four times per year. *Habitual Excessive Drinking* refers to 12 intoxications per year or under the influence more than once per week. *Alcohol Addiction* is based on either (*a*) presence of physiological withdrawal symptoms, (*b*) daily drinking, or (*c*) heavy drinking for a period of three months.

Perhaps the earliest systematic classification system was proposed by Jellinek

(1960). In this system, *Alpha* alcoholism constituted the least severe stage, with alcohol being used to cope with life but there being no evidence of loss of control. *Beta* referred to obvious physical concomitants of excessive drinking but there was no evidence of dependency. *Gamma* alcoholism was used to describe physical dependence on alcohol together with loss of control. Finally, *Delta* alcoholics are completely unable to abstain from alcohol even for short periods of time.

A more comprehensive and perhaps more objective system has been developed by the Criteria Committee of the National Council of Alcoholism (1972). Within this system alcoholics are categorized into three diagnostic levels based on the presence or absence of certain physiological, behavioral, psychological, and attitudinal factors. Included are such indicators as alcoholic "blackouts," alcoholic hepatitis, and drinking despite negative social-environmental consequences.

Historically, behaviorists have placed less emphasis on diagnosis and more on an objective baseline analysis of drinking and alcohol-related problems. Thus regardless of the label placed on him, an individual has a problem to the extent that the excessive use of alcohol consistently interferes with social, emotional, cognitive, marital, employment, or medical functioning. Specific behavioral assessment techniques are described later in this chapter.

BEHAVIORAL CONCEPTION OF ALCOHOL ABUSE

Historically, behavioral explanations of alcohol abuse have undergone developmental changes. Early theories were based on a simple drive reduction model (Conger, 1956; Kingham, 1958). This "tension reduction" hypothesis, as it came to be known, involves the notion that alcohol, through its depressant and anesthetic properties, reduces anxiety and tension related to social and environmental stress. Accordingly, chronic abusive drinking is maintained through negative reinforcement (i.e., termination of an unpleasant event). This model was based almost entirely on limited data from animal experimentation and anecdotal clinical reports. In reviewing the available evidence in this area, Cappell and Herman (1972) concluded that the "tension reduction" hypothesis has outlived its usefulness and does not offer a valid explanation of abusive drinking. In fact, numerous investigators (McNamee, Mello, & Mendelson, 1968; Mendelson, 1964; Nathan & O'Brien, 1971) have found that chronic alcoholics experience *increases* in anxiety and depression after drinking.

More recently clinical researchers in the alcoholism field have placed a moratorium on theorizing and have begun a massive data-gathering effort. Studies in which drinking behavior is observed, quantified, and analyzed have flourished over the past 10 years. Improved experimental methodologies and newly developed assessment procedures encouraged behavioral researchers to accumulate data upon which treatment could be based. As a result, the contemporary behavioral approach to alcoholism is an empirical one which has focused on a functional analysis of drinking behavior. In such an analysis, three sequentially and functionally related events are examined: (*a*) stimulus control variables (i.e., antecedent cues); (*b*) drinking behavior per se; and (*c*) outcome variables (i.e., consequent events). Within a social learning model, excessive drinking is a function of the relationship among these variables. Antecedent and consequent events usually fall into one or a combination of the following:

1. *Situational.*   Beer advertisements, neighborhood tavern.
2. *Social.*   Coaxing from friends to have a drink, discussion of exciting drinking episode by others.
3. *Emotional.*   Depression, boredom, impatience, loneliness.
4. *Physiological.*   Chronic back pain, headaches, withdrawal symptoms.

More recently the importance of mediational variables such as cognitions and attitudes has been emphasized. Marlatt (1978), Engle and Williams (1972), and Wilson and Lawson (1976) support the conclusion that positive expectations regarding the effects of alcohol exert a stronger influence on drinking behavior than the actual physiological effects themselves. Marlatt, Demming, and Reid (1973), for example, found that "loss of control" over alcohol was related to the drinker's *belief,* prior to drinking, that he had no control over the amount of his consumption. Thus cognitive factors can play a significant role in either initiating drinking or maintaining it once it begins. This *abstinence violation effect* (Marlatt, 1978), in which the alcoholic goes "off the wagon" and then thinks "Oh well, I've blown it now. I might as well get drunk," is characteristic of all types of substance abuse. For example, after one cigarette the ex-smoker labels himself as a "smoker" again and buys a whole pack. The systematic evaluation of cognitions as related to alcohol abuse has only recently begun and may provide important clues for treatment and "readiness" for treatment.

Situational, social, emotional, physiological, and cognitive antecedents to drinking rarely influence an individual as single factors. Rather, overconsumption is the result of the influence of combinations of factors occurring within a relatively brief time span. Once combinations of antecedents associated with drinking are identified, both the patient and therapist can begin to predict when drinking is likely to occur. Miller (1978) labels these combinations of factors as *High Probability Antecedent Clusters.* For example, an alcoholic may be very likely to drink on weekends, during the afternoon and evening hours, when he is alone and bored. When these factors occur together in a cluster, his chances of drinking are great. Once the therapist and client identify several clusters, behavioral strategies can be devised to either change the situation or change the client's behavior in that situation.

TREATMENT ISSUES—CRAVING

Under the disease model of alcoholism the concept of craving plays a central explanatory role in the etiology of the problem and the treatment goal (abstinence) prescribed for it. In the most comprehensive definition of craving presently available Ludwig and Wikler (1974) suggest that it is a hypothetical construct, "representing the psychological or cognitive correlate of a conditioned withdrawal syndrome" (p. 114). Craving is seen as a learned behavior with both classical and instrumental conditioning being important in its acquisition. Once it is learned it becomes a cognitive mediator for alcohol-seeking behavior and subsequent loss of control drinking. Craving is distinguished from loss of control, another core disease model concept, as follows.

Craving is the cognitive state designating ethanol consumption as a source of relief or pleasure: it need not inevitably lead to drinking. Loss of control is the behavioral state initiated by craving and characterized by activities indicative of a relative inability to modulate ethanol consumption [p. 122].

Since craving or an identifiable strong desire for drinking is a commonly reported antecedent for abusive drinking, it is a clinically relevant subjective phenomenon for those individuals who experience it. As such, clinicians must evaluate this phenomenon to determine if it indeed has relevance in terms of the prediction and control of drinking behavior. Initial attempts must be made to operationally define the term "craving." For example, craving could be defined as physiological arousal in the presence of alcohol cues. In this regard, Strickler, Bigelow, and Wells (1976) used relaxation training to reduce muscle tension responses (craving?) of abstinent alcoholics to alcohol related stimuli. Seven abstinent alcoholics (all taking Antabuse) were instructed to use relaxation procedures while listening to an audiotape recording of a problem drinker in a bar. The recording consisted of various sounds (e.g., ordering drinks, ice tinkling in glasses, etc.) typical of a barroom scene. A control group of seven abstinent alcoholics who had not received relaxation training were exposed to the same experience with instructions to relax. Electromyographic (EMG) recordings of muscle tension levels in the frontalis muscle revealed that subjects using relaxation training were able to lower their muscle tension levels significantly in response to alcohol related cues while control group subjects were not. Thus relaxation training was used to help abstinent alcoholics cope with arousal producing stimuli which would increase the likelihood of their drinking.

Hodgson and Rankin (1976) postulated that craving and addictive behavior is analogous to fear and avoidance behavior and thus is amenable to extinction procedures. Extinction may decrease arousal to alcohol cues and thus decrease the probability of drinking. They used a technique known as cue exposure with a 43-year-old manual laborer who had been drinking excessively for 17 years. Historically, the consumption of one vodka was enough to establish a strong desire for further alcohol consumption. Over several days the subject was given priming doses of either 40 ml or 80 ml of vodka with no ice or mix. Throughout the day measures were taken on mood, subjective estimates of tremor and desire to drink, pulse, and blood/alcohol concentration. After consuming the drink the subject was instructed to resist the desire to drink further. Over the period of cue exposure with no opportunity to drink further, the subject's desire for a drink after the priming dose decreased gradually. In addition his expectations of unpleasant feelings decreased over time. After the sixth session the subject experienced no further cravings in the four-hour period subsequent to receiving the priming dose. Clinically, the subject was followed up for six months. During this time he drank on only six occasions, each time terminating his drinking voluntarily soon after he began. This voluntary cessation of drinking had never occurred during the three years prior to the cue exposure procedure.

Other investigators have cautioned against assigning a causative role to the craving phenomenon (Maisto & Schefft, 1977). If a causal attribution is made, then the role of the helpless victim may be assumed by some clients. They may attribute their inappropriate drinking to "irresistible urges" over which they have little control. Focusing on the urge per se, without regard for the antecedent external and internal events that elicit it, may actually strengthen the clients perceived helplessness and further invite relinquishing responsibility for ensuing drinking behavior.

TREATMENT GOALS—ABSTINENCE OR CONTROLLED DRINKING

Under the disease model of alcoholism the only treatment goal available for alcoholics has been total abstinence. The emphasis on the progressive and irreversible aspects of the disease process, the powerful influence of Alcoholics Anonymous, and the belief that alcoholics comprise a homogeneous population are factors that have inhibited the development of alternative strategies (Briddell & Nathan, 1976; Miller, 1976). However, in the past few years many professional treatment providers and some clients have shown interest in responsible or controlled drinking as a viable alternative to total abstinence for some alcoholics. Limitations of total abstinence treatment and growing empirical support for use of a responsible drinking strategy provide the impetus for this change.

While traditional treatment programs aimed at total abstinence may offer an opportunity for significant improvement for 60–70% of those alcoholics who complete treatment, outcome studies have consistently shown that the "two-thirds improved" success rate is seldom exceeded (c.f. Armor, Polich & Stambul, 1976; Emrick, 1975). Even more significant is the fact that fewer than 20% of treated alcoholics actually remain totally abstinent (National Institute of Mental Health, 1969). Treatment that fails to intervene in the actual drinking patterns of its clients and offers only a proscription against engaging in the behavior at all seems to lack relevance to what clients actually do after treatment. Despite the fact that few programs treat the drinking response per se, it has been consistently reported that 5–15% of alcoholics treated in traditional programs become and remain nonabusive drinkers (Armor, Polich, & Stambul, 1976; Bailey & Stewart, 1967; Davies, 1962).

Reports of outcome studies in which controlled drinking training was evaluated are now available (e.g., Sobell & Sobell, 1973(a); Vogler, Compton, & Weissbach, 1975). Perhaps most importantly, these studies demonstrate that the "two-thirds improved" success rate can be met or exceeded with a radically different treatment strategy than that offered in traditional programs. These results, coupled with copious data now available refuting the simplistic "one drink, then drunk" belief about the nature of alcoholism (e.g., Cutter, Schwab, & Nathan, 1970), provide an empirical basis for the viability of controlled drinking treatment.

While the Sobell and Sobell and Vogler, et al. studies demonstrated that controlled drinking training can be successfully used with chronic alcoholics as a general population, the critical issue of identifying client characteristics that predict success under each goal remains unresolved. Certainly, client choice is probably the most important single factor in goal consideration. Recent data collected within a Veterans Administration Center alcohol program (Pachman, Foy & Van Erd, 1978) revealed that 15% of inpatient veteran alcoholics given an opportunity to choose either goal chose controlled drinking. Compared to the patient group choosing total abstinence, the controlled drinking choice group had significantly shorter abusive drinking histories (mean 11.5 years versus 6.5 years), more formal education (mean 10.8 years versus 12.5 years), and were more likely to predict that their chances of success were 100%.

Other factors to be considered by treatment providers and clients in recommending or selecting a treatment goal include the following:

1. The *client's physical condition* may be such that any further drinking would be contraindicated. Pancreatitis, diabetes, and cirrhosis are examples of chronic physical impairments that would rule out controlled drinking as a recommended goal.

2. The *social support system* available to the client in his natural environment—family, employer, and peer group—needs to be carefully evaluated and actually involved in the decision-making process. This is particularly important for a controlled drinking goal because the lay public is largely unfamiliar with it. To the extent possible, the client's goal choice should be congruent with the expectations and behavior patterns of his significant others.

3. The *client's expectations* regarding treatment success under his goal choice need to be evaluated. Important considerations are previous treatment or self-help attempts, the client's own view of alcoholism (disease, moral, or behavioral model), and major psychological problems that may decrease his ability to successfully implement a drinking management program. Chronic organic brain syndrome, psychotic history, severe depression, and psychopathic tendencies are examples of functional difficulties that impair a client's ability to follow a complex self-management regimen to control abusive drinking. Systematic provision of thorough alcohol education early in treatment is helpful to clients in setting realistic expectations for themselves.

ASSESSMENT

Two of the most important contributions of behavior modification to the field of substance abuse are the emphasis on (*a*) objective assessment of each client's problems and (*b*) systematic evaluation of treatment outcome. Assessment includes the accumulation of data on both the client's drinking behavior and his social, marital, vocational, and medical health functioning.

Behavioral clinicians have developed a number of analogue drinking measures (Marlatt, Demming, & Reid, 1978; Miller, Hersen, Eisler, Epstein, & Wooten, 1974; and Nathan & O'Brien, 1971) in which alcoholics are given access to alcoholic beverages and drinking is monitored on quantitative dimensions. Initially, these measures were used primarily in descriptive experimental studies although more recently they have been incorporated into clinical programs in which controlled drinking is an alternative treatment outcome (Foy & Simon, 1978; Sobell &

Sobell, 1973(b)). These analogue assessments take the form of taste rating tasks, operant analyses, and simulated living room or bar settings. Such techniques have been used successfully to predict a client's response to treatment (Miller, Hersen, Eisler, & Elkin, 1974).

More typical clinical assessments of drinking behavior include self-monitoring by significant others, and random breath analyses. Sobell and Sobell (1973b) describe the use of the *Alcohol Intake Sheet* as a self-monitoring form. Using this form clients are requested to keep records of drinking episodes in terms of date, time, type of drink, amount of drink consumed, and antecedent conditions. Reliability of these reports is assessed by requesting friends or relatives to observe the client and keep similar records. Such detailed records of drinking not only help to establish a therapeutic plan but also serve as a behavioral baseline needed to monitor changes in drinking patterns as treatment progresses.

Some clinical investigators have used random breath tests to determine blood/alcohol levels during and after treatment. Miller (1975) and Miller, Hersen, Eisler, and Watts (1974) have found this procedure especially useful with alcoholics who have no family, few steady friends, and irregular living habits. In one case (Miller, Hersen, Eisler, and Watts, 1974), the investigators demonstrated the utility of this technique in assessing the drinking behavior of a 49-year-old chronic alcoholic. The client lived with his elderly mother, worked sporadically, and had a history of numerous public drunkenness arrests. Self-reports of his drinking were usually vague, making it difficult to assess the extent and pattern of his alcohol consumption. Assessment involved biweekly blood/alcohol estimations based on breath analysis. Breath samples were collected randomly in the client's home, place of employment, or at the treatment facility. Arrangements for each assessment meeting were made by phone, 1 hour prior to the breath sampling procedure. Baseline blood/alcohol levels during the three weeks prior to treatment ranged from 0.00% to 0.27% with a mean of 0.11%. Using a contingency management treatment approach, the investigators reduced blood alcohol levels to 0.00% during the final treatment phase.

Social, marital, and vocational assessment and evaluation are also emphasized. Social and marital data are accumulated in a number of ways. Clients and significant others are often requested to keep daily or weekly entries in behavioral diaries. Emphasis is placed on number and types of social contacts, events precipitating episodes of emotional stress, and responses to problem situations. Observations of the client's social and recreational behavior can be assessed by such inventories as the Katz Adjustment Scale (Katz & Lyerly, 1963). Standardized social and marital interactions between the client and spouse or peer can be videotaped to provide details of interaction style (Eisler, Miller, Hersen, & Alford, 1974). Videotapes can be rated on various dimensions including frequency of positive versus negative statements, eye contact, and quality of response to problem situations. The Marital Happiness Scale developed by Azrin, Naster, and Jones (1973) is a useful inventory for the assessment of marital adjustment and pinpoints specific areas of conflict. Vocational behavior is typically assessed via reports by self and others on attempts to find employment or number of days worked per week. To corroborate self-report data, paycheck stubs can be collected on a weekly or monthly basis. For younger clients, school grades can also be obtained.

TREATMENT TECHNIQUES

While many professionals still associate behavior modification with aversion therapies, these treatments are actually used very little in contemporary alcoholism programs. While early clinical reports on these procedures appeared promising (Lemere
& Voegtlin, 1950), more recent experimental studies (Hallam, Rachman, &
Falkowski, 1972; Miller, Hersen, Eisler, & Hemphill, 1973; Wilson, Leaf, &
Nathan, 1975) have seriously questioned the efficacy of aversion therapies. Behavioral approaches to substance abuse have developed substantially since the
early use of simple conditioning approaches. Currently, emphasis is placed on
teaching alcoholics a broad range of self-management skills necessary to maintain
sobriety. The techniques used to teach these skills are described below.

Social Skills Training

Difficulty in dealing with social pressure and stressful interpersonal encounters frequently serves as a direct antecedent to substance abuse (Miller, Hersen,
Eisler, & Hilsman, 1974). The interpersonal skills needed to handle conflict
are lacking particularly in alcoholic populations. Miller and Eisler (1977)
found alcoholics to be much less socially assertive than psychiatric patients. In
addition, those alcoholics who consumed the most alcohol were the least able to
express disagreement, disapproval, or feelings of anger.

Clinical studies evaluating the efficacy of social skills training with substance
abusers are available, although in limited quantity. In one of the earliest reports,
Eisler, Miller, Hersen, and Alford (1974) demonstrated the value of assertive
training in the case of a 52-year-old outpatient alcoholic with a six-year history of
excessive drinking. Drinking episodes were usually precipitated by marital or general interpersonal conflicts. Baseline behavioral ratings of the patient's responses
to role-played interpersonal scenes indicated an inability to react directly and asser-
tively. The patient typically was unresponsive to these scenes or would respond in
a brief, mild mannered way. Using specific instructions, behavioral rehearsal, and
verbal feedback and reinforcement, the patient was trained in assertiveness. Training resulted in an enhanced ability to handle stressful interpersonal encounters and
marked improvement in his marital relationship. Both the patient and his spouse
indicated a marked decrease in alcohol consumption subsequent to training. As a
check on these reports, weekly breath alcohol levels were taken several weeks before and after training. These levels decreased from a mean of 0.08% to 0.02%.

Foy, Miller, Eisler, and O'Toole (1976) developed a more specialized assertive
training to teach alcoholics to refuse drinks under social pressure from friends.
Drug addicts and food abusers can also benefit from this treatment because of the
continual pressure to "shoot up" or to "have just one piece of cake for dessert."
The components of an appropriate refusal response include (a) direct eye contact,
(b) appropriate emotional expression, (c) offering an alternative (e.g., "I really
don't care for an alcoholic drink but I'd love some iced tea"), (d) changing the
subject of the conversation, and (e) requesting that the "pusher" discontinue his
insistence. Refusal skills were taught through the combined use of specific instructions, role playing, videotaped modeling of the appropriate behaviors, and struc-

tured practice sessions. Training resulted in effective refusal abilities and an increased sense of self-confidence and personal control over one's own behavior.

More recently, group studies (Adinolfi, McCourt, & Geoghegan, 1975; Hirsch, 1975) indicate that assertive training markedly improves alcoholics' social and occupational functioning. In turn, improved functioning in these areas is correlated with long-term maintenance of sobriety. Chaney, O'Leary, and Marlatt (1977) examined the effectiveness of social skills training with inpatient chronic alcoholics. They compared patients receiving either (a) social skills training, (b) discussion group sessions focusing on feelings, and (c) routine hospital care. A one year follow-up evaluation revealed that the duration and severity of relapse episodes were significantly lower in the social skills training group compared to the other groups.

Use of social skills training with drug abusers is rare. It is often used as an adjunct to other treatments, making it very difficult to evaluate its effectiveness apart from the overall program. Callner (1973), however, reported the exclusive use of social skills training with a group of four heroin addicts. Patients were trained in job application skills, drug refusal skills, and general communication abilities. The immediate results of the training were positive although no long-term clinical follow-up was included.

In reviewing studies in this area, Van Hasselt, Hersen, and Milliones (1978) concluded that, although the evidence is preliminary, it appears that "socially deficient alcoholics and drug addicts can be trained to perform more competently in interpersonal situations that have been distressing for them in the past" (p. 20).

Relaxation Training

Relaxation training has received increased attention from behavioral clinicians in the treatment of substance abuse. Several case studies and clinical investigations have indicated that relaxation training may be an important element of successful outcome in both treatment and prevention programs. Blake (1967) found that relaxation training combined with aversion therapy is much more effective than aversion therapy alone. Lanyon, Primo, Terrell, and Wener (1972) evaluated the efficacy of systematic desensitization (a procedure in which anxiety-producing situations are associated with relaxation) as an adjunct to aversion therapy. They compared aversion therapy, aversion therapy plus systematic desensitization, and general discussions of problems. The aversion group and the discussion group alcoholic patients were doing poorly at a one-year follow-up. The combined aversion-desensitization treatment results in a 71% abstinent rate at follow-up.

In a less extensive but more detailed experimental analysis, Steffen (1974) examined the relationship between relaxation training and drinking behavior with four chronic alcoholics. Relaxation was taught with the assistance of electromyographic (EMG) feedback. During this procedure the alcoholics received continuous feedback on the muscle activity in the frontalis muscle in the forehead. All patients learned to decrease muscle tension as a function of the training. To assess drinking behavior all patients were given access to alcohol in a controlled laboratory setting prior to and after training. The results indicated that the relaxation procedures resulted in less alcohol consumption and lower blood/alcohol levels.

Relaxation training has also been used in prevention programs designed to decrease the alcohol consumption of young social drinkers. Using nonalcoholic college students as subjects, Marlatt, Pagano, Rose, and Marques (1976) compared the effects of (*a*) meditation training as developed by Benson (1975), (*b*) progressive muscle relaxation training as developed by Wolpe (1958), (*c*) instructions to rest once per day, and (*d*) no treatment. Drinking was assessed by daily reports of alcohol consumption by the students and by an analogue drinking test known as the Taste Rating Task (Marlatt, Demming, & Reid, 1973). The results indicated that the regular practice of relaxation lowered alcohol consumption over a six-week time period. Follow-up contacts revealed that while all forms of relaxation decreased drinking, the meditation group tended to continue practicing on a regular basis for a longer period of time. The form of relaxation, then, may be related to the long-term use of relaxation skills and hence longer-term maintenance of lowered alcohol consumption. It seems doubtful that relaxation training by itself would have such a consistent effect with chronic alcoholics, but it may certainly prove to be a useful adjunct to a total behavioral treatment program. In any event, relaxation and/or meditation seem to offer promise for the prevention of alcohol abuse. In fact, Glasser (1976) has referred to these relaxation skills as "positive addictions" which when practiced as part of an individual's overall lifestyle serve as alternatives to unhealthy addictions.

Self-Management Skills

Self-management refers to a planned set of responses by which an individual modifies his own life, particularly in relationship to the antecedent and consequent events associated with substance abuse. Thus, the patient is trained to be his own behavior therapist, analyzing behavioral interactions, planning appropriate modification strategies, and implementing his plan of action. Three major aspects of these skills include (*a*) rearranging environmental cues or life routines to decrease the likelihood of excessive drinking, (*b*) utilizing thought control processes to modify cravings to drink, and (*c*) rearranging the social and environmental consequences of drinking behaviors and nondrinking alternatives to drinking so that the latter replace the former.

Unfortunately, while self-management skills have been used in the treatment of obesity and smoking, their use with alcohol and drug abusers has been rather limited. Mertens (1964) was one of the earliest behaviorists to report the use of this procedure with alcoholics. He placed particular emphasis on teaching patients to rearrange visual alcohol stimuli to make them less prominent and, hence, less likely to trigger a drinking episode. For example, a patient might be taught to plan a different route home from work to avoid passing his favorite bar or to avoid looking at liquor or beer advertisements by distracting himself in response to these cues. Patients were also taught methods of heightening the influence of potential long term consequences of alcohol abuse. In response to thoughts of drinking, patients were taught to visualize, in imagination, various ultimate *negative* consequences of drinking (e.g., loss of job and family, causing the death of another person in an automobile accident, being incapacitated because of brain damage), and the ultimate *positive* consequences of abstinence (e.g., occupational promotion, a more personally satisfying life, a feeling of personal accomplishment).

Miller (1976) reports the exclusive use of self-management skills training with a 49-year-old salesman with a history of episodic drinking. The patient never drank alcohol while at home but would overindulge on business trips. Excessive drinking on these trips was precipitated by being alone in a motel room or by social pressure to drink from customers. The patient rearranged these social and environmental cues by (*a*) arriving at out of town business meetings very close to the time of the meeting to avoid a lengthy stay in a hotel room, (*b*) avoiding business cocktail gatherings, (*c*) practicing various maneuvers to refuse drinks, and (*d*) informing all business colleagues and customers that he no longer will be drinking alcoholic beverages.

Operant Conditioning

Operant conditioning approaches to alcoholism focus on rearranging consequences of drinking so that excessive alcohol consumption is punished and more appropriate behavior is reinforced. Early applications of this approach were conducted in inpatient settings where environmental consequences of behavior are relatively easy to arrange. For example, Cohen, Liebson, & Faillace (1971) reported a series of single case design experiments in the Alcohol Research Unit of Baltimore City Hospital. A chronic alcoholic was allowed free access to 24 ounces of 95 proof ethanol each day. During contingent reinforcement weeks, the patient was placed in an "enriched ward environment" (i.e., recreation room, television, private telephone) if he drank 5 ounces or less in a day. Drinking more than 5 ounces resulted in his losing all privileges and being placed in a rather drab environment. During noncontingent reinforcement weeks, no systematic consequences were placed on drinking. Contingent reinforcement resulted in the maintenance of a pattern of moderate drinking (i.e., 5 ounces or less per day) over a five-week time period.

In the natural environment consequences are usually rearranged with the help of relatives or friends. Sulzer (1965) reported the use of peer companionship and spouse attention as reinforcers for drinking nonalcoholic beverages. Friends were advised to reinforce such behavior with increased attention and friendly conversation. On the other hand, whenever the patient drank alcohol, friends were instructed to leave his presence immediately no matter what the situation.

Miller, Hersen, Eisler, and Watts (1974) demonstrated control of an outpatient alcoholic's drinking by the use of coupons exchangeable for meals, cigarettes, and clothing. Coupons were made contingent upon a zero blood/alcohol concentration as determined by breath tests. Breath samples were collected randomly, on a biweekly basis, at the patient's home or place of employment. During the initial baseline phase, prior to the initiation of contingencies, the patient's blood/alcohol levels were high, ranging from 0.00% to 0.27%. During contingent reinforcement, the patient's blood/alcohol levels were decreased dramatically with only one sample being slightly above zero. Provision of coupons in a noncontingent fashion had no effect on the patient's drinking.

To extend these findings further, Miller (1975) applied a contingency management treatment to "Skid Row" alcoholics. All subjects in the study were chronic alcoholics who were arrested frequently for public intoxication and who worked on a sporadic basis. Under a special cooperative agreement with several social service community agencies, services such as housing, counseling, clothing, coffee, cigarettes, and meals were provided only if the alcoholic remained sober. Sobriety was determined via direct behavioral observations and by random breath tests. Excessive drinking resulted in a five-day suspension of all goods and services provided by the agencies. A control group continued to receive goods and services in a noncontingent manner. In reality, community services to "Skid Row" alcoholics inadvertantly become contingent upon *increased* alcohol consumption. That is, the more an individual is in need of assistance because of his drinking, the more assistance is provided. Social agencies may be reinforcing the exact behavior they are attempting to eliminate. This study indicated that contingent reinforcement resulted in a decreased number of public drunkenness arrests, an increased number of hours worked per week, and decreased alcohol consumption. The control group did not evidence any of these changes. In fact, during the two months of this project, only three of the contingency management alcoholics were arrested while nine of the control group subjects were arrested.

Hunt and Azrin (1973) and Azrin (1976) reported a group study of a community reinforcement program for chronic alcoholics. This program involved a rearrangement of reinforcers so that pleasurable marital, family, and peer activities occurred only as long as the patient remained sober. To promote and reinforce alternative behaviors, a social club was established where alcohol was not available. Social, vocational, and marital skills training was also provided. Over a six-month period of time these patients drank on fewer than 20% of the days as compared to 80% for a control group.

Azrin (1976) has recently improved the program by adding a planned social reinforcement system and daily reporting of drinking behavior. Antabuse is used and is taken in the presence of a wife or counselor. In this second study, the percentage of days spent drinking by patients was only 2%.

Marital Counseling

Marital problems frequently serve as precipitants for episodes of excessive drinking. Behavioral intervention in marital problems is usually a significant part of the treatment process. For example, Eisler, Miller, Hersen, and Alford (1974) decreased the alcohol consumption of an alcoholic husband by teaching him to be more assertive with his wife. Miller (1972) successfully used behavioral contracting in the treatment of an alcoholic and his wife. The contract required the alcoholic to reinforce his wife for not nagging about drinking and the wife to reinforce the husband for limiting his alcohol consumption. Reinforcement took the form of increased attention and affection. Nagging and drinking were punished by means of a response cost system in which a monetary fine of $20 was imposed for each infraction.

Hedberg and Campbell (1974) have reported the most controlled clinical research in this area. They compared the effectiveness of behavioral marital counseling, systematic desensitization, covert sensitization, and aversion therapy. At a one-year follow-up behavioral marital counseling resulted in 74% of 15 alcoholics achieving their goal (both abstinence and controlled drinking were possible goals). This was significantly higher than the success rates of any other group.

Clinically, some nonalcoholic spouses are so distraught by their partner's past and present behavior that they find it difficult to implement behavior change strategies on a consistent basis. Cheek, Franks, Laucius, and Burtle (1971) included relaxation training to assist the spouse in adopting a more positive and objective attitude.

COMPREHENSIVE BEHAVIORAL PROGRAMS

Rationale

Newer broad-spectrum behavioral approaches have emphasized teaching alcoholics methods of self-control applicable to both nondrinking and drinking conditions. Abusive drinking is viewed as a self-destructive, discriminated, operant behavior pattern maintained by its compelling short-term positive consequences (e.g., mood elevation, tension reduction). Comprehensive behavioral programs use a variety of operant, aversive, and social learning techniques in an attempt to accomplish some or all of the following:

1. Provide accurate, complete information about alcoholism to clients via comprehensive alcohol education (Stalonas, Keane, & Foy, 1979).
2. Obtain a thorough functional analysis of clients' drinking patterns so that specific drinking situational and topographical parameters may be modified (Marlatt, 1975).
3. Decrease the immediate reinforcing properties of alcohol (Miller & Eisler, 1975).
4. Teach clients new behaviors (e.g., problem-solving and drink refusal skills) that are incompatible with abusive drinking (Miller & Eisler, 1977).
5. Rearrange clients' social and vocational environments to maximize opportunities for exercising self-control of drinking (Hunt & Azrin, 1973).

These objectives are accomplished via intervention in three focal areas: (*a*) the drinking response per se; (*b*) clients' associated behavioral problems; and (*c*) clients' relationships with significant others (Briddell & Nathan, 1976).

Description of Program Components

Three different comprehensive behavioral treatment programs have been chosen to exemplify the various components that are typically offered. They also demonstrate the recent developments in behavioral approaches to alcoholism since they span a period of six to seven years. All three programs were offered in government-sponsored hospital settings; chronic male alcoholic inpatients were treated, and systematic treatment was applied to clients' drinking patterns per se. Beyond these common characteristics a wide variety of behavioral intervention strategies were employed.

The first published report of a comprehensive behavioral treatment program described "individualized behavior therapy" (I.B.T.) offered by Doctors Mark and Linda Sobell at Patton State Hospital in Southern California (Sobell & Sobell,

1973b, c). Treatment components included in I.B.T. were: (a) self-confrontation of videotaped drunken behavior; (b) stress management training; (c) discrimination training for controlled drinking, including contingent shock for inappropriate blood/alcohol levels (B.A.L.); and (d) behavior change sessions for clients' individual problems such as drinking decisions or assertiveness. Of the 17 total treatment sessions scheduled, 10 sessions were used to deliver drinking discrimination training/practice and behavior change training.

Two years after the Sobells reported on their program, Vogler, Compton, and Weissbach (1975) published data from their program of "integrated behavior change" (I.B.C.). This program was also conducted at Patton State Hospital in Southern California. The treatment components of I.B.C. were selected on the basis of five criteria: (a) inpatient residence not mandatory; (b) paraprofessionals could administer; (c) applicable to individual or group modalities; (d) cost-effective; and (e) compatible with other components. The components offered were: (a) self-confrontation of videotaped drunken behavior; (b) B.A.L. discrimination training with contingent shock for inappropriate B.A.L.; (c) discrimination avoidance practice; (d) alcohol education; (e) alternatives training; and (f) behavioral counseling for individual problems. In addition to an approximate 45-day inpatient stay, the program also offered aftercare consisting of 15 "booster" sessions in the year after discharge.

The latest example of a comprehensive behavioral program is that offered at the Veterans Administration Center, Jackson, Mississippi (Foy, Miller, Eisler, & O'Toole, 1976; Miller, Stanford, & Hemphill, 1974; Stalonas, Keane, & Foy, 1979). Since the authors of this chapter have served successively as director of this program over the past six years, the treatment components can be described in detail. The table which follows presents the current program offered in a 28-day inpatient stay. The program also offers aftercare to discharged clients via 12 scheduled outpatient visits in the first year.

Treatment Evaluation and Follow-Up

In order for gains to be made in treatment effectiveness over the gross "two-thirds" improved current standard, it is imperative that treatment programs be rigorously evaluated by empirical methods. There are several areas in which evaluation efforts need to be made. First, the individual components of a treatment program should be empirically based and undergo continuous assessment of effectiveness. Practically, this can be done using a repeated measures design at several points pre- and postintervention. This allows for within subject experimental control so that the treatment component per se is assessed. Second, the entire treatment package must be evaluated by follow-up data collected on clients' functioning. In this regard, it has been shown that treatment outcome results must be based on data collected over at least the immediate 12 months following discharge (Emrick, 1975; Gerard & Saenger, 1966).

A third area of evaluation concerns characteristics of the clients who receive the treatment package. In order for treatment outcome predictors to be identified, the salient demographic, environmental, and psychological characteristics of the treatment population must be identified. Systematic collection of these data prior to

Table 1. Jackson V.A. Hospital Alcohol Treatment Program Components

Program Component	Objectives	Staff Responsible
Psychological assessment	1. Evaluate cognitive, affective, and behavioral functioning of individual as compared to group norms	Research psychologist Psychology residents Psychology technician
Instruments		
1. Drinking profile	1. History and functional analysis of drinking pattern	
2. MAACL (Zuckerman & Lubin, 1965)	2. Anxiety, hostility, and depression scores	
3. Self-esteem Index (Barksdale, 1974)	3. Self-devaluation score	
4. Memory for design (Graham & Kendall)	4. Organic brain syndrome screening	
5. Locus of control (Rotter)	5. Self-determination score	
6. Marital Happiness Scale (Azrin, Naster & Jones)	6. 10 component marital analysis	
7. Locke-Wallace Marriage Questionnaire (Locke & Wallace)	7. Two component marital analysis	
8. M.M.P.I. (Hathaway & McKinley)	8. Personality inventory	
Alcohol education (group) (4-hour sessions total)	1. Assess patients' current knowledge of alcoholism etiology and effects	Clinical psychologist
	2. Provide empirically based information about causes and treatment of problem drinking	Clinical psychology resident Physician
	3. Educate patients about Antabuse effects and appropriate use	Psychology technician

Table 1. (Continued)

Program Component	Objectives	Staff Responsible
Behavioral group therapy (4-hour sessions/week)	1. Assess patients' interpersonal functioning on continuing basis 2. Teach personal planning, problem-solving skills 3. Assess patients' functioning within context of treatment setting 4. Teach patients self-relaxation, anxiety management	Clinical psychology resident
Drinking skills training and assessment (Group—7-hour sessions total)	1. Assess patients' capability to control alcohol consumption via external and internal methods of regulation 2. Correct skill deficits through practice drinking sessions and focused instructions 3. Teach appropriate environmental and time selection factors for drinking	Clinical psychologist Clinical psychology resident Psychology technician
Family therapy (As needed)	1. Assess present marital functioning as perceived by both patient and spouse 2. Intervene in most acute perceived problem areas 3. Teach marital problem-solving skills	Treatment coordinator
Hospital work assignments (x:8 hours/week)	1. Establish daily work responsibilities 2. Evaluate patients' vocational interpersonal functioning	Vocational specialist (via feedback from work site supervisors in pharmacy, mail room, and outpatient clinic settings)
Individual therapy (x:2 sessions/week)	1. Assess patients' psychological problems 2. Construct problem list and individual treatment plan 3. Provide additional therapy as indicated 4. Evaluate patient's progress toward treatment goals	Treatment coordinator (Vocational specialist, social worker and clinical psychology resident serve as treatment coordinator)
Job interview skills training (Group: 3-hour sessions)	1. Assess patients ability to present his history and job skills to prospective employers 2. Teach effective interview responses	Vocational specialist

Component	Objectives	Staff
Relaxation training (Group—4-hour sessions/week)	1. Teach and provide practice in progressive muscle relaxation	Clinical psychology resident
Self-management skill training (9 hours total) (There are 3 subcomponents to self-management)		
I. Self-management (5-hour sessions)	1. Teach patients about relationships between the environment (outer and inner), the individual, and his responses (S-O-R)	Clinical psychologist
	2. Teach patients how to implement stimulus-based or response-based intervention strategies to change own behavior	Clinical psychology resident
	3. Craving or urge to drink—how to elicit and extinguish it	
II. Drink refusal training (2-hour sessions)	1. Assess patients' present abilities to refuse drinks	Clinical psychology resident
	2. Teach effective refusal responses	
	3. Increase habit strength of refusal via repeated practice and peer social reinforcement	
III. General assertion training (2-hour sessions)	1. Assess patients' interpersonal problem-solving skills	Clinical psychology resident
	2. Teach effective interpersonal responses to common problems	
Vocational interpersonal skills training (Group—3-hour sessions total)	1. Assess patients present skill level	Vocational specialist
	2. Teach appropriate responses to common peer, boss-related problems	
Vocational training (Group—4-hour sessions total)	1. Discuss negative and positive aspects of the job	Vocational specialist
	2. Discuss alcohol abuse as it relates to the individual on the job	
	3. Teach job finding along with skills needed for filling out job applications	

treatment allows for a client X treatment interaction analysis when follow-up data are available. This kind of evaluation is essential in developing an effective triage system.

A methodological problem in conducting treatment evaluation concerns the choice of dependent measures used to define outcome. Focusing only on drinking amount or frequency in determining treatment success or failure is a common mistake many early investigators made (c.f. Emrick, 1974). More recent reports of alcohol treatment outcome studies (e.g., Sobell & Sobell, 1973(a); Van Dijk & Van Dijk-Koffman, 1973) have used multiple "quality of life" indicators encompassing many areas of clients' functioning in the natural environment. In a factor analytic study of potential areas related to treatment outcome, Foster, Horn, and Wanberg (1972) identified eight factors that represented critical functioning areas. These include: (a) general adequacy of adjustment; (b) abstinence; (c) observed improvement; (d) job and productivity; (e) self-acclaimed improvement and control of drinking problem; (f) decrease in sociopathy; (g) intrapersonal adjustment; and (h) social involvement. Measures selected to sample these factors provide a comprehensive evaluation of treatment.

CONCLUSIONS

Comprehensive behavioral treatment programs offered in recent years represent a broad-spectrum approach to improving the quality of life of clients who have alcohol abuse problems. By the variety of treatment components offered, it is apparent that a behavioral approach does not assume that alcoholics are a homogeneous population. Rather, the offering of multiple components allows for individualized treatment planning for each client based on his specific needs. Recent behavioral programs have emphasized intervention in clients' drinking patterns per se, in addition to treating alcohol-related behavioral problems and cilents' interactions with significant others. Behavioral programs appear to offer the potential for increasing the present "two-thirds improved" outcome standard. In this regard, offering controlled drinking training to clients who choose it and whose physical and psychological conditions permit may be an important advance over earlier abstinence only programs.

NEW DIRECTIONS AND FUTURE TRENDS

From a theoretical standpoint it is apparent that the disease theory or model of alcoholism as a progressive, irreversible process is inadequate as a comprehensive model. With ample evidence now available demonstrating that, for some alcoholics, abusive drinking is neither inevitably progressive nor irreversible, proponents of a narrow disease model have responded that those individuals were not "true" alcoholics. The tautological aspect of this reasoning is obvious. The larger issue to be addressed is whether there is a need for a comprehensive theory of alcoholism at all. The behavioral programs described earlier were not based on a single theory or model of alcoholism attempting to explain etiology and guide treatment. Rather, the problem of alcohol abuse and concommitant psychosocial and physiological problems were accepted "as is" and treated on that basis. It seems probable that future behavioral treatment efforts will continue to be atheoretical.

In the area of applied alcoholism research, the most pressing unresolved issue is developing an empirical basis for matching clients with drinking goals. Client pretreatment characteristics that can reliably serve as predictors for treatment outcome need to be identified. Perhaps the most promising focal point in this regard is objective measurement of the client's actual drinking behavior. Drinking analysis also serves as a basis for an individualized drinking treatment plan, a key component of comprehensive behavioral treatment. A second major research issue concerns the relationship of aftercare treatment to total treatment in terms of outcome effects. Future treatment outcome studies need to be designed so that aftercare effects can be independently evaluated.

Treatment areas in which increased efforts can be expected in the future include: (*a*) vocational interpersonal skills; (*b*) marital/family functioning; (*c*) decision-making or problem-solving skills training; and (*d*) self-management skills. The importance of these functional areas in behavioral treatment efforts is emphasized for several reasons. First, the frequency with which they are presented as concommitant problems by alcoholic clients makes assessment and intervention mandatory in a comprehensive treatment approach. Secondly, the outcome literature now available demonstrates that simply removing abusive drinking from the client's lifestyle does not ensure improved functioning in other areas. Treatment plans are becoming increasingly individualized to deal with clients' unique problems. Finally, the shift away from "abstinence" toward improvement in multiple "quality of life" indicators as the major objective in treatment will stimulate improvements in technology for treating problems other than the drinking response itself.

REFERENCES

Adinolfi, A. A., McCourt, W. F., & Geoghegan, S. Group assertiveness training for alcoholics. *Journal of Studies on Alcohol,* 1976, **37**, 311–320.

American Psychiatric Association. *Diagnostic and statistical manual of mental disorders* (2nd edition). Washington, D.C.: American Psychiatric Association, 1968.

Armor, D. J., Polich, J. M., & Stambul, H. B. *Alcoholism and treatment.* Santa Monica, Calif.: The Rand Corporation, 1976.

Azrin, N. H. Improvements in the community reinforcement approach to alcoholism. *Behaviour Research and Therapy,* 1976, **14**, 339–348.

Azrin, N. H., Naster, B. J., & Jones, R. Reciprocity counseling: A rapid learning based procedure for marital counseling. *Behavior Research and Therapy,* 1973, **11**, 365–382.

Bailey, M. B., & Stewart, J. Normal drinking by persons reporting previous drinking problems. *Quarterly Journal of Studies on Alcohol,* 1967, **28**, 305–315.

Benson, H. The relaxation response. New York: William Morrow, 1975.

Barkesdale, W. The Barkesdale self-esteem index. Unpublished manuscript, 1974.

Blake, B. G. A follow-up of alcoholics treated by behavior therapy. *Behaviour Research and Therapy,* 1967, **5**, 89–94.

Briddell, D. W., & Nathan, P. E. Behavior assessment and modification with alcoholics: Current status and future trends. In M. Hersen, R. M. Eisler, & P. M. Miller (Eds.), *Progress in behavior modification.* New York: Academic Press, 1976.

Callner, D. A. The assessment and training of assertive behavior in a drug addict population. Paper presented at the American Psychological Association, Montreal, 1973.

Cappell, H., & Herman, C. P. Alcohol and tension reduction: A review. *Quarterly Journal of Studies on Alcohol,* 1972, **33**, 33–64.

Chaney, E. F., O'Leary, M. R., & Marlatt, G. A. Skill training with alcoholics. Unpublished manuscript, University of Washington School of Medicine, Seattle, Washington, 1977.

Cheek, F. E., Franks, C. M., Laucius, J., & Burtle, V. Behavior modification training for wives of alcoholics. *Quarterly Journal of Studies on Alcohol,* 1971, **32**, 456–461.

Cohen, M., Liebson, I., & Faillace, L. The role of reinforcement contingencies in chronic alcoholism: An experimental analysis of one case. *Behaviour Research and Therapy,* 1971, **9**, 375–379.

Conger, J. J. Reinforcement theory and the dynamics of alcoholism. *Quarterly Journal of Studies on Alcohol,* 1956, **17**, 296–305.

Criteria Committee, National Council on Alcoholism. Criteria for the diagnosis of alcoholism. *American Journal of Psychiatry,* 1972, **2**, 127–135.

Cutter, H. S. G., Schwab, E. L., & Nathan, P. E. Effects of alcohol on its utility for alcoholics. *Quarterly Journal of Studies on Alcohol,* 1970, **30**, 369–378.

Davies, D. L. Normal drinking in recovered alcohol addicts. *Quarterly Journal of Studies on Alcohol,* 1962, **23**, 94–104.

Eisler, R. M., Miller, P. M., Hersen, M., & Alford, H. Effects of assertive training on marital interaction. *Archives of General Psychiatry,* 1974, **30**, 643–649.

Emrick, C. D. A review of psychologically oriented treatment of alcoholism: I. The use and interrelationships of outcome criteria and drinking behavior following treatment. *Quarterly Journal of Studies on Alcohol,* 1974, **35**, 523–549.

Emrick, C. D. A review of psychologically oriented treatment of alcoholism: II. The relative effectiveness of different treatment approaches and the effectiveness of treatment versus no treatment. *Quarterly Journal of Studies on Alcohol,* 1975, **36**, 88–108.

Engle, K. B., & Williams, T. K. Effect of an ounce of vodka on alcoholics' desire for alcohol. *Quarterly Journal of Studies on Alcohol,* 1972, **33**, 1099–1105.

Foster, F. M., Horn, J. L., & Wanberg, K. W. Dimensions of treatment outcome: A factor analytic study of alcoholics' responses to a follow-up questionnaire. *Quarterly Journal of Studies on Alcohol,* 1972, **33**, 1079–1098.

Foy, D. W., Miller, P. M., Eisler, R. M., & O'Toole, D. H. Social skills training to teach alcoholics to refuse drinks effectively. *Journal of Studies on Alcohol,* 1976, **37**, 1340–1345.

Foy, D. W., & Simon, S. J. Alcoholic drinking topography as a function of solitary versus social context. *Addictive Behaviors,* 1978, **3**, 39–41.

Gerard, D. C., & Saenger, G. Outpatient treatment of alcoholism: A study of outcome and its determinants. Toronto: University of Toronto Press, 1966.

Glasser, W. *Positive addictions.* New York: Harper & Row, 1976.

Graham, F. K., & Kendall, B. S. Performance of brain damage cases on a memory design card. *Journal of Abnormal and Social Psychology,* 1946, **41**, 303–314.

Hallam, R., Rachman, S., & Falkowski, W. Subjective, attitudinal, and physiological effects of electrical aversion therapy. *Behaviour Research and Therapy,* 1972, **10**, 1–13.

Hathaway, S. R., & McKinley, J. C. Minnesota Multi-phasic Personality inventory manual (Revised). New York: Psychological Corporation, 1967.

Hedberg, A. G., & Campbell, L. A comparison of four behavioral treatments of alcoholism. *Journal of Behavior Therapy and Experimental Psychiatry,* 1974, **5**, 251–256.

Hirsch, S. M. Experimental investigation of the effectiveness of assertion training with alcoholics. Doctoral dissertation, Texas Technological University, Lubbock, Texas, 1975.

Hodgson, R. J., & Rankin, H. J. Modification of excessive drinking by cue exposure. *Behaviour Research and Therapy,* 1976, **14**, 305–307.

Hunt, G. M., & Azrin, N. H. A community reinforcement approach to alcoholism. *Behaviour Research and Therapy,* 1973, **11**, 91–104.

Jackson, M., & Lubin, B. Manual for the Multiple affect objective checklist. San Diego: Educational and Individual Testing (Revised), 1965.

Jellinek, E. M. *The disease concept of alcoholism.* New Haven: College and University Press, 1960.

Katz, M. M., & Lyerly, S. B. Methods for measuring adjustment and social behaviors in the community: I. Rationale, description, discrimination validity and scale development. *Psychological Reports,* 1963, **13**, 503–535.

Kingham, R. J. Alcoholism and the reinforcement theory of learning. *Quarterly Journal of Studies on Alcohol,* 1958, **19**, 320–330.

Lanyon, R. I., Primo, R. V., Terrell, F., & Wener, A. An aversion desensitization treatment for alcoholism. *Journal of Consulting and Clinical Psychology,* 1972, **38**, 394–398.

Lemere, F., & Voegtlin, W. L. An evaluation of the aversion treatment of alcoholism. *Quarterly Journal of Studies on Alcohol,* 1950, **11**, 199–204.

Locke, H. J., & Wallace, K. M. Short marital adjustment and prediction tests: Their reliability and validity. *Marital and Family Living,* 1959, **21**, 251–255.

Ludwig, A. M., & Wikler, A. "Craving" and relapse to drink. *Quarterly Journal of Studies on Alcohol,* 1974, **35**, 108–130.

McNamee, H. B., Mello, N. K., & Mendelson, J. H. Experimental analysis of drinking patterns of alcoholics. Concurrent psychiatric observations. *American Journal of Psychiatry,* 1968, **24**, 1063–1069.

Maisto, S. A., & Schefft, B. K. The constructs of craving for alcohol and loss of control drinking: Help or hindrance to research. *Addictive Behaviors,* 1977, **2**, 207–217.

Marlatt, G. A. The drinking profile: A questionnaire for the behavioral assessment of alcoholism. In E. J. Marsh & L. G. Terdal (Eds.), *Behavior therapy assessment: Diagnosis and evaluation.* New York: Springer Publishing Co., 1975.

Marlatt, G. A. Craving for alcohol, loss of control, and relapse: A cognitive-behavioral analysis. In P. E. Nathan & G. A. Marlatt (Eds.), *Experimental and behavioral approaches to alcoholism.* New York: Plenum, 1978.

Marlatt, G. A., Demming, B., & Reid, J. B. Loss of control drinking in alcoholics: An experimental analogue. *Journal of Abnormal Psychology,* 1973, **81**, 233–241.

Marlatt, G. A., Pagano, R. R., Rose, R. M., & Marques, J. K. The effect of meditation and relaxation upon alcohol consumption in male social drinkers. Unpublished research, University of Washington, 1976.

Mendelson, J. H. Experimentally induced chronic intoxication and withdrawal in alcoholics. *Quarterly Journal of Studies in Alcohol,* Supplement no. 2, 1964.

Mertens, G. C. An operant approach to self-control for alcoholics. Paper presented at the American Psychological Association, September, 1964.

Miller, P. M. The use of behavioral contracting in the treatment of alcoholism: A case report. *Behavior Therapy,* 1972, **3**, 593–596.

Miller, P. M. A behavioral intervention program for chronic public drunkenness offenders. *Archives of General Psychiatry,* 1975, **32**, 915–918.

Miller, P. M. *Behavioral treatment of alcoholism.* New York: Pergamon Press, 1976.

Miller, P. M. *Personal habit control.* New York: Simon & Schuster, 1978.

Miller, P. M., & Eisler, R. M. Assertive behavior of alcoholics: A descriptive analysis. *Behavior Therapy,* 1977, **8**, 146–149.

Miller, P. M., Hersen, M., Eisler, R. M., & Elkin, T. E. A retrospective analysis of alcohol consumption on laboratory tasks as related to therapeutic outcome. *Behaviour Research and Therapy,* 1974, **12**, 73–76.

Miller, P. M., Hersen, M., Eisler, R. M., Epstein, L., & Wooten, L. Relationship of alcohol cues to the drinking behavior of alcoholics and social drinkers: An analogue study. *Psychological Record,* 1974, **24**, 61–66.

Miller, P. M., Hersen, M., Eisler, R. M., & Hemphill, D. P. Electrical aversion therapy with alcoholics: An analogue study. *Behaviour Research and Therapy,* 1973, **11**, 491–497.

Miller, P. M., Hersen, M., Eisler, R. M., & Hilsman, G. Effects of social stress on operant drinking of alcoholics and social drinkers. *Behavior Research and Therapy,* 1974, **12**, 65–72.

Miller, P. M., Hersen, M., Eisler, R. M., & Watts, J. G. Contingent reinforcement of lowered blood/alcohol levels in an outpatient chronic alcoholic. *Behaviour Research and Therapy,* 1974, **12**, 261–263.

Miller, P. M., Stanford, A. G., & Hemphill, D. P. A social-learning approach to alcoholism treatment. *Social Casework,* 1974, **55**, 279–284.

Nathan, P. E., & O'Brien, J. S. An experimental analysis of the behavior of alcoholics and nonalcoholics during prolonged experimental drinking: A necessary precursor of behavior therapy? *Behavior Therapy,* 1971, **2**, 455–476.

National Institute of Mental Health, Alcohol and Alcoholism. Washington, D.C.: USPHS Publication No. 1640, 1969.

Pachman, J. L., Foy, D. W., & Van Erd, M. Goal choice of alcoholics: A comparison of those choosing total abstinence versus those choosing responsible, controlled drinking. *Journal of Clinical Psychology,* 1978, **34**, 781–783.

Rotter, J. B. Generalized expectancies for internal vs. external control of reinforcement. Psychological monograph, 1966, **80**, (1, whole number 609).

Sobell, M. B., & Sobell, L. C. Alcoholics treated by individualized behavior therapy: One year treatment outcome. *Behaviour Research and Therapy,* 1973, **11**, 599–618. (a)

Sobell, L. C., & Sobell M. B. A self-feedback technique to monitor drinking behavior in alcoholics. *Behaviour Research and Therapy,* 1973, **11**, 237–238. (b)

Sobell, M. B., & Sobell, L. C. Individualized behavior therapy for alcoholics. *Behavior Therapy,* 1973, **4**, 49–72. (c)

Stalonas, P. M., Keane, T. M., & Foy, D. W. Alcohol educating for inpatient alcoholics: Comparison of live, videotape and written presentation modalities. *Addictive Behaviors,* 1979, **4**, 223–230.

Steffen, J. J. Electromyographically induced relaxation in the treatment of chronic alcohol abuse. *Journal of Consulting and Clinical Psychology,* 1974, **43**, 275–279.

Strickler, D., Bigelow, G., & Wells, D. Electromyograph responses of abstinent alcoholics to drinking related stimuli: Effects of relaxation instructions. Paper presented at the Association for the Advancement of Behavior Therapy, New York, December, 1976.

Sulzer, E. S. Behavior modification in adult psychiatric patients. In L. P. Ullman & L. Krasner (Eds.), *Case studies in behavior modification.* New York: Holt, Rinehart, & Winston, 1965, 196–199.

Van Dijk, W. K., & Van Dijk-Koffman, A. A follow-up study of 211 treated male alcoholic addicts. *British Journal of the Addictions,* 1973, **68**, 3–24.

Van Hasselt, V. B., Hersen, M., & Milliones, J. Social skills training for alcoholics and drug addicts: A review. *Addictive Behaviors,* 1978, **3**, 221–234.

Vogler, R. C., Compton, J. V., & Weissbach, T. A. Integrated behavior change techniques for alcoholics. *Journal of Consulting and Clinical Psychology,* 1975, **43**, 233–243.

Wilson, G. T., & Lawson, D. M. Expectancies, alcohol, and sexual arousal in male social drinkers. *Journal of Abnormal Psychology,* 1976, **85**, 587–594.

Wilson, T., Leaf, R., & Nathan, P. E. The aversive control of excessive drinking by chronic alcoholics in the laboratory setting. *Journal of Applied Behavior Analysis,* 1975, **8**, 13–26.

Wolpe, J. *Psychotherapy by reciprocal inhibition.* Stanford, Calif.: Stanford University Press, 1958.

Zuckerman, M., & Lubin, B. Manual for the Multiple Affect Adjective Check List. San Diego, Calif.: Educational and Industrial Testing Service, 1965.

CHAPTER 9

Disorders of Eating

Stewart Agras and Joellen Werne

Two more different entities than obesity and anorexia nervosa can hardly be imagined. Not only are there gross differences in appearance and in weight, but the one, obesity, is all too common, while the other, anorexia nervosa, is relatively rare. Anorexia nervosa, as we shall see, is a well-delineated disorder while obesity is a term applied to what will almost certainly turn out to be a heterogeneous collection of disorders. Yet both are disorders of eating and, as such, form the content of this chapter.

OBESITY

This common problem is perhaps best approached in the context of a recent conference on "Obesity and the American Public," during which investigators confessed their ignorance as to the causes of obesity or how best to treat it (Kolaka, 1977). This conclusion is a fair reflection of the literature, which is confusing and often contradictory, leading, of course, to differing interpretations of the data. Adding to the problem is the growing conviction that obesity is not one disorder but is composed of several subtypes, although, at present, there is no satisfactory way to classify these subtypes or to relate different types of obesity to treatment outcome.

Obesity is associated with a variety of hazards, both to social well-being and to health. Thus the overweight are likely to be discriminated against as was shown by Canning and Mayer (1966) in their findings of differential acceptance rates of the obese and nonobese to college, even when there were no differences in high school performance. Such discrimination may be the reason that the obese score slightly higher than the nonobese on a number of scales measuring general adjustment of neuroticism as was found in the Midtown Manhattan study (Stunkard, 1967). Other health problems include an increased incidence of varicose veins, arthritis, diabetes, gall-bladder disease, higher blood lipids and blood pressure, and a larger number of complications of surgery and anaesthesia. Such health problems are, of course, worth ameliorating by reducing overweight.

The Etiology of Obesity

The major factors involved in the etiology of obesity include inheritance; excessive caloric intake, which in turn is influenced by the availability of food and a variety of socioeconomic factors; and insufficient activity to balance caloric intake. All the work in this area suggests that obesity is a complex disorder with multiple determinants, implying that no one simple treatment will prove effective.

Socioeconomic Factors

One of the most striking features of obesity is the inverse relationship between social class and the prevalence of overweight (Goldblatt, Moore, & Stunkard, 1965). This relationship is particularly striking for women, with 30% being overweight in the lowest social class compared with 5% in the highest. Interestingly, the same relationship persists when the social class of parents was compared with the present weight of their adult offspring. This relationship with social class is found in England and other Western countries as well as in the United States and appears to exert its influence early in life. In two studies, one in England (Whitelaw, 1971) and one in America (Stunkard, d'Acquili, & Fox, 1972), an inverse relationship between social class and obesity was found in children from the ages of six or seven through adolescence.

Intriguingly, upward social mobility is linked with a decreased prevalence of obesity and downward mobility with an increased prevalence (Goldblatt, Moore, & Stunkard, 1965). What is not known is how the social environment exerts this influence, although it is probable that both the type of food eaten and eating habits within the family differ between social classes, and also that eating patterns acquired early in life will tend to persist, particularly when individuals remain in the same social circumstances. These findings in Western food-rich countries differ from those cultures in which the supply of food is not sufficient for the needs of the population. In such countries, obesity increases with rising social class.

Genetic Factors

Although obesity is clearly an inherited trait in animals, no definitive evidence exists for genetic transmission in humans. Nonetheless, individuals' weights tend to follow those of their natural parents, even in studies of adopted children (Withers, 1964). Within families, both genetic and social environmental factors are likely to influence eating patterns and weight.

Activity Levels

The only way to increase caloric expenditure is to increase activity. Unfortunately, just as food becomes more plentiful in affluent cultures, so the need to exert oneself becomes less pressing and even less possible. Difference in activity levels exist between the obese and nonobese. In an early study of this question, Chirico and Stunkard (1960) using the pedometer (an admittedly crude measure of activity) found that obese women walked less than nonobese women, a relationship that did not hold for men. Similar findings were made when activity was observed directly in a summer camp for adolescent girls, with the obese engaging in less activity than girls of normal weight (Mayer, 1955).

Weight Regulation

Animal studies and, to some extent, human studies suggest that weight is a relatively stable phenomenon, and that there is a tendency to return to previous weight despite quite dramatic alteration in diet. Thus in a study in which nonobese volunteers were fed a high calorie diet, all put on weight for an average gain of 25%. At the end of the study, when they were allowed to select their own diets, each volunteer returned to his preexperimental weight (Sims, Goldman, Gluck, Horton, Kelleher, & Rowe, 1968). However, in both short- and medium-term studies with humans fed liquid diets containing more or less calories than needed, regulation of caloric intake appears to be imprecise and relatively slow to respond to alterations in caloric density in a substantial proportion of subjects (e.g., Wooley & Wooley, 1975).

The Psychology of Obesity

One of the first psychological theories concerning overeating and obesity was that anxiety or other affective states led to overeating, perhaps because the obese tend to perceive such feelings as hunger (Bruch, 1973). Howver, as we have seen, there is not much evidence that the obese differ very significantly from normals on measures of anxiety or depression. Direct tests of this hypothesis, in which caloric intake has been measured following a laboratory-induced stress, have produced mixed results. It seems that about 30% of subjects do respond to stress either by reducing or increasing eating, and that the obese are somewhat more likely to increase than decrease their intake, although there is considerable individual variation (Meyer & Pudel, 1972).

A similar but more extended hypothesis was proposed by Schachter (1968), who suggested that obese eating is controlled by external events, while nonobese eating is controlled by inner stimuli associated with hunger and repletion. This hypothesis has provoked a considerable number of well-controlled laboratory studies, again with conflicting results. Early work suggested that there were differences between the obese and nonobese along several dimensions, including fear arousal, the salience of food cues, and time cues. However, later studies have found that both obese and nonobese eating are more under the control of the social environment than was suspected previously. Thus, in a cafeteria study, when low-calorie desserts were placed in front of high-calorie desserts and then the order reversed, normal-weighted subjects were susceptible to both maneuvers, tending to choose the most prominent dessert. The obese, on the other hand, tended to choose the low-calorie dessert under both conditions (Levitz, 1973).

One major distinguishing factor between the obese and nonobese appears to be in the response to food palatability. Nisbett (1972) found that obese and nonobese subjects ate the same amount of ice cream when it was rated as being poor in quality, but that the obese ate more when the ice cream was rated well. Similarly, in a cafeteria study, the obese were found to eat more than normals only in cafeterias serving highly palatable foods (Wooley & Wooley, 1975). In addition, when salivation to highly palatable food was used as a measure of appetite, it was found that salivation was inhibited when normals were given a high-calorie preload, but only partially inhibited in the obese (Wooley, Wooley, & Woods, 1975). Such findings suggest the possibility that the obese have learned to prefer highly palatable foods, and that in turn, when highly palatable foods are available, there is an increased probability that the obese will eat, regardless of stomach loading.

A final speculation about the obese is that their eating style might differ from that of the nonobese population. This notion, first proposed by Ferster and his colleagues in 1962, has only recently been tested by empirical research. Ferster suggested that the obese might eat more quickly than the nonobese and also that their eating might be controlled by narrowing the range of stimuli regularly associated with meals or snacks. As with all the other areas of research in obesity, the findings regarding eating style are conflicting. There is, however, growing evidence for some difference in eating style in both adults and children. In a recent study from our laboratory (Adams, Ferguson, Stunkard, & Agras, 1978), no differences in eating style were found between obese and normal-weighted women. However, as compared with a group of thin women, the obese ate the same number of calories more quickly, chewed their food less, and also spent more time drinking. Similar findings were made in a recent study of children in which it was found that obese children ate more quickly and chewed their food less than normal weighted children (Drabman, Hammer, & Jarvie, 1977).

Once more it must be emphasized that there was considerable overlap between obese and nonobese populations and that some of the obese showed styles typical of the thin and vice versa. However, it is interesting to note that in a further experiment, rapid eating was associated with greater salivation to later food cues than was slow eating in both the obese and nonobese (Wooley, Wooley, & Turner, 1975), suggesting that rapid eating is associated with less satiation and thus a tendency to eat sooner after meals.

Some Conclusions for the Clinician

Several findings from this varied body of research on obesity should be highlighted before turning our attention to treatment. First, there is a great deal of evidence that various aspects of the environment affect eating behavior both in the obese and nonobese. This augurs well for the clinician, for it suggests that by changing the enviroment, eating behavior and weight might be changed. Unfortunately, the exact nature of some of the environmental influences is not known, and, perhaps worse still, features of the Western food-rich, laborsaving culture favor the development of overweight. Second, there is evidence that the obese are less active than the nonobese, and that increasing activity should lead to weight reduction. Unfortunately, the effect of activity increase upon weight is slow, thus leading to discouragement on the part of the overweight with this approach to treatment. Third, some obese individuals have eating styles conducive to lessened satiation, suggesting that by changing eating styles weight might be lost. In line with this is the attraction of palatable foods for the obese. Last but not least is the repeated theme of conflicting findings, both within and between studies, underlining the fact that obesity is not a uniform disorder, and that there is much that we do not know. For the clinician, this means that there is individual variation and the need to assess each client's unique problems in the light of what is known.

It also seems wise to repeat here Stunkard and Mahoney's (1976) warning that, given the multiple causes of obesity, there are probably individuals who are biologically destined to become obese, for whom treatment may lead to ". . . a statistically normal but biologically abnormally low body weight. It may, in short, have simply helped him to live in a state of semi-starvation" (p. 45).

The Behavioral Treatment of Obesity

As we have seen, the behavioral approach to the treatment of obesity is based on the notions of Ferster and his colleagues (1962) concerning stimulus control and an obese eating style. These ideas were transformed into a therapeutic package by Stuart (1967), which, in turn, has led to a remarkable flurry of research.

The major elements included in most present-day treatment programs, usually applied in a group setting, are outlined in Table 1.

Self-Monitoring

The amount of food consumed, the time at which it was eaten, the circumstances under which the food was eaten, and any notable affective state is an important component of treatment, both for diagnostic assessment and at later stages of treatment for assessment of any remaining problems. Examples of forms to be used can be found in a number of manuals (e.g., Ferguson, 1975). Self-monitoring alone appears to have a transient effect upon weight (Stuart, 1971), although one study in which clients recorded the number of mouthfuls eaten at each meal and who gradually reduced the number, suggested that this method might be more successful than the more global self-monitoring in common use. Occasionally clients will be able to identify a major source of excessive caloric intake, such as three or four evening cocktails, which can be reduced or eliminated relatively easily, thus leading to satisfactory weight loss.

Stimulus Control

Attempts to change the stimulus control of eating should start with the buying and storage of food. Especially tempting snacks should be eliminated by not buying them; the amount of food kept in the house should be reduced; and all food should be kept out of sight, thus reducing the temptation to eat between meals. Meals and snacks should be eaten in one place and always sitting down at a properly laid table. This may eventually better demarcate the occasion for eating and help to reduce nibbling between meals. Other aspects of stimulus control include the use of smaller plates and deliberately leaving some food on the plate to break the habit of eating everything that is placed before one.

Eating Style

As we have seen, some obese individuals eat more quickly and chew their food less than their thinner counterparts. Thus most programs teach their clients to pause

**Table 1.   Elements of a Behavioral
Approach to Obesity**

Self-monitoring of eating behavior
Change the stimulus control of eating
Alter eating style
Caloric modification
Nutritional education
Increase activity
Reinforce new behavior

between bites. This may be accomplished by putting down one's eating utensil after each bite and not picking it up again until all the food is swallowed. In addition, the obese should be encouraged to chew their food more thoroughly and to delay taking a second helping.

Caloric Modification and Nutritional Education

The emphasis placed upon diet varies considerably between behavioral programs; some hardly mention the subject, some provide information about sensible ways to diet, and still others use caloric monitoring and dietary advice to achieve caloric restriction. Although changing stimulus control and eating style will lead to some decrease in caloric intake, clients should be encouraged to achieve some additional dietary control. Simple ways to achieve this include cutting down food intake by preplanning meals and using food exchange lists (e.g., Jeffrey & Katz, 1977) or adding a few vegetarian meals to the week's diet.

Exercise

Most behavioral programs suggest a modest increase in activity to their clients and attempt to structure such activity so that it fits into their clients' life-style. Thus walking upstairs instead of taking an elevator, parking as far away from the entrance to a building as possible, and walking instead of driving for short distances will all help to increase activity. Beyond this, a modest walking program, perhaps eventually leading to jogging or participation in sports such as tennis or swimming, may be helpful. Sudden increases in exercise are to be avoided; thus a graduated program is essential. A walk can also be used as an activity competitive with eating. For the housewife who becomes hungry, a walk may remove the temptation to eat and will diminish the attention paid to sensations of hunger.

Reinforcement

One of the advantages of a group approach to weight loss is that group members provide support and social reinforcement for each other's changes in behavior and weight loss. In addition, clients can be taught to use self-reinforcement by making pleasant events contingent upon successful completion of particular behaviors. Activities that might be used as reinforcers, often those that are engaged in frequently during leisure hours, should be listed and a few reserved for this purpose. Thus reading a book for half an hour might be made contingent on having no snacks during a 24-hour period, or weight loss of a pound might be reinforced by attending a movie, and so on.

Reinforcement can also be managed by the therapists. For example, in some programs clients write a series of checks to the charity they least would like to support. If a specific weight goal is reached, the check is returned; if not, it is mailed to the charity.

Miscellaneous Procedures

A number of programs use techniques such as relaxation training to help clients cope with feelings of anxiety that may accompany weight reduction and they generally lower feelings of stress that might lead to eating. Aversive procedures are rarely used, although covert sensitization may on occasion prove useful to help diminish the attractiveness of specific foods (e.g., Barlow, 1978).

Results of Behavioral Treatment

Stuart's (1967) description of a behavioral approach to obesity, which included most of the elements outlined above, demonstrated results that were superior to anything previously reported in the weight reduction literature. Stuart used individual therapy for between 16 and 41 sessions with 10 patients. Two patients dropped out of treatment. The remaining eight lost between 26 and 46 pounds by the end of one year. Since that time a remarkable amount of research has been generated, for the most part using a group approach to weight loss. Behavioral treatment appears to be more effective than no treatment (Harris, 1969), than various types of placebo or nonspecific therapy controls (Hagen, 1974; Wollersheim, 1970), than traditional dietary counseling (Penick, Filion, Fox, & Stunkard, 1971), and also than fenfluramine, an appetite suppressant (Öst & Götestam, 1976), at least in immediate outcome.

However, the range of outcomes, both between studies and within studies, is quite large, from about 2 to 36 pounds lost being the range between studies (Wing & Jeffrey, in press) and from 7 pounds gained to 47 pounds lost within a large clinical series of patients (Jeffrey, Wing, & Stunkard, 1978). In a recent review of behavioral weight loss programs involving more than 1000 patients, Wing and Jeffrey (1979) found a mean weight loss of some 11 pounds/client and an average rate of weight loss of about 1 pound/week. Some 15% of clients dropped out of treatment.

Maintenance of weight loss is surprisingly good in the relatively short term, with further losses of about one pound at follow-up after a few months to a year. However, the range of outcome at follow-up can be considerable, varying from a gain of 40 pounds to a loss of 80 pounds, with about half of all group participants continuing to lose weight. Nonetheless, in a number of controlled outcome studies, the early advantage of a behavioral approach over another treatment is no longer clearly discernible at follow-up (e.g., Öst & Götestam, 1976). Moreover, in the only five-year follow-up study reported to date (Stunkard & Perick, 1978), no differences were found between behavioral treatment and a more traditional treatment, even though differences had been found in favor of behavior therapy at immediate outcome and at one-year follow-up. In this study, five years after treatment, only one-quarter of the clients in both groups weighed less than at the end of treatment.

Thus, although a useful weight loss can be achieved in many clients, and results of considerable significance in a lesser number, two problems appear when the results are considered. First, there is much variability in outcome between different clients, suggesting that an omnibus treatment is not sufficient for at least some of the obese. Luckily such persons can be recognized after three or four weeks of treatment and can be given more individual attention. Second, little is known about the procedures necessary to achieve continued weight loss after treatment. However, some form of maintenance program should be instituted from the beginning of therapy, and ideas for this are considered in the following pages. First, however, we ask the question, How do the results of behavior therapy compare with more traditional treatments?

Other Approaches to Weight Loss

Excluding surgery, which is reserved for the most serious cases of obesity and which carries with it a substantial incidence of complications, the major treatment approaches to weight loss are diet, drugs—especially the anorectic agents such as dextroamphetamine sulphate—and exercise programs. As we saw, behavior therapy appears to be more successful in immediate outcome than more traditional programs, including combinations of supportive therapy and diet, and drugs, in small randomized clinical trials, although no direct comparison between behavior therapy and exercise has been made.

Diet

Despite the multitude of different diets, the hallmark of each is caloric restriction. Although diet is often viewed as an ineffective approach to achieving weight loss, a recent review of published studies (Wing & Jeffrey, 1979) suggests that diet is quite effective with mean weight losses of 1.9 pounds/week and mean overall losses of 18.4 pounds. Some of the best results of diet are associated with human chorionic gonadotrophin (HCG) programs in which a 500 calorie diet is combined with daily injections. Since placebo injections given under comparable conditions lead to similar outcomes, we can conclude that a stringent diet and extra attention are a useful combination. About one-quarter of overweight clients lose 25 pounds or more, although some weight is regained at follow-up, averaging about 4 pounds six months after the end of treatment.

One of the most vexing theoretical problems with a diet is that eating comes under the control of the stimulus conditions associated with being on a diet—eating special types of food, eliminating snacks, feeling deprived, and so on. When the diet is stopped, eating behavior should come under the control of the prediet stimuli, and thus caloric intake should increase and weight be regained. By teaching new eating behavior and altering stimulus control of eating, as is done in most behavioral programs, maintenance of diet-induced weight loss might be enhanced. Overall, it seems that behavior therapists may have minimized the importance of a dietary approach to weight control, particularly in the initial phase of their programs.

Drugs

Although, as we have seen, a behavioral treatment program proved superior to fenfluramine, an anorectic agent, in a controlled comparison the efficacy of these two disparate approaches may in practice be similar. Thus anorectic agents lead to average weight losses of about 1 pound/week and to overall mean losses of about 11 pounds, as compared with some 4 to 5 pounds for control groups given a placebo and equal amounts of attention; results very comparable to those obtained with behavior therapy. However, given the associated side effects of medication and the possibility of addiction, which is always present, it seems that behavior therapy is a preferable treatment. However, combinations of drug therapy and behavior therapy have not been examined systematically and may prove to be a promising approach to weight reduction.

Exercise

One of the most obvious complications of exercise is that the required change in life-style and overall effort involved is large. Therefore, it is no surprise that the dropout rate of nearly 25% from exercise programs (Wing & Jeffrey, 1979) far exceeds that of other approaches to weight loss. Moreover, exercise produces weight losses of about ½ pound per week and mean weight losses of some 8 pounds overall, and little is known about the long-term maintenance of weight losses achieved through exercise.

Toward the Improvement of Treatment Outcome

The marked variability in results obtained from different behavioral approaches to weight loss leads one to suspect that the use of certain procedures might enhance the outcome of treatment. In this section we examine some techniques that might be added to, or emphasized, within the standard behavioral approach to weight loss described earlier.

Maximizing Reinforcement

As we have seen, most behavioral programs rely solely upon social reinforcement provided by the therapists and group members or occasionally upon the use of self-reinforcement. However, in one pioneering study, strong incentives led to very satisfactory weight losses ($x = 32$ pounds) with five of eight subjects losing 20 pounds or more and five achieving their goal weights (Mann, 1972). In a recent replication of this study (Jeffrey, Thompson, & Wing, 1978), participants were asked to deposit $200 to be returned contingent upon performance. Subjects were randomized into three groups. In the first, $20 was returned at each group meeting at which the participant met a preset weight-loss criterion of two pounds or better. In the second, a similar refund was made for self-reported reductions in caloric intake that would lead to weight loss of 2 pounds. For the control group $20 was returned for attendance only. All groups received a standard behavioral program. The control group achieved a mean weight loss of 8.6 pounds, the calorie contract group 19.4 pounds, and the weight contract group 21 pounds. In the weight contract group, four of seven participants lost more than 20 pounds. These are impressive results, which suggest that the use of contingency management has been overlooked in the majority of behavioral weight-loss programs. However, it is to be noted that many people will not participate in such a program; thus, only half of those who agreed to take part in this experiment attended the first experimental session.

Family Involvement

Since eating is a behavior that occurs largely within the family, as in the case of anorexia nervosa, interest in family members' influence upon eating has emerged. However, unlike anorexia nervosa, there has been one experimental assessment of the influence of the spouse upon efforts to lose weight (Brownell, 1977). In this study, spouses attended all the sessions of a standard behavioral treatment package for obesity. They were taught to model appropriate eating habits, to reinforce appropriate eating behavior, and to help their partners engage in activities incompatible with eating. Comparison groups were one in which spouses who had volunteered to participate did not attend the sessions and another in which spouses had refused to cooperate. Although no clear differences were found in immediate outcome, the spouse-training group showed an advantage over the other two groups at six-months follow-up, with two-thirds of the participants losing more than 20 pounds. Thus enhanced spouse participation would seem to be a useful procedure.

Increased Frequency of Therapist Contact

As noted earlier, there is suggestive evidence that more frequent therapist contact, as seen for example in the HCG program (and its placebo control), may result in improved weight loss! This notion was investigated further in a randomized experimental design comparing groups who received two additional contacts each week in person, two contacts by telephone, or simply weekly sessions plus 30 minutes extra time to equate for therapist attention. Those contacted lost more weight than those who were not contacted (Wing & Jeffrey, 1979).

Maintenance Procedures

Since maintenance of weight loss is such a difficult problem, thought must be given to this issue in initial program design. However, in most of the research projects reported to date, such maintenance efforts have either been omitted completely or added as an afterthought. The simplest and most obvious procedure to use is a sequence of booster or follow-up sessions. In one study (Kingsley & Wilson, 1977) such sessions were found to lead to continued weight loss. However, those results have not been replicated in subsequent studies (Ashby & Wilson, 1977).

A somewhat different maintenance procedure is suggested by a study of goal setting and its effect upon weight loss (Bandura & Simon, 1977). Setting short-term goals for reduction in food consumption led to better weight loss than setting longer-term, more remote goals. Subjects who monitored their weight periodically could reinstate this procedure when a certain amount of weight had been regained and could then lose weight again.

Summary

The relatively recent increase in research in the area of obesity is beginning to enhance our understanding concerning the extent of environmental influences on the eating behavior of both the obese and those of normal weight. The behavioral approach to weight loss is a relatively well-defined multicomponent treatment package that can be administered by therapists with a variety of backgrounds and different levels of training. Although the results of such treatment are modest and long-term outcome poses a problem, behavioral treatment appears to be more effective than other approaches, including anorectic drugs, and it seems to be free of significant therapeutic complications.

It is suggested here that the addition of certain procedures such as enhanced reinforcement, more frequent therapeutic contacts, family involvement, and attention to maintenance may well strengthen the efficacy of weight-loss programs. More-over, it is to be remembered that even modest weight loss may be of significant benefit in reducing blood pressure and cholesterol levels in the obese. At the moment, the most appropriate target population for weight reduction attempts would appear to be those with moderate degrees of overweight (perhaps up to 50 pounds), since significant weight loss can be achieved with such persons.

Therapeutic research now needs to be directed toward the enhancement of initial weight loss and particularly toward identification of the procedures needed to maintain that loss. Certainly we can look forward to a continued enhancement of our therapeutic efforts as research progresses during the next few years.

ANOREXIA NERVOSA

Anorexia nervosa has intrigued both research workers and clinicians since Richard Morton's case histories, written in 1689. Gull (1888) and Lasègue (1873) independently described the syndrome with remarkable consistency. Despite the increased interest in the disorder during the last 25 years, treatment results have been uncertain; controversy surrounds the question of etiology, and the incidence of the disorder appears to be increasing among the adolescent and early adult population of affluent societies (Duddle, 1973; Crisp, Palmer, & Kalney, 1976).

Unlike obesity, anorexic patients present a relative homogeneity of behaviors including refusal to eat enough to maintain healthy body weight, with weight loss often greater than 20% of original body weight; a fear of becoming obese, which persists in spite of increasing cachexia; and a marked body image disturbance with inability to perceive body size accurately.

Patients also exhibit varying degrees of preoccupation with eating and food preparation, from secretly hoarding foodstuffs to pouring over and cooking gourmet recipes for others. Food preferences range from the idiosyncratic (one patient ate only apples and roast beef, another a diet of fish, cheese, and crackers) to more varied intake of low-caloric value. Weight loss is achieved variably through restriction of food intake, self-induced vomiting, and/or the use of laxatives and diuretics. The latter two methods are often associated with seriously disorganized eating patterns such as extreme gorging episodes or compulsive snacking followed by prolonged fasts. Persistent hyperactivity with denial of fatigue is common, although not invariably found. Second-degree amenorrhea is present in all female patients (first degree if onset occurs prior to menarche), who make up 90% of the patient population. The age of onset is also less variable than in the obese population—ranging, typically, between 12 and 25 years of age (although onset of the syndrome has been reported in prepubertal and, rarely, in middle-aged women). The presence of a medical condition explaining the weight loss or an affective or schizophrenic psychosis rules out the diagnosis of anorexia nervosa (Feighner, Robins, Guze, Woodruff, Winokur, & Munoz, 1972).

The Etiology of Anorexia Nervosa

Current literature approaches the question of etiology from three major theoretical vantage points:

Biological Factors

A variety of endocrine and other abnormalities have been reported in anorexic patients who are actively starving, including: elevated serum cholesterol (Crisp, 1965), hypercarotenemia (Warren & Van de Wiele, 1973), lowered triiodothyronine levels (Lupton, Simon, Barry, & Klawans, 1976), elevated plasma growth hormone, low plasma luteinizing hormone and follicular stimulating hormone (Russell, Loraine, Bell, et al., 1965), immature 24-hour luteinizing hormone secretory pattern (Boyar, Katz, Finkelstein, Kapen, Weiner, Weitzman, & Hellman, 1974), decreased total brain electrical activity and REM sleep (Crisp, Fenton, & Scotton, 1968), and leukopenia and pancytopenia (Warren & Van de Wiele, 1973). Cessation of menses or delayed menarche (in females, an inevitable concomitant of the syndrome) occurs most often early in the dieting behavior, sometimes even prior to reported weight loss. The changes in metabolic rate, adrenal function, growth hormone level, gonadotrophin secretion, vasopressin secretion (some patients have been reported to have mild diabetes insipidus) (Mecklenberg, Loriaux, Thompson, Anderson, & Lipsett, 1974) have all been found in subjects malnourished from other causes. Elevated cholesterol and the abnormalities of thermoregulation are more difficult to correlate directly with starvation (Mecklenberg et al., 1974).

That there is a malfunction at the hypothalamic level is widely recognized (Garfinkle, Brown, Stancer, & Moldofsky, 1975; Mecklenberg et al., 1974). Controversy now surrounds the issue of whether this is primary or secondary to starvation (Vigersky, Loriaux, Anderson, & Lipsett, 1976; Vigersky & Loriaux, 1977). The fact that practically all abnormalities return to normal once a healthy weight is achieved points toward a secondary or reactive hypothalamic dysfunction (Garfinkle, et al., 1975). However, some investigators regard the relationship between nutritional status and endocrine factors as more complicated, and they point to the time lag in return of menses and the persistent depression of urinary gonadotrophin in some patients to support their claims (Russell, Loraine, Bell, & Harkness, 1965). Mecklenberg has proposed three plausible mechanisms to explain the hypothalamic abnormalities. Inanition may directly damage the hypothalamus; the hypothalamic dysfunction may be secondary to a primary psychological abnormality; or anorexia nervosa may be a primary hypothalamic disorder that produces secondary psychological changes.

Psychological Factors

Approaches to the psychology of anorexia include psychoanalytic theories that attempt to link oral gratification with impregnation fantasies and the refusal to eat or guilt around eating as a defense against these wishes (Thoma, 1967). Others see the symptom as a phobic avoidance reaction, following a major disappointment in peer relationships or to the resurgence of sexual impulses during adolescence (Galdston, 1974). Another psychodynamic explanation views the anorexia as a weight phobia in response to the specific effects of puberty (Crisp, 1970). Bruch (1978) emphasizes the cognitive disturbance and the disordered interpersonal relationships experienced by the patient in early childhood. The distortion of body image, the inability to accurately identify both internal stimuli (hunger, satiety, fatigue) and emotional needs are "deficits" engendered by the parents' "inability" to respond to child-initiated cues in infancy (Bruch, 1962). She views the anorexic's preoccupation with not eating as a late manifestation of difficulties and a sense of overwhelming ineffectiveness, which a "pleasing compliance" has until then masked (Bruch, 1973).

The body-image distortion of the anorexic has been the subject of several recent investigations. A couple of studies reported that these patients overestimated, as measured by a caliper device, specific body areas (face, chest, waist, and hips) (Slade & Russell, 1973) and that this distortion appeared to be related to severity of weight loss (Crisp & Kalney, 1974). Another group (Garner, Garfinkle, Stancer, & Moldofsky, 1976), studying both anorexics and obese subjects using a distorting photograph technique, found also that both groups overestimated body size compared with normal controls, but that the degree of psychopathology in anorexics, rather than relative weight of the subjects, correlates with magnitude of body-image disturbance and tends to be an indicator of prognosis. Garner and his colleagues comment on the conflicting findings on the nature of body-image changes by investigators using different measurement devices and emphasize the need for a critical assessment of the reliability and validity of such instruments.

Family Influences

From this perspective the behavior of the anorexic patient is seen as a reflection of disordered family function. In this framework the anorexic is not ill but simply the symptom bearer; the functional unit to be examined is the family. Minuchin and his coworkers (Minuchin, Baker, Rosman, Leibman, Milman, & Todd, 1975; Minuchin, Rosman, & Baker, 1978) have formulated the concept of the psychosomatic family that by its unique structural characteristics facilitates the development and maintenance of the psychosomatic (anorexic) symptom in the child, whose illness then becomes an integral force in family homeostasis. Mara Selvini Palazzolli and her team at the Milan Family Therapy Center have utilized and refined the systems model approach to delineate the transactional patterns of anorexic families and some specific therapeutic approaches to induce change, including use of ritual prescriptions and paradox (Selvini, 1974). Recent publications of the Milan group have focused on the importance of parental dysfunction in the maintenance of the symptom.

The Behavioral Treatment of Anorexia Nervosa

For the most part, behavioral approaches to this complex disorder have consisted of either desensitization procedures or the use of reinforcement for eating behavior and weight gain. The Bachrach, Erwin, and Mohr (1965) initial case study successfully utilized rewards, first for eating behavior and then for weight gain in a 37-year-old woman with chronic anorexia. The procedure used was social reinforcement, which included attention, conversation, and praise made contingent upon eating. Therapists sat with the patient at every meal and talked with her only when she ate. Later, other events, such as going for walks or visits from relatives, were made contingent upon satisfactory eating behavior. With this treatment, the patient gained weight to some 28.6 kg, whereupon her weight leveled off, perhaps due to vomiting. Reinforcement was then made contingent upon weight gain rather than eating behavior. However, the effect of this change was not clear, since the patient was discharged shortly thereafter.

In an attempt to replicate this study (Leitenberg, Agras, & Thompson, 1968), it was found that providing conversation and attention during meals contingent upon eating was not successful, partly, these workers reported, because of the artificiality of the situation. On the other hand, when weight gain was rewarded directly, a steady increase both in caloric intake and weight was observed. In most subsequent studies, weight gain has been reinforced directly, although some interesting variations have been reported. For example, Blinder, Freeman, and Stunkard (1970), capitalizing upon the overactivity of the anorexic, made access to physical activity contingent upon weight gain, reporting marked success with three patients. These investigators restricted the activity of another patient by using chlorpromazine and increments of drug dosage were removed dependent upon weight gain.

In the first experimental attempt to document the efficacy of reinforcement, some rather puzzling results were obtained (Agras, Barlow, Chapin, Abel, & Leitenberg, 1974). When reinforcement was introduced contingent upon small gains in weight, both the number of calories eaten and weight increased. However, when reinforcement was stopped within a single case experimental design, eating behavior and weight gain continued unchanged instead of returning to the rates observed during the baseline phase. This finding raised questions concerning the efficacy of selective positive reinforcement and suggested that another variable or variables might be partly responsible for the therapeutic effect. Moreover, two replications of this experiment with different patients showed similar results. Interestingly the patients in each case claimed that once they realized they could gain weight, they ate in order to be able to leave the hospital—an example of the effect of negative reinforcement. To remove this effect of negative reinforcement, weight gain and leaving hospital were disconnected in the next series of experiments by contracting with the patient and her parents for a 12-week stay "for research purposes" whether or not the patient gained weight. In contrast with the three previous cases, when positive reinforcement was removed, caloric intake dropped steadily and weight gain was much slowed, while the reintroduction of reinforcement led to marked increases in both caloric intake and weight. Thus it seems reasonable to conclude that both positive and negative reinforcement effectively encourage weight gain in the anorexic.

During the baseline condition in the previous experiments patients had been told their weight, had counted the number of mouthfuls eaten during each meal, and had been told their caloric intake after each meal—all of which provide information as to progress. To test the effect of such feedback, a new baseline condition was arranged devoid of both feedback and reinforcement. Caloric intake seemed stable under this condition, and weight actually declined. When positive reinforcement was added to the therapeutic regime, no effect was observed in the absence of feedback. However, once feedback was added to reinforcement, both caloric intake and weight showed large increases.

The final variable that has been investigated, again in single case experiments, is the therapeutic effect of meal size (Elkin, Hersen, Eisler, & Williams, 1973; Agras et al., 1974). These investigators discovered that food intake was always lower by some 500 calories/day when smaller meals were served, even though the anorexic never ate all the food at any one meal. Thus we may conclude that *four* therapeutic procedures modify weight and caloric intake in patients with anorexia nervosa—positive and negative reinforcement, informational feedback, and large meals.

The effectiveness of a behavioral approach to the treatment of anorexia nervosa was recently investigated in an outcome study using a multiple baseline design with seven patients (Pertschuk, Edwards, & Pomerleau, 1978). Treatment was centered around a reinforcement program in which various activities were made contingent upon daily weight gains of ½ pound. Patients were randomly assigned to the behavioral program from the fourth through the tenth day of hospitalization. During the baseline routine hospital care, the mean weight loss was −0.09 kg/day while with behavioral treatment the gain was 0.32 kg/day with mean gains of 4.2 kg/week. Overall the results showed that behavior therapy was significantly superior to routine hospital care; this was the first experimental demonstration of the effectiveness of this treatment approach for a group of patients.

In practice, behavioral approaches to influencing weight gain in the patient with anorexia nervosa have been used almost exclusively within inpatient settings, usually within an established general hospital psychiatric unit. Since the therapeutic approach to such patients requires careful programming and sensitivity to individuals' differing problems, the treatment program in a representative unit is described in some detail.

An Inpatient Treatment Program—A Case Example

At Stanford University Hospital, a behavioral treatment program operates in the context of a therapeutic milieu. The behavioral protocol consists of, first, a *standard reinforcement paradigm* for all anorexics of free access to the ward (outside of required therapy activities) contingent upon an increment of weight gained daily, plus reinforcers for weight gain that are individualized and made concrete by a written, signed contract and, second, an *informational feedback system,* which involves daily graphing of weight and cumulative "bites" of food.

A key aspect of the program begins, however, before the decision is made to enter the hospital. Prerequisite to admission are one or more evaluation sessions which are attended by the patient and family members. During this period the principles of the treatment program are explained and its voluntary contractual nature emphasized. Care is exercised not to urge hospitalization upon the prospective patient. Moreover, attempts by family members to coerce the anorexic to agree to admission are discouraged—with the suggestion that other options for treatment (e.g., other hospitals) might be considered if all family members, including the identified patient, are not fully behind the decision.

The importance of this strategy is illustrated by the case of a 15-year-old girl who was brought by her parents to the evaluation interview, sullen and uncooperative, shortly after discharge from a two-week involuntary stay on a locked psychiatric unit. She adamantly refused to discuss the possibility of hospitalization. This was accepted without comment by the interviewer, although the program was described at the parents' request. Since the girl was markedly underweight and complaining of great fatigue and coldness, some need for weight gain was acknowledged, and a simple 1.5 pounds/week was set on an outpatient basis. The remainder of the first interview was spent discussing the family situation, which had difficulties far beyond the patient's eating disorder. At the second session, the girl participated more freely in the ongoing discussion of family troubles; she had not made her weight gain, but she had, for the first time in many weeks, not lost weight. The third session, held one week later, saw a remarkable shift. This time the 1.5 pound weight goal *had* been achieved, and the youngster was actively requesting hospitalization; it was, in her words, "too hard to gain weight at home." A working alliance had now been established, and the exploration of the family problems could continue in the more comprehensive context of the inpatient treatment program.

On the ward, the patient first spends three to five days in a "baseline" period without pressure or expectation of weight change. She is instructed in the use of graphing daily weights and the bite-counting technique—the recording of the number of mouthfuls or "bites" taken at each meal and snack with a small hand counter and the transferring of the daily total to her bite graph. If an effort is made to eat a consistent yet heterogeneous diet, patients may effectively compare one day's intake with another throughout hospitalization. By adding a number of bites to each meal until sufficient intake is maintained to gain weight, patients can predict the majority of daily weight gains. This tracking of daily weights and estimation of intake with cumulative bites is, however, not required of patients, although the majority of patients find this to be a valuable tool to facilitate control of eating over the course of weight gain (see Figure 1).

Once the patient begins to feel relatively at ease within the therapeutic community, a contingency contract is negotiated. The standard contract stipulates unlimited privileges, which include full use of the ward's facilities as well as options for passes off the unit for a daily weight gain of 0.2 kg or greater from the previous high weight. Weight gains of 0.1 kg lead to full privileges from waking until 4:00 P.M. For the remainder of the afternoon and evening patients are asked to stay in their rooms (usually a two-bed room) and to minimize contact with staff and other patients except when attending daily therapy activities (individual, group, and family sessions) which are noncontingent. While "on restriction," patients move freely about their rooms, reading, writing, listening to the radio, or exercising if they choose. They may leave their rooms once each nursing shift for gathering snacks, showering, or changing linens. They are asked to take responsibility for explaining the nature of their contract contingencies to others (roommate, new members of the community, etc.) as well as to not accept phone calls or visits from relatives and friends. A full day's restriction occurs when patients fail to gain 0.1 kg or lose weight.

At the time the individual contract is formally written up and signed, bonus reinforcers are negotiated for set-weight criteria; for example, for a patient of 75 pounds (5 feet 5 inches) who decides upon a "target" weight of 115 pounds, special events such as an afternoon driving with a friend in the country, attending a football game with father, a shopping expedition with mother, or institution of physical therapy to "get into shape" may be planned at 5- to 7-pound intervals. The target weight (which may be revised but is usually negotiated at the time of the contract's signing) is usually a couple of pounds higher than the actual weight

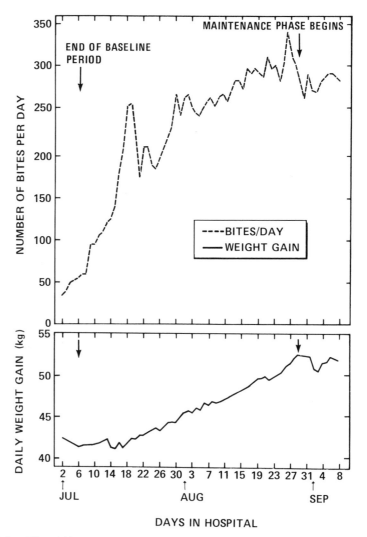

FIGURE 1. The daily number of bites of food as recorded by an anorexic patient, and daily weight gain, during the course of hospitalization. Baseline, reinforcement, and maintenance phases are shown.

at discharge and represents the beginning of the maintenance period in which the patient learns to stabilize within a 2 kg range and to begin to accept the normal, small daily fluctuations in weight that accompany even a consistently maintained caloric intake. The target weight is usually on the low side of the normal range—representing a "compromise" between the patient's ideal and the staff's preference.

Patients are served their meals alone in their rooms during the initial phase of hopsitalization. They may select any foods available in the hospital kitchen (filling out a menu the previous day and consulting with the dietician—who is part of the treatment team—as needed); however, the staff insists that patients are served 3000 calories each day at first and later up to 5000 calories a day; thus the dietician may provide additional foods beyond those requested by the patient to create a well-rounded diet. Patients are asked to sit by each meal in their room for 45 minutes. No attempt is made by staff to observe eating or to quantify amounts consumed. Later on in the treatment process patients begin to eat with the other patients, in restaurants, or at home on pass.

The Anorexia Nervosa Program operates in a milieu in which a competent staff, comfortable and experienced in working with anorexic patients, conveys an appreciation for each individual's uniqueness. Reassurance, encouragement, and genuine concern extend far beyond the area of eating and weight change. Mandatory, non-contingent attendance at all therapy meetings underlines the importance of the therapeutic tasks and relationships. Individual therapy sessions begin with entrance onto the ward. As the physical condition of the anorexic improves, therapy can change from a more strictly supportive mode to a collaborative exploration of the patient's difficulties. This invariably involves couples and/or family sessions to clarify and change dysfunctional interpersonal patterns.

Weekly anorexia conferences for the treatment team serve as a forum to present new patients, to discuss and coordinate individual treatment plans, and to deal with the anxieties and concerns of staff members. Much of the nursing staff, psychiatric residents, medical students, dieticians, and physical and occupational therapists attend these meetings, cochaired by the chief nurse, medical director of the unit, and director of the Anorexia Program. The conferences facilitate a sense of cohesion among staff and a healthy tolerance for minor infractions of the contract, with the "letter of the law" carrying far less importance than the "spirit." Control struggles, for example, around eating or adherence to room restriction, are virtually eliminated as patients assume responsibility for enforcement of their own contracts. Staff is, therefore, free to function as collaborators in the patient's efforts to change, providing guidelines and gently setting limits without becoming like police of an arbitrary or punitive system.

Results of Behavioral Treatment

A survey of the results reported for six inpatient programs using an operant approach to the treatment of anorexia nervosa show the average daily weight gain to be 0.15 kg (range 0.13 to 0.2 kg), with total weight gains of some 7.1 kg (15.6 pounds) during a hospital stay of about eight weeks (Agras & Werne, 1978). These are encouraging but not startling results. Moreover, since behavioral approaches have been in use for a relatively short time, longer-term outcome is uncertain. In five reported follow-up studies ranging from 2 to 72 months posttreatment, some 45% of patients were showing marked improvement, while 16% had not improved (Agras & Werne, 1978). It must be noted that these are findings from uncontrolled studies and that outcome was presented in global terms and was based, for the most part, on patients' self-report combined usually, but not always, with direct documentation of weight. Moreover, no studies have systematically evaluated the procedures required to maintain weight gain following inhospital treatment, or for treatment of the various interpersonal and family problems that accompany this disorder.

Other Approaches to the Treatment of Anorexia Nervosa

Since the treatment of anorexia nervosa has been of concern to medicine for many years, a variety of treatment approaches have been developed. Inhospital treatment programs are most likely to use several modalities: insistence upon eating and weight gain, intravenous therapy, feeding by a nasogastric tube, psychotherapy (from supportive to classically analytic), group and family therapy, and, often, pharmacologic agents. Rarely is any single approach used exclusively. For example, Farquarson and Hyland (1966) treated their patients with "reassurance and persuasion," "explanation and encouragement," and, occasionally, with duodenal feedings. Dally and Sargant (1966) combine bed rest, chlorpromazine, and modified insulin therapy to lower resistance to eating and stimulate appetite. Other programs rely heavily upon nursing-staff encouragement and supportive psychotherapy (Crisp, 1965; Lucas, Duncan, & Piers, 1976). Many classical psychoanalysts pay little attention to weight fluctuations in their outpatients, preferring to focus instead on their patients' fears of sexuality and bodily damage. Bruch (1978) has objected to this avoidance, emphasizing that weight correction is vital, indeed a prerequisite, to the effective exploration of the patients' other difficulties.

As noted earlier, interest in the contribution of the family to the genesis and maintenance of anorexia nervosa has led to the development of a family therapy approach that has been used in both inpatient and outpatient settings (Liebman, Minuchin, & Baker, 1974; Selvini, 1974).

For both immediate and long-term outcome such treatment approaches show more variability than behavior therapy, with a mean weight gain of 0.1 kg/day (range 0.02 to 0.29 kg) and a tendency toward longer duration of hospitalization (Agras & Werne, 1978). This variation in outcome as compared with that of behavioral approaches is graphically displayed in Figure 2. These data suggest that the major advantage of the behavioral approach is in the consistency of outcome between different centers, a consistency that is probably due to the greater precision with which the treatment procedures are specified. This is no small advantage, since such specification enhances the ease with which new therapeutic programs can be established and guarantees a more certain outcome if the protocol is carefully followed.

Although no controlled comparison of either the immediate or longer-term results of behavioral and nonbehavioral treatments have yet appeared in the literature, the average program in each modality appears to achieve similar results (Agras & Werne, 1978). One exception may be in the higher death rate reported for nonbehavioral approaches of some 8.4% as compared with 0% for behavior therapy. Such a difference may be an artifact of the shorter duration of follow-up reported for the behavioral treatments or to the more frequent use of tube feeding in the traditional approach to treatment—a procedure which has been associated with death in a small proportion of patients with anorexia nervosa.

Outpatient Treatment of Anorexia Nervosa

What of the patient who does not enter hospital for treatment? Indications for outpatient therapy include: the desire of the anorexic to attempt weight gain on an

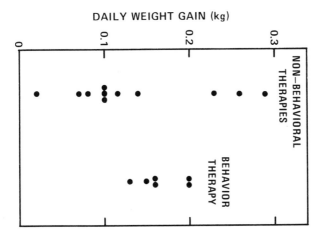

FIGURE 2.   A comparison of the short-term outcome of behavioral and nonbehavioral programs. It appears that behavioral programs show more consistency in outcome than nonbehavioral programs.

outpatient basis; financial inability to cover the costs of hospitalization; and refusal to consider inpatient treatment. If the patient is on the verge of medical collapse, medical hospitalization to correct the life-threatening situation (where intravenous or nasogastric feedings may be briefly required) is advisable. In modified form the initial approach is similar to that used in the negotiation of the inpatient contract. A case example will illustrate this approach.

Case Study

A 15-year-old sophomore in high school, second child, and oldest girl of five children, was referred by a pediatrician with a presumptive diagnosis of anorexia nervosa. Weight loss had occurred gradually over a two-year period, the onset of dieting coinciding with dissatisfaction over the fit of a new dress worn at a holiday family gathering. From a high weight of 110 pounds and 5 feet and 1 inch tall she had lost 25 pounds the first year with little comment from her family. In the past nine months, however, her pediatrician and then the parents had become concerned about continued weight loss and increasingly frantic hyperactivity expressed in compulsive housecleaning and immersion in school sports. A two-week medical hospitalization shortly before referral was remarkable only for extreme emaciation and pellagralike lesions on her hands, which cleared rapidly with vitamin therapy. At the time of the first session, her weight was 67 pounds in street clothes.

Since this patient refused hospitalization and did not consider herself to be in need of help, the first session was spent discussing possible options. Continued family sessions were made contingent upon willingness of all members to attend. Alternate facilities, referral to another psychiatrist, and commitment to a hospital (an issue raised by the parents) were discussed. With the threat of involuntary hospitalization with enforced weight gain, the patient reluctantly agreed to family sessions. Since she could not visualize a normal goal weight for herself, small increments for gain were set initially.

The family was seen twice monthly over a five-month period. They came to therapy with a common belief that their family had no problems except for the unfortunate mystery of their daughter's stubborn refusal to gain weight. For at least the past six months, all four siblings (including the seven-year-old) had been joining the parents in advising, cajoling, and threatening the patient regarding her diet. The family was instructed to let the patient make *all* dietary decisions on her own, and the parents were told to do their part in keeping the siblings from unintentionally behaving as surrogate parents. The patient agreed to be weighed daily by her father and to aim for a weight gain of 2 to 3 pounds between sessions. No specific weight contingencies were set up, although the parents were insistent that weight gain take place or else they would consider alternative treatments (i.e., negative reinforcement).

This family was not unusual in its denial of difficulties, other than the anorexia of the identified patient. Striking, however, was the degree to which the children intruded on the parents' domain, and the way in which the patient cheerfully carried virtually all the burden of the housework for her mother. It emerged only after several sessions that several years ago financial difficulties had left the father, a struggling professional, mildly depressed, and also necessitated the mother's return to work full time. While neither parent expressed negative feelings toward each other or the situation, this change in roles and relationship had coincided with the onset of their daughter's serious dieting behavior.

The therapeutic task was conceived as needing to reestablish the patient in her place as oldest *daughter* with attendant privileges, but to remove her from the position of housekeeper and cook. This involved a great deal of collaboration on the parents' part and led to a strengthening of their ability to set consistent rules for all the children as well as to restoring the mother to her rightful place as manager of the home.

By the third month of treatment, the patient was gaining well and able to set herself a realistic weight goal of 95 pounds. She was actually enjoying eating, although still exercising compulsively (however, in a more age-appropriate way with bicycle riding rather than dusting and washing dishes). She continued to deny any personal worries, except for distress at her parents' "overconcern" about her eating habits. However, she was now interacting in much more satisfying ways with her siblings who began to utilize sessions to air their own family complaints. One month after her goal weight was achieved, the family elected to discontinue treatment. The patient still had only tenuous peer relationships, although she was spending more time outside the home. However, since all members were satisfied with the results, the decision to terminate was accepted with the option to return should they wish. Four months later, the parents reported in a letter that their daughter was doing well.

Summary

Much, as we have seen, remains to be understood about the syndrome of anorexia nervosa. As in the case of obesity, the etiology is likely to be a complex blend of biologic, psychologic, and social factors. Approaches to treatment are less well developed than for obesity, and the field is remarkable for the paucity of controlled studies of the various therapeutic procedures in common use. Moreover, the literature on therapeutic outcome is noteworthy for the varying degrees of rigor with which the diagnosis is made, the identification of the various elements of the treatment regimes, and the way in which outcome is assessed.

In a previous paper (Agras & Werne, 1978), we have noted that there appears to be little difference, as far as outcome is concerned, between the effectiveness of behavioral and nonbehavioral inpatient treatments, with approximately 40 to 50% recovered or markedly improved and another 20 to 35% improved. However, the behavioral approach achieves more consistent results between different centers, probably as a result of the precise specification of the procedure.

The questions remain as to what are the key therapeutic interventions and are there specific variables, independent of treatment strategies, that influence course and prognosis? The family studies of Minuchin and Selvini offer some promising clues, although controlled research in this area is needed. Research on the body-image disturbance has led to interesting, but conflicting, findings. The arena of hypothalamic and other biologic changes continues to provide material for further investigation, but the "chicken or egg" issue of whether these represent *effect* or *cause* of starvation remains moot. In short, data derived from controlled experiments are lacking and much uncharted territory requires exploration.

REFERENCES

Adams, N., Ferguson, J., Stunkard, A. J., and Agras, W. S. The eating behavior of obese and nonobese women. *Behaviour Research and Therapy,* 1978, **16**, 225–232.

Agras, W. S., Barlow, D. H., Chapin, H. N., Abel, G. G., & Leitenberg, H. Behavior modification of anorexia nervosa. *Archives of General Psychiatry,* 1974, **30**, 279–286.

Agras, W. S., & Werne, J. Behavior therapy in anorexia nervosa: A data-based approach to the question. In J. P. Brady & K. Brodie (Eds.), *Controversy in psychiatry.* Philadelphia: W. B. Saunders, 1978.

Ashby, W. A., & Wilson, G. T. Behavior therapy for obesity: Booster sessions and long-term maintenance of weight loss. *Behaviour Research and Therapy,* 1977, **15**, 451–463.

Bachrach, A. J., Erwin, W. J., & Mohr, J. F. The control of eating behavior in an anorexic by operant conditioning techniques. In L. P. Ullman & L. Krasner (Eds.), *Case studies in behavior modification.* New York: Holt, Rinehart & Winston, 1965.

Bandura, A., & Simon, K. M. The role of proximal intentions in self-regulation of refractory behavior. *Cognitive Therapy and Research,* 1977, **1**, 177–193.

Barlow, D. H. Aversive procedures. In W. S. Agras (Ed.), *Behavior modification: Principles and clinical applications* (2nd edition). Boston: Little, Brown, 1978.

Blinder, B. J., Freeman, D. M. A., & Stunkard, A. J. Behavior therapy of anorexia nervosa: Effectiveness of activity as a reinforcer of weight gain. *American Journal of Psychiatry*, 1970, **126**, 77–82.

Boyar, R. M., Katz, J., Finkelstein, J. W., Kapen, S., Weiner, H., Weitzman, E. D., & Hellman, L. Anorexia nervosa: Immaturity of the 24-hour luteinizing hormone secretory pattern. *New England Journal of Medicine*, 1974, **291**, 861–865.

Brownell, K. D. "The effect of spouse training and partner cooperativeness in the behavioral treatment of obesity." Unpublished doctoral dissertation, Rutgers University, 1977.

Bruch, H. Perceptual and conceptual disturbances in anorexia nervosa. *Psychosomatic Medicine*, 1962, **24**, 187–194.

Bruch, H. *Eating disorders: Obesity, anorexia nervosa, and the person within*. New York: Basic Books, 1973.

Bruch, H. *The golden cage. The enigma of anorexia nervosa*. Cambridge: Harvard University Press, 1978.

Canning, H., & Mayer, J. Obesity—its possible effect on college acceptance. *The New England Journal of Medicine*, 1966, **275**, 1172–1174.

Chirico, A. M., & Stunkard, A. J. Physical activity and human obsity. *New England Journal of Medicine*, 1960, **263**, 935–946.

Crisp, A. H. Clinical and therapeutic aspects of anorexia nervosa—a study of 30 cases. *Journal of Psychosomatic Research*, 1965, **9**, 67–78.

Crisp, A. H. Anorexia nervosa—feeding disorder, nervous malnutrition, or weight phobia. *World Review of Nutrition and Dietetics*, 1970, **12**, 452–504.

Crisp, A. H., Fenton, G. W., & Scotton, L. A controlled study of the EEG in anorexia nervosa. *British Journal of Psychiatry*, 1968, **114**, 1149–1160.

Crisp, A. H., & Kalney, R. S. Aspects of the perceptual disorder in anorexia nervosa. *British Journal of Medical Psychology*, 1974, **47**, 349–361.

Crisp, A. H., Palmer, R. L., & Kalney, R. S. How common is anorexia nervosa? A prevalence study. *British Journal of Psychiatry*, 1976, **128**, 549–554.

Dally, P., & Sargant, W. Treatment and outcome of anorexia nervosa. *British Medical Journal*, 1966, **2**, 693–795.

Drabman, R. S., Hammer, D., & Jarvie, G. J. Eating styles of obese and nonobese black and white children in a naturalistic setting. *Addictive Behaviors*, 1977, **2**, 83–86.

Duddle, M. An increase of anorexia nervosa in a university population. *British Journal of Psychiatry*, 1973, **123**, 711–712.

Elkin, T. E., Hersen, M., Eisler, R. M., & Williams, J. G. Modification of caloric intake in anorexia nervosa: An experimental analysis. *Psychological Reports*, 1973, **32**, 75–78.

Farquarson, R. F., & Hyland, H. H. Anorexia nervosa. The course of 15 patients treated from 20 to 30 years previously. *Journal of the Canadian Medical Association*, 1966, **94**, 411–419.

Feighner, J. P., Robins, E., Guze, S. B., Woodruff, R. A., Winokur, G., & Munoz, R. Diagnostic criteria for use in psychiatric research. *Archives of General Psychiatry*, 1972, **26**, 57–63.

Ferguson, J. M. *Learning to eat: Behavior modification for weight control*. Palo Alto, Calif.: Bull Publishing Co., 1975.

Ferster, C. B., Nurnberger, J. I., & Levitt, E. B. The control of eating. *Journal of Mathematics,* 1962, **1**, 87–109.

Galdston, R. "Mind over matter." Observations on 50 patients hospitalized with anorexia nervosa. *Journal of the American Academy of Child Psychiatry,* 1974, **13**, 246–263.

Garfinkle, P. E., Brown, G. M., Stancer, H. C., & Moldofsky, H. Hypothalamic-pituitary function in anorexia nervosa. *Archives of General Psychiatry,* 1975, **32**, 734–739.

Garner, D. M., Garfinkle, P. E., Stancer, H. C., & Moldofsky, H. Body image disturbanches in anorexia nervosa and obesity. *Psychosomatic Medicine,* 1976, **38**, 327–336.

Goldblatt, P. B., Moore, M. E., & Stunkard, A. J. Social factors in obesity. *Journal of the American Medical Association,* 1965, **192**, 1039–1044.

Gull, W. W. Anorexia nervosa, *Lancet,* 1888, **1**, 516–517.

Gull, W. W. Anorexia nervosa. *Transactions of the Clinical Society of London,* 1974, **7**, 22–28.

Hagen, R. L. Group therapy versus bibliotherapy in weight reduction. *Behavior Therapy,* 1974, **5**, 222–234.

Harris, M. B. Self-directed program for weight control: A pilot study. *Journal of Abnormal Psychology,* 1969, **74**, 263–270.

Jeffrey, D. B., & Katz, R. C. *Take it off and keep it off: A behavioral program for weight loss and healthy living.* Englewood, Cliffs, N.J.: Prentice-Hall, 1977.

Jeffrey, R. W., Thompson, P. D., & Wing, R. R. Effects on weight reduction of strong monetary contracts for calorie restriction or weight loss. Unpublished manuscript, 1978.

Jeffrey, R. W., Wing, R. R., & Stunkard, A. J. Behavioral treatment of obesity: The state of the art 1976. *Behavior Therapy,* 1978, **2**, 189–199.

Kingsley, R. G., & Wilson, G. T. Behavior therapy for obesity: A comparative investigation of long-term efficacy. *Journal of Consulting and Clinical Psychology,* 1977, **45**, 288–298.

Kolaka, G. B. Obesity: A growing problem. *Science,* 1977, **198**, 905–906.

Lasègue, E. C. On hysterical anorexia. *Medical Times Gazette,* 1873, **2**, 265.

Lasègue, E. C. (1873) On hysterical anorexia. In M. R. Kaufman & M. Hecman (Eds.), *Evolution of psychosomatic concepts.* New York: International University Press, 1964.

Leitenberg, H., Agras, W. S., & Thompson, E. A sequential analysis of the effect of selective positive reinforcement in modifying anorexia nervosa. *Behaviour Research and Therapy,* 1968, **6**, 211–218.

Levitz, L. S. The susceptibility of human feeding behavior to external controls. Paper presented at the Fogarty International Conference on Obesity, Washington, D.C., 1973.

Liebman, R., Minuchin, S., & Baker, L. An integrated treatment program for anorexia nervosa. *American Journal of Psychiatry,* 1974, **31**, 432–436.

Lucas, R., Duncan, J. W., & Piers, V. The treatment of anorexia nervosa. *American Journal of Psychiatry,* 1976, **133**, 1034–1038.

Lupton, M., Simon, L., Barry, V., & Klawans, H. L. Minireview: Biological aspects of anorexia nervosa. *Life Sciences,* 1976, **18**, 1341–1348.

Mann, R. A. The use of contingency contracting to control obesity in adult subjects. *Journal of Applied Behavior Analysis,* 1972, **5**, 99–102.

Mayer, J. The role of exercise and activity in weight control. In E. S. Eppright, A. Swanson, & A. Iverson (Eds.), *Weight control.* Iowa: Iowa State College Press, 1955.

Mecklenberg, R. S., Loriaux, D. L., Thompson, R. H., Anderson, A. E., & Lipsett, M. B. Hypothalamic dysfunction in patients with anorexia nervosa. *Medicine,* 1974, **53**, 147–159.

Meyer, J. E., & Pudel, J. Experimental studies on food intake in obese and normal weight subjects. *Journal of Psychosomatic Research,* 1972, **16**, 305–308.

Minuchin, S., Baker, L., Rosman, B., Liebman, R., Milman, L., & Todd, T. A conceptual model of psychosomatic illness in children. *Archives of General Psychology,* 1975, **32**, 1031–1038.

Minuchin, S., Rosman, B., & Baker, L. *Psychosomatic families: Anorexia nervosa in context.* Cambridge: Harvard University Press, 1978.

Morton, R. *Phthisiologica: Or a treatise of consumptions.* London: Samuel Smith, 1689.

Nisbett, R. E. Hunger, obesity, and the ventromedial hypothalamus. *Psychological Review,* 1972, **79**: 433–438.

Öst, L., & Götestam, K. G. Behavioral and pharmacological treatments for obesity: An experimental comparison. *Addictive Behaviors,* 1976, **1**, 331–338.

Penick, S. B., Filion, R., Fox, S., & Stunkard, A. J. Behavior modification in the treatment of obesity. *Psychosomatic Medicine,* 1971, **33**, 49–55.

Pertschuk, M. J., Edwards, N., & Pomerleau, O. F. A multiple baseline approach to behavioral intervention in anorexia nervosa. Unpublished manuscript, 1978.

Russell, G. F. M., Loraine, J. A., Bell, E. T., & Harkness, R. A. Gonadotrophin and estrogen excretion in patients with anorexia nervosa. *Journal of Psychosomatic Research,* 1965, **9**, 79–85.

Schachter, S. Obesity and eating. *Science,* 1968, **161**, 751–756.

Selvini, M. P. *Self-starvation. From the intrapsychic to the transpersonal approach to anorexia nervosa.* London: Human Context Book Publishing Co., 1974.

Selvini, M. P. Recent developments in our treatment of families with anorexic patients, in press.

Sims, E. A., Goldman, R. F., Gluck, C. M., Horton, E. S., Kelleher, P. C., & Rowe, D. W. Experimental obesity in men. *Transactions of the Association of American Physicians,* 1968, **81**, 153–170.

Slade, P. D., & Russell, G. F. Awareness of body dimensions in anorexia nervosa: Cross-sectional and longitudinal studies. *Psychosomatic Medicine,* 1973, **3**, 188–199.

Stuart, R. B. Behavioral control of overeating. *Behaviour Research and Therapy,* 1967, **5**, 357–365.

Stuart, R. B. A three-dimensional program for the treatment of obesity. *Behaviour Research and Therapy,* 1971, **9**, 177–186.

Stunkard, A. J. Obesity. In A. M. Freedman, H. J. Kaplan, & H. S. Kaplan (Eds.), *Comprehensive textbook of psychiatry.* Baltimore: Williams & Wilkins, 1967.

Stunkard, A. J., d'Acquili, E., & Fox, S. The influence of social class on obesity. *Metabolism,* 1972, **21**, 599–602.

Stunkard, A. J., & Mahoney, M. J. Behavioral treatment of the eating disorders. In H. Leitenberg (Ed.), *Handbook of behavior modification and behavior therapy.* Englewood Cliffs, N.J.: Prentice-Hall, 1976.

Stunkard, A. J., & Perick, S. B. Behavior modification in the treatment of obesity: The problem of maintaining weight loss. Unpublished manuscript, 1978.

Thoma, H. *Anorexia nervosa,* (G. Brydone, trans.). New York: International Universities, 1967.

Vigersky, R., & Loriaux, D. L. Anorexia nervosa as a model of hypothalamic dysfunction. In R. Vigersky (Ed.), *Anorexia nervosa.* New York: Raven Press, 1977.

Vigersky, R., Loriaux, D. L., Anderson, A., & Lipsett, M. Anorexia nervosa: Behavioral and hypothalamic aspects. *Clinics in endocrinology and metabolism,* 1976, **5**(2), 517–535.

Warren, P., & Van de Wiele, R. L. Clinical and metabolic features of anorexia nervosa. *American Journal of Obstetrics and Gynecology,* 1973, **117**, 435–449.

Whitelaw, G. L. Association of social class and sibling number with skinfold thickness in London school boys. *Human Biology,* 1971, **43**, 414–420.

Wing, R. R., & Jeffrey, R. W. Outpatient treatments of obesity: A comparison of methodology and clinical results. *International Journal of Obesity,* 1979, **3**, 261–279.

Withers, R. F. L. Problems in the genetics of human obesity. *Eugenics Review,* 1964, **56**, 81–90.

Wollersheim, J. P. The effectiveness of group therapy based upon learning principles in the treatment of overweight women. *Journal of Abnormal Psychology,* 1970, **76**, 462–474.

Wooley, O. W., & Wooley, S. The experimental psychology of obesity. In T. Silverstone, & J. Fincham (Eds.), *Obesity: pathogenesis and management.* Lancaster, England: Technical and Medical Publishing Co., 1975.

Wooley, O. W., Wooley, S. C., & Turner, K. The effects of rate of consumption on appetite in the obese and nonobese. In A. Howard (Ed.), *Recent advances in obesity research,* Vol. 1. London: Newman Publishers, 1975.

Wooley, O. W., Wooley, S. C., & Woods, W. A. Effect of calories on appetite for palatable foods in obese and nonobese humans. *Journal of Comparative and Physiological Psychology,* 1975, **89**, 619–625.

Wooley, S. C., & Wooley, O. W. A naturalistic observation of palatability on food choices of the obese and nonobese. Unpublished manuscript, 1978.

CHAPTER 10

Treating Sleep Disorders:
Few Answers, Some Suggestions
and Many Questions

Thomas J. Coates and Carl E. Thoresen

Three perspectives guide contemporary research on sleep and sleep disorders. First, the word "sleep" is regarded as a broad description rather than a precise designation. "Sleep" refers to times during which a variety of independent processes occur sequentially and sometimes simultaneously. Although the outward appearance of the organism may not change during sleep, biological and psychological activity can vary markedly during various sleep states and stages. Second, sleep is not a passive state of quiescence but rather is characterized by varied and sometimes intense physiological and mental activity. Finally, sleep should not be studied in isolation. A thorough understanding requires that sleep be investigated using a 24-hour perspective that relates sleep to the inherent circadian rhythms governing physiological and psychological function during sleep and wakefulness alike (cf. Dement & Mitler, 1976; Webb & Cartwright, 1978).

Table 1 lists the common sleep disorders. Several assumptions, not necessarily in harmony with the contemporary perspective, have guided the study and treatment of these problems. "Sleep disorder" usually refers to: (*a*) a response or pattern of behavior occurring during sleep or associated with sleep that differs from responses and patterns observed in the majority of the population; (*b*) a complaint attributed to inadequate or excessive sleep; (*c*) a dysfunction in processes governing sleep; or (*d*) a pathology tied directly to sleep.

Contemporary perspectives on sleep demand a broadened viewpoint. These perspectives suggest that sleep be studied in relation to the entire wake-sleep (circadian) cycle of the individual. Given these new perspectives, this chapter may be discussing problems related to each other only by the fact that they are somehow associated with sleep. The behaviors and complaints in Table 1 may have little or nothing in common with each other except that they are linked traditionally and popularly with sleep. Should they, therefore, be termed "sleep disorders?" Little would be gained if encopresis or agoraphobia were called "waking disorders." Problems such as incontinence or irrational fear are seldom linked conceptually or clinically. The initiating and maintaining conditions, which in turn may call for different treatment strategies, may be different for each of the sleep disorders listed

240

Table 1. Behaviors and Complaints Associated with Sleep

Insomnia	Complaint of disturbed sleep (extended latency to sleep onset, excessive number of awakenings during the night, excessive minutes awake during the night, early morning awakening) combined with complaints of daytime fatigue
Narcolepsy	Excessive daytime sleepiness, sleep attacks (brief episodes of sleep that can occur any time during the day), and cataplexy (person loses all muscle tone). Person may also experience sleep paralysis (episodes of paralysis in transition from sleep to wakefulness), hypnagogic hallucinations and disturbed nocturnal sleep
Excessive daytime sleepiness	Person complains of excessive sleepiness and sleep episodes during the day; sleep at night may be extended; person may experience post-sleep confusion and difficulty in awakening
Somnambulism (sleepwalking)	Person walks during sleep; person usually unaware and reactivity to the environment is at a minimum
Enuresis	Bedwetting
Night terrors (Pavor nocturnus, incubus)	Intense anxiety, extreme levels of autonomic discharge, motility, vocalization, and little recall
Nightmares	Associated with REM sleep; ordinary frightening dreams; the sleeper is aroused easily and recall is vivid and detailed
Nocturnal bruxism	Clenching or grinding of the teeth during sleep; associated with headache, temporo-mandibular joint and myofascial pain, tooth motility, occlusal wear
Jactatio capitus nocturnus	Head banging sometimes accompanied by moans or talking during sleep
Somniloquy	Sleep talking; usually associated with transition from Stage 4 sleep

in Table 1. A 24-hour sleep-wake perspective suggests that it may be necessary to look beyond sleep in studying and treating these problems. Actually, some of the so-called sleep disorders may share more in common with certain "waking disorders" than with the other sleep-related problems. It is also possible that effective treatment of these problems may need to focus on the waking behavior rather than sleeping actions of the person.

Referring to the list of problems in Table 1 as disorders, disturbances, or pathologies may not be helpful. The terms "disorder," "disturbance," or "pathology" often imply (*a*) specific abnormal patterns, (*b*) causing harm to the individual, and (*c*) the need for treatment. As implied, the pathology is linked to specific initiating conditions and specific treatment and accurate prognoses can be provided once accurate diagnosis has been completed.

Some "sleep disorders" meet these criteria. Sleep apnea, for example, involves 30 or more episodes of respiratory pauses during sleep lasting more than 10 seconds. The person with sleep apnea can experience anoxia, tachycardia, high blood pressure, and can be at risk for sudden death (Guilleminault, Eldridge, & Dement, 1973).

Insomnia, on the other hand, refers to a *complaint* of daytime fatigue *attributed* to poor sleep. The complaint can be characterized by several different patterns (difficulty in falling to sleep initially, difficulty staying asleep, reduced slow wave sleep), may arise from a variety of conditions, and may respond in different ways to particular treatment strategies (Bootzin & Nicassio, 1978; Borkovec, 1979; Coates & Thoresen, 1977; Hauri, 1978). The complaint can be associated with no discernible abnormality in sleep as measured by all-night sleep recordings (Dement, 1972). Some persons can show abnormal patterns (e.g., extremely short sleep time) but fail to complain or might even enjoy the extra time they have each day to devote to waking activities (cf. Hartmann, 1973; Jones & Oswald, 1968; Meddis, Pearson, & Langford, 1973).

For these reasons we prefer to use "behaviors and complaints" as the topic of this chapter. These terms denote *responses different from those experienced by the majority*. Use of more neutral terms seems necessary considering that some deviations can cause impairment (e.g., narcolepsy), others can signify physical dysfunction (e.g., sleep apnea), and still others are transient or are experienced by many in the normal course of development (e.g., enuresis, night terrors). Finally some may be beneficial or even advantageous (e.g., short sleep time) for some persons (cf. Webb & Cartwright, 1978).

More Questions than Answers

The study of sleep has passed through the perinatal period and is now in its infancy. While continuous polygraphic monitoring of physiological functions began in 1935, Rapid-Eye-Movement (REM) sleep was identified only in the early 1950s (cf. Azerinsky & Kleitman, 1953) and its correlation with dreaming was discovered in the late 1950s (Dement & Kleitman, 1957). A decade ago, Monroe (1969) found that the numbers everyone had been reporting (e.g., minutes of Stage 4) did not have a generally reliable meaning. He distributed copies of the same all-night sleep recording to a number of laboratories; values for sleep states and stages differed significantly from lab to lab. As a result, standardized criteria for scoring all-night sleep protocols were published slightly more than 10 years ago (Rechtschaffen & Kales, 1968).

The study of sleep is still primarily descriptive and generally atheoretical (cf. Webb, 1974). Very basic descriptive work is still needed and it has not been possible to formulate more than tentative and incomplete models. Studies of behaviors and complaints associated with sleep have progressed no further. The field is beset with a variety of empirical findings, and researchers continue to poke and probe in various directions. The stranglehold of orthodox theoretical structure can inhibit progress; theoretical variety is helpful inasmuch as it keeps open a wide range of research avenues. At the same time theoretical confusion is disadvantageous because the meaning of certain empirical findings cannot be elucidated, and often promising research directions are neglected or ignored.

The phenomena of insomnia, for example, remains elusive. Persons complaining of insomnia report severely restricted amounts and quality of sleep, but indices obtained from all-night sleep recordings show generally that these persons do not sleep as badly as reported (Carskadon, Dement, Mitler, Guilleminault, Zarcone, & Spiegel, 1976). In many cases it has been difficult to discriminate insomniacs from normals on common variables used to describe sleep. Total sleep time of persons complaining of insomnia and normal sleepers, for example, may not differ (cf.

Karacan, Williams, Salis, & Hursch, 1971). Fifteen percent of the population regularly sleep between 5 and 6 hours per night, *less* than that of most persons complaining of insomnia (cf. Carskadon, et al., 1976). On the other hand, it has been reported that persons complaining of insomnia show more nocturnal arousals (Carskadon, et al., 1976), higher body temperatures, more body movements, more phasic vasoconstrictions and higher skin resistances (Monroe, 1967), and more night-to-night variability in sleep than good sleepers (Coates, Rosekind, Strossen, Thoreson & Kirmil-Gray, 1979).

While these findings are interesting, we lack a comprehensive theoretical structure to give them theoretical or practical significance. The clinical importance of these differences remains a mystery. Many treatment programs for insomnia are designed to reduce latency to sleep onset or increase total sleep time. Should they focus instead on increasing slow wave sleep, reducing body temperature, body movements, or skin resistance? The dilemma is clear. Persons need help but our current and incomplete understanding of sleep, and behaviors and complaints associated with sleep, have not permitted us to advance much beyond a "let's-see-what-would-happen-if" approach. We remain at the "trial-and-error" stage in designing and offering effective clinical treatment.

Pursuing the Need

Lack of powerful theories or definitive results does not preclude the need to develop and evaluate treatment strategies. Significant numbers of persons suffer, sometimes considerably, from these problems. Further, drugs remain the predominant treatment (Cooper, 1977). In a survey of 4358 physicians, Bixler, Kales, Scharf, Kales, and Leo (1976) found that 18% of the patient population suffered from insomnia, 4.6% experienced nightmares, and 3.1% experienced excessive sleepiness during the day. In a national prospective survey of 1,064,004 men and women, Hammond (1964) reported that 13% of the men and 26.4% of the women complained of insomnia. Complaints are not necessarily restricted to adults. Price, Coates, Thoresen, and Grinstead (1978) reported that 12% of a sample of high school students reported disturbed sleep on four or more nights per week; another 33% complained of occasional sleep disturbance. An alarming 27 million prescriptions were written for hypnotic drugs in 1976 alone; 22% of these were for barbiturate medications while 30% were for nonbarbiturates with potentially undesirable side effects (Cooper, 1977). Understandably, insomnia has been implicated in the etiology of problem drinking in some persons (Bayh, 1972).

Behavioral approaches have provided useful alternatives in many problem areas, and applications to behaviors and complaints associated with sleep show promise. However, it would be misleading to suggest that definitive and powerful treatments are available for treating these problems. A behavioral perspective may offer useful insights and procedures for examining and treating these problems. This chapter is devoted to presenting some important empirical findings on sleep and the behaviors and complaints associated with it. These findings are discussed in relation to promising theoretical notions, with an effort to integrate the diverse models into some possibly useful strategies for advancing research and treatment potency.

OBTAINING INFORMATION ABOUT SLEEP

Sleep research is conducted at present using relatively uniform and standardized settings, tools, and dependent measures. Volunteers or clinical patients participating for research or treatment typically arrive at a laboratory one to two hours prior to bedtime. At least eight electrodes are applied so that continuous polygraphic monitoring can be conducted throughout the night. The electroencephalogram (EEG) is recorded from the two central positions (C3 and C4) and sometimes the two occipital positions (01 and 02), the electrooculogram (EOG) is recorded from the outer canthi of the eyes, the electromyogram (EMG) is recorded from the digastric chin muscles, and two reference electrodes (A1 and A2) are placed on the ear lobes or mastoids. Other electrodes might be applied for a full clinical EEG or to monitor heart rate, leg movements, or breathing rate needed in specific diagnoses. Once electrodes are in place, the subject retires to a relatively quiet bedroom. The electrode leads are gathered into a ponytail behind the subject's head and plugged into a headboard that leads to a polygraph (cf. Figure 1). A technician remains on duty throughout the night to monitor the equipment and attend to subject needs. While the subject tries to sleep, a continuous record of the person's EEG, eye movements, and muscle tension is printed out on a polygraph in an adjoining room.

As might be expected, such novel sleeping arrangements can alter sleep. "First night" effects are common: sleep on the first and sometimes second nights in the laboratory is more disrupted than sleep on subsequent nights in that setting (Agnew, Webb, & Williams, 1966; Scharf, Kales, & Bixler, 1975). Persons who are accustomed to sleeping with a bed partner show more Stage 4 and less rapid eye movement (REM) sleep when they sleep alone in the laboratory. Good sleepers have reported that sleep in the lab is generally worse than at home (Frankel, Coursey, Buchbinder, & Snyder, 1976). First night effects are minimized when subjects are recorded at home.

Procedures have been developed to move the "sleep laboratory" to persons' homes so that more naturalistic and perhaps generalizable estimates of persons' sleep can be obtained. Coates, Rosekind, and Thoresen (1978), for example, developed a system for transmitting all-night EEG data from subjects' homes by telephone. A transmission unit, housed in a suitcase and powered by four 6-volt batteries, amplifies and transmits eight separate channels of biological signal over a single telephone line. The signal is received at the central laboratory where the record can be written out on a polygraph or stored on magnetic tape. A technician remains on duty to monitor the recording. The transmission unit is also equipped with a microphone for two-way voice communication between the subject at home and the technician in the laboratory.

To use this system, the technician goes to the subject's home in the evening and attaches the full electrode array needed to complete the all-night sleep recording. The individual electrodes are plugged into a master headboard that interfaces with the transmitter via a polarized plug. The technician can depart at anytime. When ready to retire, the subject goes to bed, inserts the plug, informs the lab technician the lights are being turned out, and sleeps (or stays awake) in accustomed sur-

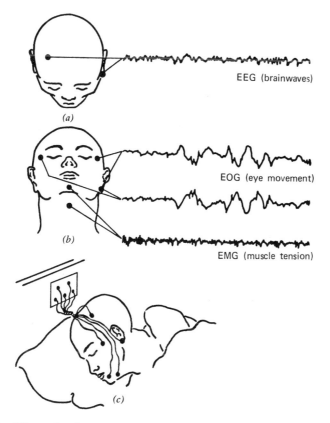

FIGURE 1. Electrode placement and standard tracings for an all-night sleep recording. Electrodes placed on the (*a*) head record brainwaves (EEG); (*b*) eyes record eye movement (EOG); and (*c*) chin record muscle tension (EMG). The electrodes are plugged into the circuit board at the head of the bed. From there, the terminals lead to the polygraph machine in another room. The person who is being recorded has complete freedom of movement while sleeping, and can be unhooked easily if he or she needs to get up in the night. (From Coates & Thoresen, 1977. Copyright, Prentice-Hall, Inc. Used with permission.)

roundings. Coates & Thoresen, 1979) compared the sleep of eight insomniacs who had received self-management training when their sleep was recorded at home and when it was recorded in a laboratory. Significant differences were found between mean values on four parameters (Minutes of Stage 3 Sleep, Percent of Stage 2 Sleep, Percent of Stage 3 Sleep, Number of REM periods). Variances on two parameters (Total Sleep Time, Latency to Sleep Onset) were greater in the laboratory than at home. These data indicated that recordings in different locations may yield different values on some variables for groups of persons and for some individuals within those groups. In contrast to usual findings in the laboratory, we found that adaptation or "first night effects in home recordings were minimal (Coates, George, Killen, Marchini, Hamilton, & Thoresen, 1980).

Findings in any field are limited by the methods used to "discover" them. The uniform methods used by separate sleep laboratories have made it possible to replicate and extend findings. At the same time, however, new findings, relationships, and theories may emerge as methods are extended beyond the lab into the natural environment.

What Do the Data Mean?

Once the all-night data are obtained, they must be interpreted. A standardized and generally accepted scoring method was adopted in 1968 (cf. Rechtschaffen & Kales, 1968). The all-night record of EEG, EMG, and EOG is divided into 30-second epochs. Each epoch is assigned a single rating if 50% or more of the biodata meet the criteria for a given stage or state of sleep or wakefulness. For example, during a given 30-second period a person may be alternating between quiet wakefulness [8–12 cycles/second (cps)] and Stage 1 (3–7 cps). The epoch would be scored as Stage 1 sleep if 50% or more of the record contained 3–7 cps activity despite the fact that considerable wakefulness also occurred during the epoch.

Sleep is divided into two major states (denoting relatively different states of being): rapid-eye-movement (REM) sleep and non-rapid-eye-movement (NREM) sleep. NREM sleep is composed of sleep stages 1, 2, 3, and 4. These are distinguished from one another primarily by EEG patterns and the subject's responsiveness to external environment. Figure 2 presents EEG, EOG, and EMG tracings from laboratory and home recordings typical of each sleep stage. Wakefulness prior to sleep onset is characterized by alpha (8–12 cps) and random eye movements. As a person enters sleep, Stage 1 appears first and is characterized by slow rolling eye movements and low-amplitude mixed-frequency (3–7 cps) EEG activity. Stage 2 sleep is characterized by sleep spindles (13–16 cps lasting ½ to 2 seconds) and K-complexes (sharp rise and fall in the brain wave pattern). Delta waves (½ to 2 cps; 75 mV in amplitude) characterize Stage 3 and 4 sleep. These slow and high amplitude brain waves signal a general slowing of brain activity. Stage 3 is scored when 20 to 50% of the epoch contains delta. Stage 4 is scored when more than 50% of the epoch contains delta waves.

A young adult in a typical night of sleep goes from wakefulness to deep sleep quite rapidly (cf. Figure 3). After 60 to 90 minutes the person experiences Stage 2 sleep, followed immediately by the first REM period of the night. As the night progresses, the cycle is repeated but the REM periods become slightly longer toward morning while Stage 3 and 4 disappear.

Table 2 demonstrates some of the interesting changes that occur as persons grow older: Total Sleep Time decreases and sleep generally becomes lighter (decreased Sleep Efficiency, increased Number of Awakenings and Frequency of Stage 1). REM period remains fairly constant, but Stage 3 and 4 drop out almost completely. There is also a noticeable increase in variability within the older age groups. A natural kind of insomnia sets in with aging.

SOME FACTS IN SEARCH OF A THEORY

Studying sleep using a biological rhythm perspective is a recent and growing trend (Webb & Cartwright, 1977). The biological clock found in all organisms accounts for such well-known phenomena in man as variations in hormone secretion, body

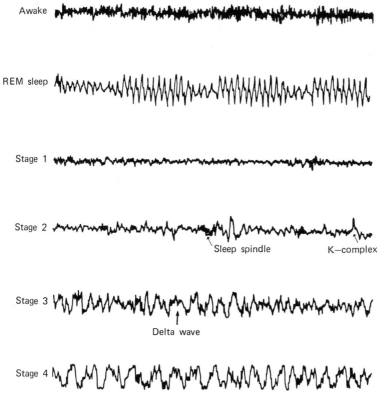

Awake

REM sleep

Stage 1

Stage 2

Sleep spindle   K—complex

Stage 3

Delta wave

Stage 4

Brainwave patterns typical of various states and stages of sleep and wakefulness.

FIGURE 2.   Brainwave tracings characteristic of wakefulness, NREM Stages 1, 2, 3, and 4, and REM sleep. (From Coates & Thoresen, 1977. Copyright, Prentice-Hall, Inc. Used with permission.)

temperature, cardiac output, veinous pressure, urine secretion, and enzyme synthesis over a 24-hour period. Factors in the environment (e.g., light and dark) termed "Zeitgebers" pace the biological rhythm but do not act as its immediate cause. Rather, the rhythm seems to be inherent in the organism (cf. Aschoff, 1965).

The "process view" of sleep suggests that sleep and sleep disorders can be understood within the context of these unlearned, inherent, species-specific cycles (Dement & Mitler, 1976). Sleep may represent the outward manifestation of a number of independent circadian processes that converge at specific times and in different relationships. REM sleep, for example, is defined by the simultaneous occurrence of three distinct processes. First is *tonic motor inhibition.* REM sleep is a time of profound motor paralysis; voluntary movement is totally impossible and the tendon reflexes cannot be elicited.

The second process is *central nervous system arousal;* during REM sleep, the EEG begins to display rapid movement characteristic of the waking state. For this reason REM sleep is sometimes referred to as "an awake brain in a paralyzed body." The third process termed *phasic activity* is short-lasting events charac-

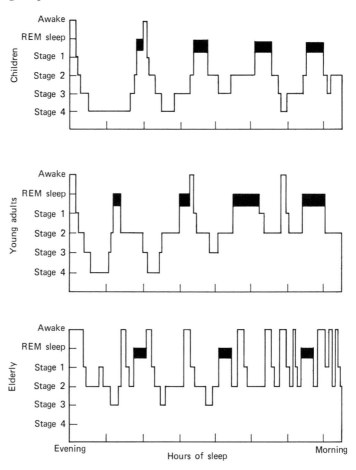

FIGURE 3.   Sleep cycles for children, young adults, and the elderly. Notice the changes that occur in Stage 3 and Non-REM sleep and in REM sleep with aging. Notice also that the elderly awaken more frequently toward morning than children and young adults. (From Coates & Thoresen, 1977. Used with permission of Prentice-Hall, Inc.)

terized by rapid movement of the eyes, muscle twitches, sudden changes in pupil diameter, fluctuations in penile tumescence, and cardiovascular irregularities.

NREM sleep is thought to result from inhibition of the reticular activating system (RAS) and activation of the sleep system. High RAS activity is needed to maintain wakefulness. Low RAS activity can lead to relaxed wakefulness and perhaps to NREM Stage 1 sleep. Stage 2 and delta sleep may require the additional active engagement of a brain-stem serotonergic system (the sleep system) (cf. Hauri, 1977). The precise roles, and interactions, and processes of these systems in regulating sleep is at present unknown (Gillin, Mendelson, Sitaram, & Wyatt, 1978).

Explanations of the "what" of sleep do not provide answers concerning the "why" of sleep. Three views are prominent currently: (a) Sleep is needed for physical and psychological restoration (Adam & Oswald, 1977; Hartmann, 1973); (b) Sleep forces the organism to conserve energy (Berger, 1975; Zepelin & Recht-

Table 2. Changes in Sleep Associated with Age[a,b]

Age Group (years)	Total Sleep Time (minutes)	Latency to Sleep Onset (minutes)	Sleep Efficiency[c]	Number of Times Awakened	Frequency of Stage 1	Percent of Time in Stages 3 and 4	Percent of Time in REM Sleep
3–5	610.6(36.6)	14.9(18.7)	0.96(.03)	1.25(1.11)	4.55(2.33)	18.9(3.9)	30.3(3.6)
6–9	572.9(20.3)**	11.1(7.5)	0.97(.02)	0.67(0.86)	4.50(1.80)	22.1(3.3)	27.3(3.5)
10–12	557.5(23.9)	16.3(9.9)	0.95(.02)	1.58(1.15)*	6.42(4.04)	22.2(3.7)	26.4(1.9)
13–15	488.8(11.9)***	16.0(7.9)	0.96(.02)	3.20(2.66)	8.15(3.59)	23.9(6.5)	26.7(3.1)
16–19	448.6(31.1)***	17.0(10.3)	0.94(.03)	2.81(1.80)	6.92(2.73)	23.0(6.5)	22.0(3.3)**
20–29	419.3(14.5)**	14.6(11.4)	0.95(.04)	3.05(2.57)	7.05(2.69)	20.8(4.8)	28.0(5.7)**
30–39	421.5(21.9)	5.8(3.8)*	0.97(.02)	2.50(1.43)	9.65(4.74)	12.5(5.6)**	23.5(3.9)*
40–49	389.1(46.5)	10.0(7.9)	0.91(.06)**	4.65 2.27)*	10.85(3.18)	8.5(6.8)	22.8(4.0)
50–59	389.8(49.5)	11.9(10.5)	0.92(.04)	5.67(1.78)	10.04(3.02)	4.92(7.7)	21.5(4.0)
60–69	407.3(44.6)	8.3(7.2)	0.90(.07)	7.55(3.69)	13.60(4.00)*	2.6(5.1)	23.1(3.6)
70–79	372.9(87.2)	32.0(27.5)*	0.77(.20)	7.09(3.22)	14.32(2.25)	1.4(2.3)	17.7(6.6)

Standard deviations are given in parentheses.
[a] Adapted from findings reported in Williams et al. (1974).
[b] Asterisks indicate significant difference from immediately younger age group.
*** Beyond .001 level.
** Beyond .01 level.
* Beyond .05 level.
[c] Proportion of time asleep divided by total time in bed.

schaffen, 1974); and (c) Sleep removes the organism from the environment and thus increases its probability of survival (Meddis, 1975; Webb, 1974). The latter two views have been combined in an interesting correlational study. Allison and Cicchetti (1976) reported that *size* (as an index of metabolism) and *probability of predation* accounted for 60% of the variance in slow wave sleep of 38 species of mammals. They hypothesized that slow wave sleep provided an enforced and adaptive rest to smaller animals with a high metabolism who are not in danger from predators. However, slow wave sleep is disadvantageous to larger animals, who need more time to forage for food and to animals who need to be alert to respond to predators. Probability of predation was also negatively correlated with amount of REM sleep. Understandably, a state of paralysis is disadvantageous to an animal likely to be devoured by other animals.

SLEEP DISORDERS AND THE PROCESS VIEW

The process view suggests that sleep disorders might represent *dis*harmonies within circadian cycles or between the circadian and sleep-wake cycles.

Disharmonies Within Circadian Cycles

Various processes oscillating on a circadian cycle might become desynchronized. Narcolepsy is a disorder characterized by excessive daytime sleepiness, sleep attacks, and cataplexy (the person loses all muscle tone but remains awake) (cf. Table 1). The person may also experience episodes of visual, auditory, or tactile hallucinations (Zarcone, 1975). Within the process view, narcolepsy may represent the intrusion into wakefulness of some of the processes associated with REM sleep (e.g., loss of muscle tone, phasic activity).

As a second example, Gastaut and Broughton (see Broughton, 1968) found that most of the episodes of enuresis began in Stage 4 sleep. Bedwetting followed a burst of rhythmic delta activity associated with a body movement and a change to Stage 2 or Stage 1. In subsequent investigations, Broughton (1968) reported from all-night studies that persons who suffered from enuresis, somnambulism, and night terrors manifested patterns of physiological changes that differed from persons not experiencing these problems. He reported, for example, that enuretic children showed similar heart rates during wakefulness and Stage 4 sleep while normals showed significantly lower heart rates during Stage 4. Individuals experiencing nightmares exhibited relative tachycardia during slow wave sleep. Broughton (1968) hypothesized that these characteristics represented general physiological arousal during sleep. When physiological activity increased, bedwetting, sleep walking, or night terrors occurred. Dissociations of some circadian processes may result in hyperarousal during sleep and ultimately some behaviors generally seen during wakefulness.

Some kinds of insomnia represent clear deviations from a normal circadian cycle. Miles, Raynal, and Wilson (1977) reported the case of a blind man with a circadian rhythm of 24.9 hours. Insomnia and excessive daytime sleepiness were experienced periodically for two to three weeks at a time and resulted in the cyclic administration of stimulants and hypnotics. When removed from his home and work environment, and allowed an ad-lib sleep-wake schedule, he spontaneously adopted a sleep-wake cycle of 24.9 hours. Body temperature, alertness, performance, and urinary potassium, sodium, and calcium also followed this 24.9-hour rhythm. Attempts to adjust the subject to a 24-hour cycle over a 10-day period using artificial Zeitgebers (i.e., stable bedtime and wake time) were unsuccessful.

Dissociations of Circadian and Sleep-Wake Cycles

Dissociations of sleep-wake and circadian cycles may also be an important source of sleep disturbance in some persons. While circadian rhythms are relatively stable, the sleep-wake cycle can deviate quite easily from a 24-hour rhythm in response to biological, environmental, or psychological pressure (cf. Aschoff, 1965). The person described in the Miles, et al. (1977) study experienced periodic insomnia; normal sleep and absence of sleepiness was experienced when circadian and enforced sleep-wake cycles were able to harmonize.

Recent evidence suggests strongly that deprivation of specific sleep stages or reductions in total sleep time can be tolerated easily but that shifts in sleep-wake cycles can impair sleep and daytime performance significantly. A recent review by a scientist actively researching the relationships between stages and states of sleep and waking performance concluded ". . . we must candidly admit that stages of sleep and the relation to performance remain a mystery" (Johnson, 1973, p. 373). The point is underlined in the dilemma of Stage 4 sleep. Several investigators have emphasized findings which suggest that the Stage 4 component of NREM sleep is of considerable biological importance. Stage 4 sleep correlates negatively with age but positively with the duration of preceding wakefulness. When Total Sleep Time is curtailed, the amount of Stage 4 sleep is preserved or increased, although there is a net loss of other sleep stages (cf. Webb, 1974). In spite of this indirect evidence of its importance, experimental deprivation of Stage 4 sleep has not produced substantial behavior deficits. Flurazepam (Dalmane) suppresses Stage 4 markedly but this suppression is not accompanied by documented side effects (Feinberg, Fein, Walker, Price, Floyd, & March, 1977).

Persons also seem to be able to reduce total sleep time without undue difficulty. Webb and Agnew (1974) engaged fifteen 18 to 21-year-old males in a long-term study of the effects of limited sleep time. Subjects' usual sleep times of 7½ to 8 hours were reduced to 5½ hours for a period of 60 days while the subjects continued a normal course load at the University of Florida. Sleep recordings and performance tests (Wilkinson Vigilance Task; Wilkinson Addition Task, Grip Strength, Word Memory, and Mood Scales) were conducted once every seven days. Subjects also kept daily sleep logs. Adherence to the regimen was increased by employing roommate pairs who might be able to monitor and also encourage each other.

Effects on sleep were minimal. Stage 4 sleep was increased initially but declined to baseline values by Week 5. Total REM time was reduced by 25% and latency to Stage 4 was reduced as well. The sleep logs showed that the subjects initially experienced difficulty in arousing from sleep in the morning and felt drowsy during the day. These effects disappeared by the third week. Only the Wilkinson Vigilance Task showed some decline over the course of study. Similar findings were reported by Johnson and McLeod (1973). When subjects were followed at eight months from the end of the study they were sleeping 1 to 1½ hours shorter than before the study.

By contrast, shifts in sleep-wake cycles are not tolerated easily. Well documented, of course, are impairments in performance and sleep produced when persons change time zones (Preston, Bateman, Short, & Wilkinson, 1973; Preston & Bateman, 1970). Preston, Bateman, Meichen, Wilkinson, & Short (1976) studied changes in performance, temperature, and menstrual cycle of a group of 12 female airline employees. Subjects were subjected to two 8-hour changes in time representing a long flight west (e.g., London to Honolulu). Body temperature and menstrual cycle remained unchanged, but sleep and performance on local time was impaired. Importantly, there was a strong correlation between performance and temperature, suggesting that circadian variations accounted for the poor performance.

Webb and Agnew (1978) summarized the effects of shift work on sleep as follows: (*a*) latency to sleep onset is reduced only minimally; (*b*) total sleep time is reduced; (*c*) time awake after sleep onset is increased; (*d*) Stage 1 may be increased; and (*e*) slow wave sleep may be decreased. Night and rotating shift workers also report greater frequency of physical disorders, complain about relationships with others, and are less satisfied with sexual relations than day workers (Rutenfranz, Colquhoun, Knauth, & Ghata, 1977). Sleep efficiency (the ratio of time asleep to time in bed) is also decreased under non-24-hour cycles. Webb and Agnew (1975), for example, studied 9, 12, 18, 30 and 36-hour sleep-wake cycles where the ratio of sleep to wakefulness was held at 1 to 2. When compared to sleep on a 24-hour cycle (8 hours of sleep for every 16 hours of wakefulness), the varied periods led to decreased sleep efficiency.

Taub and Berger (1973) studied the relative effects of extended sleep, sleep deprivation, and shifts of accustomed sleep time in 10 persons regularly sleeping from midnight to 8:00 A.M. Accuracy and speed of response were significantly poorer on a vigilance task and negative affect was increased significantly after sleep was shifted, shortened, or extended. In a more recent study, Taub and Hawkins (1977) reported that physiological arousal, psychomotor performance, and subjective mood were associated with irregular sleep schedules. Irregular sleepers (those whose retiring and awakening times and sleep duration varied by 2 hours or more) showed increases in pulse rate from morning to noon, but thereupon remained at relatively the same level. Regular sleepers' temperature, pulse rate, and performance followed a U-shaped curve; these subjects showed less negative and more positive affect than irregular sleepers.

Similar shifts or disruptions in sleep-wake cycles can be produced by persons' environments, behaviors, or thoughts. A warm or uncomfortable sleeping room, for example, causes disruptions in sleep. A stressful presleep experience can increase awakenings during sleep (Baekeland, Koulack, & Lasky, 1968), and exercise just prior to bedtime can decrease slow wave sleep during the first part of the night (Hauri, 1968). Excessive cognitive activity may prevent the person from achieving the reduced physiological or mental states necessary to experience Stage 2 or slow wave sleep (Kales, Cauldwell, Preston, Healey, & Kales, 1976).

In summary, a contemporary perspective suggests two important implications to guide our trial-and-error approaches to sleep disorders.

1. A 24-hour perspective that considers the relationships of circadian and sleep-wake cycles may provide a heuristic and useful approach in studying and treating sleep disorders. Sleep disorders may represent anomalies within circadian cycles, between various circadian cycles, or between circadian and sleep-wake cycles.
2. Biological and psychological factors may contribute to the harmonies and disharmonies within and among these various cycles.

SLEEP DISTURBANCES: A TWENTY-FOUR HOUR VIEW

Behaviors and complaints associated with sleep can be described using three general categories.

1. *Difficulty initiating or maintaining sleep.*   These persons complain of daytime fatigue, iritability, or depression that they attribute to difficulty in falling or staying asleep or because they awaken early in the morning. This is referred to typically as the complaint of insomnia.
2. *Difficulty initiating or maintaining wakefulness.*   These persons also complain of extreme sleepiness during the day but do not blame poor sleep at night. They may report that sleep at night is excessive and also report recurring sleep episodes during the day. This is sometimes referred to as hypersomnia.
3. *Abnormal nocturnal behaviors.*   This category includes activities that are normally performed during wakefulness, but which cause problems for the individual and those in his environment when performed during sleep. Sleepwalking, sleep talking, enuresis, and *jactatio capitus nocturnus* (slow-rocking head movements) are usually included in this classification. This category also includes anomalies that can cause a person to experience a physical injury (e.g., bruxism, head banging) or to experience psychological discomfort (nightmares, night terrors). These are sometimes referred to as the dyssomnias or parasomnias.

Medical Diagnosis and Behavior Analysis

Some behaviors and complaints associated with sleep can be described in useful ways using medical diagnostic procedures, while others may require other kinds of taxonomic schemes. It is tempting, at this point, to place the behaviors and complaints associated with sleep under one of the three categories above in an attempt to develop a taxonomy of sleep disorders. The nosologies that have been proposed (e.g., Hauri, 1977; Kales & Kales, 1970; Karacan et al., 1971; Oswald, 1969) have failed to gain widespread acceptance because they prove unworkable in practice. Nosologies are helpful only if they organize an apparently heterogeneous group of disorders into a logically and mutually exclusive category system based on common etiology or treatment. Systems of differential diagnosis have proven relatively helpful in medical practice, but are marginally useful for describing and treating abnormal behavior patterns (Kanfer & Saslow, 1969; Schacht & Nathan, 1977). Some deviations (e.g., sleep apnea, narcolepsy) are marked by clear symptom clusters and differential diagnosis is essential to proper medical treatment. Other deviations, such as complaints of insomnia, refer to a variety of behavior patterns that can arise from a variety of sources interacting in unique ways in specific individuals. In these cases, differentiating sleep maintenance insomnia from sleep latency insomnia may not always be possible and not necessarily useful. Further, it may not be possible to distinguish between insomnia related to excessive physical tension, excessive mental stress, or stress related to specific environments. Highly subjective and potentially unreliable judgments may be involved in making the assessments and in determining if the problem is transient, chronic, or cyclical.

Medical diagnosis may be useful in determining initially if the behavior or complaint associated with sleep is associated with a physical disorder. *The functional (behavioral-analytic) approach* may be helpful in providing an effective diagnostic system for behaviors and complaints associated with sleep when a physical disorder is not present to cause disturbed sleep. The functional approach proceeds by (*a*) describing explicitly the specific behavior or complaint, (*b*) examining a variety of physical, environmental, and psychological antecedents and consequences to determine possible causes of the behavior pattern or complaint and (*c*) designing a treatment program to modify these causes and thus improve sleep. Emphasis is placed on assessing those variables that can be modified to produce changes in the behavior or the complaint. Treatment implications follow immediately from assessment. This kind of system makes the assumption that assessment is never complete and it is possible that initial analyses may be incorrect or incomplete. The clinician interacts continuously with the client and assessment strategies to determine if initial hypotheses about the problem need changing.

Differential diagnosis remains primary. The objective of a functional analysis, like that of traditional medical diagnosis, is to match treatment to the client. But rather than assuming that matching is best accomplished by classifying symptom clusters according to presumed underlying etiology, the functional approach to diagnosis and treatment is built upon the assumption that (*a*) specific behaviors and complaints will vary from individual to individual and (*b*) the factors responsible for maintaining the problem behavior can vary markedly within and between persons. The best clues for appropriate treatment are derived from ongoing analyses, attempts at modification, and continuous evaluation (cf. Yates, 1970, 1976).

Assessment and Action: An Overview

Table 3 presents an algorithm that specifies a system by which specific treatments can be matched to individual behaviors and complaints associated with sleep. Differential diagnosis is accomplished by combining medical and functional approaches in those areas in which each approach can be most useful. The approach rests upon the possibility of collaborative working relationships between medical and behavioral scientists and practitioners. Sleep and the behaviors and complaints associated

Table 3. Assessment and Action in Sleep Disorders: An Overview

Objectives

> *Research:* Select homogeneous subsamples for assignment to treatment conditions; design dependent variables appropriate to subsample
>
> *Treatment:* Design appropriate strategy based upon analysis of individual case

Person or associates complain
of sleep disturbance

Medical examination

Physical history and medical examination to assess disturbance secondary to physical disorder	If illness is not obvious, assume that disturbance is primary complaint and continue assessment and treatment
Interview with parents, spouse, and subject to assess if disturbance may be secondary to neurological dysfunction	If neurological dysfunction is obvious or suspected (by interview, diaries, and tape recordings), refer person to competent sleep specialist for further diagnosis and appropriate treatment

Drug history and use

To determine if complaint is a result of overreliance on hypnotics, stimulants, or alcohol	If drug-dependent, design appropriate drug-withdrawal program in collaboration with medical personnel; continue to treat sleep disturbance

Behavior/personality analysis

> Use variety of assessment methods to determine physical, cognitive, behavioral, and environmental patterns potentially related to sleep disturbance

All-night sleep recording

May be needed in selected cases to provide more definitive diagnosis	If further testing reveals disturbance secondary to a neurological abnormality, refer to competent sleep specialist
Essential in research to document nature and extent of disturbed sleep of subjects	
May be helpful in clinical practice to specify the nature of sleep disturbance	

with sleep are complex. Thorough assessment and treatment require an adequate blend of specialities, each contributing unique tools and remedies.

Medical Examination

The first task involves determining if the behavior or complaint associated with sleep is secondary to a physical disorder (cf. Table 4). A variety of dysfunctions can lead to poor sleep and also daytime fatigue; the first entry in Table 4 might appear to suggest that nothing but an elaborate and complete medical examination will suffice. Guilleminault and Dement (1977), however, recommended a normal physical examination; if an illness is not obvious then the physician-behavioral scientist team can proceed with the assumption that the sleep disorder is not secondary to a medical dysfunction. Table 4 also lists four specific and not necessarily obvious dysfunctions that can be implicated directly in the complaint of poor sleep and daytime sleepiness. While these are diagnosed most reliably in all-night sleep recordings, judicious questioning of patient and bed partners is sufficient in most cases to make reasonably secure judgments about the presence of the disorder. If these disorders are suspected then the patient should be referred to a competent sleep specialist for further diagnosis and treatment. If judicious questioning does not reveal the suspicion of a problem, the assessment can continue.

Drug History

Excessive abuse of stimulants can lead to tolerance, dependence, poor sleep at night, and excessive fatigue during the day. Hypnotic medications often produce a similar result. Table 5 lists the generic and trade names of sleep medications commonly used in the United States. Over-the-counter medications usually constitute the first plan of attack. Although these highly advertised drugs have little impact on sleep beyond placebo effects (Kales, 1971; Kay, Blackburn, Buckingham, & Karacan, 1976), they can increase daytime drowsiness and possibly encourage the person's perception that sleep is becoming worse. Fortunately, the barbiturates may be losing their popularity; use of these drugs for hypnotic purposes declined by 73% from 1971 to 1976 (Cooper, 1977). Persons using these drugs rapidly fall victim to a dependence-tolerance cycle and experience considerable disruption in sleep structure and cycle (Kales & Kales, 1974; Kales, Bixler, Tan, Scharf, & Kales, 1974). The negative effects of barbiturates and related drugs are clinically significant; REM and slow wave sleep are suppressed, beta rhythm activity is increased, and persons attempting to withdraw abruptly often experience reactions as well as REM rebound in the form of severe nightmares. Thus during withdrawal a person's sleep becomes more disturbed than before the drug was used originally. Understandably, the person concludes that insomnia has worsened and that drugs are essential; to obtain some relief poor sleepers resume drug use, often at an increased level.

The nonbarbiturate hypnotics, while less detrimental in general, can affect sleep in ways similar to the barbiturates. On the positive side they decrease body movements, number of awakenings, minutes to sleep onset, and number of shifts in sleep stages. Increases in total sleep time in Stage 2 sleep are also common. However, they reduce total REM time and slow wave sleep and increase beta rhythm activity in the EEG. These medications can also lead to dependence and tolerance. With-

Disorder	Description	Assessment
Organic dysfunctions (Kales & Kales, 1974; Williams et al., 1974)	Sleep complaint is secondary to some other illness: e.g., kidney, liver, thyroid dysfunction, diabetes, heart disease (angina, myocardial infarction), illness causing pain (e.g., ulcer, arthritis), epilepsy, brain tumor	History and examination by physician; laboratory examination as indicated; if nonsleep related illness is not obvious, consider sleep disorders as primary
Sleep apnea (Guilleminault, Eldridge, & Dement, 1973)	Respiratory pauses during sleep more than 10 seconds in duration; usually more than 30 episodes in a single phase; breathing resumes following each pause only when person experiences a brief arousal to wakefulness and gasps for air	1. Bed partner reports period of nonbreathing terminated by gasp for air and loud snoring; numerous and violent body movements 2. Patient reports that daytime sleep episodes are unrefreshing, headaches and disorientation in morning are common, enuresis is common in children 3. Audiotape recordings during sleep show characteristic sounds: crescendo of snoring followed by silence
Nocturnal myoclonous (Lugaresi, Coccagna, Ceroni, & Ambrosetto, 1968)	Repetitive muscular jerks occurring in the lower limbs at sleep onset and during sleep; accompanied by brief arousals; the patient may not be aware of these arousals	1. Person reports fatigue in the morning; sleep generally not refreshing; may or may not report being awakened frequently during the night 2. Bed partner complains of being kicked in the night 3. EMG recordings of anterior fibial muscles show repetitive contractions that last about two seconds each and repeat rhythmically at intervals of approximately 30 seconds; accompanied frequently by alpha arousals in the EEG
Restless legs syndrome (Frankel, Patten, & Gillin, 1974)	Distracting and uncomfortable sensations in legs when person is resting or at sleep onset	Person complains of cramps, pain, or crawling sensation at sleep onset; relieved when person gets up and walks around
Narcolepsy (Zarcone, 1975)	1. Excessive daytime sleepiness, sleep attacks (brief episodes of sleep that can occur at any time in the day) and cataplexy (person is awake, but all muscle tone is lost) 2. Following may or may not be present: Sleep paralysis—episodes of paralysis occurring in the transition between wakefulness and sleep Hypnogogic hallucinations—episodes of visual, auditory, and tactile hallucinations that can occur in the transition between wakefulness and sleep Disturbed nocturnal sleep (frequent awakenings during the night)	Person reports sleepiness, sleep attacks, cataplexy, sleep paralysis, hallucinations, and disturbed nocturnal sleep Sleep recordings show that REM sleep occurs at sleep onset

Table 5.   Drugs Commonly Used as Hypnotic Medications[a]

Chemical Class	Compound	Brand Name	Usual Hypnotic Dose
Barbiturates	Amobarbital	Amytal®	100–200 mg
	Sodium butabarbital	Butisol®	15–30 mg
	Sodium bentobarbital	Nembutal®	100 mg
	Secobarbital	Seconal®	100 mg
	Vinbarbital	Delvinal®	
	Phenobarbital	Luminal®	100 mg
Alcohols	Chloral hydrate	Noctec®, Somos®	0.5–1.0 g
	Ethclorvynol	Placidyl®	500 mg
	Chloral betaine	Beta-Chlor®	0.87–1.7 g
	Triclofos sodium	Triclos®	1.5 g
Propyl alcohols	Meprobamate	Miltown®	1200–1600 mg
	Ethinimate	Valmid®	500–1000 mg
	Tybamate	Tybatran®	750–1000 mg
Piperidinediones	Glutethidimide	Doriden®	
	Methyprylon	Noludar®	50–400 mg
Quinazolones	Methaqualone	Quaalude®	150–300 mg
Benzodiazepines	Chlordiazepoxide	Librium®	5–25 mg
	Diazepam	Valium®	2–10 mg
	Oxazepam	Serax®	10–30 mg
	Chlorazepate	Tranxene®	3–14 mg
	Flurazepam	Dalmane®	15–50 mg

[a] Adapted from Cooper (1977).

drawal from them can be accompanied by REM rebound and other adverse reactions (cf. Kay et al., 1976). Ironically, persons complaining of insomnia who use drugs do *not* experience better sleep than persons complaining of insomnia but not using drugs (Kales et al., 1974).

Alcohol, since it is commonly available, may be the most common remedy—either by itself or in combination with accepted hypnotic medications (Spiegel, 1973). Indeed, the complaint of insomnia has been implicated as one of the factors in causing problem drinking (Bayh, 1972). Alcohol in combination with certain hypnotics can produce dangerous effects.

Flurazepam (Dalmane) is usually listed as the drug of choice because it appears to promote maximum improvement in sleep for most persons and also does not appear to lead to tolerance and dependence (Kales et al., 1974). It should be noted, however, that the long-term evaluation of the drug has included the administration of 30 mg (the usual clinical dose) more than 28 days in only two studies (Kales, Kales, Bixler, & Scharf, 1975; Dement, Zarcone, Hoddes, Smythe, & Carskadon 1973). Patients have been known to take more than the usual amount over long time periods yet the effects and side effects beyond 28 days remain unknown.

Sleep Recordings

All-night sleep recordings are expensive and time consuming to conduct but are essential for precise clinical diagnosis and research. Recordings yield plentiful data on a variety of variables, some of which are understood. However, clinical practice can probably proceed without benefit of all-night sleep recordings. Gilleminault and Dement (1977) estimated that 85% of the cases of narcolepsy, sleep apnea, nocturnal myoclonus, and restless legs can be diagnosed using judicious examination and interviews. However, *it should be remembered that information obtained from self-reports may not reflect the data that would be obtained from all-night sleep recordings.* Insomnia and daytime sleepiness are *complaints* that are not always related to one another or to poor sleep as measured in all-night sleep recordings. Persons complaining of insomnia perceive a relationship between daytime problems and nocturnal sleep disturbance. However, daytime sleepiness cannot always be attributed to disturbances in nighttime sleep. Dement (1972) has commented on the problem of "pseudoinsomnia": persons whose sleep appears normal by EEG standards but who complain of poor sleep. Pollak, McGregor, and Weitzman (1975) put normal sleeper-volunteers on a reversed sleep-wake cycle. They slept at times they were normally awake and attempted to function during normal sleep times. While their sleep was treated pharmacologically with flurazepam, daytime sleepiness was unaffected. Thus although their sleep was adequate (as measured normally) they still suffered from daytime sleepiness. Persons complaining of insomnia typically overestimate latency to sleep onset and underestimate nocturnal arousals and total sleep time (Carskadon et al., 1976; Frankel et al., 1976; Roth, Lutz, Kramer, & Tietz, 1977). Subjects receiving behavioral treatments for complaints of insomnia have reported significant improvement without significant change being found in variables derived from all-night sleep recordings (Hauri, 1978).

Two implications follow: First, the relative independence and interdependence between sleep recordings and self-reports are meaningful. Researchers need to study *both* to understand complaints associated with sleep more completely (cf. Davidson, 1978). Treatment strategies may alter the self-reported perceptions of sleep and the physiologically documented sleep behavior in different ways in different persons. Further, it seems essential to study *which* electrophysiological variables are correlated with the perception of poor sleep and fatigue and which change with treatment and the perception of improvement.

Second, when proceeding without benefit of an all-night sleep recording, the clinician needs to realize that while sleep may be the primary complaint, the person may not be experiencing a major sleep problem. Treatment may not need to focus on sleep at all. When subjects report improvement, treatment may have influenced sleep and daytime sleepiness or only the perception that each has been changed.

Behavior Analysis

A process view has suggested sleep disorders may be associated with disturbances (*a*) in the circadian cycle, (*b*) in the sleep-wake cycle, or (*c*) in disassociations between the sleep-wake and circadian cycles. Behavior analysis (cf. Table 6) is designed to illuminate various environmental, social, psychological, behavioral, or

Table 6.   Some Areas of Assessment for Treating the Complaints of Insomnia and Sleepiness

Other medications	Note side effects of other medications that are taken regularly
Physical tension	Excessive physical tension at bedtime may inhibit sleep and promote fatigue. Chronic physical tension during day may promote fatigue
Mental activity	Persistent thinking about transient problems; excessive "worries" may be a characteristic response of the person. Includes recurring thoughts about being unable to sleep well, beliefs about self-efficacy, and misattributions about causes of sleep problems
	Phobias about loss of consciousness; fear of nightmares (intermittent and/or recurring)
Diet	Specific foods, eaten prior to bedtime, may improve or diminish sleep quality (e.g., high-protein food or coffee)
	Weight loss may shorten sleep time, while weight gain may increase sleep time
	Specific foods or food allergies may promote sleepiness or fatigue
Circadian rhythm	Shifts in sleep schedule will produce sleep disturbance (e.g., travel, shift work)
	Failure to maintain regular sleep/wake schedule can result in disturbed sleep
	Person's sleep/wake cycle may be out of phase with demands of external environment (e.g., airline personnel)
	Person may have an irregular or atypical circadian rhythm
Daytime activities and environment	Person under chronic stress; can also contribute to physical and/or mental fatigue but not poor sleep
	Daytime environment that is noisy, crowded, light, hot, or humid
	Excessive exercise or lack of exercise may promote feelings of fatigue or sleepiness
Prebedtime (evening) activities	Evening activities can promote physical and mental arousal, making sleep onset difficult (e.g., family arguments, exciting television program)
Sleep environment	Bedroom may be excessively noisy, light, hot, humid
	Stimuli in the immediate sleep environment (bedroom) may evoke activities or thoughts incompatible with sleep (e.g., desk with work to be done; worry about finances)
	Activities conducted in bedroom may be incompatible or interfere with good sleep (e.g., sexual intercourse, discussions with bed partner)

physiological factors associated with these anomalies. From the analysis, various interventions can be developed and tested empirically until the therapist and client are satisfied with the outcomes. The analysis should include those areas reserved typically for personality assessment. For example, the diagnosis of "neurosis" and "psychosis" are typically correlated with disturbed sleep (Williams et al., 1974). It may be more useful, however, to conduct a behavior analysis to identify specific actions and thoughts labeled as neurotic or psychotic and to focus intervention on modifying specific patterns to reduce disturbed sleep.

PROBLEMS IN INITIATING AND MAINTAINING SLEEP

Complaints of insomnia may rank second only behind headaches as a health problem in the United States (Coates & Thoresen, 1977). The remainder of this chapter is devoted to this problem. Indeed, the clinician is more likely to encounter complaints of poor sleep than the other sleep disorders. Three topics are addressed: (*a*) current behavioral approaches to the complaint of insomnia; (*b*) the need to expand theory beyond current models and treatments to provide clinically efficacious treatments; and (*c*) the potential utility of the diagnostic framework presented in the preceding section in treating complaints of insomnia and drug-dependent insomnia.

Those occasional bouts of insomnia experienced by most persons or the frequent and chronic sleep difficulties experienced by a few are characterized by the experience of excessive physical or mental activity. This common experience has influenced contemporary behavioral approaches to the study of sleep and problems associated with it. It has been hypothesized that sleep will not occur unless the reticular activating system (RAS) acts to block stimuli to the cortex. Maintaining total sleep deprivation can require considerable external stimulation to maintain adequate RAS cortical activity. Spontaneously occurring insomnia occurs when exteroceptive and interoceptive stimulation plays on the central nervous system to maintain the waking state (Kleitman, 1963).

Heightened Physiological Arousal

Monroe's (1967) seminal study comparing good and poor sleepers is often cited to support the hypothesis that persons complaining of insomnia are more aroused physiologically than good sleepers. Monroe selected 16 good sleepers and 16 poor sleepers on the basis of responses to questionnaires about normal sleep patterns. The minimum requirement was that poor sleepers reported taking 60 or more minutes to fall asleep, usually woke up at least once during the night, and typically experienced difficulty in falling asleep. It should be noted that these poor sleepers did not perceive themselves as being insomniacs, and none used sleeping pills. Subjects slept in the lab for two consecutive nights during which their sleep and several physiological functions were monitored continuously. Poor sleepers showed significantly more time to sleep onset, a greater number of awakenings, including REM awakenings, higher percent of time in Stage 2, and more time awake after sleep onset. They also showed significantly less total sleep time and REM sleep. The poor sleepers showed considerably greater variability than good sleepers on several sleep variables (Total Sleep Time, Time Awake after Sleep Onset, Slow Wave Sleep, Time to Sleep Onset). While the two groups did not differ in heart rate per minute or pulse volume, the poor sleepers did show significantly higher rectal temperature, vasoconstrictions per minute, body movements per hour, and skin resistance. Hobson, Spagna, and Malenka (1978) more recently confirmed the findings regarding nocturnal movements. Six poor and six good sleepers were photographed at 15-minute intervals through the night. Poor and good sleepers showed no overlap on the "consolidation index" (the relative amount of time immobile during the night). Johns, Gay, Masterton, & Bruce (1971) selected two groups of male medical students on the basis of their responses to a sleep questionnaire. The poor sleepers had significantly greater levels of adrenocortical activity than did the good sleepers throughout the day and night.

Hyperarousal among poor sleepers may not be universal, however. Haynes, Follingstad, and McGowan (1974) studied the relationships between reported sleep patterns and resting frontalis EMG activity in 101 male and female college students (mean age 18.9 years). The average of four 64-second EMG measures with 20-second intertrial intervals correlated significantly but modestly with reported number of times awake ($r = .21$) and reported difficulty sleeping ($r = .22$) but not with reported time to fall to sleep ($r = .11$). Daytime EMG and global self-reports of sleep among young college students may not be an adequate test of the hyperarousal hypothesis. Good (1975) examined the relationship between frontalis muscle tension and sleep latency in nine poor and six good sleepers (21 to 61 years, mean age $= 31.4$). Each subject spent three nights in the lab. Frontalis EMG was measured while subjects relaxed in bed just prior to lights out and throughout the first sleep cycle. Poor sleepers did not show higher waking EMG levels than poor sleepers. Subjects entered Stage 2 with widely differing EMG levels (3.0 mV to 30 mV) and mean waking EMG did not correlate significantly with mean sleep latency ($r = -.23$, NS). Several studies have attempted to demonstrate positive relationships between reduction in indices of physiological arousal and improvement in sleep, using various relaxation strategies (cf. Borkovec & Hennings, 1978; Borkovec et al., 1979; Frankel et al., 1976; Haynes, et al., 1974; Lick & Heffler, 1977). None of these studies have produced evidence that improvement in sleep is correlated with reduction in physiological arousal.

The hypothesis that poor sleep results from elevated physiological arousal alone has received substantial report in only one study. The Johns et al. (1971) and the Haynes et al. (1974) studies relied on self-report to assess sleep and therefore may not be definitive tests of the hypothesis. The study by Good (1975) suggests that one common measure of arousal (frontalis EMG) is not correlated with sleep disturbance. The Monroe (1967) study clearly needs replication, especially because it has been widely used to justify physical muscle relaxation procedures in the treatment of the complaint of insomnia. The studies showed no relationship between physiological arousal and sleep-measured physiological arousal during treatment sessions and not at time of sleep onset or during sleep. Detection of relationships between arousal and sleep may require that measures with greater sensitivity be employed. This may be essential if mechanisms underlying insomnia and processes mediating treatment effects are to be found.

Personality and Psychopathology

Numerous studies have documented personality differences between good and poor sleepers. Monroe's (1967) poor sleepers, for example, scored significantly higher than good sleepers on 11 of 15 MMPI scales. Kales et al. (1976) used the MMPI to evaluate 124 subjects with the primary complaint of insomnia. Eighty-five percent of the subjects scored beyond a T-score of 70 ("pathological" range) on at least one scale. The scales most frequently elevated in rank order were: depression, hypochondriasis, psychopathic deviance, psychasthenia, schizophrenia, and hysteria. Other studies have typically found that poor sleepers scored higher on the MMPI or anxiety scales (e.g., Haynes et al., 1974; Roth et al., 1976; Carskadon et al., 1976; Karacan, Ilaria, Ware, Thornby, & Chambliss, 1978).

Kales et al. (1976) hypothesized that insomniacs are characterized by internal ways of handling stress (i.e., depression, apprehension, inhibition, rumination, and an inability to discharge anger outwardly). These unresolved psychological conflicts lead to emotional arousal and also physiological activation during sleep. This results in insomnia. Marchini, Coates, and Magistad (1980) used direct reports of behavior and mood to assess daytime functioning of insomniacs and normal sleeper controls. Subjects were issued electronic pagers and forms called the Marchini Monitoring Inventory (MMI). Over 5 days, they were paged every 1½ hours. When paged, they were required to mark down mood and activity on the MMI. Poor sleepers were less active and less involved than good sleepers. They reported considerable depression, but very little tension and anxiety. These moods seemed to be exaggerated in the morning and evening. It might be possible to improve mood, and possibly sleep, by increasing activity in the morning and evening.

Style of Thinking

Coursey, Buchsbaum, and Frankel (1975) compared 18 chronic insomniacs with 18 normals matched for age, sex, and education. Insomniacs scored significantly higher on the depression, psychasthenia, hysteria, and hypochondriasis scales of the MMPI, the Taylor Manifest Anxiety Scale, and Eyesenck's Neuroticism Scale. Subjects were also overly concerned about the past and the future on the Time-Competence Scale. The insomniacs showed lower evoked potential responses to sound. These authors hypothesized that poor sleep was not necessarily attributable to psychopathology, but rather to "thinking styles." They suggested that persons complaining of insomnia worry more and are often more depressed than good sleepers. Affectively charged ruminations result in poor sleep for these persons. It seems plausible that persons experiencing intense or ruminative thoughts prior to sleep could have difficulty falling asleep. If those thoughts recur or continue during sleep, maintaining sleep may also be difficult. Coates, Killen, Silverman, Marchini, Rosenthal, Sanchez, George, and Thoresen (1980) used the "think aloud" technique to describe the problem-solving skills of good and poor sleepers. In structured problems, good sleepers used more efficient problem-solving methods such as changing the conditions of the problem, surveying given information, and developing and generating hypotheses. In unstructured and life-related problems, poor sleepers emitted fewer problem, goal, and means statements and gave less consideration to consequences of actions or alternative solutions. Training in problem solving might be beneficial.

Mental activity continues during non-REM and REM sleep (Kamiya, 1961). Persons may vary, however, in the intensity and type of mentation experienced. Persons complaining of insomnia may experience continued cognitive activity, perhaps of an emotional nature, which (a) prevents sleep or (b) leads the person to perceive that he or she is not sleeping when they would be considered asleep by

EEG criteria. Rechtschaffen and Monroe (1969) cited data from an unpublished study comparing the mentation during sleep of good and poor sleepers. Good and poor sleepers showed no difference in dreams and nightmares. The poor sleepers, however, showed greater recall of thoughtlike mental activity during early non-REM sleep than did good sleepers. On 6 of 22 awakenings, the poor sleepers indicated that they had been awake just before being called by the experimenter. Only one good sleeper reported being awake at one awakening.

Slama (see Borkovec, 1979) tested this hypothesis using 10 poor sleepers (mean reported sleep onset of 90 minutes) and six good sleepers (mean sleep onset of 7 minutes). Subjects were placed in a sound-attenuated room during the day and asked to fall asleep. Subjects were awakened at the tenth consecutive epoch of Stage 2 sleep (an epoch equals 30 seconds), the next occurrence of Stage 2 sleep, and after five consecutive epochs of Stage 1 sleep. Poor sleepers took 18.9 minutes longer on the average to reach Stage 2 sleep than good sleepers. Upon awakening, all of the good sleepers reported being asleep, while only two of the 10 insomniacs reported being asleep. Six of the 10 insomniacs reached the second and third awakening periods; 4 of the 6 poor sleepers and none of the 6 good sleepers reported being asleep at the third awakening. The data from the first awakening suggest that poor sleepers do not preceive that they are sleeping although brain wave patterns indicate that sleep is present. Borkovec (1979) has suggested that cognitive activity may delay the onset of sleep and, if intense enough, may continue during sleep. If thoughts do continue during sleep, persons may perceive that they are not sleeping.

Borkovec and Hennings (1978), in a study involving moderately sleep-disturbed college students, found that reported cognitive intrusions but not bodily tension was associated with improvement in sleep after training in progressive muscle relaxation. Borkovec et al. (1979) replicated the findings using more severe insomniacs and all-night sleep recordings. Borkovec and Hennings (1978) also reported that poor sleepers performed less accurately in a time estimation task than subjects reporting tension during the day but undisturbed nighttime sleep. Training in progressive muscle relaxation increased accuracy of time perception that Borkovec (1979) interpreted as additional support for the cognitive intrusion hypothesis. Persons perceive that more time has passed when cognitive activity is increased. Progressive relaxation and other strategies may decrease cognitive activity prior to sleep and subsequently decrease perception of elapsed time.

Variability and Efficacy

It is also possible that marked variability in sleep from night to night is central to the complaint of insomnia. Poor sleepers, in contrast to good sleepers, show widely varying values on most sleep parameters from one night to the next (Coates et al., 1980; Karacan et al., 1971). This marked variability may dispose certain poor sleepers to interpret their sleep as a highly unpredictable phenomenon. This uncertainty might encourage a general feeling of impotence in being able to predict and produce good sleep consistently. Some indirect evidence for this view comes from comparisons of high- and low-hypnotizable nappers and nonnappers. Persons who scored higher on a scale designed to measure control of sleep fell asleep more quickly in the sleep laboratory at night and during daytime naps than those persons scoring lower on that scale (Evans, Gustafson, O'Connell, Orne, & Shor, 1970). In a subsequent study, Evans (1977) reported that persons who scored high on control of sleep also scored higher on hypnotizability. Further, hypnotizability seemed to be an important variable related to nonnapping but not to napping. Significantly more *low*-hypnotizable subjects who were nonnappers did not nap because they were unable to fall asleep; however, significantly more *high*-hypnotizable nonnappers did not nap because of time or preference. Low-hypnotizable nappers reported sleeping in the day because of fatigue, while high-hypnotizable nappers slept in the day for pleasure.

Ability to control cognitive activity (and ultimately sleep) may be one central mechanism predisposing a person to good and poor sleep. Conversely, lack of control over cognitive activity may lead not only to poor sleep but also to the perception that control is lacking. Because sleep is to them an unpredictable and uncontrollable phenomenon, it becomes something to worry about. These worries and beliefs can, in turn, make the person's sleep worse.

Arousal Associated with Sleep Stimuli

A variation on the hyperarousal hypothesis places the source of arousal on learned associations between the bed, bedroom, and bedtime and activities incompatible with sleep (e.g., reading, watching television, worrying, and arguing) (Bootzin & Nicassio (1978). Haynes et al. (1974), in one test of this hypothesis, surveyed 284 male and female college students (mean age = 20.8 years) enrolled in an introductory psychology class. Poor and good sleepers showed no differences in number of sleep-incompatible-behaviors in the bed and bedroom. Of course many college students live in one small room that is often shared by one other person. Additional tests are needed with other samples.

The Sleep System

Within the contemporary perspective the RAS and the sleep system must work in harmony for sleep to occur. Low RAS activity can result in quiet wakefulness or even Stage 1 sleep. Deeper sleep, however, may require the activation of the sleep (hypnogogic) system. Indirect evidence that the sleep system might be implicated comes from two sources. First, some patients at the Stanford University Sleep Disorder Center were found to have elevated levels of 5-hydroxyindoleactic acid (5-HIAA) in their cerebral spinal fluid (Guilleminault & Dement, 1977). Production of 5-HIAA in the brain is thought to be proportional to serotonergic neuroactivity. L-tryptophan has also been demonstrated to be an effective way of raising serotonin levels in the rat brain. Administration of L-tryptophan to some normal and mildly poor sleepers can reduce sleep latency (Hartmann, 1978).

Second, Sterman, Howe, and MacDonald (1970) reported that when cats were trained (via biofeedback) to increase sensori-motor rhythm (SMR) spindles (14 to 16 cps over the sensorimotor cortex), they also demonstrated increases in slow wave (Stage 3 and 4) sleep. Jordan, Hauri, and Phelps (1976) compared 10 good and 10 poor sleepers (age = 18 to 28) and reported that poor sleepers showed weaker SMR signal than good sleepers. The two groups did not differ in frontalis EMG. Two good sleepers and six poor sleepers (two of whom had SMR rates similar to good sleepers) were recorded for three nights in the lab. Insomniacs with high SMR rates slept like good sleepers while insomniacs with low SMR rates slept poorly. SMR correlated negatively with sleep latency ($r = -.64$) and positively with sleep efficiency ($r = .59$).

Sleep-Wake and Circadian Cycles

Hyperarousal and the inability to sleep may result from anomalies in the circadian cycles or disharmonies between the sleep-wake and circadian cycles. The Miles et al. (1977) study discussed earlier provides an example of periodic insomnia caused by an atypical (24.9 hour) circadian rhythm. No sleep problem was experienced as long as the man's imposed sleep-wake schedule and circadian cycles were in harmony. Insomnia occurred as the person was forced to try sleeping at times not favored by his circadian rhythms. Shift workers, airline personnel, and others may experience similar problems when they are forced to obtain sleep at times when circadian cycles favor their being awake, or to work when their circadian cycles favor sleep. Irregular schedules in which sleep and wake times are shifted frequently may also decrease sleep efficiency and increase daytime sleepiness.

Poor sleep may result from anomalies within the circadian cycle itself. The Monroe (1967) data, for example, might be interpreted from a different perspective. As expected, body temperature curves of good and poor sleepers fell when they retired and rose toward morning. By contrast, poor sleepers' body temperatures fell at bedtime but peaked after five hours and then began falling again. Disturbances in sleep throughout the night could represent abnormal fluctuations in rhythmic processes that then lead to disturbed sleep.

Idiopathic Insomnia, Pseudoinsomnia, and What Is Insomnia?

"Pseudoinsomnia" is used to refer to complaints of insomnia in the absence of abnormal sleep patterns as indicated by all-night sleep recordings (Dement, 1972). "Idiopathic" insomnia, on the other hand, refers to a complaint of insomnia supported by sleep recordings showing extended latency to sleep onset (greater than 30 or 60 minutes), and/or an excessive amount of wake time after sleep onset (greater than 30 or 60 minutes), an excessive number of arousals to Stage 1 or to full wakefulness, and/or short sleep time (less than 6 hours).

Borkovec (1979), see also Borkovec et al., (1979) has proposed that pseudo- and idiopathic insomniacs might represent different subtypes of insomnia characterized by different underlying mechanisms. Pseudoinsomnia is hypothesized to be a function of an overly active wakefulness system in combination with a normal sleep system. Cognitive intrusions, especially of an emotional nature, cause (a) increases in the peripheral physiological activity and (b) increases in the content and mood quality of non-REM mentation. Sleep and wakefulness became less distinguishable because the pseudoinsomniac is processing information prior to and following the occurrence of brain waves typically characteristic of sleep. By contrast idiopathic insomnia is seen as due to a weak sleep system. Peripheral physiological arousal and cognitive intrusions are considered a result of the weak sleep system.

The distinctions and hypotheses are interesting, but they should be regarded with caution. The sleep variables distinguishing idiopathic insomniacs from normal sleepers remain somewhat elusive. Table 7 presents results from six studies comparing poor sleepers who were drug-free for two or more weeks with sex and age-matched normal sleeper controls. Consistent differences between the groups emerged on latency to sleep onset, total sleep time, and percent of sleep efficiency. But the absolute magnitude of the differences is small compared to reductions in sleep that are well tolerated by normal sleepers (Webb and Agnew, 1974; Johnson & Mc-Leod, 1973). Carskadon, Mitler, Billiard, Phillips, & Dement (1975) compared 109 subjects with normal controls and reported that 38.5% of the insomniacs were within one standard deviation of the normal mean for total sleep time and 52.3% for sleep latency. In addition, 11% of the "insomniacs" were above the normal range for sleep time and 2% were below the normal range for sleep latency. One-half of the subjects could not be discriminated from normals by total sleep time nor sleep latency. The distinctions may emerge, for example, with multivariate analyses. Coates, Killen, George, Marchini, Silverman, Hamilton, & Thoresen (1980) used multiple discriminant function analysis and cross-classification tables. A combination of variables relating to REM sleep arousals and sleep efficiency percent resulted in 100% correct classification of good and poor sleepers.

"Idiopathic" insomniacs might be distinguished from normal sleepers on more subtle variables than these which have been examined. Karacan et al. (1971), Frankel et al. (1976) and Carskadon et al. (1975) suggested that persons complaining of insomnia may suffer from an intrasleep defect characterized by decreased delta or excessive arousals. From this perspective, "pseudoinsomniacs" may not be "pseudo" at all. Their complaint may have a physiological basis that cannot be documented given current methods for scoring all-night sleep recordings.

The implications are clear, however. (*a*) Physiological bases for the complaint of insomnia remain elusive and are likely to remain so until a basic understanding of physiological and psychological functions of sleep are increased. (*b*) Behavioral treatments for the complaint of insomnia may have to do with more than increase total sleep time or decrease latency to sleep onset. (*c*) "Pseudo" and "idiopathic" insomniacs may or may not differ in substantial ways. Research on process and treatment variables for both need to continue.

Treatment Strategies

Table 8 presents a variety of strategies that have been applied and evaluated in treating the complaint of insomniacs. Relaxation is designed to reduce both physical and mental arousal. Progressive muscle relaxation, autogenic training, and EMG biofeedback focus primarily on reducing muscle tension, but probably also may reduce cognitive activity because they help the person to focus on specific thoughts. Meditation and electrosleep reduce cognitive activity which, in turn, may influence physical arousal. Stimulus control treatments are designed to bring sleeping under the control of cues in the person's sleep environment: the bed, the bedroom, and bedtime. Rather than permitting these cues to initiate behaviors, mental

Table 7. Results from Studies Comparing Persons Complaining of Insomnia with Sex and Age-Matched Controls

	Monroe (1969)		Karacan et al. (1971)		Frankel et al. (1976)		Gillin et al. (1979)	Beutler et al. (1978)		Coates et al. (1980)[d]	
	Poor Sleepers	Good Sleepers	Poor Sleepers	Good Sleepers	Poor Sleepers	Good Sleepers	Poor Sleepers[a]	Poor Sleepers	Good Sleepers	Poor Sleepers	Good Sleepers
N	16	16	10	10	18	18		22	22	12	12
Age	20–40	20–40	30.55	30.55	44.5 (16.8)	45.1 (16.8)	44 (2.0)			20–60	20–60
No. of recording nights	1	1	2 or 3	2 or 3	4	4	3–6	2		3	3
Minutes to sleep onset	15.2 (15.8)	7.4 (6.9)*	37.8 (26.8)	10.6 (5.7)	54.0 (39.8)	18.2 (7.9)**	22**		9.3*	23.60	10.81**
Total sleep time (minutes)	346.5 (60.6)	388.6 (29.4)**	340.7 (87.7)	391.2 (32.4)	339.5 (29.4)	382.8 (33.0)**	380**	85.4	93.3*	360.06	390.80
Sleep efficiency percent[c]	—	—	81.0 (1.4)	93.0 (0.7)*	76.5 (6.9)	87.8 (5.9)**	88***			83.6	91.2**
Minutes awake after sleep onset	60.6 (42.1)	31.4 (29.3)**	—	—	40.5 (33.4)	30.6 (22.5)	28	4.6	4.0	30.1	19.9
Number of arousals	3.9 (1.8)	2.3 (1.6)	—	—	6.7 (3.8)	7.2 (4.0)	—	24.7%	24.8%[b]	11.9	11.7
Minutes of REM	58.7 (27.7)	95.3 (23.0)**	—	—	85.9 (12.0)	91.7 (17.7)	90 (3.0)	—	—	79.7	77.4
Latency of REM (minutes)	97.3 (32.8)	105.0 (19.5)	—	—	68.6 (16.6)	73.9 (22.2)	78.0	9.5%	8.0%	88.1	93.4
Minutes of delta sleep	—	—	—	—	9.0 (14.5)	14.9 (19.8)*	24.0*	—	—	7.14	12.07
Percent delta sleep	—	—	8.6 (11.9)	12.7 (7.8)	—	—	—	—	—	1.95	3.11
Minutes to first delta sleep	—	—	60.0 (34.2)	28.6 (16.9)*	—	—	—	—	—		

* p < .05.
** p < .01.
[a] Most values were estimated from histograms.
[b] Percent not minutes were presented in the absence of information about total sleep time; we could not calculate minutes in each sleep stage.
[c] Proportion of time asleep divided by total time in bed.
[d] Completed in subjects' homes.

Table 8. Behavioral Treatments for the Complaint of Insomnia

Progressive muscle relaxation (Bernstein & Borkovec, 1973; Borkovec et al., 1979)	Tense and relax specific muscle groups (e.g., forearms, biceps, neck) systematically; focus on feelings of relaxation; usually done prior to bedtime
Autogenic training (Nicassio & Bootzin, 1974; Traub, Jencks, & Bliss, 1973)	Systematically focus on specific muscle groups (e.g., arms, legs); self-suggestion regarding feelings of warmth or heaviness in those muscles
Meditation (cognitive focusing) (Woolfolk, Carr-Kaffashan, McNulty, & Lehrer, 1976)	Focus on single mental stimulus (e.g., word, phrase, image or sound) that is imagined subvocalized repeatedly; usually done prior to bedtime
Biofeedback (Freedman & Papsdorf, 1976; Hauri and Cohen, 1977)	EMG: to relax specific muscles (usually frontalis) EEG: to increase central or occipital alpha or theta activity
Stimulus control (Bootzin, 1972; Haynes, Price, & Simons, 1975)	Associate bed and bedroom only with sleep; eliminate or reduce activities incompatible with sleep in bedroom, while in bed, and at bedtime; person must leave bed and bedroom if not sleeping or engaged in sexual activity
Sensorimotor rhythm biofeedback (cf. Feinstein, Sterman, & MacDonald, 1974; Hauri, 1978; Jordan, Hauri, & Phelps, 1976)	Increase sensorimotor rhythm (14 cps activity over the sensorimotor cortex)
Paradoxical intention (Ascher & Efran, 1978)	Person is instructed to try to remain awake; this decreases thoughts interfering with sleep by decreasing anxiety about sleeping well and negative consequences the next day

activities, and physical arousal, the person learns to associate these cues with mental and physical states conducive to sleep. Five rules are followed: (*a*) lie down intending to go to sleep only when you are sleepy; (*b*) do not read or watch television in the bedroom; (*c*) if you find yourself unable to fall asleep (usually within 10 minutes) get up and go into another room, stay as long as you wish, and then return to the bedroom to sleep; (*d*) if you still cannot fall asleep repeat step 3—do this as often as is necessary throughout the night; and (*e*) do not nap, and arise at the same time each morning (Bootzin, 1972).

Zwart and Lisman (1979) evaluated a temporal control strategy (do not nap during the day, and arise at the same time each morning) and found it to be as effective as the complete stimulus control approach presented above with college students complaining of moderate sleep disturbance. The stimulus-control strategy may be effective, not because of the hypothesized reconditioning of responses to the physical environment, but because the person's sleep-wake and circadian cycles are consistently more harmonized.

Paradoxical instruction is a relative newcomer to the treatment of the complaint of insomnia. Ascher and Efran (1978) explored its use as an ancillary treatment with individuals for whom relaxation and desensitization seemed insufficient. Five clients who experienced severe difficulty in falling asleep were exposed to training in progressive relaxation for 10 weeks. When little improvement was noted, the clients were requested to *remain awake* for as long as possible—to exaggerate the very behavior they would like to reduce. Such instructions were designed to reduce anxiety associated with attempting to fall to sleep and to use therapeutic instructions "correctly." The strategy was reported to be successful with all five clients.

How Effective Are These Strategies?

These psychological strategies, built primarily on behavioral and biofeedback rationales, have shown *promise* in providing alternatives to hypnotic medication for treating the complaint of insomnia (cf. Bootzin and Nicassio, 1978; Knapp, Downs, & Alperson, 1976; Montgomery, Perkins, & Wise, 1975). These treatments *appear* especially strong when evaluated using self-reported estimates of sleep quantity and quality, and when efficacy is judged primarily by reductions in latency to sleep onset (cf. Coates & Thoresen, 1977). However, the apparent efficacy of behavioral strategies reported in many experimental studies must be balanced against the modest to negative outcomes obtained (*a*) in the few studies employing both self-report and all-night sleep recording data; (*b*) when strategies are evaluated with subjects who are older, who have experienced insomnia for two years or more, who present themselves at clinics for treatment, or who are referred by physicians; and (*c*) when a variety of variables relating to sleep quantity and quality (e.g., sleep efficiency, number of arousals) are monitored (cf. Thoresen, Coates, Zarcone, Kirmil-Gray, & Rosekind, 1980; Killen & Coates, in press).

Borkovec, Grayson, O'Brien and Weerts (1979) found that progressive relaxation was superior to no treatment but not to placebo in reducing latency to onset of Stage 1 sleep. However, latencies during baseline recordings averaged less than 30 minutes in each of the three treatment groups. These college students also received course credit for participation and payment for completion of all-night sleep recordings. Freedman and Papsdorf (1976) reported that frontalis EMG biofeedback and progressive muscle relaxation reduced latency to sleep onset (measured by laboratory all-night sleep recordings) relative to those of the placebo group. However, no significant reductions in other variables (e.g., minutes awake after sleep onset, number of arousals) were found. The authors questioned the clinical utility of reducing latencies alone by an average of 20 minutes.

Borkovec et al. (1979), selected college students who reported taking 60 minutes or longer to fall asleep and perceived difficulty as well. They were classified as pesudoinsomniac if the ratio of self-reported latency to physiologically recorded latency was greater than 1.5; subjects were labeled idiopathic insomniacs if they fell below this dividing line. Subjects were randomly assigned to progressive relaxation, no-tension-release relaxation, or to a no-treatment control. Progressive relaxation produced a significantly greater reduction in reported latency to sleep onset than did the other two treatments. Similarly, progressive relaxation produced significantly greater reduction in EEG latency among the idiopathic insomnia group. It should be noted, however, that the progressive relaxation idiopathic insomniacs differed at pretreatment ($\bar{X} = 63.5$) (albeit nonsignificantly) from the idiopathic insomniacs in the other two groups ($\bar{X} = 34.9$ and 34.9). Differences at posttreatment were not striking ($\bar{X} = 25.3, 30.8, 34.9$).

Age and severity of the complaints may decrease positive response to treatment. Frankel, Coursey, Gaarder, and Mott (1976) reported that EMG biofeedback and autogenic training were *ineffective* in reducing the latency to sleep onset or increasing sleep efficiency in chronic and severe insomniacs (mean age = 38). Hauri and Good (see Hauri, 1978) did not obtain positive results using biofeedback (frontalis EMG or frontalis EMG + theta). Subjects in each of these latter two studies were comparable in severity of disturbed sleep and resembled quite closely those persons commonly referred to sleep clinics for evaluation and treatment (Hauri, 1976). It was reported that Hauri's subjects were 15 years older on the average than subjects in the Freedman and Papsdorf study (Freedman et al., 1978).

Hauri (1978) reported modest effects using biofeedbacks with chronic and severe insomniacs. Centrofrontal sensorimotor rhythm (SMR) biofeedback increased sleep efficiency from 80.3 to 86.1% in 10 subjects, while frontalis EMG biofeedback increased sleep efficiency from 77.9 to 85.7% in 10 others. EMG + theta biofeedback and no-treatment control subjects showed no changes. Subjects in all three treatment groups perceived that their sleep had improved.

FINDING EFFECTIVE METHODS: SUGGESTED RESEARCH AND TREATMENT STRATEGIES

Effective treatment for the complaint of insomnia may require two significant departures from current models. First, treatments have generally focused on reducing latency to sleep onset. Much more effort is needed in reducing minutes awake after sleep onset, number of awakenings, and increasing sleep efficiency as well as increasing slow wave sleep. These variables appear to discriminate poor from good sleepers much more reliably than latency to sleep onset alone (cf. Carskadon et al., 1976; Coates et al., 1980; Frankel et al., 1976). *These variables may also be more difficult to change.*

Second, treatment programs may need to be tailored to individuals. Rather than assuming that sleep disturbance arises from a unitary source, it will be more efficacious to build treatments on the emerging view that heterogeneous sources can lead to similar complaints and disturbance patterns.

Empirical support for these points comes from three studies. While noting that EMG biofeedback and autogenic training did not affect group means, Frankel et al. (1976), did report that three of six biofeedback and two of six autogenic subjects showed significant improvement (50% decrease in laboratory sleep latency). Similarly, Traub, Jencks, and Bliss (1974) used autogenic training; three of seven subjects reduced latency to sleep onset while two increased slow wave sleep. Finally, Hauri (1978) reanalyzed his data. He concluded that EMG and SMR feedback might be useful in certain types of insomnia if patients can be matched to an appropriate treatment mode.

Treating Sleep Maintenance Insomnia: A Case Study

The following case study conducted over a five-year period reinforces the need for a flexible approach to the complaint of insomnia and suggests additional treatment leads (Coates & Thoresen, 1979). The client was a 58-year-old female with a 33-year history of insomnia accompanied by complaints of daytime sleepiness and depression. She had used a variety of sleep medications at various times including diazepam (Valium®), secobarbital (Seconal®), and meprobamate (Equanil®). These were discontinued, however, after she learned of their negative effects while participating in a Drug Evaluation Study (Year 1). The client ended her 23-year marriage with a divorce four years prior to treatment. She was currently completing a master's degree and teaching part time in a community college. She had been in Jungian psychotherapy for the previous three years and continued seeing her therapist weekly or biweekly during Year 2 of the study. Contacts were monthly or less during Years 3, 4, and 5. She reported that this therapy had no effect on her sleep but had bolstered her self-esteem. A radical mastectomy three years prior to treatment and chronic spinal arthritis caused occasional pain; recurring facial skin cancer required intermittent surgery. Prescreening physical examinations revealed no other disorders; one diagnostic all-night sleep recording prior to the Year 1 study found no evidence of sleep apnea or nocturnal myoclonus.

Treatment Program

During Year 1 the client participated as a paid subject in the short-term evaluation of a hypnotic medication (HUF-2333, Perlapine®). One year later (Year 2), she was referred to us for treatment. She had been complaining of extended minutes to sleep onset, excessive number of awakenings during the night, and daytime sleepiness and depression. She also reported being unable to return to sleep easily on about four nights per week. We began collaborating with her to develop and evaluate strategies to reduce her poor sleep and daytime sleepiness. An ongoing analysis of her problem assessed by interviews, all-night sleep recordings, and the Daily Sleep Diary shaped the strategies employed.

The sleep recordings for Years 1 through 5 were conducted in the laboratory. In Year 5 additional recordings were conducted in her home (cf. Coates et al., 1978). The Daily Sleep Diary was completed every day for 14 consecutive weeks during Year 2 and for two consecutive weeks during Years 3, 4, and 5. Each morning upon arising she estimated minutes to sleep onset, number of awakenings during the night, minutes awake during the night, and total sleep time on the Daily Sleep Diary. At every hour during the day she recorded her feelings of sleepiness on a scale of 1 (alertness) to 7 (almost asleep) on the Stanford Sleepiness Scale—SSS (Hoddes, Zarcone, Smythe, Phillips, & Dement, 1973). A sleepiness rating was computed each day by averaging the hourly ratings.

Table 9 outlines the successive treatment phases employed; Figure 4 presents weekly medians for self-reported sleep and daytime sleepiness, and the number of nights each week in which each variable exceeded a criterion judged by the client to reflect poor sleep (i.e., 30 minutes or greater latency to sleep onset and minutes awake after sleep onset; two or more wakenings per night; SSS ratings equal to or greater than 4.0). The client reported immediate reductions in sleep onset with relaxation training (Weeks 2–4). Reductions in minutes awake after sleep onset and number of arousals did not occur until Week 4. Corresponding decreases in daytime sleepiness were also reported.

The first important suggestion for departures from standard relaxation treatment emerged during Weeks 5 and 6 when reported latency to sleep onset increased dramatically (Figure 4). In exploring the reasons for this through interviews and in-

Table 9.   Treatment Components and Evaluation Time Line

Year	Phase	Days		Number of Sleep Recordings
Year 1: Drug evaluation study (Perlapine®)	Baseline to placebo	6		6
	Drug	6		6
	Recovery to placebo			3
Year 2: Self-management training	Baseline	7	One session; client begins keeping daily sleep diaries; emphasis was placed on trial-and-error approach;	2
	Relaxation training	21	Five sessions; trained in progressive relaxation, mental imagery (self-hypnosis) application to sleep onset and to awakening in the middle of the night	
	Problem-solving	70	Seven sessions devoted to solving additional problems presenting good sleep and maintenance of gains	
			Time-management: Client reported procrastinating on preparation for school and staying up late, which interfered with sleep; rearrange schedule to reduce arousing activities in evening	
			Positive self-thoughts: Negative self-thoughts increase tension; write down two positive accomplishments each day	
			Cue-controlled relaxation: Relax on cue during tension-arousing situation	2
Year 3: Follow-up		14		
Year 4: Follow-up		14		2
Year 5: Follow-up		14		3 in lab
				3 at home

spection of sleep diaries, we found that evenings preceding poor sleep were marked by intensive preparation for the next morning's classes. The client reported procrastinating until the evening before, preparing until late in the evening, and then retiring with the worry that she had not prepared her classes adequately. The time management procedures instituted in response appeared effective by client report (Table 9). At Week 9, poor sleep was blamed on doubts about teaching ability and other stresses during the day. This led to positive self-evaluation training and cue-controlled relaxation. Once all sleep variables stabilized at acceptable levels, reported daytime sleepiness declined as well.

Data from all-night sleep recordings are presented in Table 10 and Figure 5;

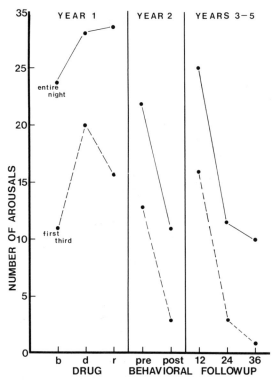

FIGURE 4. Number of arousals (to full wakefulness or Stage 1) during the baseline (*b*), drug (*d*), and recovery (*r*) phases of the Year 1 drug study; before and after self-management training in Year 2, and at the follow-up evaluations in Years 3, 4, and 5. All data are from laboratory all-night sleep recordings.

these provide convergent evidence for the reported outcomes and also demonstrate discrepancies between reported and recorded disturbance. Year 1 and Year 2 recordings showed that total sleep time and minutes to sleep onset were close to normal. By contrast, minutes awake after sleep onset and number of arousals were high, especially in the first third of the night during baseline of both years. The experimental drug reduced minutes awake after sleep onset, but the number of arousals increased and this increase persisted into the recovery phase. Year 2 baseline values are quite similar to those reported one year earlier. Training seemed especially effective in improving sleep during the first part of the night. Although minutes awake after sleep onset decreased by only 10 minutes during the entire night, a reduction of 31 minutes was found in the first third of the night. Arousals declined by 50%; again the most dramatic improvement occurred during the first third of the night.

Sleep worsened considerably Year 3, but improved again in Years 4 and 5. This provided an additional insight of potential importance. The client attributed her poor sleep in Year 3 to spinal arthritis and facial cancer; both caused pain and the latter caused worry because of impending surgery and anticipated facial scars. But a noteworthy outcome emerged from her reports about progress and apparent setbacks. At the three months' follow-up in Year 2, the client reported that sleep

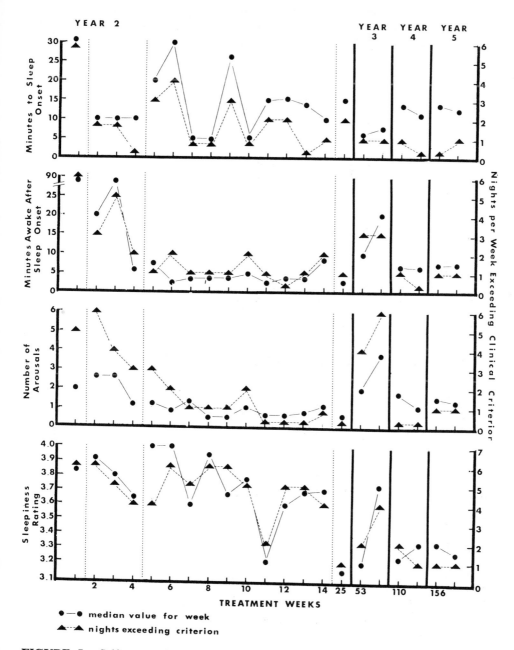

FIGURE 5. Self-report data during the treatment and follow-up evaluations. The Year 2 data are divided into four phases: baseline (Week 1), relaxation training (Weeks 2–4), problem-solving and maintenance (Weeks 5–14), and follow-up (Week 25). Data were taken daily on all variables. Triangles represent the number of nights in a given week in which the variable exceeded a value judged by the client to reflect poor sleep (30 minutes or greater minutes to sleep onset and minutes awake after sleep onset, two or more awakenings per night, a rating of 4.0 or greater on the Stanford Sleepiness Scale).

Table 10. Data on Sleep from All-Night Sleep Recordings

| Variable Statistic: | Drug Evaluation Year 1 | | | Self-Management Training Year 2 | | Follow-up Evaluations | | Year 5 | | Norms[c] |
	Baseline (6)[a]	Drug (6)	Recovery (3)	Pre (2)	Post (2)	Year 3 (2)	Year 4 (2)	Lab (2)[b]	Home (3)	Mean (S.D.)
Sleep length (minutes)										
Total sleep time	413.4	552.7	459.1	448.0	463.0	413.0	416.0	381.0*	404.5	430.8(34.9)
Latency to sleep onset	8.3	13.4	21.0*	18.0*	10.0	14.0	5.5	10.0	8.5	10.6(5.0)
Minutes awake after										
Sleep onset	54.5*	26.4	39.4*	41.0*	31.0	100.0*	28.5	50.0*	19.5	24.0(9.3)
First third only	24.7	8.6	24.0	33.0	2.0	25.0	11.5	4.5	4.3	—
Number of arousals	24.4*	31.7*	33.0*	22.0*	11.0	25.0*	11.5	10.3	11.4	13.6(2.57)
First third only	11.4	20.1	16.9	13.0	3.0	16.0	3.0	2.0	5.3	—
Sleep efficiency[d]	86.8	93.3	88.4	88.4	91.8	78.4*	92.4	87.8	93.6	93.0(7.0)
Latency to first REM (minutes)	105.7	96.8	113.6*	161.0*	83.0	165.0*	87.0	88.8	82.5	85.7(26.5)
Sleep stages										
Percent Stage 1	9.0*	6.4	6.7	4.0	6.0	4.6	8.6*	4.0	3.7	4.9(2.2)
Percent Stage 2	49.3	65.5	63.5	45.5	54.2	56.9	52.4	69.1	70.4	57.8(6.5)
Percent Stage 3	11.9	6.2	7.1	14.5	10.1	8.7	7.8	6.0	3.1	6.5(2.4)
Percent Stage 4	4.6	0.6	0.1	7.8	13.6	10.2	11.7	0.0	0.0	4.1(5.3)
Percent REM	24.6	20.7	22.1	28.1	15.9	18.4	23.5	19.7	22.2	21.8(3.3)

(From Coates & Thoresen, 1979; reprinted with permission)
[a] Numbers in parentheses refer to the number of consecutive all-night sleep recordings conducted.
[b] One recording eliminated from analysis because of technician error.
[c] Norms for 50–59-year-old women from Williams, Karacan, and Hursch (1974).
[d] Proportion of time asleep divided by total time in bed.
* Value beyond mean ± 1 standard deviation of norms.

had become rather automatic: "My body has learned to tumble into bed and to go to sleep." The physical problems experienced during Year 3 provided an unplanned reversal; sleep improved during Years 4 and 5 following improvement in physical health. Yet the client told us of periods before and after Year 3 and during Years 4 and 5 in which sleep was poor. Most important, she reported that even during these periods she no longer labeled herself an insomniac because, "I know I have the resources to manage poor sleep when it occurs." From her report, she did not experience a "cure" in the traditional sense; she still experiences some poor sleep, but she now believes that she has a variety of skills for improving sleep and believes that she can use them when necessary.

In the insomnia treatment literature it appears that biofeedback and relaxation treatments might be administered with the expectation that these procedures will work more or less automatically (much like a medication) to improve poor sleep. Bandura (1977) has proposed that all therapies are effective to the degree that they increase the client's sense of self-efficacy that he or she can perform specific actions to resolve specific problems. From this client's reports, the perception of helplessness appeared central to her complaint. Prior to treatment she never knew when good sleep might be forthcoming, much less how to produce it. Following treatment, poor sleep was of much less concern because she felt she had the resources to cope with it. Thus it may be crucial to structure treatment programs to ensure that clients acquire specific problem-solving and self-management skills, and that patients express feelings of mastery in using these skills to manage those conditions influencing their sleep.

A MULTICOMPONENT TREATMENT FOR THE COMPLAINT OF INSOMNIA

Our goal has been to develop treatment programs that (a) permit assessment of a wide variety of variables potentially related to a person's poor sleep, and (b) use this assessment in a differential application of treatment strategies. In addition, it seems important to enhance the client's sense of personal efficacy for controlling those conditions associated with poor sleep. Table 11 presents a prototype multicomponent treatment for the complaint of insomnia. Problem-solving is the key notion. Both client and therapist need to consider the potential relevance of a wide variety of variables and the importance of changes across several dimensions of the client's life, activities, and characteristic responses. (Thoresen, Coates, Kirmil-Gray, & Rosekind, in press).

Treating Drug Dependent Insomnia: Two Case Studies

Two case studies provide an example of the method by which this comprehensive treatment program can be applied to a complex sleep problem. Drug-dependent insomnia refers to disturbed sleep, maintained primarily by the chronic use of hypnotic medication. Kales et al. (1974) monitored 10 patients, each of whom had been taking hypnotic medications (chloral hydrate, glutethidimide, pentobarbital, secobarbital) chronically for 4 months to 10 years. In comparison with insomniac

Table 11.   A Self-Management Approach to Treating the Complaint of Insomnia

Assessment (2–4 weeks)	All-night sleep recording, physical and neurological examination, psychiatric examination, psychometric evaluation
	Personal, medical, sleep, and medication history
	Sleep environment, chronic stress and tension, work demands and environments, depression, other factors (e.g., eating habits, caffeine consumption, daily schedule, exercise)
	Spouse and family interview; spouse or roommate behavioral checklist
Concurrent	
Relaxation training (3–4 weeks)	Progressive muscle relaxation
	Self-hypnosis (cognitive focusing skills)
	Clients use cassette tapes for home practice
Cognition restructuring (2–3 weeks)	Basic information about sleep and sleep processes; practice using thoughts conducive to good sleep; analysis of beliefs about sleep problem; analysis of beliefs about ability to learn new skills and change behavior associated with sleep problems
Problem-solving (2–4 weeks)	Analysis of behavioral, environmental, and cognitive conditions related to poor sleep; design individualized strategies for improving disturbed sleep; evaluate and modify as needed
Maintenance (3–6 months)	Spaced sessions to note progress, promote continued use of strategies, and identify and change other behaviors, thoughts, or environments still related to poor sleep. Increased responsibility placed on client to analyze and propose solutions and evaluate progress

controls who were not receiving medication, the chronic drug users showed significantly decreased REM sleep but increased Sleep Latency and Minutes Awake After Sleep Onset. Persons on sleeping medications were sleeping *worse* than persons not taking sleep medications! When drugs have been used repeatedly over a long period, abrupt withdrawal may result in disturbed sleep and nightmares. Physical discomfort associated with withdrawal and apprehension contribute to the problem. Thus the person is trapped: sleep is poor when taking the medication but becomes even worse during withdrawal. Even if withdrawal is accomplished, there is no guarantee that sleep will improve. The strategy we have developed for treating drug-dependent insomnia combines suggestions for gradual withdrawal and close monitoring with the comprehensive self-management strategy outlined in Table 11.

The two subjects, Mary and Paula, had suffered from insomnia for a number of years and had experimented with a variety of sleep medications to improve their sleep. Mary was ingesting 600 mg of methyprylon (Noludar®) per day and 30 mg chlordiazepoxide (Librium®) initially, while Paula's bromide consisted of 15 mg of diazepam (Valium®) and 12–15 ounces of dry wine at bedtime. Withdrawal was designed to be safe, minimally disruptive to sleep, and to cause the least amount of discomfort.[1] A relatively safe hypnotic drug at a dosage that ensured sleep was prescribed (Table 12). When self-management training began, the drug was with-

---

[1] We are indebted to Vincent Zarcone, M.D., of the Stanford Sleep Disorders Clinic, for collaborating with us in this work and for supervising drug withdrawal.

Table 12.   Treatment Programs for the Two Persons with Drug-Dependent Insomnia[a]

	Mary	Paula
Description	Female, 53 years old, insomnia for 25 years	Female, 37 years old, insomnia for 20 years
Pretreatment	600 mg methyprylon + 30 mg chlordiazepoxide at bedtime; 30 mg chlordiazepoxide t.i.d.	15 mg diazepam + 12–15 ounces of wine at bedtime
Withdrawal plan	Sleep stabilized at 300 mg methyprylon + 30 mg chlordiazepoxide at bedtime; methyprylon first withdrawn by 100 mg week; chloridiazepoxide withdrawn by 10 mg/week	Stabilize sleep at 30 mg diazepam at 2.5 mg/week; stop drinking wine
Treatment sequence	1. Assessment (2 weeks) 2. Relaxation training (3 weeks) and cognitive restructuring (2 weeks) 3. Problem-solving (4 weeks) + maintenance (cue-controlled relaxation)	1. Assessment (2 weeks) 2. Relaxation training (2 weeks) and cognitive restructuring (1 week) 3. Problem solving (6 weeks) + maintenance (anticipation training; activity planning)

[a] From Thoresen, et al. (1980).

drawn at the rate of one therapeutic dose per week. Clients were informed about the mechanisms of drug action and warned about possible side effects and reactions to withdrawal. Treatment continued until they were completely withdrawn and sleep was maintained at a relatively acceptable level.

Specific withdrawal plans and treatment programs for Mary and Paula are presented in Table 12. Note that the treatment varied for each client within the general program format. Drug dosage was reduced according to the rate at which the drug could be withdrawn and reasonably good sleep maintained. Similarly, each client learned relaxation and cognitive focusing skills following assessment. However, the length of training varied in each case according to the rate at which these skills were mastered and used successfully. Finally, the program became completely individualized during the problem-solving phase.

Mary taught seventh grade English in a lower socioeconomic school. Because she attributed much of her poor sleep to the stresses imposed by students and administrators, she learned cue-controlled relaxation during problem solving. Paula, by contrast, experienced frequent mild to moderate depression. Anticipation training (Anton, Dunbar, & Friedman, 1976) was taught as one method of managing her depressive experiences.

Two consecutive all-night sleep recordings were conducted for each subject on three different occasions: prior to treatment, two weeks following final withdrawal, and six months following final withdrawal. The results are presented in Table 13. The drugs had predictable effects. Both clients reduced total sleep time but increased sleep efficiency. In addition, Mary experienced fewer arousals to wakefulness in Stage 1. Both reported needing less sleep, feeling more refreshed during the day, and having increased energy in the morning.

Table 13. Results of All-Night Sleep Recording Data While Subjects Were on Drugs, During Withdrawal, and at 6 Months Following Treatment[a]

	Mary			Paula		
	Pre-treatment	Withdrawal	6 Month Follow-up	Pre-treatment	Withdrawal	6 Month Follow-up
Total sleep time (minutes)	454.0	310.5	336.0	399.7	327.0	375.0
Latency to sleep onset (minutes)	41.5	14.0	5.5	24.7	32.0	3.0
Minutes awake after sleep onset	39.0	12.5	20.0	27.6	22.5	26.5
Sleep efficiency[b]	84.7	91.1	93.1	86.9	83.3	92.1
Number of arousals	34.0	39.5	20.0	27.6	22.5	26.5
Percent Stage 1	9.5	10.0	8.8	10.5	9.9	11.1
Percent Stage 2	69.2	36.8	56.0	69.8	51.1	31.4
Percent Stage 3	2.5	11.6	6.0	0.6	10.1	17.6
Percent Stage 4	0.0	21.3	10.7	0.0	5.8	15.6
Percent Stage REM	18.1	19.0	18.0	14.9	21.4	24.3
Onset to REM 1	129.0	75.5	66.5	209.3	98.5	123.0

[a] Data based on the average of two consecutive laboratory sleep recordings.
[b] Time asleep divided by total time in bed times 100.

WHERE DO WE GO FROM HERE?

The complaint of insomnia and other behaviors and complaints associated with sleep are not simple riddles with single answers. Some important groundwork has been laid in understanding and treating these problems. A balanced assessment of progress, however, still leaves us primarily in the dark. Major questions remain regarding physiological, psychological, and environmental processes underlying these behaviors and complaints. Some interesting empirical data have been produced but their meaning remains clouded by lack of compelling theory. Effective treatment of behaviors and complaints associated with sleep remain an important objective. Again, some interesting beginnings show promise; their efficacy and applicability await clarification of which variables to focus on in alleviating complaints of poor or disturbed sleep, as well as clarification on major processes regulating sleep and complaints about poor sleep. Moving from where we are to where we need to be can be facilitated by three key strategies: (a) encouraging theoretical flexibility; (b) conducting definitive (rather than convenient) empirical tests; and (c) using alternative research designs and dependent measures.

Theory

Theoretical flexibility is demanded by our relative ignorance of sleep in general and behaviors and complaints associated with sleep in particular. No single theory or model can, at present, explain the perplexing array of empirical findings or provide compelling rationales to shed light on complaints associated with sleep. No approach or perspective should be viewed as sacrosanct, including the 24-hour sleep-wake view we have recommended. To the contrary, every perspective and assumption should be viewed with caution lest we adopt prematurely models that inevitably shape research in subtle but important ways.

All-night sleep recording technology provides an excellent example of a rarely questioned method and theory that is highly influential in shaping thinking and research. The empirical foundation of contemporary sleep research is based on all-night sleep recordings conducted in laboratories. As we (Coates et al., 1978) and others (e.g., Monroe, 1969) have demonstrated, sleep in the laboratory may not be the same as sleep at home. Frankel et al. (1976) suggested that normal sleepers may sleep worse in the lab; studies comparing normal and poor sleepers may be less than conclusive for this reason.

The subtle influence runs deeper still. The psychophysiological literature usually regards data from all-night sleep recordings as "objective" and hence as valid data, while self and spouse reports of sleep are regarded as "subjective" data. Dement (1972) used the term "pseudoinsomnia" to describe the complaint of poor sleep in the absence of abnormal EEG patterns. Weiss, McPartland, & Kupfer (1973), entitled a paper "Once more: The *inaccuracy* of non-EEG estimations of sleep" (italics ours). Because it appeared promising quite early, because it was correlated with early advances in sleep research, and because it can provide a continuous measure over time without apparently disturbing the arousal level of the subject, EEG recordings have become regarded as *the* criterion of sleep. But the fact that all-night sleep recordings are "objective" and reliable measures may have exaggerated their biological significance. The point is underscored when sleep scoring methods are considered in detail. Each 30-second epoch of sleep is given a single rating (awake, NREM Stages 1, 2, 3, 4, or REM) if 50% or more of the biological activity during those 30 seconds is characteristic of the stage classified. Clearly this system could fail to discriminate important EEG patterns. Feinberg et al. (1977), for example, reported that while flurazepam decreased percent of time in Stage 4 sleep, the absolute number of delta waves throughout the night did not decrease significantly.

Theoretically, it seems quite promising to encourage a "daytime view" of nighttime sleep problems. As we have repeatedly suggested in this chapter, what and how a person does things during his waking hours may prove to be the major source of problems with sleeping. Daily behavior patterns characterized by a marked sense of time urgency, constant striving to succeed, and frequent experiences of anger and hostility apparently may predispose the person to experience problems in sleep onset, reawakenings, and remaining awake. The possible relationship of chronic stress and sleep complaints deserves consideration.

Definitive Studies

We urge researchers to expend energy in framing definitive rather than convenient empirical tests. Our review of the hyperarousal literature provides an example. We stated that the Monroe (1967) study is the sole source of data to support the hypothesis that persons complaining of insomnia are more aroused physiologically during the night than normal sleepers. Other studies on this question either relied on self-report or took only limited measures at a few points in time. While the results from these studies are negative, it is not clear whether the negative findings should be attributed to lack of relationship between poor sleep and physiological arousal or to the methodology employed.

A similar statement can be made in evaluation of nonpharmacological treatments for the complaint of insomnia. In a recent perusal of the literature of behavioral treatments for insomnia, we located 35 studies published in the scientific literature. Ten of the 35 used all-night sleep recordings in addition to self-reports. Only 13 of the 25 using self-reports reported any follow-up data; 6 of the follow-ups were three months or less from the end of treatment. Commendably, 8 of the 10 studies using all-night sleep recordings also reported follow-ups and 5 of these were six months or more. Most studies using self-reports provide only data on latency to sleep onset and nothing else. At most, data on one or two other variables are reported (Killen & Coates, in press). In short, fewer studies employing multiple measures and long-term follow-up might be more informative than a plethora of studies employing fewer measures at a few points in time.

It is a truism to state that no single research method or set of measures is adequate to provide full explanation of an area of inquiry. However, behavior often fails to match the belief, and important studies often generate a host of similarly designed progeny. A variety of research methods need to be employed to complement the multiple measures needed. Personality inventories, for example, have dominated comparisons of psychological characteristics between persons complaining of insomnia and normal sleepers. While interesting findings have emerged, these instruments have obvious limitations. Rather than replicating past research, investigators might expend energy in finding other ways to describe behaviors, thoughts, and feelings to expand the data base qualitatively as well as quantitatively.

Finally, a complete understanding of sleep requires multidisciplinary perspectives. Environmental, physiological, and psychological views are needed to provide a comprehensive and complete understanding of the phenomena of sleep and behaviors and complaints associated with it. Development of nonpharmacological treatment is often pursued without recognizing the importance of basic descriptive and experimental studies of sleep (Thoresen et al., 1980). We have attempted in this chapter to draw from a variety of research areas to discuss sleep and behaviors and complaints associated with sleep, and to design treatments to ameliorate behaviors and complaints associated with sleep. We believe that effective treatments will require integration of contributions from various perspectives. Clinical research designed to evaluate specific approaches or investigate processes mediating improvement will be inadequate if conducted within the insulation imposed by a single disciplinary perspective.

At present we have a great deal of ignorance to contend with, not only of empirical findings and clinical strategies, but also of useful theoretical perspectives. Because a substantial number of persons are suffering chronically and are using harmful remedies, we need to reduce our ignorance. Improving the quality of our research efforts can make the difference in the lives of these persons.

ACKNOWLEDGMENT

Preparation of this manuscript and the research reported herein were supported in part by Grant #MH-27551 from the Clinical Research Branch of the National Institute of Mental Health. We thank Joel Killen and Evelyn Marchini for helpful comments in earlier drafts. The cooperation of William Dement, M.D., Director of the Stanford Sleep Disorders Clinic, and his staff, in conducting studies cited here, is gratefully acknowledged.

REFERENCES

Adam, K., & Oswald, I. Sleep is for tissue restoration. *Journal of the Royal College of Physicians,* 1977, **11**, 376–388.

Agnew, H. W. Jr., Webb, W. B., & Williams, R. L. The first night effect: An EEG study of sleep. *Psychophysiology,* 1966, **2**, 263–266.

Allison, T., & Cicchetti, D. V. Sleep in Mammals: Ecological and constitutional correlates. *Science,* 1976, **194**, 732–734.

Anton, J. L., Dunbar, J., & Friedman, L. Anticipation training in the treatment of dedression. In J. D. Krumboltz & C. E. Thoresen (Eds.) *Counseling methods.* New York: Holt, Rinehart and Winston, 1976.

Ascher, L. M., & Efran, J. S. Use of paradoxical intention in a behavioral program for sleep onset insomnia. *Journal of Consulting and Clinical Psychology,* 1978, **46**, 547–550.

Aschoff, J. Circadian rhythms in man. *Science,* 1965, **148**, 1427–1432.

Azerinsky, E., & Kleitman, N. Regularly occurring periods of eye motility and concomitant phenomena during sleep. *Science,* 1953, **118**, 273–274.

Baekeland, F., Koulack, D., & Lasky, R. Effects of a stressful presleep experience on electroencephalograph-recorded sleep. *Psychophysiology,* 1968, **4**, 367.

Bandura, A. Self-efficacy: Toward a unifying theory of behavior change. *Psychological Review,* 1977, **84**, 1921–215.

Bayh, B. *Barbiturate abuse in the United States.* Report of the Subcommittee to Investigate Juvenile Delinquency to the Committee in the Judiciary, United States Senate, 1972.

Berger, R. J. Bioenergetic functions of sleep and activity rhythms and their possible relevance to aging. *Federation Proceedings,* 1975, **34**, 97–102.

Bernstein, D. S., & Borkovec, T. D. *Progressive relaxation training.* Champaign, Ill.: Research Press, 1973.

Beutler, L. E., Thornby, J. I., & Karacan, I. Psychological variables in the diagnosis of insomnia. In R. L. Williams & I. Karacan (Eds.), *Sleep disorders: Diagnosis and treatment.* New York: Wiley, 1978, pp. 61–100.

Bixler, E. O., Kales, J. D., Scharf, M. B., Kales, A., & Leo, L. A. Incidence of sleep disorders in medical practice: A physician survey. *Sleep Research,* 1976, **5**, 62 (*Abstract*).

Bootzin, R. R. Stimulus control treatment for insomnia. Paper presented at the meetings of the American Psychological Association, Honolulu, September 1972.

Bootzin, R. R., & Nicassio, P. Behavioral treatment of insomnia. In M. Hersen, R. M. Eisler, & P. M. Miller (Eds.), *Progress in behavior modification.* New York: Academic Press, 1978.

Borkovec, T. D. Pseudo (experiential) and idiopathic (objective) insomnia: Theoretical and therapeutic issues. In H. Eysenck & S. Rachman (Eds.), *Advances in behavior research and therapy.* New York: Pergamon, 1979.

Borkovec, T. D., Grayson, J. B., O'Brien, G. T., & Weerts, T. C. Treatment of pseudo-insomnia and idiopathic insomnia via progressive relaxation with and without muscle tension-release: An electroencephalographic evaluation. *Journal of Applied Behavior Analysis,* 1979, **12**, 37–54.

Borkovec, T. D., & Hennings, B. L. The role of physiological attention-focusing in the relaxation treatment of sleep disturbance, general tension, and specific stress reaction. *Behaviour Research and Therapy,* 1978, **16**, 7–19.

Broughton, R. J. Sleep disorders: Disorders of arousal? *Science,* 1968, **159**, 1070–1078.

Carskadon, M. A., Dement, W. C., Mitler, M. M., Guilleminault, C., Zarcone, V. P., & Spiegel, R. Self-reports versus sleep laboratory findings in 122 drug-free subjects with complaints of chronic insomnia. *American Journal of Psychiatry,* 1976, **133**, 1382–1388.

Carskadon, M., Mitler, M., Billiard, M., Phillips, R., & Dement, W. C. A comparison of insomniacs and normals: Total sleep time and sleep latency. *Sleep Research,* 1975, **4**, 212 (Abstract).

Coates, T. J., George, J., Killen, J. D., Marchini, E., Hamilton, S., & Thoresen, C. E. Minimal first night effects in good and poor sleepers when recorded at home. Unpublished manuscript, The Johns Hopkins School of Medicine, 1980.

Coates, T. J., Killen, J. D., George, J. M., Marchini, E., Silverman, S., Hamilton, S., & Thoresen, C. E. Discriminating good sleepers from persons complaining of sleep-maintenance insomnia using all-night sleep recordings conducted at home. Unpublished manuscripts, The Johns Hopkins School of Medicine, 1980.

Coates, T. J., Killen, J. D., Silverman, S., Marchini, E., Rosenthal, D., Sanchez, A., George, J., & Thorensen, C. E. Problem-solving skills of persons complaining of insomnia and matched-control good sleepers. Unpublished manuscript, The Johns Hopkins School of Medicine, 1980.

Coates, T. J., Rosekind, M. R., Strossen, R. J., Thoresen, C. E., & Kirmil-Gray, K. Sleep in the laboratory and the home: A comparative analysis. *Psychophysiology,* 1979, **16**, 339–346.

Coates, T. J., Rosekind, M. R., & Thoresen, C. E. All night sleep recordings in clients' homes by telephone. *Journal of Behavior Therapy and Experimental Psychiatry,* 1978, **9**, 157–162.

Coates, T. J., & Thoresen, C. E. *How to sleep better: A drug-free program for overcoming insomnia.* Englewood Cliffs, N.J.: Prentice-Hall, 1977.

Coates, T. J., & Thoresen, C. E. Treating arousals during sleep using behavioral self-management. *Journal of Consulting and Clinical Psychology,* 1979, **47**, 603–605.

Coates, T. J., Thoresen, C. E., Strossen, R. J., & Rosekind, M. R. Obtaining reliable all-night sleep recording data: How many nights are needed? *Sleep Research,* 1978, **7**, 235 (Abstract).

Cooper, J. R. *Sedative-hypnotic drugs: Risks and benefits.* Rockville, Md.: National Institute of Drug Abuse, 1977.

Coursey, R. D., Buchsbaum, M., & Frankel, B. L. Personality measures and evoked responses in chronic insomniacs. *Journal of Abnormal Psychology,* 1975, **84**, 239–249.

Davidson, R. J. Specificity and patterning in biobehavioral systems: Implications for behavior change. *American Psychologist,* 1978, **33**, 430–436.

Dement, W. C. *Some must watch while some must sleep.* Stanford, Ca.: Stanford Alumni Association, 1972.

Dement, W. C., & Kleitman, N. The relation of eye movements during sleep to dream activity: An objective method for the study of dreaming. *Journal of Experimental Psychology,* 1957, **53**, 339–346.

Dement, W. C., & Mitler, M. M. An overview of sleep research: Past, present, and future. In D. Hamburg & K. Brodie (Eds.), *American Handbook of Psychiatry, Vol. 6.* New York: Basic Books, 1976.

Dement, W. C., Zarcone, V. P., Hoddes, E., Smythe, H., & Carskadon, M. Sleep laboratory and clinical studies with flurazepam. In S. Grattini, E. Mussini, & L. O. Randall (Eds.), *The Benzodiazepines.* New York: Raven Press, 1973, pp. 599–611.

Evans, F. J. Hypnosis and sleep: The control of altered states of awareness. *Annals of the New York Academy of Sciences,* 1977, **296**, 162–174.

Evans, F. J., Gustafson, L. A., O'Connell, D. N., Orne, M. T., & Shor, R. E. Verbally induced behavioral responses during sleep. *Journal of Nervous and Mental Disease,* 1970, **150**, 171–187.

Feinberg, I., Fein, G. E., Walker, J. M., Price, L. J., Floyd, T. C., & March, J. D. Flurazepam effects on slow wave sleep: Stage 4 suppressed but number of delta waves constant. *Science,* 1977, **198**, 847–848.

Feinstein, B., Sterman, M. B., & MacDonald, L. R. Effects of sensorimotor rhythm biofeedback training on sleep. *Sleep Research,* 1974, **4**, 134 (Abstract).

Frankel, B. L., Coursey, R. D., Buchbinder, R., & Snyder, F. Recorded and reported sleep in chronic primary insomnia. *Archives of General Psychiatry,* 1976, **33**, 615–623.

Frankel, B. L., Coursey, R. D., Gaarder, K. R., Mott, D. E. W. EMG Feedback and Autogenic training: Is either helpful in sleep-onset insomnia? *Sleep Research,* 1976, **5**, 215.

Frankel, B. L., Patten, B. M., & Gillin, J. C. Restless legs syndrome. *Journal of the American Medical Association,* 1974, **230**, 1302–1303.

Freedman, R., Hauri, P., Coursey, R., & Frankel, B. Further studies of the behavioral treatment of insomnia. *Sleep Research,* 1978, **7**, 179 (Abstract).

Freedman, P. R., & Papsdorf, J. D. Biofeedback and progressive relaxation treatment of sleep-onset insomnia: A controlled all-night investigation. *Biofeedback and Self-Regulation,* 1976, **1**, 253–271.

Gillin, J. C., Duncan, W., Pettigrew, K. D., Frankel, B. L., & Snyder, F. Successful separation of depressed, normal, and insomniac subjects by EEG sleep data. *Archives of General Psychiatry,* 1979, **36**, 85–90.

Gillin, J. C., Mendelson, W. B., Sitaram, N., & Wyatt, R. J. The neuropharmacology of sleep and wakefulness. *Annual Review of Pharmacology and Toxicology,* 1978, **18**, 563–579.

Good, R. Frontalis muscle tension and sleep latency. *Psychophysiology,* 1975, **12**, 465–467.

Guilleminault, C., & Dement, W. C. 235 cases of excessive daytime sleepiness. *Journal of the Neurological Sciences,* 1977, **31,** 13–27.

Guilleminault, C., Eldridge, F. L., & Dement, W. C. Insomnia with sleep apnea: A new syndrome. *Science,* 1973, **181,** 856–858.

Hammond, E. C. Some preliminary findings on physical complaints from a prospective study of 1,064,004 men and women. *American Journal of Public Health,* 1964, **54,** 11–23.

Hartmann, E. *The functions of sleep.* New Haven: Yale University Press, 1973.

Hartmann, E. *The Sleeping Pill.* New Haven: Yale University Press, 1978.

Hartmann, E., Baekeland, F., Zwilling, G., & Hoy, P. Sleep need: How much sleep and what kind? *American Journal of Psychiatry,* 1971, **127,** 1001–1008.

Hartmann, E., & Brewer, V. When is more or less sleep required? A study of variable sleepers. *Comprehensive Psychiatry,* 1976, **17,** 275–284.

Hauri, P. Effects of evening activity in early night sleep. *Psychophysiology,* 1968, **4,** 267–277.

Hauri, P. A case series analysis of 141 consecutive insomniacs evaluated at the Dartmouth Sleep Lab. *Sleep Research,* 1976, **5,** 173 (Abstract).

Hauri, P. Biofeedback techniques in the treatment of chronic insomnia. In R. L. Williams, & I. Karacan (Eds.), *Sleep disorders: Diagnosis and treatment.* New York: Wiley, 1978.

Hauri, P. *Sleep.* Kalamazoo, Michigan: Upjohn, 1977.

Hauri, P., & Cohen, S. The treatment of insomnia with biofeedback: Final report of Study I. *Sleep Research,* 1977, **6,** 136 (Abstract).

Hauri, P., Phelps, P. J., & Jordan, J. B. Biofeedback as a treatment for insomnia. *Proceedings of the Biofeedback Research Society,* 1976, **7** (Abstract).

Haynes, S. N., Follingstad, D. R., & McGowan, W. T. Sleep patterns and anxiety level. *Journal of Psychosomatic Research,* 1974, **18,** 69–74.

Haynes, S. N., Price, M. G., & Simons, J. B. Stimulus control treatment of insomnia. *Journal of Behavior Therapy and Experimental Psychiatry,* 1975, **6,** 279–282.

Hobson, J. A., Spagna, T., & Malenka, R. Ethology of sleep studied with time-lapse photography: Postural immobility and sleep-cycle phase in humans. *Science,* 1978, **201,** 1251–1253.

Hoddes, E., Zarcone, V. P., Smythe, H., Phillips, R., & Dement, W. C. Quantification of sleepiness: A new approach. *Psychophysiology,* 1973, **10,** 431–436.

Johns, M. W., Gay, T. J. A., Masterton, J. P., & Bruce, D. W. Relationship between sleep habits, adrenocortical activity and personality. *Psychosomatic Medicine,* 1971, **33,** 499–507.

Johnson, L. Are stages of sleep related to waking behavior? *American Scientist,* 1973, **61,** 326–338.

Johnson, L. C., & McLeod, W. I. Sleep and awake behavior during gradual sleep reduction. *Perceptual and Motor Skills,* 1973, **36,** 87–97.

Jones, H. S., & Oswald, I. Two cases of healthy insomnia. *Electroencephalography and Clinical Neurophysiology,* 1968, **24,** 378–380.

Jordan, J. B., Hauri, P., & Phelps, P. J. The Sensorimotor Rhythm (SMR) in Insomnia. *Sleep Research,* 1976, **5** (Abstract).

Kales, A. Hypnotic drug abuse: Clinical and experimental aspects. *Medical Counterpoint,* 1971, **3,** 13.

Kales, A., Bixler, E. O., Tan, T. L., Scharf, M. B., & Kales, J. D. Chronic hypnotic drug use: Ineffectiveness, drug withdrawal insomnia, and dependence. *Journal of the American Medical Association,* 1974, **5,** 513–517.

Kales, A., Cauldwell, A. B., Preston, T. A., Healey, S., & Kales, J. D. Personality patterns in insomnia. *Archives of General Psychiatry,* 1976, **33,** 1128–1134.

Kales, A., & Kales, J. D. Evaluation, diagnosis, and treatment of clinical conditions related to sleep. *Journal of the American Medical Association,* 1970, **213,** 2229–2235.

Kales, A., & Kales, J. D. Recent findings in the diagnosis and treatment of disturbed sleep. *New England Journal of Medicine,* 1974, **290,** 487–499.

Kales, A., Kales, J. D., Bixler, E. O., & Scharf, M. G. Effectiveness of hypnotic drugs with prolonged use: Flurazepam and pentobarbital. *Clinical Pharmacology and Therapeutics,* 1975, **18,** 356–363.

Kamiya, J. Behavioral, subjective, and physiological aspects of drowsiness and sleep. In D. W. Fiske & S. R. Maddi. *Functions of varied experience.* Homewood, Ill.: Dorsey Press, 1961.

Kanfer, F. H., & Saslow, G. Behavioral diagnosis. In C. M. Franks (Ed.), *Behavior therapy: Appraisal and status.* New York: McGraw-Hill, 1969, pp. 417–444.

Karacan, I., Ilaria, R., Ware, C., Thornby, J., & Chambliss, S. Is the poor sleep of insomniacs due to anxiety? *Sleep Research,* 1978, **7,** 236 (Abstract).

Karacan, I., Williams, R. L., Salis, P. J., & Hursch, C. J. New approaches to the evaluation and treatment of insomnia. *Psychosomatics,* 1971, **12,** 81–88.

Kay, D. C., Blackburn, A. B., Buckingham, J. A., & Karacan, I. Human pharmacology of sleep. In R. L. Williams & I. Karacan (Eds.), *Pharmacology of Sleep.* New York: Wiley, 1976, pp. 83–210.

Killen, J., & Coates, T. J. The complaint of insomnia: What is it and how do we treat it? *Clinical Behavior Therapy Reviews,* in press.

Kleitman, N. *Sleep and wakefulness.* Chicago: University of Chicago Press, 1963.

Knapp, T. J., Downs, D. L., & Alperson, J. R. Behavior therapy for insomnia: A review and critique. *Behavior Therapy,* 1976, **7,** 614–625.

Lick, J. R., & Heffler, D. Relaxation training and attention placebo in the treatment of severe insomnia. *Journal of Consulting and Clinical Psychology,* 1977, **45,** 153–161.

Lugaresi, E., Coccagna, G., Ceroni, G. B., & Ambrosetto, C. Restless legs syndrome and nocturnal myoclonus. In W. Gastaut (Ed.), *The abnormalities of sleep in man.* Bologna, Italy: Aulo Gaggi, 1968, pp. 285–294.

Marchini, E., Coates, T. J., & Magistad, J. What do insomniacs do and how do they feel during the day? Unpublished manuscript, Pacific Graduate School of Psychology, 1980.

Meddis, R. On the function of sleep. *Animal Behavior,* 1975, **23,** 676–691.

Meddis, R., Pearson, A. J. D., & Langford, G. An extreme case of healthy insomnia. *Electroencephalography and Clinical Neurophysiology,* 1973, **35,** 213–214.

Miles, L. E. M., Raynal, D. M., & Wilson, M. A. Blind man living in normal society has circadian rhythms of 24.9 hours. *Science,* 1977, **198,** 421–423.

Monroe, L. J. Psychological and physiological differences between good and poor sleepers. *Journal of Abnormal Psychology,* 1967, **72,** 255–264.

Monroe, L. J. Interrater validity and the role of experience in scoring EEG sleep records: Phase I. *Psychophysiology,* 1969, **5,** 376–384.

Montgomery, I., Perkins, G., & Wise, D. A review of behavioral treatment for insomnia. *Journal of Behavior Therapy and Experimental Psychiatry,* 1975, **6**, 93–100.

Moruzzi, G. Final remarks. In O. Petre-Quadens & J. D. Schlag (Eds.), *Basic sleep mechanisms.* New York: Academic Press, 1974, pp. 415–416.

Nicassio, P., & Bootzin, R. A comparison of progressive relaxation and autogenic training as treatments for insomnia. *Journal of Abnormal Psychology,* 1974, **83**, 253–260.

Oswald, I. Human brain protein, drugs, and dreams. *Nature,* 1969, **223**, 893–897.

Pollak, C. P., McGregor, P., & Weitzman, E. D. The effects of flurazepam on daytime sleep after acute sleep-wake cycle reversal. *Sleep Research,* 1975, **4**, 112 (Abstract).

Preston, F. S., Bateman, S. C., Short, R. V., & Wilkinson, R. J. Effects of flying and time changes on menstrual cycle length and on performance in airline stewardesses. *Aerospace Medicine,* 1973, **44**, 438–443.

Preston, F. S., & Bateman, S. C. Effect of time zone changes on the sleep patterns of BOAC B-707 crews on worldwide schedules. *Aerospace Medicine,* 1970, **41**, 1409–1415.

Preston, F. S., Bateman, S. C., Meichen, F. W., Wilkinson, R., & Short, R. V. Effects of time zone changes on performance and physiology of airline personnel. *Aviation, Space, and Environmental Medicine,* 1976, **47**, 763–769.

Price, V. A., Coates, T. J., Thoresen, C. E., & Grinstead, O. The prevalence and correlates of poor sleep among adolescents. *American Journal of Diseases of Children,* 1978, **132**, 583–586.

Rechtschaffen, A., & Kales, A. (Eds.). *A manual of standardized terminology, techniques, and scoring system for sleep stages of human subjects.* Public Health Service No. 204, United States Government Printing Office: Washington, D.C., 1968.

Rechtschaffen, A., & Monroe, L. J. Laboratory studies of insomnia. In A. Kales (Ed.), *Sleep: Physiology and pathology.* Philadelphia: Lippincott, 1969, pp. 158–169.

Roth, T., Kramer, M., & Lutz, T. The nature of insomnia: A descriptive summary of a sleep clinic population. *Comprehensive Psychiatry,* 1976, **17**, 217–220.

Roth, T., Lutz, T., Kramer, M., & Tietz, E. The relationship between objective and subjective evaluations of sleep in insomniacs. *Sleep Research,* 1977, **6**, 178 (Abstract).

Rutenfranz, J., Colquhoun, W. P., Knauth, P., & Ghata, J. N. Biomedical and psychosocial aspects of shift work. *Scandinavian Journal of Work, Environment, and Health,* 1977, **3**, 165–182.

Schacht, T., & Nathan, P. E. But is it good for psychologists? Appraisal and status of DSM-III. *American Psychologist,* 1977, **12**, 1017–1025.

Scharf, M. B., Kales, A., & Bixler, E. O. Readaptation to the sleep laboratory in insomniac subjects. *Psychophysiology,* 1975, **12**, 412–415.

Spiegel, R. A survey of insomnia in the San Francisco Bay Area. Unpublished manuscript, Stanford University Sleep Disorders Clinic, Stanford, Ca., 1973.

Sterman, M. B., Howe, R. C., & MacDonald, L. R. Facilitation of spindle-burst sleep by conditioning of electroencephalographic activity while awake. *Science,* 1970, **167**, 1146–1148.

Taub, J. M., & Berger, R. J. Performance and mood following variations in the length and timing of sleep. *Psychophysiology,* 1973, **10**, 559–570.

Taub, J. M., & Hawkins, D. R. Nocturnal sleep schedules, performance, mood and diurnal rhythms. *Sleep Research,* 1977, **6**, 115 (Abstract).

Thoresen, C. E., Coates, T. J., Kirmil-Gray, K., & Rosekind, M. R. Behavioral self-management in treating sleep-maintenance insomnia. *Journal of Behavioral Medicine,* in press.

Thoresen, C. E., Coates, T. J., Zarcone, V. P., Kirmil-Gray, K. R., & Rosekind, M. R. Treating the complaint of insomnia: Self-management perspectives. In J. M. Ferguson & C. B. Taylor (Eds.), *A comprehensive handbook of behavioral medicine.* Jamaica, N.Y. Spectrum, 1980.

Traub, A. C., Jencks, B., & Bliss, E. L. Effects of relaxation training on chronic insomnia. *Sleep Research,* 1974, **3**, 164 (Abstract).

Webb, W. B. Sleep as an adaptive response. *Perceptual and Motor Skills,* 1974, **38**, 1023–1027.

Webb, W. B., & Agnew, H. W. Jr. The effects of a chronic limitation of sleep length. *Psychophysiology,* 1974, **11**, 265–274.

Webb, W. B., & Agnew, H. W. Jr. Sleep efficiency for sleep-wake cycles of varied length. *Psychophysiology,* 1975, **12**, 637–641.

Webb, W. B., & Agnew, H. W. Jr. Effects of rapidly rotating shifts on sleep patterns and sleep structure. *Aviation, Space, and Environmental Medicine,* 1978, **49**, 384–389.

Webb, W. W., & Cartwright, R. D. Sleep and dreams. In M. R. Rosenzweig & L. W. Porter (Eds.), *Annual Review of Psychology.* Palo Alto, Ca.: Annual Reviews, 1978, pp. 223–252.

Weiss, B. L., McPartland, R. J., & Kupfer, D. J. Once more: The inaccuracy of non-EEG estimations of sleep. *American Journal of Psychiatry,* 1973, **130**, 1282–1285.

Williams, R. L., Karacan, I., & Hursch, C. J. *Electroencephalography (EEG) of human sleep: Clinical applications.* New York: Wiley, 1974.

Woolfolk, R. L., Carr-Kaffashan, L., McNulty, T. F., & Lehrer, P. M. Meditation training as a treatment for insomnia. *Behavior Therapy,* 1976, **7**, 359–365.

Yates, A. *Behavior therapy.* New York: Wiley, 1970.

Yates, A. Research methods in behavior modification: A comparative evaluation. In M. Hersen, R. M. Eisler, & P. M. Miller (Eds.), *Progress in behavior modification, Vol. 2.* New York: Academic Press, 1976, pp. 279–307.

Zarcone, V. P. Narcolepsy. *New England Journal of Medicine,* 1975, **288**, 1156–1166.

Zepelin, H., & Rechtschaffen, A. Mammalian sleep, longevity, and energy metabolism. *Brain and Behavior in Evolution,* 1974, **10**, 415–470.

Zwart, C. A., & Lisman, S. A. An analysis of stimulus control treatment of sleep-onset insomnia. *Journal of Consulting and Clinical Psychology,* 1979, **47**, 113–118.

CHAPTER 11

Sexual Dysfunction (Distress and Dissatisfaction)

John P. Wincze

Although the contribution of behavior therapy to the treatment of some disorders is questionable, it is generally accepted that behavioral treatment of dysfunctional sexual problems is the treatment of choice. The strong acceptance of behavioral approaches was initially inspired by two nonbehaviorists, Masters and Johnson (1966, 1970) through their careful observations and subsequent writings on human sexual problems. These researchers did not find dynamically oriented theories useful explanations of sexual dysfunction problems. Even though they did not acknowledge learning theory per se, it is quite easy to translate their more eclectic strategies into behavioral ones. The Masters and Johnson procedures and the behavioral procedures are collectively known as "directive sex therapy," since they embody the common approach of targeting behaviors for change and programming direct behavioral changes. Regardless of the theoretical bias, the Masters and Johnson approach is easily understood by therapists and clients and raises the possibility of a relatively fast and inexpensive method of reversing sexual problems. Even clinicians of more dynamically oriented persuasions have tended to adopt sex therapy strategies based on symptom removal (Kaplan, 1974; O'Conner, 1978).

This is not to say, however, that there exists profound or substantial research evidence to support much of the clinical enthusiasm. In fact, as more and more research evidence appears, the limitations and shortcomings of clinical procedures are being defined (Kuriansky & Sharpe, 1976; Levine & Agle, 1978; Wincze, Hoon, & Hoon, 1978). For example, Wincze, et al. (1978) found that women who underwent a comprehensive sex therapy program tended to report success to the therapist while more objective behavioral, questionnaire, and physiological data tended to question the validity of their self-report. Perhaps the sex therapy model has strong demand characteristics that influence clients to report information in a therapist-pleasing direction. Levine and Agle (1978) also reported somewhat pessimistic findings when they observed, in a well-controlled study, that 68% of men who underwent therapy for chronic impotency showed improvement in erectile functioning at the end of therapy, but only 6% showed stability in sexual functioning over time in a year follow-up.

Such data are sobering, but not necessarily discouraging. We are still very much in the infancy of our science and should be reminded not to be overly enthusiastic and not to ignore complexities of human behavior. Directive sex therapy and the behavioral approaches it embodies have often been guilty of oversimplification. While it is true that there exists a large body of sexual problems for which quick and simplistic solutions are appropriate, it is also true that most clients seen in sex therapy clinics have more complex problems that demand complicated interventions. This does not mean that a behavioral model is shortsighted, inappropriate, or simplistic; in fact, such a model is strongly advocated. The purpose of this chapter is to examine the complexities of sexual problems and conceptualize their etiology and treatment within a behavioral framework. The utility of the term dysfunctional will be examined and the advantages of employing more behavioral descriptions of sexual problems will be discussed. The chapter presents a model of sexual problems, assessment, description, and finally treatment.

MODEL OF SEXUAL PROBLEMS

The term sexual dysfunction was popularized by Masters and Johnson (1970) in their book *Human Sexual Inadequacy* and may be a useful term to distinguish "normal" sexual problems from "deviant" sexual problems. In some ways, it is unfortunate that the term has become so popular, since it conveys the same inherent deficiencies that other psychiatric labels do. It implies, for example, that there is a class of dysfunctional individuals and nondysfunctional individuals rather than that there are degrees of problematic sexual behavior. The validity of labeling becomes more doubtful in light of Frank, Anderson, and Rubinstein's (1978) data which demonstrated that couples who consider themselves free of sexual problems may evidence some of the same sexual behaviors many individuals label as dysfunctional. Sexual dysfunction implies a "package" problem for which there is a "package" treatment. Use of this terminology may lead to a gross oversimplification of the complexities that sexual problems can bring and of the solutions they demand. A serious question might be raised: how useful is the term sexual dysfunction? An alternative to this term would be to simply use more behavioral descriptions of problematic sexual behavior since the term dysfunctional can be misleading and pejorative. The advantage of behavioral terminology would be to allow a more exact description of the problem and disavow a package approach.

In Figure 1 is a model of sexual problems that stresses a continuum of sexual behavior from enjoyment to distress. The model also emphasizes that individuals can have different degrees of and different combinations of areas of sexual dissatisfaction. Just as the degree of sexual enjoyment and distress may be viewed on a continuum, so too the presence of a positive or negative contributing factor should be viewed on a continuum. The idea of the continuum is important for treatment since it suggests that therapy should be tailored for each client depending on the degree and presence or absence of specific symptoms and contributing factors.

Sexual Distress

The presence of sexual distress may appear in almost any combination. An individual female, for example, could evidence little or no sexual anxiety, have little

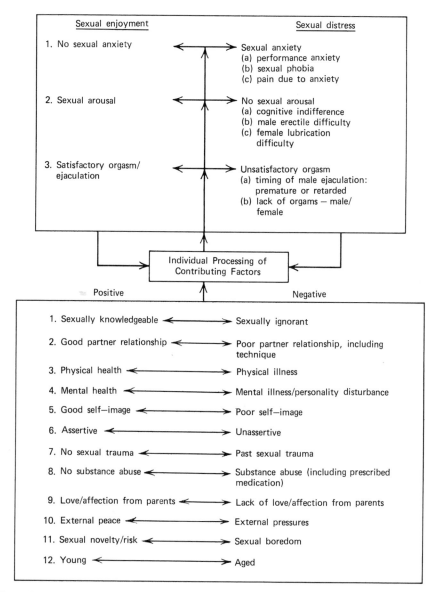

Figure 1   A Model of Sexual Problems.

or no cognitive arousal and have orgasmic problems some of the time. It is true that some of the areas of sexual distress often appear in combination (performance anxiety and impotency in males), but in terms of problem assessment and treatment, it is helpful to conceptualize the areas independently. This will allow a more comprehensive understanding of the problem and not exclude an unusual combination of problems. In addition, the model also encourages the use of behavioral descriptions of problems. Instead of labeling an individual male as sexually dysfunctional due to impotency, for example, a use of the model may describe the individual's behavior as distressing because of erectile failure on most occasions. This is not merely a semantic issue since a much more accurate description of the problem is arrived at in the second case. Also, the behavioral description does not carry the negative connotations that the word impotency does.

Individual Processing of Factors

Although there are at least 12 common contributing factors that may influence the degree that an individual will or will not enjoy sexual experiences, the processing of these factors by an individual is the key that controls whether or not these factors play a role in sexual dissatisfaction. Thus the mere presence of a negative contributing factor will not necessarily result in sexually distressing experiences. An individual's interpretation of the negative factor is an important aspect of the final sexual experience. Some individuals, for example, may be able to process a sexually traumatic experience by isolating its effect on them to a very narrow range of stimuli. On the other hand, some individuals may process the same information and overgeneralize its effect to include a wide range of stimuli and, hence, preclude all sexual behavior.

The importance of the individual client in the processing of contributing factors must be stressed since it is the individual's use and interpretation of contributing factors that leads to sexual enjoyment or sexual distress. Thus, individuals who have suffered cardiac problems, diabetes or atherosclerosis may or may not experience sexual problems; individuals who have been raped may or may not experience sexual problems; and, individuals who are 90 years old may or may not experience sexual problems. Much of a person's sexual behavior is influenced by how he or she interprets the contributing factors. For example, a woman who has been raped could say to herself "all men are creeps" or "that experience has ruined me." On the other hand, a woman could say to herself "the man who raped me is a creep, but I find great comfort and assurance in my boyfriend's sexual closeness to me." Because of the key role that an individual's interpretation of contributing factors may play, it is extremely important for a therapist to consider this when formulating a treatment approach. This aspect of the model is akin to Schacter and Singer's (1962) attribution theory or Meichenbaum's (1971) cognitive behavioral approach.

From a learning theory perspective, the processing of factors may also be greatly influenced by an individual's conditioning history. In the example of a woman who has been raped, the probability of sexual anxiety being evoked in the presence of her hubsand or lover may depend on similarities between the rapist and rape scenario to her current sexual circumstances. The rape episode may be conceptualized within a classical conditioning model. The rapist and sexual behavior associated with the rape become conditioned stimuli (CS) that may evoke a conditioned response (CR) of anxiety. Stimuli similar to the CS may also evoke anxiety through stimulus generalization.

The processing of factors may also be influenced by an individual's operant conditioning history. Thus a sexually traumatic experience may set up an avoidance chain. When an individual is confronted with a sexual opportunity, sexual anxiety increases and the individual may behave in a way to avoid sexual intimacy and, therefore, reduce sexual anxiety. If an individual is prevented from completing the avoidance behavior, anxiety may increase and also inhibit sexual responding.

In both classical and operant conditioning examples above, the person's conditioning history has contributed to the processing of stimuli associated with sexual behavior.

Contributing Factors

The collection of contributing factors underlying both enjoyable and distressing sexual experiences has been generated mainly from clinical practice and theoretical assumptions. This may not be an exhaustive list, but does represent some of the more common contributing factors presented by sexually distressed individuals. The contributing factors may be roughly divided into three main categories:

1. *Individual Characteristics.* Knowledge, health, self-image, assertiveness, and age.
2. *Past Experiences.* Trauma, parental love, and affection.
3. *Current Circumstances.* Partner relationship, substance abuse, job pressures, sexual novelty, and risk.

In clinical practice, for example, one is likely to encounter many sexually distressed persons presenting poor partner relationships and profound sexual ignorance. While this is far from proof beyond a doubt of the relationship between these negative factors and sexual distress, the occurrence is so common that it is more than mere coincidence. Similarly, a relationship exists between past sexual trauma and current sexual distress. While it is true that the therapist is unlikely to see the individual who was sexually traumatized and made a satisfactory adjustment, the relationship between past sexual trauma and current sexual difficulties is certainly common and theoretically predictable. Other contributing factors were included in the list for similar reasons, while other factors, such as physical illness and substance abuse, have been included on the basis of empirical support.

Many of the negative contributing factors are problems in and of themselves that may or may not result in sexual distress. The model is applicable to individuals who have entered therapy because of sexual distress. The therapist using this model will describe the individual's sexual problem according to the three areas delineated under sexual distress, and treatment may focus on either the appropriate negative contributing factors, or the sexual distressing behavior directly. For example, if poor partner relationship or poor self-image are assumed to be important influences in the sexual distress, then treatment may focus on these factors. If, on the other hand, the therapist determines that direct changes in the distressing behavior are important, then treatment may center on changing these behaviors. In either case, the model deemphasizes a "packaged" approach to sex therapy and emphasizes the importance of tailoring an individual treatment program for each client, regardless of the presenting complaint. More discussion of treatment approaches take place in a later section of this chapter.

ANALYTIC MODEL OF SEXUAL DYSFUNCTION

The sexual distress model points to the potential complexity of a client's sexual problems. This model, while primarily behavioral in structure, allows for alternative theoretical explanations of distressed sexual behavior. For example, sexual anxiety may be related to personality disturbance that may in turn be explained by a psychoanalytical model. In brief, the psychoanalytical model emphasizes that sexual disturbance is related to an unconscious belief that sexual activity is dangerous. The inability to carry out the sexual act is conceptualized as a defense that prevents an activity regarded as dangerous (Fenichel, 1945). For both males and females, the unresolved Oedipus complex is the underlying root of sexual disturbance; for example, a male is impotent because he sees his sexual partner as representative of his mother with whom sexual intercourse is prohibited and punishable; the female is sexually anxious because her male partner conjures up identity with her father and a prohibitive relationship. Specific symptoms of sexual disturbance may include additional underlying assumptions of unresolved childhood disturbances. Treatment programs for sexual disturbance within an analytic model involve working through the unresolved childhood conflicts. Although there are a number of case reports describing analytic treatment models, there is no strong experimental support for using this model in patients experiencing sexual distress.

ASSESSMENT OF SEXUAL PROBLEMS

There have appeared recent reviews of assessment of sexual dysfunction (Caird & Wincze, 1977) and sexual arousal (Barlow, 1977) and only a brief overview will appear here. This overview will be divided into sections describing interview procedures of assessment, paper and pencil measurement tools, and objective physiological measurement procedures. Accurate and systematic behavioral assessment of sexual problems is extremely important in order to: (a) identify specific areas of concern; (b) analyze the topography of problem behavior; and (c) analyze the environment in which the problem behavior occurs (Ferster, 1965; Kanfer & Saslow, 1969). The methodology outlined below is commonly used in a behavioral analysis of sexual problems.

Assessment by Interview

As Caird and Wincze (1977) point out, the interview is the most common and useful assessment tool for quickly obtaining a wide range of important information. In an intake interview, a therapist should be able to estimate the relative impact of each of the contributing factors on the presenting sexual problem. Furthermore, a description of the areas of sexual distress should begin to emerge. The type of initial interview and the amount of information obtained, however, is largely dependent on the client. A client may be very open and comfortable discussing sexual issues and have no difficulty revealing the most detailed and intimate aspects of his or her behavior. With such clients, the intake interview can follow a prescribed structure such as that offered by Masters and Johnson (1966), which includes specific questions and areas of query.

For many clients, however, the intake interview may represent the very first discussion and revelation of intimate sexual behavior. Embarrassment, anxiety, and even anger may be carried into the interview and will erupt if the therapist is insensitive and clumsy in his/her approach. Caird and Wincze (1977) have outlined an introduction to sexual interviewing that helps to diffuse anger and embarrassment and also serves as a thermometer for gauging a client's willingness to discuss sexual matters. Before proceeding with an interview, the therapist(s) should explain to the client in a *general* way the purpose of the interview, the range of problems the therapist(s) deals with, and the fact that many people find it difficult to discuss sexual issues. The therapist(s) should ask a client how he/she feels about discussing sexual matters and whether or not he/she is able to do this with his/her sexual partner. The client's verbal response to the therapist's introductory remarks, and careful observation of the client's nonverbal behavior should cue the therapist on how to proceed. Signs of anxiety, embarrassment, or anger should be met with a very nonspecific, nonthreatening interview, while signs of comfort and openness should signal a more direct and detailed interview. In either instance, the therapist should maintain an accepting, understanding, and warm presentation.

The interview may serve as the most important component of a thorough functional behavioral analysis. As in the case of other behavioral problems, the approach to the behavioral interview for sexual problems should seek careful and detailed descriptions of the types of problem behavior, their topography, and the stimulus conditions under which they occur. A problem initially described as impotency may under a functional behavioral analysis eventually be described as a partial erection 50% of the time while the client is with his wife. Since the stimulus situation is important, it may also be learned that full erections occur with other sexual partners and with the wife while on vacation.

Paper and Pencil Assessment

The initial and subsequent interviews with the client and his/her partner will serve as the mainstay of assessment for the clinician. In addition, clinicians may use a number of available paper and pencil assessment tools for more detailed and somewhat more objective information. Table 1 presents a list of some of the commonly used scales and the area of information they assess.

In general, all of the scales offer the clients new ways to quantify and think about their sexual experiences. The clinician may find the use of paper and pencil assessment tools a means of obtaining more detailed sexual information in general and a means of obtaining behavioral descriptions, topographies, and stimulus conditions. One should take care in explaining the purpose and content of any questionnaire before handing it to a client to fill out. In my earlier clinical experience, one woman client mailed back a sexual background questionnaire only after she had put it through a shredder. She enclosed a terse note stating she would not fill out such a filthy and offensive piece of paper and, furthermore, she wished to

Table 1.   Some Commonly Used Scales

Area of Assessment	Questionnaires
Sexual knowledge	SKAT (Lief & Reed, 1972)
Sexual experience	1. Heterosexual behavior assessment: Males—Bentler (1968a)
	2. Heterosexual behavior assessment: Females—Bentler (1968b)
Sexual attitude	Sexual Orientation Method (SOM)—Feldman, et al. (1966)
Sexual anxiety	Sexual Anxiety Scale (SAS)—Obler (1973)
Sexual arousal	Sexual Arousal Inventory (SAI) (Females only)—Hoon, et al. (1976)
Sexual behavior	Sexual Behavior Record Form—Heiman, et al. (1976)

terminate therapy. More careful interviewing and open discussion of the questionnaire may have averted this emotionally charged expression and lost case.

Assessment by Physiological Methods

One of the most exciting areas of development in recent years has been the emergence of objective physiological measures of sexual arousal. Jovanovic (1971), Zuckerman (1971), and more recently, Caird and Wincze (1977) have reviewed much of the literature in this area. Although the physiological technology has limited direct clinical use at the moment, there is enormous research potential in this methodology for helping us to better understand the process of sexual arousal in men and women. Furthermore, some preliminary research indicates that there exist quantifiable physiological differences between sexually distressed individuals and individuals not complaining of sexual problems. Wincze, Hoon, and Hoon (1977b) demonstrated significant differences between women complaining of sexual problems and women satisfied with their sexual behavior as measured by degree of vaginal vasocongestion during exposure to erotic films. Future research in this area may help to describe more effective screening procedures and treatment techniques.

Nonsexual Assessment Procedures

Discussion of assessment procedures also includes assessment of areas only indirectly related to sexual behavior (contributing factors in the model). For these other areas, the clinician can choose from a variety of assessment procedures that are described elsewhere in this text. Problems of anxiety, assertion, depression, drug abuse, marriage, and personality all have specific methodologies of assessment for evaluating their severity. A contributing factor assessed as severe, may warrant immediate clinical attention, and the sexual problem may be viewed as a secondary problem and not treated until a later time, if at all. Thorough assessment of both sexual and nonsexual behavior by both interview and paper and pencil techniques is important in the sexual distress model in order for effective treatment to proceed.

It is emphasized that a thorough medical examination should precede or be part of the assessment procedures. Since a number of disease conditions can either directly (vaginal infection, diabetes) or indirectly (angina) affect sexual functioning, it is important to rule out or evaluate the impact of a disease condition before proceeding with a behavioral intervention. A complete gynecological or urological examination is standard practice in most sex clinics.

DESCRIPTION OF SEXUAL PROBLEMS

Before discussing treatment procedures, it is important to obtain a more detailed description of the type of sexual problems commonly encountered by sex therapists. Distressing sexual problems for females and males are discussed separately in the next two sections with emphasis on a behavioral description and illustrated by case material.

FEMALE SEXUAL PROBLEMS

Early descriptions of female sexual problems relied heavily on the term frigidity for a diagnostic label. "Frigidity" like other diagnostic labels, included many more categories of behavior (symptoms) than were usually present in a single person: the inability to respond sexually, lack of arousal, high degrees of sexual anxiety, failure to lubricate, lack of orgasm, and downright disgust with sex, were all part of the syndrome. Any one or combination of these symptoms may have earned a woman the title of frigid and carried with it the negative connotation of coldness, aloofness, and even bitchiness. Through the careful work of Masters and Johnson (1966, 1970), a more meaningful and scientifically based description of sexual functioning (and hence, dysfunctioning) was presented, and it challenged the broader concept of frigidity. The sexual response cycle was described by Masters and Johnson (1966) as consisting of four phases: excitation, plateau, orgasm, and resolution. Since sexual problems could be focused at any point during the cycle, a packaged term such as frigidity became less appropriate. Masters and Johnson (1970) preferred terms such as primary and secondary erectile dysfunction, primary and secondary orgasmic dysfunction, vaginismus and dyspareunia. Although these terms are more descriptive than such terms as frigidity, a further refinement in accuracy and usefulness might be achieved through the use of behavioral descriptions that follow the model presented in Figure 1.

Female Sexual Anxiety

Description

Anxiety associated with sexual behavior in women is often described by women as a phobia in which the feared stimulus is either directly or indirectly related to sexual activity. The dreaded stimulus may be very specific such as fear of caressing of the breasts or fear of touching the male genitals. It is not unusual in such cases for a woman to be unfearful, or even excited about other aspects of sexual behavior. The more common type of sexual fear, however, is broadly defined and may include a disgust or distaste for all sexual encounters. Such women may even harbor beliefs that all men are oversexed animals and that sexual behavior is a practice that only men enjoy and that women must endure.

Symptomatically, a "mild" experience of sexual anxiety in women usually includes frequent avoidance of sexual activity and occasional feelings of panic, disgust, or extreme disinterest during sexual activity. Such an experience may lead a woman to avoid sexual contact by arguing with her mate just prior to retiring, feigning a headache, reading late to ensure that her partner is asleep, or retiring early and feigning sleep. On those infrequent occasions when the sexually anxious woman participates in sex, she may attempt to lessen her anxiety through the use of alcohol. In fact, if a female client reports that only after alcohol or drug intake she is able to let herself go and enjoy sex, then sexual anxiety is most likely present.

Avoidance behavior may also appear during sexual activity when a woman discourages foreplay and encourages rapid intercourse. Cases of premature ejaculation in males are often associated with a female partner who is uncomfortable with sexual activity. The male partner's "problem" of premature ejaculation may be subtly or not so subtly encouraged by a woman's very direct and rapid stimulation of his penis.

Some women react to sexual encounters or even the prospect of sexual encounters with an experience of "intense" anxiety. Feelings of panic, dread, loss of control, dizziness, vomiting, headache, and extreme muscle tension are sometimes described by women as being associated with actual or prospective sexual experiences. For such women, sexual encounters are rare and in extreme cases they do not occur at all. The terms dyspareunia (pain during intercourse) and vaginismus (inability to endure penetration due to vaginal muscle spasm) are used to describe conditions in which extreme sexual anxiety is often present. These terms do not convey the intensity, however, with which an individual woman may subjectively experience anxiety associated with sexual encounters. Dyspareunia and vaginismus may occur during a routine gynecological examination or insertion of a tampon, and the subjective anxiety may be much different than during sexual intercourse.

Case Study

CASE 1. Mrs. S. was 29 years old when she first sought help for her sexual problem. She had been married for nine years and during that time had experienced intercourse on only a few occasions, all of which were accompanied by extreme pain. In almost all attempts at sexual intercourse vaginal spasm occurred and penetratration was impossible. Mrs. S. reported that she had never looked at her genitals and had only occasionally viewed herself naked in a mirror. She was quite attractive and had a very good figure, but denied her attractiveness and could only think of her body as ugly. She only touched her genitals for hygienic purposes and could not insert tampons nor even the tip of her little finger into her vagina. Sexual encounters and sexual thoughts were such anathema that she could not say the word penis or vagina without blushing and avoiding eye contact.

Mrs. S. attributed her intense sexual discomfort to her parents' moralistic condemnation of sex. Rarely did they show affection to each other or to her, and they often warned her of the evils of boys (since the word sex was not spoken, this was achieved in a very circumscribed manner). Mrs. S. recalls vividly an incident as a teenager in which her mother, grandmother, and father humiliated her for buying a two-piece bathing suit. After purchasing the suit with some girlfriends, she modeled it at home and was promptly scolded and punished. She recalls feeling ashamed of her body following this incident, but readily pointed out that this was only one example of many that exemplified her parents' uncomfortable feelings about sex.

Following high school graduation, Mrs. S. dated only her present husband and married at age 20. For the most part, Mr. and Mrs. S. have been compatible in marriage with the exception of sex. Mr. S.'s approach to the problem has been "not to push things" for fear that his wife would have a neurotic breakdown.

When Mrs. S. first came for therapy, she was, in fact, experiencing deep feelings of depression accompanied by suicidal thoughts. She had made at least one serious suicide attempt and was extremely pessimistic and characterized herself as worthless.

Treatment originally focused on her depression and consisted of drug therapy (she was also seeing a psychiatrist at the time) and cognitive restructuring of negative thoughts. Over a six-month period of weekly sessions, Mrs. S. began to feel less depressed and more hopeful. As her depression lessened, treatment shifted to her sexual problem. Initially, sessions consisted of information exchange, reeducation, and challenging of myths and negative sexual attitudes. Since Mrs. S. reported strong anxiety attacks in sexual situations, systematic desensitization was applied, accompanied by home practice sessions.

The entire therapy took about 14 months, but ended successfully. Mrs. S. experienced her first orgasm following an *in vivo* home practice session and has continued to enjoy sexual relations with her husband. She is able to insert her fingers comfortably into her vagina and her husband can penetrate her without pain.

An interesting development as a result of the decrease in sexual anxiety has been Mrs. S.'s increase in and awareness of her sexual arousal. On at least one occasion, she has felt so intensely aroused that she awoke her husband at 2:00 A.M. and seduced him. In addition, she has become increasingly aware of the attention she has received from other men and has contemplated having an affair. She is now extremely interested in sex and is wondering what it would be like with another sexual partner.

Behavioral Analysis

In the above mentioned case, the distressed sexual behavior may be conceptualized within a two-process learning theory framework. Sexual stimuli associated with distressed experiences evoked conditioned responses of anxiety; these responses in turn led to patterns of avoidance behavior which were maintained by anxiety reduction. Treatment focused on reducing anxiety associated with sexual stimuli, and building in new approach responses that led to reinforcement (sexual arousal, pleasure) rather than distress.

The anxiety was conceptualized as a phobic reaction and systematic desensitization was applied since specific sexual stimuli reliably evoked anxiety responses. In addition to the possible classically conditioned anxiety stimuli it was postulated that the strong avoidance behaviors prevented satisfactory sexual behaviors from developing. The home practice sessions were designed to gradually shape up (in an operant sense) skillful sexual behaviors that would be incompatible with anxiety and lead to sexual enjoyment (relaxation, arousal, orgasm).

Lack of Sexual Arousal in Women

Description

The lack of sexual arousal is often present in women who experience anxiety associated with sexual stimuli, and, as in Case 1, reduction of anxiety can be accompanied by an increase in sexual arousal. It is of some value, however, to conceptualize lack of arousal as a separate problem needing its own unique treatment approach. In the first place, not all cases treated by anxiety reduction therapy lead to increases in sexual arousal (Caird & Wincze, 1977; Wincze & Caird, 1976) and in the second place, there are a number of women who experience lack of sexual arousal or desire with few accompanying signs or feelings of anxiety. In either case, whether anxiety is present or not, specific procedures for increasing sexual arousal may have to be utilized.

Recently, the term desire phase disorder has become popular and has been used to distinguish lack of sexual arousal from lack of orgasm. Desire phase disorder usually includes women who do not typically seek sexual experiences nor do they experience arousal once sexually involved. There are two components to this: the first can best be described as cognitive indifference to sex, and the second is a lack of early physiological concomitants of arousal, that is, tingling sensations, vaginal lubrication. In some women who do not experience anxiety or negative feelings there is a sense that the sexual "drive" has never existed. It is not a suppression of desire, but a failure to develop desire. Women often experience a similar lack of desire following the birth of a child.

Case Study

CASE 2. Mrs. H. is a 28-year-old elementary school teacher who has been married for eight years. She was the oldest child in a family of 10 children who lived in a rural village. Although her parents were not "strict" regarding sexual matters, they were very closed-mouth and never discussed sex. Menstruation was explained to her in a very clinical way, but she did not feel free to ask any questions about sex.

Mrs. H. stated that there were times in her marriage and before her marriage that she enjoyed sex, although she has never initiated sexual contacts. She has experienced orgasm, but orgasmic release was not correlated wth her rating of enjoyment. Following the birth of her son, Mrs. H. lost total desire for sexual contacts and had not enjoyed sex for two years prior to therapy. It is interesting that Mrs. H. did not enjoy foreplay at all, but would "not mind intercourse" once it was started.

Both Mr. and Mrs. H. independently reported that they had a good marriage and wanted to stay married. The lack of sexual desire on Mrs. H.'s part was the only problem. Mrs. H. denied being sexually attracted to anyone else.

Therapy was aimed at reducing the little anxiety that was associated with foreplay through a program of systematic desensitization and increasing desire through sensate focus exercises and genital pleasuring exercises. Following therapy Mrs. H.

stated that she was participating in sexual intercourse more frequently, but did not feel that her desire had increased at all.

Behavioral Analysis

In cases where anxiety reduction has led to an increase in desire it is feasible to postulate that anxiety was incompatible with arousal. Although more recent evidence challenges this reciprocal inhibition hypothesis as a model of the relationship between anxiety and arousal (Hoon, Wincze, & Hoon, 1977) it may be a feasible explanation for a subpopulation of clinical cases. Hoon, et al. (1977) have raised the possibility, however, that anxiety may in some cases facilitate sexual arousal. This area of study is relatively new and the next few years will better delineate the relationship between sexual arousal and other emotions, such as anxiety, anger, and depression.

When desire phase problems are unaccompanied by high levels of anxiety, as in the case of Mrs. H., a skill deficit hypothesis may offer the best explanation. Cognitive desire and its physiological correlates may be learned responses that require shaping. There is evidence from Heiman, LoPiccolo, and LoPiccolo (1976) that sexual desire and orgasm are behaviors that can be shaped through a graduated, structured program. The crucial ingredients of the Heiman, et al. (1976) approach seem to be instruction, graduated practice, and positive reinforcement. Pleasant tactile sensations, relaxation, feelings of closeness, pleasant verbal exchanges, and actual physiological feelings of arousal are all forms of positive reinforcement lurking in the background of each practice session. Evidence from clinical case studies that desire can be shaped in adult women, however, does not confirm that a similar process is necessary for sexual desire to develop in the first place. Throughout childhood and adolescence there may be other forces at work such as biological processes and learning experiences that are responsible for developing sexual desire. Conclusions in this area are elusive and speculative at best, and more definitive evidence may be obtained only through ethically challenging developmental studies.

Orgasmic Difficulties in Women

Description

While it is almost unheard of for a male to never achieve orgasm, it is a problem for approximately 5 to 15% of the female population (Brown, 1966). Even males who have never achieved erection report orgasmic experiences during direct penile stimulation. For many women the experience of orgasm is poorly defined, since there is not an obvious feedback mechanism, such as seminal discharge. It is not uncommon for a woman client to appear perplexed when asked whether or not she has ever achieved orgasm, and she may respond by saying "I don't know" or "I think so." That this state of affairs should exist is not surprising in light of the anatomical differences between males and females for producing orgasm. For males, the bundle of highly sensitive nerve endings that help to trigger orgasm are located in the glans and the shaft of the penis; while for women, the site of arousal and orgasmic release is located in the clitoris above the vaginal orifice. It is thus possible for a woman to participate in sexual intercourse without obtaining sufficient clitoral stimulation to produce orgasm. Even vigorous vaginal stimulation will not guarantee orgasm, whereas vigorous penile stimulation almost assuredly will.

The complexities of female orgasmic release are reflected in continuing debates over its exact psychological and physiological nature. Freudians have long maintained that there are two sites of orgasm: the clitoris and the vagina. The essence of the theory suggests that during the early stages of female psychosexual development, the clitoris is the site of arousal and orgasm, but as a female matures (becomes adult) the site shifts to the vagina. Masters and Johnson (1966) and others who have done extensive physiological work have failed to support this notion and it is now generally accepted that the clitoris is the key location of female arousal and orgasm. Kaplan (1974) points out that the source of confusion may have emanated from the fact that while clitoral stimulation produces arousal, the orgasm itself is felt by women in the smooth muscle contractions surrounding the vaginal barrel.

This controversy is of little concern to most women, however, and I have yet to have a client who is fully aware of the controversy, let alone complain about not achieving vaginal orgasm. Most women who complain of orgasmic difficulties are concerned about not experiencing orgasm at all, or about infrequent experiences. On the one hand is the woman who states that she feels nothing; there are no sensations of arousal, little or no vaginal lubrication, no build up of muscle tension, no tingling sensations, and no rhythmic releases. On the other hand, there is the woman who is close to orgasm, but does not obtain release: she is highly aroused cognitively, experiences copious lubrication, feels intense build up, but is left feeling unfulfilled and uncomfortable.

There are varied etiological considerations in orgasmic difficulties. Often lack of orgasm is present in women who have general sexual difficulties. It is not surprising to learn that the woman who is uncomfortable sexually, that is, is sexually anxious or feels disgusted with sex, has orgasmic difficulty. Other women, however, have comfort with all aspects of sex, but seem to hold back. For these women, the orgasmic release may have special psychological significance and be suppressed because of this. It is not uncommon for a woman who has been raped to experience general sexual, and particularly, orgasmic problems. Mrs. R. is an example of this problem.

Case Study

CASE 3. Mrs. R. is a highly attractive twenty-two-year-old who was married only eight months before seeking therapy for sexual difficulties. During the intake interview, Mrs. R. expressed the complaint of lack of orgasm. She had sexual experiences since age 13 and at age 16 suffered a traumatic rape. Following this incident, she was very anxious in sexual situations, but over the ensuing years was able to overcome most of her difficulties. For the past two years she has not experienced sexual anxiety and has enjoyed sexual contacts, but without orgasm. Her husband corroborated this report and felt that his wife could "go just so far, but not let go."

Mrs. R. also reported that she had never masturbated and felt hesitant to pursue this as part of therapy. Therapy initially involved discussions and readings with Mr. and Mrs. R. in conjoining sessions with a male and female cotherapist.

Through these discussions, Mrs. R. agreed to attempt the self-pleasuring program as outlined by Heiman, LoPiccolo, and LoPiccolo (1976). This proved to be highly successful and allowed Mrs. R. to enjoy self-pleasuring and experience orgasm during intercourse.

Behavioral Analysis

Orgasm in women can occur without desire through clitoral stimulation. In addition, desire and stimulation can be present but not necessarily culminate in orgasm. Although these separations do exist, it is far more common for desire and orgasm to be linked together during sexual behavior. Behavioral analysis of desire deficiencies usually applies to orgasmic problems as well. On the one hand, it can be postulated that failure to form an orgasmic platform can be a result of a significant anxiety reaction. Wincze and Caird (1976) have presented data, however, which suggest that removing sexual anxiety through desensitization procedures will not necessarily result in improved orgasmic ability. It may be that anxiety reduction procedures are appropriate only if there was orgasmic ability in the first place, which has suffered inhibition through sexual trauma.

On the other hand, a skills deficit model is perhaps more appropriate for explaining most cases of orgasmic difficulties. Women not achieving orgasm may not have developed appropriate cognitive or behavioral skills for doing so. By lack of cognitive skills it is meant that a woman has not developed a mechanism for becoming sexually aroused through the use of specific stimuli, while a lack of behavioral skills implies the inability to use tactile manipulation of the genitals in a way to produce orgasm. Indirect support for this analysis is derived from the highly successful sexual growth therapy programs which teach self-pleasuring in a graduated manner (Heiman, LoPiccolo, & LoPiccolo, 1976). Feedback and reinforcement in the form of increasing pleasurable sensations are built into this repeated practice procedure, which often results in orgasmic capability. Kolenberg (1974) has presented some very compelling data in a series of single case studies that further supports the use of self-pleasuring procedures for helping inorgasmic women achieve orgasm.

One final analysis of orgasmic problems in women was suggested by Heiman (1974) and can most aptly be described as the "out of touch" hypothesis. Heiman found that women compared to men showed less correlation between objective (physiological) and subjective (self-report) measures of sexual arousal. Women, unlike men, do not have the benefit of an observable feedback mechanism to signal their sexual arousal and, therefore, have not learned to correlate as well physiological and cognitive arousal states. The schism between physiological and cognitive arousal states may be of greater magnitude in inorgasmic women than orgasmic women, but this hypothesis awaits empirical verification. Such evidence may suggest biofeedback as a compelling treatment modality.

MALE SEXUAL PROBLEMS

There are many similarities between male and female sexual problems that allow them to be roughly categorized into three general areas as presented in Table 1.

Because of different cultural expectations between males and females and differences in anatomy and physiology, these broad categorizations readily give way to some very unique differences. LoPiccolo and Heiman (1978) have written an excellent review of the cultural influences on male and female sexual behavior in North American society. They point out that males are expected to know more about sex and are given more licenses to experiment sexually, but because more is expected of males sexually, any deficits in a male's sexual behavior are more noticed and harshly judged. Not only is the male expected to perform well, but he is also expected to arouse his female partner. This cultural pressure coupled with the more observable nature of the male sexual response places a unique burden on the male's sexual performance and, consequently, his sexual problems. In short, males are expected to perform sexually and if they do not, it cannot be kept a secret.

Male Sexual Anxiety

Description

Unlike women, men rarely express a fear of sex, per se. Rather, their expression of fear and experience of anxiety is focused on their inability to perform sexually. The basic lament is most often their sexual inability to live up to their own standards or those of their sexual partner(s). Caird and Wincze (1977) point out that a male who expresses fear or disgust at the prospect of heterosexual activity is immediately suspected of homosexuality, while women voicing similar concerns are not usually placed under such suspicion.

Typically, the male expressing performance anxiety will avoid opportunities for sexual intercourse. The single male can achieve this more easily by frequently changing partners and never allowing intimacy. If by chance he is placed in a situation likely to lead to intercourse, he may have a readily available repertoire of excuses for avoiding intercourse or explaining his failure. "I'm too tired" or "I drank too much" are commonly used. The married male is less likely to avoid sexual contacts and is usually confronted by his partner about his performance.

Performance anxiety is almost always associated with erectile failure or ejaculatory control problems and cannot be considered an isolated problem although it may demand a specific treatment approach.

Case Study

CASE 4. Mr. B. is single and a very good-looking 29-year-old, successful salesman who travels a great deal in his business. He is a very likeable and competent person with attractive social skills. His family background in all respects is quite normal and he has enjoyed a very active and successful sexual life up until six months before seeking treatment.

Mr. B. had always prided himself on his sexual skills and was shocked when he could not obtain an erection with a particularly attractive and aggressive female partner he had "picked up." His ego was shattered further when the woman's anger turned to motherly concern about what was wrong with him. The fact that he was drinking heavily did not serve to shoulder the blame, and he quickly and subsequently began asking himself what was wrong. He followed this incident with several other quick sexual experiences to further test whether or not indeed something was wrong. To his horror, he could not obtain an erection in any of these other instances and he was sent into a state of panic and avoided all sexual contacts for the next five months.

During the intake interview with Mr. B. it was apparent that he was highly anxious. His sexual anxiety had generalized to other aspects of his life, and he was having some difficulty in concentrating at work. Mr. B. underwent a program of systematic desensitization in which hierarchy items were structured around a gradual approach to intercourse. Variables of female aggressiveness and performance demand were also introduced into the scenes.

Following therapy Mr. B. started dating and was instructed to approach sex in a gradual nondemanding way. He was told to concentrate on nongenital and genital foreplay and especially aspects of pleasuring his partner. Finally, he was instructed not to rush into intercourse even if he had an erection and that it was perfectly normal for his penis to fluctuate in its degree of erectness during a sexual experience. This case was successfully treated and maintained its success at a six-month follow-up check.

Behavioral Analysis

Performance anxiety may be viewed as a conditioned emotional response (CER) following an upsetting sexual experience. As a result of erectile failure, the male experiences humiliation, embarrassment, and criticism. The subsequent emotional reaction is usually anxiety supported by negative self-statements that are evoked by real or imagined sexual stimuli. The anxiety in turn inhibits sexual arousal.

An alternative view of the role of anxiety may also be postulated. As in females, the role of anxiety in male sexual arousal is not entirely clear (Wincze, Wolchik, Beggs, & Sakheim, 1978). Anxiety not associated with sexual performance, may in fact enhance arousal while anxiety associated with sexual behavior may inhibit arousal. The facilitating or inhibiting effects of anxiety on sexual arousal may likely be under cognitive controlling factors rather than physiological factors. The CER model suggests inhibition on a physiological level à la Wolpe's reciprocal inhibition theory; while the cognitive model would suggest that focus on nonerotic stimuli (such as worry over whether or not an erection will be achieved) will inhibit arousal. In both models, the male would tend to avoid sexually arousing stimuli and, therefore, further reduce the opportunity to obtain erection.

Erectile Problems

Description

Erectile problems usually fall into two categories, acute and chronic, and they represent some of the most tragic cases facing the sex therapist. Since erection is often tied in with a man's feelings of self-esteem, loss of erection can trigger reactions of deep depression, panic, and anxiety. All men experience natural variations in the firmness of their erect penis and can readily estimate their percentage of firm or full erection. It is also common for men from time to time to achieve erection only after a great deal of stimulation or to not achieve erection at all. For some men, however, the experience of loss of erection or inability to achieve erection is devastating and is brought to the attention of health professionals.

In acute cases of erectile loss, the individual is usually panicky and describes his sexual encounters as traumatic failures. He desperately wants to achieve erection and may seek many sexual experiences in an attempt to overcome his problems. As panic grows and failure mounts, the male will begin to avoid sexual contacts and shut out erotic stimuli in defeatist resignation of his lot in life. After two years of erectile failures, he is considered chronic and often paints a tragic picture of an angry, defeated man. He may have sought medical advice and even obtained vitamin supplements or testosterone shots to desperately reverse his condition. Although there is an array of medical conditions, drugs, and physical conditions that can contribute to or directly cause loss of erections, an estimated 95% of all cases are psychogenic in origin (Kaplan, 1974). It is little consolation, however, for a man to be told by his physician (as so often is the case) that his erection loss is due to his nerves. In addition to the acute/chronic dichotomy, erectile failure can be "situational" specific or more "general."

The ability to achieve erection often varies with the stimuli one experiences; changes in sexual partners, types of sexual behaviors, or location of the sexual act may greatly influence the quality of the erectile experience. It is not uncommon to learn that a man is unable to achieve erection with his wife, but is able to with his lover; or is unable to have intercourse at home, but is able to on vacation. Such "situational" variations should be explored before advising on a therapy procedure.

Failure to attain erection can sometimes be associated with other sexual problems. A male who has a sexually uninteresting or even punitive partner may over the years gradually loose his erection capacity with that partner. Repeated experiences of suppressing arousal or of punishment following arousal (which may occur with a sexually anxious partner) may even lead to a more "general" erectile failure. That is, the male will be unable to obtain an erection in all situations with all partners. Males who experience lack of orgasmic control over long periods of time may end up with the double curse of lack of erection as well. Erectile failure in this case is most likely due to an active attempt on the part of the male to suppress arousal in order to delay ejaculation.

Finally, in fewer instances there exist males who have never obtained erections with a sexual partner. These men have earned the label of "primary" impotent by Masters and Johnson (1970) as distinguished from "secondary" impotent men who's erectile record contains incidents of successful sexual performance. The male who has never achieved successful erection is often a product of a very sexually restrictive background (Masters & Johnson, 1970). Strict moralistic teachings and condemnation of sexual behavior seem to be common ingredients leading to sexual difficulties in general and primary erectile problems in particular. While exceptions exist, these factors, nonetheless, appear prominent on the list of culprits.

Case Study

CASE 5. Mr. F is a 50-year-old, blue-collar worker who has been married 25 years. During the first 10 years of his marriage he had no erectile difficulties and for the most part had a satisfactory marriage. He comes from a very disturbed home in which his father was absent most of the time, and his mother was an explosive alcoholic. While his upbringing has left him marked with insecurities and temper control problems, he feels that he is relatively healthy compared to his two brothers and his sister.

Mrs. F. is a very unassertive woman who was raised in an extremely puritanical home. She never had experienced sexual relations before marriage and brought into the marriage sexual anxieties and feelings of disgust. Although she has participated in sexual relations with her husband throughout her marriage, she has never enjoyed sex and has steadfastly refused sexual experimentation.

Mr. F. began experiencing erectile difficulties about 15 years ago and has been totally impotent for the last 5 years. He denied experiencing nocturnal or morning erections and had not experienced erections in an extramarital affair one year ago. He claimed that he participated in the extramarital affair in order to "test out" whether or not he could achieve an erection.

When Mr. and Mrs. F. entered therapy they had not attempted intercourse for two years and were contemplating separation. Therapy initially focused on communication training and then a gradual shaping of sexual behaviors. Following six months of therapy, Mr. and Mrs. F. were participating in frequent sexual activity and were communicating very satisfactorily. Mr. F. is still unable to achieve full erection, although on some occasions he has achieved a partial erection and has used the stuff technique for completing intercourse.

Behavioral Analysis of Erectile Difficulties

Acute erectile problems very often follow psychological or physical trauma. When erectile failure occurs as a result of trauma, a male's reaction is commonly one of surprise and panic. Regardless of the initial precipitating event, he now worries a great deal over his failure and is well on his way to experiencing performance anxiety. Whether or not this anxiety inhibits erection on a physiological level is untested, but there is little doubt that concentration on performance can interfere with potentially arousing erotic stimulus cues. There are two possible ways in which this may occur. The formerly arousing cues may take on some negative properties as a result of the traumatic learning experience. Consequently, instead of evoking arousal the same stimulus cues now evoke an anxiety or unpleasant reaction. This is a higher-order classical conditioning model. A second way in which inhibition of arousal may occur is that erotic cues are not concentrated on as much as the nonerotic cue of performance; that is, "Will I or won't I achieve erection?" "If I don't achieve erection, will my partner be angry and belittle me?" In this interference model, the arousing erotic cues are not presented in sufficient intensity to evoke arousal; they are masked or eliminated almost entirely by concentration on performance cues.

Chronic erectile problems can best be conceptualized in a behavioral model as resulting from efforts to suppress arousal. During the initial stages of acute erectile failure, the male often frantically seeks out erotic cues in an attempt to "force" arousal. As sexual behavior and erotic cues are associated more and more with failure and other aversive cues, the male may stop seeking sexual experiences. This is a punishment and avoidance learning model. In order to avoid the aversive consequences associated with sexual behavior, the single male will stop dating or date women who are sexually passive or even undesirous of sex. The married male and his partner will often adopt a style of passive nonsexual coexistence. In order to help protect her husband from failure, she will not act in a seductive way. If such a couple does attempt a sexual encounter, they will not invest enthusiasm or eroticism into it. Such an investment would only heighten the disappointment and place the woman in the position of being "unfulfilled."

Finally, an analysis of "situational" erectile failure suggests a discrimination learning paradigm. Arousal is occurring in the presence of specific stimuli in which (*a*) aversive qualities are absent and/or (*b*) erotic qualities are strong for the individual. The individual who is not suffering from erectile failure, for perhaps many reasons, is able to make discriminations whereas the male suffering from more generalized erectile failure (as in the case of Mr. F.) is not. The "many reasons" may include personality variables, partner variables, and cognitive variables (what the individual says to himself). The cognitive factors may include such self-statements as "I don't love my wife, but I do love my lover" (even though the specific partner's behavior is equal) or "I can't make love in my parents' home, but I do feel free elsewhere."

Male Ejaculatory Problems

Description

The ability of the male to control ejaculation varies along a continuum from ejaculating very quickly (premature ejaculation) to not being able to ejaculate at all (retarded ejaculation). Most males are shocked to learn that the average time from intromission to ejaculation is estimated to be about two minutes (Masters & Johnson, 1970) and that long periods of intromission are not necessarily pleasurable to the female. Misinformation surrounding male ejaculation is extremely common and contributes to a great deal of unnecessary worry and mislabeling of normal behavior as problematic.

The preponderance of evidence suggests that almost all males experience great variations in their ability to control ejaculation. Younger males are especially prone to loosing control very rapidly. Fatigue, high levels of sexual excitation, and periods of abstinence can also contribute to quick ejaculatory response. The definition of a quick response varies greatly as pointed out by Caird and Wincze (1977). It is important to obtain a very accurate behavioral description of the "problem" before suggesting therapy since the cure may often be a simple information exchange.

There are some males, however, who repeatedly experience ejaculation prior to or within seconds after intromission and do not satisfy their female partner through intercourse. Males who experience such problems will often adopt a strategy of trying to suppress erotic cues by thought distraction and shortening periods of foreplay. The female may purposely avoid touching her partner's genitals or she may avoid acting in an erotic way to help prevent a disappointing experience. Such procedures do not serve a couple well and often decrease the pleasure experienced by both even more.

On the other end of the continuum there are males who cannot ejaculate without a great deal of prolonged direct stimulation and some who cannot ejaculate at all. Such behavior is rare and is frequently associated with ingestion of drugs or alcohol. For example, delayed ejaculation is a common side effect of methadone intake. Masters and Johnson (1970) see psychogenic cases of retarded ejaculation to be commonly associated with severe psychopathology. Since this problem occurs so rarely, there is less known about it than other sexual problems.

Case Study

CASE 6. Mr. V. is a typical example of a male who is experiencing difficulty in controlling his very rapid ejaculation. Mr. V. has been married less than a year and is a 22-year-old blue-collar worker. Both he and his wife are sexually experienced and enjoyed numerous sexual encounters before marriage. Mr. V. reports that he has almost always ejaculated within a few seconds after intromission and is very worried about this. Only on occasions in which he has ingested alcohol or smoked marijuana has he enjoyed longer periods of ejaculatory control.

Therapy initially concentrated on information exchange and a number of selected handouts were assigned as reading homework for both Mr. and Mrs. V. Secondly, Mr. and Mrs. V. were shown a film demonstrating the squeeze technique and a step-by-step program was advised leading to sexual intercourse.

Therapy was successful following seven sessions and the couple reported at a six-month follow-up that treatment gains had been maintained. Mr. V. was able to control ejaculation for longer periods of time and was using the squeeze technique during one-half of his sexual encounters.

Behavioral Analysis

Premature ejaculation enjoys one of the most successful treatment approaches of any sexual problem with reported success rates of 98.7% (Masters & Johnson, 1970). Unfortunately, the availability of effective treatment appears to have eclipsed research devoted to the understanding of ejaculatory control. Of the research that does exist, much of it is characterized by (*a*) poor experimental design, (*b*) inadequate control procedures, and (*c*) rudimentary assessment techniques. Recent advancements in psychophysiological assessment now make it possible to describe the psychophysiological processes that may be involved in ejaculatory control, but to date, the research has not been conducted.

Among the many unanswered questions about premature ejaculation are the specific roles of sexual anxiety and sexual arousal. It is true that most men who experience loss of ejaculation control are very anxious about their performance, but does the anxiety exacerbate loss of control? Wolpe (1969) considered conditioned anxiety to be responsible for loss of ejaculation control, whereas, Kaplan (1974) suggested that it might be due to an inability to detect excessive sexual arousal. Geer and Fuhr (1976) point out that there has been no empirical research to verify either of these hypotheses, but both hypotheses suggest a learning basis to the problem.

In the Wolpe position, it is postulated that stress associated with sexual cues via a classical conditioning process evokes anxiety that interferes with the ability to control ejaculation. The interference may be on a physiological level in which there is an overload of sympathetic arousal triggering ejaculation. The exact mechanism of action cannot be specified without further research.

Kaplan's (1974) hypothesis is similar to the "out of touch" hypothesis posited by Heiman regarding inorgasmic women. Men who lose ejaculatory control are not attentive to their arousal sensations preceding orgasm, and, consequently, do not regulate their preorgasmic sexual behavior. The orgasm occurs before their bodies have signaled them that they are aroused enough to ejaculate and/or when their bodies do signal them, they do not possess the behavioral skills to help decrease arousal to a manageable level. Increasing sexual experience may be one of the important factors related to ejaculatory control through which a male learns the necessary sexual skills by becoming more "in touch."

In contrast to the learning theory explanation of ejaculatory control, other researchers feel that the autonomic nervous system functioning of men experiencing ejaculatory problems may be fundamentally different from that of "normal" males. Rosen, Shapiro and Schwartz (1976) described a "tension" pattern of autonomic nervous system activity, characterized by unusual variability of respiratory, heart rate, and penile circumference measures in certain subjects and they feel that this may be a precursor to premature ejaculation. If this is true, it would lend credence to a theory of premature ejaculation that proposes a biological substrate (Johnson, 1968).

TREATMENT

As outlined earlier, the conceptualization of sexual difficulties is very complex and often involves many-faceted problems. Although sexual symptoms may appear similar in various individuals, the etiology of their difficulties may be very different and the treatment approaches demanded may also differ greatly. In dealing with sexual problems, a therapist should adopt a very flexible approach to treatment and be prepared to use combinations of techniques and focus on nonsexual problems if necessary. All too often, sexual problems and their treatment are simplified and described in a manner that almost ensures their misuse. In a recent review article, Wright, Perreault, and Mathieu (1977) note that although there have been tremendous advances in the treatment of sexual dysfunction in the last 15 years, there is "a clear danger that some of these promising treatment procedures are being applied indiscriminately with inadequately selected populations" (p. 890). The desire for a clear understanding of sexual problems and a quick effective treatment has proven seductive and has misled individual therapists to overlook complexities in the problems they face.

Controlled research evaluating the effectiveness of sex therapy is sorely lacking. Wincze, Hoon, and Hoon (1978) have indicated that as evaluation becomes more objective, there is less observable change in a patient's sexual problems following treatment. It matters very much just what criterion will be used to evaluate change in a sexual problem; Wincze and Caird (1976) and Levine and Agle (1978) have noted that change in one sexual problem, such as performance, will not necessarily change desire or even sexual satisfaction.

In discussing various treatment approaches for sexual problems, it is important for the reader to keep in mind that the efficacy of the methodology is largely untested in a strict experimental research sense. A convergence of clinical evidence and uncontrolled or poorly controlled research studies comprise our major source of treatment knowledge. The behavioral treatment approaches outlined below may be evaluated on a different plane, however, since much of the support comes from applications to other problems. It is not a question, for example, of whether or not systematic desensitization works, but rather how it can be applied to sexual problems. The treatment approaches outlined below fall into three major areas: anxiety reduction, skill acquisition, and decreasing problem behaviors. Application to "pure" sexual problems are discussed since behavioral treatment of other non-sexual problems are reviewed elsewhere in this text.

Treatment of Sexual Anxiety Problems

It has long been recognized by most researchers and clinicians that anxiety is strongly implicated in sexual difficulties either as a precursor to the problem or as a by-product of it. The earliest applications of behavioral approaches to the treatment of sexual difficulties have been anxiety reduction procedures (Brady, 1966; Friedman, 1968; Lazarus, 1963; Wolpe, 1969). Systematic desensitization and its variations has been the mainstay of the anxiety reduction procedures and has enjoyed support from numerous clinical case reports and uncontrolled studies as well as more controlled research studies (Obler, 1973; Wincze & Caird, 1976). For the most part, systematic desensitization has been applied to cases of women experiencing sexual anxiety although there are some reports of its application to men experiencing erectile difficulties (Cooper, 1969a) and ejaculation problems (Cooper, 1969b).

There are surprisingly few controlled studies that have looked at the effectiveness of systematic desensitization as applied to sexual problems. Although some studies have reported encouraging results with systematic desensitization, Wright, Perreault, and Mathieu (1977) felt after reviewing the literature that no strong claims could be made for the effectiveness of directive therapies, including systematic desensitization with sexual problems. Their somewhat pessimistic point of view is based on the following observations:

(1) Most of the studies reported to date are based on unsystematic case reports and, consequently, are open to all possible experimental confounds; (2) Success notes vary widely from study to study (39% to 98%); (3) The three studies that include a control condition found a wide variation in rate of change in untreated patients; and (4) Most studies either provided little data on the degree and type of psychopathology in their patients or are highly selective, ruling out all patients with nonsexual psychopathology [p. 888].

The application of systematic desensitization procedures to sexual problems is basically the same as it would be applied to other anxiety problems. Relaxation is taught, a hierarchy is constructed, and scenes from the hierarchy are systematically presented to the client in imagination or through audiovisual means (Wincze & Caird, 1976). For women, the theme of the hierarchy usually focuses on a gradual approach to sexual behavior. The most anxiety-evoking item is usually intercourse, but may for some women be breast or genital stimulation. For men, the hierarchy theme may be similar to that for women, but it almost always includes the suggestion of performance demand and the experience of sexual failure.

In addition to systematic desensitization, operant procedures can be used to help sexually anxious clients relax. Masters and Johnson (1970) describe a procedure they labeled "sensate focus" that is essentially a gradual step-by-step approach to sexual intercourse. This carefully programmed approach is akin to the operant procedure of reinforced practice (Callahan & Leitenberg, 1970). Approach behavior is rewarded while avoidance behavior is extinguished through nonreward. In the sensate focus procedure, couples are instructed to create a nondemanding atmosphere (therefore, nonpunishing) and to concentrate on pleasurable (rewarding) sensations. This procedure is an important one for the treatment of both male and female sexual problems in which anxiety plays an important role.

One final anxiety-reducing procedure is cognitive restructuring. It may matter a great deal what a person is saying to herself or himself when approaching and engaging in a sexual experience. For a male confronted with erectile difficulties, it may be especially crucial for him to say to himself something that is self-supporting as opposed to self-depreciating. For example, in Tahiti, where sexual difficulties are almost unknown, males who experience erectile difficulties attribute their lack of arousal to the female's inability to turn them on rather than their own inadequacy.

If a man starts to caress a woman and finds that he does not have an erection, he will decide that the woman is not attractive to him and make some excuse to avoid proceeding. This is not considered a failure, nor is it considered that in spite of this desire for intercourse, he cannot perform. He simply concludes that he does not want to have intercourse. [Levy, 1973, p. 129].

Such an interpretation by the Tahitian male may help ensure future sexual success and protect him against sexual trauma. Another example of cognitive restructuring may be in the interpretation of physiological response. Since almost all of the physiological signs of anxiety are present during sexual arousal (i.e., increased heart rate, increased respiration, and sweating) it may be of value to teach an individual to relabel anxiety symptoms as signs of sexual arousal. This may be of special value to women who deny experiencing sexual arousal, yet experience sexual anxiety. Cognitive restructuring may hold promise as a treatment approach for sexual anxiety problems, but this is largely speculative and awaits future research support.

Sexual Skill Acquisition

Skillful sexual behavior is not something that one is born with, rather, it is a learned skill as is playing the piano or soccer. Unlike the learning of piano or soccer, however, there are no organized and institutionalized mechanisms in our society for learning sexual skills, and most individuals are left to their own trial and error learning experiences. For some, the trial and error of these experiences may be very good; if one finds a patient and competent teacher and has exposure to sensible educational material, then he or she is likely to develop adequate sexual skills. Many individuals, however, have not had beneficial sexual training and may have deficits in a number of areas, such as orgasmic control, ability to become aroused, sexual knowledge, and timing of behaviors. Such deficits may lead to awkward and disappointing sexual experiences that in turn may result in feelings of inadequacy and anxiety.

Behaviorists have conceptualized many areas of sexual difficulties as skill deficits. The most notable behaviorally oriented program is the "Sexual Growth Program" developed by Heiman, LoPiccolo, and LoPiccolo (1976). This program is based on operant shaping in which complex behavioral chains are broken down into simpler components through a step-by-step procedure. As early components of the chain are mastered, they become the building blocks for more complex sexual behaviors. A sexual growth program approach may be applicable to male and female orgasmic and arousal difficulties. The Masters and Johnson (1970) programs of sensate focus and squeeze technique may also be viewed as skill acquisition programs although behavioral terminology is not used.

One important point about sexual skill training is that there are constitutional factors that may enhance or limit a person's ability to benefit from training. Just as there are Van Cliburns and Péles in music and sports, so too there exist sexual athletes whose skills may far surpass those of most individuals. And, conversely, there are musical and sporting bumblers and sexual bumblers as well who can't quite get their act together in spite of training.

Occasionally, individuals have incorporated behaviors within their sexual repertoir that lead to unsatisfactory sexual experiences. For example, an individual may ritualistically bathe just before or immediately after a sexual encounter. Although cleanliness is next to godliness in most instances, such behavior can prove to be handicapping in sexual situations if it is compulsive in nature. When behavioral excesses are present, they may be dealt with through a behavioral training program. In the case of a compulsive bather, increasing amounts of time between bathing and intercourse can be outlined as the goal behavior. The person's sexual partner can provide feedback and reinforcement for meeting the set criterion of each sexual experience.

SUMMARY

Although very specific behavioral treatment approaches have been outlined, it should be emphasized that these procedures are often limited. In a great many cases, discussion with the therapist and reading assignments will account for significant changes in a client's attitude and behavior and should be capitalized on whenever possible.

A behavioral approach to sexual problems can be employed as a therapy in and of itself or it may be used as an adjunct procedure for short-term or long-term therapy. A therapist's skills comes in knowing how to assess the problem thoroughly and accurately, and then orchestrating the appropriate sequence of therapeutic procedures. The model of sexual enjoyment and distress presented in Table 1 helps to underscore the complexity of assessment and treatment approaches and strongly argues against "package" approaches to "sex therapy" popularized in traveling cross-country workshops. A functional behavioral analysis of an individual's sexual problem is advocated. This approach will help the therapist to individually tailor therapy to the client's needs and employ behavioral procedures when they are indicated.

As a final cautionary note, there are clients who have difficulty in accepting a learning theory explanation of their sexual problems and may be looking for either a medical explanation or a more insight-oriented one. Such clients would most probably find working within a behavior therapy approach troublesome. The directed sexual exercises may be viewed as awkward, intrusive, unnatural, offensive, and unimportant. A therapist should thoroughly explore a client's feelings about a directed behavioral approach before launching into such a program.

REFERENCES

Barlow, D. H. Assessment of sexual behavior. In R. A. Ciminero, K. S. Calhoun, and H. E. Adams (Eds.), *Handbook of behavioral assessment.* New York: Wiley, 1977.

Bentler, P. Heterosexual behavior assessment I. Males. *Behaviour Research and Therapy,* 1968, **6**, 21–25. (a)

Bentler, P. Heterosexual behavior assessment II. Females. *Behaviour Research and Therapy,* 1968, **6**, 27–30. (b)

Brady, J. P. Brevital relaxation treatment of frigidity. *Behaviour Research and Therapy,* 1966, **4**, 71–77.

Brown, D. G. Female orgasm and sexual inadequacy. In R. Brecher and E. Brecher (Eds.), *An analysis of human sexual response.* New York: Signet Books, 1966.

Caird, W. K., & Wincze, J. P. *Sex therapy: A behavioral approach.* Hagerstown, MA.: Harper & Row, 1977.

Callahan, E. J., & Leitenberg, H. Aversion therapy for sexual deviation: contingent shock and covert sensitization. *Journal of Abnormal Psychology,* 1973, **81**, 60–73.

Cooper, A. J. A clinical study of coital anxiety in male potency disorders. *Journal of Psychological Research,* 1969, **13**, 143–147. (a)

Cooper, A. J. Clinical and therapeutic studies in premature ejaculation. *Comprehensive Psychiatry,* 1969, **10**, 285–294. (b)

Feldman, M., MacCullough, M., Mellor, V., & Pinschof, J. The application of anticipatory avoidance learning to the treatment of homosexuality III: The sexual orientation method. *Behaviour Research and Therapy,* 1966, **4**, 289–299.

Fenichel, O. *The psychoanalytic theory of neurosis.* New York: W. W. Norton, 1945.

Ferster, C. B. Classification of behavioral pathology. In L. Krasner & L. D. Ullmann (Eds.), *Research in behavioral modification.* New York: Holt, Rinehart & Winston, 1965.

Frank, E., Anderson, C., & Rubenstein, D. Frequency of sexual dysfunction in "normal" couples. *New England Journal of Medicine,* 1978, **299**, 111–115.

Friedman, D. The treatment of impotency by Brevital relaxation therapy. *Behaviour Research and Therapy,* 1968, **6**, 257–261.

Geer, J., & Fuhr, R. Cognitive factors in sexual arousal: The role of distraction. *Journal of Consulting and Clinical Psychology,* 1976, **44**, 238–243.

Heiman, J. "Use of the vaginal photoplethysmograph as a diagnostic and treatment aid in female sexual dysfunction." Paper presented at the annual meeting of the American Psychological Association, Illinois, 1975.

Heiman, J., LoPiccolo, L., & LoPiccolo, J. *Becoming orgasmic: a sexual growth program for women.* Englewood Cliffs, N.J., Prentice-Hall, 1976.

Hoon, E., Hoon, P., & Wincze, J. The SAI: An inventory for the measurement of female sexual arousal. *Archives of Sexual Behavior,* 1976, **5**, 291–300.

Hoon, P. W., Wincze, J. P., & Hoon, E. F. A test of reciprocal inhibition: Are anxiety and sexual arousal in women mutually inhibitory? *Journal of Abnormal Psychology,* 1977, **86**, 65–74.

Jovanovic, V. The recording of physiological evidence of genital arousal in human males and females. *Archives of Sexual Behavior,* 1971, **1**, 309–320.

Johnson, J. *Disorders of sexual potency in the male.* Oxford: Pergamon Press, 1968.

Kanfer, F. H., & Saslow, G. Behavioral diagnosis. In C. M. Franks (Ed.), *Behavior therapy: Appraisal and status.* New York, McGraw-Hill, 1969.

Kaplan, H. S. *The new sex therapy: Brief treatment of sexual dysfunction.* New York: Brunner/Mazel, 1974.

Kolenberg, R. Directed masturbation and the treatment of primary orgasmic dysfunction. *Archives of Sexual Behavior,* 1974, **3**, 349–356.

Kuriansky, J. B., & Sharpe, L. Guidelines for evaluating sex therapy. *Journal of Sex and Marriage,* 1976, **2**, 303–308.

Lazarus, A. A. The treatment of chronic frigidity by systematic desensitization. *Journal of Nervous and Mental Diseases,* 1963, **136**, 272–278.

Lief, H., & Reed, D. Sexual Knowledge and Attitude Test (SKAT). University of Pennsylvania, School of Medicine: Division of Family Study, Department of Psychiatry. 2nd edition, 1972.

Levine, S. B., & Agle, D. "The effectiveness of sex therapy for chronic secondary psychological impotence." Paper presented at the Eastern Association for Sex Therapists' Convention, New York, 1978.

Levy, R. I., Bodies. In Levy, R. I., *Tahitians: Mind and experience in the society islands.* Chicago: University Press, 1973.

Masters, W. H., & Johnson, V. E. *Human sexual response.* Boston: Little, Brown, 1966.

Masters, W. H., & Johnson, V. E. *Human sexual inadequacy* Boston: Little, Brown, 1970.

Meichenbaum, D. Examination of model characteristics in reducing avoidance behavior. *Journal of Personality and Social Psychology,* 1971, **17**, 298–307.

Obler, M. Systematic desensitization in sexual disorders. *Journal of Behavior Therapy and Experimental Psychiatry,* 1973, **4**, 93–101.

O'Connor, J. "The relationship of sex therapy and psychodynamics." Paper presented at Eastern Association for Sex Therapists' Convention, New York, 1978.

Rosen, R. C., Shapiro, D., & Schwartz, G. E. Voluntary control of penile tumescence. *Psychosomatic Medicine,* 1976, **37**, 479–483.

Schacter, S., & Singer, J. E. Cognitive, social and physiological determinants of emotional state. *Psychological Review,* 1962, **69**, 379–399.

Wincze, J. P. & Caird, W. K. The effects of systematic desensitization and video desensitization in the treatment of essential sexual dysfunction in women. *Behavior Therapy,* 1976, **7**, 335–342.

Wincze, J. P., Hoon, E. F., & Hoon, P. W. Physiological responsivity of normal and sexually dysfunctional women during erotic stimulus exposure. *Journal of Psychosomatic Research,* 1976, **20**, 445–451.

Wincze, J. P., Hoon, E. F. & Hoon, P. W. Multiple measure analysis of women experiencing low sexual arousal. *Behaviour Research and Therapy,* 1978, **16**, 43–49.

Wincze, J. P., Wolchik, S., Beggs, V., & Sakheim, D. "The influence of various emotional states on sexual arousability in males and females." Paper presented at the American Psychological Association Convention, Toronto, 1978.

Wolpe, J. *The practice of behavior therapy.* Oxford: Pergamon Press, 1969.

Wright, J., Perreault, R., & Mathieu, M. The treatment of sexual dysfunction: A review. *Archives of General Psychiatry,* 1977, **34**, 881–890.

Zuckerman, M. Physiological measures of sexual arousal in the human. *Psychological Bulletin,* 1971, **75**, 347–356.

CHAPTER 12

Behavior Therapy
with Sexual Deviations

Henry E. Adams, C. David Tollison, and Tracey Potts Carson

Sexual deviations are usually defined as sexual arousal to inappropriate persons, objects, or activities. Constituent disorders range from innocuous erotic attachment to women's shoes (a fetish) to vicious assault on others for the purpose of sexual gratification. The Diagnostic and Statistical Manual II (DSM-II, APA, 1968) reserves this classification "for individuals whose sexual interests are directed primarily toward objects other than people of the opposite sex, toward sexual acts not usually associated with coitus, or toward coitus performed under bizarre circumstances as in necrophilia, pedophilia, sexual sadism, and fetishism" (p. 44). Although many of these individuals are disgusted with their sexual practices, they remain unable to find gratification through normal sexual activity. The DSM-II further notes that diagnosing an individual as a sexual deviant is not appropriate when engagement in deviant sexual acts is caused by an unavailability of normal sexual objects.

The DSM-III (APA, 1980) has substantially modified the classification criteria for sexual deviations. These conditions have been relabeled as "paraphilias." According to the DSM-III, paraphilias are characterized by repetitive and persistent sexually arousing fantasies—often of an unusual nature—that are associated with either: (*a*) preference for use of a nonhuman object for sexual arousal, (*b*) repetitive sexual activity with humans involving real or simulated suffering or humiliation, or (*c*) repetitive sexual activity with nonconsenting partners. It is noted that the paraphiliac fantasy or activity is not always unusual (such as viewing women's underwear) but becomes deviant when it is the focal rather than peripheral goal of sexual activity. The DSM-III further specifies that homosexuality is not a sexual deviation unless the individual's sexual values are inconsistent with his/her sexual behavior (referred to an ego-dystonic homosexuality). Of course, the classificatory category of ego-dystonic homosexuality raises the question of whether subjective distress should be a defining characteristic for any or all sexual deviations.

Sexual deviations have often been labeled as a personality disorder because they usually develop during childhood or adolescent years, tend to be stable over time, and may be associated with a lack of anxiety or guilt. However, unlike personality disorders, sexual deviations do not necessarily involve a pervasive disturbance of interpersonal functioning. Impairment is often restricted to the area of sexual relations.

Paraphilias, or sexual deviations, must be differentiated from sexual dysfunctions. While both deviations and dysfunctions usually involve a disruption of heterosexual activity associated with coitus, only for sexual deviations is sexual arousal elicited, maintained, and increased by persons, activities, or objects not typically associated with coitus. The defining characteristic of sexual dysfunctions is a suppression of sexual arousal caused by negative emotions (i.e., anxiety, disgust, pain, etc.). Sexual deviations, on the other hand, involve a lack of sexual arousal to appropriate heterosexual stimuli and may or may not include negative emotions.

Many individuals with sexual deviations do engage in heterosexual practices. However, the occurrence or nonoccurrence of heterosexual activity is not diagnostically significant. Sexual performance, even in males, can occur in situations that are not intrinsically sexually arousing if the individual fantasizes about another situation to arouse himself. For example, a homosexual male may successfully engage in heterosexual intercourse by using homosexual fantasy. Sexual orientation must therefore be defined in terms of *preferred* sexual stimuli and activity.

Behavior therapy for modification of sexual deviations can be discussed in a variety of ways. One approach is to organize discussion of treatment strategies around traditional psychiatric categories of the sexual deviations. This approach is inherently problematical. First, the diagnostic categories used by the psychiatric classification system convey very little specific information about the target problem(s) and consequently are extremely heterogeneous. Pedophilia, for example, may be heterosexual or homosexual, may or may not involve sadism or rape, and may include only exhibitionistic and/or voyeuristic behavior. There are many types of pedophilia whose only common characteristic is the occurrence of sexual activity with an individual who is not legally of age. Second, this type of approach focuses on deviant sexual arousal as the major characteristic of sexual deviation, at the expense of ignoring other crucial aspects of sexual behavior. Simplistic attempts to modify only deviant sexual arousal, while ignoring other crucial elements of sexual behavior, are not likely to render a successful therapeutic outcome (Adams & Sturgis, 1978). Unfortunately, this narrow focus of treatment efforts has been the common practice (Adams & Sturgis, 1978).

Alternatively, behavior therapy with sexual deviations may be discussed as an overall approach to the assessment and modification of aberrant sexual arousal, gender behavior, heterosocial behavior, and heterosexual behavior. This approach encompasses multiple components of sexual orientation and thereby avoids the limitations of many standard diagnostic categories. A careful assessment along these lines involves the identification and delineation of specific problem behaviors, and it facilitates the development of an individualized treatment program for each patient, tailored to his personal therapeutic needs.

In the remainder of this chapter, assessment and modification of deviant sexual functioning is discussed from a multicomponent, behavioral perspective. As the literature to date has focused almost exclusively on *males* with these problems, this discussion does not address the assessment and modification of inappropriate sexual orientation in females.

ASSESSMENT OF DEVIANT SEXUAL BEHAVIOR

In behavior therapy, adequate assessment of sexual behavior requires continuous monitoring across three channels of data: subjective report, behavioral observation, and physiological measurement. While there are obvious advantages to collecting such data in the patient's natural environment where the problems occur, the clinician is usually required to develop analog or contrived situations within the clinic setting for assessment and treatment purposes. A major problem of these analog situations is that they are often highly artificial, at best. Of course, it is difficult to capture all parameters of the environment and patient behavior with clinical simulations. Along this line, analogs must incorporate as many features of the natural behavioral/environmental context as possible to maximize their utility. The validity and reliability of any analog, in turn, must be continuously monitored to ensure that it is yielding accurate information concerning the individual's behavior in the natural environment (Barlow, 1977).

There are obvious limitations to direct behavioral observation of sexual activity. Some sex therapists, however, do observe and record individuals engaging in overt sexual behavior, including intercourse (Hartman & Fithian, 1972; Serber, 1974). Masters and Johnson (1966, 1970) have observed several hundred couples involved in sexual activity, and the data obtained from these observations have been of monumental importance in the field of human sexuality and sexual therapy. Because of the private nature of sexual functioning in our society, assessment of sexual arousal and behavior through direct behavioral observation is generally considered questionable, especially from an ethical perspective. Thus, the clinician usually employs analog situations to measure early components in the sequence of sexual activities, with emphasis on the component of sexual arousal.

In what follows, we discuss assessment procedures relative to the commonly recognized components of sexual orientation, beginning with the assessment of sexual arousal itself.

Assessment of Sexual Arousal

Masters and Johnson (1966) have noted that such nongenital measures as increased blood pressure, heart rate, respiration, skin conductance, and pupillary dilation correlate with *active* sexual behaviors of masturbation and coitus. However, a majority of sexual deviant individuals evidence abnormalities in sexual arousal much earlier in the chain of sexual behaviors—much earlier than the climatic phase. Consequently, physiological data collected in assessment must tap into the earlier stage of arousal.

The physiological responses most frequently employed in the investigation of male sexual arousal fall into five categories: (*a*) electrodermal responses; (*b*) cardiovascular responses; (*c*) respiratory responses; (*d*) pupillary responses; and (*e*) penile erection. Of these, the most accurate indices of male sexual arousal in both psychological and medical research has been penile erection, as measured by various types of penile transducers (Abel, Blanchard, Barlow, & Mavissakalian, 1975). The specific devices employed are of two distinct types: (*a*) volumetric; and (*b*) circumferential. Exactly which type of apparatus is preferable remains a subject of debate. McConaghy (1974) claims that the less cumbersome and more durable volumetric devices are more sensitive and capable of detecting smaller penile changes. According to Barlow (1977), both types of devices are capable of detecting low levels of arousal that the subject is not aware of; however, volumetric devices are more accurate when extremely low arousal level recordings are necessary. Barlow (1977) has concluded that more investigation of these devices is necessary before a final comparative evaluation can be made. (For a more extensive discussion of penile transducers, see Barlow [1977].)

The patient's sexual arousal pattern should be physiologically assessed with reference to a variety of stimuli. The ultimate goal is to determine those specific stimuli that elicit sexual arousal. First, stimuli that are *likely* to elicit inappropriate arousal are identified from the patient's self-report of situations, objects, and people that are associated with deviant arousal and behavior. These stimuli are then sequentially presented to the patient (with pictures, slides, audio tapes, reading material, guided imagery, etc.) to determine which of them elicit a physiological arousal response. The percentage of arousal elicited by various stimuli can be determined by comparing the degree of arousal to a particular stimulus to the degree of arousal attained during a full erection. Self-report ratings of arousal level are also obtained from the patient during this physiological assessment to determine the correlation between self-report and physiological measures of arousal. Finally, this same procedure is administered with reference to heterosexual stimuli—to identify which, if any, heterosexual stimuli are arousal-eliciting for the patient.

Verbal report information should also be collected in the assessment of sexual arousal. Frequently, subjective information is gathered through the use of self-report inventories and self-monitoring devices. Self-report information may be obtained with questionnaires that attempt to assess sexual attitudes or patterns of sexual arousal. Commonly, these questionnaires are used for one of two purposes: intrasubject comparison with repeated administrations over time; or the comparison of an individual with a standardized group as, for example, on the Sexual Anxiety Scale (Obler, 1973). Self-monitoring procedures require the individual to record the occurrences of a specified behavior, the events that precede and follow the behavior, and the parameters of situations in which the behavior occurs.

We have already commented on direct behavioral observation of sexual activity by the clinician. If the patient has a sexual partner, she of course will be an important source of observational data. If the patient lacks a partner, observational data may be obtained through the participation of a sexual surrogate, a practice that has recently been a topic of considerable publicity. While at first glance the use of surrogates for patients without sexual partners seems a viable, logical approach, some have labeled this practice as "thinly veiled prostitution" (Holden, 1974). Most disturbing is the current trend for sexual surrogates to move toward becoming independent therapists and to operate without professional supervision (LoPiccolo, 1977).

Assessment of Gender Behavior

The most recently investigated and probably the least understood of the four major components of sexual behavior is gender role behavior. Barlow (1977) defines deviation of gender role as "some degree of incongruence between one's biological and genetic sex and the behavior accompanying that sex as defined by a given culture" (p. 494). Although a formal assessment of gender role behavior is not necessary with every patient, it is not uncommon to find that some sexual deviants draw attention to themselves by displaying opposite-sex gender behaviors, which may sabotage their efforts at successful sexual reorientation.

One self-report instrument for assessing gender role behavior is the Body-Image Scale developed by Lindgren and Pauly (1975). Although this scale is designed to assess gender role behavior in general, it is specifically constructed to assess and evaluate transsexuals. The body-image scale, as the name implies, supposedly assesses a subject's satisfaction with the physical appearance of his/her various body parts. Another verbal-report scale of gender role behavior is the Sex Role Inventory (Bem, 1974). The Sex Role Inventory attempts to assess orientation to the masculine or feminine sex role by asking subjects to choose items that best describe themselves. Feminine items include such descriptives as "cheerful" and "affectionate," while masculine descriptive items include "aggressive" and "ambitious." Bem considers masculinity and femininity as two separate and distinct entities and believes it is possible to categorize individuals as either masculine, feminine, or androgynous—androgynous being a category that incorporates aspects of both sex roles.

The assessment of gender role behavior through observation of overt behavior is accomplished largely with the use of behavioral checklists and coding systems. Barlow, Reynolds, and Agras (1973) approached the assessment of gender role behavior by directly assessing the motor behaviors of sitting, standing, and walking for both sexes. According to the authors, females tend to sit with their lower back and buttocks close to the back of a hard-back chair and cross their legs with one knee resting on the other. On the other hand, males tend to sit with the lower back and buttocks away from the back of a chair and cross their legs with one ankle resting on the opposite knee. Barlow (1977) has claimed that the checklist demonstrates that females have a much greater variety of behaviors while sitting, standing, and walking than do males, who are limited to a very narrow range of behaviors, which are considered characteristically masculine.

Assessment of Heterosocial Skills

The importance of adequate heterosocial skills has been recognized by clinicians of various theoretical persuasions as germaine to successful heterosexual functioning. For example, believing that homosexuality is a result of fear or avoidance of the opposite sex, some behavioral clinicians have long been engaging in some form of heterosocial skills training with their homosexual patients (Barlow, 1977). Most research on the assessment of heterosocial skills has involved analog studies with college students. This is not surprising, since most psychological research is conducted within the university setting, and college students represent a convenient subject pool for the psychology academician. These studies typically involve students presumed to be deficient in heterosocial skills when their self-report indicates minimal dating.

Two somewhat different theoretical positions have been postulated to account for deficits in heterosocial functioning. The first position postulates that maladaptive heterosocial functioning is a result of conditioned anxiety that inhibits the expression of normal feelings and the performance of adaptive heterosocial behavior (Borkovec, Stone, O'Brien, & Kaloupek, 1974). The second position views low-frequency dating (i.e. minimal heterosocial contact) as a function of the individual's failure to learn adaptive heterosocial skills (Twentyman & McFall, 1975). These somewhat contrasting approaches to etiology are also reflected in the choice of assessment technique. For example, Borkovec et al. (1974) utilized self-report measures of anxiety and subjective awareness of internal autonomic cues in the assessment of heterosocial functioning. Twentyman and McFall (1975), on the other hand, conducted a direct assessment of behaviors representing social skill. When possible, it is wise to obtain self-report and physiological indices of anxiety as well as behavioral measurement of patient interactional behavior. Anxiety may be blocking the expression of acceptable heterosocial behavior, but it also may have prevented sufficient acquisition of heterosocial skills.

Self-monitoring data may be useful in assessing heterosocial behavior. Generally, self-recording techniques require a person to record instances and parameters of heterosocial interactions. Table 1 is an example of a self-recording form we used with a 19-year-old homosexual college male who presented minimal heterosexual dating and significant heterosocial anxiety.

Heterosexual skills are directly measured by assessing specific behaviors that presumably comprise heterosocial skills, relative to specific situations in which these target behaviors are typically observed (Hersen & Bellack, 1977). Assessment situations usually involve either role playing or *in vivo* heterosocial interactions within the clinical setting. Unfortunately, most of the work in this area to date has been of limited usefulness for clinical purposes. For example, Barlow, Abel, Blanchard, Bristow, and Young (1975) have developed a behavioral observation checklist of three heterosocial behaviors that supposedly differentiate heterosocially successful males from socially incompetent males having sexual problems. These authors claim that voice, form of conversation, and affect differentiate

Table 1.   Daily Heterosocial Recording Form

NAME: Tommy Shy
DATE: Tuesday, March 10

Partner	Time	Antecedent	Consequence
1. Girl in history class	30 seconds	She asked to borrow my notes	I gave her my notes for overnight study
2. Girl who lives next door	9 minutes	I went over to ask her to the movies	She already had date
3. Girl in my chemistry class	26 minutes	I met her in cafeteria and had lunch with her. Also asked her out for Friday night	She accepted
4. Roommate's girlfriend	30 seconds	I asked her to get me a date sometime	She said she didn't know anyone that I would like

heterosocially competent from incompetent males; but it is doubtful that these variables alone adequately measure heterosocial behavior.

Assessment of Heterosexual Behavior

Heterosexual behavior refers to those behaviors that are specifically sexual in nature yet are heavily influenced by each of the other three components of sexual orientation. Assessment of heterosexual skills is important in determining whether the patient has the required knowledge and skills necessary for successful sexual interaction. An individual may have adequate and appropriate heterosexual arousal, evidence appropriate gender behavior, and be skilled in interacting socially with the opposite sex, yet he may lack the sexual knowledge and skills necessary to initiate and maintain an adequate sexual encounter.

Assessment of heterosocial behavior by means of verbal report is conducted primarily during clinical interviews. A complete sexual history is important for determination of how and where the patient first learned and applied knowledge about sex and standards for sexual conduct. Equally important is questioning about the patient's first deviant sexual experience and its immediate consequences, as well as initial attempts, if any, at nondeviant sexual interaction. Other topics of assessment include: patient knowledge of the functioning of male and female sexual anatomy, awareness of appropriate sexual behavior, and knowledge of techniques to elicit sexual arousal in the opposite-sex partner.

Assessment of heterosexual skills via observational data is usually limited to questioning the individual's sexual partner. In the absence of a willing sexual partner, as discussed previously, some therapists employ the services of sexual surrogates for their patients. Observational data should provide specific information about the individual's sexual skills, covering sexual approach behavior and foreplay through intercourse.

MODIFICATION OF DEVIANT SEXUAL ORIENTATION

Elimination of Deviant Arousal

The major procedures employed to directly decrease inappropriate sexual arousal are collectively referred to as aversion therapy. Aversion therapy involves the presentation of an aversive stimulus contingent upon the occurrence of maladaptive responses. The goal of such procedures is to develop a strong association between undesirable target behaviors and aversive reinforcement (Rachman & Teasdale, 1969). Aversion therapy is applicable to the treatment of behavioral disorders in which the patient's behavior is undesirable to himself and/or society but nevertheless self-reinforcing (Rachman & Teasdale, 1969). Consequently, it is not surprising that deviant sexual patterns have been frequent targets for these procedures. Although a sexually deviant individual may regard his sexual activity as repugnant and may actually desire alteration of his sexual orientation, his deviant sexual behavior has acquired reinforcing properties by virtue of its connection with orgasmic pleasure. It should be noted that aversion therapy is designed to eliminate undesirable responses but does not ensure the development of alternative, desirable behaviors. As we have indicated earlier, eliminating an undesirable sexual response is not sufficient unless the patient has learned alternative, appropriate means of gratifying sexual urges. Thus the effectiveness of aversion therapy is enhanced when there is training for the patient in a satisfactory, alternative form of sexual arousal and behavior.

Most behavioral scientists who have systematically investigated aversion treatment techniques have concluded that aversion, when administered correctly, is effective in modifying human behavior (Azrin & Holtz, 1966; Baer, 1971; Forgione, 1976). Even those who view it less favorably admit that aversion therapy has been very promising in areas where other therapeutic techniques have failed (Rachman & Teasdale, 1969). Of course, careless administration of aversive stimulation (or any treatment technique, for that matter) is likely to have deleterious effects. Unfortunately, aversive therapeutic techniques are easy to abuse and can be employed for unethical, punitive purposes. The harmful consequences of careless practice, though, should not subtract from the potential benefits accrued from careful application of aversive procedures. Furthermore, aversive techniques should not be labeled unethical or cruel simply because they are experienced as noxious by the patient. Many beneficial therapeutic procedures, including psychotherapy, may cause distress to a patient.

All therapeutic techniques—especially those that induce pain and discomfort—should be performed in a manner that facilitates expedient and maximal success. To this end, variables that affect the efficacy of aversion therapy are worthy of careful consideration. For example, with punishment techniques, low or intermediate levels of intensity often produce adaptation, and the frequency and/or intensity of the stimulus must be increased to even greater proportions before behavioral suppression is achieved (Arzin & Holtz, 1966). Thus it may be more humane as well as more effective to use a relatively high intensity of negative stimulation at the beginning of treatment to prevent adaptation effects. The contingency arrangement between deviant responses and negative stimulation is also an important factor. That is, the closer the aversive stimulus follows the undesired response, the more effective the suppression of the response. The therapist should ensure that escape from contact with the aversive stimulus is not possible, as this will reduce the impact of aversive stimulation. Finally, patient motivation to engage in deviant behavior can be decreased by reinforcing alternative, competing responses (e.g., reinforcement of heterosexual arousal). Programming contingent, positive consequences for alternative responses may also reduce the total amount of aversive stimulation required to modify deviant behavior.

Time is an important consideration in treating many sexual deviant individuals. If a patient's behavior is unlawful (e.g., rape, pedophilia, etc.) and the therapist uses a treatment procedure that requires an extended period of time, the possibility of the patient committing a crime does not rapidly decrease. Given this situation, the typically expedient results produced by aversion therapy may make it preferable to other therapeutic procedures requiring longer periods of time to take effect.

Although the efficacy of aversion therapy has been demonstrated, researchers and clinicians should continue to investigate less painful and discomforting techniques for achieving desired behavioral change. As an alternative to physically aversive techniques (e.g., chemical, olfactory, and electrical aversion), many clinicians recommend the use of covert sensitization. We would only comment that in selecting a particular type of aversion therapy for a patient, the therapist should consider the amount of pain or discomfort the patient will experience relative to the effectiveness of the procedure.

Let us now briefly discuss the major types of aversion therapy.

Chemical and Olfactory Aversion

Chemical aversion therapy involves the production of an aversive physical state via administration of certain emetic or nausea-inducing pharmacological agents. If successful, such therapy establishes a connection between induced physical discomfort and deviant response patterns. Morganstern, Pearce, and Linford-Rees (1965) have illustrated the approach. These researchers treated 13 transvestites by administering apomorphine injections and then requiring each subject to cross-dress while experiencing the drug-induced nausea. Treatment for each subject consisted of 39 such sessions, at a rate of three sessions per day. A detailed follow-up ranged in duration from eight months to four years posttreatment. As the results indicated, cross-dressing was completely eliminated in 7 of the 13 subjects, while the other 6 transvestites showed improvement but periodic relapses. Follow-up data led to three additional observations. First, a majority of the subjects reported that they were no longer sexually aroused by formerly exciting clothing. Second, no symptom substitution was observed for any of the subjects. And third, the relapses that occurred tended to be episodic, as well as provoked by specific stressful events in the subject's life such as sexual deprivation during wife's pregnancy.

There are a number of problems inherent in the practice of chemical aversion therapy. First, individuals significantly differ in the speed and extent of their physiological and psychological reaction to drugs. As a consequence, precise control over the effects of a given pharmacological agent is extremely difficult, if not impossible, to achieve. Second, the drugs indicated for chemical aversion therapy may be contraindicated because of the possibility of harmful side effects. In fact, many clinicians agree that the potentially dangerous side effects of drug administration warrant discontinuation of this type of therapy. Of course, medically trained personnel must be present to administer any drug and monitor its effects. Third, the complicated and possibly harmful nature of chemical aversion techniques also limits the frequency of aversion sessions for any patient. As a result, the pairing of the conditioned and unconditioned stimuli may be weak because of limited associations. And finally, some evidence indicates that chemical aversion techniques increase patient aggressiveness and hostility (Morganstern et al., 1965).

Olfactory aversion therapy employs an odiferous chemical substance as the aversive stimulus to be paired with deviant responses. Maletzky (1977) reported the successful use of this type of therapy in treating 12 exhibitionists. In this study, subjects utilized imagery and photographs of exhibitionistic behavior to achieve sexual arousal, at which point they were exposed to a noxious odor. Levin, Barry, Gambaro, Wolfinsohn, and Smith (1977) treated a pedophiliac male with a combination of olfactory aversion and covert sensitization. Fumes from a vile of valeric acid were used to augment the aversiveness of noxious imagery. Specifically, the vial was uncorked as the patient became sexually aroused by deviant fantasy, just before he was instructed to imagine nauseating scenes. The vial was then covered immediately with the termination of the aversive imagery. This combined procedure effected a significant decrease in the patient's sexual response to young girls, with a concommitant increase in sexual arousal to mature women. Additionally, follow-up assessment at 2.5, 4.5, and 10 months posttreatment indicated that therapeutic effects were maintained over time.

Many problems have been reported in connection with olfactory aversion therapy. As with chemical aversion therapy, it is difficult to control for the parameters and the effects of the aversive stimulus.

Covert Sensitization

Covert sensitization in the treatment of sexual deviancy requires that the patient incorporate personally noxious images and scenes into deviant sexual fantasies. Noxious imagery thus functions as the aversive stimulus. Many clinicians consider this form of aversion therapy to be less unpleasant for the patient than chemical, olfactory, or electrical aversion techniques (Brownell & Barlow, 1976). While research to date does not conclusively demonstrate its effectiveness, there is evidence suggesting that covert sensitization may be a viable technique in the treatment of sexual deviations.

As early as 1965, Gold and Neufeld utilized covert sensitization in treating a 16-year-old boy convicted of homosexual soliciting. This technique was reportedly successful in eliminating the boy's homosexual behavior. In 1968, Davison successfully treated a case of sadistic fantasy with a combination of covert sensitization and counterconditioning procedures. Hayes, Brownell, and Barlow (1978) reported the successful modification of fetish behavior in a 14-year-old boy consequent to covert sensitization therapy, while Cautela (1967) claimed similar results in treating a homosexual male.

Cautela (1967) has observed that the effectiveness of covert sensitization is enhanced when the technique is employed with a highly motivated person who possesses an ability to vividly imagine aversive scenes and who is above-average in intelligence. The procedure definitely requires that the patient be able to engage in imagery/fantasy. Cautela (1967) also emphasizes the importance of between-session practice; that is, the patient should be instructed to rehearse at home the covert procedure taught to him during therapy sessions.

A case study by Harbert, Barlow, Hersen, and Austin (1974) exemplifies the use of covert sensitization to treat sexual deviancy. This case involved a 52-year-old male convicted of incestuous behavior, who had a 12-year history of kissing, fondling, and mutual masturbation with his 17-year-old daughter. During treatment, the patient was first trained in a muscular relaxation technique. Once the relaxation technique was mastered, covert sensitization sessions were initiated. The patient was instructed to imagine being discovered by his wife, father-in-law, or family priest while engaging in incestuous behavior. For this patient, the possibility of such discovery was extremely noxious and threatening. One of the scenes during covert sensitization for this man follows below:

You are alone with your daughter in your trailer. You get the feeling that you want to caress your daughter's breasts. So you put your arm around her, insert your hand in her blouse and begin to caress her breasts. Unexpectedly the door to the trailer opens and in walks your wife with Father X (the family priest). Your daughter immediately jumps up and runs out the door. Your wife follows her. You are left alone with Father X. He is looking at you as if to ask for some explanation of what he has just seen. You think of what Father X must be thinking as he stands there staring at you. You are very embarrassed; you want to say something, but you can't seem to find the right words. You realize that Father X can no longer respect you as he once did. Father X finally says, "I don't understand this; this is not like you." You begin to cry. You realize that you may have lost the love and respect of both Father X and your wife, which are very important to you. Father X asks, "Do you realize what this has done to your daughter?" You think about this and you hear your daughter crying; she is hysterical. You feel like you want to run, but you can't. You are miserable and disgusted with yourself. You don't know if you will ever regain the love and respect of your wife and Father X [p. 82].

Treatment for this patient consisted of 150 covert sensitization trials during a 15-day period. He was then discharged from the hospital and seen for follow-up booster sessions at two week, one month, two month, three month, and six month intervals. Follow-up sessions revealed only a slight indication of deviant sexual arousal at the three month follow-up, as measured by a penile strain gauge. Otherwise the patient evidenced no deviant arousal during follow-up sessions.

Electrical Aversion

In electrical or faradic aversion, a mild but painful electrical shock serves as the aversive stimulus. Electrical shock is delivered contingent upon the occurrence of targeted deviant responses—typically, the occurrence of deviant sexual fantasy. As a consequence of this procedure, the sexually deviant individual should learn to associate deviant sexual responses with the pain of shock.

Marshall (1973) employed electrical aversion in sexual reorientation programs with two fetishists, two rapists, two homosexual pedophiliacs, two heterosexual pedophiliacs, one mixed pedophiliac, and three homosexuals. A classical conditioning paradigm was used with all subjects, in which relevant deviant fantasies and slides were paired with shock. Shock was in turn immediately preceded by the command, "Stop!" The schedule of shock administration was varied across the total 27 treatment sessions. Posttreatment results indicated that deviant sexual arousal had been eliminated in 11 of 12 subjects. Follow-ups, ranging from 3 to 16 months in duration and completed on eight subjects, indicated that one pedophiliac relapsed once following treatment, and one homosexual relapsed completely.

Forgione (1976) used electrical aversion in the treatment of two males with histories of pedophiliac behavior. Interestingly, he required these men to demonstrate their deviant sexual behavior with life-sized mannequins of children, and he photographed their sexual interactions with these mannequins. The photographs were then used as deviant arousal stimuli in electrical aversion therapy. This procedure was reportedly successful in eliminating the pedophiliac behavior of both males.

Electrical aversion is a relatively simple procedure that allows the therapist to precisely control the intensity, extent, and duration of aversive stimulation. Individual differences in reactivity to noxious stimulation are controlled by determining for each patient the level of electrical stimulation that the therapist judges to be at, or just above, his pain threshold. Additionally, there is no restriction on the frequency of electrical aversion sessions and no need for surveillance by a physician—unlike chemical aversion therapy discussed above. The therapist is in direct control of the contingency relationship between the aversive stimulus and deviant behavior, probably more than with other types of aversion therapy. For all of these reasons, electrical aversion may be preferable to other aversion techniques. Of course, shock aversion should not be used with patients who have cardiovascular difficulties. The appropriateness of electrical aversion for any patient must be determined through careful evaluation of his psychological and medical status. Research to date does not associate any harmful side effects with the careful application of this procedure.

Shame Aversion

Shame aversion therapy employs shame or humiliation as the critical aversive stimulus. With this procedure, the sexually deviant individual is required to engage in his deviant behavior while in front of a number of observers. Behavior in front of the audience must be as similar as possible to the patient's deviant sexual activity in the natural environment, and should continue for a duration of 15 to 35 minutes. Wickramasekera (1972) has found this procedure to be effective with a subset of exhibitionists whom he describes as "neurotic patients with high manifest anxiety, fundamentalist religious backgrounds, and strong motivation" (p. 207). Serber (1971) has applied shame aversion therapy to long-standing cases of exhibitionism, frotteurism, pedophilia, transvestism, and voyeurism. Among a group of eight patients whom he treated for a variety of sexual deviations, five remained free of their deviant sexual behavior at a six month follow-up.

Wickramasekera (1972) developed a variation of shame aversion after having noticed that, for some sexually deviant patients, rehearsal of the deviant behavior in front of observers could be more aversive than electric shock therapy. According to Wickramasekera, with some exhibitionists the secrecy and anonymity surrounding enactment of their deviant behavior are important sources of reinforcement. Additionally, some exhibitionists seem to enter a state of dissociation prior to and during an exhibitionistic episode; that is, they do not seem to be focusing their attention on their exhibitionistic behavior or its situational context (Wickramasekera, 1972).

The treatment technique devised by Wickramasekera requires the patient to demonstrate his exhibitionistic behavior in the presence of one, two, and then three female observers who are carefully selected for their similarity to the patient's typical deviant sexual target. While enacting his deviant behavior, the patient must: verbalize an introspective dialogue between himself and his penis, describe his bodily sensations, tell the observers what his fantasies and assumptions are regarding their reactions to his behavior, and verbalize what he thinks the female observers are feeling, perceiving, and thinking about him. Observers are trained to stare expressionlessly at the patient. Further, the impact of this procedure has been enhanced by having the female observers ask the patient brief, direct questions during his demonstration and by videotaping the patient during this procedure, for his future viewing.

According to Wickramasekera (1972), this treatment is effective in disrupting patient fantasies of secrecy and anonymity, as well as being effective in eliciting considerable anxiety from the patient. The patient is forced to recognize the way his deviant behavior looks to himself and others, in a context that removes the reinforcing element of privacy. Videotapes of the treatment sessions may be used in follow-up booster sessions.

Serber (1971) first reported the successful use of shame aversion with a 23-year-old transvestite who enjoyed dressing in his mother's undergarments. Assessment indicated that each cross-dressing episode had been followed and reinforced by masturbatory orgasm, at a frequency of two to three times per week over a period of 10 years. During treatment, the patient was observed and photographed while engaging in cross-dressing. The procedure caused him considerable anxiety and distress, and at its termination he reported that he was completely turned off by his cross-dressing behavior.

Although the literature on shame aversion therapy for sexual deviations is still somewhat limited, our preliminary impression is that this technique provides a promising approach to deviant sexual behavior.

Increase of Heterosexual Arousal

Major goals in the behavioral treatment of deviant sexual arousal are suppression or elimination of inappropriate arousal patterns *and* enhancement of appropriate sexual arousal. According to most behavioral researchers, successful suppression of deviant sexual arousal requires the development of an alternative mode of gratifying the sexual drive. While suppression of deviant arousal patterns may in turn facilitate or increase appropriate sexual arousal, the enhancement of appropriate sexual arousal should not be left to chance.

What constitutes an "appropriate" pattern of sexual arousal is currently a topic of active debate among mental health professionals, politicians, and society. Traditionally, "normal" sexuality has referred to, and been limited to, heterosexual arousal and behavior. However, the gay rights movement has recently challenged this limited conception of normal sexual behavior and has succeeded in persuading the American Psychiatric Association to remove homosexuality from the classification of deviant sexual orientations. We do not address here the question of whether or not homosexuality is an appropriate or normal sexual orientation. Since most research dealing with arousal modification focuses on the development of a heterosexual orientation, we follow suit in our discussion but note that the treatment techniques to be described may be utilized—with obvious modifications—to develop or enhance either a heterosexual or homosexual arousal pattern.

Aversion Relief

Aversion relief is a treatment procedure frequently used in combination with aversion therapy, as it involves establishing an association between heterosexual stimuli and relief from an aversive stimulus. Heterosexual stimuli thereby become paired with escape from noxious stimulation and acquire positive reinforcement properties.

Thorpe, Schmidt, Brown, and Castell (1964) introduced aversion relief to the treatment of sexual deviations in an outcome study with three homosexuals, one transvestite, and one fetishist. Initially, each subject was presented a number of words that functioned as stimuli for deviant sexual behavior. Then, as the subjects read each arousing word, they received an electrical shock. The last word of each word series represented "normal" sexual behavior (for example, "heterosexual") and signified the termination of a shock sequence. As might be expected, the word "heterosexual" soon became associated with relief. At termination of treatment, all subjects reported increased heterosexual interests; however, the investigators did not directly assess this interest and did not complete a follow-up. Thorpe et al. (1964) speculated that the aversion relief technique modified heterosexual interest through either inhibition of heterosexual anxiety or positive reinforcement of heterosexual approach behavior.

According to Barlow (1974), in numerous case studies since this pioneering effort the heterosexual relief stimulus has taken two forms: verbal—usually words associated with heterosexual interest such as "intercourse" (Gaupp, Stern, & Ratliff, 1971); or pictorial—such as slides or films of nude females (Larson, 1970). A number of patients subjected to this procedure have reported increased heterosexual interest and responsiveness following treatment.

A procedure developed by Feldman and MacCulloch (1965) has been utilized in over 150 reported cases and probably remains the most popular aversion relief technique (Barlow, 1974). It was initially applied by these authors in a study with male homosexual patients. In this study, each patient first identified a level of electrical shock that he experienced as "very unpleasant." Then he was shown one of several slides depicting semiclothed and unclothed males and was informed that he could terminate the slide whenever he no longer found it to be sexually arousing by pressing a switch. Electrical shock was administered to the patient 8 seconds after the onset of the male slide, and shock intensity was then increased until he switched off the slide. Aversion was terminated when the patient removed the male slide. After a few pairings of shock and male slides, the patient was placed on a predetermined schedule of shock (i.e., only a certain proportion of male slides resulted in shock after 8 seconds). Following termination of male slides, female slides were presented, signaling shock-free "relief" periods.

A study by Abel, Levis, and Clancy (1970) included continual physiological measurement of heterosexual arousal during, and following, aversion relief treatment of sexual deviation. Results from this study do not support the effectiveness of aversion relief techniques as a treatment modality for increasing heterosexual arousal. Actually, there is little evidence that aversion relief procedures reduce heterosexual anxiety or enhance heterosexual arousal. Barlow (1974) has questioned why, in the empirical field of behavior therapy, with little evidence to demonstrate the efficacy of aversion relief, this treatment has been utilized in so many published cases and continues to be used in the clinical setting.

Shaping

Shaping involves the strategic dispensation of positive reinforcement for gradual approximations to appropriate behavior. This technique has been used by a number of investigators, including Quinn, Harbinson, and McAllister (1970) and Harbinson, Quinn, and McAllister (1970) to increase the level of heterosexual arousal in homosexual individuals. The forementioned researchers attempted to increase penile response to heterosexual stimuli with the following procedure. Initially patients were treated with aversion therapy for elimination of deviant sexual arousal. Next, after a significant period of dehydration, each patient was positively reinforced with a drink of lime juice for (*a*) heterosexual fantasies of progressively increasing duration and elaboration, and (*b*) increased penile tumescence in reaction to slides and pictures of nude females. Penile responses to heterosexual stimuli increased over the course of treatment, as did heterosexual scores on an attitude scale. Results also indicated a decline in homosexual scores on the attitude scale during treatment, although no report on sexual behavior outside the laboratory was obtained.

The technique of directly shaping sexual responses by contingent reinforcement seems to hold much promise. Unfortunately, the results of the Quinn, Harbinson, and McAllister research have largely been ignored.

Orgasmic Reconditioning

Orgasmic reconditioning is one of several techniques that attempts to increase heterosexual arousal through pairing heterosexual stimuli with elicited sexual arousal. This technique has also been referred to as masturbation training and masturbatory conditioning.

Orgasmic reconditioning rests on the assumption that various stimuli acquire erotic, arousal properties by virtue of their association with orgasmic pleasure. Even neutral stimuli, according to this premise, can be conditioned to elicit sexual arousal. For example, Lovibond (1963) conditioned autonomic responses associated with sexual arousal to previously neutral stimuli by means of repeated association with sexual arousal. McConaghy (1970) paired slides of sexual stimuli with geometrical configurations and thereby produced penile erectile responses to the configurations in 10 heterosexual and 15 homosexual subjects. Rachman (1966), in turn, paired a slide of a woman's boot with slides of nude females and found penile erection increases to the slide of the boot in three heterosexual subjects. Rachman and Hodgson (1968) later replicated these findings with an additional five subjects.

The procedure for orgasmic reconditioning has been fairly well standardized. First, the patient is instructed to masturbate, using deviant fantasy, until he closely approximates the point of orgasm. When he feels the inevitability of orgasm, he is to switch to, and concentrate on, appropriate heterosexual fantasy. Not infrequently during the first few practices with the procedure, a patient will lose his arousal consequent to this switch. If arousal is lost, he must briefly switch back to deviant fantasy until he achieves a higher level of arousal, at which point he is to try again to introduce heterosexual fantasy. Over successive practices with this procedure, the switch from deviant to appropriate fantasy is gradually moved backward in time from the point of orgasm, toward the beginning of masturbation. Eventually, arousal and release of sexual tension should be associated with the heterosexual fantasy, such that the patient can masturbate to orgasm with exclusive reliance on the heterosexual fantasy. It is extremely important that the patient never attend to deviant imagery or fantasy during the occurrence of orgasm; this rule applies throughout treatment to both his masturbatory activity and overt sexual interactions. (Note that the procedure of orgasmic reconditioning also involves fading, a procedure discussed in the next section.)

Unfortunately, orgasmic reconditioning has rarely been investigated as a treatment technique in isolation. Thus the singular efficacy of this technique for establishing and enhancing heterosexual arousal has yet to be conclusively determined. While further research is needed, it does appear promising as a method of altering sexual preference and arousal.

Fading

The technique of fading was derived from operant work on errorless discrimination (Terrace, 1966). It involves the introduction or "fading in" of heterosexual stimuli while the patient is aroused, in an attempt to change arousal-eliciting stimuli (Barlow & Agras, 1973). Barlow and Agras developed a procedure whereby one male and one female slide were superimposed on one another. Through the use of an adjustable transformer, a decrease in the brightness of the male slide resulted in concomitant increased brightness of the female slide. More specifically, the female stimulus was gradually faded in contingent upon the subject's maintaining 75% of a full erection (measured by a penile strain gauge), through a 20-step progression ranging from 100% male brightness to 100% female brightness. This technique was successfully applied with male homosexuals in three controlled, single case experiments involving reversal designs.

The rationale behind fading is that the arousal elicited by deviant stimuli can be gradually transferred to appropriate stimuli through the pairing procedure. At this point, the various parameters, theoretical implications, and techniques of fading are in need of additional scientific exploration. It seems possible that an individual could become sexually aroused to both heterosexual and deviant stimuli (as with the bisexual person, if that sexual orientation truly exists) through the singular application of this procedure.

Exposure

Exposure is a technique whereby the individual is exposed to explicit heterosexual stimuli in an effort to directly elicit heterosexual arousal. Herman and his colleagues (Herman, 1971; Herman, Barlow, & Agras, 1971) have exemplified the exposure procedure in three single case designs involving the treatment of two homosexuals and one pedophiliac. During the first phase of this treatment, subjects were shown an 8-mm movie of a nude, seductive female for 10 minutes daily. During the control phase, a movie of a nude, seductive male was presented on a daily basis. The third and final phase reinstated the female exposure condition. For all three subjects, exposure to the female film during the first and third phases resulted in increased heterosexual arousal, while exposure to the male film resulted in decreased heterosexual arousal. Additionally, each subject reported that enhancement of heterosexual arousal generated to fantasies and behavior in the natural environment. Homosexual arousal had been previously decreased for one subject through aversion therapy. For the other two subjects, homosexual arousal did not decrease during exposure treatment. Follow-ups ranging from three months to one year posttreatment revealed that two subjects had difficulty with heterosexual relations, despite continued heterosexual arousal, due to deficient social skills. This reminds us of the importance of a multicomponent treatment approach.

Although an experimental analysis of the above mentioned results attributed the subjects' enhanced heterosexual arousal to exposure, the mechanism of change is not clear (Barlow, 1974). It may be that exposure is similar to "flooding," and it results in a decrease in heterosexual anxiety rather than a direct increase in heterosexual arousal. It is also possible that exposure provides novel material for fantasy that is then associated with sexual arousal outside of treatment (Barlow, 1974)— one of several rationales also reported to explain video desensitization.

We now turn to various techniques that focus on the enhancement of heterosexual arousal via reduction of heterosexual anxiety. These techniques are most appropriate when arousal to heterosexual stimuli is inhibited by anxiety responses. Imaginal desensitization, in vivo desensitization, and video desensitization can be utilized to indirectly enhance heterosexual arousal and are discussed below.

Imaginal Desensitization

In contrast to in vivo desensitization, where the patient must actually go into "real life" anxiety-producing situations, imaginal or classical systematic desensitization (developed by Wolpe, 1958) takes the patient through imagery representations of the feared situations. The goal of desensitization in the treatment of sexual disorders is the neutralizing of anxiety and other negative emotions associated with the sexual situation that are inhibiting sexual arousal. Repeated presentation of anxiety-eliciting imaginal scenes, during which the patient engages in a competing response (relaxation), supposedly "neutralizes" anxiety-eliciting properties of the scenes. This neutralization of anxiety-arousing stimuli then reportedly generalizes to "real life" situations.

The most systematic attempt to evaluate the efficacy of imaginal desensitization for the treatment of sexual deviations was conducted by Bancroft (1970), in a study involving two 15-subject groups of homosexual males. The first group was treated with systematic desensitization using imagery of heterosexual content, while the second group received electrical aversion therapy. Dependent measures included verbal report of homosexual and heterosexual behavior and the physiological assessment of sexual arousal with a penile strain gauge. Results of this investigation indicated no significant difference between groups in heterosexual arousal at the conclusion of treatment or at a six-month follow-up. Both treatments increased heterosexual arousal (as measured by degree of penile engorgement); whereas, only aversion therapy significantly reduced homosexual arousal at posttreatment.

Interestingly, Bancroft (1970) next divided the groups into improved and unimproved, on the basis of subjects' verbal report at the six-month follow-up. He then found that significant increases in reported heterosexual arousal were evidenced only in the improved group. This latter result again indicates that suppression of deviant arousal is not sufficient for change in sexual orientation unless heterosexual arousal is enhanced—a finding verified by Adams and Sturgis (1978). Stated otherwise, if an alternate means of sexual gratification is not provided to replace extinguished deviant arousal, the probability of relapse is high.

In vivo Desensitization

With in vivo desensitization for sexual disorders, therapist and patient together construct a hierarchy of anxiety-producing sexual situations that the patient will gradually get into with the help of a consenting partner (e.g., spouse, girlfriend). Primary goals of in vivo desensitization include the elimination of heterosexual anxiety and the increase of heterosexual arousal. Additionally, heterosexual skills may be improved by this procedure.

A number of clinicians and researchers have documented the effectiveness of in vivo desensitization in the treatment of sexual deviation. In an early study, Cooper (1963) successfully treated a fetishist with a combination of chemical aversion and in vivo desensitization. Regarding the desensitization procedure, the patient was first instructed to lie in bed naked with his wife until he felt comfortable. Then, he was encouraged to gradually follow a format of small steps progressively leading to—and eventually including—intercourse. The patient was instructed to advance one step in the sexual hierarchy only when he had completed all prior steps without experiencing anxiety. Gray (1970) employed a similar procedure in conjunction with covert sensitization for the treatment of a homosexual male. Successful in vivo desensitization in the absence of aversion therapy has also been reported by numerous researchers, including Barlow and Agras (1973) with a homosexual and Wickramasekera (1968) with an exhibitionist.

Video Desensitization

The procedure of video desensitization, similar to that of imaginal and systematic desensitization, involves relaxation training, hierarchy construction, and graduated patient exposure to anxiety-producing events. However, with video desensitization the patient is exposed to visual representations of the anxiety-eliciting situations. The technique is largely based on research in which slides and movies depicting models engaging in feared or phobic behavior have successfully reduced the anxiety of observers (Bandura, Blanchard, & Ritter, 1969; Bandura & Menlove, 1969). Through observation, an individual can vicariously learn to perform activities demonstrated by models, including relaxed engagement in sexual activity.

Caird and Wincze (1977) have specifically applied the technique of video desensitization to the treatment of sexual disorders. These investigators have prepared an extensive library of 140 video cassettes, depicting a wide variety of sexual interactions. The content of these 4 minute cassettes ranges from a couple merely talking to each other to a nude intercourse scene. Cassettes are presented to the patient in a hierarchical order. The patient is instructed to view each film while imagining the same-sex actor as himself and the opposite-sex actor as his partner. Once the patient has viewed a film without any experience of anxiety, he advances to the next scene on the hierarchy.

Video desensitization, while inherently a viable and promising technique, suffers from a lack of research replicating the effectiveness demonstrated by early investigations. Obviously, the time and equipment necessary to construct a video hierarchy of sexual scenes are considerable. Additionally, there is some risk involved in showing homosexual patients films of heterosexual scenes, as the homosexual individual can become aroused to such scenes by identifying with the female actor and imagining himself in sexual contact with the male actor (Tollison, Adams, & Tollison, 1979).

Modification of Deviant Gender Role Behavior

Surprisingly, the presence of opposite-sex role behavior has received minimal attention in the treatment of sexual deviancy. While the development of inappropriate gender role behavior has itself been a topic of interest for some time (e.g., Brown, 1958), its relationship to deviant sexual orientation has seldom been examined. The transsexual individual, whose gender role identification is so pervasively deviant that he or she requests sex reassignment surgery, represents the extreme in adoption of opposite-sex role behavior. Few patients encountered in clinical practice, however, will evidence such a complete predominance of opposite-sex identification and behavior. Nevertheless, some degree of gender role deviation and opposite-sex behavior is present in many sexually deviant persons.

The presence of gender role deviation makes it more difficult to successfully modify deviant sexual arousal (Barlow, 1974). For example, Gelder and Marks (1969) have observed that, unlike "simple" transvestites who respond well to aversion therapy, transvestites with opposite-sex role behavior respond poorly to such treatment. In fact, the one patient in their study who fit Stoller's (1971) definition of a true transsexual showed no improvement at all. Bieber, Bieber, Dain, Dince, Drellich, Grand, Frundlach, Kremer, Wilber, and Bieber (1963) have also found that homosexuals with a history of childhood gender role problems do not respond as well to psychoanalytically oriented therapy as do those without an early history of such problems. Barlow (1974) has appropriately concluded from these results that it is necessary to modify deviant gender role behavior early in the treatment of sexual deviations.

Modeling

Barlow, Reynolds, and Agras (1973) employed modeling and videotape feedback in modifying the inappropriate gender role behavior of a 17-year-old transsexual, and analyzed treatment effects with a multiple-baseline design across targeted deviant behaviors. Pretreatment assessment showed that this patient's motor behavior was almost exclusively feminine, with only an occasional instance of masculine behavior. After a five-day baseline period, daily 30-minute treatment sessions were begun, focusing initially on the patient's sitting behavior. Prior to each treatment session—while the patient was in the waiting room—daily measures of masculine and feminine components of sitting, standing, and walking were taken by an experimentally blind rater. After sitting behavior had been successfully modified, treatment procedures focused on standing behavior, and finally on walking behavior.

The components of appropriate gender behavior were broken down and taught to the patient step-by-step. Each behavior was first modeled by a male therapist and then practiced by the patient. Therapist reinforcement was contingently administered to the patient to shape successful rehearsal of target behaviors. The final trial of each session was videotaped, to be shown at the beginning of the next session. Results indicated that, with this treatment, the patient learned and successfully performed the masculine prototypes of sitting, standing, and walking. Furthermore, the experimental design demonstrated that the treatment program was the causal agent of change, for no target behavior changed prior to it being the focus of treatment.

Rekers and Varni (1977) used similar modeling and feedback techniques to modify inappropriate gender role behaviors in children. Aside from these two studies, there is very little discussion or experimental implementation of techniques to directly modify opposite-sex gender behavior.

Improvement of Heterosocial Functioning

Failure in heterosocial interactions may lead to a high degree of social anxiety, which has in turn been associated with homosexuality (Feldman & MacCullough, 1971), sexual dysfunction (Bandura, 1969), sexual deviation (Quinsey, 1977), and various "mental disorders" (Argyle, 1969). Therefore, techniques that are effective in decreasing heterosocial anxiety may be useful in the modification of heterosocial behavior as well as the overall treatment of sexual deviations.

As stated earlier, ineffective heterosocial skills may be the result of conditioned anxiety in which the previously neutral cues of heterosocial interactions have become associated with aversive stimuli, and/or a skills deficit in which the patient has never learned appropriate interaction skills. Further, the conditioning of anxiety to heterosocial exchanges may occur independent of the adequacy of the individual's behavioral repertoire.

Much of the following discussion is extrapolated from an excellent review of heterosocial skill techniques prepared by Curran (1977). We will first examine those techniques that focus on heterosocial anxiety, and then turn to those procedures that directly modify heterosocial behavior.

Self-Reinforcement

Rehm and Marston (1968) hypothesized that the anxiety some males experience in heterosocial situations is not the result of an inadequate behavioral repertoire. They further reasoned that if they could increase the approach behavior of heterosocially anxious males toward females and teach them to self-reinforce such attempts, a decrease in heterosocial anxiety as well as positive changes in self-concept would result. The investigators assigned 24 male college students who complained of discomfort in dating situations to one of three groups: (a) self-reinforcement; (b) nonspecific therapy control (nondirective counseling); or (c) contact control (in which subjects were instructed to think about their problem and its possible solution, but no recommendations or suggestions were given by therapists). Subjects in the self-reinforcement group were asked to work up a systematic hierarchy of in vivo heterosocial interactions, to evaluate their performance relative to individualized goals, and to reward themselves with self-approval for each successful interaction. For a five-week period, subjects received one 30-minute session per week of individualized treatment. Each subject was assessed at pretreatment, posttreatment, and at a seven- to nine-month follow-up. The assessment battery included self-report measures of anxiety and dating frequency and behavioral measures of heterosocial skills.

Results of this investigation indicated that only the self-reinforcement group evidenced a significant decrease in self-reported anxiety. The self-reinforcement group also showed a greater increase from baseline in dating frequency than the other two groups. However, very few significant differences were found between groups on behavioral measures, including observer ratings of anxiety, adequacy of response, likability, and latency of response. Thus the self-reinforcement procedure led to a reduction of self-reported heterosocial anxiety but did not produce a change in the behavioral measures chosen to assess heterosocial skills.

Response Practice

The response practice approach is appropriate for those heterosocially anxious individuals who possess an adequate repertoire of social skills and only need practice in when and how to apply those skills. This approach assumes that repeated exposure to heterosocial encounters will eventually result in appropriate utilization of heterosocial skills and decreased heterosocial anxiety.

Martinson and Zerface (1970) examined the therapeutic impact of practice dating on subsequent dating behavior and comfort. Twenty-four male subjects were randomly assigned to either a five-week practice dating program, individual counseling program, or delayed treatment control. All subjects included in this study reported having had no dates during the month prior to this investigation and described themselves as fearful of dating situations. The practice dating program followed a format of semistructured, arranged interactions with female volunteer confederates. Results indicated that the practice dating program was significantly more effective than either other condition in reducing subjective fear of dating, as well as significantly more effective than the delayed control condition in increasing dating frequency. No significant posttreatment differences were found between groups on a measure of general manifest anxiety.

Christensen and Arkowitz (1974) found that a practice dating program that included a feedback exchange from dating partners successfully decreased self-reported heterosocial anxiety as well as increased heterosocial skills and dating frequency. However, in a study that examined the relative effects of practice dating with and without partner feedback, partner feedback did not improve on the benefits of practice dating alone. It should be noted that neither of these studies screened subject volunteers for average dating frequency or heterosocial skills.

As Curran (1977) has noted, the exchange of information and in vivo exposure gained through practice dating may indeed prove therapeutic. However, there is always the risk that the arranged dates will be experienced as failures by the subject and will therefore consequent in increased heterosocial anxiety (Curran, 1977). Curran appropriately suggests:

Perhaps instead of randomly matching program members, the subjects could be matched with a surrogate date trained in techniques to elicit pleasant interchanges [p. 145].

Curran (1977), after reviewing the literature on practice dating, has concluded that this approach has considerable therapeutic potential, but its effectiveness must be validated through more rigorous investigation.

Response Acquisition

Numerous investigations have examined the effectiveness of such behavioral techniques as modeling, behavioral rehearsal, self-observation, and assertiveness training for improvement of heterosocial skills. Heterosocial skill deficiencies indirectly produce reactive anxiety (Kanfer & Phillips, 1969) as well as avoidance of hetero-social interactions (Curran & Gilbert, 1975). With response acquisition techniques, new social skills are taught to those individuals who, because of avoidance or behavioral deficiencies, are unable to function effectively in heterosocial and heterosexual situations (Barlow, 1974). Such procedures may also be referred to as social retraining procedures.

Melnick (1973) investigated the additive effectiveness of various behavioral techniques in the modification of minimal dating behavior. Pre- and postassessment involved both self-report and behavioral measures. Subjects were randomly assigned to one of four treatment groups or to one of two control groups. Treatment groups consisted of: (a) vicarious learning; (b) vicarious learning plus participant modeling; (c) vicarious learning plus participant modeling plus self-observation (via videotape); and (d) vicarious learning plus participant modeling plus self-observation plus therapist reinforcement. Control groups included a minimal contact group and a nonspecific therapy control group (insight-oriented individual therapy).

Because of inadequate sample sizes, Melnick (1973) collapsed his original treatment groups. As a result, the two treatment groups not receiving self-observation feedback, the two treatment groups receiving self-observation feedback, and the two control groups were left for final comparisons. The investigator concluded that participant modeling plus self-observation (via videotape) was an effective procedure for inducing behavioral change, whereas participant modeling alone was not. Interestingly, no differences between groups were found with respect to dating frequency during treatment. However, the two self-observation groups were significantly more effective than the other two treatment groups on behavioral ratings of assertion and anxiety. Curran (1977) identifies several methodological flaws in Melnick's study that make interpretation of the data somewhat hazardous.

McGovern, Arkowitz, and Gilmore (1975) compared the effectiveness of three behavioral training programs for dating-inhibited males. Thirty-four males were assigned to either a discussion group, a waiting list control group, or to one of two types of behavioral rehearsal groups. Each subject was required to read a dating manual. In the discussion group, material from the manual was presented, and female experimental assistants elicited concerns from the subjects, provided feedback, and suggested alternative strategies for problematic interactions. In the behavioral rehearsal groups, male subjects actually rehearsed with the female assistants various dating interactions described in the manual; further, they received verbal feedback consequent to rehearsed interactions.

Assessment consisted of a battery of self-report questionnaires administered pre- and posttreatment. Results indicated that a discussion group focusing on dating problems and behavioral strategies may be therapeutic with dating problems. Surprisingly, the addition of a behavioral rehearsal component to the discussion format did not significantly enhance therapeutic effects. However, as with Melnick's (1973) investigation, several methodological flaws in this study make conclusions somewhat tentative (Curran, 1977).

In a series of three studies, Curran and his colleagues (Curran, 1975; Curran & Gilbert, 1975; Curran, Gilbert, & Little, 1976) evaluated the effectiveness of a replication training program (Kanfer & Phillips, 1970) for alleviation of heterosocial anxiety. The program consisted of information-giving, modeling, behavioral rehearsal, coaching, video and group feedback, and *in vivo* assignments. Target skills included: the provision and receipt of compliments, nonverbal communicative behavior, assertive behavior, and feeling talk. Additionally, subjects were taught to handle silence during social interactions, plan and ask for dates, enhance their physical appearance, and handle physical intimacy problems. Results from the three investigations combined indicated that groups receiving the replication skills training program showed more improvement than various control groups at posttest and follow-up, and showed equal or greater improvement than those groups receiving systematic desensitization (Curran, 1975; Curran & Gilbert, 1975) or sensitivity training (Curran et al., 1976) at posttreatment or follow-up assessment. Curran (1977) concludes that the three investigations taken as a whole demonstrate the effectiveness of the response acquisition model as a comprehensive approach to heterosocial anxiety. The major weaknesses of these studies relate to the lack of physiological measurement of anxiety, direct measures of transfer to the environment, and validity data on some of the assessment instruments (Curran, 1977).

The clinical implications of various response acquisition studies are limited by their reliance on college student populations. Additionally, these studies typically focus on dating skills, only one component of heterosocial behavior.

Numerous cases of sexual deviation (e.g., Edwards, 1972; Stevenson & Wolpe, 1960) and sexual dysfunction (e.g., Wolpe, 1973; Yulis, 1976) have been successfully treated with assertiveness training, particularly in conjunction with other techniques. Subjects are typically taught general assertive skills that enable them to be more successful in heterosocial situations and, in turn, facilitate successful heterosexual relations. Assertiveness training is geared toward teaching individuals to emit behaviors that are personally satisfying and which enhance the probability of obtaining reinforcement from interpersonal exchanges.

Modification of Heterosexual Skill Deficiencies

In this section, we are concerned with those heterosexual skill deficiencies resulting from misconceptions about sexual functioning and behavior and/or heterosexual inexperience. Deficient heterosexual skills may of course accompany a nonheterosexual orientation as well as heterosexual anxiety or phobias, but in such cases heterosexual behavior would not become a major focus of treatment until the primary problems involving deviant arousal and excessive anxiety have been modified.

When working with the heterosexually naïve individual or couple, the therapist usually assumes the role of sex-educator and permission-giver. The actual content of therapist instruction is of course determined by the specific needs of the patient; however, some discussion about the anatomy and physiology of male/female sexual responses is usually included. Other topics of discussion may cover: typical sequences of various heterosexual behaviors, from initial advances and foreplay through sexual intercourse; behavior that facilitates arousal in the opposite-sex partner; demographic data on sexual activities; and the effects of age, drugs, alcohol, anxiety, and illness on sexual functioning. Excessively restrictive attitudes about sexuality may change as a result of the therapist, an authority figure, condoning or labeling as "normal" sexual fantasy and activity previously considered taboo by the patient. Additionally, it is often helpful to augment direct advice, guidance, information, reassurance, and instruction with educational aids, such as nontechnical but authoritative literature (e.g., Ellis, 1959; McCary, 1967).

As Kolvin (1967) indicates, sexual education, counseling, and reassurance may alone generate behavior change. However, modification of heterosexual skills very often requires the prescription of *in vivo* sexual interactions to be completed by the patient with the assistance of an opposite-sex partner. This usually entails between-session practice by the patient of those behaviors discussed with the therapist during office sessions.

Unfortunately, numerous patients requiring heterosexual skill training lack a sexual partner. This is unfortunate in as much as *in vivo* learning experience requires a sexual partner who will cooperate in the physical application of sexual activities assigned in therapy and who will exemplify different levels of opposite-sex response (Reckless & Geiger, 1978). In an attempt to meet the needs of the patient who has no cooperative partner, some therapists and clinics have experimented with sexual group therapy, in which all group members are without partners. Usually, the group format includes the presentation of erotic films and some erotic stimulation between group members. Frequently, heavy emphasis is placed on masturbation (Kaplan, 1974). Other techniques for partnerless patients have included nudity and massage between patient and therapist (Hartman & Fithian, 1971) and "body-work therapy," in which the patient engages in active sexual behavior with an opposite-sex therapist (Williams, 1978). As might be expected, these techniques have not been systematically evaluated. Further, a sexual relationship between therapist and patient violates professional ethical standards for psychologists and physicians. Clinically and ethically, these latter techniques are unacceptable.

In working with patients who lacked sexual partners, Masters and Johnson (1970) found that the use of a cooperative and skilled surrogate partner who had no prior association with the patient was as effective as participation by marital partners in conjoint treatment of sexual difficulties. The utilization of sexual surrogates for therapeutic purposes has created a controversy and certainly warrants serious examination on ethical and legal grounds. However, it remains a standard practice with a number of therapists and patients. We are unaware of any legal restrictions regarding the use of surrogates, but law enforcement officers may regard the practice as a form of prostitution. Typically, the women employed as surrogate partners are not prostitutes by profession.

Proponents of therapy using sexual surrogates defend the practice as being the best of limited options in working with a partnerless patient who has sexual difficulties. Additionally, they contend that surrogate partners are carefully screened as well as trained in appropriate reactions to the patient (e.g., discouraging development of an emotional attachment between patient and surrogate, preventing patient engagement in deviant sexual behavior, etc.). In the final analysis, the decision to use or not use sexual surrogate partners is usually based on an estimation of potential benefit to the patient, the availability of other options, the therapist's and patient's personal value systems, and legal considerations.

REFERENCES

Abel, G., Blanchard, E., Barlow, D., & Mavissakalian, M. Identifying specific erotic cues in sexual deviations by audiotaped descriptions. *Journal of Applied Behavior Analysis,* 1975, **8**, 247–260.

Abel, G., Levis, D., & Clancy, J. Aversion therapy to taped sequences of deviant behavior in exhibitionists and other sexual deviations: A preliminary report. *Journal of Behavior Therapy and Experimental Psychiatry,* 1970, **1**, 59–66.

American Psychiatric Association. *Diagnostic and statistical manual of mental disorders* (2nd edition). Washington, D.C.: American Psychiatric Association, 1968.

American Psychiatric Association. *Diagnostic and statistical manual of mental disorders* (3rd edition). Washington, D.C.: American Psychiatric Association, 1980.

Adams, H. E., & Sturgis, E. T. Status of behavioral reorientation techniques in the modification of homosexuality: A review. *Psychological Bulletin,* 1978, **84**, (6), 1171–1188.

Argyle, M. *Social interaction.* London: Methuen, 1969.

Azrin, N. H., & Holtz, W. C. Punishment. In W. K. Honig (Ed.), *Operant behavior: Areas of research and application.* New York: Appleton-Century-Crofts, 1966.

Baer, D. M. Let's take another look at punishment. *Psychology Today,* 1971, **9**, 19–25.

Bancroft, J. A comparative study of aversion and desensitization in the treatment of homosexuality. In L. E. Burns and J. L. Worsley (Eds.), *Behavior therapy in the 1970's.* Bristol, England: Wright, 1970.

Bandura, A. *Principles of behavior modification.* New York: Holt, Rinehart & Winston, 1969.

Bandura, A., Blanchard, E. B., & Ritter, R. The relative efficacy of desensitization and modeling approaches for inducing behavioral, affective, and attitudinal changes. *Journal of Personality and Social Psychology,* 1969, **13**, 173–199.

Bandura, A., & Menlove, F. L. Factors determining vicarious extinction of avoidance behavior through symbolic modeling. *Journal of Personality and Social Psychology,* 1967, **8**, 99–108.

Barlow, D. H. The treatment of sexual deviation: Toward a comprehensive, behavioral approach. In K. S. Calhoun, H. E. Adams, & K. M. Mitchell (Eds.), *Innovative treatment methods in psychopathology,* New York: Wiley, 1974.

Barlow, D. H. Assessment of sexual behavior. In A. R. Ciminero, K. S. Calhoun, & H. E. Adams (Eds.), *Handbook of behavioral assessment.* New York: Wiley, 1977.

Barlow, D. H., Abel, G. G., Blanchard, E. B., Bristow, A. R., & Young, L. D. A heterosocial skills checklist for males. *Behavior Therapy,* 1977, **8**, 229–239.

Barlow, D. H., & Agras, W. S. Fading to increase heterosexual responsiveness in homosexuals. *Journal of Applied Behavior Analysis,* 1973, **6**, 355–367.

Barlow, D. H., Reynolds, E. H., & Agras, W. S. Gender identity change in a transsexual. *Archives of General Psychiatry,* 1973, **28**, 569–576.

Bem, S. L. The measurement of psychological androgyny. *Journal of Consulting and Clinical Psychology,* 1974, **42**, 155–162.

Bieber, B., Bieber, I., Dain, H. J., Dince, P. R., Drellich, M. G., Grand, H. G., Frundlach, R. H., Kremer, M. W., Wilber, C. B., & Bieber, T. D. *Homosexuality.* New York: Basic Books, 1963.

Borkovec, T. D., Stone, N. M., O'Brien, G. T., & Kaloupek, D. Evaluation of a clinically relevant target behavior for analog outcome research. *Behavior Therapy,* 1974, **5**, 503–513.

Brown, D. G. Sex-role development in a changing culture. *Psychological Bulletin,* 1958, **35**, 232–242.

Brownell, K. D., & Barlow, D. H. Measurement and treatment of two sexual deviations in one person. *Journal of Behavior Therapy and Experimental Psychiatry,* 1976, **7**, 349–354.

Caird, W. K., & Wincze, J. P. *Sex therapy: A behavioral approach.* Hagerstown, Md.: Harper & Row, 1977.

Cautela, J. R. Covert sensitization. *Psychological Record,* 1967, **20**, 459–468.

Christensen, A., & Arkowitz, H. Preliminary report on practice dating and feedback as treatment for college dating problems. *Journal of Counseling Psychology,* 1974, **21**, 92–95.

Cooper, A. A. A case of fetishism and impotence treated by behavior therapy. *British Journal of Psychiatry,* 1963, **109**, 649–652.

Curran, J. P. Skills training as an approach to the treatment of heterosexual-social anxiety: A review. *Psychological Bulletin,* 1977, **84**, 140–157.

Curran, J. P., & Gilbert, F. S. A test of the relative effectiveness of a systematic desensitization program and an interpersonal skills training program with date anxious subjects. *Behavior Therapy,* 1975, **6**, 510–521.

Curran, J. P., Gilbert, F. S., & Little, L. M. A comparison between behavioral training and sensitivity training approaches to heterosexual dating anxiety. *Journal of Counseling Psychology,* 1976, **23**, 190–196.

Davison, G. Elimination of a sadistic fantasy by a client-controlled counter-conditioning technique: A case study. *Journal of Abnormal Psychology,* 1968, **73**, 84–90.

Edwards, N. B. Case conference: Assertive training in a case of homosexual pedophilia. *Journal of Behavior Therapy and Experimental Psychiatry,* 1972, **3**, 55–63.

Ellis, A. The effectiveness of psychotherapy with individuals who have severe homosexual problems. *Journal of Consulting Psychology,* 1959, **20**, 191–195.

Feldman, M. P., & MacCulloch, M. J. The application of anticipatory avoidance learning and the treatment of homosexuality: Theory, technique and preliminary results. *Behaviour Research and Therapy,* 1965, **2**, 165.

Feldman, M. P., & MacCulloch, M. J. *Homosexual behavior: Therapy and assessment,* Oxford: Pergamon Press, 1971.

Forgione, A. G. The use of mannequins in the behavioral assessment of child molesters: Two case reports. *Behavior Therapy,* 1976, **7**, 678–685.

Gaupp, L. A., Stern, R. M., & Ratliff, R. G. The use of aversion-relief procedures in the treatment of a case of voyeurism. *Behavior Therapy,* 1971, **2**, 585–588.

Gelder, M. G., & Marks, I. M. Aversion treatment in transvestism and transsexualism. In R. Green and J. Money (Eds.), *Transsexualism and sex reassignment,* Baltimore: John Hopkins Press, 1969.

Gold, S. A., & Neufeld, I. L. A learning approach to the treatment of homosexuality. *Behaviour Research and Therapy,* 1965, **2**, 201–204.

Gray, J. J. Case conference: Behavior therapy in a patient with homosexual fantasies and heterosexual anxieties. *Journal of Behavior Therapy and Experimental Psychiatry,* 1970, **1**, 225–232.

Harbert, T. L., Barlow, D. H., Hersen, M., & Austin, J. B. Measurement and modification of incestuous behavior: A case study. *Psychological Reports,* 1974, **34**, 79–86.

Harbison, J. J., Quinn, J. T., & McAllister, H. An attempt to shape human penile response. *Behaviour Research and Therapy,* 1970, **9**, 286–290.

Hartman, W. A., & Fithian, M. A. *Treatment of sexual dysfunction.* Long Beach, Calif.: Center for Marital and Sexual Studies, 1972.

Hayes, S. H., Brownell, K. D., & Barlow, D. H. The use of self-administered covert sensitization in the treatment of exhibitionism and sadism. *Behavior Therapy,* 1978, **9**, 283–289.

Herman, S. H. An experimental analysis of two methods of increasing heterosexual arousal in homosexuals. Unpublished doctoral dissertation, University of Mississippi, 1971.

Herman, S. H., Barlow, D. H., & Agras, W. H. Exposure to heterosexual stimuli: An effective variable in treating homosexuality? *Proceedings of the 79th Annual Convention of the American Psychological Association,* American Psychological Association, 1971, pp. 699–700.

Hersen, M., & Bellack, A. S. Assessment of social skills. In A. R. Ciminero, K. S. Calhoun, & H. E. Adams (Eds.), *Handbook for behavioral assessment.* New York: John Wiley, 1977.

Holden, C. Sex therapy: Making it as a science and an industry. *Science,* 1974, **186**, 330–334.

Kanfer, J. H., & Phillips, J. S. *Learning foundations of behavior therapy.* New York: Wiley, 1969.

Kaplan, H. S. *The new sex therapy.* New York: Brunner/Mazel, 1974.

Kolvin, I. Aversion imagery treatment in adolescent. *Behaviour Research and Therapy,* 1967, **5**, 245–248.

Larson, D. E. An adaptation of the Feldman and MacCulloch approach to the treatment of homosexuality by the application of anticipatory avoidance learning. *Behaviour Research and Therapy,* 1970, **8**, 209–210.

Levin, S. M., Barry, S. M., Gambaro, S., Wolfinsohn, L., & Smith A. Variations of covert sensitization in the treatment of pedophilic behavior: A case study. *Journal of Consulting and Clinical Psychology,* 1977, **10**, 896–907.

Lindgren, T. N., & Pauly, I. B. A body-image scale for evaluating transsexuals. *Archives of Sexual Behavior,* 1975, **4**, 639–656.

LoPiccolo, J. The professionalism of sex therapy: Issues and problems. *Society,* 1977, **14**, 60–68.

Lovbond, S. H. The mechanism of conditioning treatment of enuresis, *Behaviour Research and Therapy,* 1963, **1**, 17–21.

McCary, J. L. *Human sexuality.* New York: D. Van Nostrand, 1973.

McConaghy, N. Penile response conditioning and its relationship to aversion therapy in homosexuals. *Behavior Therapy,* 1970, **1**, 213–221.

McConaghy, N. Measurements of change in penile dimensions. *Archives of Sexual Behavior,* 1974, **3**, 381–388.

McGovern, K., Arkowitz, H., & Gilmore, S. Evaluation of social skills training programs for college dating inhibitions. *Journal of Counseling Psychology,* 1975, **22**, 505–512.

Maletzky, B. M. "Booster" sessions in aversion therapy: The permanency of treatment. *Behavior Therapy,* 1977, **8**, 460–463.

Marshall, W. L. The modification of sexual fantasies: A combined treatment approach to the reduction of deviant sexual behavior. *Behaviour Research and Therapy,* 1973, **11**, 557–564.

Martinson, W. D., & Zerface, J. P. Comparison of individual counseling and a social program with non-daters. *Journal of Counseling Psychology,* 1970, **17**, 36–40.

Masters, W. H., & Johnson, V. E. *Human sexual inadequacy.* Boston: Little, Brown, 1970.

Melnick, J. A comparison of replication technique in the modification of minimal dating behavior. *Journal of Abnormal Psychology,* 1973, **81**, 51–59.

Morganstern, F. S., Pearce, J. F., & Linford-Rees, W. Predicting the outcome of behavior therapy by psychological tests. *Behaviour Research and Therapy,* 1965, **3**, 191–200.

Obler, M. Systematic desensitization in sexual disorders. *Journal of Behavior Therapy and Experimental Psychiatry,* 1973, **4**, 93–101.

Quinn, J. T., Harbison, J. J., & McAllister, H. An attempt to shape penile response. *Behaviour Research and Therapy,* 1970, **8**, 212–216.

Quinsey, V. L. The assessment and treatment of child molesters: A review. *Canadian Psychological Review,* 1977, **18**, 204–220.

Rachman, S. J. Studies in desensitization: I. The separate effects of relaxation and desensitization. *Behaviour Research and Therapy,* 1966, **3**, 245–252.

Rachman, S. J., & Hodgson, R. J. Experimentally induced sexual fetishism: Replication and development. *Psychological Record,* 1968, **18**, 25–27.

Rachman, S. J., & Teasdale, J. *Aversion therapy and behaviour disorders: An analyses.* London: Routledge and Kegan, 1969.

Reckless, J., & Geiger, N. Impotence as a practical problem. In H. F. Dowling (Ed.), *Disease-a-month,* Chicago: Year Book Medical Publishers, 1975.

Rehm, L. P., & Marston, A. R. Reduction of social anxiety through modification of self-reinforcement: An instigation therapy technique. *Journal of Consulting and Clinical Psychology,* 1968, **32**, 565–574.

Rekers, G. A., & Varni, J. W. Self-monitoring and self-reinforcement process in a pre-transsexual boy. *Behaviour Research and Therapy,* 1977, **10**, 211–216.

Serber, M. Shame aversion therapy. *Journal of Behavior Therapy and Experimental Psychiatry,* 1971, **1**, 213–215.

Serber, M. Videotape feedback in the treatment of couples with sexual dysfunction. *Archives of Sexual Behavior,* 1974, **3**, 377–380.

Stevenson, I., & Wolpe, J. Recovery from sexual deviations through overcoming non-sexual neurotic responses. *American Journal of Psychiatry,* 1960, **116**, 739–742.

Stoller, R. J. Referenced personal communication, in Barlow, D. H.: The treatment of sexual deviation: Toward a comprehensive behavioral approach. In K. S. Calhoun, H. E. Adams, & K. M. Mitchell (Eds.), *Innovative treatment method in psychopathology,* New York: Wiley, 1974.

Terrace, H. S. Stimulus control. In W. K. Honig (Ed.), *Operant behavior: Areas of research and application,* New York: Appleton-Century-Crofts, 1966.

Thorpe, J. G., Schmidt, E., Brown, P. T., and Castell, D. Aversion relief therapy: A new method for general application. *Behaviour Research and Therapy,* 1964, **2**, 71–82.

Tollison, C. D., Adams, H. E., & Tollison, J. W. Physiological measurement of sexual arousal in homosexual, bisexual, and heterosexual males. *Journal of Behavioral Assessment,* 1979.

Twentyman, C. T., & McFall, R. M. Behavioral training of social skills in shy males. *Journal of Consulting and Clinical Psychology,* 1975, **43,** 394–395.

Wickramasekera, I. The application of learning theory to a case of sexual exhibitionism. *Psychotherapy: Theory, Research and Practice,* 1968, **5,** 108–112.

Wickramasekera, I. A technique for controlling a certain type of sexual exhibitionism. *Psychotherapy: Theory, Research and Practice,* 1972, **9,** 207–210.

Williams, M. H. "Individual sex therapy." Paper presented to second annual meeting of the Eastern Association for Sex Therapy, Phil., Pennsylvania, March, 1976.

Wolpe, J. *Psychotherapy by reciprocal inhibition.* Stanford: Stanford University Press, 1958.

Wolpe, J. *The practice of behavior therapy (2nd edition).* New York: Pergamon, 1973.

Yulis, S. Generalization of therapeutic gain in the treatment of premature ejaculation. *Behavior Therapy,* 1976, **7,** 355–358.

CHAPTER 13

Behavioral Treatment of Victims of Sexual Assault

Judith V. Becker and Gene G. Abel

The 1976 Federal Bureau of Investigation's Uniform Crime Report indicates that there were 56,730 forcible rapes reported in that year, but the actual number of rapes committed is unknown, since it is generally assumed that a very high percentage go unreported. Curtis (1975), for example, estimates the incidence of rape to be from 2.2 to 5 times greater than that reported to the police.

Any person may be the victim of a sexual attack. A widely held myth is that only young, attractive women are raped. Yet the data indicate that rape victims can range in age from two months to 100 years. The incidence of sexual abuse of young children is unknown. However, De Francis (1969) estimates that 100,000 children are sexually abused yearly.

Until recently, the subject of rape was taboo. In the past five years, the situation has changed considerably, partly due to the activities of the feminist movement in this country. Books, articles, and television programs have discussed the topic extensively. The new attitude toward rape is evident in many spheres. For example, rape laws are being changed. Several states, such as Wisconsin, have revised their rape laws to include a nongender specific definition and to define the various degrees of sexual assault. Since most states are in the process of revising their rape laws, the mental health clinician needs to review his/her state's laws regarding rape; this information will be helpful in the event that the patient wishes to prosecute, and these laws can usually be obtained from the Sex Crime Squad Division of the police department or police division that routinely investigates sexual assaults.

Many police departments have instituted specifically trained sex crimes squads and a number of hospitals are implementing special programs for the medical and the psychological treatment of rape victims. A National Center for the Prevention and Control of Rape has been established to support research in the area of sexual assault. Numerous phone-line crisis centers and walk-in rape counseling centers have developed throughout the country. These centers, usually staffed by volunteer paraprofessionals and former victims, provide counseling to the victim and the victim's family, and they educate the public about the problem (Burgess & Holmstrom, 1974; Connell & Wilson, 1974; Csida & Csida, 1974; Horos, 1974; Medea & Thompson, 1974; Walker, 1975).

THE VICTIMS

Mary is a three-year-old, attractive, very bright child who allegedly was assaulted by her father during a visit (the parents are divorced). Four months after the assault the mother brings Mary for counseling and relates the following symptoms: (*a*) 6-pound weight loss during the past four months; (*b*) onset of self-injurious behavior (constantly falling and injuring legs and arms) following the assault; (*c*) fear of males; (*d*) general unhappiness; and (*e*) regression to early developmental stage behavior.

Sue is a 29-year-old female who was raped at age 13. Prior to the rape she had led a normal life and had engaged in consensual sexual behavior that led to orgasm. Sixteen years after the assault and following numerous psychiatric hospitalizations, she presents the following symptoms: (*a*) inability to orgasm since the assault; (*b*) painful intercourse (dyspareunia); (*c*) constant, intrusive thoughts of being raped.

Deluce is a 20-year-old college junior who was awakened in the middle of the night by a man holding a knife to her throat, threatening to kill her if she did not submit sexually. He terrorized her for nearly an hour before she was successful in deterring a rape by feigning an epileptic seizure. She requests therapy several months later and relates the following symptoms: (*a*) inability to sleep in a room by herself; (*b*) constant thoughts about being raped; and (*c*) loss of concentration at school.

Alyce is a 22-year-old senior in college who was raped by two men while she was walking from the school parking lot to the library. Several days following the assault she requests therapy for anxiety that is crippling and inhibiting her from returning to the college campus to take her exams.

Helen is a 50-year-old grandmother who was born and lived all her life in a ghetto. She was raped by a fellow parishioner after he walked her home from church. Following the assault, Helen relates having spells during which she experiences temporary amnesia. In the course of the interview, she reports having been raped on two other occasions.

Arlene, in her mid-twenties, requests therapy two days after her employer attempted to rape her. She experiences feelings of "losing control," is unable to sleep or concentrate, and wonders if she's "going crazy." At the close of the interview, she verbalizes "something I've never told anyone before." She was kidnapped and gang raped by a motorcycle gang several years previously.

Both males and females can be the victim of a sexual assault; however, the majority of the cases we have treated and those reported in the literature are female victims. Consequently, those reactions observed in female victims and treatment techniques employed are elaborated on.

The consequences of a sexual assault to a victim vary as a function of the interaction between the victim's developmental level and her current rape experience (Burgess & Holmstrom, 1974). The meaning of a sexual assault to a young child, for example, will differ markedly from that of an adult victim and will significantly influence the type of treatment modality implemented. For example, a very young child who has been raped vaginally will not focus on the "sexual" nature of the assault. To her, a part of her body has been injured. Children may be more in-hibited in talking about the incident than an adult victim. To facilitate verbalization with children, it is helpful to have them draw pictures or demonstrate with toys what occurred.

Two Models of Victim Response

Even though there is considerable variability across victims, a number of common responses have been observed. Sutherland and Scherl (1970) have described three sequential phases of a victim's emotional response to rape. The first stage, lasting from a few hours to a week, is characterized by a feeling of numbness where the victim may actually be in a state of physical and emotional *shock* and may express disbelief over the assault. During this stage, the victim may express fear, terror, disgust, humiliation, vulnerability, powerlessness, and anxiety. Few mental health practitioners actually witness the victim in this stage. Usually, police, close friends, family members, medical personnel, or rape counselors are the first to come into contact with a victim following an assault.

The second stage involves a period of *outward adjustment* during which the vic-tim attempts to reorganize her life and appears to be adjusting to the assault. This state is characterized by denial. The victim does not want to discuss or be re-minded of the assault. This stage appears to be self-protective and enables the vic-tim to deal with her everyday life functions, such as working, going to the hospital for medical care, and so on. However, should she completely stop all expression of feelings regarding the rape during this stage, she is very likely to have difficulty later. A similar consequence of denial is seen in individuals who have not accepted a loved one's death. Later emotional dysfunctions surround the issue of death (Kubler-Ross, 1969). With rape, emotional dysfunctions usually surround the area of sex.

The third stage is termed *integration*. The victim is sensitive to any stimulus that reminds her of the assault. Depression, anger, and excessive ruminations about the assault are common during this stage. Stimulus generalization is quite frequent and the victim may withdraw from stimuli associated with the rape, such as contact with unknown males, environments similar to that in which the rape occurred, and people in general. A number of victims may seek or are encouraged to seek ther-apy or counseling while in this stage.

Burgess and Holmstrom (1974; 1978), as a result of their counseling rape vic-tims in the emergency room of Boston City Hospital, have also described a cluster of symptoms consistently described by most rape victims. They defined these as the "Rape Trauma Syndrome." This syndrome, which includes physical, emo-tional, and behavioral concomitants, has two stages. During the acute stage, the majority of the victim's coping and life-functioning processes are disrupted. She is hit by the immediate reaction of the trauma and undergoes strong physical and emotional reactions. Stage two, during which the victim tries to reorganize her life, is often filled with nightmares about the assault and strong avoidance responses, to situations and people, that take the form of phobias. Drastic changes in life-styles may be evidenced during this stage.

Our clinical experience in treating victims of sexual assault has confirmed the predominance of avoidance behaviors in victims having difficulty coping. We see the victim as going through three stages. During the first stage, she is stunned, shocked, and unable to organize a coping plan. This stage can last from 1 to 10 days. As the victim attempts to deal with the rape, vascillation of mood occurs with an attenuation of emotional responses and avoidance behaviors. This second stage usually lasts 1 to 7 weeks and normally ends with the victim reestablishing a steady state of functioning. During a possible third stage, the victim is unable to resolve stage two issues and the symptoms seen in stage two can develop into a chronic condition. This lack of resolution frequently results from a lack of a support system, significant personal and emotional losses in the years preceding the rape with which the victim has not adequately dealt, or previous psychological disturbances that are exacerbated by the rape. Stage three victims are usually able to function physically but a strong emotional response to the rape persists, leading to sexual dysfunctions, persistent phobias, and/or high anxiety levels. Bart (1975), for example, in a study of 1000 rape victims, found that one-third experienced sexual problems from the rape, such as vaginismus, secondary nonorgasmia, decreases in sexual drives, and fear of any type of sexual involvement. In a study of 20 victims and 20 attempted rape victims one year following a sexual assault, Becker, Abel, Bruce, and Howell (1978) found that 45% of both groups continued to have nightmares, and 66% of the attempted victims and 70% of the victims continued to experience some form of trauma or phobia. These results indicate that therapists should realize that attempted or completed rape victims develop significant emotional problems and both groups need treatment. Table 1, then, summarizes the typical reactions of adult rape victims or attempted rape victims.

Childhood Victims

Child victims of sexual assault have special needs. For example, care must be taken in the medical exam of child victims to not further traumatize them by focusing on the genitals. The context of the exam should be that of an overall physical exam (Sgroi, 1978). It is essential that an alliance is established with the child. If the child has difficulty trusting the physician or counselor, interviewing and treatment will be difficult (Burgess and Holmstrom, 1978). Frequently, in incest

Table 1.   Adult Victims' Reactions and Sequelae to Rape

---

1. Immediate reaction: expressed (crying, anxious); controlled (little affect)
2. Feelings of: vulnerability, helplessness, hopelessness, anger, shame, guilt, and embarrassment
3. Physiological disturbances: appetite disturbance, sleep disturbance, genitourinary problems (chronic vaginal infections), and diffuse anxiety
4. Sexual dysfunctions: arousal dysfunctions, nonorgasmia, dyspareunia, and vaginismus
5. Phobias: fear of people, fear of being alone, fear of indoor or outdoor locations, and fear of men
6. Cognitive disturbances: nightmares (homicidal or rape), and chronic ruminations of the assault

---

cases, children are made to feel responsible for the involvement. This "weight" must be lifted from them.

Klemmack (1977), in an analysis of child victims of sexual assault, reports that society is uncomfortable with the idea of dealing with any aspect of sexuality and/or violence with children. She states because of this discomfort ". . . all too often the focus is on the complicity of the child rather than on the trauma of the event and the irresponsibility of the offender" (p. 58).

As cited previously, the incidence of sexual assaults and molestation of children is unknown. However, there is evidence to suggest that the incidence is grossly underestimated (DeFrancis, 1969). The data available indicates that child victims are predominantly female, and typically between 10 to 11 years of age. The offender is almost always male (Gagnon & Simon, 1970). DeFrancis (1973), in a three-year study of sexual abuse in children, found that 25% of the offenders were members of the child's household (father, stepfather, mother's boyfriend). Eleven percent of the offenders did not live in the child's home but were friends or acquaintances of the child or the child's family. Twenty-five percent were strangers.

Studies that have focused on the psychological trauma sustained by the child have not been consistent in defining the exact type of sexual contact. Klemmack (1977) addresses this issue: "any discussion of the effect of sexual assault on long-term functioning has to take into account the type of assault. Confusion results because there is no clear definition of what constitutes sexual assault, sexual abuse, or sexual misuse of children" (p. 61). This distinction should be made in the literature in regard to reported cases, since the psychological functioning of the child's postrape symptomatology may be related to the type of sexual assault.

Research findings regarding the impact of a sexual assault on a child vary. DeFrancis (1973) found that two-thirds of sexually exploited children showed signs of emotional disturbance. He acknowledges, however, that pathology may have existed preassault. Gagnon (1976) notes that forced sexual activity over a prolonged period of time may contribute to later psychological adjustment problems. Burton (1968), by contrast, states that sexual assaults on children do not seriously affect their later adult adjustment. Gibbons and Prince (1963), in a study of 82 victims, found that 43% showed no outward disturbance, 16% were "unsettled" and manifested behavior problems, 14% were in need of therapy, and 6% were confined to a correctional institute. Several researchers have defined the response of the parents to their child's assault as an important variable in the child's adjustment postassault (Burgess & Holmstrom, 1974; Peters, 1976). The extent of violence used and the relationship of the offender to the child are also important variables (Schultz, 1975).

Our knowledge of the impact of a sexual assault on a child is slowly growing. Although the impact may vary from child to child, variables that affect the child's reaction include: reaction of the parents, the relationship of the offender to the victim, the type of assault and any preexisting pathology in the victim. Additional research should elucidate these issues further.

A child or adolescent's reaction to a sexual assault is basically similar to that of an adult. However, since their development is not completed, there are some differences. Table 2 summarizes the typical reactions seen in child and adolescent victims.

Table 2.   Child and Adolescent Victim's Reactions and Sequelae to Rape

1. Immediate reaction: expressed or controlled
2. Feelings of: loss of ability to trust parents to protect them, fearfulness, and embarrassment
3. Physiological disturbances: gastrointestinal (appetite disturbance, stomach pains), sleep disturbance, enuresis, and hyperactivity
4. Phobias: fear of people, fear of leaving the home, fear of being left alone, and fear of sex
5. Avoids: school, friends, and dates
6. Cognitive disturbances: nightmares and chronic rumination about the assault

Family and friends of victims are also affected by the sexual assault. If the victim is a child, very often the parents feel guilty because they believe they did not adequately protect their child. Parents may also blame the child. This is more common in incest cases when a mother is torn between her loyalty to the child and her loyalty to her spouse. In incest cases, the mother may also become jealous of the victim after discovery of the assault.

Parents frequently verbalize wanting to take revenge and may become overzealous in their attempts to gain retribution. Parents need to be told that their excessive reactions may further traumatize their child and prolong the child's coping with the assault.

It is common for parents to express concern for their child's psychosexual development. This concern may take the form of: (a) becoming very restrictive regarding the child's social interactions because they fear the sexual assault will lead to sexual promiscuity at a later age; (b) concern that the child will become homosexual in her sexual orientation; or (c) overprotecting the child and, thereby, reinforcing some of the avoidance behaviors resulting from the assault.

Parents frequently experience cognitive disturbances similar to the actual victim's. It is extremely important that parents receive counseling to help alleviate their own guilt feelings as well as to educate them as to how to respond to their child after the assault. Saperstein (1975) provides the following guidelines in working with child victims: (a) assess the cognitive, life experience age of the child; (b) determine the meaning of the rape to the child and deal with the rape on the child's level; and (c) give the child information about their medical examination. The needs of the parents are also addressed by Saperstein who recommends to: (a) help parents to focus on the child's needs; (b) help parents channel their anger appropriately (not on the child); (c) teach parents how to meet the child's needs; and (d) give parents information on medical and legal resources.

In working with sexual assault victims, clinicians have begun to develop models and apply existing models to meet their treatment needs. The following describes such models:

TREATMENT MODELS

Crisis Model

The National Organization for Women (NOW) and other women's organizations have been instrumental in directing the nation's concern to the serious problem of rape in this country. There are presently more than 200 NOW Rape Task Forces in the United States, actually involved in providing crisis intervention and public education, lobbying for changes in legislation, teaching prevention and self-defense to women, and assessing the services presently being provided by police, hospital personnel, and the court system.

The model for counseling victims used by these centers is based on the crisis intervention model. Lindenmann's (1944) study of the survivors of the Coconut Grove Fire is an excellent example of the impact of a trauma on its human participants. He found that following a disaster or trauma, individuals experience sensations of somatic distress, intense subjective distress that they label tension or mental pain, avoidance of the distressing event. We see a very similar pattern in women postsexual assault.

Caplan (1964), recognized as an expert in crisis theory, defines crisis in terms of the psychological disequilibrium experienced by the person and the method of coping used by the person to resolve the crisis. Coping with a severe illness, a death of a significant other, a sexual assault, or transitions—such as moving, starting a new job—exert stress on an individual with which he/she has to cope. If the individual is facing a specific developmental task at that time, the coping process may be compounded. For example, Burgess and Holmstrom (1974) discuss the impact an assault has on victims as they pass through various developmental phases. For young adults the task involves acquiring a sense of intimacy. A sexual assault can generate ambivalence in a young adult regarding who to tell about the assault, her feelings about her own sexuality, and what to do about dating in the future.

The major goal in rape crisis counseling is to aid the victim in regaining control of her life. Counselors are taught to listen and help the victim express her feelings. As with any type of crisis counseling, the victim is given information to help her gain control and make decisions. Empathy is expressed toward the victim, with counselors being trained in becoming aware of their own feelings and prejudices regarding rape that may interfere with counseling (Burgess and Holmstrom, 1974; Largen, 1975; Lyons, 1975). Many victims feel responsible for the attack and they are reassured that this and other feelings that they may be experiencing are normal (Halleck, 1962). Counselors also encourage the victim to express her feelings but do not force her to disclose them. Counseling thus involves support while the victim regains control of her life, without challenging the defenses she has constructed during her self-protective period. Counseling also includes a "working through" of the victim's feelings about herself and about the assailant and helps her gain self-respect. The reader is directed to the following sources for further information on victims' responses to sexual assault and crisis counseling: Burgess and Holmstrom, 1974, 1978; Csida and Csida, 1974; Hilberman, 1976; Notman and Nadelson, 1976; MacDonald, 1971; Sutherland and Scherl, 1970.

Based on the case reports of victims treated using the crisis model, this appears to be an effective treatment. There is, however, a clear need for the development of dependent measures and systematic follow-up to determine the efficacy of this model as well as which elements of counseling are critical and which are not. Furthermore, if victims fail to respond to this model one needs to know what other approaches might be used. Although some possible measures of response to therapy exist (such as number of days not functioning as a student, employee, home-maker; extent of nightmares; social withdrawal; fear of males; and avoidance of social settings), these have not been used systematically.

Another issue that needs evaluation is the significance of the counselor's sex. Rape counseling centers for the most part utilize female counselors for a number of reasons. Many centers are staffed by previous victims who have a better under-standing of what it is to be assaulted and can accurately empathize with the vic-tim. Additionally, some have considered rape a political issue (Brownmiller, 1975) and believe that since rape is a crime committed almost exclusively against women by men, only women can understand the psychological and physical trauma and, therefore, women would be better able to lead other women through their resolu-tion of the crisis. Silverman (1977) in an article entitled, "First Do No More Harm; Female Rape Victims and the Male Counselor," addresses some of the male counselors' responses to victims, which include; (a) anxiety and a feeling of "making up" to the victim; (b) overzealousness in showing how liberated or non-sexist a therapist he is; (c) displaying more interest in the sex trauma rather than the actual violent act; and (d) having the same stereotypes of rape as the rest of society. He concludes that the male counselor should: (a) confront his own myths and stereotypes; (b) help the victim gain control of her life (not take control for her); (c) not feel responsible for her assault or a need to make up for the assault; and (d) help the victim's significant other (father, boyfriend) understand the problem.

The use of female counselors exclusively may be inappropriate based on our understanding of fear–phobia development (Rachman, 1968). Since the victim has been traumatized by a brutal, insensitive male, it is not surprising that the vic-tims generalize this experience to other males, constantly fearing social contact with males, known or unknown. The common element in the treatment of fears is exposure (Agras, 1972; Marks, 1972). Contact with female counselors, however, removes the victim from the opportunity to interact on a close interpersonal level with a warm, empathic male. This would be the very treatment identified as effec-tive for reducing the victim's fears. Clearly, controlled studies are needed to ex-plore this issue further.

Assessment

The knowledge we have about the impact of sexual assault is based on case reports rather than empirical data. There are several explanations for this fact. (a) His-torically, our society has not seen rape as an issue that warranted much concern; (b) Those individuals who focused attention on rape—the political, physical, and psychological traumas experienced by its victims—were not clinical researchers and were interested primarily in providing treatment services to women; and (c) Some rape crisis centers have been reluctant to work with clinical researchers, fearing that the victim may be exposed to added stress or unnecessary intrusion. There has also been some professional rivalry in the field as various professions muster their expertise in dealing with the problem. However, with the establishment of the Na-tional Center for the Prevention and Control of Rape, there are now monies available for rape crisis centers and for interested mental health professionals to, either individually or through pooled resources, investigate the issue of rape.

Measurement Issue

All research requires the development of dependent measures and observable or recordable observations that can be replicated by others. Our prior studies in developing dependent measures for other patient populations (Abel, 1976; Abel, Barlow, & Blanchard, 1973) exemplifies such work. Without objective dependent measures, any treatment method with rape victims can not be validated and, subsequently, the development of such measures are critical to the investigation of any treatment for rape victims.

Research dealing with anxiety and emotions has used two categories of dependent measures to assess patients' symptoms and the response of those symptoms to treatment: objective and subjective measures.

Subjective Measures

Although providing greater flexibility in assessment than objective measures, subjective measures are the most easily distorted by the research patient or subject. There are five commonly used types of subjective measures: verbal report, frequency counts, card sorts, audiovisual tape ratings, and paper and pencil tests.

1. *Verbal Report.* Almost all studies dealing with rape victims rely on this method of data collection. The reported occurrence or absence of behaviors associated with continued functioning after a rape attack (days at work; presence or absence from home or residence; tasks performed) are obtained, but usually not systematically, and thus comparisons across victims become difficult since unequal data collection has occurred.

2. *Frequency Reports.* In the treatment of a sexual deviate, Mees (1966) used the subject's self-report of frequencies of various fantasies and behaviors to measure change in a victim's response to treatment. This same method can be used with rape victims; that is, the victim is asked to record the frequency of a variety of events, such as: thoughts about the rape, fear of being alone, or number of avoidance responses. The frequency of occurrence of each of these events is then totaled and plotted daily, giving an ongoing measure of the victim's progress. Wolff (1977) for example, used a victim's self-report of "checking behaviors" and average hours of sleep as the dependent measures in the systematic desensitization and negative practice treatment of a rape victim whose symptoms (fear of being alone and checking behavior) persisted seven years after the assault.

3. *Card Sort.* Card sorts are attitudinal measures that allow further quantification of treatment progress. Examples of their use are available for other emotional problems (Abel, 1976; Abel, Barlow, & Blanchard, 1973) and it appears to be easily adaptable to dealing with rape victims. For example, victims can be asked to rate daily on a seven-point scale ranging from a −3 (very anxious) to a +3 (very pleasant), various scenes that are rape and

nonrape related. The ratings, -3 through $+3$, are totaled daily for each category of scenes and plotted, reflecting the patient's attitudes toward her trauma and environment.

Table 3 depicts the frequency count and card sort used with a 45-year-old woman who was abducted from her parking lot and raped by two men. Since that time, the victim developed a fear of entering a parking lot when it was dark and has become socially withdrawn.

4. *Audiovisual Tape Ratings.* Rape prevention is an important topic in the area of sexual assault. One means of successful rape prevention is by the potential victim emitting certain behaviors that disrupt the rapist's intent to rape. Giacinti and Tjaden (1973) report that one-third of rape attacks are successfully thwarted by victim-controlled behaviors, such as screaming out, fleeing, or offering verbal or physical resistance. Unfortunately, information about which rape deterrence behaviors are successful are sketchy because:

Table 3.   Victim's Frequency Count and Card Sort

In the last 24 hours, how many times have you:

1a.   Asked someone to accompany you home _____?

1b.   Thought about rape or injurious acts _____?

1c/d.   Left your apartment building to do something other than work, in the evening or night, alone _____? with someone else _____?

1e.   Thought about what could have happened that night _____?

1f.   Thought about the rape _____?

1g.   Looked out your window toward car, spot _____?

1h.   Number of nonwork related social contacts you made today _____? (List who and activity on back).

1i.   Rate yourself on the average level of social facility you showed today with 0 = wall flower and 10 = comfortable and adept _____?

Instructions: Rate yourself on the scale, indicating how anxious each statement makes you feel today:

Extremely anxious			*Neutral*		*Extremely relaxed*	
-3	-2	-1	0	$+1$	$+2$	$+3$

____ 2.   You are at a party and a male stranger comes over to talk with you

____ 3.   You read about a rape or violent crime in the newspaper

____ 4.   You imagine your own rape as it actually occurred

____ 5.   A male stranger knocks on your door when you are at home, alone, at night

____ 6.   You are unlocking your car in a grocery parking lot during the day when a man approaches you

____ 7.   You are alone in an elevator when a man begins to enter it

____ 8.   You are walking to your car, alone, during the day, at a shopping center and you do not see anyone nearby

____ 9.   You are walking to your car, alone, at night, and you see a man along your path

____10.   An unknown man appears to be following you to your car at night; you are alone

____11.   A car appears to be following your car during the day; you are alone

(*a*) information regarding this behavior has been gathered in a haphazard fashion; (*b*) when collected, information is not detailed since this has not been a special area of concern to most data sources; and (*c*) information depends on victim's recall, which may be poor.

Mastria (1976) has approached the evaluation of successful rape deterrence behavior in a novel way. Women who had expressed an interest in learning self-defense were assigned to one of five conditions: (*a*) a police department's self-defense course, (*b*) assertiveness training, (*c*) self-defense plus assertiveness training; (*d*) waiting list controls; and (*e*) a group comprised of females who had not expressed an interest in learning self-defense. All groups received a series of personality and assertiveness paper and pencil tests pre- and posttreatment. Each subject also had her verbal responses to male-female, escalating social-sexual encounters audiotaped, pre- and post-assault. Results indicated that assertiveness training alone was the most effective in increasing the frequency of rape deterrence behavior. The implications of this research are far-reaching since self-defense training is frequently advocated as a means of deterring rape. Mastria found that self-defense training may have served to *increase* the women's fear levels. Further use of such dependent measures will help evaluate the effectiveness of various forms of rape-deterrence and self-defense training that are being taught to women but are lacking in empirical documentation.

5. *Paper and Pencil Tests.*   Since fear is a prominent response in victims of rape, it would be advantageous to utilize pre- and posttreatment instruments that would assess the types of fears experienced and the degree to which the patient is experiencing anxiety. The Fear Survey Schedule (Wolpe and Lang, 1964) is such an instrument. Veronen and Kilpatrick (1977) have modified the original fear survey schedule to include a rape subscale. Their MFS (Modified Fear Survey) contains a 120-item list of events, objects, and situations that are rated on a five-point scale in regard to the amount of fear or disturbance they produce in the victim. Twenty recent rape victims (one week to four months postrape) were administered the instrument. The control group consisted of 12 college coeds. The MFS was then scored for seven subscales. While no mean differences were observed between victims and nonvictims in overall fearfulness, the victim group had significantly larger variances on two subscales of the MFS. Those items for the victim group that were rated as the most fear engendering were oral intercourse, veneral disease, guns, weapons, knives, walking on dimly lighted streets, suffocation, testifying in court, feeling disappointed, and dead people. The authors acknowledge the limitations of their study in terms of the unmatched control group. However, this study is significant in that it is the first study conducted with rape victims that has utilized a comparison group, and it has documented the differential response frequencies between victims and a control group on rape-related stimuli.

Other paper and pencil tests that are presently being used as dependent measures with rape victims are the Profile of Mood States Scale (McNare, Lorr, & Droppleman, 1971); Self-Report Inventory (Brown, 1961); and the State-Trait Anxiety Inventory (Spielberger, Gorsuch, & Lushene, 1970).

Objective Measures

A woman's rape frequently affects her sexual life with an avoidance of sexual behavior and, sometimes, the development of sexual dysfunctions. It thus becomes critical to be able to objectively evaluate a woman's sexual responding. Until recently, there has not been a valid and reliable physiological measure of sexual arousal in females. While the technique for directly monitoring sexual arousal in males is quite sophisticated (Zuckerman, 1971), the measurement of the sexual responsiveness of women has been far slower in development because of a possible lack of interest in female sexuality as well as the problem of devising an instrument that can accurately measure a woman's sexual arousal. Various devices have been developed with limited success, including a thermal flowmeter (Cohen & Shapiro, 1970; Shapiro, Cohen, DiBianco, & Rosen, 1968), a clitoroplethysmograph (Tart, 1973); and a method of measuring uterine contractions (devised by Bardwick & Behrman, 1967).

VAGINAL PROBE. Sintchak and Geer (1975) developed a photoplethysmographic probe that serves as a photoelectric transducer measuring changes in the optical density of the vaginal tissues. The device is a clear acrylic probe the shape of a menstrual tampon that the subject inserts into the outer one-third of the vagina so that it measures the highly vascular vaginal tissues. The probe is instrumented with a light source and photosensitive cell, both embedded in the acrylic. The voltage used is quite low so that minimal thermal stimulation occurs. Relative pulse pressure and relative blood volume are each measured by the device.

With increased sexual arousal, two physiologic changes are recorded: (a) increased relative pulse pressure; and (b) increased pooling of blood in the vagina. Initial validating work with the device indicates that it is highly sensitive to sexual arousal (Geer, Morokoff, & Greenwood, 1974; Heiman, 1974, 1975). Our modification of the Sintchak device arranges the photocell so that it records irrespective of the probe's position in the vagina and thereby lessens movement artifact. This device has been used to record sexual arousal in both victims of sexual assault and nonvictims with minimal difficulties. The details of its use as a dependent measure in the treatment of a sexual assault victim are presented later.

OTHER PSYCHOPHYSIOLOGIC MEASURES. Kilpatrick & Veronen (1978) are presently conducting a group outcome study comparing the efficacy of systematic desensitization, stress innoculation, and a peer-counseling support group, in treating rape-induced fear and anxiety. To evaluate the outcome of these treatments, electrodermal and cardiovascular activity are monitored while victims listen to audio taped descriptions of three target behavior scenes. Target behavior scenes vary from victim to victim, depending upon the specifics of her assault. They are based on three separate behaviors that are associated with fear and avoidance as a result of the rape. For example, three target behaviors may be (a) fear of men, (b) fear of cars, and (c) fear of guns, if the woman was raped in a car while being held at gunpoint. Data from this study are yet to be published, but should prove helpful in elucidating the psychophysiologic responses experienced by victims listening to these fantasized experiences.

MOTOR-SKILLS ASSESSMENT. Avoidance behavior by victims is frequently motivated by their fear of once again encountering the rapist. Moving from her prior residence, avoiding heterosocial gatherings, and staying with female friends are typical examples of attempts to escape the rapist again. One approach to helping victims overcome these rape-induced behavioral changes is to teach the victim social skills and/or assertiveness skills that are inconsistent with a sustained, fear-avoidance response (Alberti & Emmons, 1974; Osborn & Harris, 1975; Serber, 1972). The specific application of skills training to rape victims would be the training of rape deterrence behaviors; that is, what specifically to do if she encounters a rapist again. Technology already exists to evaluate the successful training of such rape deterrence behaviors as reflected in the assessment of social skills (Abel, et al., 1977). Assessment would involve videotaping scenes from situations where the potential victim successfully or unsuccessfully thwarted the rapist. Scales similar to social skills could then be developed that separate successful from unsuccessful deterrence behaviors. These scales could then be used to evaluate whether women have been successfully taught rape deterrence skills.

Behavioral Treatments

Behavioral intervention focuses on teaching the victim to alter her maladaptive or nonfunctional behaviors that were learned as a result of the rape experiences. "A therapeutic goal of the behavioral model is to deflate the fears, stresses, and anxieties the victim experiences after the rape and to help inflate her own self-esteem and self-confidence in dealing with the world again" (Burgess & Holmstrom, 1974, p. 228).

Although behavioral treatment is frequently viewed as a treatment for discrete symptoms, complex problems can also be treated by breaking them down into smaller, more discrete components. Each of these components can then be dealt with by the treatment most effective for that specific component (Abel, 1975). This involves looking at the verbal, motoric, and physiological components of a patient's behavior and applying treatments that decrease excesses or correct deficits in each of the component areas.

Such a model has begun to be applied to the treatment of rape victims. Systematic desensitization has been utilized to mitigate the victim's avoidance responses to feared stimuli or to decrease her fearful thoughts of the rapist returning. Negative practice training is useful in treating compulsive behaviors resulting from a sexual assault. Sexual dysfunction counseling has helped women who have developed sexual problems as a result of the rape. Biofeedback training has proven to be successful in treating victims with severe physiological arousal responses following their rape. Social skills and assertiveness training has helped the victim who manifests social, phobic avoidance or who feels helpless interpersonally.

The abovementioned treatments might be viewed as components of an overall treatment package for the victim. Which method to use would depend on the individual victim's specific symptomatology. A few behavioral methods are now reviewed to demonstrate their applicability for treating special problems displayed by rape victims.

Biofeedback

The literature contains only one study using biofeedback with a rape victim. Blanchard and Abel (1976) treated a patient with a 15-year history of a rape-induced psychophysiologic cardiovascular disorder, episodic sinus tachycardia and subsequent syncope using biofeedback. The patient reported that her symptoms had developed shortly after she was raped at age 14. Her subsequent medical history as an endless repetition of organic evaluations, resulting in a diagnosis that her frequent bouts of tachycardia were precipitated by her recall of the emotional factors surrounding her rape. Treatment involved presenting the patient the tachycardia-eliciting stimuli (audiotape descriptions of society's attitude regarding her rape) while concomitantly providing her with a visual display of her cardiac rate, using a single case experimental design. The investigators systematically demonstrated that biofeedback training enabled her to control her tachycardia while attending to the tachycardia-eliciting stimuli. Generalization of the effectiveness of biofeedback from the laboratory to the patient's natural environment further supported the biofeedback's effectiveness. Although biofeedback would not be an appropriate treatment for many victims, it does have applicability when a specific physiologic system is involved, and that system can be fed back to the victim, as demonstrated in this case.

Systematic Desensitization

Systematic desensitization, developed by Wolpe (1958), is a commonly used behavioral treatment technique. Its main use has been reported with a wide variety of problems for which there was some anxiety-based problem (Paul, 1969; Wolpe, 1969).

Controversy exists as to the actual mechanism by which systematic desensitization works. Wolpe (1958, 1969) and others (Davison, 1968) propose a counterconditioning or reciprocal inhibition explanation. That is, the response of arousal initially present to the hierarchy stimuli is replaced by a response of relaxation or at least nonarousal. Others (Agras, 1972; Marks, 1972) have proposed an extinction explanation. That is, it is exposure to the anxiety-arousing cues, with no adverse consequences befalling the patient, that leads to the eventual diminution of arousal. Regardless of the theoretical explanation, empirically, this method has been documented as effective with various fears.

There have been several reports in the literature of the successful use of systematic desensitization in the treatment of women having heterosexual fears (Lazarus, 1963; Wolpe, 1958). The application of systematic desensitization with a rape victim has been reported by Wolff (1977). His patient was a 20-year-old, female victim of an attempted rape at age 13. She had fallen asleep on a couch while babysitting and was awakened by a rapist who threatened to harm her and the children under her care if she did not submit. Since the rape attempt, the patient had never spent a night sleeping alone because of her fear of his return.

Systematic desensitization was completed in seven sessions with the result that the patient had increased the amount of time she was able to sleep at night (dependent variable). Although the patient reported she was no longer fearful when alone in the apartment, she reportedly continued to engage in compulsive checking of the rooms looking for an intruder. Negative practice was utilized to extinguish the compulsive checking.

Examples of Systematic Desensitization

In our work with rape victims, we have utilized both systematic desensitization and in vivo desensitization to reduce phobic behaviors. Our application involved the use of systematic desensitization with a college student who was raped one night in the parking lot of her university library. The patient had left her car and was approaching the building when she was pulled into a vacant car by two men. One held her down while the other raped her. The penetration had been so brutal that the patient's vaginal wall had been torn, necessitating the frequent application of ice packs to stop the hemorrhaging. The patient had been a virgin at the time of the rape. Prior to the rape, her heterosexual relationships were limited; she had broken an engagement and she viewed intercourse as animalistic. The rape was not reported to the police because of a movie the patient had seen on television (*A Case of Rape*). She saw what the TV victim was put through by both the police and the court and did not want to expose herself to further trauma.

Our first contact with the victim was two months after the attack. At that time her symptoms included constant nightmares, which included being held down and raped, fear of remaining alone in her apartment (she had two roommates), and fear of returning to the campus to complete her academic program. The patient had not returned to the campus since the rape nor would she drive on the main street of the town on which the campus was located.

The first component of treatment consisted of teaching the patient progressive muscle relaxation. We then constructed a hierarchy of fearful stimuli and desensitization began on the second session. The patient was requested to complete a card sort (containing 10 items) at the close of each session. The cards were to be sorted into four categories: zero (no anxiety); one (somewhat anxious); two (much anxious); three (very anxious). The patient was instructed to read each card and place it in the appropriate category. A score was obtained by multiplying the number of cards in each category by the number assigned to that category and totaling the scores for that day. For example, if 3 cards were placed in category 3 and 7 cards in category 2, the patient's score would be 23 (3 × 3 plus 7 × 2).

The task for each session, the patient's card sort score, and the topography of her nightmares are presented in Table 4.

Although the patient was able to return to the campus following her sixth session and take the required exams to finish her course, she continued to maintain a high level of anxiety. The therapy helped her since she was able to return to the campus and drive on the main street of the town. However, her fear of social-sexual situations and her nightmares remained. Additionally, she continued to experience anxiety to her last two hierarchy items. The systematic desensitization was not completed because she had to leave town. There was subsequently a four-week interim between session eight and nine. When she did return her card sort was back to a pretreatment level. After relocating she continued her systematic desensitiza-

Table 4.   Results of Systematic Desensitization With A Rape Victim

Session	Goal	Card Sort	Nightmare
1	History and relaxation training	–	Constant nightmares, screams, but cannot awaken quickly
2	History and relaxation training	20	Nightmare but did not scream and woke up instantly
3	Began systematic desensitization	17	Unchanged
4	Patient presented with an impending crisis in regard to visit from mother. Did not do systematic desensitization	No Card Sort	Unchanged
5	Continued systematic desensitization	19	Unchanged
6	Desensitization and *in vivo* (drove to parking lot on campus with patient)	17	Unchanged
7	Continued systematic desensitization	17	Nightmare usually occurred every night at 1:30 A.M., changed one night, occurred at 5:30 A.M.
8	Began assertiveness and anger training	18	Unchanged
9	Patient returned to town to handle some business, came in to see therapist	20	Unchanged

tion treatment and also received social skills and assertive training. She has since married and is functioning both socially and sexually. Unfortunately, systematic follow-up data is not available to us.

Systematic desensitization was used to treat another woman who had been the victim of an attempted rape. As a college coed she was awakened by a man standing over her holding a knife. She tried to deter the rapist and was successful by feigning an epileptic seizure. The patient had not been able to spend a night alone since the rape attempt nor could she fall asleep alone at night. She was able to sleep in the daytime and early evening. However, if she awoke and it was dark, she could not fall back asleep. This was especially problematic to her since she was presently residing with a man with whom she no longer wanted to live. She was phobic to the extent that she could not go to sleep until he returned from work. Since he was employed as a bartender and did not return home until 2 A.M., the subject would not get much rest. A second major symptom was her strong fear of walking to and from her car.

Therapy first involved using the standard crisis model of intervention to deal with her two crises: (*a*) the attempted rape; and (*b*) the recent death of a male friend. This form of therapy had no impact on her fear as measured by self-report. She was then taught relaxation training and aided in the development of a fear hierarchy (see Table 5).

The actual attempted rape scene was not included in the hierarchy since the goal of systematic desensitization with victims of sexual assault should not be to decrease anxiety to being raped. The goal, instead, is to reduce her paralyzing anxiety to those events that have come to elicit anxiety as a result of the sexual assault. The fear of being raped is not an irrational fear for women in our society to have. Consequently, systematic desensitization should not be used to desensitize women

Table 5. Rape Victim's Hierarchy

1. You think about having to deal with your fears in therapy
2. You are walking to a building from the parking lot
3. You are lying on the couch at home with your eyes closed at night
4. You enter your apartment and make only a minimal check of the rooms
5. You enter your apartment and do not check to see if someone is hiding in it
6. You receive an obscene phone call
7. You are walking around your apartment in the dark
8. You enter your apartment, alone, at night and the lights are out
9. A customer at work tells you he is going to follow you home
10. You are walking to your car, alone, at night, and you do not see anyone along your path
11. You are at home, alone, at night, in a part of the apartment where you cannot see either entrance
12. You are in your old apartment the night of the attempted rape, just before anything happened
13. You are alone in your current apartment, at night, taking a bath
14. You think about the woman's body that was found in the car near your apartment
15. You are walking to your car, alone, at night, and see a man along your path
16. You are driving alone when you see a car that appears to be following you
17. You are lying in bed at night with your eyes closed
18. A male stranger knocks on your door when you are at home, alone, at night
19. You are at home alone, and it sounds like someone is in the house
20. You think about your friend's recent rape
21. You approach your car and see that someone is in the back seat

to something that is a potential reality. Instead, women should be taught verbal and physical assertion skills that could be utilized to deter an assault.

The subject's frequency count and card sort are presented in Table 6.

The victim's card sort and frequency count data collected during systematic desensitization are presented in Table 7. Each data point represents four days of data collection. Pre A and B scores represent the two weeks respectively of baseline data collection. Change scores were computed by averaging the two weeks of baseline and comparing them with the final week of treatment. At the end of the eleventh week, the subject had completed all the items on her hierarchy. (The subject failed to collect data during week six.)

Although the subject did not manifest a significant change on her frequency count items, she did show a slight increase in the expected direction for thoughts about being alone, being startled by sudden noises, and not checking her apartment for the presence of an intruder. There was no change in the frequency of nightmares or thoughts about rape. The subject actually increased the frequency of the remaining items; this is in contrast to what we had predicted.

It is important to note, however, that there is a considerable amount of variability in this subject's data. For example, during week 10, she was able to fall asleep, alone, at night. During week 11, however, she did not fall asleep.

This subject's card sort did show a change in the expected direction on all items. There is, however, a considerable amount of variability, as was found in the fre-

Table 6.   Attempted Rape Victim's Card Sort and Frequency Count

In the last 24 hours, how many times have you:

    1a.   Invited someone over just so you would not have to be alone _____?

    1b.   Fallen asleep alone in the apartment _____? (Time of day _____?)

    1c.   Thought about being alone in the apartment _____?

    1d.   Had a nightmare _____?

    1e.   Thought about other rape or injurious acts _____?

    1f.   Left your home to go do something by yourself (other than work) during the day _____? During the night _____?

    1g.   Been startled by sudden noises _____?

    1h.   Thought about the attempted rape _____?

    1i.   Entered the apartment and checked to see if someone was hiding _____?

    1j.   Entered but did not check _____?

Rate how anxious each statement makes you feel today, if −3 = extremely anxious, 0 = neutral; and +3 = extremely relaxed.

_____ 2.   You are at a party and a male stranger comes over to talk with you

_____ 3.   You think about your friend's recent rape

_____ 4.   You imagine that attempted rape as it actually occurred

_____ 5.   You're entering your apartment, alone, at night

_____ 6.   A male stranger knocks on your door when you are at home, alone, at night

_____ 7.   You are at home, alone, and it sounds like someone's in the house

_____ 8.   You are home, alone, at night, in a part of the apartment where you cannot see either entrance

_____ 9.   You are walking to your car, alone, at night and you do not see anyone along your path

_____10.   You are walking to your car, alone, at night and you see a man along your path

_____11.   A strange man appears to be following you to your car at night; you're alone

quency count. It is important to note that during the last week of treatment the subject moved into an apartment with a female roommate. This may explain some of the variability during week 11 on the frequency count data.

Although the subject failed to rate her items as not anxiety-producing in most cases, she did experience some reduction in overall anxiety. The subject's verbal report indicated that she felt much less anxious and that the systematic desensitization had helped her. However, this subject continued to have intrusive thoughts about rape. Consequently, a third component of treatment, an extinction procedure, was used to help reduce the frequency of intrusive rape thoughts.

It is possible that a victim of a sexual assault or an attempted sexual assault has been so traumatized by the assault that they may never rate a behavior in relation to the assault as neutral on an anxiety scale. Another explanation of the lack of significant change relates to the measures themselves. It has been our experience with one victim that reading the card sort and frequency count served to generate anxiety because the victim was "forced" to recount the assault. Finally, it is pos-

Table 7. Attempted Rape Victim Data on Card Sort and Frequency Treatment Weeks[a]

	Pre^A	Pre^B	1	2	3	4	5	6	7	8	9	10	11	Δ
Frequency count items[b]														
1.a	2	0	0	0	0	0	0		0	0	0	0	2	−1
1.b	2	1	1	2	2	2	1		3	2	1	4[c]	0	−1.5
1.c	5	4	0	2	1	3	1		3	1	1	3	4	+0.5
1.d	0	0	0	1	0	2	0		0	0	0	2	0	0
1.e	1	1	0	2	0	1	2		2	1	2	4	3	0
1.f	1	5	4	6	6	3	2		3	2	1	2	0	−1
1.f″	3	1	0	1	0	0	0		0	0	0	0	2	−0.5
1.g	2	2	0	1	2	2	2		1	1	1	7	3	+1
1.h	0	0	0	0	0	0	1		0	0	0	2	0	0
1.i	6	5	2	5	5	2	3		2	0	1	2	4	+1.5
1.j	1	1	2	3	1	0	0		1	2	0	2	0	0
Card sort items[b]														
2.	+1.0	+1.0	+2.0	+2.0	+1.75	+1.0	+1.0		+1.0	+1.75	+2.0	+1.25	+2.0	+1.0
3.	−2.75	−2.5	−2.0	−2.0	−1.75	−1.5	−1.75		−1.5	−1.25	−1.0	−2.25	−2.0	+.62
4.	−2.0	−1.5	−2.0	−2.0	−1.0	−0.75	−1.0		−1.0	−1.0	−1.0	−1.5	−1.0	+.75
5.	−2.25	−2.0	−1.0	−1.25	−1.25	−1.25	−1.0		−1.0	−1.0	−1.25	−1.75	−1.0	+1.12
6.	−3.0	−3.0	−2.0	−3.0	−1.25	−1.5	−1.25		−1.25	−1.75	−1.75	−2.0	−1.75	+1.25
7.	−3.0	−3.0	−3.0	−3.0	−1.75	−1.5	−1.5		−1.25	−1.25	−1.5	−2.25	−1.5	+1.5
8.	−2.25	−2.0	−1.25	−1.25	−1.0	−1.5	−1.0		−1.25	−1.5	−1.5	−1.5	−1.0	+1.12
9.	−2.0	−2.0	−1.25	−1.25	−1.0	−1.5	−1.0		−1.0	−1.0	−1.5	−1.25	−0.5	+1.5
10.	−3.0	−2.75	−2.25	−2.25	−1.25	−2.0	−1.5		−2.0	−2.0	−2.0	−2.0	−1.5	+1.38
11.	−3.0	−3.0	−3.0	−3.0	−3.0	−2.5	−1.75		−2.0	−2.0	−2.0	−2.25	−2.0	+1.0

[a] + = increase in desired behavior; − = decrease in desired behavior.
[b] Each data point is the total of four days of data collection.
[c] Two times this treatment week victim fell asleep alone, at night. All other times that she fell asleep alone were during daylight hours.

365

sible that the systematic desensitization was somewhat helpful in reducing anxiety, but further treatment components are necessary.

Kilpatrick (1978), in his work with victims of sexual assault, has found that high fear and anxiety ratings by victims are sustained for as long as three months postrape. Furthermore, he acknowledges that systematic desensitization might not be very effective with victims of sexual assault in extinguishing anxiety since their fears are rational ones, as opposed to irrational ones, which are seen in phobic disorders that have proved amenable to desensitization. Kilpatrick asserts that stress innoculation, which serves to elicit coping mechanisms, may prove a more effective treatment.

Finally, the passive nature of systematic desensitization may be a variable. Victims feel out of control and need assistance in gaining control of their lives. Systematic desensitization is something a therapist does to his/her client. The victim is passive and again being "acted upon." Systematic desensitization appears to be effective in reducing anxiety somewhat but in and of itself it may not be the most clinically efficient treatment. Research which is ongoing (Kilpatrick, 1978; Turner, 1978) should help clarify this issue.

Sexual Dysfunction Therapy

Bart (1975) reported that a significant number of rape victims develop sexual problems following a rape experience. We have made similar observations in our treatment of rape victims. The problem can vary from secondary orgasmic dysfunction, to vaginismus, decreased libido, or having to control the sexual act in order to enjoy it. The treatment of sexual dysfunction in females has been reviewed by Annon (1975), Hoon (in press), Kaplan (1974), and Masters and Johnson (1966). Recently, we have successfully utilized a behavioral approach (Lobitz & LoPiccolo, 1972) in the treatment of orgasmic dysfunction in a 29-year-old rape victim.

Clinical Example of Sexual Dysfunction

Sue was 13 years of age when she was raped. She was returning home from a football game when a car pulled beside her and one of the occupants pulled her into it. There were four teenage boys in the car (one of whom was known to the victim). The boys proceeded to tie her up with coat hangers and rape her. The experience lasted approximately one hour. The boy who knew Sue threatened to kill her mother if she disclosed the assault to anyone. Several months after the rape, she became very ill and was hospitalized. Sue was diagnosed as having gonorrhea. It was at this time that Sue revealed to her mother and physician that she had been raped. Medical treatment consisted of three D and C's and it was necessary to remove her right ovary.

Prior to the sexual assault, Sue had limited sexual experience. She was dating one boy regularly, enjoyed sex, and was orgasmic. Following the sexual assault, she reported experiencing no pleasure from sex, was unable to orgasm, and experienced dyspareunia. At age 18 Sue married. Her marriage was an unhappy one. Her husband beat her severely on several occasions. She had attempted to divorce him but he would not consent. During the course of this marriage, she underwent numerous psychiatric hospitalizations.

At the time of our first contact with Sue, she was separated from her husband, unemployed, and was being seen as an outpatient at a local mental health center. When asked to elaborate her problems, she listed them as follows: (*a*) inability to have children; (*b*) nonorgasmia; (*c*) dyspareunia; (*d*) nightmares about the rape; and (*e*) intrusive thoughts about the rape. She reported being involved in a relationship with a man about whom she cared a great deal. However, sex continued to be a problem with them. Her present sexual partner refused to be interviewed or participate in her therapy.

A treatment program was designed, based on the Lobitz and LoPiccolo (1972) model. Prior to and during treatment the patient completed a card sort and frequency count and underwent vaginal probe measures to evaluate the effectiveness of the treatment for her sexual functioning.

During the first therapy session we discussed Sue's views on sexuality and corrected any misinformation or myths she had regarding her sexual responding. The treatment program was described to her as a method by which she would learn what she finds pleasurable by exploring and stimulating her body. She could then communicate this information to her present sexual partner. Her homework assignment involved taking a bath at least three times during the following week followed by looking at herself in a mirror (using a hand mirror to explore her genitals) and touching her body all over to discover what parts "felt good" when stimulated. Since Sue had related that her most erotic thoughts were of Don touching her, she was instructed to fantasize about Don as she was exploring her body.

Sue returned for her second session (one week later) and reported that she had carried out the exercise only one time. She gave the following account of her exercise: ". . . it felt good when I touched my breasts, but I had some funny feelings when I touched my genitals. I felt silly about touching myself and so I stopped."

Further discussion revealed that Sue had never stimulated her genitals, and as a youngster had been instructed by her parents that after urinating she was to "wipe very quickly." She also recalled being very modest to the extent that it took her a year before she could be naked in front of her present sexual partner. She had also limited herself in terms of the sexual positions used during intercourse. Again, her parents had instructed her that the only "acceptable" position was the "missionary" position. Her present sexual partner had helped her overcome her inhibitions regarding varied sexual positions. We took this opportunity to discuss how sexual behavior is learned and how it can be relearned.

Prior to the rape, Sue had perceived intercourse as a pleasurable experience. However, since the rape, intercourse represented sex plus fear and pain. In short, sex had come to represent something aversive. We gave her the expectation that through her exercises she could be reeducated and again come to view sex as pleasurable and reinforcing. While indicating that it would take her some time to get comfortable with her own body, we wanted her to continue the exercises.

During the third session Sue indicated that she was able to carry out the exercises that we had given to her. She related having 30-minute sessions every day and found that her breasts and the area behind her ears were the most sensitive parts of her body. She continued to rate sensations in the genital area as aversive. We told her that for the next week she was to focus on the genital area and to evaluate the clitoral, vaginal, and genital areas separately. That is, she was to note any sensations positive or negative that she had in these areas.

At our next session she reported that she had continued the exercises but had some difficulty with them because she was angry with Don and could not use him as a source for fantasy material. We discussed other options and she was again encouraged to continue using clitoral and vaginal stimulation. The subject of using a vibrator was broached but she was most adamant about not wanting to use one. We did not make any further recommendations regarding the vibrator (in working with victims of sexual assault, it is most important that they feel in control and they do not view any of the therapist's recommendations as being aggressive; should we have pushed the issue of using a vibrator the patient may have terminated therapy).

During the fifth session Sue reported that she had experienced an orgasm. She stated that she stimulated her clitoris while thinking about Don. She was most pleased by the feeling of orgasm. The experience was so reinforcing that she related that she would continue doing her exercises.

At our next session, she related that she did not have any more orgasms. She was having realtionship difficulties with Don and felt that this problem was interfering with her ability to orgasm.

Both objective and subjective assessment instruments were used. Sue completed a card sort and frequency count. We monitored changes in vaginal blood volume using our intravaginal photoplethysmograph, as described previously (Sintchak & Geer, 1975), while Sue listened to a 2-minute audio taped description of a heterosexual-sexual scene. Figure 1 reflects the results of Sue's treatment.

Vaginal probe measures were not taken after each treatment session for the following reasons: (a) subject was in menses; and (b) subject was unable to remain for lab session because of other appointments; therefore, subjective data are only reported for those days on which probe measures were taken. During baseline her relative average vaginal blood volume to the heterosexual scene was 8. Card sort averaged a negative 0.8. Frequency of sexual thought averaged 6.5. Higher levels of arousal were achieved as more focused, genital stimulation exercises were produced, with a mean relative blood volume index of 19 during treatment. The one low data point (6.5) during genital stimulation corresponded with her boyfriend's incarceration; Sue was depressed that day. However, the following data points show an increase in relative vaginal blood volume. The noncoercive card sort and frequency count also showed an increase in expected direction during treatment. The rape card sort and frequency count remained fairly constant throughout treatment.

This victim's history reveals that a rape attack can so traumatize a woman that her sexual functioning can be impaired for years. Furthermore, although the victim had received a significant amount of therapy during the years following the assault and her first contact with the present writers, her sexual dysfunction persisted. It was not until a specific treatment intervention, which focused on her sexual problem, was initiated that change occurred.

This study also demonstrates that both subjective and objective measures can

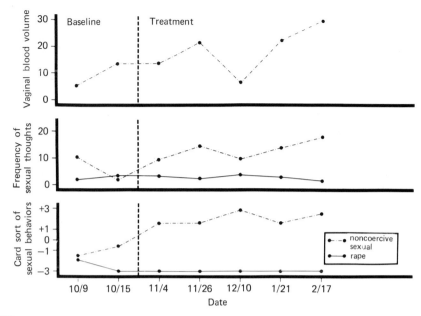

FIGURE 1. Rape victims sexual dysfunction treatment.

be employed with sexual assault victims. Sue was most conscientious about recording her card sort and frequency count data. She reported no adverse psychological or physical problems in relation to the objective measure (vaginal probe).

In conclusion, the results of this single case study provide initial support for the use of a specific behavioral treatment technique to modify a sexual dysfunction resulting from a sexual assault. In working with sexual dysfunction in females we have found the following books helpful: *Liberating Masturbation* (Dodson, 1974); *My Secret Garden* (Friday, 1974); *Becoming Orgasmic: A Sexual Growth Program for Women* (Heiman, LoPiccolo, & LoPiccolo, 1976).

Extinction Procedures

There are a number of behaviors problematic to victims that develop following a rape. For example, a considerable number of victims have reported having consistent, disturbing, intrusive thoughts about the sexual assault. Frequently victims who have been raped in their own homes, engage in checking behaviors. That is, before they retire at night they must check all the locks on the doors and all of the rooms to ascertain whether or not it is safe to remain in the house. A review of the literature revealed only one study involving a rape victim as a subject that utilized an extinction procedure (Wolff, 1977). Negative practice was used to decrease the frequency of occurrence of ritualistic checking behavior in a 20-year-old rape victim who felt compelled to check her apartment for the presence of an intruder. This checking behavior included 13 steps ranging from looking into the kitchen to opening closets and looking under beds. Negative practice involved having the subject perform the checking behaviors five times in succession. Treatment reduced the occurrence of this behavior from a baseline range of from zero to two times a day to a zero occurrence at the end of treatment and at 6- and 12-month follow-up.

Further research is indicated to investigate the effectiveness of other types of extinction procedures to decrease the frequency of problematic behaviors that develop postrape.

Skills Training

We have seen a number of females who have been raped on more than one occasion in their lifetime. One patient had been sexually assaulted 3 times over a period of 20 years. Therefore, teaching victims rape prevention skills or assertiveness skills is another approach to aid the victim in dealing with her fear and avoidance responses. The theoretical assumption underlying assertiveness training is that expressing one's feelings is incompatible with anxiety associated with social interactions. Learning appropriate skills would thus inhibit social anxiety (Wolpe, 1966). This procedure has been demonstrated to be effective with a diverse patient population.

Burgess and Holmstrom (1974) report that the loss of the ability to control her life and the feelings of helplessness during the attack generate anxiety in the victim after the attack. Furthermore, Kolias (1974) feels that the sense of helplessness in a woman and her passivity may influence a rapist in selecting her as a target. He stated that rapists expect nonassertive, passive women.

In examining the rape literature we could not locate any studies reporting skills training as a treatment for victims of sexual assault. Mastria (1976), however, reports on the effectiveness of assertiveness training as a method to deter rape in an analogue study. A group of women were given four assertiveness training sessions (Alberti and Emmons, 1973), consisting of didactic information on assertiveness and modeled situations to role play. Pre- and postassessments using the Behavioral Assertiveness Test (Eisler, et al., 1973) were used as dependent measures as well as various paper and pencil tests. Assertiveness training proved to be a valid deterrence technique.

We propose the specific application of such skills training to rape victims to help them gain a feeling of control and overcome their sense of helplessness. Familiarity with what to expect, knowledge of rape prevention tactics, and practice in emitting rape deterrence behaviors would provide the victim with a behavioral repertoire inconsistent with anxiety responses.

A number of steps are required in such training. Since rape attacks begin in a variety of situations, the victim first has to learn to identify the situational determinants of an attack. This is especially critical since many completed rapes occur during the shock phase of a sexual attack when the victim is attempting to "pull herself together" so as to mobilize a response. Step one could require role playing the frequent situations where an attack first becomes identifiable by the victim.

The second step would involve teaching her to emit rape deterrence behaviors. Although there is not one style of rape prevention behavior, but multiple styles—depending on the environment, the rapist's tactics, and the victim's skills—the victim can be taught a repertoire of responses (Abel, 1976).

Equally as important as demonstrating that such rape deterrence training is successful would be to examine its impact on the victim's fears and avoidance behaviors. This could be accomplished by concomitantly measuring the acquisition of skills using the dependent measures cited under the measurement section (i.e., frequency counts, videotape, vaginal probe, EMG, etc.). We are presently conducting research to evaluate the effectiveness of this technique.

RAPE PREVENTION

We conceptualize rape prevention as falling into three areas. The first involves changing society's attitudes and behaviors toward women. We live in a male-dominated, sexist society in which women are victimized and discriminated against in almost all levels of life. Although this has been changing of late, the pace at which this has been occurring has been a slow one. If we were to abolish differential child-rearing practices and women were no longer defined as sexual objects, the weaker sex, or portrayed through the media as helpless victims, then, perhaps over time, we would see a decrease in the number of sexual assaults against women. Whether this would facilitate the amelioration of sexual assault entirely or whether there would be an increase in sexual assault against males is an empirical question.

A second method of prevention involves treating those men who engage in sexual aggressive behavior. The classification, characteristics, and treatment of rapists have been described by numerous researchers (Abel, Blanchard, Becker, 1976; Amir, 1971; Cohen, Garofalo, Boucher, and Seghorn, 1971; MacDonald, 1971; Vuocolo, 1969). A third area of prevention relates to the rapist-victim interface. That is, what occurs between the rapist and his victim and, specifically, what kind of rape prevention methods might the potential rape victim use to prevent the rape. Of course, a number of individuals have spoken about the rape prevention skills. However, their suggestions have been "armchair" suggestions as to what can be done rather than material based upon scientific evidence. To prevent rape adequately, however, we must maximize our knowledge on this complicated interchange between the rapist and his victim so that specific guidelines based upon scientific evidence can be developed for the rape victim to use.

What women can do to deter a rapist has been explored from two vantage points. Giacinti and Tjaden (1973) retrospectively examined police records of 915 rapes or attempted rapes. A surprisingly large percentage of these rapes were successfully thwarted (33%). Of these, 68% were prevented by the victim's own behavior; that is, she initiated an action at the time of the assault that stopped her own rape. Since a large percentage of sexual attacks are preventable by what the victim can do, a much higher percentage of rapes could be thwarted, with a concomitant reduction in human suffering, if potential victims could be provided with scientifically based information on how to prevent rape. The problem, however, is how to obtain the best advice possible for victims.

A second means of evaluating the effectiveness of various victim-initiated techniques has been reported by Brodsky (1976). After reviewing the literature, Brodsky collected nine categories of victim behaviors that had been reported as successful rape deterrents. (Examples of these categories can be found in Table 8).
Scenes depicting these specific interactions between a potential rapist and a victim were constructed and videotaped. The scenes were then rated by 35 hospitalized rapists as to which methods would be most effective (rated as 5) and least effective (rated as 1) with them. Results indicated the following degrees of effec-

Table 8.   Examples of Rape Deterrence Behaviors

Verbal attack

"Let go of me, you son of a bitch, you pervert, you sex deviate. Stop this. Let me go, you bastard."

Body weakness

"I've got cancer. I just had a pap smear and I have cancer in my vagina and you're probably going to catch it."

Virginity

"Don't rape me, I'm a virgin. I've never had sex before, I'm about to get married and I want to be a virgin."

Moral appeal

"You shouldn't rape me. What would God think? This is against his commandments. God wouldn't approve of this."

Interpersonal liaison

"Why are you doing this? My name is Mary. I'm just a person like you. You must have trouble meeting girls if you have to try to rape them. Let's talk about it."

Self-punitiveness

"If you rape me, I'll never get over this. I'll probably get ill and never be well again. I'll never be the same person."

External influence

"If you rape me, the cops will catch you and put you in jail. You're going to spend time in jail. The cops will get you and you'll rot in jail."

Ambivalent refusal

The woman fights against you and, at other times, stops fighting you. She tells you not to rape her but sometimes puts up no resistance.

Acquiescence

The woman does not say anything and does not fight you. She just lies there and does not move.

Physical resistance

The woman fights you by kicking, hitting, scratching, biting, or spitting.

---

tiveness: self-punitiveness (2.63); external influence (2.36); moral appeals (2.27); claiming bodily weakness (2.98); acquiescence (2.15); ambivalent refusal (2.10); verbal attack (2.03); virginity (1.84) and interpersonal liaison (1.76). Although these two studies are a good first step toward collecting effective data as to what potential victims might do to prevent rapists' attacks, identical data is yet to be collected from both rapists and rape victims. If one is to investigate the rapist-victim interface, it is essential that identical data be collected from both groups so that we can adequately compare and contrast the conclusion of both groups in evaluating identical methods of rape prevention.

We have recently used objective measures of the sexual arousal in rapists and child molesters to determine which rape deterrence behaviors would be most effective at reducing their arousal. To date, 6 rapists and 11 pedophiliac-subjects have listened to 2-minute audiotaped descriptions of rape encounters that include 1 of 10 different victim deterrent behaviors. While the rapists and child molesters listened to these descriptions, we were able to measure the actual percent of a full erection each sexual aggressive developed in response to the various means of preventing a rape. Additionally, each offender was individually interviewed about victim responses that would be effective in supporting a sexual assault. Table 8 describes the 10 audiotaped scenes. The authors have concomitantly measured the effectiveness of these rape deterrence behaviors as reported by 10 rape victims referred by our local rape crisis center. This preliminary study thus provides us with information pertaining to rape deterrence behaviors from both rapist and victim. On the basis of the data collected to date, the relative effectiveness of the 10 possible rape deterrence behaviors is presented in Table 9. A comparison of the four dependent measures across all victim response categories for rapists indicates that the most effective victim response was to claim body weakness, a finding consistent with 100% of the rapists reporting little or no sexual arousal to this type of rape prevention behavior and only 17% of the rapists having significant sexual arousal to this particular category of rape prevention technique.

To further compare the reports of rapists and rape victims as to which type of deterrence behaviors were used in attempts to prevent rapes, examples of each of the 10 possible victims' prevention behaviors were written on cards and evaluated by sexual aggressives and rape victims as to whether they were attempted by the victim. Table 10 illustrates the responses of both groups. A high correlation occurred between these two sources of self-reports, with the exception of the victim behavior described as acquiescence (in essence, the victim does nothing because she is shocked and stunned by the attack). While only 20% of the rape victims reported acquiescing during their assault, 60% of the rapists indicated that their victims acquiesced. The discrepancy may be a function of the misperception of the rape victim's behavior as seen by the rapist. Collecting identical data from both groups helps us identify more closely how each group sees themselves and each other, and further studies would appear to profit from this cross-examination.

Currently, advice is given by police and rape crisis agencies as to what women or children can do to prevent their own rapes. Unfortunately, this information has not been collected systematically, but it is usually based on subjective impressions of each of these groups. What is needed is a systematic, comprehensive examination of this issue from the vantage point of both the rapist and the rape victim, with identical information being gathered to improve the validity of the conclusions so derived. Armed with this information, law enforcement agencies, rape crisis centers, and mental health professionals could more accurately suggest to potential victims means of preventing their own rapes. Once this information is obtained, the behavioral therapist can then role play appropriate rape deterrence behaviors with the victim and, thereby, help her gain further control of her life and gain a sense of ability to protect herself in the face of an impending sexual assault.

Table 9. Percent of Rapists and Pedophiles Indicating High-Effectiveness of or Low-Induced Sexual Arousal by Victim Response

Rape Deterrence Behavior	Rapists[a]				Pedophiles[b]			
	Interview Report of Effectiveness	Report[g] of Effectiveness in Laboratory Setting	Erection Measures	Subjective[h] Arousal	Interview Report of Effectiveness	Report[g] of Effectiveness in Laboratory Setting	Erection Measures	Subjective[h] Arousal
Verbal attack	17	50	33	83	91[d]	55	44	88
Body weakness	67	50	83	100	55[d]	88	22	100
Virginity	17	0	0	67	36[d]	77	44	66
Moral appeal	33	33	17	83	45[d]	77	33	66
Interpersonal liaison	50	17	17	67	36[d]	77	44	77
Self-punitiveness	67	50	50	67	55[d]	66	33	66
External influence	67	33	50	83	70[e]	55	44	77
Ambivalent refusal	17	0	17	67	10[e]	66	33	55
Acquiescence	33	0	17	67	0[e]	55	22	55
Physical resistance	50[c]	67	17	100	80[f]	77	33	77

Note: Percentages can exceed 100% as the rank ordering was within subjects across the 10 response categories and some subjects rated responses equally.

[a] N = 6.
[b] N = 9.
[c] N = 4.
[d] N = 11.
[e] N = 10.
[f] N = 5.
[g] All scores of 100% were ranked as 1.
[h] All scores of 0% were ranked as 1.

Table 10. Percent of Rapists and Rape Victims
Reporting the Occurrence of Rape Deterrence
Behaviors

	Rapists	Rape Victims
Verbal attack	40	40
Body weakness	20	20
Virginity	0	10
Moral appeal	40	40
Interpersonal liaison	40	50
Self-punitiveness	0	0
External influence	40	30
Ambivalent refusal	25	10
Acquiescence	60	20
Physical resistance	0	0

CONCLUSION

Sexual assault is the most rapidly increasing assaultive crime in the United States. This country has already taken some steps to deal with the problem. The rape crisis model has already been suggested as an appropriate victim treatment model, but lacks documentation of its effectiveness. Sexual assault victims, due to the acuteness of their emotional conflicts, pose special problems in the collection of dependent measures. Frequently victims want to forget the assault. Requesting that a victim keep records of the frequency of her thoughts or behaviors is occasionally seen as intrusive by victims. It is difficult for them to "forget" if they are requested to complete a card sort or paper and pencil test, which ask specific questions about the assault. A second issue relates to the reactivity of the collection of dependent measures. Follow-up studies in which victims are interviewed at predetermined intervals to assess the impact of an assault are often viewed as "therapy" by victims. Consequently, the "natural process" is disrupted. In our work in interviewing victims we have had several comments that they felt "much better" after the interview and felt a "weight had been lifted," or that they had never been able to "tell all" as they had with us. Lastly, the rape crisis counseling centers where researchers frequently seek research subjects are often very protective of the victims they counsel. Research in general and behavioral treatments specifically are areas with which they have not had much exposure and, consequently, they may show reluctance to involve their centers and clients. Therefore, it is imperative that clinical researchers be both sensitive and innovative in their attempts at working with victims and in documenting the effectiveness of various treatment techniques.

There is a dearth of literature related to the application of proven behavioral techniques in the area of sexual assault. Further pilot work is suggested to evaluate the effectiveness of behavioral techniques with victims of sexual assault. By utilizing single case designs and controlled group outcome studies our knowledge of the most effective treatments for victims will be broadened.

Prevention of rape must be emphasized as much as treatment of the victim. This can be accomplished by establishing more empirically based treatment programs for offenders and providing education to the community about sexual assault. The victimization of women by men appears to be directly related to our sexist society, in which male supremacy is reinforced at the cost of the female members. The form that victimization takes may vary from subtle discrimination in hiring practices to blatant physical and sexual assaults on females. Gender role stereotyping and lack of equal rights for women are at the core of the victimization of women. Changes in this condition need to be addressed by social scientists and policymakers.

Preliminary data is already available regarding successful rape-victim deterrence behaviors. Attempts are being made to quantify and qualify some of the existing data. We encourage more behavioral scientists to investigate the area of prevention of sexual aggression and treatment of victims of sexual assault.

REFERENCES

Abel, G. Assessment of sexual deviation in the male. In M. Hersen & A. Bellack (Eds.), *Behavioral assessment: A practical handbook.* New York: Pergamon Press, 1976.

Abel, G., Barlow, D., & Blanchard, E. Developing heterosexual arousal by altering masturbatory fantasies: A controlled study. Paper presented at the meeting of the Association for the Advancement of Behavior Therapy, Miami Beach, December 1973.

Abel, G., Blanchard, E., & Becker, J. Psychological treatment for rapists. In M. Walker & S. Brodsky (Eds.), *Sexual assault.* Lexington, Ma.: Lexington Books, 1976.

Abel, G., Blanchard, E., & Becker, J. An integrated treatment program for rapists. In R. Rada (Ed.), *Clinical aspects of the rapist.* New York: Grune & Stratton, 1977, 161–214.

Agras, S. *Behavior modification: Principles and clinical application.* Boston: Little, Brown, 1972.

Alberti, R., & Emmons, M. *Your perfect right: A guide to assertive behavior.* San Luis Obispo, Ca.: Impact, 1974.

Amir, M. *Patterns in forcible rape.* Chicago: University of Chicago Press, 1971.

Annon, J. *The behavioral treatment of sexual problems,* Vol. 1. Honolulu: Enabling Systems, 1975.

Bardwick, J., & Behrman, S. Investigation into the effects of anxiety, sexual arousal and menstrual cycle phase on uterine contraction. *Psychosomatic Medicine,* 1967, **29,** 468–482.

Bart, P. Rape alert. *Newsweek,* 10 November 1975: 70–79.

Becker, J., Abel, G., Bruce, K., & Howell, J. Follow-up and comparison of victims of attempted rape and rape one year following a sexual assault. Unpublished manuscript, University of Tennessee, 1978.

Blanchard, E., & Abel, G. An experimental case study of the biofeedback treatment of a rape induced psychophysiological cardiovascular disorder. *Behavior Therapy,* 1976, **7,** 113–119.

Brodsky, S. Prevention of rape: Deterrence by the potential victim. In M. Walker & S. Brodsky (Eds.), *Sexual assault.* Lexington, Ma.: Lexington Books, 1976.

Brown, O. The development of a self-report inventory and its function in a mental health assessment battery. *American Psychologist,* 1961, **16**, 402.

Brownmiller, S. *Against our will: Men, women and rape.* New York: Simon & Schuster, 1975.

Burgess, A. W., & Holmstrom, L. L. *Rape: Victims of crisis.* Bowie, MD: Robert J. Brady Co., 1974.

Burgess, A. W., Groth, A. N., Holmstrom, L. L., & Sgroi, S. M. *Sexual assault of children and adolescents.* Lexington, Ma.: Lexington Books, 1978.

Burton, L. *Vulnerable children.* New York: Schocken, 1978.

Caplan, S. *Principles of preventive psychiatry.* New York: Basic Books, 1964.

Cohen, H., & Shapiro, A. A method for measuring sexual arousal in the female. *Psychophysiology,* 1970, **8**, 251 (abstract).

Cohen, M., Garofalo, L., Boucher, R., & Seghorn, T. The psychology of rapists. *Seminars in Psychiatry,* 1971, **3**, 307–327.

Connell, N., & Wilson, C. *Rape: The first sourcebook for women.* New York: New American Library, 1974.

Csida, J. B., & Csida, J. *Rape: How to avoid it and what to do about it if you can't.* Chatworth, Ca.: Books for Better Living, 1974.

Curtis, L. Victimization: Hidden people, hidden statistics. Paper presented at the Sixth Alabama Symposium on Justice and the Behavioral Sciences, University of Alabama, Tuscaloosa, Alabama, January, 1975.

Davison, G. Elimination of sadistic fantasy by a client-controlled counter-conditioning technique: A case study. *Journal of Abnormal Psychology,* 1968, **73**, 84–90.

DeFrancis, V. *Protecting the child victim of sex crimes committed by adults.* Denver: The American Humane Association, 1969.

Dodson, B. *Liberating masturbation.* New York: Body Sex Designs, 1974.

Eisler, M., Miller, P., & Hersen, M. Components of assertive behavior. *Journal of Clinical Psychology,* 1973, **29**, 295–299.

Federal Bureau of Investigation. *Uniform Crime Report, 1976.* Government Printing Office, Washington, D.C.: 1976.

Friday, N. *My secret garden: Women's sexual fantasies.* New York: Pocket Books, 1974.

Gagnon, J. Female child victims of sex offenses. *Social Problems,* 1965, **13**, 176–192.

Gagnon, J., & Simon, W. Sexual encounters between adults and children. In S.I.E.C.U.S. (Ed.), *Sexuality in man.* New York: Scribners & Sons, 1970.

Geer, J., Morokoff, P., & Greenwood, P. Sexual arousal in women: The development of a measurement device for vaginal blood volume. *Archives of Sexual Behavior,* 1974, **3**, 559–564.

Giacinti, T. A., & Tjaden, C. The crime of rape in Denver: A report submitted to the Denver High Impact Anti-Crime Council, Denver, 1973.

Gibbons, T., & Prince, J. *Child victims of sexual offenses.* London: Nell, 1963.

Halleck, S. The physician's role in management of victims of sexual offenses. *J.A.M.A.,* 1962, **180**, 273.

Heiman, J. Facilitating erotic arousal: Towards sex positive research. Paper presented at the annual meeting of the American Psychological Association, New Orleans, September, 1974.

Heiman, J. The physiology of erotica. *Psychology Today,* April, 1975: 91–94.

Heiman, J., LoPiccolo, J., & LoPiccolo, L. *Becoming orgasmic: Sexual growth program for women*. Englewood Cliffs, N.J.: Prentice-Hall, 1976.

Hilberman, E. *The rape victim*. New York: Basic Books, 1976.

Hoon, P. The assessment of sexual arousal in women. In M. Hersen, R. Eisler, & P. Miller (Eds.), *Progress in behavior modification* (vol. 7). New York: Academic Press, 1979.

Horos, C. V. *Rape*. New Canaan, Conn.: Toby, 1974.

Kolias, K. Women and rape. *Medical Aspects of Human Sexuality*, 1974, **8**, 183–197.

Kaplan, H. *The new sex therapy*. New York: Brunner/Mazel, 1974.

Kilpatrick, D. Personal communication, June 1978.

Kilpatrick, D., & Veronen, L. Personal communication, June 1978.

Klemmack, S. H. Child victims. In Brodsky, S. L., Klemmack, S. H., Skinner, L. J., Bender, L. Z., & Polyson, A. M. K. *Sexual assault: A literature analysis*. Report no. 33. Tuscaloosa, Alabama: Center for Correctional Psychology, 1977.

Kubler-Ross, E. *On death and dying*. New York: MacMillan, 1969.

Largen, M. A. History of women's movement in changing attitudes, law and treatment toward rape victims. In M. Walker (Ed.), *Rape: Research, action, prevention*. Proceedings of the Sixth Symposium on Justice and the Behavioral Sciences, University of Alabama: reprint 29 May 1975.

Lazarus, A. The treatment of chronic frigidity by systematic desensitization. *Journal of Nervous and Mental Disease*, 1963, **136**, 272–278.

Lindenmann, E. Symptomatology and management of acute grief. *American Journal of Psychiatry*, 1944, **101**, 141–418.

Lobitz, W., & LoPiccolo, J. New methods in the behavioral treatment of sexual dysfunctions. *Journal of Behavior Therapy and Experimental Psychiatry*, 1972, **3**, 265–271.

Lyons, B. A model for the training of rape crisis center counselors. Unpublished manuscript, University of Tennessee, 1975.

MacDonald, J. *Rape offenders and their victims*. Springfield, Ill.: C. Thomas, 1971.

McNare, D., Lorr, M., & Droppleman, L. *The manual profile of mood states*. San Diego: Educational and Industrial Testing Service, 1971.

Marks, I. Flooding in a lot of treatments. In W. S. Agras (Ed.), *Behavior Modification: Principles and clinical application*. Boston: Little, Brown, 1972.

Masters, W., & Johnson, V. *Human sexual response*. Boston: Little, Brown, 1966.

Mastria, M. A study of assertiveness as a function of training in rape prevention and assertive training. Unpublished doctoral dissertation, 1976.

Medea, A., & Thompson, K. *Against rape*. New York: Farrar, Straus & Giroux, 1974.

Mees, H. L. Sadistic fantasies modified by aversive conditioning and substitution: A case study. *Behaviour Research and Therapy*, 1966, **4**, 317–320.

Notman, M., & Nadelson, C. The rape victim: Psychodynamic considerations. *American Journal of Psychiatry*, 1976, **133**, 408–413.

Osborn, S., & Harris, G. *Assertive training for women*. Springfield, Ill.: Charles C. Thomas, 1970.

Paul, G. Outcome of systematic desensitization. In C. Franks (Ed.), *Behavior Therapy: Appraisal and status*. New York: McGraw-Hill, 1969.

Peters, J. Children who are victims of sexual assault and the psychology of offenders. *American Journal of Psychotherapy*, 1976, **30**, 398–421.

Rachman, S. *Phobias: Their nature and goal.* Springfield, Ill.: Charles C. Thomas, 1968.

Saperstein, A. Child rape victims and their families. In L. G. Schultz (Ed.), *Rape victimology.* Springfield, Ill.: Charles C. Thomas, 1975.

Serber, M. Teaching the non-verbal components of assertive training. *Journal of Behavior Therapy and Experimental Psychiatry,* 1972, **3**, 179–183.

Shapiro, A., Cohen, J., DiBianco, T., & Rosen, G. Vaginal blood flow changes during sleep in sexual arousal. *Psychophysiology,* 1968, **4**, 394 (abstract).

Silverman, D. First do no more harm: Female rape victims and the male counselor. *American Journal of Orthopsychiatry,* 1977, **47**, 91–96.

Sintchak, G., & Geer, J. A vaginal plethysmograph system. *Psychophysiology,* 1975, **12**, 113–115.

Spielberger, C., Gorsuch, R., & Lushene, R. *The state-trait anxiety inventory.* Palo Alto: Consulting Psychologist Press, 1970.

Sutherland, S., & Scherl, D. Patterns of response among victims of rape. *American Journal of Orthopsychiatry,* 1970, **40**, 503–511.

Tart, C. Personal communication, 1973.

Turner, S. Personal communication, June, 1978.

Veronen, L., & Kilpatrick, D. Conditioned fear and anxiety in victims of rape. Paper presented at the Eleventh Annual Convention of the Association for the Advancement of Behavior Therapy, Atlanta, December, 1977.

Vuocolo, A. The repetitive sex offender. Abilene, Tx.: Quality Printing, 1969.

Walker, M. (Ed.). *Rape, Research, Action, Prevention.* Report no. 29. Tuscaloosa, Alabama: Center for Correctional Psychology, 1975.

Wolff, R. Systematic desensitization and negative practice to alter the aftereffects of a rape attempt. *Journal of Behavior Therapy and Experimental Psychiatry,* 1977, **8**, 423–425.

Wolpe, J. *Psychotherapy by reciprocal inhibition.* Stanford, Ca.: Stanford University Press, 1958.

Wolpe, J. *The practice of behavior therapy.* New York: Pergamon Press, 1969.

Wolpe, J., & Lang, P. A fear survey schedule for use in behavior therapy. *Behaviour Research and Therapy,* 1964, **2**, 27–30.

Zuckerman, M. Physiological measures of sexual arousal in the human. *Psychological Bulletin,* 1971, **75**, 297–329.

CHAPTER 14

Vascular Disorders

W. M. Kallman and J. D. Gilmore

Recently developed behavioral treatments for vascular disorders have proved to be valuable adjuncts to traditional medical interventions. The most common form of extracranial cephalic vascular problem is the migraine headache. Typically treated with analgesics such as Fiorinal® or vasoconstrictors such as the ergotamine drugs, migraine headache patients frequently do not achieve relief from their symptoms. New procedures to teach the patient to control his or her own bodily processes have provided relief from symptoms for extended periods without the use of medication.

Raynaud's disease, which is manifest by cold hands and feet, discoloration, and even necrosis and gangrene in severe cases has been treated with vasodilators and, in intractable cases with a sympathectomy. Even such radical measures as the sympathectomy often fail to bring relief to the patient. Again, procedures aimed at teaching the client to control his own physiological responses have been demonstrated to produce satisfactory reduction in symptoms.

Essential hypertension is currently one of the most serious health problems in this country. Although antihypertensive medications produce reductions in blood pressure for the majority of patients, most medications produce uncomfortable side effects, or for some patients they are ineffective. Additionally, hypertensive patients frequently do not maintain their prescribed medical regimen because the disorder is usually symptomless. Recent psychological interventions involving biofeedback, deep-muscle relaxation, and cognitive restructuring have been shown to be invaluable adjunct or primary treatments for essential hypertension.

Finally, several types of cardiac arrhythmias have been partially controlled using biofeedback. The ability of patients to learn to alter the rate of their heartbeat is well established experimentally. Clinical evidence suggests that here again the role of nonmedical treatments can prove to be a valuable addition to the traditional medical interventions.

This chapter deals with behavioral interventions to teach patients suffering from vascular disorders how to produce the desired vascular response in a localized area that will eliminate or reduce symptoms. The procedures are discussed from a historical perspective. The role of these procedures as part of a complete therapy program will be emphasized. Two migraine headache cases are presented to illustrate case management issues.

380

HISTORICAL PERSPECTIVE

Skinner (1938) differentiated between voluntary or operant responses mediated by the skeletal muscles and involuntary or respondents mediated by the autonomic nervous system and directed psychology away from efforts to use operant conditioning principles to bring about changes in physiological systems. It was not until the late 1950s that the psychological community began to question the notion that bodily processes were, for the most part, controlled at a level of involuntary control and hence opened up an interest in the use of psychological intervention with physical problems. In the late 1950s researchers in the Soviet Union began to look at the feasibility of using operant conditioning principles to shape and maintain changes in visceral functions. Lisina (1958) reported that subjects in her laboratory were able to reverse the normal vasomotor response to mild skin shock if they were shown the ongoing strip chart record of their vasomotor responses. When Lisina's article was translated by Razran in 1961, American psychologists began to reevaluate the distinction between voluntary skeletal muscle responses and involuntary visceral responses. With the earliest published work there was controversy over whether control of the autonomic nervous system was really done directly via the use of reinforcement, or whether we were simply conditioning a skeletal muscle response that was mediating a change in the involuntary system.

Within only five years this debate had reached a prominent position in the literature. Miller and his associates had used Curare (a muscle paralyzing agent) to block all skeletal muscle activity and had shown that by using electrical stimulation of the median forebrain bundle as a reinforcer, laboratory animals could learn to control a wide variety of internal, visceral functions including heart rate, peripheral blood flow, gastric motility, and any number of other organ functions previously thought to be purely automatic in nature (Miller, 1968).

Brener (1973) proposed that the argument about whether control of internal processes was learned directly or through skeletal muscle mediation was unimportant. At that point the fact that humans as well as animals could learn to control bodily processes was an important discovery. The question of the method of control was one of basic research. The use of these new procedures to treat a variety of medical problems appeared promising, and behavioral scientists began to apply the new procedures to clinical populations that had not responded adequately to standard medical treatments.

The relevance of this perspective for current treatments is substantial. The present use of psychological treatments with vascular problems follows two distinct models. Biofeedback treatments assume that direct control over the biological response is efficacious. Other treatment approaches such as deep-muscle relaxation and positive imagery assume that the best way to change an internal process is by teaching a specific voluntarily mediated response.

THE VASCULAR SYSTEM AND SPECIFIC VASCULAR DISORDERS

The cardiovascular system represents a closed hydraulic system with the heart continuously pumping blood to the lungs for oxygenation and back to the body tissues through the arteries to deliver the oxygen and other vital nutrients. Various parameters of the system have been identified as being relevant to a healthy-functioning organism. Among these are the rate at which the heart pumps, the rhythm of the chambers of the heart as it pumps, the pressure of the blood going through the vessels, the residual pressure in the system that resists the flow of blood back to the heart, and the relative distribution of the blood to various parts of the body.

Numerous physical variables have been identified that can produce unhealthy changes in the cardiovascular system via any one of the above-mentioned parameters. For example, the internal pacing cells or the parasympathetic controls of the heart can be disturbed chemically or physically to produce an arrythmia. Clogging of the vessels by an embolism or atherosclerosis can produce an increase in blood pressure or decrease in the volume of blood that reaches specific regions of the body. Diseases such as scleraderma can cause the tissues to lose their elasticity and thus reduce blood flow to the periphery.

Friedman (1964) has noted that approximately 90% of all chronic headaches are vascular headaches of the migraine type, muscle contraction headaches, and combinations of the two. Migraine is a unilateral, extracranial headache that often involves a number of other symptoms. It is one of the most common psychosomatic disorders, with an estimated incidence of at least 5% (Childes & Sweetnam, 1961; Lyght, 1966), and the severity, frequency, and duration of attacks vary widely within and between patients (Friar & Beatty, 1976).

Migraine headaches are thought to be a function of autonomically mediated changes in the cephalic vascular system. In the classical migraine there is a period of intense intracranial and extracranial vasoconstriction prior to the onset of the headache (Skinhoj & Paulson, 1969), although with the common migraine headache this phase may not be evident. In both forms of migraine, however, the associated pain is the result of the subsequent vasodilation of the extracranial vessels. Initially there is a pulsating head pain resulting from increased amplitude of the blood volume pulse (BVP). It is believed that the increased BVP distends the pain receptors surrounding the blood vessel. Inflammation and edema produced in the extracranial arteries makes them thicken and become rigid, producing a steady rather than pulsating pain (Friar & Beatty, 1976). Wolff (1946) described a cluster of symptoms that usually accompany the classic migraine headache. Migraine headaches are usually associated with increased irritability and periods of nausea, and are often accompanied by photophobia, constipation, vomiting, diarrhea, and visual changes such as scotomata and hemianopia. Other common accompaniments of migraine include unilateral paresthesia and speech disorders (Wolff, 1946). Although there is some evidence that migraine headaches are associated with a defect in the neurological pathways that control vasoconstriction and dilation (Dalessio, 1972), there appears to be no physiological problem with the blood vessel itself that can account for the headache.

Raynaud's disease is a functional disorder of the peripheral vascular system in which the patient experiences painful episodes of vasoconstriction in the hands and sometimes the feet, resulting in a low skin temperature, subjective feelings of coldness, discoloration, and in severe cases, necrosis and gangrene. Exposure to cold temperatures as well as emotional factors appear to play a role in the precipitation of Raynaud symptoms (Mittelmann & Wolff, 1939; Spittell, 1972).

Elevated blood pressure, or hypertension, is a relatively common disorder that has come to represent a major health problem in the United States. It has been estimated that approximately 20% of the adult population in the United States suffers from hypertension (National Health Survey, 1964), using as the criteria 160 mm Hg or more systolic and 95 mm Hg or more diastolic (World Health Organization, 1959). Essential hypertension, in which the elevations in blood pressure cannot be directly attributed to an organic or physiological problem, comprises nearly 90% of all diagnosed cases of hypertension.

Essential hypertension is not only a common disorder, but is also considered to be a major contributor to cardiovascular disease, with individuals diagnosed as hypertensive being much more susceptible to congestive heart failure and coronary heart disease, and experiencing a higher incidence of strokes and occlusive peripheral arterial disease than similar individuals whose blood pressure lies within the normal limits (Dawber, Kannel, Revotskie, & Kagan, 1962; Kannel & Dawber, 1974).

Although the introduction of a variety of antihypertensive medications has greatly reduced the incidence of these complications and made it possible to maintain relatively good long-term control over high blood pressure (Wolff & Lindeman, 1966), the problems associated with requiring often symptomless hypertensive patients to continue taking medication that often produces unpleasant side effects remain (Brook & Appel, 1973; Langfeld, 1973). These considerations, along with the extremely high incidence of hypertension in this country, would seem to make the development of an effective, nonpharmacological treatment highly desirable.

A cardiac arrhythmia refers to any regular or episodic interruption of the normally rhythmic and synchronized contractions of the heart and represents potentially serious conditions that can often lead to death if left untreated. While there are a number of distinguishable arrhythmias, each involving a somewhat unique disruption of the patterning of heart rate activity, the two that have been most widely investigated in relation to biofeedback treatment are premature ventricular contractions (PVCs) and sinus tachycardia.

In the normal-functioning heart, contractions of the upper chambers, or atria, are stimulated by impulses from the sinoatrial node (S-A node), a group of specialized conducting cells located in the right atrium. The S-A node initiates each heartbeat and is often referred to as the pacemaker of the heart. As the atria contract, the impulses from the S-A node are transmitted to the lower chambers of the heart, or ventricles, by way of the atrioventricular node (A-V node) located at the junction of the right atrium and right ventricle. The impulse is delayed for a brief period of time at the A-V node, which allows time for the atria to empty their contents into the ventricles before the ventricles are stimulated to contract.

During PVCs, the ventricles are stimulated prematurely and contract prior to or during the atrial contractions rather than contracting after a brief delay. Since the atria have not yet fully emptied their contents, the ventricles are incompletely filled and overall cardiac output is reduced. PVCs are thought to be due to some localized area of the heart initiating the contractions rather than the A-V and S-A nodes.

TREATMENT OF MIGRAINE HEADACHES

Since the cause of the pain associated with migraine is recognized as being due to the intense dilation of the extracranial vasculature that results from increased sympathetic activity, biofeedback treatment has typically focused on training the individual to control his sympathetic activity by having him monitor his peripheral or cephalic blood volume. One result of the increased sympathetic reactivity that is characteristic of migraine is peripheral vasoconstriction, as well as cephalic vasodilation. Constriction of the peripheral blood vessels during stress is part of an adaptive biological pattern that has the effect of preparing the body for action by moving blood out of the periphery, into the deep muscles and up the head (Mittleman & Wolff, 1939). Because skin temperature is thought to be directly related to peripheral blood flow, a convenient, indirect measure of the degree of vasoconstriction, and therefore of sympathetic activity, is the surface skin temperature of the hands. Skin temperature can be readily measured using a thermistor. This device consists of a material whose electrical properties (resistance) change with fluctuations in skin temperature, and thus translates temperature to an electrical signal that can then be amplified and displayed. Typically, thermistors are attached to either the index finger of one hand (Turin & Johnson, 1976), or to the index finger and the midforehead (Keefe, 1975). The subject is then provided with visual and/or auditory feedback that reflects changes in finger temperature or changes in the finger-forehead differential temperature. In either case, the subject is instructed to try any nonphysical means to change his finger temperature in the desired direction.

A more direct measure of the degree of vasoconstriction or vasodilation is obtained with a photoplethysmograph, a device that measures either the amount of light transmitted by, or the amount and wavelength of light reflected by, a particular section of tissue. Since tissue is relatively transparent to infrared light, while blood is relatively opaque, the amount of light that passes through or is reflected by a particular section of tissue is directly proportional to the amount of blood underlying that tissue. The photoplethysmograph allows for the detection of blood volume and blood volume pulse, with the former representing the level of blood in a particular section of tissue (e.g., finger) and the latter referring to the blood flow through the tissue with each cardiac contraction.

In addition to using peripheral blood volume changes in the biofeedback treatment of migraine, cephalic blood volume change has also been employed. As migraine is characterized by intense extracranial vasodilation, individuals can be trained to decrease the pulse amplitude in these arteries (usually the temporal artery) through the use of a photoplethysmograph and the appropriate visual and/or auditory feedback. A reduction in the blood pulse amplitude results in decreased dilation of the targeted artery.

Autogenic training is a system of psychosomatic self-regulation that has as its goal the gradual acquisition of autonomic control. This control is not active, but rather is thought to develop out of a "passive concentration" on phrases or certain preselected words (Schultz & Luthe, 1969). Through this "passive concentration," the subject attempts to move toward certain states (e.g., relaxation), while at the same time remaining detached as to his actual progress (Fahrion, 1977). The specific somatic responses that are brought under voluntary control include heaviness in the limbs, warmth in the extremities, control of heart rate, sense of warmth in the abdomen, and cooling of the forehead (Sargent, Green, & Walters, 1973). Autogenic training is presumed to produce changes that are directly opposite to those evoked by stress (e.g., migraine) and are therefore thought to promote healthy autonomic functioning. Sargent, Green, and Walters (1973) employed 20 migraine, 6 tension headache, and 2 questionable migraine patients and provided them with autogenic-feedback training for hand warming. There were two groups of autogenic phrases that the subjects were instructed to repeat during training. The first group of phrases helped the subjects attain "passive concentration" and were aimed at achieving relaxation of the whole body. These included statements such as "I feel quiet," "I feel relaxed," and "my whole body feels quiet, heavy, comfortable, and relaxed." The second group of phrases focused on achieving warmth in the hands and included statements such as "my hands are relaxed," "my hands are warm," and "my whole body is relaxed and my hands are warm, relaxed, and warm." These autogenic phrases were used together with a "temperature trainer" that indicated changes in the differential temperature between the right index finger and the mid-forehead. A positive response on the trainer was obtained by increasing the temperature of the hands relative to the forehead, and although the absolute temperature of the two sites was not recorded, the authors noted that a positive response on the trainer was "always associated with a feeling of increased warmth in the hands without any apparent change of feeling in the forehead." The subjects were first seen on a weekly or biweekly basis until they were able to maintain a consistent feeling of warmth in their hands and could reliably obtain positive responses on the temperature trainer. Following this, they practiced on alternate days without the trainer, which was later withdrawn entirely. After the termination of treatment, an independent assessment of improvement was provided for each subject by an internist and two psychologists in terms of the severity of the headaches, the sum of the potency of the analgesics being used, and the total number of analgesics being used. Agreement among the three judges was obtained on 19 of the original 28 subjects, and these included 15 cases of migraine and 4 tension headaches. Of the 15 migraine patients, 12 were rated as improved and 3 as unimproved. Additionally, a "majority of the patients" had the ability to produce warmth in their hands one to eight weeks following treatment. In a more recent study, Fahrion (1977) employed autogenic phrases and auditory feedback for hand warming in a group of 11 migraine patients, and reported that a majority of the patients showed a significant reduction in headache activity.

The exact role played by autogenic phrases in the treatment of migraine is not altogether clear. Bertelson and Klein (1974) found that autogenic phrases had little effect on controlling hand temperature, while Wickramasekera (1973) reported the successful treatment of migraine through hand temperature biofeedback alone. Additional support for the use of hand temperature feedback alone comes from a study by Reading and Mohr (1976) in which they trained six migraine patients in the voluntary regulation of hand temperature without the use of autogenic phrases. The results indicated statistically and clinically significant improvement on several indices of headache activity for all of the patients. In addition, there was evidence of an improvement in the ability of the subjects to produce voluntary increases in hand temperature, and improvement in headache activity continued through the two-month follow-up. Turin and Johnson (1976) trained seven individuals suffering from migraine in the usual finger-warming procedure with the omission of autogenic phrases. Additionally, in order to control for placebo-expectancy effects, three of the subjects were trained in finger cooling prior to finger warming. While headache activity either remained at baseline levels or increased during the cooling phase, the activity decreased substantially with training in finger warming. Similarly, in a study by Johnson and Turin (1975), a migraine patient was trained to first lower and then raise her peripheral skin temperature. The patient's migraine activity was observed to increase during cooling, but decreased substantially during the warming period.

A somewhat contradictory finding with regard to placebo effects in the hand-warming treatment of migraine has been reported by Mullinex, Norton, Hack, and Fishman (1978). They employed two groups of migraine patients and provided the experimental group with auditory feedback that was contingent on skin temperature changes in their fingers. A control group received a similar signal that was independent of skin temperature changes and was controlled by the experimenter. Although the experimental group increased their skin temperature significantly more than the control group, both groups exhibited similar improvements in headache activity. The authors interpreted these results as indicating that the mechanism underlying the biofeedback treatment of migraine is a placebo effect that is independent of actual changes in peripheral skin temperature. Somewhat in support of this interpretation, Andreychuck and Skriver (1975) found that highly suggestible subjects (as determined by the Hypnotic Induction Profile) showed significantly greater reductions in migraine activity than low-suggestible subjects following either hand warming or EEG alpha biofeedback training, or training for self-hypnosis.

The results of these studies seem to suggest, therefore, that biofeedback training in hand warming, without autogenic training, is effective in reducing migraine headache activity. Numerous studies have found that subjects appear to employ a number of idiosyncratic tactics such as the use of imagery or self-verbalizations in order to aid increases in peripheral skin temperature, and thus do not have to be provided with autogenic phrases. Despite the apparent effectiveness of hand temperature biofeedback in the treatment of migraine, however, placebo and expectancy effects appear to play a rather large part in the success of these procedures. In addition, several studies (e.g., Blanchard, Theobald, Williamson, Silver, & Brown, 1978) have shown standard relaxation training to be equally as effective in reducing total headache activity and intensity as thermal biofeedback.

A number of studies have been reported that employed direct cephalic blood volume biofeedback in the treatment of migraine headaches. Feuerstein and Adams (1977) treated several migraine patients with cephalic vasomotor feedback and, although there was some evidence of learning to reduce the cephalic vasomotor response, the reduction in headache activity was not impressive and was not statistically significant within single subjects. Zamani (1975) trained a group of migraine patients to constrict the extracranial temporal artery with pulse amplitude feedback, and as a control, employed progressive deep-muscle relaxation with a second group. The results indicated that the feedback group exhibited significant reductions in terms of the duration and frequency of headaches and medication usage, while the relaxation group showed no significant changes on any of these variables. Friar & Beatty (1976) trained migraine patients to decrease the amplitude of the pulse in the temporal artery. Following eight training sessions, they were able to reduce their pulse amplitude to 80% of that exhibited prior to training, and this reduction was significantly greater than that for control subjects trained to reduce hand pulse amplitude. The patients were instructed to continue the response at home in order to abort headaches, and the results of a 30-day follow-up showed that the experimental subjects had significantly fewer migraine headaches than did the controls, although headache intensity and medication usage were not significantly reduced. Sturgis, Tollison, and Adams (1978) investigated the effects of blood volume pulse (BVP) and frontalis EMG feedback on the control of vasoconstriction in the temporal artery and frontalis muscle activity in two subjects with combined migraine-muscle contraction headaches. The results indicated that both subjects learned to control BVP during BVP feedback and EMG during EMG feedback. Furthermore, both of the subjects experienced decreases in migraine frequency during the BVP feedback and decreases in muscle contraction headaches during EMG feedback.

It thus appears that both peripheral skin temperature and cephalic vasomotor feedback are viable procedures for the treatment of migraine headaches. While there is a considerable amount of evidence supporting the effectiveness of skin temperature feedback, the data on cephalic vasomotor feedback appears to be somewhat more sparse and inconsistent, although it tends to support the use of this procedure as well. At this point, no one has adequately demonstrated why dilating the blood vessels in the hands has any effect on the vasomotor responses of the cranial blood vessels. Although it is assumed to be through some form of autonomic nervous system mediation, the actual mechanism is as yet unclear (Blanchard & Epstein, 1978). Several studies (e.g., Sargent, Walters, & Green, 1973) have proposed a reduction in sympathetic nervous system activity as being responsible for the alleviation of migraine symptoms, although none of these have included adequate measures of sympathetic activity. Additionally, the shunting of blood away from the cranial vessels and the reduction of the vasodilation thought to be responsible for the pain, does not appear to be supported by the physiological data. A reduction in forehead skin temperature, which should be correlated with a decreased extracranial blood flow, and concomitant hand temperature increases also has not been adequately demonstrated (Mullinex, et al., 1978). It has been suggested (Blanchard & Epstein, 1978) that the "final common pathway of action" in the biofeedback treatment of migraine is a generalized relaxation response that includes peripheral vasodilation and skin temperature increases.

TREATMENT OF RAYNAUD'S DISEASE

Since Raynaud's disease is associated with episodes of vasoconstriction in the extremities, biofeedback treatment typically consists of those same procedures aimed at increasing peripheral blood flow in the treatment of migraine. Thus thermistors may be applied to the affected area (i.e., the hands and/or the feet), and the individual can be trained to increase the temperature in his extremities by displaying the appropriate visual or auditory analogue feedback. A photoplethysmograph may also be employed in order to increase either the blood volume or the blood volume pulse in the hands or the feet.

In an early application of temperature biofeedback to the treatment of Raynaud's disease, Surwit (1973) treated a female patient who had already received two sympathectomies in unsuccessful attempts to relieve the disorder. After six months of treatment and over 50 feedback sessions, this patient exhibited an increase in skin temperature from her pretreatment level of 23°C to 26.6°C, and showed other signs of marked clinical improvement. Surwit reported, however, that the patient lost her ability to control her hand temperature shortly after the treatment ended. Jacobson, Hackett, Surman, and Silverberg (1973) reported the successful treatment of a male with a three-year history of Raynaud's disease who had failed to respond to an initial treatment of hypnosis and suggestions of warmth. During five sessions of thermal feedback training, he rapidly learned to increase his fingertip temperature by as much as 4°C, and this increase in temperature was accompanied by an improvement in symptomatology that was maintained through a seven-month follow-up. In another single case, Blanchard & Haynes (1975) employed differential hand-forehead temperature biofeedback in the successful treatment of a patient with a chronic, moderately severe case of Raynaud's disease. Not only was the patient able to consistently increase the temperature of her hands during feedback, but the latency with which the maximum increase occurred decreased throughout training. Overall, there was an average increase of 3.4°F in hand temperature during the feedback phase of treatment from pretraining to posttraining. At the end of the seven-month follow-up, the patient reported that both of her hands become warm when she tried to warm them mentally and that she was even getting some transfer to her feet. There was an increase in the absolute temperature of her hands from 79°F prior to treatment to 88.3°F at the follow-up. In another clinical case study (Peper & Grossman, 1974), using differential hand-forehead temperature feedback training, further support is found for the use of the treatment methodology with patients suffering from Raynaud's disease.

May & Weber (1976) administered temperature feedback training for finger skin temperature to four women with primary Raynaud's disease, four women with secondary Raynaud's disease, and three control subjects. The training consisted of 16 fifty-minute sessions over an eight-week period and resulted in symptomatic improvement in each of the Raynaud's patients. The patients recorded significantly fewer vasospastic attacks during the last two weeks of training than during the first two weeks, as well as a significant increase in the number of days completely free from symptoms. In addition, the degree of improvement was found to be significantly correlated with the patient's success at temperature raising. In a variation on the standard hand temperature feedback procedure, Sedlacek (1976a) combined skin temperature and EMG feedback in the treatment of three chronic Raynaud's patients. Each of these patients was also given home exercises that included progressive relaxation and autogenic phrases. Following treatment, the symptoms of all the patients were improved and they were able to voluntarily increase their hand temperature by 5°F within 5 minutes, as well as maintain a hand temperature of 90°F for at least 15 minutes. Similarly, Stephenson (1976) combined finger temperature feedback, frontalis EMG feedback, autogenic training, and deep muscle relaxation in the successful treatment of two Raynaud's patients.

While a majority of the studies pertaining to Raynaud's disease have employed hand temperature biofeedback as the method of treatment, several studies have been reported in which blood volume feedback was used. Schwartz (1972) employed blood volume biofeedback in the treatment of two cases of Raynaud's, one of which was successful and the other unsuccessful. In the successful case, a man with Raynaud's disease in his feet was given 10 feedback sessions to increase the blood volume in his big toe. Following treatment, he remained symptom-free for a year-and-a-half at which time he returned for additional booster sessions. This patient also reported that he had developed certain images that enabled him to warm his feet away from treatment. The other case was a woman with Raynaud's disease of the hands, who dropped out of treatment before she had completed 10 sessions. At the time of termination, she showed no evidence of controlling blood volume nor any reduction in Raynaud symptoms. In evaluating several biofeedback procedures for the treatment of Raynaud's disease in a single subject, Kallman, Roberts, & Adams (1976) found that, while an avoidance procedure (i.e., keeping a feedback tone turned off) was effective in stabilizing blood volume in the finger, it was not effective in increasing blood pulse amplitude. Another procedure, which provided pulse by pulse feedback for both stable blood volume and relative increases in blood pulse volume, was effective and enabled the subject to stabilize his blood volume while at the same time increasing blood pulse amplitude. Although there was no change in the self-reported frequency of symptoms following training with this procedure, the subject did report a decreased latency to recover from symptom attacks.

As can be seen from this relatively brief review, most of the published reports on the biofeedback treatment of Raynaud's disease consist of single case studies and are characterized by a general lack of procedural sophistication and control. Few of the studies report the specific procedures employed in sufficient detail to make them clinically useful or to allow comparisons of the procedures across studies in terms of outcome. Additionally, the combining of temperature feedback with other procedures (e.g., EMG feedback) in several studies makes it somewhat difficult to evaluate the relative efficacy of these techniques in treating Raynaud's disease. While there does seem to be a paucity of well-controlled studies investigating the biofeedback treatment of Raynaud's disease, the available research appears to point suggestively to at least skin temperature feedback as an efficacious procedure in the treatment of this disorder. The status of blood volume biofeedback is even more tentative, although several studies would seem to support its use as well. In both cases, however, more conclusive evidence depends upon further research that employs a larger number of subjects, institutes the proper control procedures, and publishes the specific procedures and methods in enough detail to permit an objective evaluation of the effectiveness of biofeedback in the treatment of Raynaud's disease.

TREATMENT OF ESSENTIAL HYPERTENSION

Early studies in the direct treatment of essential hypertension with biofeedback were promising. A group at the Harvard Medical School used an automated constant cuff-pressure transducer to provide patients with continuous feedback of either systolic or diastolic blood pressure (Benson, Shapiro, Tursky, & Schwartz, 1971). Previous work with normotensives had suggested that subjects could learn to both raise and lower their blood pressure with feedback (Shapiro, Tursky, Gershon, & Stern, 1969; Shapiro, Tursky, & Schwartz, 1970) using the constant cuff pressure system. In addition, Blanchard, Young, Haynes, and Kallman (1974) found similar results by giving blood pressure feedback at 1-minute intervals.

One of the first applications of blood pressure biofeedback to the treatment of hypertension was reported by Benson, Shapiro, Tursky, and Schwartz (1971) using their automated constant cuff-pressure procedure. Seven hypertensive patients, all on stabilized doses of antihypertensive medication, received daily feedback training sessions for lowering systolic blood pressure until no further reduction occurred over five consecutive sessions. Reductions in systolic pressure for all seven patients averaged 16.5 mm Hg following training, with five patients showing significant reductions of 16 mm Hg or more. However, an informal follow-up (Benson, 1975), indicated that the pressures of all patients gradually returned to their previous levels. Miller (1972) reported the successful treatment of a hypertensive woman who was able to reduce her diastolic pressure by as much as 21 mm Hg following 37 biofeedback training sessions. During training, she received feedback for both raising and lowering blood pressure, and she was able to produce increases of up to 20 mm Hg and decreases of up to 10 mm Hg. Following treatment, her diastolic pressure stabilized from its baseline average of 97 mm Hg to about 76 mm Hg. Additionally, she was withdrawn from antihypertensive medication and discharged from the hospital during training, both of which would have presumably resulted in an increase in blood pressure. Despite this apparent success, however, Miller noted that factors other than the biofeedback may have contributed to the reductions in blood pressure, and later (Miller, 1975) reported that the patient had lost her ability to control her blood pressure and had to be reinstated on medication. Some degree of control was later recovered through additional feedback sessions. Despite the early promise, it is evident from a review of the literature that patients typically do not maintain therapeutic gains beyond a few weeks if only biofeedback is used for treatment.

The only study of blood pressure feedback reported thus far with adequate follow-up data is that of Kristt & Engel (1975), in which data was systematically collected over a two- to three-month period following treatment. Five patients, all with at least a 10-year history of hypertension and all on antihypertension medication, monitored their own blood pressure at home four times daily for seven weeks prior to the start of treatment and regularly mailed these results to the investigators. Following this baseline period, patients were hospitalized for three weeks for treatment during which they received blood pressure biofeedback training. During the first week, patients were taught to raise their blood pressure, while training in blood pressure reductions was carried out in the second week. The third week consisted of training patients to alternately raise and lower their blood pressure. Following treatment, patients continued to practice lowering their blood pressure at home, as well as regularly monitoring their blood pressure levels and sending in the results. Among the four patients for whom baseline data were available, reductions in systolic pressure ranged from 9 to 36 mm Hg, with an average decrease of 18 mm Hg. Two of these patients also showed significant reductions of 7 mm Hg and 20 mm Hg in diastolic pressure. All five patients exhibited an ability to lower their blood pressure at home, and three were able to lower their antihypertension medication. At the follow-up, three of the four patients who obtained sizable reductions in blood pressure during training were able to maintain these gains.

The study of Kristt & Engel (1975) represents a departure from the majority of investigations pertaining to blood pressure biofeedback, not only in terms of their excellent follow-up data, but also in terms of the training procedure itself. The combination of intensive biofeedback training, including training in both blood pressure raising and lowering, and instruction in certain self-management skills such as regular home practice and blood pressure monitoring would seem to be responsible for the good follow-up results, and they certainly seem to have implications for the clinical application of blood pressure biofeedback. It has been noted elsewhere (Epstein & Blanchard, 1979) that self-control training followed by a program of self-management is probably the most effective approach for controlling a tonic physiological response.

A rather large body of recent research on hypertension (Blanchard, Haynes, Kallman, & Harkey, 1976; Blanchard, Miller, Abel, Haynes, & Wicker, 1977; Hager & Surwit, 1978; Shoemaker & Tasto, 1975; Surwit, 1976; Surwit, Shapiro, & Good, 1978; Walsh, Dale, Brethauer, Eagan, Frick, Ostrowski, Walberg, & Weiss, 1976) seems to indicate that various relaxation procedures may be equal or superior to blood pressure biofeedback in producing reductions in systolic and diastolic blood pressure levels. This research has led at least one pair of investigators (Blanchard & Epstein, 1978) to concede that blood pressure biofeedback may be "only an elaborate means of teaching subjects to relax" (p. 60), and it has prompted a move away from the use of direct feedback of blood pressure as the sole treatment for hypertension to investigations of various relaxation techniques alone or in combination with feedback. All of these investigations seem to have centered around efforts to obtain reductions in elevated levels of blood pressure either by reducing sympathetic nervous system activity or by reducing the overall level of muscle tension (Blanchard, 1979).

Studies by Patel (Patel, 1973; Patel, 1975a; Patel, 1975b; Patel & North, 1975) are perhaps the most outstanding in the whole area of clinical biofeedback and provide strong support for the combined effectiveness of biofeedback, passive relaxation, and meditation in the treatment of hypertension. In the first of these studies, Patel (1973) employed each of these techniques in the treatment of 20 hypertensive patients. All patients had at least a one-year history of high blood pressure and 19 were receiving antihypertensive medication at the start of treatment. Average blood pressure levels at the time of diagnosis were 201.5 mm Hg systolic and 121.8 mm Hg diastolic, while the same readings prior to treatment measured 160 mm Hg and 102 mm Hg, respectively, reflecting the influence of the antihypertensive medications. Patients were seen individually in three half-hour sessions per week over a period of three months, and blood pressure levels were checked both prior to and following each session.

Continuous GSR biofeedback in the form of an auditory analogue signal was provided throughout each session. Each patient was first instructed to attend closely to his breathing and to make it as smooth and regular as possible. Once this was achieved, the patient attempted to attain a state of complete physical relaxation by mentally going over the various parts of the body and making them as limp and relaxed as possible. This process was facilitated by the use of various phrases similar to those employed in autogenic training (Schultz & Luthe, 1969). Additionally, patients were given copies of these phrases and instructed to practice relaxation at home. Following physical relaxation, mental relaxation was introduced in the form of yoga exercises and meditation. At the end of each treatment session, patients were given information on their pre- and postsession blood pressure levels.

Results showed that 16 of the 20 patients exhibited reductions in blood pressure, averaging 26 mm Hg systolic and 16 mm Hg diastolic. Antihypertensive medication was stopped completely in five of these patients, while medication was reduced by 33 to 60% in seven others. Among the four patients who did not show reductions in blood pressure, at least one derived some indirect benefits from the treatment. This patient was able to stop her antidepressant drug therapy completely, and the frequency and severity of her migraine had been reduced considerably.

Following these rather impressive results, Patel (1975a) undertook a controlled-group outcome study in which the blood pressure reductions of patients in the previous group were compared with 20 age- and sex-matched hypertensive controls so as to eliminate the effects of increased medical attention and repeated blood pressure measurements. Moreover, patients in the Patel (1973) group were followed up monthly for a period of 12 months, while the control group was followed up similarly for 9 months after the initial 3 months of the control study. Control group patients were treated in a manner identical to the earlier patients (e.g., total number of attendances, time spent in each session, and blood pressure measurements), but they did not receive any of the specific treatment techniques, being required instead to rest comfortably on a couch throughout each session. Though no additional training sessions were given during the follow-up period, patients who had received treatment were encouraged to continue to practice the relaxation and meditation techniques at home.

In contrast to the marked reductions displayed by the treatment groups mentioned earlier, patients in the control group showed nonsignificant reductions in blood pressure levels, averaging 0.5 mm Hg systolic and 2.1 mm Hg diastolic, and their drug requirement remained undiminished. At the follow-up, patients who had received treatment maintained their post-training reductions and antihypertensive medication had to be increased for only one patient. The control group, on the other hand, exhibited only nonsignificant changes in blood pressure levels during the follow-up period and increased their medication requirement by 5.5% in the first three months following the last session.

In a third study, Patel and North (1975) randomly assigned 34 hypertensive patients to either a treatment or a control group. The training period was reduced from the previous studies to two sessions per week for six weeks and the treatment procedure was also modified somewhat.

Patients in the treatment group received verbal instruction in the relaxation technique employed previously during the first 10 to 12 minutes of each session and then tried to achieve and maintain a relaxed state for the duration of the session. This was again followed by the passive mental concentration and meditation procedures. Though GSR biofeedback was provided as before during the first six sessions, EMG feedback from an unspecified site was employed in later sessions. Patients were also verbally reinforced for correct responding and were provided with information about their blood pressure levels at the end of each session. Throughout treatment, patients were instructed to practice the relaxation techniques at home at least twice a day and were encouraged to gradually incorporate more "relaxed attitudes" into their daily lives.

Patients in the control group attended the same number of sessions for the same length of time, but they did not receive any specific instructions or feedback and spent each session relaxing in a reclined position.

At the end of the six-week period, patients from both groups were followed up every two weeks for three months. Results showed that the treated patients exhibited significantly greater declines in blood pressure following training, averaging 26.1 mm Hg systolic and 15.2 diastolic, than did control patients, who showed corresponding reductions of 8.9 mm Hg and 4.2 mm Hg. Though the latter figures represent significant reductions in both systolic and diastolic pressures for the control group, this was not true for all patients. Eight patients in the control condition showed a rise in either systolic or diastolic pressure, while none of the treated patients showed such an increase.

At the end of the three-month follow-up period, blood pressure levels had risen slightly among patients in the treatment group, from 141.4 to 148.8 systolic and from 84.4 to 87.9 diastolic. Control patients, however, exhibited substantial increases, rising from 160.0 to 176.6 systolic and from 96.4 to 104.3 diastolic.

A second phase of this study was begun two months after the end of the follow-up. During this phase, patients in the control group received treatment, while patients who had been treated previously served as the controls and were seen only at the beginning and end of the phase to provide blood pressure readings for comparison purposes. The same treatment procedures and the same number of sessions were employed with the control patients as had been used before. The results for the newly treated group were similar to those obtained previously, with the patients showing significant reductions in both systolic (28.1 mm Hg) and diastolic (15.0 mm Hg) blood pressure. As in the first part of the study, no member of the treatment group showed a rise in blood pressure levels, while patients in the previously treated group maintained their lowered levels of blood pressure throughout the second phase.

Patel's work provides rather impressive evidence for the effectiveness of a treatment regimen combining biofeedback, relaxation, and meditation, and her research is supported further by a number of other similar studies. Love, Montgomery, and Mueller (1974), and Mueller and Love (1974) found moderate reductions in blood pressure levels among hypertensive patients following treatment with EMG biofeedback and relaxation training. Moreover, Love, et al. (1974) found further blood pressure reductions in their treated patients at an eight-month follow-up. Sedlacek and Cohen (1978) reported significant reductions in both systolic and diastolic blood pressure among 20 hypertensive patients following training in EMG and thermal biofeedback and relaxation. Additional reports have indicated relatively good results using a variety of other biofeedback and relaxation procedures, including temperature regulation (Datey, 1976), EMG and thermal biofeedback (Sedlacek, 1976b), and hypnosis (Datey, 1978).

Considered together, these studies would seem to show that relaxation training utilizing biofeedback procedures is an effective form of treatment for lowering elevated levels of blood pressure. It is uncertain at this point, however, what the biofeedback component of these programs contributes to the effectiveness of the treatment. Patel (1978) has commented that biofeedback is only a small part of her treatment package and that the relaxation procedures employed probably play the more important role. In support of this contention, Datey (1977) obtained moderate reductions in blood pressure among hypertensive patients through the use of a yoga exercise alone. Similarly, Benson and his colleagues (Benson, 1975; Benson, Rosner & Marzetta, 1973; Benson, Rosner, Marzetta, & Klemchuk, 1974a, 1974b) have shown that relaxation techniques, employing passive relaxation training and meditation, can alone lead to significant reductions in the high blood pressure levels of hypertensive patients.

The evidence at this point does not seem to support the use of direct blood pressure biofeedback as an effective alternative treatment for hypertension. The evidence does show, however, that relaxation training, either alone or in combination with biofeedback training, is effective in producing significant reductions in blood pressure levels and affords promise as a viable adjunct or alternative to the standard pharmacological treatment of hypertension. A rather consistent finding throughout this research seems to be that regular home practice is an integral part of the treatment process, and that discontinuation of practice invariably results in a gradual return to the previously high levels of blood pressure. This observation further implicates the necessity of instituting a program of self-management following training in order to maintain the benefits accrued during treatment. While this suggests a compliance problem similar to that encountered with antihypertensive medication, the relatively positive side effects experienced with relaxation training might better serve to facilitate such a program of self-maintenance (Blanchard, 1979).

HEART RATE

Like the area of blood pressure biofeedback, the initial work with heart rate demonstrates that this response can be increased or decreased and reduced in variability in normal individuals by providing them with the appropriate biofeedback (Brener & Hothersall, 1966; Brener & Hothersall, 1967; Brener, Kleinman, & Goesling, 1969; Hnatiow & Lang, 1965; Engel & Hansen, 1966; Engel & Chism, 1967; Levene, Engel, & Pearson, 1968; Lang, Sroufe, & Hastings, 1967; Sroufe, 1969). Though a rather sizable amount of research has been done investigating the parameters of biofeedback control of heart rate among normals, much less work has been presented that applies these principles to specific clinical problems and disorders. For the most part, these applications have employed heart rate biofeedback as a treatment methodology for various cardiac arrhythmias.

The first and perhaps the best reports of the clinical application of heart rate biofeedback are those of Engel and his colleagues. Following several initial studies (Engel & Melmon, 1968; Weiss & Engel, 1970), Weiss & Engel (1971) reported a study in which eight patients experiencing PVCs received training in heart rate biofeedback. The number of training sessions varied considerably, from 22 to 53 depending upon the individual's progression through the program, but each phase of the program typically lasted for about 10 sessions. Sessions were held one to three times daily, with approximately 34 minutes of each session being devoted to biofeedback training. All patients were hospitalized during training, and each patient had his ECG monitored while in bed throughout the training period.

Training consisted of providing feedback for several types of cardiac control. Patients were first taught to increase their heart rate, followed by training in heart rate lowering, and then training in alternately raising and lowering heart rate for 1 to 3 minute intervals. During the next phase, the patient was taught to reduce heart rate variability by holding it within a certain specified range. Biofeedback consisted of a binary visual signal that also provided patients with direct feedback of PVCs. The last phase of treatment consisted of self-control training during which the patient attempted to keep his heart rate within the specified range while feedback was gradually faded out.

Only three of the original eight patients completed the entire training program, while two others had progressed at least as far as the first part of feedback fading procedure. Two patients had received feedback for increasing and decreasing heart rate and range training, and the final patient had received training in heart rate lowering and in reducing heart rate variability.

Results showed that five of the eight patients exhibited marked reductions in PVC rate, going from 10–20 PVCs/min. to less than 1 PVC/min. following training. An independent check confirmed these reductions in four of the five patients. The remaining three patients showed virtually no reductions in PVC rate. Follow-up data gathered from 3 to 21 months after treatment indicated that the patients had maintained their improvement and continued to display lowered rates of PVCs.

In a subsequent study, Engel and Bleecker (1974) replicated these findings in a single patient with a pretreatment PVC rate of approximately 15 PVCs/minute. Training sessions were held two to three times per day for 16 days and were similar to those employed in the Weiss and Engel (1971) study. The patient received training in heart rate lowering, heart rate increasing, alternately lowering and increasing heart rate, and range training. During the lowering phase, PVC rate was reduced to about 5 PVCs/minute and dropped to nearly zero during alternation training. Though the time span was not specified, the patient showed continued improvement at follow-up.

Pickering and Gorham (1975) employed a biofeedback treatment procedure with a patient whose PVC rate appeared to be directly related to her cardiac rate. As her heart rate increased, particularly above 78 bpm, her rate of PVCs also increased. Sixteen training sessions were held over a period of six weeks and consisted primarily of teaching the patient to alternately raise and lower her heart rate. During training, the patient learned to increase her heart rate by as much as 25 bpm, but did not show much evidence of learning to lower her heart rate level.

Additionally, the heart rate level at which the PVCs began increased to nearly 106 bpm. As a result, the patient was able to engage in a great many nonstrenuous activities and when the PVCs began, she was able to reduce her heart rate level to a point where they were reduced considerably.

Blanchard and Epstein (1978) reported a less successful case of heart rate biofeedback in the treatment of a woman with a baseline PVC rate of approximately 10 PVCs/minute. Throughout a training program similar to that employed by Weiss and Engel (1971), the patient was unable to demonstrate any consistent ability to reduce her PVC rate. Though moderate reductions were obtained during alternation training, they did not hold up during the later sessions.

The second cardiac arrhythmia that has been treated through biofeedback procedures is sinus tachycardia. In this case, the heart beats with its normal rhythmic contractions, or sinus rhythm, but the rate at which it beats is accelerated to an abnormally high level.

Engel and Bleecker (1974) employed binary visual feedback of heart rate along with instructions to lower it in the treatment of a patient with a four-year history of chronic sinus tachycardia. Though the patient's history indicated her resting heart rate to be 106 bpm, first session recordings showed it to be only 86 bpm. Twelve daily biofeedback sessions were followed by nine fading sessions in which the feedback was gradually withdrawn in a manner similar to that employed by Weiss and Engel (1971). Following training, heart rate was reduced by approximately 18 bpm, to 68 bpm in the laboratory and 75 bpm as measured by her own physician.

Scott, Blanchard, Edmundson, and Young (1973) have reported on two single subject experiments in which patients with sinus tachycardia received heart rate biofeedback training. In the first case, a 46-year-old male with a 20-year history of tachycardia was able to reduce his heart rate level to within the normal range following training with binary heart rate biofeedback. The change in heart rate was also accompanied by other signs of clinical improvement. The man was able to obtain employment, reduce his use of minor transquilizers, and report feeling less anxious. An 18-month follow-up showed that the patient was still employed. In the second case, biofeedback training resulted in a reduction of 18 bpm, from a baseline level of 96 bpm to 78 bpm after 19 feedback sessions. Though this patient was unable to return to work, he did report feeling less anxious and was able to begin doing more chores at home.

As is evidenced by the brevity of this review, there has been relatively little work reported pertaining to the clinical applications of heart rate biofeedback, and those studies which are available are generally at a less sophisticated level than those in the areas of migraine and hypertension. As Blanchard (1979) has pointed out, this state of affairs is probably attributable to the fact that there are far fewer patients available with diagnosed arrhythmias than with migraine or hypertension, and since arrhythmias tend to be viewed as somewhat more serious, they are more likely to be treated by the standard pharmacological interventions.

The available research does, however, suggest that biofeedback be considered as a possible treatment procedure for cardiac arrhythmias, particularly PVCs and sinus tachycardia. More definitive conclusions are impossible at this point and must await further controlled clinical research.

We have discussed a number of treatment strategies for a wide variety of cardio-vascular problems from hypertension to migraine headaches. It is clear from the published research that there is no single "best" treatment for any of the problems we have explored. In the following section there are two case reports of treatment of migraine headaches. In each case a different treatment strategy was found to be effective. The cases are presented to illustrate important issues in case management rather than a how-to "cookbook" of treatment. Dealing with a population that suffers from serious physical symptoms is challenging and should be done with caution. Close communication between the behavioral scientist and physician is critical if safe and successful psychological interventions are to be applied to persons with serious cardiovascular problems.

CLINICAL CASE REPORTS

CASE 1

Presenting problem: The client was a 24-year-old single female. She referred herself to our clinic for biofeedback treatment of migraine headaches after discussing the possibility of finding an alternative to medication with her family doctor. She reported that her headaches occurred almost daily for the past two years. The client reported a long history of somatic complaints including colitis and a "nervous stomach" from age 10 through 16. During college she had no physical complaints until her senior year when the headaches began. She reported that the headaches never occurred during times of stress but usually began after a stressful event such as an exam or job interview. There is no history of headaches in the client's family. The headaches were described as unilateral, usually starting over the right eye and lasting from 2 to 24 hours. There was no report of nausea or visual problems except on rare occasion (twice in the past six months). Evaluations by an allergist, neurologist, and dentist (to rule out Temperomandibular Joint Syndrome) had resulted in a diagnosis of common type migraine headaches.

At the time of referral the client was controlling the headache pain with Fiorinal® (P.R.N.) and Valium® (H.S.). Although the medication reduced the pain to a "tolerable" level it did not eliminate the headaches. Trial use of vasoconstricting drugs had been unsuccessful because of severe allergic reactions of the client.

Treatment: Initial assessment of the client involved several stages including a psychophysiological profile of the client. Following the first interview the client was asked to monitor her daily headache activity on an hourly basis. A simple self-monitoring form was used that allows the client to rate the intensity of her headaches. The client is instructed in the use of the forms and asked to describe a situation in which she had no headache pain; this is labeled zero on the scale. She is then asked to remember the most intense headache she has ever had and to label this a 10 on the scale. Self-monitoring serves to help the client and therapist identify relevant environmental stressors related to the headaches and provides a relatively precise measure of the frequency, intensity, and duration of the symptom. In addition to rating headache intensity the client was asked to indicate an F or V in any hour when she took medication for pain.

A physiological assessment (Kallman & Feuerstein, 1977) was completed with measures of finger temperature, temporal artery blood pulse volume, and frontalis muscle tension. The evaluation identified several clear, eliciting stressors including interpersonal relations with her boyfriend and incidents requiring assertive responses at work. These situations, presented in imagination, produced increased frontalis tension from a resting level of 3–4 uv to 10–12 uv. In addition there was a 0.5–1.0°F drop in finger temperature.

A contract was written with the client specifying types of treatment that would be tried, and time limits were set for intermediate and long-range goals. The first plan called for finger temperature feedback to be used for four sessions. A Cyborg P442 thermal feedback device was used with proportional auditory feedback. After four sessions there was no evidence of control by the client of finger temperature. Additional use of autogenic phrases also failed to produce changes in skin temperature or headache intensity or frequency (Table 1).

The second treatment phase involved teaching the client deep-muscle relaxation (Jacobson, 1938). The client was taught to relax in three, 30-minute sessions and was given a tape recorded set of relaxation instructions to use at home. Following the second relaxation session the client's self-reported frequency and intensity of headaches was drastically reduced (Table 1).

At this point the client decided that she did not wish to deal with the interpersonal problems that were related to the headaches. However, a follow-up of the client suggests continued relief from headache pain and a complete cessation of medication use for six months following termination.

CASE 2

Presenting problem: This client was a 32-year-old married female advertising agent. Her headaches were of the classic type. She reported unilateral pain, nausea, and blurred vision. The headaches occurred approximately three to four times per month and usually lasted for 5 to 12 hours. The headaches had first occurred during puberty (age 13). Current medication was Fiorinal® and Cafergot®. These medicines successfully reduced the headache pain enough to allow the client to work, but she was distressed about having to take medication and complained of coldness and discoloration in her hands and feet from the vasoconstricting drugs.

Treatment: A physiological assessment of this client revealed severe vasoconstriction in the hands (surface skin temperature always less than 76°F) but neither

Table 1. **Weekly Monitoring of Headache, and Use of Medication Across Treatment Phases and Follow-Up for Relaxation of Migraine Headaches**

Week	1	2	3	4	5	6	7	8	9	10	11	12 . . . 6 months
% of days with no headache	0	20.0	36.4	18.2	9.1	58.3	16.7	62.5	62.5	66.7	60.5	58.2	59.7
Frequency of use of Fiorinal	18	7	9	16	30	23	12	3	0	0	0	0	0

	Baseline	Biofeedback	Deep-muscle relaxation	Follow-up

Table 2. **Weekly Monitoring of Headache Frequency, and Change in Finger Temperature Within Sessions for Biofeedback Treatment of Migraine Headaches**

Week	1	2	3	4	5	6	7	8	9	10	11	12 . . . 16
Frequency of headaches	1	1	2	1	1	2	5	1	0	0	0	0 . . . 0
Temperature change in session		Baseline		+6.5	+3.0	+4.2	No Session	+1.3	+3.4	+2.8	Terminated therapy continued self-monitoring headaches	

frontalis muscle tension nor temporal artery blood pulse volume appeared to be reactive to stressful or relaxing situations presented in imagination. The client was also nonreactive to images or autogenic phrases designed to alter skin temperature. As in the previous case the client was asked to self-monitor her headaches.

A contract for four sessions of thermal biofeedback with a goal of a 2 degree increase in temperature was established with the client. Table 2 shows that during the first session the client was able to increase her finger temperature by 4 degrees after a 20-minute adaptation period. Following this session the client was questioned about any cognitive strategies she used to raise her temperature. She reported that images of the beach and the sun had been moderately successful but when she began to use procedures learned in yoga classes the temperature rose dramatically. By the fourth session the client was able to increase her finger temperature significantly (2.5°F) within 5 minutes. She was then instructed to raise her temperature without feedback. She was able to increase her finger temperature an additional 4°F within 15 minutes. The client reported she was using a procedure learned in yoga that involved "seeing" a white spot in the center of the visual field and concentrating on the spot. She reported that she had been unable to ever "see" this white spot prior to the feedback sessions.

Table 2 shows the course of the headaches following treatment. The initial increase in headaches may have been due to an illness in the family that had forced the client to spend several weeks out of town caring for her sick mother. Following the third session the client reported that she was able to abort any headache in its early stages. The client voluntarily terminated therapy following the fifth session. A four-month follow-up shows the client remains headache-free and is no longer using medication. When mild symptoms occur she reports relaxing and focusing on the "white spot" to eliminate the headache.

Discussion

These anecdotal case reports are presented as illustrations of two approaches to the treatment of migraine headaches. Similar procedures have been used successfully with Raynaud's disease and are reviewed in the earlier section of this paper.

There are several relevant issues to evaluating these two cases. In one case the problem was not a clear classical migraine and was a relatively chronic problem (two years), while in the other the symptoms were classical and the problem was more acute. Although some authors such as Blanchard and Epstein (1978) suggest that deep-muscle relaxation and thermal biofeedback work equally well with migraine headache patients, others such as Sturgis, Tollison, and Adams (1978) note that self-report of mixed tension-migraine headaches responds differentially to deep-muscle relaxation and blood pulse volume feedback. The problem of classification of headache types is immense and until it is solved little can be said about whether relaxation or biofeedback works best with any particular patient. It is important therefore that the therapist be willing to spell out alternative treatment strategies with the client and set intermediate goals. Ongoing evaluation of self-reported headache and physiological responses allows the therapist and client to logically select the most efficacious treatment modality for the given client. If it is argued that treatment of headaches is no more than teaching a generalized relaxation response (Blanchard & Epstein, 1978), then it might be assumed that different clients learn this response via different modalities of treatment. The "myth of homogeneity of clients" (Kiesler, 1966) prevents us from identifying client characteristics that may be very relevant to the process of designing an effective treatment for vascular disorders. Certainly, in the cases reported here it can be argued that both women learned to relax or reduce autonomic nervous system activity. However, each learned it in a different way and neither woman was particularly responsive to other treatment modalities.

As a final note it should be pointed out that the cases reported here are greatly abbreviated. Deep-muscle relaxation and temperature control via biofeedback are simple skills that can be readily mastered by most people. Teaching the skill however is not usually sufficient for elimination of the presenting complaint even though symptom severity may be reduced. The functional nature of any physical symptom must be evaluated. Issues of "secondary gain" either directly with attention from others, prescribed medication, and disability income, or indirectly through avoidance of aversive stimuli must be addressed. In the chronic cases the functional nature of the problem becomes more evident and the likelihood of success without intervention in the client's family system may be poor (Kallman, Hersen, & O'Toole, 1975). Clients should be made aware from the start that an understanding of their life situation and environmental events is important. Frequently clients with physical symptoms are resistant to dealing with "psychological things," since they do not want to see themselves as "mental patients." A straightforward discussion of the notion of functionality of symptoms in the beginning stages of therapy will allow the therapist to treat the vascular problem within the context of any other behavior problem.

REFERENCES

Andreychuck, T., & Skriver, C. Hypnosis and biofeedback in the treatment of migraine headache. *International Journal of Clinical and Experimental Hypnosis*, 1975, **23**, 172–183.

Benson, H. *The relaxation response*. New York: William Morrow, 1975.

Benson, H., Rosner, B. A., & Marzetta, B. R. Decreased systolic blood pressure in hypertensive subjects who practiced meditation. *Journal of Clinical Investigation,* 1973, **52**, 8.

Benson, H., Rosner, B. A., Marzetta, B. R., & Klemchuk, H. M. Decreased blood pressure in borderline hypertensives who practiced meditation. *Journal of Chronic Diseases,* 1974, **27**, 163–169. (a)

Benson, H., Rosner, B. A., Marzetta, B. R., & Klemchuk, H. M. Decreases blood pressure in pharmacologically treated hypertensive patients who regularly elicited the relaxation response. *Lancet,* 1974, **1**, 289–291. (b)

Benson, H., Shapiro, D., Tursky, B., & Schwartz, G. E. Decreased systolic blood pressure through operant conditioning techniques in patients with essential hypertension. *Science,* 1971, **173**, 740–742.

Bertelson, A., & Klein, M. "The effects of autogenic and anti-autogenic phrases on ability to increase and decrease hand temperature." Paper presented at the Biofeedback Research Society Annual meeting, Colorado Springs, Col., 1974.

Blanchard, E. B. Biofeedback and the modification of cardiovascular dysfunctions. In H. J. Gatchel, & K. P. Price, *Clinical applications of biofeedback: Appraisal and status.* New York: Pergamon Press, 1979.

Blanchard, E. B., & Epstein, L. H. *A Biofeedback Primer.* Reading, Mass.: Addison-Wesley, 1978.

Blanchard, E. B., & Haynes, M. R. Biofeedback treatment of a case of Raynaud's disease. *Journal of Behavior Therapy and Experimental Psychiatry,* 1975, **6**, 230–234.

Blanchard, E. B., Haynes, M. R., Kallman, M. D., & Harkey, L. A comparison of direct blood pressure feedback and electromyographic feedback on the blood pressure of normatensives. *Biofeedback and Self-Regulation,* 1976, **1**, 445–451.

Blanchard, E. B., Miller, P. M., Abel, G. G., Haynes, M. R., & Wicker, R. "The failure of blood pressure feedback in treating hypertension." Unpublished manuscript. State University of New York: Albany, N.Y., 1977.

Blanchard, E. B., Theobald, D. E., Williamson, D. A., Silver, B. V., & Brown, D. A. *Archives of General Psychiatry,* 1978.

Blanchard, E. B., & Young, L. D. Clinical application of biofeedback training: Review of evidence. *Archives of General Psychiatry,* 1974, **30**, 573–589.

Blanchard, E. B., Young, L. D., & Haynes, M. R. A simple feedback system for the treatment of elevated blood pressure. *Behavior Therapy,* 1975, **6**, 241–245.

Blanchard, E. B., Young, L. D., Haynes, M. R., & Kallman, M. D. A simple feedback system for self-control of blood pressure. *Perceptual and Motor Skills,* 1974, **39**, 891–898.

Brener, J., "Biofeedback—Current status." Colloquim, University of Georgia, 1973.

Brener, J., & Hothersall, D. Heart rate control under conditions of augmented sensory feedback. *Psychophysiology,* 1966, **3**, 23–27.

Brener, J., & Hothersall, D. Paced respiration and heart rate control. *Psychophysiology,* 1967, **4**, 1–6.

Brener, J., Kleinman, R. A., & Goesling, W. J. The effects of different exposures to augmented sensory feedback on the control of heart rate. *Psychophysiology,* 1969, **5**, 510–516.

Brook, R. H., & Appel, R. A. Quality-of-care assessment: Choosing a method for peer review. *New England Journal of Medicine,* 1973, **288**, 1323–1329.

Childes, A., & Sweetnam, M. Study of 104 cases of migraine. *British Journal of Industrial Medicine,* 1961, **18**, 243.

Dalessio, D. *Wolff's headache and other pain* (3rd ed.). New York: Oxford Univ. Press, 1972.

Datey, K. K. Temperature regulation in the management of hypertension. *Biofeedback and Self-Regulation,* 1976, **1,** 308.

Datey, K. K. Biofeedback training and Shavasan in the management of hypertension. *Biofeedback and Self-Regulation,* 1977, **2,** 303.

Datey, K. K. Biofeedback training and hypnosis in the management of hypertension. *Biofeedback and Self Regulation,* 1978, **3,** 206–207.

Dawber, T. R., Kannel, W. B., Revotskie, N., & Kagan, A. The epidemiology of coronary heart disease—The Framingham enquiry. *Proceedings of the Royal Society of Medicine,* 1962, **55,** 265.

Engel, B. T., & Bleecker, E. R. Application of operant conditioning techniques to the control of cardiac arrhythmias. In P. A. Obrist, A. H. Black, J. Brener, & L. V. DiCara (Eds.), *Cardiovascular psychophysiology.* Chicago: Aldine, 1974.

Engel, B. T., & Chism, R. A. Operant conditioning of heart rate speeding. *Psychophysiology,* 1967, **3,** 418–426.

Engel, B. T., & Hansen, J. P. Operant conditioning of heart rate slowing. *Psychophysiology,* 1966, **3,** 176–187.

Engel, B. T., & Melmon, L. Operant conditioning of heart rate in patients with cardiac arrhythmias. *Conditional Reflex,* 1968, **3,** 130.

Epstein, L. H., & Blanchard, E. B. Biofeedback, self-control, and self-management: An integration and reappraisal. *Biofeedback and Self-Regulation* (in press).

Fahrion, S. L. Autogenic biofeedback treatment for migraine. *Mayo Clinic Procedures,* 1977, **52,** 776–784.

Feuerstein, M., & Adams, H. E. Cephalic vasomotor feedback in the modification of migraine headaches. *Biofeedback and Self-Regulation,* 1977, **2,** 241–254.

Friar, L. R., & Beatty, J. Migraine: Management by trained control of vasodilation. *Journal of Consulting and Clinical Psychology,* 1976, **44,** 46–53.

Friedman, A. P. Reflection on the problem of headaches. *Journal of the American Medical Association,* 1964, **190,** 445–447.

Hager, J. L., & Surwit, R. S. Hypertension self-control with a portable feedback unit or meditation-relaxation. *Biofeedback and Self-Regulation,* 1978, **3,** 269–276.

Hnatiow, M., & Lang, P. J. Learned stabilization of cardiac rate. *Psychophysiology,* 1965, **1,** 330–336.

Jacobson, E. *Progressive relaxation.* Chicago: Univ. of Chicago Press, 1938.

Jacobson, A. M., Hackett, T. P., Surman, O. S., & Silverberg, E. L. *Journal of American Medical Association,* 1973, **225,** 739–740.

Johnson, W. G., & Turin, A. Biofeedback treatment of migraine headache: A systematic case study. *Behavior Therapy,* 1975, **6,** 394–397.

Kallman, W. M., & Feuerstein, M. Psychophysiological procedures. In A. R. Ciminero, K. S. Calhoun, & H. E. Adams (Eds.), *Handbook of behavioral assessment.* New York: John Wiley, 1977.

Kallman, W. M., Hersen, M., & O'Toole, D. H. The use of social reinforcement in a case of conversion reaction. *Behavior Therapy,* 1975, **6,** 411–413.

Kallman, W. M., Roberts, M., & Adams, H. E. "An experimental analysis of three biofeedback procedures with a case of Raynaud's disease." Paper presented at the Southeastern Psychological Assoc. Annual Meeting, New Orleans, La., 1976.

Kannel, W. B., & Dawber, T. R. Hypertension as an ingredient of a cardiovascular risk profile. *British Journal of Hospital Medicine,* 1974, **11,** 508–528.

Keefe, F. J. Conditioning changes in differential temperature. *Perceptual and Motor Skills,* 1975, **40,** 283–288.

Kiesler, D. J. Some myths of psychotherapy research and the search for a paradigm. *Psychological Bulletin,* 1966, **65,** 110–136.

Kristt, D. A., & Engel, B. T. Learned control of blood pressure in patients with high blood pressure. *Circulation,* 1975, **51,** 370–378.

Lang, P. J., Sroufe, L. A., & Hastings, J. E. Effects of feedback and instructional set on the control of cardiac rate variability. *Journal of Experimental Psychology,* 1967, **75,** 425–431.

Langfeld, J. B. Hypertension: Deficient care of the medically served. *Annals of International Medicine,* 1973, **78,** 19–23.

Levene, H. I., Engel, B. T., & Pearson, J. A. Differential operant conditioning of heart rate. *Psychosomatic Medicine,* 1968, **30,** 837–845.

Lisina, cited in Razran, G. The observable unconscious and the inferable conscious in current Soviet psychophysiology: Interceptive conditioning, semantic conditioning, and the orienting reflex. *Psychological Review,* 1961, **68,** 81–147.

Love, W. A., Montgomery, D. D., & Mueller, T. A. "Working paper no. 1." Unpublished manuscript. Nova University: Ft. Lauderdale, Fla., 1974.

Lyght, C. *The Merck Manual.* Rahway, N.J.: Merck, Sharp and Dohme, 1966.

May, D. S., & Weber, C. A. Temperature feedback training for symptom reduction in primary and secondary Raynaud's disease. *Biofeedback and Self-Regulation,* 1976, **1,** 317.

Miller, N. E. Learning of visceral and glandular responses. *Science,* 1968, **163,** 434–445.

Miller, N. E. Postscript. In D. Dingh, & C. T. Horgan (Eds.), *Current status of physiological psychology: Readings.* Monterey, Calif.: Brooks-Cole, 1972.

Miller, N. E. Clinical applications of biofeedback: Voluntary control of heart rate, rhythm, and blood pressure. In H. I. Russek (Ed.), *New horizons in cardiovascular practice.* Baltimore: University Park Press, 1975. Pp. 245–246.

Mittelmann, B., & Wolff, H. G. Affective states and skin temperature: Experimental study of subjects with "cold hands" and Raynaud's syndrome. *Psychosomatic Medicine,* 1939, **1,** 271–292.

Mueller, T. A., & Love, W. A. A method to reduce arterial hypertension through muscular relaxation. Unpublished manuscript. Nova University: Ft. Lauderdale, Fla., 1974.

Mullinex, J. M., Norton, B. J., Hack, S., & Fishman, M. A. Skin temperature biofeedback and migraine. *Headache,* 1978, **17,** 242–244.

National Health Survey, National Center for Health Statistics. Series 11, No. 6, U.S. Department of Health, Education and Welfare. Public Health Service: Washington, D.C.: 1964.

Patel, C. H. Personal communication reported in, Blanchard, E. B., & Epstein, L. H. *A Biofeedback Primer,* Reading, Mass.: Addison Wesley, 1978.

Patel, C. H. Yoga and biofeedback in the management of hypertension. *Lancet,* 1973, **2,** 1053–1055.

Patel, C. H. 12-month follow-up of yoga and biofeedback in the management of hypertension. *Lancet,* 1975, **1,** 62–65. (a)

Patel, C. H. Yoga and biofeedback in the management of "stress" in hypertensive patients. *Clinical Science and Molecular Medicine,* 1975, **48**, Suppl., 171–174. (b)

Patel, C. H., & North, W. R. S. Randomized controlled trial of yoga and biofeedback in management of hypertension. *Lancet,* 1975, **2**, 93–95.

Peper, E., & Grossman, E. R. Preliminary observations of thermal biofeedback training in children with migraine. Abstract in the proceedings of the Biofeedback Research Society, Denver, University of Colorado Medical Center, 1974, p. 63.

Pickering, T., & Gorham, G. Learned heart-rate controlled by a patient with a ventricular parasystolic rhythm. *Lancet,* 1975, **1**, 252–253.

Razran, G. The observable unconscious and the inferable conscious in current Soviet psychophysiology: Interceptive conditioning, semantic conditioning and the orienting reflex. *Psychological Review,* 1961, **68**, 81–147.

Reading, C., & Mohr, P. D. Biofeedback control of migraine: A pilot study. *British Journal of Social and Clinical Psychology,* 1976, **15**, 429–433.

Sargent, J. D., Green, E. E., & Walters, E. D. Preliminary report on the use of autogenic feedback training in the treatment of migraine and tension headaches. *Psychosomatic Medicine,* 1973, **35**, 129–235.

Sargent, J. D., Green, E. E., & Walters, E. D. Psychosomatic self-regulation of migraine headaches. In L. Birk (Ed.), *Biofeedback: Behavioral medicine.* New York: Grune & Stratton, 1973.

Schwartz, G. E. Biofeedback as therapy: Some theoretical and practical issues. *American Psychologist,* 1972, **28**, 666–673.

Schultz, J. H., & Luthe, W. *Autogenic therapy (Vol. 1).* New York: Grune & Stratton, 1969.

Scott, R. W., Blanchard, E. B., Edmundson, E. D., & Young, L. D. A shaping procedure for heart rate control in chronic tachycardia. *Perceptual and Motor Skills,* 1973, **37**, 327–338.

Sedlacek, K. W. EMG and thermal feedback as a treatment for Raynaud's disease. *Biofeedback and Self-Regulation,* 1976, **1**, 318. (a)

Sedlacek, K. W. EMG, GSR, and thermal biofeedback in the treatment of hypertension. *Biofeedback and Self-Regulation,* 1976, **1**, 311–312. (b)

Sedlacek, K. W., & Cohen, J. Biofeedback treatment of essential hypertension. *Biofeedback and Self-Regulation,* 1978, **3**, 207.

Shapiro, D. Operant-feedback control of human blood pressure: Some clinical issues. In P. A. Obrist, A. H. Black, J. Brener, & L. V. DiCara (Eds.), *Cardiovascular psychophysiology.* Chicago: Aldine, 1974.

Shapiro, D., Schwartz, G. E., & Tursky, B. Control of diastolic blood pressure in man by feedback and reinforcement. *Psychophysiology,* 1972, **9**, 296–304.

Shapiro, D., Tursky, B., Gershon, E., & Stern, M. Effects of feedback and reinforcement on control of human systolic blood pressure. *Science,* 1969, **163**, 558–590.

Shapiro, D., Tursky, B., & Schwartz, G. E. Control of blood pressure in man by operant conditioning. *Circulation Research,* 1970, **26** (Suppl. 1:27–32).

Shoemaker, J. E., & Tasto, D. L. The effects of muscular relaxation on blood pressure of essential hypertensives. *Behaviour Research and Therapy,* 1975, **13**, 29–43.

Skinhoj, E., & Paulson, O. Regional blood flow in internal carotid distribution during migraine attack. *British Medical Journal,* 1969, **3**, 569.

Skinner, B. F. *The behavior of organisms: An experimental analysis.* New York: Appleton-Century-Crofts, 1938.

Spittell, J. A. *Peripheral vascular disease.* Philadelphia: W. B. Saunders, 1972.

Stephenson, N. L. Two successful cases of treatment of Raynaud's disease. *Biofeedback and Self-Regulation,* 1976, **1**, 318.

Sturgis, E. T., Tollison, D. D., & Adams, H. E. Modification of combined migraine-muscle contraction headaches using BVP and EMG feedback. *Journal of Applied Behavioral Analysis,* 1978, **11**, 215–223.

Sroufe, L. A. Learned stabilization of cardiac rate with respiration experimentally controlled. *Journal of Experimental Psychology,* 1969, **81**, 391–393.

Surwit, R. S. Biofeedback: A possible treatment for Raynaud's disease. *Seminars in Psychiatry,* 1973, **5**, 483–490.

Surwit, R. S. Cardiovascular biofeedback, muscle activity in biofeedback, and meditation-relaxation training in borderline essential hypertension. *Biofeedback and Self-Regulation,* 1976, **1**, 312.

Surwit, R. S., Shapiro, D., & Good, M. I. A comparison of cardiovascular biofeedback, neuromuscular biofeedback, and meditation in the treatment of borderline essential hypertension. *Journal of Consulting and Clinical Psychology,* 1978, **46**, 252–263.

Turin, A., & Johnson, W. G. Biofeedback therapy for migraine headaches. *Archives of General Psychiatry,* 1976, **33**, 517–519.

Tursky, B., Shapiro, D., & Schwartz, G. E. Automated constant cuff-pressure system to measure average systolic and diastolic blood pressure in man. *IEEE Transactions in Bio-Medical Engineering,* 1972, **19**, 217–276.

Walsh, P., Dale, A., Brethauer, L., Eagan, R., Frick, J., Ostrowski, N., Walberg, M., & Weiss, S. A comparison of pulse waves velocity feedback coupled with verbal sphygmomanometric feedback vs. deep relaxation treatments in drug-controlled and nondrugged essential hypertensives. *Biofeedback and Self-Regulation,* 1976, **1**, 313.

Weiss, T., & Engel, B. T. Voluntary control of premature ventricular contractions in patients. *American Journal of Cardiology,* 1970, **26**, 666.

Weiss, T., & Engel, B. T. Operant conditioning of heart rate in patients with premature ventricular contractions. *Psychosomatic Medicine,* 1971, **33**, 301–321.

Wickramasekera, I. Temperature feedback for the control of migraine. *Journal of Behavior Therapy and Experimental Psychiatry,* 1973, **4**, 343–345.

Wolff, H. G. Headache mechanisms. *McGill Medical Journal,* 1946, **15**, 130–169.

Wolff, F. W., & Lindeman, R. D. Effects of treatment in hypertension: Results of a controlled study. *Journal of Chronic Diseases,* 1966, **19**, 227–240.

World Health Organization. Hypertension and coronary heart disease: Classification and criteria for epidemiological studies. *Technical Report series 168,* Geneva, 1959.

Zamani, R. Treatment of migraine headache: Biofeedback versus deep-muscle relaxation. Cited in S. L. Fahrion, *Autogenic biofeedback treatment for migraine. Mayo Clinic Procedures,* 1975, **52**, 776–784.

CHAPTER 15

Behavioral Medicine for Muscular Disorders

Bruce L. Bird, Michael F. Cataldo, and Lynn Parker

In the fifteenth century, the noted physician Paracelsus, in studying chorea—a dancelike writhing of the limbs—differentiated among "natural" chorea, "imaginary" chorea, and the chorea of "lacivious desire." Throughout the history of medicine, disorders of muscle tone or musclar control have posed significant problems in diagnosis and treatment (Bruyn, 1968). During this century, like other disorders with uncertain etiologies, neurologists and psychiatrists have respectively classified muscular disorders as problems of the brain or of the mind. During the past decade, behavioral therapists and researchers have entered the perilous "borderland" of neurology and psychiatry (Geschwind, 1975; Williams, 1975) and have developed promising treatments for various disorders under the rubric of behavioral medicine.

The purposes of this chapter are to review current behavioral treatments for muscular disorders, and to provide a resource to clinicians on current medical and behavioral conceptualizations of and treatments for these disorders. Issues that appear to be critical for improved study and treatment of behavioral aspects of muscular disorders are briefly discussed. Reviews of current literature which illustrates principles and procedures support the value of an interdisciplinary behavioral medicine approach to these disorders.

DIAGNOSTIC CATEGORIES

Table 1 lists diagnostic categories of muscle disorders treated by behavioral medicine programs. The nature of these disorders and diagnostic procedures are detailed in a following review of the reported behavioral treatments for each.

Several general issues related to the categories in Table 1 are worth noting: (*a*) categories are quite heterogeneous, in behavioral topography and suspected pathological mechanisms; (*b*) diagnostic procedures and values vary across disorders, service disciplines, and practitioners, and are especially problematic in the borderland disorders; (*c*) mechanisms for the borderland and neurological disorders are very poorly understood; (*d*) clinical medical literature clearly recognizes the interactive effects of learning and emotional factors with physiology in exacer-

Table 1.   Classification of Muscular Disorders

Psychosomatic
Tension headaches
Tension-related pain
Miscellaneous tension disorders

Borderland
Tension-induced migraines
Tics
Spasmodic torticollis

Neurological
Spinal injuries
Cerebral trauma
Extrapyramidal disorders
Cerebral palsy
Peripheral neuromuscular disorders
Smooth muscle disorders

bating or improving symptoms; and (*e*) behavioral technology may contribute to understanding the borderland and neurological disorders by improving quantification of symptoms to correlate with anatomical, biochemical, and electrophysiological measures.

In current practice, diagnostic differentiation of organic versus psychogenic causes does not indicate for or against behavioral medicine treatments. However, proper diagnosis is important for consideration of alternative medical treatments. Comprehensive behavioral assessments may also differentially indicate certain treatment components, as detailed below.

DEMOGRAPHICS AND SCOPE

The disorders listed in Table 1 have enormous impact on health and medicine in this country. For example, although the reliance of tension headache sufferers on over-the-counter drugs makes estimates of prevalance difficult, estimates are in the millions (Lance, 1975), as corroborated by the amount of advertising in all forms of popular media for drug remedies of tension headaches. Stroke has been estimated to afflict over 1.5 million Americans annually, a large proportion of whom will require therapy or care for motor dysfunctions (Thompson & Green, 1977). Over 700,000 individuals in the United States have cerebral palsy, many of whom require substantial care, and have severe social and emotional problems (Molnar & Taft, 1975). The obvious severity of personal and psychosocial difficulties related to the physical disabilities of these disorders are well detailed in the clinical literature (Arieti, 1975; Cooper, 1969; Dalessio, 1973; Eldridge & Fahn, 1976; Fordyce, 1976; Keats, 1965; Krusen, 1971; Shapiro, Shapiro, & Wayne, 1973).

These disorders as a class are prevalent, and carry medical and psychosocial impacts varying from mild to most severe. Moreover, even in the cases of the severest neurological disorders such as dystonia, life-span is rarely shortened, and the individual is faced with a chronic disorder with severely handicapping effects. Therefore, behavioral treatments may be applied to both primary and secondary psychosocial aspects of muscular disorders.

TRADITIONAL MEDICAL TREATMENTS

Traditional medical treatments, for muscular disorders include psychotherapy, psychopharmacology, neuropharmacology, neurosurgery, orthopedic surgery, and physical therapy. The goals, methods, and reported risks and benefits of these treatment modalities differ across muscular disorders. However, some summary statements about these approaches appear to be appropriate.

Psychotherapeutic approaches have generally received little research attention. Patients with muscular disorders of all varieties may be referred for psychotherapy if they present secondary psychiatric problems or if their disorder is considered functional (Arieti, 1975). Referral and acceptance for direct treatment of these disorders also occurs when hysteria is suspected (Ford, 1973), but these cases appear to be rare, and cautionary notes on overdiagnosis of hysteria have appeared in recent literature on organic disorders (Eldridge, Riklan, & Cooper, 1969).

Direct pharmacological treatment for neurological and borderland muscular disorders include muscle relaxants such as diazepam (Blackwell, 1973), dantrolene sodium (Basmajian & Super, 1973), dopamine agonists, and antagonists (Yahr & Duvoisin, 1968), and many others (Calne, 1973). A review of the literature reveals that significant long-term effects have not been established for most agents, and even in the case of the longest and most promising drug-disorder relationship—levodopa for Parkinsonism—beneficial effects have not been as great as hoped, and risks and side effects are considerable (Fahn & Calne, 1978).

The recent increase in pharmacological treatment for psychosomatic disorders (Solow, 1977) has paralleled increasing interest in and evidence for biochemical mechanisms in psychiatric and pain disorders (Halpern, 1974; Bonica, 1974). The problems and benefits involved in medication regimens for chronic pain and interactions with behavioral variables have been well reviewed by Fordyce (1976). A major problem in traditional drug regimens for pain is that the agent is usually administered at the patient's request, after some minimal time period. If the agent reduces pain, a behavioral analysis suggests that a potent reinforcer is being administered contingent on pain complaints. Fordyce's (1976) solution is to alter the regimen to dispense the agent on a fixed time schedule. Other aspects of behavioral medicine for pain related to muscle dysfunction are discussed in a following section.

Neurosurgical treatments are available for borderland and organic muscular disorders. Major forms of neurosurgery for these disorders are lesions (Cooper, 1969; Sorenson & Hamby, 1966), and neural stimulators (Cooper, 1976). Lesions are performed in attempts to destroy or block abnormal neuronal activity, allowing residual motor systems to function more efficiently. Stimulators are implanted in an attempt to activate neural circuits that may block or inhibit abnormal activity. Similar treatments have been reported for chronic pain (Ebersold, Laws, Stonnington, & Stillwell, 1975; Stravino, 1970). However, critical reviews have questioned the evidence for consistent benefits of these procedures (Medical News, 1978; Black, 1975; Swanson, Swenson, Manuta, & McPhee, 1976).

Physical therapies offer a wide range of programs for a similarly wide range of disorders, all aimed at improving abnormal posture and motor control. Procedures include passive and active exercising, stimulating or inhibiting reflexes, and teaching patients to use residual motor skills to maximize adaptive functions (Krusen, 1971; Pearson & Williams, 1972). Despite a long history of recognized clinical benefits, the field has been self-critical for lack of sufficient procedural detail for replication and lack of documentation of therapeutic effects (Wolf, 1969; Wright & Nicholson, 1973).

The lack of potent, widely applicable medical treatments has been attributed to poor understanding of the mechanisms of muscular disorders and probable heterogeneous etiologies and pathophysiologies within traditional categories (cf: A.M.A., 1978; Eldridge & Fahn, 1976). However, although the literature has not indicated that any traditional therapy is generally effective for a selected disorder, it has reported, and our experiences have corroborated, dramatic benefits of neurosurgery, pharmacology, or physical therapy in individual cases. It has also been our experience that current trends toward interdisciplinary evaluation and management of patients is an optimal approach (Batshaw & Haslam, 1976; Diamond & Dalessio, 1978; Gottlieb, Strite, Koller, Madorsby, Hockersmith, Kleeman, & Wagner, 1977). The rationale that neurosurgical or pharmacological interventions often improve a patient's benefits from a learning-based treatment provides a logical basis for combined behavioral and medical therapies.

For reasons of ethics and efficacy, practitioners of behavioral medicine should be well aware of alternative medical treatments for the disorders they treat. In the case of muscular disorders, the available alternative treatments have not been proven to be consistently effective, and behavioral treatments offer viable alternatives or compliments to traditional biomedical treatment programs. As progress occurs in understanding the mechanisms of these disorders, and in improving both medical and behavioral treatments, increases in interactive treatments are clearly predicted.

BEHAVIORAL TREATMENTS

Table 2 presents a list of behavioral treatments that have been attempted for one or more muscular disorders. Prior to reviewing the literature on behavioral treatments for each disorder, a brief description of the types of treatment appears warranted.

Relaxation Training

Several types of relaxation training have been developed for a variety of clinical uses. Most techniques are variations of the procedures pioneered by Jacobsen

**Table 2.   Behavioral Treatments for
Muscular Disorders**

Behavioral
Relaxation training
Contingency management
Cognitive strategies
Adjunctive programs

Biofeedback
EMG relaxation
EMG inhibition
EMG recruitment
EMG bidirectional
Force feedback

(1938, 1967), who worked with a broad range of psychosomatic problems. Jacobsen's progressive relaxation used an exercise of sequential tensing and then relaxing major muscle groups, eventually involving all parts of the skeletal musculature. Wolpe (1958) adapted Jacobsen's procedures to use in systematic desensitization. This use of relaxation for counterconditioning anxiety and tensing to specific environmental stimuli has since become a widely used tool in the behavior therapist's repertoire (Rachman, 1967).

Other prominent models of relaxation are: (*a*) autogenic training, which combines musculoskeletal, autonomic, and cognitive exercises and has a long history of successful application to psychiatric, psychosomatic, and a wide range of medical problems (Luthe, 1969; Schultz & Luthe, 1959); (*b*) Benson's (1975) relaxation response, a modified version of Jacobsen's exercises; and (*c*) various forms of meditation (Nanjo & Ornstein, 1971).

It is worth noting that the Luthe and Benson models have in common a strong emphasis on regulation of the rate and volume of breathing as a key component in producing relaxation. The extent and range of physiological responses affected by these relaxation procedures are a continuing subject for research. In contrast to proposed specific effects of biofeedback training on targeted responses, relaxation training procedures may diffusely affect skeletomuscular and autonomic responses throughout the body (Schwartz, 1977).

The relationships among autonomic and somatic response systems in pathological conditions and relaxation training are complex, poorly understood, and not the focus of this chapter. The interested reader is referred to recent reviews and research on somatic and autonomic interactions (Benson, 1975; Schwartz, 1977; Stoyva, 1977) and on procedures for producing relaxation (Harris, Katkin, Lick, & Halberfield, 1976; Schandler & Grings, 1976; Michaels, Haber, & McCann, 1976).

For the practitioner, three points are worthy of special note. (*a*) Evidence continues to grow suggesting that relaxation training is an effective treatment modality for a variety of psychosomatic and medical disorders, including muscular disorders; (*b*) The mechanisms of these effects are not understood; and (*c*) The literature is weakest in the assessment of generalization of relaxation effects to extraclinic situations and in the long-term follow-up of patients.

Contingency Management

Contingency management has been found to be useful in improving muscle control in psychogenic disorders, such as chronic pain (Fordyce, 1976), borderland disorders such as tics (Barret, 1962), and even in severe neurological disorders such as cerebral palsy (Rugel, Mattingly, & Eichinger, 1971). Perhaps more importantly, almost all treatment programs that utilize alternative procedures such as relaxation training or biofeedback employ some form of contingency management either as a working component of the treatment or in order to obtain compliance with prescribed treatments (i.e., Finley, Niman, Standley, & Ender, 1976). Likewise, well-designed contingency management programs are increasingly evident in medical disciplines such as physical therapy (Ince, 1976). It is becoming clear that a major role of behavioral medicine will develop in the area of contingency management programs directed to target symptoms or as adjuncts to other treatments, for example, as in obtaining treatment compliance (Epstein & Masek, 1978).

Cognitive and Self-Control Strategies

The past five years have evidenced an increasing interest in behavioral control of cognition and the use of cognitive behavior modification in therapies (Goldiamond, 1965, 1976; Lazarus, 1972; Meichenbaum, 1976; Thorsen & Mahoney, 1974). The clinical literature in muscular disorders has offered support for the value of such strategies in treating psychogenic and borderland problems including pain (Chaves & Barber, 1976), tics (Varni, Boyd, & Cataldo, in press), and tension headaches (Reeves, 1976). The literature on neuromuscular disorders indicates that often cognitive strategies either develop as patients progress through treatment or are encouraged by therapists in an unsystematic manner (Singer, 1974). The relaxation-training literature clearly has attempted to utilize strategies of cognitive behavior modification, but it has not systematically assessed their contributions to treatment effects (Schwartz, 1977). Research and issues in behavioral cognitive strategies have been reviewed in the context of self-control (Epstein & Blanchard, 1977), biofeedback and self-regulation (Meichenbaum, 1976; Stoyva, 1977) and hypnosis (Chaves & Barber, 1976). Meichenbaum (1974) has discussed the value of "self-control" procedures applied to a variety of maladaptive behaviors, including anxiety and stress-related symptoms. Important components of these procedures include training the patient to discriminate stress-related symptoms as cues for emitting competing responses such as relaxation, and they include training the patient to utilize self-instruction and self-administered reinforcement. Meichenbaum (1976) has also reviewed the theoretical and practical relationship between biofeedback and cognitive behavior modification, and he has pointed out that such self-control procedures may be most useful in producing transfer of clinic effects to the real world.

It appears that increasingly these procedures will be utilized in treating psychosomatic and medical disorders, and that clinical research attention will continue to focus on these processes. Our clinical experience in behavioral and biofeedback treatments for psychosomatic and medical disorders has indicated that using cognitive stimuli, such as images or self-instructions, as discriminative stimuli often enhance reported generalization of learned adaptive responses to the natural environment.

Adjunctive Behavioral Programs

The clinical literature in physical rehabilitation (Anderson & Kottke, 1978; Ince, 1976) and psychosomatic medicine (Arieti, 1975; Wittkower & Warnes, 1977) has traditionally argued for treatment programs that serve the whole patient. General trends in clinical medicine and a growth in "Holistic" medicine support this argument (Halstead & Halstead, 1978).

In the previous section on diagnostics, the need for a comprehensive behavioral assessment was stressed. As noted previously, muscular disorders often produce significant psychosocial problems. It has been our impression from clinical work in several areas of behavioral medicine that behavioral programs for targeted problems such as a particular muscular disorder will succeed only if sufficient attention is given to serious problems in the patient's psychosocial environment. Clinical findings described in the review of individual disorders illustrate this principle. Although there is almost no literature on applying traditional behavioral techniques to adjustment problems in muscular disorders, the rationale for such application is clear, and any direct behavioral treatment for muscular disorders should be developed in the context of the patient's psychosocial needs.

Biofeedback: Electromyographic

Procedures and rationale for, and research reviews of biofeedback have been provided elsewhere (Basmajian, 1978; Beatty & Legewie, 1977; Miller, 1969, 1977), as have reviews of electromyographic (EMG) biofeedback (Inglis, Campbell, & Donald, 1976; Keefe & Surwit, 1978). Electromyographic feedback involves using electronic apparatus to monitor and amplify muscular activity, and to provide additional sensory feedback (usually visual or auditory signals) to a motivated patient who practices some forms of muscular control. As will be evident in the following section on selected disorders, EMG biofeedback has been reported to be successful in treating almost all types of muscular disorders.

Types of EMG feedback training that may be used include: (*a*) training for general, whole-body relaxation using forehead or other muscle groups; (*b*) training for inhibition of undesirable muscular activity in selected muscle groups; (*c*) training for increasing voluntary contractions in selected muscles; and (*d*) training for both increases and inhibition in muscle activity, which may be proposed as training for improved discrimination or for improved control. Two techniques that have not been researched but appear to be promising include training for stabilization of muscle activity in disorders producing variable tone, and training for synergistic coordination in disorders producing excessive antagonism or tremor in muscles serving selected joints.

Three cautionary notes are evident in the EMG feedback literature. (*a*) Little research exists demonstrating that EMG feedback procedures are the contributory factors in improving muscle control (this point is especially noteworthy since almost all EMG feedback treatment programs use some additional form of reinforcement, e.g., Finley, Niman, Standley, & Wansley, 1977); (*b*) Very little data exists documenting generalization of therapeutic effects to adaptive functions in the natural environment; and (*c*) Little data exists on maintenance of achieved gains over long periods. Despite these cautions, the clinical literature is most promising, suggesting that EMG feedback is a potent therapy for disorders traditionally found to be resistant to other therapies (Fernando & Basmajian, 1978).

Biofeedback: Force or Pressure

In addition to EMG feedback, recent reports have suggested that providing augmented visual or auditory feedback for changes in force or pressure in the head, neck, or limbs affected by muscular disorders produces significant clinical benefit (cf. Wooldridge & Russell, 1975). In addition, pressure feedback has been successfully used in training continence in patients with disorders of the anal sphincter (Engel, Nikoomanesh, & Schuster, 1974). Herman (1978) has cogently argued that force provides a much simpler but very sensitive type of feedback to the patient, for example, transforming the complicated interactions of several muscle groups around a joint into a unitary signal. This type of treatment merits further evaluation, and appears promising for any of the disorders that produce displacements or impairments of the limb, head, or body position.

SPECIFIC DISORDERS

In the following section, behavioral and biofeedback treatments for selected muscular disorders are reviewed in detail. General issues in behavioral treatments are discussed in a subsequent section.

Pain

During the past decade, advances in several areas of science have improved our understanding and treatment of pain (Bonica, 1977). Evidence from neurophysiology and psychophysiology (Melzack & Wall, 1970; Sternbach, 1978; Tursky, 1976) has contributed to development of the view that pain involves both sensing pain and reacting to or elaborating upon pain sensations. Behavioral medicine strategies consonant with such a proposal and involving sophisticated contingency management programs have been developed and well detailed by Fordyce (1976). Relaxation training and EMG feedback have been reported successful as direct treatments for tension problems associated with pain disorders (cf: Stoyva, 1977). Before reviewing the literature on tension related to headaches and other pain disorders, a few cautionary points are merited.

The role of increased muscle tension in tension headaches and other purported tension-related pain disorders has been questioned by several authors. Haynes,

Griffin, Mooney, and Parise (1975), in addition to finding equivalent effects of forehead EMG feedback and relaxation exercises in treating headaches, also reported poor correlations of EMG and headache occurrence. Epstein and Abel (1977) noted similar findings and also found poor generalization of control of muscle tension from feedback to no-feedback conditions in the clinic. Basmajian (1978) has reported that in patients with pain-related spasms in the neck and lumbar back areas, increases in EMG activity were not accompanied by clinical spasms. He has also reported that drug-produced improvements in spasms were accompanied by increased activity in back muscles during prescribed movements.

Evidence supporting the direct relationship of muscle tension and headache has been reported by Wolff (Dalessio, 1972). Wolff found that muscle tension was elevated at the site of headache as described by 28 of 37 patients studied. He proposed that the mechanism of pain in tension headaches is vasoconstriction occurring during increased muscular contractions. Rodbard (1975) has conducted systematic research on mechanisms of pain in contracting muscles, manipulating variables such as force loads on muscles, duration and frequency of required contractions, intervals between required contractions, arterial and venous pressures, and vascular supplies while measuring motor performance and verbal descriptions of pain. Rodbard's conclusions are that excessive muscular contractions produce some as yet unidentified catabolite that activates nerve fibers conducting pain information.

A related issue concerns the cause-effect sequence in pain disorders. Increased localized tension may be proposed as a response of the patient to some pain-producing phenomena in the same or a distant area of the skeletomuscular system due to referred pain from visceral tissue or due to a problem with the local or distant nervous tissue. It is also reasonable to suspect that in some cases, increased tensions may exacerbate pain, and such a tension-vascular sequence has been proposed to occur in some migraine patients (Dalessio, 1972).

The literature reveals, and the experience of our clinic has shown, that relaxation and EMG feedback procedures are often helpful in tension-related pain. Usually patients with such disorders present with increased EMG levels in identified muscle groups, and in many the abnormalities are striking. In some cases that do not present increased muscle tension levels in the clinic, careful history and self-observations suggest that controlling physical or psychosocial stimuli may produce increased tension in selected extraclinic conditions. In some patients, we have not found that EMG levels in the clinic are always correlated with verbal reports of patient responsiveness to EMG feedback or to relaxation training. A corollary finding has been that relaxation training is sometimes helpful to patients who do not present increased tension as measured in the clinic. In some cases therefore, EMG feedback or relaxation training may produce effects by teaching the patient skills (either discriminating or reducing tension) that can be used in extraclinic situations which set the occasion for symptoms.

One additional cautionary note is warranted in discussing pain. Several authors have noted the sensitivity of patients with chronic pain to placebo effects (Barber, 1959; Bonica, 1977). During recent years placebo effects have been the subject of some research and much discussion (Shapiro, 1960, 1971). In behavioral terms, if placebo effects are those which after an initial period of change wane even though maintenance procedures are attempted, then it is probable that the therapist has not identified variables critical for effective change or for maintenance of beneficial effect. Comprehensive assessments, adequate controls in designing intervention strategies, and long-term maintenance programs may reduce the probabilities of placebo effects.

Tension Headaches

Estimates of the incidence of severe headaches occurring sometime in a person's life range from 50 to 92% of the population studied (Ziegler, 1976). Headache may be related to a variety of medical disorders. Graham (1976) has identified eight currently recognized mechanisms responsible for head pain: (a) intrinsic disorders of pain neurons (e.g., *tic douloureaux*); (b) direct pressure on pain nerves or pain-sensitive structures (e.g., acoustic neuroma pressing on Vth ganglion); (c) traction on pain sensitive structures (e.g., on veins by a space-occupying tumor or abcess); (d) excessive dilation of intracranial arteries; (e) excessive dilation of extracranial arteries; (f) inflammation of meninges at the base of the brain or of blood vessel walls in the brain or scalp; (g) prolonged contractions of scalp, facial, and neck muscles; and (h) hysteria. Diamond (1976) has estimated that approximately 50% of patients seen in his large urban headache clinic have strong psychogenic components affecting their headaches.

The two most common forms of headache, both of which have been recognized as having psychogenic components, are tension headaches and migraine (and migraine-variant) headaches. Although there has been some debate in recent years on the symptoms identifying and separating these two types of headache (Lance, 1975; Ziegler, 1976), they are traditionally considered different disorders which may in some cases occur together. Behavioral medicine treatments for vascular migraines are discussed in a subsequent section of this chapter.

Tension headaches have been reported to be products of excessive muscle contractions in forehead, scalp, and neck muscles and are considered to be largely psychogenic (Dalessio, 1972; Lance, 1975). Topographies vary across individuals, with tightness, pressure, or bands of dull pain being described in forehead, temporal or posterior head areas. Kudrow (1976) has estimated the incidence to be about 25% of the general population, although chronic tension headaches are estimated as less prevalent. Approximately 67% of the Kudrow clinic's 1000 tension headache patients suffered from chronic headaches, with an average duration of 8.7 years and a range of from 1 to 55 years in duration. Approximately 40% of Lance's (1975) and 44% of Kudrow's (1976) general headache clinic populations were tension headache sufferers. Most prominent clinicians have noted that medical treatments (i.e., analgesics, tranquilizers, physical therapies) are often not effective in alleviating tension headaches, and that relaxation training procedures offer great benefit for these patients (Diamond & Dalessio, 1978; Kudrow, 1976; Lance, 1975).

Deep-muscle relaxation training has been reported successful in treating tension headaches (Tasto & Hinkle, 1973). In recent years, several authors reported successful use of EMG feedback for tension headaches. In these studies feedback was provided for forehead or frontalis muscles in frequent clinic sessions, and daily relaxation practice sessions were part of the treatment regimen (Budzynski, Stoyva,

& Adler, 1970; Budzynski, Stoyva, Adler, & Mullaney, 1973; Raskin, Johnson, & Rondestvedt, 1973; Wickramasekera, 1972). Follow-ups to lengths of three months indicated successful maintenance in the Budzynski et al. studies.

Phillips (1977) has noted that prevalent views of muscle tension headaches may be too simplistic, and they do not recognize variations in muscles involved or response abnormality. Phillips (1977) reported on research in which EMG feedback training was conducted to reduce tension in the most abnormal muscle group (either frontalis or temporalis in this series) as measured in resting baseline. Results indicated that these programs were successful in treating tension headaches but unsucessful for mixed tension-migraine patients. A control group of similar patients treated with false biofeedback signals did not show improvement. Poor correlation was noted between headache pain and tension levels in both groups.

Reinking and Hutchings (1976) conducted controlled group comparisons of forehead EMG feedback, modified Jacobson–Wolpe relaxation training, and combined EMG plus relaxation training. Their results suggest that the groups that also received EMG feedback showed better results than the relaxation-only groups. In contrast, Chesney and Shelton (1976) found that relaxation and relaxation plus forehead feedback were significantly more effective in reducing headache frequency than feedback only and control no-treatment groups, which did not differ. Haynes, Griffin, Mooney, and Parise (1975) reported that EMG feedback and relaxation training were equally effective compared to a control group in reducing headaches.

As noted in the previous section, the relationship of EMG measures of muscle tension to verbal reports of pain has not been consistently reported. Significant positive correlations of frontalis muscle EMG and pain reports have not been found in some proportion of patients with tension headaches (Epstein & Abel, 1977; Epstein, Abel, Collins, Parker, & Cinciripini, 1978; Haynes et al., 1975; Phillips, 1977). However, positive effects of EMG feedback training for frontalis muscle relaxation on headache reports has been noted even in cases in which correlations were poor (Epstein & Abel, 1977; Epstein et al., 1978). As previously discussed, one proposal for these effects is that controlling stimuli may not be in evidence in the clinic. Training patients to discriminate changes in tension and to relax may provide patients with adaptive responses to make in the presence of tension-controlling stimuli.

Despite a lack of information on mechanisms and key procedures of treatment effects, sufficient clinical evidence for beneficial effects has accrued and the Biofeedback Society of America's Task Force on Tension Headaches has recommended that EMG feedback and associated relaxation techniques can be considered viable alternatives to traditional medical treatments (Budzynski, 1978).

Other Pain-Related Tension Disorders

Temporomandibular joint (TMJ) pain syndrome (sometimes termed myofascial pain-dysfunction syndrome) is characterized by pain over the masseter muscles in the preauricular area. Pain frequently extends over the face and head, and there is often associated jaw dysfunction. TMJ syndrome has been considered to be a functional disorder (Alberman, 1971; Bessett, Mohl, & Duda, 1973), and it has been estimated to affect about 20% of the general population (Agerberg & Carlsson,

1972). Traditional treatments have included psychotherapy (Pomp, 1974) and procedures aimed at improving dental structure and mandibular function such as ensuring correct occlusion (Greene, 1973).

Relaxation training procedures have been reported successful in treating TMJ syndrome. Gessel and Alderman (1971) reported successful treatment of 6 of 11 TMJ patients with Jacobsonian progressive relaxation. The nonresponsive patients were assessed as indicating higher levels of "social disability," and more severe depression. The failure of relaxation treatments with five patients may have been due to a failure to provide behavioral programs for pervasive and severe associated behavior problems.

Gessel (1975) has also reported successful use of temporalis-masseter EMG feedback in 15 of 23 TMJ patients. Interestingly, Gessel's (1975) approach to EMG nonresponders has not been to provide more comprehensive behavioral programs. Rather, antidepressant medications have been used with reported success.

Dohrmann and Laskin (1976) reported successful biofeedback treatment of 12 to 16 TMJ patients, and Rosenthal (1976) reported successful frontalis EMG feedback treatment in 5 of 7 TMJ patients. Carlsson and Gale (1977) utilized masseter EMG feedback, and they reported that 8 of 11 patients for whom previous dental treatments had failed experienced successful treatment, 5 of whom were totally symptom-free at a one-year follow-up. This study emphasized discrimination training in which patients practiced increasing and reducing masseter tension, guessing levels of tension without feedback, relaxing with feedback, and estimating tension at home. Failures were ascribed to personality problems or possible nonmuscular etiology. The possibility of nonmuscular (and possibly structural) etiologies producing symptoms was also noted by Rosenthal (1976) whose two failures demonstrated long silent periods in masseter EMG.

Peck and Kraft (1977) reported that the utility of EMG feedback was greater in tension headaches ($n = 18$) than in temporomandibular joint (TMJ) syndrome ($n = 6$) and shoulder and back pain patients ($n = 8$). Interpretation of the results of this study were complicated by several factors, including the use of similar training protocols and lengths of training for different disorders, and unequal numbers of patients in each group.

Applications of behavioral and biofeedback treatments to other pain disorders have also appeared in the rehabilitation literature. Gottlieb et al. (1977) have reported that EMG feedback made a significant contribution in a large-scale comprehensive management program for chronic back pain. This study did not report sufficient data to clearly demonstrate the utility of feedback, but the program was notable in providing a comprehensive assessment and treatment of a number of behaviors relevant to rehabilitation.

Grzesiak (1977) has reported successful application of relaxation training techniques to chronic pain in four spinal-cord injured patients. Although controls and data were not provided, the long-term gains reported by three of four patients were encouraging.

The nature and mechanisms of pain in these disorders are poorly understood. Caution is therefore in order when assessing behavioral medicine approaches. The developing literature on behavioral and biofeedback treatments of pain-related tension suggests reasonable therapeutic benefits. Most importantly, tension-related treatments for pain disorders appear to be most effective when components of comprehensive behavioral intervention strategies for pain disorders of the type detailed by Fordyce (1976) are indicated.

Miscellaneous Psychosomatic Disorders of Tension

Lance, Cohen, and Rickles (1976) have reported successful EMG feedback treatment of a severely debilitating condition of esophageal, neck and facial spasms in a middle-aged woodwind musician. This case study was exemplary from several aspects: detailed reports were presented on the patient's long history of disorder and unsuccessful alternative medical treatments; associated behavioral problems were clearly identified by a comprehensive assessment and addressed initially by an individual behaviorally oriented psychotherapy; generalization of relaxed throat muscles to functional woodwind playing was programmed in stages in clinic and extraclinic environments; and amounts of training and EMG voltages were reported quantitatively.

In another interesting study, Haynes (1976) successfully used frontalis EMG feedback to alleviate severe spasms of the pharynx and esophagus in a 25-year-old female who had a previous history of unsuccessful medical treatment. Home practice involved the patient's attempting to practice relaxation as she had learned it in feedback training, and self-reported difficulty in swallowing was monitored. Follow-up at six months posttreatment showed continuing beneficial effects. Although Haynes' treatment program did not use formal relaxation training, the patient had previously been taught such procedures, and their effects may have been contributed to the biofeedback program.

Spastic dysphonia is a complex speech disorder including stuttering, whispering, hoarseness, and halting, with possible behavioral/emotional etiology (Brodnitz, 1976) and debatable medical treatment (Strong, 1977). Boone (1971) has reported some success in spastic dysphonia with contingency management, but also Boone reported a high rate of remissions. Henschen and Burton (1978) successfully treated two cases with alternating frontalis and throat EMG feedback and progressive relaxation. Improved relaxation was achieved with slight improvement in speech. At termination of therapy, the authors conducted standard personality tests, revealing what they interpreted as rigidity and psychosomatic expression of anger. This may have represented an example of an incomplete behavioral medicine approach, in that treatment resulting in reduction of tension failed to generalize to improved speech function in the natural environment. Two apparent deficiencies in the Henschen and Burton (1978) treatment program were lack of adjunctive behavioral programming for associated problems and poor attempts to assess and program generalization in the natural environment.

Other applications of biofeedback and behavioral treatments for tension-related disorders that are beyond the scope of this chapter include: insomnia (Montgomery, Perkin, & Wise, 1975; Nicassio & Bootzin, 1974), bruxism (Solberg & Rugh, 1972), bronchial asthma (Davis, Saunders, Creer, & Chai, 1973; Kotee, Glans, Broncel, Edwards, & Crawford, 1978), hyperactivity (Braud, 1978) stuttering (Brady, 1971; Hanna, Wilfling, & McNeill, 1975), and undesired subvocal speech (Hardyck, Petrinovich, & Ellsworth, 1966). In these disorders, the relationship of tension to evident dysfunctions has often been suggested and the role of reduced tension was proposed as contributory to beneficial effect. However, firmly established evidence on mechanisms for tension effects and for treatment effects is lacking.

Tension-Induced Migraines

The term migraine is ultimately derived from the Greek *hemicrania,* referring to the frequently reported unilateral nature of the pain and associated neurological symptoms. The mechanisms causing migraine headaches are currently not fully understood, and they involve some interaction of emotional, neural, pharmacological, and vascular phenomena. The most frequently proposed mechanism of migraine includes a two-state alteration in intracranial and/or extracranial blood vessels, in which: (*a*) vessels initially constrict for a period of minutes, in some cases producing temporary neurological dysfunctions with symptoms such as visual scotomas or abberrations, dizziness, paresis, auditory disturbances, or somatosensory disturbances; and (*b*) vessels then dilate, causing severe pain, nausea, and an infrequently neurological sequela (Dalessio, 1972). The vascular nature of migraines has been proposed based on clinical and experimental studies in humans (Dalessio, 1972; Wolff, 1963). Recent findings have suggested that significant structural malformations may occur in intracranial blood vessels in chronic migraine patients (Hungerford, du Boulay, & Zilkha, 1976). Genetic factors also have been proposed, as strong family histories are frequently found (Ziegler, 1976). Traditional medical management has utilized drugs that produce vasoconstriction (such as ergotamine) and dietary prescriptions to avoid agents that have been proposed to precipitate migraines in some patients (such as histamine), all with moderate success (Dalessio, 1972; Lance, 1975). The incidence of migraine has been estimated to affect from 2 to 30% of the general population (Ziegler, 1976). Females by far have higher reported incidences, and the years from puberty to middle-age have the highest incidences (Dalessio, 1972; Lance, 1975).

During the past 10 years, several clinical researchers have reported successful reductions in migraines using relaxation training and/or biofeedback training for increasing skin temperature in the hands or increasing vasoconstriction in the scalp (Friar & Beatty, 1976; Sargent, Green, & Walters, 1973; Turin & Johnson, 1976; Wickramasekera, 1973). Proposed mechanisms for these reported successes involve increasing blood supply to peripheral vessels, diverting it from vessels in and around the head. Sufficient evidence supporting positive clinical outcomes has been collected by the Biofeedback Society of America Task Force on Migraine Headaches to warrant proposing behavioral and biofeedback treatments to be clinically efficacious alternatives or complements to traditional therapies (Diamond, 1978).

Approximately 10% of the migraine headache population also suffers from tension headaches (Lance, 1975), and a significant proportion suffers from migraines that may be precipitated by or exacerbated by excessive tension (Dalessio, 1972; Diamond, 1978). Additionally, recent evidence has suggested that vascular migraines may be responsive to frontalis EMG relaxation (Cohen, 1978).

Sargent, Green, and Walters (1972) have reported that the use of a combined temperature feedback and autogenic relaxation training procedure successfully alleviated headaches in not only 12 of 15 migraine, but also 2 of 4 tension headache patients. This effect has been ascribed to general relaxation and has been noted in surveying clinicians practicing behavioral medicine for headaches (Diamond, 1976, 1978).

As noted in the section on tension headaches, Phillips (1977) has evaluated EMG feedback treatment of tension and combined tension-migraine patients. Differences in the two groups were noted. Positive correlations between headache intensity and muscle tension levels were found for the tension headache cases, whereas low or negative correlations were found for patients with combined headaches. As noted previously, the details of procedures and data presented and the small numbers of patients in this study render its interpretation problematic. Phillips (1977) concludes that EMG feedback may not be effective for combined tension-migraine patients. A more important question would seem to be why EMG feedback did not successfully reduce tension levels in these patients, and whether or not effective reductions in tension would have produced better results.

In a recent study, Sturgis, Tollison, and Adams (1978) evaluated the utility of frontalis EMG and temporal artery blood volume pulse feedback in treating two patients with combined tension and migraine headaches. A multiple baseline across responses design was used. Remarkable specificity of treatment effect was found for type of biofeedback on type of headache in both patients. Migraines were reduced only after vascular feedback was begun, and tension headaches were reduced only after EMG feedback. No relaxation training was attempted, but both patients, after demonstrating control in the clinic, were instructed to practice the learned response for 10 minutes daily at home, and to practice whenever a headache was beginning.

In a previous study, Feurstein and Adams (1977) had reported similar specificity of results, with EMG biofeedback reducing headaches in two tension patients and vascular biofeedback reducing headaches in two migraine patients. In this study, no general relaxation training was used and patients were instructed to practice at home daily for 10 minutes by "reproducing the strategies" used in the clinic. The lack of EMG training effects on migraine patients and similar lack of vascular training on tension headache patients was significant.

Some prominent researchers have argued that biofeedback training for specific responses may produce changes only in targeted responses, whereas others have noted that multiple system changes may be effected by particular types of training (Schwartz, 1977). Many clinicians, including those in our own clinic, have reported using relaxation with or without EMG biofeedback to successfully reduce headache frequencies and/or intensities in combined tension-migraine patients. The training protocols used by Sturgis et al. (1978) and Feurstein and Adams (1977) may have produced an effect that was more specific than that generally achieved with relaxation training.

Although further research is needed on behavioral medicine treatments for migraine headaches, the current literature suggests that biofeedback or behavioral procedures aimed at producing general relaxation or targeted to reduce vascular or tension mechanisms are clinically effective in a large (50% or more) proportion of headache patients (Diamond, 1976, 1978).

Tics

Tics are frequent, sudden, rapid, unexpected, purposeless, stereotypic, motor or verbal responses. Tics may occur singly or in groups, and they have long been considered a controversial set of disorders with uncertain etiologies (Shapiro, Shapiro, Bruun, Sweet, Wayne, & Solomon, 1976). Certain subclasses, such as Gilles de la Tourette's syndrome have traditionally been considered to have neurological etiologies, and have recently received additional attention for possible etiologies and relationship to dystonia and torticollis (Eldridge, 1976). Traditional treatment modalities for tics have included psychotherapy, and pharmacological modalities, the latter of which has been reported helpful, but they are not without some risks (Shapiro, Shapiro, & Wayne, 1973).

Learning theory explanations for tics have been proposed by Yates (1958). Control of tics has been achieved using aversive contingencies (Rafi, 1962), reinforcing low rates of tics (Rosen & Wesner, 1973), combined aversive and positive contingencies (Doleys & Kurtz, 1974), procedures designed to correct habit-behaviors (Azrin & Nunn, 1973), and combination relaxation and self-monitoring procedures (Thomas, Abrams, & Johnson, 1971).

In a recent case study in the Hopkins Behavioral Medicine Center, Varni, Boyd, and Cataldo (in press), have successfully utilized a combined contingency management and self-control program to reduce tics in a seven year old with a diagnosis of minimal brain dysfunction and hyperactivity. This youngster had a history of multiple tics from Year 2, and was developing a profile that fit Gilles de la Tourette's syndrome (Shapiro, et al., 1976). He initially presented four tics, including facial grimaces with squinting, shoulder shrugging, rump protrusions, and vocalizing a noise, "huh." After operationalizing these behaviors and obtaining baseline in clinic and home settings, a behavioral treatment program was implemented, consisting of: teaching the child to label and self-monitor his own tics, allowing access to preferred activities contingent upon an increasingly lower rate of facial tics, and applying time-out contingent upon a high rate of facial tics. The child's parents were taught in turn to identify and record facial tics and to apply the treatment program; parental reliability was checked in the clinic.

Figures 1 and 2 illustrate the results of treatment, which showed successful remission of not only the targeted facial, but also the other tics, in both environments, through a 32-week follow-up. Also noteworthy was a reversal of the decreasing trend, with the initial reversal to baseline condition. In addition to demonstrating the effectiveness of a behavioral treatment package, the finding of response generalization in this case is worthy of special note. Generalization of treatment effects across responses has important implications for cost-efficiency and mechanisms of treatments (Wahler, 1975), and it has also been demonstrated to be important in neurological disorders (Bird & Cataldo, 1978).

Blepharospasm is a ticlike winking involving frontalis, orbicularis oculi, and occasionally associated facial muscles. Psychotherapy and psychopharmacological treatments have been reported successful for blepharospasm (Reckless, 1972). Sharpe (1974) has reported success of a well-sequenced behavioral treatment program utilizing relaxation training, practicing blinking and reinforcing responses incompatible with blepharospasms. Peck (1977) has found that frontalis-orbicularis

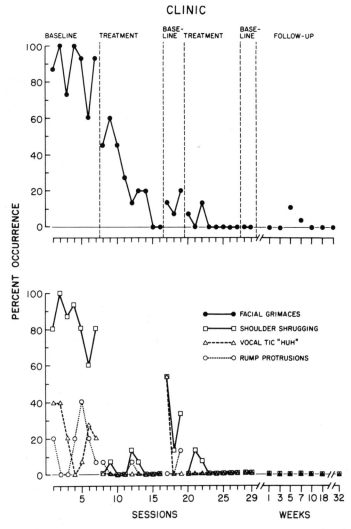

FIGURE 1. Percent occurrence of the tic behaviors across successive baseline and treatment reversals in the clinic. Only facial grimace tics were directly treated (Varni, Boyd, & Cataldo, in press).

oculi EMG feedback was successful in reducing blepharospasms in a 50-year-old woman with a several-year history. Follow-up to four months indicated continuing success in this case.

We have recently experienced successful reduction in blepharospasms in a 27-year-old adult with mild cerebral palsy, treated with both biofeedback and relaxation training procedures. Of note in this case was the patient's clear discrimination of anxiety-provoking social stimuli that drastically increased involuntary blepharospamodic and choreoathetoid responses. The treatment program utilized systematic desensitization, including *in vivo* desensitization to novel social stimuli in the clinic. Success has been maintained for over three months with home relaxation exercises.

HOME

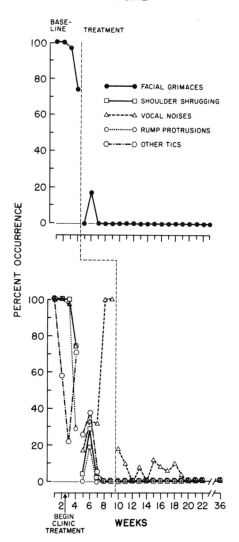

FIGURE 2. Percent occurrence of the tic behaviors during baseline and treatment in the home. Facial grimaces were initially treated, then vocal noises. Shoulder shrugging, rump protrusions, and other tics were not directly treated (Varni, Boyd, & Cataldo, in press).

An added component of assertion and self-confidence problems were also addressed with behavioral strategies, and by report they have been important for success.

As noted in other disorders, the contribution of biofeedback procedures in treating tics or ticlike responses as compared to behavioral programs is currently questionable and should be addressed in further studies. Several behavioral strategies, including self-monitoring, contingency management, and relaxation training, all deserve consideration as potentially effective treatments for tics.

Spasmodic Torticollis

Spasmodic torticollis is a disorder affecting the neck and/or shoulder muscles that produces spasmodic or sustained twisting of the neck and head to one side. Podivinsky (1968) has detailed several types of torticollis, according to the particular groups of neck and/or shoulder muscles involved. Neurological and psychiatric etiologies have been proposed, but causes and mechanisms remain uncertain (Podivinsky, 1968). Cases are diagnosed as organic or functional based on histories and clinical exam (Couch, 1976). Traditional treatments have included neurosurgery (Cooper, 1964; Sorenson & Hamby, 1966) and pharmacology (Gilbert, 1972), with varying success (Mears, 1970).

Brierly (1967) proposed that torticollis might be considered to be a habit and reported successful treatment of two patients using contingent aversive stimuli (shock), detected by a head position monitor. One patient was symptom-free after only 2 sessions and the second was largely symptom-free after 10. The generalization and long-term maintenance of this procedure was remarkable, despite little reported systematic programming for these effects.

Cleeland (1973) provided auditory EMG biofeedback and mild electric shock for sternocleidomastoid spasms in 10 patients, some with long histories of refractoriness to traditional treatments. Six of these 10 showed long-lasting benefits of several months' duration, whereas in 2 others initial gains were not maintained. Although his procedures and data were not well detailed, Cleeland (1973) also reported that in clinic trials in 8 of 10 patients, shock produced a significant effect above that of feedback alone.

Brudny, Grynbaum, and Korein (1974) reported successful EMG biofeedback treatment of nine spasmodic torticollis patients with durations of 9 months to 15 years and refractoriness to previous treatments. Four of these patients had additional organic symptoms, suggesting that their disorder was a segmental dystonia (see below). Specific procedures included providing feedback for sternocleidomastoid or trapezius muscle groups, or both. However, training procedures and home exercises were not well detailed. Seven of the 10 patients were reported to have voluntary (no-feedback) control of spasmodic muscles and significant clinical improvements. Three were still in training at the end of the study. In subsequent reports updating their original paper, this clinic has reported significant benefits for additional patients (Brudny, Korein, Levidow, Grynbaum, Lieberman, & Friedmann, 1974; Brudny, Korein, Grynbaum, Friedmann, Weinstein, Sachs-Frankel, & Belandres, 1976). The Brudny group (e.g., Brudny, et al., 1976) have also noted that some patients need continuing infrequent EMG biofeedback training sssions to maintain therapeutic effects.

Recently, Jankel (in press) has reported successful treatment of a 39-year-old female with spasmodic torticollis of 12 years duration and previous resistances to medical treatments. The study is noteworthy for its demonstration of EMG feedback effects using both a reversal design and bidirectional training for increases and decreases in tension while monitoring affected left and unaffected right sternocleidomastoids. Unfortunately, follow-up was only available for a period of weeks, although the patient was reported to be symptom-free at that time.

The research to date strongly argues for effects of behavioral and biofeedback treatments. Based on collated reports from a number of prominent clinics, biofeedback has been estimated to be effective in about 60% of referred cases (Fernando & Basmajian, 1978). Relaxation training applied to spasmodic torticollis appears to have been somewhat neglected in recent years. Especially in light of the recognized exacerbation of torticollis in stressful situations (Podivinsky, 1968), there is a clear rationale for utilizing relaxation training, and further clinical research should address this question.

Spinal Cord Injuries

Spinal injuries, depending upon the level and completeness of the lesion, produce complicated and severe muscular, and in some cases, autonomic dysfunctions (Brucker & Ince, 1977). Ince (1976) has discussed the utility of behavioral treatments in rehabilitation of spinal cord injuries. A following section in this chapter on smooth muscle disorders describes behavioral and biofeedback approaches to bowel and bladder disorders in these patients. Biofeedback has also been evaluated in treating neuromuscular dysfunctions in spinal cord injuries.

Jacobs and Felton (1969) have compared the relaxation of trapezius muscles in 10 normals and 10 patients with "neck injuries" with and without visual (oscillocope) EMG feedback. Using feedback, the patients were able to significantly reduce trapezius EMG. This study was experimental in intent and did not attempt to produce or to assess clinical gains. A lack of information on patient pathophysiology, procedural details, and controls renders interpretation somewhat difficult. Some reviewers have considered these patients to have peripheral nerve disorders (Keefe & Surwit, 1978).

Owen (1974) described a paraplegia due to an incomplete spinal lesion, and she reported successful recovery of some motor functions such as improved ability to stand and to pedal an exercise bike after several months of biofeedback treatment. Although her report was promising, especially in light of her 10-year history of no recovery of function, neither the role of feedback nor the specific effects on various muscles were described in detail.

Brudny et al. (1974, 1976) have reported successful treatment of two C-5 and C-6 quadriplegics with some function but severe spasticity in the arms. One patient reportedly had sufficient response to EMG feedback training such that spasticity in one arm was reduced and functions significantly increased, including typing and manipulating a lever to drive an electric wheelchair. However, the Brudny et al. (1974, 1976) reports do not offer sufficient information on subjects, procedures, or data, and they do not assess the contribution of biofeedback to therapeutic effects.

Dunn, Davis, and Webster (1978) have reported successful training for reduced EMG levels in rectus abdominus (one case) and gastrocnemius (two cases) muscles in patients with spinal cord injuries (quadriplegics). Using within session baseline-feedback-baseline reversals, decreases in EMG microvolts and muscular spasms were noted during feedback periods. The extent and maintenance of gains outside of the training environment were not reported.

As in the case of other disorders, more controlled evidence is needed to judge the clinical efficacy of biofeedback in spinal injuries. Also important to acceptance of biofeedback treatments in these disorders will be development of sound neurophysiological rationales. For example, the proposal that patients with "complete" spinal lesions might respond to biofeedback training (Dunn, David, & Webster, 1978) is neurologically difficult. However, there are experimental data on conditioning motor functions in "spinal" animals (Buerger & Fennessy, 1970).

In addition to skeletal muscular disorders in spinal injuries, behavioral treatments have been applied to a variety of other physiological and psychological problems as reviewed by Ince, Brucker, and Alba (1976). The potential for growth in behavioral medicine in this area is enormous.

Cerebral Trauma

A significant number of persons are estimated to be affected by cerebral trauma each year. For example, approximately 80% of the estimated deaths due to automobile accidents involve brain injury and 60% of the 1.5 million annual strokes produce physical problems related to spasticity (Hook, 1976; Thompson & Klonoff, 1976). Spasticity due to cerebral trauma (or upper motor neuron syndromes) may be produced by injuries, anoxia, cerebrovascular accidents (CVAs), and diseases affecting the CNS (Vinken & Bruyn, 1976). Posttraumatic motor disorders often follow predictable patterns of recovery, with hemiplegias resolving in proximal to distal sequence to some end point after stroke and many other forms of trauma (Licht, 1975). Associated psychological and emotional problems are evident in significant proportions of posttrauma patients, and design of rehabilitation programs must obviously address such issues (Anderson & Kottke, 1978). Mechanisms of spasticity have traditionally been ascribed to motor cortex or pyramidal tract dysfunction, although both clinical and experimental evidence challenges the "pyramidal-extrapyramidal" dichotomy as too simplistic (Bucy, 1957), and "extrapyramidal" symptoms have been noted in about 10% of this population (Arne, 1976). Problems in the definition of spasticity and traditional medical therapies for spasticity have been cogently presented by Landau (1974).

Designing treatments for muscular dysfunction due to stroke often requires consideration of a number of associated deficits. Postcerebrovascular accident patients often present cognitive, perceptual, and higher-level motor difficulties (e.g., apraxia). Recent reviews discussing issues and methods in stroke rehabilitation are available to therapists focusing on motor function (Anderson & Kottke, 1978; Lichts, 1975; Mossman, 1976). Several reports have described successful reduction in spasticity or improvement in voluntary muscle control in patients with cerebral spasticity through biofeedback (Amato, Hermsmeyer, & Kleinman, 1973; Andrews, 1964; Brudny et al., 1974, 1976; Johnson & Garton, 1973; Nafpilotis, 1976). These studies are characterized as clinically promising but poorly controlled.

A few reports have attempted more systematic evaluations of biofeedback effects on spasticity and warrant closer review. Harrison and Connolly (1971), using unspecified amounts of bidirectional training, reported that spastics eventually reached normal levels of EMG control. These procedures are not described in quantitative or replicable terms, and their data are reported in complicated trials-to-criteria format, which renders interpretation of the effectiveness of controls on results difficult. Lee, Hill, Johnston, and Smiehorowski (1976), counterbalanced conditions of true EMG feedback, false feedback, and no feedback. In this study hemiplegic subjects were divided into two subgroups according to age, after the study was completed, when it was noted that data changed over sessions as a function of the subject's age. In view of this strategy, reconsiderations of the proposed positive results seem warranted. No significant differences due to feedback were reported on data for the entire group of hemiplegics. Swaan, van Wieringen and Fokkema (1974), using counterbalanced conditions of EMG feedback and physical therapy treatments within sessions, presented descriptive EMG data and quantitative muscle function data (angle of knee at which the peroneus longus muscle's spike activity was at least 7/sec.) which was reported as indicating significant differences in favor of biofeedback. However, their statistical calculations as presented are more accurately described as approaching significant differences in improvement favoring the biofeedback group.

Basmajian, Takebe, Kukulka, and Narayan (1975) have reported a controlled study comparing the effects of physical therapy procedures with and without EMG biofeedback in 20 patients with foot drop due to cerebrovascular accidents. Mean data for strength in ankle dorsiflexion and active range of motion showed significant differences in improvement favoring the biofeedback group. However, it is interesting to note that $\frac{5}{10}$ of the subjects in the physical-therapy-only group showed improvements in strength and $\frac{4}{10}$ of the subjects in range of motion about equal to the average improvements in the biofeedback groups. No statistical significances were reported. In follow-up testing, biofeedback patients reportedly exhibited better retention of ankle dorsiflexion, with three able to walk with a short leg brace at follow-up. In general, this paper is methodologically sound and presents scientifically acceptable conclusions, but the conclusions raise questions about the importance of biofeedback in therapeutic success.

Wannstedt and Herman (1978) have recently reported on the use of feedback from a device called a Limb Load Monitor, which is sensitive to weight applied by the foot. Symmetry of stance improved initially in 23 of 30 hemiplegic patients and 14 of 20 who completed training maintained symmetrical stance one month after training. The authors noted that performance in the initial session predicted long-term success.

The literature on biofeedback training for spasticity of cerebral trauma may be characterized as promising, but needing additional controlled studies. Therapists who attempt to use biofeedback for motor disturbances in traumatic spasticity should be cautioned by discussions of Harrison (1977) and Mroczek, Halpern, and McHugh (1978) who have noted that counterproductive effects may be obtained. In preliminary clinical research in our laboratory, we have found that a combined EMG feedback and contingency program improved motor control of patients with cerebral spasticity (Bird, Parker, & Cataldo, 1979), but more extensive study of the role of contingency programs using behavioral shaping are indicated.

Extrapyramidal Disorders

The term movement disorders has been commonly used to describe disorders of normal posture and/or movement produced by damage to the "extrapyramidal" motor systems of the cerebellum and/or basal ganglia (Cooper, 1969; Vinken &

Bruyn, 1976.) Included are the variants of Parkinson's disease, chorea, dystonia, choreoathetoid cerebral palsy, hemiballismus and cerebellar disorders (such as intention tremor), among others. Spasmodic torticollis, discussed in detail previously, is also often considered in this category (Podivinsky, 1968). These disorders are characterized by involuntary movements or posturing, elevations in tone, and lack of normal synergistic muscle action around joints. Treatments have included traditional neurosurgery (Cooper, 1969), pharmacology (Fahn & Calne, 1978; Yahr & Duvoisin, 1968) and physical therapy (Wolf, 1969). Little documented success has been reported in these disorders, with the exception of levodopa treatment in Parkinson's disease (Fahn & Calne, 1978). Mechanisms for extrapyramidal movement disorders have been admitted to be very poorly understood and the ascription of pathophysiology to "extrapyramidal" systems has been challenged (Bucy, 1957; Myers, 1953).

Biofeedback and behavioral treatments have been evaluated for improving motor control in several extrapyramidal movement disorders with considerable promise. Brudny et al. (1974, 1976) have reported successful EMG feedback treatment of four patients with dystonia. As in their report of other disorders, lack of controls and procedural details render interpretation of the role of feedback difficult.

We have previously reported successful EMG feedback training of a 20 year old with dystonia musculorum deformans (autosomal recessive subtype) to reduce tension in forehead and facial muscles and improve facial posture (Bird & Cataldo, 1978). Controlled single subject analyses clearly indicated the contribution of biofeedback to relaxation, and generalization of effects across muscle groups was found. Reliable data indicated clinically significant effects occurred in the extratraining environment. Our experience with dystonics has suggested that biofeedback may offer significant therapeutic benefit when used as a component of interdisciplinary management of dystonia (Batshaw & Haslam, 1976). This disorder is particularly difficult from a behavioral perspective, as it progresses in spurts and produces severe physical handicaps with resulting psychoemotional sequelae. However, given the acknowledged problems in traditional therapies (Eldridge & Fahn, 1976) and promise of EMG feedback studies to date, biofeedback offers an attractive addition to the management repertoire.

Nusselt and Legewie (1975) have reported reduction in tremor during feedback (from tremor) in two patients with Parkinsonism. Also, Petajan and Jarcho (1975) have utilized EMG biofeedback training for single motor unit control to study levodopa effects in Parkinson's patients. Netsell and Cleeland (1973) have reported on successful reductions in hypertonicity of facial muscles in a 64-year-old patient with Parkinson's and a status of six years post-bilateral thalamotomies. The patient responded dramatically in the first session, and facial posture and dysarthria were significantly clinically improved.

Clearly, more clinical research in this population with a variety of behavioral treatments is suggested. This is an especially fruitful area to assess interactions with pharmacological treatments, which have significantly reduced mortality and modestly remediated motor control over the past decade (Fahn & Calne, 1978).

Cerebral Palsy

Cerebral Palsy (CP) can be defined as a nonprogressive motor disorder occurring in pre- or perinatal periods (Keats, 1965). Major subcategories include spastic and extrapyramidal (choreoathetoid) CP (Keats, 1965). Spastic cerebral palsy has been considered to be due to cerebral trauma or anoxia during pre- or perinatal periods and may take the form of hemiplegia, paraplegia, or quadriplegia (Crothers & Paine, 1969). Extrapyramidal or choreoathetoid CP has been similarly associated with early brain damage, but the nature of the movement disorder is very different than that of spastic CP, and intelligence is often spared (Keats, 1965). Major subtypes of choreoathetoid CP include choreiform, characterized by rapid, jerky movements, most frequently in distal limb and/or facial muscles, and athetoid, characterized by slow, writhing movements in proximal limbs, trunk, and facial muscles. Traditional therapies include: (*a*) orthopedic surgery to correct or improve bone, joint, or tendon problems; (*b*) pharmacology; (*c*) neurosurgery; and (*d*) physical therapy (Vining, Accardo, Rubenstein, Farrell, & Roizen, 1976). Success of these therapies has indicated much room for improvement (Wolfe, 1969). Physical therapy, which often involves procedural components of conditioning, has been primarily criticized for poor documentation of efficacy (Wolfe, 1969; Wright & Nicholson, 1973).

Several studies have shown that behavior modification may improve motor functions in children with CP (Block, 1978; Garber, 1974; Martin & Sachs, 1973; Rugel, Mattingly, & Eichinger, 1971; Sachs & Mayhall, 1971; 1972). Several authors have also utilized feedback devices that provide signals and/or reinforcement when an involuntary movement or posture occurs (Ball, McCrady, & Hart, 1975; Halpern, Kottke, & Burrill, 1970; Harris, Spelman, & Hymer, 1974; Spearing & Poppen, 1974; Wooldridge & Russell, 1976).

Finley, Niman, Standley, and Ender (1976) have reported using EMG biofeedback to reduce frontalis muscle tension in six adults with athetoid CP. Six weeks of training produced improved speech in four mildly retarded patients and less improvement in two severely retarded patients. A second study by Finley, Niman, Standley, and Wansley (1977) represents an approximation of a controlled within-subjects experiment. The subject population was well defined, the procedures were described in replicable terms, and an ABAB quasi-reversal design was employed. In the study, six week periods of EMG feedback were separated by a six week period of no treatment. The design might be more approximately termed a BAB, with the actual sequence having been test-treatment-test-no treatment and no observations-test-treatment-test. EMG and motor function results were quantified and well described, and significant improvements in speech and motor functions were found after treatment conditions.

In our laboratory, using single subject research designs, the effects of EMG feedback training on EMG activity (Cataldo, Bird, & Cunningham, 1978), and/or involuntary and functional responses in extratreatment environments (Bird, Cataldo, Parker, Baker, & Francis, 1979), have been assessed as beneficial to patients with choreoathetoid cerebral palsy. However, additional data have indicated that contingency management can be used to improve some functional responses (Bourland, Bird, Ciulla, & Cataldo, unpublished manuscript).

The issues involved in selecting treatment strategies and integrating behavioral procedures with physical therapy programs have been discussed by Harrison (1975, 1978). This area appears to be most fruitful, and especially offers potential benefits to the choreoathetoid population who have been refractory to other treatments (Vining et al., 1976).

Peripheral Nerve Disorders

Peripheral neuromuscular disorders may be divided into categories of myopathies, neuropathies, and injuries. Depending upon etiology and pathophysiology, a variety of medical and surgical treatments are indicated (Griggs & Moxley, 1977). Biofeedback procedures have been utilized in neuromuscular reeducation in several of the peripheral disorders, although these reports may be characterized as showing clinical promise without presenting controlled evidence.

Marinacci (1968), a pioneer in EMG feedback in neuromuscular rehabilitation, reported improvement of motor function in cases with Bell's Palsy, poliomyelitis, neuromuscular substitution after injury, regeneration after injury, causalgia, and reversible blockage of peripheral nerves. Although patients, procedures, and results in these cases were not fully described, they represent most promising reports based on reasonable neurophysiological foundations.

Brudny et al. (1974, 1976) have reported that EMG feedback treatment "potentiated" the rate and degree of recovery of muscular performance in six patients with peripheral nerve injuries. Although the abbreviated descriptions of patients, procedures, and results render detailed evaluation impossible, the nature and duration of the problems were such that the reported positive results were most encouraging.

Booker, Rubow, and Coleman (1969) reported successful training of a patient to control unilateral surgically reinnervated facial muscles. By recording and displaying EMG from the normal contralateral muscles, and training the patient to match the normal EMG with EMG from the reinnervated side, the patient's facial tone and movements and blinking were clinically improved. Although controls were lacking, the case was notable for ingenuity in training and dramatic clinical results. Jankel (1978) has subsequently used a similar biofeedback procedure to improve facial muscle control in a patient with Bell's Palsy, by training the affected muscles to match EMG levels on the unaffected side of the face. A follow-up at one year has indicated continuing maintenance of effects (personal communication). Swaan, van Wieringer, and Fokkema (1974) trained three patients with poliomyelitis to reduce excessive peroneus muscle activity during knee extension. After six 25-minute sessions spread over three weeks, all patients showed significant increases in size of the angle of knee extension attainable without excessive peroneus EMG activity. Data on maintenance were not reported.

Recently Cohen, Crouch, and Thompson (1977) reported EMG biofeedback to be a useful adjunct in physical therapy for Gullian-Barre syndrome. However, because the report was based upon a case study with no controls, and recovery from the syndrome has been notoriously unpredictable, it is questionable that EMG feedback provided any direct therapeutic benefit. The authors appropriately cited the benefits of EMG feedback as: (a) allowing quantitative assessment of progress;

(b) allowing the therapist to work simultaneously with more than one patient; and (c) maintaining patient interest.

The current literature on biofeedback and behavioral treatments for peripheral neuromuscular disorders is sparse and uncontrolled, but generally promising. Further controlled studies will be critical to progress. Additionally, as in the case of spinal injuries, mechanisms for potential biofeedback effects are currently speculative, and will require careful study and development for neurological and rehabilitative medicine audiences. For example, Marinacci (1968) has presented an excellent rationale for neuromuscular reeducation in muscular disorders evident after some temporary neurophysiological problem has been reversed or compensated.

Disorders of Smooth Muscle

Fecal incontinence, a common sequela of spinal injuries, neurological diseases, or spina bifida (congential open spine) is a problem that dramatically and adversely affects the lives of many individuals (Schuster, 1977). In recent years, biofeedback has been reported to be of great benefit for improving bowel control in these patients. Kohlenberg (1973) in a case study of an incontinent adolescent, utilized visual feedback and monetary rewards for increases in external anal sphincter pressure. Results indicated significant reductions in soiling and obviated surgical treatment. Engel, Nikoomanesh, and Schuster (1974), employing a similar strategy, found significant and long-lasting improvement in sphincter control and continence in six ambulatory patients with various disorders.

Briefly, the training procedures developed by Engel et al. (1974) and since that have proven extremely effective (Schuster, 1977) involve monitoring responses of internal and external sphincters on pressure balloons while presenting a simulated fecal stimulus (rectal distention) with a third balloon. The procedures involve a combination of discrimination training for improved sensitivity to rectal distention and shaping, increasing voluntary contractions of the external sphincter using feedback, and social and sometimes tangible rewards. The most impressive aspect of this procedure is that many patients experience complete continence after only a few training sessions. The beneficial results of this treatment appear to be largely determined by neurological status, and they are predicted by the patient's response to initial discrimination training.

Traditional treatments of neurogenic disorders of bladder control, which affects a large population, have recently been critically reviewed, with the suggestion that "mobilization of innate biologic resources is the best form of management" (Abramson, 1976, p. 20). Behavioral treatments not involving chronic catheterization would seem to be most helpful additions to the traditional repertoire.

Pearne, Zigelbaum, and Peyser (1977) have recently reported a successful EMG frontalis relaxation treatment for a 27-year-old woman with a history of urinary retention that was resistant to several medical and surgical procedures. Home relaxation was also employed, in which the patient was instructed to "do the same thing" as in EMG training. Frontalis EMG, residual urine, and number of urinary accidents all dropped significantly over an eight-month treatment, while voluntary urinations increased. At four months posttreatment, effects were maintained.

Data on the relationship of other muscles to bladder control have suggested alternative considerations for behavioral treatments, including abdominal muscle relaxation (LaJoie, Cosgrove, & Jones, 1976) and stretching of anal sphincter muscles (Donovan, Clowers, Kivial, & Marci, 1977). Ince, Brucker, and Alba (1977) have recently reported successful classical conditioning of two patients with lumbar spinal injuries and neurogenic bladders to achieve independent bladder functioning. Their procedures involved using mild electrical stimulation to abdominal muscles as an unconditioned stimulus and a mild electrical stimulation of the thigh as a conditioned stimulus. Independence in bladder functioning was reported improved in both cases, as the patients were able to apply the conditioned stimulus themselves to produce micturition.

Recently in our Center, Russo, and Fuller (1978) have found contingency management techniques to improve emptying of the bladder in children with bladder dysfunctions of unknown etiology. These data, and our clinic experiences using Foxx and Azrin's (1973) contingency-based toilet-training procedures to successfully train urinary continence in cases strongly suspected to have neurogenic bladders, argue for further examination of contingency programs for urinary continence in patients with bladder control problems.

ISSUES IN BEHAVIORAL TREATMENTS

As Basmajian (1976) has noted in reviewing EMG biofeedback, behavioral treatments for muscular disorders require expertise in several areas. It is not the purpose of this chapter to provide detailed information on behavior therapy, neurology, psychiatry, electromyography, nor on basic nor clinical neurophysiology. A brief list of pertinent knowledge and skills that we have found useful is proved in Table 3. Other authors and the Biofeedback Society of America have provided detailed guidelines on competency in therapist or researcher use of electromyographic biofeedback (Fernando & Basmajian, 1978).

The philosophy of behavioral medicine applied to this area is worth restating. The nonmedical clinician or researcher should be acquainted with sufficient knowledge and skill in areas of medicine and technology, or should have access to those areas through consulting staff. The reasons for these areas of expertise are a clear patient protection and a choice of appropriate therapy. For example, consider the case of a patient referred to a behavioral medicine clinic for treatment of headaches. The behavior therapist who assesses and treats such a patient should have sufficient knowledge of and confidence in the referring physician's diagnostic skills in ruling out organic causes of the headaches (e.g., brain tumor) that require alternative medical treatments, or the therapist should seek additional diagnostics. Risks for both the behavior therapist and the patient will be reduced if: (a) the therapist is sufficiently skilled to question a nonorganic diagnosis (this does *not* suggest the opposite—that a behavior therapist should be confident to *make* or *confirm* a medical diagnosis); (b) the therapist is knowledgeable about the methods and skills of the referring physician in making such diagnoses; and (c) medical consultation and supervision is routinely available to the behavior therapist. In our experience, the use of all three has helped to ensure ethical and appropriate treatment. Moreover, a written statement of clinic policy for both patient and referring

Table 3. Knowledge and Skills Useful in
Behavioral and Biofeedback
Treatment of Muscular
Disorders

Electrophysiology
Patient safety
Artefact detection

Electromyography
Electrode placement
Normal activity

Neurology and rehabilitation medicine
Pathological activity
Neuropathophysiology
Clinical diagnostics
Alternative treatments
Adjunctive treatments

Psychiatry and clinical psychology
Primary or associated psychiatric disorders
Hysterical (conversion) symptoms
Alternative treatments

Behavioral medicine
Functional assessment
Behavioral and biofeedback treatments
Program evaluation
Maintenance programs

physician helps to define the responsibilities of the clinic staff, which are not to make or confirm medical diagnoses, and are based on the presumption that a referring physician's diagnosis is accurate.

In many instances, medical and technical information will also be critical to designing effective treatment programs. For example, in treating patients with hemiplegia due to stroke, knowledge about the neuromuscular deficits, their predicted recovery rates, the steps that must necessarily be programmed to move the patient toward normal functioning, and associated neurological and psychological difficulties in poststroke patients should all be considered in designing an effective treatment program (Lichts, 1975). Close collaboration with physical therapists is obviously most desirable for the neurological disorders.

While a behaviorist treating muscular disorders should possess medical and technical knowledge, as mentioned previously, the most important set of skills should be a comprehensive repertoire in behavior therapy. Many of our adolescent and adult cases for which biofeedback training is the primary mode of therapy require some additional form of behavior therapy. For example, poor assertiveness and lack of self-confidence found in mildly involved cerebral palsied clients have been remediated with assertion training based on behavioral rehearsal. In several cases of neurological movement disorders, motor control has been found to be adversely affected by novel persons entering the treatment environment, and adequate treatment has required desensitization (c.f. Bird & Cataldo, 1978). Stress, conflicts, and other problems in the social environment may require programming for successful transfer of learned muscular control from clinic to home environment.

A full repertoire of skills in behavioral assessment and treatment appears to be important for competence in this area. This point is not as trivial as it may initially seem, as indicated by three current trends. (a) The predominance of simplistic behavioral treatment programs for muscular disorders in the literature; (b) The emphasis on medical and technical aspects of procedures in most training workshops for behaviorists; and (c) The current lack of published data on behavioral, as opposed to physiological, aspects of treatment. The importance of providing a program for the whole patient has been stressed in clinically oriented reviews of specific disorders (Diamond, 1978; Fernando, 1978; Fordyce, 1976). Moreover, this issue will acquire added importance as the very positive trend of medical professionals using behavioral techniques increases, and as behaviorists working within the various medical disciplines participate in service and training.

FUTURE DIRECTIONS

Progress in behavioral medicine for muscular disorders will depend upon continued demonstrations of treatment efficacy and continued development of rationales for behavioral treatments. This chapter has surveyed the literature extensively, and is meant to serve as a resource, and not a critical review. However, in light of the repeated cautions and critical issues noted in previous sections, a brief discussion of a few salient points appears merited.

As indicated throughout this chapter, the literature can be characterized as clinically promising but generally lacking in controlled outcome studies. The relative contributions of reinforcement contingencies, biofeedback, and other procedures have often been left unclear. Generalization and maintenance of treatment effects have been particularly neglected. Our research efforts to date have been directed at: (a) documenting contributions of EMG biofeedback to muscle control in the laboratory; and (b) studying response and stimulus generalization processes in EMG biofeedback training. Initial studies in cerebral palsy (Cataldo et al., 1978; Bird et al., 1979) and dystonia (Bird & Cataldo, 1978) found evidence for biofeedback effects in the laboratory, and evidence for both generalization across responses (i.e., improved control of one muscle group was accompanied by improvements in control of others) and stimulus situations (i.e., to no feedback conditions in the laboratory, and to extralaboratory situations). Further research on generalization will also provide insight into mechanisms for biofeedback or behavior therapy effects.

Also noted throughout the chapter were rationales for behavioral and/or biofeedback effects in muscular disorders. The behavioral and biofeedback principles developed in other areas have been applied to muscular disorders with reasonable arguments. However, neurophysiological bases for behavioral medicine treatments have been speculative (cf. Finley et al., 1977). In our experience, the traditional medical audience has responded well to a data-based documentation of treatment effects. It is widely recognized that traditional treatments are often ineffective, and some carry severe risks. It is also widely recognized that current treatments fail because mechanisms of most muscular disorders are so poorly understood (cf: Eldridge & Fahn, 1976). Research on behavioral aspects of these disorders will therefore have two benefits: acceptance by interdisciplinary medical audiences of the value of behavioral medicine treatments, and advancements in the understanding of neurophysiological mechanisms of muscular disorders.

SUMMARY

In 1907 Sir William Gowers, a renowned neurologist, published a manuscript entitled "The Borderland of Epilepsy" (Williams, 1975). In the paper, he discussed difficulties in diagnosing and treating seizures and related disturbances of consciousness as neurological or psychiatric phenomena. These difficulties are still acknowledged in current medicine (Williams, 1975). The "Borderland" of neurology and psychiatry also contains most muscular disorders, for which definitive organic or psychiatric diagnostics and efficacious treatments are sorely lacking. It is apparent that during the past decade, behaviorists have entered both the borderland of neurology and psychiatry, and neurology proper, treating psychosomatic, borderland, and neurological muscular disorders with most encouraging results.

This chapter has reviewed the first generation of behavioral medicine for muscular disorders and found the results to be clinically promising. Current behavioral and biofeedback treatments offer comparable outcomes with far smaller risks than traditional therapies. Further progress will require increased scientific evidence on efficacy, generalization, and maintenance of behavioral treatments, and development of treatment rationales that are both behaviorally and physiologically sound. An increasing role for behavioral medicine in treatment for and research on muscular disorders is clearly predicted.

ACKNOWLEDGMENTS

Preparation of this manuscript and research reported were supported by Grants #917 and MC-R-24014 of the Maternal and Child Health Service, and #R-294-78, United Cerebral Palsy Foundation, and the resources of the Behavioral Medicine Center, Department of Neurology, Department of Psychiatry and Behavioral Sciences, and John F. Kennedy Institute of the Johns Hopkins University School of Medicine.

The authors gratefully acknowledge the assistance of Margaret Weigel in preparing this manuscript.

REFERENCES

Abramson, A. S. Management of the neurogenic bladder in perspective. *Archives of Physical Medicine and Rehabilitation*, 1976, **57**, 197–201.

Agerberg, G., & Carlsson, G. E. Functional disorders of the masticatory system, I: Distribution of symptoms according to age and sex as judged by investigation by questionnaire. *Acta Odontologica Scandinavica,* 1972, **30**, 597–613.

Amato, A., Hermsmeyer, C. A., & Kleinman, K. M. Use of electromyographic feedback to increase inhibitory control of spastic muscles. *Physical Therapy,* 1973, **53**, 1063–1066.

Anderson, T. P., & Kottke, F. J. Stroke rehabilitation: A reconsideration of some common attitudes. *Archives of Physical Medicine and Rehabilitation,* 1978, **59**, 175–181.

Andrews, T. Neuromuscular re-education of the hemiplegic with the aid of the electromyograph. *Archives of Physical Medicine and Rehabilitation,* 1964, **45**, 530–532.

Arieti, S. (Ed). *American handbook of psychiatry, vol. 4: Organic disorders and psychosomatic medicine.* New York: Basic Books, 1975.

Arne, L. Post-traumatic cerebellar signs and symptoms. In P. Vinken & G. Bruyn (Eds.), *Handbook of clinical neurology, vol. 23: Injuries to brain and skull part I.* New York: Elsevier, 1976.

Azrin, N. H., & Nunn, R. G. Habit-reversal: A method of eliminating nervous habits and tics. *Behaviour Research and Therapy,* 1973, **11**, 619–628.

Ball, T. S., McCrady, R. E., & Hart, A. D. Automated reinforcement of head posture in two cerebral palsied retarded children. *Perceptual and Motor Skills,* 1975, **40**, 619–622.

Barrett, B. H. Reduction in rate of multiple tics by free operant conditioning methods. *Journal of Nervous and Mental Disorders,* 1962, **135**, 187–195.

Basmajian, J. V. Cyclobenzaprine hydrochloride effect on skeletal muscle spasm in the lumbar region and neck: Two double-blind controlled clinical and laboratory studies. *Archives of Physical Medicine and Rehabilitation,* 1978, **59**, 58–63.

Basmajian, J. V. Facts vs. myths about EMG biofeedback. *Biofeedback and Self Regulation,* 1976, **4**, 369–371.

Basmajian, J. V. *Biofeedback: Principles and practice for clinicians.* Baltimore: Williams & Wilkins, 1978.

Basmajian, J. V., & Super, G. A. Dantrolene sodium in treatment of spasticity. *Archives of Physical Medicine and Rehabilitation,* 1973, **54**, 60–65.

Basmajian, J. V. Takebe, K., Kukulka, C. G., & Narayan, M. G. Biofeedback treatment of foot drop after stroke compared with standard rehabilitation technique. *Archives of Physical Medicine and Rehabilitation,* 1976, **57**, 9–11.

Batshaw, M. L., & Haslam, R. H. Multidisciplinary management of dystonia misdiagnosed as hysteria. In R. Eldridge & S. Fahn, (Eds.), *Advances in neurology, vol. 14: dystonia,* New York: Raven, 1976.

Beatty, J., & Legewie, H. (Eds.). *Biofeedback and behavior,* New York: Plenum, 1977.

Benson, H. *The relaxation response.* New York: Avon Books, 1975.

Bessett, R., Mohl, N., & Duda, L. Differential diagnosis of the pain dysfunction syndrome. *Journal of Dental Research,* 1973, **52**, 116–119.

Bird, B. L., & Cataldo, M. F. Experimental analysis of EMG feedback in treating dystonia. *Annals of Neurology,* 1978, **3**, 310–315.

Bird, B. L., Cataldo, M. F., Parker, L. H., Baker, T., & Francis, D. "Generalization of EMG biofeedback in choreathetoid cerebral palsy." Paper presented at the Tenth Meeting of the Biofeedback Society of America, San Diego, February, 1979.

Bird, B. L., Parker, L. H., & Cataldo, M. F. "Experimental analysis of EMG biofeedback in cerebral spasticity." Paper presented at the Tenth Meeting of the Biofeedback Society of America, San Diego, February, 1979.

Black, R. G. The chronic pain syndrome. *Surgical Clinics of North America,* 1975, **55,** 999–1011.

Blackwell, B. Psychotropic drugs in use today: the rote of diazepam in medical practice. *Journal of the American Medical Association,* 1973, **225,** 1637–1641.

Block, J. D. Teaching reading and writing skills to teenaged spastic cerebral palsied person: A long-term case study. *Perceptual and Motor Skills,* 1978, **46,** 31–41.

Bonica, J. J. (Ed.). *Advances in neurology, vol. 4: International symposium on pain.* New York: Raven Press, 1974.

Booker, H., Rubow, R., & Coleman, P. Simplified feedback in neuromuscular retraining: An automated approach using electromyographic signals. *Archives of Physical Medicine and Rehabilitation,* 1969, **50,** 621–625.

Boone, D. *The voice and voice therapy.* Englewood Cliffs, N.J.: Prentice-Hall, 1971.

Bourland, G., Ciulla, R., Bird, B. F., & Cataldo, M. F. "Generalization of behavioral interventions in cerebral palsy." Manuscript in preparation.

Brady, J. P. Metronome-conditioned speech retraining for stuttering. *Behavior Therapy,* 1971, **2,** 129–150.

Braud, L. W. The effects of frontal EMG biofeedback and progressive relaxation upon hyperactivity and its behavioral concomitants. *Biofeedback and Self-Regulation,* 1978, **3,** 69–90.

Brierly, H. The treatment of hysterical spasmodic torticollis by behavior therapy. *Behaviour Research and Therapy,* 1967, **5,** 139–142.

Brodnitz, F. S. Spastic dysphonia. *Annals of Otology, Rhinology, and Laryngology,* 1976, **85,** 210–214.

Brucker, B. S., & Ince, L. P. Biofeedback as an experimental treatment for postural hypotension in a patient with a spinal cord lesion. *Archives of Physical Medicine and Rehabilitation,* 1977, **58,** 49–53.

Brudny, J., Grynbaum, B., & Korein, J. Spasmodic torticollis: Treatment by feedback display of the EMG. *Archives of Physical Medicine and Rehabilitation,* 1974, **55,** 403–408.

Brudny, J., Korein, J., Grynbaum, B. B., Friedman, L. W., Weinstein, S., Sachs-Frankel, G., & Belandres, P. V. EMG feedback therapy: Review of treatment of 114 patients. *Archives of Physical Medicine and Rehabilitation,* 1976, **57,** 55–61.

Brudny, J., Korein, J., Levidow, L., Grynbaum, B., Lieberman, A., & Friedman, L. W. Sensory feedback therapy as a modality of treatment in central nervous system disorders of voluntary movement. *Neurology,* 1974, **24,** 925–932.

Bruyn, G. W. Huntington's chorea: Historical, clinical, and laboratory synopsies. In P. J. Vinken & G. W. Bruyn (Eds.), *Handbook of clinical neurology, vol. 6: Diseases of the basal ganglia.* New York: John Wiley, 1968.

Bucy, P. C. Is there a pyramidal tract? *Brain,* 1957, **80,** 376–392.

Budzynski, T. *Report of the task force on biofeedback treatment of tension headache.* Denver, Colorado: Biofeedback Society of America, 1978.

Budzynski, T. H., Stoyva, J. M., & Adler, C. S. Feedback-induced muscle relaxation: Application to tension headache. *Behavior Therapy and Experimental Psychiatry,* 1970, **1,** 205–211.

Budzynski, T. H., Stoyva, J. M., Adler, C. S., & Mullaney, D. J. EMG biofeedback and tension headache: A controlled outcome study. *Psychosomatic Medicine,* 1973, **35**, 484–496.

Buerger, A., & Fennessy, A. Learning of leg position in chronic spinal rats. *Nature,* 1970, **225**, 751–752.

Calne, D. B. *Progress in the treatment of Parkinsonism.* New York: Raven Press, 1973.

Carlsson, S. G., & Gale, E. N. Biofeedback in the treatment of long-term temporomandibular joint pain: An outcome study. *Biofeedback and Self-Regulation,* 1977, **2**, 161–172.

Carlsson, S. G., Gale, E. N., & Ohman, A. Treatment of temporomandibular joint syndrome with biofeedback training. *Journal of American Dental Association,* 1975, **91**, 602–605.

Cataldo, M. F., Bird, B. L., & Cunningham, C. Experimental analysis of EMG feedback in treating cerebral palsy. *Journal of Behavioral Medicine,* 1978, **1**, 311–322.

Cataldo, M. F., Russo, D. C., Bird, B. L., & Varni, J. W. Assessment and management of chronic disorders. In J. Ferguson & C. B. Taylor (Eds.), *Advances in Behavioral Medicine,* Holliswood, N.Y.: Spectrum Publications, in press.

Chaves, J. F., & Barber, T. X. Hypnotism and surgical pain. In D. Mostofsky (Ed.), *Behavioral control and modification of physiological activity,* Englewood Cliffs, N.J.: Prentice-Hall, 1976.

Chesney, M. A., & Shelton, J. L. A comparison of muscle relaxation and electromyogram biofeedback treatments for muscle contraction headache. *Journal of Behavior Therapy and Experimental Psychiatry,* 1976, **7**, 221–225.

Cleeland, C. S., Behavior techniques in modification of spasmodic torticollis. *Neurology* (Minneapolis), 1973, **23**, 1241–1247.

Cohen, B. A., Crouch, R. H., & Thompson, S. N. Electromyographic biofeedback as a physical therapeutic adjunct in Guillain-Barre Syndrome. *Archives of Physical Medicine and Rehabilitation,* 1977, **58**, 582–584.

Cooper, I. S. *Involuntary movement disorders,* New York: Harper & Row, 1969.

Cohen, M. J. Psychophysiological studies of headache: Is there similarity between migraine and muscle contraction headaches? *Headache,* 1978, **18**, 189–196.

Cooper, I. S. Effects of thalamic lesions upon torticollis. *New England Journal of Medicine,* 1964, **270**, 967–972.

Cooper, I. S., Rikland, M., & Snider, R. S. (Eds.), *The cerebellum, epilepsy, and behavior,* New York: Plenum Press, 1974.

Couch, J. R. Dystonia and tremor in spasmodic torticollis. In R. Eldridge, & S. Fahn (Eds.), *Advances in neurology, vol. 14: Dystonia.* New York: Raven Press, 1976.

Crothers, B., & Paine, R. S. *The natural history of cerebral palsy.* Cambridge, Mass.: Harvard University Press, 1959.

Dalessio, D. J. *Wolff's headache and other head pain.* (3rd edition). New York: Oxford University Press, 1972.

Davis, M. H., Saunders, D. R., Creer, T. L., & Chai, H. Relaxation training facilitated by biofeedback apparatus as a supplemental treatment in bronchial asthma. *Journal of Psychosomatic Research,* 1973, **17**, 121–128.

Diamond, S. Psychogenic headache. In O. Appenzeller (Ed.), *Pathogenesis and treatment of headache.* New York: Spectrum, 1976.

Diamond, S. *Report of the task force on biofeedback treatment of migraine headache.* Denver, Colorado: Biofeedback Society of America, 1978.

Diamond, S., & Dalessio, D. J. *The practicing physician's approach to headache*. Baltimore: Williams & Wilkins, 1978.

Doleys, D. M., & Kurtz, P. S. A behavioral treatment program for Gilles de la Tourette," syndrome. *Psychological Reports,* 1974, **35,** 43–48.

Donovan, W. H., Clowers, D. E., Kivial, M. D., & Marci, P. Anal sphincter stretch: A technique to overcome detrusor-sphincter dyssynergia. *Archives of Physical Medicine and Rehabilitation,* 1977, **58,** 320–324.

Dohrmann, R. J., & Laskin, D. M. Treatment of myofacial pain dysfunction syndrome with EMG biofeedback. *Journal of Dental Research,* 1976, **55,** B249.

Dunn, M. E., Davis, J., & Webster, J. "Voluntary control of muscle spasticity in three spinal cord injured patients." Paper presented at the Annual Meeting of the Biofeedback Society of America, Albuquerque, February 1978.

Ebersold, M. J., Laws, E. R., Stonnington, H. H., & Stillwell, G. K. Transcutaneous electrical stimulation for treatment of chronic pain: A preliminary report. *Surgical Neurology,* 1975, **4,** 96–99.

Eldridge, R. Discussion of Gilles de la Tourette's syndrome. In R. Eldridge, & S. Fahn (Eds.), *Advances in neurology, vol. 14: Dystonia.* New York: Raven Press, 1976.

Eldridge, R., & Fahn, S. (Eds.). *Advances in neurology, vol. 14: Dystonia.* New York: Raven Press, 1976.

Eldridge, R., Riklan, M., & Cooper, I. S. The limited role of psychotherapy in torsion dystonia: Experience with 44 cases. *Journal of American Medical Association,* 1969, **210,** 705–712.

Engel, B. T., Nikoomanesh, P., & Schuster, M. M. Operant conditioning of rectosphincteric responses in the treatment of fecal incontinence. *New England Journal of Medicine,* 1974, **290,** 646–649.

Engstrom, D. R. Hypnotic susceptibility, EEG alpha, and self-regulation. In G. E. Shwartz, & D. Shapiro (Eds.), *Consciousness and self regulation, vol. 1.* New York: Plenum Press, 1976.

Epstein, L. H., & Abel, G. Analysis of biofeedback training effects for tension headache patients. *Behavior Therapy,* 1977, **8,** 34–47.

Epstein, L. H., & Blanchard, E. B. Biofeedback, self-control, and self-management. *Biofeedback and Self-Regulation,* 1977, **2,** 201–211.

Epstein, L. H., & Masek, B. T. Behavioral control of medicine compliance. *Journal of Applied Behavior Analysis,* 1978, **11,** 1–9.

Epstein, L. H., Abel, G. G., Collins, F., Parker, L., & Cinciripini, P. M. The relationship between frontalis muscle activity and self-reports of headache pain. *Behaviour Research and Therapy,* 1978, **16,** 153–160.

Fahn, S., & Calne, D. P. Considerations in the management of parkinsonism. *Neurology,* 1978, **23,** 5–7.

Fernando, C. K., & Basmajian, J. V. "Report of the task force on application of biofeedback in physical medicine and rehabilitation." Denver, Colorado: Biofeedback Society of America, 1978.

Feurstein, M., & Adams, H. E. Cephalic vasomotor feedback in the modification of migraine headache. *Biofeedback and Self-Regulation,* 1977, **2,** 241–254.

Finley, W. W., Niman, C., Standley, J., & Ender, P. Frontal EMG-biofeedback training of athetoid cerebral palsy patients: A report of six cases. *Biofeedback and Self-Regulation,* 1976, **1,** 169–182.

Finley, W. W., Niman, C. A., Standley, J., & Wansley, R. A. Electrophysiologic behavior modification of frontal EMG in cerebral palsied children. *Biofeedback and Self-Regulation,* 1977, **2,** 59–79.

Ford, F. R. *Diseases of the nervous system in infancy, childhood, and adolescence.* Springfield, Ill.: Charles C. Thomas, 1973.

Fordyce, E. *Behavioral methods for chronic pain and illness.* Saint Louis: C. V. Mosby, 1976.

Foxx, R. M., & Azrin, N. H. *Toilet training the retarded.* Champaign, Ill.: Research Press, 1973.

Friar, L. R., & Beatty, J. Migraine: Management by trained control of vasoconstriction. *Journal of Consulting and Clinical Psychology,* 1976, **44,** 46–53.

Garber, N. B. Operant procedures to eliminate drooling behavior in a cerebral palsied client. *Journal of Nervous and Mental Disease,* 1974, **159,** 148–151.

Gatchel, R. J., Korman, M., Weis, C. B., Smith, P., & Clarke, L. A multiple response evaluation of EMG biofeedback performance during training and stress-induction conditions. *Psychophysiology,* 1978, **15,** 253–258.

Geschwind, N. The borderland of neurology and and psychiatry. Some common misconceptions. In F. Benson, & D. Blumer (Eds.), *Psychiatric aspects of neurological disease.* New York: Grune & Stratton, 1975.

Gessel, A. H. Electromyographic biofeedback and tricyclic antidepressants in myofascial pain-dysfunction syndrome: Psychological predictors of outcome. *Journal of the American Dental Association,* 1975, **91,** 1048–1052.

Gessel, A. H., & Alderman, M. M. Management of myofascial pain dysfunction syndrome of the temporomandibular joint by tension control training. *Psychosomatics,* 1971, **12,** 302–309.

Gilbert, G. J. The medical treatment of spasmodic torticollis. *Archives of Neurology,* 1972, **27,** 503–506.

Goldiamond, I. Self-control procedures in personal behavior problems. *Psychological Reports,* 1965, **17,** 851–868.

Goldiamond, I. Self-reinforcement. *Journal of Applied Behavior Analysis,* 1976, **9,** 509–514.

Gottlieb, H., Strite, L. C., Koller, R., Madorsby, A., Hockersmith, V., Kleeman, M., & Wagner, J. Comprehensive rehabilitation of patients having chronic low back pain. *Archives of Physical Medicine and Rehabilitation,* 1977, **58,** 101–108.

Graham, J. R. Headache related to a variety of medical disorders. In O. Appenzeller (Ed.), *Pathogenesis and treatment of headache.* New York: Spectrum, 1976.

Greene, C. S. A survey of current professional concepts and opinions about the myofascial pain-dysfunction (MPD) syndrome. *Journal of the American Dental Association,* 1969, **79,** 1168–1172.

Griggs, R. C., & Moxley, R. T. (Eds.). *Advances in neurology, vol. 17: Treatment of neuromuscular diseases.* New York: Raven Press, 1977.

Grzesiak, R. C. Relaxation techniques in treatment of chronic pain. *Archives of Physical Medicine and Rehabilitation,* 1977, **58,** 270–272.

Halpern, D., Kottke, F. J., & Burrill, C. Training of control of head posture in children with cerebral palsy. *Developmental Medicine and Child Neurology,* 1970, **12,** 290–305.

Halpern, L. M. Treating pain with drugs. *Minnesota Medicine,* 1974, **57,** 176–184.

Halstead, L. S., & Halstead, M. G. Chronic illness and humanism. Rehabilitation as a model for teaching humanistic and scientific health care. *Archives of Physical Medicine and Rehabilitation,* 1978, **59,** 53–57.

Hanna, R., Wilfling, F., & McNeill, B. A biofeedback treatment for stuttering. *Journal of Speech and Hearing Disorders,* 1975, **4,** 270–273.

Hardyck, C., Petrinovich, L. F., and Ellsworth, D. W. Feedback of muscle activity during silent reading: Rapid extinction. *Science,* 1966, **154,** 1467–1468.

Harris, F. A., Katkin, E. S., Lick, J. R., & Halberfield, T. Paced respiration as a technique for the modification of autonomic response to stress. *Psychophysiology,* 1976, **13,** 386–391.

Harris, F. A., Spelman, F. A., & Hymer, J. W. Electronic sensory aids as treatment for cerebral palsied children. *Physical Therapy,* 1974, **54,** 354–365.

Harrison, A. Training spastic individuals to achieve better neuromuscular control using electromyographic feedback. In V. K. Holt (Ed.), *Movement and child development.* London: Heinemann Medical, 1975.

Harrison, A. Augmented feedback training of motor control in cerebral palsy. *Developmental Medicine and Child Neurology,* 1977, **19,** 75–78.

Harrison, A., & Connolly, K. The conscious control of fine levels of neuromuscular firing in spastic and normal subjects. *Developmental Medicine and Child Neurology,* 1971, **13,** 762–771.

Haynes, S. N. Electromyographic biofeedback treatment of a woman with chronic dysphagia. *Biofeedback and Self-Regulation,* 1976, **1,** 121–126.

Haynes, S. N., Griffin, P., Mooney, D., & Parise, M. Electromyographic biofeedback and relaxation instructions in the treatment of muscle contraction headaches. *Behavior Therapy,* 1975, **6,** 672–678.

Henschen, T. L., & Burton, N. G. Treatment of spastic dysphonia by EMG biofeedback. *Biofeedback and Self-Regulation,* 1978, **3,** 91–96.

Herman, R. "Biofeedback in neuromuscular reeducation." Paper presented at the Annual Meeting of the Biofeedback Society of America, Albuquerque, February 1978.

Hook, O. Rehabilitation. In P. Vinken & G. Bruyn (Eds.), *Handbook of clinical neurology, vol. 24: Injuries to brain and skull, part II.* New York: Elsevier, 1976.

Hungerford, G. D., du Boulay, G. H., & Zilkha, K. J. Computerized axial tomography in patients with severe migraine: A preliminary report. *Journal of Neurology, Neurosurgery, and Psychiatry,* 1976, **39,** 990–994.

Ince, L. P. *Behavior modification in rehabilitative medicine.* Springfield, Ill.: Charles C. Thomas, 1976.

Ince, L. P., Brucker, B. S., & Alba, A. Behavioral techniques applied to the care of patients with spinal cord injuries. *Behavioral Engineering,* 1976, **3,** 87–95.

Inglis, J., Campbell, D., & Donald, M. V. Electromyographic biofeedback and neuromuscular rehabilitation. *Canadian Journal of Behavioral Science,* 1976, **8,** 299–323.

Jacobs, A., & Felton, G. S. Visual feedback of myoelectric output to facilitate muscle relaxation in normal persons and patients with neck injuries. *Archives of Physical Medicine and Rehabilitation,* 1969, **50,** 34–39.

Jacobson, E. *Progressive relaxation.* Chicago: University of Chicago Press, 1938.

Jacobson, E. (Ed.), *Tension in medicine.* Springfield, Ill.: Charles C. Thomas, 1967.

Jankel, W. R. Electromyographic biofeedback in Bell's Palsy. *Archives of Physical Medicine and Rehabilitation,* 1978, in press.

Jankel, W. R. EMG feedback in spasmodic torticollis. *Journal of Clinical Biofeedback,* in press.

Johnson, H. E., & Garton, W. H. Muscle re-education in hemiplegia by use of electromyographic device. *Archives of Physical Medicine and Rehabilitation,* 1973, **54,** 320–322.

Keats, S. *Cerebral palsy.* Springfield, Ill.: Charles C. Thomas, 1965.

Keefe, F. J., & Surwit, R. S. Electromyographic biofeedback: Behavioral treatment of neuromuscular disorders. *Journal of Behavioral Medicine,* 1978, **1,** 13–24.

Kohlenberg, R. J. Operant conditioning of human and anal sphincter pressure. *Journal of Applied Behavior Analysis,* 1973, **6,** 201–208.

Kotee, H., Glans, K. O., Boncel, S. K., Edwards, J. E., & Crawford, P. L. Operant muscular relaxation and peak expiratory flow rate in asthmatic children. *Journal of Psychosomatic Research,* 1978, **22,** 17–23.

Krusen, F. (Ed.). *Handbook of physical medicine and rehabilitation.* Philadelphia: W. B. Saunders, 1971.

Kudrow, L. Tension headache. In O. Appenzeller (Ed.), *Pathogenesis and treatment of headache.* New York: Spectrum, 1976.

LaJoie, W. J., Cosgrove, M. D., & Jones, W. G. Electromyographic evaluation of human detrusor muscle activity in relation to abdominal muscle activity. *Archives of Physical Medicine and Rehabilitation,* 1976, **57,** 382–386.

Lance, J. W. *Headache.* New York: Charles Scribner's Sons, 1975.

Landau, W. M. (Editorial). Spasticity: The fable of a neurological demon and the Emperor's new therapy. *Archives of Neurology,* 1974, **31,** 217–218.

Lazarus, A. *Behavior therapy and beyond.* New York: McGraw-Hill, 1972.

Lee, K. H., Hill, E., Johnston, R., & Smiehorowski, T. Myofeedback for muscle retraining in hemiplegic patients. *Archives of Physical Medicine and Rehabilitation,* 1967, **57,** 588–591.

Levee, J. R., Cohen, M. J., & Rickles, W. H. Electromyographic biofeedback for relief of tension in the facial and throat muscles of a woodwind musician. *Biofeedback and Self-Regulation,* 1976, **1,** 113–122.

Lichts, S. (Ed.). *Stroke and its rehabilitation.* New Haven, Conn.: Elizabeth Licht Publisher, 1975.

Luthe, W. *Autogenic therapy, vols. 1–5.* New York: Grune & Stratton, 1969.

Marinacci, A. *Applied electromyography.* Philadelphia: Lea and Feiberger, 1968.

Martin, J. E., & Sachs, D. A. The effects of visual feedback on the fine motor behavior of a deaf cerebral palsied child. *Journal of Nervous and Mental Disease,* 1973, **157,** 59–62.

Meares, R. Features which distinguish groups of spasmodic torticollis. *Journal of Psychosomatic Research,* 1970, **19,** 1–11.

Medical News. Brain stimulation for seizures, spasticity needs better evaluation. *Journal of the American Medical Association,* 1978, **239,** 915–927.

Meichenbaum, D. *Cognitive behavior modification.* Morristown, N.J.: General Learning Press, 1974.

Meichenbaum, D. Cognitive factors in biofeedback therapy. *Biofeedback and Self-Regulation,* 1976, **1,** 201–216.

Melzack, R., & Wall, P. D. Psychophysiology of pain. *International Anesthesiology Clinics,* 1970, **8,** 3–34.

Michaels, R. R., Haber, M. J., & McCann, D. S. Evaluation of transcendental meditation as a method of reducing stress. *Science,* 1976, **192**, 1242–1244.

Miller, N. E. Learning of visceral and glandular responses. *Science,* 1969, **163**, 434–445.

Miller, N. E. Biofeedback and visceral learning. *Annual Review of Psychology,* 1978, **29**, 373–404.

Molnar, G. A., & Taft, L. T. Cerebral Palsy. In J. Wortis (Ed.), *Mental retardation and developmental disabilities: An annual review.* New York: Brunner/Mazel, 1975, pp. 85–112.

Montgomery, I., Perkin, G., & Wise, D. A review of behavioral treatments for insomnia. *Journal of Behavior Therapy and Experimental Psychiatry,* 1975, **6**, 93–100.

Mossman, P. L. *A problem oriented approach to stroke rehabilitation.* Springfield, Ill.: Charles C. Thomas, 1976.

Mroczek, N., Halpern, D., & McHugh, R. Electromyographic feedback and physical therapy for neuromuscular retraining in hemiplegia. *Archives of Physical Medicine and Rehabilitation,* 1978, **59**, 258–267.

Myers, R. The extrapyramidal system. *Neurology,* 1952, **24**, 627–655.

Nafpliotis, H. Electromyographic feedback to improve ankle dorsiflexion, wrist extension, and hand grasp. *Physical Therapy,* 1976, **56**, 821–825.

Nanjo, C., & Ornstein, R. E. *On the psychology of meditation.* New York: Viking Press, 1971.

Netsell, R., & Cleeland, C. S. Modification of lip hypertonia in dysarthria using EMG feedback. *Journal of Speech and Hearing Disorders,* 1973, **38**, 131–140.

Nicassio, P., & Bootzin, R. A comparison of progressive relaxation and autogenic training as treatments for insomnia. *Journal of Abnormal Psychology,* 1974, **83**, 253–260.

Nusselt, L., & Legewie, H. Biofeedback and systematische desensibilisierung bei Parkinson-tremor: Eine fallstudie. *Zeitschrift fur Klinische Psychologie,* 1975, **4**, 112–123.

Owens, S. Biofeedback in rehabilitation. *Rehabilitation Gazette,* 1974, **17**, 46–49.

Pearne, D. H., Zigelbaum, S. D., & Peyser, W. V. Biofeedback-assisted EMG relaxation for urinary retention and incontinence. *Biofeedback and Self-Regulation,* 1977, **2**, 213–217.

Pearson, P. H., & Williams, C. E. *Physical therapy services in the developmental disabilities.* Springfield, Ill.: Charles C. Thomas, 1972.

Peck, C. L., & Kraft, G. H. Electromyographic biofeedback for pain related to muscle tension. *Archives of Surgery,* 1977, **112**, 889–895.

Peck, D. F. The use of EMG biofeedback in the treatment of a severe case of blepharospasm. *Biofeedback and Self-Regulation,* 1977, **2**, 273–277.

Petajan, J., & Jarcho, L. Motor unit control in Parkinson's disease and the influence of levodopa. *Neurology,* 1975, **25**, 866–869.

Phillips, C. The modification of tension headache pain using EMG biofeedback. *Behaviour Research and Therapy,* 1977, **15**, 119–129.

Podivinsky, F. Torticollis. In P. J. Vinken & G. W. Bruyn (Eds.), *Handbook of clinical neurology, vol. 6: diseases of the basal ganglia.* New York: John Wiley, 1968.

Pomp, A. M. Psychotherapy for the myofascial pain-dysfunction syndrome. *Journal of the American Dental Association,* 1974, **89**, 629–632.

Rachman, S. Systematic desensitization. *Psychological Bulletin,* 1967, **67**, 93–103.

Rafi, A. A. Learning theory and the treatment of tics. *Journal of Psychosomatic Research,* 1962, **6,** 71–76.

Raskin, M., Johnson, G., & Rondestvedt, J. W. Chronic anxiety treated by feedback-induced muscle relaxation. *Archives of General Psychiatry,* 1973, **28,** 263–267.

Reckless, J. B. Hysterical blepharospasm treated by psychotherapy and conditioning procedures in a group setting. *Psychosomatics,* 1972, **13,** 263–264.

Reeves, J. L. EMG biofeedback reduction of tension headache: A cognitive skills training approach. *Biofeedback and Self-Regulation,* 1976, **1,** 217–226.

Reinking, R. H., & Hutchings, D. F. Tension headaches: What forms of therapy is most effective? *Biofeedback and Self-Regulation,* 1976, **1,** 183–190.

Rodbard, S. Pain in contracting muscle. In B. L. Crue (Ed.), *Pain: research and treatment.* New York: Academic Press, 1975.

Rosen, M., & Wesner, C. A behavioral approach to Tourette's syndrome. *Journal of Consulting and Clinical Psychology,* 1973, **41,** 308–312.

Rugel, R. P., Mattingly, J., & Eichinger, M. Use of operant conditioning with a physically disabled child. *American Journal of Occupational Therapy,* 1971, **25,** 247–249.

Russo, D. C., & Fuller, E. F. "Behavioral management of genitourinary disorders." Paper presented at the Conference on the Vulnerable Child, the Johns Hopkins University School of Medicine, Baltimore, October 1978.

Sachs, D. A., & Mayhall, B. Behavioral control of spasms using aversive conditioning with a cerebral palsied adult. *Journal of Nervous and Mental Disease,* 1971, **152,** 362–363.

Sachs, D. A., & Mayhall, B. The effects of reinforcement contingencies upon pursuit rotor performance by a cerebral palsied adult. *Journal of Nervous and Mental Disorders,* 1972, **155,** 36–41.

Sargent, J. D., Green, E. E., & Walters, E. D. Preliminary report on the use of autogenic feedback training in the treatment of migraine and tension headaches. *Psychosomatic Medicine,* 1973, **35,** 129–135.

Schandler, S. L., & Grings, W. W. An examination of methods for producing relaxation during short-term laboratory studies. *Behaviour Research and Therapy,* 1976, **14,** 419–426.

Schultz, J. H., & Luthe, W. *Autogenic training: A psychophysiological approach in psychotherapy.* New York: Grune & Stratton, 1959.

Schuster, M. M. Biofeedback treatment of gastrointestinal disorders. *Medical Clinics of North America,* 1977, **61,** 907–912.

Schwartz, G. E. Biofeedback and physiological patterning in human emotion and consciousness. In J. Beatty & H. Legewie (Eds.), *Biofeedback and behavior.* New York: Plenum, 1977.

Shapiro, A. K. Contribution to a history of the placebo effect. *Behavior Science,* 1960, **5,** 109–135.

Shapiro, A. K. Placebo effects in medicine, psychotherapy, and psychoanalysis. In A. Bergin & S. Garfield (Eds.), *Handbook of psychotherapy and behavior change.* New York: John Wiley, 1971.

Shapiro, A. K., Shapiro, E. S., Bruun, R. D., Sweet, R., Wayne, H., & Solomon, G. Gilles de la Tourette's syndrome: summary of clinical experience with 250 patients and suggested nomenclature for tic syndromes. In R. Eldridge & S. Fahn (Eds.), *Advances in Neurology, Vol. 14: Dystonia.* New York: Raven Press, 1976, pp. 277–283.

Shapiro, A. K., Shapiro, E. S., & Wayne, H. Treatment of Tourette's syndrome with haloperidol: Review of 34 cases. *Archives of General Psychiatry,* 1973, **24,** 92–97.

Sharpe, R. Behavior therapy in a case of blepharospasm. *British Journal of Psychiatry,* 1974, **124,** 603–604.

Singer, J. *Imagery and day dream methods in psychotherapy and behavior modification.* New York: Academic Press, 1974.

Solberg, W. K., & Rugh, J. D. The use of biofeedback devices in the treatment of bruxism. *Journal of Southern California Dental Association,* 1972, **40,** 892-853.

Solow, C. Psychotropic drugs in somatic disorders. In Z. J. Lipowski, D. R. Lipsitt, & P. C. Whybrow (Eds.), *Psychosomatic medicine:* New York: Oxford University Press, 1977.

Sorensen, B. F., & Hamby, W. B. Spasmodic torticollis. *Neurology,* 1966, **16,** 867–878.

Spearing, D. L., & Poppen, R. Single case study: The use of feedback in reduction of foot dragging in a cerebral palsied client. *The Journal of Nervous and Mental Disease,* 1974, **159,** 148–151.

Sternbach, R. A. (Ed.). *The psychology of pain.* New York: Raven Press, 1978.

Stoyva, J. Why should muscular relaxation be useful? In J. Beatty & H. Legewie (Eds.), *Biofeedback and behavior.* New York: Plenum, 1977.

Stravino, V. D. The nature of pain. *Archives of Physical Medicine and Rehabilitation,* 1970, **51,** 37–44.

Strong, M. S. Spastic dysphonia. *The Yearbook of Otolaryngology.* Chicago: Year Book Medical Publishers, 1977.

Sturgis, E. T., Tollison, C. D., & Adams, H. E. Modification of combined migraine-muscle contraction headaches using BVP and EMG feedback. *Journal of Applied Behavior Analysis,* 1978, **11,** 215–223.

Swaan, D., van Wieringen, P. C., & Fokkema, S. D. Auditory electromyographic feedback to inhibit undesired motor activity. *Archives of Physical Medicine and Rehabilitation,* 1974, **55,** 251–254.

Swanson, D. W., Swenson, W. M., Manuta, T., & McPhee, M. C. Program for managing chronic pain 1: Program description and characteristics of patients. *Mayo Clinic Proceedings,* 1976, **51,** 401–408.

Tasto, D. L., & Hinkle, J. E. Muscle relaxation treatment for tension headache. *Behaviour Research and Therapy,* 1973, **11,** 347–349.

Thomas, E. J., Abrams, K. S., & Johnson, J. B. Self-monitoring and reciprocal inhibition in the modification of multiple tics with Gilles de la Tourette's syndrome. *Journal of Behavior Therapy and Experimental Psychiatry,* 1971, **2,** 159–171.

Thompson, R. A., & Green, J. R. (Eds.). *Advances in neurology, vol. 16: Stroke.* New York: Raven Press, 1977.

Thompson, G. B., & Klonoff, H. Epidemiology of head injuries. In P. Vinken & G. Bruyn (Eds.), *Handbook of clinical neurology, vol. 23: Injuries to brain and skull, part I.* New York: Elsevier, 1976.

Thorsen, C. E., & Mahoney, M. J. *Behavioral self-control.* New York: Holt, Rinehart & Winston, 1974.

Turin, A., & Johnson, W. G. Biofeedback therapy for migraine headaches. *Biofeedback and Self-Regulation,* 1976, **33,** 517–519.

Tursky, B. Laboratory approaches to the study of pain. In D. Mostofsky (Ed.), *Behavior control and modification of physiological activity.* Englewood Cliffs, N.J.: Prentice-Hall, 1976.

Varni, J. W., Boyd, E. F., & Cataldo, M. F. Self-monitoring, external reinforcement, and time-out procedures in the control of high rate tic behaviors in a hyperactive child. *Behavior Therapy,* in press.

Vining, E. P. G., Accardo, P. J., Rubenstein, J. E., Farrell, S. E., & Roizen, N. J. Cerebral Palsy: A pediatric developmentalist's overview. *Archives of American Journal of Diseases of Children,* 1976, **130**, 643–649.

Vinken, P., & Bruyn, G. (Eds.). *Handbook of clinical neurology, vol. 23: Injuries to brain and skull, part I.* New York: Elsevier, 1976.

Whaler, R. G. Some structural aspects of deviant child behavior. *Journal of Applied Behavior Analysis,* 1975, **8**, 27–42.

Wannstedt, G. T., & Herman, R. M. Use of augmented sensory feedback to achieve symmetrical standing. *Physical Therapy,* 1978, **58**, 553–559.

Wickramasekera, I. Electromyographic feedback training and tension headache: Preliminary observation. *The American Journal of Clinical Hypnosis,* 1972, **15**, 83–85.

Wickramasekera, I. The application of verbal instructions and EMG feedback training to the management of tension headaches: Preliminary observations. *Headache,* 1973, **13**, 74–75.

Williams, D. The borderland of epilepsy revisited. *Brain,* 1975, **98**, 1–12.

Wittkower, E. D., & Warnes, H. *Psychosomatic Medicine.* New York: Harper & Row, 1977.

Wolfe, J. M. (Ed.). *The results of treatment in cerebral palsy.* Springfield, Ill.: Charles C. Thomas, 1969.

Wolff, H. G. *Headache and other head pain.* New York: Oxford University Press, 1963.

Wolpe, J. *Psychotherapy in reciprocal inhibition.* Stanford: Stanford University Press, 1958.

Wooldridge, C. P., & Russell, G. Head position training with the cerebral palsied child: An application of biofeedback techniques. *Archives of Physical Medicine and Rehabilitation,* 1976, **57**, 407–414.

Wright, T., & Nicholson, J. Physiotherapy for the spastic child: An evaluation. *Developmental Medicine and Child Neurology,* 1973, **15**, 146–163.

Yahr, M. D., & Duvoisin, R. C. Drug therapy of the extrapyramidal disorders. In P. J. Vinken, & G. W. Bruyn (Eds.), *Handbook of clinical neurology, vol. 6: Diseases of the basal ganglia.* New York: John Wiley, 1968.

Yates, A. J. The application of learning theory to the treatment of tics. *Journal of Abnormal and Social Psychology,* 1958, **56**, 175–182.

Ziegler, D. K. Epidemiology and genetics of migraine. In D. Appenzeller (Ed.), *Pathogenesis and treatment of headache.* New York: Spectrum, 1976.

CHAPTER 16

Recurrent Paroxysmal Disorders of Central Nervous System

David I. Mostofsky

It would be difficult, if not impossible, to cover a discussion of behavior therapy of all "central nervous system (CNS) disorders" within the limits of a single chapter. Such a chapter would require inclusion of the many reports in the behavior therapy literature dealing with neuromuscular impairment, cerebral vascular accidents, cord damage, cerebral palsy, and numerous other neuropathological conditions. While reports of such therapeutic efforts have been published in professional journals and books, they are usually incomplete and few in number; therefore, it would seem premature at this time to attempt to review or to integrate the data from these diverse sources. In general, the use of behavior therapy techniques with neurological disorders is relatively recent, and except for a few select classes of disorders, its acceptance by the majority of patients and clinicians has been met with caution, skepticism, and at times hostile rejection. This chapter focuses on the *paroxysmal* CNS disorders, which present a distinctively qualitative difference from the chronic behavioral impairments and which suggest great promise in the experimental analysis of the situation as well as in the remedial opportunities.

The pervasive nature of the CNS in physiological and psychological functioning is overwhelming, and even considerations of classic nonsensory or autonomic activities cannot be properly understood without an appreciation of CNS involvement. The histories of basic research and clinical practice in physiology, medicine, and behavior have repeatedly affirmed the central role that the nervous system, and especially cortical functioning, plays in the modulation of normal and dysfunctional behavior. In recent years, however, there has been an increased interest in delineating the extent of the interdependencies among the physiological machineries and the behavior systems (particularly learning, cognition, and psychodynamics). The hallmark of this interest has been to give serious attention to the bidirectional nature of these interdependencies; that is, to demonstrate that not only can physiological manipulations affect behavior, but that behavioral operations can bring about nontrivial changes in physiology (cf. Mostofsky, 1977). To some extent this position had been advanced in the early days of both medicine and psychology and was given greater credence with the development of psychosomatic medicine and with the seminal research by Pavlov. The rediscovery of this position, and the aggressive advocacy for reconceptualizations of health and sickness in this context has been largely the result of investigations and clinical services in the behavior therapies and biofeedback. The following two important realizations have been derived from these efforts: (*a*) It is possible to contrive environmental and behavioral interventions that can provide meaningful remedies for dysfunctional physiological consequences; and (*b*) The extent of nondrug, nonsurgical treatment protocols need not be restricted to conventional "mental health" symptomatologies, but can be applied to a wide range of disorders, including those formerly viewed as being exclusively medical, organic, and not subject to change except by application of chemical or anatomical interventions. The importance of the latter has been to admit to examination the practical utilization of behavioral strategies as primary or adjunctive treatment alternatives in the management of disorders presumed to be governed by insult or imperfection in brain structure or chemistry. The clinical demonstrations in this regard have been encouraging, although not conclusive. Many patients have realized a measure of relief that was not otherwise available, and in many instances the larger profile of personal functioning and quality of life has been considerably improved, separate from the primary condition for which they were referred for therapy. These demonstrations, while tremendously gratifying, have also pointed to our stark ignorance about the problem's origin and to our inability to formulate viable theoretical accounts of why we succeed and why we fail. Nonetheless, they offer encouragement for continued study and refinement, mindful of Lovass' observation that:

Behavior therapy proceeds independent of etiology. A treatment based on etiology rests on very tenuous grounds . . . Behavior therapy can offer systematic demonstrations that its treatment variables are in fact operating to produce the desired changes. Limited as these changes may be, it (may often be) the only treatment which at the present time has demonstrated effectiveness. It may therefore be considered the treatment of choice [1970].

While these comments were primarily addressed to problems of retardation and neurosis-psychosis, they are no less valid in discussions of somatic and organic disorders. Because the developments and applications of the behavior therapies relative to CNS problems may be largely unfamiliar to most physicians and therapists, this chapter first considers the perspectives and rationale that guide the various clinical designs, and which have been comfortably accommodated in the popular arena of "Behavioral Medicine." As illustrative and representative of the clinical cases (usually seen first in neurological practice) for which behavior therapy protocols have been implemented, a discussion of the patient's suffering from the epilepsies as well as a discussion of those with movement disorders are presented, together with a review of the behavioral techniques and elements that have been shown to be necessary for a proper analysis and treatment plan. Finally, the chapter considers the necessary ingredients for establishing behavior therapy programs for such clients in both inpatient and outpatient settings.

BEHAVIORAL MEDICINE

"Behavioral Medicine" is essentially a point of view. The formal definition, proposed at the Yale Conference and affirmed by the Academy of Behavioral Medicine

Research regards it as an interdisciplinary field "concerned with the development of behavioral science knowledge and techniques relevant to the understanding of physical health and illness and the application of this knowledge and techniques to prevention, diagnosis, treatment, and rehabilitation (Schwartz & Weiss, 1978). The definition bestows a major role for all health-related disciplines, and embraces descriptive, predictive, and therapeutic activities. The behavior therapist, perhaps more than any other, occupies a prominent position in his/her ability to contribute significantly to the formulation of treatment and clinical services. In my view the range of involvement for behavioral therapy includes three broad classes of objectives: symptom reduction, compliance, and relief from unavoidable and uncomfortable diagnostic or treatment procedures (see Table 1). For purposes of our discussion with respect to the epilepsies and movement disorders, only the first two objectives are considered.

The objective of symptom reduction does not refer only to a decrease in the manifest frequency of a particular symptom or symptom complex. While the ideal goal may be the complete elimination of a disruptive episode of motor spasm or seizure, a significant clinical service is rendered if the duration of the episode can be altered, or if it can be brought under sufficient stimulus control to assure that its occurrence will be restricted to locations or times that are both physically and psychologically "safe" for the patient. The person with epilepsy who experiences interruptions of consciousness only in the evening in the privacy of the bedroom will suffer little from the stigmata of the disorder, from barriers to employment, and from restraints on personal and interpersonal growth. The implication of this objective is, however, that the therapy program is directed toward an alteration of the presenting intrusion of the illness (e.g., a seizure) whether or not any accompanying indices of dsyfunctional physiology are correspondingly altered (e.g., normalization of the EEG). Treatment plans for pain, sleep disorder, and encopresis would fall into this category.

On numerous occasions, the treatment sought is related to symptom control only indirectly. Diabetics may avoid crisis by observing their food and insulin intake; asthmatics may prevent attacks by avoiding allergenic agents and/or by effectively coping with their breathing problem at the first suggestion of an impending difficulty; persons with epilepsy cannot be cavalier with their anticonvulsant medications, and so forth. The thrust of the compliance objective is to provide the patient with a behavioral repertory of sufficient habit strength to ensure that the CNS disorder will not be exacerbated. Most often this will take the form of compliance to medication or sleep, but it will often involve considerations of life-style, coping with a chronic condition, and counteracting behavior patterns generated by condi-

Table 1. Behavior Therapy in Behavioral Medicine

Objectives	Example	Approaches	Kanfer Variables
1. Symptom reduction	Seizure	A. Reward management	α
2. Compliance	Medication	B. Self-control	β
3. Relief from uncomfortable medical procedure	Endoscopy examination	C. Psychophysiological technique	λ

tions of "learned helplessness." To be sure not infrequently symptom reduction will also be achieved, although the emphasis in the course of therapy will have been directed elsewhere.

The variety of behavioral strategies that are available to the therapist can be clustered in three major groups: reinforcer management (which utilizes the undisguised administration of contingent reinforcement and punishers), self-control (which includes relaxation, "thought-stopping" and psychotherapy), and psychophysiological techniques (which are primarily represented by biofeedback and less frequently by physiological habituation and desensitization). These three categories correspond to Kanfer and Koraly's (1972) formulation of alpha, beta, and gamma variables in which behavior change is modulated by external environmental factors, internal and intrapsychic factors, and physiological factors, respectively. The selection of a particular technique is not only defined by the treatment objective, but rather by the training and temperamental persuasion of the therapist; the specific characteristics of the disorder, the patient, and the patient's environment; and by the realities of available resources to properly implement the therapy program. The published literature suggests that each category of treatment has achieved a measure of success in treating disorders of the CNS. In a later section we examine specific instances of the application of these techniques.

THE DIMENSIONS OF SICKNESS

The reluctance by both behavioral and medical specialists to consider treatment of disorders for which an organic etiology is established (or is presumed to exist) is attributable, in part, to the ingrained training and traditions of "medical" versus "psychological" models. Despite an espousal of a monistic conceptualization of human functioning, the hyphen separating mind and body has largely been retained to indicate the existence of purely somatic conditions that are beyond the pale of interaction with nonsomatic processes. Admittedly, the epistomological position is subject to harsh criticism and flies in the face of empirical results, but the views persist.

Lacking from discussions of disorders, disabilities, and disease processes has been a careful delineation of the dimensions of sickness. Such an analysis might be profitable in clarifying the status of a learning model in sick behavior (Fordyce, 1976; Wooley, Blackwell, Epps, & Harper, 1975) and the parsimony of applying learning-based treatment designs for frank neurological disorders. It would also allow for an appreciation of the need to consider treatment programs that provide for coping skills and contingency management in the large and natural environment—where the patient's sick behavior is often supported and maintained.

It is proposed that the dimensions of sickness are disease, illness, and predicament. They are not equivalent terms. The distinction is best seen when they are compared along nine separate factors. A summary of the comparison is given in Table 2.[1]

[1] I am indebted to Dr. David Taylor (University of Oxford, England) who has graciously permitted me to draw from his presentation at the Colby Epilepsy Course (Colby College, July 1977) where the basis for this discussion was first developed.

Table 2. Dimensions of Sickness

Disease	Illness	Predicament
1. A physical reality not necessarily organ specific	1. A declaration of disease in symptomatic form that is organ specific	1. A complex of social ramifications with immediate bearing on the individual
2. Produces specific change in organ or tissues	2. Results in limitation of behavior	2. Diffuse, multifactorial and personal—but not necessarily unique
3. May be trivial	3. May change for better or worse	3. Very unstable structure
4. Valid without illness	4. Valid without discoverable disease	4. Valid without disease or illness
5. Amoral	5. Probably judged "morally"	5. Highly charged with moral implications
6. Diagnosis is discovery; specifies structural/ functional change	6. Diagnosis is description and semantic reattribution	6. Diagnosis is discernment
7. Space, place, time are irrelevant	7. Space, place, time are relevant	7. Space, place, time are paramount
8. Knowledge grows with investigation	8. Knowledge grows with classification	8. Knowledge grows with understanding
9. Search for specific therapy	9. Search for palliation and for personal change	9. Search for social and political remedies

Definition

Disease is a physical reality, although not necessarily organ specific (e.g., blood pressure or EEG indices may reflect disease processes without locus of a pathological organ). *Illness* is the observable and behavioral consequences of disease. The manifestation of symptomatology *is* organ specific. *Predicament* refers to the "fix"—the sad state of affairs that the illness has created and that denies the patient optimal functioning in social family, and personal affairs. The emphasis of behavior therapy will be seen to be most concerned with illness, while traditional psychotherapy has paid more of its attention to predicament. Whether successful treatment of either illness or predicament can reverse the physical realities of disease is unclear at this time, but not particularly relevant. The important point is that the presence of disease does not, *ipso facto,* rule out treatment by behavioral means. Unfortunately, traditional medical practice has been unable to offer help to a patient who suffers without benefit of a documented disease.

Our culture defines disease as an entity with objective clinical and laboratory signs that produce discomfort and lack of productivity. Unfortunately, this is not always the way people become sick. A patient can have a disease or several diseases and have no symptoms, or be terribly symptomatic and have no disease. This can be a severe problem if there are symptoms associated with a loss in comfort and productivity but laboratory tests show no demonstrable significant reduction in (physiological) function [Rowlett & Dudley, 1978].

Consequences

While the disease will produce a specific chemical or anatomical change in an organ or tissue, the consequence of illness is seen as a restriction on behavior. Illness is a commentary on how one's navigation in, and operations on, the environment has been limited and is both specifiable and quantifiable. The predicament in which the person finds him/herself is describable in less specific terms.

Training in behaviors mutually incompatible with those imposing limitations constitute treatments for the clinical illness. Improving the quality of life and restructuring the life-style in the face of the chronic illness provides yet other forms of treatment. The treatment of predicament—as conceptualized here—is beyond the specific activities of a therapist, and it implies change in the larger system and culture, with its attending values.

Stability and Importance

The consequences of disease may be irreversible and permanent, yet trivial. Illness, however, will almost by definition be nontrivial. The severity of its intrusion will be controlled by environmental contingencies and throughout its various transitions and states, illness nonetheless never reclassifies the disease. Predicament, subject not only to disease and illness factors, will be most unstable in character.

Validity of Existence

Disease does not depend on implications for its existence. It may be valid without illness (e.g., spike discharges in the EEG, while abnormal, do not mandate medical or behavioral intervention and need not be correlated with any functional loss or impairment). Similarly, illness and predicament do not require preconditions of disease (i.e., a physical reality of pathology) for their existence (e.g., the reality of a headache does not require confirmation of vascular or neurophysiological impairment). Behavior therapy has long been comfortable with a position in which defined observable responses, target behaviors, or symptom complaints are proper subjects for manipulation without the necessity for specifying reductionistic causal agents or states.

Morality

Disease is amoral in nature. For many persons afflicted with disorders, their illness does carry moral judgments (e.g., epilepsy). While this further complicates the plan for therapy, it is necessary to be sensitive to these demands and to recognize that psychosocial processes modify the judgments of morality. Predicament is highly dependent on social mores, and the acceptability of sickness is highly charged with moral complications. To the extent to which societal biases accompany the illness or the predicament, they must be recognized as added aversive consequences of one disorder that may well be maintaining undesirable stress, avoidance, or escape behaviors by the patient. The potential for symptom aggravation under these conditions cannot be easily disregarded.

The Nature of Diagnosis

To discover structural or functional change is to diagnose a disease. To describe and to assign a semantic label for a behavior syndrome is to diagnose an illness. Little changes in the diagnostic process for the child who cannot read and who is "diagnosed" as dyslexic. Descriptions and psychometric determinations are important, but they differ in kind from disease diagnosis on the one hand and from the skilled discernment of complex environments and the forces they exert, which are the parallels for diagnosis of predicament.

Stimulus Control

Space, place, and time are irrelevant in disease, critical in illness, and paramount in predicament. The significance of the illness expands and contracts in response to environmental and developmental variables. Judicious application of behavioral management (including the conventional psychotherapies) can do much to attenuate the ravages of predicament and to improve the quality of life, but the diffuse nature of the system that constitutes the setting for the predicament renders it less responsive to one-on-one treatment than is possible when the target objective is the illness.

Knowledge

The frontiers of knowledge about disease are extended with investigation. In illness, knowledge grows with the refinement of classification and with the reliability of predictive and covariational outcomes, which such classifications imply. To know about predicament is to understand the range of forces that confront the sick person, and on that basis to strive for solution, which most often is remotely attainable at best.

Treatment Objectives

One searches for specific reversibility of the structural or functional change brought on by the disease. One searches for behavior change in the case of illness. To affect amelioration of predicament, one must work for social and political remedies, since predicament is more a function of the system external to the patient than it is of his/her limited personal life space.

The distinctions among the dimensions of sickness serve to highlight the distinctions in the kind and form of treatments that are appropriate for the respective attributes of sickness. Without the need to invoke holistic medicine or faith healing it should be patently convincing that the roles of the behavior therapist and the physician can and must coexist to provide the comprehensive management of physiological disorders; the practice of either is likely to affect the mandates of the other. Neither denies the visible somatic ingredients that produce symptoms, and neither denies the plasticity and adaptive capabilities for relatively permanent changes in behavior. The anecdotes of medical practice allude to personal and environmental control in sick behavior, while the behavior therapies have provided in the learning-based framework the principles that allow for the systematic introduction of such control.

In the discussions to follow, the sucess or failure of a behavior therapy approach must be evaluated, in part, in the context of each of the dimensions of sickness. Furthermore, it would be well advised to incorporate in the therapeutic plan tactics that can address more than a single dimension of the sickness problem. One's faith in the role of learned acquisition and maintenance of disease and illness must be met by corresponding efforts to provide appropriate occasions for their extinction, change in the probability of their occurrence, or substitution by incompatible and acceptable alternatives.

EPILEPSY

The technical literature on epilepsy is vast, but it has remained a relatively obscure topic for most nonmedical specialists.[2] Epilepsy embodies features of disease (although epilepsy, i.e., the seizure, is itself not a disease, but only a symptom complex), illness, and predicament. The distinguishing property of epileptic disorders is the recurring seizure.

A seizure is defined as any interruption of consciousness which is accompanied by changes in motor, sensory, or behavioral activity. At least two seizures occurring at random intervals as well as a detailed clinical evaluation is necessary before a diagnosis of epilepsy can be made.

Seizures are the clinical manifestations of a malfunction within the central nervous system. There is no specific cause for seizures. Rather, a number of different factors including metabolic disorders, anoxia, tumors, head injuries, and drug withdrawal can all precipitate clinical seizures. Because of the common presentation of recurrent seizures with diverse etiologies in many patients, seizure disorders are grouped under the broad term classification of "The Epilepsies."

Physiologically, seizures are believed to be precipitated by excessive repetitive firing of a single or small group of neurons (focus) in the brain. As these neurons continue to fire, the adjacent neurons also become overactive. As more and more neurons fire excessively, the seizure activity spreads until the entire electrical system of the brain is completely out of control. As the various neuronal circuits become overloaded, they cease to carry out their designated function until the entire system fails due to a massive "short circuit." An analogy would be the overloading of a city's power lines. A malfunction in the circuit of one small area results in cascading of load to other circuits. As these circuits become overloaded, they also fail and the remaining circuits pick up even a greater load until eventually a blackout occurs as the entire system fails. The system is then brought back to full activation a unit at a time.

The brain, in the presence of excessive neuronal activity, is constantly trying to maintain its normal functioning level to keep the excessive neuronal activity from spreading. If it does so, the seizure is limited in both duration and clinical manifestation. For example, a major (grand mal) seizure involves the firing of all neurons within the brain whereas in an absence (petit mal) seizure only a limited number of neurons are firing

---

[2] Two inexpensive and articulate monographs on the epilepsies of value to behavior therapists are: *The epilepsy fact book*, H. Sands & F. C. Minters, Phila.: Davis, 1977; *The epilepsies: Modern diagnosis and treatment*, J. M. Sutherland, H. Tait, & M. J. Eadie (2nd edition), London: Churchill Livingstone, 1974.

excessively and they cannot succeed in overloading the other neuronal circuits. This is analogous to throwing a circuit breaker to prevent the spread of an overload in an entire system [EFA, 1978].

The person with epilepsy suffers from the consequences of recurrent, abnormal electrical discharges from nerve-cell aggregates in the brain. The pathophysiology creating this paroxysmal electroneurophysiological condition produces motor, cognitive, or affective changes that may last from a few seconds to several minutes (in most cases). The changes need not appear to the observer as ugly convulsions (although they may); they need not be more than transient interruptions in normal activity (although they may); they need not lead to alterations in mental health or personality (although they may). It is true that some epileptic disorders can mean deterioration and can be fatal, but these incidences are rare. Unfortunately, in the public mind, and often the patient's, it is these very infrequent occurrences that strengthen rather than weaken such irregular and unpredictable associations. The prevailing reaction is to reconstruct in the mind's eye the epileptic as "an excursion through madness into death" (Taylor, 1973). There is ever present the stigmata of pills, the restrictions on activity, the days missed from school or work, the occasional injury, and the sense of helplessness. Indeed, the public relations effort to create an image of normalcy about epilepsy may be misguided. As a symptom-complex it is strikingly different from most other medical disabilities, and it cannot be simplistically considered only as the psychosocial sequelae of an organic disorder. A review of the psychological consequences can be found elsewhere (Hermann, 1977).

The varieties of seizures have been classified according to an internationally defined taxonomy (see Table 3). This arrangement departs from the older—and perhaps still more familiar—labelling scheme in which epilepsy was primarily identified as petit mal, grand mal, temporal lobe, and so on. The accepted nomenclature points to the local versus total involvement of the spread of hyperneuronal activity and the corresponding impairments in consciousness, affect, and motor functioning. Such a rational classification is eminently supported by the utility it has provided, namely to identify meaningful commonalities in the EEG and to suggest the class of anticonvulsant drug therapy that will be most effective.

Of particular interest to behavior therapy is what *is not* contained in the classification. Nothing in the taxonomic structure suggests whether one symptom class is likely to be more subject to stress and anxiety than another; whether one is more disabling than another (how can one assess the severity of 30 petit mal attacks per day compared to a single grand mal episode every two months?), or whether one will be more responsive to behavioral management than another. At this time, alternative classifications that are able to embrace these non-EEG characteristics of epileptic disorders do not exist, and indeed no argument is advanced here to reject the international classification. What is noted is that the neurological diagnostics are incomplete, and that behavior therapy must proceed with its independent determinations of relevant diagnostic indices.[3]

---

[3] Descriptions of the patients' perceptions about his/her disease or content analyses of verbal behaviors suggest possible directions in alternative formulations. The reports by Luborsky et al. (1975), Jenkins (1970), and Ben-Sira (1977) are representative of this literature.

Table 3.   International Classification of Epileptic Seizures[a]

I. Partial seizures (seizures beginning locally)
   - A. Partial seizures with elementary symptomatology (generally without impairment of consciousness)
     1. With motor symptoms [includes Jacksonian seizures]
     2. With special sensory or somatosensory symptoms
     3. With autonomic symptoms
     4. Compound forms
   - B. Partial seizures with complex symptomatology (generally with impairment of consciousness) [temporal lobe or psychomotor seizures]
     1. With impairment of consciousness only
     2. With cognitive symptomatology
     3. With affective symptomatology
     4. With "psychosensory" symptomatology
     5. With "psychomotor" symptomatology (automatisms)
     6. Compound forms
   - C. Partial sezures secondarily generalized

II. Generalized seizures (bilaterally symmetrical and without local onset)
     1. Absences [petit mal]
     2. Bilateral massive epileptic myoclonus
     3. Infantile spasms
     4. Clonic seizures
     5. Tonic seizures
     6. Tonic-clonic seizures [grand mal]
     7. Atonic seizures
     8. Akinetic seizures

III. Unilateral seizures (or predominantly)

IV. Unclassified epileptic seizures (due to incomplete data)

---

[a] Abstracted from H. Gastaut, Clinical and electroencephalographical classification of epileptic seizures, *Epilepsia,* 1970, **11,** 102–113.

Most of the behavior treatment efforts to date have been undertaken without the guidance of specific theoretical formulations. They have often resulted from the rare encounter by a therapist with an epileptic client. The literature reports are generally of single cases, commonly without demonstrations of control by reversal or multiple baseline designs or descriptions of statistical analysis, and often with questionable validity of a "true" epileptic abnormality. While treatment of "illness" does not require such preconditions, it is nonetheless important that such data be accurately represented. The empirical findings are nonetheless most encouraging and, considering that, in general, most patients referred for behavioral treatment have either been refractory to medication or are "controlled" at an unacceptable level; these data deserve careful and aggressive programs of replication.

Behavioral Treatment

In an earlier publication we have reviewed the published literature concerned with nondrug, nondiet, and nonsurgical treatment applications to seizure disorders (Mostofsky & Balaschak, 1977). Although we identified 12 different classes of behavioral strategies, each procedure may be recognized as a familiar and accepted tactic for changing behavior. In general, each procedure is more likely to be encountered in the context of classroom, mental health, or garden variety behavior management. The novelty is largely in extending these techniques to the "behavior" of seizures. The necessary requirements for their adaptation to the epilepsy problem are relatively simple, given that the therapist has a competent grasp of the behavioral methodology and a comfortable familiarity with the nature of the epilepsies. The premise underlying the various procedures is that seizures may be regarded as "another kind" of behavior that will be responsive to environmental contingencies and that, with judicious selection, new learned behaviors in the patients' repertory will acquire sufficient strength and permanence to provide a reduction of seizures either by extinction of those "behaviors," by shifting stimulus control in the triggering of seizures, or because the newly acquired skills will be incompatible and mutually exclusive with the conditions necessary for provoking or allowing the development of epileptic seizures.

As noted earlier, the classes of treatment into which the 12 separate procedures may be collapsed, can be identified as (*a*) reward management, (*b*) self-control; and (*c*) psychophysiological methods. In practice, a given protocol will be seen to contain features descriptive of another class, and indeed a treatment plan will often be designed so that the protocol will consist of a number of phases and operations that draw from the separate classes of treatment. A summary of the major features representative of the treatment classes follows.

Reward Management

These techniques are designed to address seizure problems as a variant of a standard learning problem. Reward is administered or made available following the execution of some behavior (or the nonemission of a seizure), with the hope that it will be followed by an increased probability in the strengthening of that behavior (or nonbehavior); that is, it will reappear with a shorter latency, it will be emitted more frequently, and it will become part of the performing repertory with some degree of permanence. If, however, the behavior in question is *not* rewarded, or even punished, the predicted outcomes are reversed. The speculation that epileptic seizures are at least in part learned phenomena does not imply that it is ncessarily voluntary or hysterical, but rather that (*a*) it is not inconceivable that learning principles apply to cells and their aggregates, and (*b*) that under certain conditions where rewards for seizures are available (secondary gain, socially acceptable "acting out," avoidance of or escape from stress, punishment, or uncomfortableness) they tend to reoccur and, in the course of their emission and subsequent consequences, are actually "rewarded." The reward management procedures rely on the judicious introduction, elimination, and timing of reinforcers (both positive and negative) to effect appropriate learning. A major goal is often to enable the patient to efficiently discriminate relevant environmental conditions which, from baseline observations, have demonstrated correlations with seizure onset, and then to cope with those situations without producing a seizure. Environmental conditions, as used in this context, include not only external trigger stimuli but also subtle private, covert, sensory, autonomic, or other physiological and nonverbal activity. Clinical improvement may, however, result even without the patient's ability to report awareness of personal change.

Examples of studies in this category include simple withholding of reinforcement on the occasion of a seizure (Gardner, 1967); time-out (Adams, Klinge, & Keiser, 1973); avoidance of noxious substance (Dorcus & Schaffer, 1945); contingent punishment (Efron, 1956); positive (overt) reward (Balaschak, 1975); covert reward (Daniels, 1975). The specific features of a treatment program for seizure control are dictated by the unique character of the patient, symptomatology, and his/her life space. Equally important are factors such as the presence of another handicap, discriminable prodromes or auras, and whether the program is carried out as an outpatient or inpatient effort. For a child, reward usually takes the form of money or a special privilege; for an adolescent it may be the promise of a reduction in medication. For an adult, the ultimate reward of job employment or improvement in family living may still require the administration of smaller and more frequent pleasures. These procedures do not appear to be selectively attractive nor contraindicated for any subgroup of persons with epilepsy stratified by sex, diagnostic category, cognitive or intellectual patency, or presence of a multiple handicap. In our own work we have been successful in a few cases with establishing a contract stipulating that if an agreed upon minimum number of seizures occur in any week, some valued consequence decided upon by both patient and parent will be forthcoming. In this case the patient provides his/her own technique for seizure control and defines the necessary discrimination tasks without instructions from the therapist. Of interest is that while the consequences of any single seizure are neither rewarded nor punished, the reinforced cumulation of desired behaviors distributed over a longer time period are able to gain control.

Clearly the armamentarium of possible behavior therapy strategies has not been exhausted. One can only speculate on the utility of attempting techniques such as implosion and flooding, negative practice, or paradoxical intention. Furthermore, one should be cautious in ascribing major biobehavioral improvements to the unitary reinforcer employed in the therapeutic situation. There are always the countless other conditions of the patient's life space that may benefit from a "multiplier effect" originating from the restricted objectives of the experimental intervention. Consider, for example, that some arrangement of reward conditions results in bringing about a meaningful reduction of seizure frequency. With this outcome, the patient's personal and interpersonal functioning may be correspondingly improved, and a host of other unprogrammed sources of rewards enter (self-esteem, peer interaction, job opportunity, increased alertness due to decreased medication, etc.). Ultimately the credit for seizure control may be better attributed to the *collection* of the various illness and predicament components that, by elimination, have contributed to maintaining nonseizure behavior, rather than to a simplistic attribution of control mechanisms via the limited therapy program alone.

Self-Control

The treatment styles represented by this category are designed to effect control of behavior via gaining control of cognitive processes. Cognitions, self-control, coping, and similar mediating behaviors are regarded as the critical operative variables in bringing about necessary changes. The practical translation of this approach ranges from relatively simple training in relaxation exercises and stress reduction (with or without biofeedback devices) to the shaping of various cognitive variables. By monitoring thought processes and emotional states and by learning to appreciate the role of conflicts and anxieties, the patient is taught to deal appropriately with situations suspect of being provocative, threatening, or catalytic in precipitating seizures. Even with patients who cannot report prodromal or aura symptoms, these techniques have been stated to produce successful clinical management of seizures. Among such studies are those emphasizing relaxation (Ince, 1976); Wolpian desensitization (Cabral & Scott, 1976); and dynamic psychotherapy (Williams, Spiegel, & Mostofsky, 1978).[4]

A recent report by Muthén (1978) is particularly noteworthy. Using relaxation procedures, the author was able to provide a dramatic improvement in petit mal patients—a class that is generally seen as most refractory to behavioral techniques because of the brevity and frequency of the attacks and also because correlations with environmental elements are almost always impossible to be found; nor can the subject report an aura predictive of the attack onset. In addition, Muthén (personal communication) noted that as the course of therapy proceeded, the subjects' ability to predict whether they would experience a petit mal attack during the course of a day was greatly improved.

These techniques have long been recognized as effective in the clinical management of a broad range of health-related goals, including life-style adjustment, coping with a chronic disorder, and compliance with drugs and other medical orders. Particularly since these strategies have been most effective in stress reduction and the elimination of anxiety (both long regarded as nasty culprits by epileptologists) their adaptation to the seizure control problem is both relevant and important.

Psychophysiological Methods

The techniques represented in this category are essentially of two forms: (a) psychophysiological habituation to critical parameters of a physical stimulus known to trigger a seizure (e.g., light or sound frequency and intensity); and (b) cortical biofeedback. The first of these procedures have been extensively studied by Forster (1977) and require long and repeated exposures to the stimuli as they are presented from subthreshold levels through the range of suprathreshold (hopefully extinguished or habituated) values. Despite these limitations they are probably the treatments of choice for patients in whom the trigger is clearly demarcated in an external physical stimulus. While the incidence of such idiosyncratic disorders is

---

[4] The language and descriptions of treatment procedures are those used by traditional psychotherapists. Neither compellingly contradicts or refutes a behavior therapy position. Indeed, when reduced to an operational level, the translation of the "dynamic" interpretations are seen as equivalent to and compatible with a behavior oriented approach. The inclusion of citations from "psychotherapy" is provided to allow an appreciation of the breadth of disciplinary, theoretical, and conceptual systems that have formulated behavioral medicine treatment alternatives.

rare and accounts for but a fraction of the persons with epilepsy (i.e., startle, photosensitive, musicogenic, etc.), the treatment solution is most promising.

The second form of treatment in this category is best represented by the original work of Sterman and Friar (1972) in which a patient was trained to generate EEG within a specified beta range without accompanying slow wave or EMG activity. The results, taken from numerous laboratories, are as yet unclear, difficult to interpret and costly, but indisputably remarkable.

In his most recent controlled study Sterman and McDonald (1978) reports six of eight patients with statistically significant and sustained seizure reductions (which averaged 74%) following rewarded cortical biofeedback. Whether a nonspecific theory or (as Sterman proposes) an EEG normalizing hypothesis will best account for these outcomes remains to be established. It is clear, however, that as the complicated and expensive hardware that the technique requires becomes more available to properly trained researchers, the integration of such biofeedback into larger-scale clinical service settings will be forthcoming. The elephant's trunk is in the tent, and in the meantime it is well to remember Neal Miller's caveat that "we should be bold in what we try, and cautious in what we say."

SOME SPECULATIONS ON BEHAVIORAL ANALYSIS AND THEORETICAL ISSUES

Although epilepsy is generally excluded from discussions on psychosomatic disorders, both anecdotal and laboratory data suggest that it would properly qualify for such consideration (see Bird, Chapter 15). The grand mal seizure, in particular, is a dramatic and serious intrusion on normal functioning, yet not the random event it is usually thought to be. It is quite different in kind from the detached retina in which vision is permanently impaired or the severed muscle for which function is irreversible. The problem has been noted by Rodin (1968):

The great majority of neurophysiological and neurochemical investigations still deal with the "epileptic focus" or the properties of the "epileptogenic neuron." These are important studies but they are likely to be insufficient in providing the final answer to the problem. (One should also ask) what are the factors that are responsible for the spread of abnormal electrical activity in this particular patient? Even more important would be the question: How does the patient's condition differ on the five days of the week when he is seizure-free from that of the sixth day when he has an attack? [p. 343].

However tentative, it may be profitable to offer some guidelines that may contribute to a better understanding of behavioral control in epilepsy, and open avenues of research in this area.

Operant-Respondent Processes

If we examine the epileptic crisis as a segment in the stream of behaviors, we might indicate the beginning of the seizure period with the onset of prodromal symptoms (on those occasions when they are present). Commonly, such "premonitions" are only vaguely expressed and will precede the seizure itself often hours before. The seizure (ictus) is represented in Figure 1 together with the aura, since the popular

Presumed Physiology	ANS/CNS	CNS		?	
Developmental Stages	Prodromata	Aura	Ictus	Post Ictus 1	Post Ictus 2
Behavior Analysis	Operant	Respondent		?	

FIGURE 1.   Representation of the possible behavioral and physiological processes that accompany the time course of a seizure episode.

view is that the aura already represents the initiation of the seizure. When the seizure has run its course the patient in the postictal period will first be seen in a comatose state, unresponsive to the environmental surroundings. In the postictal state, patients report a clouded contact with what is happening—sometimes able to hear but not talk, sometimes appearing confused and drawn. Behaviorally, it seems appropriate to consider the presence of two separate postictal periods.

It has been suggested that behavior therapy, if it is beneficial at all, can only be expected to operate on the preictal periods; once the seizure begins there is no possibility for its termination. In the broadest sense, such a pronouncement is inaccurate. The ability to abort a Jacksonian March by application of a tourniquet or the use of noxious stimulation in the case of an "uncinate fit" (Efron, 1956) stand in clear contradiction to such an assertion. To be sure, most behavior therapy attempts appear to exert control prior to the ictus. Perhaps, if the ictal period is conceived of as respondent, operant procedures will indeed be ineffective at that time. Even if the entire seizure period is regarded as a respondent phenomenon, Goldiamond's analogy to operant control of sunburn merits consideration; namely, getting in the sun may be respondent, but the behavior of entering the risk environment of the sun is under operant control (personal communication). Using operant procedures it is possible to develop the necessary discriminations to teach a patient appropriate behaviors that will not allow him to enter the chain leading to a seizure. One needs also to refer to the common sight in which a child will experience seizures upon having a protective helmet (S^D?) put in place.

Perhaps, too, we should consider a reply to Gannt's observation (1970) that the aversive consequences of the seizure should by themselves be expected to lead to seizure reduction, which apparently they do not.

Excessive claims may lead to false hopes and produce the same kind of damage as the excessive claims of J. B. Watson . . . As an example of one of the fallacies of the Miller school is the prediction of the control of anxiety and grand mal epilepsy through operant conditioning. Such control is extremely doubtful, because as the epileptic has cues (aura) just before the attack, the disagreeable effect of one fit would be more potent in eliminating the attack than would any small operant reinforcers that could be introduced . . . If one were familiar with the distinction between conditioned reflexes and unconditional reflexes and with *grand mal* epilepsy one would know that the epileptic convulsion is an unconditional reflex and therefore not extinguishable as are the conditioned reflexes [p. 65].

While it is difficult to propose a rigorous rebuttal, it is possible to regard the aversive consequences in a backward conditioning paradigm, occurring to the patient during the postictal period. One would not be very surprised at the ineffectiveness of sparsely programmed trials of this sort. One could also regard the aversive consequences as being overshadowed by other consequences or as part of a sequence which, like fear, is represented by the maintenance of behavior by both classical and instrumental elements. Finally, one may consider that the discomforting and punishing properties of the seizure occur as autonomic system events during which time the seizure itself is under CNS control, and that such a combination allows for the continued nonextinction of the seizure problem. Above all, one must reconcile the Gannt argument with the reality that there are reliable demonstrations in which behavior therapy led to control of grand mal seizures. Charcot phrased it succinctly: *"La théorie c'est bon, mai ça n'empêche pas exister."*

Careful examination of the operant-respondent issue will, I suspect, become of considerable importance as animal analogue studies are undertaken. But such an examination will also be of great value in replication attempts which may, upon appropriate control, demonstrate success when initial efforts failed. In a study by Stevens (1962), subjects trained to suppress abnormal EEG spike activity when preceded by a tone were unable to maintain such suppression once the tone was eliminated. It is too early to conclusively infer that such EEG activity is not discriminable, for it remains a possibility that if the condition was gradually faded out (instead of being abruptly absent) the desired outcomes might be obtained. Finally, the variables that are separately responsible for seizure acquisition and initiation must be separated from those that maintain seizures and seizure-prone times.

Relaxation Therapies

From our own experience as well as from various published reports, the inclusion of relaxation protocols in the behavioral treatment of epilepsy often produces gratifying results. The explanation is not clear. To the extent that relaxation procedures eliminate (or provide coping responses) for anxiety and stress, the consequence of improved seizure control would be consistent with the suspicion held by many epileptologists that these conditions are serious contraindications for patients in whom a background predisposition for seizures is ever present. The ability to relax on self command may also enable patients with an aura "to do something about it," rather than to randomly attempt escaping or blocking the seizure progression at the first sign of its onset. It is always easier to supply a patient with an executable behavior than to try to teach the behavior of "not doing."

The research on relaxation and its effects allows some speculation on the possible mechanics by which it may contribute to inhibiting clinical seizures. I submit that at least four (4) proposals can be formulated:

1. *Direct Physiochemical Change.* Relaxation training has been shown to alter corticosteroids, cerebral blood flow, acidosis-alkalosis, and lactose levels in

the blood. These changes may be critical in providing some measure of control at the epileptogenic site.

2. *Indirect Neurophysiological Modulation.*   The affective, emotional, and musculoskeletal concomitants of "tenseness" may, through provocation of remote cortical sites (e.g., limbic cortex) ennervate electroneurophysiological propagation and stimulation of epileptogenic foci, from which there ultimately will develop frank clinical seizures.

3. *Psychophysiological Aggravation.*   Consequences of anxiety states are often discernable by alterations in respiration, pulse rate, and so on. Often hyperventilation may be a subtle accompaniment. Any of these outcomes may satisfy the minimum conditions for the seizure threshold.

4. *Scheduled-Induced Behavior.*   Commonly persons with epilepsy will bear well under the immediate conditions of stress and anxiety and experience seizures only after an abrupt shift in emotional level or after a period of delay. Relaxation may (*a*) provide a means for gradual transition of emotional states or (*b*) may alter a critical component in some undefined schedule which, though not directly programmed to the reinforcement of seizures, can no longer support their "off-schedule" control (as for example may be shown in schedule-induced polydipsia).

Comprehensive Epilepsy Management

The person with epilepsy, however severe, usually is referred for treatment on an outpatient basis. Even when provision for asylum or short-term respite care can be provided, the constellation of behavioral interactions significant in achieving relief and maintaining health exist outside the limited intensive care environment.

The incidence of epilepsy is between 1–2% of the population. The problems for the patient, family, and community are often great, and the burdens can in part be shared. The therapist who accepts responsibility for delivering clinical services to this population should recognize the complexity of disease, illness, and predicament factors that often mitigate against his/her efforts, but which may also be engineered to be of positive service. The major elements are schematized in Figure 2. The figure is not intended to reflect the complete system, but it is offered as a reminder to the therapist that there is a big world out there that may be exploited, used improperly, or not at all.

The rigorous and defined behavior therapy protocol that may be designed should ideally bring into its activities these elements. At the very least, both therapist and client should proceed with attempts at normalization fully sensitized to the range of resources and obstacles that will often determine the success of the therapeutic program. Behavior therapy has already contributed to demolishing some of the myths about epilepsy, but it remains a cruel social-psychological disability with attitudes remarkable for their negativism.

The history of epilepsy—probably the longest in medical literature to which any single disease, unless it can be malaria, can lay claim—might well be said to stand as a monument to human fallibility; as lamentable evidence of the unnumberness of those whispers of fancy to which the human mind has ever listened with credulity [Bunker, 1947, p. 1].

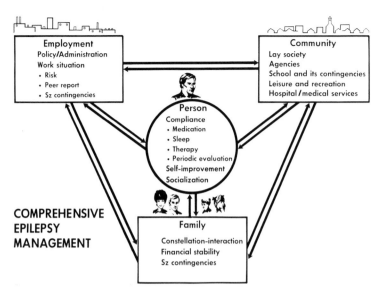

FIGURE 2. Elements in the design of a comprehensive management program for seizure problems.

In addition to patient therapy, social, family, and communal support are requisite elements for habilitation.

MOVEMENT DISORDERS

A comprehensive review of neurological movement disorders as they are of concern to behavioral movement disorders treatment and analysis remains an uncompleted task. It is beyond the scope of this chapter to attempt a complete discussion, and instead the focus is on the major disorders that have received at least some attention in the behavioral literature (cf. Leitenberg, 1976). The reference sections of the respective reports cited provide access to the larger body of writings on this subject.

Movement disorders are best classified into several broad categories: choreas, tics, tremors, and dystonias. As with epilepsy—with which they often share suspicions of common origin—the onset of the symptom pattern is often sudden, sometimes preceded by an aura, most often without confirmation of organicity for the disease etiology. In contrast to the epilepsies, loss of consciousness or abnormal EEG are absent. Medical treatment is usually limited to drug treatment by Haldol, Valium, and L-dopa.

Choreas

Among the choreas, Sydenham's Chorea (St. Vitus' Dance) occurs most commonly in children between ages 5 to 15. It is associated with rheumatic fever and is twice as frequent in girls (Weiner, Bresnan, & Levitt, 1977). A chorea is a series of involuntary "jerklike movements" that are aggravated during periods of agitation or activity and are diminished when the patient is quiet. During sleep they usually disappear. Fingers, hands, extremities, face, or even diaphragm may be involved. In extreme cases the illness may make the patient bedridden. Personality changes and even psychotic reactions have been reported by parents prior to onset of the illness. During the illness the emotionality of the child is usually described as labile. The onset may be abrupt or insidious; at times there may be only a one-sided weakness and movement disorder (hemichorea). Periods of remission may last weeks and even months and years. Longin, Kohn, and Macurik (1974) report a decrease in the spasmodic movements of Sydenham's Chorea by training the patient to make an incompatible response. Other reports of treatment with chorea patients only infrequently are concerned with the movement problem itself and research in this area has been hardly substantial. Paroxysmal choreoathetosis, though known for over 100 years and quite commonly subtitled "A form of reflex epilepsy" (Stevens, 1966), is poorly understood and only infrequently treated by behavior therapists. We are currently monitoring a two-year follow-up of a teenage female presenting this symptom; namely, movements beginning in the distal portions of the limbs and eventually implicating all or most of the musculature in a "bizarre writhing movement [with] grotesque posturing. The violence of the movement may hurl the patient to the floor, but there is no tonic-clonic pattern, no loss of consciousness and no amnesia" (Stevens, 1966). The disability, which severely restricted her school activity, finally resulted in a hospital admission. In the course of several days, contingent reward for reduced episodes coupled with training to practice normal movements without chorea (including walking with a coin carried in a mouth-held spoon) led to a remarkable decrease in such movements. Hospital passes were granted following days in which no choreas were reported by either patient or staff. Subsequently, she has been receiving extended psychotherapeutic support. After 18 months, some choreic movements have returned, but their frequency and severity are considerably below their baseline levels. Whether the behavioral intervention was real or had any sustaining effect is difficult to establish, but its remarkable initial effects (in the face of an otherwise collapsed medical management) were impressive. Reports such as those by Bird and Cataldo (1978), Cleeland (1973), and others point to the promise of biofeedback techniques for these disorders.

Tics (Gilles de la Tourette's Syndrome)

Perhaps the most dramatic form of a paroxysmal motor dyscontrol syndrome is the "nervous affliction characterized by motor incoordination, accompanied by echolalia and coprolalia" first described in detail by Gilles de la Tourette (1885) on six cases that he had collected; two others were originally described by Itard (1825). The Tourette syndrome, or *maladie de* Gilles de la Tourette, on occasion has gone by other names, among them: *maladie des tics* (Chabbert, 1893), *maladie des tics confulsifs* (Guinon, 1886), *maladie des tics impulsifs* (Koster, 1899; Wilson, 1941), *maladie des tics des degeneres* (Kanner, 1942), *koordinierte Erinnerungskraempfe* (quoted by Koester) and *myospasia impulsiva* (quoted by Gilles de la Tourette). As a clinical problem resting uncomfortably between neurology and psychiatry, the requirements essential for the diagnosis of the syndrome are said to consist of a number of pathognomonic features, namely: (*a*) childhood onset (below age 16), (*b*) multiple motor tics, and (*c*) unprovoked loud utterances, which may progress to the forced shouting of obscenities (coprolalia). In practice among an increasing number of clinical neurologists, the requirement for coprolalia as a necessary condition for differential diagnosis has been all but set aside. Jerking and motor movements of the face, arms, neck, or other parts of the body are characterized by suddenness of onset and rapidity of disappearance. They are frequently brought on by strong emotional stimuli, and usually disappear during sleep. An accurate appreciation of our current understanding of this syndrome is provided by excellent reviews of the literature by Kelman (1965), Fernando (1967), Hersen and Eisler (1973) and Shapiro, Shapiro, Brown, and Sweet (1978) as well as individual case reports by neurologists (Stevens & Blachly, 1966), psychiatrists (Ascher, 1948; Shapiro, 1970) and psychologists (Rosen & Wesner, 1973; Morphew & Sim, 1969; Tophoff, 1973). Tourette's syndrome, however, is devoid of specific, consistent antecedents or specific morphology. Reports on patients suffering from Tourette's syndrome are usually concerned with three broad areas of interest: (*a*) etiology, (*b*) psychopathological manifestations, and (*c*) treatment.

Behavior therapy programs usually consist of adaptations from the reward management variety, although Tophoff (1973) incorporated assertive training and relaxation as the primary approach. In our own practice we have met with moderate success even when relaxation training was used as the single treatment mode.

Though the disorder is severely disabling, parents are often resistant to treatment, which suggests psychiatric overtones; the implication of organic brain disorder seems more attractive—until the undesirable effects of medication and lack of progress begins to persuade otherwise. We are encouraged that behavior therapy offers a meaningful alternative, and we find comfort in the observation by Birk (1978) who stands apart in the medical community by noting that Tourette's syndrome is "eminently treatable behaviorally" (p. 439).

Theoretical accounts on the development of the Gilles de la Tourette syndrome include two extreme positions; namely, either that it is exclusively the result of a neurophysiological impairment with the likely suspects being the basal ganglia and/or the absence or appropriate inhibitory mechanisms, or the result of a psychopathologic history (akin to the evolution of stuttering or hysterical conversions). The separate positions clearly dictate quite separate approaches to the formulation of a desired treatment program. While each, in part, has met with success, each also is vulnerable to significant demonstrations of failure. Like the blind men of Indostan, each is probably partly in the right and partly in the wrong. Indeed, support for the separate conceptual formulations derives circularly from the efficacy of the "treatment of choice." The organicity position draws upon the effectiveness of Haldol, a butyrophenone (haloperidol) that antagonizes stereotyped hyperactivity, exhibits a pronounced inhibitory effect on conditioned avoidance behavior (presumably by blocking dopaminergic receptors), and leads to EEG arousal. The functional intrapersonal position finds support in the success of behavioral intervention for symptom control.

Extensive psychometric evaluations have failed to be dramatically convincing of any unique constellation of predisposing or consequential personality characteristics. The data, however, do suggest a parallel with other psychiatric patients (although not significantly different from them). Further, the rich collection of clinical descriptions of Tourette's syndrome are quite suggestive of behavior problems, separate from the inability to properly control muscular activity or the insensitivity of standard psychiatric procedures to quantify them. These data have been of considerably less value for formulating procedures for either differential diagnosis or potentially differential treatments. Proponents of a psychopathology theory have been less passionate in their claims than the vigorous voices of their critics who would echo Shapiro et al.:

Our impression was that psychological factors are unrelated to the etiology, useless for diagnosis, and irrelevant to the treatment of Tourette's syndrome. Our conclusion from other data was that the etiology of Tourette's syndrome is a subtle organic impairment of the central nervous system. We do not believe that further research on the psychopathology of Tourette's syndrome will prove to be useful [1978, p. 434].

The history of behavioral attempts to control tics is old, and a renewed interest in an alternative treatment mode of behavior modification has been reported by a number of investigators (Browning & Stover, 1971; Clark, 1966; Hutzell, Platzek, & Loque, 1974; Sand & Carlson, 1973; Thomas et al., 1971). The report by Clark is notable in that the author takes great pains to provide a rationale for implementing a learning-based extinction approach, and it provides an analytic framework for integrating learning processes and neurophysiological mechanisms as they relate to the control of the Tourette tic syndrome. The author's discussion is particularly important in questioning several critical assumptions, namely:

ASSUMPTION 1. *The singularity of a clinical entity of Tourette's syndrome*

The value of specially delineating any particular syndrome should be that a particular prognosis and specific treatment are associated with it. Neither the literature nor the cases described above demonstrated any of these benefits from separating the Gilles de la Tourette syndrome from other tics [p. 11].

Indeed, a similar view is expressed by Erikson and Persson:

We believe that we have here a group of disorders, all characterized by excito-motor symptoms, and that one of these has attracted particular attention because of its striking constellation of abnormalities, and has been called Gilles de la Tourette's syndrome. Disorders of the same group which do not meet the usual criteria have not attracted so much attention and their nature has undoubtedly often been misunderstood [p. 352].

If, in fact, this syndrome can legitimately be considered a variant of the more general problem of tics, then the therapist is able to draw on the documented experiences of other behavior control attempts that have responded well to such protocols (Barret, 1962; Yates, 1958; Walton, 1961; Abi-Rafi, 1962, and others).

ASSUMPTION 2. *The necessity for an organic treatment mode because of the organic substrate responsible for Tourette's syndrome*

The related notion that it may bear relationship to Syndenhams chorea and encephalities lethargica with all its attendant cerebral change also seems to be only of academic importance in view of a success of treatment based on a modification of function only. That such functioning may be mediated biochemically as well as by processes of learning is not precluded and is indeed indicated by the successful use of phenothiazines in similar cases, it being known that the latter drugs act in the area of the corpus striatum [p. 10] . . . A treatment based on learning theory has the effect of generating new functional connections at a corticothalamic level which achieve a new dynamic equilibrium between resting states of autonomic and cortical arousal [p. 11] . . . It is likely that even if the tic syndrome should result from structural defect of the basal ganglia, a learning theory approach can justifiably be made in order to increase arousal of cortical suppressor areas or otherwise set up new functional interrelationships between thalamu cortex and basal ganglia [p. 14].

An analysis of the published literature leads to an impressive conclusion that learning plays a central (if not exclusive) role in the development of the Tourette syndrome. This position may also be defended by those adopting the "psychopathology" and "organic damage" theories.

Behavioral analyses of these theoretical positions can be illuminating. For example, the orthodox/psychoanalytical account by Fenichel (1945) attributing unconscious meanings in children's games and making faces (and by extension the exhibitionistic components in stuttering and tics) provides an insightful formulation when cast in behavioral perspectives. Fenichel suggests four dynamic explanations for the child engaging in making ugly faces: First, the child enjoys this activity as proof of control over beauty and ugliness (or psychodynamically, that castration is not final and that it can be brought about or undone at will). Second, that being ugly means the ability to frighten others. Third, to play ugly (i.e., to feign castration) misleads the attacker (the castrator). Finally, the ugliness serves as an attack on the spectator. In behavioral terms, the first explanation can be viewed as a discriminated positive reinforcer having been learned because it supports environmental adaptation (i.e., it is not directed to any specific stimulus, but rather it appears as a coping skill for gaining other available reinforcers and for warding off "learned helplessness"). The other explanations are all special cases of behaviors encountered in aversive situations, which generate avoidance responses, escape responses, and aggressive responses. The value of such a translation is not merely academic gymnastics, but rather once seen in behavioral terms, appropriate treatment strategies suggest themselves. With respect to dealing with a behavior developed because of positive reinforcing mechanisms, an appropriate treatment might properly rely on developing a competing positive reinforced-based response that would acquire greater response strength sufficient to dominate in the response elicitation hierarchy. If, however, the need is to extinguish behavior developed because of a history of avoidance, escape, or aggression, the treatment of choice would also have to concern itself with ensuring that those response-eliciting stimuli or their generalized variants do not continue to support the avoidance or escape behaviors in the future. Whereas extinction, counterconditioning, or desensitization might not be required for the first hypothesized causal factor, it would be unthinkable not to guarantee its incorporation in designs premised on the other hypothesized causal factors. Acceptance of the learning model carries testable implications about the design of an optimum treatment program (at least for the immediate amelioration of the symptoms) and suggests guidelines for the selection among alternative strategies of learning-based interventions.

Tremors and Dystonias

The largest source of data on behavioral control in these conditions will likely be found in the literature on cerebral palsy, Parkinsonism, and traumatic disorders (Cooper & Riklin, 1973). These, however, do not easily qualify as paroxysmal to the same degree as the other examples in this section. There is, however, a strong suggestion of relief attributable to relaxation training, reward, biofeedback programs, and self-control treatment. Other conditions such as writers cramp and torticollis have been similarly investigated with moderate success, although well-controlled behavioral protocols are lacking. Chapter 15 by Bird provides an extended discussion of the problem.

PROGRAM DEVELOPMENT

While there are few unusual elements in the design and administration of behavior therapy protocols for these illness complexes, it would seem appropriate at this time to rehearse some of the major considerations. The demands of working with somatic-based complaints, and often in the close contact of traditional medical practice, warrants such a review.

At the outset it is noteworthy to remember that behavioral treatment for "medical" disorders will usually be sought only after the "treatment of choice" (usually pharmacomanagement) has proven refractory or unsatisfactory. It should also be remembered that while a large proportion of behavioral medicine treatments were performed on subjects with multiple handicaps or retardation, their application for otherwise "normal" subjects deserves most favorable consideration.

I submit that four areas of the total treatment effort can be identified: baseline, intervention, evaluation, follow-up.

Baseline

Because of each of these illnesses is notoriously subject to periods of remission and seemingly biorhythmic effects, the need for a reasonable baseline period is mandatory. Often this position is compromised, but it should not be viewed as a research nicety; it is very much more of a clinical necessity.

A proper baseline period presupposes that the necessary inventories, intake or interview protocols, psychodiagnostic determinations, and summary medical information are available. Standard hospital forms will often prove inadequate for the clinician's behavioral objectives and tailor-made paper-and-pencil batteries will need to be developed. To the extent possible, every effort should be made in collaboration with the attending physician that the drug regimen not be altered during this time.

Finally, the format for data recording and organization should be considered. In many instances individual capture of single symptoms will either be too rapid for manual recording (tics) or unobservable (petit mal). Most serious, however, will be the dependence upon self-report. If possible, multiple sources of baseline behavior should be sought, and to objectively evaluate subsequent changes in topography or severity, a video recording of the symptoms prior to treatment is most valuable.

Intervention

With a decision by the therapist to proceed with one or more of the tactical alternatives, the incorporation of a multiple baseline design is desirable. It is likely that reversal or no-treatment conditions will be impossible to introduce (not only do regulations take a dim view of such procedures, but in the case of seizures occurring with great frequency, the consequences can be risky). The treatment phase, although primarily directed to the patient, must be equally concerned with assuring adequate training and cooperation by staff, family, and others. Since most patients with these disorders will only rarely be subject to 24-hour monitoring, the outpatient population must be serviced with the next best approximations to the ideal treatment environment. For example, we have found that the use of telephone contact during treatment not only increases the probability of compliance and goodwill but can, in many instances, be used as a reinforcer for those behaviors as well.

Evaluation

Analysis of the data is almost certain to focus on the attenuation of the presenting symptom. It is equally important that other parameters of the symptom also be examined—namely, severity, duration, and pattern. Similarly, treatment effects on changes in environmental control (person, time, location) should be carefully noted. It is also more than for simple curiosity to suggest that changes in other indices or the status of the patient be correlated with the phases of the treatment program. Changes in serum level concentrations of anticonvulsants, EEG characteristics, and general conduct and behavior will often accompany the course of behavior therapy and should be appropriately reported.

Finally, not only should statistical quantification of the results draw upon measures of central tendency and variability but, where appropriate, the use of serial correlational techniques, scaling procedures, and other multidimensional analyses will often be most illuminating.

Follow-Up

It is the position of this writer that the follow-up period constitutes a part of the treatment program itself. As noted earlier, it is important first to ascertain that changes are independent from any background cycles of good and bad, and then to evaluate whether any changes are transient or have been maintained once the course of intensive treatment has been terminated. If indeed the changes do not appear to last for any appreciable time, a valuable clinical service can nonetheless be claimed for the temporary relief—or relief that requires ongoing "behavioral prosthesis"—that can be demonstrated. A follow-up period of 12 to 24 months is hardly unreasonable for these symptom complaints. Occasionally, "booster treatments" interspersed during the follow-up period will be of great value. Similarly, many patients (and their families) might benefit during this period from therapy programs not directly focused on the referral illness. And most important, the information provided from the follow-up can enable or convince the physician to consider pharmacological adjustments, reduction, or even elimination.

SUMMARY

There is excitement, confidence, and documentation that the behavior therapy treatment programs in behavioral medicine offer measures of relief not otherwise attainable for paroxysmal disorders of the CNS. The research and clinical experience is relatively new, and claims for successes must be tempered with the realization that only infrequently have appropriate controls and analyses been used. This is particularly true of studies concerned with movement disorders. It is probably a fair guess that for the near term, research and clinical experience will continue this way, but progress (not only in the rejection of wrong hypotheses) is sure to result. Behavior therapy applications to disorders of the central nervous system, while in many ways the more difficult of the species, hold much untested promise for medicine, behavior science, and the patient in a predicament.

ACKNOWLEDGMENT

Ideas for portions of this chapter were generated at the Switzer Conference (Denver, 1978) and in presentations at various epilepsy conferences. The continued support of Cesare T. Lombroso, Chief, Seizure Unit (Children's Hospital Medical Center) and Barbara A. Balaschak, and their contributions to the Behavioral Neurology Program, is most appreciatively acknowledged.

REFERENCES

Abi Rafi, A. Learning theory and the treatment of tics. *Journal of Psychosomatic Research,* 1962, **6**, 71–76.

Adams, K. M., Klinge, V., & Keiser, T. W. The extinction of a self-injurious behavior in an epileptic child. *Behaviour Research and Therapy,* 1973, **11**, 351–356.

Ascher, E. Psychodynamic considerations in Gilles de la Tourette's disease (maladie des tics). *American Journal of Psychiatry,* 1948, **105**, 267–276.

Balaschak, B. A. Teacher-implemented behavior modification in a case of organically based epilepsy. *Journal of Consulting and Clinical Psychology,* 1976, **44**, 218–223.

Barret, B. H. Reduction in the rate of multiple tics by free operant conditioning methods. *Journal of Nervous and Mental Disease,* 1962, **135**, 187–195.

Ben-Sira, Z. The structure and dynamics of the image of diseases. *Journal of Chronic Diseases,* 1977, **30**, 831–842.

Bird, B. L., & Cataldo, M. Experimental analysis of EMG feedback in treating dystonia. *Annals of Neurology,* 1978, **3**, 310–315.

Birk, L. Behavior Therapy and Behavioral Psychotherapy. In Armand M. Nicholi (Ed.), *The Harvard guide to modern psychiatry,* Harvard University Press, Cambridge, 1978.

Browning, R. M., & Stover, D. D. *Behavior modification in child treatment: An experimental and clinical approach.* Chicago: Aldine, 1970.

Bunker, H. A. Epilepsy: A brief historical sketch. In P. H. Hoc & R. P. Knight (Eds.), *Epilepsy.* New York: Grune & Stratton, 1947.

Cabral, R. J., & Scott, D. F. Effects of two desensitization techniques, biofeedback, and relaxation, on intractable epilepsy: Follow-up study. *Journal of Neurology, Neurosurgery and Psychiatry,* 1976, **39**, 504–507.

Chabbert, L. De la maladie des tic. *Archives de Neurologie,* 1893, **25**, 10.

Clark, D. F. Behavior therapy of Gilles de la Tourette syndrome. *British Journal of Psychiatry,* 1966, **112**, 771–778.

Cleeland, C. S. Behavioral techniques in the modification of spasmodic torticollis. *Neurology,* 1973, **23**, 1241–1247.

Cooper, I. S., & Riklin, M. Organic and psychogenic factors in tremor. *Psychiatric Annals,* 1973, **3**, 50–53.

Daniels, L. K. The treatment of grand mal epilepsy by covert and operant conditioning techniques: A case study. *Psychosomatic Medicine,* 1975, **16**, 65–67.

Dorcus, R. M., & Schaffer, G. W. *Textbook of abnormal psychology* (3rd edition). Baltimore: Williams & Wilkins, 1945.

Efron, R. The effect of olfactory stimuli in arresting uncinate fits. *Brain,* 1956, **79**, 267–282.

Epilepsy Foundation of America. A guide to the therapeutic monitoring of antiepileptic drug levels. Washington, D.C.: EFA, 1977.

Erikson, B., & Persson, T. Gilles de la Tourette syndrome. *British Journal of Psychiatry,* 1969, **115**, 351–353.

Fenichel, O. *The psychoanalytic theory of neurosis.* New York: Norton, 1945.

Fernando, S. J. M. Gilles de la Tourette's syndrome. *British Journal of Psychiatry,* 1967, **113**, 607–617.

Fordyce, W. E. *Behavioral methods for chronic pain and illness.* St. Louis: Mosby, 1976.

Forster, F. M. *Reflex epilepsy, behavioral therapy, and conditional reflexes.* Springfield, Ill.: C. C. Thomas, 1977.

Gannt, W. H. B. F. Skinner and his contingencies. *Conditional Reflex,* 1970, **5**, 63–74.

Gardner, J. E. Behavior therapy treatment approach to a psychogenic seizure case. *Journal of Consulting Psychology,* 1967, **31**, 209–212.

Gilles, de la Tourette. Etude sur une affection nerveuse caractérisée par de l'incoordination motrice, accompagnée d'écholalie et de coprolalie. *Archives de Neurologie,* 1885, **9**, 158–200.

Goldiamond, I. Personal communication.

Guinon, G. Sur la maladie des tics convulsifs. *Revue de Médicaine,* 1886, **6**, 54.

Hermann, B. P. Psychological effects and epilepsy: A review. *American Psychological Assoc. Journal Supplement,* MS. 1430, 1977.

Hersen, M., & Eisler, R. M. Behavioral approaches to the study and treatment of psychogenic tics. *Genetic Psychology Monographs,* 1973, **87**, 289–312.

Hutzell, R. R., Platzek, D., & Loque, P. E. Control of symptoms of Gilles de la Tourette's syndrome by self-monitoring. *Journal of Behavior Therapy and Experimental Psychiatry,* 1974, **5**, 71–76.

Ince, L. P. The use of relaxation training and a conditioned stimulus in the elimination of epileptic seizures in a child: A case study. *Journal of Behavior Therapy and Experimental Psychiatry,* 1976, **7**, 39–42.

Itard, J. M. G. Mémorie sur quelque fonctions involuntaires des appareils de la locomotion, de la préhension et de la voix. *Archives of Géneral Médicaine,* 1825, **8**, 385–407.

Jenkins, C. D. The semantic differential for health. *Public Health Report,* 1966, **81**, 549–558.

Kanfer, F. H., & Karoly, P. Self-control: A behavioristic excursion into the lion's den. *Behavior Therapy,* 1972, **3**, 398–416.

Kanner, L. *Child psychiatry.* Springfield, Ill.: C. C. Thomas, 1942.

Kelman, D. H. Gilles de la Tourette's disease in children: A review of the literature. *Journal of Child Psychology and Psychiatry,* 1965, **6**, 219–226.

Koster, G. Über die Maladie des tics impulsifs (mimische krampfneurose). *Dtsch. Z Nervenheilk,* 1965, **6**, 298–305.

Leitenberg, H. (Ed.), *Handbook of behavior modification and behavior therapy,* New Jersey: Prentice-Hall, 1976.

Longin, H. E., Kohn, J. P., & Macurik, K. M. The modification of choreal movements. *Journal of Behavior Therapy and Experimental Psychiatry,* 1974, **5**, 263–265.

Lovaas, I. Letter to the editor. *Psychology Today,* Nov. 1970.

Luborsky, L., Docherty, J. P., Todd, T. C., Knapp, P. H., Mirsky, A. F., & Gottschalk, L. A. A context analysis of psychological states prior to petit-mal EEG paroxysms. *Journal of Nervous and Mental Diseases,* 1975, **160**, 282–298.

Morphew, J. A., & Sim, M. Gilles de la Tourette's syndrome: A clinical and psychopathological study. *British Journal of Medical Psychology,* 1969, **42**, 293–301.

Mostofsky, D. I. (Ed.), *Behavioral control and modification of physiological activity.* New Jersey: Prentice-Hall, 1977.

Mostofsky, D. I., & Balaschak, B. A. Psychobiological control of seizures. *Psychological Bulletin,* 1977, **84**, 723–750.

Muthén, J. Psychological treatment of epileptic seizures. Thesis, Institute of Applied Psychology, Uppsala University, Sweden, 1978.

Rodin, E. A. *Prognosis of patients with epilepsy.* Chicago: C. C. Thomas, 1968.

Rosen, M., & Wesner, C. A behavioral approach to Tourette's syndrome. *Journal of Consulting and Clinical Psychology,* 1973, **41**, 308–312.

Rowlett, D. B., & Dudley, D. D. COPD: Psychosocial and psychophysiological issues. *Psychosomatics,* 1978, **19**, 273–279.

Sand, P. L., & Carlson, C. Failure to establish control over tics in Gilles de la Tourette syndrome with behaviour therapy techniques. *British Journal of Psychiatry,* 1973, **122**, 665–670.

Sands, H., & Minters, F. C. *The epilepsy fact book.* Philadelphia: Davis, 1977.

Schwartz, G. E., & Weiss, S. M. Yale Conference on behavioral medicine: A proposed definition and statement of goals. *Journal of Behavioral Medicine,* 1978, **1**, 3–12.

Shapiro, A. K. Symposium on Gilles de la Tourette's syndrome. *New York State Journal of Medicine,* 1970, **70**, 2193–2214.

Shapiro, A. K., Shapiro, E. S., Brown, R. D., & Sweet, R. D. *Gilles de la Tourette syndrome.* New York: Raven Press, 1978.

Sterman, M. B., & Friar, L. Suppression of seizures in an epileptic following sensorimotor EEG feedback training. *Electroencephalography and Clinical Neurophysiology,* 1972, **33**, 89–95.

Sterman, M. B., & MacDonald, L. R. Effects of central cortical EEG feedback training on incidence of poorly controlled seizures. *Epilepsia,* 1978, **19**, 207–222.

Stevens, H. Paroxysmal choreoathetosis. *Archives of Neurology,* 1966, **14**, 415–420.

Stevens, J. R. Endogenous conditioning to abnormal cerebral electrical transients in man. *Science,* 1962, **137**, 974–976.

Stevens, J. R., & Blachly, P. H. Successful treatment of the maladie des tics. *American Journal of Diseases of Children,* 1966, **112**, 541–545.

Taylor, D. C. Aspects of seizure disorders: II On prejudice. *Developmental Medicine and Child Neurology,* 1973, **15**, 91–94.

Thomas, E. J., Abrams, K. S., & Johnson, J. B. Self-monitoring and reciprocal inhibition in the modification of multiple tics of Gilles de la Tourette syndrome. *Journal of Behavior Therapy and Experimental Psychiatry,* 1971, **2**, 159–171.

Tophoff, M. Massed practice, relaxation and assertion training in the treatment of Gilles de la Tourette's syndrome. *Journal of Behavior Therapy and Experimental Psychiatry,* 1973, **4**, 71–73.

Walton, D. Experimental psychology and the treatment of a tiquer. *Journal of Child Psychology and Psychiatry,* 1971, **2**, 159–171.

Weiner, H. L., Bresnan, M. J., & Levitt, L. P. *Pediatric Neurology for the House Officer.* Baltimore: Williams & Wilkins, 1977.

Williams, D. T., Spiegel, H., & Mostofsky, D. I. Neurogenic and hysterical seizures in children and adolescents: Differential diagnostic and therapeutic considerations. *American Journal of Psychiatry,* 1978, **135**, 82–86.

Wilson, S. A. K. *Neurology.* New York: Williams & Wilkins, 1941.

Wooley, S. C., Blackwell, B., Epps, B., & Harper, R. A learning treatment model for illness behavior. American Psychosomatic Society, New Orleans, 1975 (mimeograph).

Yates, A. J. The application of learning theory to the treatment of tics. *Journal of Abnormal and Social Psychology,* 1958, **56**, 175–182.

CHAPTER 17

Behavioral Perspectives in Preventive Medicine

Bruce J. Masek, Leonard H. Epstein, and Dennis C. Russo

Health care is America's third largest industry, consuming $160 billion in 1977 and representing 8.6% of the gross national product (Culliton, 1978). The phenomenal development and expense of medical technology, increased construction costs, expanded public subsidy of health care, and the current awareness and interest in the use of health services by the average citizen have partly been responsible for such increases. Although costs are increasing (Walsh, 1978), there is little evidence that such increases produce significantly better health in the general population (Culliton, 1978). For this reason, a number of knowledgeable sources have called for the renovation and extension of the health care system (Breslow, 1978; Hamburg & Brown, 1978; Schwartz & Weiss, 1978). A major movement in renovation is a shift in emphasis from curative medicine to prevention and health promotion (Ball, 1978; Saward & Sorenson, 1978).

The emphasis on preventive medicine in the United States is reflected in the statement on prevention in The Forward Plan for Health FY 1978–82 (1976):

In the absence of a major scientific breakthrough (e.g., cancer cure), further expansion of the Nation's health system is likely to produce only marginal increases in the overall health status of the American people. Obviously, we must continue efforts to correct the inequalities and the maldistribution of services in the current system, but in the long run, the greater benefits are likely to accrue from efforts to improve the health habits of all Americans and the environment in which they live and work [p. 69].

Similarly, Lalonde (1975) has indicated that the future level of health for Canadians will be determined by improvements in the environment, modification of self-imposed health risks, and expansion of our knowledge of human biology. Medical science will continue the attempt to improve the quality of life and to increase longevity. The long-range importance of this medical research for future advances in the diagnosis, treatment, and prevention of disease must be kept in the perspective that acknowledges the growing importance of preventive medicine (Comroe, 1978). It is clear within preventive medicine that a mandate for research and effective strategies for the prevention of disease and maintenance of health is being issued to the behavioral sciences (Kane, 1977; Saward & Sorenson, 1978; Weiss, 1975).

PREVENTION AND THE BEHAVIORAL SCIENCES

From a behavioral perspective, preventive medicine is concerned with the development of behavior that promotes optimal health through the identification and modification of maladaptive behavior that is likely to produce illness, and the prevention of further disability after the onset of disease. Historically, medical science has conceptualized preventive medicine in terms of primary, secondary, and tertiary prevention (Clark, 1967). Primary prevention refers to interventions designed to prevent the occurrence of disease. Examples of primary prevention include immunization against poliomyelitis or the prescription of iron tablets during pregnancy to prevent iron-deficiency anemia. Secondary prevention involves efforts for the early detection and treatment of disease through such measures as routine physical examination, X-ray screening, pap smears, and so on. Tertiary prevention focuses on rehabilitation; for example, antihypertensive medication therapy to reduce the risk of coronary heart disease.

Prevention programs that utilize behavioral science components have been, principally, primary prevention efforts (Kasl & Cobb, 1966). More recently, several articles have suggested the expansion of behavioral approaches to other aspects of prevention. Breslow (1978) has defined the role of behavioral science in terms of primary and secondary prevention. He suggests that primary prevention efforts, aimed at reducing the occurrence of known or suspected causative factors of chronic diseases such as obesity, cigarette smoking, sedentary life-style, improperly balanced diet, and psychological stress, be stepped up through the implementation of behaviorally based programs. Likewise, secondary prevention programs designed to halt the progression of chronic disease once detected through procedures such as compliance with medication regimens (e.g., antihypertensive medication in asymptomatic heart disease) are viewed as a second area of great potential. Cataldo, Russo, Bird, and Varni (in press) have further suggested the importance of the role of behavioral science in tertiary prevention. In cases of long-term chronic diseases, such as chronic pain, epilepsy, and neuromuscular disease, they argue that rehabilitative efforts should focus not only toward the return of normal physical function but also on the modification of inappropriate behavior that is likely to be learned in conjunction with long-term chronic disease. These suggested expansions of behavioral science inquiry into preventive medicine fit well within the context of recent developments and concerns in health care.

The use of behavioral procedures in preventive medicine for risk factor intervention and health maintenance is a relatively recent development (Berkanovic, 1976; Pomerleau, Bass, & Crown, 1975). The potential use of behavioral interventions to modify risk-taking behaviors and make a significant impact on the health status of the citizenry of this country has been formulated (Blackly, 1977; Haggerty, 1977; McAlister, Farquhar, Thorsen, & Maccoby, 1976). Yet, little empirical research exists to evaluate the direct contribution of the procedures of behavior therapy and behavior modification to preventive medicine. However, behavior therapy will undoubtedly contribute more to preventive medicine as the developing field of behavioral medicine is integrated into medical training (cf. Stoeckle, 1977) and services (Cataldo et al., in press).

Preparing a general review of the contributions of behavioral science to preventive medicine is a considerable undertaking. For the purposes of this chapter, we have chosen to focus specifically on the role of behavior modification and behavior therapy. A brief review of risk factor identification as a basis for prevention programs is undertaken first. The translation of these risk factors into viable treatment strategies within a behavioral conceptualization follows. Based upon these considerations, two courses of treatment may be called for. (*a*) Treatment based upon knowledge of risk factors associated with a particular disease; and (*b*) Treatment based upon the development of patient skills and compliance, irrespective of the disease. Finally, a discussion of some general considerations for future research is presented.

RISK FACTORS IN CHRONIC DISEASE

Behavioral approaches to prevention of cardiovascular disease have been the most researched of any areas in behavioral approaches to prevention. This literature will serve as the focus for defining intervention strategies for risk factor identification and modification, treatment strategies, and conceptual issues.

The identification of risk factors represents an initial step in the prevention of disease and the development of strategies for health maintenance. Risk factors are those circumstances (e.g., occupation or environment), behaviors (e.g., smoking), or conditions (e.g., obesity) that place an individual in increased jeopardy to develop a particular disease. A number of other factors, such as genetic predisposition, also influence risk. Epstein and LaPorte (1978) have suggested that since many of these risk factors are behaviors, or have behavioral components, behavioral strategies appear appropriate for the study of their epidemiology and their treatment.

Risk factor identification is a primary component of traditional approaches to prevention (Wilner, Walkley, & O'Neill, 1978). It can also have great value as a basis for assessment of relevant behaviors for modification. While behavioral analysis has typically been conducted with small numbers of individuals, risk factor identification is usually based upon population characteristics. Traditional studies may therefore be used as a basis for the selection of target responses for behavioral prevention programs. Additionally, since epidemiological methods are able to assess the relative contribution of each factor in the development of disease, the sequence of target modification may also be suggested.

Prevention of disease requires control of well-documented risk factors (Stamler & Epstein, 1972). For cardiovascular disease, a number of behaviors have been identified that are associated with increased mortality. A review of these factors will serve to provide the background for an analysis of the current conceptualization and treatment technology for behavioral primary prevention programs in cardiovascular disease.

Belloc (1973) presents data to suggest that the presence or absence of certain behaviors can significantly modify average life expectancy. In a sample of 6298 adult Californians, the relationships among mortality, physical health status, income level, and seven specific health behaviors were studied over the course of

5½ years. Mortality was found to be strongly associated with poor health practices much more so than with physical health status or income level. The behavioral factors that were most predictive of mortality were obesity, smoking, alcohol use, and physical inactivity. Hours of sleep and regularity of meals were also predictive of mortality but to a lesser degree. Most importantly, there was a strong relationship between the number of health practices an individual engaged in and his or her chances of dying within 5½ years as depicted in Figure 1. This study is representative of a number of prospective studies conducted since 1950 that have indicated that several physical and behavioral characteristics are predictive of developing cardiovascular disease.

The "Framingham Study" (Dowber, Kannel, & Lyell, 1963) is another epidemiological study designed to identify risk factors for cardiovascular disease. The incidence of Coronary Heart Disease (CHD) was studied over a 12-year period in a population of 2187 men and 2669 women initially free of coronary disease from the community of Framingham, Massachusetts. Seven risk factors were investigated as they related to the development of CHD: (*a*) age; (*b*) serum cholesterol; (*c*) diastolic blood pressure; (*d*) relative weight (adjusted for sex and height); (*e*) cigarettes per day; (*f*) hemoglobin; and (*g*) electrocardiogram (ECG). Truett, Cornfield, and Kannel (1967) analyzed the data from the Framingham Study using a multivariate procedure. They reported that the combined effect of all risk factors in predicting CHD was precise despite the marked de-

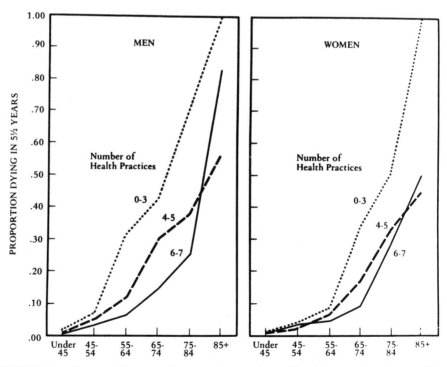

FIGURE 1.   Age-specific mortality rates by number of health practices, by sex (From N. B. Belloc, *Preventive Medicine*, 1973, **2**, 67–81. Copyright 1973 by Academic Press, Inc. Reprinted by permission).

partures of the actual distributions from multivariate normality. Individual risk factors found to be most important were elevated cholesterol, cigarette smoking, ECG abnormality, and blood pressure. Evidence for the causative role of these factors and several others (e.g., physical inactivity and diet) continues to mount.

The role of psychological stress as a risk factor for CHD has also received considerable attention in recent years, but it is less clearly understood (Jenkins, 1971; Russek & Russek, 1976). The coronary-prone behavior pattern or "Type A" behavior deserves special mention because of its relationship to CHD. Type A behavior is described as an overt behavior pattern that is characterized by exaggerated competitiveness, need for achievement, explosiveness of speech, hyperalertness, tenseness of facial musculature, and feelings of chronic time pressure (Friedman & Rosenman, 1974). Type B individuals are described as more easy-going, less competitive, and less reactive. The best evidence for the relationship between the Type A behavior pattern and coronary heart disease comes from the Western Collaborative Group Study. This was a prospective study of the predictive value of various cardiovascular risk factors in healthy adult males on subsequent development of CHD. The results from the Western Collaborative Group Study (WCGS) have been reported at intervals (Rosenman, Friedman, Straus, Wurm, Kositchek, Hahn, & Werthessen, 1964; Rosenman, Friedman, Straus, Wurm, Jenkins, & Messinger, 1968; Rosenman, Friedman, Straus, Jenkins, Zyzanski, & Wurm, 1970) with the final follow-up at 8½ years recently being reported (Rosenman, Brand, Jenkins, Friedman, Straus, & Wurm, 1975). The results of 3154 subjects at risk were presented, with the sample being approximately equally divided into 1589 Type A subjects and 1565 Type B subjects. At the final follow-up, 257 subjects were observed to have CHD. Factors that were related to the development of CHD across both decades studied (40–49, 50–59) were schooling, current cigarette smoking, systolic and diastolic blood pressure, serum cholesterol, triglyceride, beta/alpha lipoprotein ratios, and behavior pattern. The relative effects of behavior pattern in relationship to the other risk factors were assessed. For the younger subjects, the results indicated a 2.21 relative risk ratio for Type A persons as compared to Type B persons. After adjustment for independent contribution of other major risk factors, this ratio was reduced to 1.87. For older subjects, the unadjusted and adjusted risk rates were 2.31 and 1.98, respectively. The results suggest that Type A persons are twice as likely to have CHD than Type B subjects, and that this important risk factor operates independently of other risk factors. Further analyses of these data by Brand (1977) show relative risk for all Type A versus B subjects to be 2.31 as great for A's and B's, while the adjustment for other major risk factors reduces risk to 1.97. Brand then attempted to identify the effect modification of interaction of Type A versus B on the basis of the level of other risk factors. Effect modification refers to the possibility that CHD risk as a function of behavior pattern may be moderated by other risk factors. Subjects at risk were divided on the basis of behavior pattern and four major risk factors (age, systolic blood pressure, cigarette smoking, serum cholesterol) into 32 subgroups (2^5). Linear and logistic coefficients of risk were developed, with the additive logistic model fitting the observed data better, suggesting that any risk factor may have a multiplicative effect applied to the background level determined for the other risk factors by multivariate statistical procedures, Rosenman, Brand, Scholtz, and Friedman (1976), indicated that behavior pattern was the second most important factor after cholesterol in the younger subjects, and the most important for the older subjects.

The predictive value of risk factors obtained by the WCGS was recently compared to similar data (without behavior pattern as a risk factor) obtained in the Framingham Study (Brand, Rosenman, Sholtz, & Friedman, 1976). The results indicated that the risk factors were comparable across the two studies. For example, risk predictions were made for each WCGS subjects for both Framingham and WCGS risk equations. Results showed correlations of .82 and .89 between risk predictions obtained by Framingham and WCGS risk equations for subjects in younger and older decades. In addition, the incidence of CHD in the WCGS study was predicted by establishing deciles at risk using the Framingham risk factors. The results also showed that the relative risk for Type A versus Type B subjects was increased as the subjects' relative risk for other risk factors increased, again suggesting the effect of modification noted by Brand (1977).

In addition to predicting the incidence of CHD, Type A behavior has been related to the prognosis for developing a second myocardial infarction (MI). Jenkins, Zyzanski, and Rosenman (1976) assessed the role of Type A behavior and other risk factors on risk of recurrent MI in patients with CHD. Results showed Type A behavior, cigarettes smoked daily, and serum cholesterol differentiated the subjects in a combined prospective-retrospective design. A stepwise discriminant function analysis indicated that Type A was the best single predictor of a new MI. Bruhn, Paredes, Adsett, and Wolf (1973) showed that Type A behavior was predictive of sudden death in a population of patients who had a previous MI.

The Type A behavior pattern has been characterized as an overt behavior pattern. However, very little research has been performed to reliably quantify differences in behavior patterns of Type A or Type B subjects. In addition, the conditions that elicit or maintain Type A behavior are not well understood. The research by Glass and associates has begun to address these issues, and the recent book by Glass (1977) should be useful to those interested in behavioral aspects of the Type A behavior pattern.

Data are slowly accumulating to indicate that it is feasible to intervene and modify risk behavior. Primary prevention requires the development and maintenance of behaviors necessary for cardiovascular health including: (a) controlled intake of saturated fats, cholesterol, sugar, and salt; (b) restriction of caloric intake for maintenance of optimal body weight; (c) regular physical activity; (d) avoidance of cigarette smoking; (e) relaxation skills for management of stress; and (f) adherence to antihypertensive or antihyperlipidemia medication regimens.

BEHAVIORAL APPROACHES TO DISEASE PREVENTION

The tactics of intervention for the prevention of disease by traditional means are based upon a large and expanding literature (Breslow, 1976; Hughes & Kane, 1977). Major behavior change efforts have traditionally centered on health education, environmental modification, and group and individual interventions to reduce risk (Berkanovic, 1976). While the value of behavior modification in primary prevention programs has been recognized, the procedures developed in applied behavior analysis for use with other populations and problems are only now beginning to be modified and assessed.

Cataldo et al. (in press) suggest that efforts aimed at the treatment of chronic disease by the behavioral model be undertaken within the context of the medical environment and the knowledge of its practices. While this rationale was developed for existing disease states, a similar approach to guide behavioral approaches into preventive medicine may also be appropriate. Areas of study such as epidemiology (Epstein & LaPorte, 1978) and health education (Breslow, 1978) may provide productive existing bases for the development of behavioral methodology.

Behavioral procedures are well suited to modify risk-taking behavior and promote health maintenance (Epstein & Ossip, in press; Schwartz & Weiss, 1978). Promotion of improved health is largely a matter of getting individuals to engage in a lifestyle that promotes the healthful behavior. Where learned patterns of maladaptive health behavior are identified, they may be modified so they no longer pose a risk for the individual to develop chronic illness. Within this framework, several approaches may be taken. Since maladaptive behaviors such as smoking and overeating represent behavioral excesses, procedures may be designed to reduce or eliminate these behaviors directly. Contingencies placed directly on the response or its frequency of occurrence may be of benefit. For example, programs to reduce the number of cigarettes smoked per day (Marston & McFall, 1971; Schmahl, Lichtenstein, & Harris, 1972) may be developed using response cost or positive reinforcement.

A second approach might therefore focus on the development of alternative or competing behaviors rather than, or in conjunction with, maladaptive response reduction. As an example, programs for obesity often focus on weight reduction as a primary dependent variable (Hall, Hall, Borden, & Hanson, 1975; Horan, Baker, Hoffman, & Shute, 1975). Clearly, weight loss is the major concern of the general public. Behaviorally, modification of eating patterns and food choices may be the more efficacious strategy, with weight loss seen as a secondary and long-term goal (Stuart & Davis, 1972; Stunkard, 1976). Using this strategy, persons may be frequently reinforced for small positive changes in behavior. Additionally, maintenance may be facilitated since these responses are easier for the individual to monitor than weight change.

Development of empirically based prevention programs may be best accomplished in two stages. As an initial step, small groups or individuals are studied to assess antecedents of both adaptive and maladaptive health behaviors in at-risk individuals (Zifferblatt, 1975). In this same analysis, identification of consequences that are effective in maintaining current health behaviors may also be examined. The methodologies for this type of evaluation currently exist (cf. Hersen & Bellack, 1976), although these methods have typically been applied to other problems with other populations. Through the study of small groups and individuals the most efficacious, as well as the range of potentially utilizable treatment methodologies, may be defined. The results of these investigations could then be used in the design of primary prevention behavior change packages which would be applicable to large numbers of individuals. Based upon empirical outcome of the initial small group studies, these packages would provide empirically pretested treatment. Applied behavior analysis as well as group statistical methodologies could then be used to evaluate the impact of the packages and, particularly, specific cases in which the treatment failed to produce effect.

Self-monitoring for breast cancer is a case in point. Breast self-examination requires the regular emission of a fairly complex chain of behaviors for which the consequences of successful performance (detection of a node) frequently results in the removal of a breast. If one is willing to assume that the threat of the ultimate long-term consequence of death from cancer controls very little present-day behavior, then it is understandable why breast cancer screening programs in the United States have largely been failures (Kushner, 1978). The short-term aversive consequences of mastectomy are potent events in maintaining the avoidance response for most women. In other words, most women do not engage in routine breast self-examination for the very simple reason that they would rather not know if a node is present. Data by Fink, Shapiro, and Levison (1968) provided indirect support for this analysis. A free-screening program for breast cancer for women at risk (between the ages of 40 and 64) was conducted. Of the 11,500 women in the original sample, over 4000 failed to attend despite repeated individual contacts. Of the women who did participate, 65% attended after receiving one notice, 17% required a second notice or phone contact, and 18% required multiple additional phone contacts. The development of innovative behavioral procedures to promote early detection of breast cancer will require just such an analysis of the antecedents and consequences of the targeted health behavior before this situation is likely to change.

Table 1 presents behavioral procedures currently in use to modify risk-taking behavior and promote health maintenance. As can be seen, behavioral approaches include procedures for direct reduction of risk behaviors (e.g., self-punishment) as well as those designed to facilitate the development and maintenance of appropriate health behavior (e.g., relaxation training). Appropriate behavioral intervention should be based upon the realization that the relationship between behavior and illness is varied and complex (Cataldo et al., in press; Fabrega, 1974; Fordyce, 1976; Stroebel, 1977). The application of behavioral procedures to preventive medicine requires the consideration of a number of variables, including the empirical evaluation of risk factors, the identification of antecedents and the consequences of health behavior, determination of the unit of intervention (i.e., the individual, the family, the school, etc.), and concern for the long-term maintenance of change. Attention to these factors will very likely influence the outcome and widespread applicability of behavioral approaches to prevention.

In the remainder of this chapter, we focus on two areas of behavioral treatment; direct treatment designed to produce a reduction in risk-taking behavior and facilitate health behavior maintenance, and procedures designed to supplement traditional methods of prevention in the improvement of patient compliance. Both areas provide opportunities for the application of behavioral technology in primary, secondary, and tertiary prevention programs. While thus far, the majority of behavioral effort has been seen in primary prevention of cardiovascular risk, secondary and tertiary programs in cardiovascular and other chronic diseases are currently underway and they provide examples of the range of treatment potential that behavioral approaches bring to preventive programs. Therefore, while the preponder-

Table 1.   Behavioral Intervention Strategies for Health Maintenance

---

Aversive conditioning procedures to eliminate risk-taking behaviors
1. Covert sensitization
2. Electric shock
3. Noxious chemicals

Biofeedback
1. Management of hypertension
2. Relaxation training adjunct

Contingency management procedures
1. Behavioral contracts to modify risk-taking or to promote maintenance of health behaviors
2. Reinforcement
    (a) Social reinforcement of acquisition of health behaviors
    (b) Token economies, lotteries, monetary rewards, and other incentives to participate in health care system
3. Response cost for noncompliance

Modeling principles to facilitate learning to appropriate health behaviors

Self-control procedures for acquisition and maintenance of health behaviors
1. Self-monitoring
2. Self-punishment
3. Self-reinforcement

Stimulus control of environment to facilitate acquisition and maintenance of health behaviors

Stress Management
1. Assertive training
2. Behavioral rehearsal
3. Relaxation techniques
    (a) Autogenic control
    (b) Meditation (Yoga)
    (c) Muscle relaxation
4. Social skills training
5. Systematic desensitization

---

ance of studies cited deal with primary prevention of cardiovascular disease, noteworthy examples of behavioral programs in secondary and tertiary prevention, and treatment of other chronic conditions are also discussed when they are suggestive of the potential efficacy of behavioral intervention in preventive medicine.

DIRECT TREATMENT OF HEALTH BEHAVIOR

Direct treatment strategies focus on the reduction of risk behaviors and the establishment of behaviors to promote health maintenance. The development of behavioral procedures for inclusion in preventive medicine programs has been advocated in a number of areas such as periodontal disease (Horner & Keilitz, 1975; Martens, Frazier, Hirt, Meskin, & Proshek, 1973), cancer (Cullen, Fox, & Isom, 1976; Fox

& Goldsmith, 1976), obstructive lung disease (Goldsmith, 1972), diabetes (Lenner, 1976) and renal failure (Magrab & Papadoipoulou, 1977). This list is not exhaustive but represents some of the more challenging chronic illnesses that are likely to receive concentrated research efforts from behavioral scientists in the next two decades.

The prevention of cardiovascular disease appears to be one of the most important areas in which the direct application of behavioral procedures promises to yield positive results. Coronary heart disease is epidemic in the United States (Ball & Turner, 1975). It has been estimated that one male in five will develop clinical CHD before age 60 (Paffenbarger, 1972). The death rate of CHD victims (usually as a result of MI) is approximately 600,000 annually (Cooper, Pollock, Martin, White, Linnerud, & Jackson, 1976), and major advances in control may ultimately depend on advances in prevention. Behavioral scientists are just beginning to conduct well-organized research on the use of behavioral procedures to modify risk-taking behavior in the prevention of cardiovascular disease. As previously indicated, the empirical research in this area is sparse. However, several important investigations have been conducted and deserve mention in detail because of the conceptual and, in some instances, methodological advances they represent. Hopefully, they will collectively serve to stimulate further research.

Innovative behavioral programs for the primary prevention of cardiovascular disease have precedence in the "Know Your Body" program developed by the American Health Foundation in New York City (Williams, Arnold, & Wynder, 1977). The "Know Your Body" program represents the first comprehensive attempt to identify risk factors for later chronic disease in children and test an intervention package aimed at children exhibiting multiple risk behavior. Approximately 4600 children between the ages of 11 and 14 served as the target population to determine whether selected risk factors for chronic disease can be reduced through health screening, feedback of results, and health education. Screening was conducted in school and consisted of: (a) height; (b) weight; (c) three resting blood pressures; (d) plasma cholesterol; (e) nonfasting glucose level; (f) hematocrit; (g) modified Harvard Step Test; (h) a health knowledge survey; and (i) a health habits questionnaire. Following screening, the results were returned to students to be recorded in a "Health Passport" as well as to their parents and physicians. A health education program was then implemented in which modeling of appropriate health behaviors, personalized educational materials, continued self-monitoring of health behaviors, and classroom-learning activities were a central feature.

The preliminary results of the "Know Your Body" program indicated that risk factors for CHD are highly prevalent in pediatric and adolescent populations. Serum cholesterol levels were abnormally high in 43% of the students using 160 mg% as the upper normal limit. Approximately 10% of the students admitted to smoking, although consumption was widely varied. An average of 12% of the students were overweight (120% or more of ideal weight for height). Blood pressure determinations showed that 2% of the students had elevated average systolic ($\geq$ 140 mm Hg) or diastolic ($\geq$ 90 mm Hg) pressures. Health knowledge was typically poor, with blood pressure being the least understood factor.

The "Know Your Body" program is an ongoing project and screening will be conducted annually for the next several years to evaluate the impact of intervention in risk factors for chronic diseases at an early age. The program merits further investigation as it may prove to be a most cost-efficient model for preventive medicine (Boyer, 1975) and is an important first effort in this area. The contributions that a more rigorous application of behavioral methodology could make to a study such as this are severalfold, particularly in the area of behavioral assessment for personal behaviors.

Two studies conducted by the Stanford Heart Disease Prevention Program present evidence that cardiovascular risk factors can be modified using behavior modification strategies and a mass-media campaign. In one study (Meyer & Henderson, 1974), 240 employees of a local corporation were screened for risk of heart disease. The initial screening identified 36 persons as being at high risk for cardiovascular disease. Risk factors included in the evaluation were: (a) cigarette smoking; (b) overweight; (c) family history of premature cardiovascular disease; (d) elevated blood pressure; (e) physical inactivity; and (f) elevated serum cholesterol and triglyceride levels. The risk factors targeted for modification were overweight, physical inactivity, smoking, and improper diet. Twelve subjects received a behavioral treatment, 10 subjects received individual counseling, and 14 subjects received a one-time only physician consultation. The behavioral treatment consisted of 12 sessions conducted over an 11-week period which subjects and their spouses attended. The treatment package included the use of modeling of appropriate dietary behavior, a $50 refundable deposit to assure attendance, weekly weigh-ins, a token reward system for progress toward established goals, self-monitoring of risk behavior, and instructional materials. In the individual counseling treatment, each subject met for nine 15-minute sessions with a health educator. Information on risk reduction was elaborated, and subjects were encouraged to make modifications in their behavior. A weekly weigh-in was also conducted. The physician consultation consisted of a 20-minute lecture on cardiovascular risk factors, and a prescription for modification of the targeted behaviors.

The results of this study are important and suggest a fruitful area of research for behavioral scientists to pursue in the prevention of CHD. The results were analyzed in terms of change scores on the dependent variables between pre- and posttesting during the 12-week experimental period. Scores obtained at a three-month follow-up interval were also analyzed. The results showed that the behavioral strategies and the individual counseling procedure produced significantly greater change in the targeted behaviors than did the physician consultation. The follow-up data were suggestive (but not statistically significant) of a better maintenance effect of the behavioral procedures than the other two treatments, particularly with regard to serum cholesterol levels.

However, this study has methodological weaknesses. One weakness was the fact that no attempt was made to control for differences in the amount and quality of experimenter contact received by the three groups. More importantly, the assessment of cigarette smoking, dietary pattern (with the exception of triglyceride and serum cholesterol levels), and physical activity relied solely on self-report. Hence, these data must be interpreted with caution. The study could have benefited from the inclusion of a brief, objective physical fitness measure such as forced vital capacity or a maximal treadmill stress test as recommended by Cooper et al. (1976). A study by Evans (1976) suggests that inclusion of an objective nicotine-in-saliva analysis results in more accurate self-report of cigarette smoking, and such a procedure would have also been well-suited for inclusion in this study.

The study indicates that further investigation is needed to determine whether various components of the behavioral approach or of individualized counseling are sufficient to produce the magnitude of change observed. For that matter, adding procedures to each treatment without sacrificing cost effectiveness may result in further beneficial change in risk-taking behavior and a better maintenance effect. The technology of behavioral assessment (Hersen & Bellack, 1976) has a clear application in future studies of this type regarding the measurement of risk behavior. Longer follow-up should be conducted to further test the durability of the treatments.

The "Stanford Three Community Study" (Stern, Farquhar, Maccoby, & Russell, 1976) is an example of a large-scale intervention trial in risk reduction. A bilingual mass-media health education campaign was conducted in two communities, with a third serving as a control. The targeted risk factors were serum cholesterol and saturated fat levels in high risk individuals identified, using the procedures of Truett et al. (1967). The treatment package consisted of direct mailing of educational materials, exposure to radio and television advertisements, billboards, posters and newspaper columns all directed toward health education. The mass-media campaign was conducted for two 9-month intervals during the two years of the study. In addition, two-thirds of one of the experimental communities were exposed to the behavioral and counseling procedures of Meyer and Henderson (1974). Risk factors were assessed at the beginning of the study and at one-year and two-year intervals.

The results indicated that both the media campaign and the individual treatment procedures produced only moderate decreases in plasma cholesterol levels in men (triglyceride levels were not reported) in the two experimental communities. This effect was maintained over the course of two years. Only women in the intensive individual treatment subgroup showed a substantial decrease in cholesterol levels. Women in the other experimental groups and both men and women in the control group showed an increase in cholesterol levels over the two-year period. The authors attributed these somewhat inconsistent findings to a methodological problem with the first baseline serum cholesterol determination, and the fact that women have lower plasma low-density lipoprotein concentrations than men, which may result in underestimation of dietary behavior. In this study, major emphasis was placed on the self-report of cholesterol and saturated and unsaturated fat intake as measured by a dietary questionnaire, which may have produced more favorable experimental findings. The authors argue for the validity of the dietary questionnaire on the basis of comparison of their observed changes with predicted changes based on equations derived from precise metabolic assessment in a controlled environment (Keys, Anderson, & Grande, 1965). There are limitations in making this type of comparison that the authors clearly point out, and a more direct method of assessing dietary behavior would have been extremely helpful in substantiating their findings.

Cardiovascular Risk Factors

The Multiple Risk Factor Intervention Trial (MRFIT) (*Journal of the American Medical Association,* 1976) is currently underway and represents the most ambitious attempt at large-scale modification of CHD risk factors to date. Twenty clinical centers nationwide are participating in the study with the goal of making significant modifications in three risk factors: serum cholesterol, diastolic blood pressure, and cigarette smoking. Males between the ages of 37 to 57 comprise the subject pool of 12,866 individuals. Treatment consists of 10 intensive group sessions emphasizing health education, principles of behavior modification (as yet, not clearly outlined), and the dynamic process of group therapy. The MRFIT has been underway too short a period of time to permit anything but a preliminary evaluation. The results of the initial screening indicate an average serum cholesterol of 257 mg/dl, average diastolic blood pressure of 99 millimeters of mercury (mm Hg), and an average of 22 cigarettes/day. There were essentially no differences between the experimental and control (half of the subjects) groups. The proposal calls for a six-year clinical trial, and a number of ancillary investigations are also being conducted that would provide important information in the prevention of CHD.

There are numerous examples of the use of behavioral procedures in modifying risk factors such as obesity (Stunkard & Mahoney, 1976), smoking (Epstein & McCoy, 1975), and hypertension (Blanchard & Miller, 1977; Jacob, Kraemer, & Agras, 1977). The outcomes of large-scale research projects may, in the future, be greatly enhanced by inclusion of procedures validated in small group studies. Two examples will be presented in greater detail. Patel and Carruthers (1977) studied the effects of biofeedback-aided relaxation training, meditation, and cursory health education in the modification of cigarette smoking, hypertension, and hyperlipidemia. Four groups were studied: smokers (10 cigarettes or more per day for a minimum of five years), normotensives receiving treatment, hypertensives (12 of which were receiving antihypertensive medication), and a control group. There were 18 subjects in each group, except for the hypertensive group that contained 22 subjects. Relaxation training was accomplished in six sessions using electromyographic and galvanic skin resistance feedback. A cassette tape with relaxation instructions was provided for home practice. Blood pressure, plasma lipids, pulse rate, weight, and number of cigarettes per day (by self-report) were recorded at the beginning of the study and at six weeks. The results showed that in the control group none of the measures changed significantly. In the hypertensive group, the mean systolic blood pressure was reduced by 20 mm Hg and the mean diastolic pressure was reduced by 11 mm Hg. In addition, significant decreases also occurred in pulse rate, cholesterol, and triglyceride levels without any significant change in weight. Significant changes in blood pressure were also observed in the smokers and the normotensive groups. The smokers group reported an average of 60% reduction in cigarettes per day which was maintained at six-months follow-up.

Suinn (1974) studied the effects of a stress management training program on 10 postcardiac patients identified as Type A individuals in modifying serum cholesterol and triglyceride levels. Treatment consisted of discrimination training to recognize overt physical (tics, bruxism, etc.) and physiological cues of tension, relaxation training, and imagery training of adaptive behaviors for stressful situations. Ten control patients undergoing traditional rehabilitation were also studied. The preliminary results indicated that the control group showed no changes in serum cholesterol over the course of eight weeks. The experimental subjects experienced a decrease in median cholesterol level of 21 points (215 mg% for pre- and 194 mg% for posttest). Triglyceride levels decreased by a total of 39 points (median of 143 mg% for pre- and 104 mg% for posttest). The control group declined 16 points from a median of 146 mg% for pre- to 130 mg% for posttesting.

The results of these initial behavioral studies in the primary prevention of cardiovascular disease suggest some promise. Further research is necessary to evaluate contributory factors of the development of disease as well as the conditions for their maintenance. While cardiovascular risk has been most thoroughly studied, a number of other chronic conditions with behavioral precursors have also begun to receive attention.

Periodontal Disease

Martens et al. (1973) report a successful outcome using a token reinforcement program and instruction from a dental hygienist to increase dental hygiene in six- to eight-year-old children. Plaque scores were reduced by 30% in the experimental group as compared with a 15% reduction in the control group. Horner and Keilitz (1975) successfully trained retarded children in tooth-brushing skills using token reinforcement and prompting techniques. The program was implemented using a multiple baseline design with a systematic replication, and the high degree of performance achieved by the subjects was demonstrated to be simply not due to practice, but rather to the 15-step training sequence. This study is particularly important because recent evidence suggests the retarded individual may be at greater risk for periodontal disease (Miller, 1965).

Liver Disease

A carefully executed assessment study by Goldstein, Stein, Smolen, and Perlina (1976) evaluated the reliability of patient self-monitoring in a tertiary prevention program to control a number of risk factors associated with chronic liver disease. Thirteen cirrhotic patients were required to make daily measurements in various combinations of weight, alcohol ingestion, medication, general activity, ounces of liquid consumed, and abdominal girth, which they telephone reported daily. Regular clinic visits were also required of the subjects to corroborate the self-report data and included were blood alcohol determinations. Spouses were also asked to record alcohol consumption daily. The results showed, first of all, that compliance with the data collection procedures averaged 90% in the first six months of monitoring. Blood test corroboration of prior day self-report data on alcohol consumption was 80%. Self-reported weights correlated with weights obtained on physical examination to a high degree ($r = .99$). Alcohol consumption was maintained at low levels in 6 subjects and decreased in 2 others out of the 10 subjects checked for daily alcohol use. The procedures described in this study are important in that they indicate that patients can reliably engage in the assessment and potentially the management of their own chronic disease.

Kidney Disease

In another example of tertiary prevention, Barnes (1976) reported the results of a token reinforcement program to maintain appropriate dietary restrictions in a hemodialysis patient prone to fluid overload. Tokens were exchanged for water up to a maximum of 800 cc/day. Tokens also were awarded for minimal daily weight gain. The results showed a decrease in weight gain and blood pressure with maintenance of therapeutic effects at the six-month follow-up. Magrab and Papadopoulou (1977) reported the successful application of a similar program in the modification of dietary behavior in seven children on hemodialysis.

In summary, the recent research on the prevention of cardiovascular and other diseases shows promise in the reduction of risk factors and in the development of health maintenance strategies. Programmed reductions in cholesterol intake, cigarette smoking, and blood pressure, along with changes in physical activity and dietary patterns suggest the initial efficacy of behavioral treatments. However, long-term follow-up of patients in these programs as well as the future application of procedures to large segments of the "at risk" population will, in the final analysis, best determine the future of behavioral methods in preventive medicine.

COMPLIANCE WITH HEALTH CARE PRESCRIPTION

In all areas of preventive medicine, the treatment of risk-taking behavior and programming for healthful behavior requires that the patient comply with the procedures prescribed. Behaviorally, compliance monitoring evidence suggests that noncompliance with medical advice and procedures is a serious problem. One area, compliance to medication regimens, has been particularly well studied with respect to the problem of noncompliance (Sackett & Haynes, 1976). The problem of noncompliance affects not only the outcome of individual programs in prevention, but the evaluation of the outcomes of pharmacological intervention as well. In this section, we consider compliance to medication regimens as an example of how behavior technology might be used to increase the cost-effectiveness of programs within the current practice of preventive medicine.

Magnitude of the Problem

Patient noncompliance with prophylactic medication regimens is considered to be one of the major problems in health care (Sackett & Haynes, 1976). Several reviews of the literature have produced estimates of noncompliance ranging from 4–92% (Marston, 1970) and averaging from 30–35% (Davis, 1966). The magnitude of the problem has led to the suggestion that poor medical outcomes resulting from noncompliance may account for much of the current general dissatisfaction with the delivery of health care (Korsch & Negrete, 1972). In addition, noncompliance with oral medication regimens may affect the results of clinical drug trials. Soutter and Kennedy (1974) reviewed 768 studies on drug efficacy published over a three-year period in *The Lancet* and the *British Medical Journal*. Only 19% of the 324 studies requiring an objective measure of compliance to ensure that the drug(s) were being taken according to the research protocol actually included such an assessment. The importance of an objective assessment of compliance in clinical drug trials cannot be overstated, as poor compliance can result in misinterpretation of the results, lead to underestimation of the efficacy of the drug being studied, and reduce the effectiveness of prevention efforts in which drug therapy is an essential component.

Noncompliance with prophylactic medication regimens presents a particularly difficult challenge for the behavioral scientist. Prophylactically prescribed medication may have a lower probability of being taken by a person than medication prescribed for symptomatic relief. There are no short-term reinforcing consequences associated with the intake of prophylactically prescribed medication. Lack of compliance with antihypertensive medications is a common clinical problem (Sackett & Haynes, 1976) and serves to illustrate the complexity of the problem. Regular ingestion of antihypertensive medication does not afford the person any immediate symptomatic relief because the disease process is typically insidious. Discriminable symptoms are usually absent. The negative consequences of noncompliance, although quite serious, are usually delayed in time, and as already indicated, probably control very little present-day behavior. On the other hand, the patient prescribed an analgesic for pain is more likely to adhere to the medication regimen to avoid pain. The symptomatic relief afforded by the medication serves to negatively reinforce medication-taking behavior. Zifferblatt (1975) indicated that there are a number of antecedents and consequences influencing medication-taking behavior in addition to the ones mentioned above. He also argued that noncompliance is essentially a behavioral problem that requires a treatment strategy based on the principles of applied behavior analysis. The research on behavioral control of medication compliance has resulted in the development of some very promising approaches to the problem.

Behavioral Approaches

Azrin and Powell (1969), in one of the first applications of behavioral engineering to the problem of noncompliance, developed a portable timer-dispenser to effect compliance. The apparatus sounded a tone that was terminated by turning a knob which then ejected a pill into the user's hand. The signal was programmed to occur at the times the pills were to be taken. The authors tested the efficacy of this device in establishing compliance to a placebo regimen requiring ingestion of tablets at half-hour intervals. Subjects were observed by participant observers, and the results showed that significantly fewer doses were missed by subjects when using the experimental apparatus as opposed to the use of a simple pill container. Further investigations employing this apparatus have not been published, probably because less elaborate technologies and procedures have been shown to be effective in establishing compliance. However, this device could have important clinical applications in cases where other procedures have failed to establish compliance, and the problem is of sufficient magnitude to warrant the cost.

Providing feedback to subjects has been shown to be an effective procedure in establishing compliance. Gundert-Remy, Remy, and Weber (1976) mailed the results of serum digoxin level determinations to 33 cardiac patients at eight-week intervals on two successive occasions. The mean serum concentration at baseline was 0.52 mg/ml. (The lower therapeutic limit is 0.5 mg/ml and half the subjects were well below this limit.) The mean serum concentration following the two mailings were 0.88 mg/ml and 0.89 mg/ml, respectively. These results were statistically significant, but more importantly, only 3 of the 33 patients had a serum level less than 0.5 mg/ml at the time of the last serum level determination. Lund, Jorgensen, and Kuhl (1964) conducted a controlled investigation of the effects of feedback on serum diphenylhydantoin (Dilantin) levels. Subjects were 76 epileptic patients who, upon discharge from the hospital, were assigned to one of two groups. The experimental group ($n = 36$) was required to return at 2, 6, and 12 weeks after discharge for serum diphenylhydantoin level determinations. If the levels were too low the subjects were informed of this fact and requested to take their medication as prescribed. The control group ($n = 40$) was required to return 12 weeks after discharge for a serum level determination. The results indicated that of the 22 subjects in the experimental group who completed the study, 17 showed serum levels within the therapeutic range by the twelfth week. Of the 29 subjects who remained in the control group, only 10 showed serum levels within the therapeutic range. Another study in the use of feedback to increase serum levels of the anticonvulsant ethosuximide (Zanrontin) demonstrated the efficacy of the procedure (Sherwin, Robb, & Lechter, 1973). The only shortcoming to the above-mentioned study was the lack of follow-up to assess whether feedback produces durable changes in compliance behavior.

Two studies on the use of behavioral procedures to maintain regular Antabuse intake successfully used negative consequences to effect compliance. Haynes (1973) implemented a program designed to keep habitual offenders of public intoxication laws in Antabuse treatment. Subjects were given a choice of entering a year of Antabuse therapy or going to jail for 90 days. Choosing Antabuse therapy meant that the person was required to take his/her Antabuse in the presence of a probation officer twice weekly. After a maximum of two subsequent violations, the person was sent to jail. The results showed almost one-half of the chronic offenders were still on Antabuse after one year, and the arrest rate for the sample had dropped from 3.8 to 0.3 arrests per year. Bigelow, Strickler, Liebson, and Griffiths (1976) tested a response cost procedure to effect compliance with Antabuse therapy in 20 chronic problem drinkers. A security deposit that averaged $71.25 was required of each participant. Failure to report to the clinic for a scheduled dose of Antabuse resulted in forfeiture of between $5 and $10 per visit. Patients were required to come daily for the first two weeks, and then every other day. The results showed that the patients were abstinent for 95% of the treatment days in the initial contract (at least three months). Only 7.8% of the scheduled clinic visits were missed by the patients. Seventy percent of the patients reenlisted in a second contract and 76.9% of those patients were successfully abstinent throughout their second contract.

Compliance with antihypertensive medications has been studied fairly extensively by Sackett, Haynes, and their colleagues. In one study (Sackett, Haynes, Gibson,

Hackett, Taylor, Roberts, & Johnson, 1975) a combination of augmented convenience for hypertensive care and mastering the learning of facts about hypertension was largely unsuccessful in improving compliance in 230 Canadian steelworkers with hypertension.

This unsuccessful outcome prompted a second study in which 38 of the subjects were exposed to a behavioral program to improve compliance. Treatment consisted of self-monitoring of blood pressure and medication ingestion. In addition, suggestions were made as to how to tie the pill-taking response to daily rituals performed by the subjects. Every two weeks the subject's pressure was checked and criterion performance (diastolic: < 90 mm Hg) resulted in a $4 credit toward the purchase of the blood pressure recording equipment. Urine specimens were collected randomly without warning at home and at the subject's place of employment. Unobstrusive pill counts of unused medication as a further assessment of compliance were also made. The results indicated that compliance was 80% in the experimental group ($n = 20$) and 39% in the control group ($n = 18$) after six months. A decrease in blood pressure of 5.4 mm Hg was observed in the experimental group as compared to a 1.9 mm Hg drop in the control group. These results suggest that behavioral procedures can be used effectively to counter maladaptive health behavior and they can salvage a clinically significant portion of hypertensives.

Epstein and Masek (1978) compared several behavioral procedures in the modification of Vitamin C intake in college students. Subjects were informed that they were participating in a study of the effects of Vitamin C in preventing the common cold. In this way Vitamin C served as an analogue to medicine typically prescribed prophylactically or for asymptomatic disorders. A $9 deposit was required of each subject at the start of the study. A three-week baseline indicated that 56 subjects were noncomplaint subjects, 20 were randomly assigned to one of four groups: a nontreatment control group; a self-monitoring group in which subjects recorded time of pill ingestion; a taste group in which subjects were provided pills flavored neutral, orange, or quinine to increase their saliency as suggested by Zifferblatt (1975); and a self-monitoring plus taste group in which subjects recorded the flavor of the pill they were ingesting. Results after three weeks indicated the two self-monitoring groups were significantly better than the other groups in improving compliance. During the final three weeks of the study, one-half of the subjects in each group were exposed to a response cost procedure. One dollar of the initial deposit was subject to forfeiture if weekly compliance did not reach a criterion level. Results of this phase showed significant improvements in all response cost groups, independent of prior history. The self-monitoring plus taste subjects also showed compliance levels equal to the response cost subjects, while self-monitoring only proved to be a less durable treatment. This study was unique in that a new assessment procedure for compliance was also tested. In addition to pill counts of unused medication returned each week by the subjects, a variation of the urine tracer method was employed. In each week's supply of pills, subjects were provided with three pills that contained phenazopyridine in a programmed sequence. Phenazopyridine is a urinary tract analgesic that discolors the urine a bright reddish-orange. Subjects were required to record the occasions they noticed urine discolorations, and compliance to the four times per day regimen could be estimated by comparing these times to the programmed intervals for urine discolorations.

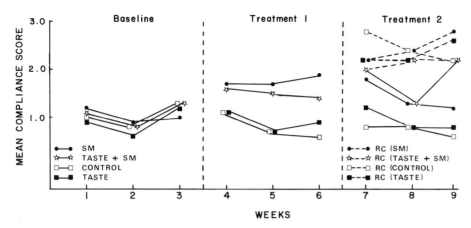

FIGURE 2. Mean compliance score for subjects in all groups during baseline and the two treatment phases (from Epstein & Masek, *Journal of Applied Behavior Analysis,* 1978, **11**, 1–9. Copyright 1978 by the Society for the Experimental Analysis of Behavior. Reprinted by permission.)

This procedure was useful and appears to be even more accurate in assessing compliance in less complex regimens. The results of the compliance data for subjects in the four groups are presented in Figure 2.

Studies of medication compliance suggest that behavioral procedures may be beneficial in establishing therapeutic drug levels for prophylactic medication. These studies have demonstrated that knowledge of disease alone is not sufficient to produce compliance in many patients, and contingency management procedures may be an important adjunct. Clearly, what is needed is continued research, not only in the procedures that affect compliance, but also in the development and evaluation of efficient and effective procedures utilizable within the context of current practice. Similar procedures have been designed to evaluate current practice and develop increased compliance to other procedures, such as clinic visits (Hagen, Foreyt, & Durham, 1976; Turner & Vernon, 1976), participation in hospital activities (Tracey, Briddell, & Wilson, 1974), and management of fear and avoidance of medical care (Machen & Johnson, 1974; Melamed, Hames, Heiby, & Glick, 1975), in which regular patient participation may be a necessary precursor to medical outcome.

IMPLICATIONS FOR FUTURE RESEARCH

This chapter was designed to stimulate reader interest in one area of the rapidly developing field of behavioral medicine. Behavioral medicine has been broadly conceived of as a field devoted to the interface of behavioral and medical sciences for the purpose of developing knowledge and procedures relevant to prevention, diagnosis, treatment, and rehabilitation of disease (Schwartz & Weiss, 1977). The focus of this chapter was on the application of behavioral procedures in the prevention of chronic disease. This is a new area for behavioral science, but one of potentially incalculable benefit as approximately 1 of every 10 persons in the

United States suffers from a chronic disease or disability severe enough to limit activity (Cataldo et al., in press). The majority of research in this area has investigated the application of principles of applied behavior analysis in the modification of cardiovascular risk factors. However, other chronic diseases are beginning to receive the attention of behavioral scientists. The problem of noncompliance with medication regimens prescribed as a preventive measure has been thoughtfully researched using behavioral assessment and treatment, and it will likely produce cost-beneficial treatments to effect compliance with a variety of medications within the next few years.

Much of the future research in this area should be initially conducted on a small scale using single subject methodology or small group intervention. The reasons for this are twofold. First, much of the research reviewed in this chapter relied mainly on self-report measures of risk factors. The behavioral assessment axiom: "Assess as many of the response systems concurrently that a given evaluation situation will permit" (Hersen & Bellack, 1976, p. 16) should be strongly considered when planning future prevention studies requiring risk factor assessment. Self-report data alone must be interpreted cautiously. Coupled with physiological measures and direct observation of behavior, self-report data can be a valuable addition to the data base. Although the area of behavioral assessment is new, a vast array of assessment techniques have already been developed and further innovation and refinement should add sophistication to future studies. Second, the procedures of behavior therapy and behavior modification are just beginning to be applied to the problem of modifying risk factors and promoting learning of alternative healthful behaviors. A thorough understanding based upon empirical analysis of the phenomena involved in risk factor modification and healthful behavior patterns will proceed from programmatic research on a small scale. Hopefully, this will lead to parsimonious assessment and treatment packages that can then be applied on a large scale complementing existing methodologies for the prevention of chronic disease.

ACKNOWLEDGMENTS

This work was supported by Grant #917 from the Maternal and Child Health Service and the resources of the Behavioral Medicine Program, Department of Psychiatry and Behavioral Sciences, Johns Hopkins University School of Medicine, and the Department of Behavioral Psychology, John F. Kennedy Institute.

REFERENCES

Arguments over behavior and heart disease continue. *Journal of the American Medical Association,* 1975, **232**, 691–700.

Azrin, N. H., & Powell, J. Behavioral engineering: The use of response priming to improve prescribed self-medication. *Journal of Applied Behavior Analysis,* 1969, **2**, 39–42.

Ball, K. P., & Turner, R. Realism in the prevention of coronary heart disease. *Preventive Medicine,* 1975, **4**, 390–397.

Ball, R. M. National health insurance: Comments on selected issues. *Science,* 1978, **200**, 864–870.

Barnes, M. R. Token economy control of fluid overload in a patient receiving hemo-dialysis. *Journal of Behavior Therapy and Experimental Psychiatry,* 1976, **7**, 305–306.

Belloc, N. B. Relations of health practices and mortality. *Preventive Medicine,* 1973, **2**, 67–81.

Berkanovic, E. Behavioral science and prevention. *Preventive Medicine,* 1976, **5**, 92–105.

Bigelow, G., Strickler, D., Liebson, I. & Griffiths, R. Maintaining disulfiram ingestion among outpatient alcoholics: A security-deposit contingency contracting procedure. *Behaviour Research and Therapy,* 1976, **14**, 378–381.

Blackly, P. H. How to decrease the self-destructive behaviors that threaten the goals of preventive medicine. In R. L. Kane (Eds.), *The behavioral sciences and preventive medicine: Opportunities and dilemmas,* (DHEW Publication No. (NIH) 76–876). Washington: U.S. Government Printing Office, 1977.

Blanchard, E. B., & Miller, S. T. Psychological treatment of cardiovascular disease. *Archives of General Psychiatry,* 1977, **34**, 1402–1413.

Boyer, J. Coronary heart disease as a pediatric problem: Prevention through behavior modification. *American Journal of Cardiology,* 1974, **33**, 784–786.

Brand, R. J. An examination of the association between A-B behavior and coronary heart disease incidence. Paper presented at the NHLBI Forum on Coronary Prone Behavior, St. Petersburg, Florida, June, 1977.

Brand, R. J., Rosenman, R. H., Sholtz, R. J., & Friedman, M. Multivariate prediction of coronary heart disease in the western collaborative group study compared to the findings of the Framingham study. *Circulation,* 1976, **53**, 348–355.

Breslow, L. Task force report. Theory practice and application of prevention in personal health services. In *Preventive medicine USA.* New York: Prodist, 1976.

Breslow, L. Risk factor intervention for health maintenance. *Science,* 1978, **200**, 908–912.

Bruhn, J. G., Paredes, A., Adsett, C. A., & Wolf, S. Psychological predictors of sudden death in myocardial infarction. *Journal of Psychosomatic Research,* 1974, **18**, 187–191.

Cataldo, M. F., Russo, D. C., Bird, B. L., & Varni, J. W. Assessment and management of chronic disorders. In J. Ferguson, & C. B. Taylor (Eds.), *Comprehensive hand-book of behavioral medicine.* Jamaica, N.Y.: Spectrum Publications, in press.

Clark, D. W. A vocabulary for preventive medicine. In D. W. Clark, & B. MacMahon (Eds.), *Preventive medicine.* Boston: Little, Brown, 1967.

Comroe, J. H. The road from research to new diagnosis and therapy. *Science,* 1978, **200**, 931–936.

Cooper, K. H. *The new aerobics.* New York: Bantam, 1970.

Cooper, K. H., Pollock, M. L., Martin, R. P., White, S. T., Linnerud, A. C., & Jackson, A. Physical fitness levels vs. selected risk factors: A cross-sectional study. *Journal of the American Medical Association,* 1976, **236**, 166–169.

Cullen, J. W., Fox, B. H., & Isom, R. H. (Eds.), *Cancer: The behavioral dimensions.* New York: Raven Press, 1976.

Culliton, B. J. Health care economics: The high cost of getting well. *Science,* 1978, **200**, 883–885.

Davis, M. S. Variations in patient's compliance with doctor's orders: Analysis of congruence between survey responses and results of empirical investigations. *Journal of Medical Education,* 1966, **41,** 1037–1048.

Dowber, T. R., Kannel, W. B., & Lyell, L. P. An approach to longitudinal studies in a community: The Framingham study. *Annals of the New York Academy of Science,* 1963, **107,** 539–556.

Epstein, L. H., & McCoy, J. F. Issues in smoking control. *Addictive Behaviors,* 1975, **1,** 65–72.

Epstein, L. H., & Masek, B. J. Behavioral control of medicine compliance. *Journal of Applied Behavior Analysis,* 1978, **11,** 1–9.

Epstein, L. H., & Ossip, D. J. Health care delivery. In J. R. McNamara (Ed.), *Behavioral medicine.* New York: Plenum, in press.

Epstein, L. H. & LaPorte, R. Behavioral epidemiology. *Association for the Advancement of Behavior Therapy Newsletter,* 1978, **1,** 3–5.

Evans, R. I. Smoking in children: Developing a social psychological strategy of deterrence. *Preventive Medicine,* 1976, **5,** 122–127.

Fabrega, J., Jr. *Disease and social behavior: An interdisciplinary perspective.* Cambridge: MIT Press, 1974.

Fink, R., Shapiro, S., & Levinson, J. The reluctant participant in a breast cancer screening program. *Public Health Reports,* 1968, **83,** 479–489.

Fordyce, W. E. *Behavioral methods for chronic pain and illness.* St. Louis: C. V. Mosby, 1976.

Forward plan for health FY 1978–82. (DHEW Publication No. OS 76–50046). Washington, D.C.: U.S. Government Printing Office, 1976.

Fox, B. H., & Goldsmith, J. R. Behavioral issues in prevention of cancer. *Preventive Medicine,* 1976, **5,** 106–121.

Friedman, M., & Rosenman, R. H. *Type A behavior and your heart.* New York: Knopf, 1974.

Glass, D. C. Behavior patterns, stress, and coronary disease. New York: Lawrence Erebaum, 1977.

Goldsmith, J. R. Prevention of chronic lung disease. *Postgraduate Medicine,* 1972, **51,** 74–78.

Goldstein, M. K., Stein, G. H., Smolen, D. M., & Perlina, W. S. Bio-behavioral monitoring: A method for remote health measurement. *Archives of Physical Medicine and Rehabilitation,* 1976, **57,** 253–258.

Gundert-Remy, U., Remy, C., & Weber, E. Serum digoxin levels in patients of a general practice in Germany. *European Journal of Clinical Pharmacy,* 1976, **10,** 97–100.

Hagen, S. M., Foreyt, J. P., & Durham, T. W. The dropout problem: Reducing attrition in obesity research. *Behavior Therapy,* 1976, **7,** 463–471.

Haggerty, R. J. Changing lifestyles to improve health. *Preventive Medicine,* 1977, **6,** 276–289.

Hall, S. M., Hall, R. G., Borden, B. L., & Hanson, R. W. Follow-up strategies in the behavioral treatment of overweight. *Behaviour Research and Therapy,* 1975, **13,** 167–172.

Hamburg, D. A., & Brown, S. S. The science base and social context of health maintenance: An overview. *Science,* 1978, **200,** 847–849.

Haynes, R. B., Sackett, D. L., Gibson, E. S., Taylor, D. W., Hackett, B. C., Roberts,

R. S., & Johnson, A. L. Improvement of medication compliance in uncontrolled hypertension. *The Lancet,* 1976, **1**, 1265–1268.

Haynes, S. N. Contingency management in a municipally-administered Antabus program for alcoholics. *Journal of Behavior Therapy and Experimental Psychiatry,* 1973, **4**, 31–32.

Hersen, M., & Bellack, A. S. (Eds.), *Behavior assessment: A practical handbook,* Elmsford, New York: Pergamon, 1976.

Horan, J. J., Baker, S. B., Hoffman, A. M., & Shute, R. E. Weight loss through variations in the coverant control program. *Journal of Consulting and Clinical Psychology,* 1975, **43**, 68–72.

Horner, R. D., & Keilitz, I. Training mentally retarded adolescents to brush their teeth. *Journal of Applied Behavior Analysis,* 1975, **8**, 301–310.

Hughes, C. C., & Kane, R. L. The behavioral sciences and community medicine: Intersection, interaction or interpenetration. In R. L. Kane (Ed.), *The behavioral sciences and preventive medicine: Opportunties and dilemmas.* (DHEW Publication No. (NIH) 76–876). Washington, D.C.: U.S. Government Printing Office, 1977.

Jacob, R. G., Kraemer, H. C., & Agras, W. S. Relaxation therapy in the treatment of hypertension. *Archives of General Psychiatry,* 1977, **34**, 1417–1427.

Jenkins, C. D. Psychologic and social precursors of coronary disease. *The New England Journal of Medicine,* 1971, **284**, 307–317.

Jenkins, C. D., Zyzanski, S. J., & Rosenman, R. H. Risk of new myocardial infarction in middle-aged men with manifest coronary heart disease. *Circulation,* 1976, **53**, 342–347.

Kasl, S. V., & Cobb, S. Health behavior, illness behavior, and sick role behavior. *Archives of Environmental Health,* 1966, **12**, 246–266.

Keys, A., Anderson, J. T., & Grande, F. Serum cholesterol response to change in diet. IV. Particular saturated fatty acids in the diet. *Metabolism,* 1965, **14**, 776–784.

Korsch, B. M., & Negrete, V. F. Doctor-patient communication. *Scientific American,* August, 1972, 66–74.

Kushner, R. Personal communication, March, 1978.

Lalonde, M. *A new perspective on the health of Canadians: A working document.* Ottawa: Government of Canada, 1975.

Lenner, R. A. The importance of motivation in adherence to dietary advice. A one-year follow-up study of middle-aged women with a supposed risk to develop diabetes. *Nutrition and Metabolism,* 1976, **20**, 243–253.

Lund, M., Jorgensen, R. S., & Kuhl, V. Serum diphenylhydantoin (Dilantin) in ambulant patients with epilepsy. *Epilepsy,* 1964, **5**, 51–58.

McAlister, A. L., Farquhar, J. W., Thorsen, C. E., & Maccoby, N. Behavioral science applied to cardiovascular health: Problems and research needs in the modification of risk taking habits in adult populations. *Health Education Monographs,* 1976, **4**, 45–73.

Machen, J. B., & Johnson, R. Desensitization, model learning, and the dental behavior of children. *Journal of Dental Research,* 1974, **53**, 83–87.

Magrab, P. R., & Papadopoulou, Z. L. The effect of a token economy on dietary compliance for children on hemodialysis. *Journal of Applied Behavior Analysis,* 1977, **10**, 573–578.

Marston, M. V. Compliance with medical regimens: A review of the literature. *Nursing Research,* 1970, **19**, 312–323.

Marston, A. R., & McFall, R. M. Comparison of behavior modification approaches to smoking reduction. *Journal of Consulting and Clinical Psychology*, 1971, **37**, 80–86.

Martens, L. V., Frazier, M. A., Hirt, K. J., Meskin, L. H., & Proshek, J. Developing brushing performance in second graders through behavior modification. *Public Health Reports*, 1973, **88**, 818–823.

Melamed, B. G., Hames, R. R., Heiby, E., & Glick, J. Use of filmed modeling to reduce uncooperative behavior of children during dental treatment. *Journal of Dental Research*, 1975, **54**, 797–801.

Meyer, A. J., & Henderson, J. B. Multiple risk factor reduction in the prevention of cardiovascular disease. *Preventive Medicine*, 1974, **3**, 225–236.

Miller, S. L., Dental care for the mentally retarded: A challenge to the profession. *Journal of Public Health Dentistry*, 1965, **25**, 111–115.

Moss, N. H., & Mayer, J. (Eds.), Food and nutrition in disease. *Annals of the New York Academy of Science*, 1977, **300**, 1–474.

Paffenbarger, R. S. Prevention of heart disease. *Postgraduate Medicine*, 1972, **51**, 74–78.

Patel, C., & Carruthers, M. Coronary risk factor reduction through biofeedback-aided relaxation and medication. *Journal of the Royal College of General Practitioners*, 1977, **27**, 401–405.

Pomerleau, O., Bass, F., & Crown, V. Role of behavior modification in preventive medicine. *The New England Journal of Medicine*, 1975, **292**, 1277–1282.

Rosenman, R. H., Brand, R. J., Jenkins, C. D., Friedman, M., Straus, R., & Wurm, M. Coronary heart disease in the western collaborative group study. *Journal of the American Medical Association*, 1975, **232**, 872–877.

Rosenman, R. H., Brand, R. J., Scholtz, R. I., & Friedman, N. Multiprediction of coronary heart disease during 8½ years follow-up in the western collaborative group study. *American Journal of Cardiology*, 1976, **37**, 903–910.

Rosenman, R. H., Friedman, M., Straus, R., Jenkins, C. D., Zyzanski, S. J., & Wurm, M. Coronary heart disease in the western collaborative group study: A follow-up experience of 4 and one-half years. *Journal of Chronic Diseases*, 1970, **23**, 173–190.

Rosenman, R. H., Friedman, M., Straus, R., Wurm, M., Jenkins, C. D., & Messinger, H. B. Coronary heart disease in the western collaborative group study: A follow-up experience of two years. *Journal of the American Medical Association*, 1968, **195**, 130–136.

Rosenman, R. H., Friedman, M., Straus, R., Wurm, M., Kositchek, R., Hahn, W., & Werthessen, N. A predictive study of coronary heart disease: The western collaborative group study. *Journal of the American Medical Association*, 1964, **189**, 103–110.

Russek, H. I., & Russek, L. G. Is emotional stress an etiologic factor in coronary heart disease? *Psychosomatics*, 1976, **17**, 63–67.

Sackett, D. L., & Haynes, R. B. *Compliance with therapeutic regimens*. Baltimore: Johns Hopkins University Press, 1976.

Sackett, D. L., Haynes, R. B., Gibson, E. S., Hackett, B. C., Taylor, D. W., Roberts, R. S., & Johnson, A. L. Randomized clinical trial of strategies for improving medication compliance in primary hypertension. *The Lancet*, 1975, **1**, 7818–1920.

Saward, E., & Sorenson, A. The current emphasis on preventive medicine. *Science*, 1978, **200**, 889–894.

Schmahl, D. P., Lichtenstein, E., & Harris, D. E. Successful treatment of habitual smokers with warm, smokey air and rapid smoking. *Journal of Consulting and Clinical Psychology,* 1972, **38**, 105–111.

Schwartz, G. E., & Weiss, S. M. *Yale conference on behavioral medicine* (DHEW Publication No. (NIH) 78–1424). Washington, D. C.: U.S. Government Printing Office, 1977.

Sherwin, A. L., Robb, J. P., & Lechter, M. Improved control of epilepsy by monitoring plasma ethosuximide. *Archives of Neurology,* 1973, **28**, 1978–1981.

Soutter, R. B., & Kennedy, M. C. Patient compliance assessment in drug trials: Usage and methods. *Australian and New Zealand Journal of Medicine,* 1974, **4**, 360–364.

Stern, M. P., Farquhar, J. W., Maccoby, N., & Russell, S. H. Results of a two-year education campaign on dietary behavior: The Stanford three community study. *Circulation,* 1976, **54**, 826–833.

Stoeckle, J. D. The politics of prevention in medical education, practice, and research. In R. L. Kane (Ed.), *The behavioral sciences and preventive medicine: Opportunities and dilemmas.* (DHEW Publication No. (NIH) 76–876). Washington, D.C.: U.S. Government Printing Office, 1977.

Stroebel, C. Ethics and responsibilities of therapists in biofeedback and behavioral medicine. Symposium presented at the Eighth Annual Meeting of the Biofeedback Society of America, Orlando, 1977.

Stuart, R. B., & Davis, B. *Slim Chance in a fat world: Behavioral control of obesity.* Champaign, IL.: Research Press, 1972.

Stunkard, A. J. *The pain of obesity,* Palo Alto, Calif.: Bull Publishing Co., 1976.

Stunkard, A. J., & Mahoney, M. J. Behavioral treatment of the eating disorders. In H. Leitenberg (Ed.), *Handbook of behavior modification and behavior therapy.* Englewood Cliffs, N.J.: Prentice-Hall, 1976.

Suinn, R. M. Behavior therapy for cardiac patients. *Behavior Therapy,* 1974, **5**, 569–571.

The multiple risk factor intervention trial (MRFIT): A national study of primary prevention of coronary heart disease. *Journal of the American Medical Association,* 1976, **235**, 825–827.

Tracey, D. A., Briddell, D. W., & Wilson, G. T. Generalization of verbal and nonverbal behavior: Group therapy with psychiatric patients. *Journal of Applied Behavior Analysis,* 1974, **7**, 391–402.

Truett, J., Cornfield, J., & Kannel, W. A multivariate analysis of the risk of coronary heart disease in Framingham. *Journal of Chronic Diseases,* 1967, **20**, 511–524.

Turner, A. J., & Vernon, J. C. Prompts to increase attendance in a community mental health center. *Journal of Applied Behavior Analysis,* 1976, **4**, 141–146.

Walsh, J. Federal spending passes the $50-billion mark, *Science,* 1978, **200**, 886–887.

Weiss, S. M. (Ed.), *Proceedings of the national heart and lung institute working conference on health behavior* (DHEW Publication No. (NIH) 77–868). Washington: U.S. Government Printing Office, 1975.

Williams, C. L., Arnold, C. B., & Wynder, E. L. Primary prevention of chronic disease beginning in childhood. The "Know Your Body" program. *Preventive Medicine,* 1977, **6**, 344–357.

Wilner, D. M., Walkley, R. P., & O'Neill, E. J. *Introduction to public health.* New York: Macmillan, 1978.

Zifferblatt, S. M. Increasing patient compliance through the applied analysis of behavior. *Preventive Medicine,* 1975, **4**, 173–182.

CHAPTER 18

A Guideline for Planning
Behavior Modification Programs
for Autistic Children

Laura Schreibman and Robert L. Koegel

Autism was first described as a distinctive disorder by Leo Kanner in 1943. Since then others, both clinicians and researchers, have elaborated upon this definition (e.g., Ferster, 1961; Goldfarb, 1961; Kanner, 1973; Ornitz & Ritvo, 1968; Rutter, 1978; Schopler, 1978). In general, autism is described as a severe form of mental disorder that greatly affects the lives of the (autistic) children, their parents, and their community. About one child out of every 2500 births is likely to be diagnosed autistic. Typically, the disorder is not diagnosed until about age two to five years. However, there is a general consensus among most researchers that the disorder was probably present from birth. In general, the population of autistic children exhibit a cluster of symptoms, although each individual child is likely to exhibit only a majority (but not all) of the symptoms. Each symptom is discussed separately below.

BEHAVIORAL EXCESSES

There are certain behaviors exhibited by autistic children that are abnormal primarily because of their excess. These include *tantrums* and *self-stimulatory behavior*. These behaviors are bad enough at home, but are particularly disruptive when the parents take the children into public places. Tantrums, for example, are common when demands are placed on the children. Therefore, asking them to walk quietly through a supermarket, sit in a restaurant, or stand in a line at the zoo may result in the child's screaming, kicking, biting, scratching, and so on. Occasionally, in the more extreme cases, these tantrums may become so extreme that the child may do actual physical injury to himself. In these cases, the children are described as exhibiting *self-destructive,* self-injurious, or self-mutilatory behavior.

Self-stimulatory behavior refers to behaviors that appear to provide little other than sensory input for the child. These behaviors include rhythmic body rocking, arm or hand flapping, gazing intently at their hands, and so forth. The primary problems presented by such behaviors are that: (*a*) they look quite bizarre and frequently intimidate strangers in public places; and (b) at least some of these behaviors appear to interfere with learning (as is discussed below in the section on discriminative stimuli).

BEHAVIORAL DEFICIENCIES

In addition to the behavioral excesses described above, autistic children typically exhibit marked deficiencies in many behaviors. For example: (a) They typically lack appropriate *speech*. They may be nonverbal, expressing many sounds but very few, if any, words. Other autistic children are echolalic and repeat words they have heard (either immediately or after a delay), but they do not use these words to communicate in the normal manner. For example, in immediate echolalia, when asked, "What is your name?" the child may respond by saying, "What is your name" rather than giving the appropriate answer. In delayed echolalia, one may observe a child seated at the dinner table repeating his teacher's commands verbatim from earlier in the day at school. (b) The children may lack appropriate social behavior. That is, they may react to people more as if they were objects than as if they were people. For example, a child may climb into his mother's lap, not for affection, but in order to reach a cookie jar. (c) The children may show apparent sensory deficits. That is, frequently the children are incorrectly suspected of being blind or deaf. However, hearing and vision examinations to date usually have not revealed sensory impairment (at least at the receptor level). The children seem to respond quite normally at some times, but not at all at others (cf. Koegel & Schreibman, 1976). (d) The children often lack appropriate play. For example, instead of driving a toy truck along the ground, an autistic child may completely ignore the truck, or turn it upside down and spin one of the wheels for hours in a perseverative manner. (e) The children often show inappropriate emotions. Some scream and/or laugh with little or no provocation. Others show almost no emotional behavior at all, exhibiting generally flat affect. For example, the child may simply sit and stare into space if someone attempts to tickle him. (f) Many diagnosticians have described a demand for sameness in the children's environments. For example, they may become quite upset if furniture is rearranged, if familiar routes are departed from, and so forth.

DIFFERENTIAL DIAGNOSIS: AUTISM VERSUS CHILDHOOD SCHIZOPHRENIA, MENTAL RETARDATION

Both autistic and mentally retarded children tend to score low on IQ tests. However, while retarded children tend to show even delays across the board, autistic children are different. Although many autistic children perform intellectually below their age level overall, they usually show isolated areas of exceptionally high-level functioning. Typically, these "splinter" areas include normal or above-normal musical, mechanical, or mathematical skills. For example, a child who has not learned to talk or eat appropriately may yet be able to play complicated musical pieces on the piano (cf. Rimland, 1978).

Comparing autism with schizophrenia is somewhat difficult since some investigators use the terms interchangeably. However, there appears to be a fairly regular distinction between the two diagnoses with respect to variables such as age of onset and level of language functioning. In general, autistic children are seen as having had a much earlier age of onset (prior to 30 months) and a much lower level of language functioning. For example, schizophrenic children may first be diagnosed in adolescence and may show irregular periods of recovery and regression. These children may speak in a bizarre manner, drifting across topics (as in the case of thought disorder), whereas autistic children rarely attempt to communicate verbally at all (usually being either nonverbal or echolalic).

CAUSATION

In the past, parents of autistic children have been implicated in the cause of the disorder (Bettelheim, 1967). However, no empirical evidence has been provided to support this contention. At this point in time there are many other theories relating to causation. However, there is no solid evidence to support any one of these theories. The general consensus now among most professionals is that the disorder is probably organic in nature, and most likely does not have an environmental cause. However, to attempt to be more specific than that at this time is to move completely into the realm of speculation.

There are other characteristics of autism described in the literature. The description above gives a thumbnail sketch. For more detailed descriptions of the population of autistic children, the reader is referred to (among others) Rimland (1964), Ritvo and Freeman (1978), and Rutter (1978).

TREATMENT

The disorder has been very resistant to most forms of treatment intervention. This is probably true because many of the symptoms preclude the typical application of most treatments. For example, the lack of appropriate speech and social behavior makes most traditional forms of psychotherapy impossible. Similarly, the lack of appropriate play makes play therapy difficult. Partly because of this, behavior modification treatment procedures have become quite prevalent for this population because they do not depend on the child's verbal skills, nor the therapist's knowledge of the etiology of the disorder (see below).

MAJOR PROBLEMS IN THE DIAGNOSIS OF AUTISM

When one examines the definition of autism, it immediately becomes apparent that one is faced with a tremendous amount of heterogeneity. First of all, there is more than one definition, and these definitions are not in complete agreement (cf. Churchill, Alpern, & DeMyer, 1971; Ritvo & Freeman, 1978; Rutter, 1978; Schopler,

1978). Secondly, within any one of the existing definitions there is still a tremendous amount of variability in the way the diagnosis is applied. That is, the term autism usually refers to a syndrome that is composed of a majority of a list of symptoms. Not all symptoms need to be present. As such, one child may exhibit an almost totally different set of behaviors from another child, and yet both children may be diagnosed as autistic because both exhibit a majority of the symptoms.

The resultant heterogeneity among children bearing the diagnosis of autism leads to at least three major problems. First, the diagnosis does not facilitate communication. Professionals argue about whose definition should be used, and even when they agree on a given definition, the definition only summarizes the behaviors of the group, but it does not specify the behaviors of any individual child. Second, the diagnosis of autism per se does not suggest a treatment. There is no consensus among professionals as to what specific treatment to use for "autism." Where there is occasional agreement on a treatment technique, the technique is usually for a specific symptom (e.g., self-destructive behavior) and not for the syndrome as a whole. As such, the term "autism," by itself, does not serve a function with respect to suggesting a treatment procedure. Third, the term "autism" does not suggest a prognosis. It is true that without treatment most autistic children do not improve. However, a few autistic children do improve without treatment (Rutter, 1968). With treatment, some improve a great deal, others not much at all (Lovaas, Koegel, Simmons, & Long, 1973). The term autism, by itself, does not specify which children will improve and which ones will not.

BEHAVIORAL ASSESSMENT

In an attempt to solve some of the above-mentioned problems many researchers have de-emphasized the importance of defining the entire syndrome at this time and have instead focused on assessing individual behaviors. There is still an attempt to group, but in this case it is toward grouping *behaviors* according to those that covary and/or have common controlling variables. The approach rests on the assumption that an empirical definition of autism is necessary if it is going to be functional. According to this approach, a functional definition of autism is gradually developed as the individual behaviors accompanying the disorder each become understood.

In general, the approach proceeds as follows. In the *first step,* individual behaviors are operationally defined. For example, instead of merely saying autistic children exhibit self-stimulatory behavior, this behavior is spelled out in such a way that independent observers can reliably record it. For example, in the following table self-stimulatory behavior was defined for each of two children in terms of the exact behaviors each child exhibited (from wiggling toes inside of tennis shoes to swishing saliva in the mouth, etc.).

The *second step* in a behavioral assessment involves identifying the variables that control the behavior. Typically this involves a library search for research articles dealing with each behavior. For example, Carr (1977) has reviewed an extensive body of research dealing with self-injurious behavior and has identified the

Table 1.   Complete List of Self-Stimulatory Responses for Two Children[a]

Child 1

1. Eye crossing
2. Finger manipulations (moving the hands with continuous flexion and extension)
3. Repetitive vocalizations (excluding recognizable words)
4. Feet contortions (tight sustained flexions)
5. Leg contortions (tight sustained flexions)
6. Rhythmic manipulation of objects (repeatedly rubbing, rotating, or tapping objects with fingers)
8. Staring or gazing (a fixed glassy-eyed look lasting more than 3 seconds)
7. Grimacing (corners of mouth drawn out and down, revealing the upper set of teeth)
9. Hands repetitively rubbing mouth
10. Hands repetitively rubbing face
11. Mouthing of objects (holding nonedible objects in contact with the mouth)
12. Locking hands behind head
13. Hands pressing on or twisting ears

Child 2

1. Staring or gazing (a fixed glassy-eyed look lasting more than 3 seconds)
2. Grimacing (corners of mouth drawn out and down, revealing the upper set of teeth)
3. Hand waving vertically or horizontally with fingers outstretched in front of eyes
4. Hands vigorously and repetitively rubbing eyes
5. Hands vigorously and repetitively rubbing nose
6. Hands vigorously and repetitively rubbing mouth
7. Hands vigorously and repetitively rubbing ears
8. Hands vigorously and repetitively rubbing hair
9. Hands vigorously and repetitively rubbing clothes
10. Hands vigorously and repetitively rubbing objects
11. Hand flapping in air
12. Hand wringing (hands alternately rubbing and clutching each other)
13. Finger contortions (tight sustained flexions)
14. Tapping fingers against part of body or an object
15. Tapping whole hand against part of body or object
16. Mouthing of objects (holding nonedible objects in contact with the mouth)
17. Rocking (moving the trunk at the hips rhythmically back and forth or from side to side)
18. Head weaving (moving head from side to side in a figure-eight pattern)
19. Body contortions (sustained flexions or extensions of the torso)
20. Repetitive vocalizations (excluding recognizable words)
21. Teeth clicking (audibly and rapidly closing teeth together)
22. Tongue rolling and clicking
23. Audible saliva swishing in mouth
24. Repetitive tapping feet on floor
25. Repetitive tapping toes inside shoes (visible through canvas tennis shoes)
26. Leg contortions (tight sustained flexions)
27. Repetitive knocking knees against each other
28. Repetitive knocking ankles against each other
29. Tensing legs and suspending feet off the ground
30. Head shaking (rapid small movements from side to side)
31. Tensing whole body and shaking

[a] Based upon Koegel, Firestone, Kramme, & Dunlap, 1974. Copyright by the Society for the Experimental Analysis of Behavior, used by permission.

major variables known to control this behavior (more detailed descriptions of several of these variables are provided below).

The *third step* in a behavioral assessment is to *group the behaviors* according to common controlling variables. Note that this is much different from *grouping children* according to similarities in behaviors. In a behavioral assessment the label is not applied to the child or to groups of children (e.g., self-stimulatory children or for that matter, broken-leg children) but rather to behaviors and groups of behaviors (e.g., self-stimulatory behaviors). Relatively large numbers of behaviors can be easily grouped. For example, in Table 1 above, the individual behaviors can easily be grouped together and referred to by the same name since they appear to be controlled, as a group, by the same variables. At some point in time we may find that larger categories of behaviors may also be grouped. For example, Lovaas, Varni, Koegel, and Lorsch (1977) have argued that self-stimulatory behaviors and certain types of delayed echolalia may be controlled by the same variables (e.g., a need for sensory input—cf. also, Koegel & Felsenfeld, 1977). Eventually with this approach an empirically defined limit is reached, where all of the behaviors controlled by a given set of variables have been identified. At that time, one of these sets of behaviors (which perhaps most closely fits one of the existing global definitions of autism) could be labeled as autism. That definition of autism would be an extremely functional one.

1. It would facilitate communication. For example, the definition of self-stimulatory behavior in Table 1 has been shown to be highly reliable. That is, any two independent observers recording the self-stimulatory behavior of those children come up with essentially the same percentage. Phrased differently, it is easy to read the definition and then visualize the behavior (although probably not to visualize the entire child).

2. The definition suggests a treatment (when the variables controlling the behavior are known). The "therapist" merely manipulates the controlling variables, and accordingly changes the behavior in a desirable and predictable direction.

3. The definition suggests a prognosis. If most of the variables controlling the behavior are known (as appears to be the case with self-injurious behavior) then the prognosis for that behavior is extremely good. On the other hand, when most of the variables controlling a behavior are unknown (as appears to be the case with self-stimulatory behavior) then the prognosis for that behavior is extremely guarded.

In summary, the behavioral approach to assessment is at once: (*a*) both immediately useful; and (*b*) has the potential to evolve gradually a functional definition of autism. At this time we would prefer not to define the entire syndrome. Naturally since the behavior modification approach to the treatment of "autism" has dealt with changing individual behaviors, it has relied heavily on the behavioral method of assessment. The remainder of this chapter describes how many of the behaviors (from language through perception through tantrums) of children who bear the label of autism can be changed in a therapeutic direction. The following is a description of our therapy procedures.

AN EMPIRICALLY BASED TREATMENT APPROACH

Many people have argued that autistic children cannot learn. This argument, however, appears to be in error. Autistic children can learn, but they only seem to do so if considerable care is taken in the learning situation. Autistic children do not seem to learn very much unless specific teaching rules, identified through research in the area of learning, are closely followed. Slight deviations on the part of the teacher's behavior produce major disruptions in the autistic child's learning. While it is obvious that there is still much to learn about the effective teaching of autistic children, there is currently a considerable amount of information known and published.

In order to provide a generalized therapy program, we have found it necessary to train therapists in the general procedural rules of behavior modification rather than in many individual treatment programs (Koegel, Glahn, & Nieminen, 1978; Schreibman & Koegel, 1975). When implementing a treatment program for autistic children, it appears to be important to take care to maximize the clarity with which stimuli are delivered. The training format that we usually follow in executing clinical programs helps present things in a clear manner, and it seems to maximize the rate at which the children acquire new skills.

The generalized format for a training trial is as follows:

1. The teacher (parent) presents a clear stimulus (command or question) to the child who is quietly attending to the teacher or the task at hand.
2. This stimulus may optionally be followed by a prompting cue designed to evoke the desired response.
3. The child responds correctly or incorrectly.
4. The teacher responds (with a reward or punishment).

Problems can take place at any point within a trial. For purposes of clarity, it is probably best to describe each component separately.

Discriminative Stimuli

A trial begins by presenting a signal for the child to respond. This signal, a discriminative stimulus (S^D), is a stimulus that one desires to establish as discriminative for the child to respond. In explaining this to new therapists we typically point out that questions and commands are both examples of S^D's; that when therapists say, "Touch your nose," or ask, "What color is this?" they are presenting an S^D.

In order for an autistic child to learn, it is desirable that the S^D be presented in a certain way. The S^D should be: (a) presented when the child is attending; and (b) easily discriminable. Each of the characteristics of an effective S^D is considered separately below.

Child Attending

Frequently, the autistic child does not attend to the learning situation. He may be jumping around on his chair, pulling the therapist's hair, screaming, and so forth.

In many cases it turns out to be practically useless to present the S^D while the child is not attending. All "off-task," nonattending behavior must be eliminated before the S^D is presented. Eliminating off-task behaviors is done in the same way as working with any other behavior. In other words, before attempting to teach the child the S^D "Touch red," it would be better first to make sure that the child responds appropriately to the S^D's "Look at me," "Hands down," "Sit quietly," "No screaming," and so on. In any case, the major point here is that the S^D should preferably not be presented if the child is engaging in self-stimulatory or other off-task behavior, since it often takes much longer for the child to learn under such conditions (see Koegel & Covert, 1972; Risley, 1968).

Easily Discriminable

This means that the S^D must be presented in such a way that it stands out from everything else. The S^D is the stimulus that eventually is to acquire control over the child's behavior. Eventually, the child is going to learn the "meaning" of the S^D. Therefore, in the case of autistic children, it is frequently necessary for the therapist to take considerable precautions to ensure that the child does discriminate the specific S^D that the therapist desires to become meaningful.

The reason for taking care in presenting S^D's is that there is a growing literature suggesting that autistic children have difficulty responding appropriately when multiple stimuli are presented. Under such conditions the children typically respond to only a restricted portion of the total stimulus complex. This characteristic has been called *stimulus overselectivity* (Lovaas, Schreibman, Koegel, & Rehm, 1971). In the first study showing this finding, autistic and normal children were taught to respond to a complex stimulus display containing three elements: (*a*) a moderately bright visual stimulus (consisting of a 160-watt red floodlight); (*b*) an auditory stimulus consisting of white noise at a moderately high (65 db level) intensity; and (*c*) a tactile stimulus on the child's leg delivered by a pressure cuff at 20 mm mercury (Hg). These stimuli appeared quite noticeable to the children since they often oriented to them (e.g., turned around to look at the light, touched their legs when the cuff was inflated). This complex S^D was presented to the child and he was reinforced for responding (bar-pressing) in the presence of the display, and he was not reinforced for responding in its absence. After training had established this stimulus display as functional for the children's response, single-cue test trials were presented where each component (auditory, visual, tactile) was presented separately.

The results showed that the normal children responded to each of the components equally. In other words, each of the separate cues became equally functional in controlling the child's behavior. The performance of the autistic children was quite different. Each child responded primarily to only *one* of the component cues. (The retarded children responded at a level between these two extremes.) Three of the autistic children responded primarily to the auditory component while two of the autistic children responded primarily to the visual cue. None of the autistic children responded to the tactile stimulus. It was striking to observe the autistic children attentively respond to one of the component cues (e.g., the sound), only to remain motionless in the presence of the other (e.g., the light), even though that stimulus had been presented as discriminative for reinforcement.

Subsequently, two of the autistic children were trained to respond to the component that had remained least functional for them during test sessions. Both children quickly learned to respond to the previously nonfunctional component, *when that component was presented alone*. This helped to ensure that the problem was not one of some relatively "simple" sensory deficit (as in the case of being blind or deaf) but rather was a problem of responding to the cue in the context of other cues.

It was concluded from this first study that the data could best be understood as the autistic child's difficulty in responding to stimuli in context, a problem pertaining to the quantity rather than to the quality of simulus control. The data failed to support any notion that a particular sense modality was impaired in autistic children or that any particular sense modality was a "preferred" modality.

The finding that autistic children respond overselectively has been replicated with auditory and visual cues (Koegel & Schreibman, 1977; Lovaas & Schreibman, 1971; Rincover & Koegel, 1975), with multiple visual cues (Koegel & Rincover, 1976; Koegel & Wilhelm, 1973; Schreibman, 1975; Schreibman & Lovaas, 1973), and with multiple auditory cues (Koegel & Rincover, 1976; Reynolds, Newsom, & Lovaas, 1974; Schreibman, 1975).

While responding to selective aspects of a complex situation is a normal adaptive, and necessary response, autistic *stimulus overselectivity* is much more restrictive. There is now a large corpus of data indicating that stimulus overselectivity might be the basis for much of the impoverished behavioral repertoire of these children and for the difficulty they have in learning new behaviors.

For example, restrictions on the number of stimuli that acquire control over behavior can cause serious problems in stimulus generalization; that is, the extent to which a behavior learned in one environment transfers to other new environments. This relates to the familiar problem of "undergeneralization" of therapeutic gains—the failure of a behavior, acquired in a therapeutic setting, to transfer to a new "outside" environment.

This problem of limited generalization has been clinically observed in all our work on autistic children. It was shown in a study by Rincover and Koegel (1975) where stimulus overselectivity seemed directly to limit generalization. In this experiment, one teacher taught autistic children to perform a simple behavior upon request (e.g., "Touch your nose"). Immediately after each child had learned this behavior, a second teacher took the child into another environment and made the same request. Four of the 10 autistic children did not perform the relatively simple behavior in the new environment. Tests showed that the children had failed to generalize the learned behavior because they had selectively responded to irrelevant stimuli during training. In one case, for example, the child's responding was controlled by incidental movements of the first teacher's hand. Subsequently, when the second teacher simply raised his hand in a similar way in the outside setting, the child did respond appropriately. That is, generalized responding occurred only after the systematic exploration and isolation of relevant "stimuli" in the treatment environment and the introduction of these stimuli to new (outside) environments.

In order to prevent such problems from occurring in the first place, we have tried to reduce the number of irrelevant stimuli present when we teach the children. We do this even when we present verbal S^D's. This is easily done if the S^D is short and has a clear start and end. Examples of such discriminable S^D's are "Touch red" and "Sit down."

Examples of presenting S^D's that are hard for the child to discriminate follow. "Okay, now we are going to learn all about colors: reds, greens, blues, oranges, and other pretty colors. What you are supposed to do is touch the color I name. Don't touch any other color, only the one I name. If I say touch red, then you touch red, not green or blue. Okay? Now touch red. Remember what I told you, now."

In this example, the words that are supposed to signal the child's response (touch red) are easily lost in the barrage of other stimuli. That is, one might readily expect the autistic child to overselect on the wrong word(s). A much better S^D might be simply to say "Touch red."

Another example: "First, I'm going to put down a square block, and then I'm going to put down a round block. Now you tell me which block I put down first." This S^D contains too many cues and again is likely to result in overselectivity to the wrong cue. A better S^D would be to say "Which is first?" or in the case of a nonverbal child, the S^D might be "Touch first."

Prompts

There are many occasions when the clinician wishes to teach a behavior that is not elicited by the S^D nor is likely to occur spontaneously. On these occasions it is advisable to use a "prompt" to bring about the correct response. A prompt, as we are using the term, is a stimulus presented along with the S^D that guides the child to the correct response. In behavior modification, prompts are very frequently used in teaching situations of all kinds. For example, if the S^D "Touch your nose" is presented and the child does not respond, the therapist may prompt the response by manually moving the child's hand to his nose while presenting the S^D "Touch your nose." Or if the therapist is trying to teach the child to imitate the sound "mm" but the child is not responding correctly, the therapist may prompt by holding the child's lips together as the S^D "mm" is presented. This could very likely lead the child to say the "mm" sound. If the child is echolalic and the therapist holds up a red block and says "What color is this?", the child may echo the S^D, saying "What color is this?" In this case the therapist can prompt a correct response by holding a hand over the child's mouth during the S^D presentation, preventing the echo. Then, immediately after the S^D, the therapist can say "red" and uncover the child's mouth permitting the echo "red." Thus the prompt would look like this: therapist (with hand over child's mouth): "What color is this?" One second pause. "Red." (Therapist then uncovers child's mouth.) Child's response: "Red."

In the use of prompts at least two things are critical. First, a prompt is only a prompt if it works. That is, it *must* bring about a correct response. In the examples above, if the child pulls away when the therapist attempts to hold closed the child's lips or if the child echoes the entire sequence "What color is this? Red.", then the prompts are ineffective and must be abandoned in favor of other, more effective prompts. One of the most common errors therapists make is to try an ineffective prompt repeatedly merely because it seems logical, or because it worked with another child.

The second major point to remember in prompting is that the prompt must eventually be removed. That is, once the prompted response has been established, the therapist seeks to reduce the child's dependency on the prompt by gradually "fading" the prompt until the child responds solely on the basis of the S^D. For example, in the above example where the therapist manually places the child's hand on his nose to prompt the response to "Touch your nose," the prompt may be faded by gradually reducing the manual guidance. Thus, the therapist may lift the child's hand halfway to the nose while saying "Touch your nose" so the child completes the response on his own. When the child will do this reliably, the therapist may merely lift the child's arm slightly. Then he may just touch the child's arm, and so on. It is not just that the therapist is doing less guiding, but also as the prompt is faded the child is doing more and more on his own. Eventually the prompt is completely faded such that the child correctly touches his nose when the verbal S^D is presented. It appears to be important to fade the prompt slowly enough so that the child makes few errors (cf. Terrace, 1963). Yet, it is important to fade the prompt completely so that the child's response comes under the control of the S^D and does not remain under the control of the prompt.

Special Points to Remember in Prompting with Autistic Children

This last point, total removal of the prompt, can be problematic in the case of autistic children. Whereas prompt-fading procedures have proven effective with normal children (e.g., Cheney & Stein, 1974; Storm & Robinson, 1973; Taber & Glaser, 1962), retarded children (e.g., Dorey & Zeaman, 1973; Sidman & Stoddard, 1966, 1967; Touchette, 1968, 1969, 1971); and autistic children (e.g., Ferster & DeMyer, 1962; Koegel & Rincover, 1974; Metz, 1965; Risley & Wolf, 1967), many studies have pointed out difficulties encountered when trying to fade the prompt completely with autistic children (e.g., Acker, 1966; Koegel & Rincover, 1976; Lovaas, Schreibman, Koegel, & Rehm, 1971; Schreibman, 1975).

It appears that many autistic children do not learn with typical prompt-fading procedures. The reasons for this failure to learn may be due to the stimulus overselectivity phenomenon discussed earlier. This can be seen when one considers that the use of a prompt typically requires response to two simultaneous cues, the prompt stimulus and the training stimulus (S^D) (Fields, Bruno, & Keller, 1976). The child must shift responding from the prompt to the training stimulus, and in doing so he/she must associate the two cues. One can readily see that if the child responds only to one cue the necessary association of the two cues will not take place. More likely, since the prompt is the only reliable cue for reinforcement at the start of training, the autistic child overselectively responds to this cue and fails to respond to the training stimulus. In working with these children several investigators have indeed found that autistic children, when presented with a discrimination task involving prompt-fading, typically responded only to the prompts and did not learn the discrimination (e.g., Koegel & Rincover, 1976; Rincover, 1978; Schreibman, 1975). For example, if the therapist first trained the child to respond to the color blue, and then prompted response to a particular word by underlining the word with a blue line, the child might continue to respond to very faded color cues as the prompt was faded, but never respond to the word when the color was completely absent.

However, since prompt-fading is such a useful technique for bringing about correct responding, it is a tool the therapist can ill do without. Thus some investigators

(Rincover, 1978; Schreibman, 1975) have approached the problem by developing prompts that allow the autistic child to be overselective, yet transfer from the prompt to the training stimulus when the prompt is removed. These investigators have developed "within-stimulus" and "distinctive feature" prompt-fading procedures.

For our purposes, these procedures can be discussed together. The basic principle is that rather than providing an extra stimulus as a prompt (thus requiring response to two cues), the therapist exaggerates the one component stimulus that is relevant for distinguishing S+ from S− in a discrimination task. This exaggeration is then slowly faded until the child can reliably respond correctly to the final discrimination. Figure 1 illustrates fading steps for such a prompt. In looking at the original discrimination (Part c, Step 5 in Fig. 1), the only relevant component of the discrimination is the position (horizontal or vertical) of the dots. The "X" is redundant. Thus if the child is to learn the discrimination, he must respond to the orientation of the dots and *not* exclusively to the "X." The first step in within-stimulus prompting involves pretraining an exaggerated presentation of the S+ relevant component; the horizontal dots (Fig. 1, Part a, Step 1). In this step only the horizontal dots are presented, ensuring that the child can only respond on the basis of this cue. Once the child learns this step, the S− component (vertical dots) are slowly faded in (Steps 2–5). The child is now reliably discriminating S+ and S−. The exaggerated size of the dots is now gradually faded to their normal size (Part b of Fig. 1). At this point (Part c, Steps 1–5) the redundant component of the discrimination (X) is slowly faded in.

Schreibman (1975) reported that using this procedure, autistic children were able to learn discriminations they had failed to learn either without a prompt or with an extra-stimulus (therapist pointing to S+ card) prompt. The strength of this within-stimulus prompting procedure lies in that the child is *never required to respond to more than one cue* (in this case, dot orientation) and response to this cue is guaranteed by the initial prompt steps. Rincover (1978) elaborated on this work and pointed out the necessity of exaggerating the "distinctive feature" of the discrimination. Figure 2 presents a possible fading progression for teaching the discrimination "JAR" versus "SON." Note the emphasis on:

(*a*) exaggerating the distinctive feature of the discrimination (here there is a cross bar on "J" and none on "S" while the bottom curve on both letters is the same); and (*b*) exaggerating within that component as a prompt, and fading within that component.

While "within-stimulus" and "distinctive feature" fading have proven to be effective in teaching autistic children certain types of discriminations, their use is definitely limited. They cannot be used to teach all types of discriminations. For example, when attempting to teach a discrimination involving multiple modalities, a within stimulus distinctive feature prompt may be impossible. Another limitation is that although the autistic children are learning with the prompts, they are still overselective in their approach to learning situations. Thus, the basic learning deficit is unchanged and the children still fail to learn from their normal environment as do children who are not overselective.

Recent research has suggested that autistic children *can* learn to respond to discriminations on the basis of multiple cues (Koegel & Schreibman, 1977). In this study, autistic children were presented with a conditional discrimination task neces-

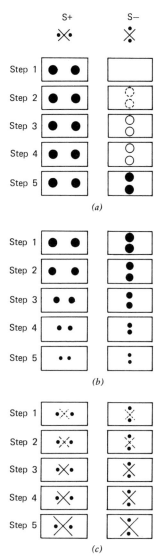

FIGURE 1. An example of a within-stimulus prompt fading progression to teach the discrimination X vs. X . (a) Fade in S−. (b) Fade out size and position prompts. (c) Fade in redundant components. (Redrawn from Schreibman, 1975. Copyright by the Society for the Experimental Analysis of Behavior, used by permission.)

sitating response to two cues. All of the children learned the task (although it took them much longer than it did for the normal controls). Further, preliminary data for one child suggested that after training on a series of successive conditional discriminations, this child ceased to be overselective on new tasks. Thus, it appears that the child learned to approach new tasks on the basis of multiple cues. The implications of this finding for prompting are obvious. If we can teach an autistic child to respond on the basis of multiple cues, then the child should learn with traditional (extra-stimulus) prompting procedures. We are currently investigating

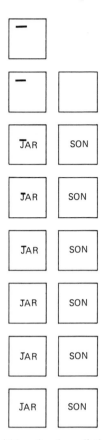

FIGURE 2. An example of a within-stimulus, distinctive feature prompt fading progression to teach the discrimination JAR versus SON. (Redrawn from Rincover, 1978. Copyright by the American Psychological Association, used by permission.)

this possibility in our laboratory, and preliminary findings suggest that we can teach autistic children to learn with traditional prompts.

Gradual Approximations—Shaping and Chaining

The techniques of shaping and chaining are invaluable tools for a therapist working with autistic children. The basic principles of these procedures are relatively easy to communicate to new practitioners. To illustrate, here is how we instruct parents in the use of these procedures:

There are many behaviors that a therapist would want to teach an autistic child that do not lend themselves to some of the techniques we have discussed thus far. Some behaviors would be unlikely to occur spontaneously and thus the frequency of their occurrence could not be increased by differential reinforcement of the response. An example of such a behavior is putting on a shirt. One could conceivably wait forever for the child to emit this response spontaneously. Thus, there are some complex behaviors that are best trained by breaking down the target behavior into smaller, gradual steps. approximations that are emitted by the child) and *chaining* (if the therapist breaks Such procedures are called *shaping* (if the therapist breaks down a response into rough down a complex response into a series of component responses that, when performed in sequence, lead to the target behavior).

Shaping

Shaping is a procedure whereby a complex response is taught by rewarding successive approximations to that response. Initially, even the smallest approximation to the desired behavior is reinforced. Gradually, reinforcement is withheld until the child emits a response that more closely approximates the target response. When the child reliably performs this response, reinforcement is again withheld until the child emits an even closer approximation, and so on. It is essential that the child only be rewarded for responses at least as good as those made on previous trials. This ensures forward progress. If the child seems to perseverate for several trials at a particular level without progress, the therapist should not back up and reward a less-accurate response. Instead, he should switch to a more familiar task for a few trials to allow the child to receive reinforcement and thus remain motivated. Then he may return to the shaping sequence.

The use of shaping can be illustrated by an example. If the therapist desires the child to imitate the vocalization "ah," the response could be shaped in the following manner. The child is seated opposite the therapist, is exhibiting no off-task behavior, and is attending to the therapist's face. The therapist then says "ah." Initially the child will probably make no response. Since in shaping we begin by reinforcing even the smallest approximation to the goal behavior we may wish to begin by reinforcing *any* vocalization the child makes, even if it is a grunt, babble, cough, and so on. Sometimes initial vocalizations can be prompted or elicited by tickling or fondling. As soon as a sound is emitted, the child is reinforced. This rewarding of sounds is continued until the child's rate of spontaneous vocalization is quite high (about one every 5 seconds). When the child reliably vocalizes, reinforcement can now be withheld so that only vocalizations occurring right after the therapist's vocalization ("ah") are reinforced. All other vocalizations are not reinforced. When the child reliably vocalizes (with any sound) only after the therapist's "ah," the demands can be increased so that reinforcement is withheld until the child's vocalization more closely resembles "ah." For example, if the child has been saying "gee," reinforcement might be withheld until the child's vocalization is closer to the sound "ah." This procedure is continued until the child says "ah" after the therapist's "ah."

Chaining

We can conceive of any complex behavior as being made up of a chain of simpler responses. To teach a behavior using chaining we break down a complex behavior into smaller progressive component parts and teach the parts one at a time. We begin by rewarding the first response in the chain, selecting a first response that is so simple that the child can successfully perform it and thus be reinforced. The first step may be a long way from the target behavior but we are building a foundation for the progression toward that target behavior. Once the child reliably performs this first response, we slightly increase the demand by progressing to the next step. Now reinforcement is available only for successful performance on the next step. Ideally, the next step will be such that, again, the child is likely to be successful.

(By breaking the behavior down into these small steps we minimize the number of errors the child makes during the chaining procedure.) When the child is proficient at this step the therapist uses the same method to require advancement to the next step, and so on. (Note the close similarity to the shaping procedure.)

Of great importance to the success of the chaining procedure is the determination of when the child is proficient enough at one level before progressing to the next. A good rule of thumb for the therapist is to make sure that the child can perform correctly on at least 8 of 10 consecutive trials on a step before advancing; however, if the child happens to emit a response that is a closer approximation than the present level, the child should be immediately reinforced. The child is now at this new level. As with shaping, the emphasis is always on *forward* progress since only responses that are at least as good as those made previously are reinforced.

EXAMPLE OF CHAINING. Dressing is a behavior that is unlikely to be spontaneously emitted by the child and is one that is often taught using a chaining procedure. To begin, only a very simple response is required as the first step in the chain. For example, the child may be presented with the verbal S^D "pants up" while being handed a pair of underpants. If the first step of the chain is "holding the pants," the child is rewarded for taking the pants from the therapist and holding them. When he will hold the pants each time, the therapist increases the requirement to the next step, which may be that the child must hold the pants with both hands before he is reinforced. When he will reliably do this, the next step may be that he be required to hold them right side up. Further steps might include: (*a*) bending over holding the pants close to feet; (*b*) placing one foot in leg hole; (*c*) placing foot in correct leg hole; (*d*) placing first one foot, then the other in the appropriate leg holes; (*e*) raising pants to ankles; (*f*) raising pants to mid-calf; (*g*) raising pants to knees; and (*h*) raising pants to waist.

Sometimes a "backward" chaining procedure is employed. In this procedure, the steps are taken in reverse order so that the last step in the behavior sequence is the first trained, and the therapist moves backward down the sequence of steps. In the previous example, the same behavior ("pants up") could be taught using backward chaining by placing the pants on the child and reinforcing him for touching the waistband when the S^D "pants up" is presented. After the child has reached criterion at this step, the therapist may pull the pants down a few inches and require that the child pull the pants to the waist when the S^D "pants up" is presented. Next the child may be required to pull the pants up from the knees, and so forth. Note that the sequence of steps here may be identical to those used in forward chaining.

There are two essential points the therapist must recognize when using a chaining procedure. First, each of these steps is *cumulative,* meaning that to get rewarded at Step 7, the child must correctly perform the entire previous sequence (Steps 1–6). Second, the size of step increments will ultimately be determined by the child's performance. If he is having great difficulty, the step increments will have to be smaller than if he is progressing rapidly. If the child begins to make errors (which do not seem to be due to inattention or lack of motivation) it will be necessary to back up to the previous step at which the child was successful. After the child performs correctly at this level, he should be again advanced, but at a smaller step increment than before when he erred.

Shaping and Chaining with Autistic Children

Therapists working with autistic children will find that whereas the *principles* involved in shaping and chaining are relatively simple and logical, the *practice* can be more difficult with some of these children. The training session never seems to go as smoothly as described in the procedural description. We can point to some of the problems frequently encountered when attempting to use shaping or chaining with autistic children.

First, the children often progress so slowly that improvement increments are infrequent and small. This, in turn, makes it very difficult for the therapist to discriminate the occurrence of these improvements. For example, if the therapist is shaping the sound "ga" and the child is saying "gee," the therapist needs to listen for any sound that is a closer approximation to "ga." Yet, if the child has gone several trials with no improvement, the therapist may have trouble remembering the last best approximation and thus be unable to tell if the next one is indeed a further improvement.

Another problem is that a child may be progressing along at an early stage of the shaping process, when he, by chance, happens to make a response that is very close to the target behavior. By principle, the child should now be moved up to this more advanced level, yet the therapist knows that the child may not spontaneously make this response again for thousands of trials, and is therefore likely to cease responding long before another reward can be presented. What does he then do—reinforce the response but go back to the child's previous best approximation to continue shaping, or advance the child to the new high level? In practice therapists have developed their own plans for handling this situation. One way seems to be to reinforce the good response and end the session for the day as an extra reward. (This also reduces the immediacy of allowing the child to be reinforced for less-accurate responses.) Others just treat the response as a lucky fluke and go back to the earlier stage of shaping where the progress had been more gradual and steady.

These situations point to a glaring hole in our knowledge of the use of gradual approximations with autistic children. We do not have a solid empirical basis for *how* to use these procedures. Now we rely heavily on clinical intuition to handle these problems. What we need is some research on just how to do shaping and chaining. Hopefully, the use of shaping and chaining will be treated in the same manner as the prompting research discussed earlier. In that case, problems with prompting were identified and research conducted to understand causal variables and to design alternative, more effective prompting procedures. This is the kind of research we await to help in developing more effective shaping and chaining procedures.

Consequences

The most important determinant of an individual's behavior may be the consequences the environment presents for that behavior (cf. Skinner & Ferster, 1957). Thus the therapist's most powerful tool for accomplishing behavior change is the effective use of consequences. This, in turn, requires that the therapist possess a sophisticated knowledge of the principles involved in consequating behavior. This is particularly essential in the case of autistic children since we know that the typical "rewards and punishments" that are effective with other children often do not work with autistic children. In this section we discuss techniques of behavioral consequences as they relate to the treatment of these children.

The use of consequences can be broadly divided into two main areas for consideration. First, is the *type* of consequence. Second, is the *manner* in which the consequence is presented. We address each of these areas below.

Type of Consequence

Behaviorally the type of consequence is defined solely by the effect its presentation has on the behavior immediately preceding it (Skinner & Ferster, 1957). If the strength of a behavior is increased when a particular stimulus is presented contingent upon its occurrence, the stimulus is defined as a *positive reinforcer*. Typically, we see the use of positive reinforcement when someone says "good boy" or gives the child a cookie when the child does something desirable. In the case of autistic children, one often needs to be particularly resourceful and imaginative when trying to find potent positive reinforcers. This is the case because, as discussed earlier, these children typically are socially unresponsive and, consequently, typical social reinforcers such as "good boy/girl" or a hug may be ineffective. With these children the therapist often must resort to primary reinforcers such as edibles (Lovaas, Freitag, Kinder, Rubenstein, Schaeffer, & Simmons, 1966). Sometimes even food is not a potent enough reinforcer and the therapist must seek alternatives (cf. Rincover, Newsom, Lovaas, & Koegel, 1977). This process can be difficult. For example, one boy with whom the authors worked presented a particularly difficult motivational problem. He was not socially responsive and rejected any attempts to use social approval as a positive reinforcer. He was also a poor eater and would not work for food. He did not play, thus ruling out the use of toys as a reward. Finally, it was discovered that he loved a particular song. We reasoned that the song might serve as a reinforcer and recorded it on a cassette tape. During therapy sessions, 5-second intervals of the song were presented to the child contingent upon correct responding. Indeed, correct responding increased dramatically using this procedure.

A therapist must also be able to identify positive reinforcers that may not be intuitively obvious and, indeed, may seem very unlikely. It is often the case with autistic children that stimuli that we may consider to be aversive have positively reinforcing effects on the child's behavior. For example, verbally chastising a child (e.g., "no," "stop that") may lead to an increase in the undesirable behavior even though the opposite effect is intended. But the therapist *is* attending to the child and attention like this can be reinforcing, especially if the child has few other sources of reinforcement, and/or if the child has some minimal social behavior. A particularly good example of an unexpected positive reinforcer was recently demonstrated by Favell, McGimsey, and Jones (1978). These investigators reported on three self-abusive subjects for whom physical restraint served as a positive reinforcer. When physical restraint was presented contingent upon increasing periods of time with no self-abuse, the self-abuse was eliminated.

The use of *negative reinforcement* has also proven to be effective with autistic children, particularly in those instances where an appropriate positive reinforcer cannot be found. Since a negative reinforcer is a stimulus that when removed or avoided serves to strengthen a behavior, we are typically dealing with an aversive stimulus. Thus, if the therapist cannot identify a positive reinforcer for which the child will work, an alternative is to use a negative reinforcer that the child will work to escape or avoid. For example, if trying to teach the child to look at the therapist, one method is for the therapist to hold a piece of food up in front of his/her eyes while saying, "Look at me." If the child cannot be enticed by the food (positive reinforcer) an alternative is to say, "Look at me" and hold the child's head firmly. Most likely this will be unpleasant to the child. When he looks at the therapist, the head is released. The child should quickly learn that the way to avoid or escape the head-holding is to look at the therapist when asked.

Besides applying negative reinforcement to increase a desirable behavior, one needs to be alert to the possibility of negative reinforcement operating to maintain undesirable behavior. An example will serve to illustrate this problem. Carr, Newsom, and Binkoff (1976) presented the case of an institutionalized psychotic boy, Tim, with a long history of severe self-abuse. Tim's teacher was reporting that his self-abuse was interfering with his treatment. During his treatment sessions, he would slap his face repeatedly. The teacher, being careful not to present attention (positive reinforcement) to him when he self-abused, immediately stopped speaking to him and turned away. Soon Tim would stop hitting himself. Yet, when the teacher resumed her instruction (which consisted of having Tim respond to commands and questions) his self-abuse recurred. Carr et al. hypothesized that the commands and questions constituted an aversive situation that Tim was escaping by engaging in self-abuse. A systematic analysis conducted by the authors confirmed the hypothesis. Thus, Tim could avoid having to work by hitting himself. The teacher had inadvertently negatively reinforced the self-abuse.

Extinction is a frequently used consequence and one of the most effective tools in a therapist's repertoire. Basically, extinction means that a stimulus known to be a reinforcer is no longer presented contingent on a behavior. If a child has been receiving attention for tantrums and if the attention has been maintaining the tantrums because it is a positive reinforcer, an effective way to eliminate the tantrums is to no longer provide the attention. Since there is no longer any reinforcement forthcoming for the disruptive behavior, the child will cease to tantrum. To take another example we can discuss the Carr et al. (1977) study involving the child whose self-abuse was being maintained by the negative reinforcement of avoiding the teacher's commands. One would suspect that this behavior could be put on extinction by no longer presenting the negative reinforcer (teacher stopping the commands) when self-abuse occurred. Thus, in this case a potentially effective treatment procedure would be to *continue* the commands when the child self-abused so that he would learn that hitting himself would not lead to escape from the work situation. This would remove the "pay off" for such behavior.

This last point serves to bring us to some important characteristics of the extinction procedure. First, extinction is effective but it typically involves a gradual reduction in the strength of the behavior rather than a sharp, dramatic drop (as is more characteristic of punishment). In the case of Tim, his self-abuse consisted of fairly mild self-abuse and thus extinction might be used since he would not really do serious damage to himself. However, a child with more severe self-abuse might not be a good candidate for extinction because of the serious harm that might be inflicted during the extinction process. Second, at the onset of extinction there is usually an initial *increase* in the strength of the target behavior as the child "tries harder" to reinstate the reinforcer. Thus, the child might cry harder during a tantrum or nag harder for a cookie. After this initial extinction "burst" the behavior gradually extinguishes. It is important that the therapist expect this initial increase in the strength of the behavior or he may prematurely abandon an effective treatment procedure. Third, the therapist can expect an increase in the variability of the response at the onset of extinction. Thus, the child may be more "creative" in his attempts to gain attention for his tantrum. He may now kick the door or throw himself on the floor, and so forth. Again, it is important to anticipate the occurrence of these effects during the initial stages of extinction.

Punishment refers to the presentation of a (usually aversive) stimulus contingent upon an undesirable behavior with the effect of reducing the strength of that behavior. Forms of punishment can range from a mild verbal "no" to a spank or other physical aversive stimuli. Punishment has been shown to be an effective means of decreasing problem behaviors.

Punishment with autistic children has received much attention over the years, both pro and con. Punishment has proved necessary with these children in instances where it would not be necessary with normal children. This is primarily due to the fact that autistics are typically nonverbal and rather than verbally describing the contingencies to the child ("Don't engage in self-stimulation because it interferes with your learning") the contingencies must be directly applied. Further, punishment has been demonstrated to be effective with forms of behavior that are very resistant to other forms of treatment such as self-abuse (e.g., Baroff & Tate, 1968; Lichstein & Schreibman, 1976; Lovaas & Simmons, 1969; Tate & Baroff, 1966).

It is important for the therapist to remember that punishment serves only to suppress a behavior temporarily. If the child is not taught another, more acceptable behavior, then the undesirable behavior will recur after the punishment is removed. Thus, one of the advantages of punishment is that it suppresses an undesirable behavior, allowing the therapist to reinforce concurrently (increase the strength of) an incompatible, desirable behavior. For example, if a child is receiving attention for self-abuse and this attention is maintaining the behavior, the therapist may elect to punish the self-abuse. While this behavior is suppressed, the child can be taught another, more appropriate response that will similarly serve to gain attention. Perhaps the child can be taught to talk. Under these conditions, the child should not and typically does not revert to self-abuse for attention.

The use of punishment should be governed by several considerations. First, is the nature of the response suppression desired. Punishment is often the treatment of choice when it is deemed undesirable to allow the behavior to continue any longer. Such would be the case of a severe self-abusive child or a very aggressive child. Second, is the fact that punishment may be used when other procedures such as extinction or rewarding incompatible behaviors have failed. Third, is the fact that some therapists are more comfortable with one approach than another. If the therapist is not comfortable with punishment or with the particular punishing stimulus being used, he probably will not be consistent with the procedure. This would, of course, render the procedure ineffective. Fourth, one would typically opt for the mildest punisher that will prove effective for a particular behavior.

Time-out is a form of punishment often used with autistic children. This procedure involves removing the child from the opportunity to receive reinforcement. This is done contingent upon engaging in an undesirable behavior. For example, if a child is engaging in disruptive behavior in a classroom or therapy setting, the therapist may remove the child to another small room where there are no toys, people, or other potentially reinforcing objects or activities. In addition, the child is no longer in the treatment environment where reinforcement is available. After the child has ceased the undesirable behavior, he is again brought back to the treatment setting.

While time-out can be a very effective procedure, it is only effective when the time-out environment is less reinforcing than the environment the child is being removed from (cf. Solnick, Rincover, & Peterson, 1977). For example, removing the child from the classroom to another playroom will probably not be effective because the child might prefer to be in the playroom rather than in the classroom. In fact, the child may be engaging in the undesirable behavior just to get to the playroom.

When using consequences, the therapist must remember that a particular consequence may not always be identified beforehand. A consequence is defined by the *effect* it has on the behavior and by no other definition.

Manner of Presenting Consequences

As mentioned earlier, the manner in which a consequence is delivered is as important as the type of consequence. One can look at four basic rules when applying consequences.

1. *The consequence must be contingent upon the behavior.*   This means that to be effective a consequence must follow *only* the specific target behavior and be presented *immediately* upon the behavior's occurrence. Thus, if the therapist is using candy to reinforce a child positively for saying "mama," he/she should be careful to present the candy immediately when the child says "mama" and not after other responses.

2. *The consequence delivery must be consistent.*   If a consequence is to be effective it must be presented in the same manner and contingent upon the same behavior across trials. For example, one must be careful not to punish some instances of a behavior while allowing the child to "get away" with the behavior on other occasions just because the therapist is tired or occupied elsewhere.

3. *The consequence must be delivered in an unambiguous manner.*   The nature of the consequence must always be clear to the child. If the reinforcer is positive it should be delivered in a positive fashion. For example if the child gives a correct response, the therapist might say "Good boy!," smile, present a piece of candy, and sound happy. Thus, several positive cues are being delivered and even if the child is responding to only one of the cues, he will know it was positive. On the other hand, an example of an ambiguous posi-

tive consequence would be where the child has made several errors and finally responds correctly only to have the therapist feed him and angrily state "Well, it's about time!" The food is positive but the affect and verbal statement are negative. Similarly, another ambiguous consequence would be one in which a punisher is delivered simultaneously with a sympathetic statement (e.g., "No, no, no, but I know you're trying, you cutie you").

4. *The consequence should be easily discriminable.* The therapist must make the consequence obvious to the child. The best way to do this is to present the stimulus strongly and to minimize extraneous cues at the time. For example, if the consequence "Good boy" is presented amid a running conversation, it is unlikely the child will discriminate it as a consequence. Again, this may be because of stimulus overselectivity (see above). A good idea is to keep the consequence short, present it in a stronger tone than the regular conversation, and minimize other interactions at that time.

Curriculum

As stated, we have found the above-mentioned behavioral procedures to be generally effective across a wide variety of behaviors. In general we have selected target behaviors according to a very simple rule. If the behavior was abnormal (e.g., self-destructive behavior) and the child did it, then we worked on reducing or eliminating the behavior; conversely, if the behavior was normal (e.g., appropriate speech) and the child did not exhibit it, then we worked on increasing the behavior. As pointed out in the introduction, the behavioral characteristics of autistic children can be divided into two categories: behavioral excesses and behavioral deficiencies. Accordingly, we have designed our treatment curriculum along these lines. Typically, since the behavioral excesses shown by these children are disruptive to learning situations, these are the behaviors we work on first. Once these behaviors are under some elementary stimulus control we concurrently begin focusing on the behavioral deficits. This is an important point to remember, since merely eliminating the excesses without providing any alternative behaviors could lead to some of the problems discussed above in the section on consequences. For example, a child who had stopped tantruming, but merely sat with nothing to do might be particularly susceptible to the paradoxical effect of time-out actually becoming a positive reinforcer. The details of several behaviors we have emphasized are included for illustrative purposes in Table 2.

As one examines this table, one may notice a heavy emphasis on language behaviors, since many experts in the field of autism view the deficits in language as being the autistic child's most severe problem. Further, some view the language deficits as central to many of the other problems, such as the failure to develop social behavior.

Literally all of our attempts to compile lists of behaviors have resulted in thousands of individual behaviors, and yet they have left us with the feeling that we were barely scratching the surface. Thus, it is quite likely that the future will result in a more efficient curriculum than we have used in the past (cf. Rincover & Koegel, 1977). Nevertheless, because we have experienced considerable success even with an unsystematic target behavior selection procedure, it may be useful to give some

Table 2. List of Examples of Target Behaviors

Categories	Examples
Behavioral excesses	
Self-abusive behaviors	Eliminate hitting, biting, scratching oneself, and so forth.
Aggression towards others	Eliminate kicking, hitting, biting, pinching, and so forth.
Tantrums	Eliminate yelling, crying, jumping up, and down, and so forth.
Gets into or messes up things	Eliminate getting into cabinets, scattering books and toys, playing in water, and so forth.
Self-stimulatory behaviors	Eliminate staring at fingers, rocking, handflapping, and so forth.
Behavioral deficits	
Learning readiness	Eye contact on request; follows simple commands such as "Close the door," "Sit down," and so forth.
Gross motor skills	Plays ball; rides tricycle; and so forth.
Fine motor skills	Copies lines; colors; uses scissors; prints; and so forth.
Nonverbal imitation	Claps hands; points to body parts; imitates mouth movements or positions; and so forth.
Verbal imitation	Emits speech sounds spontaneously; imitates vowels and consonants; imitates syllables; imitates stress or inflection in phrase; and so forth.
Simple functional speech	Answers questions with at least one word; asks for things with one or more words; answers "I don't know" to question he does not know; is able to request and transfer information; and so forth.
Identifying, labeling, and describing (receptive and expressive)	Follows commands; identifies familiar people; labels body parts; labels colors; labels common objects; labels alphabet; labels numbers 1 to 20; labels different money values; labels big and little; describes shape of object; describes objects by size and color; identifies emotions; and so forth.
Using general concepts and relationships	Matches alike (similar) versus dissimilar; identifies many action verbs; uses prepositions; uses genetive pronouns; uses nominal case pronouns; uses pronouns to describe personal characteristics; uses "and"; understands "don't"; understands the order command of "then"; understands relationship of "first" and "last"; understands relationship of "before" and "after"; answers "yes" or "no" to questions involving desires; recalls what's missing when an object is removed from a group; recalls what he did in the immediate past; recalls a few things from the remote past; discriminates right and left; discriminates singular and plural; counts up to 10 objects; relates a written number to a number of objects; understands simple money exchange; tells time; knows days of week in order; and so forth.
Using functional concepts	Identifies function of many personal objects; describes function of many personal objects; identifies function of different body parts; identifies function of many common objects; describes function of common objects; identifies pairs of objects that belong together; understands concepts cold, tired, hungry; answers "why" questions with "because"; and so forth.
Story telling	Comprehends sentences; describes picture of an activity; makes up story with beginning, middle, and end; makes up story about a topic or subject; and so forth.

Table 2. (Continued)

Categories	Examples
Socialization	Follows commands of other children in a group; answers questions asked by other children; initiates nonverbal interaction with other children; initiates verbal interaction with other children; and so forth.
School readiness	Works independently on a task for at least 5 minutes without being distracted; participates in small group activities; seeks help when can't solve problem; and so forth.
Self-help skills	Dresses self; drinks from cup or glass unassisted; uses eating utensils properly; washes hands unaided; washes face unaided; bathes self unassisted; is toilet-trained; and so forth.

examples of the target behaviors we have focused on in our clinical work. Table 2 provides a list of some of the categories and examples of target behaviors we have frequently become involved with.

ACKNOWLEDGMENT

The preparation of this manuscript was supported by U.S. Public Health Service grants MH 28231 and MH 28210 from the National Institute of Mental Health and by U.S. Office of Education Research Grant No. G007802084 from the Bureau of Education for the Handicapped. The authors also express appreciation to Dean Alexander, Jon Killion, and Vera Bernard-Opitz for their work in compiling the curriculum, and to Glen Dunlap for comments on an earlier draft.

REFERENCES

Acker, L. Errorless discrimination training in autistic and normal children. Unpublished doctoral dissertation, University of California, Los Angeles, 1966.

Baroff, G. S., & Tate, B. G. The use of aversive stimulation in the treatment of chronic self-injurious behavior. *Journal of the American Academy of Child Psychiatry,* 1968, **7**, 454–470.

Bettelheim, B. *The empty fortress.* New York: The Free Press, 1967.

Carr, E. G. The motivation of self-injurious behavior: A review of some hypotheses. *Psychological Bulletin,* 1977, **84**, 800–816.

Carr, E. G., Newsom, C. D., & Binkoff, J. A. Stimulus control of self-destructive behavior in a psychotic child. *Journal of Abnormal Child Psychology,* 1976, **4**, 139–153.

Cheney, T., & Stein, N. Fading procedures and oddity learning in kindergarten children. *Journal of Experimental Child Psychology,* 1974, **17**, 313–321.

Churchill, D. W., Alpern, G. D., & DeMyer, M. K. (Eds.), *Infantile autism.* Springfield, Ill.: Charles C. Thomas, 1971.

Dorey, G. W., & Zeaman, D. The use of a fading technique in paired-associate teaching of a reading vocabulary with retardates. *Mental Retardation,* 1973, **11**, 3–6.

Favell, J. E., McGimsey, J. S., & Jones, M. L. The use of physical restraint in the treatment of self-injury and as positive reinforcement. *Journal of Applied Behavior Analysis,* 1978, **11**, 225–241.

Ferster, C. B. Positive reinforcement and behavioral deficits of autistic children. *Child Development,* 1961, **32**, 437–456.

Ferster, C. B., & DeMyer, M. A method for the experimental analysis of the behavior of autistic children. *American Journal of Orthopsychiatry,* 1962, **32**, 89–98.

Fields, L., Bruno, V., & Keller, K. The stages of acquisition in stimulus-fading. *Journal of the Experimental Analysis of Behavior,* 1976, **26**, 295–300.

Goldfarb, W. *Childhood schizophrenia.* Cambridge: Harvard University Press, 1961.

Kanner, L. *Childhood psychosis: Initial studies and new insights.* Washington, D.C.: V. H. Winston & Sons, 1973.

Koegel, R. L., & Covert, A. The relationship of self-stimulation to learning in autistic children. *Journal of Applied Behavior Analysis,* 1972, **5**, 381–387.

Koegel, R. L., & Felsenfeld, S. Sensory deprivation. In S. Gerber (Ed.), *Audiometry in infancy.* New York: Grune & Stratton, 1977.

Koegel, R. L., Firestone, P. B., Kramme, K. W., & Dunlap, G. Increasing spontaneous play by suppressing self-stimulation in autistic children. *Journal of Applied Behavior Analysis,* 1974, **7**, 521–528.

Koegel, R. L., Glahn, T. J., & Nieminen, G. S. Generalization of parent-training results. *Journal of Applied Behavior Analysis,* 1978, **11**, 95–109.

Koegel, R. L., & Rincover, A. Treatment of psychotic children in a classroom environment: I. Learning in a large group. *Journal of Applied Behavior Analysis,* 1974, **7**, 45–59.

Koegel, R. L., & Rincover, A. Some detrimental effects of using extra stimuli to guide learning in normal and autistic children. *Journal of Abnormal Child Psychology,* 1976, **4**, 59–71.

Koegel, R. L., & Schreibman, L. Identification of consistent responding to auditory stimuli by a functionally "deaf" autistic child. *Journal of Autism and Childhood Schizophrenia,* 1976, **6**, 147–156.

Koegel, R. L., & Schreibman, L. Teaching autistic children to respond to simultaneous multiple cues. *Journal of Experimental Child Psychology,* 1977, **24**, 299–311.

Koegel, R. L., & Wilhelm, H. Selective responding to the components of multiple visual cues by autistic children. *Journal of Experimental Child Psychology,* 1973, **15**, 442–453.

Lichstein, K. L., & Schreibman, L. Employing electric shock with autistic children: A review of the side effects. *Journal of Autism and Childhood Schizophrenia,* 1976, **6**, 163–173.

Lovaas, O. I., Freitag, G., Kinder, M. I., Rubenstein, B. D., Schaeffer, B., & Simmons, J. Q. Establishment of social reinforcers in two schizophrenic children on the basis of food. *Journal of Experimental Child Psychology,* 1966, **4**, 109–125.

Lovaas, O. I., Koegel, R. L., Simmons, J. Q., & Long, J. S. Some generalization and follow-up measures on autistic children in behavior therapy. *Journal of Applied Behavior Analysis,* 1973, **6**, 131–166.

Lovaas, O. I., & Schreibman, L. Stimulus overselectivity of autistic children in a two stimulus situation. *Behaviour Research and Therapy,* 1971, **9**, 305–310.

Lovaas, O. I., Schreibman, L., Koegel, R., & Rehm, R. Selective responding by autistic children to multiple sensory input. *Journal of Abnormal Psychology,* 1971, **77,** 211–222.

Lovaas, O. I., & Simmons, J. Q. Manipulation of self-destruction in three retarded children. *Journal of Applied Behavior Analysis,* 1969, **2,** 143–157.

Lovaas, O. I., Varni, J. W., Koegel, R. L., & Lorsch, N. Some observations on the nonextinguishability of children's speech. *Child Development,* 1977, **48,** 1121–1127.

Metz, J. P. Conditioning generalized imitation in autistic children. *Journal of Experimental Child Psychology,* 1965, **2,** 389–399.

Ornitz, E. M., & Ritvo, E. R. Perceptual inconstancy in early infantile autism. *Archives of General Psychiatry,* 1968, **18,** 76–98.

Reynolds, B. S., Newsom, C. D., & Lovaas, O. I. Auditory overselectivity in autistic children. *Journal of Abnormal Child Psychology,* 1974, **2,** 253–263.

Rimland, B. *Infantile autism.* New York: Appleton-Century-Crofts, 1964.

Rimland, B. Inside the mind of the autistic savant. *Psychology Today,* 1978, **12,** 68–80.

Rincover, A. Variables affecting stimulus-fading and discriminative responding in psychotic children. *Journal of Abnormal Psychology,* 1978, **87,** 541–553.

Rincover, A., & Koegel, R. L. Setting generality and stimulus control in autistic children. *Journal of Applied Behavior Analysis,* 1975, **8,** 235–246.

Rincover, A., & Koegel, R. L. Research on the education of autistic children: Recent advances and future directions. In B. B. Lahey & A. E. Kazdin (Eds.), *Advances in clinical child psychology, Volume 1.* New York: Plenum Press, 1977.

Rincover, A., Newsom, C. D., Lovaas, O. I., & Koegel, R. L. Some motivational properties of sensory stimulation in psychotic children. *Journal of Experimental Child Psychology,* 1977, **24,** 312–323.

Risley, T. R. The effects and side effects of punishing the autistic behaviors of a deviant child. *Journal of Applied Behavior Analysis,* 1968, **1,** 21–34.

Risley, T. R., & Wolf, M. M. Establishing functional speech in echolalic children. *Behaviour Research and Therapy,* 1967, **5,** 73–78.

Ritvo, E. R., & Freeman, B. J. National Society for Autistic Children definition of the syndrome of autism. *Journal of Autism and Childhood Schizophrenia,* 1978, **8,** 162–167.

Rutter, M. Concepts of autism: A review of research. *Journal of Child Psychology and Psychiatry,* 1968, **9,** 1–25.

Rutter, M. Diagnosis and definition of childhood autism. *Journal of Autism and Childhood Schizophrenia,* 1978, **8,** 139–161.

Schopler, E. On confusion in the diagnosis of autism. *Journal of Autism and Childhood Schizophrenia,* 1978, **8,** 137–138.

Schreibman, L. Effects of within-stimulus and extra-stimulus prompting on discrimination learning in autistic children. *Journal of Applied Behavior Analysis,* 1975, **8,** 91–113.

Schreibman, L., & Koegel, R. L. Autism: A defeatable horror. *Psychology Today,* 1975, **8,** 61–67.

Schreibman, L., & Lovaas, O. I. Overselective response to social stimuli by autistic children. *Journal of Abnormal Child Psychology,* 1973, **1,** 152–168.

Sidman, M., & Stoddard, L. T. Programming perception and learning for retarded children. In N. R. Ellis (Ed.), *International review of research in mental retardation, volume II.* New York: Academic Press, 1966.

Sidman, M., & Stoddard, L. T. The effectiveness of fading in programming a simultaneous form discrimination for retarded children. *Journal of the Experimental Analysis of Behavior,* 1967, **10**, 3–15.

Skinner, B. F., & Ferster, C. B. *Schedules of reinforcement.* New York: Appleton-Century-Crofts, 1957.

Solnick, J. V., Rincover, A., & Peterson, C. R. Some determinants of the reinforcing and punishing effects of time-out. *Journal of Applied Behavior Analysis,* 1977, **10**, 424.

Storm, R. H., & Robinson, P. W. Application of a graded choice procedure to obtain errorless learning in children. *Journal of Applied Behavior Analysis,* 1973, **20**, 405–410.

Taber, J. I., & Glaser, R. An exploratory evaluation of a discriminative transfer program using literal prompts. *Journal of Educational Research,* 1962, **55**, 508–512.

Tate, B. G., & Baroff, G. S. Aversive control of self-injurious behavior in a psychotic boy. *Behaviour Research and Therapy,* 1966, **4**, 281–287.

Terrace, H. S. Errorless transfer of a discrimination across two continua. *Journal of the Experimental Analysis of Behavior,* 1963, **6**, 223–246.

Touchette, P. E. The effects of graduated stimulus change on the acquisition of a simple discrimination in severely retarded children. *Journal of the Experimental Analysis of Behavior,* 1968, **11**, 39–48.

Touchette, P. E. Tilted lines as complex stimuli. *Journal of the Experimental Analysis of Behavior,* 1969, **12**, 211–214.

Touchette, P. E. Transfer of stimulus control: Measuring the moment of transfer. *Journal of the Experimental Analysis of Behavior,* 1971, **15**, 347–354.

CHAPTER 19

Childhood Behavior Problems in the Home

Karen C. Wells and Rex Forehand

Traditional approaches to disturbed families have focused on treating the parent(s) and child in the consulting room or child guidance clinic. The parent and child may be seen individually or together, and treatment focuses on strengthening the self-concepts, "ego," and personality structures of the respective family members and providing them with insight into the nature of their particular problems. It is usually left to the family members to translate their newly acquired knowledge and insight into more adaptive patterns of behavior (Russo, 1964). Although this is the approach followed by many child guidance clinics, reviews of the literature on traditional psychotherapy with children indicate that the improvement rate associated with this kind of approach is almost identical to that of untreated control groups (Levitt, 1957, 1963).

This apparent failure of traditional approaches to deal effectively with the problems of children, coupled with the early pioneering work of empirical child researchers such as Sidney Bijou and Don Baer, led to a surge of interest in the 1960s in behavioral approaches to the treatment of children. Initially, as noted by Berkowitz and Graziano (1972), claims for the effectiveness of this approach were made for all child diagnostic categories. However, reports of the effectiveness of behavioral approaches through about 1967 were mainly limited to single subject descriptive case studies dealing with single problem behaviors and reporting little "hard" data. Since that time, research methodology with children has improved considerably, and we can now be more confident in stating that behavioral approaches do indeed appear to be effective in many cases. Fortunately, the early (grandiose) claims which seemed to suggest that behavioral approaches were a virtual panacea for the problems of children have fallen by the wayside, and we are now willing to evaluate our work more critically and to determine *what* techniques are best for *whom,* and under what conditions are they *not* the most effective. We have even begun publishing negative results (e.g., Weathers & Liberman, 1975) and seem much more willing to admit in the face of competently collected data that nonbehavioral interventions on occasion may be equally or more efficient and/or effective with some diagnostic categories. Thus, behavior therapy with children appears to be moving away from dogmatic adherence to its early claims without losing its empirical underpinnings.

The purpose of this chapter is to describe those areas of child psychopathology displayed in the home for which behavioral approaches do appear to be the most effective and to briefly review the literature evaluating treatment outcome. In addition, the treatment approaches are presented in sufficient detail to hopefully allow for clinical application. Areas of major childhood psychopathology, such as childhood schizophrenia and mental retardation, are not reviewed here as chapters 18 and 22 deal with these areas.

CONDUCT DISORDERS

In surveying the presenting problems of children described in the behavioral literature, it is quite clear that the vast majority of studies deal with children whose behavior can generally be described as "out-of-control" of the parents and/or community. Chief complaints of these children's parents include: aggressiveness toward others (hitting, kicking, fighting); physical destructiveness; disobedience to adult authorities; temper tantrums; high rate annoying behaviors (e.g., yelling, whining, high activity level, and threatening others); and, to a lesser extent, community rule violations such as stealing or fire setting (Bernal, Duryee, Pruett, & Burns, 1968; Hawkins, Peterson, Schweid, & Bijou, 1966; O'Leary, O'Leary, & Becker, 1967; Patterson, 1974; Peed, Forehand, & Roberts, 1977; Wahler, 1969). Typically, these behaviors do not occur in isolation but as a complex or "class," and children displaying such behaviors have been labeled oppositional, socially aggressive, and conduct disordered by various authors (e.g., Patterson, 1974; Wahler, 1969). Furthermore, factor analytic studies of children's behavior problems have repeatedly isolated a primary factor that is often labeled conduct disorders, adding validity to the clinical descriptions of this behavioral "syndrome" (Conners, 1970; Jenkins, 1966; Patterson, 1964; Quay, Morse, & Cutler, 1966; Sines, Pauker, Sines, & Owen, 1969).

The need for developing and evaluating effective treatment approaches for the conduct-disordered child and adolescent is evidenced by the fact that these children are the most common referrals to mental health centers. Surveys indicate that from ⅓ to ½ of all child referrals from parents and teachers concern these kinds of problems (Patterson, Reid, Jones, & Conger, 1975; Roach, 1958; Wolff, 1961). Furthermore, longitudinal studies of childhood behavior disorders demonstrate that aggressive, conduct-disordered children are likely to exhibit similar patterns of behavior into adulthood if left untreated (Morris, 1956; Robins, 1966). Given the frequency with which these families present themselves to mental health facilities for help, the gloomy statistics on outcome of traditional psychotherapy, and the consequences of doing nothing, it is not surprising that much of the research on behavioral approaches with children has been focused on this target population.

Before reviewing the various treatment approaches with conduct-disordered children, it may be useful to describe the clinical picture presented by these families in more detail. Several behavior-analytic studies have been conducted describing the behavioral characteristics of conduct-disordered children and their families, as well as comparing these families to matched normal control groups. In one study conducted by Patterson (1976), 14 behaviors were identified that field observations indicated occurred with a high frequency for boys labeled "aggressive." Multiple observations were conducted in the homes of 27 "aggressive" and 27 nonproblem boys using a complex behavioral coding system and revealed that boys labeled "aggressive" displayed significantly higher rates of "coercive behavior," such as negative commands, disapproval, humiliation, noncompliance, negativism, teasing, physically negative acts, and yelling. Validity studies have indicated that all of these behaviors are considered deviant by parents (Adkins & Johnson, 1972). A comparative study by Lobitz and Johnson (1975) employed a coding system similar to that used by Patterson and indicated that conduct-disordered children displayed a significantly higher proportion of deviant behavior (a summary score consisting of the combined rates of 15 behaviors similar to those listed above), high intensity deviant behavior (low rate, highly objectionable behavior such as destructiveness), and a significantly lower proportion of positively valanced behavior, such as approval expressed to others, positive attention, independent activity, laughing, and talking. Studies by other investigators have essentially replicated these findings (Delfini, Bernal, & Rosen, 1976; Forehand, King, Peed, & Yoder, 1975; Green, Forehand, & McMahon, 1979; Moore, 1975).

In addition to the differences in child behavior obtained in studies comparing normal and deviant families, many studies also report significant differences in the behavior of parents toward their children. Forehand et al. (1975) found that mothers referred to a clinic for treatment of their oppositional children emitted a significantly higher rate of commands and criticisms to their children than did a group of nonclinic mothers. Delfini et al. (1976) replicated these findings and showed that a significantly greater proportion of commands emitted by parents of deviant children were posed in a threatening, angry, or nagging way. Finally, in addition to replicating the data on commands, Lobitz and Johnson (1975) found that parents of referred children responded with a greater proportion of negative behavior in general and supplied more negative consequences to deviant as well as nondeviant child behavior than parents of nonreferred children.

These studies indicate that the families of conduct-disordered children are characterized by a high rate of what Patterson (1976) has called "coercive" interactions among family members. Children engage in excessive rates of behaviors aversive to parents (e.g., noncompliance, physically aggressive behavior, and temper tantrums), and parents retaliate with equally excessive rates of aversive responses (e.g., threatening commands and criticisms) designed to "turn off" their children's negative behavior. The validity of these conclusions is evident as similar results have been obtained from four different laboratories using different coding systems, subjects, and operational definitions (Delfini et al., 1976; Forehand et al., 1975; Lobitz & Johnson, 1975; Patterson, 1976).

On the other hand, the results of these behavior-analytic studies must not be interpreted too rigidly. Each study demonstrated that *statistically* significant differences existed between referred and nonreferred families on the child and parent behavioral variables. However, in the Delfini et al. (1976) and Lobitz and Johnson (1975) studies considerable overlap existed between the distributions of scores for each group on behavioral variables. That is, a considerable number of children in the referred groups could not be differentiated from children in the normal groups on behavioral measures and vice versa. In contrast, the overlap between groups of referred and nonreferred children using questionnaires assessing parental *perception* of child deviance was much smaller (i.e., clear-cut differences between the groups were obtained). Thus, it appears that some children's parents perceive them as deviant even though behaviorally they cannot be differentiated from normal children. Methodological problems could account for this apparent lack of convergence between behavioral and parental report measures (e.g., parental manipulation of child behavior during observations). Nevertheless, as Lobitz and Johnson (1975) have suggested, it is also possible that in some cases factors other than actual child deviance may be contributing to negative parent attitudes and the subsequent referral of the child for treatment. With respect to this issue, recent research has demonstrated relationships between personal and marital adjustment of parents and observed child deviance (Johnson & Lobitz, 1974; Oltmanns, Broderick, & O'Leary, 1977), suggesting that such variables may be an integral component of the clinical picture in many disturbed families. Our clinical experience suggests that excessively high parental standards for child behavior may be another variable to consider in the assessment of these families. Failure to assess and treat each of the salient variables contributing to the presenting clinical picture of conduct disordered children and their families could lead to inappropriate or incomplete treatment, resulting in treatment failure or relapse.

BEHAVIORAL FORMULATION OF CONDUCT DISORDERS

Behavioral formulations on the development of conduct disorders in children have been offered by Patterson (1976), Wahler (1976), and others. As mentioned earlier, Patterson emphasizes the "coercive" or controlling nature of oppositional behaviors and has developed a "coercion hypothesis" to account for their development and maintenance. According to this hypothesis, rudimentary aversive behaviors, such as crying, may be instinctual in the newborn infant. Such behaviors could be considered highly adaptive in the evolutionary sense, in that they quickly shape the mother in the skills necessary for the infant's survival (i.e., feeding and temperature control). Presumably, as most infants grow older, they substitute more appropriate verbal and social skills for the rudimentary coercive behaviors. However, according to Patterson (1976), a number of conditions might ensure that some children continue to employ aversive control strategies. For example, parents might fail to model or reinforce more appropriate prosocial skills and/or may continue to respond to the child's coercive behavior. As far as this latter point is concerned, Patterson and Reid (1973) have emphasized the role of negative reinforcement in the escalation and maintenance of coercive behaviors. In the negative reinforcement model, coercive behavior on the part of one family member is reinforced when it results in the removal of an aversive event being applied by another family member. The following examples illustrate how parent and child are negatively reinforced for engaging in coercive behavior.

Application of Aversive → →	*Child Coercive* → →	*Removal of Aversive*
Event	*Response*	*Event*
Mother gives command	Whine, scream, non-comply	Mother gives up (withdraws the command) rather than listen to whining and screaming child.

In this example, the child's coercive behaviors are negatively reinforced when mother withdraws the aversive stimulus (command). In the following example, coercion escalates.

Application of Aversive → →	*Coercive Child* → →	*Application of Aversive*
Event 1	*Response*	*Event 2* → →
Mother gives command	Child whines, non-complies	Mother raises her voice; repeats command.

Child Response 2 → → → →	*Aversive Event 3* → →	*Removal of Aversive*
Child yells louder, non-complies	Mother begins to yell; repeats command again	*Child Response* Child complies

In this example, the mother's escalating coercive behavior is reinforced by the child's eventual compliance.

It is apparent in the preceding examples how negative reinforcement functions to increase the probability of the occurrence of aggressive control techniques by both child and parent. In addition, as this "training" continues over long periods of time, significant increases in rate and intensity of these coercive behaviors occur as both family members are reinforced for higher amplitude aggression. Thus, in this system the child is reinforced for engaging in coercive behaviors. Furthermore, he also observes his parents engage in coercive responses that provide the opportunity for the modeling of aggression to occur (Patterson, 1976; Patterson & Reid, 1973).

Although the "negative reinforcement trap" delineated above is probably the most powerful process contributing to deviant child behavior, Wahler (1976) has also emphasized the role of positive reinforcement in shaping these behaviors. In this model the parent applies positive reinforcers, such as verbal or physical attention, to the child's deviant behaviors. In a common scenario, the child might throw a tantrum at bedtime. A typical parental response to this coercive behavior might be to approach the child and spend several minutes talking with the child trying to "understand" his anger or reason with him. Assuming that parental verbal attention is a reinforcing event for the child, the parent has in effect spent several minutes rewarding the very behavior she is trying to eliminate.[1] In our experience this is a very difficult point to drive home to parents as well as child care workers. Coercive

---

[1] Throughout this chapter the parent is identified as "she" and the child as "he." The pronouns are used as mothers and boys have typically been the parent and child involved in treatment.

behavior is often viewed by these adults as symptomatic of underlying hostility and a sign that the child "needs to talk it out." Successful treatment of children often involves the very difficult task of convincing these critical social agents that it is certainly appropriate to talk to children, but *not* contingent upon their coercive behaviors.

INTERVENTIONS FOR CONDUCT-DISORDERED CHILDREN AND ADOLESCENTS

Our survey of the literature revealed that four major approaches have been investigated in the research dealing with conduct-disordered children and adolescents. By far, most of the literature deals with procedures aimed at reprogramming the social environment of the child via parent behavior training. Other approaches include the use of token economies in the home, behavioral contracting, and conflict resolution skills training. The first two approaches have been used most often with younger children (ages 3 to 8); the latter two approaches with older adolescents (ages 9 to 18). Although some overlap may exist between the techniques employed in each of these approaches, they nevertheless appear to represent conceptually distinct areas of inquiry, and each will be presented here.

Before turning to a discussion of treatment strategies, however, it is necessary to mention the critical role of a complete behavioral assessment prior to embarking on any treatment program. Indeed, it is impossible to select the most appropriate treatment strategy without first completing an adequate functional analysis that includes a behavioral description of the problems presented by the family as well as an analysis of the variables maintaining their occurrence. As complete guidelines for the behavioral assessment of children's problems exist elsewhere (Doke, 1976; Evans & Nelson, 1977; Mann, 1976), these strategies are not presented in detail here. Suffice it to say that the minimal requirements of an adequate assessment include an ecological interview with the involved family members, followed by behavioral observations, definitely in the clinic and preferably at home as well. Wahler and Cormier (1970) have provided a guide for conducting an ecological interview with members of the child's social community (parents, teachers, etc.) that is designed to gather information on the topography of the child's deviant behavior(s), the setting(s) in which it occurs, and the consequences that "contingency dispensers" in the environment provide (or fail to provide). Emphasis is placed on avoiding mentalistic or abstract descriptions of behavior; rather, the parent is directed to provide specific descriptions of concrete actions and their antecedents and consequences. Thus not only does the interview function as an information gathering tool, it also sets the stage for the intervention to follow by sensitizing the parents to become more accurate observers of their child's actual behavior, a necessary prerequisite for effective contingency management.

Although the interview will provide much useful information, many authors have noted the low correlation that often exists between parent report and actual behavioral data (e.g., Schnelle, 1974). For this reason behavioral observations of the parent-child interaction in the clinic or during a high probability problem time at home (e.g., mealtime) should be conducted. The coding system employed must include clear definitions of the child's presumed target behaviors as well as parent antecedents and consequences (see Doke, 1976; Evans & Nelson, 1977; Mann, 1976, for guidelines on constructing coding systems). Behavioral observations will provide critical information identifying those events that appear to elicit deviant child behavior and those that may be maintaining it. Rearranging these environmental events then becomes the object of intervention. On the other hand, extensive behavioral observations may reveal that the child's rate or topography of deviant behavior is not different than normal children. In that case further assessment is needed to identify conditions contributing to negative parental attitudes (e.g., problems with personal or marital adjustment); modifying these conditions becomes the object of intervention.

Reprogramming The Social Environment

As indicated in an earlier section, behavioral approaches with children emphasize that deviant behavior is shaped and maintained through maladaptive patterns of family communication and behavioral interchange that reinforce (positively or negatively) coercive behavior. As a logical outgrowth of this formulation, most of the behavioral treatment strategies employed with this population involve teaching the parents to change their behavior toward the problem child. Berkowitz and Graziano (1972) have noted several reasons for this approach. First, since most of the child's coercive behavior is acquired and maintained in the natural environment (i.e., family), it is unlikely that clinically significant changes can be obtained by treating the child "out-of-context." Second, even if changes are achieved in the child's behavior in the clinic, these will most likely dissipate if the child is returned to the natural environment that produced the problems in the first place. Finally, parents have the greatest contact with the child and the greatest control over his environment and, by virtue of their parenthood, have the major moral, ethical, and legal responsibility to care for the child. This approach obviously represents a major departure from traditional child therapy that treats only the child in a highly artificial setting (the consulting room or office) and focuses little attention on directly altering those conditions maintaining the deviant behavior.

As mentioned earlier, most of the initial research aimed at reprogramming the social environment of children via training the parents was limited to descriptive case studies or single case designs with data collected in the laboratory or home. In one of the first-known attempts to teach parents to alter coercive child behavior, Williams (1959) instructed parents in a simple ignoring (extinction) procedure to modify bedtime tantrums of a 21-month-old boy. The parents put the child to bed and did not reenter the room regardless of the child's tantruming. Tantrums were completely eliminated by the eighth night, reappeared when an aunt put the child to bed and reinforced tantruming, and decreased again when the aunt was instructed to apply the extinction procedure. No further tantrums were reported during a two-year follow-up.

The next papers published between the years 1964 and 1969 varied greatly with respect to the complexity of behavior problems treated, the setting in which training occurred, the degree of parental involvement, and the methodological sophistication of the study (Berkowitz & Graziano, 1972). Russo (1964) reported two descriptive case studies of a six-year-old aggressive, oppositional girl and an eight-year-old "hyperactive," aggressive boy. Training of the parents occurred in the clinic and consisted of teaching them to ignore their children's deviant behavior (extinction) and to apply differential attention to adaptive behaviors. These techniques were first modeled for the parents. Later the parents received supervised practice in the clinic and were instructed to practice the new procedures at home. Russo anecdotally reported substantial improvement in both children but presented no data to corroborate these conclusions.

Wahler, Winkel, Peterson, and Morrison (1965) treated three boys who engaged in coercive behaviors, such as excessive shouting, crying, noncompliance, and demanding, by training parents in differential attending and ignoring procedures. Training occurred in the clinic and was facilitated by signal lights that cued the parents when to ignore and attend to their children's behaviors. Independent observers scored the mother-child interactions from behind a one-way mirror and variants of reversal and withdrawal designs (Hersen & Barlow, 1976) were used to demonstrate experimental control. Results indicated improvement in mother behavior as well as child behavior as a function of training. Again, parents were instructed to employ the procedures at home; however, no measures were taken in the home.

In the first of three studies which employed parent-training procedures directly in the home environment, Patterson and Brodsky (1967) treated an extremely deviant five-year-old boy who displayed separation anxiety, aggression, destructive behavior, and extreme tantruming in the clinic, home, and school. Training of the mother commenced in a clinic-laboratory and consisted of modeling differential attending and ignoring techniques as well as a holding procedure for extreme tantrums. A therapist later visited the home on several occasions and prompted the mother in her use of these procedures in this setting. Treatment also occurred in the school setting. Unfortunately, no data were collected in the clinic or home settings. Data collected in school revealed substantial reductions in temper tantrums, negativistic, and isolative behavior.

Two studies that appeared at about the same time as the Patterson and Brodsky (1967) study also employed home training of mothers but in addition were the first to report data from observations of the target behaviors collected directly in the home environment. O'Leary, O'Leary, and Becker (1967) reported a treatment program for two male siblings, ages six and three, one of whom had been under psychiatric treatment for two years with little improvement in his destructiveness, temper tantrums, aggressiveness, and noncompliance. During the first treatment phase, the therapist administered candy and social reinforcers to the children contingent on cooperative play in the home. Later, a home token reinforcement system was added. During the second phase, the mother was trained to take over the treatment program by attending to the children's positive behavior, ignoring minor deviant behavior, and using a time-out procedure for aggressive and destructive behavior. She also learned to administer the token program. The therapist prompted the mother to employ each of these procedures in the home during problematic situations using a prearranged cueing system. Data from the home observations collected during baseline and treatment phases showed improvements in cooperative play behavior and decreases in deviant behavior as a function of these procedures. Using a similar approach, Hawkins, Peterson, Schweid, and Bijou (1966) trained the mother of a four-year-old boy to modify nine "objectionable" behaviors, such as biting, name calling, kicking, hitting, and removing his clothing. The mother was cued by a therapist to utilize one of three procedures: (*a*) telling the boy to stop engaging in an objectionable behavior; (*b*) using a time-out procedure for the second occurrence of the objectionable behavior; and (*c*) praising and talking to the boy whenever he behaved appropriately. Training occurred in the home and resulted in decreases in the boy's objectionable behaviors.

Other single case studies conducted prior to 1970 essentially replicated many of the procedures and results already described (Bernal, 1969; Bernal, Duryee, Pruett, & Burns, 1968; Holland, 1969; Johnson & Brown, 1969; Zeilberger, Sampen, & Sloane, 1968). The fact that similar positive results were obtained by many different investigators indicated that parent-training interventions had great potential usefulness with conduct-disordered children. Therefore, after 1969, studies employing more sophisticated experimental methodology (e.g., groups of subjects, naïve independent observers in the home, and complex behavioral coding systems with demonstrated reliability and validity) were conducted to assess the effectiveness of parent-training in a more rigorous fashion. In the first such study, Patterson, Cobb, and Ray (1973) treated 13 consecutive referrals of conduct-disordered boys and their families. Behavioral observations were conducted in the homes before and during treatment using professional observers trained in a complex coding system. Results indicated that 9 of the 13 families showed improvements equal to or greater than 30% reduction from baseline in scored deviant behavior following treatment. In subsequent replication studies in which a total of 27 consecutive referrals were treated, similar effects of parent training were reported (Patterson, 1974; Patterson & Reid, 1973). Generalization data across time and siblings also have been reported (Arnold, Levine, & Patterson, 1975; Patterson, 1974) as well as studies comparing groups of families receiving parent training for deviant child behavior to a waiting list control (Wiltz & Patterson, 1974) and an attention placebo control group (Walter & Gilmore, 1973). In the former studies the authors concluded that generalization did occur, while in the control group studies it was concluded that environmental reprogramming via parent training led to significantly greater improvement than occurred in the control group. Attempts by other investigators to replicate Patterson's procedures and methodology have met with mixed results (Eyberg & Johnson, 1974; Ferber, Keeley, & Shemberg, 1974).

Before describing the research of other investigators, it may be helpful to review the treatment procedures used by Patterson and his colleagues in some detail. The program can be loosely divided into three stages with progression to each successive stage contingent on successful completion of the one before. The first phase of treatment focuses on teaching parents the basic language and concepts of social-learning theory. Parents are asked to read one of two programmed texts (Patterson, 1971; Patterson & Gullion, 1968) and answer questions on each chapter. They are then required to pass a test assessing knowledge of concepts before treatment formally begins. Patterson et al. (1975) have stated that knowledge of concepts facilitates acquisition of parenting skills as well as generalization across behaviors and time. Although such a statement appears logical, at the present time there are no empirical data to support it. During the first treatment sessions in the clinic, the parents are taught to define, track, and record behavior and are asked to delineate two deviant and two prosocial behaviors of their child. The parents then record these behaviors in the home for a three-day period. Daily phone calls to the home occur during this time to prompt parents to do their "homework" as well as to collect their data for the day. This phase can be particularly useful in clearing up parental misperceptions about the frequency, intensity, or severity of presenting problems. In the third phase, the parent is trained to develop intervention programs beginning with two or three easily tracked behaviors. A point system is set up whereby the child earns and loses points contingent on positive and negative behaviors, respectively. Points are then exchanged *daily* for back-up rewards selected by the child. In addition, parents are taught to use positive social reinforcers, such as verbal-labeled rewards ("I really like the way you cleaned up your room just now") for positive behaviors and to implement a time-out procedure (5 minutes of isolation in a corner or bathroom) for negative behaviors. Thus, the child is earning multiple reinforcers for positive behavior (e.g., praise and points for compliance) and multiple negative consequences for deviant behavior (e.g., loss of points and time-out for noncompliance).[2]

A similar line of research has been followed by Forehand and his associates at the University of Georgia using a program initially developed by Hanf for the treatment of child noncompliance. Although based on the same set of social-learning principles, this program differs from Patterson's in a number of important respects. First, the program is not limited to changing single discrete behaviors but focuses on modifying the general parent-child interaction. Second, training occurs in a controlled-learning environment in which parent behaviors are directly shaped during *in vivo* interactions with the child. Third, parents are required to demonstrate changes in *their own* as well as their child's behavior before treatment termination. Fourth, whereas the Patterson program has focused on children in the 5- to 13-year-old range, the Hanf program is designed for children in the 2- to 8-year-old range.

During the first phase of this two-part program, parents learn a specific set of verbal attending and following skills that can be used in ongoing interactions with their children. These skills are modeled for the parent who subsequently practices them with a therapist and then with her child while receiving bug-in-the-ear feedback from the therapist. In addition, the parent is taught to reduce her use of commands, questions, and criticisms directed toward the child. Only after the parent becomes facile with this set of skills in a wide variety of situations is emphasis placed on the differential application and withdrawal of attention for positive and negative child behaviors. After training in attending and following, parents learn to use verbal (e.g., "You did such a good job picking up your blocks") and physical (i.e., hug, kiss, pat on the head) rewards. Daily homework assignments are given to the parent to spend at least one 15-minute period with her child attending and rewarding appropriate behavior. In addition, the parent is instructed to "catch your child being good" all throughout the day and attend and reward on these occasions.

Many younger children will evidence decreases in oppositional behavior after

---

[2] See Patterson et al. (1975) for a detailed description of Patterson's treatment program.

the parent learns these skills. However, research has clearly demonstrated that with severe or longstanding oppositional behavior, differential attending and ignoring (extinction) procedures will not be sufficient to reduce these behaviors (Herbert, Pinkston, Hayden, Sajwaj, Pinkston, Cordua, & Jackson, 1973; Wahler, 1969). Thus, in the second phase of the Hanf program, parents are taught a punishment procedure that can be used contingent upon noncompliance to parental commands. First, as used by Forehand and his associates, at least one session is spent teaching parents good commanding behavior since research has demonstrated that poor commanding contributes to a significant portion of the variance of child noncompliance (Budd, Green, & Baer, 1976; Roberts, McMahon, Forehand, & Humphreys, 1978). Following this, the parent is taught to administer a 3 to 5 minute time-out procedure (confinement to a chair in a corner) contingent upon noncompliance to a clearly stated parental command and warning of impending consequences. Training in these procedures continues until the parent can administer the time-out procedures perfectly and the child shows a noncompliance rate no greater than 10% in clinic observations. (See Forehand and Peed, 1979 for a detailed outline of the procedures).

Using this parent-training program, Hanf and Kling (1973) treated 40 mothers of physically handicapped, noncompliant children. Although no control group was employed, a comparison of pre- and posttreatment data indicated that the mothers significantly increased verbal rewards and decreased commands and questions and, as a result, children displayed increases in compliance. Similar results were achieved by Forehand and King (1974) who treated eight noncompliant preschoolers and by Forehand, Cheney, and Yoder (1974) who treated a noncompliant deaf child.

In a more recent study, Forehand and King (1977) applied the program to 11 oppositional children and compared this group to a group of *normal* control children using behavioral measures collected in the clinic as well as parent-report inventories. Results indicated that mothers of the referred children used significantly more rewarding statements and fewer commands and questions following treatment than before treatment. The children improved significantly on a behavioral measure of compliance; in addition, mothers perceived their children to be significantly improved. When these treated children were compared to the matched group of normal children, the referred children were less compliant prior to treatment and more compliant following treatment; in addition, mothers of referred children perceived their children as more maladjusted before treatment than did the mothers of normal children. After treatment, there were no differences between the treated group and normal control group in parent-perceived adjustment of their children.

None of the studies using the Hanf program reported thus far used a control group of *referred* children or behavioral observations collected *in the home* by trained, independent observers. A recent study by Peed, Roberts, and Forehand (1977) was designed to address these methodological issues. In this study three clinic and five home observations were collected pre- and posttreatment for six mother-child pairs who received the training program. A waiting list control group of six referred mother-child pairs underwent the same observation procedures but received no treatment. Mothers and children in the treatment group evidenced significant improvement in their respective targeted behaviors (increases in general parental positive statements and in positive attention contingent upon compliance;

decreases in parental poor commanding behavior; and increases in child compliance) in the clinic and home setting. No improvement occurred for waiting list parents and children. Interestingly, improvement occurred in parental perception measures taken pre and post for *both* of the groups even though behavioral improvement occurred only in the treatment group. This last finding provides supportive data for the conclusion reached by Atkeson and Forehand (1978) in their review of parent-training studies: behavioral measures collected by independent observers are a more rigorous and conservative outcome measure than parent-completed questionnaires or parent-collected data on child behavior problems.

Forehand and his colleagues have provided additional data to support the utility of the Hanf program by examining the generality of the treatment effects. Humphreys, Forehand, McMahon, and Roberts (1978) found that parent training was associated with significant changes in the behavior of siblings of the treated child whereas Forehand, Sturgis, McMahon, Aguar, Green, Wells, and Breiner (1979) reported no adverse or contrast effects in the school behavior of children when they were treated by parent training. Furthermore, Forehand et al. (1979) found evidence to suggest that behavior and attitude changes resulting from parent training were maintained at a one-year follow-up. Current research is focusing on procedures to enhance generality of treatment effects. Wells, Griest, and Forehand (in press) have recently reported that the addition of self-control procedures (i.e., parents monitor their use of parenting skills and reinforce themselves for appropriate use of the skills) to parent training enhances the change in child behavior at follow-up beyond that achieved by parent training alone.

All of the studies reviewed in this section demonstrate that reprogramming the social environment via parent behavioral training is an effective treatment approach for many conduct-disordered children. A review of these studies demonstrates that most of the treatment procedures focus on altering the immediate parental antecedents and consequences of deviant and positive child behaviors. Procedures employed to alter antecedents include teaching parents good commanding behavior, teaching parents to issue clear warnings of impending consequences if misbehavior occurs a second time, and the use of clearly stated rules and responsibilities as part of token or point systems. Procedures employed to alter consequences of negative child behavior include teaching parents to use ignoring (extinction) procedures, time-out procedures, and the withdrawal of points or tokens for negative behavior. Procedures employed to alter consequences of positive child behavior include teaching parents how to deliver positive social and physical attention and points or tokens exchangeable for back-up rewards. As mentioned earlier, the Hanf program also teaches parents to employ positive social attention in a more generalized way.

With so many procedures available, the question becomes one of choosing the procedure or combination of procedures most appropriate for any given case. The answer to the question is, of course, dependent on what is revealed in the initial behavioral assessment. If behavioral observations of the parent-child interaction reveal that certain parent behaviors frequently precede deviant child behavior, one goal of treatment would obviously be to alter those parental behaviors. For example, in a very innovative series of studies Patterson has shown that for some families, parental and sibling antecedent responses of disapproval, teasing, and laughing all function to increase the probability that a coercive child response will follow (Patterson, 1975, 1976). For such families, parents should be taught to decrease their use of these responses. Similarly, certain parental consequences, such as hitting, talking, or disapproving delivered contingently on coercive child behavior have been demonstrated to *increase* the chances that a coercive child behavior will occur again (Patterson, 1975, 1976). This is a paradoxical effect since parents often use these tactics to punish negative child behavior. These parents must learn to inhibit their use of these consequences since they have an effect opposite of the one that is intended. They must be taught other procedures of demonstrated effectiveness for reducing coercive behavior (e.g., ignoring, time-out, and loss of points in a token system).

A final treatment decision involves whether or not teaching parents to ignore deviant behavior while rewarding positive behavior will be sufficient to decrease coercive child responses. Indeed, some of the studies reported earlier used ignoring as the only parental response to deviant behavior (e.g., Russo, 1964). Our clinical experience suggests that for children who engage in high rate or very intense oppositional behavior, differential attention and ignoring procedures alone will not be sufficient to decrease coercive behavior. Some form of time-out or token reinforcement procedure will usually be required for these children. Data collected by Wahler (1969) and Herbert et al. (1973) substantiate the need for time-out with these children. The reasons for this are not entirely clear; however, it may be related to the fact that for some children who have been engaging their parents in coercive interaction patterns for a long period of time, positive parental attention (when it occurs) is no longer rewarding. The parents of these children seem to have lost their reinforcing value (Herbert et al., 1973). Interestingly, Wahler (1969) has demonstrated that when parents learn to set firm limits on coercive child behavior, their reinforcing value to the child increases.

In closing this section, it is important to note that some parent trainers have now begun to look beyond the immediate parent-child interaction to identify variables that contribute to conduct disorders. Wahler (1978) has identified high risk families who are "insulated" from their surrounding social context. In these families the parents have few contacts with friends and neighbors. Preliminary data *suggest* that increasing social contacts decreases deviant parent-child interactions. If future systematic research substantiates this finding, treatment of parents and their children by way of parent training may not be limited to changing immediate parental antecedents and consequences of child behavior.

Home Token Economy

The development of the token economy was one of the first systematic attempts to apply behavioral principles to the treatment of adult psychiatric populations (Ayllon & Azrin, 1968). However, it was not until the 1970s that this technology was applied to family problems. As mentioned earlier, Patterson and his colleagues (e.g., Patterson et al., 1973) use point systems in the home as one part of the total program, which also focuses on differential attention and time-out procedures. Another group of researchers at the University of Kansas has refined this technology and developed a family training program based primarily on the use of token economies administered by parents. Home token economies essentially involve the systematic rewarding of desirable behavior and punishment of undesirable behavior via the contingent application and withdrawal of tokens that are used by the child to "purchase" certain privileges. The tokens acquire secondary reinforcing value for the child by being paired with the back-up rewards in the same way that money acquires secondary reinforcing value for adults due to its exchange value in the national economic system.

Alvord (1971) has noted several advantages of home token economies over conventional methods of parental discipline with conduct-disordered children. First, the parents' behavioral expectations and prearranged consequences are clearly specified. This helps to mitigate arguing by the child and emotional overreactions by the parents when target behaviors occur. Second, the use of tokens as secondary reinforcers allows for immediate consequation of desirable and undesirable behavior. Texts (e.g., Patterson & Gullion, 1968; Rimm & Masters, 1974) on successful use of behavior principles uniformly stress the importance of the *immediate* consequences of behavior. Since natural reinforcers often cannot be delivered by parents immediately, the use of tokens solves this problem. Third, token economies provide children with a clearly discriminable and consistent environment.

In constructing a home token economy, the parents are first asked to generate a list of target deviant behaviors they would like to decrease, prosocial behaviors they would like to increase, and privileges for which the child should work. These are usually naturally occurring reinforcers that the child is currently obtaining noncontingently (e.g., TV time, desserts, and access to use of a bicycle). Unit values are assigned to each of the behaviors and the "price" of each of the privileges is specified. With younger children tangible tokens, such as poker chips, are often used as the medium of exchange, while with older children and adolescents points or stars recorded on charts or cards serve this purpose. In either case a large chart or contract sheet is posted in a public place defining the targeted behaviors and privileges and the values/prices of each. For preschool children, pictures of the behaviors and privileges in question might be drawn on the chart or cut and pasted from magazines. With young children it is important to keep the economy as simple as possible and, at least initially, to provide for the daily exchange of tokens for back-up reinforcers.

Christophersen and his colleagues (Christophersen, Arnold, Hill, & Quilitch, 1972; Christophersen, Barnard, Ford, & Wolf, 1976) have emphasized the importance of home training in the implementation of token economies. In their work, the therapist goes into the home and actively intervenes with the children (in the presence of the parents), thereby establishing initial control with the children and modeling correct application of the procedures. Parents are taught to deliver or withdraw the tokens or points in the child's presence immediately when the target behaviors occur. The presence of the therapist allows for immediate instructions and feedback in the actual environment in which the behavior problems occur. However, it should be noted that data are not available to substantiate the hypothesis that intervention in the actual home environment is more effective than planning the token program in the clinic and having the parents implement the system at home.

We are aware of three studies investigating the use of token economies administered by parents for home problems. In one of these, Alvord (1971) applied home token economies to 63 children in 28 families. The outcome measures consisted of global ratings of parent-reported success. No independent objective measures were collected and no control groups were employed. According to the author, all but four parents who implemented the program thought it succeeded in giving them additional control over their children's behaviors and resulted in more harmony in the home. Of the four adjudged failures, each was a child over 14 years of age whose parents were unable to enforce the economy by denying privileges when the child had insufficient tokens. This 93% success rate appears encouraging; however, the conclusions of the author are tenuous in the absence of adequate experimental methodology.

The remaining two studies have been more rigorous in design. The first of these (Christophersen et al., 1972) used AB and multiple baseline designs to evaluate the effects of home token economies with five children in two families. Primary observations of target behaviors were done by the parents in the home with occasional reliability checks by an experimenter. Results clearly demonstrated that the token economy was responsible for increases in prosocial and decreases in deviant child behaviors. The authors concluded that the token economy can be a very useful and efficient treatment strategy (average therapist time for those families was 10 hours) given *cooperative* parents who are willing to take primary responsibility for implementing the program.

The final study conducted by Christophersen et al. (1976) examined the effects of home token economies versus traditional child outpatient therapy. Twenty-seven children in 10 families were assigned to a token economy group and 10 children in nine families were assigned to a traditional treatment group. The treatment outcome measures consisted of parental recordings of the occurrence or nonoccurrence of targeted behaviors for one week before and after treatment. These daily parent evaluations showed an average decrease in problem behaviors of 67% for the token economy subjects but only a 34% decrease for child guidance referrals. The authors concluded that their family-training program using token economies was more effective than traditional outpatient therapy for the treatment of oppositional child behavior.

Contingency Contracting

While the home token economy has been shown to be an effective treatment approach with children in the 5 to 12 age range, it has not been as effective with adolescents (e.g., Alvord, 1971), prompting researchers and clinicians to search for other treatment strategies for this older population. The one home-based program that has been tried with some success is contingency contracting.

As is true of token economies, contingency contracts provide a mechanism by which privileges enjoyed by the adolescent occur in exchange for prosocial behaviors targeted in the contract. However, Stuart (1971) has emphasized the critical importance of reciprocity among family members in contingency contracting. According to Stuart, reciprocity implies that *"each party* has rights and duties and further that items of value in an interchange must be exchanged on an equity or *quid pro quo* basis" (p. 3). It is this principle of reciprocity that distinguishes contingency contracting from token economies in clinical practice. In token economies, parents essentially function as administrators; their primary role is to decide which child behaviors will be targeted for treatment and to function as contingency dispensers. In contrast, contingency contracting usually involves much more active negotiation and reciprocal interchange between the parent and adolescent. Oftentimes, the adolescent will be invited to target behaviors for change in his parents and will have an active voice in deciding how privileges will be dispensed. Thus, in contingency contracting both the parent and the adolescent are actively involved in negotiating the treatment plan with the therapist.

According to Stuart (1971) and Weathers and Liberman (1975), good contingency contracts include five basic elements. Contracts must: (*a*) detail the privileges that each party (parent and adolescent) expects to gain after fulfilling their respective responsibilities; (*b*) detail the responsibilities (behaviors) essential to securing each privilege; (*c*) contain a system of sanctions for failure to meet responsibilities; (*d*) contain a bonus clause that provides for reinforcement of compliance to the contract; and (*e*) provide a monitoring system in which each party cues the other when responsibilities have been fulfilled. Table 1 from Stuart (1971) provides an example of a contract negotiated between an adolescent and her parents that illustrates each of the five points.

Three studies have evaluated the effects of contingency contracting with groups of subjects. In a report of the first year of a four-year project, Stuart and Tripodi (1973) treated 79 families of junior high school predelinquents and delinquents with a 15, 45, or 90 day time-limited program focusing on contingency contracting, and they compared these families to 15 referred families who declined therapeutic contact. At posttreatment, families in the contracting group outperformed those in the control groups on several of the measures collected in the school, home, and community; the length of treatment was unrelated to treatment outcome. In a later report from this same project, Stuart, Tripodi, Jayaratne, and Camburn (1976) compared 57 referred families of predelinquent adolescents treated with contingency contracting to 45 waiting list control families. Results indicated that, relative to the controls, the adolescents treated with contingency contracting displayed small but significantly greater improvement on five measures of school and home behavior, including parental ratings of the parent-adolescent behavior in the home.

A final study conducted by Weathers and Liberman (1975) did not yield such positive results. These authors treated six families with contingency contracting and training in negotiation skills using multiple baseline experimental designs. In addition, these families were compared to 16 families who consented to an initial home visit but later dropped out of treatment. Of the four measures monitored during baseline and intervention (completion of chores, curfew compliance, verbal abusiveness, and school attendance), only verbal abusiveness showed any systematic treatment effect. Data from a behavior checklist and school grades collected before treatment and three months following treatment revealed no difference between the contracting and control groups. The authors concluded that contingency contracting as applied in this study was not effective. Possible variables mitigating against positive outcome were the use of adjudicative delinquents as subjects and

Table 1. Behavioral Contract

Privileges	Responsibilities
General	
In exchange for the privilege of remaining together and preserving some semblance of family integrity, Mr. and Mrs. Bremer and Candy all agree to	concentrate on positively reinforcing each other's behavior while diminishing the present overemphasis upon the faults of the others
Specific	
In exchange for the privilege of riding the bus directly from school into town after school on school days	Candy agrees to phone her father by 4.00 P.M. to tell him that she is all right and to return home by 5.15 P.M.
In exchange for the privilege of going out at 7.00 P.M. on one weekend evening without having to account for her whereabouts	Candy must maintain a weekly average of "B" in the academic ratings of all of her classes and must return home by 11.30 P.M.
In exchange for the privilege of going out a second weekend night	Candy must tell her parents *by 6.00* P.M. of her destination and her companion, and must return home by 11.30 P.M.
In exchange for the privilege of going out between 11.00 A.M. and 5.15 P.M. Saturdays, Sundays, and holidays	Candy agrees to have completed all household chores *before* leaving and to telephone her parents once during the time she is out to tell them that she is all right
In exchange for the privilege of having Candy complete household chores and maintain her curfew	Mr. and Mrs. Bremer agree to pay Candy $1.50 on the morning following days on which the money is earned
Bonsuses and Sanctions	
If Candy is 1–10 minutes late	she must come in the same amount of time earlier the following day, but she does not forfeit her money for the day
If Candy is 11–30 minutes late	she must come in 22–60 minutes earlier the following day and does forfeit her money for the day
If Candy is 31–60 minutes late	she loses the privilege of going out the following day and does forfeit her money for the day
For each half hour of tardiness over one hour, Candy	loses her privilege of going out and her money for one additional day
Candy may go out on Sunday evenings from 7.00 to 9.30 P.M. and either Monday or Thursday evening	if she abides by all the terms of this contract from Sunday through Saturday with a total tardiness not exceeding 30 minutes which must have been made up as above
Candy may add a total of two hours divided among one to three curfews	if she abides by all the terms of this contract for two weeks with a total tardiness not exceeding 30 minutes which must have been made up as above, and if she requests permission to use this additional time by 9.00 P.M.

Monitoring

Mr. and Mrs. Bremer agree to keep written records of the hours of Candy's leaving and coming and of the completion of her chores

Candy agrees to furnish her parents with a school monitoring card each Friday at dinner a very limited intervention (three sessions per family). The authors make the point that "in working with families that are decimated by divorce, crime, drug abuse, and woefully inadequate communication and negotiation skills, the introduction of a contingency contract is worth about as much as the paper it's printed on" (p. 365). The negative results obtained with such families emphasize the importance of comprehensive assessment and, when needed, subsequent intervention strategies directed toward the total family.

Conflict Resolution Skills Training

The final treatment strategy that has been employed with conduct-disordered adolescents is training in conflict resolution skills. These strategies are based on the notion that much of the disruptive behavior of ad scents occurs as an inappropriate reaction to conflict situations with parents. The assumption is made that by teaching these adolescents and their parents more appropriate conflict resolution skills, their inappropriate responses will decrease. Thus, training in conflict resolution skills alters coercive behavior indirectly by teaching and strengthening more appropriate, incompatible responses to these situations.

We are aware of six reports that focus primarily on conflict resolution skills training with adolescents and their parents. Martin and Twentyman (1976) reported a strategy aimed at teaching parents to minimize the use of arbitrary power, direct and indirect blaming, and long lectures. Specifically, parents were taught to express their feelings and desires directly and briefly, listen to their children and make reflective statements, and reach specific agreements with their children. Parents first listened to an audiotaped model engaging in feeling expression and listening reflection with a child. The parent then practiced these skills in hypothetical situations with the therapist and later with her own child. Finally, the parent and child were taught to generate as many solutions as possible to their particular problem(s) and choose the one most acceptable to both of them.

Martin (1975) used the strategies outlined above in treating 28 families (14 in a father-included group and 14 in a father-not-included group) and compared these families to 15 families in a waiting list control group. The primary outcome measures were the average *estimated* weekly rate of target problems and parent-recorded descriptions of problem situations collected daily for seven consecutive days. Both types of assessment occurred before treatment, three weeks following treatment, and at a six-month follow-up. Results indicated that both treatment groups displayed significant improvement on parent-recorded and parent-estimated data compared to the control group; the two treatment groups did not differ significantly from each other. Treatment effects were maintained at the six-month follow-up.

Kifer, Lewis, Green, and Phillips (1974) utilized a S.O.C.S. (Situations-Options-Consequences-Simulation) model originated by Roosa (1973) to train two mother-daughter pairs and one father-son pair in conflict negotiation skills. The parent-child pairs were trained to evaluate all possible options and their related consequences to hypothetical problem situations and to employ specific negotiation behaviors such as the use of complete communication (statements that clearly indicate one's own position followed by a request for the other person to state his position), identification of issues (statements that identify the point of conflict between the two parties), and suggestion of options (statements that suggest action to resolve the conflict) to solve the problem. Audiotapes of conflict situations were collected in the training session and at home. A multiple baseline across subjects experimental design was employed and results indicated that all three pairs of subjects increased their use of the negotiation behaviors over baseline levels during the training sessions. Pre-post audiotaped assessments in the home also showed increases in the performance of negotiation behaviors as well as agreements reached.

Robin, Kent, O'Leary, Foster, and Prinz (1977) applied the problem-solving model of D'Zuilla and Goldfried (1971) to six mother-daughter and six mother-son dyads and compared these to a matched waiting list control group. Treatment group dyads were taught to define the problem, list the solutions, evaluate each option by reviewing positive and negative consequences of each, and plan the implementation of the chosen solution. Dependent measures were collected pre- and posttreatment; they consisted of frequencies of these behaviors collected from audiotapes of hypothetical and real conflict situations conducted in the clinic and a behavior checklist on communication at home. Results indicated significant improvement for the treatment group on measures collected in the clinic; however, ratings on the communication checklist failed to yield substantial evidence of improvement at home. The authors concluded that this lack of generalization of effects to the home should prompt a search for procedures to enhance generalization, such as use of homework assignments and incorporation of other relevant family members into treatment.

In a different approach, Blechman has recently investigated the use of a Family Contracting Game to reduce family conflict and facilitate effective problem-solving behavior between parent and child. Before playing the game, parent and child each select problems to solve and potential rewards from a card sort. These are then entered into the game's problem card deck and reward card deck. The game consists of a board with 14 squares that contain instructions prompting problem-solving behaviors, such as selecting a problem, agreeing on a replacement behavior, and writing a contract targeting changes in these behaviors. The game requires about 10 minutes to play and terminates in a written contract between parent and child. Using the Family Contracting Game, Blechman, Olson, and Hellman (1976) treated six children, ages 8–15, and their mothers who were experiencing disruptive parent-child conflict. Baseline and treatment sessions were videotaped, and videotapes were scored for the occurrence of on-task problem-solving behavior and off-task behavior. Use of the Family Contract Game resulted in significant decreases in off-task behavior and significant increases in on-task behavior from baseline to treatment phases. However, these behaviors returned to their baseline levels of occurrence in a posttreatment reversal phase in which the game was removed and family members were asked to solve a problem in an unstructured setting.

In another study Blechman, Olson, Schornagel, Halsdorf, and Turner (1976) used the Family Contracting Game to treat a 14-year-old boy and his mother. Videotaped assessment occurred in the clinic before, during, and after treatment; in addition, the mother and son self-monitored the frequency of problem behaviors in the home. Results of the videotaped assessments showed significant improvement in problem-solving behavior by mother and son from baseline to treatment phases. Unlike the previous study, improvements were maintained on the post-treatment reversal phase. In addition, contracts that were carried out in the home were associated with a significant pregame to postgame decline in problem behavior.

Although each of the above procedures (reprogramming the social environment, home token economies, contingency contracting, and conflict resolution skills training) have been reported separately, we should reemphasize that considerable overlap of treatment approaches often exists in clinical practice. For example, Welch (1976) recently reported a clinical study of a family that failed in contingency contracting because attempts to discuss the contract degenerated into verbal and physical abuse within minutes, a behavioral style typical of the family's interactions at home. The therapist successfully initiated a course of conflict resolution skills training after which the family was capable of negotiating a contingency contract. This case illustrates that multiple impact treatment approaches may succeed where single component strategies fail. Thoughtful treatment planning and implementation should consist of the systematic assessment and treatment of each of the problem areas presented by each individual family.

CROSS-GENDER BEHAVIOR

In the course of normal development, children often explore the various aspects of the same and opposite sex roles. For example, two little girls might be observed playing "house" with one taking the role of the "daddy." By the time children reach school age, however, most will predominantly display behavior patterns that might be predicted by the child's sex (Wahler, 1976). Occasionally, a child will continue to engage in opposite sex role behaviors into the school age years. This can range from "tomboy" behavior on the part of some little girls to a pathological insistence by the child that he or she is actually a member of the opposite sex. This latter condition is most often seen in boys who sometimes state that they feel like a girl and want to bear children. The excessive use of cross-gender behavior patterns has been referred to as childhood gender disturbance.

Recent research exploring methods of treatment for cross-gender disturbed children has been prompted by large-scale retrospective studies of adults with severe gender identity problems. These studies have shown that the gender problems usually begin to develop in early childhood (Money & Primrose, 1968; Walinder, 1967). Furthermore, treatment methods recently have received attention because of the adjustment problems of these children. For example, Rekers and Lovaas (1974) have indicated that gender-disturbed children often suffer social isolation and ridicule and adults with gender problems frequently experience intermittent depression with suicidal ideation (Pauly, 1965, 1969), self-mutilation (Pauly, 1965), and a high proportion of criminal or other antisocial behavior (Hoenig, Kenner, & Youd, 1970). At this time assessment and treatment of gender disturbances have been limited to males in part because the sex ratio of males to females demonstrating this problem is 15 to 1 (Rekers, Bentler, Rosen, & Lovaas, 1977). Consequently, our discussion focuses only on boys.

Rosen, Rekers, and Friar (1977) have distinguished between two different but closely related syndromes of child gender disturbance and have outlined a diagnostic/assessment process that should be accomplished when these children are seen. The first syndrome, *gender behavior disturbance,* is characterized by the adoption of behaviors primarily shown by the female sex in the absence of identification with the opposite sex. *Cross-gender identification* involves a wish or belief on the part of the child that he is a girl and can bear children. According to Rosen et al. (1977), this latter syndrome typically involves

cross gender clothing preferences, actual or imaginal use of cosmetic articles, feminine gestures and behavior mannerisms, aversion to masculine sex-typed activities, preference for assuming a female role, feminine voice inflection and predominantly feminine speech content, and verbal statements about the desire or preference to be a girl or a mother and to bear children and breast-feed infants [p. 91].

Based on their intensive clinical experience with many gender-disturbed children, Rosen et al. (1977) have suggested several areas that are important to assess in the formulation of an accurate diagnosis. Assessment should occur via interviews with the parents and child exploring the development and current status of the child's problem behavior, as well as through direct observations in the clinic and home. The first and most important area to assess is the presence of cross-gender identity statements such as "I am a girl" or "I want to grow up and be a mommy." These are most often seen in younger boys. While older boys might hold such beliefs, they frequently learn by age eight not to verbalize them because of social criticism and rejection. Thus other areas, such as cross-dressing, cross-gender play behavior, and preference for female rather than male playmates are also important to assess, particularly in older boys. With respect to cross-gender role play, a recent study assessed the play of five cross-gender identified boys in several different stimulus situations ranging from playing alone to playing in the presence of an adult family member or stranger. Results indicated that while each boy played a predominantly feminine role (i.e., with toys usually preferred by girls) in most of the conditions, at least one condition was found for each child in which he played a predominantly masculine role. The only condition that consistently elicited feminine play across all five boys was the "alone" condition (Rekers, 1975). These results suggest that it is important to assess the play behaviors of referred boys in a number of settings in order to obtain an accurate picture of their play patterns.

In addition to child behaviors, Rosen et al. (1977) indicate that it is important to assess certain parental variables, such as parental attitudes toward the child's cross-gender behaviors and the nature of the parent-child relationship. With respect to the first issue, failure to perceive anything abnormal until pointed out by some outside person often exists on the part of parents. Indeed, some mothers have reported thinking their son's feminine behaviors were "cute" until neighborhood or school children began to tease the child. With respect to the second issue, the mother-child relationship is often characterized by extremely intimate physical and psychological contact, while the father tends to be either physically or psychologically distant from the son (Rosen et al., 1977; Rosen & Teague, 1974). Interestingly, strong mother-son attachments, along with cross-gender identity statements, are the most important diagnostic indicators of gender-identity disturbance (Rosen et al., 1977).

As mentioned earlier, the choice of the areas of assessment mentioned above was based on the clinical observations of Rosen, Rekers, and their colleagues. Empirical investigations are needed to validate the importance of these areas, in differentiating gender-disturbed from normal children. At the present time data are available from only one study; the toy play of randomly selected normal boys and girls (ages three to eight) and referred "feminoid" boys (ages four to nine) was observed in a laboratory playroom. Masculine and feminine sex-typed toys, such as masculine and feminine clothing and cosmetic articles, baby dolls, baby bottles, toy dart guns, and plastic cowboys and Indians, were present in the room. Each child was observed continuously in four 5-minute play periods. Results indicated that the sex-typed play of the "feminoid" boys significantly differed from the play of normal boys and was not significantly different from the play of normal girls in terms of duration of play with masculine versus feminine toys (Rekers & Yates, 1976).

Formulations of Cross-Gender Behavior

Formulations on the development of gender disturbances in children have occurred from two perspectives: biological and social-learning theory. Results of research on the influence of biological variables are equivocal with some data supporting (Evans, 1972) and other data not supporting (Money, Hampson, & Hampson, 1955) biological influences. Speculations on the development of gender disturbances from a social-learning perspective have been offered by Wahler (1976). Appealing to the work of Bandura and Walters (1963) and Michel (1968), Wahler emphasizes the importance of imitative learning and modeling in the development of gender appropriate as well as cross-gender behaviors. Of particular interest here are our previous descriptions of the close psychological and physical attachment of gender-disturbed boys to their mothers and the lack of attachment to the father. From a social-learning perspective, these mothers would hold much greater reinforcement value for their sons and thus would be more likely to be imitated by them. In addition, anecdotal data (e.g., Rosen et al., 1977) suggest that these mothers often provide social and physical reinforcement to certain cross-gender behaviors. While some naturalistic and laboratory analogue studies support these speculations (cf. Wahler, 1976), it is clear that more research is needed to validate the importance of imitative and reinforcement processes as well as to tease out the unique or combined influences of environmental and biological variables on the development of cross-gender behavior in children.

Treatment of Cross-Gender Disorders

We have located five single case studies that report the successful treatment of childhood gender disturbances (Rekers & Lovaas, 1974; Rekers, Lovaas, & Low, 1974; Rekers & Varni, 1977; Rekers, Yates, Willis, Rosen, & Taubman, 1976; Rekers, Willis, Yates, Rosen, & Low, 1977). The five children in these studies ranged in age from 4 years, 11 months to 8 years, 8 months. Each had a history of actual or simulated cross-dressing, played predominantly with feminine toys, preferred to play with little girls, and used mannerisms and behavioral characteristics usually considered feminine. Three of the boys had directly stated their desire to be a girl and the other two made statements that "implied" their desire to be girls. Three of the children were evaluated at a department of pediatric genetics. Evaluations included physical examination, chromosomal analysis, and sex chromation studies. No physical or chromosomal abnormalities were found in any of these three children.

The treatment strategies were similar in each study with some minor variations across studies, depending upon the idiosyncratic needs of each child. Four of the children were treated in the clinic and home environments. Treatment in the clinic was mediated by the mother, another family member, or a research assistant who sat in a playroom containing masculine and feminine toys with the child and provided differential attention (smiles, praise, etc.) to the boys' masculine play and ignored feminine play and verbal behavior (extinction). Mothers were provided with instructions and feedback during this training from therapists, observing from behind a one-way mirror. Treatment in the home involved a parent-mediated token economy. Blue tokens were given for appropriate gender behaviors, such as playing with brother. Red tokens, which represented either a response cost (loss of blue tokens) or time-out procedure, were administered for cross-gender behaviors, such as doll play, feminine gestures, and feminine speech content. Mothers first read a text on social-learning principles and were later visited in their homes at least three times a week for four months by assistants who helped them appropriately administer the program. A verbal prompt and token reinforcement system was also administered in the clinic for one boy who could not readily discriminate occurrences of his own effeminate behavior.

Rekers and his colleagues have reported remarkable success treating the five gender-disturbed boys with the procedures described above. Positive results have been obtained not only on objective behavioral measures but also on more global clinical measures. Using multiple baseline and reversal designs, the five studies have clearly demonstrated functional relationships between the treatment procedures utilized and changes in targeted behaviors. In addition, one study (Rekers et al., 1976) included pre- and posttreatment independently administered psychological evalautions that revealed a pretreatment diagnosis of childhood cross-gender identification and a posttreatment diagnosis of normal male with mildly effeminate behavior. In another study (Rekers et al., 1974) the subject had been evaluated by two separate psychiatric agencies as having a severe cross-gender identity problem prior to treatment. After 15 months of treatment, the child was referred by the authors to two independent psychologists who administered a battery of tests and interviews and found no evidence of cross-gender identification.

These results are indeed remarkable given the range of inappropriate behaviors displayed by these children. The steps taken by Rekers and his colleagues to obtain such clinically significant gains bear repeating. In their initial studies in which treatment was introduced first, there was no generalization to the home environment, even for those children whose mothers were involved in the treatment in the clinic. For this reason, in subsequent studies home treatment was introduced simultaneously with clinic treatment in order to avoid setting specificity of treatment effects. In one study (Rekers et al., 1974) treatment also occurred in the school environment. This multi-setting intervention is exemplary of the type of treatment that should occur for children who display chronic, pervasive behavior problems. Second, the length of treatment provided to these five children ranged from six to

15 months. This is a longer treatment period than is reported in most studies of outpatient behavior therapy and represents an intensive treatment effort. Finally, in two cases intensive adjunctive treatments occurred to teach boys appropriate athletic and masculine play skills where these were deficient. (Rekers et al., 1974; Rekers, Willis, Yates, Rosen, & Low, 1977). In addition, in one case a male research assistant built a buddy relationship with a boy who lacked a stable father-son relationship (Rekers et al., 1974). This relationship appeared to provide the boy with a stable adult-male model with whom the child could associate. While some might question whether such interventions could be called "therapy," these may be the very ingredients necessary to promote generalization of treatment effects across time.

Before leaving the area of gender disturbances, two issues must be brought to the attention of the reader. First, the studies by Rekers and his colleagues are the only reports of successful behavioral intervention with these children. While the results obtained by the authors are very impressive, their work must be replicated by other researchers in other laboratories before sweeping generalizations about the efficacy of behavioral interventions with this population can be made. Second, serious ethical issues have been raised regarding treatment with cross-gender children (Nordyke, Baer, Etzel, & Leblanc, 1977; Winkler, 1977). One of the first and most fundamental issues addresses the assumption that boys should be treated early because they will *necessarily* grow up to be unhappy and maladjusted as a result of gender disturbance or homosexuality. Critics (e.g., Nordyke et al., 1977) cite examples of homosexuals and transsexuals who are happy with their sexual adjustment. This issue basically reduces to the question of who has the right and/or responsibility to make a decision for or against treatment of childhood gender disturbance. The second issue involves what behaviors should be targeted for modification once a decision to treat has been made. Specifically, critics (Nordyke et al., 1977) have suggested that rather than punishing boys for displaying so-called feminine behaviors (e.g., play with girls) and reinforcing them for so-called masculine behaviors (e.g., aggressive play with war toys), a better and more judicious outcome might be achieved by suppressing behaviors that are inappropriate for both sexes (e.g., dependency on mother, avoidance of brother, male playmates or certain types of play activities), and reinforcing behaviors that might be considered appropriate for both sexes (e.g., skills, self-defense, and cooperative play with boys and girls). Considerable attention has been devoted to these issues and the reader is referred to that literature for further discussion (e.g., Nordyke et al., 1977; Rekers, 1977; Rekers, Bentler, Rosen, & Lovaas, 1977; Rosen, Rekers, & Bentler, 1978; Winkler, 1977). It is our intention to alert the reader to these ethical issues and suggest that any treatment decision with children be based on thoughtful consideration of all the issues involved.

DISORDERS INVOLVING SOMATIC SYSTEMS

Children often display disorders involving bodily systems that traditionally have been viewed as within the realm of medical practitioners. Enuresis, encopresis, and asthma are examples of these types of disorders. Often in response to the failure of a medical intervention to affect desirable change, behavioral interventions also have been used for many of these disorders. As a result of space considerations, this section cannot constitute a comprehensive review of all the somatic disorders that have been treated with various behavioral approaches. However, the reader is exposed to major interventions and disorders that have received the most empirical evaluation.

Before embarking on this discussion, it should be noted that even though behavioral interventions have been used successfully with many seemingly physical disorders, this does not necessarily imply that these disorders are psychological in origin. Indeed, it is increasingly becoming evident that most disorders involving somatic systems are the result of an interaction of genetic-constitutional, environmental, and psychosocial factors, with each component contributing relatively more or less weight in any given disorder and individual (Davison & Neale, 1974; Siegel & Richards, 1978). Following from this multifactorial formulation, it is clear that behavioral interventions should be used in conjunction with or following medical examination and intervention if these are indicated. For example, 10% of enuresis in children is caused by urinary tract defects, urinary tract infections, or neurological disorders (Campbell, 1970). Thorough medical examination of the child should occur to rule out or eliminate these factors. Even in cases of clear organic etiology, bed-wetting often will persist after the organic illness has been eliminated as a result of environmental factors that maintain its occurrence independent of the organic precipitant (Siegel & Richards, 1978). Thus, even in those cases of clear organic etiology, behavioral interventions can serve as useful collaborative or adjunctive procedures. Behavioral procedures also may be the treatment of choice in those cases for which medical interventions are inadvisable, ineffective, or unavailable.

As noted above, the behavioral model of somatic disorders in children emphasizes that, in addition to constitutional or physical factors that may be present, conditioning processes can contribute significantly to the development or maintenance of many somatic disorders. It is well established that through classical conditioning processes neutral stimuli acquire the ability to elicit autonomic responses (cf. Bandura, 1969). More recent research has demonstrated that these autonomic responses, previously thought to be "involuntary" also can be affected by operant conditioning processes (e.g., Miller, 1969). As an example in which both classical and operant conditioning processes were operative, Siegel and Richards (1978) cite the case of a child who experienced stomachaches during a viral infection. Stomach pains intensified whenever the child drank milk. As a function of this association between milk and intensified pain during the illness, the child continued to experience pain when drinking milk after the virus had subsided. This is obviously a classical conditioning paradigm in which, through repeated pairings, the neutral stimulus (milk) continued to elicit the response (stomach pain) when the unconditioned stimulus (virus) was no longer present. Siegel and Richards (1978) noted that operant processes (e.g., attention and comfort from adults, staying home from school) also appeared to be contributing to the maintenance of the symptomatic response. It should be emphasized that in such problems the patients are not malingering (faking the symptom) but genuinely experience the symptomatic behavior, which nevertheless is maintained by social and environmental variables.

Enuresis

Persistent nighttime bed-wetting occurs in about 20% of 3-year-old children, 15% of 6 year olds and 3% of 14 year olds. In "primary enuresis" the child has never attained consistent nighttime dryness. In "secondary enuresis" bed-wetting reappears after a period of nocturnal bladder control. As mentioned earlier, about 10% of enuresis in children is caused by organic factors while 90% occurs in the absence of neurologic or urologic pathology (Campbell, 1970). The disorder occurs twice as often in boys as in girls (Oppel, Harper, & Rowland, 1968).

There are no firmly established age limits beyond which bed-wetting is defined as pathological. The definition changes from culture to culture. In our society, most children attain nocturnal bladder control by three to four years of age. Intervention probably should occur for children whose bed-wetting persists beyond the age of four. Our clinical experience suggests that enuresis certainly should be treated before the child enters school since bed-wetting into school age can have negative social consequences for the child.

Assessment of enuresis first should entail a medical screening. In addition, sphincter control should be assessed by having the child stop the flow of urine in midstream and try to void when he does not feel the urge. Lack of control in these areas may indicate that sphincter control exercises are needed (Starfield, 1967). In the clinical interview with the parents, information regarding toilet-training procedures, previous interventions, and other medical or behavioral problems, such as noncompliance, should be collected. This latter point is extremely important, since many of the available treatment procedures require the child's cooperation and obedience. If noncompliance is a significant problem area, this behavior may have to be treated before the enuresis can be treated. Finally, parameters of the child's wetting behavior should be determined. Parents should record nightly wetting episodes for three weeks. Optimally, because many children wet more than once during the night, bed checks should occur at the parents' bedtime, halfway through the night, and in the morning. During each check the parents should record the approximate time of the wetting episode and estimate the size of the wet spot. Changes in these two parameters often precede changes in actual frequency of wetting as treatment progresses. Measures of the child's bladder capacity also should be obtained, since significant correlations have been obtained between functional bladder capacity and enuresis (Muellner, 1960; Starfield, 1967). Average bladder capacity is obtained by measuring the amount of urine passed each time the child voids for a seven-day period and determining the mean amount per void. Maximum bladder capacity is represented by the largest void obtained when assessing the average bladder capacity. (The reader is referred to Ciminero and Doleys, 1976 for a comprehensive discussion of assessment.)

Following a thorough assessment, a treatment program should be formulated based on information gathered in the assessment process. Several procedures currently are available for treatment of enuresis. The most frequently used method, the bell-and-pad, was first introduced in 1938 by Mowrer and Mowrer. In this method the child sleeps upon a sensing or detecting mechanism (urine alarm) that is activated when urination occurs. A buzzer or bell sounds, waking the sleeping child, who then turns off the alarm, goes to the toilet, and completes the act of micturition. The treatment effect that occurs with this method has been related to a classical conditioning paradigm in which the conditioned response (awakening) is elicited by the conditioned stimulus (full bladder) through repeated pairings with an unconditioned stimulus for waking (loud bell or buzzer).

In terms of treatment efects, dozens of studies indicate success rates of 70 to 90% with the bell-and-pad (Doleys, 1977; Yates, 1970). Nevertheless, several problems are associated with the method. Treatment duration ranges from 5 to 12 weeks, therefore requiring much persistence on the part of the parent and child (Young, 1965). Probably because of this lengthy treatment period, the dropout rate is around 30% (Turner, Young, & Rachman, 1970; Young, 1965; Young & Morgan, 1972). Of those who do stay in treatment, 32% eventually relapse (Doley, 1977); however, reinstatement of treatment usually eliminates the problem.

Because of the problems with the bell-and-pad, other treatment methods recently have received attention. Many children and adults neither awaken to urinate in the toilet during the night nor wet the bed but rather sleep throughout the night while withholding urination. Based on this fact, Kimmel and Kimmel (1970) developed and tested a procedure aimed at teaching the child to increase his bladder capacity. It was hypothesized that this would allow the child to retain urine with or without discriminable bladder distension and thus terminate bed-wetting. The method is basically one in which the child is required to increase his liquid intake and then is reinforced for retaining urine for successively longer periods of time. Retention intervals, which usually start at 5 minutes and gradually increase to a maximum of 30 minutes, are initiated when the child reports an urge to urinate.

Kimmel and Kimmel (1970) reported three case studies in which Retention Control Training (RCT) was used successfully. Two 4-year-old females were reported to be completely dry in seven days, and a 10-year-old psychotic female stopped bed-wetting in two weeks. Attempts to replicate the effectiveness of RCT in a more rigorous manner have produced equivocal results. Using ABAB designs, Miller (1973) evaluated the effects of RCT on two secondary enuretics. Results revealed that both childrens' bed-wetting episodes decreased to zero levels in the second treatment phase. Daily urination frequency also decreased, supporting the hypothesis that RCT increased the functional bladder capacity of these two children. Using a group design, Doleys, Ciminero, Tollison, Williams, and Wells (1977) compared RCT to an operant conditioning-based treatment program. No improvement was noted for the RCT group during six weeks of treatment. Also, no change was noted in functional bladder capacity for this group. In another group study, Paschalis, Kimmel, and Kimmel (1972) treated 35 Cypriot children with RCT. After 15 to 20 days of treatment, less than half of the 35 children were dry at night for seven consecutive days. Rocklin and Tilker (1973) found no differences between an RTC group, a noncontingent reinforcement group, and a control group. The equivocal results obtained in these studies suggest that further research is needed to conclusively demonstrate the effectiveness of RCT. At the present time, the procedure would appear to be useful as a primary or adjunctive procedure for cases in which a small bladder capacity is associated with bed-wetting.

The final major procedure that has been used in treating enuresis is Dry Bed Training (DBT), first introduced by Azrin, Sneed, and Foxx (1974). This method combines a variety of techniques, including *nightime awakening* of the child, *cleanliness training* contingent upon wetting in which the child cleans and changes his own wet pajamas and sheets, *positive practice* in which the child intensively practices the responses necessary for appropriate nighttime toileting behavior (rising from the bed, walking to the bathroom, etc.), and *positive reinforcement* for dry nights. Treatment involves one night of intensive practice in which a therapist stays in the home and conducts practice with the child hourly through the night. Thereafter, the parents monitor the program during a "posttraining supervision" period. (The method is quite detailed and the reader is referred to Azrin et al. (1974) for a complete outline.)

Using this program, Azrin et al. (1974) treated 24 enuretics who all achieved a dryness criterion of 14 consecutive dry nights within four weeks. Seven subjects required further training during the six-month follow-up period. Doleys et al. (1977) treated 13 enuretics with DBT and found substantial decreases in wetting episodes during the six-week treatment program. However, only 5 of the 13 subjects had 14 or more consecutive dry nights by the end of the treatment phase. Recently, in an attempt to reduce the training inconveniences involved in the original procedure, Azrin and Thieves (1978) modified the DBT program to provide intensive training in the afternoon and evening rather than all night long. A retention training component also was included. Twenty-eight children received this modified treatment program. Within two weeks these children reduced their wetting behavior from 90 to 15% of the nights for which data were collected. In this study a bell-and-pad "control" group was compared to the DBT. After two weeks, wetting behavior in the bell-and-pad group still occurred in 76% of the nights.

In summary, at least three methods are available for treatment of enuresis in children. Although a clear link between assessment and selection of the most appropriate treatment procedure does not exist at the present time, a few guidelines can be offered. First, the bell-and-pad method requires the least effort on the part of the parent and child and may be more convenient for that reason. However, the therapist should be aware and should caution the parent regarding the length of treatment required for this method as well as the danger of dropout and relapse. In cases of poor functional bladder capacity and/or frequent daytime urination, RCT should be employed as a primary or adjunctive treatment procedure. For children who are clearly deficient in the set of responses necessary for appropriate nighttime toileting behavior (e.g., rising from the bed and walking to the bathroom), DBT would appear to be the treatment of choice. Of course, some children who display a number of deficiencies (e.g., poor bladder capacity and poor toileting behavior) may profit most from a multicomponent approach consisting of practice in appropriate toileting behavior plus RCT (Azrin & Thieves, 1978; Doleys & Wells, 1975).

Encopresis

Encopresis has been defined as any voluntary or involuntary fecal soiling of clothing beyond the time when the child should have been successfully toilet trained (Siegel & Richards, 1978). "Discontinuous" encopretics are children who begin to soil after a period of fecal continence, while "continuous" encopretics are children who have never attained fecal continence.

In some cases of encopresis, organic pathology resulting in diarrhea is responsible for forceful expulsion of feces into the clothing. In most cases of functional (inorganic) encopresis, rather than fecal material being forcefully expelled, small quantities of feces escape at short intervals without ever producing a complete evacuation (cf. Neale, 1963). In some encopretic children the syndrome of dyschezia develops in which chronic fecal retention results in the rectum being constantly filled and distended; the anus also may become dilated without the patient being aware of it, resulting in overflow incontinence (Gaston, 1948; Neale, 1963). Wright and Walker (1978) reported that 80 of 102 cases of functional encopresis seen at a Children's Hospital had stool impaction accompanying their incontinence, while Fitzgerald (1975) indicated that 95% of encopretic patients are impacted.

At least two authors have delineated distinct subtypes of encopresis based on etiology. Ashkenazi (1975) distinguished between phobic and nonphobic encopretics. The first group consists mainly of young children who respond to the toilet with phobic behaviors such as crying, clinging to the mother, and refusal to approach the toilet. The history of these children often reveals at least one episode of constipation or diarrhea resulting in painful bowel movements or extremely coercive toilet-training procedures employed by the parents. The second group of children display no anxiety reactions but report being unaware when fecal elimination is about to occur. In addition to these subtypes, Ayllon, Simon, and Wildman (1975) have distinguished between children who are completely lacking in appropriate toileting skills and those who possess the requisite skills but display them infrequently. With respect to selection of the most appropriate treatment procedure, it would appear important to identify the particular subtype in the initial assessment. Phobic children should be treated with an *in vivo* desensitization procedure in which graduated approaches to the toilet are reinforced (Ashkenazi, 1975). If the child is lacking in toileting behaviors, these skills must be shaped (Azrin & Foxx, 1974). Finally, for children who possess the requisite skills, procedures aimed at increasing the frequency of bowel movements in the toilet in response to physiological cues for elimination should be used.

Most of the research on behavioral treatment of encopresis consists of single case reports in which various forms of contingent reinforcement were used for appropriate elimination in the toilet. The type of reinforcements used has included contingent delivery of money, toys, sweets, outings, and/or praise for attempts to eliminate in the toilet (Plachetta, 1976), successful toilet eliminations (Bach & Moylan, 1975; Gelber & Meyer, 1965; Neale, 1963; Plachetta, 1976), or days in which no soiling occurred (Ayllon et al., 1975). In many of these studies, the authors attempted to establish an association between cues of rectal fullness and elimination in the toilet by having the children sit on the toilet at regular intervals— usually afer each meal and at bedtime (Ashkenazi, 1975; Gelber & Meyer, 1965; Neale, 1963; Plachetta, 1976). Ashkenazi (1975) prompted the urge to eliminate by using glycerine suppositories after each meal. Others also have suggested that before instituting treatment an initial purge with suppositories, laxatives, or mineral oil may be necessary due to the disruption that has occurred in reflexive elimination and the pain associated with impaction (Neale, 1963). Other approaches to treatment of encopresis have included withdrawal of maternal attention to soiling episodes (Balson, 1973; Conger, 1970), time-out contingent upon soiling (Edelman, 1971), and Full Cleanliness Training—consisting of regular pant checks, 20 minutes each of clothes washing and a cool water bath contingent upon soiling, and positive reinforcement for appropriate toileting behavior (Doleys, McWhorter, Williams, & Gentry, 1977).

Recently, Wright and Walker (1978) described a systematic treatment program that can be applied in a step by step fashion to many cases of psychogenic encopresis. The program begins with a complete evacuation of the child's colon with an enema. Thereafter, a time is chosen when the child is required to defecate in the toilet on a regular, daily basis, usually after breakfast and before the child leaves for school. If the child does not defecate on his own, a suppository is used, followed by an enema if he is still unsuccessful. The child receives a reward for defecation in the toilet and another reward at the end of the day for not soiling. This program continues uninterrupted until 14 consecutive days of nonsoiling have occurred at which time it is gradually phased out. The program also involves parental record keeping and weekly phone calls to maintain the parent's motivation. Wright and Walker (1978) report that this program, which has been used with over 100 cases, is virtually 100% successful within four months if properly applied. While the program certainly appears promising, further empirical research collected in well-controlled studies is needed to substantiate the author's claim.

In summary, behavioral procedures appear to be quite useful in the treatment of psychogenic encopresis. Group studies have found these procedures to be 88 to 100% effective (Ashkenazi, 1975; Wright & Walker, 1978), with treatment ranging from about two to six months. Single case studies typically also have reported positive outcomes with behavioral treatment (e.g., Doleys et al., 1977). Systematic comparisons of various treatment procedures or component analyses of complex programs (Wright & Walker, 1978) have not been undertaken at this time.

OTHER SOMATIC DISORDERS

Although enuresis and encopresis have been the major somatic disorders for which systematic programs have been designed and evaluated, behavioral procedures also have been used for several other disorders. These include obesity and asthma among others.

Obesity

Obesity is characterized by calorie intake that exceeds energy expenditure. While extensive research has occurred on behavioral approaches to adult obesity (Leon, 1976), childhood obesity has been largely ignored until recently. In one of the first attempts to study this problem in children, Argona, Cassady, and Drabman (1975) trained the parents of two groups of 5 to 10-year-old obese girls to administer a response cost or a response cost plus reinforcement program to their children. Both groups of parents received information on nutrition, exercise, and stimulus control procedures, established weight loss goals for their children, and set up a deposit contract with the experimenter. After 12 weeks of treatment, there were no differences between the two groups on weight lost by the children; however, both groups lost more than a no-treatment control group. Wheeler and Hess (1976) designed individualized behavioral programs for obese 2 to 11-year-old children aimed at altering children's eating habits. Each program was based on information gathered in the assessment and included such procedures as eliminating high calorie foods from the home, providing low-calorie snacks, and increasing the child's activity level. This treatment group demonstrated a significant improvement and approximated age-appropriate weight while a no-treatment control group failed to change.

Kingsley and Shapiro (1977) treated three groups of 10 to 11-year-old obese children using procedures similar to those described by Stuart and Davis (1972) for treatment of adult obesity. In addition, parents implemented a token economy program to reinforce the child for following the procedures. Following treatment each group of children lost significantly more weight than a control group. No differences in weight lost existed between the three treatment groups that varied with respect to group membership (i.e., mothers only, children only, and mothers plus children). Finally, Epstein, Masek, and Marshall (1978) recently have developed a nutritionally based program to regulate food intake in obese children. Based on nutritional standards, foods available to six school children were placed in three categories—red, yellow, and green—according to whether the children should decrease, maintain, or increase intake of these foods. If they ate amounts of food appropriate to the nutritional criteria, the children were given red, yellow, or green stars that were exchangeable for toys. Results of this simple but innovative program indicated a decrease in caloric intake and positive changes in food selection in five of the six obese school children. A general discussion of obesity is provided in Chapter 9 of this book.

Asthma

Asthma is a disorder of breathing due to constriction of the bronchial passage and characterized by wheezing, coughing, gasping for air, and a feeling of suffocation (Siegel & Richards, 1978). Various behavioral approaches have been applied to the treatment of this disorder based on operant and classical conditioning paradigms. Neisworth and Moore (1972) had parents withdraw attention from their seven-year-old son's bedtime asthma attacks. Creer (1970) had hospital staff withdraw attention and privileges from two boys with a history of repeated admissions to the hospital for asthma attacks. In both studies, frequency and/or duration of asthma attacks were reduced.

Other studies have investigated the use of relaxation training alone (Alexander, 1972; Alexander, Miklich, & Hershkoff, 1972) and in conjunction with systematic desensitization (Moore, 1965). Both the single and combined procedures have been found to improve respiratory functioning and to decrease the reported number of wheezing episodes in asthmatic children. Finally, biofeedback procedures also have been found to be useful in treatment of asthma. Davis, Saunders, Creer, and Chai (1973) found greater improvement in respiratory airflow for children treated with biofeedback-induced relaxation than in children treated with relaxation alone. In a slightly different approach, Kahn, Staerk, and Bonk (1973) used biofeedback procedures to train asthmatic children to dilate their bronchial passages. Children in the experimental group were significantly more improved than the control group children on measures of bronchial dilation, frequency of asthmatic attacks, use of medication, and emergency hospital visits.

In summary, innovative behavioral programs have been used in the treatment of childhood somatic disorders previously thought to be amenable only to medical interventions. While most research has occurred in the areas of enuresis and encopresis, treatment procedures recently have been extended to eating disorders and asthma. Behavioral procedures have been found to facilitate the treatment effect obtained with medical interventions alone and have frequently been effective in cases for which medical procedures have failed. The collaborative effort of medical and behavioral scientists would appear to be a promising approach in alleviating some distressing somatic disorders in children.

CONCLUSIONS

Behavioral intervention procedures have been utilized with a wide variety of childhood behavior problems that occur in the home setting. The majority of these problems fit into the conduct disorders category. As this is the most prevalent reason for referral of children to a clinic for psychological treatment, it is not surprising that the majority of the research has addressed behaviors that typically are classified under this category. Furthermore, the number of studies in this area is not unexpected as the category is a broad one that includes a number of problem behaviors. From the studies reviewed, it is clear that behavioral interventions are effective with conduct disorders. This appears to be the case even though the actual procedures utilized to affect behavior change have varied greatly.

The use of behavioral procedures with cross-gender behavior and psychosomatic disorders represents a major extension of our technology to behaviors typically viewed as being beyond the scope of psychological treatment. With the exception of enuresis, extensive systematic research efforts have not been undertaken with these disorders. However, the preliminary data suggest that the principles of behavior therapy can be effective with these childhood problems.

The apparent effectiveness of behavior modification should not lead us to believe that all childhood behavior problems in the home have been resolved. The data reported in journals represent a biased, positive view of the field, as negative results are rarely accepted for publication. Therefore, there are many instances in which our approaches that fail are not reported. In addition, generalization of treatment effects across time, settings, behaviors, and siblings has received minimum attention and, when the issue is addressed, the outcome data would appear to be far from optimal (e.g., Forehand & Atkeson, 1977). Furthermore, multiple outcome measures (i.e., behavioral measures collected by independent observers, parent-collected data, parent questionnaire reports, and physiological measures) are critical for the evaluation of treatment effects but rarely have been used when childhood home problems are addressed (e.g., Atkeson & Forehand, 1978). Finally, the effects of parental adjustment (e.g., depression and marital satisfaction) and family relationships with outside contacts (e.g., friends and helping agencies) on therapy outcome with children have only begun to be examined (e.g., Oltmanns et al., 1977; Wahler, 1978). Continued efforts by behavioral researchers are needed; such efforts should lead to happier and more productive family lives for our children and their parents.

ACKNOWLEDGMENT

Preparation of this chapter was supported in part by NIMH grant MH-22859-01.

REFERENCES

Adkins, D. A., & Johnson, S. M. What behaviors may be called deviant for children? A comparison of two approaches to behavior classification. Paper presented at the Western Psychological Association Convention, Portland, Oregon, April, 1972.

Alexander, A. B. Systematic relaxation and flow rates in asthmatic children: Relationship to emotional precipitants and anxiety. *Journal of Psychosomatic Research,* 1972, **16**, 405–410.

Alexander, A. B., Miklich, D. R., & Hershkoff, H. The immediate effects of systematic relaxation training on peak expiratory flow rates in asthmatic children. *Psychosomatic Medicine,* 1972, **34**, 388–394.

Alvord, J. R. The home token economy: A motivational system for the home. *Corrective Psychiatry and Journal of Social Therapy,* 1971, **17**, 6–13.

Argona, J., Cassady, J., & Drabman, R. S. Treating overweight children through parental training and contingency contracting. *Journal of Applied Behavior Analysis,* 1975, **8**, 269–278.

Arnold, J. E., Levine, A. G., & Patterson, G. R. Changes in sibling behavior following family intervention. *Journal of Consulting and Clinical Psychology,* 1975, **43**, 683–688.

Ashkenazi, Z. The treatment of encopresis using a discriminative stimulus and positive reinforcement. *Journal of Behavior Therapy and Experimental Psychiatry,* 1975, **6**, 155–157.

Atkeson, B. M., & Forehand, R. Parent behavioral training for problem children: An examination of studies using multiple outcome measures. *Journal of Abnormal Child Psychology,* 1978, **6**, 449–460.

Ayllon, T., & Azrin, N. H. *The token economy: A motivational system for therapy and rehabilitation.* New York: Appleton-Century-Crofts, 1968.

Ayllon, T., Simon, S. J., & Wildman, R. W. Instructions and reinforcement in the elimination of encopresis: A case study. *Journal of Behavior Therapy and Experimental Psychiatry,* 1975, **6**, 235–238.

Azrin, N. H., & Foxx, R. M. *Toilet training in less than a day.* New York: Simon & Schuster, 1974.

Azrin, N. H., Sneed, T. J., & Foxx, R. M. Dry bed: Rapid elimination of childhood enuresis. *Behaviour Research and Therapy,* 1974, **12**, 147–156.

Azrin, N. H., & Thieves, P. M. Rapid elimination of enuresis by intensive learning without a conditioning apparatus. *Behavior Therapy,* 1978, **9**, 342–354.

Bach, R., & Moylan, J. J. Parents administer behavior therapy for inappropriate urnination and encopresis: A case study. *Journal of Behavior Therapy and Experimental Psychiatry,* 1975, **6**, 239–241.

Balson, P. M. Case study: Encopresis: A case with symptom substitution? *Behavior Therapy,* 1973, **4**, 134–136.

Bandura, A. *Principles of behavior modification.* New York: Holt, Rinehart & Winston, 1969.

Bandura, A., & Walters, R. H. *Social learning and personality development.* New York: Holt, Rinehart & Winston, 1963.

Berkowitz, B. P., & Graziano, A. M. Training parents as behavior therapists: A review. *Behaviour Research and Therapy,* 1972, **10**, 297–317.

Bernal, M. E. Behavioral feedback in the modification of brat behaviors. *Journal of Nervous and Mental Diseases,* 1969, **148**, 375–385.

Bernal, M. E., Duryee, J. S., Pruett, H. L., & Burns, B. J. Behavior modification and the brat syndrome. *Journal of Consulting and Clinical Psychology,* 1968, **32**, 447–455.

Blechman, E. A., Olson, D. H. L., & Hellman, I. D. Stimulus control over family problem-solving behavior: The family contract game. *Behavior Therapy,* 1976, **7**, 686–692.

Blechman, E. A., Olson, D. H. L., Schornagel, C. Y., Halsdorf, M., & Turner, A. J. The family contract game: Technique and case study. *Journal of Consulting and Clinical Psychology,* 1976, **44**, 449–455.

Budd, K. S., Green, D. R., & Baer, D. M. An analysis of multiple misplaced parental social contingencies. *Journal of Applied Behavior Analysis,* 1976, **9**, 459–470.

Campbell, M. F. Neuromuscular uropathy. In M. F. Campbell & J. H. Harrison (Eds.), *Urology,* Vol. 2. Philadelphia: Saunders, 1970.

Christophersen, E. R., Arnold, C. M., Hill, D. W., & Quilitch, H. R. The home point system: Token reinforcement procedures for application by parents of children with behavior problems. *Journal of Applied Behavior Analysis,* 1972, **5**, 485–497.

Christophersen, E. R., Barnard, J. D., Ford, D., & Wolf, M. M. The family training program: Improving parent-child interaction patterns. In E. J. Mash, L. C. Handy, & L. A. Hamerlynck (Eds.), *Behavior modification approaches to parenting.* New York: Brunner/Mazel, 1976.

Ciminero, A. R., & Doleys, D. M. Childhood enuresis: Considerations in assessment. *Journal of Pediatric Psychology,* 1976, **4**, 17–20.

Conger, J. C. The treatment of encopresis by the management of social consequences. *Behavior Therapy,* 1970, **1**, 386–390.

Conners, C. K. Symptom patterns in hyperkinetic, neurotic, and normal children. *Child Development,* 1970, **41**, 667–682.

Creer, T. L. The use of time-out from positive reinforcement procedure with asthmatic children. *Journal of Psychosomatic Research,* 1970, **14**, 117–120.

Davis, M. H., Saunders, D., Creer, T., & Chai, H. Relaxation training facilitated by biofeedback apparatus as a supplemental treatment in bronchial asthma. *Journal of Psychosomatic Research,* 1973, **17**, 121–128.

Davison, G. C., & Neale, J. M. *Abnormal psychology: An experimental clinical approach.* New York: Wiley, 1974.

Delfini, L. F., Bernal, M. E., & Rosen, P. M. Comparison of deviant and normal boys in home settings. In E. J. Mash, L. A. Hamerlynck, & L. C. Handy (Eds.), *Behavior modification and families.* New York: Brunner/Mazel, 1976.

Doke, L. Assessment of children's behavioral deficits. In M. Hersen & A. S. Bellack (Eds.), *Behavioral assessment: A practical handbook*. Oxford: Pergamon, 1976.

Doleys, D. M. Behavioral treatments for nocturnal enuresis in children: A review of the recent literature. *Psychological Bulletin*, 1977, **84**, 30–54.

Doleys, D. M., Ciminero, A. R., Tollison, J. W., Williams, C. L., & Wells, K. C. Dry-bed training and retention control training: A comparison. *Behavior Therapy*, 1977, **8**, 541–548.

Doleys, D. M., McWhorter, A. Q., Williams, S. C., & Gentry, W. R. Encopresis: Its treatment and relation to nocturnal enuresis. *Behavior Therapy*, 1977, **8**, 77–82.

Doleys, D. M., & Wells, K. C. Changes in functional bladder capacity and bed-wetting during and after retention control training. *Behavior Therapy*, 1975, **6**, 685–688.

D'Zurilla, T. J., & Goldfried, M. R. Problem solving and behavior modification. *Journal of Abnormal Psychology*, 1971, **78**, 107–126.

Edelman, R. I. Operant conditioning treatment of encopresis. *Journal of Behavior Therapy and Experimental Psychiatry*, 1971, **2**, 71–73.

Epstein, L. H., Masek, B. J., & Marshall, W. R. A nutritionally based school program for control of eating in obese children. *Behavior Therapy*, 1978, **9**, 766–778.

Evans, R. B. Physical and biochemical characteristics of homosexual man. *Journal of Consulting and Clinical Psychology*, 1972, **39**, 140–147.

Evans, I. M., & Nelson, R. O. Assessment of child behavior problems. In A. R. Ciminero, K. S. Calhoun, & H. E. Adams (Eds.), *Handbook of behavioral assessment*. New York: Wiley, 1977.

Eyberg, S. M., & Johnson, S. M. Multiple assessment of behavior modification with families: Effects of contingency contracting and order of treated problems. *Journal of Consulting and Clinical Psychology*, 1974, **42**, 594–606.

Ferber, H., Keeley, S. M., & Shemberg, K. M. Training parents in behavior modification: Outcome of and problems encountered in a program after Patterson's work. *Behavior Therapy*, 1974, **5**, 415–419.

Fitzgerald, J. F. Encopresis, soiling, constipation: What's to be done? *Pediatrics*, 1975, **56**, 348–349.

Forehand, R., & Atkeson, B. M. Generality of treatment effects with parents as therapists: A review of assessment and implementation procedures. *Behavior Therapy*, 1977, **8**, 575–593.

Forehand, R., Cheney, T., & Yoder, P. Parent behavior training: Effects on the noncompliance of a deaf child. *Journal of Behavior Therapy and Experimental Psychiatry*, 1974, **5**, 281–283.

Forehand, R., & King, H. E. Preschool children's noncompliance: Effects of short-term therapy. *Journal of Community Psychology*, 1974, **2**, 42–44.

Forehand, R., & King, H. E. Noncompliant children: Effects of parent training on behavior and attitude change. *Behavior Modification*, 1977, **1**, 93–108.

Forehand, R., King, H. E., Peed, S., & Yoder, P. Mother-child interactions: Comparison of a noncompliant clinic group and a nonclinic group. *Behaviour Research and Therapy*, 1975, **13**, 79–84.

Forehand, R., & Peed, S. Training parents to modify noncompliant behavior of their children. In A. J. Finch, Jr. & P. C. Kendall (Eds.), *Treatment and research in child psychopathology*. New York: Spectrum, 1979.

Forehand, R., Sturgis, E. T., McMahon, R., Aguar, D., Green, K., Wells, K. C., & Breiner, J. Parent behavioral training to modify child noncompliance: Treatment generalization across time and from home to school. *Behavior Modification,* 1979, **3**, 3–25.

Gaston, E. A. The physiology of fecal continence. *Surgery, Gynecology and Obstetrics,* 1948, **87**, 280–290 and 669–678.

Gelber, H., & Meyer, V. Behaviour therapy and encopresis: The complexities involved in treatment. *Behaviour Research and Therapy,* 1965, **2**, 227–231.

Green, K. D., Forehand, R., & McMahon, R. J. Parental manipulation of compliance and noncompliance in normal and deviant children. *Behavior Modification,* 1979, **3**, 245–266.

Hanf, C., & Kling, F. Facilitating parent-child interaction: A two stage training model. Unpublished manuscript, University of Oregon Medical School, 1973.

Hawkins, R. P., Peterson, R. F., Schweid, E., & Bijou, S. W. Behavior therapy in the home: Amelioration of problem parent-child relations with the parent in a therapeutic role. *Journal of Experimental Child Psychology,* 1966, **4**, 99–107.

Herbert, E. W., Pinkston, E. M., Hayden, M. L., Sajwaj, T. E., Pinkston, S., Cordua, G., & Jackson, C. Adverse effects of differential parental attention. *Journal of Applied Behavior Analysis,* 1973, **6**, 15–30.

Hersen, M., & Barlow, D. H. *Single-case experimental designs: Strategies for studying behavior change.* Oxford: Pergamon, 1976.

Hoenig, J., Kenner, J., & Youd, A. Social and economic aspects of transsexualism. *British Journal of Psychiatry,* 1970, **117**, 163–172.

Holland, C. J. Elimination by the parents of fire-setting behavior in a seven-year-old boy. *Behaviour Research and Therapy,* 1969, **7**, 135–137.

Humphreys, L., Forehand, R., McMahon, R., & Roberts, M. Parent behavioral training to modify child noncompliance: Effects on untreated siblings. *Journal of Behavior Therapy and Experimental Psychiatry,* 1978, **9**, 235–238.

Jenkins, R. Psychiatric syndromes in children and their relation to family background. *American Journal of Orthopsychiatry,* 1966, **36**, 450–457.

Johnson, S. M., & Brown, R. A. Producing behavior change in parents of disturbed children. *Journal of Child Psychology and Psychiatry,* 1969, **10**, 107–121.

Johnson, S. M., & Lobitz, G. K. The personal and marital adjustment of parents as related to observed child deviance and parenting behaviors. *Journal of Abnormal Child Psychology,* 1974, **2**, 193–207.

Kahn, A. V., Staerk, M., & Bonk, C. Role of counterconditioning in the treatment of asthma. *Journal of Psychosomatic Research,* 1973, **17**, 389–392.

Kifer, R. E., Lewis, M. A., Green, D. R., & Phillips, E. L. Training predelinquent youths and their parents to negotiate conflict situations. *Journal of Applied Behavior Analysis,* 1974, **7**, 357–364.

Kimmel, H. D., & Kimmel, E. An instrumental conditioning method for the treatment of enuresis. *Journal of Behavior Therapy and Experimental Psychiatry,* 1970, **1**, 121–123.

Kingsley, R. G., & Shapiro, J. A. A comparison of three behavioral programs for the control of obesity in children. *Behavior Therapy,* 1977, **8**, 30–36.

Leon, G. R. Current directions in the treatment of obesity. *Psychological Bulletin,* 1976, **83**, 557–578.

Levitt, E. E. The results of psychotherapy with children: An evaluation. *Journal of Consulting Psychology,* 1957, **21**, 189–196.

Levitt, E. E. Psychotherapy with children: A further evaluation. *Behaviour Research and Therapy,* 1963, **1**, 45–51.

Lobitz, G. K., & Johnson, S. M. Normal versus deviant children: A multimethod comparison. *Journal of Abnormal Child Psychology,* 1975, **3**, 353–374.

Mann, R. A. Assessment of behavioral excesses in children. In M. Hersen & A. S. Bellack (Eds.), *Behavioral assessment: A practical handbook.* Oxford: Pergamon, 1976.

Martin, B. Brief family intervention: Effectiveness and the importance of including father. Unpublished manuscript, University of North Carolina, 1975.

Martin, B., & Twentyman, C. Teaching conflict resolution skills to parents and children. In E. J. Mash, L. C. Handy, & L. A. Hamerlynck (Eds.), *Behavior modification approaches to parenting.* New York: Brunner/Mazel, 1976.

Michel, W. *Personality and assessment.* New York: Wiley, 1968.

Miller, N. E. Learning of visceral and glandular responses. *Science,* 1969, **163**, 434–445.

Miller, P. M. An experimental analysis of retention control training in the treatment of nocturnal enuresis in two institutionalized adolescents. *Behavior Therapy,* 1973, **4**, 288–294.

Money, J., Hampson, J. G., & Hampson, J. L. An examination of some basic sexual concepts: Evidence of human hermaphroditism. *Bulletin of the Johns Hopkins Hospital,* 1955, **97**, 301–319.

Money, J., & Primrose, C. Sexual dimorphism and dissociation in the psychology of male transsexuals. *Journal of Nervous and Mental Disease,* 1968, **147**, 472–486.

Moore, D. R. Determinants of deviancy: A behavioral comparison of normal and deviant children in multiple settings. Unpublished manuscript, University of Tennessee, 1975.

Moore, N. Behavior therapy in bronchial asthma: A controlled study. *Journal of Psychosomatic Research,* 1965, **9**, 257–276.

Morris, H. H. Aggressive behavior disorders in children: A follow-up study. *American Journal of Psychiatry,* 1956, **112**, 991–997.

Mowrer, O. H., & Mowrer, W. M. Enuresis: A method for its study and treatment. *American Journal of Orthopsychiatry,* 1938, **8**, 436–459.

Muellner, R. S. Development of urinary control in children. *Journal of the American Medical Association,* 1960, **172**, 1256–1261.

Neale, D. H. Behavior therapy and encopresis in children. *Behaviour Research and Therapy,* 1963, **1**, 139–149.

Neisworth, J. R., & Moore, F. Operant treatment of asthmatic responding with the parent as therapist. *Behavior Therapy,* 1972, **3**, 95–99.

Nordyke, N. S., Baer, D. M., Etzel, B. C., & Leblanc, J. M. Implications of the stereotyping and modification of sex role. *Journal of Applied Behavior Analysis,* 1977, **10**, 553–557.

Oltmanns, T. F., Broderick, J. E., & O'Leary, K. D. Marital adjustment and the efficacy of behavior therapy with children. *Journal of Consulting and Clinical Psychology,* 1977, **45**, 724–729.

O'Leary, K. D., O'Leary, S., & Becker, W. C. Modification of a deviant sibling interaction in the home. *Behaviour Research and Therapy,* 1967, **5**, 113–120.

Oppel, W., Harper, P., & Rowland, V. The age of attaining bladder control. *Journal of Pediatrics,* 1968, **42**, 614–626.

Paschalis, A., Kimmel, H. D., & Kimmel, E. Further study of diurnal instrumental conditioning in the treatment of enuresis nocturna. *Journal of Behavior Therapy and Experimental Psychiatry,* 1972, **3**, 253–256.

Patterson, G. R. An empirical approach to the classification of disturbed children. *Journal of Clinical Psychology,* 1964, **20**, 326–337.

Patterson, G. R. *Families: Applications of social learning to family life.* Champaign, Ill.: Research Press, 1971.

Patterson, G. R. Interventions for boys with conduct problems: Multiple settings, treatments, and criteria. *Journal of Consulting and Clinical Psychology,* 1974, **42**, 471–481.

Patterson, G. R. A three-stage functional analysis for children's coercive behavior: A tactic for developing a performance theory. In B. C. Etzel, J. M. LeBlanc, & D. M. Baer (Eds.), *New developments in behavioral research: Theory, methods and applications.* Hillsdale, N.J.: Lawrence Erlbaum, 1975.

Patterson, G. R. The aggressive child: Victim and architect of a coercive system. In E. J. Mash, L. A. Hamerlynck, & L. C. Handy (Eds.), *Behavior modification and families.* New York: Brunner/Mazel, 1976.

Patterson, G. R., & Brodsky, G. A. Behavior modification programme for a child with multiple problem behaviors. *Journal of Child Psychology and Psychiatry,* 1967, **7**, 277–295.

Patterson, G. R., Cobb, J. A., & Ray, R. S. A social engineering technology for retraining aggressive boys. In H. E. Adams & P. Unikel (Eds.), *Issues and trends in behavior therapy.* Springfield, Ill.: Charles C. Thomas, 1973.

Patterson, G. R., & Gullion, M. E. *Living with children.* Champaign, Ill.: Research Press, 1968.

Patterson, G. R., & Reid, J. B. Reciprocity and coercion: Two facets of social systems. In C. Neuringer & J. Michaels (Eds.), *Behavior modification in clinical psychology.* New York: Appleton-Century-Crofts, 1970.

Patterson, G. R., & Reid, J. B. Intervention for families of aggressive boys: A replication study. *Behaviour Research and Therapy,* 1973, **11**, 383–394.

Patterson, G. R., Reid, J. B., Jones, R. R., & Conger, R. E. *A social learning approach to family intervention: Families with aggressive children.* Eugene, Oregon: Castalia Press, 1975.

Pauly, I. Male psychosexual inversion: Transsexualism: A review of 100 cases. *Archives of General Psychiatry,* 1965, **13**, 172–181.

Pauly, I. Adult manifestations of male transsexualism. In R. Green, & J. Money (Eds.), *Transsexualism and sex reassignment.* Baltimore: The Johns Hopkins Press, 1969.

Peed, S., Roberts, M., & Forehand, R. Evaluation of the effectiveness of a standardized parent training program in altering the interaction of mothers and their noncompliant children. *Behavior Modification,* 1977, **1**, 323–350.

Plachetta, K. E. Encopresis: A case study utilizing contracting, scheduling, and self-charting. *Journal of Behavior Therapy and Experimental Psychiatry,* 1976, **7**, 195–196.

Quay, H. C., Morse, W. C., & Cutler, R. T. Personality patterns of pupils in special classes for the emotionally disturbed. *Exceptional Children,* 1966, **35**, 297–301.

Rekers, G. A. Stimulus control over sex-typed play in cross-gender identified boys. *Journal of Experimental Child Psychology,* 1975, **20**, 136–148.

Rekers, G. A. Atypical gender development and psychosocial adjustment. *Journal of Applied Behavior Analysis,* 1977, **10**, 559–571.

Rekers, G. A., Bentler, P. M., Rosen, A. C., & Lovaas, O. I. Child gender disturbances: A clinical rationale for intervention. *Psychotherapy: Theory, Research and Practice,* 1977, **14**, 2–11.

Rekers, G. A., & Lovaas, O. I. Behavioral treatment of deviant sex-role behaviors in a male child. *Journal of Applied Behavior Analysis,* 1974, **7**, 173–190.

Rekers, G. A., Lovaas, O. I., & Low, B. The behavioral treatment of a "transsexual" preadolescent boy. *Journal of Abnormal Child Psychology,* 1974, **2**, 99–116.

Rekers, G. A., & Varni, J. W. Self-monitoring and self-reinforcement processes in a pre-transsexual boy. *Behaviour Research and Therapy,* 1977, **15**, 177–180.

Rekers, G. A., Willis, T. J., Yates, C. E., Rosen, A. C., & Low, B. P. Assessment of childhood gender behavior change. *Journal of Child Psychology and Psychiatry,* 1977, **18**, 53–65.

Rekers, G. A., & Yates, C. E. Sex-typed play in feminoid boys versus normal boys and girls. *Journal of Abnormal Child Psychology,* 1976, **4**, 1–8.

Rekers, G. A., Yates, C. E., Willis, T. J., Rosen, A. C., & Taubman, M. Childhood gender identity change: Operant control over sex-typed play and mannerisms. *Journal of Behavior Therapy and Experimental Psychiatry,* 1976, **7**, 51–57.

Rimm, D. C., & Masters, J. C. *Behavior therapy: Techniques and empirical findings.* New York: Academic, 1974.

Roach, J. L. Some social-psychological characteristics of child guidance clinic caseloads. *Journal of Consulting Psychology,* 1958, **22**, 183–186.

Roberts, M. W., McMahon, R. J., Forehand, R., & Humphreys, L. The effect of parental instruction-giving on child compliance. *Behavior Therapy,* 1978, **9**, 793–798.

Robin, A. L., Kent, R., O'Leary, K. D., Foster, S., & Prinz, R. An approach to teaching parents and adolescents problem-solving communication skills: A preliminary report. *Behavior Therapy,* 1977, **8**, 639–643.

Robins, L. N. *Deviant children grown up: A sociological and psychiatric study of sociopathic personality.* Baltimore: Williams & Wilkins, 1966.

Rocklin, N., & Tilker, H. Instrumental conditioning of nocturnal enuresis. *Proceedings of the 81st Annual Convention of the American Psychological Association,* 1973, 915–916.

Roosa, J. B. SOCS: situations, options, consequences, and simulation: A technique for teaching social interaction. Paper presented at American Psychological Association, Montreal, 1973.

Rosen, A. C., Rekers, G. A., & Bentler, P. M. Ethical issues in the treatment of children. *Journal of Social Issues,* 1978, **34**, 122–136.

Rosen, A. C., Rekers, G. A., & Friar, L. R. Theoretical and diagnostic issues in child gender disturbances. *The Journal of Sex Research,* 1977, **13**, 89–103.

Rosen, A. C., & Teague, J. Case studies in development of masculinity and femininity in male children. *Psychological Reports,* 1974, **34**, 971–983.

Russo, S. Adaptations in behavioral therapy with children. *Behaviour Research and Therapy,* 1964, **2**, 43–47.

Schnelle, J. F. A brief report on the invalidity of parent evaluations of behavior change. *Journal of Applied Behavior Analysis,* 1974, **7**, 341–343.

Siegel, L. J., & Richards, C. S. Behavioral intervention with somatic disorders in children. In D. Marholin (Ed.), *Child behavior therapy.* New York: Gardner Press, 1978.

Sines, J. O., Pauker, J. D., Sines, L. K., & Owen, K. D. R. Identification of clinically relevant dimensions of children's behavior. *Journal of Consulting and Clinical Psychology,* 1969, **33**, 728–734.

Starfield, B. Functional bladder capacity in enuretic and nonenuretic children. *Journal of Pediatrics,* 1967, **70**, 777–781.

Stuart, R. B. Behavioral contracting within the families of delinquents. *Journal of Behavior Therapy and Experimental Psychiatry,* 1971, **2**, 1–11.

Stuart, R. B., & Davis, B. *Slim chance in a fat world: Behavioral control of obesity.* Champaign, Ill.: Research Press, 1972.

Stuart, R. B., & Tripodi, T. Experimental evaluation of three time-constrained behavioral treatments for predelinquents and delinquents. In R. D. Rubin, J. P. Brady, & J. D. Henderson (Eds.), *Advances in behavior therapy.* New York: Academic Press, 1973.

Stuart, B., Tripodi, T., Jayaratne, S., and Camburn, D. An experiment in social engineering in serving the families of pre-delinquents. *Journal of Abnormal Child Psychology,* 1976, **4**, 243–261.

Turner, R. K., Young, G. C., & Rachman, S. Treatment of nocturnal enuresis by conditioning techniques. *Behaviour Research and Therapy,* 1970, **8**, 367–381.

Wahler, R. G. Oppositional children: A quest for parental reinforcement control. *Journal of Applied Behavior Analysis,* 1969, **2**, 159–170.

Wahler, R. G. Deviant child behavior within the family: Developmental speculations and behavior change strategies. In H. Leitenberg (Ed.), *Handbook of behavior modification and behavior therapy.* Englewood Cliffs, N.J.: Prentice-Hall, 1976.

Wahler, R. G. General processes in child behavior change. Invited address presented at the Midwestern Association of Behavior Analysis, Chicago, May, 1978.

Wahler, R. G., & Cormier, W. H. The ecological interview: A first step in out-patient child behavior therapy. *Journal of Behavior Therapy and Experimental Psychiatry,* 1970, **1**, 279–290.

Wahler, R. G., Winkel, G. H., Peterson, R. F., & Morrison, D. C. Mothers as behavior therapists for their own children. *Behaviour Research and Therapy,* 1965, **3**, 113–124.

Walinder, J. *Transsexualism: A study of forty-three cases.* Goteborg: Scandinavian University Books, 1967.

Walter, H., & Gilmore, S. D. Placebo versus social learning effects in parent training procedures designed to alter the behaviors of aggressive boys. *Behavior Therapy,* 1973, **4**, 361–377.

Weathers, L., & Liberman, R. P. Contingency contracting with families of delinquent adolescents. *Behavior Therapy,* 1975, **6**, 356–366.

Welch, G. J. Verbal communication training: A procedure to augment contingency contracting. *Journal of Behavior Therapy and Experimental Psychiatry,* 1976, **7**, 301–304.

Wells, K. C., Griest, D. L., & Forehand, R. The use of a self-control package to enhance temporal generality of a parent training program. *Behaviour Research and Therapy,* in press.

Wheeler, M. E., & Hess, K. W. Treatment of juvenile obesity by successive approximation control of eating. *Journal of Behavior Therapy and Experimental Psychiatry,* 1976, **7**, 235–241.

Williams, C. D. The elimination of tantrum behaviors by extinction procedures. *Journal of Abnormal and Social Psychology,* 1959, **59**, 269–270.

Wiltz, N. A., & Patterson, G. R. An evaluation of parent training procedures designed to alter inappropriate aggressive behavior of boys. *Behavior Therapy,* 1974, **5**, 215–221.

Winkler, R. C. What types of sex-role behavior should behavior modifiers promote? *Journal of Applied Behavior Analysis,* 1977, **10**, 549–552.

Wolff, S. Symptomatology and outcome of preschool children with behaviour disorders attending a child guidance clinic. *Journal of Child Psychology and Psychiatry,* 1961, **2**, 269–276.

Wright, L., & Walker, C. E. A simple behavioral treatment program for psychogenic encopresis. *Behaviour Research and Therapy,* 1978, **16**, 209–212.

Yates, A. J. *Behavior therapy.* New York: Wiley, 1970.

Young, G. C. Conditioning treatment of enuretics. *Developmental Medicine and Child Neurology,* 1965, **7**, 557–562.

Young, G. C., & Morgan, R. T. T. Overlearning in the conditioning treatment of enuresis: A long-term follow-up study. *Behaviour Research and Therapy,* 1972, **10**, 419–420.

Zeilberger, J., Sampen, S. E., & Sloane, H. N. Modification of a child's problem behaviors in the home with the mother as therapist. *Journal of Applied Behavior Analysis,* 1968, **1**, 47–53.

CHAPTER 20

Childhood Behavior Problems in the School

Russell T. Jones and Alan E. Kazdin

Childhood problems in the schools encompass a variety of behaviors varying in severity and clinical importance. Many problems such as mild disruptiveness in class are identified as problems because they are bothersome to the teacher or interfere with classroom functioning but usually are of minor importance clinically. Other problems such as social withdrawal might be overlooked and not identified as a problem at all by the teacher but may be clinically significant because of their relation to subsequent adjustment problems. Broadly defined, the full gamut of problems at school include primarily deportment, academic behaviors, and social interactions. In addition, avoidance reactions, in the form of school phobia, often cause major problems for children functioning at school.

Until recently, few techniques have been available for intervening in classroom settings. Of course, many techniques have been suggested but little research has attested to the efficacy of the procedures. Recent developments in behavior modification have generated several techniques that have been shown to alter behavior. The present chapter reviews behavioral techniques that are designed to treat a wide range of problems and discusses advances that have been achieved.

CLASSROOM INTERVENTION TECHNIQUES

A variety of techniques have been used effectively in the classroom to alter deportment and academic performance. The techniques vary in complexity and in the extent to which they alter the classroom environment and teacher behavior from what they ordinarily would be without intervention. Major techniques include the use of teacher attention, token reinforcement, response cost, time-out from reinforcement, and programmed instruction.

Teacher Attention

Smiles, nods, a pat on the back, a handshake, and verbal praise are all examples of positive teacher attention. If reinforcing appropriate responses is made contingent upon children's appropriate behavior, an increase in the frequency of the desired behavior should follow. Teacher attention must be applied systematically if desired outcome is to follow. For example, raising hands to talk during circle time may be immediately followed by handshakes and M & M's, while talking prior to raising hands is ignored. This technique is still widely used in classroom settings due to its ease of application as well as its effectiveness in modifying behavior in a variety of situations.

Modification of social behavior by means of teacher attention has been well documented by several investigators. Behaviors altered include: playmate choice (Bijou & Baer, 1967), cooperative behavior (Hart, Reynolds, Baer, Brawley, & Harris, 1968), talking out and turning around behavior (McAllister, Stachowiak, Baer, & Conderman, 1969), aggressive behavior (Brown & Elliot, 1965), and disruptive behavior (Ward & Baker, 1968). Although teachers refer children for exhibiting undesired behavior, they often fail to recognize that their own inappropriate responses to such behavior are a major factor in the development and maintenance of this behavior. Madsen, Madsen, Saudargas, Hammond, and Egar (1970) provide documentation for this assertion after surveying a large number of public school teachers in Florida. They found that 77% of the teachers' interactions with their students were negative and that a mere 23% of the interactions were positive. Responding to children by saying "shut up," "be quiet," "sit down," are all examples of commonly used inappropriate attention that foster inappropriate behavioral patterns.

In the late 1960s, Becker at the University of Illinois—spurred by the success of Bijou (1963) at the University of Washington Laboratory Preschool—devised procedures where elementary school teachers were taught to apply attention systematically to children's undesired behavior. In a series of studies, Becker and his colleagues systematically trained elementary school teachers to praise appropriate behavior contingently while ignoring inappropriate behavior. Through this process a number of classroom problem behaviors were modified (Becker, Madsen, Arnold, & Thomas, 1967; Madsen, Becker, & Thomas, 1968; Madsen, Becker, Thomas, Koser, & Plager, 1968; Thomas, Becker, & Armstrong, 1968).

For example, Becker et al. (1967) employed the selective use of teacher attention and praise to social and academic behavior. Deviant behavior emitted by children was defined as behavior incompatible with learning, including gross motor behavior, disruptive noise with objects, talking, and disrupting others. Following a five-week baseline, teachers were instructed to employ a set of rules when interacting with pupils. The rules included being explicit in expectancies for children during each period, ignoring inappropriate behavior that interfered with learning or teaching, and administering praise and attention to desired behavior. Following an unsuccessful procedure where teachers were provided prompts via hand signals, the above mentioned explicit instructions were given in conjunction with daily feedback. Teachers were also provided with training to facilitate their appropriate delivery of positive reinforcement.

After eight weeks of treatment, average rate of "deviant" behavior for 10 children in five classrooms declined from previous baseline levels. It can be concluded from this investigation that teachers can be taught to apply teacher attention effectively to alter inappropriate classroom behavior of children.

Likewise, teacher attention has been found to be effective in modifying academic as well as adaptive behavior. Successful applications of this technique have altered the following behaviors: spelling scores (Zimmerman & Zimmerman, 1962), digit reversal behavior (Kirby & Shields, 1972), task relevant behavior (Ward & Baker, 1968), attending behavior (Broden, Bruce, Mitchell, Carter, & Hall, 1970), attentiveness (Hawkins, McArthur, Rinaldi, Gray, & Schaftenaur, 1967), studying behavior (Hall, Lund, & Jackson, 1968), and adaptive skills (Jones 1980a; Jones & Kazdin, in press). Variations of this procedure where teacher and peer attention were manipulated have similarly proven to be effective in reducing problem behavior (Hall & Broden, 1967; Patterson, 1965).

In the management of classroom behavior, teachers should be cognizant of the fact that inappropriate behavior often is the only way to gain teacher attention. Teachers can obviate such negative patterns of behavior by providing the child with a variety of reinforcing activities contingent upon desired performance. In addition to teacher attention, consideration should be given to reinforcing activities such as field trips to airports, museums, YMCAs, and sporting events. These activities should be lavishly interspersed with daily educational activities to make children's learning experiences fun.

Token Reinforcement Programs

Although teacher attention is an effective procedure for modifying classroom behavior, token reinforcement techniques are somewhat more powerful (see Drabman, 1976; Kazdin & Bootzin, 1972; McLaughlin, 1975; O'Leary & Drabman, 1971 for reviews). The token economy is a program where desired behavior is reinforced with tokens (e.g., poker chips, points, stars) that at a later time can be exchanged for back-up reinforcers (e.g., candy, food, cereal, free time, or small toys).

The earliest published investigation employing token reinforcement in a classroom situation was carried out at the Rainier State School in Washington by Birnbrauer and Lawler (1964). Attentive behavior of severely retarded children was modified when tokens were made contingent upon entering the classroom quietly, hanging up coats, paying attention while sitting at desks, and working hard on tasks. Tokens were then exchanged for candy and trinkets. The large-scale use of this technique is, in part, due to its adaptability to diverse populations as well as its variations in application (Jones, in press).

The token economy has successfully enhanced academic achievement. Many programs have focused on deportment to enhance students' academic performance. It is reasoned that academic attainment will improve if students are taught to follow directions, work quietly, attend to teacher and relevant task, and not disrupt the class. Generally, students are given tokens redeemable for privileges or candy contingent upon such desired responses.

Following the initial classroom token program by Birnbrauer and Lawler (1964), later studies at Rainier School evaluated the effects of token reinforcement on academic performance and cooperation (Birnbrauer, Bijou, Wolf, & Kidder, 1965; Birnbrauer, Wolf, Kidder, & Tague, 1965). In the study by Birnbrauer et al. (1965), program effectiveness was shown by employing an ABA design where during the A phase token reinforcement was first made contingent upon the number

and accuracy of items completed on academic assignment and upon cooperative behavior; during the B phase the program was withdrawn; and during the second A
phase the program was reinstituted. The target population consisted of 15 retarded
students who were having difficulty in academic and cooperative behavior. Although the results of this investigation are confounded with social reinforcement
and time-out, both target behaviors were changed systematically in 10 of the 15
students.

A wide range of academic subjects, including reading, writing, arithmetic, vocabulary, and spelling have served as target behaviors in token programs (Ayllon &
Roberts, 1974; Chadwick & Day, 1971; Ferritor, Buckholdt, Hamblin, & Smith,
1972; Glynn, 1970; Hopkins, Schutte, & Garton, 1971; Knapczyk & Livingston,
1973; Lahey & Drabman, 1974; Lovitt & Curtiss, 1969; McLaughlin & Malaby,
1972; Miller & Schneider, 1970; Rickard, Melvin, Creel, & Creel, 1973; Salzberg,
Wheeler, Devar, & Hopkins, 1971; Surratt, Ulrich, & Hawkins, 1969; Wilson &
McReynolds, 1973).

An early study by Wolf, Giles, and Hall (1968) illustrates a remedial program
designed to aid slow readers. Sixth-grade students, at least two years below the
norm for grade level in reading ability, were given tokens contingent upon correct
completion of classroom assignments, completion of extra work, cooperation, grade
averages, and attendance. Tokens were redeemable for food, clothes, candy, field
trips, and other items. Although systematic evaluation of these behavioral contingencies was lacking, a one-year follow-up showed that these students performed
significantly higher on achievement test performance than did control students.

More complex academic behaviors have also been developed and enhanced
through the use of token programs. Complex behaviors that were increased include
several aspects of compositional writing (Brigham, Graubard, & Stans, 1972; Van
Houten, Morrison, Jarvis, & McDonald, 1974) and creativity in writing skills
(Maloney & Hopkins, 1973).

One other area where token reinforcement has been successfully applied is
standardized test performance. Notwithstanding a number of methodological confounds (e.g., attending remedial sessions and differential regression among treatment and control groups), significant increases on achievement test scores have
been noted when compared to untreated controls (Ayllon & Kelly, 1972; Bushell,
1974; Clark, Lachowicz, & Wolf, 1968; Edlund, 1972; Kaufman & O'Leary,
1972; Wolf et al., 1968). Token reinforcement has been found to raise performance
on several standardized tests, including the Metropolitan Readiness Test, the Stanford Achievement Test, the Wide Range Achievement Test, and the Wechsler Intelligence Scale for Children. Maintenance of increased academic performance has
been found in follow-up sessions, extending as far as one year following the program's withdrawal (Dalton, Rubino, & Hislop, 1973).

Although the major focus of the token economy program in regular classroom
settings has been on deportment, several investigations have been carried out to
modify social behaviors. The modifications of several types of social interaction
have been successfully demonstrated in the following areas: modifications of cooperative play (Hart et al., 1968) and increasing nonaggressive play (Horton, 1970).
A procedure where overt interracial social interaction of first grade children was
altered was presented by Hauserman, Walen, and Behling (1973). In an ABA de-

sign all children in a predominantly white classroom were given token and social reinforcement for interracial interaction. Target subjects were five first-grade black children who isolated themselves from white members of the class during social activities. Following a nine-day baseline, children were administered tokens redeemable for a snack and social reinforcement was contingent upon making new friends by "sitting and eating with a new friend" during 30-minute lunch periods. Although some generalization was found during a free-play period immediately following lunch, where children continued to interact even though no training had been carried out in this setting, the return to the baseline phase evidenced a decline in interracial interactions. This study does, however, speak to the potential use of token reinforcement for a highly relevant social problem. Additionally, a host of similar studies have subsequently been carried out, attesting to the worth of token reinforcement in decreasing the frequency of disruptive behavior and increasing attentiveness in classrooms (Broden, Hall, Dunlap, & Clark, 1970; Bucher & Hawkins, 1973; Bushell, Wrobel, & Michaelis, 1968; Drabman, Spitalnik, & Spitalnik, 1974; Herman & Tramontana, 1971; Jones & Kazdin, 1975; Kaufman & O'Leary, 1972; Medland & Stachnik, 1972; O'Leary, Becker, Evans, & Saudargas, 1969; Schmidt & Ulrich, 1969; Schwartz & Hawkins, 1970; Wagner & Guyer, 1971). Behaviors other than academic, social, and disruptive have been taught by employing token reinforcement, including instructional control (Baer, Rowbury, & Baer, 1973), response latency (Fjellstedt & Sulzer-Azaroff, 1973), and emergency telephone dialing (Jones, 1980a).

Although the efficacy of token reinforcement has been well demonstrated in the modification of children's classroom behavior, the classroom teacher needs to be aware of the complexities and idiosyncracies of his pupils. Not all children's behavior improves as a result of token reinforcement (Kupers, Becker, & O'Leary, 1968; Kazdin, 1977). Therefore, knowledge of procedures to facilitate desired responding, such as reinforcer sampling, response priming, and modeling of target behaviors, are of paramount importance.

Response Cost

While the abovementioned techniques are of a positive nature—desired behavior is reinforced—response cost is an aversive procedure. Typically, response cost consists of contingently withdrawing reinforcers following an undesirable response (see Kazdin, 1972 for a review). This procedure represents a form of punishment by withdrawal of positve events as does time-out. In response cost, however, there are no necessary time restrictions for available reinforcement as in time-out (Kazdin, 1972; Weiner, 1962).

Response cost may be particularly useful for at least three reasons. First, response cost programs have been used in their own right as a special variation of token programs. For example, Hall, Axelrod, Foundopoulos, Shellman, Campbell, and Cranston (1972) used a response cost procedure where tokens (in the form of slips of paper) were contingently withdrawn upon whining, complaining, and crying rather than administered contingent upon desired behavior. The response cost procedure suppressed the target behaviors. Second, inasmuch as tokens can be used to administer reinforcement or punishment (in the form of response cost), response cost can be implemented in token programs with relative ease. Third, the utility of response cost has been demonstrated in a number of therapeutic programs other than the token economy (Kazdin, 1977). These and numerous other reasons make response cost a particularly valuable procedure for the modification of problem behavior.

Although there have been relatively few studies where response cost has been used as the sole technique in decreasing undesired behavior (Burchard & Barrera, 1972; Weiner, 1962), successful outcomes have been frequently noted when response cost is combined with other behavioral techniques (i.e., token economy). Academic behaviors that have been altered successfully by procedures coupled with response cost include inappropriate verbalizations (McLaughlin & Malaby, 1972), rule violation and off task (Iwata & Bailey, 1974), out of seat (Wolf, Hanley, King, Lachowicz, & Giles, 1970), and rate and percentage of correct responses in reading and spelling tasks (Sulzer, Hunt, Ashby, Koniarski, & Krams, 1971). Similarly, positive findings have been evidenced in the modification of social classroom behavior. An illustration of a response cost procedure combined with a group contingency employed in a classroom setting is provided by Sulzbacher and Houser (1968). The disruptive behavior of 14 six- and seven-year-old educably mentally retarded children was changed. The target response was "naughty finger" behavior, defined as a raised fist with the middle finger extended. This response was especially annoying because it was followed by distractive verbalization. A contingency between the opportunity to engage in a "special 10-minute recess" and the nonoccurrence of the naughty finger or verbalizations resulting from it was established. Occurrence of the undesired behavior resulted in a loss of 1 minute of recess for all children. Flipping down a card by the teacher signified a loss of 1 minute of recess. Results showed an immediate deceleration of the undesired behaviors. These findings, along with those reviewed earlier, indicate the usefulness of response cost in modifying a number of significant problem classroom behaviors.

Time-Out From Reinforcement

Time-out from reinforcement, also commonly referred to as time-out, is defined as the removal of positive reinforcers for a specified period of time. Following the subject's placement into time-out, there is no access to positive reinforcers. Because of the latter requirement, this technique in its "pure form" is seldom achieved. That is, children often are able to gain access to reinforcers during the time-out interval. The situation where a child watches TV when sent to his room due to inappropriate behavior, illustrates this point. For example, setting aside a period of time when the child cannot earn reinforcers is a variation of time-out where the child remains in the social situation (Foxx & Shapiro, 1978).

An example of time-out procedure is provided by Zeilberger, Sampen, and Sloane (1968), where they utilized parents to escort a 4½-year-old child to a time-out room immediately following aggressive acts or disobedience. The child was to remain there for 2 minutes if neither a tantrum nor crying behavior was emitted during this time. Following the 2 minutes, the child was taken out of the time-out room and placed back into his regular activity. The child's inappropriate behavior was decreased following this program.

As in the area of response cost, time-out has most often been used in conjunction with other behavioral programs. Support for the claim that time-out can be an effective reductive procedure is derived from a host of studies reported in the literature. To modify social behavior, Sibley, Abbott, and Cooper (1969) successfully reduced social isolation, assaultive behavior, and resisting authority, while Wasik, Senn, Welch, and Cooper (1969) decreased resisting authority behavior as well as behavior aimed at criticizing others. Wolf, Risley, and Mees (1964) provide an excellent demonstration of the effects of time-out in reducing tantrum behavior of an autistic boy. Temper tantrums were followed by the boy being isolated from his peers and aides, by being placed in a room for a specified period of time. Tantrum behavior was observed to decrease to a near zero level. Academic behaviors including attending behaviors (Walker, Mattson, & Buckley, 1968) and behavior incompatible with academic achievement such as out of seat and aggressive behavior (Drabman, Spitalnik, & O'Leary, 1973), have also been successfully reduced.

Aside from the apparent effectiveness of both response cost and time-out, a word of caution is warranted. Many teachers, principals, parents, and social groups have objected to the use of these techniques, largely because of the negative overtone resulting from their gross misuse. For example, the convenience of response cost, where a token is removed quickly, quietly, and with little physical effort, contingent upon an undesired response, often leads to overusage. When classroom teachers view these procedures as the only mode of behavior intervention, a gross error is made. Punishment procedures including response cost and time-out should rarely be used unless they are accompanied with reinforcement procedures for alternative appropriate responding. It should be remembered that desired alternative behaviors need to be provided in order for children to gain reinforcement effectively. The overall goal of these programs should be to maximize the reinforcing and minimize the punishing aspects of the child's environment. Finally, teachers and clinicians should be familiar with variables influencing the effectiveness of punishment procedures (Azrin & Holtz, 1966) as well as important safeguards to obviate negative public reactions, as described by Sulzer-Azaroff and Mayer (1977).

Programmed Instruction

A procedure employed as early as 1920 and later researched by Skinner (1958), programmed instruction was designed to make learning a relatively fun and easy experience, as well as efficient. Programmed instruction is defined as a selection and arrangement of educational content based on principles of human learning. Programmed instruction provides the child with information, requires the child to respond to the information, and provides immediate feedback for performance. For example, Sulzer et al. (1971) trained a group of slow readers who were reinforced for producing correct answers in a programmed task designed by Sullivan (1965) to increase correct responses in reading and spelling. Subjects were provided with the opportunity to respond to information, followed by immediate feedback. The findings showed that better school performance resulted.

Widespread use of programmed instruction is largely a function of its diversity in application. That is, programmed instructions can be presented in several fashions, including teaching machines, booklets, manuals, computers, and talking typewriters. These various systems have served a helpful adjunctive role in the classroom in altering academic performance.

Programmed instruction has been employed across a number of populations, including normal children (Lumsdaine & Glaser, 1960; Stolurow, 1961; Becker, 1963), disadvantaged children (Williams, Gilmore, & Malpass, 1968), and educably mentally retarded children (Blackman & Capobianco, 1965; Malpass, Hardy, Gilmore, & Williams, 1964; Smith & Quackenbush, 1960). These programs have been found to be particularly effective in enhancing children's academic performances in settings where conventional classroom procedures fail to maximize results (see Greene, 1966; Malpass, 1968; Jamison, Suppes, & Wells, 1974 for reviews). Areas of performance increased include word acquisition, simple reading skills, and arithmetic (Atkinson, 1968; Birnbrauer, Kidder, & Tague, 1964; Blackman & Capobianco, 1965; Malpass et al., 1964).

In a study by Williams et al. (1968), the usefulness of programmed verbal materials for slow learners was assessed, comparing the effectiveness and feasibility of the teaching machine and programmed textbooks to conventional classroom learning methods. The subject population includes 48 "slow-learning" and "culturally deprived" 6- to 10-year-old second graders. These children were randomly divided into three groups of 16 and placed into teaching machine, programmed textbook, and conventional classroom groups. Instructions were provided via filmstrips. Following examination of a given item, the subject makes a response after which the correct answer is provided by simply pressing a lever. Pressing a button marked "advance" presents a new item. This mechanical optical device was found to be easily operated by all subjects.

The programed textbook group received instructions via workbook of linear programmed printed material. Multiple-choice questions were presented on 19 pages of the workbook. Answers to questions were provided on a file card. A subject's responses were represented by a circle or "X" indicating his choice. Following this response, the correct answer was obtained by simply sliding the card approximately one-half inch down the page. In both teaching procedures, subjects were given immediate feedback as well as the opportunity to compare their answer to the correct answer. The authors noted that the major difference between these two groups was the format of teaching and not the substance. In the third group (conventional classroom), subjects were provided with "the regular classroom routine" where programmed instructional materials were also used.

Results showed that after approximately one month, significant differences between both the teaching machine and programmed textbook groups and the classroom group on word gains were obtained. During a 30-day follow-up, over 90% of the words learned in the teaching machine and programmed textbook groups were retained. Although the classroom group showed significant gains in verbal performance, they were of much lower magnitude. These findings suggest that both programmed instruction methods facilitate learning of verbal material and motivation for "slow learning children." Notwithstanding these encouraging results, many of the promises made concerning programmed instructions are yet to materialize. When employing such techniques, teachers should remain aware of the fact that programmed instructions are not to be viewed as a substitute, but a valuable adjunct to those unique qualities and ideas that they bring to the classroom.

RECENT TRENDS AND ADVANCES IN CLASSROOM INTERVENTIONS

Classroom techniques mentioned to this point have evolved over the last 15 years. A number of program options have been investigated, particularly in recent years, to increase the overall efficacy or efficiency of the procedures outlined earlier and to provide alternatives for altering classroom behaviors. Recent research has investigated the utility of self-reinforcement techniques, group contingencies, peer reinforcement, and home-based contingencies. Moreover, attention has been given to teacher training techniques to ensure that child behaviors can be sustained long after any particular intervention has been withdrawn.

Self-Reinforcement Techniques

In most classroom programs, reinforcers such as praise or tokens are administered by the teacher or an aide. Considerable research has shown that children can administer consequences to themselves, a procedure often referred to as "self-reinforcement." Although definitions have varied considerably, self-reinforcement usually refers to determining for oneself the criteria for earning reinforcers and actually administering the reinforcers to oneself (cf. Glynn, 1970; Jones, Nelson, & Kazdin, 1977).

In the typical application of self-reinforcement in the classroom, tokens serve as reinforcers. The primary reason for using tokens is that they provide a discrete event that can be delivered and later exchanged for back-up events, as discussed earlier. Also, token earnings are easily observed by teachers, who can monitor the extent to which the students are rewarding their own behavior.

As a typical example of self-reinforcement in the classroom, Glynn and Thomas (1974) allowed elementary school students to administer points (check marks) to themselves for attentive behavior. Intermittent tape-recorded "beeps" sounded randomly in the classroom. The beep served as a signal for the child to decide whether he or she was attending and, hence, earned a point. To help the children decide exactly what the appropriate behavior was, the teacher displayed a chart at the front of the room that clarified whether children should be working on their assignment or paying attention to her. Points earned through self-administration were later exchanged for free time in class. Overall, self-administration of points markedly improved on-task behavior relative to baseline levels.

Several other studies have demonstrated that students can reward themselves and that behavior improves as a result (Bolstad & Johnson, 1972; Glynn, 1970; McLaughlin & Malaby, 1974). Comparisons of self-reinforcement with teacher administered reinforcement have tended to show that the programs are equally effective (Felixbrod & O'Leary, 1973, 1974; Glynn, Thomas, & Shee, 1973; Kaufmann & O'Leary, 1972). For example, Frederiksen and Frederiksen (1975) compared teacher and self-determined reinforcement in a junior high school class. During the self-determined phase, each student was approached periodically by the teacher, who asked whether he or she had earned a token for appropriate deportment. If the student replied affirmatively, a token was given. This procedure was as effective as the one in which the teacher made the decision as to whether behavior had been appropriate.

A few practical problems have emerged in the implementation of self-reinforcement programs. First, research has suggested that children may become increasingly lenient in the standards they invoke for deciding whether they have earned a reinforcer (e.g., Felixbrod & O'Leary, 1974; Frederiksen & Frederiksen, 1975; Santogrossi, O'Leary, Romanczyk, & Kaufman, 1973). If students really are free to administer consequences without constraints, one might expect a reduction in the response requirements they invoke for self-reward. In light of the demonstrations of increased leniency over time, relatively few classroom programs in fact allow students complete decision-making capacity in setting the criterion for performance, evaluating whether the criterion has been met, and actually administering consequences.

A second issue, related to the above, pertains to the role of the teacher in self-reinforcement programs. Programs referred to as self-reinforcement occasionally appear to have a strong teacher influence in determining behavior (Jones, 1980b; Jones & Evans, in press; Jones & Ollendick, in press; Jones et al., 1977). In most programs, teachers model how consequences are to be administered, and in a subsequent phase children are allowed to self-reward. Essentially, teacher administration has provided the criterion to which children are expected to adhere. In addition, direct teacher consequences are often invoked during the "self-reinforcement" phase so that approval, reprimands, and even token reinforcement may be given by the teacher according to whether students are administering reinforcers to themselves for appropriate behavior (Drabman, et al., 1973; Turkewitz, O'Leary, & Ironsmith, 1975). This research has suggested that teacher consequences may be needed to sustain adequate student adherence to the contingencies. Even so, self-reinforcement offers considerable advantage because it involves students directly in the contingencies. Self-reinforcement programs may even be a desirable transition to wean students off teacher-administered consequences, leading ultimately to the withdrawal of all of the contingencies that normally are not present in the classroom.

Group Contingencies

In most classroom behavior modification programs, students receive reinforcing consequences based entirely upon their own performance. However, programs have been designed to involve the group. Group contingencies are used in which the criterion for reinforcement depends upon the performance of the group as a whole. Several types of group contingencies have been identified, depending upon whether the criterion for reinforcement depends upon one or many individuals within the group or the entire group as a whole (see Greenwood, Hops, Delquadri, & Guild, 1974; Litow & Pumroy, 1975).

Typically, performance of the group as a whole serves as the basis for deciding whether reinforcing or punishing consequences are administered. Although the collective performance determines the consequences, any individual can influence the final outcome. As an illustration of the typical group contingency, Schmidt and Ulrich (1969) designed a reinforcement program to control excessive noise in a fourth-grade classroom. Students were told that when a timer sounded at the end of a 10-minute period, they would receive 2 extra minutes of gym plus a 2-minute break to talk if the class had not been noisy. The noise level was recorded automatically by a sound-level meter and monitored by an observer. If the noise level surpassed the criterion, the timer was reset. Any individual student, any subgroup, or the class as a whole could be responsible for resetting the timer. On the other hand, earning the reinforcer depended upon cooperative efforts among all of the students. When the group contingency was in effect, noise decreased substantially.

Occasionally, group contingencies are used in a slightly different fashion. A large group, such as a classroom, is divided into two subgroups. Each subgroup operates as a team and functions as the single group contingency, described above. The difference is that the teams compete. Consequences are not only given to the subgroups, but additional consequences can be earned if one subgroup surpasses the other or meets a particular criterion first.

For example, Maloney and Hopkins (1973) utilized a team contingency to improve the writing skills of elementary school students attending a remedial summer school program. Students in class were assigned to one of the teams. The contingency involved earning extra recess and candy for such writing behaviors as the use of different adjectives, action verbs, and novel sentence beginnings within a composition. The team that earned the higher number of points for these behaviors, based upon accumulated performance of individual members, earned early recess and extra candy. To ensure that high levels of performance were reinforced, both teams could win on a given day if performance on each team had met a prespecified high criterion. The team contingency improved the specific writing skills mentioned above. Other studies have shown that the team contingency enhances performance (Barrish, Saunders, & Wolf, 1969; Medland & Stachnik, 1972). Apparently, dividing a group into separate teams enhances performance over and above the use of the group as a single unit (Harris & Sherman, 1973).

Many advantages accrue when using group contingencies. First, group contingencies are useful when peer contingencies seem to compete with teacher contingencies. For example, students may provide socially reinforcing consequences to each other for disruptive behavior, talking without permission, and slowing in general. On the other hand, the teacher may reserve delivery of social consequences for working and ignore those behaviors fostered by the peer group. A group contingency often aligns the opposing contingencies. With a group contingency, peers tend to support those behaviors the teacher has identified as appropriate.

Another advantage of group contingencies is that they often are easier to administer than programs based upon individual contingencies for each student. The teacher can periodically evaluate performance of the class as a whole and deliver consequences to the group as a single unit (e.g., marking points on the board). The entire class can earn or not earn the consequences based upon daily or weekly point totals. A group program requires considerably less effort than the usual program because the separate earnings and expenditures need not be monitored. In addition, research has suggested that group contingencies are no less effective than are individually based programs. Indeed, some studies have suggested that group contingencies may be more effective than individual contingency programs (Brown, Reschly, & Sabers, 1974; Hamblin, Hathaway, & Wodarski, 1974; Long & Williams, 1973), but other studies have shown the programs to be equally effective (Axelrod, 1973; Grandy, Madsen, & DeMersseman, 1973). In passing, it is worth noting that team-based group contingencies, mentioned earlier, have been shown to enhance group contingencies (Harris & Sherman, 1973). Thus adding competition to the incentive system may be useful when the group can be divided into approximately equally skilled units.

Although group contingencies offer many advantages, they are not necessarily applicable to all classroom situations. In many programs, the goals may be highly individualized, and similar performance among members of the group would not be expected or desired. In such cases, individualized reinforcement contingencies are likely to be more appropriate. Possibly, aspects of the group contingency can be retained if special group consequences are provided when all students meet their individualized criteria. However, such a contingency loses some of the ease of application that characterizes group contingencies. In any case, selection of group contingencies for the classroom may depend upon the setting and the specific goals of the behavior change program.

Peer Reinforcement

One of the benefits of group contingencies is that they incorporate the child's peers in the program. Another way to involve peers in the program is to use *consequence sharing*. This is a special type of contingency in which reinforcing consequences earned by one or a few individuals are shared by a larger group. Consequence sharing involves peers in the program only in the sense that they receive reinforcers for someone else's performance. The advantage of this technique is that it often leads to peer support for the target behaviors.

As an example, Kazdin and Geesey (1977) used consequence sharing in a special education class to improve the attentive behavior of two educably retarded boys. During different portions of the program, the boys could earn reinforcers either for themselves or for the class as a whole. The behaviors that received reinforcing consequences, the criteria for earning consequences, and the consequences themselves did vary. Nevertheless, in separate simultaneous-treatment designs for the two children, performance was shown to be greater when the children earned for their peers than when they earned for themselves alone. Several other studies have demonstrated the effectiveness of consequence sharing (Kubany, Weiss, & Sloggett, 1971; Patterson, 1965; Wolf et al., 1970).

Occasionally, consequence sharing has been noted to evoke social consequences from the peers who earn reinforcers (Axelrod, 1973; Schmidt & Ulrich, 1969). Peers may provide prompts, reinforcing, and even aversive consequences (e.g., threats) to enhance performance of the target subject. The coercive tactics that peers may use might be a function of the specific contingencies and students for whom the program is designed. Coercive tactics might be especially likely if peers lose reinforcers, rather than merely gain extra ones, depending upon performance of the target subject.

Consequence sharing is not the only way in which peers are involved in classroom programs. Occasionally, peers are responsible for directly administering consequences and, hence, for changing classroom behavior. For example, in a sixth-grade elementary school classroom program reported by Solomon and Wahler (1973), peers reinforced appropriate classroom behavior such as working on assignments, talking appropriately, and staying at one's desk. After baseline observations of disruptive behavior, some of the students in class were trained, through discussion and practice in monitoring behavior, to implement reinforcement contingencies. These individuals were instructed to attend to appropriate behavior of the target subjects in the classroom. Problem behavior decreased when peers carried out the program and reverted to baseline levels when peers withdrew their contingent attention.

Peers have been used as behavior change agents in other ways. For example, Winett, Richards, and Krasner (1971) used a peer to deliver tokens in the classroom. The child who served this function varied daily and was given the maximum number of tokens on the day he or she was selected as monitor. Occasionally, students elect a peer who administers the contingencies (Drabman, 1973). In such cases, the peer administers reinforcers to each student and receives reinforcers on the basis of how well this task is performed. Other research has shown that reinforcing the performance of the peer who administers the consequences is an important ingredient to ensure that the peers administer reinforcers contingently (Greenwood, Sloane, & Baskin, 1974).

Involving peers in the administration of the classroom contingencies is important because it is likely to bring target behavior under the control of cues from the peer social environment as well as under the control of the teacher, who ordinarily administers the contingencies. Moreover, peers usually are very interested in serving as the agent who dispenses reinforcers and often will even purchase the privilege of dispensing reinforcers with tokens they have earned (Phillips, Phillips, Wolf, & Fixsen, 1973). From a practical standpoint, peers apparently represent an enthusiastic resource to help administer the program. Moreover, use of peers as reinforcing agents does not reduce the efficacy of the program relative to teacher-administered contingencies (Drabman, 1973). Indeed, peer-administered consequences,occasionally are superior to those administered by staff.

A potential disadvantage with consequence sharing, mentioned earlier, is the form that peer support may take to encourage the target subject to perform the desired behaviors. It is essential to devise the contingency so that peers have a great deal to gain from the performance of the target subject. If peers lose privileges or other reinforcers for performance of the target subject, this may generate undesirable and coercive interactions. In general, it may be useful to monitor peer interactions with the target subject to ensure that the contingency is fostering prosocial behavior.

Home-Based Contingencies

A significant advance in classroom programs has been to involve the children's parents directly in the program. The usual way in which this is accomplished is by implementing the classroom program in such a way that the child's behaviors at school earn reinforcers that are delivered to the child at home. For example, Schumaker, Hovell, and Sherman (1977) devised a daily report card system for problem junior high school students. The students took home a report card each day, in which the teacher simply noted (by a check mark) whether the child had followed the rules of the classroom, and the teacher gave points for completion of classwork. Parents were instructed to administer praise and privileges at home for improvements at school. A list of privileges and rules for exchanging teacher ratings for these events were devised. In a multiple baseline design across children, the home-based contingency was shown to accelerate adherence to classroom rules and to increase earnings for classroom work. Moreover, students in the home-based program tended to surpass comparison children in semester grades in junior high school. The effectiveness of home-based contingencies has been shown in other elementary classrooms as well (Todd, Scott, Bostow, & Alexander, 1976).

Home-based contingencies require that the teachers have a way of informing parents about classroom performance. The format for providing this information should be relatively simple to ensure that its meaning can be immediately and accurately conveyed. It is also important to ensure that parents actually administer consequences and do so contingently. Because aspects of the program are implemented in the classroom and the home, contact between teacher and parent is needed to ensure that efforts are coordinated in behalf of the child.

Home-based contingencies serve many useful purposes. To begin with, they maintain continuity of training of the child between the classroom and home. Programs begun in one setting are rarely supported and actively pursued in the other setting. Both teachers and parents lament the fact that their behavior change goals may not be continued when the child is away from them. Home-based contingencies help teachers and parents cooperate in developing a specific set of behaviors.

Another advantage is that parents often can provide a wider set of reinforcers for children than the teacher has available in the classroom. Daily privileges, weekend activities, money, and even special foods can be used at home but are either unavailable or very much restricted at school. In addition, the fact that parents need only consider one child gives them greater flexibility than a classroom teacher who must consider several different children simultaneously.

Finally, another advantage of home-based programs is that many parents may be better able to sustain the program than teachers. Teachers have many activities and obligations that compete with considering the individual need of a particular child. The extra work entailed by conducting a classroom-based contingency program is difficult to sustain. Parents often are greatly motivated to assist the teacher and may continue the program because of its importance for their individual child. Of course, many parents often have little involvement with the classroom or the teachers of their children, and home-based contingencies might not be effective at all. In such cases, programs that are conducted completely at school might be superior because that is the only way to ensure adherence to the contingencies.

Teacher Training

Training teachers to administer reinforcement contingencies is one of the major obstacles in effectively implementing a classroom program. Under most circumstances, the success of a classroom program depends upon the skills of the teacher in specifying target behaviors, monitoring these behaviors, shaping approximations of appropriate behavior, and providing consequences contingently.

A number of different techniques have been applied to train teachers to implement behavior change programs. Most programs have relied upon instructional methods such as lectures, discussions, workshops, and inservice training. Evidence suggests that teachers or other agents such as parents and hospital aides are not greatly influenced by instructional methods (Kazdin & Moyer, 1976). Although instructions convey information about the procedures, by themselves they tend not to teach the requisite skills to sustain an effective program in the classroom.

Many other methods of teacher training have been used. Verbal or written feedback has been given during or after class to convey how well teachers are attending to appropriate behavior. Such feedback has produced changes in teacher behavior in some programs, but has tended to have weak or inconsistent effects among different teachers (Breyer & Allen, 1975; Cooper, Thomson, & Baer, 1970; Cossairt, Hall, & Hopkins, 1973).

Modeling and role playing have been used by having a teacher see someone else administer the program or by having the teacher practice taking the role of the teacher or student in simulated situations to learn how reinforcement contingencies actually are implemented. For example, Ringer (1973) provided a model for the teacher in a fourth-grade classroom. The model was completely responsible for administering verbal and token reinforcement to maintain appropriate behavior. Gradually, the teacher assumed increasing responsibility for the program after seeing how it had been implemented by the model. Role playing was used by Jones and Eimers (1975), who trained elementary school teachers by demonstrating specific skills that teachers would need (e.g., use of praise, disapproval, instructions, and time-out), and by having teachers practice these skills. Participants in the sessions alternated playing the role of the teacher and a well-behaved or problem student. Training was associated with changes in inappropriate student behaviors in the teachers' original classrooms.

By far, reinforcement techniques for teachers have been the most effective manner of ensuring that the teachers perform the desired behaviors in the classroom. Both social and token reinforcement have been used to alter teacher behavior. Social reinforcement usually refers to the positive comments made to a teacher about his performance. For example, Cossairt et al. (1973) altered teacher behavior by praising teachers for using praise in the classroom. Not only did teacher use of praise increase, but student attending behavior improved as well.

An especially interesting use of social consequences to alter teacher behavior was reported by Graubard and his colleagues (Graubard, Rosenberg, & Miller, 1971; Gray, Graubard, & Rosenberg, 1974). These investigators trained students in a special education class to provide consequences for teachers depending upon the type of teacher behaviors that were performed. Students increased positive student-teacher contacts by smiling, making eye contact, sitting up straight, and making appropriate comments about how well they liked class when the teacher made positive contact with them. In an ABA design, teacher positive contacts with the students were shown to vary as a function of student comments.

Aside from social consequences, token reinforcement has been used to train teachers. For example, McNamara (1971) provided teachers with points for attending to appropriate child behavior. The points were later exchanged for cans of beer, a contingency that improved teacher behavior. Other forms of tokens have been used to alter staff behavior. For example, in institutions for psychiatric patients and the retarded, where staff training raises issues and objectives parallel to those raised in teacher training, green stamps and money have been quite effective in developing staff behavior (e.g., Bricker, Morgan, & Grabowski, 1972; Pomerleau, Bobrove, & Smith, 1973).

Over the years, evidence has emerged indicating how to best train teachers effectively. Programs that combine incentives, instructions, feedback, and models for teacher performance can accomplish the training tasks with considerable success. Regrettably, the feasibility of executing such programs on a large scale in most educational settings is slight. The incentives normally available to teachers rarely are administered for teacher behavior in relation to the student. When teacher behavior is noticed, often credit is given to skills in managing classroom behavior rather than in teaching academic material. In short, the rewards allocated to teachers are not contingent upon specific behaviors that would necessarily maximize student performance.

Even if teacher behavior is altered in the classroom, evidence suggests that incentives of some sort would be needed to sustain such performance (Kazdin & Moyer, 1976). The technology for altering teacher and child behavior has advanced considerably. However, implementing behavior change techniques on a large scale so that they are maintained by the contingencies operating in the system (e.g., contingencies that normally influence teacher behavior) remains to be resolved.

ISSUES AND PROBLEMS

Maintenance and Transfer of Training

Two of the most significant difficulties in classroom programs develop after behavior change has been accomplished. The maintenance of changes after the classroom program is withdrawn and the transfer of new behaviors to settings beyond the one where the program was implemented present formidable problems, referred to respectively as maintenance and transfer of training. In general, classroom programs have demonstrated that incentive systems alter behavior but that gains usually are lost once the program is withdrawn. Indeed, the experimental designs used to demonstrate the effects of the contingencies often rely on the fact that behavioral gains are lost during phases where the program is temporarily withdrawn. Similarly, once behavior is changed in one setting, the improvements usually are restricted to that setting. Here too, some experimental demonstrations capitalize upon the fact that behavioral changes usually are situation specific and that changes are unlikely to occur across settings until specific contingencies are implemented in each setting (Hartmann & Atkinson, 1973).

Maintenance of behavior is an issue because in most classrooms or schools, contingencies used in a particular program are not likely to be continued. Certainly, as the child continues through the educational system, few single themes and teacher practices are consistent over time. Hence, once behaviors are developed, specific practices are needed to attempt to maintain them. Similarly, after a program is withdrawn, children change settings in which they are assigned. Hence, it is important to ensure that behaviors are not restricted to the specific setting in which they may have been developed. Even while a program is in effect in one setting (e.g., classroom), it may be very important to program transfer to other settings (e.g., the playground, at home).

Only recently has much attention been given to procedures designed to develop maintenance and transfer of training. Several procedures have been explored, only a few of which can be mentioned here (see Kazdin, 1977; Marholin, Siegel, & Phillips, 1976; Stokes & Baer, 1977). One procedure is to continue programs in new settings to facilitate transfer of performance and maintenance after the program ultimately is withdrawn. For example, Walker, Hops, and Johnson (1975) developed token reinforcement programs in a special education classroom. Once children were returned to their regular classrooms, the reinforcement contingencies were altered slightly but continued. The gains developed in the special classrooms were maintained in the new program implemented in the regular classroom. More importantly, up to four months after the new program had been terminated, children still showed high levels of the appropriate behavior. Other programs have shown that continuing contingencies across settings often facilitates transfer and maintenance (Lovaas, Koegel, Simmons, & Long, 1973).

Another procedure to develop maintenance is to withdraw the classroom program gradually. For example, Drabman et al. (1973) provided token reinforcement to children in an adjustment class. Tokens were delivered for conduct and academic performance. After appropriate behavior developed, the program was gradually withdrawn. This was accomplished by giving the children greater control over their own behavior. Children rated themselves for appropriate behavior and received consequences if these ratings corresponded to teacher evaluations. Gradually, the teachers monitored fewer of the children's ratings and eventually stopped checking altogether. Although the teacher's control over the contingencies was gradually decreased, the gains made during the teacher-implemented program tended to be sustained for the 12-day period in which all checks of child behavior were eliminated.

In fading the contingencies in the above example, children were given greater control over administering consequences. Self-reinforcement, as discussed earlier, occasionally has been used to help develop sustained performance (Turkewitz et al., 1975). Self-reinforcement has not been shown to sustain long-term performance as a technique in its own right. Investigations have suggested that self-reinforcement may produce little or no improvement in maintenance over externally managed contingencies or influence maintenance for only brief follow-up periods, for example, several days (Bolstad & Johnson, 1972; Felixbrod & O'Leary, 1973; Johnson & Martin, 1972). However, considerably more research is needed because variations of self-reinforcement have shown promise in altering behavior in general and in fading the contingencies, as noted above.

Another technique for developing maintenance and transfer consists of varying the conditions in which the contingencies are implemented. Part of the problem in most programs is that the reinforcement contingencies are restricted to a narrow range of stimulus conditions and children readily discriminate when the contingencies are in effect and when they are not. If the contingencies can be implemented across several settings or agents, behavior is more likely to extend to new settings and over time where the contingencies are not in effect.

For example, Koegel and Rincover (1974) found that training autistic children to pay attention in a one-to-one situation did not extend to classroom performance. Hence, training shifted to expand the stimulus conditions of training so that training increasingly resembled the classroom situation. More children were trained together, approximating the group situation of the classroom. The teacher and teacher aide were brought into training, and reinforcement was administered increasingly intermittently. Behaviors transferred to the classroom when training was conducted in this fashion.

A number of other procedures have been used to maintain and enhance maintenance and transfer. Parameters of reinforcement such as schedules and delay periods have been varied to wean individuals from the program (e.g., Greenwood et al., 1974; Kazdin & Polster, 1973). Also, individuals have been trained to provide self-instructions so that appropriate behavior can be prompted in diverse settings (e.g., Robin, Armel, & O'Leary, 1975). In many programs that attempt to develop maintenance and/or transfer, several techniques mentioned above are combined. For example, Jones and Kazdin (1975) developed response maintenance in a special education classroom for retarded children. Token reinforcement was delivered for attentiveness. After behavior change had been evident, several different procedures were combined to develop sustained performance. First, natural reinforcers (peer praise and activities) were substituted for token reinforcement. Second, reinforcers were later given only intermittently rather than daily. Third, a group contingency for the class as a whole was put into effect even though only four children in class were actually in the program. After two weeks of maintenance procedures all contingencies were withdrawn. Behaviors were maintained up to 12 calendar weeks (9 school weeks) after the program had been terminated.

In general, maintenance and transfer of classroom behaviors constitute extremely important issues for the field. One of the reasons that many procedures are combined to effect maintenance and transfer is that relatively little is known about the necessary and sufficient conditions for maintenance. Hence, several components are combined to maximize the chances for sustained performance. However, much more attention is needed in this area. Part of the problem consists of developing a technology for maintaining behavior so that specific maintenance and transfer techniques can be implemented. Another part of the problem consists of the structure of schools. If schools developed consistent classroom incentive programs to maximize student performance, there would be less immediate need to be concerned about maintenance and transfer. The problems arise because programs are in effect for a single term or a single classroom among several that students attend during a school term. The discontinuity of school programs or lack of consistency in achieving classroom behaviors has made the need for maintenance and transfer procedures crucial.

Limitations of Classroom Programs

Several issues can be identified that constitute limitations of classroom behavioral programs. Some of the limitations refer to the difficulties in their long-term success or the behaviors focused upon; others refer to difficulties encountered in implementing these programs.

One limitation of classroom programs pertains to the absence of long-term follow-up assessment attesting to their effectiveness. Few studies have assessed whether changes in classroom deportment or academic performance are sustained over protracted periods. Indeed, the majority of investigations demonstrate that changes are not sustained as soon as the contingencies are withdrawn. Research examining long-term follow-up raises issues about the technology of maintenance and transfer, and hence has been addressed as an issue in the previous section.

Another limitation of classroom programs has been the target focus. Most investigations have focused upon classroom deportment, which includes a variety of behaviors such as attending to the teacher or to one's assignment, remaining in one's seat, not talking without permission, not disrupting others, not playing with materials while working, rocking in one's seat, and so on. The focus on deportment is understandable in part because management problems are the first complaints that teachers have about their classrooms and, unfortunately, the area where teacher efforts, by necessity, often seem to be the greatest. To meet teacher concerns, investigators have designed programs to make children more manageable and more attentive to the classroom tasks.

After several years of classroom research, questions were raised about the appropriateness of focusing on management (Winett & Winkler, 1972). In many classes deportment may not even be a problem. Along with general criticisms about the focus, an increasing body of literature emerged suggesting that improving deportment had little or no relation to academic behaviors such as productivity and accuracy on assignments. For example, Ferritor et al. (1972) demonstrated that providing token reinforcement for attentive behavior did not improve academic performance. Similarly, focusing on academic behaviors did not necessarily improve attentive behavior. However, each behavior improved when contingencies were directly provided for those behaviors.

Several other studies have corroborated part of the above mentioned findings. In general, improving deportment in the classroom usually has little or no bearing on academic behaviors. On the other hand, increasing academic performance has been shown in several studies to improve attentive behavior and to reduce disruptive behavior (e.g., Ayllon, Layman, & Burke, 1972; Ayllon & Roberts, 1974; Winett & Roach, 1973). Hence, programs interested in developing improved deportment might be designed to focus on academic behaviors, since these latter behaviors presumably serve as the ultimate focus in any event. In light of the studies above, deportment should improve. If it does not, perhaps separate contingencies should be designed for attentive behavior as well. However, the initial focus on deportment would not seem to be warranted in most programs where improvements are desired in academic activities as well.

Perhaps one of the greatest limitations of effective classroom programs pertains to the structure of the settings in which they are implemented. Of course, behavioral programs are designed to be implemented in existing settings. Many of the limitations that such programs encounter are not a function of the technology of changing behavior but a result of the execution of programs in settings that do not always foster behavior change.

Different levels of analysis illustrate influences that may compete with designing and implementing effective programs. One of the problems of classroom programs already mentioned pertains to teacher training. It is difficult to implement the contingencies necessary to have teachers carry out effective programs for sustained periods. Research has suggested that incentives, in the form of increased attention or tokens of some kind, sustain high levels of teacher performance of behavior change techniques. Yet, the contingencies existing in contemporary education do not provide rewards for teacher effectiveness in the classroom, as noted earlier. When effectiveness is important, educators often have global dimensions in mind rather than concrete accomplishments in the academic attainment of the children. If contingencies in education helped foster teacher accountability in the classroom and explicitly examined what teachers do in relation to their children, the matter of staff training could be more readily resolved. The problem with staff training is implementing a program in a system that does not normally support teacher efforts to improve concrete child behaviors. Salaries, vacations, promotions, recognition, and improved conditions of teaching are some of the normally available teacher rewards that might be tied to student performance. If these naturally available reinforcers were made contingent for teachers, problems in sustaining teacher performance might be reduced.

The problem above essentially criticizes the overall system in which the classroom is present. At other levels, additional factors can be identified that compete with effective programming. For example, most individuals who have been elementary students are familiar with the general fact that escape from school is a reinforcer (e.g., leaving school early, having days cancelled, and being let out for summer). Indeed, research has shown that leaving the classroom early is a reinforcer and staying late is an aversive event (e.g., Harris & Sherman, 1973).

The fact that behavior modification programs have used escape from the classroom as a reinforcer, whether it is going home early or staying out for extra recess, is a comment about the classroom itself. If one were able to restructure the classroom rather than design behavioral programs to fit into poorly designed classrooms, it would be important to establish firmly the positive nature of the situation. Escape from the class should not be a reward; it should be a punisher. If the classroom structure, learning procedures, and academic skills were better programmed, they would enhance the probability of positive classroom situations. In such a classroom, behavioral programs would be less likely to be needed because many of the problems of deportment might even be eliminated. When programs were needed, they probably would be very effective because mild punishment or special incentives would be superimposed upon a richly rewarding environment.

The contingencies for teacher behavior and valence of the classroom for students are not the only problems that interfere with maximally effective programs. The relative absence of the teacher, the absence of existing evaluative criteria based upon classroom progress, and the failure of contingencies throughout the administrative hierarchy of the education system compete with effective programs. It should be noted that identification of these problems as a limitation of classroom programs is not merely an attempt to make areas outside of the field a scapegoat for inadequacies of classroom behavior modification. In fact, the classroom technology has developed reasonably well in terms of demonstrating improvement in academic skills, deportment, and social behavior. Many improvements in the technology no doubt will emerge. However, even with existing knowledge, major advances might be made in the classroom if the programs could be implemented and disseminated on a wider basis. Some of the limitations for such dissemination pertain to the structure of education as an institution and the nature of classroom instruction as it often is practiced.

SCHOOL PHOBIA

The focus of programs discussed to this point entails classroom behavior, primarily management problems and academic performance. The techniques devised for these behaviors have been based primarily upon operant conditioning and include variations elaborated upon earlier in the chapter. Another problem that often arises in relation to children's functioning in class is a phobic reaction toward school.

School phobia is a childhood disorder that occurs at a significant rate among school-aged children. Kennedy (1965) has documented the incidence of school phobia to be 1.7% of school-age children each year. Kahn and Nursten (1962) estimated the incidence of this disorder to range from 5 to 8% in the general population. These data attest to the significant occurrence of this disorder. As a result, a rapidly growing literature examining the etiology and treatment of school phobia has appeared (see Berecz, 1968; Gelfand, 1978; Kahn, 1958; Klein, 1945; Hersen, 1971; Miller, Barrett, & Hampe, 1974; Waldfogel, Coolidge, & Hahn, 1957; for excellent reviews). This disorder has presented an array of problems for parents, school personnel, and mental health professionals. Unfortunately, unequivocal findings regarding its development, maintenance, and treatment have yet to appear in the literature. Recently, empirical findings occurring from behavioral approaches have provided much promise in the modification and arrest of this disorder. A selected review of behavioral studies is presented to provide concrete examples of empirically tested procedures for treating this childhood disorder.

Fear in one form or another is not an uncommon experience for children at some point during childhood. Fear of dogs, heights, and darkness are certainly minor fearful situations faced by each of us during our early years of development. Fear, on many occasions serves an essential survival role, as in the case of avoiding encounters with certain types of dangerous animals, individuals, or objects. However, most minor fears are usually overcome without the aid of professional intervention. Several authors have noted that the vast majority of childhood phobias are substantially improved or completely recovered in a few years without professional treatment (Agras, Chapin, & Oliveau, 1972; Kessler, 1966). However, when fear leads to extreme degrees of anxiety and consequently leads to a breakdown of normal behavior functioning, it becomes the concern of mental health professionals. Those children who exhibit unwarranted fear in reaction to certain animals, individuals, or situations usually require clinical assistance in overcoming such fear.

Definition

One factor that has led to difficulty in the assessment and subsequent treatment of school phobia is the lack of a clear definition. Ambiguity arising from the definition of school phobia stems largely from confusion surrounding the broader definition of the word "phobia." Unfortunately, an unequivocal definition of the term "phobia" has been jeopardized by the tremendously diverse meaning and usage of the term. For example, Terhune (1949) listed 107 specific phobias employed in the literature. Similarly, Redlich & Freedman (1966) reported that Hinsie and Campbell's dictionary lists 200 phobic reactions. Additional areas of confusion contributing to problems preventing clear definition stem from the influence of etiological variables, theoretical biases, and differences in the meaning of the term during various periods of history (Berecz, 1968). Consequently, the term "school phobia" is yet to be unequivocally defined in the literature.

The term "school phobia" first appeared in the literature in 1941 (Johnson, Falstein, Szurek, & Svendsen, 1941). At that time it was depicted by psychiatrists as a type of emotional disturbance associated with extreme anxiety that resulted in serious absence from school. The phobic child was said to be suffering from "deepseated neuroses of the obsessional type" where he felt that something terrible was happening to his mother resulting in him feeling a need to run home. It was maintained that children who left school usually returned to their mothers. These children were seldom if ever able to verbalize their fears and frequently refused to leave the house. Since the introduction of the term "school phobia," there has been continued controversy regarding all aspects of the disorder.

To define school phobia as a child's lack of school attendance is to oversimplify the term grossly. Similarly, labeling a child's refusal to attend school, independent of additional information, misrepresents its meaning. A child may repeatedly refuse to attend school for any number of reasons that may or may not concern the school, ranging from avoiding a test to going fishing. Whether a child's frequent nonattendance to school is to be labeled as a school phobia or simple truancy is dependent upon the basis of the behavior. The literature attests to a fairly good consensus differentiating truancy and school phobia. Broadwin (1932) emphasized the fact that the school phobic child stays near home or with the mother. In 1957 Vaughan claimed that the school phobic child differs from the truant child in that he is terrified of school.

Coolidge, Hahn, & Peck (1957) generated data specifying two types of school phobia. Kennedy (1965), commenting on these findings, states that the Type I school phobia (the neurotic crisis), and Type 2 phobia (the way of life phobia) share the following common symptoms:

(*a*) morbid fears associated with school attendance; a vague dread of disaster; (*b*) frequent somatic complaints: headaches, nausea, drowsiness; (*c*) symbiotic relationship with mother, fear of separation; anxiety about many things: darkness, crowds, noises; (*d*) conflict between parents and the school administration [p. 285].

From an operant perspective, Ayllon, Smith, and Rogers (1970) operationally defined the term "school phobia as zero or low probability of school attendance" (p. 125). In conclusion, from the above mentioned conceptualization, the term school phobic would appear to be most appropriately applied to those children possessing characteristics that relate to fear and anxiety resulting from an irrational fear of school or home-related events or objects and not simply delinquent behavior.

Traditionally, school phobia has been viewed as a disorder related primarily to separation anxiety (Eisenberg, 1958). That is, psychodynamic writers claim separation anxiety is the true cause of fear in the phobic child and not any real fear of school. The major issue here is the anxiety resulting from the child's fear of leaving the mother. Jarvis (1964), operating within the psychoanalytic framework, for example, traces this problem to the hostile impulses of sadomasochistic school personnel toward the child, which he (the child) perceives as similar to the relationship between himself and his mother. Johnson et al. (1941), when introducing the term "school phobia" described it as an anxiety reaction in the child, resulting in his/her persistent absence from school.

Leventhal and Sills (1964), with a somewhat contrary interpretation, view the causes of school phobia as a result of a child's unrealistic perceptions of himself and his academic ability. Thus anxiety, somatic complaints, and avoidance behavior appear when a child is confronted with the school situation and his self-perceptions are threatened. This pattern of behavior is said to be reinforced and maintained by a permissive mother. Unfortunately, these conceptualizations are yet to provide adequate techniques or guidelines for treatment.

An alternative interpretation of the causes of phobia in general and school phobia in particular stems from a learning theory conceptualization. For example, Eysenck (1960) states: "neurotic symptoms are learned patterns of behavior which for some reason or another are unadaptive" (p. 5). When viewing this disorder from a conditioning perspective, a counterconditioning model where conditioned fear and avoidance responses can be modified provides a plausible mode of treatment. This approach not only provides a parsimonious explanation of school phobia, but it also affords the clinician with a variety of treatment strategies in which to alter the behavior effectively.

Yates (1970), in an effort to consider both the child's self-perceptions and principles of conditioning, proposes an integrative interpretation of school phobia. He maintains that the child's mother becomes a very potent reinforcing stimulus during the child's early development. The child comes to rely on her and look to her for safety and comfort. When he is separated from her, the resulting anxiety leads him to engage in a variety of inappropriate behaviors in quest of security. The development and maintenance of the child's phobic behavior pattern will largely be determined by the mother's reaction to such behavior. The development and maintenance of phobic behavior patterns are similarly viewed by Ayllon et al. (1970), where they too posit environmental causes.

Despite varying positions directed toward the explanation and interpretation of school phobia from traditional views, behavioral intervention appears most promising in providing effective modes of treatment. In the following section, a description of behavioral programs implemented to modify school phobic behavior is presented.

Treatment

One of the earliest behavioral treatments of school phobia was carried out by Lazarus (1960), when a 9½-year-old girl was treated with systematic desensitization. Prior to treatment, this subject exhibited a variety of symptoms, including enuresis, night terrors, fear of school. Following three traumatic events, including a friend drowning, a friend dying of meningitis, and observing a man in a tragic automobile accident, a seven-item hierarchy based on the child's fear was employed. Items on the hierarchy were centered around her fear of separation from her mother, undesired symptoms, and return to school. Treatment extended for five short sessions. Behavioral maintenance of desired behavior was obtained at a five-month follow-up. Although specific information concerning school adjustment and success was not provided, this case study suggests the potential effectiveness of behavioral intervention in the management of this disorder.

In a similar report, Lazarus, Davison, and Polefka (1965) employed both classical and operant conditioning procedures (*in vivo* desensitization and positive reinforcement) to increase the school attendance of a nine-year-old boy. After preliminary interviews designed to assess the history of the problem and possible maintaining factors, treatment was implemented. Following the unsuccessful application of a number of techniques in the consulting room, *in vivo* desensitization was employed. A number of increasingly difficult situations related to school phobia were exposed to the subject. These situations ranged from the subject walking from his house to the school on Sunday afternoon while accompanied by a therapist to the subject attending school independent of the therapist's presence. This behavior change was facilitated by making token reinforcement contingent upon attending school and remaining there alone.

The goal of regular school attendance was obtained over a 4½ month period through the combined use of *in vivo* desensitization coupled with "emotive imagery." A 10 month and nine year-follow-up revealed that Paul's school attendance was regular, and, as a student, he was making significant progress. The authors underscored the importance of going beyond the confines of the consulting office in carrying out the treatment of school phobia. The inclusion of the school setting in the treatment procedure appears to have contributed significantly to treatment effectiveness.

In a cleverly designed and detailed investigation, Kennedy (1965) treated a series of Type 1 school phobic children. In what he called a "rapid treatment procedure for returning a child to school," Kennedy treated 50 school phobics over a period of eight years. An early identification and treatment of school phobic children was developed with the school and the Human Development Clinic at Florida State University.

In his conceptualization of this problem, Kennedy similarly differentiated Type 1 and Type 2 phobics as did Coolidge et al. (1957). In addition to this differentiation, Kennedy spelled out 10 different symptoms, each characterizing the two types of phobics. Although reliability data are yet to appear in the literature, Table 1 provides a detailed list of these characteristics.

The treatment procedure for Type 1 phobia is briefly detailed below:

1. *Good Professional Public Relations.*   To facilitate referral of school phobics and provide a sound communication network between the schools, physicians, and parent groups, good public relations need to be established.

2. *Avoidance of Emphasis on Somatic Complaints.*   Emphasis on somatic complaints should be avoided if the child exhibits 7 of the 10 symptoms.

3. *Forced School Attendance.* Significant others are encouraged to force the phobic child to attend school by practically any means necessary.
4. *Structured Interview with Parents.* An interview is designed to provide the parents with sufficient confidence in this treatment procedure, as well as its components and, additionally, to spell out parents' role as major change agents.
5. *Brief Interview with the Child.* A short interview is carried out by the therapist in order to describe the transitory nature of the phobia to the child.
6. *Follow-up.* Data are gathered concerning the child's progress in relation to school attendance, school performance, and the absence of school phobia symptoms.

Following the implementation of this treatment procedure, complete remission was found in all 50 cases reported in this article. Follow-up data revealed the effectiveness of this treatment program in maintaining treatment gains. The benefit of this program in the treatment of Type 1 phobics is noteworthy.

A behavioral procedure was implemented by Patterson (1965) to treat a seven-year-old school phobic boy named Karl. Karl was referred by the school nurse to the university clinic for treatment of reluctance to stay in school and inability to deal with his mother's absence. During a year of nursery school, as well as the first grade, this subject exhibited a number of behaviors suggestive of school phobia. For example, he would remain in his classroom only when one of his parents was present. Previous attempts to modify this behavior via punishment or bribes proved to be unsuccessful. Treatment began with Karl's behavior being reinforced with M & M's paired with verbal reinforcement in an attempt to shape independence

Table 1. Ten Differential School Phobia Symptoms[a]

Type 1	Type 2
1. The present illness is the first episode	1. Second, third, or fourth episode
2. Monday onset, following an illness the previous Thursday or Friday	2. Monday onset following minor illness not a prevalent antecedent
3. An acute onset	3. Incipient onset
4. Lower grades most prevalent	4. Upper grades most prevalent
5. Expressed concern about death	5. Death theme not present
6. Mother's physical health in question: actually ill or child thinks so	6. Health of mother not an issue
7. Good communication between parents	7. Poor communication between parents
8. Mother and father well adjusted in most areas	8. Mother shows neurotic behavior; father, a character disorder
9. Father competitive with mother in household management	9. Father shows little interest in household or children
10. Parents achieve understanding of dynamics easily	10. Parents very difficult to work with

[a] Reprinted from Wallace A. Kennedy, 1965. School phobia; rapid treatment of fifty cases. *Journal of Abnormal Psychology*, 1965, **70**, 286. Copyright 1965 by the American Psychological Association. Reprinted by pemission.

from his mother. A "doll play" situation was employed where a little boy named "Henry" was being taken to visit a doctor by his mother. During this procedure, Karl's behavior was reinforced when attributing independent and assertive behavior to the doll in the play situation. For example, when "Henry" was separated from his mother for increasingly longer periods of time, Karl was rewarded when responding to the question "How the boy felt" with "not afraid." Subsequent to this initial session, reinforcement was administered contingent upon independent behavior where he would agree to stay in the playroom while his mother was in the reception room. Several themes depicting independent behavior of "Little Henry" were presented to enhance Karl's progress. Following 10 sessions of treatment in the clinic setting, treatment took place in the school. Karl was now reinforced for remaining in the classroom without the presence of a special teacher for increasingly longer periods of time. Marked improvement was noted within a one-week period of this treatment phase. The author pointed out that this behavior was totally under social control, as opposed to primary reinforcers. On a three-month follow-up, Karl's "classroom adjustment" was said to have dramatically improved. Thus 10 hours of staff time and 20 bags of M & M's were sufficient to modify this subject's phobic behavior. Following the success of this procedure, Patterson treated a similar school phobic case. Employing the same procedures as in the first case study, success was found in treating similar symptoms. Less than six hours of treatment produced dramatic changes in target behavior.

Hersen (1970) similarly treated a school phobic case with a behavioral treatment program and in doing so provided guidelines for therapists who treat such cases. The subject was a 12½-year-old white male named Bruce. During a careful behavioral assessment of Bruce, it was found that his phobic behavior was fostered by a "model" for school-avoidant behavior previously established by five school-age siblings. A "model of separation-anxiety" presented by his mother had been provided on several occasions. Also, Bruce's phobic behavior, as well as other deviant behavior, was inadvertently reinforced by both his mother and father as well as a school guidance counselor. Bruce's phobic behavior developed over the school year to the point where one month prior to psychological assessment, "he typically cried and sobbed about two and one-half hours preceding his leaving for classes each morning and was beginning to refuse to attend school altogether" (p. 129).

During the first phase of treatment, the subject's mother was seen in 15 one-half hour weekly consultation sessions. During these sessions reinforcement patterns maintaining Bruce's inappropriate behavior were pointed out, discussed, and modified. That is, she was taught not to reinforce the subject's inappropriate behavior, such as crying and complaining about school each morning, and to reinforce appropriate behavior, including coping responses in the form of achievements. She was also taught to be aware of other modes of "substitute behavior" that were to be nonreinforced. Moderate success was evidenced following five treatment sessions. A significant decline in crying behavior was noted. These treatment gains were maintained at a six-month follow-up.

The second phase of treatment consisted of teaching the school guidance counselor appropriate ways of reinforcing desired behavior and extinguishing inappropriate behavior. The counselor was told to have Bruce return to class when he consulted him during the school day and to limit contact to 5 minutes. As a result of this procedure, the frequency of Bruce's visits plummeted and his crying behavior during classes was eliminated.

The third phase of treatment entailed 15 one-half hour counseling sessions with Bruce alone. The purpose of these meetings was threefold:

(a) to provide the therapist with an opportunity of verbally reinforcing the expression of coping responses, (b) to enable the therapist to extinguish deviant behaviors via nonreinforcement methods (silence in reaction to crying and sobbing), and (c) to provide the patient with opportunity of venting hostile feelings concerning alteration in attitude at home and school [p. 131].

By the sixth visit, crying behavior during the course of therapy sessions had extinguished completely.

In summary, this three-component treatment strategy extending over a period of 15 weeks was found to eliminate school phobic behavior in a 12½-year-old boy. A six-month follow-up evidenced the maintenance of treatment gains. It is interesting to note that this author involved significant others as major components of the treatment procedure. By modifying the behavior of the mother and guidance counselor, successful modification of the child's behavior was enhanced. The importance of eliciting support from parents and school officials is noted.

Perhaps the most elegant treatment procedure designed to treat a school phobic was carried out by Ayllon et al. (1970). In designing this treatment strategy to modify school phobia in an eight-year-old black girl, these authors behaviorally redefined school phobia as the absence of school attendance, as noted earlier. Rationale for this redefinition of school phobia and the implementation of an operant approach was provided by previous empirical validation of this approach and by the benefits of objectively defining school phobia. Treatment was carried out in the school setting rather than a clinic setting in hopes of maximizing treatment effectiveness.

The subject had an extensive history of nonattendance as evidenced by 41 absences in the second grade. Her mother's attempts to take her to school resulted in violent temper tantrums. Following several unsuccessful efforts to produce sufficient help from mental health personnel, the subject was brought to the local hospital and diagnosed as a school phobic by the pediatric staff. Further evaluation revealed a consistent variability in her overall functioning related to a low level of concentration in classroom activities. Shortly following this diagnosis, treatment was begun. The procedure was broken down into the following three components: (*a*) a redefinition of school phobia to "a low or near zero level of school attendance" (p. 127); (*b*) establishing contingencies between reinforcement and attending school; and (*c*) reprogramming the environmental consequences to enhance the probability of school attendance. Following systematic observation in three primary environments—home, a neighbor's home, and school—it was ascertained that the child's phobic behavior was maintained by the reinforcing atmosphere of the neighbor's apartment where she was free to do whatever she pleased. Subsequent to this thorough behavioral assessment, four distinct procedures were employed over a 45-day period to increase school attendance:

1. *Prompting-shaping of School Attendance.* During this phase, the subject's behavior was shaped by means of reinforcing successive approximations of

the target behavior (attending school). Reinforcement was made contingent upon spending longer and longer periods of time in the school classroom while fading the presence of an assistant.

2. *Withdrawal of Social Consequences on Failure to Attend School.* This phase was designed to eliminate positive consequences resulting from the child staying away from school. The subject's mother was instructed to leave the house at the same time the children (Val and her three siblings) left for school each morning, resulting in little incentive for the subject to remain at home.

3. *Prompting School Attendance Combined with a Home-based Motivational System.* Following little or no improvement from procedures 1 and 2, this strategy was designed and implemented as a reinforcement system in the home to increase school attendance. Stars redeemable for a special treat or reinforcing activity were made contingent upon school attendance.

4. *The Effects of Aversive Consequences on the Mother.* After having some success with procedure 3, procedure 4 was implemented in combination with this procedure to further increase the probability of voluntary school attendance. This was done by introducing a mild aversive consequence in the form of requiring the subject's mother to leave the house 10 minutes early and reinforcing her children when they arrived at the school. If Val did not show up at the school, this response would require the mother to return home and escort her to school. Requiring the mother to return to the house and escort her to school meant her walking an extra three miles daily. This procedure was employed to shape the mother's behavior to become more active and interested in her daughter's attendance.

Procedure 4 was found to be effective in increasing and maintaining voluntary school attendance. Following a one-month treatment session, this procedure was gradually withdrawn over a one-month period. A 135-day follow-up revealed maintenance of perfect attendance behavior. Additional follow-ups at six and nine months continued to reveal normal school attendance as well as gains in academic and social behavior.

In summary, the treatment of school phobia has been briefly reviewed by employing select cases of detailed behavior treatment strategies. In designing treatment strategies to modify school phobic behavior, we stress the importance of several elements that may contribute to the success of behavioral intervention. These variables include: (*a*) involvement of significant others (e.g., mother, father, teacher) in carrying out the program; (*b*) extension of the treatment across a number of settings (e.g., school, clinic, home); and (*c*) the need to observe overt phobic behavior. The latter element is of paramount importance in the initial stages of any behavioral program. Objectification of target behavior in a treatment paradigm provides the change agent with a sound set of behaviors to observe and subsequently modify and/or eliminate.

Another variable to be considered in designing an effective treatment strategy is awareness of the apparent transient nature of Type 1 phobias. For example, Kennedy (1965), in his treatment of 50 Type 1 cases, pointed out the extremely high probability of spontaneous remission when stating that: "There is little reason to doubt that the majority of cases would eventually return to school whatever treatment was undertaken" (p. 289). Future research efforts should focus on the treatment of individuals exhibiting characteristics of the Type 2 phobia. Again, Kennedy (1965) points out that the success in treating such cases has not been encouraging and thus suggests the need for future research attention. Lastly, the need for methodological and clinical scrutiny in looking at component parts of treatment packages as well as the production of comparative data is mandatory if a greater degree of prediction and treatment of school phobia is to be forthcoming.

SUMMARY

This chapter presented a number of meaningful ways of dealing with childhood problems in the school. Mild disruptiveness, deportment, academic behaviors, and social interaction were areas discussed in light of their potentially negative effects on children's development. Aside from pointing out the application and worth of several well-established procedures, including teacher attention, token reinforcement, response cost, time-out from reinforcement, and programmed instruction, recent trends in classroom techniques were addressed. Recently investigated program options, including self-reinforcement techniques, group contingencies, peer reinforcement, home-based contingencies, and teacher training were described and their overall effectiveness in modifying undesired classroom behavior was pointed out.

A brief section elucidated the problems concerning maintenance of behavior gains and transfer of classroom behaviors with current behavioral techniques. Additional issues surrounding the long-term success, behaviors focused upon, and difficulties encountered in implementing such techniques were discussed as well. The chapter concluded with a discussion of the relatively frequent problem of children's phobic reactions toward school. Examples and illustrations of experimentally tested techniques were presented in hopes of providing the classroom teacher, parents, and mental health professionals with assistance in dealing with these problem areas more adequately.

REFERENCES

Agras, W. S., Chapin, H. N., & Oliveau, D. C. The natural history of phobia. *Archives of General Psychiatry,* 1972, **26,** 315–317.

Atkinson, R. C. Computerized instruction and the learning process. *American Psychologist,* 1968, **23,** 225–239.

Axelrod, S. Comparison of individual and group contingencies in two special classes. *Behavior Therapy,* 1973, **4,** 83–90.

Ayllon, T., & Kelly, K. Effects of reinforcement on standardized test performance. *Journal of Applied Behavior Analysis,* 1972, **5,** 477–484.

Ayllon, T., Layman, D., & Burke, S. Disruptive behavior and reinforcement of academic performance. *Psychological Record,* 1972, **22,** 315–323.

Ayllon, T., & Roberts, M. D. Eliminating discipline problems by strengthening academic performance. *Journal of Applied Behavior Analysis,* 1974, **7,** 71–76.

Ayllon, T., Smith, D., & Rogers, M. Behavioral management of school phobia. *Journal of Behavior Therapy and Experimental Psychiatry,* 1970, **1**, 125–138.

Azrin, N. H., & Holz, W. C. Punishment. In W. K. Honig (Ed.), *Operant behavior: Areas of research and application.* New York: Appleton, 1966, 380–447.

Baer, A. M., Rowbury, T., & Baer, D. M. The development of instructional control over classroom activities of deviant preschool children. *Journal of Applied Behavior Analysis,* 1973, **6**, 289–298.

Barrish, H. H., Saunders, M., & Wolf, M. M. Good behavior game: Effects of individual contingencies for group consequences on disruptive behavior in a classroom. *Journal of Applied Behavior Analysis,* 1969, **2**, 119–124.

Becker, J. L. *A programmed guide to writing auto-instructional programs.* Camden: Radio Corporation of America, 1963.

Becker, W. C., Madsen, C. H., Arnold, C. R., & Thomas, D. R. The contingent use of teacher attention and praising in reducing classroom problems. *Journal of Special Education,* 1967, **1**, 287–307.

Berecz, J. M. Phobias of childhood: Etiology and treatment. *Psychological Bulletin,* 1968, **70**, 694–720.

Bijou, S. W. Theory and research in mental (developmental) retardation. *Psychological Record,* 1963, **13**, 95–110.

Bijou, S. W., & Baer, D. M. (Eds.), *Child development: Readings in experimental analysis,* New York: Appleton, 1967.

Birnbrauer, J. S., Bijou, S. W., Wolf, M. M., & Kidder, J. D. Programmed instruction in the classroom. In L. P. Ullmann, & L. Krasner, (Eds.), *Case studies in behavior modification.* New York: Holt, Rinehart & Winston, 1965, 350–363.

Birnbrauer, J. S., Kidder, J. K., & Tague, C. E. Programming reading for the teacher's point of view. *Programmed Instruction,* 1964, **3**, 1–2.

Birnbrauer, J. S., & Lawler, J. Token reinforcement for learning. *Mental Retardation,* 1964, **2**, 275–279.

Birnbrauer, J. S., Wolf, M. M., Kidder, J. D., & Tague, C. E. Classroom behavior of retarded pupils with token reinforcement. *Journal of Experimental Child Psychology,* 1965, **2**, 219–235.

Blackman, L. S., & Capobianco, R. J. An evaluation of programmed instruction with the mentally retarded utilizing teaching machines. *American Journal of Mental Deficiency,* 1965, **70**, 262–269.

Bolstad, O. D., & Johnson, S. M. Self-regulation in the modification of disruptive behavior. *Journal of Applied Behavior Analysis,* 1972, **5**, 443–454.

Breyer, N. L., & Allen, G. J. Effects of implementing a token economy on teacher attending behavior. *Journal of Applied Behavior Analysis,* 1975, **8**, 373–380.

Bricker, W. A., Morgan, D. G., & Grabowski, J. G. Development and maintenance of a behavior modification repertoire of cottage attendants through TV feedback. *American Journal of Mental Deficiency,* 1972, **77**, 128–136.

Brigham, T. A., Graubard, P. S., & Stans, A. Analysis of the effects of sequential reinforcement contingencies on aspects of composition. *Journal of Applied Behavior Analysis,* 1972, **5**, 421–429.

Broadwin, I. A. A contribution to the study of truancy. *American Journal of Orthopsychiatry,* 1932, **2**, 253.

Broden, M., Bruce, C., Mitchell, M. A., Carter, V., & Hall, R. V. Effects of teacher attention on attending behavior of two boys at adjacent desks. *Journal of Applied Behavior Analysis,* 1970, **3**, 199–203.

Broden, M., Hall, R. V., Dunlap, A., & Clark, R. Effects of teacher attention and a token reinforcement system in a junior high school special education class. *Exceptional Children,* 1970, **36**, 341–349.

Brown, P., & Elliot, R. Control of aggression in a nursery school class. *Journal of Experimental Child Psychology,* 1965, **2**, 103–107.

Brown, D., Reschly, D., & Sabers, D. Using group contingencies with punishment and positive reinforcement to modify aggressive behaviors in a Head Start classroom. *Psychological Record,* 1974, **24**, 491–496.

Bucher, B., & Hawkins, J. Comparison of response cost and token reinforcement systems in a class for academic underachievers. In R. D. Rubin, J. P. Brady, & J. D. Henderson (Eds.), *Advances in behavior therapy, Volume 4.* New York: Academic Press, 1973.

Burchard, J. D., & Barrera, F. An analysis of time-out and response cost in a programmed environment. *Journal of Applied Behavior Analysis,* 1972, **5**, 271–282.

Bushell, D., Jr. The design of classroom contingencies. In F. S. Keller, & E. Ribes-Inesta (Eds.), *Behavior modification: Applications to education.* New York: Academic Press, 1974.

Bushell, D., Wrobel, P. A., & Michaelis, M. L. Applying "group" contingencies to the classroom study behavior of preschool children. *Journal of Applied Behavior Analysis,* 1968, **1**, 55–61.

Chadwick, B. A., & Day, R. C. Systematic reinforcement: Academic performance of underachieving students. *Journal of Applied Behavior Analysis,* 1971, **4**, 311–319.

Clark, M., Lachowicz, J., & Wolf, M. M. A pilot basic education program for school drop-outs incorporating a token reinforcement system. *Behaviour Research and Therapy,* 1968, **8**, 183–188.

Coolidge, J. C., Hahn, P. B., & Peck, A. L. School phobia: Neurotic crisis or way of life. *American Journal of Orthopsychiatry,* 1957, **27**, 296–306.

Cooper, M. L., Thomson, C. L., & Baer, D. M. The experimental modification of teacher attending behavior. *Journal of Applied Behavior Analysis,* 1970, **3**, 153–157.

Cossairt, A., Hall, R. V., & Hopkins, B. L. The effects of experimenter's instructions, feedback, and praise on teacher praise and student attending behavior. *Journal of Applied Behavior Analysis,* 1973, **6**, 89–100.

Dalton, A. J., Rubino, C. A., & Hislop, M. W. Some effects of token rewards on school achievement of children with Down's Syndrome. *Journal of Applied Behavior Analysis,* 1973, **6**, 251–259.

Drabman, R. S. Child versus teacher administered token programs in a psychiatric hospital school. *Journal of Abnormal Child Psychology,* 1973, **1**, 68–87.

Drabman, R. S. Behavior modification in the classroom. In W. E. Craighead, A. E. Kazdin, & M. J. Mahoney (Eds.), *Behavior modification: Principles, issues, and applications.* Boston: Houghton Mifflin, 1976.

Drabman, R. S., Spitalnik, R., & O'Leary, K. D. Teaching self-control to disruptive children. *Journal of Abnormal Psychology,* 1973, **82**, 10–16.

Drabman, R. S., Spitalnik, R., & Spitalnik, K. Sociometric and disruptive behavior as a function of four types of token reinforcement programs. *Journal of Applied Behavior Analysis,* 1974, **7**, 93–101.

Edlund, C. V. The effect on the test behavior of children, as reflected in the IQ scores, when reinforced after each correct response. *Journal of Applied Behavior Analysis,* 1972, **5**, 317–319.

Eisenberg, L. School phobia: A study in the communication of anxiety. *American Journal of Psychiatry,* 1958, **114**, 712–718.

Eysenck, H. J. (Ed.), *Behavior therapy and the neuroses.* Oxford: Pergamon Press, 1960.

Felixbrod, J. J., & O'Leary, K. D. Effects of reinforcement on children's academic behavior as a function of self-determined and externally imposed contingencies. *Journal of Applied Behavior Analysis,* 1973, **6**, 241–250.

Felixbrod, J. J., & O'Leary, K. D. Self-determination of academic standards by children: Toward freedom from external control. *Journal of Educational Psychology,* 1974, **66**, 845–850.

Ferritor, D. E., Buckholdt, D., Hamblin, R. L., & Smith, L. The noneffects of contingent reinforcement for attending behavior on work accomplished. *Journal of Applied Behavior Analysis,* 1972, **5**, 7–17.

Fjellstedt, N., & Sulzer-Azaroff, B. Reducing the latency of a child's responding to instructions by means of a token system. *Journal of Applied Behavior Analysis,* 1973, **6**, 125–130.

Foxx, R. M., & Shapiro, S. T. The time-out ribbon: A nonexclusionary time-out procedure. *Journal of Applied Behavior Analysis,* 1978, **11**, 125–136.

Frederiksen, L. W., & Frederiksen, C. B. Teacher-determined and self-determined token reinforcement in a special education classroom. *Behavior Therapy,* 1975, **6**, 310–314.

Gelfand, D. M. Social withdrawal and negative emotional states: Behavior therapy. In B. B. Wolman, J. Egan, & A. O. Ross (Eds.), *Handbook of treatment of mental disorders in childhood and adolescence.* Englewood Cliffs, N.J.: Prentice-Hall, 1978.

Glynn, E. L. Classroom applications of self-determined reinforcement. *Journal of Applied Behavior Analysis,* 1970, **3**, 123–132.

Glynn, E. L., & Thomas, J. D. Effect of cueing on self-control of classroom behavior. *Journal of Applied Behavior Analysis,* 1974, **7**, 299–306.

Glynn, E. L., Thomas, J. D., & Shee, S. M. Behavioral self-control of on-task behavior in an elementary classroom. *Journal of Applied Behavior Analysis,* 1973, **6**, 105–113.

Grandy, G. S., Madsen, C. H., Jr., & DeMersseman, L. M. The effects of individual and interdependent contingencies on inappropriate classroom behavior. *Psychology in the Schools,* 1973, **10**, 488–493.

Graubard, P. S., Rosenberg, H., & Miller, M. B. Student applications of behavior modification to teachers and environments or ecological approaches to social deviancy. In E. A. Ramp, & B. L. Hopkins (Eds.), *A new direction for education: Behavior analysis.* Lawrence, Kansas: Support and Development Center for Follow Through, 1971.

Gray, F., Graubard, P. S., & Rosenberg, H. Little brother is changing you. *Psychology Today,* 1974, **7**, March, 42–46.

Greene, F. M. Programmed instruction techniques for the mentally retarded. In N. R. Ellis (Ed.), *International review of research in mental retardation, Volume 2.* New York: Academic Press, 1966, 209–239.

Greenwood, C. R., Hops, H., Delquadri, J., & Guild, J. Group contingencies for group consequences in classroom management: A further analysis. *Journal of Applied Behavior Analysis,* 1974, **7**, 413–425.

Greenwood, C. R., Sloane, H. N., & Baskin, A. Training elementary aged peer-behavior managers to control small group programmed mathematics. *Journal of Applied Behavior Analysis,* 1974, **7**, 103–114.

Hall, R. V., Axelrod, S., Foundopoulos, M., Shellman, J., Campbell, R. A., & Cranston, S. S. The effective use of punishment to modify behavior in the classroom. In K. D. O'Leary, & S. G. O'Leary (Eds.), *Classroom management: The successful use of behavior modification.* New York: Pergamon Press, 1972.

Hall, R. V., & Broden, M. Behavior changes in brain-injured children through social reinforcement. *Journal of Experimental Child Psychology,* 1967, **5**, 463–479.

Hall, R. V., Lund, D., & Jackson, D. Effects of teacher attention on study behavior. *Journal of Applied Behavior Analysis,* 1968, **1**, 1–12.

Hamblin, R. L., Hathaway, C., & Wodarski, J. Group contingencies, peer tutoring, and accelerating academic achievement. In R. Ulrich, T. Stachnik, & J. Mabry, *Control of human behavior, Volume 3.* Glenview, Illinois: Scott, Foresman & Company, 1974.

Harris, V. W., & Sherman, J. A. Effects of peer tutoring and consequences on the math performance of elementary classroom students. *Journal of Applied Behavior Analysis,* 1973, **6**, 587–597.

Hart, B. M., Reynolds, N. J., Baer, D. M., Brawley, E. R., & Harris, F. R. Effect of contingent and noncontingent social reinforcement on the cooperative play of a preschool child. *Journal of Applied Behavior Analysis,* 1968, **1**, 73–76.

Hartmann, D. P., & Atkinson, C. Having your cake and eating it too: A note on some apparent contradictions between therapeutic achievements and design requirements in N = 1 studies. *Behavior Therapy,* 1973, **4**, 589–591.

Hauserman, N., Walen, S. R., & Behling, M. Reinforced racial integration in the first grade: A study in generalization. *Journal of Applied Behavior Analysis,* 1973, **6**, 193–200.

Hawkins, R., McArthur, M., Rinaldi, P., Gray, D., & Schaftenaur, L. "Results of operating conditioning techniques in modifying the behavior of emotionally disturbed children." Paper presented at the 45th Annual International Council for Exceptional Children, St. Louis, 1967.

Herman, S. H., & Tramontana, J. Instructions and group reinforcement in modifying disruptive group behavior. *Journal of Applied Behavior Analysis,* 1971, **4**, 113–119.

Hersen, M. Behavior modification approach to a school phobia case. *Journal of Clinical Psychology,* 1970, **26**, 128–132.

Hersen, M. The behavioral treatment of school phobia. *Journal of Nervous and Mental Disease,* 1971, **153** (2), 99–107.

Hopkins, B. L., Schutte, R. C., & Garton, K. L. The effects of access to a playroom on the rate and quality of printing and writing of first- and second-grade students. *Journal of Applied Behavior Analysis,* 1971, **4**, 77–87.

Horton, L. E. Generalization of aggressive behavior in adolescent delinquent boys. *Journal of Applied Behavior Analysis,* 1970, **3**, 205–211.

Iwata, B. A., & Bailey, J. S. Reward versus cost token systems: An analysis of the effects on students and teacher. *Journal of Applied Behavior Analysis,* 1974, **7**, 567–576.

Jamison, D., Suppes, P., & Wells, S. The effectiveness of alternative instructional media: A survey. *Review of Educational Research,* 1974, **44,** 1–67.

Jarvis, V. Countertransference in the management of school phobia. *Psychoanalytic Quarterly,* 1964, **33,** 411–419.

Johnson, A. M., Falstein, E. I., Szurek, S. A., & Svendsen, M. School phobia. *American Journal of Orthopsychiatry,* 1941, **11,** 702–707.

Johnson, S. M., & Martin, S. Developing self-evaluation as a conditioned reinforcer. In B. Ashem, & E. G. Poser (Eds.), *Behavior modification with children.* New York: Pergamon, 1972.

Jones, F. H., & Eimers, R. C. Role playing to train elementary teachers to use a classroom management "skill package." *Journal of Applied Behavior Analysis,* 1975, **8,** 421–433.

Jones, R. T. Academic improvement through behavioral intervention. In S. M. Turner, & R. T. Jones (Eds.), *Behavior Modification In Black Populations: Psychosocial Issues and Empirical Findings.* New York: Plenum, in press.

Jones, R. T. Teaching children to make emergency telephone calls. *Journal of Black Psychology,* 1980, **6,** 81–93. (a)

Jones, R. T. The role of external variables in self-reinforcement. *American Psychologist,* 1980, **35,** 102–104. (b)

Jones, R. T., & Evans, H. Self-Reinforcement: A Continuum of External Cues. *Journal of Educational Psychology,* in press.

Jones, R. T., & Kazdin, A. E. Programming response maintenance after withdrawing token reinforcement. *Behavior Therapy,* 1975, **6,** 153–164.

Jones, R. T., & Kazdin, A. E. Teaching children how and when to make emergency telephone calls. *Behavior Therapy,* in press.

Jones, R. T., Nelson, R. E., & Kazdin, A. E. The role of external variables in self-reinforcement: A review. *Behavior Modification,* 1977, **1,** 147–178.

Jones, R. T., & Ollendick, T. H. Self-reinforcement: An assessment of external influences. *Journal of Behavioral Assessment,* in press.

Kahn, J. H. School refusal—some clinical and cultural aspects. *Medical Officer,* 1958, **100,** 337.

Kahn, J. H., & Nursten, S. P. School refusal: A comprehensive view of school phobia and other failures of school attendance. *American Journal of Orthopsychiatry,* 1962, **32,** 707–718.

Kaufman, K. F., & O'Leary, K. D. Reward, cost and self-evaluation procedures for disruptive adolescents in a psychiatric hospital. *Journal of Applied Behavior Analysis,* 1972, **5,** 293–309.

Kazdin, A. E. Response cost: The removal of conditioned reinforcers for therapeutic change. *Behavior Therapy,* 1972, **3,** 533–546.

Kazdin, A. E. *The token economy: A review and evaluation.* New York: Plenum Press, 1977.

Kazdin, A. E., & Bootzin, R. R. The token economy: An evaluative review. *Journal of Applied Behavior Analysis,* 1972, **5,** 343–372.

Kazdin, A. E., & Geesey, S. Simultaneous-treatment design comparisons of the effects of earning reinforcers for one's peers versus for oneself. *Behavior Therapy,* 1977, **8,** 682–693.

Kazdin, A. E., & Moyer, W. Training teachers to use behavior modification. In S. Yen, & R. McIntire (Eds.), *Teaching behavior modification.* Kalamazoo, Michigan: Behaviordelia, 1976.

Kazdin, A. E., & Polster, R. Intermittent token reinforcement and response maintenance in extinction. *Behavior Therapy,* 1973, **4**, 386–391.

Kennedy, W. A. School phobia: Rapid treatment of fifty cases. *Journal of Abnormal and Social Psychology,* 1965, **70**, 285–289.

Kessler, J. W. *Psychopathology of childhood.* Englewood Cliffs, N.J.: Prentice-Hall, 1966.

Kirby, F. D., & Shields, F. Modification of arithmetic response rate and attending behavior in a seventh-grade student. *Journal of Applied Behavior Analysis,* 1972, **5**, 79–84.

Klein, E. The reluctance to go to school. *Psychoanalytic Study of the Child,* 1945, **1**, 263–279.

Knapczyk, D. R., & Livingston, G. Self-recording and student teacher supervision: Variables within a token economy structure. *Journal of Applied Behavior Analysis,* 1973, **6**, 481–486.

Koegel, R. L., & Rincover, A. Treatment of psychotic children in a classroom environment: I. Learning in a large group. *Journal of Applied Behavior Analysis,* 1974, **7**, 45–59.

Kubany, E. S., Weiss, L. E., & Sloggett, B. B. The good behavior clock: A reinforcement/time-out procedure for reducing disruptive classroom behavior. *Journal of Behavior Therapy and Experimental Psychiatry,* 1971, **2**, 173–179.

Kupers, D. S., Becker, W. C., & O'Leary, K. D. How to make a token system fail. *Exceptional Children,* 1968, **35**, 101–109.

Lahey, B. B., & Drabman, R. S. Facilitation of the acquisition and retention of sight-word vocabulary through token reinforcement. *Journal of Applied Behavior Analysis,* 1974, **7**, 307–312.

Lazarus, A. A. The elimination of children's phobias by deconditioning. Medical Proceedings, South Africa, 1959, Reprinted in H. J. Eysenck (Ed.), *Behavior therapy and the neuroses,* New York: Pergamon Press, 1960.

Lazarus, A. A., Davison, G. C., & Polefka, D. A. Classical and operant factors in the treatment of school phobia. *Journal of Abnormal Psychology,* 1965, **70**, 225–229.

Leventhal, T., & Sills, M. Self-image in school phobia. *American Journal of Orthopsychiatry,* 1964, **34**, 685–695.

Litow, L., & Pumroy, D. K. A brief review of classroom group-oriented contingencies. *Journal of Applied Behavior Analysis,* 1975, **8**, 341–347.

Long, J. D., & Williams, R. L. The comparative effectiveness of group and individually contingent free time with inner-city junior high school students. *Journal of Applied Behavior Analysis,* 1973, **6**, 465–474.

Lovaas, O. I., Koegel, R., Simmons, J. Q., & Long, J. S. Some generalization and follow-up measures on autistic children in behavior therapy. *Journal of Applied Behavior Analysis,* 1973, **6**, 131–166.

Lovitt, T. C., & Curtiss, K. Academic response rate as a function of teacher- and self-imposed contingencies. *Journal of Applied Behavior Analysis,* 1969, **2**, 49–53.

Lumsdaine, A. A., & Glaser, R. *Teaching machines and programmed learning.* Washington, D.C.: National Education Association of the United States, 1960.

McAllister, L. W., Stachowiak, J. G., Baer, D. M., & Conderman, L. The application of operant conditioning techniques in a secondary school classroom. *Journal of Applied Behavior Analysis,* 1969, **2**, 277–285.

McLaughlin, T. F. The applicability of token reinforcement systems in public school systems. *Psychology in the Schools,* 1975, **12**, 84–89.

McLaughlin, T. F., & Malaby, J. E. Reducing and measuring inappropriate verbalizations in a token classroom. *Journal of Applied Behavior Analysis,* 1972, **5**, 329–333.

McLaughlin, T. F., & Malaby, J. E. Note on combined and separate effects of token reinforcement and response cost on completing assignments. *Psychological Reports,* 1974, **35**, 1132.

McNamara, J. R. Teacher and students as a source for behavior modification in the classroom. *Behavior Therapy,* 1971, **2**, 205–213.

Madsen, C. H., Becker, W. C., & Thomas, D. R. Rules, praise, and ignoring: Elements of elementary classroom control. *Journal of Applied Behavior Analysis,* 1968, **1**, 139–150.

Madsen, C. H., Becker, W. C., Thomas, D. R., Koser, L., & Plager, E. An analysis of the reinforcing function of "sitdown" commands. In R. K. Parker (Ed.), *Readings in educational psychology.* Boston: Allyn & Bacon, 1968.

Madsen, C. H., Madsen, C. K., Saudargas, R. A., Hammond, W. R., & Egar, D. E. "Classroom raid (rules, approval, ignore, disapproval): A cooperative approach for professionals and volunteers." Unpublished manuscript, University of Florida, Tallahassee, Florida, 1970.

Maloney, K. B., & Hopkins, B. L. The modification of sentence structure and its relationship to subjective judgments of creativity in writing. *Journal of Applied Behavior Analysis,* 1973, **6**, 425–433.

Malpass, L. F. Programmed instruction for retarded children. In A. A. Baumeister (Ed.), *Mental retardation.* London: University of London Press, 1968, 212–231.

Malpass, L. F., Hardy, M. W., Gilmore, A. S., & Williams, C. F. Automated instruction for retarded children. *American Journal of Mental Deficiency,* 1964, **69**, 405–412.

Marholin, D., II, Siegel, L. J., & Phillips, D. Treatment and transfer: A search for empirical procedures. In M. Hersen, R. M. Eisler, & P. M. Miller (Eds.), *Progress in behavior modification, Volume 3.* New York: Academic Press, 1976.

Medland, M. B., & Stachnik, T. J. Good-behavior game: A replication and systematic analysis. *Journal of Applied Behavior Analysis,* 1972, **5**, 45–51.

Miller, L. C., Barrett, C. L., & Hampe, E. Phobias of childhood in a prescientific era. In A. Davids (Ed.), *Child personality and psychopathology: Current topics.* New York: John Wiley, 1974.

Miller, L. K., & Schneider, R. The use of a token system in project Head Start. *Journal of Applied Behavior Analysis,* 1970, **3**, 213–220.

O'Leary, K. D., Becker, W. C., Evans, M. B., & Saudargas, R. A. A token reinforcement program in a public school: A replication and systematic analysis. *Journal of Applied Behavior Analysis,* 1969, **2**, 3–13.

O'Leary, K. D., & Drabman, R. Token reinforcement programs in the classroom: A review. *Psychological Bulletin,* 1971, **75**, 379–398.

Patterson, G. R. An application of conditioning techniques to the control of a hyperactive child. In L. P. Ullmann, & L. Krasner (Eds.), *Case studies in behavior modification.* New York: Holt, Rinehart & Winston, 1965.

Phillips, E. L., Phillips, E. A., Wolf, M. M., & Fixsen, D. L. Achievement place: Development of the elected manager system. *Journal of Applied Behavior Analysis,* 1973, **6**, 541–561.

Pomerleau, O. F., Bobrove, P. H., & Smith, R. H. Rewarding psychiatric aides for the behavioral improvement of assigned patients. *Journal of Applied Behavior Analysis,* 1973, **6**, 383–390.

Redlich, F. C., & Freedman, D. X. *The theory and practice of psychiatry.* New York: Basic Books, 1966.

Rickard, H. C., Melvin, K. B., Creel, J., & Creel, L. The effects of bonus tokens upon productivity in a remedial classroom for behaviorally disturbed children. *Behavior Therapy,* 1973, **4**, 378–385.

Ringer, V. M. The use of a "token helper" in the management of classroom behavior problems and in teacher training. *Journal of Applied Behavior Analysis,* 1973, **6**, 671–677.

Robin, A. L., Armel, S., & O'Leary, K. D. The effects of self-instruction on writing deficiencies. *Behavior Therapy,* 1975, **6**, 178–187.

Salzberg, B. H., Wheeler, A. A., Devar, L. T., & Hopkins, B. L. The effect of intermittent feedback and intermittent contingent access to play on printing of kindergarten children. *Journal of Applied Behavior Analysis,* 1971, **4**, 163–171.

Santogrossi, D. A., O'Leary, K. D., Romanczyk, R. G., & Kaufman, K. F. Self-evaluation by adolescents in a psychiatric hospital school token program. *Journal of Applied Behavior Analysis,* 1973, **6**, 277–287.

Schmidt, G. W., & Ulrich, R. E. Effects of group contingent events upon classroom noise. *Journal of Applied Behavior Analysis,* 1969, **2**, 171–179.

Schumaker, J. B., Hovell, M. F., & Sherman, J. A. An analysis of daily report cards and parent-managed privileges in the improvement of adolescents' classroom performance. *Journal of Behavior Analysis,* 1977, **10**, 449–464.

Schwartz, M. L., & Hawkins, R. P. Application of delayed reinforcement procedures to the behavior of an elementary school child. *Journal of Applied Behavior Analysis,* 1970, **3**, 85–96.

Sibley, S., Abbott, M., & Cooper, B. Modification of the classroom behavior of a "disadvantaged" kindergarten boy by social reinforcement and isolation. *Journal of Experimental Child Psychology,* 1969, **4**, 281–287.

Skinner, B. F. Teaching machines. *Science,* 1958, **128**, 969–977.

Smith, E. A., & Quackenbush, J. Devereux teaching aids employed in presenting elementary mathematics in a special education setting. *Psychological Reports,* 1960, **7**, 333–336.

Solomon, R. W., & Wahler, R. G. Peer reinforcement control of classroom problem behavior. *Journal of Applied Behavior Analysis,* 1973, **6**, 49–56.

Stokes, T. F., & Baer, D. M. An implicit technology of generalization. *Journal of Applied Behavior Analysis,* 1977, **10**, 349–367.

Stolurow, L. M. Teaching by machine. Office of Education, OE-34010, Cooperative Research Monograph, No. 6, U.S. Department of Health, Education, and Welfare, Washington, D.C.: U.S. Government Printing Office, 1961.

Sullivan Associates Program, *Programmed reading book.* (Ed.), C. D. Buchanan. New York: McGraw-Hill, 1965.

Sulzbacher, S. I., & Houser, J. E. A tactic to eliminate disruptive behaviors in the classroom: Group contingent consequences. *American Journal of Mental Deficiency,* 1968, **73**, 88–90.

Sulzer, B., Hunt, S., Ashby, E., Koniarski, C., & Krams, M. Increasing rate and percentage correct in reading and spelling in a fifth grade public school class of slow readers by means of a token system. In E. A. Ramp, & B. L. Hopkins (Eds.), *A new direction for education: Behavior analysis.* Lawrence: University of Kansas, 1971.

Sulzer-Azaroff, B., & Mayer, G. R. *Applying behavior-analysis procedures with children and youth.* New York: Holt, Rinehart & Winston, 1977.

Surratt, P. R., Ulrich, R. E., & Hawkins, R. P. An elementary student as a behavioral engineer. *Journal of Applied Behavior Analysis,* 1969, **2**, 85–92.

Terhune, W. The phobic syndrome: A study of 86 patients with phobic reactions. *Archives of Neurology and Psychiatry,* 1949, **62**, 162–172.

Thomas, D. A., Becker, W. C., & Armstrong, M. Production and elimination of disruptive classroom behavior by systematically varying teacher's behavior. *Journal of Applied Behavior Analysis,* 1968, **1**, 35–45.

Todd, D. D., Scott, R. B., Bostow, D. E., & Alexander, S. B. Modification of the excessive inappropriate classroom behavior of two elementary school students using home-based consequences and daily report card procedures. *Journal of Applied Behavior Analysis,* 1976, **9**, 106.

Turkewitz, H., O'Leary, K. D., & Ironsmith, M. Generalization and maintenance of appropriate behavior through self-control. *Journal of Consulting and Clinical Psychology,* 1975, **43**, 577–583.

Van Houten, R., Morrison, E., Jarvis, R., & McDonald, M. The effects of explicit timing and feedback on compositional response rate in elementary school children. *Journal of Applied Behavioral Analysis,* 1974, **7**, 547–555.

Vaughan, F. School phobias (Original publication, 1954). Cited by M. Talbot, Panic in school phobia. *American Journal of Orthopsychiatry,* 1957, **27**, 286–295.

Wagner, R. F., & Guyer, B. P. Maintenance of discipline through increasing children's span of attending by means of a token economy. *Psychology in the Schools,* 1971, **8**, 285–289.

Waldfogel, S., Coolidge, J. C., & Hahn, P. Development and management of school phobia. *American Journal of Orthopsychiatry,* 1957, **27**, 754–780.

Walker, H. M., Hops, H., & Johnson, S. M. Generalization and maintenance of classroom treatment effects. *Behavior Therapy,* 1975, **6**, 188–200.

Walker, H., Mattson, R., & Buckley, N. Special class placement as a treatment alternative for deviant behavior in children. In F. Benson, (Ed.), *Modifying deviant social behavior in various classroom settings.* Eugene, Oregon: University of Oregon, 1968.

Ward, M. H., & Baker, B. L. Reinforcement therapy in the classroom, *Journal of Applied Behavior Analysis,* 1968, **1**, 323–328.

Wasik, B. H., Senn, K., Welch, R. H., & Cooper, B. R. Behavior modification with culturally deprived children: Two case studies. *Journal of Applied Behavior Analysis,* 1969, **2**, 181–194.

Weiner, H. Some effects of response cost upon human operant behavior. *Journal of Experimental Analysis of Behavior,* 1962, **5**, 201–208.

Williams, C. F., Gilmore, A. S., & Malpass, L. F. Programmed instruction for culturally deprived slow-learning children. *The Journal of Special Education,* 1968, **2,** 421–427.

Wilson, M. D., & McReynolds, L. U. A procedure for increasing oral reading rate in hard of hearing children. *Journal of Applied Behavior Analysis,* 1973, **6,** 231–239.

Winett, R. A., Richards, C. S., & Krasner, L. Child-monitored token reading program. *Psychology in the Schools,* 1971, **8,** 259–262.

Winett, R. A., & Roach, E. M. The effects of reinforcing academic performance on social behavior. *Psychological Record,* 1973, **23,** 391–396.

Winett, R. A., & Winkler, R. C. Current behavior modification in the classroom: Be still, be quiet, be docile, *Journal of Applied Behavior Analysis,* 1972, **5,** 499–504.

Wolf, M. M., Giles, D. K., & Hall, V. R. Experiments with token reinforcement in a remedial classroom. *Behaviour Research and Therapy,* 1968, **6,** 51–64.

Wolf, M. M., Hanley, E. L., King, L. A., Lachowicz, J., & Giles, D. K. The timer-game: A variable interval contingency for the management of out-of-seat behavior. *Exceptional Children,* 1970, **37,** 113–117.

Wolf, M. M., Risley, T., & Mees, H. Application of operant conditioning procedures to the behaviour problems of an autistic child. *Behaviour Research and Therapy,* 1964, **1,** 305–312.

Yates, A. J. *Behavior therapy,* New York: Wiley, 1970.

Zeilberger, J., Sampen, S. E., & Sloane, H. N. Modification of a child's problem behaviors in the home with the mother as the therapist. *Journal of Applied Behavior Analysis,* 1968, **1,** 47–54.

Zimmerman, E. H., & Zimmerman, J. The alteration of behavior in a classroom situation. *Journal of the Experimental Analysis of Behavior,* 1962, **5,** 59–60.

CHAPTER 21

Intervention Strategies with Hyperactive and Learning-Disabled Children

Benjamin B. Lahey, Alan Delamater, and David Kupfer

Until the early 1970s, learning disabled and hyperactive children were the "black holes" of child behavior therapy: they were there, presenting problems of significant magnitude, but they simply were not "seen" by most professionals. Even though they represented a combined population of 5–10% of all children, little attention was given to this group by behaviorists until quite recently. Perhaps more surprising is the fact that *no* professional recognition was made of this group before 1960 (Lahey, 1976). In 200 years of public education in the United States, their existence has been recognized only for the past 20 years.

Today the terms still cause difficulties for most professionals as considerable confusion and lack of specificity exists in the definitions. Hyperactivity is typically defined as an excessive level of motor activity, distractability, and impulsivity that brings the child into conflict with his or her environment (Ross & Ross, 1976). The primary difficulty in dealing with this definition has been in determining what "excessive" meant in this context. Another difficulty is the as of yet unresolved issue of whether the excessive activity is situation-specific or generalized to many environments. Some evidence suggests, however, that "hyperactive" behavior is specific to situations in which significant performance demands are placed on the child that require "sustained attention," such as doing classwork or completing household chores (Ross & Ross, 1976). There is also much doubt as to whether or not hyperactivity exists as a syndrome of maladaptive behavior that is independent from the conduct problems dimension (Lahey, Green, & Forehand, in press).

Learning disabilities are defined by low academic performance relative to measured intelligence in children who are not mentally retarded, handicapped by severe sensory deficits, are not from seriously disadvantaged backgrounds, and do not have other serious behavior problems. This definition is clear enough in the abstract, but it is quite difficult to apply in practice for two reasons. First, there are no clear guidelines as to how much discrepancy between achievement and expected performance must exist at each age level before the term is to be applied. Second, there is considerable overlap of one-third or more between the diagnostic populations of learning disabilities, hyperactivity, and conduct problems (Rutter, 1976). Again, no clear guidelines exist as to what degree of hyperactivity or other behavior problems may exist before the term learning disability is not applicable.

These difficulties are germane only to the problem of differential diagnosis. The real question is how to intervene with children who show serious problems of academic underachievement and hyperactivity. Over the years, there has been a rapid succession of basic changes in the way learning disabilities have been conceptualized and treated. Lahey, Hobbs, Kupfer, and Delamater (1978) likened this series of new conceptualizations to the paradigm shifts that characterize scientific revolutions (Kuhn, 1962).

Working from a medical model paradigm, earlier scientists assumed that hyperactivity and learning disabilities were disease entities that resulted from minimal brain damage (Strauss & Lehtinen, 1947). Although not considered serious enough to produce full mental retardation, this damage was seen as disabling enough to cause academic difficulties and/or overactivity. The notion of minimal brain damage was grounded in the apparent similarity between hyperactive, underachieving children and some wartime neuropsychiatric patients who were known to have suffered physical trauma to the brain.

When researchers determined that hard evidence of even minimal brain damage could not usually be found in learning-disabled and hyperactive children, minimal brain dysfunction was seen as the problem. Although structurally intact, the child's brain was thought to be dysfunctional in certain specific ways. Educators translated these theories of neurological damage or dysfunction into treatment programs emphasizing the reduction of environmental stimulation and tightly structured, step-by-step academic instruction. Reviews of the literature, however, report no data that support the efficacy of these neurologically based treatment approaches (Lahey, 1976).

More recent work by Conners (1975) and others has again implicated physiological variables in the etiology of hyperactivity and learning disabilities. It is still too early to evaluate the validity of this work, but the theory has recently been translated into treatment methods that offer some promise. These are discussed in a later section.

Another dominant traditional theory viewed perceptual disorders as responsible for learning disabilities and hyperactivity. Psychologists have noted that these children often perform inadequately on school-related tasks that seem to be based on efficient use of perceptual mechanisms. Numerous studies, finding that learning-disabled children perform relatively poorly on visual discrimination and intersensory integration tasks, have suggested a lag in perceptual development (e.g., Silver, Hagin, & Hersh, 1967; Van de Voort, Senf, & Benton, 1972).

Based on this apparent correlation between learning disorders and perceptual dysfunction, assessment and training programs have been designed and used with various groups of children. In the Frostig and Horne (1964) program, children draw abstract forms, practice writing within a set of lines, locate and trace embedded figures, and place themselves in certain specified positions around the classroom. The Getman program (Getman & Kane, 1964), emphasizing perceptual-motor development, includes body movement exercises performed while lying on the floor, walking on balance beams, copying geometric figures, and practicing eye movements by quickly alternating visual fixations from nearby to faraway objects.

These and other remedial programs were based on the assumption that therapy aimed directly at the underlying problem (perceptual dysfunction) would result in improved academic performance. After describing these treatment procedures, however, Hallahan and Kauffman (1976) concluded that "visual perceptual training programs as they are usually employed are of questionable benefit" (p. 75). Hammill (1972) reviewed the literature on perceptual training procedures and found that they have "no positive effect on reading and possibly none on visual perception" (p. 552).

Those who have criticized the use of perceptual training programs have also pointed out that they violate basic learning principles (Ross, 1976). Ross (1976) asserted that "the problem of the disabled reader is one of reading, so it would follow that the remedial programs should concentrate not on learning to balance on a walking beam but on learning to decode written material" (p. 143). All too often, treatment programs based on a medical model paradigm aimed their interventions at underlying processes *presumed* to cause learning and activity disorders, rather than targeting the behaviors actually observed to be deficient.

More recent theories have focused on cognitive and attentional factors in learning disabilities and hyperactivity. Cognitive and attentional processes have been considered in an attempt to understand academic and behavioral disturbances. In this view, the child's learning problems may be caused by problems that fall within the realm of information processing and memory. Academic failure has thus been linked to the learning-disabled child's purported inability to use organized and structured cognitive strategies. In support of this view, research has shown that learning-disabled children are relatively deficient in their use of verbal rehearsal and self-verbalized encoding strategies that help normally achieving children perform in school (Tarver, Hallahan, Kauffman, & Ball, 1976). The possible treatment implications of this view is examined later in this chapter.

Another cognitive dimension considered relevant to these disorders is that of "cognitive tempo." Most hyperactive and some learning-disabled children have been noted to use an impulsive cognitive style. Employing Kagan's Matching Familiar Figures test (Kagan, 1966) as a measure of conceptual tempo, hyperactive children have generally been found to be impulsive (as opposed to reflective) in their problem-solving strategies (Douglas, 1972). On this match-to-sample task, children observed to be hyperactive in the classroom exhibit short decision-making times and numerous errors. In Douglas' (1972) terms, these children are unable to "stop, look, and listen;" that is, they are unable to inhibit hasty responding, unable to plan and organize their responses.

Williams and Lahey (1977) have demonstrated that errors in match-to-sample tasks can be modified using operant techniques *independent* of response latency. They suggest a deemphasis on the concept of impulsivity and a focus instead on methods for eliminating errors in academic settings.

In an effort to explain both learning and activity disorders, other investigators have suggested that attention deficits may be the primary problem (Hallahan & Kauffman, 1976; Keogh & Margolis, 1976; Ross, 1976). The learning-disabled child with reading problems, for example, may be suspected of having perceptual or information-processing deficits, but the child could actually be reading poorly because he/she fails to properly pay attention to reading stimuli. For this reason, Hallahan and Kauffman (1976) refer to attentional deficits as an "overriding disability" (p. 153). Ross (1976) has proposed that the hyperactive child's impulsivity is a function of problems in sustaining attention. In class, a child may "impulsively" blurt out the first (often wrong) answer that occurs to him, simply because he or she fails to maintain attention long enough to produce a correct answer.

Despite the difficulty in defining a broad hypothetical construct such as attention, a multitude of research has shown a correlation between attentional variables and learning disabilities and hyperactivity. Ross (1976) has pointed to a developmental delay in the ability to sustain selective attention as a key problem for these children. When using the term selective attention, Ross is referring to an admittedly unobservable process, by which we distribute our attention among the various elements in the stimulus field. In research employing Hagen's measures of central (task-relevant) and incidental (irrelevant) recall (Hagen & Sabo, 1967), learning-disabled children seem to attend to fewer relevant, and more irrelevant stimuli (Hallahan, Kauffman, & Ball, 1973; Tarver, Hallahan, Kauffman, & Ball, 1976; Hallahan, Gajar, Cohen, & Tarver, 1978; Pelham & Ross, 1977). Similar deficits have been noted for both hyperactive and learning-disabled children tested on vigilance tasks in which subjects were required to report the occurrences of an infrequent visual stimulus (Doyle, Anderson, & Halcomb, 1976; Kirchner & Knopf, 1974; Kirchner, 1976; Knopf & Mabel, 1975; Noland & Schuldt, 1971). Compared to normal control groups, the hyperactive and learning-disabled children were less accurate in noticing the relevant stimulus while ignoring irrelevant distracting stimuli.

The theories mentioned thus far constitute only a sample of the numerous medical model paradigm attempts to link learning disabilities and/or hyperactivity to a single underlying deficit. Commenting on this research, Torgesen (1977) has noted that these "labeled" children have traditionally been compared to normals on tasks that are assumed to be accurate measures of a specific underlying ability. When a child performs poorly on these tasks, medical model paradigm researchers have concluded that he lacks the supposedly measured ability. As a result, learning-disabled and hyperactive children have appeared to be handicapped by "a whole catalog of discrete disabilities" (Torgesen, 1977, p. 33).

An alternative conceptualization, more in accord with a behavior analysis, has also emerged. Within this paradigm, academic and activity problems are not conceptualized as symptoms of underlying disorders, rather poor performance in the school and home is seen as maladaptive, but modifiable, behavior. Instead of attributing all learning and activity problems to a single deficient underlying process, a behavioral approach begins with the realization that both the learning-disabled and the hyperactive populations are quite heterogeneous. These children manifest many different academic and behavioral problems, and the search for causative agents has not led to effective treatment programs. It can, however, be safely expected that these "labeled" groups of children, like all other children, are homogeneous in that their behavior is governed by the known principles of behavior change. It follows that behavior therapy with learning-disabled and hyperactive children consists of the therapeutic application of these principles to the specific problems presented by the children. In other words, the "cause" of their problems is that they have not yet learned to learn and behave effectively and acceptably under typical classroom conditions. The solution is to arrange environmental conditions that will help the child learn and behave more adaptively.

In implementing this solution, the first and most crucial step is a comprehensive behavioral assessment of the children. Merely knowing that a child has been labeled learning disabled or hyperactive does not provide sufficient information for designing a treatment program. Additional, more treatment relevant data must be gathered through evaluating each individual child's particular strengths and weaknesses.

Assessment of the learning-disabled or hyperactive child begins with a description of both the child's academic and social behavior based on direct observation and achievement testing. A functional analysis of behavior will note antecedents and consequences of the child's problem behaviors, when assessment is conducted under the classroom conditions where the child's learning problem actually occurs (Kauffman & Hallahan, 1978).

Recent researchers have begun to identify subcategories within the broad groupings of hyperactivity and learning disabilities (Bugental, 1977; Doyle, Anderson, & Halcomb, 1976; Ross, 1976). It is hoped that this effort will lead to empirically based knowledge that certain treatment strategies will be most effective with children in certain subcategories. At present, however, the clinician must rely on individualized assessment information to guide the selection of treatment strategies.

BEHAVIORAL APPROACHES

Soon after learning disabilities and hyperactivity were first conceptualized within a behavioral paradigm, therapeutic applications of learning principles appeared in the research literature. From the beginning, these applied programs were based on fundamental behavioral notions, that is, contingent reinforcement of desirable behavior and precise, objective measurement of selected target behaviors. Although sharing these common features, behavioral programs have since become diversified, in attempts to meet the needs of the heterogeneous samples of learning-disabled and hyperactive children.

Direct Approaches

Positive teacher attention, in the form of verbal praise or a smile, is a basic method of modifying a child's behavior. Empirical studies have confirmed that when teachers contingently attend to and praise desirable classroom behavior, a wide range of disruptive behaviors are reduced (Becker, Madsen, Arnold, & Thomas, 1967). Unfortunately, most people, school teachers included, have a natural tendency to give their attention to undesirable behavior while taking "good" behavior for granted. Teacher attention has not only been shown to be related to such clearly attention-getting responses such as disruption, but even to specific learning disabilities. Hasazi and Hasazi (1972) worked with an eight-year-old boy who frequently reversed the digits of two-digit numbers when adding, a problem traditionally attributed to underlying perceptual disorders. They observed that the boy's teacher would give him extra help and attention when he reversed digits. Believing that teacher attention was maintaining the boy's errors, the authors urged the teacher to betray "common sense" and mark all digit reversals correct, giving him no special help at those times. When his answers were correct, the teacher smiled, patted him on his back, and praised his correct responses. This treatment dramatically decreased the digit reversals.

In a similar application of differential teacher attention, Stromer (1977) reported on a flashcard instruction program used with learning disabled children who had difficulty discriminating "reversible" letters and numbers (for example, b and d, 13 and 31). Instructors significantly reduced these errors by verbally praising correct responses and simply ignoring improperly reversed responses. Most importantly, Stromer found that by fading from a continuous to a variable ratio reinforcement schedule, the children's academic improvements generalized to related schoolwork in their regular classroom settings.

Differential teacher attention, although often effective, has not always proven to be a sufficiently powerful technique in classroom settings. It is possible that some children have not had learning histories that lead them to be strongly motivated by their teachers' attention and approval. For these children, who may have grown accustomed to failure under typical classroom conditions, a token economy may be beneficial.

Although token economy programs take many different forms, they generally include:

1. instructions to the children clarifying the behaviors to be reinforced
2. rules for making tokens contingent upon those behaviors
3. rules governing the exchange of tokens for back-up reinforcers

Broden, Hall, Dunlap, and Clark (1970) empirically demonstrated that a token economy can be more effective than a program relying on differential teacher attention alone. Working with junior high school students who were disruptive and academically deficient, the authors followed a baseline observation period with a phase in which the teacher verbally praised study behavior, then a token economy period, followed by a return to the use of verbal praise alone. In this case, the token program simply involved the teacher putting check marks on cards contingent upon in-seat studying. The check mark points were exchangeable for free time and longer lunch periods. Study behavior was highest during the token reinforcement period, dropping to lower levels when verbalized teacher attention was the sole reinforcer. Later in this study, even more impressive increases in studying were observed when the token program was expanded to include points gained for completed schoolwork assignments and good grades, as well as the loss of points for disruptive behavior.

Haring and Hauck (1969) have also reported on the use of token programs with learning-disabled boys who were seen as not responding to the typical classroom social reinforcement conditions. These third- through fifth-graders had normal IQs but were reading below their grade level. Using programmed reading texts, they earned points for improved oral reading and reading comprehension responses. The token points were exchanged for tangible back-up reinforcers on a gradually thinning schedule. Reading achievement scores accelerated quickly and appeared to be effectively maintained.

Viewing the learning-disabled child as "unmotivated," Wadsworth (1971) reasoned that increased motivation does not arise from within the person, but it must be arranged through environmental manipulation. A token program was designed for 10 third-grade learning-disabled boys, who were initially assigned to a special resource room and then gradually faded back into their regular classroom. Points were earned for both academic and prosocial behaviors, and they could be exchanged for tangible reinforcers as well as free time. After the children were reintegrated into their regular class, statistically and clinically significant gains in reading and social behavior were maintained through the remainder of the school year.

In addition to modifying broad categories of classroom behavior, token programs have also been applied to the specific academic weaknesses that cause some children's schoolwork to appear inconsistent or disabled. Reading, the most critical academic skill, has been the focus of an extensively researched behavioral treatment package designed by Staats and his colleagues (e.g., Camp & Van Doorninck, 1971; Staats, Minke, Goodwin, & Landeen, 1967; Staats, Staats, Schutz, & Wolf, 1962). Throughout his program, plastic discs are contingently rewarded to more effectively motivate the child's progress through several essential steps in the reading process. The child is first taught to pronounce new vocabulary words, until all new words can be pronounced without prompting. Next, he/she reads each work in a paragraph aloud, until it can be read properly as a unit. The child then reads an entire story silently and replies to questions designed to evaluate his/her reading comprehension. Periodic vocabulary reviews help the child assimilate his/her advances. In this system, a child learns at his/her own rate, mastering one step before moving on to the next. Independent learning is encouraged, since more token points are awarded for correct responses that do not require an instructor's help or prompting. Progressively more reading responses are required per unit or reinforcement to prevent dependency upon extrinsic reinforcement. Research reports indicate that children make fewer and fewer errors as the program continues, with reading improvements being reflected on most measures of reading achievement.

An added advantage of the Staats reading program is its ease of implementation. In several studies (Minke, Goodwin, & Landeen, 1967; Ryback & Staats, 1970), parents have successfully administered the program with minimal training time.

Similar operant reading programs have eased teachers' burdens by employing other students as tutors. Willis, Morris, and Crowder (1972) taught eighth-grade student volunteers to use a token reinforcement system aimed at fourth-grader's reading problems. The 10 fourth-graders progressed rapidly through this program, all of them making gains on standardized reading tests. A particularly convincing demonstration of a token program's utility was provided by Drass and Jones (1971). In their study, the tutors themselves were learning-disabled children. These "tutors" learned to use verbal, token, and tangible reinforcement procedures to successfully teach younger learning disabled students to initiate and complete more assignments and to improve reading skills. The tutors, in turn, were reinforced by their teachers for their own effective work.

Deficits in reading comprehension were modified by Lahey, McNees, and Brown (1973), working with sixth-graders whose oral reading was acceptable but whose reading comprehension was poor. Using an ABAB design, the authors reported a clear treatment affect on reading comprehension. When pennies and praise were awarded contingent upon correct answers to reading comprehension questions, the proportion of correct answers climbed dramatically. Since no direct training in reading skill was given, these results raise the possibility that many specific learning disabilities can be remedied through basic operant programs.

Handwriting difficulties have also been treated using positive reinforcement. Lahey, Busemeyer, O'Hara, and Beggs (1977) designed a program for learning-disabled children who made numerous letter orientation, sequencing, and mirror-image reversal errors in their writing. Treatment involved delivery of tokens (redeemable for pennies) and verbal praise after accurate writing responses, with the instructor giving corrective feedback following inaccurate responses. Subjects made substantially fewer handwriting errors when this contingency was introduced, with the improved writing generalizing to unreinforced probe trials. Similarly successful results were found by Fauke, Burnett, Powers, and Sulzer-Azaroff (1973), who combined modeling, instructions, and contingent reward into an effective treatment package for a young boy with deficient handwriting and letter recognition skills.

The rapid success of behavior modification with these specific academic problems ("mirror-writing," reading comprehension, etc.) is important not only for pragmatic educational reasons, but it also has relevance to theoretical explanations of learning disabilities. The subjects of these studies may have appeared to be disabled by deficits in "information processing," but their schoolwork was quickly remedied by behavioral management procedures.

Token reinforcement programs have also been used in work with hyperactive children. A customary behavioral approach viewed hyperactive behaviors (leaving one's desk, fidgeting) as the problem, and the reinforcement of incompatible behavior (sitting still, visually attending) as the solution. In an early study, Patterson (1965) rewarded a hyperactive boy's "attending" responses by turning on a light contingent upon his attending. These "light tokens" were counted and later exchanged for M & M's or pennies. Under the experimental conditions, hyperactive behaviors were significantly reduced. Generalization to other situations or to academic progress, however, was not measured in this case.

Early token economies received criticism for their "briberylike" reliance on extrinsic material rewards, their cost in terms of staff time and money, and their failure to have generalized effects (across time, on nontarget behaviors, and in other settings). Although it is true that some experimental token programs reported costs as high as $250 per student for a year (Wolf, Giles, & Hall, 1968), other programs with "problem children" have provided responses to those criticisms. Rather than using tangible back-up rewards such as toys, or food, the Premack Principle has been successfully applied with learning-disabled children (Nolen, Kunzelmann, & Haring, 1967). Children in this study performed academic work in order to gain free time privileges and engage in more preferred classroom activities. Gains in several academic areas were maintained for a considerable length of time. Emphasizing the power of "intrinsic" reinforcers, McLaughlin and Malaby (1972) improved fifth- and sixth-graders' academic and social behavior by allowing them to choose their own naturally occurring reinforcers. Token points were exchanged for the opportunity to play favorite games and to listen to preferred music. The authors reported a teacher time cost of only 20 minutes a week and approval of the token program by teachers and students alike. In order to enhance generalization across time, token programs have progressed gradually from continuous to intermittent reinforcement schedules (Haring & Hauck, 1969). Writers have pointed out that a teacher's verbal approval can become a more potent reinforcer after being repeatedly paired with the giving of tokens or tangible rewards. In this way, even temporary token programs can produce enduring effects, by increasing a teacher's value as a reinforcing agent (Chadwick & Day, 1971; O'Leary & Drabman, 1971).

Further enhancement of a token economy effect has been demonstrated by involving parents and the home environment in the program. With learning-disabled, hyperactive, or disruptive children, who have experienced failure at school, the most effective reinforcers may be found at home rather than at school. Several studies have examined the benefits of linking school behavior to home-based consequences.

Ayllon, Garber, and Pisor (1975) reported on a third grade class of disruptive learning-disabled children. Initial token programs, using school-based rewards as back-up reinforcers, failed to produce enduring decreases in disruptive classroom behavior. Deciding that school-related reinforcement was just not strong enough, the experimenters arranged a 2-hour meeting with these children's parents. They were told to expect their children to bring a "good behavior letter" home after each nondisruptive, well-behaved day at school. Since the parents were most familiar with their child's likes and dislikes, they were allowed to select rewards and punishments analogous to the back-up reinforcers in school-based token programs. Good behavior letters were typically greeted with praise, extended television privileges, or allowance money. The failure to receive a letter sometimes meant the withholding of allowances, earlier bedtime, or even a spanking. Unlike the previously attempted school-based token programs, this home-based system resulted in lasting reduction of disruptive school behavior.

Similar home-based programs have been shown to reduce inappropriate behavior in kindergarten children (Lahey, Gendrich, Gendrich, Schnelle, Gant, & McNees, 1977) as well as learning-disabled adolescents (McKenzie, Clark, Kothera, & Benson, 1968; Schumaker, Howell, & Sherman, 1977). The latter study utilized a "daily report card" that informed the parents how well their child had behaved that day. Good report cards brought the child privileges that had been negotiated with the parents. Not only did this approach reduce disruption in class, but semester grades and general teacher satisfaction also improved. In relation to other classroom management procedures, these home-based efforts required very little teacher time, no school costs, and no classroom procedure changes.

Treatment programs for hyperactive children in home settings have been based on the assumption that high rates of inappropriate behavior form the core characteristic of the disorder in the home. Indeed, the same parent-training programs developed for parents of conduct problem children have been successfully used with hyperactive children (O'Leary, Pelham, Rosenbaum, & Price, 1978). These children are rated by their parents as being both less active and less troublesome. Apparently, special parent-training procedures are not needed for children given this label.

Indirect Approaches

Many of the behavioral strategies discussed so far have aimed intervention at schoolroom behaviors that have been believed to be incompatible with efficient academic work. Particularly with those children diagnosed hyperactive or learning disabled, it was assumed that their frequent inattention, disruption, and impulsivity was responsible for their failure to learn and behave acceptably. As a result of this assumption, contingency management programs often attempted to reduce the frequency of these inappropriate behaviors, expecting that either accelerated appropriate or inattentive classroom behavior would not necessarily lead to actual learning improvements.

Early studies of operant conditioning with these children focused on their ability to increase attending and decrease disruptive behaviors, but they did not evaluate concurrent effects on academic work (Novy, Burnett, Powers, & Sulzer-Azaroff, 1973; Walker & Buckley, 1968; Wolf, Giles, & Hall, 1968). When the relationship between classroom behavior and academic work was empirically studied, some key assumptions were questioned. Wagner and Guyer (1971), for example, used a token economy program to successfully lengthen learning-disabled student's attention spans. Reading achievement tests, however, revealed no significant improvements as a result of their increased attending. These authors concluded that "operant conditioning of span of attending does not seem to have a positive effect on academic performance (reading) since the fact that learning-disabled children attend to a task does not imply they are able to concentrate" (Wagner & Guyer, 1971, p. 288). Supporting this same point, Ferritor, Buckholdt, Hamblin, and Smith (1972) showed that reinforcement of attending behaviors led to improved attending and less disruption, but it had little effect on the quality of academic exercises. They found that academic work would improve only when reinforcement was made directly contingent upon improved academic work.

In addition to these empirical data, Winett and Winkler (1972) have criticized those behavior modification procedures targeting "inappropriate" classroom behaviors. Their review of the behavioral literature revealed consistent attempts to produce a model child who is silent, attentive, and docile. Behaviors that lead a child to be labeled hyperactive or disruptive—leaving one's seat, jumping, tapping feet, laughing, peer interaction—were often the "inappropriate" behaviors targeted by behavior modifiers, without investigation of their relationship to academic work. As Winett and Winkler suggested, "it may be that learning can take place more effectively if it can be accompanied by singing and laughing and whistling and that a quiet, controlled, docile classroom may not only be unnecessary but destructive" (p. 500).

As a result of these empirical and humanistic considerations, an alternative behavioral approach has emerged. In this approach, behaviors that are conducive to academic learning are considered to be linked in a behavioral chain, with accurate academic performance the terminal response in the chain. Reinforcement of accurate academic performance will result in both a strengthening of any responses that are necessary components of the chain, as well as elimination of any responses in the chain that are incompatible with accurate academic work. As set forth by Ayllon and Rosenbaum (1977), this view leads to a different method of selecting target behaviors for intervention. "If this reasoning is correct, then the major behavioral targets for measurement and modification are not concentration, interest, or attention per se, but the academic performances that require those components for their successful completion" (Ayllon & Rosenbaum, 1977, p. 192).

The reinforcement of terminal academic behaviors has an additional advantage, in allowing the child to determine for himself what behaviors are truly incompatible with his academic progress. If a reinforcement procedure is effective in increasing the rate of correct academic work, then any behaviors that had actually been interfering with learning must have been effectively eliminated from the chain. If behaviors such as talking quietly to peers, humming, laughing, or fidgeting do not drop out of the chain, then by definition, they were not incompatible with academic work.

A clear illustration of this approach can be found in Kirby and Shields' (1972) work with a 13-year-old distractible learning-disabled boy. Frequently appearing inattentive in class, this boy was performing poorly in arithmetic. The authors decided to make reinforcement contingent upon improvement in the boy's arithmetic work, viewing inattentive behavior as incompatible with adequate academic performance. When his arithmetic work improved, his inattentive behavior was concurrently decreased.

In a study relevant to several issues discussed in this chapter, Ayllon, Layman, and Kandel (1975) demonstrated the power of reinforcing terminal academic responses with three elementary school children. These children, labeled both hyperactive and learning disabled, had been taking Ritalin but were performing poorly on academic work. After discontinuing the stimulant medication, each child showed higher rates of inappropriate, hyperactive behavior. When a token program then made reinforcement contingent upon specific academic accomplishments (first in mathematics, then in both mathematics and reading), academic accuracy increased and hyperactive behavior was concurrently decreased. Equally convincing applications of this approach have been reported with disruptive children (Ayllon & Roberts, 1974), emotionally disturbed and low-achieving children (Marholin, Steinman, McInnis, & Heads, 1975), educably mentally handicapped children (Aaron & Bostow, 1978), and inattentive children in remedial mathematics classes (Broughton & Lahey, 1978). In each case, reinforcement of terminal academic responses resulted in decreased inappropriate behavior as well as improved academic work.

Behavioral Self-Management

After considering the therapeutic attempts of teachers, parents, and others, it is interesting to examine the possibility of the child himself assuming a central role in his own behavior therapy. Self-control procedures, already applied to a wide range of clinical problems for adults, may have applicability in these areas.

A number of factors have led behavioral psychologists to see the promise of teaching learning-disabled and hyperactive children the management of their own behavior. As discussed earlier, externally controlled management programs such as token economies have often failed to maintain their beneficial effects over periods of time. A self-managed program may affect a child longer, since he "carried around" his own control, rather than becoming dependent upon external tokens or teacher attention. Based on this reasoning, there have been efforts to produce more enduring effects through self-management techniques, used either by themselves or as an adjunct to externally controlled programs. Frederikson and Frederikson (1975), working with a special education class, first initiated a teacher-controlled token economy designed to promote on-task behavior and reduce disruptive behavior. During this phase of the experiment, the teacher would stop and award redeemable tokens to deserving students after every half hour. Next, the teacher allowed the students to determine for themselves whether they should have earned a token during the preceding half hour. If a student indicated that he had met the criteria for reinforcement, he was awarded a token. This self-determined reinforcement program proved effective in maintaining the children's behavioral improvements.

Self-management programs such as this one raise an obvious question. How accurate and demanding will children be in evaluating their own behavior? Felixbrod and O'Leary (1974) found that academically deficient children consistently chose close to the maximum rewards available, when given the opportunity. Other studies, however, have not confirmed this expected finding. Glynn (1970), in a study of normal ninth grade girls, found that the girls in a self-reinforcement condition required more performance of themselves than did girls in an externally imposed reinforcement group. Drabman, Spitalnik, and O'Leary (1973) confronted the issue of accurate self-evaluation in a study conducted with highly disruptive children with academic problems. After establishing a teacher-controlled token reward system, they began to reward children for self-evaluations of their academic and social behavior. Bonus token points were awarded if the child's self-evaluation approximated the teacher's ratings. The teacher's checking was gradually faded out, having found a .70 correlation between student and teacher ratings. After improving their academic and social behavior under the initial teacher-determined token procedure, these pupils performed even better academically when they themselves did the evaluating. In addition, their disruptive behavior was lowered even more during the self-evaluation period, and these beneficial decreases generalized well to nonreinforced class periods. Although children will certainly vary in the accuracy and honesty of their self-assessment, this study indicates that accurate self-evaluation can be taught.

Explaining his own preference for self-management procedures, Lovitt (1973) has suggested an analysis of the type of school system whose failures are labeled learning disabled and hyperactive. The educational process aims toward the production of self-reliant students, expecting children to evolve from passive first-graders to independent college students. As Lovitt points out, however, these steps toward self-management are not systematically programmed. Learning-disabled and hyperactive children may be among those most in need of training in the general skill of self-managed classroom learning. This rationale for the application of self-management procedures to these particular children is in accord with Torgesen's (1977) view of the learning-disabled child as an "inactive" learner. With a self-management system in effect, these children could be helped to become more actively involved in the learning process.

Programs of many different types fall under the heading of self-management, making research comparisons tentative at this point. Moreover, it is often difficult to determine which parts of a multifaceted program are most potent. One particularly unsettled issue is the effect of self-monitoring alone as opposed to self-reinforcement. Aware of the reactive effects of self-monitoring with adults, Broden, Hall, and Mitts (1971) proposed a self-recording technique for an eighth-grade girl who had received poor grades. Whenever she thought of it, she wrote down either a plus or a minus, indicating whether or not she was studying at the moment. Her study behavior improved with the introduction of this procedure and was maintained by her teacher's unprogrammed praise and attention after the self-recording therapy was terminated. The same authors also reported a successful self-recording project with an eighth-grade underachieving boy. When asked to self-record every time he talked out, his frequency of talking out decreased substantially. These results, therefore, seem to indicate that self-recording alone can be a useful procedure with academically deficient pupils. Adding even more support, Sagotsky, Patterson, and Lepper (1978) instructed fifth and sixth graders to concurrently record their on-task (vs. off-task) behavior as well as the number of math problems completed. When self-monitoring, these students improved on both academic and behavioral measures concurrently.

Ballard and Glynn (1975), however, found self-monitoring alone to be insufficient in their attempts to improve regular third graders' performance on writing tasks. Only when they were allowed to award themselves token points for proper writing (self-reinforcement) did their performance improve. Hopefully, further research will clarify the particular contributions of self-recording and self-reinforcement.

Lovitt (1973) has reported success with a variety of self-management techniques with learning and behavior-disordered children. He has allowed some children to determine the sequence of academic areas covered during a day, correct their own answers, and graph the rate of their academic progress, with resulting improvements in academic performance. Since self-management techniques have the potential of saving teacher management time, maintaining improvement in a more permanent way, and giving prompt feedback to children, this would appear to be a profitable area for more research.

Cognitive Self-Instruction

A behavioral self-control strategy which theoretically addresses itself directly to the particular deficits of hyperactive and learning-disabled children is cognitive self-instruction (SI). Such an approach attempts to involve "higher-order" cognitive variables such as task approach, cognitive style, and information processing and would theoretically subsume the "lower-order" behavior dealt with through self-monitoring and self-reward procedures.

Palkes, Stewart, and Freedman (1972) investigated the effects of verbal training procedure upon the Porteus maze performance of hyperactive boys. One group of children was taught by the experimenter in the use of verbal self-instructions, which involved approaching a task situation in the following manner: stop, listen to directions, look, and think before doing. Another experimental group used similar, but silently read self-directive commands; both experimental groups were compared to a no-treatment control group. The results indicated that with two short training sessions in which tasks similar to the mazes were used, hyperactive children who engaged in verbal self-instruction improved their Porteus maze performance relative to baseline measures obtained the day before. The performance improvements, however, were not maintained at a two-week follow-up test.

Meichenbaum and Goodman (1971) used a similar approach in attempting to modify the behavior of hyperactive, impulsive second-graders in a remedial class. Five children received four one-half hour individual training sessions over a two-week period in cognitive self-instructions that included modeling by the experimenter, and the fading of overt to covert verbalizations concerning the nature of the task, answers to questions concerning the task, self-instructions, and self-reinforcement. This group of children was compared to two control groups on measures of performance (Porteus maze, Matching Familiar Figures, WISC performance subtests) and direct observations of on-task behavior in the classroom. The only significant result to emerge was that the experimental group showed a greater latency on the Matching Familiar Figures test, indicating increased reflectivity. It is noteworthy, however, that the training situation was very similar to the testing situation, and that no transfer from the experimental tasks to the classroom was found.

The effects of a self-instructional procedure on three overactive preschool boys was investigated by Bornstein and Quevillon (1976) in a multiple baseline design across subjects. The boys were described as having a "short attention span" and being "disruptive and noncompliant." The treatment procedure was similar to that employed by Meichenbaum and Goodman (1971) but differed in that Bornstein and Quevillon dealt with younger children, used massed versus spaced practice, briefly used material rewards, and used "storylike" self-instructional training. On-task behavior increased significantly immediately after the introduction of the training, and treatment gains were maintained 22 weeks after the baseline condition. Behavioral observations of the three subjects indicated transfer of training effects from the experimental tasks to the classroom. This well-controlled study (which utilized an expectancy control condition) provides evidence for the efficacy of cognitive self-instructional procedures in the treatment of children with "hyperactive" behavior.

Other studies (Bender, 1976; Egeland, 1974; Zelniker & Oppenheimer, 1976) have demonstrated the short-term efficacy of SI procedures in modifying latency and accuracy of performance in tasks similar to training tasks. These studies, though, have used subjects selected as "impulsive" on the basis of the Matching Familiar Figures (MFF) test, and they have not looked at the application of the SI procedures to significant classroom behaviors.

Other studies have looked at the effects of SI on remediation of deficient academic performance. Grimm, Bijou, and Parsons (1973) report case studies with two handicapped children (one hyperactive, the other cerebral palsied), in which accurate math responding was maintained through the use of a cognitive SI strategy. This study is important in suggesting the utility of this approach, especially after continuous reinforcement of correct academic responding failed.

Robin, Armel, and O'Leary (1975) compared the effectiveness of SI and direct training (feedback and social reinforcement) on writing deficiencies in young children. SI training was similar to that employed by Meichenbaum and Goodman (1971) except that Robin et al. did not fade their subjects to covert self-instruction, having them whisper so that their verbalizations could be recorded. Their results indicated that SI proved more effective than direct training in correcting writing deficiencies, while both treatments were superior to the no-treatment control group. However, a generalization test from the training letters to other letters and forms revealed that the training effect was limited to only those letters that were specifically trained. The authors noted that high rates of SI verbalizations were not correlated with improved performance. They also discussed the procedure in terms of the difficulty involved in teaching the children to self-instruct, and they conclude that, while the procedure is statistically effective, it remains cumbersome and of limited practical value. Nevertheless, their study replicates earlier work (e.g., Meichenbaum & Goodman, 1971; Paulkes et al., 1972) and provides additional evidence for applicability to the practical issues faced by clinicians and educators.

Another recent study, reported by Cullinan, Epstein, and Silver (1977), looked at the application of SI procedures to the treatment of learning-disabled males, selected on the basis of their impulsive performance on the MFF test. The children were treated using modeling plus self-verbalization. Both treatment groups showed reduced errors on a posttest, relative to control children, but their gains were not maintained on follow-up obtained after three weeks.

In the largest study to date using diagnosed hyperactive children, Douglas, Parry, Marton, and Garson (1976) investigated the effects of modeling and cognitive self-instruction on improving attention and reducing impulsivity. Eighteen subjects were given two 1-hour sessions per week for 12 weeks in training procedures similar to that used by Meichenbaum and Goodman (1971). Their performance on a number of performance measures (including Porteus mazes and Matching Familiar Figures) as well as ratings of classroom behavior was compared to a control group of 11 subjects. The authors' conclusion that there is "substantial evidence for the efficacy of cognitive training with hyperactive children" (p. 402) is somewhat premature in that the only measures to demonstrate significant change as a result of treatment were reductions in errors and increased latency on the Matching Familiar Figures test, indicating an enhancement of reflectivity. This result is qualified by the general criticism concerning similarity of training and assessment materials found in this and other studies of its kind. It is noteworthy that no significant results were obtained in ratings of classroom behavior, indicating that behavior did not generalize to the natural environment.

Another study that has investigated the use of SI procedures with hyperactive children was reported by Bugental, Whalen, and Henker (1977). In this study, the authors suggest that behavior change is maximized when childrens' casual attributions are matched to the implicit attributional emphasis of the particular treatment they receive. In the terms of their sudy, children in the high-personal-casuality/ self-control and low-personal-casuality/social reinforcement conditions improved significantly more than children in the noncongruent conditions. The authors also note that the SI procedure was difficult to teach and maintain.

Based on review of the available data to date, the following conclusions regarding the use of SI procedures seem warranted:

1. The procedures appear to be difficult to implement and seem to require repeated training sessions as well as persistence on the part of both child and trainer.
2. Generalization across both tasks and time has been consistently weak.
3. The treatment package has not been analyzed at this point. Component analyses are indicated to determine the potent features of the procedure.
4. More research aimed at well-defined hyperactive/learning-disabled samples is needed, using meaningful measures of classroom behavior and academic achievement.

Behavior Therapy and Stimulant Drug Treatment

That stimulant drugs exert influence upon the behavior of hyperactive children is documented in the literature, notwithstanding serious methodological problems. Whether such procedures should be used in preference to behavior therapy is another issue altogether, particularly in light of recent findings that implicate possibly serious physical side effects of such medication—increased heart rate and blood pressure (Knights and Hinton, 1969), reductions in height and weight gain (Safer & Allen, 1973), and anorexia and insomnia (Conners, 1972). In addition, there have been reports of undesirable causal attributions associated with stimulant drug usage (Bugental, Whalen, & Henker, 1977; Whalen & Henker, 1976), unreliable prediction of drug responsivity (Barkley, 1977), and failure to find beneficial long-term effects of drug therapy alone (Weiss, Minde, Werry, Douglas, & Nemeth, 1971). Thus, although stimulants have long been the treatment of choice for hyperactivity, and there is much data to support its short-term effectiveness in reducing hyperactive behavior, it is important to consider the use of behavioral treatment strategies as alternatives to, or in conjunction with, stimulant drug therapy. Such an approach involves the investigation of comparative efficacy by assessing independent and combined effects of both behavior therapies and stimulant drugs. Several recent studies have addressed these issues.

Sprague, Christensen, and Werry (1974) investigated the effects of conditioning procedures alone and in conjunction with methylphenidate (Ritalin) in reducing the seat activity of conduct problem children who showed hyperactive behavior in the classroom. Stabilimetric cushions were used to measure seat activity. After baseline, one group of children received the drug while the other group received placebo; in the next phase all children received token reinforcement for decreased activity in addition to pills; in the last phase only pills were administered. Methylphenidate significantly decreased seat activity compared to placebo; reinforcement modified the activity of both groups, but the children receiving medication showed greater reductions. In addition, it was found that placebo-treated children showed an immediate increase in activity once the reinforcement was discontinued, while methylphenidate-treated children showed no such extinction effect. Thus the combined drug-behavior modification treatment was found to be superior. These results, however, are limited to the narrowly defined dependent variable, the restricted subject sample and contrived setting, and the fact that the groups differed with respect to baseline measures of seat activity.

Christensen (1975) further explored the combined effects of behavior modification with methylphenidate or placebo in a crossover study involving 13 mentally retarded students who demonstrated hyperactive behavior. No differences were found between the two conditions and the author concluded that there appeared to be little benefit in the additive use of stimulant medication. However, in view of the fact that drug, placebo, and reinforcement effects were not evaluated separately, and that standarized, low dosages were used for all subjects in this particular clinical sample, it would appear that this study did not sufficiently address the notion that additive effects of the two treatments could be useful in the treatment of hyperactive children.

Wulbert and Dries (1977) investigated the relative efficacy of drug and placebo with contingency management in the treatment of a boy referred for hyperactive behavior and poor school achievement. Measures of several different target behaviors were obtained by direct measurement in both the home and clinic setting. A token reinforcement program was administered by the parents in the home, while token reinforcement was applied in the clinic for appropriate behavior and task performance. Results indicated that ritualistic behavior decreased with token reinforcement of incompatible behavior, while no drug effects on any problem behaviors were demonstrated in the structured clinic setting; in the home setting, direct observations obtained by the mother indicated increased ritualistic behavior with medication, but decreased aggression. The authors attribute this finding to situation-specific effects, and they conclude that there were no interactive effects between drug and contingency management. One could question whether this child was an appropriate subject for such a study, since he demonstrated motor deficits, an abnormal EEG, idiosyncratic bizarre behavior, and a long history of other behavioral deviancy, in addition to "hyperactivity."

Ayllon, Layman, and Kandel (1975) investigated the effects of stimulant drugs and behavior modification on both hyperactive behaviors and academic performance in the classroom setting. Three children, diagnosed as hyperactive, were the subjects of this study, which took place in a learning-disabilities class of 10 children. Hyperactivity and academic performance across two academic periods, math and reading, were the dependent measures. The measures were obtained during four conditions: (a) on medication, (b) off medication, (c) on medication, reinforcement of math, and (d) no medication, reinforcement of math and reading. Thus a multiple baseline design across academic tasks was employed to assess the relative effectiveness of the token reinforcement system. Results indicated that when methylphenidate was discontinued, the level of hyperactivity for all subjects dramatically increased; when reinforcement for academic performance was systematically administered, hyperactivity for all the children decreased to the drug baseline level. Moreover, academic performance, which was initially near zero, dramatically and systematically increased concurrent with reinforcement. The authors concluded that "contingency management techniques provided a feasible alternative to medication for controlling hyperactivity in the classroom while enabling the children to grow academically" (p. 137).

Gittelman-Klein, Abikoff, Katz, Gloisten, and Kates (1976) addressed the issue of relative efficacy of methylphenidate and behavior therapy in a well-controlled study using an objectively defined group of hyperactive children. Three treatments were compared: methylphenidate alone, methylphenidate and behavior therapy, and placebo and behavior therapy. Drug dosages were individually monitored, and behavior therapy consisted of individually tailored token reinforcement programs for both home and school. Measures included parent, teacher, and psychiatric ratings, as well as blind, direct observations of classroom behavior. The results indicated that ratings of behavioral deviance were significantly reduced by all treatments. There was, however, a significant advantage for the groups receiving methylphenidate over the group receiving placebo and behavior therapy. Though there was not a statistically significant difference between the combined methylphenidate and behavior therapy group and the methylphenidate only group, teacher ratings comparing the children in the groups to normals suggested that the strongest effect was a result of the combined treatment.

While there is much evidence to indicate that stimulant medication decreases hyperactive behavior in the school setting, there is little data to support the contention that it enhances academic learning. There is, on the other hand, a growing body of literature to suggest that behavior modification procedures may favorably affect academic achievement. Rie, Rie, Stewart, and Ambuel (1976) reported in a well-controlled and replicated study that the typical suppressive behavioral effects were observed in hyperactive children treated with methylphenidate, but that no beneficial effects on achievement were noted. Other research (Ayllon, Layman, & Kandel, 1975; Gittelman-Klein & Klein, 1976; Rapoport, Quinn, Bradbard, Riddle, & Brooks, 1974) supports the contention that stimulant drugs have little impact on the academic performance of hyperactive and learning-disabled children.

One recent study is worth describing in some detail since it addresses these issues in a well-controlled fashion. Woolraich, Drummond, Salomon, O'Brien, and Sivage (1978) investigated the effects of methylphenidate alone and in combination with behavior modification on the behavior and academic performance of 20 hyperactive children. The children were placed in two experimental classrooms for a six-week period. The design was an A-B-A reversal in which B was the behavioral intervention phase. Half of the subjects in each class were randomly assigned to medication or placebo for the duration of the study.

The behavioral and academic measures were discrete, reliable, and obtained in double-blind fashion during individual and group work in the classroom. Importantly, this study used the dosage level (0.3 mg/kg) previously determined by Sleator and Sprague (1974) to be most effective in improving cognitive rather than behavioral performance. The results indicated that both drugs and the reinforcement procedure favorably affected classroom behavior, but only the latter had a significant effect on academic performance. Interestingly, while both procedures were effective in decreasing hyperactive behavior, they were not equally effective in all situations. The drugs had a greater effect during individual work, and reinforcement was most effective during group work. While the authors note the limitations of the study (e.g., limited number of subjects and duration of the study, contrived setting of the experimental classroom), they seem justified in concluding that methylphenidate will not directly enhance academic achievement. Thus, if scholastic achievement is the goal, it would seem that a behavior modification procedure is the treatment of first choice. Given the lack of uniformity among the studies reviewed above, concerning subjects, dosages, types of behavior modification procedures, kinds of measures, and so forth, it is difficult to draw definite conclusions. It appears at this time, however, that both drugs and behavior therapies have effects specific to certain classes of behavior, and that the combined treatment may act in synergistic fashion above the effects of separate treatments for the more severely disturbed hyperactive children. The very real risk of iatrogenic effects from pharmacological treatments must always be weighed in the choice of treatments. This fact would suggest that, in most cases at least, drugs should be added to the treatment regimen only when behavior therapy does not produce satisfactory effects, and then only when potential benefits outweigh potential risks.

While drugs do seem to manage hyperactive behavior, they exert no effect on academic learning per se. If learning is the specific target behavior, then behavior therapy aimed toward that end would seem the most appropriate choice of treatment. It is always important to consider subject variables, though, in determining at what point in the chain of behaviors leading to correct academic responding one may begin to reinforce. For some children, particularly those whose hyperactive behavior severely interferes with accurate performance, it may be necessary to move down the chain. At that point, other strategies, including stimulant medication may be indicated. This point is supported by data from a recent study by Wells, Conners, Delamater, and Imber (1978) in which the academic behavior of two severely hyperactive boys in an acute residential treatment facility deteriorated while on placebo or off medication, following success with combined stimulant and self-control treatment. Studies such as this, as well as others already mentioned (e.g., Wulbert & Dries, 1977), convincingly argue for the use of single subject methodology, both as a research technique and as an applied clinical approach to determine optimal individual treatment procedures. In addition, systematic studies exploring the environmental and subject variables related to differential responding to drug and/or behavior therapy interventions are clearly indicated.

INNOVATIVE TREATMENT APPROACHES

Recent basic research has deemphasized the importance of motor restlessness as the major factor in hyperactivity, considering it to be a reflection of the inability to inhibit response and maintain goal-directed behavior. Psychophysiological studies investigating the autonomic correlates of hyperactivity (Cohen & Douglas, 1972; Conners & Rothschild, 1973; Satterfield & Dawson, 1971; Zahn, Abate, Little, & Wender, 1975) implicate a defect in the orienting response, particularly in habituation tasks. Conners (1975) discusses the "sluggish" response, noting that the nature of the defect is probably not chronic underarousal, but the inability to evidence phasic increases in arousal associated with task demands; he suggests that central control mechanisms involving the basic voluntary and inhibitory functions, independent of tonic arousal, are implicated.

The "immature" cortical functioning of hyperactive children has been demonstrated with averaged evoked response (AER) measures, and the stimulant drugs have been shown to increase the amplitude of AER's (Buchsbaum & Wender, 1973; Satterfield, Lesser, Saul, & Cantwell, 1973). Furthermore, Conners (1975), in an elegant series of AER studies suggested "The major effect of the drug is to increase the capacity of the subject to maintain an alert, active, and controlled state while being subjected to multiple stimuli from the environment" (p. 150). Conners goes on to suggest that built-in limits on "channel capacity" in children with central processing abnormalities (associated with maturational lag) may interact with situational stress, such that the effects of distraction become more crucial as the information load in the environment increases. This notion has received empirical support in that stimulant-treated hyperactive children show improved task performance under stress (Conners, 1966), and such children typically perform better in self-paced, rather than experimenter-paced vigilance tasks (Douglas, 1974).

Several theorists have questioned whether behavior modification directly changes the selective attention deficit that they believe underlies learning and activity problems. On the basis of available evidence demonstrating weak or nonexistent generalization, they conclude that it does not. Innovative treatment strategies aimed at modifying the inferred attention deficit itself have therefore been suggested. Braud, Lupin, and Braud (1975) for example, reported a case study in which a six-year-old hyperactive boy was taught to reduce muscular activity and tension through electromyographic biofeedback training. Throughout the 11 training sessions, the child evidenced decreased levels of muscle tension, which were maintained at follow-up. Global ratings of behavior at school and at home also indicated improvement as long as the child practiced the relaxation techniques. This study, although lacking methodological sophistication, at least demonstrates the feasibility of such an approach.

Another study investigating the effects of EMG biofeedback training was recently reported by Bryant and Hunter (1977). Twenty children, described by their teachers as "severe attention-problems," received either EMG training, pseudofeedback, or no-treatment in this well-controlled study providing measures of cognitive task performance and classroom behavior, as well as physiological activity. Both biofeedback and pseudofeedback subjects learned to decrease EMG activity, with a greater reduction occurring among biofeedback subjects. Distractibility decreased and on-task behavior increased for biofeedback subjects, but not significantly so. Posttests of cognitive task performance also revealed no significant changes in the ability of the children to focus attention.

Investigators have reported in recent years an association between voluntary motor inhibition and increases in the sensorimotor rhythm (SMR). Although originally stemming from applications to various forms of epilepsy, recent studies have focused on SMR training in its application to reducing hyperactive behavior. Lubar and Shouse (1976) reported a case study in which hyperactivity was successfully modified via SMR training. Increases in SMR were associated with enhanced motor inhibition during the training task; furthermore, such inhibition generalized to the classroom situation, as measured by global behavioral assessment. Lubar and Shouse (1978) extended their findings by reporting that the combined effects of stimulant drug treatment and SMR training resulted in significant improvements in direct observations of classroom behavior, which were greater than the effects of the drug alone, and which were maintained after the drug was withdrawn. These findings support the concept of the role of central motor-system functions in both the development and treatment of hyperactive behavior. However, findings from these studies are too sparse and inconsistent to do more than encourage further research in this area.

CONCLUSIONS

Hyperactivity and learning disabilities are labels given to two large, underserviced populations of children. The populations have distinctive characteristcs, but they overlap considerably with each other and with conduct problems.

Behavior therapy with these children does, and does not, involve the use of special methods. First, the basic tools of behavior therapy (reinforcement, modeling, self-monitoring, etc.) are used in the same ways as with any other children with behavior problems. Second, the major treatment strategies of parent-training and classroom token economies (especially those focusing on academic behavior) seem to work with hyperactive and learning-disabled children with the same benefits as afforded children given other diagnostic labels. On the other hand, some adaptations of reinforcement procedures to specific academic deficits are necessary, and cognitive and psychophysiological treatment methods may be shown by future research to be of special benefit to these populations.

Stimulant medications generally have been shown to result in short-term benefits to hyperactive children, but they do not seem to improve academic learning. Behavior therapy generally seems to be comparable to drug treatments, except for behavior therapy's clear superiority with academic deficits, but both treatments are probably most effective with certain response classes and in certain situations. The combined use of these methods seems to be appropriate, therefore, but must be restricted because of possible iatrogenic drug effects. Drugs should be combined with behavior therapy only when the potential benefits outweigh the medical risks.

REFERENCES

Aaron, B. A., & Bostow, D. E. Indirect facilitation of on-task behavior produced by contingent free time for academic productivity. *Journal of Applied Behavioral Analysis,* 1978, **11,** 197.

Ayllon, T., Garber, S., & Pisor, K. The elimination of discipline problems through a combined school-home motivational system. *Behavior Therapy,* 1975, **6,** 616–626.

Ayllon, T., Layman, D., & Kandel, H. J. A behavioral-educational alternative to drug control of hyperactive children. *Journal of Applied Behavior Analysis,* 1975, **8,** 137–146.

Ayllon, T., & Roberts, M. Eliminating discipline problems by strengthening academic performance. *Journal of Applied Behavior Analysis,* 1974, **7**, 71–76.

Ayllon, T., & Rosenbaum, M. S. The behavioral treatment of disruption and hyperactivity in school settings. In B. B. Lahey, & A. E. Kazdin (Eds.), *Advances in Clinical Child Psychology,* Vol. 1. New York: Plenum Press, 1977.

Ballard, K. D., & Glynn, E. L. Behavioral self-management in story writing with elementary school children. *Journal of Applied Behavioral Analysis,* 1975, **8**, 61–72.

Barkley, R. A. The effects of methylphenidate on various types of activity level and attention in hyperkinetic children. *Journal of Abnormal Child Psychology,* 1977, **5**, 351–369.

Becker, W. C., Madsen, C. H., Arnold, C. R., & Thomas, D. R. The contingent use of teacher attention and praising in reducing classroom behavior problems. *Journal of Special Education,* 1967, **1**, 287–307.

Bender, N. N. Self-verbalization versus tutor verbalization in modifying impulsivity. *Journal of Educational Psychology,* 1976, **68**, 347–354.

Bornstein, P. H., & Quevillon, R. P. The effects of a self-instructional package on overactive preschool boys. *Journal of Applied Behavior Analysis,* 1976, **9**, 179–188.

Braud, L. W., Lupin, M., & Braud, W. G. The use of electromyographic biofeedback in the control of hyperactivity. *Journal of Learning Disabilities,* 1975, **8**, 21–26.

Broden, M., Hall, R. V., Dunlap, A., & Clark, R. Effects of teacher attention and a token reinforcement system in a junior-high special education class. *Exceptional Children* 1970, **36**, 341–349.

Broden, M., Hall, R. V., & Mitts, B. The effect of self-recording on the classroom behavior of two eighth grade students. *Journal of Behavior Analysis,* 1971, **4**, 191–199.

Broughton, S. F., & Lahey, B. B. Direct and collateral effects of positive reinforcement, response code, and mixed contingencies for academic performance. *Journal of School Psychology,* 1978, **16**, 126–136.

Bryant, D. M., & Hunter, S. H. Is biofeedback training really beneficial for attention-problem children? Paper presented at the annual convention of the Association for Advancement of Behavior Therapy, Atlanta, GA, 1977.

Buchsbaum, M., & Wender, P. Averaged evoked response in normal and minimal brain dysfunction children treated with amphetamine. *Archives of General Psychiatry,* 1973, **29**, 764–770.

Bugental, D. B., Whalen, C. K., & Henker, B. Causal attributions of hyperactive children and motivational assumptions of two behavioral change approaches: Evidence for an interactment position. *Child Development,* 1977, **48**, 874–884.

Camp, B. W., & Van Doornick, W. J. Assessment of "motivated" reading therapy with elementary school children. *Behavior Therapy,* 1971, **2**, 214–222.

Chadwick, B. A., & Day, R. C. Systematic reinforcement: Academic performance of underachieving students. *Journal of Applied Behavior Analysis,* 1971, **4**, 311–319.

Christensen, D. E. Effects of combining methylphenidate and a classroom token system in modifying hyperactive behavior. *American Journal of Mental Deficiency,* 1975, **80**, 266–276.

Cohen, N. J., & Douglas, V. I. Characteristics of the orienting response in hyperactive and normal children. *Psychophysiology,* 1972, **9**, 238–245.

Conners, C. K. The effect of dexedrine on rapid discrimination and motor control of hyperkinetic children under mild stress. *Journal of Nervous and Mental Diseases,* 1966, **142**, 429–433.

Conners, C. K. Pharmacotherapy of psychopathology in children. In H. Quay, & J. Werry (Eds.), *Psychopathological disorders in childhood.* New York: John Wiley, 1972.

Conners, C. K. Minimal brain dysfunction and psychopathology in children. In A. Davids (Eds.), *Child personality and psychopathology,* Vol. 2. New York: John Wiley, 1975.

Conners, C. K., & Rothschild, G. The effect of dextroamphetamine on habituation of peripheral vascular response in children. *Journal of Abnormal Child Psychology,* 1973, **1**, 16–25.

Cullinan, D., Epstein, M. H., & Silver, L. Modification of impulsive tempo in learning-disabled pupils. *Journal of Abnormal Child Psychology,* 1977, **5**, 437–443.

Douglas, V. I. Stop, look, and listen: The problem of sustained attention and impulse control in hyperactive and normal children. *Canadian Journal of Behavior Science,* 1972, **4**, 259–281.

Douglas, V. I. Differences between normal and hyperkinetic children. In C. K. Conners (Ed.), *Clinical use of stimulant drugs in children.* Amsterdam: Excerpta Medica, 1974.

Douglas, V. I., Parry, P., Marton, P., & Garson, C. Assessment of a cognitive training program for hyperactive children. *Journal of Abnormal Child Psychology,* 1976, **4**, 389–410.

Doyle, R. B., Anderson, R. P., & Halcomb, C. G. Attention deficits and the effects of visual distraction. *Journal of Learning Disabilities,* 1976, **9**, 59–65.

Drabman, R. S., Spitalnik, R., & O'Leary, K. D. Teaching self-control to disruptive children. *Journal of Abnormal Psychology,* 1972, **82**, 10–16.

Drass, S. D., & Jones, R. L. Learning disabled children as behavior modifiers. *Journal of Learning Disabilities,* 1971, **4**, 418–425.

Egeland, B. Training impulsive children in the use of more efficient scanning techniques. *Child Development,* 1974, **45**, 165–171.

Fauke, B. S., Burnett, M. A., Powers, M. A., & Sulzer-Azaroff, B. Improvement of handwriting and letter recognition skills: A behavior modification procedure. *Journal of Learning Disabilities,* 1973, **6**, 296–300.

Felixbrod, J. J., & O'Leary, K. D. Self-determination of academic standards by children: Toward freedom from external control. *Journal of Educational Psychology,* 1974, **66**, 845–850.

Ferritor, D. E., Buckholdt, D., Hamblin, R. L., & Smith, L. The noneffects of contingent reinforcement for attending behavior on work accomplished. *Journal of Applied Behavior Analysis,* 1972, **5**, 7–17.

Frederikson, L. W., & Frederikson, C. B. Teacher-determined and self-determined token reinforcement in a special education classroom. *Behavior Therapy,* 1975, **6**, 310–314.

Frostig, M., & Horne, D. *The Frostig program for the development of visual perception.* Chicago: Follet Educational Corporation, 1964.

Getman, G. N., & Kane, E. R. *The physiology of readiness: An action program for the development of perception for children.* Minneapolis: Programs to Accelerate School Success, 1964.

Gittelman-Klein, R., & Klein, D. F. Methylphenidate effects in learning disabilities. *Archives of General Psychiatry,* 1976, **33**, 655–664.

Gittelman-Klein, R., Klein, D. F., Abikoff, H., Katz, S., Gloisten, A. C., & Kates, W. Relative efficacy of methylphenidate and behavior modification in hyperkinetic children: An interim report. *Journal of Abnormal Child Psychology,* 1976, **4**, 361–379.

Glynn, E. L. Classroom application of self-determined reinforcement. *Journal of Applied Behavior Analysis,* 1970, **3**, 123–132.

Grimm, J. A., Bijou, S. W., & Parsons, S. A. A problem-solving model for teaching remedial arithmetic to handicapped young children. *Journal of Abnormal Child Psychology,* 1973, **1**, 26–39.

Hagen, J. W., & Sabo, R. A developmental study of selective attention. *Merrill-Palmer Quarterly,* 1967, **13**, 159–172.

Hallahan, D. P., Gajur, A. H., Cohen, S. B., & Tarver, S. F. Selective attention and locus of control in learning disabled and normal children. *Journal of Learning Disabilities,* 1978, **11**, 231–236.

Hallahan, D. P., & Kauffman, J. M. *Introduction to learning disabilities: A psychobehavioral approach.* Englewood Cliffs, N.J.: Prentice-Hall, 1976.

Hallahan, D. P., Kauffman, J. M., & Ball, D. W. Selective attention and cognitive tempo of low-achieving and high-achieving sixth grade males. *Perceptual and Motor Skills,* 1973, **36**, 579–583.

Hammill, D. Training visual perceptual processes. *Journal of Learning Disabilities,* 1972, **5**, 553–559.

Haring, N. G., & Hauck, M. A. Improved learning conditions in the establishment of reading skills with disabled readers. *Exceptional Children,* 1969, **35**, 341–351.

Hasazi, J. E., & Hasazi, W. E. Effects of teacher attention of digit-reversal behavior in an elementary school child. *Journal of Applied Behavior Analysis,* 1972, **5**, 157–162.

Kagan, J. Reflection-impulsivity: The generality of conceptual tempo. *Journal of Abnormal Psychology,* 1966, **71**, 17–24.

Kauffman, J. M., & Hallahan, D. P. Learning disabilities and hyperactivity. In B. B. Lahey, & A. E. Kazdin (Eds.), *Advances in child clinical psychology,* Vol. 2. New York: Plenum, 1978.

Keogh, B. K., & Margolis, J. S. A component analysis of attentional problems of educationally handicapped boys. *Journal of Abnormal Child Psychology,* 1976, **4**, 349–359.

Kirby, F. D., & Shields, F. Modification of arithmetic response rate and attending behavior in a seventh grade student. *Journal of Applied Behavior Analysis,* 1972, **5**, 29–84.

Kirchner, G. L. Differences in the vigilance performance of highly active and normal second-grade males under four experimental conditions. *Journal of Educational Psychology,* 1976, **6**, 696–701.

Kirchner, G. L., & Knopf, I. J. Differences in the vigilance performance of second grade children as related to sex and achievement. *Child Development,* 1974, **45**, 490–495.

Knights, R. M., & Hinton, G. G. The effects of methylphenidate (ritalin) on the motor skills and behavior of children with learning and behavior problems. *Journal of Nervous and Mental Diseases,* 1969, **148**, 643–649.

Knopf, I. J., & Mabel, R. M. Vigilance performance in second graders as a function of interstimulus intervals, socioeconomic levels, and reading. *Merrill-Palmer Quarterly,* 1975, **21**, 195–203.

Kuhn, T. S. *The structure of scientific revolutions.* Chicago: University of Chicago Press, 1962.

Lahey, B. B. Behavior modification with learning disabilities and related problems. In M. Hersen, R. M. Eisler, & P. M. Miller (Eds.), *Progress in Behavior Modification,* Vol. 3. New York: Academic Press, 1976.

Lahey, B. B., Busemeyer, M. K., O'Hara, C., & Beggs, V. E. Treatment of severe perceptual-motor disorders in children diagnosed as learning disabled. *Behavior Modification,* 1977, **1**, 123–140.

Lahey, B. B., Gendrich, J. G., Gendrich, S. I., Schnelle, J. F., Gant, D. S., & McNees, M. P. An evaluation of daily report cards with minimal teacher and parent contacts as an efficient method of classroom intervention. *Behavior Modification,* 1977, **1**, 381–394.

Lahey, B. B., Green, K. D., & Forehand, R. L. On the independence of ratings of hyperactivity, conduct problems, and attention deficits: A multiple-regression analysis. *Journal of Consulting and Clinical Psychology,* in press.

Lahey, B. B., Hobbs, S. A., Kupfer, D., & Delamater, A. Current perspectives on hyperactivity and learning disabilities. In B. B. Lahey (Ed.), *Behavior therapy with hyperactive and learning disabled children.* New York: Oxford, 1978.

Lahey, B. B., McNees, M. P., & Brown, C. C. Modification of deficits in reading for comprehension. *Journal of Applied Behavioral Analysis,* 1973, **6**, 475–480.

Lovitt, T. C. Self-management projects with children with behavioral disabilities. *Journal of Learning Disabilities,* 1973, **6**, 138–150.

Lubar, J., & Shouse, M. EEG and behavioral changes in a hyperkinetic child concurrent with training of the sensorimotor rhythm (SMR): A preliminary report. *Biofeedback and Self-Regulation,* 1976, **1**, 293–298.

Lubar, J., & Shouse, M. Use of biofeedback in the treatment of seizure disorders and hyperactivity. In B. B. Lahey, & A. E. Kazdin (Eds.), *Advances in clinical child psychology,* Vol. 1. New York: Plenum, 1977.

McKenzie, H., Clark, M., Wolf, M., Kothera, R., & Benson, C. Behavior modification of children with learning disabilities using grades as tokens and allowances as back-up reinforcers. *Exceptional Children,* 1968, **34**, 745–752.

McLaughlin, T. F., & Malaby, J. Intrinsic reinforcers in a classroom token economy. *Journal of Applied Behavioral Analysis,* 1972, **5**, 263–270.

Marholin, D., Steinman, W. M., McInnis, E. T., & Heads, T. B. The effect of a teacher's presence on the classroom behavior of conduct problem children. *Journal of Abnormal Child Psychology,* 1975, **3**, 11–25.

Meichenbaum, D., & Goodman, J. Training impulsive children to talk to themselves: A means of developing self-control. *Journal of Abnormal Psychology,* 1971, **77**, 115–126.

Noland, E. C., & Schuldt, W. T. Sustained attention and reading retardation. *Journal of Experimental Education,* 1971, **40**, 73–75.

Nolen, P. A., Kunzelmann, H. P., & Haring, N. G. Behavioral modification in a junior high learning disabilities classroom. *Exceptional Children,* 1967, **34**, 163–168.

Novy, P., Burnett, J., Powers, M., & Sulzer-Azaroff, B. Modifying attending-to-work behavior of a learning disabled child. *Journal of Learning Disabilities,* 1973, **6,** 217–221.

O'Leary, K. D., & Drabman, R. Token reinforcement in the classroom: A review. *Psychological Bulletin,* 1971, **75,** 379–398.

O'Leary, K. D., Pelham, W. E., Rosenbaum, A., & Price, G. H. Behavioral treatment of hyperkinetic children. *Clinical Pediatrics,* 1976, **15,** 510–515.

Patterson, G. R. An application of conditioning techniques to the control of hyperactive children. In L. Ullmann, & L. Krasner (Eds.), *Case studies in behavior modification,* New York: Holt, Rinehart & Winston, 1965.

Paulkes, H., Stewart, M., & Freedman, J. Improvement in maze performance of hyperactive boys as a function of verbal training procedures. *Journal of Special Education,* 1972, **5,** 337–342.

Pelham, W. E. Withdrawal of a stimulant drug and concurrent behavioral intervention in the treatment of a hyperactive child. *Behavior Therapy,* 1977, **8,** 473–479.

Pelham, W. E., & Ross, A. O. Selective attention in children with reading problems: A developmental study of incidental learning. *Journal of Abnormal Child Psychology,* 1977, **5,** 1–8.

Rapoport, S., Quinn, P., Bradbard, G., Riddle, D., & Brooks, E. Imipramine and methylphenidate treatments of hyperactive boys. *Archives of General Psychiatry,* 1974, **30,** 789–793.

Rie, H. E., Rie, E. D., Stewart, S., & Ambuel, J. Effects of methylphenidate on underachieving children. *Journal of Consulting and Clinical Psychology,* 1976, **44,** 250–260.

Robin, A. L., Armel, S., & O'Leary, K. D. The effects of self-instruction on writing deficiencies. *Behavior Therapy,* 1975, **6,** 178–187.

Ross, A. O. *Psychological aspects of learning disabilities and reading disorders.* New York: McGraw-Hill, 1976.

Ross, D. M., & Ross, S. A. *Hyperactivity: Research theory and action.* New York: Wiley, 1978.

Rutter, M. *Helping troubled children.* York: Oxford, 1976.

Ryback, D., & Staats, A. W. Parents as behavior therapy-technicians in treating reading deficits (dyslexia). *Journal of Behavior Therapy and Experimental Psychiatry,* 1970, **1,** 109–115.

Safer, D. M., & Allen, R. P. Factors influencing the suppressant effects of two stimulant drugs on the growth of hyperactive children. *Pediatrics,* 1973, **51,** 660–667.

Sagotsky, G., Patterson, C. J., & Lepper, M. R. Training children's self-control: A field experiment in self-monitoring and goal-setting in the classroom. *Journal of Experimental Child Psychology,* 1978, **25,** 242–253.

Satterfield, J. H., & Dawson, M. E. Electrodermal correlates of hyperactivity in children. *Psychophysiology,* 1971, **8,** 191–197.

Satterfield, J. H., Lesser, L. I., Saul, R. E., & Cantwell, D. P. EEG aspects in the diagnosis and treatment of minimal brain dysfunction. *Annals of the New York Academy of Science,* 1973, **205,** 274–282.

Schumaker, J. B., Howell, M. F., & Sherman, J. A. An analysis of daily report cards and parent-managed privileges in the improvement of adolescents' classroom performance. *Journal of Applied Behavior Analysis,* 1977, **10,** 449–464.

Silver, A. A., Hagin, R. A., & Hersh, M. F. Reading disability: Teaching through stimulation of deficit perceptual areas. *American Journal of Orthopsychiatry,* 1967, **37**, 744–752.

Sleator, E. K., & Sprague, R. L. Dose effects of stimulants in hyperkinetic children. *Psychopharmacology Bulletin,* 1974, **10**, 29–31.

Sprague, R. L., Christensen, D. E., & Werry, J. S. Experimental psychology and stimulant drugs. In C. K. Conners (Ed.), *Clinical use of stimulant drugs in children.* Amsterdam: Excerpta Medica, 1974.

Staats, A. W., Minke, K. A., Goodwin, W., & Landeen, J. Cognitive behavior modification: "Motivated learning" reading treatment with subprofessional therapy technician. *Behaviour Research and Therapy,* 1967, **5**, 283–299.

Staats, A. W., Staats, C. K., Schutz, R. E., & Wolf, M. M. The conditioning of reading response utilizing "extrinsic" reinforcers. *Journal of the Experimental Analysis of Behavior,* 1962, **5**, 33–40.

Strauss, A., & Lehtinen, L. *Psychopathology and education of the brain-injured child.* New York: Grune & Stratton, 1947.

Stromer, R. Remediating academic deficiencies in learning disabled children. *Exceptional Children,* 1977, **43**, 432–440.

Tarver, S. G., Hallahan, D. R., Kauffman, J. M., & Ball, D. W. Verbal rehearsal and selective attention in children with learning disabilities: A developmental lag. *Journal of Experimental Child Psychology,* 1976, **22**, 375–385.

Torgesen, J. K. The role of nonspecific factors in the task performance of learning disabled children: A theoretical assessment. *Journal of Learning Disabilities,* 1977, **10**, 33–40.

Vandevoort, L., Senf, G. M., & Benton, A. L. Development of audiovisual integration in normal and retarded readers. *Child Development,* 1972, **43**, 1260–1272.

Wadsworth, H. G. A motivational approach toward the remediation of learning disabled boys. *Exceptional Children,* 1971, **38**, 32.

Wagner, R. F., Guyer, B. P. Maintenance of discipline through increasing children's span of attending by means of a token economy. *Psychology in the Schools,* 1971, **8**, 285–289.

Walker, H. M., & Buckley, N. K. The use of positive reinforcement in conditioning attending behavior. *Journal of Applied Behavior Analysis,* 1968, **1**, 245–250.

Weiss, G., Minde, K. K., Werry, J. S., Douglas, V. I., & Nemeth, E. Studies on the hyperactive child VII: Five-year follow-up. *Archives of General Psychiatry,* 1971, **24**, 409–414.

Wells, K., Conners, C. K., Imber, L., & Delamater, A. M. An evaluation of stimulant medication and behavioral self-control procedures. Paper presented at the Twenty-fifth Annual Convention of the Southeastern Psychological Association, New Orleans, March, 1979.

Whalen, C. K., & Henker, B. Psychostimulants and children: A review and analysis. *Psychological Bulletin,* 1976, **83**, 1113–1130.

Williams, M., & Lahey, B. B. The functional independence of response latency and accuracy: Implications for the concept of conceptual tempo. *Journal of Abnormal Child Psychology,* 1977, **5**, 371–378.

Willis, J. W., Morris, B., & Crowder, J. A remedial reading technique for disabled readers that employs students as behavioral engineers. *Psychology in the Schools,* 1972, **9**, 67–70.

Winett, R. A., & Winkler, R. C. Current behavior modification in the classroom: Be still, be quiet, be docile. *Journal of Applied Behavior Analysis,* 1972, **5**, 499–504.

Wolf, M. M., Giles, D. K., & Hall, R. V. Experiments with token reinforcements in a remedial classroom. *Behaviour Research and Therapy,* 1968, **6**, 51–64.

Woolraich, M., Drummond, T., Solomon, M. K., O'Brien, M. L., & Sivage, C. Effects of methylphenidate alone and in combination with behavior modification procedures on the behavior and academic performance of hyperactive children. *Journal of Abnormal Child Psychiatry,* 1978, **6**, 149–161.

Wulbert, M. & Dries, R. The relative efficacy of methylphenidate (Ritalin) and behavior modification techniques in the treatment of a hyperactive child. *Journal of Applied Behavior Analysis,* 1977, **10**, 21–32.

Zahn, T. P., Little, B. C., & Wynder, P. H. Minimal brain dysfunction, stimulant drugs and autonomic nervous system activity. *Archives of General Psychiatry,* 1975, **32**, 381–387.

Zelniker, T. & Oppenheimer, L. Effect of different training methods on perceptual learning in impulsive children. *Child Development,* 1976, **47**, 492–497.

CHAPTER 22

Mental Retardation

Bruce Wetherby and Alfred A. Baumeister

In the broadest sense, mental retardation is a culturally defined concept; it is a behavioral syndrome characterized by a lack of adaptive responding. A mentally retarded individual is thus said to be developmentally disabled in that important and, consequently, expected behaviors (e.g., dressing, eating, communication) are not performed. Because societies emphasize the survival of their particular cultures through the dissemination of group expectancies, those individuals who do not meet the basic set of qualifications for membership in society, and who have exhibited a lack of adaptive behavior from an early age, are often said to be mentally retarded.

A great deal of attention has been addressed in recent years toward new methods of diagnosis and treatment of mental retardation. Much of this interest has been spawned, in particular, by recent advances in the areas of behavior research and therapy. In this chapter, we review the role of behavior research and therapy in the treatment of retarded behavior. Our presentation is divided into five major sections. The first addresses more specifically the clinical diagnosis and definition of mental retardation, while the second section addresses the nature of the remediation perspective inherent in clinical behavior therapy. A third major section provides a model for effective research and therapy concerned with mental retardation. The fourth section provides a short review of two areas of current behavior therapy research concerned with mental retardation. Finally, in the last major section, we discuss the future of behavior research and therapy in mental retardation as it relates to developmental psychology.

THE DEFINITION AND DIAGNOSIS OF MENTAL RETARDATION

Although in a formal sense, mental retardation is usually construed in psychometric terms, in its broadest sense it is a cultural concept. That is, people who are identified as mentally retarded are those who fail to conform to certain cultural expectations for a particular age group. Although minor departures are usually tolerated within a cultural group, extreme deviation from expected patterns of behavior typically results in the assignment of diagnostic labels and the designation of the individual as exceptional. According to the definition advanced by the American Association on Mental Deficiency, three criteria are employed for making a diagnosis of mental retardation: (*a*) significantly subaverage intellectual functioning; (*b*) deficits in adaptive behavior; and (*c*) problems manifested before the 18th birthday (Grossman, 1977). This particular definition is widely used throughout this country and, in fact, has achieved, in many instances, official status.

The term "intellectual functioning" is defined by scores from a standardized measure of general intelligence, usually the Stanford-Binet or one of the Wechsler scales. "Subaverage" refers to a performance two or more standard deviations below the mean, that is, a score of around 70 or below.

The second major dimension involved in the definition concerns *adaptive behavior*—how effectively and to what extent an individual exhibits social responsibility and personal independence that is typical for his age peers and cultural group. During the periods of infancy and early childhood, adaptive behavior includes such attributes as sensorimotor function, communication, and self-help skills. During childhood and early adolescence emphasis is placed upon school-related behaviors, particularly academic skills. In late adolescence and adulthood the emphasis is shifted to vocational performance. In all cases, of course, stress is placed upon appropriate social responding.

The concept of adaptive behavior differs from that of general intelligence in a number of respects, and it is a rather nebulous concept that defies easy definition. In general, measurement has taken a largely pragmatic approach based upon a rational set of expectations about what is appropriate or inappropriate behavior in a given context. Over 100 different scales, more or less formally constructed, are recorded in the literature (Meyers, Nihira, & Zetlin, 1979). In addition, numerous others, mostly of a checklist variety, have been developed for local use in institutions. Probably the most widely used (and carefully constructed) scale is the Adaptive Behavior Scale developed under the auspices of the American Association on Mental Deficiency. Originally designed for use with institutional populations, a recent version of the scale has been developed for public school children. The Adaptive Behavior Scale consists of two parts, one measuring positive competencies and the other retarded behavior. In effect, it consists of abnormally low response rates in certain classes of behavior and excessive responding in others.

There are some significant distinctions between the constructs of adaptive behavior and intelligence. For one, adaptive behavior stresses current performance in skills required for meeting the daily exigencies of living; that is, coping skills. Adaptive behavior is a descriptive concept in this sense, rather than a measure of behavioral potential as the IQ is usually purported to be. The IQ is primarily predictive of academic performance, while adaptive behavior is much more varied and specific with respect to the behaviors that comprise adaptation to the environment. One might say that adaptive behavior is the more criterion-referenced measure.

A related consideration is that the IQ is a unitary or general conception of ability, while adaptive behavior measures reflect more specific and varied attributes. In fact, most measures of adaptive behavior yield scores in a variety of behavioral domains, rather than one overall score representative of performance.

The intelligence quotient is usually (but not always) thought of as a trait of the individual, while the various adaptive behavior measures usually (but not always) eschew any reference to competence, dispositions, capacity, or any other term that connotes a trait. Therefore, the two differ upon the relative importance of construct and concurrent validity. In a sense, most domains of adaptive behavior are defined beforehand as socially significant and require no further validation. This is not to say, however, that the concept of adaptive behavior cannot be viewed as an individual trait.

Another difference between intelligence, on the one hand, and adaptive behavior, on the other, involves the means by which they are obtained. Tests of individual intelligence typically require the active participation of the subject, whereas measures of adaptive behavior rely upon informants to provide information about the subject. There may be exceptions in both respects, however.

In addition, while general population norms are imperative to the interpretation of IQ scores, the norming procedure for adaptive behavior scales is usually much more limited, applying to a particular subgroup of individuals. Indeed, for some programmatic purposes normative data are not useful at all in that the individual's behavior provides its own frame of reference. In this sense, measures of adaptive behavior are of much greater value to the practitioner than IQs.

In summary the IQ and adaptive behavior are the two basic dimensions by which mental retardation is defined. On the other hand, the diagnostic implications are not quite as clear. Despite the requirement that individuals exhibit relatively poor performance in both dimensions, the fact is that most clinicians rely upon the IQ for inferring mental retardation (Adams, 1973). Moreover, the adaptive behavior scales, to the extent that they are psychological tests, possess shortcomings inherent in all psychometric procedures.

THE SPECIFICATION OF CONTROLLING
ENVIRONMENTAL EVENTS

The diagnosis and determination of the clinical syndrome of mental retardation ideally is followed by the prescription of appropriate treatment. For some forms of mental retardation known to be caused by biochemically determined factors (e.g., phenylketonuria (PKU)), treatment may require a change in dietary intake or the prescribed use of a particular chemical agent. Such relatively straightforward treatments, however, are rare. By far the most common prescribed treatment involves some form of behavior modification through teaching.

The behavioral component of a mental retardation treatment strategy is likely to be based upon the principles of behavior change proposed by Skinner (e.g., Skinner, 1938, 1953). The basic premise underlying this approach is that our behavior is under the control of the world around us. If we want to document how a child may be taught to speak, for example, we will need to isolate the events in the child's environment that appear to bring about a change in behavior. We might see that a child will imitate his mother's speech if the mother is careful to ensure that she congratulates her child everytime he produces an utterance, or that particular words may be removed from a linguistic repertoire if the child is told "no" everytime these words are uttered. In short, we see that behavior is often controlled by the environmental events that surround a young child.

The methodological perspective outlined by Skinner suggests that educational programs can be devised that will benefit each individual, no matter how seriously affected. Based upon this perspective, Lindsley (1964) provided an influential model for approaching the remediation of developmental disability. Basically, the model described by Lindsley specifies that there is more to the remediation of mental retardation than merely specifying behavioral deficiencies; an attempt must be made to determine the variables that functionally control the behavior in question. The model he provides can be thought of as an equation, of which the behavior in question is one variable. Figure 1 is a representation of this model.

When attempting to remediate the behavior of a mentally retarded individual, attention to each of the four components is required. First, as indicated by R, the nature of the response we desire must be specified. This is the terminal response. For instance, we may wish to decrease the probability of an undesirable behavior. Because we have chosen to focus our remediation attempt on this behavior, the undesirable response becomes the dependent variable in the behavior equation. This means that our attempts to change the frequency of undesirable behavior will occur as a function of manipulating one of the three variables shown in the equation.

One event that needs to be controlled by the therapist is the stimulus conditions that set the occasion for a response. These are indicated by S_D in the figure. For instance, specific discriminative stimuli (e.g., presence of the mother soon after eating) may appear to control the occurrence of a rumination response. Thus, in order to stop rumination, we may need to prevent the child's mother from interacting with the child immediately after the child has eaten. However, such a solution to the problem may not be appropriate or desirable, so the therapist may wish to establish a more desirable response (e.g., talking) when the mother is present. An advantage to teaching an alternative behavior is that this response may be incompatible with the one we wish to replace (i.e., they cannot occur at the same time). Consequently, should we decide to choose this latter treatment alternative, we shall also need to be aware of the specific conditions that control the occurrence of the vocalization response.

Making the mother a discriminative stimulus to control the vocalizations of a mentally retarded child does not ensure the rumination will decrease. We need to be aware of two other variables in the behavior equation that affect whether or not the presence of the mother will control vocalization and not rumination. The primary variable of the two, the consequent stimulus (S_C), is important because it provides us with the information as to whether the mother is making it desirable for the child to ruminate or vocalize. That is, by closely evaluating whether the

$$R = S_D + S_C + C$$

where R = the response
$=$ = is a function of
S_D = discriminative stimuli
S_C = consequent stimuli
C = stimulus-response relationships
(contingencies)

FIGURE 1.   The behavior equation. Adapted from Lindsley (1964). Reprinted with permission.

mother's attention, fondling, and so forth, occurs after rumination or after vocalization, the therapist can determine whether the mother's attention is contributing to the occurrence or nonoccurrence of either behavior. This information is useful for informing the mother whether she needs to stop attending to rumination, start attending to vocalization, or both.

But a child's environment (mother included) does not always consistently attend to certain behaviors. This is where a knowledge of the contingency portion (C) of the behavior equation may help one understand the conditions that control the frequency of any particular response. For instance, Ferster and Skinner (1966) have suggested how a behavior that is not attended to every time it occurs may actually remain in a child's repertoire longer than some other behavior that was previously attended to continuously. Such knowledge of stimulus-response relationships is useful for the therapist in explaining why our mentally retarded child continues to ruminate although we have not followed this behavior with a desirable event for a long time.

Together, knowledge of the four portions of the behavior equation serves to provide the behavior therapist with a tool for approaching and evaluating the functional variables that determine the behavior of a mentally retarded individual. If we can show that the frequency of a particular response varies as a function of the manipulation of one of the three variables shown in Figure 1, then we have demonstrated an understanding of what controls the behavior. Clinical behavior therapy is based upon the assumption that a manipulation of a child's environment may prove beneficial to the remediation of mental retardation.

THE CURRICULUM-PROCESS REMEDIATION MATRIX

The information contained in the operant learning paradigm developed by Skinner provides the behavior therapist/researcher interested in the remediation of retarded behavior with a means for evaluating specific intervention strategies once they have been instigated. As should be obvious, however, more is involved in the remediation of mental retardation than a knowledge of operant psychology. In a previous section (Definition and Diagnosis) we indicated that mental retardation is typically defined in terms of normative processes. Mental retardation can only be evaluated in regard to that which constitutes normal development. Normal development refers to the idealized sequence of performances and skills that humans will typically demonstrate at different chronological ages.

Information collected during assessment and diagnosis can be summarized into one or both of two classes of behaviors: (a) those that are absent from a child's adaptive repertoire and require establishment or *acceleration;* or (b) those that exist in a child's repertoire, are maladaptive, and require removal or *deceleration.* In other words, assessment and diagnosis is not just a simple matter of determining what a child does. The collection of this information also involves the making of assumptions about what the child's treatment program should involve. Basically, this means that a mentally retarded child should be taught to exhibit or approximate the behavior of a normal child. Thus, the very diagnosis of mental retardation carries with it an implied prescription for the content or *curriculum* of remediation.

But curriculum is not the only component of an effective remediation program for mental retardation. Corresponding to the need to either increase or decrease a particular behavior of a retarded child is the need to specify the behavioral techniques that are most likely to result in the change of behavior desired. Although these techniques can all be evaluated in terms of their effectiveness with the behavioral equation developed by Lindsley (1964), they too can be broken down into one of two types: (*a*) techniques that result in acceleration of behavior; or (*b*) deceleration of behavior. Together, the techniques developed to either increase or decrease behavior can be said to represent the manner or *process* of a remediation program.

The dual acceleration-deceleration considerations for the curriculum and process components of a behavioral remediation program for mental retardation can be combined into the model shown in Figure 2. This model specifies that the identification of mental retardation will automatically dictate the remediation techniques that one should consider for the program intervention. Thus, if deceleration of a particular behavior is called for, behavioral techniques that have been effective in decelerating the same or similar behavior should be reviewed for potential adoption. Subsequently, with the adoption of these techniques for their specified purpose, we may say that we have provided a therapeutic intervention (i.e., we have aligned curriculum needs directly with those instructional techniques that have proven to be most effective with similar problems). Note, however, that a therapeutic program for mental retardation may involve both acceleration and deceleration components. This simply means that at least two different behavioral performances were selected for remediation during the assessment and diagnosis portion of the child's treatment program.

The curriculum-process remediation matrix may be used to organize intervention strategies for mentally retarded individuals. The matrix provides a two-step procedure for approaching behavior therapy. The first step recognizes the importance of assessment and diagnosis in mental retardation, and acknowledges the concept that diagnosis must carry with it prescriptions for behavior change. This prescription involves increasing and/or decreasing the frequencies of particular behavioral performances. A second step in the curriculum-process model for behavior therapy makes the assumption that behavioral techniques exist for the accelera-

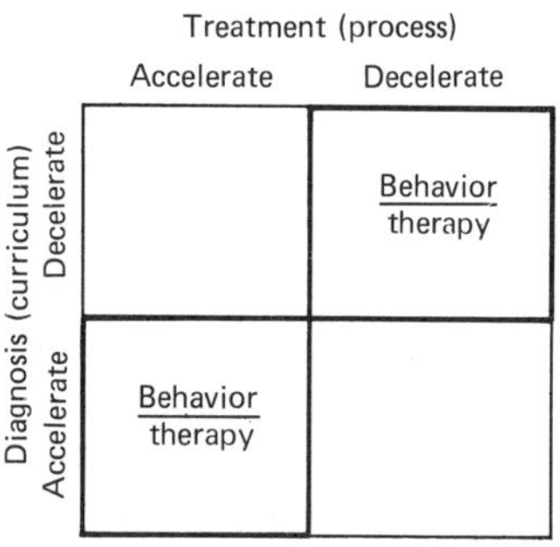

FIGURE 2. The curriculum-process remediation matrix. Remediation of developmental disabilities is accomplished by (*a*) diagnosis of the nature of the behavior pathology and (*b*) application of appropriate treatment procedures.

tion and deceleration of behavior, and that these procedures may be adopted for the programming needs specified by the curriculum. When the technology matches the specifications of the curriculum, a behavioral intervention has occurred. Together, the interaction between curriculum needs and the utilization of process variables for therapeutic change specify a universal approach to the remediation of mental retardation.

The curriculum-process remediation matrix can also be used to approach a short review of remediation techniques that have proven useful for accelerating and decelerating the behavior of mentally retarded people. As implied by the model provided in Figure 2, the development of curriculum and behavior change technologies occurs as a function of an interactive process between the two components. Thus we find that recent research has provided the field of mental retardation with better assessment tools and behavior change technologies. If these two psychologies in mental retardation did not develop in relation to one another, then it would mean that they were not a part of the same solution. It is as if better assessment techniques are developed as a function of our increased ability to remediate behavioral differences, and as if more refined behavior change technologies evolve as our ability to detect behavioral differences becomes more sophisticated. The remediation of mental retardation is an interactive and evolutionary science.

What follows is a short listing of some of the procedures that have been used by behavior therapists to remediate various aspects of the clinical manifestation of mental retardation. Realize, however, that all of the behavior change technologies identified below were either adopted for use from previous behavior research and/or therapy or developed in response to previously unsuccessful attempts at remediation. There is no guarantee that any of the treatment processes described below would work with similar problems. The effectiveness (and thus validity) of each remediation technology is left solely to the individual therapist.

Increase Behavior

A primary feature of mental retardation is the absence or low frequency of appropriate behavior. Consequently, a major focus of behavior therapy with the mentally retarded is to establish or accelerate the frequency with which certain behaviors are emitted. How are these behaviors organized or grouped? Unfortunately, there is no systematic method for the development of a behavioral curriculum with the mentally retarded. The primary strategy is simply to compare how mentally retarded people behave in relation to normally developing individuals. Thus to the degree that the behaviors of normal people can be organized into types or classes of behavior, we can specify behavioral deficiencies in the mentally retarded.

Watson (1977) has specified five basic behavioral areas that may be scheduled for acceleration in the mentally retarded. These include (*a*) self-help, (*b*) motor, (*c*) language, (*d*) academic and, (*e*) social-recreational skills. Of course, other curriculum divisions may be made, but the point is that there are many ways in which behavior can be classified.

A primary assumption of the behavior therapist is that the behavior is performed because it is ultimately adaptive; that is, behavior is followed by an event or outcome that serves to maintain it. Given in this perspective, any "undesirable" behavior that is emitted by an individual is undesirable to someone other than the person exhibiting it. Thus procedures designed to increase the behavior of a mentally retarded individual have been adopted by the therapist for the purpose of providing the client with behaviors the therapist thinks will be more adaptive in the future.

The primary concept that underlies the strategies of behavior therapists is that of *reinforcement*. In general, this concept specifies that a change in the environment of a mentally retarded individual contingent upon the demonstration of a desired behavior may result in an increased probability that the behavior will be exhibited again in the future. The word "may" should be stressed in that there is no guarantee that a specific event following a behavior will ensure that the rate or probability of this response will increase in the future.

Two methods for increasing the rate of desired behavior with reinforcement procedures are *positive* and *negative* reinforcement. With positive reinforcement, an increase in the frequency of a behavior is sought through the presentation of events that the therapist has reason to believe will be desired by the client. For example, access to television may be presented as a consequence for appropriate verbal behavior, while nonappropriate verbalizations would result in no such "positive" consequence. Thus if it was shown that presentation of a specific event results in a behavior increase, the therapist may assume that this event served as a positive reinforcer for the subject. If no such differential responding occurs, the therapist should conclude that the contingent environmental event was not a positive reinforcer and seek another positively reinforcing event.

A second, although less frequently emphasized, mechanism used to increase desired behavior involves the application of negative reinforcement. In this procedure, which is often confused with the presentation of a negative stimulus or punishment, removal of a hypothesized negative event is made contingent upon the occurrence of a desirable behavior. Because removal of an undesired event is thought to be a positive outcome, such procedures may be used to establish desirable behavior in the mentally retarded. Because of ethical considerations involved in subjecting an individual to an undesirable event for the purpose of ultimately removing it, and because positive reinforcement procedures are more desirable, extensive application of negative reinforcement procedures is not recommended.

The use of reinforcement procedures to increase the rate of desired behavior is a primary tool of the behavior therapist interested in the remediation of mental retardation. For a particular behavior to be desirable it must be contextually appropriate. That is, various events or stimuli in the environment of a retarded individual are said to control or set the occasion for a response. If desirable behavior is truly appropriate, then it is emitted when specific stimuli are present and is not emitted when these stimuli are absent. For example, it would generally be inappropriate for a retarded individual to talk when there is no other individual present.

One way to gain control over appropriate behavior is to reinforce this behavior differentially in the presence of a particular stimulus. In this way, a specific discriminative stimulus may gain *stimulus control* over the production of a desirable response. The use of such a teaching strategy, however, may not be the most effective method for the establishment of appropriate responding. Frequently called a trial-and-error teaching strategy, differential reinforcement is often not sufficient to teach desirable behavior to retarded people. In this case, the use of one of three procedures to establish stimulus control may be warranted.

In *stimulus shaping,* the teacher establishes control over responding by initially teaching a subject to discriminate a very obvious stimulus and by modifying the configuration of the stimulus over time so that a "new" form of this configuration controls the response. In *stimulus fading,* an obvious stimulus that is paired with the target discriminative stimulus is gradually removed over time so that the client's behavior is eventually controlled by the target stimulus. In a final transfer of stimulus control procedure, the *time-delay procedure,* control over desirable responding is shifted to the target stimulus by gradually increasing the length of time between presentation of the target stimulus and the stimulus currently controlling responding. Together, all three procedures for establishing stimulus control provide an effective technology for the establishment of appropriate behavior.

An additional means to control the occurrence of appropriate behavior in the mentally retarded is simply to change the frequency with which reinforcement may be obtained. Although the frequency with which reinforcement can be obtained may vary as a function of time and/or the number of responses a subject exhibits, the basic point is that desired rates of responding may be established by modifying the nature of the reinforcement schedule. As a general statement, partial reinforcement schedules produce more durable responding than a continuous schedule.

Decrease Behavior

A secondary feature of mental retardation, one that often interferes with the therapists' efforts to increase appropriate responding, is the individual's inappropriate behavior. Although it is clear that mental retardation is defined primarily in terms of behavioral impoverishment, the fact also remains that many of these individuals behave excessively in a variety of maladaptive ways. Thus common problems among retarded individuals include the presence of stereotyped mannerisms, self-injurious behaviors, and aggressive responding. Indeed, in many cases maladaptive responding dominates the behavior repertoire to the extent that any type of programming directed at increasing rates of positive responding must often involve suppression of high rate aberrant behavior. This is not to say that the two goals of behavior control—increasing one class and decreasing another—are programmatically incompatible, but it does suggest that priorities often dictate greater emphasis in one domain than in the other.

Many of the behavioral methods used for decelerating responding are similar to those employed for increasing response rates. At the very least, the essential principles of behavior management are the same—that behavior is under the control of identified stimuli, both antecedent and consequent, and the strategy for altering response strength lies in the manipulation of the contingent relationships between stimuli and responses.

A variety of methods are available for decelerating undesirable responses that are atypically high in strength. Although, in practice, the actual application of these procedures usually consists of "packages" or combinations of treatments, it is possible to classify these methods into fairly distinctive categories based upon their major defining features.

One method that, in principle, should be highly useful to the practitioner is that of extinction; that is, permitting the behavior to occur in the absence of a reinforcing stimulus. While there are an abundance of laboratory data showing that, in fact, response deceleration does occur under conditions of nonreinforcement, in practice this procedure is difficult to apply for two reasons: (*a*) it is usually not possible to specify the reinforcing stimulus; and (*b*) the behavior is free to occur, a condition that may be intolerable in many situations. With respect to the former situation, we should make a distinction between initiating and maintaining conditions. That is, a response may become part of the repertoire through a rather straightforward learning mechanism. This is not to say that all aberrant behavior is the product of learning, but over a long history a response may be practiced in such a variety of stimulus contexts that considerable generalization has occurred; consequently, many cues, through continuity, may become capable of maintaining high-response rates over a long period of time. In fact, there is some evidence that some secondary reinforcing stimuli may effectively displace the original reinforcing stimulus. If that is the case, then in any particular situation it may be difficult to specify the controlling stimulus. In our own work with two self-injurious subjects, for example, we have been unable to identify a critical reinforcing stimulus, although we carefully observed the subjects for hundreds of hours over a two-year period.

The second point noted above concerning extinction procedures is rather self-evident. Considering the nature of many aberrant behaviors, it would be inadvisable to allow responding to occur, either because the behavior is disruptive or because of the possibility of immediate harm to the individual. In a rather vivid demonstration of this effect, Lovaas and Simmons (1969) were successful in extinguishing self-injurious behaviors of two of their subjects, but only after thousands of responses had occurred.

Another disadvantage of the extinction paradigm is that response rates often actually accelerate initially when a subject is placed in a nonreward situation. That is, assuming that we can identify the reinforcing stimulus, and, further, that it can be effectively withdrawn (another assumption that is not always tenable), the subject may exhibit increased responding either in terms of rate or amplitude or both. Clearly, that can be an undesirable outcome.

Finally, we should note that if some response strength remains, and if the reinforcement contingency is put back into place (as is often the case with naturally occurring events), then in effect we have inadvertently created a schedule of reinforcement that will sustain behavior over even longer periods of time. In terms of a conventional conditioning paradigm, we may have created the well-known partial reinforcement effect.

The extinction procedure is essentially passive in nature and, within most practical contexts, is governed more by hope than by certain knowledge of the contingencies. Although it is certainly a treatment approach that ought to be considered by the practitioner, for most practical purposes it is ineffective. More direct measures are usually called for, particularly when the undesirable behavior has bad consequences.

A primary method of direct treatment for inappropriate behaviors has involved the principle of aversive conditioning. In this paradigm, undesirable behavior exhibited by a retarded indiviual is subject to either the presentation of a potentially undesirable event or the withdrawal from a previously reinforcing event. Respectively, these procedures have been labeled *punishment* and *time-out from reinforcement*. In both cases, however, the expected behavioral outcome is that a client will cease the undesirable behavior. If such an outcome is not obtained, then the therapist has not determined a functional punishment event or removed the subject from an event that was reinforcing.

The more direct approach is that of punishment; that is, contingent application of a stimulus that (*a*) either decreases response rate of the target behavior, or (*b*) increases rates of behaviors that terminate the stimulus. There is an enormous experimental literature on punishment that provides some useful guidelines for the practitioner. In general, we may say that punishment is an effective means for decelerating response rates in certain cases. Nevertheless, by itself simple punishment of a response is not likely to bring about generalized and durable response suppression.

There are basically two kinds of stimuli the practitioner can use in a punishment situation: (*a*) those that are already available in the environment, and (*b*) the application of new punishing stimuli. It is the latter class (e.g., electric shock) that has been the more frequently used, particularly for controlling highly undesirable behavior.

As we mentioned earlier, two of the problems regarding punishment concern the extent to which generalization is achieved and the durability of the suppression effects. Notwithstanding, that punishment is sometimes reported to be a good method for controlling deviant behavior, there is considerable question as to the overall effectiveness of punishment per se. Even profoundly retarded subjects are capable of forming some very keen discriminations as to when the punishment contingency is in effect. Thus subjects will discriminate "safe" from "unsafe" conditions on the basis of location, people, time, and the device itself (Baumeister, 1978). These considerations do not necessarily mean that punishment will be ineffective as a method of behavior control, but we do suggest that it is important to take into account these problems and to design intervention strategies accordingly. For example, if the procedure is to apply electric shock contingently upon a self-inflicted head pound, one should attempt to program the behavior out immediately and completely. It is not uncommon for practitioners to begin with a very mild stimulus and then "escalate" the intensity over training trials. While such a procedure is understandable, in the long run it is probably better to begin training with a relatively strong stimulus.

We should point out, as well, that it is often the case that punishment suppresses behavior generally, not just the target response for which the punishment was delivered. Avoidance behavior is, often, in fact, the most adaptive response available to the subject in the face of a punishment contingency. The principal goal of any behavior modification strategy should be to increase rather than to suppress behavior variability. These considerations suggest that a punishment treatment strategy should be accompanied by procedures designed to teach a subject how to behave appropriately in a given context. That is, punishment tells the individual what not to do. We should, at the same time, provide the individual with another way of behaving.

In a general sense, another method for decreasing inappropriate behavior is merely to prevent an opportunity for such behavior to occur. Specifically, in this case, a desirable behavior that is not currently in the subject's repertoire is chosen to be established with proper acceleration techniques. Such a strategy is based upon the assumption that the establishment of a new behavior in an individual's repertoire will either "replace" an undesirable behavior or make the production of inappropriate behavior "conflict" with the production of appropriate behavior. A subject can only exhibit a finite set of behaviors in any situation; therefore, the establishment of appropriate behavior in addition to what the subject already may possess perhaps might have the effect of "crowding out" an inappropriate behavior. Thus it is for this reason, instead of using a direct intervention upon the inappropriate behavior, that many behavior therapists have recommended that treatment be directed toward the establishment of behaviors that can be reinforced. Although punishment can be very effective for the deceleration of particular behaviors, there is no guarantee that the individual will not substitute other undesirable behaviors.

Overall, therapeutic attention directed at the decrease of specific behaviors appears to be a primary activity of those interested in the remediation of mental retardation. The decision-making process as to whether aversive conditioning (e.g., punishment) should be provided for undesirable behaviors or whether a more indirect approach (e.g., the establishment of competing behaviors) should be incorporated has yet to be completely satisfied.

EXAMPLES OF CURRENT BEHAVIOR RESEARCH AND THERAPY CONCERNED WITH THE REMEDIATION OF MENTAL RETARDATION

The various behavior change methods covered in the previous section were reviewed in an attempt to draw a general picture of the various procedures that have been used to modify the behavior of mentally retarded people. Although the review of these procedures was gleaned from a large body of experimental and therapeutic research with the retarded, no attempt was made to address the wide range of specific behaviors that have been successfully modified with these techniques. A primary rationale for not providing such a breakdown is based upon the conceptualization that mental retardation represents such a wide range of behavioral deficits that to simply list them all would be a nearly impossible task.

But what are the criteria that dictate the successful remediation of mental retardation? This question is essentially unanswerable, as all people have and will continue to differ from one another. What is significant about this question, however, is the perspective it places upon those concerned with the remediation of mental retardation; new behavior change technologies will be required to replace the old as new behavioral deficits and definitions of mental retardation are introduced into the literature. This orientation suggests that mental retardation is a relative phenomenon, and that behavior therapists must keep abreast of new conceptualizations of human behavior and the technologies responsible for their development. Two areas that have received recent attention for their importance to mental retardation are (*a*) the establishment of generalized language, and (*b*) the removal of undesirable behavior. We are going to review some current research and conceptualization in these areas in order to illustrate the need to build upon previous behavior change technologies for increasing and/or decreasing behaviors exhibited by the mentally retarded.

The Establishment of Generalized Language

Although the need to identify and remediate language and communication skills in the mentally retarded has been documented for a long time (e.g., Spradlin, 1963), recent theoretical perspectives have raised the issue that many conceptualizations of the structure of language are too narrow in their focus (e.g., Harris, 1975). Basically, this position has stated that language is a complex system of behavior that is characterized by the ability of the language user to either respond to or produce a large number of linguistic utterances that have not been directly taught. The implication of this conceptualization is that language is a repertoire of behavior that is characterized by a large degree of *generalization* or the ability to respond appropriately in "new" or "novel" linguistic environments.

Such a conceptualization of language specifies that methods of training to establish, in retarded individuals, language and communication skills that are not reflective of the "generalizable" nature of language are inappropriate training models, regardless of their effectiveness in establishing the targeted behavior. Thus, in recent years, experimental research concerned with the establishment of language skills in the mentally retarded has begun to focus upon ways in which generalized responding may be obtained. This trend is exemplified in recent research concerned with establishing emergent or untrained language and conceptual skills in the retarded.

A review of the literature reveals the identification of at least four processes that may be responsible for the development of generalized language and conceptual skills. Although others (e.g., Baer & Stokes, 1977; Stokes & Baer, 1977) have not used a similar terminology in their reviews of basic techniques for establishing generalized behavior, their analysis is consistent with the current formulation. The reader is referred to these works and others (e.g., Wehman, Abramson, & Norman, 1977) for additional perspectives in the area of establishing generalized behavior.

A first mechanism that is responsible for generalization, or the occurrence of an untrained and appropriate response in a situation where no other response existed previously, is the notion of *stimulus generalization*. Basically, this concept, which was utilized by Guess, Keogh, and Sailor (1978) in their analysis of generalization mechanisms in language, refers to the notion that a trained response will occur to new or novel stimuli that are in some way *similar to* the stimulus that originally controlled this response. Thus, generalization is defined by the nature of the stimuli

that are present in an organism's environment; a generalized response will not occur to stimuli that are not similar to the original discriminative stimulus. The basic
paradigm is shown in Figure 3.

An example of stimulus generalization is the situation in which a child who was
previously taught to provide the word "ball" to a round object is now able to provide this same response to other balls of a similar size. The child is behaving in a
manner that would suggest that he/she cannot discriminate the difference between
the original ball and subsequent ones. Nevertheless, such a response pattern is an
adaptive one; the child is able to provide an appropriate response in a novel environment without the necessity of being formally trained to do so.

Traditionally, stimulus generalization has been a passive concept; that is, generalized response is said to occur simply because the organism has a tendency to
respond to stimuli that exhibit similar characteristics. Unfortunately, this conceptualization of stimulus generalization has resulted in a passive orientation by many
behavior therapists; generalization is thought to occur by itself, automatically;
moreover, there is nothing that the therapist can do to facilitate this process. Stokes
and Baer (1977) have called this the "train and hope" method of establishing a
generalized response. They have also suggested that it is an inappropriate orientation to take when addressing the problem of generalization.

A primary strategy to assume, when attempting to take advantage of the process
of stimulus generalization and program the occurrence of a generalized response,
is to ensure that the stimulus situations assessed for the occurrence of a novel response are sufficiently similar to the situation in which the original response was
trained. This principle dictates, for example, that if we wish to establish the use of
language in a child's natural environment, that this training should either occur in
the natural environment or under "simulated" conditions that attempt to capture
as many of the salient characteristics of the natural environment as possible. In
this way, the therapist becomes an environmental engineer who attempts to arrange
for the occurrence of generalization by making environments as similar as possible.

However, the establishment of homogeneous environments is not always the ultimate desire of most behavior therapists. It is obvious that we must be able to respond appropriately in a number of novel environmental situations, and that adaptive behavior reflects the ability of the organism to provide appropriate responses

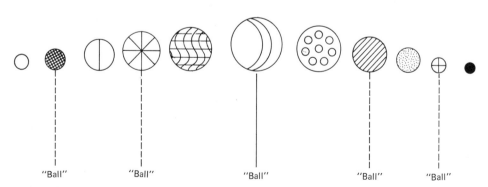

FIGURE 3. A *stimulus generalization* analysis of generalized responding.

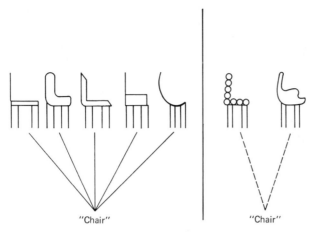

FIGURE 4.   An *abstraction* analysis of generalized responding.

in a changing environment. In this case, a behavioral process called *abstraction* may be responsible for the occurrence of generalization. This paradigm is shown in Figure 4.

Abstraction refers to the ability of an organism to pinpoint invariant characteristics of divergent environmental situations and to respond in a consistent fashion across these situations. In this manner, it is similar to stimulus generalization because similarity plays a role in the determination of a particular response; but, abstraction differs from stimulus generalization in that an active discrimination of the discriminative stimulus from other stimuli in the environment is required. Thus the concept of abstraction acknowledges the diversity of environments while attempting to specify the conditions that control appropriate responding.

Although the process of abstraction was studied by Hull (1920) and Smoke (1932) many years ago, a more current example of abstraction as a behavioral process was suggested by Skinner (1957). He provided a hypothetical analysis of how a child may come to emit the productive label, *chair*. At first, the child is confronted with the requirement to label appropriate instances of the chair concept. All manner of complex stimulus objects can be enumerated in the child's environment. For example, there are big objects, small objects, colored objects, covered objects, and so forth. Which are to be labeled a chair, and what is the criterion for the production of this response? Obviously, an answer to this question comes from experience. The child learns that all objects that have certain features (e.g., an upright back on four legs) are to be labeled as a chair, while other stimulus characteristics (e.g., color, size, texture, etc.) are irrelevant to the correct identification of this object.

The same analysis holds true for the establishment of concepts in mentally retarded people. To program the occurrence of a particular response across divergent environments (i.e., environments that possess many different stimuli), the behavior therapist must be willing to attempt to establish specific environmental cues as discriminative stimuli for the response in question. This is done by specifically requesting the organism to discriminate the conditions calling for a particular response from among a wide range of potential stimuli in the environment. For example, to establish a concept such as *animal,* a number of exemplars must be provided before a subject can determine the stimulus features responsible for the identification of animal. The Becker, Engelmann, and Thomas (1975) concept training program provides an example of such a teaching strategy.

A third generalization mechanism, and one that can be illustrated by recent research investigating the parameters of generalized receptive language in the mentally retarded, is the concept of *rule induction.* In short, this notion specifies, unlike the previous stimulus generalization and abstraction concepts, that language cannot be simply characterized as a unitary event governed by simple discrimination and generalization mechanisms. Rather, a concept of rule induction specifies that language is composed of a relationship between a series of discriminative stimuli, each of which controls the occurrence of a particular response that may be classified as belonging to a specific type or class of response events. These discriminative stimuli may be combined in a "novel" fashion to control the occurrence of generalized behavior.

The discovery of rule induction as a generalization mechanism has occurred because of increased attention by behavioral researchers toward the factors that control the development of speech and language. Wetherby (1978) has argued that rule induction or "combinative" generalization is the conceptual basis of all successful attempts to teach generalized language to adults, children, mentally retarded people, and animals. Wetherby and Striefel (1978) have suggested that this has been especially true in the area of teaching receptive language to retarded people. A short synopsis of this area in this latter research should serve to illustrate the clinical use of the concept of rule induction for establishing generalized responding.

Citing the need to establish generalized receptive language skills in the retarded, Whitman, Zakaras, and Chardos (1971) suggested that such a strategy may be based upon previous motor imitation research indicating that "untrained" imitations of modeled behavior could be taught by teaching mentally retarded children to imitate a sufficient number of imitative behaviors (e.g., Baer & Sherman, 1964; Baer, Peterson, & Sherman, 1967). This research demonstrated that if a number of imitative behaviors were taught mentally retarded individuals with shaping and reinforcement techniques, these people would soon begin to imitate models of behavior that were never trained or reinforced by the experimenter. Consequently, these findings suggested to Whitman et al. that perhaps all they needed to do to establish generalized instruction-following behavior in the mentally retarded was to teach their subjects to follow a sufficient number of instructions.

Whitman et al. proceeded by teaching two severely retarded adolescents to respond to approximately a dozen instructions. For the most part, these instructions did not have any common components; that is, verbs and nouns, for example, were not recombined with other verbs and nouns. Nevertheless, Whitman et al. found that the subjects behaved like normal children who were taught to imitate—they provided correct responses to untrained exemplars. This finding suggested that generalized instruction following and imitation could be conceptualized as being similar behaviors, and that teaching mentally retarded subjects generalized behavioral repertoires could be accomplished by teaching a sufficient number of exemplars. Only a potential artifact, involving differential motivation across conditions, prevented the authors from concluding that procedures similar to those used for establishing imitation skills should be incorporated for teaching receptive language.

Whitman et al. (1971) reported that because they did not evaluate their subjects' instruction-following skills directly, but instead used reports from the teachers that indicated that the subjects were not currently following instructions, the possibility existed that the subjects already knew the generalization instructions and that the use of reward for compliance to the training instructions simply informed the subjects that these skills were now being reinforced. Consequently, the subjects began to provide correct responses to the generalization items under conditions of reinforcement because their previous environment (including the assessment) did not maintain instruction-following behavior.

A study by Striefel and Wetherby (1973) demonstrated that this motivational interpretation was true when they systematically replicated the Whitman, et al. (1971) experiment without the motivational confound. Whereas Whitman, et al. asked teachers for an evaluation of each subject's instruction-following competence, Striefel and Wetherby directly assessed this skill by requesting each subject to follow the instructions and by reinforcing any correct response they may have exhibited. This procedure ensured that the subjects provided what they knew at all times. Unlike the Whitman et al. (1971) results, however, Striefel and Wetherby (and subsequently, Striefel, Bryan, & Aikins, 1974) found no generalization to new combinations of instructions. Striefel and Wetherby (1973) concluded that a critical variable in language training was probably the manner with which one taught receptive language skills and not the number of instructions that were taught.

This hypothesis was tested and shown to be reasonable by Striefel, Wetherby, and Karlan (1976). Using what has come to be called a matrix training procedure (Wetherby & Striefel, 1978), they taught generalized instruction-following skills to severely retarded adolescents with the training paradigm shown in Figure 5. In short, instead of teaching instructions in a haphazard fashion, the training strategy

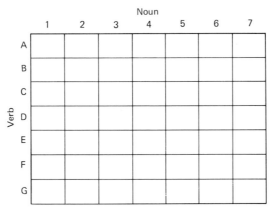

FIGURE 5.   A *rule induction* analysis of generalized responding.

shown in the figure taught the subjects that verbs and nouns were presented in a specified sequence, and that individual constituents from one class could be combined with all constituents from the second class. The subjects were presented with the task of learning a linguistic system that could be said to contain a simple rule for the recombination of constituents.

Results of the Striefel, Wetherby, and Karlan (1976) experiment, in contrast to the results of Striefel and Wetherby (1973), indicated that the mentally retarded subjects learned to behave as though they were aware of the linguistic combination rule; both subjects were able to respond to a large percentage of the instructions without having to be directly taught. These findings indicated to Striefel et al. (1976) that language training procedures incorporating the overlap of linguistic constituents were more effective for establishing generalized responding. Striefel, Wetherby, and Karlan (1978) have since expanded the parameters of their basic training strategy, while Wetherby (1978) and Wetherby and Striefel (1978) have attempted to draw the basic implications of this line of research for those interested in the experimental analysis of language development and language remediation.

A final generalization process, and one that may eventually be shown to be related to rule induction, is the concept of *stimulus equivalence*. Basically, this concept refers to the development of untrained stimulus-response relationships as a function of the prior establishment of a systematic relationship with a second response. The significance of this concept is that it may help to pinpoint the nature and organization of conceptual development. The fundamental paradigm is shown in Figure 6.

If two stimuli are taught to control the occurrence of a common response, and one of these stimuli is subsequently taught to control the occurrence of a second response, there will be a tendency for the second stimulus to control the production of the second response without any direct training. Descriptive evidence for this concept has been shown in the work of Sidman (1971), Sidman and Cresson (1973), Spradlin et al. (1973) and Van Biervliet (1977).

In an attempt to teach printed word-picture reading to a severely retarded adolescent, Sidman (1971) incorporated the training strategy shown in Figure 7. After initial testing, it was determined, for example, that the subject could respond to the spoken word "cat" by selecting the picture of the cat, but that remaining auditory-visual or visual-visual performances could not be performed by the subject. This included the eventual target response, pointing to the picture of cat when presented with the word *cat*. With differential reinforcement, Sidman was successful in teaching the subject to select the printed word when presented with the printed word, and point to the printed word when the auditory label was presented. This sequence of training, however, also resulted in the sudden occurrence of printed word-picture reading without any direct training, leading Sidman to con-

$$
\begin{array}{c}
A - C \\
B - C \\
\underline{A - D} \\
B - D
\end{array}
$$

FIGURE 6.   A *stimulus equivalence* analysis of generalized responding.

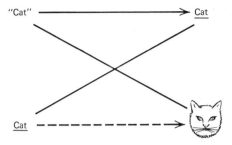

FIGURE 7.   Use of the stimulus equivalence concept by Sidman (1971) to teach an elementary reading skill.

clude that systematic training procedures incorporating basic stimulus class concepts may be useful for establishing generalized behavior in the mentally retarded.

Although pointing the way to an experimental analysis of generalized behavior, the work of Sidman (1971) has yet to have its full impact. Only recently have we seen published reports addressing the applied significance of this work. For example, Van Biervliet (1977) demonstrated how a concept of stimulus equivalence could be used to establish sign-object, sign-word production, spoken word-object selection, and object-word production skills in the mentally retarded. Future research should serve to determine the range of untrained performances that may be established with a concept of stimulus equivalence, while other areas of research may strive to make a connection between this generalization process and that represented by rule induction.

In summary, four concepts currently exist that may be fruitful for an understanding of how to establish generalized language and conceptual skills in the retarded. These represent the concepts of stimulus generalization, abstraction, rule induction, and stimulus equivalence. Although experimental research has yet to identify all of its parameters of these concepts, attention to these notions should serve to specify the nature of educational programs interested in the establishment of generalized behavior in the mentally retarded.

The Removal of Undesirable Behaviors

High-rate aberrant behavior such as stereotypy and self-injurious behavior pose serious problems of adaptation for many retarded and/or autistic children. A large variety of intervention strategies have been designed to bring these kinds of behaviors under control. These methods have covered a wide range of variables, from brain ablation to massages. Those methods that seem to produce the best effects fall within the rubric of behavior modification; that is, applications of principles derived from operant psychology. The volume of research literature dealing with modification of aberrant responding has increased enormously over the past decade. As a result, the practitioner has available a fairly substantial array of treatment methods, the major ones of which we have already identified. Johnson and Baumeister (1978) in their review of the treatment of self-injurious behavior found over 20 different methods described in the literature.

Nevertheless, questions remain about the efficacy of these various treatment methods, notwithstanding that positive results have been reported with all of them. At the most general level, we may assume a bias in the literature, in which favorable outcomes are more likely to be reported than negative ones. Of course, this is a problem that confronts all research reporting, but it is one that may be particularly acute with respect to the treatment of deviant behavior. The fact is that an investigator is unlikely to report failures, particularly using a method that someone else has shown to work. As great as such a reluctance is on the part of the investigator, it is even greater among editors for whom negative results are typically regarded as anathema. There are, of course, all manner of reasons for obtaining negative results. Nevertheless, we can be fairly sure that benefits claimed for any particular method are probably exaggerated.

Moreover, an examination of the technical qualities of the research that has been reported in this area should not be a source of jubilation on the part of the practitioner. Of course, it is much easier to criticize than it is to do good research, particularly when the behaviors under consideration are so individually unique. Nevertheless, our enthusiasm for behavior modification methods should be tempered by an appreciation of the procedural shortcomings that are painfully evident in much of the relevant research.

Most of the research studies in this area are of the single subject, case study variety. One can hardly dispute the power of the single subject experiment, when it is properly conducted. The problem, in this case, is that the target behaviors and the circumstances that control them are typically highly idiosyncratic. Thus, measurement and intervention strategies must inevitably be tailored to fit the behavior, producing a lack of standardization that makes application in any new instance problematical. Although the same method may obstensibly be employed from one study to the next, a close examination of the actual procedures reported reveals that significant discrepancies usually exist. In short, the problem of generalization of a particular treatment method across individuals has not really been dealt with adequately. There are, of course, some notable exceptions.

The typical study involves obtaining baseline measures on some target behavior, say body rocking, in some particular context, and then imposing some sort of treatment, usually involving a manipulation of consequences. The context in which the treatment is carried out is usually quite restricted, often to a laboratory situation. Baselines obtained in such a context may be quite unrepresentative of the naturally occurring ebb and flow of the behavior. This produces a different type of problem concerning generalization—across situations and time. In Figure 8 observational data are presented for two stereotyping (body rocking and hand waving) children for several sessions within a variety of different school settings. Three facts are immediately clear: (a) setting makes an enormous difference with respect to the expression of stereotyped movements; (b) there is marked variability across sessions even within the same setting; and (c) the two children display different patterns of responding. These data illustrate the importance of multiple baseline designs in intervention studies, a consideration that has been largely ignored.

Another type of control in the single subject design that is considered important for establishing the nature of cause and effect is the reversal condition. That is, subsequent to baseline a treatment is then imposed, effects observed, treatment

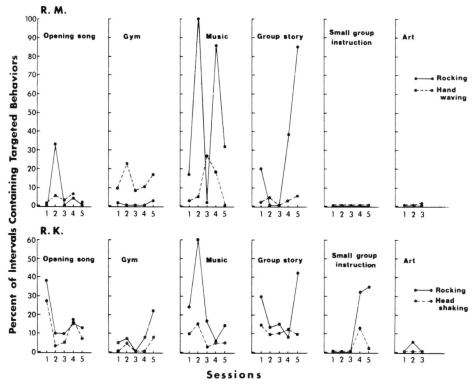

FIGURE 8.   Frequencies of stereotyped movements across settings and over time.

withdrawn, and so on. The logic behind this design is eminently simple: if in a succession of reversal rates of behavior there is systematic change as a function of the treatment, then one can be fairly certain that it is the treatment and not some extraneous factor that is exerting control over the behavior. Unfortunately, this design strategy has not been universally employed in studies of aberrant responding. This omission is perhaps understandable in view of the practical and ethical constraints that often exist in applied research. If one has succeeded, for whatever reason, in bringing down the rate of some aberrant behavior, particularly one that is harmful to the subject, it simply may be unwise to permit the behavior to reoccur. Nevertheless, this reluctance to employ the reversal strategy, no matter how highly motivated, leaves us with an ambiguous situation as to inferring about the relative effectiveness of various types of interventions.

Another problem is that the interventions themselves are usually complicated packages of treatments involving a number of distinct components, the separate effects of which are difficult to disentangle. This problem, too, has a very practical origin in that the therapist, in an effort to deal with a serious behavior problem, may simultaneously employ a number of different treatments under the well-founded assumption that the greater the diversity of events the greater the likelihood that something will work. Nevertheless, when response suppression occurs it is frequently the case that one cannot attribute the effect to any specific manipulation. We may conclude that component analysis has been generally neglected, although lately there have been some encouraging attempts to conduct more refined experiments.

A less understandable flaw in this literature has to do with the lack of attention to matters that are under the control of the researcher. For example, it is not uncommon to find that the subjects and their target behaviors are inadequately described. This can be a serious deficiency for the practitioner who, in sorting through the various intervention strategies that have been reported, is seeking to find the one most suitable for his own client(s). Other problems include failure to specify why and under what conditions the subject was assigned to a treatment, confounding of treatments with alternations in other aspects of the environment (e.g., staff ratios), failure to test for generalization effects, lack of follow-up, inadequate description of procedures. For instance, in their review of the literature on self-injurious behavior, Johnson and Baumeister (1978) found that fully one-half of the research reports contained no mention whatsoever of interobserver reliability measurements.

Another more complicated problem is that researchers have generally neglected to consider the effects of suppression of one response upon rates of other responses. Only recently have researchers begun to pay systematic attention to the problem of collateral behaviors or "side effects" as they are sometimes called. Earlier reports of collateral behaviors were primarily of an anecdotal nature and tended to accentuate their positive characteristics. Thus, for example, several workers have reported increased sociability, eye contact, and cooperativeness concomitant with suppression of aberrant responding. However, more recently reports have been made of increased maladaptive behaviors that accompany efforts to modify inappropriate responding (e.g., Doke & Epstein, 1976). In some cases the collateral behavior may be as severe or worse than the target. For instance, Rollings, Baumeister, and Baumeister (1977) were successful in suppressing body rocking by a retarded subject, but at the same time they observed increases in rates of head nodding and self-slapping. We venture the generalization that decreases in the rate of one behavior are always accompanied by increases in the rates of other behaviors. Because in any situation there are more ways to behave inappropriately than appropriately and because the adaptive response repertoire of many retarded individuals is so severely restricted, we can expect these individuals to exhibit other forms of maladaptive behavior. This is not to say that efforts to modify aberrant behavior should not be undertaken, but rather to indicate the advisability to be alert to the possibility of collateral responding and the importance of multiple baseline data collection.

The most pervasive problem of all concerns the generalization of suppression effects across situations and time. Perhaps the most discouraging aspect of behavior modification technology is that we have yet to devise methods to ensure that both the positive and negative response rate changes that have been taught achieve generality, that is, are under appropriate and durable stimulus control in all contexts. The literature is replete with demonstrations of successful response suppression; but it is hard to find studies that show successful transfer of stimulus control to new situations and over time.

This is not to say that we do not have the theory and the empirical knowledge that would tell us how to accomplish such generalization of training. But, for whatever reasons, the practical application of this knowledge has not been accomplished to any meaningful extent.

We do fairly well in behavior modification when we can control the major sources of stimulation that impinge upon a subject. That is why, of course, behavior control achieved in a laboratory is usually more complete than control achieved in more naturalistic contexts. To the extent that the behavior modifier loses control of discriminative and reinforcing stimuli, his ability to affect response rates diminishes.

Even if we are successful in teaching an individual an appropriate form of behavior to replace an undesirable one, we can be fairly certain that once the new contingencies are lifted and the individual is returned to old contingencies, the aberrant behavior will reappear. Indeed, most behavior modification techniques involve the structuring of new contingencies upon old ones, apparently on the assumption that the new ones will overpower or replace the old ones. Thus, for instance, a child who head bangs may be exposed to contingent electrical shock. Supposedly the shock is more powerful as a negative consequence than the naturally occurring positive consequences (e.g., social reinforcement) that are maintaining the behavior. Quite obviously, this strategy has an artificiality to it that fails to take into account the events in the ecology of the environment that set the conditions for and maintain the behavior. Once the artificial contingencies are removed and nothing is done to alter the basic ecology, then it should not be surprising to find that the suppression effects are not maintained.

An alternative is to focus attention on naturally occurring controlling stimuli. If we can understand the conditions that support the expression of a behavior, we may be in a better position to intervene by manipulation of the discriminative cues that set the occasion for the behavior. That is, if these relationships can be isolated, quantified, and manipulated, it may be possible to bring aberrant behaviors under control of naturally occurring contingencies.

In order to accomplish this goal, however, another type of methodology is required, one that goes well beyond conventional description. That is, we must be concerned with the order or sequence in which behaviors occur in relation to events in the environment. The assumption is that behaviors do not happen randomly and that there is an identifiable recurring pattern of events representing a "stream" of behavior.

One alternative approach is to be found in the lag sequential analysis (Bakeman, 1978). In brief, this method is designed to answer the question: given that behavior "X" has occurred, what events will follow in a sequence at different points (lags)? A list of behavior categories is devised that captures the interactive and transactive nature of events surrounding the behavior in question. Sequences are generated by using each behavior category as the beginning of the sequence, thereby determining the probability of occurrence of each of the other events or behaviors following the criterion. The lag sequential analysis model is thus a method for determining whether sequences of behaviors and contingencies among behaviors occur more frequently or less frequently than would be expected on the basis of chance.

A system such as this has been utilized by Patterson in a series of studies (1973,

1974, 1976, 1977a, 1977b) designed to identify those events that control aggressive behavior of children. Patterson employs an observation system that allows him to identify complex sequences of social interactions. Conditional probabilities (if X then Y) that correspond to components within these sequences are calculated. These conditional probabilities, then, suggest the most meaningful points of intervention. In one experiment, Patterson altered the discriminative and maintaining stimuli for certain aggressive acts with the result that the children decreased their rates of aggressive responding. Similar studies involving the lag sequential analysis have been conducted with retarded children who exhibit stereotyped movements (Baumeister, MacLean, Kelley & Kasari, in press) and retarded adults who injure themselves (Johnson, 1979).

The attractiveness of this system lies in its potential for quantitatively specifying both the antecedent and consequent natural events that control rate of responding. Given this information the teacher or practitioner has a better understanding of the natural contingencies and, thus, a better chance of producing durable behavior change.

This observational methodology has only recently been used in applied contexts, although its basic elements have been used for years in the naturalistic study of animal behavior. For the practitioner, the method, as powerful as it may potentially be, does have a number of significant limitations: (a) a fairly extensive coding system must be devised that incorporates the key variables; (b) observational time is considerable; and (c) the analysis although not conceptually complicated may involve so much data that without a computer, the analysis could not be accomplished. It is fair to characterize this approach as "experimental" in that for most school and institutional settings its application is impractical.

Nevertheless, there is one main principle inherent in the observational approach that should be taken seriously by the practitioner. It is that careful consideration of the events surrounding the behavior may offer clues for intervention that may be more meaningful than the precipitous imposition of artificial contingencies, as is typical in most behavior change methodologies.

FUTURE DIMENSIONS OF BEHAVIOR RESEARCH AND THERAPY IN MENTAL RETARDATION

The current chapter represents an attempt to outline the defining characteristics of mental retardation and to sketch some of the basic behavior change processes that have been isolated by psychologists working with this population. Information from both of these areas was forwarded as being useful during the design of educational and remedial programs for the mentally retarded. We have not found it possible to specify clinical techniques for the total range of behavioral involvement exhibited by this population. Rather, general guidelines for diagnosis and treatment as well as a more in-depth look at two areas of current research concerned with the functional remediation of mental retardation have been outlined. For a more detailed analysis of some of these issues, the reader is referred to recent edited work by Bialer and Sternlicht (1977) and Meyers (1978).

A fundamental theme has been that the ontogenesis and treatment of mental retardation as a behavior pathology can often be specified by environmental factors. In particular, work derived from operant psychology has primarily been reviewed to exemplify the type of behavior change questions that must be asked if society can begin to effectively remediate the behavioral manifestations of mental retardation. Although some have suggested that operant psychology, or behavior modification, is only a part of the equation to solve mental retardation, a more concrete and futuristic discussion of this clinical perspective is warranted.

Mental retardation is a developmental disability; that is, those who are retarded do not develop in the same manner as nonretarded individuals. This developmental disability is diagnosed primarily as a function of behavioral deficiencies exhibited by the individual who is suspected to be mentally retarded. Most often, the cause of mental retardation is simply left to be a matter of speculation.

Generally, depending upon the theoretical background of the individual therapist or researcher, the cause of mental retardation is said to occur either inside or outside the individual. For example, we may specify that either biochemical deficiencies determined by a missing gene or environmental deficiencies determined by an unresponsive society may be at fault. To speculate as to the location of the cause of mental retardation, however, does not ensure that means can be derived to treat the syndrome.

The opportunity to treat mental retardation is provided to medical and psychological science by society, in the hope that the specific variables that contribute to mental retardation can be specified. It is only through the *manipulation* of variables that may be responsible for mental retardation that society can be sure it will find a treatment for mental retardation. Thus, it is only under the pretext of remediation that society will accept and condone the manipulative efforts of the genetic counselor, drug-prescribing physician, and behavior therapist as being erstwhile endeavors.

The fact that many educational attempts at remediation based upon learning principles may not seem adequate to remediate all behavioral deficiencies associated with mental retardation should not be a source of discouragement for therapists. Behavior therapy is a terminology devised to refer to a general attempt to specify the variables that are responsible for the development (and thus remediation) of mental retardation. There is no guarantee that previously successful treatment procedures will work with different problems. Other than criticism, what is needed in the case where a previously successful treatment procedure fails should be the understanding that an area for future research has been stumbled upon. The innovative therapist is one who takes advantage of such a situation by providing research documentation concerning the effectiveness of an experimental treatment procedure. In this regard, the innovative therapist is a basic researcher—someone who questions the viability of traditional distinctions between basic and applied science.

Because many of the basic behavior change processes documented in the current manuscript have been reviewed elsewhere (e.g., Baumeister & Forehand, 1973; Baumeister & Rollings, 1976; Forehand & Baumeister, 1977; Spradlin, Karlan, & Wetherby, 1976), a more in-depth discussion of recent research representing both the acceleration and deceleration areas of the curriculum-process remediation matrix was emphasized. These areas were represented by interests in the removal of stereotyped behavior and the establishment of generalized language. Basically, researchers and practitioners in these areas have determined two general findings. First, as documented, new behavioral treatment procedures and/or processes of behavior change can be specified for the treatment of mental retardation. Second, the nature of these techniques appear to differ as a function of changes in the behaviors we select to study. Specifically, what this later finding suggests is that the curriculum and process portions of the remediation matrix cannot be separated. If we are looking at new problems, we must be prepared to seek new solutions. In this sense, the nature of behavior therapy in mental retardation changes over time, and responsive therapists either keep up with new findings or seek new solutions by themselves.

One issue that will probably remain with the behavior therapist interested in the remediation of mental retardation is concerned with the ethics of developing a behavior change technology. The basic issue that behavior therapists must currently address is the concern forwarded about treatment side effects. The issue is a difficult one. On the one hand, if innovative treatment methodologies are to be devised, the freedom to explore potential developmental variables is necessary. On the other hand, however, if the experimental remediation of mental retardation results in an exacerbated condition, one may question the degree of freedom that should be allowed the therapist. The effective therapist should be sensitive to this issue.

A second issue that will surround future behavior therapy research concerned with mental retardation is the question of how new diagnostic procedures and behavior change methodologies become a part of the clinical field. If the researcher/therapist is concerned with potential side effects, how can manipulations be performed to gain new treatment information? An answer to this question is contained in the relationship mental retardation diagnosis and therapy should hold with the field of developmental psychology.

Developmental psychology is concerned with specifying the variables responsible for the growth of an organism. To be effective practitioners, therapists in the area of mental retardation should attempt to keep abreast of current developmental research documenting the variables responsible for behavior change. There are two reasons for doing so. First, knowledge of normal development will always be useful for specifying delayed or abnormal development; and second, behavior change information may come from many other sources. As an example of the latter, recent advances in teaching behavioral skills to chimpanzees, including language and communication skills (e.g., Savage-Rumbaugh, Rumbaugh, & Boysen, 1978), have been instrumental in designing communication programs for the profoundly retarded. In a related area, skills taught to normal children and adults (e.g., a second language) may also become effective intervention models for the behavior therapist concerned with mental retardation (Wetherby & Striefel, 1978). In summary, it is likely that many areas of developmental research may provide valuable insights into the variables that may be responsible for growth in mentally retarded persons. The behavior therapist concerned with the remediation of mental retardation should be aware of the significance of developmental research conducted with normally developing individuals and with other populations. It would appear prudent that scholarship activities in both areas be read and supported by their counterparts.

Overall, the current chapter has outlined some of the basic diagnostic and therapeutic concerns that should be addressed by those interested in the clinical remediation of mental retardation. The research and/or concepts reviewed in this chapter were chosen both for their historical contributions to mental retardation and for their potential future significance in understanding the developmental aspects of this syndrome. To facilitate the interaction between the diagnostic and behavior change factions of behavior therapy concerned with mental retardation, however, a curriculum-process remediation matrix was derived in an attempt to specify the fundamental conceptual questions that need to be addressed in the remediation of mental retardation. Attention to this model should serve to crystalize effective therapeutic interventions for mentally retarded people.

A final section addressed the future status of behavior therapy in the area of mental retardation and suggested means for ensuring the continued refinement of the therapeutic activity in this area. A primary focus of this attention was to draw a picture of the conceptual similarities between behavior therapy and developmental psychology. It was suggested that behavior therapists in mental retardation may be able to derive effective treatment procedures from the developmental psychology literature without the potential risk associated with experimentation upon the clinical population. Thus, attention to the relationship that the field of mental retardation holds with developmental psychology should ultimately serve the best interests of the mentally retarded individual.

ACKNOWLEDGMENT

Preparation of this chapter was supported by P.H.S. Grant HD00973 awarded to the John F. Kennedy Center for Research on Education and Human Development, George Peabody College for Teachers of Vanderbilt University, Nashville, Tennessee, 37203. The authors would like to thank Ms. Judy Hanna for her valuable and friendly assistance.

REFERENCES

Adams, J. Adaptive behavior and measured intelligence in the classification of mental retardation. *American Journal of Mental Defic ency,* 1973, **78,** 77–81.

Baer, D. M., Peterson, R. F., & Sherman, J. A. The development of imitation by reinforcing behavioral similarity to a model. *Journal of the Experimental Analysis of Behavior,* 1967, **10,** 405–416.

Baer, D. M., & Sherman, J. A. Reinforcement control of generalized imitation in young children. *Journal of Experimental Child Psychology,* 1964, **1,** 37–49.

Baer, D. M., & Stokes, T. F. Discriminating a generalization technology: Recommendations for research in mental retardation. In P. Mittler (Ed.), *Research to practice in mental retardation, Vol. II: Education and training.* Baltimore: University Park Press, 1977.

Bakeman, R. Untangling streams of behavior: Sequential analyses of observation data. In G. P. Sackett (Ed.), *Observing behavior, Vol. II: Data collection and analysis methods.* Baltimore: University Park Press, 1978.

Baumeister, A. A. Origins and control of stereotyped movements. In C. E. Meyers (Ed.), *Quality of life in severely and profoundly retarded people: Research foundations for improvement. Monographs of the American Association on Mental Deficiency,* 1978, **3**, 353–384.

Baumeister, A. A., & Forehand, R. Stereotyped behaviors. In N. R. Ellis (Ed.), *International review of research in mental retardation.* Vol. II. New York: Academic Press, 1973. Pp. 55–96.

Baumeister, A. A., & MacLean, W. E., Jr. Brain damage and mental retardation. In N. R. Ellis (Ed.), *Handbook of mental deficiency: Psychological theory and research.* Hillsdale, New Jersey: Lawrence Erlbaum Associates, 1979. Pp. 197–230.

Baumeister, A. A., MacLean, W. E., Kelley, J., & Kasari, C. Observational studies of retarded children with multiple stereotyped movements. *Journal of Abnormal Child Psychology,* in press.

Baumeister, A. A., & Rollings, J. P. Self-injurious behaviors. In N. R. Ellis (Ed.), *International review of research in mental retardation.* Vol. 8. New York: Academic Press, 1976. Pp. 223–278.

Becker, W. C., Engelmann, S., & Thomas, D. R. *Teaching 2: Cognitive learning and instruction.* Chicago: Science Research Associates, 1975.

Bialer, I., & Sternlicht, M. *The psychology of mental retardation: Issues and approaches.* New York: Psychological Dimensions, 1977.

Doke, L. A., & Epstein, L. H. Oral overcorrection: Side effects and extended applications. *Journal of Experimental Child Psychology,* 1975, **20**, 496–511.

Ferster, C. B., & Skinner, B. F. *Schedules of reinforcement.* Englewood Cliffs, N.J.: Prentice-Hall, 1957.

Forehand, R., & Baumeister, A. A. Deceleration of behaviors with mentally retarded individuals. In M. Hersen (Ed.), *Progress in behavior modification.* Vol. 2. New York: Academic Press, 1976. Pp. 223–278.

Guess, D., Keogh, W., & Sailor, W. Generalization of speech and language behavior. In R. L. Schiefelbusch (Ed.), *Bases of language intervention.* Baltimore: University Park Press, 1978.

Grossan, H. J. (Ed.), *Manual on terminology and classification in mental retardation.* Washington, D. C.: American Association on Mental Deficiency, 1977.

Harris, S. L. Teaching language to nonverbal children—with emphasis on problems of generalization. *Psychological Bulletin,* 1975, **82**, 565–580.

Hull, C. L. Quantitative aspects of the evolution of concepts: An experimental study. *Psychological Monographs,* 1920, **28** (No. 123).

Johnson, W. L. Maladaptive and other behaviors of two profoundly retarded, institutionalized women and related staff and peer interactions. Unpublished masters thesis, George Peabody College for Teachers, 1979.

Johnson, W. L., & Baumeister, A. A. Self-injurious behavior: A review and analysis of methodological details of published studies. *Behavior Modification,* 1978, **2**, 465–487.

Lindsley, O. R. Direct measurement and prosthesis of retarded behavior. *Journal of Education,* 1964, **147**, 62–81.

Lovaas, O. I., & Simmons, J. Q. Manipulation of self-destruction in three retarded children. *Journal of Applied Behavior Analysis,* 1969, **2**, 143–157.

Meyers, C. E. Quality of life in severely and profoundly retarded people: Research foundation for improvement. *Monographs of the American Association on Mental Deficiency,* 1978, No. 3.

Meyers, E. C., Nihira, K., & Zetlin, A. The measurement of adaptive behavior. In N. R. Ellis (Ed.), *Handbook of mental deficiency: Psychological theory and research.* Hillsdale, New Jersey: Lawrence Erlbaum Associates, 1979.

Patterson, G. R. Changes in states of family members as controlling stimuli: A basis for describing treatment process. In L. A. Hamerlynck, L. C. Handy, & E. J. Mash, (Eds.), *Behavior change: Methodology, concepts, and practice.* Champaign, Ill.: Research Press, 1973.

Patterson, G. R. A basis for identifying stimuli which control behaviors in natural settings. *Child Development,* 1974, **45,** 900–911.

Patterson, G. R. The aggressive child: Victim and architect of a coercive system. In L. A. Hammerlynck, E. J. Mash, & L. C. Handy (Eds.), *Behavior modification and families. I. Theory and research. II. Applications and developments.* New York: Brunner/Mazel, 1976.

Patterson, G. R. Naturalistic observation in clinical assessment. *Journal of Abnormal Child Psychology,* 1977, **5,** 309–322. (a)

Patterson, G. R. Accelerating stimuli for two classes of coercive behaviors. *Journal of Abnormal Child Psychology,* 1977, **5,** 335–350. (b)

Rollings, J. P., Baumeister, A. A., & Baumeister, A. A. The use of overcorrection procedures to eliminate the stereotyped behaviors of retarded individuals: An analysis of collateral behaviors and generalization of suppressive effects. *Behavior Modification,* 1977, **1,** 29–46.

Savage-Rumbaugh, E. S., Rumbaugh, D. M., & Boysen, S. Symbolic communication between two chimpanzees. *Science,* 1978, **201,** 641–644.

Sidman, M. Reading and auditory-visual equivalences. *Journal of Speech and Hearing Research,* 1971, **14,** 5–17.

Sidman, M., & Cresson, O. Reading and cross modal transfer of stimulus equivalences in severe retardation. *American Journal of Mental Deficiency,* 1973, **77,** 515–523.

Skinner, B. F. *The behavior of organisms.* New York: Appleton-Century-Crofts, 1938.

Skinner, B. F. *Science and human behavior.* New York: Macmillan, 1953.

Skinner, B. F. *Verbal behavior.* New York: Appleton-Century-Crofts, 1957.

Smoke, K. L. An objective study of concept formation. *Psychological Monographs,* 1932, **42** (No. 191).

Spradlin, J. E. Assessment of speech and language of retarded children: The Parsons language sample. In R. L. Schiefelbusch (Ed.), *Language studies of mentally retarded children. Journal of Speech and Hearing Disorders.* Monograph Supplement No. 10, 1963.

Spradlin, J. E., Cotter, V. W., & Baxley, N. Establishing a conditional discrimination without direct training: A study of transfer with retarded adolescents. *American Journal of Mental Deficiency,* 1973, **77,** 556–566.

Spradlin, J. E., Karlan, J. E., & Wetherby, B. Behavior analysis, behavior modification, and developmental disabilities. In L. L. Lloyd (Ed.), *Communication assessment and intervention strategies.* Baltimore: University Park Press, 1976.

Stokes, T. F., & Baer, D. M. An implicit technology of generalization. *Journal of Applied Behavior Analysis,* 1977, **10,** 349–367.

Striefel, S., Bryan, K. S., & Aikins, D. A. Transfer of stimulus control from motor to verbal stimuli. *Journal of Applied Behavior Analysis,* 1974, **71,** 123–135.

Striefel, S., & Wetherby, B. Instruction-following behavior of a retarded child and its controlling stimuli. *Journal of Applied Behavior Analysis,* 1973, **6**, 663–670.

Striefel, S., Wetherby, B., & Karlan, G. R. Establishing generalized verb-noun instruction-following skills in retarded children. *Journal of Experimental Child Psychology,* 1976, **22**, 247–260.

Striefel, S., Wetherby, B., & Karlan, G. R. Developing generalized instruction-following behavior in the severely retarded. In C. E. Meyer (Ed.), Quality of life in severely and profoundly retarded persons: Research foundation for improvement. *Monographs of the American Association on Mental Deficiency,* 1978, **3**, 267–326.

Van Biervliet, A. Establishing words and objects as functionally equivalent through manual sign training. *American Journal of Mental Deficiency,* 1977, **82**, 178–186.

Watson, L. S. Issues in behavior modification of the mentally retarded individual. In I. Bialer, & M. Sternlicht (Eds.), *The psychology of mental retardation: Issues and approaches.* New York: Psychological Dimensions, 1977.

Wehman, P., Abramson, M., & Norman, C. Transfer of training in behavior modification programs: An evaluative review. *Journal of Special Education,* 1977, **11**, 217–231.

Wetherby, B. Miniature languages and the functional analysis of verbal behavior. In R. L. Schiefelbusch (Ed.), *Bases of language intervention.* Baltimore: University Park Press, 1978.

Wetherby, B., & Striefel, S. Application of miniature linguistic system or matrix–training procedures. In R. L. Schiefelbusch (Ed.), *Language intervention strategies.* Baltimore: University Park Press, 1978.

Whitman, T. L., Zakaras, M., & Chardos, S. Effects of reinforcement and guidance procedures on instruction-following behavior of severely retarded children. *Journal of Applied Behavior Analysis,* 1971, **4**, 283–290.

CHAPTER 23

Sociopathy and Antisocial Behavior: Theory and Treatment

Patricia B. Sutker, Robert P. Archer, and Dean G. Kilpatrick

A number of therapeutic approaches have been undertaken to modify antisocial behaviors often associated with the diagnostic labels of sociopathy, psychopathy, or antisocial personality. It hardly seems necessary to enumerate the references that report or predict a pessimistic outcome in attempting to bring the behavior of deviant individuals into line with societal expectations. However, with increasing sophistication of therapeutic techniques extrapolated from learning theory and research, scientific investigators and traditionally oriented psychotherapists have looked to behavioral strategies for more effective management and control of antisocial expression, if not its prevention. In examining application of any mode of therapeutic intervention, it becomes necessary to describe and evaluate a complex interplay of critical variables, including personal characteristics of patients and therapists, methodology of therapeutic intervention, and conditions under which such are implemented. This chapter reviews the development of the concept of sociopathy, defines the behavioral and psychological characteristics of individuals so classified by clinical description and experimental findings, outlines the major hypotheses related to the origins of sociopathy, and discusses the application of behavioral and related treatment approaches to the description, modification, control, and prevention of antisocial expressions.

LABELING OF ANTISOCIAL BEHAVIOR

Observation and interpretation of antisocial behaviors often classified under the label of sociopathic or psychopathic personality have provoked interest and argument since the early nineteenth century. Clinical accounts described individuals who failed to conform to moral and ethical expectations and found themselves in open conflict with legal restraints. Lacking a symptom picture easily classified by psychotic or neurotic descriptors, antisocial behavior was explained by references to evil spirits, moral defects, intellectual ignorance, or other maladies, as indicated by well-known reviews of the history of the concept of psychopathy (Cleckley, 1971; Maughs, 1961; McCord & McCord, 1964; Ullmann & Krasner, 1969; Whiteley, 1975). Briefly summarized, the concept was earliest defined in 1801 when Pinel identified a disorder, *mania sans delire,* which referred to a symptom constellation including undisturbed reasoning but damaged affective abilities and capacity for instinctual rage. Other descriptive precursors to the term sociopathy were "moral derangement," "moral insanity," and "psychopathic inferiority" (see Cleckley, 1971). Underlying many of these labels was the pervasive belief that antisocial behaviors resulted from organic or constitutional defect, possibly of genetic origin.

More recent attempts to label individuals characterized by persistent antisocial behavior are as diverse as early explanations. Confusion remains as to which among such terms as "psychopath," "sociopath," and "antisocial personality" is most appropriate. The majority of research and clinical articles are written about the psychopath; however, the label psychopathic personality has been officially discarded by the American Psychiatric Association (DSM-II, 1968; DSM-III, 1980) in favor of antisocial personality. With emphasis on the social and environmental forces hypothesized to shape and maintain behavior, the term sociopath has been used to describe many of the symptoms subsumed under the older and perhaps less productive rubric of psychopathy (Partridge, 1930). Recently, Vaillant (1975) discussed the concept of sociopathy as a human process and attempted to distinguish the sociopath from what he called that "incurable entity of psychopath." Others use such labels synonymously (Ullmann & Krasner, 1969). Although the designation sociopath is preferred for this chapter, terms appropriate to the writer cited, for example, sociopath, psychopath, or antisocial personality, are maintained with an understanding that in most cases they describe similar constellations of psychopathology.

Given the disparity of labels noted above, it might be asked if diagnoses describing sociopathic, psychopathic, or antisocial behavior represent anything more than a wastebasket category. However, Gray and Hutchison (1964) found that as many as 84% of 677 Canadian psychiatrists who responded to survey questionnaires viewed the diagnosis of psychopathic personality as a meaningful one. That its use remains popular is evident by data reported by Robins, Gentry, Munoz, and Marten (1977) who found antisocial personality to be the third most common diagnosis assigned to psychiatric emergency room patients, following affective disorder and alcoholism. Other clinicians have eschewed use of the term sociopathy and its synonyms because they are convinced that it hinders search for other kinds of symptomatology, especially among youth, and creates a situation in which patients may be denied treatment or offered that which is inadequate (Lewis & Balla, 1975; Rotenberg, 1975).

CLASSIFICATION OF ANTISOCIAL BEHAVIOR

Issues in Diagnosis

Differences of opinion exist regarding the extent to which the concept of sociopathy refers to a typology of symptoms and/or behaviors or a continuum of characteristics along which individuals may be represented. Most commonly, sociopathy has been conceptualized as a psychiatric symptom cluster of genetic and/or learned origins that is maladaptive in nature and manifested in inappropriate antisocial behaviors (Cleckley, 1971; Thorne, 1959; Vaillant, 1975). With few exceptions, definitions of sociopathy have been associated with samples of individuals who engage in blatantly antisocial behaviors, such as criminals (Hare, 1970, 1978; Schmauk, 1970; Widom, 1976a,b), institutionalized juvenile delinquents (Johns & Quay, 1962; Skrzypek, 1969; Stewart, 1972), and alcohol and opiate addicts (Astin, 1959; Hill, Haertzen, & Davis, 1962; Painting, 1961). Regardless of criteria used for classification, the literature supports considerable overlap among groups described in terms of dyssocial reaction and psychopathy (Robins, 1967), hysteria and sociopathy (Cloninger & Guze, 1970), alcoholism and sociopathy (Caster & Parsons, 1977; Tarter, McBride, Buonpane, & Schneider, 1977), drug use, sociopathy, and psychiatric illness (Westermeyer & Walzer, 1975), drug dependence and sociopathy (Sutker, 1971; Vaillant, 1975), and criminality, sociopathy, alcoholism, and drug addiction (Guze, Goodwin, & Crane, 1969).

From a different perspective, sociopathy has been viewed as represented by some behavioral or psychological characteristics which, though perhaps defined as socially aberrant, have adaptive value (Rotenberg, 1975; Smith, 1973). Sociopathy may also be described as a system of cognitive styles and/or psychological characteristics that are neither necessarily nor inevitably associated with blatant antisocial displays. For example, Widom (1977) identified a sample of psychopaths by newspaper advertisement who were more successful in avoiding the negative consequences of antisocial behaviors than their counterparts in prisons, drug abuse programs, or psychiatric hospitals. Extending this reasoning one step further, it should be possible by means of psychological criteria alone to identify yet even more "successful" sociopaths, that is, those who share assumed cognitive and psychological characteristics with a concomitant disposition to behavioral deviance but maintain their conduct within the bounds of sociolegal expectations. Description of these more adaptable sociopaths could well provide an important source for specification of motivational drives and appropriate reinforcers to initiate and maintain socially approved behaviors among those less successful.

Assumptions that sociopathy represents a unitary concept or describes a group of relatively homogeneous individuals have been seriously questioned. Eysenck and Eysenck (1978) argued that psychopathy, like other psychiatric diagnoses, is in no sense a category at all. They proposed that psychopathy, described in terms of hypothesized major and independent personality dimensions, be represented as a point in space around which concentric multidimensional spheres can be drawn. Among others, Lykken (1957), Karpman (1961), Hare (1970), and Widom (1976a) contended that at least two dimensions, those of neurotic symptomatology and antisocial behavior, must be separated so that psychopaths who are behaviorally or psychologically antisocial without complicating anxiety, guilt, depression, or other neurotic manifestation are identified. Spielberger, Kling, and O'Hagan (1978) also suggested that anxiety and sociopathy appear to be relatively independent constructs. A third dimension, that of a thinking disorder or subtle psychosis, has been suggested as important by Sutker, Moan, and Swanson (1972) who point to the necessity of identifying individuals who combine blatantly antisocial behavior and subtle schizophrenic thinking, which may be masked by seemingly appropriate reasoning processes and social skills. Although other distinctions are too numerous for elaboration, Arieti's (1967) differentiation of simple and complex types on the basis of intellectual sophistication deserves mention. Pointing to level of intelligence as an important determinant of manifestation of antisocial behavior, Arieti characterized the complex sociopath as one who, having average to superior intelligence, exhibits sufficient judgment to achieve self-determined goals while disregarding social morality.

In addition to problems in diagnosing an inadequately defined entity—limited populations from which subjects or patients have been identified and potential for classification overlap—considerable disagreement exists as to the most appropriate methods by which to define the range, frequency, and severity of antisocial behavior or psychological characteristics represented by this category. Hence, clinicians and researchers have assumed a variety of postures when defining sociopathic patients or subjects. Classification systems differ in the extent to which diagnosis is made dependent upon recording of observable behavior or family description of such, interpretation of deviant behavior as reflective of underlying psychiatric or psychological symptomatology, and inferences of psychological and behavioral potential from psychometric or psychophysiological data. The diversity of classification approaches is reviewed below with focus on clinical, behavioral checklist, and test instrument descriptions of sociopaths.

Clinical Descriptions

Despite concerns regarding the appropriateness and utility of diagnoses of sociopathy, there is surprising agreement in listing the characteristics of individuals so classified. In a content analysis of approximately 70 publications regarding the psychopathic personality, Albert, Brigante, and Chase (1959) found consensus about symptom patterns ascribed but striking disagreement as to possible etiologies and capacity for change. Clinicians agreed that psychopaths shared such features as inability to identify with others, absence of conflict, anxiety, guilt, or insecurity, inadequate superego functioning, low ego strength, and a host of behavioral deviations. Gray and Hutchison (1964) also found clinical agreement about such features as inability to profit from experience, early onset, irresponsibility, inability to form meaningful relationships, and lack of impulse control and moral sense. Thus, there appears to be a core constellation of characteristics inferred from behavioral manifestations that suggest a basis for classification.

In five editions of his book, *The Mask of Sanity* (see Cleckley, 1976), and several articles (e.g., 1971), Hervey Cleckley provided one of the most complete clinical descriptions of the psychopath. His concepts have been theoretically criticized, and experimental findings do not always support his claims. However, there is little question of the significance of his pioneering work in delineating behavioral and symptom patterns. Cleckley noted that psychopaths suffer from what he called "semantic dementia," or failure to react appropriately to words and phrases that elicit emotional responses in normals. He also described 16 distinguishing characteristics:

Superficial charm and good intelligence; absence of delusions and other signs of irrational thinking; absence of "nervousness" or other psychoneurotic manifestations;

unreliability; untruthfulness and insincerity; lack of remorse or shame; inadequately motivated antisocial behavior; poor judgment and failure to learn by experience; pathologic egocentricity and incapacity for love; general poverty in major affective reactions; specific loss of insight; unresponsiveness in general interpersonal relations; fantastic and uninviting behavior, with drink and sometimes without; suicide rarely carried out; sex life impersonal, trivial, and poorly integrated; and failure to follow any life plan [1976; pp. 337–338].

The 1968 American Psychiatric Association description of "personality disorder, antisocial personality" is strikingly similar and reads as follows:

This term is reserved for individuals who are basically unsocialized and whose behavior pattern brings them repeatedly into conflict with society. They are incapable of significant loyalty to individuals, groups, or social values. They are grossly selfish, callous, irresponsible, impulsive, and unable to feel guilt or to learn from experience and punishment. Frustration tolerance is low. They tend to blame others or offer plausible rationalization for their behavior [1968, p. 43].

Among others who described correlates of sociopathy is Thorne (1959) who viewed it as a life-style disorder in which initially normal persons are conditioned to depend upon unhealthy mechanisms for need gratification. In emphasizing such unhealthy defense mechanisms as acting out, Thorne's reasoning is similar to that of Vaillant (1975). In focusing on learning or conditioning etiologies, his theories resemble the hypotheses of Maher (1966). Despite affirmation of behavior reversibility, Thorne's view of the sociopath is almost as negative as that of Cleckley as he wrote:

The sociopath leaves a swath of disillusioned, hurt, and seriously damaged people in his wake . . . does not emerge unscathed from his irregularities. At heart, he knows what he is, and this causes an increasing burden of self-hate, however well disguised or repressed. In the beginning, the sociopath can escape from anxiety by simply leaving the site of failure and securing ego inflation from the spurious security of new sexual conquests. But gradually it becomes necessary to consume increasing amounts of alcohol or drugs to anesthetize anxiety . . . also the sociopath is getting older, less physically attractive, and outwardly ravaged by the wages of sin . . . gravitates socially downward until finally ending in the slums, broken financially, in and out of delirium tremens, shunted from prison to hospital, and finally expiring in the poor house or mental hospital [1959, p. 325].

On a more positive note, Vaillant (1975) reasoned that the Cleckley characterization of the psychopath represents a mythical beast. Using the histories of four narcotic addicts restricted to a controlled environment, he attempted to illustrate the underlying dynamics associated with sociopathy and thus the "humanness" and treatability of individuals so classified. Where sociopaths have been described by an apparent absence of anxiety and depression, he reasoned that they conceal negative affective states by such immature defenses as conversion symptoms, acting out, passive-aggressiveness, and projection. Rather than characterized by lack of motivation for change or inability to learn from experience, he described them as more adolescent than ineducable.

Behavioral and Checklist Descriptions

Eli Robins (1967) asserted that descriptions of antisocial reaction emphasizing such inferred qualities as inability to learn from experience, callousness, lack of responsibility, poor conscience, and pregenital fixation make the concept difficult to define. Robins argued that more precise analysis is required for definition of the syndrome such that reliably observable symptoms and behaviors are identified and used to select homogeneous groups of patients. Much has been done toward this end by L. N. Robins and O'Neil (see Robins, 1966) who specified childhood antisocial symptoms and behaviors for patients given the diagnosis of antisocial reaction as adults. Describing results of a 30-year follow-up study of 524 child guidance clinic patients and 100 controls, these investigators listed the following characteristics of antisocial children:

> Theft, incorrigibility, truancy, running away overnight, bad associates, staying out late, physical aggression, poor employment record, impulsivity, recklessness and irresponsibility, slovenly appearance, enuresis, lack of guilt, premarital sexual relations, pathological lying, homosexual activity [see E. Robins, 1967, p. 952].

Future diagnosis of antisocial reaction was related to number of childhood symptoms observed. Forty-three percent of adults with 10 or more childhood symptoms were ultimately labeled antisocial reaction, as opposed to 4% with less than three symptoms. Of the remaining antisocial children, 90% were psychiatrically ill at follow-up. Adulthood symptoms were also specified by L. N. Robins (1966) who listed 19 possible life areas that could provide evidence for diagnosis of psychopathy, including work or marital history, arrest record, excessive alcohol use, school problems, armed forces difficulties, use of drugs, and use of aliases. More recent summaries of this and related work are provided by L. N. Robins (1970, 1978).

Attempts to define the behavioral manifestations of sociopathy using global and checklist rating approaches, many of which derived from the observations of Cleckley, have been described in detail by Hare and Cox (1978). Quay and his collaborators (Peterson, Quay, & Cameron, 1959; Peterson, Quay, & Tiffany, 1961; Quay, 1964) developed the Behavior Problem Checklist based upon factor analytic studies to classify delinquent behavior into unsocialized-psychopathic, neurotic-disturbed, and socialized-subcultural types. Quay and Parsons (1970) also developed the Checklist for the Analysis of Life History Data, which distinguished among four delinquent groups: inadequate-immature, neurotic-disturbed, unsocialized-psychopathic, and socialized-delinquent. A number of research studies have used these approaches to define subject samples, particularly to contrast neurotic and psychopathic delinquents (Bryan & Kapche, 1967; Johns & Quay, 1962; Orris, 1969; Skrzypek, 1969; Stewart, 1972). Other behavior checklists have been devised by Craddick (1962), Jenkins (1964), and Ziskind (1978). Investigators have also used Cleckley or Robins classification criteria directly by rating potential subjects on specific dimensions (Hare, 1970, 1978; Lykken, 1957; Widom, 1977) or by combining behavioral ratings with psychometric techniques for group selection (Gendreau & Suboski, 1971; Steinberg & Schwartz, 1976; Widom, 1976a,b). Dinitz, Goldman, Allen, and Lindner (1973), however, criticized selection procedures that rely on subjective criteria, such as interpretations by raters or on psychiatric evaluations, as insufficient to isolate a homogeneous group of sociopaths. Nevertheless, correlations among checklist instruments have been reported to be relatively high, ranging from 0.51 to 0.88 (Ross & Hundleby, 1973).

Test Instrument Descriptions

Clinicians and researchers who routinely use self-report instruments for personality assessment have reasoned that the assumed cognitive and personality correlates of sociopathy should be logically represented on certain objective measures, such as Scales 4 and 9 of the MMPI, the Socialization Scale of the California Psychological Inventory (CPI), Hogan's (1969) measure of moral maturity, or the Empathy Scale, the Machiavellianism Scale (Mach V: Christie & Geis, 1969), Extraversion, Psychoticism, and Neuroticism dimensions of the Eysenck Personality Inventory (EPI: Eysenck & Eysenck, 1968, 1978), the Activity Preference Questionnaire (Lykken, Tellegen, & Katzenmeyer, 1973), the Sociopathy Scale (SPY: Spielberger et al., 1978), and the Personal Opinion Survey (Quay & Parsons, 1970). Others have argued that specific diagnostic clues can be observed in projective test protocols (Wagner, 1974). However, many studies have classified clinical or research subjects on the basis of multiple MMPI criteria, using scores on Scales 4 and 9 to identify sociopathy and Scales A or 7 to discriminate between primary and secondary categories. These and other approaches are based on assumptions that scores on specific scales are correlated with cognitive, emotional, and/or behavioral characteristics definitive of the sociopathic personality. Such assumptions have been questioned most recently by Hundleby and Ross (1977) who found no substantial agreement among "psychopathy" scales that could lead to a factor interpretation of the concept.

Gilberstadt and Duker (1965) acknowledged difficulty in equating spike 4 or 4–9 MMPI profile code types with diagnosis of sociopathy, but their definitions of the profile types are strikingly reminiscent of Cleckley's characterizations. The cardinal features of the spike 4 profile are stated as follows:

Irresponsible, immature, demanding, egocentric, impulsive. Childish, careless, restless, emotionally unstable. Babied by mothers. Divorce infrequent because patients elicit succorrant, motherly attitude of forbearance from wives but have severe marital conflict. Sexual maladjustment including perverse sexual behavior and acting-out. Become tense, moody, and depressed because of low frustration tolerance. Suicide attempts, aggressive outbursts toward wives, and alcoholism most frequent causes for admission [p. 58].

Similarly, Gilberstadt-Duker correlates of the 4–9 profile code type include immaturity, hostility, rebelliousness, impulsivity, low frustration tolerance, poor work and marital adjustment, and poor socialization of morals and standards with further elaboration by such adjectives as superficially friendly, outgoing, likable, self-centered, grandiose, haughty, moody, irritable, and unaffectionate to adults. According to Marks and Seeman (1963), most characteristic of the 4–9 profile type are verbal flippancy, impulsiveness, egocentricity, insecurity, need for attention, and self-indulgence; however, also descriptive are tendencies to act out and to be excitable, provocative, resentful of authority, and conflicted about emotional dependency.

Use of the MMPI for classification of sociopaths is certainly not uniformly rec-ommended (Hare, 1970), and psychopathic behavioral correlates have not always been associated with expected scale scores. Gynther, Altman, and Warbin (1973) found 4–9 code type psychiatric inpatients less maladjusted than patients in general with little support for a relationship between antisocial behaviors and 4–9/9–4 code types. Comparing hospitalized mental patient communications about them-selves and expected correlates of the Gilberstadt-Duker and Marks-Seeman code types, Payne and Wiggins (1972) found response homogeneity among patient types and high congruence between content of patient self-report and code-type de-scriptions. The one striking exception was produced by 4–9 patients who saw them-selves as less deviant than other groups and symptom-free in almost every area. There is also evidence to suggest that spike 4 or 4–9/9–4 scale elevations appear more frequently than expected in what are considered behaviorally nondeviant groups. Hawk and Peterson (1974) found that up to 23% of college students and 53% of helping professionals in a therapeutic collective, as opposed to 73% of delinquents, earned T-scores of 70 or greater on Scale 4. The extent to which such subgroups share common psychological characteristics and propensities for social deviance, with conventionally defined sociopaths, is yet to be specified.

The 4–9/9–4 or spike 4 profile has been found characteristically typical of groups of male and female narcotic addicts (Gilbert & Lombardi, 1967; Olson, 1964; Sutker, 1971; Sutker & Moan, 1972; Zuckerman, Sola, Masterson, & An-gelone, 1975), criminals (Megargee & Dorhout, 1977; Sutker & Moan, 1973), and alcoholics (Hill, Haertzen, & Davis, 1962; Kammeier, Hoffman, & Loper, 1973). However, the social deviance represented by Scale 4 has not always been found to be the primary component in alcoholic profile patterns (Overall, 1973). Other re-searchers have also identified typical code-type correlates for Scales 4 and 9, such as irritability and quick anger among psychiatric inpatients (Lewandowski & Gra-ham, 1972) and academic and legal difficulties for college students seeking psy-chological services (King & Kelley, 1977). Similarly, Hedlund (1977) found scores on Scale 4 positively related to hostile and angry outbursts, assaultive or homicidal thoughts, and depressive thoughts and feelings, and negatively related to blatant psychosis among psychiatric inpatients. In this study, Scale 4 correlates were significantly associated with Scales F, 8, and 9, suggesting the importance of differentiating between code types 4–9/9–4 and types in which high scores on Scales 4, 9, F, and 8 are combined. It might be speculated that individuals repre-sented by the latter are characterized by underlying schizophrenic patterns of think-ing masked by seemingly intact social skills or superficial sociopathy associated with elevations on Scale 4.

Eysenck and Eysenck (1978) suggested that primary or criminal psychopathy is related to high positive values on the independent personality dimensions of psy-choticism, extraversion, and neuroticism. Some research findings are in support of this notion (Sigal, Star, & Franks, 1958; Widom, 1977). Widom found noninsti-tutionalized psychopaths recruited by newspaper ads were characterized by a com-bination of high extraversion and neuroticism scores, as might be predicted for sec-ondary psychopaths. Evidence is also contradictory (Foulds, 1961), and Hughes and Johnson (1975) found no significant differences between neurotic and psycho-pathic psychiatric inpatients in extraversion-introversion scores. Psychopaths have also been compared with groups of controls on the Mach V Scale, purported to measure attitudes focusing on concepts of power, control, and manipulation, but no differences were found between psychopaths and other groups (Widom, 1977) or among groups of psychopathic subjects (Saruk, 1975). In contrast, there are indications that the Socialization and Empathy Scales are of more value in distinguishing psychopathic from nonpsychopathic groups (Widom, 1977).

Of some promise is the SPY Scale that was developed by Spielberger and his associates (1978) to identify persons with sociopathic tendencies who are impulsive, egocentric, repeatedly in conflict with the law, less inhibited by rules and customs of society, as well as virtually free of anxiety and other neurotic symptoms. These investigators conceived of sociopathy as a dimension reflecting individual differences in the disposition to exhibit antisocial attitudes and behaviors. They further reasoned that a comprehensive theory of sociopathy must account for differences in inclination to manifest antisocial and aggressive behavior and for the role of anxiety as a determinant of the behaviors of individuals so diagnosed. Preliminary work in construction of the SPY Scale from MMPI items yielded some success in measurement of individual differences in antisocial behavior tendencies. Inmates with high SPY scores, compared to low scorers, were characterized by stronger antisocial attitudes and values and manifested more behavioral characteristics typically associated with sociopathic personality disturbance. They were also less socialized and adjusted more poorly to prison life. Contrary to expectations, no relationship was found between SPY scores and responses to measures of anxiety and neuroticism, suggesting that tendencies to exhibit aggressive, antisocial behaviors are unrelated to level of trait anxiety and neurotic personality disturbance.

EXPLANATORY MODELS OF ANTISOCIAL BEHAVIOR

Learning theory or conditioning models accounting for sociopathic behavior can be contrasted with those that place more emphasis on genetic or constitutional factors. As emphasized by Cloninger, Reich, and Guze (1978), any plausible model of the pathogenesis of antisocial behavior must allow for genetic and environmental factors without making unwarranted assumptions about their relative importance. Over the past few years, there has been renewed interest in studying the biological bases of personality (Buss & Plomin, 1975; Dworkin, Burke, Maher, & Gottesman, 1976) and the hereditary transmission of personality and behavior disorders (Hill & Hill, 1973). The notion that sociopathy may be genetically transmitted has been discussed by Hare (1970) with reference to data on EEG slow wave activity and patterns of autonomic functioning.

Reviewing results of concordant studies, Eysenck and Eysenck (1978) concluded that 55% of monozygotic twins are concordant for criminal conduct as opposed to 13% of dizygotic twins. Studies of adopted children (Crowe, 1972, 1974; Hutchings, 1972; Schulsinger, 1972) also suggest that genetic factors are important in the etiology of sociopathy. For example, in a Danish investigation of 854 biological and adoptive relations of 57 psychopathic adoptees and 57 matched controls, Schulsinger reported a higher frequency of mental and sociopathic disorders in biological relatives of sociopathic probands than among their adoptive relatives or either group of control relatives. Sociopathy occurred more than five times as frequently among sociopathic proband biological fathers as among adoptive fathers or the biological fathers of controls, with an overall tendency to appear more frequently among male than female relatives. Winokur and his associates (1974, 1975) found male relatives were not necessarily so defined. Goodwin and his colleagues (1973, 1977) also suggested that genetic factors play a role in development of alcohol and psychiatric problems among men; whereas in women, environmental factors may assume greater importance. Finally, Crowe (1974) reported a higher rate of antisocial personality among probands born to female felons than to controls; however, antisocial probands also experienced unfavorable infancy conditions, indicating the importance of genetic-environmental interactions.

Assuming that the pathogenetic factors associated with antisocial behavior are multiple and additive, Cloninger et al. (1978) pointed to the value of a multifactorial explanatory model in which contributing factors constitute a continuous underlying and normally distributed variable, termed the "liability" to develop the disorder. As these authors note, two main reasons compel the use of a multifactor conceptualization: (*a*) Individuals with the disorder aggregate within particular families though transmission does not follow Mendelian patterns; and (*b*) Both genetic and environmental factors are relevant to transmission of the disorder with unknown relative contributions. Related to these issues is a study by Guze, Goodwin, and Crane (1969) which showed that wives of convicted felons came from similarly disturbed backgrounds as their husbands and tended to show psychopathology exhibited among their husbands' first degree female relatives. Hence, assortative mating combined with other genetic and environmental factors expose children to a double dose of whatever may predispose them to sociopathy. Importance of the home environment is seen in the observation that criminality aggregates among siblings more often than can be accounted for by genetic factors alone (Cloninger et al., 1978).

One theory attempting to incorporate behavioral and psychophysiological findings has derived from the concept of an optimal level of arousal, such that arousal level and sensory intake are seen as dynamically related. The most explicit statements of arousal theory are those of Quay (1965) and Hare (1970, 1978) who suggest that psychopathy is related to pathologically low levels of autonomic and cortical arousal. However, as reviewed later in this chapter, it has been shown that sociopaths do not necessarily demonstrate uniformly low or fixed levels of arousal and are not uniformly hyporeactive. Rather, they may demonstrate greater inter- or intravariability in CNS and autonomic arousal and reactivity than normal individuals. Mawson and Mawson (1977) identified some of the weaknesses of low-arousal theories and presented a dual, neurochemical model for understanding the patterns of behavioral and physiological activity manifested in sociopathy. Their theory emphasized a dynamic equilibrium between neural systems characterized by rhythmic fluctuations in the relative dominance of two groups of neurotransmitters whose overall functions are sympathomimetic (epinephrine and dopamine) and parasympathomimetic (acetylcholine and serotonin). Also focusing on neurotransmitter functioning, Dinitz, Dynes, and Clarke (1975) postulated that psychopaths are characterized by a defect in catecholamine-secreting neurons, primarily in the sympathetic nervous system, which makes it difficult for them to produce graded responses to environmental stimuli and renders them behaviorally non- or over-responsive. Similarly, Porges (1976) reasoned that psychopathy is an example of behavioral pathology dominance linked to neurotransmitter activity.

Inseparable from genetic and learning theory perspectives is attention devoted to developmental-familial variables and parent-child relationships (Hetherington, Stouwie, & Ridberg, 1971; L. Robins, 1978). Early disturbances in the family environment such as parental loss, parental rejection, or emotional deprivation have been linked to development of antisocial behaviors (McCord & McCord, 1964). However, Cleckley (1976) was unable to associate specific parental characteristics with sociopathy among many of his patients who frequently seemed to have had healthy family environments. Hare (1970) observed that severe forms of family disturbance might be related to a variety of types of psychopathology and concluded there is little evidence to suggest familial disturbances are either specific to or necessary for development of sociopathy. In contrast, Hetherington et al. (1971) stressed that certain types of family interactions might be related to specific delinquent subtypes. The prevalence of antisocial behaviors has also been shown to vary with community socioeconomic level and population density (Cloninger et al., 1978).

Learning theory explanations for antisocial behavior, though not necessarily exclusive of acknowledgments of genetic involvement, rest upon assumptions that sociopathy is the result of individual histories of reinforcement for antisocial behavior resulting in failure to learn prosocial behaviors necessary for appropriate cultural adjustment. Buss (1966) and Maher (1966) argued that sociopathic behavior has origins in childhood reinforcement patterns that reward avoidance of punishment. Maher postulated that sociopaths encounter success in producing verbal and nonverbal behaviors that serve to ward off unpleasant consequences of personal actions. Similarly, Buss (1966) suggested that the sociopathic child, faced with inconsistent parental expectations, learns to avoid punishment by use of lying or superficial apology. Based upon animal studies, Solomon, Turner, and Lessac (1968) suggested that sociopaths may have received delayed punishment as children, leading to development of minimal resistance to temptation and capacity for generalization from punishing situations. Others (Eysenck, 1957; Ullmann & Krasner, 1969) argued that sociopaths failed to become conditioned to social stimuli or the secondary reinforcing properties of human contact and interaction. Thus sociopaths are said to find interpersonal relationships reinforcing only in terms of resulting tangible reinforcements, for example, status, sex, or money. However, Eysenck's theories emphasize genetic over learning factors in that deficits in learning are related to genetic characteristics.

L. Robins (1966) found that the best single predictor of psychopathy in adulthood was childhood antisocial behavior. Robins also found, consistent with reports by Andry (1957), Marcus (1960), and Archer, Sutker, White, and Orvin (1978) that parental sociopathic characteristics were related to the presence of similar psychopathology in male and female offspring. Childhood antisocial behavior has also been shown to be the best predictor of adult narcotic abuse (Egger, Webb, & Reynolds, 1978). Interestingly, maternal characteristics have not been significantly related to antisocial behavior in children. Robins attributed this finding to the traditional role of the father as the main disciplinarian in the home. However, the extent to which children model parental figures, whether of the same or opposite sex, is yet unspecified, particularly among children who become antisocial. In fact, research suggests that opposite-sex individuals are perhaps of more reinforcing value than those of the same sex (Bernard & Eisenman, 1967; Stewart & Resnick, 1970). Hence, the mechanism of modeling or imitative learning, an intriguing procedure for transmission of information, may serve to facilitate as well as discourage antisocial behaviors. Sarason (1978) reasoned that many of the problems of delinquent youth seem to be manifestations of undesirable histories of social-learning experiences, including lack of opportunity for constructive modeling experiences. Thus, in terms of cognitive social learning, behavior may be viewed as a function of interactions with others and the cognitive effects of these interactions, including the development of thought processes, attitudes, problem-solving strategies, and perceptions of reality. Studies that have applied modeling techniques to rehabilitation of delinquents and other groups are discussed in more detail later in this chapter.

EMPIRICAL TESTS OF CLINICAL THEORY

Despite a host of clinical explanations for the phenomena associated with sociopathy, it is only over the past two decades that researchers have subjected clinical notions to controlled investigation. Review of the literature reveals an amazing number of studies specifically designed to test hypotheses generated by Cleckley. In fact, practically every distinguishing characteristic proposed by Cleckley has been subjected to experimentation in one form or another. There are now numerous studies that attempt to test the concept of sociopathy by defining the characteristics of members assigned to that class, studying learning and conditioning behavior, identifying unusual components of physiological responsiveness, specifying unique types of interpersonal interactions and cognitive construct systems, and delineating special types of performances under varying conditions. Investigations in these and other areas summarized below shed light on the characteristics of sociopaths as well as provide a mechanism for speculation regarding the origins of their characteristic psychological, behavioral, and physiological features, and they offer directions for cognitive and behavioral change.

Sensation Seeking and Sociopathy

Assuming that impulsivity, the need to create excitement, and inability to tolerate even minimal amounts of sameness are distinctive characteristics of psychopathy. Quay (1965) hypothesized that these are manifestations of an inordinate need for increases or changes in the pattern of stimulation. Tying together the work of Hebb (1949), sensory deprivation studies (Heron, 1957; Zubek, Pushkar, Sansom, & Gowing, 1961), and earlier research with psychopaths (Fairweather, 1954; Fox & Lippert, 1963; Lindner, 1942, 1943; Lykken, 1957), Quay suggested two possibilities to account for this situation: lowered basal reactivity to stimulation such that more sensory input is required to produce efficient and subjectively pleasurable cortical functioning; or more rapid adaptation to stimulation causing the need for stimulation variation to occur more rapidly and with greater intensity. Quay reasoned that the psychopath is found in an affectively unpleasant condition of stimulus deprivation that motivates sensation seeking. These speculations have fostered a number of research studies dealing with psychosocial and physiological parameters of sensation seeking, but only those related to psychosocial behavior are reviewed in this section.

The relationship between stimulus seeking and antisocial behavior has been demonstrated in studies that showed that antisocial children exhibited less time viewing boring material, more rapid habituation to boring material, and higher initial gain in attention to novel stimuli than children classified as neurotic (DeMyer-Gapin & Scott, 1977; Whitehill, DeMyer-Gapin, & Scott, 1976). DeMyer-Gapin and Scott (1977) also noted that antisocial children engaged in more extraneous behaviors during task administration than did neurotics. Similarly, Skrzypek (1969) described adolescent psychopaths as lacking tolerance for short periods of inactivity or sameness and being highly motivated to seek varied stimulation following sensory restriction. Skrzypek identified groups of psychopathic and neurotic juvenile delinquents and studied their preferences for complex versus simple and novel versus familiar stimuli before and after subjection to sensory deprivation and arousal conditions. As anticipated, psychopathic delinquents were initially less anxious and more inclined to prefer novel and complex stimuli than neurotics. They also showed significant increases in preference for novel and complex stimuli following sensory deprivation; whereas, neurotics exhibited increases in anxiety and decreases in complexity preference following arousal treatment.

Widom (1976a) found that primary or nonanxious psychopaths were as able as normals to tolerate sameness in a Prisoner's Dilemma (PD) game, but secondary or anxious psychopaths showed difficulty under these conditions. The role of situational variables is highlighted in a study by Orris (1969) who required psychopathic, neurotic, and subcultural delinquents to perform a vigilance task involving two 100-minute sessions. There were no obvious reinforcements for continued accurate performance (measured by signals detected and detection latency), and psychopathic subjects performed significantly poorer than did other groups. Orris also noticed a variety of self-stimulating behaviors, probably self-reinforcing, such as singing and talking among psychopaths. Hence, it is possible that decrements in performance were related to requirements for sustained attention and performance without adequate motivational or reward conditions as well as self-imposed distractions.

Attempts to understand the relationship between antisocial behavior and sensation seeking have taken other forms as indicated by recent reviews (Blackburn, 1978; Zuckerman, 1978). Scores on sensation-seeking measures (SSS: Zuckerman, 1972b) have been shown to be related to such antisocial activities as prison escapes and disobedience to authorities among female delinquents (Farley & Farley, 1972), drug use in male veteran and college student samples (Kilpatrick, Sutker, Roitzsch, & Miller, 1976; Zuckerman, 1972a), and earlier and more varied drug use among chronic illicit users (Sutker, Archer, & Allain, 1978). In the latter study, drug abusers classified as high sensation seekers scored higher on MMPI scales reflecting sociopathy, attitudinal deviance, and heightened activity and lower on measures indicating denial, hypochondriacal preoccupation, hysteria, and social introversion. On the other hand, SSS scores did not differentiate between hospitalized alcoholics and employee controls (Kish & Busse, 1969) or psychopaths and nonpsychopaths in a maximum security hospital (Blackburn, 1969). More recently, however, Blackburn (1978) reported that primary psychopathic offenders in a security hospital scored higher on all SSS scales than nonpsychopathic offenders, with secondary psychopaths showing attenuation of stimulus-seeking tendencies by social avoidance. From this evidence, it seems apparent that a penchant for sensation seeking is closely related to cognitive and behavioral dimensions of sociopathy or antisocial behaviors in general; that sociopaths tend to become more easily bored and require more novel stimulation than others; and, that avoidance of boredom and pursuit of sensation seeking can be altered by important motivational properties of a given situation.

Delay of Gratification and Sociopathy

Inability to delay gratification and concomitant impulsiveness are features that have long been considered integral to sociopathy. The sociopath has been described as the epitome of short-range hedonism, and Shapiro (1965) suggested that such an individual, with an aim of quick concrete gain, is the prototype for the impulsive style. This impulsivity has been the topic of much speculation (Buss, 1966; Cleckley, 1976; Maher, 1966), largely because of the relationship between impulsivity and antisocial behaviors, as well as Mischel's (1966) suggestion that the ability to learn delay of gratification in favor of later reward is highly important for socialization. Nevertheless, few studies have attempted to verify that sociopaths share an inability to delay gratification or inhibit impulsive displays—deficits potentially predictive of pessimistic treatment outcome.

Exploring this hypothesis in a situation where psychopaths were asked to choose lesser monetary rewards for study participation or greater rewards after time delay, Widom (1977) found that psychopaths generally tended to delay gratification. However, their decisions appeared to be a complex function of situational variables (employment vs. unemployment) and individual personality characteristics (degree of elevation on MMPI Scale 4). Taking a different approach, Gullick, Sutker, and Adams (1976) investigated the effects of delay of reinforcement (information feedback) on acquisition rate in paired-associate learning among nonaddict prisoner sociopaths, addict prisoner sociopaths, and normal prisoners defined by MMPI criteria that excluded anxious or secondary sociopaths. Although delay did not interfere with performance in normals, rate of acquisition was significantly impaired under the most extreme condition of reinforcement delay in both sociopaths and sociopathic addicts. In sociopathic nonaddict and sociopathic addict groups, investigators noticed a variety of extraneous behaviors (e.g., complaining, conversation, arguing). Again, as in the Orris (1969) study, there were no added enticements to encourage subjects to perform well under conditions of extended delay.

Looking at inability to delay gratification as integrally related to impulsivity, studies have investigated Porteus Maze Test performance among sociopaths to assess the extent of difficulty in inhibiting impulsive errors, carelessness, and disregard for details of instructions. Comparing incarcerated MMPI-defined groups of pure sociopaths, antisocial psychotics, and normals, Sutker et al. (1972) found that incarcerated sociopaths showed better qualitative Porteus Maze Test performance than prison normals or incarcerated antisocial psychotics, although groups did not differ on Shipley or Porteus measures of intelligence. Similarly, Widom (1977) found relatively fewer qualitative errors for psychopaths than those reported in earlier studies (Doctor & Winder, 1954; Fooks & Thomas, 1957; Schalling & Rosen, 1968). Such findings cast doubt on the notion that sociopaths are unable or unwilling to control their impulses or regard the arbitrary limits of instruction. In fact, Stumphauzer (1972) showed that exposure to high-delay peer models resulted in an increased percent of delay choices immediately and after a period of one month among juvenile delinquents.

Learning and Sociopathy

Clinical observations have led to conclusions that sociopaths are unable to profit from experience or acquire certain forms of behavior necessary for socialization. Learning theorists, however, have described situations in which behaviors assumed under the rubric of sociopathy became functional and even adaptable (Buss, 1966; Maher, 1966). It would seem important, therefore, to examine the assumption that sociopaths find difficulty in acquiring learned responses. Consistent with Cleckley's (1971) speculation that psychopaths cannot profit from experience, Eysenck (1964) hypothesized that psychopaths acquire conditioned responses slowly and extinguish rapidly. Similarly, Hare (1965b) characterized psychopaths as having steeper and lower than normal gradients of avoidance tendencies because of their relative inferiority in developing and retaining conditioned fear responses and their low degree of emotional reactivity. The literature relating to arousal, conditioning of emotional responses, and physiological anticipation of punishing events is reviewed at a later point; however, the following section is devoted to an examination of learning phenomena across a variety of cognitive and psychomotor tasks.

The notion that psychopaths seem unable to profit from experience has been supported by studies that found them inferior in verbal conditioning (Johns & Quay, 1962; Quay & Hunt, 1965; Stewart, 1972), avoidance of punished responses (Lykken, 1957), and classical conditioning of autonomic responses (Hare & Quinn, 1971). Reviewing the literature, Hare (1970) commented that psychopaths perform well on verbal conditioning, rote learning, and other tasks that are not dependent upon acquired fear. For example, no significant differences have been reported between sociopaths and controls on tasks involving serial learning (Fairweather, 1954; Kadlub, 1956), paired-associate learning without significant time delay (Gullick et al., 1976), learning sets (McCullough & Adams, 1970), verbal conditioning with social approval (Bryan & Kapche, 1967), and probability learning in a card game where punishment was a near certainty (Siegel, 1978). A number of studies have also shown that sociopaths were not necessarily deficient in avoidance conditioning (Gendreau & Suboski, 1971; Persons & Bruning, 1966; Schmauk, 1970). Further, exploration of the parameters of reinforcement among sociopaths has revealed that performance may be significantly enhanced, or unexpectedly impaired, by experimenter manipulations of reinforcement conditions, even though such may have little or no effect among controls.

Illustrating this point, Schmauk (1970) varied type of reinforcers (e.g., electric shock, money, and negative social comment) and demonstrated that primary sociopaths learned to anticipate and avoid punishment as well as normals if the punishment (particularly threat of monetary loss) were appropriate to their value system. An older study by Painting (1961) illustrated the complexity in attempting to explain why psychopaths may encounter difficulty in responding to avoidance conditions and yet, under other circumstances, make significant behavioral alterations. Painting showed that when correct responses served to avoid loss of a cigarette, primary sociopaths made fewer errors than nonpsychopaths or controls. Under reward conditions with close proximity between stimulus and response, primary psychopaths adopted superior strategies and alternated to the correct answer more frequently than other groups. However, psychopaths showed stereotyped and rigid tendencies to display strong positive recency effects and deficits in performance with more remote stimulus-response associations. Recently, Siegel (1978) found that diminished responsiveness to punishment among psychopathic offenders was greatest when the probability of punishment was uncertain, which he interpreted in terms of cognitive (superstitious logic) rather than affective (anxiety, guilt, depression) factors. In contrast, Fairweather (1954) reported that psychopaths performed better with uncertain reward than for certain or no reward.

To summarize, situational factors, cognitive variables, and yet unspecified situation-person interactions are of particular significance in influencing response to experimental situations among sociopaths. Further, dimensions of reward versus punishment seem to be critical in terms of predicting response patterns. The degree to which sociopaths will expend efforts in task performance or acquisition of new material is highly dependent upon such situational conditions as type of reward, timing of reinforcement, probability of punishment or reward, and perceptions of tasks and their surrounding conditions. For example, other factors inherent in the experimental situation such as content of task material (Sutker, Gil, & Sutker, 1971), experimenter gender (Bernard & Eisenman, 1967; Stewart & Resnick, 1970), and reward timing (Gullick et al., 1976) have been shown to affect sociopathic performance. As Lykken (1978) stated, it is critically important to consider the entire experimental setting as well as the extent to which the "game" strikes the fancy of psychopathic subjects. Yet, details of the experimental environment and conditions, experimenter characteristics, and other variables such as the subject's perceptions of, attitudes toward, or expectancies regarding the situation have been infrequently assessed. Thus it might be speculated that psychopathic delinquents in the Orris (1969) study were relatively uninspired to perform a vigilance task for two 100-minute sessions and hence performed relatively poorly. However, psychopathic deficiencies in task acquisition or performance are infrequently explained by reference to reports from those who are studied, or the subjects themselves.

Interpersonal Performance and Sociopathy

Gough (1948) speculated that psychopaths are pathologically deficient in the ability to role play, to foresee the social consequences of personal behavior, and to judge such behavior from the perspective of another. This description is related to Cleckley's notion of *semantic dementia* and the claim that psychopaths are unempathetic to the suffering of others, despite the capacity to mimic appropriate emotional expressions. Both theorists assume that sociopathy is related to deficiency in socialization skills, insensitivity to the reactions of others, and inability to understand interpersonal expectations. However, Ullmann and Krasner (1969) as well as Gough (1948) noted that sociopaths may be more skilled than average in influencing others to reinforce them or to do what they wish. Ullmann and Krasner (1969) claimed that people have not become effective reinforcing stimuli for sociopaths, a circumstance necessary for normal development. In an interesting theoretical article, Smith (1973) questioned these and other assumptions regarding sociopathy.

No studies have directly tested the hypothesis that people are inadequate reinforcers for sociopathic subjects. Nevertheless, it has been shown that serial learning is enhanced by the social content of material to be learned, and results of investigations reviewed above suggest that sex of the experimenter (surely a social stimulus) as well as social reward are effective in influencing behavior. Further, in a study designed specifically to investigate the interpersonal posture of sociopaths, Widom (1976a) reported that psychopaths did not behave more selfishly or egocentrically, show more concern with personal gain, or act less responsively than normal subjects. She found that they can and will cooperate with one another over a period of time if the stakes are high enough and performance feedback is immediate. Thus, she concluded that psychopaths are not always impulsive, aggressive, or antisocial, and that their behaviors are clearly influenced by situational and motivational demands.

Widom's results were qualified by partial support for the notion that secondary psychopaths were less able to tolerate routine and boredom or to perform efficiently and responsively. Secondary psychopaths were less accurate in predicting the behavior of others in the PD game, though primary psychopaths did not show a deficiency. While primary psychopaths exhibited highest frequencies for mutually cooperative and mutually competitive intentions, this was reversed for controls. In fact, it was observed that primary psychopaths intended complete cooperation or complete lack of cooperation. This is an important point related to the authors' assumption that a core characteristic of sociopathy is the strong relationship between degree of willingness to perform a task and affective response to the reinforcement parameters inherent in the situation. That sociopaths in the Widom (1976a) study most frequently chose competitive, gambling, and opponent roles is interesting, in that controls most often chose collaborator, accomplice, cooperator, partner, and team worker roles. These results suggest that more work must be undertaken to identify meaningful reward parameters for those completely successful sociopaths who have adapted sufficiently to societal expectations such that they do not interact with law enforcement systems.

Using the repertory grid technique to explore interpersonal and personal construct systems, Widom (1976a) found that the construct systems of primary psychopaths were lopsided and idiosyncratic but highly consistent, suggesting that primary psychopaths make no distinctions between their own conceptualizations and those of people in general. Secondary psychopaths and controls manifested less lopsidedness, consistency, and social discrepancy; and, psychopaths showed a significant degree of misperception than people in general and a more specific misperception along the dull-exciting construct dimension. Widom concluded that psychopaths do not think that other people construe events differently from them;

hence, they make little effort to modify their own construct system. Finally, there have been few attempts to test the notion that sociopaths are deficient in empathy, but using a framework of vicarious instigation of electrodermal activity, Sutker (1970) found that sociopaths demonstrated vicarious instigation at the sight of another individual shocked. In this situation, observing another individual in immediate discomfort elicited measureable changes in electrodermal activity in both sociopaths and normals, and sociopaths were as likely to relinquish subject monetary payments to prevent shock to the other individual as were normals.

Sociopathy and Arousal

Arousal theory has attracted the attention of several investigators attempting to explain the behavior of sociopaths (Blackburn, 1978; Hare, 1970, 1978; Petrie, 1967; Quay, 1965; Zuckerman, 1978). Generally, it is reasoned that sociopaths are characterized by low levels of cortical and autonomic arousal as well as hyporesponsiveness to stimulation that result in a constellation of sensation-seeking behaviors. Prior to reviewing related evidence, it is necessary to make several comments about methodological issues in psychophysiological research with sociopaths. Problems with the use of varied criteria for identification of sociopathic subjects have already been discussed, but the importance of obtaining homogeneous samples in order to ensure replicability of findings (Dinitz et al., 1973) cannot be overemphasized. Slight differences in selection of response measures, methodology of response measurement, and data reduction procedures may also influence study findings (Kilpatrick, 1972). Another important issue is the extent to which the demand characteristics of the experimental situation, inclusive of subject expectancies and motivations, affect study results (Lykken, 1978). Most data on the psychophysiology of sociopathy have been generated in experimental paradigms with low-sensory stimulation and minimal subject activity. As Hare (1978) observed, psychopaths tend to become drowsy and bored under such conditions, and psychophysiological responses may be reflective of these states. When more activity is required, the situation may resemble a "game" or artificial creation, such that results could be compromised (Lykken, 1978). At present, little is known about sociopaths in realistic situations of high stimulation or threat where opportunities for eliciting a high rate of active behaviors exist.

The term arousal refers to an hypothesized dimension of activation ranging from sleep to extreme excitation. As stated by Hebb (1955), there are optimal levels of arousal, and deviations from these levels may result in decrements in performance and/or affective mood states. Therefore, organisms may attempt to maintain adaptive levels of arousal by augmenting or decreasing sensory input. The role of the reticular brain stem formation was identified as the neuroanatomical structure most heavily involved in maintenance of arousal level (Moruzzi & Magoun, 1949), and as used by Hebb, the term arousal referred to cortical activation. However, the assumption that a variety of psychophysiological variables—including electroencephalographic (EEG), electrodermal, electromyographic, and cardiovascular responses—are highly correlated with and may, in fact, directly represent cortical activation (e.g., Duffy, 1972; Kilpatrick, 1972; Lindsley, 1951; Malmo, 1972) led to a broadened use of the concept. This and other assumptions have been questioned by Mawson and Mawson (1977) who pointed to the following issues: (*a*) the outmoded view of neuroanatomical functioning related to the reticular system and arousal; (*b*) evidence that there may be little synchrony between autonomic, EEG, behavioral, and motor systems (Lacey, 1967); and (*c*) evidence that individuals show characteristic patterns of autonomic responding that vary as a function of situational stimuli (Lacey, 1967).

Whether sociopaths exhibit EEG abnormalities or deficiencies in cortical arousal has been a subject for research investigation and review (Dongier, 1974; Ellingson, 1954; Hill, 1963; Syndulko, 1978). Syndulko (1978) concluded that a subset of subjects labeled sociopaths show excessive incidence of EEG abnormalities, but Blackburn (1978) argued that some psychopaths show no deficit in cortical arousal in resting situations. With respect to measures of cortical activation in response to stimulation, several investigators have studied the contingent negative variation (CNV) response. McCallum (1973) found reduced CNV amplitude among sociopaths, but subsequent studies failed to replicate this finding (Fenton, Fenwick, Ferguson, & Lam, 1975; Syndulko, Parker, Jens, Maltzman, & Ziskind, 1975; Timsit-Berthier, Rouseau, & Delaunoy, 1971). Cortical-evoked potentials have also been investigated in sociopaths with somewhat mixed results. Studies have shown slower-evoked potential recovery rate in sociopaths than schizophrenics (Shagass & Schwartz, 1962), lower-amplitude P 300 auditory-evoked potential responses among sociopaths as opposed to controls (Syndulko, Parker, Maltzman, & Ziskind, unpublished manuscript, see Syndulko, 1978), and no differences in evoked potentials between sociopaths and controls (Dobbs & Speck, 1968; Syndulko et al., 1975).

Hypoarousal theories of sociopathy have generated considerable psychophysiological research with efforts foused primarily on cardiovascular and electrodermal systems. Evidence is reasonably clear that sociopaths and nonsociopaths do not differ in cardiovascular activity in resting situations (Aniskiewicz, 1973; Blackburn, 1978; Blankstein, 1969; Fenz, 1971; Hare & Craigen, 1974; Hare, Frazelle, & Cox, 1978; Hare & Quinn, 1971; Steinberg & Schwartz, 1976). In contrast, studies using electrodermal response measures have yielded mixed results. Some investigators showed significantly lower resting levels of skin conductance among sociopaths (Blankstein, 1969; Dengerink & Bertilson, 1975; Hare, 1965c, 1968; Laycock, 1968; Mathis, 1971; Schalling, Lidberg, Levander, & Dahlin, 1973), and others reported no significant differences (Borkovec, 1970; Goldstein, 1965; Hare, 1972; Hare & Craigen, 1974; Hare et al., 1978; Lippert & Senter, 1966; Schalling, Lidberg, Levander, & Dahlin, 1968; Schmauk, 1970; Sutker, 1970). With regard to nonspecific electrodermal responses in resting situations, there are reports of decreased frequency in sociopaths (Fox & Lippert, 1963; Hare, 1968; Hare & Quinn, 1971; Lippert & Senter, 1966; Schalling et al., 1973), no differences (Hare et al., 1978; Steinberg & Schwartz, 1976), and higher frequency of nonspecific responses (Blankstein, 1969).

Such contradictory findings do not provide strong support for the notion that sociopaths as a group are more electrodermally underaroused than nonsociopaths. However, Hare (1978) argued that basal skin conductance in psychopaths is lower in absolute magnitude in several studies where significant differences were not observed and that when data were pooled for comparisons from eight of his studies, psychopaths showed significantly lower skin conductance but no differences in frequency of nonspecific responses. In contrast, Mawson and Mawson (1977) postulated a dual, neurochemical model to account for patterns of physiological and behavioral activity manifested in psychopathy and suggested that psychopaths were characterized by considerable intraindividual variability, but not higher or lower levels of arousal per se. It is, however, also possible that there may be significant interindividual variation within groups of defined sociopaths in terms of arousal level and therefore that sociopaths as a group may be neither under- nor over-aroused.

Hare (1978) suggested that there are considerable differences between situations in which stimuli are preceded by a warning stimulus and those in which no signal is given. Investigations of electrodermal responses to unsignaled stimuli have yielded contradictory findings, with some researchers reporting no differences between psychopaths and nonpsychopaths (Blackburn, 1978; Hare, 1975c; Hare et al., 1978; Lippert & Senter, 1966) and others showing psychopaths to be less responsive (Blankstein, 1969; Hare, 1972, 1978; Mathis, 1971). Of perhaps more significance are situations in which a signal precedes presentation of a stimulus permitting evaluation of anticipatory autonomic responses. That anticipatory responses are important for avoidance learning has been suggested by Hare (1975a) who cited Mowrer's (1947) two-process theory of avoidance learning. In this scheme, classical conditioning of autonomic fear responses to cues associated with punishment is a necessary precursor to avoidance behavior; therefore, cues that signal the onset of punishment should also elicit anticipatory autonomic activity. Although review of supporting evidence for this statement is beyond the scope of this chapter, studies by Katkin (1965, 1975), Kilpatrick (1972), Miller and Shmavonian (1965), and Szpiler and Epstein (1976) suggest that nonspecific or spontaneous electrodermal responses are reasonable indices of emotional arousal or anxiety.

Studies investigating electrodermal responses prior to onset of noxious stimulation have produced relatively consistent results. Conditioning experiments using a noxious UCS have shown deficient electrodermal conditioning among sociopaths (Hare, 1965a; Hare & Quinn, 1971; Lykken, 1957; Syndulko et al., 1975). Similarly, studies in which subjects were instructed to expect to receive an aversive stimulation showed evidence of diminished anticipatory electrodermal responding among sociopaths (Hare, 1965c; Hare & Craigen, 1974; Hare et al., 1978; Lippert & Senter, 1966; Schalling & Levander, 1967). This has also been the case in vicarious situations in which anticipatory electrodermal responses to threat of shock to other individuals have been measured (Aniskiewicz, 1973; Hare & Craigen, 1974; Sutker, 1970). However, results reported by Hare and Quinn (1971) suggested that poor electrodermal conditioning may be limited to situations that use noxious stimuli, since sociopaths conditioned normally to other types of stimuli.

Contrary to reports of diminished anticipatory electrodermal activity, recent reviews concluded that sociopaths exhibit no deficit in heart rate conditioning or anticipatory heart rate responses preceding noxious stimulation (Hare, 1975b, 1978; Schalling, 1978). In fact, studies indicate that sociopaths exhibit greater heart rate increases to signals of impending noxious stimulation than controls. Hare and Craigen (1974) requested psychopathic and nonpsychopathic prisoners to administer electric shock, preceded by a 10-second tone, to themselves and other prisoners. In anticipation of shock to themselves or others, psychopaths showed initial heart rate acceleration in contrast to nonpsychopaths whose heart rate decelerated. In another study, Hare et al. (1978) used the CPI Socialization Scale to subdivide groups of psychopathic and nonpsychopathic prisoners into high and low scorers and expose them to a series of 120-db tones, preceded by a 12-second countdown. Subjects defined as most psychopathic, or with the lowest socialization scores, differed from the other three groups in showing marked heart rate acceleration and small increases in electrodermal activity prior to tone presentation. Summarizing these findings, sociopaths manifested specific patterns of heart rate acceleration and decreased electrodermal activity in anticipation of noxious stimulation, although there was considerable variability within groups.

Overall results suggest that sociopaths are characterized by highly effective, though perhaps maladaptive, resources for coping with the threat of punishment. Although minimum levels of anxiety can be maintained, mechanisms may be maladaptive in that failure to attend to cues that signal impending punishment could interfere with normal avoidance learning. Incorporating Lacey and Lacey's (1974) notions about the relationship between cardiovascular responding and sensory processing of environmental stimulation, Hare (1978) developed a theory to explain the findings reported above. Lacey and Lacey (1974) argued that perception of stimuli is markedly influenced by the state of the cardiovascular system, such that with heart rate acceleration there is increased pressure in the baroreceptors of the carotid artery that results in decreased cortical arousal and receptivity to environmental stimulation. Conversely, heart rate deceleration reduces baroreceptor pressure and increases both cortical arousal and receptivity to stimulation. Hare (1978) suggested that the pattern of heart rate acceleration among psychopahs in anticipation of noxious stimulation represents an effective psychophysiological coping process that inhibits fear arousal. Further, he reasoned that electrodermal responses, particularly nonspecific responses, provide a sensitive measure of the successfulness of the coping process.

TREATMENT APPROACHES TO ANTISOCIAL BEHAVIOR

Reports of success in modifying behaviors associated with sociopathy using traditional therapeutic methods have been largely negative. Only 18% of Canadian psychiatrists surveyed viewed sociopathy as a treatable disorder (Albert et al., 1959). In keeping with notions that sociopaths were incapable of profiting from experience, Cleckley (1976) and others (Bender, 1947; McCord & McCord, 1956) saw psychotherapeutic and correctional programs as failing to achieve substantial personality or behavioral change. Maughs (1961) examined such interventions as chemotherapy, electric shock treatment, and psychosurgery and reached a similarly pessimistic view. On the more positive side are the clinicians who found intensive psychotherapy to be effective, when combined with highly controlled outpatient or inpatient situations (Lion, 1972; Thorne, 1959; Vaillant, 1975; Whiteley, 1975). Their views are compatible with approaches initiated over the past two decades to establish residential settings, therapeutic communities, and token economies within correctional settings to manage the behavior problems of antisocial children and adults. It is beyond the scope of this chapter to review the variety of psychological, sociological, legal, and medical approaches that have been used with sociopathic patients (see Suedfeld & Landon, 1978). However, the following section provides an overview of behavioral treatment interventions employed in attempts to modify antisocial behaviors among groups of children, adolescents, and adults.

Behavioral approaches to modification of antisocial behavior among youthful and adult populations have gained increased popularity. It is reasonable to assume that this trend has resulted from continued pessimism regarding the effectiveness of traditional psychotherapeutic approaches, a growing literature indicating that antisocial individuals or sociopaths can profit from experience, and a tendency to use behavioral techniques with an ever-widening range of disorders. Although not always evident from review of therapeutic interventions, underlying the application of behavioral principles and technology to antisocial behaviors are the following assumptions: (a) that individualized target behaviors among delinquents and sociopaths or related environmental factors are subject to modification by systematic and contingent use of reinforcing and punishing events; (b) that specified behavior changes have relevance for reducing the presenting problems of delinquency or sociopathy as reflected by observable events; and (c) that behavior changes are monitored in the treatment situation and response maintenance and generalization occur over time as evidenced by outcome data. Most behavioral interventions have focused on identifiable deficits or excesses of so-called maladaptive behavior; however, more recently, emphasis has also been given to targeting behaviors for change reasoned to be incompatible with delinquency or at least of value in adapting to the demands of the societal whole (Bassett, Blanchard, & Koshland, 1975). Questions have arisen regarding learning phenomena among deviant groups, but the literature reviewed in this chapter lends support to the contention that antisocial behaviors, even among so-called primary sociopaths, are amenable to change. Evidence also suggests that the special conditions of the learning situation (Subject X Situation interactions) are of critical significance in determining whether the behavior of antisocial individuals may be altered in the predicted direction.

Approaches to Child and Adolescent Antisocial Behaviors

Over the past 20 years, significant effort has been expended to application of behavior modification techniques to the modification and prevention of delinquent behavior (see reviews by Braukmann & Fixsen, 1975; Burchard & Harig, 1976; Davidson & Seidman, 1974; Emery & Marholin, 1977; Stumphauzer, 1973). Davidson and Seidman (1974) critically analyzed studies employing applied behavior analysis to modification of specific classes of behavior, for example, educational, program, delinquent. More recently, Burchard and Harig (1976) evaluated the effectiveness of therapeutic efforts classified in terms of institutional, community-based residential, and social-learning programs. These authors concentrated on application of behavior techniques among populations of adjudicated adolescents as well as children or adolescents who, not yet in conflict with the criminal justice system, nevertheless exhibited a range of antisocial behaviors. As Patterson (1974) pointed out, conduct disorders constitute a class of problems that frequently lead both teachers and parents to refer children for professional assistance. Assuming that the more extreme forms of conduct disorders are not easily "out-grown" (Robins, 1966), it is these children who will be institutionalized in training schools or as adults in prisons as a result of more blatant forms of deviance. Therefore, the undertaking of treatment for antisocial behavior among children and adolescents seems a reasonable place to initiate and evaluate treatment approaches for modification of antisocial behaviors, despite pessimism expressed by Robins (1978).

Application of behavior modification approaches to delinquent behavior within institutional, residential, or outpatient settings de-emphasizes verbal therapies in favor of such techniques as operant and classical conditioning, modeling frameworks for imitative learning, behavior shaping, contingency contracting, and combinations of behavioral and other strategies. What constitutes behavioral treatment for antisocial individuals has been described at length (Burchard & Harig, 1976; Ullmann & Krasner, 1969). However, it might be reiterated that treatment focus is directed toward modification of clearly defined problem behaviors or environmental conditions, identified most often through direct observations, with emphasis on interobserver reliability and continued measurement of outcome effectiveness. Modification efforts involve, then, the systematic, consistent, and contingent application of reinforcing or punishing consequences, so that the likelihood of desirable responses is increased and the probability of specific undesirable behaviors is decreased. Token economies for institutionalized settings, mild forms of punishment combined with positive reinforcement approaches, response cost techniques, and time-out from positive reinforcement are among specific strategies used.

Characterizing a traditional institutional environment as reflecting primarily contingent punishment and noncontingent reward, Nay (1974) described an assessment of institutional needs, development of a comprehensive behavioral treatment program, and evaluation of therapeutic success. The goal of this and other behavioral programs within institutions is to create an environment with prescribed contingencies such that predetermined behaviors can be reinforced, ignored, or punished in accordance with a treatment plan. Token economies and behavioral contracting are most frequently employed in a framework resting on assumptions that behaviors can be changed within the institutional setting and that such changes can be maintained in the natural environment. The disagreement as to whether tokens, which allow access to privileges, are more reinforcing than social stimuli is not addressed in this section. Using an institutional approach based upon the theoretical model that psychopaths are pathological sensation-seekers, Ingram, Gerard, Quay, and Levinson (1970) separated psychopathic young offenders and provided them a therapeutic milieu that emphasized action-oriented, novel activities as opposed to verbal therapeutic approaches. As predicted, these investigators found more successful adaptation to the institutional environment for psychopathic as opposed to control groups and stressed the effectiveness of such innovative aspects as novelty combined with competition, controversial movies and debates, and time-out techniques.

In a comprehensive investigation of therapeutic effectiveness, Jesness (1975) used the Youth Center Research Project to study the impact of two different treatment programs with 983 adjudicated delinquents assigned at random to two different institutions, with programs based on transactional analysis or behavior modification. Covering a wide range of outcome and process data, Jesness found that subjects at both institutions experienced positive attitudinal and behavioral changes, and both programs seemed equally effective as measured by parole criteria. However, each program generated specific treatment effects. For example, improvement on psychological measures favored transactional analysis, while behavior ratings favored the behavioral program. Subjects from both programs fared significantly better on parole than comparison groups assigned to different institutions. An important finding in this investigation was that the nonspecific factor of client positive regard for staff potentiated whatever specific treatment effects were present and contributed about as much to outcome as did type of treatment. Related to this point, Sutker, Allain, Smith, and Cohen (1978) found that attitudes of opiate addicts toward staff varied significantly depending upon type of treatment program and that clients with the most positive attitudes toward themselves also exhibited the most favorable attitudes toward staff.

Community-based residential programs offer an alternative to incarceration for delinquent adolescents. The growth of residential programs has become sufficiently extensive such that it would be impossible to describe them in detail. Programs can be built around a family unit with few residents as is done in Achievement Place (Fixsen, Wolf, & Phillips, 1973; Phillips, Phillips, Fixsen, & Wolf, 1973) or may accommodate larger numbers, either in homogeneous groups or integrated into adult communities—options available in the Odyssey House system (Densen-Gerber, 1973; Densen-Gerber & Drassner, 1974). Theoretically, residential communities differ from incarceration alternatives in that the focus for behavior change can more easily be shifted to learning to live a productive life within a defined and structured social community. The question of whether what is learned can be generalized to the real world, once the support of the community is removed, remains largely unanswered. Essential components of behaviorally oriented therapeutic community approaches ideally include design of individualized treatment plans, continual structure and supervision, increasing patient involvement in responsibility and decision making, punishment for excessive or inappropriate behaviors, social and other rewards for desired changes or newly developed response alternatives, and long-term follow-up.

A well-known example of community-based behavioral intervention for adolescents is Achievement Place in Lawrence, Kansas, a family-style program incorporating foster care for small groups of adjudicated or neglected youths. Program strategy incorporates modeling, practice, instruction, and feedback mechanisms mediated by a motivational system that is based upon a token economy and administered by professionally trained teaching parents (Phillips et al., 1973). Oriented around rules, consequences, fines, and rewards, with emphasis on academic achievement, cooperation, and responsibility, the program has as its goal to teach youngsters how to recognize the predictable consequences of behaviors. Residents are placed in a multilevel motivational system of behavior modification in which the first stage of program activity is governed by a point system of reinforcement. With points earned in the first phase, residents are able to buy out of the token economy into the merit phase in which no points are used and privileges are freely given. When the child is able to demonstrate ability to perform in this system, transfer is made to the home environment. The token economy system is reinstituted only if difficulties arise in maintaining behavioral change. Proponents of community-based approaches contend that they are more cost effective than institutional programs and lend themselves better to generalization of behavior changes (Phillips et al., 1973). However, as indicated recently by Emery and Marholin (1977), demonstration of changes in target behaviors among delinquent populations is not necessarily evidence of modification of delinquency itself. Indeed, in their survey of behavioral studies reported from 1968–1976, they found as many as 70% failed to show a relationship between target behavior change and reductions in delinquency.

Approaches to treatment of adolescent behavioral problems or their ultimate prevention have often taken a systems perspective in which such strategies as direct behavior observations, contingency contracting, shaping, modeling, and follow-up of expected outcome changes are used to modify home or school interactions. Patterson and his colleagues (1974, 1977) have invested considerable effort in devising effective treatment interventions for the antisocial behaviors of adolescents or children labeled deviant and their family members. Most characteristic are such procedures as direct observations of child and family interactions by trained observers, instructional periods for parental or school shaping of behaviors, and measurement of outcome by direct observations before, during, and subsequent to treatment interventions (see Patterson, 1977). In a 1974 report, observational data of home interactions by trained observers, parental reports, and classroom behavior showed significant reductions from baseline for stated criteria in both classroom and family environments. However, whether changes persisted over time has been the subject of controversy (Kent, 1976; Reid & Patterson, 1976). Interestingly, Arnold, Levine, and Patterson (1975) reported that teaching child management procedures to parents of identified problem children was followed by significant reductions in rates of deviant behavior for siblings of such children, which were maintained over a six-month period.

Noticing that the parents of deviant children might not have the social repertoire to apply contingencies effectively, Tharp and Wetzel (1969) used a formal contract arrangement that stated specific expectations and contingencies for all parties. Based on the assumption that the etiology of delinquency stems from a paucity of opportunities for positive home reinforcement, Stuart (1971) defined elements of good behavioral contracts and advocated their use with families in which parent-child interactions were oriented toward negative feedback. Employing family strategies developed by Patterson and his colleagues, as well as a system for behavioral contracting, Alexander and Parsons (1973) executed a well-designed comparison of short-term behavior intervention, other therapeutic intervention, and no therapeutic intervention with families of delinquents. Results showed that families receiving behaviorally oriented intervention demonstrated significant improvement on three family interaction measures at the end of therapy and reduced recidivism rates at follow-up compared to families receiving alternative forms of family therapy and no treatment.

Another dimension critically relevant to therapeutic success is the process through which training agents are able to motivate parents, nurses, teachers, and institutions to apply behavioral principles. Although the importance of this issue was suggested by others (Stuart, 1971; Thorne, Tharp, & Wetzel, 1967), Alexander, Barton, Schiavo, and Parsons (1976) called attention to the need for intratherapy identification and evaluation of variables that differentially contribute to changes in therapy process and outcome. They designed a study to investigate degree of outcome variance accounted for by therapist characteristics while holding constant the formal aspects of the treatment program and therapist training. Results suggested that the global quality of relationship skills contributed most significantly to outcome variance. However, as Alexander et al. (1976) clarified, relationship skills alone were apparently ineffective in modifying family behavior. Thus the effects of therapist relationship skills were most likely enhanced or elicited by a well-structured therapeutic agenda and operational framework. Further illustrating the importance of relationship variables and positive contingency conditions, Fo and O'Donnell (1974) showed that school attendance among behavior and academic problem students increased under conditions of social or social material contingencies, while no changes occurred in noncontingent relationship and control conditions. Social material contingency was effective in decreasing assorted problem behaviors, such as fighting and returning home late, but it produced no effects when grade improvement was the target goal.

Approaches to Antisocial Behavior in Adults

Despite seemingly endless possibilities, the technology of behavior modification has not been widely used among populations of adult sociopaths. For the most part, applications have been limited to individual clinical or isolated experimental situations and tailored to such groups as criminal offenders, alcoholics, homosexuals, and opiate addicts—all of whom may share antisocial characteristics. Examples observed in the literature include the use of operant conditioning, self-monitoring, classical conditioning, covert therapies, punishment, contingency contracting, systematic desensitization, progressive relaxation, hypnosis, avoidance and escape learning, thought-stopping, and social skills training. Behavior modification is also becoming an interdisciplinary effort characterized by increasing sophistication and creativity, with advances in such areas as biofeedback training, telemetry, and computer technology (see Dinitz et al., 1975).

In operant conditioning paradigms, a specified consequence is made contingent upon spontaneous emission of a carefully defined behavior. In positive reinforcement, an event such as verbal praise, knowledge of results, or presentation of tokens follows the occurrence of a behavior targeted for increase. Maintaining or increasing desired behavior by withdrawing an aversive stimulus such as electric shock, negative verbal comment, or an unpleasant physiological state is termed negative reinforcement. Two negative reinforcement paradigms are escape conditioning, in which a response terminates an aversive stimulus after the stimulus has begun, and avoidance conditioning, in which a response avoids or postpones aversive stimulus presentation. Operant procedures may also take the form of punishment paradigms in which an undesired response is followed by an aversive stimulus to reduce the rate of response occurrence. As reviewed earlier, there is consensus that sociopaths can alter behavior in the operant framework subsequent to presentation of a variety of reinforcers, for example, money, social approval, and even negative stimulation. One example is a study by Doctor and Craine (1971) who reported use of verbal operant conditioning procedures to modify dialectic drug language of primary and neurotic psychopaths toward more conventional verbiage.

Results showed that primary psychopaths conditioned better than those who were neurotic. Conditioning performances were highly correlated with reports of contingency awareness, and changes in language were maintained in extraexperimental behavior. In view of evidence suggesting that humans are able within the operant framework to alter responses associated with the autonomic nervous system and data indicating a uniqueness of psychophysiological response among some subcategories subsumed under the umbrella of sociopathy, it is likely that the operant paradigm will prove increasingly useful for investigation of potential behavior changes.

Results summarized by Steinberg and Schwartz (1976) indicated that psychopaths, though perhaps idiosyncratic in their responses, are as able as controls to modify spontaneous skin resistance responses with instructions and biofeedback. Interestingly, psychopaths achieved control by learning to decrease electrodermal response production, while normals were capable of increasing and decreasing responses. Upon first consideration, it might seem reasonable to initiate treatment efforts designed to increase electrodermal activity in response to threat; however, upon closer examination, this strategy might not be most effective. If, as Hare (1978) hypothesized, cardiac acceleration reduces perception of cues signaling impending punishment, then biofeedback training focused on this aspect of autonomic behavior might be more productive. Sociopaths could be subjected to biofeedback conditions and reinforced for heart rate deceleration to facilitate rather than reduce sensory input. One might predict that, if the cardiac response to threat of punishment became normalized through such training, patterns of avoidance behavior might become more normal as well. Conceivably, the cardiovascular process of "tuning out" environmental cues may be the first part of a chain that results in maladaptive avoidance learning. Indeed, biofeedback could prove useful in raising maladaptively low levels of arousal for sociopaths so characterized on psychophysiological assessment.

A classical conditioning paradigm has been used frequently with antisocial patients to eliminate inappropriate approach responses. Classical conditioning is operationalized by repeated pairing of an initially neutral stimulus with reference to a specific response (the conditioned stimulus or CS) with a stimulus that is known to elicit a specific response (the unconditioned stimulus or UCS). Antisocial subjects have most frequently been subjected to aversive classical conditioning paradigms in which a CS for the inappropriate approach response is paired with a strong, noxious UCS. Evidence has been reviewed suggesting that sociopaths tend to be defective conditioners when negative stimulation is used (Johns & Quay, 1962; Quay & Hunt, 1965), but other studies showed that sociopaths are not necessarily inferior conditioners under these circumstances (Gendreau & Suboski, 1971; Persons & Bruning, 1966; Schmauk, 1970). Reports of success in applying conditioning techniques for therapeutic purposes with alcoholic patients, for example, vary from those of overwhelming success to marginal improvement. Summing up, Miller (1976) indicated that aversion therapy was most useful for temporarily suppressing alcohol abuse when combined with positive instructions for rearrangement of environmental contingencies, teaching of alternative modes of responding, and aspects of covert sensitization.

Working with two opiate addicts in a clinical setting, Liberman (1968) followed the prohibited behavior of self-administration of morphine with administration of apomorphine, a negative stimulus, over 38 treatment sessions. In this pilot investigation, "booster" sessions were used as well as allowance for occasional free-choice situations in which the patient could choose between morphine and interaction with therapist or nurse figures. Results showed that aversive conditioning did occur in both patients, and effects generalized outside the treatment setting. Similarly, Lesser (1967) undertook a program of 33 one-hour individual therapy sessions with a morphine addict. Using a combination of relaxation training, assertive training, and aversive conditioning, he reported initial success and continued nondrug use at 7 and 10 months subsequent to termination of treatment. Recently, Lesser (1976) noted that this client had not resumed narcotic use over a period of 10 years and that he had established successful marital and work situations.

As an alternative to aversive conditioning with faradic or other stimulation, Cautela (1967, 1969, 1970) described several covert conditioning techniques (e.g., covert sensitization, covert reinforcement, and covert extinction) that have shown particular applicability for eliminating negative behaviors such as drug abuse. The term "covert" was used because procedures involved presentation of neither the undesirable nor aversive stimulus, except by imaginary processes. Of course, the advantages of covert procedures include the design of imaginary situations aptly suited to the therapeutic need and avoidance of direct application of noxious physical stimulation. Looking at examples, covert sensitization has been applied with relative success among alcoholics (Ashem & Donner, 1968; Cautela, 1970), LSD users (Duehn & Shannon, 1973), narcotic addicts (Steinfeld, 1970; Wisocki, 1973), and barbiturate abusers (Polakow, 1975). More recently, Copemann (1977) described a variation of covert techniques that incorporated hypnosis to achieve continuous imagery of aversive scenes.

Although the approaches reviewed above have gained popularity for treatment of behavioral excesses, few attempts to alter behavior have used self-reporting, baseline assessment, or contingency contracting as primary intervention strategies. Recently, Hay, Hay, and Angle (1977) reported dramatic reduction in the frequency of drug-related behaviors following three weeks of an assessment self-monitoring procedure with a young chronic amphetamine user. Whether changes in drug-taking behaviors were related to a high level of personal motivation, recording prior to drug-taking behavior, or other factors is not apparent. Using unobtrusive baseline recordings, reactive baseline recordings, and contingency procedures in a forensic psychiatry institution, McNamara and Andrasik (1977) found the greatest change in self-improvement and self-maintenance behaviors during the reactive baseline phase where no consequences were attached to behavior; however, decrease of inappropriate behaviors was greatest during the contingency phase. Thus it is reasonable to assume that even among antisocial individuals, self-monitoring or observer-monitoring with no obvious contingencies has an important effect on behavior.

To illustrate the use of contingency contracting, several examples are cited. Polakow and Doctor (1972) showed that contingency contracting could be used to accelerate prosocial behaviors in a group of criminal offenders in the natural environment. Subsequently, these same investigators (1973) reported the use of contingency contracting and behavioral rehearsal for treatment of outpatients who displayed habitual use of marijuana and barbiturates. Their work was based on a counterconditioning model where low-frequency behaviors incompatible with habitual drug use were accelerated. In this study, Polakow and Doctor (1973) attempted to treat marijuana and barbiturate dependence in a husband-wife dyad who were both on probation for drug offenses. Social reinforcement contingencies were applied to accelerate behaviors incompatible with drug abuse, and behavioral rehearsal was used to reduce aversive consequences in social situations which were previously anxiety provoking. Both procedures were applied for a nine-month period with complete cessation of drug use, and a one-year follow-up showed no return to drug use as well as continued employment and improvement in the marital relationship. Similarly, Frederiksen, Jenkins, and Carr (1976) using contingency contracting to modify the relationship between a polydrug abusing adolescent and his family found marked decrease in drug use.

As may be noted for this review, there is ever-increasing diversity in the application of behavior modification techniques to antisocial behavior, but the underlying theory of operation always includes systematic functional analysis, identification of individualized target behaviors, specified therapeutic design, immediate evaluation of progress, and long-term follow-up. As advised by Schwitzgebel (1975), procedures for changing behavior that rely upon unique, nontransferrable characteristics of therapists or change agents lie outside the domain of scientific behavior modification. Although many psychotherapists now strive to control the patient environment while applying intensive psychotherapy of a personal variety, their efforts would not be considered behavior modification per se. The therapeutic community approach may, however, be considered at least a partial attempt to control the environment in a specified manner so as to modify a class of antisocial behaviors. The principles of therapeutic community development were early articulated by Maxwell Jones (1952), who established a community for treatment of psychopaths at Henderson Hospital, which has been in operation for over two decades. Use of the therapeutic community for sociopaths has also been recommended by Whiteley (1975), who suggested that the aim of communal living is to produce a context in which all interpersonal reactions, feelings, and communications can be examined, misperceptions corrected, and mislearned social behavior replaced by more adaptive habits. Of those approaches applied to the problem of drug abuse, the therapeutic community has been regarded as the most successful over time (Collier & Hijazi, 1974; Sugarman, 1974) as well as the modality that engenders the most positive attitudes toward staff and clients (Sutker et al., 1978). For greater detail, one might refer to Platt and Labate's (1976) description of the more well-known therapeutic communities designed to manage drug abuse problems.

As in the case of therapeutic or residential living communities, there is the possibility that the introduction and application of the principles of applied behavior analysis can be used without significant advantage and perhaps to resident disadvantage, particularly in a penal or highly restricted, potentially punitive setting. Probably one of the first targets for action within therapeutically designed prison units has been to increase resident academic skills and to motivate continued academic achievement. There is no question that the use of incentive systems directed toward these ends were successful with predelinquents (Phillips, 1968), delinquents (Cohen, Filipczak, & Bis, 1967), and adult offenders (Milan, Wood, Williams,

Rogers, Hampton, & McKee, 1965). For an example, Kandel, Ayllon, and Roberts (1976) reported that two adult inmates passed academic tests in math and English as much as nine times faster under an enriched incentive schedule. Describing a more broadly based program encompassing target behaviors in addition to academics, Jones, Stayer, Wichlacz, Thomes, and Livingstone (1977) found that an operant system in which specification of stimulus conditions, preferred behaviors, and contingencies of reinforcement yielded positive changes in military adjustment after 4 and 11 months.

Despite such dramatic gains, there is often no demonstration of a relationship between increased or decreased rates of responding on a certain parameter and reduced levels of crime or antisocial behavior (see Emery & Marholin, 1977). Further, Milan and McKee (1976) pointed to a number of problems that may be inherent in conducting behavioral research for treatment purposes within institutional settings (e.g., coercion of inmate participation, faulty treatment design, lack of on-site professional supervision). At least some of these concerns seem well-founded as demonstrated by Bassett and Blanchard (1977) who studied the effect of the absence of close supervision on the use of response cost in a prison token economy where close supervision was initiated and removed. These investigators found that during the director's absence, behavioral technicians not only withheld contingent points when an individual failed to reach target criteria but levied a response cost and further increased the response cost when inmates failed to respond appropriately. They also noted considerable variation in response costs among behavioral technicians. It was concluded that without continuing supervision a behavioral program may deteriorate naturally from an intentionally reinforcing environment into a punitive response cost system. Probably then the greatest potential disadvantage of behavioral programs within correctional or forensic institutions is the misuse of punishment—an already familiar problem in such settings. And, as Milan and McKee (1976) suggest, it is undoubtedly more effective and humane to schedule and award incentives available in the criminal justice system systematically to encourage productive behavior than it is to threaten and withdraw or withhold reinforcements to discourage undesirable behaviors.

Similar to the social-learning projects initiated with adolescent delinquents, such procedures as assertiveness training, instructional control, and the building of interpersonal skills have been applied to populations of behaviorally deviant adults, though sparingly. For the most part, these techniques have been used with alcoholics to teach refusal of drinks after return to the home environment (Foy, Miller, Eisler, & O'Toole, 1976), modification of abusive verbal outbursts (Frederiksen, Jenkins, Foy, & Eisler, 1976), instructional control of drinking behavior (Miller, Becker, Foy, & Wooten, 1976), and appropriate assertiveness (O'Neil & Roitzsch, 1977). Miller (1976) summarized other skills-building approaches to maladaptive drinking behavior, but few studies report their use among drug abusers (Cheek, Tomarchio, Standen, & Albahary, 1973) or defined sociopaths. Nevertheless, based upon the premises that deviant behaviors occur within a social context and that significant and sustained changes depend upon execution within that framework, social-skills training holds considerable promise. Of further advantage is minimal emphasis on aversive stimulation or other maneuvers that would result in ethical controversy. Hence, social-skills training may fill an important gap in the repertoire of behavioral methodology, that is, provide additional mechanisms for replacement of negative activity with positive alternatives. Future research is needed to explore its effectiveness in changing cognitive styles and behavior among sociopaths.

Techniques sometimes included under the label of behavioral strategies, depending upon their design for use, are electrical brain stimulation and psychopharmacology. Such procedures are also clearly highly controversial in terms of raising ethical, theoretical, and moral issues, which must eventually be evaluated and judged by the societal whole. Obviously, it may be possible to effect such complete behavioral control in some cases that the values of a free society are seriously compromised. A full description of these methods is beyond the scope of this chapter (see Suedfeld & Landon, 1978); however, it is interesting to cite several examples. As noted above, behavioral treatment has frequently incorporated pairing cues to undesirable behavior with aversive stimulation. However, Moan and Heath (1972) found that a program of midseptal stimulation and encouragement of heterosexual behavior was effective in initiating new behaviors in a homosexual man. Septal stimulation was also reported to result in improved mood, self-confidence, general muscle relaxation, and other positive psychological states.

Psychopharmacological approaches designed to alter autonomic nervous system activity and/or neurotransmitter functioning have been advocated by several investigators, particularly for that subset of sociopaths who can be identified to demonstrate parasympathetic dominance and attenuated sympathetic activity. Porges (1976), Satterfield (1978), and Tarter (1977) reasoned that hyperactive children and psychopaths share common features. For example, Satterfield (1978) reviewed evidence which suggested that hyperactive children who respond well to stimulant medication show the greatest deficits in electrodermal and/or cortical arousal. Pharmacological modification of behavior pathologies has also been attempted by Allen, Dinitz, Foster, Goldman, and Lindner (1976) who reported improvement in nine incarcerated psychopaths administered imipramine pamoate, an antidepressant drug with stimulant properties. However, evidence suggesting the proclivity of sociopaths to modify their own arousal level by self-medication, for example, illicit drug and/or excessive alcohol use (Kilpatrick, Sutker, & Smith, 1976; Sutker et al., 1978), obviously raises issues of concern regarding the necessity of other therapeutic intervention to manage these specific maladaptive behaviors.

TREATMENT SUMMARY

As may be noted, few studies have investigated the process and outcome of various forms of treatment among sociopathic adolescents or adults. Further, the literature is characterized by pessimism with regard to treatment outcome, despite experimental findings that many of Cleckley's hypothesized psychopathic personality traits have not been demonstrated. In one of the few studies that investigated both patient characteristics and treatment outcome, Sloane, Staples, Cristol, Yorkston, and Whipple (1976) compared the effectiveness of analytically oriented psychotherapy, behavior therapy, and waiting list treatment among 94 psychoneurotic or personality-disordered patients. Neither form of active treatment was more effective than the other, though both were more effective than the waiting list condition. Further, these investigators found relatively greater success with psychotherapy associated with less overall pathology, measured by the MMPI and higher socioeconomic status, whereas outcome was least effective with patients who scored high on MMPI Scales 4 and 3. There was also a trend for behavior therapy to be more successful with hysterical and psychopathic subjects. Results are compatible with those of Jesness (1975), who found that neither transactional analytic nor behavior modification approaches was more successful than the other, but that both were more successful than other kinds of institutional treatment.

After review of the varieties of therapeutic approaches to the problem of psychopathy, Suedfeld and Landon (1978) remarked that results are "not much to show for the amount of money, time, and effort spent." These conclusions are somewhat reminiscent of those of Eysenck (1961), who found the recovery rate of neurotics who received psychotherapy was no better than that for neurotic untreated patients. Even those reports that indicate success may be tempered by the possibility that sociopaths become less deviant with age or experience, or what has been called the "burning out" phenomenon, somewhere during the years of middle life. For example, Weiss (1973) found that antisocial behaviors and attitudes evidenced by MMPI and medical records decreased by age groups with decline in middle and later life. However, Maddocks (1970) followed 50 psychopathic psychiatric outpatients for approximately five years and found that only 10 appeared to have settled down. He concluded that maturation alone does not eliminate psychopathy. In a 12-year follow-up of narcotic addicts, Vaillant (1966) also found no evidence of burning out, but addicts seemed to recover for reasons relatively unrelated to treatment, for example, discovery of gratifying alternative activities, relationships with significant others. In few, if any, cases did opiate addicts attribute significant help to professional intervention. In another study, Robins et al. (1977) identified 57 antisocial patients in an 18-month follow-up and found no evidence of significant remission, even in one patient who was as old as 61 years.

Review of evidence reported in this chapter suggests that so-called sociopathic behavior, ranging from idiosyncratic to highly maladaptive, is subject to the same principles of acquisition and modification as any behaviors that might be described in categorical terms. The behavioral contingencies controlling antisocial expressions may be infrequently apparent; however, this does not mean that they are nonexistent or inexplicable. Further, it appears crucial that certain events are not reasoned a priori to be punishing or reinforcing for antisocial individuals, but that rather the characteristics of classes of punishing and rewarding stimuli be carefully identified and tested. A study reported by Boren and Colman (1970) in which principles of reinforcement were tested within a psychiatric ward for delinquent soldiers provides a good example of the point made above. Testing the effects of certain behavioral procedures to hospital-ward behavior of antisocial patients, Boren and Colman showed that the type of reinforcement or behavioral strategy was critical to making desired changes. For example, delinquent soldiers were more likely to run a half-mile when rewarded by points that they could exchange for privileges than under conditions where a live model demonstrated the run. Further, the effect of contingent punishment significantly reduced the likelihood of desired behavior, and again points were more effective in eliciting personal discussion than approval from psychiatrists on the ward. Antisocial soldiers seemed to prefer individual contingencies as opposed to group contingencies, and they initiated desired behaviors with a chaining reinforcement technique that made one meet requirements of the first schedule and then a second schedule in order to receive point reinforcement.

In terms of individual treatment, it is important to reiterate that sociopathy is obviously inclusive of a heterogeneous group with respect to numerous salient characteristics and that individuals so labeled should not be expected to respond similarly across a set of environmental conditions. For example, studies have shown that some sociopaths share moderate to severe levels of depression and anxiety, whereas others evidence no neurotic symptomatology. Similarly, there are sociopaths who are bright and adaptable within most environments, and others of less intelligence find themselves in constant difficulty. Additionally, the existence of possible behavioral or cognitive differences between male and female sociopaths has been virtually unexplored. Finally, the cognitive styles and/or psychological characteristics associated with sociopathy may exist for individuals who do not exhibit expected behavioral excesses or responses under inappropriate stimulus control. The extent to which such individuals permeate various occupational or social groups, as well as identification of their mechanisms for behavior control, are potentially intriguing areas for research. These points are made to suggest that any treatment program must be prefaced by functional analysis, specification of individualized targeted behaviors for change, flexibility for a multifaceted treatment plan, and appropriate behavior monitoring and follow-up.

Reviewing results of a representative sample of behavioral interventions with delinquents from 1968–1976, Emery and Marholin (1977) indicated that there is little doubt that behavior modification strategies are effective in impacting on target behaviors for individuals or groups. Whether demonstrated changes can be shown to have direct relevance to delinquency or sociopathy, or are maintained and generalized over time, remain subjects for continued investigation. Self-reporting of behavioral excesses, contingency contracting, covert conditioning procedures, and aversive conditioning are examples of techniques used with success on an individual level. Thompson and Conrad (1977) have also called attention to the need for multifaceted behavioral treatment. In their own study, they reported success across several parameters with an opiate-dependent man using contingency contracting, self-observation, systematic desensitization, covert sensitization, assertion training, rational emotive therapy, and thought-stopping techniques during in- and outpatient sessions. Highly structured therapeutic communities offering immediate rewards for behaviors considered incompatible with antisocial activity or drug abuse, withholding of reward or contingent punishment for inappropriate behaviors, and minimal opportunity to practice or be rewarded for behavioral excesses also constitute a viable treatment context. Such programs may incorporate behavioral shaping techniques to delay reinforcement for specified performances and offer an opportunity for vicarious learning of prosocial cognitions and behaviors. Similarly, involvement of offenders in constructive, novel, and exciting activities seems to be of value in attenuating sensation-seeking needs that might otherwise be gratified in inappropriate ways. Probably the greatest deficiencies with therapeutic community programs, whether in residential homes or prison settings, are the potential for punitive measures to be excessive and inappropriate, lack of sufficient individualizing in terms of treatment plans, and minimal attention to interrater reliability for observation of change and adequate follow-up.

Although there has been controversy regarding the effectiveness of aversive stimulation in modifying the behavior of sociopaths, punishment may prove valuable in discouraging so-called undesirable behaviors when combined with positive reinforcement of alternative adaptive responses. As noted above, a multifaceted approach is most frequently the methodology of choice as individualized target behaviors will inevitably necessitate varying strategies. The continuing use of covert conditioning techniques also allows one to be as innovative and individualized as is possible in presentation of appropriate noxious stimuli in aversive condition procedures. In fact, its use might well be pursued among individuals who exhibit the earliest signs of alcohol and drug abuse or behavioral excesses, such as repeated sexual acting out and theft. Social skills training and physical fitness programs, often restricted to the treatment of alcoholics and some types of drug abusers, also offer significant potential benefit for providing sociopathic patients with meaningful alternatives to antisocial involvement. The extent to which behaviors labeled sociopathic are related to parental or peer modeling has yet to be determined; nevertheless, interpersonal skills-building mechanisms may prove of great value in facilitating acquisition of more adaptive behaviors as well as modification of those regarded as undesirable. For example, seemingly aggressive sociopaths may have as much need for assertive training as do individuals labeled passive-dependent.

In summary, the extent to which personal variables, cognitive sets, or environmental factors influence the development of antisocial behavior or sociopathy and its variations is unknown. Further, aspects of typically sociopathic thinking and behavior may be highly adaptive under certain circumstances and thus might represent inappropriate targets for behavior change. In some cases then, behavioral strategies might more productively focus on effecting cognitive and attitudinal changes within societal subgroups to facilitate development of greater tolerance and acceptance of social deviance. That few of the treatment approaches reviewed above, their underlying assumptions, or other suggested strategies have been systematically explored or evaluated over time for sociopathic offenders or patients is indeed an understatement. However, in keeping with recent research findings descriptive of the characteristics of sociopaths, evaluations of treatment outcome may also yield evidence to dispel some of the pessimism surrounding their treatment.

REFERENCES

Albert, R. S., Brigante, T. R., & Chase, M. The psychopathic personality: A content analysis of the concept. *The Journal of General Psychology*, 1959, **60**, 17–28.

Alexander, J. F., Barton, C., Schiavo, R. S., & Parsons, B. V. Systems-behavioral intervention with families of delinquents: Therapist characteristics, family behavior, and outcome. *Journal of Consulting and Clinical Psychology*, 1976, **44**, 656–664.

Alexander, J. F., & Parsons, B. V. Short-term behavioral intervention with delinquent families: Impact on family process and recidivism. *Journal of Abnormal Psychology*, 1973, **81**, 219–225.

Allen, H. E., Dinitz, S., Foster, T. W., Goldman, H., & Lindner, L. A. Sociopathy. *American Behavioral Scientist,* 1976, **20**, 215–226.

American Psychiatric Association. *Diagnostic and Statistical Manual of Mental Disorders* (2nd edition). Washington, D.C.: American Psychiatric Association, 1968.

American Psychiatric Association. *Diagnostic and Statistical Manual of Mental Disorders* (3rd edition). Washington, D.C.: American Psychiatric Association, 1980.

Andry, R. G. Faulty paternal- and maternal-child relationships, affection, and delinquency. *British Journal of Delinquency,* 1957, **8**, 34–48.

Aniskiewicz, A. S. "Autonomic components of vicarious conditioning and psychopathy." Doctoral dissertation, Purdue University, 1973. *Dissertation Abstracts International,* 1973, **34**, 2295B. (University Microfilms No. 73–28,040).

Archer, R. P., Sutker, P. B., White, J. L., & Ovin, G. H. Personality relationships among parents and adolescent offspring in inpatient treatment. *Psychological Reports,* 1978, **42**, 207–214.

Arieti, S. *The intrapsychic self.* New York: Basic Books, 1967.

Arnold, J. E., Levine, A. G., & Patterson, G. R. Changes in behavior following family intervention. *Journal of Consulting and Clinical Psychology,* 1975, **43**, 683–688.

Ashem, B., & Donner, L. Covert sensitization with alcoholics: A controlled replication. *Behaviour Research and Therapy,* 1968, **6**, 7–12.

Astin, A. W. A factor study of the MMPI psychopathic deviate scale. *Journal of Consulting Psychology,* 1959, **23**, 550–554.

Bassett, J. E., & Blanchard, E. B. The effect of the absence of close supervision on the use of response cost in a prison token economy. *Journal of Applied Behavior Analysis,* 1977, **10**, 375–379.

Bassett, J. E., Blanchard, E. B., & Koshland, E. Applied behavior analysis in a penal setting: Targeting "free world" behaviors. *Behavior Therapy,* 1975, **6**, 639–648.

Bender, L. Psychopathic behavior disorders in children. In R. M. Lindner, & R. V. Seliger (Eds.), *Handbook of correctional psychology,* New York: Philosophical Library, 1947.

Bernard, J. L., & Eisenman, R. Verbal conditioning in sociopaths with social and monetary reinforcement. *Journal of Personality and Social Psychology,* 1967, **6**, 203–206.

Blackburn, R. Sensation seeking, impulsivity, and psychopathic personality. *Journal of Consulting Psychology,* 1969, **33**, 571–574.

Blackburn, R. Psychopathy, arousal, and the need for stimulation. In R. D. Hare, & D. Schalling (Eds.), *Psychopathic behavior: Approaches to research.* New York: Wiley, 1978.

Blankstein, K. R. Patterns of autonomic functioning in primary and secondary psychopaths. Unpublished master's thesis, University of Waterloo, 1969.

Boren, J. J., & Colman, A. D. Some experiments on reinforcement principles within a psychiatric ward for delinquent soldiers. *Journal of Applied Behavior Analysis,* 1970, **3**, 29–37.

Borkovec, T. Autonomic reactivity to stimulation in psychopathic, neurotic and normal juvenile delinquents. *Journal of Consulting and Clinical Psychology,* 1970, **35**, 217–222.

Braukmann, C. J., & Fixsen, D. L. Behavior modification with delinquents. In

M. Hersen, R. M. Eisler, & P. M. Miller (Eds.), *Progress in behavior modification.* New York: Academic Press, 1975.

Bryan, J. H., & Kapche, R. Psychopathy and verbal conditioning. *Journal of Abnormal Psychology,* 1967, **72**, 71–73.

Burchard, J. D., & Harig, P. T. Behavior modification and juvenile delinquency. In H. Leitenberg (Ed.), *Handbook of behavior modification and behavior therapy.* Englewood Cliffs, N.J.: Prentice-Hall, 1976.

Buss, A. H. *Psychopathology.* New York: Wiley, 1966.

Buss, A. H., & Plomin, R. *A temperment theory of personality development.* New York: Wiley, 1975.

Caster, D. U., & Parsons, O. A. Relationship of depression, sociopathy, and locus of control to treatment outcome in alcoholics. *Journal of Consulting and Clinical Psychology,* 1977, **45**, 751–756.

Cautela, J. R. Covert sensitization. *Psychological Reports,* 1967, **20**, 459–468.

Cautela, J. R. Behavior therapy and self control: Techniques and implications. In C. M. Franks (Ed.), *Behavior therapy: Appraisal and status.* New York: McGraw-Hill, 1969.

Cautela, J. R. The treatment of alcoholism by covert sensitization. *Psychotherapy: Theory, research and practice,* 1970, **7**, 83–90.

Cheek, R. E., Tomarchio, T., Standen, J., & Albahary, R. S. Methadone plus—a behavior modification training program in self-control for addicts on methadone maintenance. *The International Journal of the Addictions,* 1973, **8**, 969–996.

Christie, R., & Geis, F. *Studies in Machiavellianism.* New York: Academic Press, 1969.

Cleckley, H. Psychopathic states. In S. Arieti (Ed.), *American handbook of psychotherapy and behavior change.* New York: Wiley, 1971.

Cleckley, H. *The mask of sanity* (5th edition). St. Louis: Mosby, 1976.

Cloninger, C. R., & Guze, S. Female criminals: Their personal, familial, and social backgrounds (the relation of those to the diagnoses of sociopathy and hysteria). *Archives of General Psychiatry,* 1970, **23**, 554–558.

Cloninger, C. R., Reich, T., & Guze, S. B. Genetic-environmental interactions and antisocial behavior. In R. D. Hare & D. Schalling (Eds.), *Psychopathic behavior: Approaches to research.* New York: Wiley, 1978.

Cohen, H. L., Filipczak, J., & Bis, J. *Case I: An initial study of contingencies applicable to special education.* Silver Springs, MD: Educational Facility Press-IBR, 1967.

Collier, W. V., & Hijazi, Y. A. A follow-up study of former residents of a therapeutic community. *The International Journal of the Addictions,* 1974, **9**, 805–826.

Copemann, C. D. Treatment of polydrug abuse and addiction by covert sensitization: Some contraindications. *The International Journal of the Addictions,* 1977, **12**, 17–23.

Craddick, R. Selection of psychopathic from nonpsychopathic prisoners within a Canadian prison. *Psychological Reports,* 1962, **10**, 495–499.

Crowe, R. R. The adopted offspring of women criminal offenders: A study of their arrest records. *Archives of General Psychiatry,* 1972, **27**, 600–603.

Crowe, R. R. An adoption study of antisocial personality. *Archives of General Psychiatry,* 1974, **31**, 785–791.

Davidson, W. S., & Seidman, E. Studies of behavior modification and juvenile delinquency: A review, methodological critique, and social perspective. *Psychological Bulletin,* 1974, **81**, 998–1011.

DeMyer-Gapin, S., & Scott, T. J. Effect of stimulus novelty on stimulation seeking in antisocial and neurotic children. *Journal of Abnormal Psychology,* 1977, **86**, 96–98.

Dengerink, H. A., & Bertilson, H. S. Psychopathy and physiological arousal in an aggressive task. *Psychophysiology,* 1975, **12**, 682–684.

Densen-Gerber, J. *We mainline dreams: The Odyssey House story.* Garden City, N.Y.: Doubleday, 1973.

Densen-Gerber, J., & Drassner, D. Odyssey House: A structural model for the successful treatment and re-entry of the ex-drug abuser. *Journal of Drug Issues,* 1974, **4**, 414–427.

Dinitz, S., Dynes, R. R., & Clarke, A. C. *Deviance: Studies in definition, management, and treatment* (2nd edition). New York: Oxford University Press, 1975.

Dinitz, S., Goldman, H., Allen, H. E., & Lindner, L. A. Psychopathy and autonomic responsivity: A note on the importance of diagnosis. *Journal of Abnormal Psychology,* 1973, **82**, 533–534.

Dobbs, D. S., & Speck, L. B. Visual evoked response and frequency density spectra of prisoner-patients. *Comprehensive Psychiatry,* 1968, **9**, 62–70.

Doctor, R. F., & Winder, C. L. Delinquent versus nondelinquent performance on the Porteus Qualitative Maze test. *Journal of Consulting Psychology,* 1954, **18**, 71–73.

Doctor, R. M., & Craine, W. H. Modification of drug language usage of primary and neurotic psychopaths. *Journal of Abnormal Psychology,* 1971, **77**, 174–180.

Dongier, M. Mental diseases. In A. Remond (Editor-in-chief), *Handbook of electroencephalography and clinical neurophysiology* (Vol. 13: H. Gaustaut (Ed.), *Clinical EEG,* III). Amsterdam: Elsevier, 1974.

Duehn, W., & Shannon, C. Covert sensitization in the public high school: Short-term group treatment of male adolescent drug abusers. Paper presented at the National Conference on Social Welfare, 1973.

Duffy, E. Activation. In N. S. Greenfield & R. A. Steinbach (Eds.), *Handbook of psychophysiology.* New York: Holt, Rinehart & Winston, 1972.

Dworkin, R. H., Burke, B. W., Maher, B. A., & Gottesman, I. I. A longitudinal study of the genetics of personality. *Journal of Personality and Social Psychology,* 1976, **34**, 510–518.

Egger, G. J., Webb, R. A. J., & Reynolds, I. Early adolescent antecedents of narcotic abuse. *The International Journal of the Addictions,* 1978, **13**, 773–781.

Ellingson, R. J. The incidence of EEG abnormality among patients with mental disorders of apparently nonorganic origin: A critical review. *American Journal of Psychiatry,* 1954, **111**, 263–275.

Emery, R. E., & Marholin, D. An applied behavior analysis of delinquency: The irrelevancy of relevant behavior. *American Psychologist,* 1977, **32**, 860–873.

Eysenck, H. J. *The dynamics of anxiety and hysteria.* New York: Praeger, 1957.

Eysenck, H. J. Classification and the problem of diagnosis. In H. J. Eysenck (Ed.), *Handbook of abnormal psychology.* New York: Basic Books, 1961.

Eysenck, H. J. *Crime and personality.* London: Methuen, 1964.

Eysenck, H. J., & Eysenck, S. B. G. *Eysenck personality inventory* (Form A). San Diego: Educational and Industrial Testing Service, 1968.

Eysenck, H. J., & Eysenck, S. B. G. Psychopathy, personality, and genetics. In R. D.

Hare & D. Schalling (Eds.), *Psychopathic behavior: Approaches to research.* New York: Wiley, 1978.

Fairweather, G. W. The effect of selected incentive conditions on the performance of psychopathic, neurotic, and normal criminals in a serial rote learning situation. (Doctoral dissertation, University of Illinois, 1953). *Dissertation Abstracts International,* 1954, **14**, 394–395 (University Microfilms No. 6940).

Farley, F. H., & Farley, S. V. Stimulus-seeking motivation and delinquent behavior among institutionalized delinquent girls. *Journal of Consulting and Clinical Psychology,* 1972, **39**, 94–97.

Fenton, G. W., Fenwick, P. B. C., Ferguson, W., & Lam, C. T. The CNV and antisocial behavior: A pilot study of Broadmoor patients. *Electroencephalography and Clinical Neurophysiology,* 1975, **38**, 214.

Fenz, W. Heart rate responses to a stressor: A comparison between primary and secondary psychopaths and normal controls. *Journal of Experimental Research in Personality,* 1971, **5**, 7–13.

Fixsen, D. L., Wolf, M. M., & Phillips, E. L. Achievement Place: A teaching family model of community-based group homes for youth in trouble. In L. A. Hammerlynck, L. C. Handy, & E. J. Mash (Eds.), *Behavioral change: Methodology, concepts and practice.* Champaign, Ill.: Research Press, 1973.

Fo, W. S. O., & O'Donnell, C. R. The buddy system: Relationship and contingency conditions in a community intervention program for youth with nonprofessionals as behavior change agents. *Journal of Consulting and Clinical Psychology,* 1974, **42**, 163–169.

Fooks, G., & Thomas, R. R. Differential qualitative performance of delinquents on the Porteus Maze. *Journal of Consulting Psychology,* 1957, **21**, 351–353.

Foulds, G. A. The logical impossibility of using hysterics and dysthymics as criterion groups in the study of introversion and extraversion. *British Journal of Psychology,* 1961, **52**, 385–387.

Fox, R., & Lippert, W. Spontaneous GSR and anxiety level in sociopathic delinquents. *Journal of Consulting Psychology,* 1963, **27**, 368.

Foy, D. W., Miller, P. M., Eisler, R. M., & O'Toole, D. H. Social skills training to teach alcoholics to refuse drinks effectively. *Journal of Studies on Alcohol,* 1976, **37**, 1340–1345.

Frederiksen, L. W., Jenkins, J. O., & Carr, C. R. Indirect modification of adolescent drug abuse using contingency conditions. *Journal of Behavior Therapy and Experimental Psychiatry,* 1976, **7**, 377–378.

Frederiksen, L. W., Jenkins, J. O., Foy, D. W., & Eisler, R. M. Social skills training to modify abusive verbal outbursts in adults. *Journal of Applied Behavior Analysis,* 1976, **9**, 117–125.

Gendreau, P., & Suboski, M. D. Classical discrimination eyelid conditioning in primary psychopaths. *Journal of Abnormal Psychology,* 1971, **77**, 241–246.

Gilberstadt, H., & Duker, J. *A handbook for clinical and actuarial MMPI interpretation.* Philadelphia: Saunders, 1965.

Gilbert, J. G., & Lombardi, D. N. Personality characteristics of young male narcotic addicts. *Journal of Consulting Psychology,* 1967, **31**, 536–538.

Goldstein, I. B. The relationship of muscle tension and autonomic activity to psychiatric disorders. *Psychosomatic Medicine,* 1965, **27**, 39–52.

Goodwin, D. W., Schulsinger, F., Hermansen, L., Guze, S. B., & Winokur, G. Alcohol problems in adoptees raised apart from alcoholic biological parents. *Archives of General Psychiatry,* 1973, **28**, 238–243.

Goodwin, D. W., Schulsinger, F., Knop, J., Mednick, S., & Guze, S. B. Alcoholism and depression in adopted-out daughters of alcoholics. *Archives of General Psychiatry,* 1977, **34**, 751–755.

Gough, H. G. A sociological theory of psychopathology. *American Journal of Sociology,* 1948, **53**, 359–366.

Gray, K. G., & Hutchison, H. C. The psychopathic personality: A survey of Canadian psychiatrists' opinions. *Canadian Psychiatric Association Journal,* 1964, **9**, 452–461.

Gullick, E. L., Sutker, P. B., & Adams, H. E. Delay of information in paired-associate learning among incarcerated groups of sociopaths and heroin addicts. *Psychological Reports,* 1976, **38**, 143–151.

Guze, S. B., Goodwin, D. W., & Crane, J. B. Criminality and psychiatric disorders. *Archives of General Psychiatry,* 1969, **20**, 583–591.

Gynther, M. D., Altman, H., & Warbin, R. W. Behavioral correlates for the Minnesota Multiphasic Personality Inventory 4–9/9–4 code types: A case of the emperor's new clothes? *Journal of Consulting and Clinical Psychology,* 1973, **40**, 259–263.

Hare, R. D. Acquisition and generalization of a conditioned-fear response in psychopathic and nonpsychopathic criminals. *Journal of Psychology,* 1965, **59**, 367–370. (a)

Hare, R. D. A conflict and learning theory analysis of psychopathic behavior. *Journal of Research in Crime and Delinquency,* 1965, **2**, 12–19. (b)

Hare, R. D. Temporal gradient of fear arousal in psychopaths. *Journal of Abnormal Psychology,* 1965, **70**, 442–445. (c)

Hare, R. D. Psychopathy, autonomic functioning and the orienting response. *Journal of Abnormal Psychology, Monograph Supplement,* Part 2, June 1968. Pp. 1–24.

Hare, R. D. *Psychopathy: Theory and research.* New York: Wiley, 1970.

Hare, R. D. Psychopathy and physiological responses to adrenalin. *Journal of Abnormal Psychology,* 1972, **79**, 138–147.

Hare, R. D. Anxiety, stress and psychopathy. In I. Sarason, & C. Spielberger (Eds.), *Anxiety and stress,* Vol. 2. Washington, D.C.: Hemisphere, 1975. (a)

Hare, R. D. Psychopathy. In P. Venables & M. Christie (Eds.), *Research in psychophysiology,* New York: Wiley, 1975. (b)

Hare, R. D. Psychophysiological studies of psychopathy. In D. C. Fowles (Ed.), *Clinical applications of psychophysiology.* New York: Columbia University Press, 1975. (c)

Hare, R. D. Electrodermal and cardiovascular correlates of psychopathy. In R. D. Hare & D. Schalling (Eds.), *Psychopathic behavior: Approaches to research.* New York: Wiley, 1978.

Hare, R. D., & Cox, D. N. Clinical and empirical conceptions of psychopathy, and the selection of subjects for research. In R. D. Hare & D. Schalling (Eds.), *Psychopathic behavior: Approaches to research.* New York: Wiley, 1978.

Hare, R. D., & Craigen, D. Psychopathy and physiological activity in a mixed-motive game situation. *Psychophysiology,* 1974, **11**, 197–206.

Hare, R. D., Frazelle, J., & Cox, D. N. Psychopathy and physiological responses to threat of aversive stimulus. *Psychophysiology,* 1978, **15**, 165–172.

Hare, R. D., & Quinn, M. J. Psychopathy and autonomic conditioning. *Journal of Abnormal Psychology,* 1971, **77**, 223–235.

Hawk, S. S., & Peterson, R. A. Do MMPI psychopathic deviancy scores reflect psychopathic deviancy or just deviancy? *Journal of Personality Assessment,* 1974, **38**, 362–368.

Hay, L. R., Hay, W. M., & Angle, H. V. The reactivity of self recording: A case report of a drug abuser. *Behavior Therapy,* 1977, **8**, 1004–1007.

Hebb, D. O. *Organization of behavior.* New York: Wiley, 1949.

Hebb, D. O. Drives and the CNS (conceptual nervous system). *Psychological Review,* 1955, **62**, 243–254.

Hedlund, J. L. MMPI clinical scale correlates. *Journal of Consulting and Clinical Psychology,* 1977, **45**, 739–750.

Heron, W. The pathology of boredom. *Scientific American,* 1957, **196**, 52–56.

Hetherington, E. M., Stouwie, R. J., & Ridberg, E. H. Patterns of family interaction and child-rearing attitudes related to three dimensions of juvenile delinquency. *Journal of Abnormal Psychology,* 1971, **78**, 160–176.

Hill, D. The EEG in psychiatry. In J. D. N. Hill & G. Parr (Eds.), *Electroencephalography: A symposium on its various aspects.* London: Macdonald, 1963.

Hill, H. E., Haertzen, C. A., & Davis, H. An MMPI factor analytic study of alcoholics, narcotic addicts, and criminals. *Quarterly Journal of Studies on Alcohol,* 1962, **23**, 411–431.

Hill, M. S., & Hill, R. N. Hereditary influence on the normal personality using the MMPI, I. Age-corrected parent-offspring resemblances. *Behavior Genetics,* 1973, **3**, 133–144.

Hogan, R. Development of an Empathy Scale. *Journal of Consulting and Clinical Psychology,* 1969, **33**, 307–316.

Hughes, R. C., & Johnson, R. W. Introversion-extraversion and psychiatric diagnoses: A test of Eysenck's hypothesis. *Journal of Clinical Psychology,* 1975, **31**, 426–427.

Hundleby, J. D., & Ross, B. E. Comparison of measures of psychopathy. *Journal of Consulting and Clinical Psychology,* 1977, **45**, 702–703.

Hutchings, B. Environmental and genetic factors in psychopathology and criminality. Thesis, University of London, 1972.

Ingram, G. L., Gerard, R. E., Quay, H. C., & Levinson, R. B. An experimental program for the psychopathic delinquent: Looking in the "correctional wastebasket." *Journal of Research in Crime and Delinquency,* 1970, **7**, 25–30.

Jenkins, R. L. Diagnosis, dynamics, and treatment in child psychiatry. *Psychiatric Research Reports,* 1964, **18**, 91–120.

Jesness, C. F. Comparative effectiveness of behavior modification and transactional analysis programs for delinquents. *Journal of Consulting and Clinical Psychology,* 1975, **43**, 758–779.

Johns, J. H., & Quay, H. C. The effect of social reward or verbal conditioning in psychopathic and neurotic military offenders. *Journal of Consulting Psychology,* 1962, **26**, 217–220.

Jones, F. D., Stayer, S. J., Wichlacz, C. R., Thomes, L., & Livingstone, B. L. Contingency management of hospital diagnosed character and behavior disorder soldiers. *Journal of Behavior Therapy and Experimental Psychiatry,* 1977, **8**, 333.

Jones, M. *Social psychiatry: A study of therapeutic communities.* London: Tavistock, 1952.

Kadlub, K. J. The effects of two types of reinforcements on the performance of psychopathic and normal criminals. Unpublished doctoral dissertation, University of Illinois, 1956.

Kammeier, M. L., Hoffman, H., & Loper, R. G. Personality characteristics of alcoholics as college freshmen and at time of treatment. *Quarterly Journal of Studies on Alcohol,* 1973, **34**, 390–399.

Kandel, H. J., Ayllon, T., & Roberts, M. D. Rapid educational rehabilitation for prison inmates. *Behaviour Research and Therapy,* 1976, **14**, 323–331.

Karpman, B. The structure of neurosis: With special differentials between neurosis, psychosis, homosexuality, alcoholism, psychopathy, and criminality. *Archives of Criminal Psychodynamics,* 1961, **4**, 599–646.

Katkin, E. S. Relationship between manifest anxiety and two indices of autonomic responses to stress. *Journal of Personality and Social Psychology,* 1965, **2**, 324–333.

Katkin, E. S. Electrodermal lability: A psychophysiological analysis of individual difference in response to stress. In I. Sarason, & C. Spielberger (Eds.), *Anxiety and stress,* Vol. 2. Washington, D.C.: Hemisphere, 1975.

Kent, R. A methodological critique of Interventions for boys with conduct problems. *Journal of Consulting and Clinical Psychology,* 1976, **44**, 297–299.

Kilpatrick, D. G. Differential responsiveness of two electrodermal indices to psychological stress and performance of a complex cognitive task. *Psychophysiology,* 1972, **9**, 218–226.

Kilpatrick, D. G., Sutker, P. B., Roitzsch, J. C., & Miller, W. C. Personality correlates of polydrug use. *Psychological Reports,* 1976, **38**, 311–317.

Kilpatrick, D. G., Sutker, P. B., & Smith, A. D. Deviant drug and alcohol use: The role of anxiety, sensation seeking, and other personality variables. In M. Zuckerman & C. D. Spielberger (Eds.), *Emotions and anxiety: New concepts, methods, and applications.* Hillsdale, N.J.: Lawrence Erlbaum, 1976.

King, G. D., & Kelley, C. K. Behavioral correlates for spike-4, spike-9, and 4–9/9–4 MMPI profiles in students at a university mental health center. *Journal of Clinical Psychology,* 1977, **33**, 718–724.

Kish, G. B., & Busse, W. MMPI correlates of sensation-seeking in male alcoholics: A test of Quay's hypothesis applied to alcoholism. *Journal of Clinical Psychology,* 1969, **25**, 60–63.

Lacey, B., & Lacey, J. Studies of heart rate and other bodily processes in sensorimotor behavior. In P. Obrist, A. Black, J. Brener, & L. Dicara (Eds.), *Cardiovascular psychophysiology.* Chicago: Aldine, 1974.

Lacey, J. I. Somatic response patterning and stress: Some revisions of activation theory. In N. H. Appleby & R. Trumbell (Eds.), *Psychological stress: Issues in research.* New York: Appleton-Century-Crofts, 1967.

Laycock, A. L. Vascular change under stress in delinquents and controls. *British Journal of Criminology,* 1968, **8**, 64–69.

Lesser, E. Behavior therapy with a narcotics user: A case report. *Behaviour Research and Therapy,* 1967, **5**, 251–252.

Lesser, E. Behavior therapy with a narcotics user: A case report: Ten-year follow-up. *Behaviour Research and Therapy,* 1976, **14**, 381.

Lewandowski, D., & Graham, J. R. Empirical correlates of frequently occurring two-point MMPI code types: A replicated study. *Journal of Consulting and Clinical Psychology,* 1972, **39**, 467–472.

Lewis, D. O., & Balla, D. "Sociopathy" and its synonyms: Inappropriate diagnoses in child psychiatry. *American Journal of Psychiatry,* 1975, **132**, 720–722.

Liberman, R. Aversive conditioning of drug addicts: A pilot study. *Behaviour Research and Therapy,* 1968, **6**, 229–231.

Lindner, R. M. Experimental studies in constitutional psychopathic inferiority. Part I. Systemic patterns. *Journal of Clinical Psychopathology,* 1942, **4**, 252–276.

Lindner, R. M. Experimental studies in constitutional psychopathic inferiority. Part II. *Journal of Criminal Psychopathology,* 1943, **4**, 484–500.

Lindsley, D. B. Emotion. In S. S. Stevens (Ed.), *Handbook of experimental psychology.* New York: Wiley, 1951.

Lion, J. R. The role of depression in the treatment of aggressive personality disorders. *American Journal of Psychiatry,* 1972, **129**, 347–349.

Lippert, W. W., & Senter, R. J. Electrodermal responses in the sociopath. *Psychonomic Science,* 1966, **4**, 25–26.

Lykken, D. T. A study of anxiety in the sociopathic personality. *Journal of Abnormal and Social Psychology,* 1957, **55**, 6–10.

Lykken, D. T. The psychopath and the lie detector. *Psychophysiology,* 1978, **15**, 137–142.

Lykken, D. T., Tellegen, A., & Katzenmeyer, C. *Manual for the activity preference questionnaire.* Minneapolis: Department of Psychiatry, University of Minnesota, 1973.

McCallum, W. C. The CNV and conditionability in psychopaths. *Electroencephalography and Clinical Neurophysiology,* 1973, **33**, 337–343.

McCord, W. M., & McCord, J. *Psychopathy and delinquency.* New York: Grune & Stratton, 1956.

McCord, W. M., & McCord, J. *The psychopath.* Princeton, N.J.: Van Nostrand, 1964.

McCullough, J. P., & Adams, H. E. Anxiety, learning sets, and sociopathy. *Psychological Reports,* 1970, **27**, 47–52.

McNamara, J. R., & Andrasik, F. Systematic program change—its effects on resident behavior in a forensic psychiatry institution. *Journal of Behavior Therapy and Experimental Psychiatry,* 1977, **8**, 19–23.

Maddocks, P. D. A five-year follow-up of untreated psychopaths. *British Journal of Psychiatry,* 1970, **116**, 511–515.

Maher, B. A. *Principles of psychopathology.* New York: McGraw-Hill, 1966.

Malmo, R. B. Overview and indices. In N. S. Greenfield & R. A. Steinbach (Eds.), *Handbook of psychophysiology.* New York: Holt, Rinehart & Winston, 1972.

Marcus, B. A. A dimensional study of a prison population. *British Journal of Criminology,* 1960, **1**, 130–153.

Marks, P. A., & Seeman, W. *Actuarial description of abnormal personality.* Baltimore: Williams & Wilkins, 1963.

Mathis, H. Emotional responsivity in the antisocial personality. (Doctoral dissertation, The George Washington University, 1970). *Dissertation Abstracts International,* 1971, **31**, 6907B–6908B. (University Microfilms No. 71–12,299)

Maughs, S. B. Current concepts of psychopathology. *Archives of Criminal Psychodynamics,* 1961, **4**, 550–557.

Mawson, A. R., & Mawson, C. D. Personality and arousal: A new interpretation of the psychophysiological literature. *Biological Psychiatry,* 1977, **12**, 49–74.

Megargee, E. I., & Dorhout, B. Revision and refinement of the classificatory rules. *Criminal Justice and Behavior,* 1977, **4**, 125–148.

Milan, M. A., & McKee, J. M. The cellblock token economy: Token reinforcement procedures in a maximum security correctional institution for adult male felons. *Journal of Applied Behavior Analysis,* 1976, **9**, 253–275.

Milan, M. A., Wood, L., Williams, R., Rogers, J., Hampton, L., & McKee, J. M. *Applied behavior analysis and the imprisoned adult felon, Project I: The cellblock economy.* Montgomery, Ala.: Rehabilitation Research Foundation, 1965.

Miller, L. H., & Shmavonian, B. M. Replicability of two GSR indices as a function of stress and cognitive activity. *Journal of Personality and Social Psychology,* 1965, **2**, 753–756.

Miller, P. M. *Behavioral treatment of alcoholism.* New York: Pergamon Press, 1976.

Miller, P. M., Becker, J. V., Foy, D. W., & Wooten, L. S. Instructional control of the components of alcoholic drinking behavior. *Behavior Therapy,* 1976, **7**, 472–480.

Mischel, W. Research and theory on delay of gratification. In B. A. Maher (Ed.), *Progress in experimental personality research,* Vol. 2. New York: Academic Press, 1966.

Moan, C. E., & Heath, R. G. Septal stimulation for the initiation of heterosexual behavior in a homosexual male. *Journal of Behavior Therapy and Experimental Psychiatry,* 1972, **3**, 23–30.

Moruzzi, G., & Magoun, H. Brain stem reticular formation and activation of the EEG. *Electroencephalography and Clinical Neurophysiology,* 1949, **1**, 455–473.

Mowrer, O. H. On the dual nature of learning—a reinterpretation of "conditioning" and "problem-solving." *Harvard Educational Review,* 1947, **17**, 102–148.

Nay, W. R. Comprehensive behavioral treatment in a training school for delinquents. In K. S. Calhoun, H. E. Adams, & K. M. Mitchell (Eds.), *Innovative treatment methods in psychopathology.* New York: Wiley, 1974.

Olson, R. W. MMPI sex differences in narcotic addicts. *Journal of General Psychology,* 1964, **71**, 257–266.

O'Neil, P. M., & Roitzsch, J. C. Assertiveness training for alcohol abusers: Rationale and application. *British Journal on Alcohol and Alcoholism,* 1977, **12**, 107–113.

Orris, J. B. Visual monitoring performance in three subgroups of male delinquents. *Journal of Abnormal Psychology,* 1969, **74**, 227–229.

Overall, J. E. MMPI personality patterns of alcoholics and narcotic addicts. *Quarterly Journal of Studies on Alcohol,* 1973, **34**, 104–111.

Painting, D. H. The performance of psychopathic individuals under conditions of positive and negative partial reinforcement. *Journal of Abnormal Psychology,* 1961, **62**, 352–355.

Partridge, G. D. Current conceptions of psychopathic personality. *American Journal of Psychiatry,* 1930, **10**, 53–99.

Patterson, G. R. Interventions for boys with conduct problems: Multiple settings, treatments, and criteria. *Journal of Consulting and Clinical Psychology,* 1974, **42**, 471–481.

Patterson, G. R. Naturalistic observation in clinical assessment. *Journal of Abnormal Child Psychology,* 1977, **5**, 309–322.

Payne, F. D., & Wiggins, J. S. MMPI profile types and the self-report of psychiatric patients. *Journal of Abnormal Psychology*, 1972, **79**, 1–8.

Persons, R. W., & Bruning, J. L. Instrumental learning with sociopaths: A test of clinical theory. *Journal of Abnormal Psychology*, 1966, **71**, 165–168.

Peterson, D. R., Quay, H. C., & Cameron, G. E. Personality and background factors in juvenile delinquency as inferred from questionnaire responses. *Journal of Consulting Psychology*, 1959, **23**, 395–399.

Peterson, D. R., Quay, H. C., & Tiffany, T. L. Personality factors related to juvenile delinquency. *Child Development*, 1961, **32**, 355–372.

Petrie, A. *Individuality in pain and suffering.* Chicago: University of Chicago Press, 1967.

Phillips, E. L. Achievement Place: Token reinforcement procedures in a home-style rehabilitation setting for "predelinquent" boys. *Journal of Applied Behavior Analysis*, 1968, **1**, 213–223.

Phillips, E. L., Phillips, E. A., Fixsen, D. L., & Wolf, M. W. Behavior shaping works for delinquents. *Psychology Today*, June 1973. Pp. 75–79.

Platt, J. J., & Labate, C. *Heroin addiction: Theory, research, and treatment.* New York: Wiley, 1976.

Polakow, R. L. Covert sensitization treatment of a probationed barbiturate addict. *Journal of Behavior Therapy and Experimental Psychiatry*, 1975, **6**, 53–54.

Polakow, R. L., & Doctor, R. M. A behavior modification program for adult probationers. Paper presented at the 25th annual convention, California Psychological Association, Los Angeles, January, 1972.

Polakow, R. L., & Doctor, R. M. Treatment of marijuana and barbiturate dependency by contingency contracting. *Journal of Behavior and Experimental Psychiatry*, 1973, **4**, 375–377.

Porges, S. W. Peripheral and neurochemical parallels of psychopathology: A psychophysiological model relating autonomic imbalance to hyperactivity, psychopathy, and autism. In H. W. Reese (Ed.), *Advances in child development and behavior*, Vol. 2. New York: Academic Press, 1976.

Quay, H. C. Personality dimensions in delinquent males as inferred from the factor analysis of behavior ratings. *Journal of Research in Crime and Delinquency*, 1964, **1**, 33–37.

Quay, H. C. Psychopathic personality as pathological stimulation-seeking. *American Journal of Psychiatry*, 1965, **122**, 180–183.

Quay, H. C., & Hunt, W. A. Psychopathy, neuroticism and verbal conditioning. A replication and extension. *Journal of Consulting Psychology*, 1965, **29**, 283.

Quay, H. C., & Parsons, L. *The differential behavioral classification of the juvenile offender.* Washington, D.C.: Bureau of Prisons, U.S. Department of Justice, 1970.

Reid, J. B., & Patterson, G. R. Follow-up analyses of a behavioral treatment program for boys with conduct problems: A reply to Kent. *Journal of Consulting and Clinical Psychology*, 1976, **44**, 299–302.

Robins, E. Personality disorders. II: Sociopathic type: Antisocial disorders and sexual deviations. In A. M. Freedman & H. I. Kaplan (Eds.), *Comprehensive textbook of psychiatry*. Baltimore: Williams & Wilkins, 1967.

Robins, E., Gentry, D. A., Munoz, R. A., & Marten, S. A contrast of the three more common illnesses with the ten less common in a study and 18-month follow-up of

314 psychiatric emergency room patients. II. Characteristics of patients with the three more common illnesses. *Archives of General Psychiatry,* 1977, **34**, 269–281.

Robins, L. N. *Deviant children grown up.* Baltimore: Williams & Wilkins, 1966.

Robins, L. N. The adult development of the antisocial child. *Seminars in Psychiatry,* 1970, **2**, 420–434.

Robins, L. N. Aetiological implications in studies of childhood histories relating to antisocial personality. In R. D. Hare & D. Schalling (Eds.), *Psychopathic behavior: Approaches to research.* New York: Wiley, 1978.

Ross, B. E., & Hundleby, J. D. A comparison of measures of psychopathy on a prison sample. *Proceedings of the 81st annual convention of the American Psychological Association,* 1973, **8**, 535–536.

Rotenberg, M. Psychopathy, insensitivity, and sensitization. *Professional Psychology,* 1975, **6**, 283–292.

Sarason, I. G. A cognitive social-learning approach to juvenile delinquency. In R. D. Hare & D. Schalling (Eds.), *Psychopathic behavior: Approaches to research.* New York: Wiley, 1978.

Saruk, S. A comparison study of Machiavellianism, values, and locus of psychopathic subgroups. (Doctor dissertation, United States International University, 1975). *Dissertation Abstracts International,* 1975, **36**, 458B. (University Microfilms No. 75-14, 344)

Satterfield, J. H. The hyperactive child syndrome: A precursor of adult psychopathy– In R. D. Hare & D. Schalling (Eds.), *Psychopathic behavior: Approaches to research.* New York: Wiley, 1978.

Schalling, D. Psychopathy-related personality variables and the psychophysiology of socialization. In R. D. Hare & D. Schalling (Eds.), *Psychopathic behavior: Approaches to research.* New York: Wiley, 1978.

Schalling, D., & Levander, S. *Spontaneous fluctuations in skin conductance during anticipation of pain in two delinquent groups differing in anxiety proneness.* Reports from the Psychological Laboratories, University of Stockholm, 1967, No. 238.

Schalling, D., Lidberg, L., Levander, S. E., & Dahlin, Y. Relations between fluctuations in skin resistance and digital pulse volume and scores on the Gough *De* Scale. Unpublished manuscript, University of Stockholm, 1968.

Schalling, D., Lidberg, L., Levander, S. E., & Dahlin, Y. Spontaneous autonomic activity as related to psychopathy. *Biological Psychology,* 1973, **1**, 83–97.

Schalling, D., & Rosen, A. Porteus Maze differences between psychopathic and non-psychopathic criminals. *British Journal of Social and Clinical Psychology,* 1968, **7**, 224–228.

Schmauk, F. J. Punishment, arousal, and avoidance learning in sociopaths. *Journal of Abnormal Psychology,* 1970, **76**, 325–335.

Schulsinger, F. Psychopathy: Heredity and environment. *International Journal of Mental Health,* 1972, **1**, 190–206.

Schwitzgebel, R. K. Behavior modification programs. In S. Dinitz, R. R. Dynes, & A. C. Clarke (Eds.), *Deviance: Studies in definition, management, and treatment* (2nd edition). New York: Oxford University Press, 1975.

Shagass, C., & Schwartz, M. Observations on somatosensory cortical reactivity in personality disorders. *Journal of Nervous and Mental Disease,* 1962, **135**, 44–51.

Shapiro, D. *Neurotic styles.* New York: Basic Books, 1965.

Siegel, R. A. Probability of punishment and suppression of behavior in psychopathic and nonpsychopathic offenders. *Journal of Abnormal Psychology*, 1978, **87**, 514–522.

Sigal, J. J., Star, K. H., & Franks, C. M. Hysterics and dysthymics as criterion groups in the study of introversion-extraversion. *Journal of Abnormal and Social Psychology*, 1958, **57**, 143–148.

Skrzypek, G. J. Effect of perceptual isolation and arousal on anxiety, complexity preference, and novelty preference in psychopathic and neurotic delinquents. *Journal of Abnormal Psychology*, 1969, **74**, 321–329.

Sloane, R. B., Staples, F. R., Cristol, A. H., Yorkston, N. J., & Whipple, K. Patient characteristics and outcome in psychotherapy and behavior therapy. *Journal of Consulting and Clinical Psychology*, 1976, **44**, 330–339.

Smith, R. J. Some thoughts on psychopathy. *Psychotherapy: Theory, research, and practice*, 1973, **10**, 354–358.

Solomon, R. L., Turner, L. H., & Lessac, M. S. Some effects of delay of punishment on resistance to temptation in dogs. *Journal of Personality and Social Psychology*, 1968, **8**, 233–238.

Spielberger, C. D., Kling, J. K., & O'Hagan, S. E. J. Dimensions of psychopathic personality: Antisocial behavior and anxiety. In R. D. Hare & D. Schalling (Eds.), *Psychopathic behavior: Approaches to research*. New York: Wiley, 1978.

Steinberg, E. P., & Schwartz, G. E. Biofeedback and electrodermal self-regulation in psychopathy. *Journal of Abnormal Psychology*, 1976, **85**, 408–415.

Steinfeld, G. J. The use of covert sensitization with institutionalized narcotic addicts. *The International Journal of the Addictions*, 1970, **5**, 225–232.

Stewart, D. J. Effects of social reinforcement on dependency and aggressive responses of psychopathic, neurotic, and subculture delinquents. *Journal of Abnormal Psychology*, 1972, **79**, 76–83.

Stewart, D. J., & Resnick, H. J. Verbal conditioning of psychopaths as a function of experimenter-subject sex differences. *Journal of Abnormal Psychology*, 1970, **75**, 90–92.

Stuart, R. B. Behavioral contracting within the families of delinquents. *Journal of Behavior Therapy and Experimental Psychiatry*, 1971, **2**, 1–11.

Stumphauzer, J. S. Increased delay of gratification in young prison inmates through imitation of high-delay peer models. *Journal of Personality and Social Psychology*, 1972, **21**, 10–17.

Stumphauzer, J. S. (Ed.). *Behavior therapy with delinquents*. Springfield, Ill.: Charles C. Thomas, 1973.

Suedfeld, P., & Landon, P. B. Approaches to treatment. In R. D. Hare & D. Schalling (Eds.), *Psychopathic behavior: Approaches to research*. New York: Wiley, 1978.

Sugarman, B. S. Evaluating drug treatment programs: A review and critique of some studies on programs of the concept house type. *Drug Forum*, 1974, **3**, 149–153.

Sutker, P. B. Vicarious conditioning and sociopathy. *Journal of Abnormal Psychology*, 1970, **76**, 380–386.

Sutker, P. B. Personality differences and sociopathy in heroin addicts and nonaddict prisoners. *Journal of Abnormal Psychology*, 1971, **78**, 247–251.

Sutker, P. B., Allain, A. N., Smith, C. J., & Cohen, G. H. Addict descriptions of therapeutic community, multimodality, and methadone maintenance treatment clients and staff. *Journal of Consulting and Clinical Psychology*, 1978, **46**, 508–517.

Sutker, P. B., Archer, R. P., & Allain, A. N. Drug abuse patterns, personality characteristics, and relationships with sex, race, and sensation seeking. *Journal of Consulting and Clinical Psychology,* 1978, **46**, 1374–1378.

Sutker, P. B., Gil, S. H., & Sutker, L. W. Sociopathy and serial learning of CVC combinations with high and low social content ratings. *Journal of Personality and Social Psychology,* 1971, **17**, 158–162.

Sutker, P. B., & Moan, C. E. Personality characteristics of socially deviant women: Incarcerated heroin addicts, street addicts, and nonaddicted prisoners. In J. M. Singh, L. H. Miller, & H. Lal (Eds.), *Drug addiction,* Vol. 2. Mt. Kisco, N.Y.: Futura, 1972.

Sutker, P. B., & Moan, C. E. A psychosocial description of penitentiary inmates. *Archives of General Psychiatry,* 1973, **29**, 663–667.

Sutker, P. B., Moan, C. E., & Swanson, W. C. Porteus Maze Test qualitative performance in pure sociopaths, prison normals and antisocial psychotics. *Journal of Clinical Psychology,* 1972, **28**, 349–353.

Syndulko, K. Electrocortical investigations of sociopathy. In R. D. Hare & D. Schalling (Eds.), *Psychopathic behavior: Approaches to research.* New York: Wiley, 1978.

Syndulko, K., Parker, D. A., Jens, R., Maltzman, I., & Ziskind, E. Psychophysiology of sociopathy: Electrocortical measures. *Biological Psychology,* 1975, **3**, 185–200.

Szpiler, J. A., & Epstein, S. Availability of an avoidance response as related to autonomic arousal. *Journal of Abnormal Psychology,* 1976, **85**, 73–82.

Tarter, R. E. *Etiology of alcoholism: Interdisciplinary integration.* Manuscript presented at the NATO International Conference, Bergen, Norway, September, 1977.

Tarter, R. E., McBride, H., Buonpane, N., & Schneider, D. U. Differentiation of alcoholics: Childhood history of minimal brain dysfunction, family history, and drinking patterns. *Archives of General Psychiatry,* 1977, **34**, 761–768.

Tharp, R. G., & Wetzel, R. J. *Behavior modification in the natural environment.* New York: Academic Press, 1969.

Thompson, M. S., & Conrad, P. L. Multifaceted behavioral treatment of drug dependence: A case study. *Behavior Therapy,* 1977, **8**, 731–737.

Thorne, F. C. The etiology of sociopathic reactions. *American Journal of Psychotherapy,* 1959, **13**, 319–330.

Thorne, G. L., Tharp, R. G., & Wetzel, R. J. Behavior modification techniques: New tools for probation officers. *Federal Probation,* 1967, **31**, 21–27.

Timsit-Berthier, M., Rousseau, J. C., & Delaunoy, J. *Revue d' Electroencephalographic et de Neurophysiologic Clinique,* 1971, **1**, 245–248.

Ullmann, L. P., & Krasner, L. *A psychological approach to abnormal behavior.* Englewood Cliffs, N.J.: Prentice-Hall, 1969.

Vaillant, G. E. A twelve-year follow-up of New York narcotic addicts: IV: Some characteristics and determinants of abstinence. *American Journal of Psychiatry,* 1966, **123**, 573–585.

Vaillant, G. E. Sociopathy as a human process: A viewpoint. *Archives of General Psychiatry,* 1975, **32**, 178–183.

Wagner, E. E. The nature of the psychopath: Interpretation of projective findings based on structural analysis. *Perceptual and Motor Skills,* 1974, **39**, 563–574.

Weiss, J. M. A. The natural history of antisocial attitudes: What happens to psychopaths? *Journal of Geriatric Psychiatry,* 1973, **6**, 236–242.

Westermeyer, J., & Walzer, V. Sociopathy and drug use in a youth psychiatric population. *Diseases of the Nervous System,* 1975, **36**, 673–677.

Whitehill, M., DeMyer-Gapin, S., & Scott, T. J. Stimulation seeking in antisocial pre-adolescent children. *Journal of Abnormal Psychology*, 1976, **85**, 101–104.

Whiteley, J. S. The psychopath and his treatment. *Contemporary Psychiatry*, 1975, Special Publication No. 9, 159–169.

Widom, C. S. Interpersonal conflict and cooperation in psychopaths. *Journal of Abnormal Psychology*, 1976, **85**, 330–334. (a)

Widom, C. S. Interpersonal and personal construct systems in psychopaths. *Journal of Consulting and Clinical Psychology*, 1976, **44**, 614–623. (b)

Widom, C. S. A methodology for studying noninstitutionalized psychopaths. *Journal of Consulting and Clinical Psychology*, 1977, **45**, 674–683.

Winokur, G. The division of depressive illness into depression spectrum disease and pure depressive disease. *International Pharmacopsychiatry*, 1974, **9**, 5–13.

Winokur, G., Cadoret, R., Baker, M., & Dorzab, J. Depression spectrum disease versus pure depressive disease: Some further data. *British Journal of Psychiatry*, 1975, **127**, 75–77.

Wisocki, P. The successful treatment of heroin addiction by covert conditioning techniques. *Journal of Behavior Therapy and Experimental Psychiatry*, 1973, **4**, 55–61.

Ziskind, E. The diagnosis of sociopathy. In R. D. Hare & D. Schalling (Eds.), *Psychopathic behavior: Approaches to research*. New York: Wiley, 1978.

Zubek, J. P., Pushkar, D., Sansom, W., & Gowing, J. Perceptual changes after prolonged sensory isolation (darkness and silence). *Canadian Journal of Psychology*, 1961, **15**, 83–100.

Zuckerman, M. Drug usage as one manifestation of a "sensation seeking trait." In W. Keup (Ed.), *Drug abuse: Current concepts and research*. Springfield, Ill.: Charles C. Thomas, 1972. (a)

Zuckerman, M. *Manual and research report for the sensation seeking scale (SSS)*. Newark, N.J.: University of Delaware, 1972. (b)

Zuckerman, M. Sensation seeking and psychopathy. In R. D. Hare & D. Schalling (Eds.), *Psychopathic behavior: Approaches to research*. New York: Wiley, 1978.

Zuckerman, M., Sola, S., Masterson, J., & Angelone, J. V. MMPI patterns in drug abusers before and after treatment in therapeutic communities. *Journal of Consulting and Clinical Psychology*, 1975, **43**, 286–296.

CHAPTER 24

Ethical Guidelines for Behavior Therapy

Richard B. Stuart

Individuals who enter either a behavior therapy or behavior modification undertaking, as with any other therapeutic encounter, expose themselves to a range of risks and inconvenience from which they are normally protected. These include: (*a*) openness to invasion of privacy; (*b*) the necessity to "sacrifice personal resources such as time, attention, dignity, and physical, mental or emotional energy" (Wolfensberger, 1967); (*c*) submission of at least some measure of their personal autonomy; (*d*) exposure to procedures that may involve mental or physical pain or discomfort; and (*e*) exposure to procedures that may lead to lasting physical or emotional injury. By the same token, those who offer treatment or conduct research assume a position from which they have unusual power to help or to hinder those who partake of the service they offer. To protect the rights of the participants and to constrain the powers of the purveyors of these services, a series of laws, ethical codes, and sets of moral principles have gradually evolved. After briefly reviewing the nature of these three sets of guidelines, this paper offers a comparatively objective method for protecting what many regard as the most basic right of therapeutic clients and research subjects, the right to participation only through informed consent (e.g., Denzin, 1970; Freund, 1969; Wolfensberger, 1967).

LAWS, ETHICS, AND MORALITY

All professionals must seek guidelines for their actions in order to be able to answer questions such as:

1. Under what circumstances can I offer my services?
2. How shall I know that the service I have offered is sufficient?
3. Are there circumstances in which I might be guilty of rendering too little service?

One source of these guidelines is law, whether by statute or by case. Laws are principles laid down or accepted as governing conduct, action, or procedure. Laws represent a compromise between the frequently competing interests of various fac-

713

tions in the community (Foster, 1975). Therefore, they vary from jurisdiction to jurisdiction: for example, 5 states do but 45 do not license the practice of marriage and family counseling (Dorkin & Associates, 1976), while all but 3 states regulate the practice of psychology, 21 through certification and 26 through licensure (Van Hoose & Kottler, 1977). In addition, laws are generally proscriptive rather than prescriptive: that is, they are more likely to specify penalties for misbehavior than to set guidelines for acceptable actions. Laws are also characteristically reactive rather than being proactive: that is, they are promulgated after some misdeed rather than being passed in anticipation of their need. For these various reasons, laws generally represent the lowest common denominator of behavioral guides and are at best an incomplete patchwork with respect to the practice of behavior therapy. Therefore, codes of ethics are formulated as behavioral guides to supplement laws (Reubhausen & Brim, 1965).

Like laws, ethics are also principles that guide behavior. Unlike laws, however, they are codifications that are logically deduced from sets of assumptions about human behavior. Ethical codes are generally the work of associations of individuals, and, unfortunately, they are as apt to protect the needs of association members as to address the rights of consumers of their services (Barclay, 1968; Bersoff, 1975; McGowan & Schmidt, 1962). In addition to their tendency to be arbitrary, ethical codes also tend to be vague. They generally express professionals' views about how they and their peers "ought" to practice in rather imprecise terms. Van Hoose and Kottler (1977) concluded their review of ethical codes with the observation that: "For the most part . . . the standards are ambiguous, nonspecific, and quite deficient in procedures for determining unethical practice" (p. 7).

Both the American Psychological Association (1977) and the Association for Advancement of Behavior Therapy (1977; reprinted in Table 1) have promulgated ethical codes relevant to the activities of behavior therapists. The former code makes an attempt to specify practice while the latter code is expressed in the form of a series of questions that practitioners can ask themselves in planning intervention and research and that peers can ask of the practitioner in the event of any challenge to the ethical standards of the programs in question.

Friedman (1975) has argued that behavior modification poses special problems not raised by other therapies and therefore requires special regulation. His sentiments are echoed by others who view behavior modifiers as having a unique ability to control the behavior of others (e.g., Pines, 1973; Szasz, 1975), an incorrect set of therapeutic assumptions that are likely to lead to suboptimal results (e.g., Arieti, 1974), and a set of value premises that are antithetical to the freedom and growth of individual action (e.g., Kapfer, 1970; Winett & Winkler, 1972). Other arguments for special controls of behavior therapy cite its specificity which would permit regulation, its occasional use of aversive techniques, and its occasional withholding of privileges as in the early stages of the use of token economies. In response to these views, however, the Commission on Behavior Modification of the American Psychological Association took the position that:

it would be unwise for the American Psychological Association to enunciate guidelines for the practice of behavior modification. The procedures of behavior modification appear to be no more or less subject to abuse and no more or less in need of ethical regu-

Table 1.   Ethical Issues for Human Services[a]

In 1975, the Board of Directors of the Association for Advancement of Behavior Therapy appointed a committee to consider the development of a statement on ethical practice for the organization. The committee consisted of Nathan H. Azrin (Anna Mental Health and Developmental Center, Anna, Illinois) and Richard B. Stuart (University of Utah, Salt Lake City), co-chairpersons; Todd R. Risley (University of Kansas, Lawrence); and Stephanie B. Stolz (National Institute of Mental Health, Rockville, Maryland). The Board of Directors adopted this statement at its May 22, 1977 meeting.

Rather than recommending a list of prescriptions and proscriptions, the committee agreed to focus on critical ethical issues of central importance to human services.

On each of the issues described below, ideal interventions would have maximum involvement by the person whose behavior is to be changed, and the fullest possible consideration of societal pressures on that person, the therapist, and the therapist's employer. The committee recognizes that the practicalities of actual settings sometimes require exceptions, and that there certainly are occasions when exceptions can be consistent with ethical practice. Even though some exceptions may eventually be necessary, the committee feels that each of these issues should be explicitly considered.

The questions related to each issue have deliberately been cast in a general manner that applies to all types of interventions, and not solely or specifically to the practice of behavior therapy. The committee felt strongly that issues directed specifically to behavior therapists might imply erroneously that behavior therapy was in some way more in need of ethical concern than nonbehaviorally oriented therapies.

In the list of issues, the term "client" is used to describe the person whose behavior is to be changed; "therapist" is used to describe the professional in charge of the intervention; "treatment" and "problem," although used in the singular, refer to any and all treatments and problems being formulated with this checklist. The issues are formulated so as to be relevant across as many settings and populations as possible. Thus, they need to be qualified when someone other than the person whose behavior is to be changed is paying the therapist, or when that person's competence or the voluntary nature of that person's consent is questioned. For example, if the therapist has found that the client does not understand the goals or methods being considered, the therapist should substitute the client's guardian or other responsible person for "client" when reviewing the issues below.

A. **Have the goals of treatment been adequately considered?**
   1. To ensure that the goals are explicit, are they written?
   2. Has the client's understanding of the goals been assured by having the client restate them orally or in writing?
   3. Have the therapist and client agreed on the goals of therapy?
   4. Will serving the client's interests be contrary to the interests of other persons?
   5. Will serving the client's immediate interests be contrary to the client's long-term interest?

B. **Has the choice of treatment methods been adequately considered?**
   1. Does the published literature show the procedure to be the best one available for that problem?
   2. If no literature exists regarding the treatment method, is the method consistent with accepted practice?
   3. Has the client been told of alternative procedures that might be preferred by the client on the basis of significant differences in discomfort, treatment time, cost, or degree of demonstrated effectiveness?
   4. If a treatment procedure is publicly, legally, or professionally controversial, has formal professional consultation been obtained, has the reaction of the affected segment of the public been adequately considered, and have the alternative treatment methods been more closely reexamined and reconsidered?

Table 1.   (Continued)

C. Is the client's participation voluntary?

1. Have possible sources of coercion on the client's participation been considered?
2. If treatment is legally mandated, has the available range of treatments and therapists been offered?
3. Can the client withdraw from treatment without a penalty or financial loss that exceeds actual clinical costs?

D. When another person or an agency is empowered to arrange for therapy, have the interests of the subordinated client been sufficiently considered?

1. Has the subordinated client been informed of the treatment objectives and participated in the choice of treatment procedures?
2. Where the subordinated client's competence to decide is limited, have the client as well as the guardian participated in the treatment discussions to the extent that the client's abilities permit?
3. If the interests of the subordinated person and the superordinate persons or agency conflict, have attempts been made to reduce the conflict by dealing with both interests?

E. Has the adequacy of treatment been evaluated?

1. Have quantitative measures of the problem and its progress been obtained?
2. Have the measures of the problem and its progress been made available to the client during treatment?

F. Has the confidentiality of the treatment relationship been protected?

1. Has the client been told who has access to the records?
2. Are records available only to authorized persons?

G. Does the therapist refer the clients to other therapists when necessary?

1. If treatment is unsuccessful, is the client referred to other therapists?
2. Has the client been told that if dissatisfied with the treatment, referral will be made?

H. Is the therapist qualified to provide treatment?

1. Has the therapist had training or experience in treating problems like the client's?
2. If deficits exist in the therapist's qualifications, has the client been informed?
3. If the therapist is not adequately qualified, is the client referred to other therapists, or has supervision by a qualified therapist been provided? Is the client informed of the supervisory relation?
4. If the treatment is administered by mediators, have the mediators been adequately supervised by a qualified therapist?

---

[a] From *Behavior Therapy* 8, 763–764 (1977). Copyright © 1977 by Association for Advancement of Behavior Therapy. Reprinted by permission.

lation than intervention procedures derived from any other set of principles and called by other terms [Stolz & Associates, 1978, p. 104].

In short, the commission shied away from the practice of imposing special controls on behavior therapy simply because of its effectiveness (see: Holland, 1973), recognized that behavior therapy is neither more nor less value governed nor aimed at interpersonal influence than other psychological approaches (Bandura, 1969; Benjamin, 1974; Frank, 1961), and heeded Agras' (1973) admonition that the imposition of special controls could have a chilling effect on innovation both within and beyond behavior modification.

Moral principles are a third source of guides for professional behavior, and a source that potentially transcends the local concerns of laws and the potential conflicts of interest in professional associations' codes of ethics. Moral principles are concerned with some absolute assumptions about the rights and responsibilities of individuals. Because they are subjective, morals tend to be overlooked by scientists whose search for objectivity has led them away from moral discourse. As an added consequence of their subjectivity, disputes about moral principles are not readily resolved. For example, Monod (1967) has asserted that the moral precept of science is the acquisition of knowledge. He wrote:

The only goal, the sovereign good, is not, we must admit, the happiness of man, even his temporal power or comfort . . . —it is objective knowledge itself. This is a rigid and constraining ethic which, if it respects man as a supporter of knowledge, nevertheless defines a value superior to man himself [p. 31: cited by Cournand, 1977, p. 703].

But Cournand (1977) has correctly viewed this as "inimical to the liberal and democratic traditions that we prefer to uphold" (p. 704), and he favors the more humanistic viewpoint of Masse (1973) who wrote:

The first exigencies of those who uphold such an ethic are: to defend freedom, to will justice, to respect all men. These exigencies characterize development, since there is no emergence without freedom, no humanization without justice, no fraternity without respect [pp. 121–123; cited by Cournand, 1977, p. 704].

Only the deductive methods of philosophy rather than the inductive method of science can resolve a difference such as this. But when each person has evolved a set of moral precepts that he or she accepts, those precepts can serve as very generalized guides to behavior that transcend omissions in the law and inconsistencies in codes of ethics. Indeed, it is in the response to moral principles that professional practice can move beyond the letter of law or ethical code and achieve the spirit of genuine respect for the rights of individuals. Therefore, every professional practice is as much answerable to moral questions as to statute, case, and code.

THE RIGHT TO INFORMED CONSENT

There is no legal or ethical consideration that comes closer to a universal moral precept than respect for the right to informed consent to participation in therapeutic and research endeavors. The Nuremberg Code (1946) is one of the hallmark documents in the evolution of modern therapeutic practice and research. Growing from public dismay over the chilling abuses of experimentation perpetrated during the Second World War, the code recognizes as inalienable the individual's right to self-determination with regard to participation in both experimental and therapeutic programs. The protection of this right is spelled out in the requirement that all such participation be preceded by a consent procedure that has three basic elements. In the language of the court, these three elements are as follows:

The voluntary consent of the human subject is absolutely essential. This means that the person involved should have legal capacity to give consent; should be so situated as to be able to exercise free power of choice . . . ; and should have sufficient knowledge and comprehension of the elements of the subject matter involved as to enable him to make an understanding and enlightened decision [*United States* v. *Karl Brandt,* cited in Katz, 1972, p. 16].

The court further ruled that the individual has the right to know the nature, duration, and purpose of the proposed procedure, as well as its possible benefits and risks. On the basis of the information supplied, the framers of the code envisioned a contract between the intervenor and the participant. This contract specifies the privileges and responsibilities of both parties and serves as a frame of reference against which to assess their evolving relationship.

While the concept of informed consent is compelling and endorsed in principle, at least, by mostly all contemporary researchers and clinicians, it is clear that in some settings the process of obtaining informed consent is no more than an elaborate ritual that meets the letter but falls far short of the spirit of the law (Ingelfinger, 1972). For example, Gray (1975) found that the requirements of obtaining informed consent were ignored in some settings and only partially met in others. In one study, they found that fully 39% of the participants in a double-blind evaluation of labor-inducing drugs did not even know that they were participating in research, while most of the others failed to understand one or more important aspects of the research—all of this despite the fact that the investigator was well intended and did attempt to obtain informed consent. In another study of the conditions under which college students are solicited as volunteers for research, it was found that only 2 of 124 volunteers were able to correctly describe the major elements of the research in which they agreed to participate (Stuart, 1978). Findings such as these lend strong support for the contention of Gray (1975) and others (e.g., Barber, Lally, Makarushka, & Sullivan, 1973; Friedman, 1975; Katz, 1972; Pappworth, 1967) that the formal process of obtaining a signature on a consent form is often incorrectly confused with the ethically sound process of obtaining fully informed consent.

Every behavior therapy and research program must have a formal way of assuring the voluntary consent of its participants. This must be a *standardized* procedure and not a simple matter of *de novo* negotiation, as determined by recent court rulings (e.g., *Canterbury* v. *Spence,* 1972). It should be *written* in order to be available as evidence in any subsequent litigation. It should be *specific to the procedures that are applied,* because so-called blanket consent forms that give generalized approval have long been held to be insufficient (e.g., *Moore* v. *Webb,* 1961; *Rogers* v. *Lumberman's Mutual Casualty Co.,* 1960; *Valdez* v. *Percy,* 1939). Also ruled invalid are consent forms that ask individuals to waive their right to consent (e.g., *Tunkl* v. *Regents of the University of California,* 1963).

Even with these caveats, efforts to protect individuals' rights to informed consent may be met in a cursory and indifferent manner. To guard against this, it is essential to have objective means of determining when the three cardinal provisions of this right have been satisfied. While Gergen (1973) has asserted that the "vast majority of instances in which these principles have been violated [are] inconsequential to subjects" (p. 908), and that promulgating specific ethical guidelines is tantamount to "mounting a very dangerous cannon to shoot a mouse" (loq. cit.), respect for human rights demands adherence to precise guidelines for determining how to best effect this fundamental guarantee.

1. *Competency to Give Consent.* The concept of competency has a long legal, social, and psychological history (Shaw, 1975). Unfortunately, the determination of competency is somewhat subjective and very much influenced by the circumstances under which the judgment is made. In general, individuals are considered to be competent if they seem to know what they are doing in a layman's sense (Meisel, Roth, & Lidz, 1977), and they are considered to be legally competent unless proven otherwise (*Lotman* v. *Security Mutual Life Insurance Co.,* 1973). Words like "responsible" (In re Yetter, 1973), "knowingly" (Friedman, 1975) and "capable" (*New York City Health and Hospital Corporation* v. *Stein,* 1972) have appeared in case law as synonyms for competence, but no clear test of its presence or absence has emerged. Hardisty (1973) has defined competence as the appearance that the individual knows what he or she is doing. Others define competence according to status such as that of child or mental patient. But the "mature child rule" of Mississippi (Mississippi Code Annotated, 1977) that has been upheld in New York (*Bach* v. *Long Island Jewish Hospital,* 1966) has held that under some circumstances the wishes of legal minors must be respected, and the "Model Patients' Bill of Rights" (Annas, 1975) addresses the conditions under which general and mental hospital patients must be allowed to be the arbiters of their own fates. Because it is far from easy to determine whether an action does indeed appear to be competent and because status alone is not a clear guide to competence, other criteria are needed.

Roth, Meisel, and Lidz (1977) have reviewed five different methods for determining competence. In one test, the person may be judged competent simply because a decision has been made—irrespective of the quality of that decision. This test can be passed if an individual shows—by word or deed—a clear desire to participate in the procedure being offered. For example, almost a century ago it was ruled that a woman who stood in a vaccination line seeing others being treated and subsequently presenting her arm for innoculation constructively consented to the procedure (*O'Brien* v. *Cunard S. S. Co.,* 1891). In the same vein, an adult requesting treatment at a community mental health center might be construed by the act of competently making this request to have consented to participate in the treatment that is subsequently offered. Second, competence can be inferred from the fact that the individual has made what is considered to be a "reasonable" choice (Friedman, 1975). This test rests upon a cost/benefit analysis of the consequences of the decision by those concerned. For example, the courts have ruled that refusal of blood transfusions on religious grounds may be unreasonable, and therefore this refusal can be construed as constructive proof of the individual's incompetence to make the decision (Cantor, 1973). Thus competence has also been inferred from the belief that a decision to enter into or decline participation in a particular program may be based upon "rational" reasons (Stone, 1975). A reasoning process is considered rational if it has a logical flow and is free of non sequiturs. The ability to understand the nature of an intervention is a fourth criterion of competence. This can be determined by asking the individual a series of questions about the details of the procedure and its potential risks and benefits, and by determining whether or not any misunder-

standings are remediable (Ingelfinger, 1972). Finally, competence can also
be evaluated by estimating the actual level of understanding of the procedure
evidenced by the individual. Demonstration of understanding would be taken
as constructive proof of the individual's competence.

Several sets of guidelines have been proposed for selection of one of these
tests of competence ranging from the least stringent (implied consent through
participation) through the most stringent (demonstration of the fact of understanding). Roth, Meisel, and Lidz (1977) suggest that the strenuousness
of the test of competency that is used should be determined by evaluating the
interaction of the direction of the individual's decision (consent or refusal)
and the relative balance of costs and benefits (favorable, questionable, or unfavorable). They suggest that minimum tests of competence suffice when the
individual consents to participate in a program with a positive risk/benefit
ratio. In the same vein, they would not set stringent demands for demonstrating competence when individuals refuse treatments with unfavorable bene-
fit/risk ratios. In these instances, their second criterion—reasonableness of the
decision—would seem to be their choice. However, when treatments with high
benefit/risk ratios are rejected or those with low benefit/risk ratios are accepted, they would require the more stringent test of a clear demonstration of
the individual's understanding of his or her decision. Annas (1975), in a
summary of recommendations of the American Civil Liberties Union, asserts
the belief that more stringent tests must be used when the procedure being offered is elective as opposed to having a life-saving benefit. This is consistent
with Stuart's (1971) view that greater caution is needed when the goals of
treatment are elective (e.g., improved school performance) rather than seeking minimally necessary social behavior (such as interacting noninjuriously
with classmates at school). From yet another perspective, Davison and Stuart
(1975) express the view that competency tests must be more stringent when
the procedures to be used are more experimental as opposed to having been
well tested.

Unfortunately, the critical terms in each of these frameworks—benefit/risk
ratio, elective, minimal, and experimental—are all open to considerable inter-
pretive debate. Before the bar, any assertions by a defense attorney appealing
to these concepts could easily be challenged by counsel for the plaintiff.
Moreover, in his or her defense, the burden of proof would rest with the
therapist-defendant who must be able to establish the fact that the client was
in fact competent to make the decision to accept or refuse either the treatment
or research participation that had been offered. Therefore, the conservative
approach of adopting all of the competence tests would seem warranted. That
would mean that the individual would be considered to be competent: (a) if
he or she made a decision, (b) that appears to be reasonable, (c) through
what seemed to be a rational process, (d) based upon an accurate understanding of the nature of the procedure and its potential benefits and risks.
Where the person is a minor, a person deemed to be legally incompetent to
act on his or her own behalf, or a resident in a total institution in which participation is solicited, this test of competence would apply to the individual's
legal guardian or advocate.

2. *Freedom from Constraint.*   The dictionary defines "coercion" as "the act of restraining or dominating by nullifying individual will . . . [usually] by froce or by threat." Coercion can occur when false or incomplete information is given about a proposed procedure, when nonparticipation is punished in a way other than by simple loss of the potential benefits of participation, or when compliance is obtained through physical coercion. If constraint enters into the process of obtaining participation in a research or therapeutic offering, the contract for that participation is invalid (Schwitzgebel & Kolb, 1974) and the rights of the participant are seriously undermined. Two groups are especially vulnerable to coercion; those who are not competent to understand the nature of the procedure being offered and those who are residents of total institutions wherein the potential for coercion is high.

Davison and Stuart (1975) have proposed a hierarchy of protections for the freedom of consent that varies with the function of the potential benefits and risks of the procedure, the level of its empirical validation, and the potential for institutional pressure to participate. An adaptation of their approach offers the following range of possibilities:

a. No consent by the subject is necessary because normally unhidden behaviors are anonymously observed in public places, such as observation of traffic flow on city streets.

b. Subject is simply asked to sign a consent form for participation in a program without full disclosure of its objectives. A study of buying preferences in supermarkets might fall into this category if the process of disclosure would invalidate the data and if post-observation debriefing were judged to be noninjurious in any way.

c. Subject is asked to sign a consent form following full disclosure, as is the normal process.

d. Subject is asked to sign a consent form following full disclosure in the presence of a guardian or advocate. This might be the practice for competent individuals who are asked to participate in a therapeutic or research endeavor with a high-risk potential in a setting in which the potential for coercion is minimal.

e. Subject is asked to sign a consent form following full disclosure in the presence of a guardian or advocate, with review of the consent-giving process by an intrainstitutional committee prior to administration of the procedure. This might be the practice when competent individuals are asked to participate in low-risk procedures in settings in which the coercive process is likely.

f. Subject is asked, or his guardian or advocate is asked, in the presence of witnesses and following full disclosure, to enter into a high-risk procedure, with the consent process reviewed by both intrainstitutional and community-based review committees. This level of caution would be indicated in settings in which the presence of coercive potential is clearly present.

In attempting to make a determination of the level of coercion present in any effort to secure acceptance of a treatment or research procedure, review committees are likely to address the following kinds of issues: first, they will be interested in knowing whether any *direct physical force* was used to secure participation. Second, they will be interested in knowing whether potential participants were *denied access to any privileges that they would ordinarily have been allowed to enjoy.* For example, if an institutional work program wished to evaluate varied incentive systems as a means of improving participant output, they might seek to make participation in preferred work programs contingent upon willingness to accept involvement in the experimental effort. This could be construed as a form of coercion. In the same vein, a school child who is denied access to certain programs unless he accepts counseling might also be the victim of coercion. Third, review committees might wish to determine whether the *level of inducement* to participate in research can be considered to be coercive. For example, Stuart (1978) found that undergraduates were more willing to participate in research involving electric shock when offered $20 for their participation as opposed to $5. Residents of institutions whose lives are dull might likewise agree to participate in experiments that are fraught with risk if this participation introduces some stimulation into their lives. Review committees could determine whether or not the rewards for participation were so great as to cloud the judgment of the decision-making individual. Fourth, the *conditions under which the individual's participation is invited* can be highly coercive. Annas (1975) has indicated that hospital patients, particularly those with acute conditions, are likely to agree to sign anything, and they require very special handling to make certain they do not act in a manner contrary to their own best interests. School children who are asked orally and individually in a group to participate in a research project might feel constrained to agree to do so more because of their wish to avoid peer pressure than because of a strong desire to become research subjects. Finally, the *language of the request for participation* can be coercive, and that is the subject of the next section.

The foregoing are just some of the ways in which coercion can enter into the process of obtaining consent to participation in treatment and/or research. Rather than relying upon their own feelings that the solicitation process is unconstrained, behavior modifiers are urged to develop a set of questions like those above, but adapted to their own professional setting, so that the coercive level of each activity can be determined. These questions could be put in the form of a checklist such as that proposed by Schwartz (1978) for review of the consent-giving process for dispensing psychoactive drugs in mental health clinics.

3. *Clarity in the Information Given.*   Manipulation of the kind, quality, and amount of information given about an experiment can have a material effect upon the individual's understanding of the program being offered. While it may be argued that every minute detail of the program should be explained to the individual, it has also been recognized that the provision of too much information can obscure understanding. This was found by Epstein and Lasagna (1969) who asked for volunteers in an experiment aimed at evaluating

the effects of a new pain-control drug. Prospective participants were asked to volunteer for a double-blind study in which they would take just one time either "acetylhydroxybenzoate" or a placebo sugar pill. Prospects were offered three different levels of information about the use, actions, side effects, warnings, precautions, types of people at high risk from the drug, and drug dosage—with all the information based on the standard pharmacological textbook dosage for aspirin. Form B provided about twice the amount of information as Form A, while Form C doubled the amount of information contained in Form B. The language used in all three forms was essentially the same. Comprehension of the information given was then tested through the use of an objective quiz about the forms. Results indicated that the comprehension level for the minimum information condition was 66.69%, as opposed to 44.67% and 34.95% for the second and third forms, respectively. The authors concluded that "Subjects who read the short form of the protocol in which the pertinent information was included without detailed elaboration retained significantly more important facts than did subjects shown either the intermediate or long protocol forms" (p. 684). The experimenters thereby demonstrated that overkill is a distinct possibility in consent forms.

While longer is not necessarily better, completeness is a must. Omission of salient aspects of an experiment or therapeutic offering has the obvious potential for compromising the judgment of prospective participants. Stuart (1978) demonstrated that subjects who were alerted to the inclusion of shock in an experiment were less willing to participate than those who were not so informed, although elsewhere it was found that complete information did not discourage patients who were about to undergo angiography (Alfidi, 1973).

In addition to the amount of information given and its completeness as regards important aspects of the proposed intervention, the level of wording of the information can also have a biasing effect. Courts have ruled that consent forms must be worded in language understandable to the average lay person (*Cobbs* v. *Grant,* 1972). Fortunately, there are two standard tests for estimating the level of language (Grunder, 1978). Both tests call for collection of 100-word samples of the consent form, after which total syllables in each sample are counted and average word and sentence length are determined. In the first test, reading ease is determined by subtracting from 206.835, 0.846 times the average word length minus 1.015 times the average sentence length (Flesch, 1948). The resulting number between 0 and 100 can be rated as very difficult (0.30), difficult (31–50), fairly difficult (51–60), standard (61–70), and either fairly easy, easy, or very easy for each of the last three deciles. The other system uses a nomogram to calculate approximate grade level from the same data (Fry, 1968). While essentially sensitive to reading levels below Grade 12, both systems can be very useful in making certain that the jargon level of consent forms is kept within the reach of prospective participants.

Even when the amount of information given, its completeness, and the level of sophistication of its verbiage has been evaluated, there is no necessary guarantee that the consent form will do its job. Review committees can monitor each of these three formal aspects of the form, but only the participant can judge whether he or she has in fact been fully informed. Therefore, as an important behavioral test—as an opportunity for the participant to show "through positive acts that he understands the significance of the information given him" (Martin, 1975, p. 30)—both clinicians and *researchers are strongly advised to use a multiple-part consent form.* Miller and Willner (1974) have suggested use of a two-part form. The first part would describe the "purposes, procedures, risks, discomforts, alternatives and rights" (p. 965), while the second would ask objective questions covering "six basic categories of information: benefits; departures from ordinary . . . practice; risks; inconveniences and tasks; purposes; and rights" (loq. cit.). Stuart (1978) has suggested that a third part be added to this form: one in which participants are asked to describe in their own words the nature of the program in which they are being asked to volunteer. He found that many potential subjects did not demonstrate a clear understanding of the proposed program. Those who fail to show understanding could be contacted for a discussion of any inaccuracies in their view as a core dimension of the true process of negotiation that underlies the contractual nature of ethically sound treatment and research undertakings. Moreover, this negotiation process would help to make a reality of the standard proposed by Annas (1975) for an adequate consent solicitation process. He proposes that the therapist:

always inform the patient of all material information, but that the manner in which the information is conveyed (time, place, language used, etc.) be permitted to vary depending upon the patient's circumstances [p. 68].

This lends special strength to the realization that it is not merely the process of seeking to obtain informed consent, but the reality of such consent that is sought by the ethical codes governing professional behavior. Therefore, no formal procedure of any kind can in and of itself stand in place of a cogent demonstration of the fact that the participant was competent to decide, was free to decide, and was given all of the information needed to decide whether or not to participate in a therapeutic or research offering.

STRUCTURING THE NEGOTIATION PROCESS

Commenting on the process of psychotherapy, Hans Strupp (1975) recently stressed the fact that "the client has a right to know what he is buying, and the therapist, like the manufacturer of a product or the seller of a service, has a responsibility to be explicit on this subject" (p. 39). The therapist, no less than the researcher, has the responsibility to help the client come to the wisest possible choice about whether or not to participate in therapy, and if so, which methods to accept as offering the best chances for a positive outcome. This must naturally include both information about the generally reported benefits and risks associated with the treatment as well as the therapist's personal rate of success using the technique at issue (Annas, 1973). Both the therapist and the researcher are obliged to convey the necessary information through a two-way exchange with their prospective clients and subjects. It is only through this negotiation process that the true spirit of the right to informed consent can be realized.

Stuart (1975) has offered a framework for this negotiation process through the format of a treatment contract. In discussing information contained in this form, therapists and clients can reach clear and accurate understandings of their reciprocal privileges and responsibilities. For example, the contract form obliges the therapist to give the client one or two references to recent validations of the techniques whose use is being contemplated. Through discussion of these techniques, the therapist and client together can decide the relative benefit/cost ratios of each and can decide together which of the techniques is the least intrusive (May, Risley, Twardosz, Friedman, Bijou, Wexler, et al., 1975; Wexler, 1973). They can also decide the optimum conditions under which these techniques are to be used and the best framework in which their results can be evaluated.

Some might argue that this negotiation process might give the client more information than is needed or appropriate, cutting into the placebo value of the treatment that is offered. Indeed, any weakening of expectation of therapeutic gain might erode the potential for change. However, it can also be argued that the negotiation process in which candid ideas are exchanged can build a more effective good faith and collaborative relationship between therapist and client, and this, in turn, may more than compensate for any therapeutic power lost through lowered expectancy—particularly when expectation is unrealistically high and destined to lead to disappointment when treatment ends.

CONCLUSION

It has been argued that the right to informed consent to participate in treatment and research is the cornerstone of the modern conception of human rights. While laws and ethical codes offer guides to the best way to respect this right, they are imprecise and incomplete. Therefore, every therapist and researcher must adopt a set of moral precepts that bridges the gaps between these various behavioral guides.

It is essential to use the most objective possible criteria in efforts to effect informed consent through asking capable individuals to freely give consent to participate in programs whose nature, benefits, and risks they fully understand. Some of the best criteria currently available have been reviewed in this paper. But the criteria are necessarily incomplete, for it is impossible to envision all of the possible legal, ethical, and moral implications of all of the conceivable therapeutic and research situations. When questions arise concerning ethical practice, they are most likely to be answered by reference to what is considered to be currently acceptable professional practice. Nash (1975) correctly recognizes this to be a peer review process, and he advises that everyone "seek the opinion of colleagues *before* [offering treatment or] running an experiment" (p. 780). While peer discussion of ethical practice is not a guarantee of manifest respect for the rights of clients and subjects, it clearly reflects a concern for and sensitivity to those rights that cannot but help to improve both the quality of the program offered and its ethical, legal, and moral stature.

REFERENCES

Agras, W. S. Toward the certification of behavior therapists. *Journal of Applied Behavior Analysis.* 1973, **6**, 167–171.

Alfidi, A. Informed consent. In R. Meaney & Associates (Eds.), *Complications and legal implications of radiologic special procedures.* St. Louis: Mosby, 1973.

Annas, G. J. Informed consent: When good medicine may not be good law. *Mediolegal News,* 1973, **3**, 1.

Annas, G. J. The rights of hospital patients: *The basic ACLU guide to hospital patients' rights.* New York: Avon Books, 1975.

American Psychological Association. *Ethical standards of psychologists:* 1977 Revision. Washington, D.C.: American Psychological Association, 1977.

Arieti, S. Psychiatric controversy: Man's ethical dilemma. *American Journal of Psychiatry,* 1974, **132**, 39–42.

Association for Advancement of Behavior Therapy. Ethical issues for human service. *Behavior Therapy,* 1977, **8**, 763–764.

Bach v. Long Island Jewish Hospital, 29 Misc. 2nd 207 (S. Ct. Nassau Co., 1966).

Bandura, A. *Principles of behavior modification.* New York: Holt, Rinehart & Winston, 1969.

Barber, B., Lally, J. J., Makarushka, J., & Sullivan, D. *Research on human subjects: Problems of social control in medical experimentation.* New York: Russell Sage, 1973.

Barclay, J. *Counseling and philosophy: A theoretical exposition.* Boston: Houghton Mifflin, 1968.

Benjamin, A. *The helping interview.* Boston: Houghton Mifflin, 1974.

Bersoff, D. N. Professional ethics and legal responsibilities: On the horns of a dilemma. *Journal of School Psychology,* 1975, **13**, 359–376.

Canterbury v. Spence, 464 F2nd 772 (D.C. Cir., 1972).

Cantor, N. L. A patient's decision to decline life-savings medical treatment: Bodily integrity versus the preservation of life. *Rutgers Law Review,* 1973, **26**, 228–264.

Cobbs v. Grant, 8 Cal. 3rd 229, 502 P.2nd 1 (1972).

Cournand, A. The code of the scientist and its relationship to ethics. *Science,* 1977, **198**, 699–705.

Davison, G. C., & Stuart, R. B. Behavior therapy and civil liberties. *American Psychologist,* 1975, **30**, 775–763.

Denzin, N. K. (Ed.). *The values of social science.* Chicago: Aldine Publishing Co., 1970.

Dorkin, H., & Associates. *The professional psychologist today: New developments in law, health insurance, and health practice.* San Francisco, Ca: Jossey-Bass, 1976.

Epstein, I. C., & Lasagna, L. Obtaining informed consent. *Archives of Internal Medicine,* 1969, **123**, 682–688.

Flesch, R. A new reliability yardstick. *Journal of Applied Psychology,* 1948, **32**, 221–233.

Foster, H. M. The conflict and reconciliation of the ethical interests of therapist and patient. *Journal of Psychiatry and Law,* 1975, **3**, 39–48.

Frank, J. Persuasion and healing. New York: Schocken, 1961.

Freund, P. A. *Experimentation with human subjects.* New York: George Braziller, 1969.

Friedman, P. R. Legal regulation of applied behavior analysis in mental institutions and prisons. *Arizona Law Review,* 1975, **17**, 39–104.

Fry, E. A readability formula that saves time. *Journal of Reading,* 1968, **11**, 513–516; 575–578.

Gergen, K. J. The codification of research ethics: Views of a doubting Thomas. *American Psychologist,* 1973, **28**, 907–912.

Gray, B. H. An assessment of institutional review committees in human experimentation. *Medical Care,* 1975, **13**, 318–328.

Grunder, T. M. Two formulas for determining the readability of subject consent forms. *American Psychologist,* 1978, **33**, 773–775.

Hardisty, J. H. Mental illness: A legal fiction. *Washington Law Review,* 1973, **48**, 735–762.

Holland, J. G. Ethical considerations in behavior modification. In M. F. Shore & S. E. Golann (Eds.), *Current ethical issues in mental health.* Rockville, Md.: National Institute of Mental Health, 1973.

Ingelfinger, F. J. Informed (but uneducated) consent. *New England Journal of Medicine,* 1972, **287**, 465–466.

In re Yetter, 62 D & C 2nd 619, 624 (CP Northampton County, Pa., 1973).

Kapfer, P. Behavioral objectives and the processor. *Educational Technology,* 1970, **3**, 116–121.

Katz, J. *Experimentation with human beings.* New York: Russell Sage Foundation, 1972.

Lotman v. Security Mutual Life Insurance Co., F2nd 868 (3rd Cir., 1973).

McGowan, J. F., & Schmidt, L. D. *Counseling: Readings in theory and practice.* New York: Holt, Rinehart & Winston, 1962.

Martin, R. *Legal challenges to behavior modification.* Champaign, Ill.: Research Press, 1975.

Masse, P. *La crise du developpement.* Paris, France: Gallinard, 1973.

May, J. G., Risley, T. R., Twardosz, S., Friedman, P., Bijou, S. W., Wexler, D., et al. Guidelines for the use of behavioral procedures in state programs for retarded persons. *Mental Retardation Research,* 1975, **1**, entire issue.

Meisel, A., Roth, L. H., & Lidz, C. W. Toward a model of the legal doctrine of informed consent. *American Journal of Psychiatry,* 1977, **134**, 285–289.

Miller, R., & Willner, H. S. The two-part consent form: A suggestion for promoting free and informed consent. *The New England Journal of Medicine,* 1974, **290**, 964–966.

Mississippi Code Annotated, Art. 41-41-3 h (1977).

Monod, J. *Lecon inaugurale au College de France.* 3 November 1967 (College de France, Paris, 1968).

Moore v. Webb, 345 S. W. 2nd. 239 (Mo., 1961).

Nash, M. M. Nonreactive methods and the law. Additional comments on legal liability in behavior research. *American Psychologist,* 1975, **30**, 777–780.

New York City Health and Hospital Corp. v Stein, 335 NYS 2nd 461, 465 (N.Y., 1972).

Nuremberg Code. *Journal of the American Medical Association,* 1946, **132**, 1090.

O'Brien v. Cunard S.S. Co., 154 Mass. 272, 28 N.E. 266 (1891).

Pappworth, M. H. *Human guinea pigs: Experimentation on man.* Boston: Beacon Press, 1967.

Pines, M. *The brain changers.* New York: New American Library, 1973.

Reubhausen, O. M., & Brim, O. J. Privacy and behavioral research. *Columbia Law Review,* 1965, **65**, 1190–1198.

Rogers v. Lumbermans' Mutual Casualty Co., 119 So. 2nd. 649 (La., 1960).

Roth, L. H., Meisel, & Lidz, C. W. Tests of competency to consent to treatment. *American Journal of Psychiatry,* 1977, **134**, 279–284.

Schwartz, E. D. The use of a checklist in obtaining informed consent for treatment with medication. *Hospital and Community Psychiatry,* 1978, **29**, 97–98.

Schwitzgebel, R. K., & Kolb, D. A. *Changing human behavior: Principles of planned intervention.* New York: McGraw-Hill, 1974.

Stolz, S. B., & Associates. *Ethical issues in behavior modification.* San Francisco, CA: Jossey-Bass, 1978.

Stone, A. A. *Mental health and law: A system in transition.* Rockville, Md.: U.S. Dept. of Health, Education, and Welfare, 1975.

Stuart, R. B. Behavioral control of delinquency: Critique of existing programs and recommendations for innovative programming. In L. A. Hammerlynck & F. C. Clark (Eds.), *Behavior modification for exceptional children and youth.* Calgary, Alberta: University of Calgary Press, 1971.

Stuart, R. B. *Treatment contract.* Champaign, IL: Research Press, 1975.

Stuart, R. B. Protection of the right to informed consent to participate in research. *Behavior Therapy,* 1978, **9**, 73–82.

Shaw, S. A. Dangerousness and civil commitment of the mentally ill: Some policy considerations. *American Journal of Psychiatry,* 1975, **132**, 501–505.

Strupp, H. H. On failing one's patient. *Psychotherapy: Theory, Research and Practice,* 1975, **12**, 39–41.

Szasz, T. S. The control of conduct: Authority vs. autonomy. *Criminal Law Bulletin,* 1975, **11**, 617–622.

Tunkl v. Regents of University of California, 60 Cal 2nd 92, 32 Cal. Reporter 33, 383 P. 2nd 441 (1963).

Valdez v. Percy, 35 Cal. App. 2nd 485, 96 P. 2nd 142 (1939).

Van Hoose, W. H., & Kottler, J. A. *Ethical and legal issues in counseling and psychotherapy.* San Francisco, CA: Jossey-Bass, 1977.

Wexler, D. B. Token and taboo: Behavior modification, token economies, and the law. *California Law Review,* 1973, **61**, 81–109.

Winett, R. A., & Winkler, R. C. Current behavior modification in the classroom: Be still, be quiet, be docile. *Journal of Applied Behavior Analysis,* 1972, **5**, 499–505.

Wolfensberger, W. Ethical issues in research with human subjects. *Science,* 1967, **155**, 47–51.

Author Index

Subject Index

759

Psychology and Psychiatry in Courts and Corrections: Controversy and Change
  by Ellsworth A. Fersch, Jr.
Restricted Environmental Stimulation: Research and Clinical Applications
  by Peter Suedfeld
Personal Construct Psychology: Psychotherapy and Personality
  edited by Alvin W. Landfield and Larry M. Leitner
Mothers, Grandmothers, and Daughters: Personality and Child Care in
Three-Generation Families
  by Bertram J. Cohler and Henry U. Grunebaum
Further Explorations in Personality
  edited by A. I. Rabin, Joel Aronoff, Andrew M. Barclay, and Robert A. Zucker
Handbook of Clinical Behavior Therapy
  edited by Samuel M. Turner, Karen S. Calhoun, and Henry E. Adams
Handbook of Clinical Neuropsychology
  edited by Susan B. Filskov and Thomas J. Boll
Hypnosis and Relaxation: Modern Verification of an Old Equation
  by William E. Edmonston, Jr.